T0336729

Research and Applications in Global Supercomputing

Richard S. Segall
Arkansas State University, USA

Jeffrey S. Cook
Independent Researcher, USA

Qingyu Zhang
Shenzhen University, China

A volume in the Advances in Systems Analysis,
Software Engineering, and High Performance
Computing (ASASEHPC) Book Series

Information Science
REFERENCE
An Imprint of IGI Global

Managing Director:	Lindsay Johnston
Managing Editor:	Austin DeMarco
Director of Intellectual Property & Contracts:	Jan Travers
Acquisitions Editor:	Kayla Wolfe
Production Editor:	Christina Henning
Typesetter:	Mike Brehm
Cover Design:	Jason Mull

Published in the United States of America by
Information Science Reference (an imprint of IGI Global)
701 E. Chocolate Avenue
Hershey PA, USA 17033
Tel: 717-533-8845
Fax: 717-533-8661
E-mail: cust@igi-global.com
Web site: http://www.igi-global.com

Copyright © 2015 by IGI Global. All rights reserved. No part of this publication may be reproduced, stored or distributed in any form or by any means, electronic or mechanical, including photocopying, without written permission from the publisher. Product or company names used in this set are for identification purposes only. Inclusion of the names of the products or companies does not indicate a claim of ownership by IGI Global of the trademark or registered trademark.

Library of Congress Cataloging-in-Publication Data

Research and applications in global supercomputing / Richard S. Segall, Jeffrey S. Cook, and Qingyu Zhang, editors.
     pages cm
  Includes bibliographical references and index.
  Summary: "This book investigates current and emerging research in the field, as well as the application of this technology to a variety of areas by highlighting a broad range of concepts"-- Provided by publisher.
  ISBN 978-1-4666-7461-5 (hardcover) -- ISBN 978-1-4666-7462-2 (ebook) 1. High performance computing 2. Super-computers. I. Segall, Richard, 1949- II. Cook, Jeffrey S., 1966- III. Zhang, Qingyu, 1970-
  QA76.88.R48 2015
  004.1'1--dc23
                                        2014045462

This book is published in the IGI Global book series Advances in Systems Analysis, Software Engineering, and High Performance Computing (ASASEHPC) (ISSN: 2327-3453; eISSN: 2327-3461)

British Cataloguing in Publication Data
A Cataloguing in Publication record for this book is available from the British Library.

All work contributed to this book is new, previously-unpublished material. The views expressed in this book are those of the authors, but not necessarily of the publisher.

For electronic access to this publication, please contact: eresources@igi-global.com.

Advances in Systems Analysis, Software Engineering, and High Performance Computing (ASASEHPC) Book Series

Vijayan Sugumaran
Oakland University, USA

ISSN: 2327-3453
EISSN: 2327-3461

MISSION

The theory and practice of computing applications and distributed systems has emerged as one of the key areas of research driving innovations in business, engineering, and science. The fields of software engineering, systems analysis, and high performance computing offer a wide range of applications and solutions in solving computational problems for any modern organization.

The **Advances in Systems Analysis, Software Engineering, and High Performance Computing (ASASEHPC) Book Series** brings together research in the areas of distributed computing, systems and software engineering, high performance computing, and service science. This collection of publications is useful for academics, researchers, and practitioners seeking the latest practices and knowledge in this field.

COVERAGE

- Metadata and Semantic Web
- Computer Graphics
- Virtual Data Systems
- Storage Systems
- Engineering Environments
- Computer System Analysis
- Enterprise Information Systems
- Human-Computer Interaction
- Computer Networking
- Software Engineering

IGI Global is currently accepting manuscripts for publication within this series. To submit a proposal for a volume in this series, please contact our Acquisition Editors at Acquisitions@igi-global.com or visit: http://www.igi-global.com/publish/.

The Advances in Systems Analysis, Software Engineering, and High Performance Computing (ASASEHPC) Book Series (ISSN 2327-3453) is published by IGI Global, 701 E. Chocolate Avenue, Hershey, PA 17033-1240, USA, www.igi-global.com. This series is composed of titles available for purchase individually; each title is edited to be contextually exclusive from any other title within the series. For pricing and ordering information please visit http://www.igi-global.com/book-series/advances-systems-analysis-software-engineering/73689. Postmaster: Send all address changes to above address. Copyright © 2015 IGI Global. All rights, including translation in other languages reserved by the publisher. No part of this series may be reproduced or used in any form or by any means – graphics, electronic, or mechanical, including photocopying, recording, taping, or information and retrieval systems – without written permission from the publisher, except for non commercial, educational use, including classroom teaching purposes. The views expressed in this series are those of the authors, but not necessarily of IGI Global.

Titles in this Series

For a list of additional titles in this series, please visit: www.igi-global.com

Challenges, Opportunities, and Dimensions of Cyber-Physical Systems
P. Venkata Krishna (VIT University, India) V. Saritha (VIT University, India) and H. P. Sultana (VIT University, India)
Information Science Reference • copyright 2015 • 328pp • H/C (ISBN: 9781466673120) • US $200.00 (our price)

Human Factors in Software Development and Design
Saqib Saeed (University of Dammam, Saudi Arabia) Imran Sarwar Bajwa (The Islamia University of Bahawalpur, Pakistan) and Zaigham Mahmood (University of Derby, UK & North West University, South Africa)
Information Science Reference • copyright 2015 • 354pp • H/C (ISBN: 9781466664852) • US $195.00 (our price)

Handbook of Research on Innovations in Systems and Software Engineering
Vicente García Díaz (University of Oviedo, Spain) Juan Manuel Cueva Lovelle (University of Oviedo, Spain) and B. Cristina Pelayo García-Bustelo (University of Oviedo, Spain)
Information Science Reference • copyright 2015 • 745pp • H/C (ISBN: 9781466663596) • US $515.00 (our price)

Handbook of Research on Architectural Trends in Service-Driven Computing
Raja Ramanathan (Independent Researcher, USA) and Kirtana Raja (IBM, USA)
Information Science Reference • copyright 2014 • 759pp • H/C (ISBN: 9781466661783) • US $515.00 (our price)

Handbook of Research on Embedded Systems Design
Alessandra Bagnato (Softeam R&D, France) Leandro Soares Indrusiak (University of York, UK) Imran Rafiq Quadri (Softeam R&D, France) and Matteo Rossi (Politecnico di Milano, Italy)
Information Science Reference • copyright 2014 • 520pp • H/C (ISBN: 9781466661943) • US $345.00 (our price)

Contemporary Advancements in Information Technology Development in Dynamic Environments
Mehdi Khosrow-Pour (Information Resources Management Association, USA)
Information Science Reference • copyright 2014 • 410pp • H/C (ISBN: 9781466662520) • US $205.00 (our price)

Systems and Software Development, Modeling, and Analysis New Perspectives and Methodologies
Mehdi Khosrow-Pour (Information Resources Management Association, USA)
Information Science Reference • copyright 2014 • 365pp • H/C (ISBN: 9781466660984) • US $215.00 (our price)

Handbook of Research on Emerging Advancements and Technologies in Software Engineering
Imran Ghani (Universiti Teknologi Malaysia, Malaysia) Wan Mohd Nasir Wan Kadir (Universiti Teknologi Malaysia, Malaysia) and Mohammad Nazir Ahmad (Universiti Teknologi Malaysia, Malaysia)
Engineering Science Reference • copyright 2014 • 686pp • H/C (ISBN: 9781466660267) • US $395.00 (our price)

DISSEMINATOR OF KNOWLEDGE
www.igi-global.com

701 E. Chocolate Ave., Hershey, PA 17033
Order online at www.igi-global.com or call 717-533-8845 x100
To place a standing order for titles released in this series, contact: cust@igi-global.com
Mon-Fri 8:00 am - 5:00 pm (est) or fax 24 hours a day 717-533-8661

List of Reviewers

Tianxing Cai, *Lamar University, USA*
Gerard G. Dumancas, *Oklahoma Medical Research Foundation, USA*
Venkat N. Gudivada, *Marshall University, USA*
Neha Gupta, *Northeastern University, USA & Osmania University, India*
Kim Grover-Haskin, *University of North Texas, USA*
Jeremy Horne, *International Institute of Informatics and Systemics, Mexico*
Russ Jones, *Arkansas State University, USA*
Manzoor Ahmed Khan, *Technische Universität Berlin, Germany*
Shen Lu, *SoftChallenge LLC, USA*
Randall Maples, *Oklahoma State University, USA*
Alan Olinsky, *Bryant University, USA*
Dan Ophir, *Ariel University, Israel & Tel Aviv University, Israel*
Liviu Popa-Simil, *Los Alamos Academy of Sciences, USA*
Jollean Sinclaire, *Arkansas State University, USA*
Anamika Singh, *University of Delhi, India*

Table of Contents

Section 3
Supercomputer Theory

Section 4
Supercomputing Leadership and Philosophy

Detailed Table of Contents

Section 1
Overview to Global Supercomputing and its Current Challenges

Chapter 1
Overview of Global Supercomputing 1
Richard S. Segall, Arkansas State University, USA
Neha Gupta, Northeastern University, USA & Osmania University, India

In this chapter, a discussion is presented of what a supercomputer really is, as well as of both the top few of the world's fastest supercomputers and the overall top 500 in the world. Discussions are also of cognitive science research using supercomputers for artificial intelligence, architectural classes of supercomputers, and discussion and visualization using tables and graphs of global supercomputing comparisons across different countries. Discussion of supercomputing applications and overview of other book chapters of the entire book are all presented. This chapter serves as an introduction to the entire book and concludes with a summary of the topics of the remaining chapters of this book.

Chapter 2
History of Supercomputing and Supercomputer Centers 33
Jeffrey S. Cook, Independent Researcher, USA
Neha Gupta, Northeastern University, USA & Osmania University, India

This chapter begins with the definition of supercomputers and shifts to how the supercomputers have evolved since the 1930s. Supercomputing need is stressed, including issues in time and cost of resources currently faced by the researchers. The chapter transitions to an overview of the supercomputing era with a small biography of Seymour Cray. The timeline of Cray's history and various Cray inventions are discussed. The works of Fujitsu, Hitachi, Intel, and NEC are clearly demonstrated. A section on Beowulfs and S1 supercomputers is provided. A discussion on applications of supercomputing in healthcare and how Dell is emerging in its supercomputing abilities in 21st century are cohesively explained. The focus is shifted to the petaflop computing in the 21st century, current trends in supercomputing, and the future of supercomputing. The details of some of the global supercomputing centers in the Top500 list of fastest supercomputers in the world are also provided.

Supercomputing is a contemporary solution to enhance the speed of calculations in nanoseconds. Presently, there are different aspects of supercomputing like Cloud Computing, High Performance Computing, Grid Computing, etc. provided by companies like Amazon (Amazon Web Services), Windows (Azure), Google (Google Cloud Platform). Supercomputers play an important role in the field of Computer Science and are used for a wide range of computationally intensive tasks across domains like Bioinformatics, Computational Earth and Atmospheric Sciences, Computational Materials Sciences and Engineering, Computational Chemistry, Computational Fluid Dynamics, Computational Physics, Computational and Data Enabled Social Sciences, Aerospace, Manufacturing, Industrial Applications, Computational Medicine, and Biomedical Engineering. However, there are a lot of issues that need to be solved to develop next generation supercomputers. In this chapter, the potential applications and current challenges of supercomputing across these domains are explained in detail. The current status of supercomputing and limitations are discussed, which forms the basis for future work in these areas. The future ideas that can be applied efficiently with the availability of good computing resources are explained coherently in this chapter.

Section 2
Supercomputing Applications

The accelerated development of nano-sciences and nano-material systems and technologies is made possible through the use of High Performance Scientific Computing (HPSC). HPSC exploration ranges from nano-clusters to nano-material behavior at mezzo-scale and specific macro-scale products. These novel nano-materials and nano-technologies developed using HPSC can be applied to improve nuclear devices' safety and performance. This chapter explores the use of HPSC.

Present High Performance Scientific Computing (HPSC) systems are facing strong limitations when full integration from nano-materials to operational system is desired. The HPSC have to be upgraded from the actual designed exa-scale machines probably available after 2015 to even higher computer power and storage capability to yotta-scale in order to simulate systems from nano-scale up to macro scale as a way to greatly improve the safety and performances of the future advanced nuclear power structures. The road from the actual peta-scale systems to yotta-scale computers, which would barely be sufficient for current calculation needs, is difficult and requires new revolutionary ideas in HPSC, and probably the large-scale use of Quantum Supercomputers (QSC) that are now in the development stage.

# Chapter 6

In the modern era of science, bioinformatics play a critical role in unraveling the potential genetic causes of various diseases. Two of the most important areas of bioinformatics today, sequence analysis and genome annotation, are essential for the success of identifying the genes responsible for different diseases. These two emerging areas utilize highly intensive mathematical calculations in order to carry out the processes. Supercomputers facilitate such calculations in an efficient and time-saving manner generating high-throughput images. Thus, this chapter thoroughly discusses the applications of supercomputers in the areas of sequence analysis and genome annotation. This chapter also showcases sophisticated software and algorithms utilized by the two mentioned areas of bioinformatics.

# Chapter 7

Population genetics is the study of the frequency and interaction of alleles and genes in population and how this allele frequency distribution changes over time as a result of evolutionary processes such as natural selection, genetic drift, and mutation. This field has become essential in the foundation of modern evolutionary synthesis. Traditionally regarded as a highly mathematical discipline, its modern approach comprises more than the theoretical, lab, and fieldwork. Supercomputers play a critical role in the success of this field and are discussed in this chapter.

# Chapter 8

Modeling of biological systems has become an important facet in today's scientific community because it has aided in the simulation of the minute biological entities comprising a living individual. With the advent in the advances of supercomputers, most challenges in understanding the complexities of biological networks and processes occurring in the human body can now be understood. Proteins, which are large biomolecules comprised of amino acids, play a critical role in the proper functioning of a living organism, and, thus, the prediction of its structure is essential in medicine for drug design or in biotechnology, such as in the designing of novel enzymes. This chapter focuses on how supercomputers facilitate in the prediction of protein structures in its different forms, modeling of protein-ligand binding site identification, as well as in the protein-surface interactions modeling.

Anamika Singh, Department of Botany, Maitreyi College, University of Delhi, India
Rajeev Singh, Division of RCH, Indian Council of Medical Research, India
Neha Gupta, Northeastern University, USA & Osmania University, India

Due to the involvement of effective and client-friendly components (i.e. supercomputers), rapid data analysis is being accomplished. In Bioinformatics, it is expanding many areas of research such as genomics, proteomics, metabolomics, etc. Structure-based drug design is one of the major areas of research to cure human malady. This chapter initiates a discussion on supercomputing in sequence analysis with a detailed table summarizing the software and Web-based programs used for sequence analysis. A brief talk on the supercomputing in virtual screening is given where the databases like DOCK, ZINC, EDULISS, etc. are introduced. As the chapter transitions to the next phase, the intricacies of advanced Quantitative Structure-Activity Relationship technologies like Fragment-Based 2D QSAR, Multiple-Field 3D QSAR, and Amino Acid-Based Peptide Prediction are put forth in a manner similar to the concept of abstraction. The supercomputing in docking studies is stressed where docking software for Protein-Ligand docking, Protein-Protein docking, and Multi-Protein docking are provided. The chapter ends with the applications of supercomputing in widely used microarray data analysis.

Tianxing Cai, Lamar University, USA
Neha Gupta, Northeastern University, USA & Osmania University, India

Power delivery has become more dissimilar with that of the previous era. Conventional power and energy materials, such as relic fuels, nuclear power, and renewable energy (solar power, geothermal, hydroelectric, wind power, and biomass), are already present. The energy network operation becomes complicated because the integration of power generation, energy conversion, power transportation, and power utilization should be considered. There is an intricate assignment for us to perform swift power transmission for the extremely urgent situations. These situations are the results of regional lack of energy that needs to be brought back as soon as possible. Advanced supercomputing has already been one of the powerful solutions to work out these issues. This chapter initially presents an introduction of some of the supercomputing techniques and then the potential applications and demonstration examples follow to give the readers some hint on the handling of energy network operation.

Section 3
Supercomputer Theory

Dan Ophir, Ariel University, Israel & Tel Aviv University, Israel

Supercomputers and cloud computing seem to be competing paradigms. Supercomputing focuses on increasing CPU speed, thus significantly increasing the speed of its associated memory access and its capacity. Conversely, cloud computing increases the computing throughput by parallel computing, spreading computing tasks over unused nodes and platforms. Steganography, the art of concealing a message within a message, is a type of encoding whose operations are required to remain secret. Steganography encoding requires data manipulation and is linked to data mining methodologies. Data mining reveals concealed data that is embedded in exposed data. Encoding by steganography is reverse data mining, hiding data among visible data. Conventionally, encryption methods are used to successfully hide the data. Cloud computing can take the data and disperse it in a way that even without any encryption, each individual packet of data is meaningless, thus hiding the message as like by steganography. This chapter explores steganography encoding as inverse data mining.

# Chapter 12

The growth pattern of mobile devices and wireless network technologies leads to revolutionized communication markets with constant advancements (e.g., partly realized 4G and yet-awaited 5G wireless networks, content centric networking, and mobile cloud computing). From the thin-client paradigm of the early computing history, where the bulk of the computing power was on the server side, we have witnessed a rapid transformation to powerful mobile end-user devices with ubiquitous connectivity. The cloud-computing paradigm is now promising to bridge those two ends in order to combine the best of both worlds. This chapter presents: 1) basic concepts of cloud computing in examining the different perspectives of stakeholders in the cloud market, 2) survey of existing approaches and solutions, 3) applications of cloud computing, 4) architectural approaches to cloud computing, including traditional and mobile cloud architectures, and 5) an overview of the related Software-Defined Networking and Network Function Virtualization concepts.

# Chapter 13

Availability of multiprocessor and multi-core chips and GPU accelerators at commodity prices is making personal supercomputers a reality. High performance programming models help apply this computational power to analyze and visualize massive datasets. Problems which required multi-million dollar supercomputers until recently can now be solved using personal supercomputers. However, specialized programming techniques are needed to harness the power of supercomputers. This chapter provides an overview of approaches to programming High Performance Computers (HPC). The programming paradigms illustrated include OpenMP, OpenACC, CUDA, OpenCL, shared-memory based concurrent programming model of Haskell, MPI, MapReduce, and message-based distributed computing model of Erlang. The goal is to provide enough detail on various paradigms to help the reader understand the fundamental differences and similarities among the paradigms. Example programs are chosen to illustrate the salient concepts that define these paradigms. The chapter concludes by providing research directions and future trends in programming high performance computers.

With the development of information technology, the size of the dataset becomes larger and larger. Distributed data processing can be used to solve the problem of data analysis on large datasets. It partitions the dataset into a large number of subsets and uses different processors to store, manage, broadcast, and synchronize the data analysis. However, distributed computing gives rise to new problems such as the impracticality of global communication, global synchronization, dynamic topology changes of the network, on-the-fly data updates, the needs to share resources with other applications, frequent failures, and recovery of resource. In this chapter, the concepts of distributed computing are introduced, the latest research are presented, the advantage and disadvantage of different technologies and systems are analyzed, and the future trends of the distributed computing are summarized.

Section 4
Supercomputing Leadership and Philosophy

Present day and projected labor demands forecast a need for minds to comprehend in algorithm in order to leverage computing developments for real world problem resolutions. This chapter focuses not so much on solutions to the preparation of the learners and the scientists, but on the future leadership that will advocate and open doors for the high performance computing community to be funded, supported, and practiced. Supercomputing's sustainable future lies in its future of leadership. Studies over the last ten years identify a shift in leadership as the Baby Boomers enter retirement. The talent pool following the Baby Boomers will shrink in numbers between 2010-2020. Women continue to be under represented in IT leadership. This chapter provides information on the talent pool for supercomputing, discusses leadership and organizational culture as influenced by gender, and explores how a mentoring community fosters leaders for the future.

Supercomputers solve very large-scale complex problems efficiently and expediently – simulating societies, modeling the weather, or mapping genes, etc. Perhaps the most complex task of all is simulating our brains. The physical mapping of organic components to an artificial architecture is daunting, but more so is identifying the mental content referred to as "consciousness." Creating a human mind is not impossible; what appeared out of reach yesterday is near reality now – a mind embodied in a machine. More profoundly, we may become our own gods, religion merging with science, a "supercomputer brain" encapsulating consciousness, reason, rationality, intelligence, etc. Can we overcome human bias in looking at ourselves, humans creating their own minds, our living as simulations in a virtual world, and computers actually solving social problems? If ultimately these developments amount to creating ourselves as a god, humanity looking at itself through itself, we may not like what we see.

Chapter 17

Jeremy Horne, International Institute of Informatics and Systemics, Mexico

Binary logic is the language of supercomputers. Programming applications do work more rapidly, efficiently, and accurately than humans, with supercomputers doing thermodynamic modeling, simulation of societies, and other large number-crunching projects. More recently, the supercomputer is taking on human brain functions, with increasing attention to actually replicating the human brain. Elsewhere in this book, the author has written about the philosophy underpinning these developments, but he now focuses on how computers communicate with us. The binary language computers use has an underpinning philosophy that may help explain at least one aspect of consciousness. When we probe deeply into the philosophy of bivalent systems, radical issues emerge that embrace the nature of our very being, such as completeness, certainty, process, the very nature of our universe, and possibly a consciousness pervading it.

Preface

Supercomputers are the fastest computers and the backbone of Computational Sciences. By processing and generating vast amounts of data with unparalleled speed, they make new developments and research possible. The hardware structure or the architecture of supercomputers determines to a large extent the efficiency of supercomputing systems. Another important element that is considered is the ability of the compilers to generate efficient code to be executed on a given hardware platform.

While the supercomputers of the 1970s used only a few processors and the supercomputers by the end of the 20th century were massively parallel computing systems composed of tens of thousands of processors, the supercomputers of the 21st century can use over 100,000 processors connected by fast connections.

This book is designed to cover a broad range of topics in the field of supercomputing. As a result, it will be an excellent source on this topic. It is primarily intended for professionals, researchers, students, and practitioners who want to more fully understand the realm and technology of supercomputing and how it has been used to solve large-scale research problems in a multitude of disciplines. Because each chapter is designed to be stand-alone, the reader can focus on the topics that most interest him/her.

Supercomputers are used today for highly intensive calculation tasks for projects ranging from quantum physics, weather forecasting, molecular modeling, and physical simulations. Supercomputers can be used for simulations of airplanes in wind tunnels, detonations of nuclear weapons, splitting electrons, and helping researchers study how drugs combat the swine flu virus. Supercomputing can be in the form of grid computing, in which the processing power of a large number of computers is distributed, or in the form of computer clusters, in which a large number of processors are used in close proximity to each other.

In 2012, the Cray XK7 "Titan" at the United States Department of Energy (DOE) at Oak Ridge National Laboratory (ORNL) located in Tennessee was the fastest supercomputer in the world at 17.59 petaflops, consuming 8209 kilowatts of power using 560,640 cores (Top500, 2012). However, in 2014, according to the Top500 listing of November 2013, China outplaced the United States with the fastest supercomputer named Tianhe-2 for the "MilkyWay-2" built by NUDT and located at National Super Computer Center in Guangzhou with 33.86 petaflops consuming 17,808 kilowatts of power with 3,120,000 cores (Top500, 2013; see Appendix).

According to Wikipedia webpages titled "Supercomputing in India," the Indian Government has proposed to commit 2.5 billion in Unites States Dollars (USD) to supercomputing research during the 12th five-year plan period (2012-2017). The project will be handled by Indian Institute of Science (IISc), Bangalore. Additionally, it was later revealed that India plans to develop a supercomputer with processing power in the exaflop range (Supercomputing in India, n.d.).

The objective of this book is to present the concepts of supercomputing, explore its technologies and their applications, and develop a broad understanding of issues pertaining to the use of supercomputing in multidisciplinary fields. The book aims to highlight the historical and technical background; architecture; programming systems; storage, visualization, analytics, state of practice in industry, universities, and government; and numerous applications ranging from such areas as computational earth and atmospheric sciences to computational medicine.

Readers would utilize this book as a unified presentation of a spectrum of up-to-date research and applications topics on supercomputing. The collection of chapters could interest the readers to do subsequent research in supercomputing, as well as be used in teaching courses in supercomputing.

The book is focused on the structure, practice, and applications of supercomputing such as represented by the following topics: background of supercomputing; supercomputing architecture; clouds, clusters, and grids; programming systems for supercomputers; storage, visualization, and analytics for supercomputers including data mining for high performance computing; state of practice of supercomputers; and applications of supercomputers from bioinformatics to data-enabled social science.

A special novel feature of this book is that it contains an elaborate and descriptive Appendix of the "Top 500 Supercomputers in the World" and their rankings at the time of the publication of this book.

Section 1 consists of three chapters on "Overview to Global Supercomputing and its Current Challenges."

Chapter 1, "Overview of Global Supercomputing," by Richard S. Segall and Neha Gupta, provides an overview of global supercomputing and also as an introduction to the entire book of edited chapters. The subsequent chapters of this book include further discussion of Seymore Cray, the father of supercomputing, and the history of supercomputing from past to present to year 2050, and a history of supercomputing and supercomputer centers. The subsequent chapters include detailed studies of applications of supercomputing to nuclear power, nano-materials, steganography, cloud computing, leadership, sequence analysis and genome annotation, population genetics, programming paradigms, modeling of biological systems, renewable energy network design and optimization, data mining, philosophical logic perspective, a philosophy of their language, and current challenges across multiple domains of computational science. The reader is referred to the Appendix of this book for more information about each of the top 500 supercomputers in the world.

Chapter 2, "History of Supercomputing and Supercomputer Centers," by Jeffrey Cook and Neha Gupta, discusses various aspects of supercomputing, including the need for supercomputing and the challenges associated with supercomputing in terms of the cost and time. The chapter also presents the evolution of Seymour Cray's research beginning with the discovery of CDC 1604, CDC 6600, and CDC 7600 in 1960s to Star 100 in 1974, Cray 1 in 1976, CMOS ETA-10 in 1987, ILLIAC IV in 1976, Cray X-MP in 1982, Cray 2 in 1985, Cray Y-MP in 1988, Cray 3, and then the Cray era during the time period of years 2000 until today. Later, a discussion of the contributions of companies like Fujitsu, Hitachi, Intel, and NEC in supercomputing are provided.

Supercomputing and its dominance in healthcare are displayed by a brief discussion of a section on this topic. History of Supercomputing Center at Florida State University, Minnesota Supercomputing Center, and Moscow University Supercomputing Center are discussed among various equally important supercomputing centers globally. Dell's contributions in the evolution of supercomputing is also discussed in this chapter. A section on Petaflop supercomputing in 21st century and current exascale computing challenges are described coherently. The chapter highlights in a positive direction the current global supercomputing centers in the Top 500 list, the current trends in supercomputing, and the bright future of supercomputing.

Chapter 3 is titled "Applications and Current Challenges of Supercomputing across Multiple Domains of Computational Sciences," by Neha Gupta. Supercomputing has been of utmost importance since it was discovered because it has enabled crucial advances in national defense and safety, scientific discovery, manufacturing, etc. The current challenges of supercomputers across most of the computational sciences domains are discussed here that would enable a positive future direction. It is therefore obvious that the supercomputers are super smart digital computers having various achievements both in the past and in the bright future. For instance, a simple Google search is built on the usage of MapReduce™ paradigm that is a useful application of supercomputing. However, despite consistent increases in the capability, supercomputing systems are still inadequate to meet the computational needs of various projects.

The challenges discussed in this chapter are achievable by devising new architectures of supercomputers, something that is much faster, portable, and adaptable to most of the projects of all the subjects. Hence, it becomes imperative that novel research is applied that can produce more and more powerful supercomputing systems. The current status of supercomputing and limitations that forms the basis for future work are discussed in this chapter for computational areas ranging from bioinformatics and computational biology to computational design optimization for manufacturing. The future ideas which can be applied efficiently with the availability of good computing resources are explained coherently in this chapter.

Section 2 consists of seven chapters on "Supercomputing Applications."

Chapter 4, "Accelerated Discovery and Design of Nano-Material Applications in Nuclear Power by Using High Performance Scientific Computing," by Liviu Popa-Simil, presents a summary of nano-materials, nano-technologies, and associated physics and engineering capable of improving nuclear power performance, motivation to use high performance scientific computing, and examples of different nuclear energy-related problems and their solutions that led to accelerated development of high-performance scientific computing.

Chapter 5, "Using High Performance Scientific Computing to Accelerate the Discovery and Design of Nuclear Power Applications," by Liviu Popa-Simil, discusses available architectures and solution approaches, presentation of the common sense, and practicality of developing the supercomputer architectures, issues in current supercomputing landscape, modern trends in high performance scientific computing with respect to nuclear power applications, and examples of future extreme-scale, multi-process, multi-phenomena high performance supercomputing. This chapter indicates that the future belongs to quantum computers, with far greater capabilities, if we succeed to understand some fundamental problems that are now hot research subjects. The author of this chapter feels that the term Central Processing Unit (CPU) might be replaced by a Quantum Processing Unit, and the terms memory and communication interface might be replaced by their quantum equivalents, respectively.

Chapter 6, "Applications of Supercomputers in Sequence Analysis and Genome Annotation," by Gerard G. Dumancas, discusses that sequence alignment and genome annotation are among the most commonly used techniques in the area of genetics and bioinformatics. With the emergence of a large sequence of genomic data, scientists are confronted with computational burden in these two fields. Supercomputers facilitate in the ease of analyses in these two areas by reducing computational time. Synchronizing the threads in supercomputing processes and the use of massively parallel, distributed memory supercomputers enable researchers to do comparative genomics on large datasets, eventually reducing computational time.

Chapter 7, "Applications of Supercomputers in Population Genetics," by Gerard G. Dumancas, discusses how supercomputers play a critical role in the success of the field of population genetics. This field is the study of the frequency and interaction of alleles and genes in populations and how this allele frequency distribution changes over time as a result of evolutionary processes such as natural selection, genetic drift, and mutation. This field has become essential in the foundation of modern evolutionary synthesis. Traditionally regarded as a highly mathematical discipline, its modern approach comprises more than the theoretical, lab, and fieldwork.

Chapter 8, "Supercomputers in Modeling of Biological Systems," by Randall Maples, Sindhura Ramasahayam, and Gerard G. Dumancas, discusses computational methods for protein structure prediction, including that of homology modeling, and fold recognition or threading, and computational methods for protein-ligand binding site identification, including that of protein-surface interactions. This chapter discusses that protein modeling is playing a more and more important role in protein and peptide sequences due to improvements in modeling methods, advances in computer technology, and the huge amount of biological data becoming available. These modeling tools can pave the way to future research directions in predicting the structure, functions, and mechanisms of novel proteins.

This chapter discusses that although there has been progress in using supercomputers for the prediction of biological systems (i.e. proteins), there have been challenges facing the scientists today, which include refining comparative models so that these could match experimental accuracy, search for more algorithms that can predict the structure of very large proteins, calculations of absolute binding free energies in protein-ligand binding, as well as the issues of protein folding structure prediction. Further, since protein-ligand interactions are dynamic and complex; the issue of capturing these molecular movements over relatively long periods of time can be a great challenge. With the advent of advanced supercomputers and the development of algorithms, these challenges have been met in course of time.

Chapter 9, "Role of Supercomputers in Bioinformatics," by Anamika Singh, Rajeev Singh, and Neha Gupta, discusses supercomputing in sequence analysis, virtual screening, Quantitative Structure-Activity Relationship (QSAR), macro-molecular docking studies, micro-array data analysis, and applications of DNA microarray technology. Software and Web-based programs used for sequence analysis area also discussed.

Chapter 10, "Energy Network Operation in the Supercomputing Era," by Tianxing Cai and Neha Gupta has the objective to help the reader understand the idea of the applications of advanced computing techniques, especially for high performance and cloud computing technique applications in the energy network operation. The included application demonstration of environment protection and energy recovery are just the references for the readers. The real application can be extended but not limited to the above-mentioned topics. The technique significance and application demonstration have been presented in this chapter in order to attract more engineers, scientists, researchers, and the other related stakeholders to dedicate to the future research of this field.

Section 3 consists of four chapters on "Supercomputing Theory."

Chapter 11 "Steganography Encoding as Inverse Data Mining," by Dan Ophir, presents an introduction on the picture of steganography and its applications and historical development, and its linkage with cloud architectures and supercomputers, and other alternatives to supercomputers such as nCUBE, which is the machine's ability to build an order-ten hypercube supporting 1024 CPUs in a single machine.

This chapter also discusses that supercomputers do not have to oppose cloud computing. They both can become an integrated entity where the cloud-computing methodology is superimposed onto supercomputers. The beginning of this chapter alludes to the apparent competition between the two paradigms of supercomputing and cloud computing. The author of this chapter indicates that in the future the strengths of both systems will undergo a complementary integration, exploiting the powerfulness of the supercomputers and optimally using their idle time.

Chapter 12, "Cloud Computing: Future of the Past," by Manzoor Ahmed Khan and Fikret Sivrikaya, discusses basic concepts and motivation to use cloud computing, traditional cloud computing architectures of distributed storage architectures, computational services, higher infrastructure services, and mobile cloud computing architecture. This chapter introduced the concept of cloud computing, its components, applications, and architectural aspects. It also provides an overview of the stakeholders in the cloud market, with their corresponding perspectives to cloud computing. Software-Defined Networking (SDN) and Network Function Virtualization (NFV) concepts are covered as related technologies and enablers for both realization and utilization of cloud computing.

Chapter 13, "Programming Paradigms in High Performance Computing," by Venkat N. Gudivada, Jagadeesh Nandigam, and Jordan Paris, provides a fairly comprehensive introduction to various programming paradigms used in high-performance computing. Each paradigm is illustrated with a concrete programming example. The programs were chosen to illustrate the fundamental concepts of the paradigms rather than to demonstrate their esoteric or advanced features. The reader should consult the bibliography and additional resources sections for advanced and comprehensive exposition to the topics.

Chapter 14, "Data Mining for High Performance Computing," by Shen Lu, discusses how to use High-Performance Computing (HPC) in data mining. The basic concepts of data mining are discussed and several data mining algorithms are tested in a high-performance computing environment. In order to perform data mining on high-performance computing, several high-performance computing technologies need to be adjusted, such as process management, naming mechanism, message passing, remote procedure calls, distributed shared memory, and synchronization. Existing data-mining algorithms can be used in high-performance computing environments after choosing the proper mechanisms.

Experiments in this chapter used supercomputer Lonestar Server from the Extreme Science and Engineering Discovery Environment (XSEDE) Computing Center at Texas Advanced Computing Center (TACC) to do experiments. The Extreme Science and Engineering Discovery Environment (XSEDE) is the most powerful and robust collection of integrated advanced digital resources and services in the world. It is a single virtual system that scientists can use to interactively share computing resources, data, and expertise.

Lonestar is a Dell Linux Cluster, a powerful, multi-use cyberinfrastructure High-Performance Computer (HPC) and remote visualization resource. Lonestar is intended primarily for parallel applications scalable to thousands of cores so that normal batch queues will enable users to run simulations up to 24 hours. Experiments performed as shown in this chapter were for testing 7 data mining algorithms on a large lymphoma microarray gene expression data set with 240 instances and 522 attributes, and used several evaluation measurements to show the performance of each data-mining algorithm.

Section 4 consists of three chapters on "Supercomputing Leadership and Philosophy."

Chapter 15, "Super Leaders: Supercomputing Leadership for the Future," by Kim Grover-Haskin, discusses that the latest EDUCAUSE Center for Analysis and Research (ECAR) report on research computing states explicitly the need for collaboration between IT and faculty to perpetuate a dynamic environment for supercomputing to thrive in academia. Recommendations include developing research computing services infrastructure with researchers on grants, partner with other institutions, provide research staffing personnel, and be proactive in uncovering research computing needs.

If IT leadership recognizes the value of computational research, potential demand for research intensive study and support emerges for consideration. The strength of the vision relies on partnership and relationship, fundamental transformational leadership attributes most notable of women's leadership styles. Tomorrow's supercomputing leadership faces no shortage of talent. The challenge to the leadership is in preparing its future, readying a diverse, gendered, and global community of leaders for supercomputing.

Chapter 16, "Supercomputers: A Philosophical Perspective," by Jeremy Horne, discusses a supercomputer as thinking organism. This chapter provides somewhat of an overview of how supercomputer technological development may apply in recreating the human mind-brain, and also focuses on provoking discussion about emergence in an artificial brain by interweaving ideas somewhat repetitive but in different contexts. In other words, it is not the fascination of a brain's construction and how the architecture of a supercomputer might be mapped to it that is the focal point here but the implications. Neuroimaging advances and nanotechnology are two areas that may make at least a physical replication possible. The principle issue in producing a fully functioning brain is knowing precisely what the supercomputer will emulate, and what we think is a mind, thinking, and consciousness. Many times it is safer just to ask the question, but one cannot act on questions. When we find the answer we must be prepared for more dramatic problems, such as those concerning policy.

Chapter 17, "Supercomputers: A Philosophy of Their Language," by Jeremy Horne, explores the idea that binary logic as both a structure and the processes within it is innate in the universe. That is, what we set forth on paper as binary logic describes the essence of the universe. At its most fundamental level, it is a two-valued system, and binary logic displays all that happens with these values. The substance of the system may at first not appear to be elegant, but there appears to be an irreducible empirical truth in what constitutes order and how it translates into mind. The most immediate technical aspect of interfacing with a supercomputer is the language by which a supercomputer communicates: binary logic. The supercomputer has a potential of being a sentient entity.

All chapters went through a blind refereeing process at the initial phase, and then revised manuscripts were reviewed multiple times by the editor before final acceptance.

Richard S. Segall
Arkansas State University, USA

Jeffery S. Cook
Independent Researcher, USA

Qingyu Zhang
Shenzhen University, China

REFERENCES

Supercomputing in India. (n.d.). In *Wikipedia*. Retrieved from http://en.wikipedia.org/wiki/Supercomputing_in_India

Top500. (2012, November). Retrieved from http://www.top500.org/lists/2012/11/

Top500. (2013, November). Retrieved from http://www.top500.org/lists/2013/11/

Acknowledgment

Each of the authors of the contributing chapters had been asked to referee chapter manuscripts of those submitted by others. Each of the authors of the contributing chapters need to be acknowledged for their careful reviews of the submitted chapter manuscripts that the editors then subsequently reviewed for the many versions of the revisions.

Additional reviewers need to be acknowledged: Professor Jollean Sinclair of Arkansas State University, Professor Russ Jones of Arkansas State University, and Professor Alan Olinsky of Bryant University. Acknowledgements need to be made to Dr. Henry Neeman, Director of University of Oklahoma Supercomputer Center for Education and Research (OSCER) at University of Oklahoma in Norman, for the many postings of the Call for Chapters on the numerous list servers of computer societies and Chris Hempel, the Director of User Services at Texas Advanced Computing Center (TACC) located at the University of Texas at Austin, for providing supercomputing account support to Editor Dr. Richard Segall.

Numerous personnel at supercomputing centers around the world that are too many to individually mention need to be acknowledged for the countless e-mail communications made with each of them in facilitating the visibility of the announcements for the Call for Chapters of this book.

Great appreciation needs to be expressed to the late Professor Dr. Hans Meuer, co-founder of Top500.com, for his kindness of providing us and IGI Global written permission to include the listing of the Top500 supercomputers in the world as an Appendix of this book. Dr. Hans Meuer did this act of generosity and kindness by e-mails sent to us and his associates at Top500 while he was out of his home country of Germany before his untimely death due to a brief battle with cancer in January 2014.

Appreciation also needs to be made to University Distinguished Professor Dr. Jack Dongarra in the Department of Electrical Engineering and Computer Science at the University of Tennessee at Knoxville, who is one of the other co-founders of the Top500, who after the untimely death of Professor Dr. Hans Meuer, graciously provided us and IGI Global continuation and extension of the written permission for use of the updated version of the Top500 supercomputers in the world to use in the Appendix as it appears in this published book.

Acknowledgements definitely need to be made to Ms. Neha Gupta of Northeastern University, USA, and Osmania University, India, for not only contributing a chapter on her own but who also provided support beyond the call of duty by assisting authors of several other chapters to complete their chapters, and who in addition graciously accepted and completed the horrendous task of word processing the pages for the entire Appendix of the Top 500 Supercomputers in the World. It is clear to state that without the help of Ms. Neha Gupta this book would not have been completed.

Recognition needs to be made to the College of Business at Arkansas State University for awarding Dr. Richard Segall a Summer Faculty Research Grant for purposes of supporting the completion of this book.

Dr. Qingyu Zhang would like to acknowledge the support from the National Science Foundation of SZU (grant no. 836) and the Research Institute of Business Analytics and Supply Chain Management at Shenzhen University.

Finally, last but not least, Austin Demarco, the Managing Editor, and entire Editorial staff at IGI Global need to be acknowledged for their support and communication throughout the writing process; without their help this project would not have been possible.

Richard S. Segall
Arkansas State University, USA

Jeffery S. Cook
Independent Researcher, USA

Qingyu Zhang
Shenzhen University, China

Section 1
Overview to Global Supercomputing and its Current Challenges

Chapter 1
Overview of Global Supercomputing

Richard S. Segall
Arkansas State University, USA

Neha Gupta
Northeastern University, USA & Osmania University, India

ABSTRACT

In this chapter, a discussion is presented of what a supercomputer really is, as well as of both the top few of the world's fastest supercomputers and the overall top 500 in the world. Discussions are also of cognitive science research using supercomputers for artificial intelligence, architectural classes of supercomputers, and discussion and visualization using tables and graphs of global supercomputing comparisons across different countries. Discussion of supercomputing applications and overview of other book chapters of the entire book are all presented. This chapter serves as an introduction to the entire book and concludes with a summary of the topics of the remaining chapters of this book.

INTRODUCTION

Supercomputers are the fastest computers till date and hence the backbone of Computational Sciences. By processing and generating vast amounts of data with unparalleled speed, they make new developments and research possible. The hardware structure or the architecture of supercomputers determines to a larger extent the efficiency of supercomputing systems. Another important element that is considered is the ability of the compilers to generate efficient code to be executed on a given hardware platform. While the Supercomputers of the 1970s used only a few

processors, supercomputers of the 21st century can use over 100,000 processors connected by fast connections.

In 1929, New York World newspaper coins the term "Super Computer" when talking about a giant tabulator custom-built by IBM for Columbia University (Gardner, 2014). In 1966, Seymour Cray developed the world's first "real" supercomputer, the CDC 6600: the first computer specifically designed for science and engineering calculations (Gardner, 2014).

A supercomputer is a computer at the frontlines of current processing capacity and speed of calculations. (Wikipedia, 2014) First introduced in

DOI: 10.4018/978-1-4666-7461-5.ch001

Copyright © 2015, IGI Global. Copying or distributing in print or electronic forms without written permission of IGI Global is prohibited.

the 1960s, the supercomputers of the 1970s used only few processors, and in the 1990s machines with thousands of processors began to appear.

By the end of the 20th century supercomputers were massively parallel computing systems composed of tens of thousands of processors. In contrast, supercomputers of the 21st century can use over 100,000 processors including those with graphic capabilities. For example, Sequoia, ranked as world's third system in 2103 (Top500, 2013) is a third-generation Blue Gene machine from IBM, and runs on 1.6 million processor cores. It can reach speeds of up to 20 petaflops. A petaflop, equals 1015 operations per second, which means that Sequoia can perform 20 x 1015 operations every second. Sequoia requires 3,000 gallons of water per minute to cool it down. It uses 6 or 7 megawatts on average with peak usage approaching 9 1/2 megawatts. (One megawatt equals 1 million watts), and that's $6 or $7 million a year in power. The 1.6 million cores of supercomputer Sequoia are located on 96 different racks, each of which weigh nearly 5,000 pounds and gives off an average of 100 kilowatts of energy, the amount needed to power about 50 single-family homes (Wagstaff, 2012).

Titan, a Cray XK7 system installed at the U.S. Department of Energy's (DOE) Oak Ridge National Laboratory and previously the No. 1 system, is now ranked No. 2 as of November 2013 (Top500, 2013). Titan achieved 17.59 petaflop/s on the Linpack benchmark using 261,632 of its NVIDIA K20x accelerator cores. Titan is one of the most energy efficient systems on the list, consuming a total of 8.21 MW and delivering 2,143 Mflops/W.

Tianhe-2, a supercomputer developed by China's National University of Defense Technology, is as of November 2013 the world's new No. 1 system (Top500, 2013) with a performance of 33.86 petaflop/s on the Linpack benchmark, according to the 42nd edition of the twice-yearly TOP500 list of the world's most powerful supercomputers. The list was announced November 18, 2013 during the opening session of the 2013 Supercomputing Conference (SC13) in Denver, Colorado USA.

Tianhe-2, or Milky Way-2, was deployed at the National Supercomputer Center in Guangzho, China in 2013. The surprise appearance of Tianhe-2, two years ahead of the expected deployment, marks China's first return to the No. 1 position since November 2010, when Tianhe-1A was the top system. Tianhe-2 has 16,000 nodes, each with two Intel Xeon Ivy Bridge processors and three Xeon Phi processors for a combined total of 3,120,000 computing cores.

The Indian government has stated that it has committed about $940 million to develop what could become the world's fastest supercomputer by 2017, one that would have a performance of 1 exaflop, which is about 61 times faster than today's fastest computers (PTI, 2012).

Table 1 lists the top ten supercomputer sites in the world as of November 2013 along with number of cores and other performance measures. The Appendix of this book provides complete information for each of the Top500 supercomputer sites in the world as of November 2013. The authors gratefully acknowledge the permission granted to the co-editors of this book for reprinting this detailed information as one of the Appendices of this book. A more complete discussion of the Tianhe-2 or Milk Way-2, Titan, Sequoia, and other supercomputers are also presented in the following sections of this chapter.

APPLICATIONS OF SUPERCOMPUTERS

Supercomputers are used today for highly-intensive calculation tasks for projects ranging from quantum physics, weather forecasting, molecular modeling, and physical simulations. Supercomputers can be used for simulations of airplanes in wind tunnels, detonations of nuclear weapons, splitting electrons, and helping researchers study how drugs

Table 1. Top 10 Supercomputer Sites in the World as of November 2013 (Source: http://www.top500. org/list/2013/11//#.U3_DUCjRhCg)

Rank	Site	System	Cores	Rmax (TFlop/s)	Rpeak (TFlop/s)	Power (kW)
1	National Super Computer Center in Guangzhou China	Tianhe-2 (MilkyWay-2) - TH-IVB-FEP Cluster, Intel Xeon E5-2692 12C 2.200GHz, TH Express-2, Intel Xeon Phi 31S1P NUDT	3,120,000	33,862.7	54,902.4	17,808
2	DOE/SC/Oak Ridge National Laboratory United States	Titan - Cray XK7, Opteron 6274 16C 2.200GHz, Cray Gemini interconnect, NVIDIA K20x Cray Inc.	560,640	17,590.0	27,112.5	8,209
3	DOE/NNSA/LLNL United States	Sequoia - BlueGene/Q, Power BQC 16C 1.60 GHz, Custom IBM	1,572,864	17,173.2	20,132.7	7,890
4	RIKEN Advanced Institute for Computational Science (AICS) Japan	K computer, SPARC64 VIIIfx 2.0GHz, Tofu interconnect Fujitsu	705,024	10,510.0	11,280.4	12,660
5	DOE/SC/Argonne National Laboratory United States	Mira - BlueGene/Q, Power BQC 16C 1.60GHz, Custom IBM	786,432	8,586.6	10,066.3	3,945
6	Swiss National Supercomputing Centre (CSCS) Switzerland	Piz Daint - Cray XC30, Xeon E5-2670 8C 2.600GHz, Aries interconnect, NVIDIA K20x Cray Inc.	115,984	6,271.0	7,788.9	2,325
7	Texas Advanced Computing Center/ Univ. of Texas United States	Stampede - PowerEdge C8220, Xeon E5-2680 8C 2.700GHz, Infiniband FDR, Intel Xeon Phi SE10P Dell	462,462	5,168.1	8,520.1	4,510
8	Forschungszentrum Juelich (FZJ) Germany	JUQUEEN - BlueGene/Q, Power BQC 16C 1.600GHz, Custom Interconnect IBM	458,752	5,008.9	5,872.0	2,301
9	DOE/NNSA/LLNL United States	Vulcan - BlueGene/Q, Power BQC 16C 1.600GHz, Custom Interconnect IBM	393,216	4,293.3	5,033.2	1,972
10	Leibniz Rechenzentrum Germany	SuperMUC - iDataPlex DX360M4, Xeon E5-2680 8C 2.70GHz, Infiniband FDR IBM	147, 456	2,897.0	3,185.1	3,423

combat the swine flu virus. Supercomputing can be in the form of grid computing, in which the processing power of a large number of computers is distributed, or in the form of computer clusters, in which a large number of processors are used in close proximity to each other. Jungle computing refers to the use of diverse [vague], distributed

and highly non-uniform [vague] high performance computer systems to achieve peak performance (Wikipedia, 2014d).

Application areas for supercomputers also include their use for solving large-scale computational problems in earth and atmospheric sciences, materials sciences and engineering, chemistry, fluid dynamics, physics, design optimization for aerospace, and manufacturing and industrial applications. Chapter by co-editor of this book can be found in Cook (2011) on supercomputers and supercomputing.

Supercomputers have been used in bioinformatics and computational biology, and especially are useable for intensive data sets such as at the genetic level. Previous work of the lead co-editor of this book and of this chapter in this area of supercomputing for bioinformatics and computational biology can be found in publications cited in references of this chapter as (Segall, 2013b), (Segall and Cook, 2014), (Segall and Zhang, 2013) and (Segall et al., 2013, 2011, 2010a, 2010b, 2009), and (Segall, 2013a) that are web links for video posted on the web and YouTube for Invited Plenary Address at 17th World International Institute of Informatics and Systemics (IIS) Conference presented by lead co-editor of this book and co-author of this chapter.

In this Invited Plenary Address (Segall, 2013a) presented discussion of applications of supercomputers and video of the Human Brian Project. The human brain is a complicated machine that neuroscientists continually try to understand, and the Human Brian Project is a new scientific endeavor that hopes to unravel some of these mysteries by creating a highly detailed simulation and working replica of the human brain using a supercomputer. With $1.6 billion in funding and more than 200 researchers, the Human Brain Project is the largest, most ambitious cooperative experiment of its kind. Serious hardware is necessary for a project of this kind — to pack the simulation into a single computer would require a system 1,000 times more powerful than today's supercomputers. The Human Brain Project began in 2012. It will take Europe 10 years to map all of the 100 billion neurons connected by 100,000 billion synapses that make up a human brain (Human Brain Project, 2012) (Wikipedia, 2014c).

COMPUTER ARCHITECTURAL CLASSES

The classification of high performance supercomputers comprises four main architectural classes known as Flynn's taxonomy (Steen, 2005) and (Wikipedia, 2014b).

Single Instruction, Single Data Stream (SISD)

These are the conventional systems that contain one CPU and can accommodate one instruction stream that is executed serially (Steen, 2005). These days, many large mainframes can have more than one CPU but each of these executes instruction streams that are unrelated. Such systems should still be regarded as a couple of SISD machines acting on different data spaces. Examples are HP, IBM, SGI (Steen, 2005).

Single Instruction, Multiple Data Streams (SIMD)

Such systems have a large number of processing units ranging from 1,024 to 16,384 that all may execute the same instruction on different data in lock-step (Steen, 2005). So, a single instruction manipulates many data items in parallel. Examples of SIMD machines in this class are the CPP Gamma II and the Quadrics Apemille which are not marketed currently (Steen, 2005).

Mutiple Instruction, Single Data Stream (MISD)

In these systems, multiple instructions should act on a single stream of data. As yet no practical machine in this class has been constructed nor are such systems easy to conceive (Steen, 2005).

Multiple Instruction, Multiple Data Stream (MIMD)

These execute several instruction streams in parallel on different data. The difference with the multi-processor SISD machines mentioned above lies in the fact that the instructions and data are related because they represent different parts of the same task to be executed (Steen, 2005). So, MIMD machines may run many sub-tasks in parallel in order to shorten the time for the main task to be executed. There is a large variety of MIMD systems. Another important distinction between classes of systems is shown as below (Steen, 2005):

1. Shared–memory systems.
2. Distributed-memory systems.

OVERVIEW OF TIANHE-2 (MILKYWAY-2) SUPERCOMPUTER

This is the first ranked fastest supercomputer in the world as of November 2013. This supercomputer in China has around 100 petaflops system speed. It has a hybrid architecture (Xeon CPU and Xeon Phi). Memory is 1.4 PB in total. Storage system is 256 I/O nodes and 64 storage servers with a total capacity of 12.4 PB. It has 16000 compute nodes in total (Lu, 2014). It has TH Express-2 interconnection network. Cooling type is Close-coupled chilled water cooling and a high cooling capacity of 80kW. Programming languages used for compiling are C/C++/Fortran, OpenMP, OpenMC, MPI/GA, Intel Offload (Lu). The supercomputer also has extended Map Reduce framework on CPU/MIC heterogeneous architecture for big data processing. Automatic fault management is another feature (Lu, 2014) (Wikipedia, 2104g).

TITAN III SUPERCOMPUTER

Titan is ranked second in the world's Top500 list of supercomputers as of November 2013. Titan was developed as the archetype of a class of machines better suited than a linked workstation for interactive visualization in supercomputing applications (Miranker, 1992).

Architecture

The computational engine of Titan III is a 64 bit vector multiprocessor. Each CPU of the multiprocessor consists of a trio of co-executing processors: a general purpose, RISC-based integer unit or IPU; a low-latency, pipelined floating point unit or FPU; and a multi-pipelined vector floating-point unit or VPU (Miranker, 1992). Each titan integer processor attains 20 Mips average performance; each vector floating-point processor a 32 Mflop peak. It is the only commercially available, desktop supercomputer (Miranker, 1992). It consists of 1 to 4 CPUs, a graphics processor, I/O processor and memory.

The principle features are:

1. **Multiprocessing:** It provides scalability, upgradeability and lower entry price for a machine. Algorithmic and compilation techniques to take advantage of such architectures are well established for the class of computations for which Titan was constructed (Miranker, 1992), (Wikipedia, 2014e).

2. **Vector Processing:** This reflects the nature of the applications targeted for the system. These applications are described as "interactive simulations" requiring both numerical computation and visualization of real-world phenomena (Miranker, 1992), (Wikipedia, 2014i).

3. **Special Graphics Engine:** Titan provides a graphics subsystem with a high resolution, 1,280 X 1,024 pixel display and full color (Miranker, 1992).

IBM's SEQUIOA SUPERCOMPUTER

It is the world's third largest supercomputer after China's Tianhe-2 and US's Titan. It has achieved 16.32 petaflops/s on the Linpack benchmark using 1,572,864 cores (Whittaker, 2012). It will be used to carry out simulations in order to prolong the life of nuclear weapons. The supercomputer is 1.55 times faster than the Japanese Fujitsu model. It also has less than half the number of CPUs than IBM's number crunching behemoth. Sequioa is an IBM/BlueGene Q system which was installed at the Department of Energy's National Nuclear Security Administration at the Lawrence Livermore National Laboratory (LLNL) (Whittaker, 2012).

K COMPUTER

K Computer ranks 4th in the world's Top500 list of supercomputers as of November 2013 (Wikipedia, 2014h). Fujitsu has been actively developing and providing advanced supercomputers for over 30 years since its development of the FACOM 230-75 APU, Japan's first supercomputer in 1977 (Miyazaki, 2012). Their technical expertise has been applied to developing a massively parallel computer system – the K Computer which has been ranked as the top performing supercomputer in the world (Miyazaki, 2012).

The K Computer was developed jointly by RIKEN and Fujitsu as a part of the High Performance Computing Infrastructure (HPCI) initiative. One objective of this project was to achieve a computing performance of 10^{16} FLOPS (Miyazaki, 2012).

Architecture

It consists of an 8-core CPU with a peak performance of 128 GFLOPS called the "SPARC64 VIIIfx". Commercially available DDR3-SDRAM-DIMM is used as the main memory (Miyazaki,

2012). An interconnect architecture called "Tofu" in excess of 80000 nodes was used. The Tofu interconnect constitutes a direct interconnection network that provides scalable connections. The K Computer system consists of 864 compute racks in total. Two adjacent compute racks are connected by a Z-axis cable (Miyazaki, 2012).

MIRA SUPERCOMPUTER

One of the fastest supercomputers, ranked 5th in Top500 list as of November, 2013, Mira, 10-petaflops IBM Blue Gene/Q system is capable of 10 quadrillion calculations per second. With this computing power, what Mira can do in one day, it would take an average personal computer 20 years to achieve. Mira is helping researchers to tackle more complex problems and create more robust models of everything from jet engines to the human body (Argonne National Laboratory, 2014).

It consists of 48 racks 786,432 processors and 768 terabytes of memory. Mira is 20 times faster than Intrepid, its IBM Blue Gene/P predecessor. In addition to being one of the fastest computers, Mira is also among the most energy efficient. By fitting more cores onto a single chip, Mira speeds the communication between cores and saves the energy lost when transporting data across long distances (Argonne National Laboratory, 2014).

Mira's water-cooling system uses copper tubes to pipe cold water directly alongside the chips, saving power by eliminating an extra cooling step (Argonne National Laboratory, 2014).

PIZ DAINT SUPERCOMPUTER

This is ranked 6th in the world's Top500 list as of November 2013 (Wikipedia, 2014h). It is developed by Swiss National Supercomputing Centre. This supercomputer is based on Intel Xeon E5 processors, has 28 cabinets and has been upgraded to a hybrid architecture featuring NVIDIA Tesla K20X graphical processing units (Swiss National Supercomputing Centre, 2014). With a total of 5272 hybrid compute node, it is possible for real simulations to sustain petaflops (10^{15} FLOPS) performance (Swiss National Supercomputing Centre, 2014).

STAMPEDE SUPERCOMPUTER

It is ranked 7th fastest in the world's Top500 list as of November 2013. Texas Advanced Computing Center (TACC) operates many of the most powerful and capable high performance computing systems in the world (Barth, 2013). Stampede is one of the world's most comprehensive systems for the open science community as a part of the National Science Foundation's (NSF) XSEDE program. It is a Dell PowerEdge C8220 cluster with Intel Xeon Phi coprocessors. The scale of Stampede delivers opportunities in computational science and technology research, from highly parallel algorithms to high-throughput computing, from scalable visualization to next generation programming languages (Barth, 2013).

SuperMUC PETASCALE SYSTEM

SuperMUC is the 10th fastest supercomputer in the Top500 list as of November 2013. SuperMUC is the new supercomputer at Leibniz-Rechenzentrum (Leibniz Supercomputing Centre, 2014) in Garching near Munich. With more than 155.000 cores and peak performance of 3 Petaflop/s, superMUC is one of the fastest supercomputers in the world (Leibniz Supercomputing Centre, 2014).

System Overview

There are 155,656 processor cores in 9400 compute nodes with > 300 TB RAM. Infiniband FDR10

interconnect is present. 4 PB of NAS-based permanent disk storage. 10 PB of GPFS-based temporary disk storage. > 30 PB of tape archive capacity (Leibniz Supercomputing Centre, 2014). Powerful visualization and highest energy efficiency.

Energy Efficiency

SuperMUC uses a new form of warm water cooling developed by IBM. Active components like processors and memory are directly cooled with water that can have an inlet temperature of up to 40 degrees Celsius (Leibniz Supercomputing Centre, 2014). The "High Temperature Liquid Cooling" together with very innovative software cuts the energy consumption of the system.

Typically, water used has an inlet temperature of approximately 16 degrees Celsius and after leaving the system, an outlet temperature of approximately 20 degrees Celsius (Leibniz Supercomputing Centre, 2014). To make water with 16 degrees Celsius requires complex and energy-hungry cooling equipment. Also, there is hardly any use of the warmed-up water as it is too cold to be used in any process (Leibniz Supercomputing Centre, 2014).

SuperMUC allows an increased inlet temperature. It is easily possible to provide water having 40 degrees Celsius using simple "free-cooling" equipment as outside temperatures in Germany hardly ever exceed 35 degrees. At the same time, the outlet water can be made quite hot (up to 70 degrees C) and re-used in other technical processes.

System Configuration

SuperMUC consists of 18 Thin Node Islands and one Fat Node Island. Each island contains more than 8,192 cores. All compute nodes within an individual island are connected via a fully Infiniband Network (FDR10 for thin nodes/ QDR for fat nodes) (Leibniz Supercomputing Centre, 2014).

System Software

Suse Linux Enterprise Server. For system management, xCat from IBM is used. For Batch processing, Loadleveler from IBM is used.

Permanent storage for data and programs is provided by a 16-node NAS cluster from Netapp. This cluster has a capacity of 2 petabytes. Data is regularly replicated to a separate 4-node Netapp cluster with another 2 PB of storage for recovery purposes (Leibniz Supercomputing Centre, 2014).

PANGEA SUPERCOMPUTER

Pangea supercomputer is ranked number 14 in the top 500 list of world's fastest supercomputers. Total Exploration production inaugurated its new Pangea supercomputer on March 22, 2013 in France (Total inaugurates its new Pangea supercomputer, 2013). The supercomputer represents an investment of 60 million pounds over four years. It will be used as a tool to assist decision-making in the exploration of complex geological areas and to increase the efficiency of hydrocarbon production complying the safety standards (Total inaugurates its new Pangea supercomputer, 2013).

It is designed by SGI (Silicon Graphics International). The Pangea supercomputer has a computing capacity of 2.3 Pflops. Its unique computing architecture is based on over 110,000 calculation cores, 7 Pb^2 storage capacity and an innovative cooling system (Total, 2013). Requiring 2.8 MW of electric power, the heat generated by this supercomputer is recovered making it possible to heat the Scientific and Technical Centre (Total, 2013).

PLEIADES SUPERCOMPUTER

Pleiades, one of the world's most powerful supercomputers ranked 16th fastest, represents NASA's

state-of-the-art technology for meeting the agency's supercomputing requirements (Biswas, 2014). This distributed-memory SGI ICE cluster is connected with InfiniBand in a dual-plane hypercube technology. The system contains the following Intel Xeon Processors: E5-2680v2 (Ivy Bridge), E5-2670 (Sandy Bridge), and X5670 (Westmere) (Biswas, 2014).

System Architecture

Manufacturer is SGI. There are 11,176 nodes (163 racks). 3.59 Pflop/s peak cluster, 1.54 Pflop/s LINPACK rating, 2 racks (64 nodes total) enhanced with NVIDIA graphics processing unit (GPU): 43 teraflops total, Total cores: 184,800 (32,768 additional GPU cores), Total memory: 502 TB (Biswas, 2014).

Interconnects

Internode: InfiniBand with all nodes connected in a partial hypercube topology. There is also Gigabit Ethernet management network (Biswas, 2014).

Storage

SGI Infinite Storage NEXIS 9000 home file system. There is 15 PB of RAID disk storage configured over several cluster-wide Lustre file systems. Operating system is SUSE Linux. Job scheduler is PBS. Compilers are Intel and GNU, C, C++, Fortran (Biswas, 2014).

BLUE WATERS SUPERCOMPUTER

Blue Waters is one of the most powerful supercomputers in the world. It can complete more than 1 quadrillion calculations per second on a sustained basis and more than thirteen times that at peak speed (Kramer, 2014). The peak speed is almost 3 million times faster than the average laptop. The machine architecture balances processing speed with data storage, memory and communication within itself and to the outside world in order to cater to a wide variety of scientific endeavers (Kramer, 2014). Many of the projects require a large portion of the thousands of processors that constitute Blue Waters and would be impossible to run elsewhere. Blue Waters is supported by the National Science Foundation and the University of Illinois (Kramer, 2014).

Three programming environments are available on Blue Waters, namely the Cray Programming Environment, the PGI programming environment and the Gnu programming environment. The environment is managed effectively by the module command (Kramer, 2014).

Compiling and Linking

Multiple compiler suites are available for building and linking application codes. Depending on the type of application, one set of compilers may produce code that performs better than the other (Kramer, 2014). The compilers currently available in this system are Cray (Wikipedia, 2014a), The Portland Group (PGI) and GNU (Kramer, 2014).

System Summary

The Blue Waters system is a Cray XE/XK hybrid machine composed of AMD 6276 "Interlagos" processors (nominal clock speed of at least 2.3 GHz) and NVIDIA GK110 "Kepler" accelerators all connected by the Cray Gemini torus interconnect (Kramer, 2014).

Storage

All file systems on Blue Waters are Lustre based. The home directory has 2.2 PB. Scratch has 22 PB for running batch jobs generating large amounts of data. Projects directory has 2.2 PB. This space is used for sharing frequently used large files within a team.

SUPERCOMPUTING WITH PARALLELLA

Packing impressive supercomputing power inside a small credit card-sized board running Ubuntu, Adapteva's $99 ARM-based Parallella system includes the unique Ephiphany numerical accelerator that promises to unleash industrial strength parallel processing on the desktop at a low price (Lucifredi, 2013).

The board is properly structured like a Supercomputer, with a host side powered by a 667 MHz Zynq 7020 ARM A9 System-on-Chip manufactured by Xilinx (Lucifredi, 2013). This is an interesting chip that includes alongside a dual-core ARM v7 CPU a full-fledged programmable logic facility equivalent to an Artix-7 FPGA. The number-crunching side is powered by a 600 MHz, 16-core Adapteva Epiphany-III numerical accelerator, which is replaced by a 64-core version in more expensive configurations (Lucifredi, 2013).

It is built of Linaro 12.10 Ubuntu derivative and hence is extremely standard. The kernel is 3.6.0 with patches additionally and the system runs the SSH daemon. Apt-get has access to the full Linaro 12.10 repositories, so the choice of software is infinite. The board comes loaded with GCC 4.6, Perl 15.4.2 and Python 2.7. Cross-compile is not necessary (Lucifredi, 2013). Man pages are also installed by default. The interesting part is programming the numerical accelerator, binaries for which are created with e-gcc (Lucifredi, 2013). For instance, comparison of performance of the ARM CPU (2 cores) with that of the Epiphany accelerator (16 cores) can be done. The 16-core matrix outpaces the general purpose CPU by 11X (Lucifredi, 2013).

SYMBOLIC SUPERCOMPUTER FOR ARTIFICIAL INTELLIGENCE AND COGNITIVE SCIENCE RESEARCH

Supercomputers are invaluable resources in many areas of science and engineering. However, artificial intelligence and cognitive science research has not benefited from supercomputing because traditional supercomputers are aimed at numerical simulation (Forbus, n.d.). A symbolic supercomputer is built in order to address this. This cluster machine is carefully designed to support the creation and modeling of intelligent systems (Forbus, n.d.). This supercomputer is created in order to support research being conducted on two ONR projects:

- The Artificial Intelligence Project, Qualitative Reasoning for Intelligent Agents.
- The Cognitive Science Project, Analogical Learning and Case-Based Instruction.

The supercomputer is made of Linux Networx Evolocity cluster with 67 nodes and a gigabit switch. Each node has two 3.2 Ghz Pentium Xeon Processors, with 4 GB RAM and 80 GB of disk (Forbus, n.d.). This machine, known as mk2, became operational in 2004.

COMPARISON OF SUPERCOMPUTING ABILITIES ACROSS DIFFERENT COUNTRIES

Visualization of Global Supercomputing Comparisons by Tables and Graphs

This section provides tables and graphs to illustrate the comparisons of supercomputer abilities across the world as of November 2013. The following sections will provide a more detailed description of the supercomputing in the countries of China, India and Japan and those in Europe of Belgium, Bulgaria, Finland, France, Germany, Italy, Norway, Netherlands, Poland, Russia, Slovenia, Spain, Sweden, Switzerland, and United Kingdom.

Table 2 lists each of the countries in the world that have at least one supercomputer and ranks them accordingly to their system share of the top 500. Performance measures of Rmax and Rpeak are also provided as well as number of cores. Figure 1 provides a frequency curve for the count of the number of supercomputers for each of the countries presented in Table 2. This statistic shows the locations of the world's 500 most powerful supercomputers as of November 2013. As of this date, 264 of the world's leading supercomputers were located in the United States.

Figure 2 provides the teraflops per country and log teraflops per country. Log teraflops per country is provided as additional bar graph because of the magnitude of the numbers a more convenient scale is needed to compare these. As Figure 2 illustrates, the United States is the leader with China, Japan, Germany and France lagging behind.

Figure 3 provides a comparison by introducing the factor of average country income by country of the top 500 supercomputers in the world by comparing the megaflops per capita by country. As Figure 3 illustrates the country of Switzerland outpaces all other countries, including the United States, Japan, and Germany in both megaflops and log megaflops per capita.

Figure 4 illustrates the number of people (in millions) per supercomputer by country as of November 2013 in bar graphs, and shows that the India is the leader with 103.06 million because of its population followed by Brazil with 66.72 million and Russia with 28.71 million. Figure 4 also overlays the bar graph with a connected line graph of the number of supercomputers and shows that United States is leader in number of supercomputers of 264 but the lowest in number of people per supercomputer with 1.19 million.

Table 2. Count by country and performance statistics of the 500 most powerful computers in the world as of November 2103 (Source: Top500, http://www.top500.org/statistics/list/#.U30G4SjRhCh)

Countries	Count	System Share (%)	Rmax (GFlops)	Rpeak (GFlops)	Cores
United States	264	52.8	118,261,596	169,499,661	9,837,537
China	63	12.6	48,549,093	89,432,561	4,925,804
Japan	28	5.6	22,472,218	28,925,862	1,558,880
United Kingdom	23	4.6	9,058,329	11,380,215	627,120
France	22	4.4	9,489,912	11,228,571	720,416
Germany	20	4	13,696,834	16,426,807	1,033,252
India	12	2.4	3,040,297	3,812,719	188,252
Canada	10	2	2,077,842	2,627,756	190,752
Korea, South	5	1	1,258,060	1,760,092	154,224
Sweden	5	1	1,067,767	1,297,036	95,680
Russia	5	1	1,846,613	3,242,736	166,432
Australia	5	1	2,180,151	2,635,546	145,036
Italy	5	1	2,665,609	3,212,697	221,120
Switzerland	5	1	7,765,418	9,632,162	253,904
Netherlands	3	0.6	511,071	671,160	47,544
Brazil	3	0.6	626,000	1,182,104	58,880
Norway	3	0.6	735,400	873,164	54,400
Saudi Arabia	3	0.6	1,165,315	1,827,011	128,272
Ireland	2	0.4	268,565	343,310	30,996
Israel	2	0.4	314,056	736,819	35,424
Finland	2	0.4	378,000	436,301	20,976
Hong Kong	2	0.4	352,937	658,368	47,520
Poland	2	0.4	455,909	583,605	41,852
Spain	2	0.4	1,199,031	1,357,824	65,280
Belgium	1	0.2	152,348	175,718	8,448
Austria	1	0.2	152,900	182,829	20,776
Denmark	1	0.2	162,098	183,676	15,672
Taiwan	1	0.2	177,100	231,859	26,244

Table 3 provides the aggregation of the statistics in Table 2 for each geographical region of North America, Western Europe, Northern Europe, Southern Europe, Eastern Europe, Eastern Asia, South-central Asia, Western Asia, Australia and New Zealand, and South America. Table 3 shows a count of 274 supercomputers for North America,

and 99 in Eastern Asia, and 52 in Western Europe to account for 85% of the world's supercomputers.

Table 4 provides a count of how many of the top 500 supercomputers use cluster versus massively parallel processors (MPP) and indicates that 84.6% of the world's supercomputers use a cluster architecture.

Figure 1. Locations of the 500 most powerful supercomputers in the world as of November 2013 by country (Source: http://www.statista.com/statistics/264445/number-of-supercomputers-worldwide-by-country/)

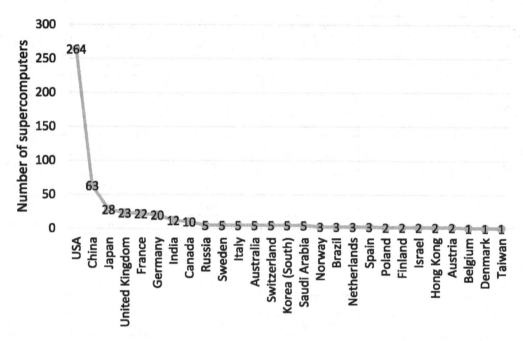

Figure 2. Teraflops and Log Teraflops per country of the world's top 500 supercomputers (Source: top500.org/list/2013/11)

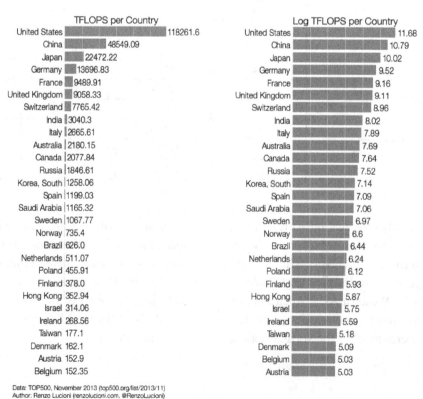

Figure 3. Megaflops and Log Megaflops per capita by country of the world's top 500 supercomputers. (Source: top500.org/list/2013/11)

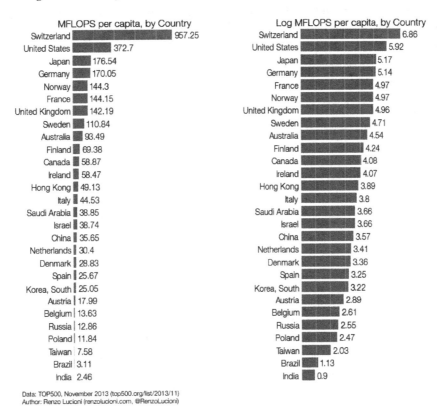

As of that date the operating system family Linux held a system share of 96.4 percent.

Table 5 shows the counts of operating systems for the top 500 supercomputers in the world.

Table 6 shows the number of supercomputers of the top 500 in the world per processor generation and the system share and other performance measures.

Table 7 shows the counts of the operating system families of Linux, Unix, Mixed and Windows for the Top 500 supercomputers in the world as of November 2013. As Table 6 indicates, 96.4% (482) of the top 500 supercomputers in the world use a Linux Operation System.

Figure 5 shows a bar graph of the aggregated counts for the operating systems of Table 5. The statistics of Figure 5 show a breakdown of the 500 most powerful supercomputers around the world as of November 2013, by operating system family.

Table 8 shows the numerical counts of the number of supercomputers used for each of the listed application areas as of November 2013. As Table 7 illustrates, 82% (410) of the top 500 supercomputers in the world had a non-specified application area, followed by 11.2% (56) for research, and 1.8% (9) for weather. Figure 6 from Statista shows an aggregated distribution of the 500 most powerful supercomputers as of November 2013 into only 7 categories instead of the 12 categories of Table 7, and thus showing a greater number and percentage (20.6%) of supercomputers being used for research area.

Figure 7 shows the system share of interconnect families used in the 500 most powerful supercom-

Figure 4. Number of people per supercomputer (bar graph) and number of supercomputers by country (line graph) as of November 2013 (Source: http://imgur.com/r/dataisbeautiful/xvsmNbc) also posted at: http://www.reddit.com/r/dataisbeautiful/comments/1tftbr/number_of_people_per_supercomputer_by_country_oc/)

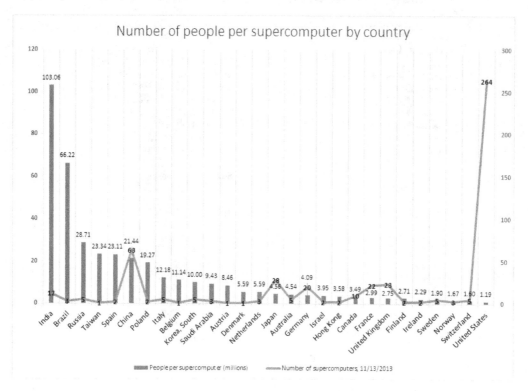

Table 3. Count by geographical region and performance statistics of the 500 most powerful computers in the world as of November 2013 (Source: http://www.top500.org/statistics/list/#.U30G4SjRhCh)

Geographical Region	Count	System Share (%)	Rmax (GFlops)	Rpeak (GFlops)	Cores
North America	274	54.8	120,339,438	172,127,417	10,028,289
Eastern Asia	99	19.8	72,809,408	121,008,742	6,712,672
Western Europe	52	10.4	31,768,483	38,317,247	2,084,340
Northern Europe	36	7.2	11,670,158	14,513,703	844,844
South-central Asia	12	2.4	3,040,297	3,812,719	188,252
Southern Europe	7	1.4	3,864,640	4,570,521	286,400
Eastern Europe	7	1.4	2,302,522	3,826,340	208,284
Western Asia	5	1	1,479,371	2,563,830	163,696
Australia and New Zealand	5	1	2,180,151	2,635,546	145,036
South America	3	0.6	626,000	1,182,104	58,880

Table 4. Architecture classifications of the Top 500 supercomputers in the world as of November 2013 (Source: http://www.top500.org/statistics/list/#.U30G4SjRhCh)

Architecture	Count	System Share (%)	Rmax (GFlops)	Rpeak (GFlops)	Cores
Cluster	423	84.6	156,485,694	244,434,097	13,409,693
MPP	77	15.4	93,594,774	120,124,072	7,311,000

Table 5. Types of operating systems for the Top 500 supercomputer in the world as of November 2013 (Source: http://www.top500.org/statistics/list/#.U30G4SjRhCh)

Operating System	Count	System Share (%)	Rmax (GFlops)	Rpeak (GFlops)	Cores
Linux	414	82.8	158369073	230603624	14277307
Cray Linux Environment	20	4	30911722	43804792	1302984
SUSE Linux Enterprise Server 11	13	2.6	9174795	13081620	432150
CentOS	11	2.2	2685015	3654410	192552
AIX	11	2.2	3496347	4208920	137536
CNK/SLES 9	4	0.8	1184521	1420492	417792
Bullx Linux	4	0.8	1103827	1330204	50960
RHEL 6.2	4	0.8	1738900	2132582	102528
Redhat Enterprise Linux 6	4	0.8	2571639	3388905	321976
bullx SUperCOmputer Suite A.E.2.1	3	0.6	2942070	3583180	165888
Redhat Linux	2	0.4	327834	424760	26636
SLES10 + SGI ProPack 5	2	0.4	398000	439910	38400
Super-UX	1	0.2	122400	131072	1280
Windows Azure	1	0.2	151300	167731	8064
CNL	1	0.2	165600	201216	20960
Windows HPC 2008	1	0.2	180600	233472	30720
Scientific Linux	1	0.2	188725	199680	9600
RHEL 6.1	1	0.2	230600	340915	37056
SUSE Linux	1	0.2	274800	308283	26304
Kylin Linux	1	0.2	33862700	54902400	3,120,0

puters around the world as of November 2013. As of this date Infiniband was the interconnect family used in 41.4 percent of the leading supercomputers.

Figure 8 shows the number of computer cores in the 10 fastest supercomputers in the world (current to November 2009).

1. The "Jaguar" (XT5 HC, Six Core Opteron 2.6 GHz) from Cray is in the Oak Ridge National Laboratory.
2. "Nebulae" (TC3600 Blade, Intel X5650, NVIDIA Tesla C2050 GPU) from Dawning in in the National Supercomputing Centre Shenzhen.

Table 6. Processor generation for the Top 500 supercomputers in the world as of November 2013 (Source: http://www.top500.org/statistics/list/#.U30G4SjRhCh)

Processor Generation	Count	System Share (%)	Rmax (GFlops)	Rpeak (GFlops)	Cores
Intel Xeon E5 (SandyBridge)	307	61.4	87,073,127	136,737,345	6,730,764
Xeon 5600-series (Westmere-EP)	55	11	16,727,544	30,902,871	1,565,654
Intel Xeon E5 (IvyBridge)	34	6.8	45,699,316	70,380,755	3,764,390
Power BQC	24	4.8	46,402,484	54,316,237	4,243,456
Opteron 6100-series "Magny-Cours"	17	3.4	5,295,469	7,163,629	773,640
Opteron 6200 Series "Interlagos"	16	3.2	23,462,905	35,054,646	1,303,280
POWER7	12	2.4	5,011,347	6,153,312	200,896
Xeon 5500-series (Nehalem-EP)	10	2	2,507,531	3,278,734	228,788
Opteron 4100-series "Lisbon"	5	1	691,960	1,057,795	125,928
Xeon 5400-series "Harpertown"	4	0.8	687,264	939,327	81,673
PowerPC 450	4	0.8	1,184,521	1,420,492	417,792
Opteron Quad Core	3	0.6	477,800	596,888	69,904
SPARC64 IXfx	2	0.4	1,209,700	1,317,077	89,088
Opterons 6300 Series ("Abu Dhabi")	1	0.2	119,300	157,286	16,384
NEC	1	0.2	122,400	131,072	1,280
Xeon 5300-series "Clovertown"	1	0.2	132,800	172,608	14,384
ShenWei	1	0.2	795,900	1,070,160	137,200
Opteron Six Core	1	0.2	919,100	1,173,000	112,800
Xeon 5500-series (Nehalem-EX)	1	0.2	1,050,000	1,254,550	138,368
SPARC64 VIIIfx	1	0.2	10,510,000	11,280,384	705,024

Table 7. Operating system family for the Top 500 supercomputers in the world as of November 2013 (Source: http://www.top500.org/statistics/list/#.U30G4SjRhCh)

Operating System Family	Count	System Share (%)	Rmax (GFlops)	Rpeak (GFlops)	Cores
Linux	482	96.4	244,945,300	358,396,482	20,125,301
Unix	11	2.2	3,496,347	4,208,920	137,536
Mixed	4	0.8	1,184,521	1,420,492	417,792
Windows	2	0.4	331,900	401,203	38,784
BSD Based	1	0.2	122400	131072	1280

Figure 5. Distribution of the 500 most powerful supercomputers worldwide as of November 2013, by operating system family (Source: http://www.statista.com/statistics/249270/distribution-of-leading-supercomputers-worldwide-by-operating-system-family/)

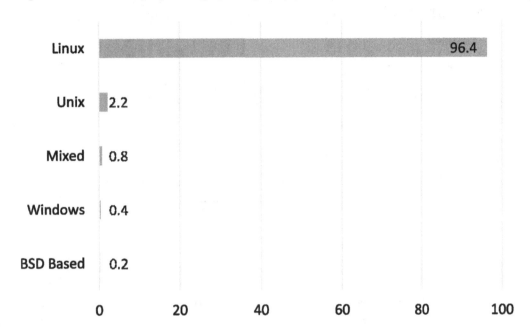

Table 8. Application areas for top 500 supercomputers in the world as of November 2013 (Source: http://www.top500.org/statistics/list/#.U30G4SjRhCh)

Application Area	Count	System Share (%)	Rmax (GFlops)	Rpeak (GFlops)	Cores
Not Specified	410	82	197,710,899	297,627,905	16,061,176
Research	56	11.2	38,576,766	49,804,226	3,589,245
Weather and Climate	9	1.8	3,682,699	4,428,772	295,844
Energy	6	1.2	2,299,298	2,803,536	182,108
Defense	5	1	1,873,434	2,246,243	217,248
Benchmarking	5	1	2,092,440	2,624,667	103,632
Environment	3	0.6	746,307	885,441	43,984
Aerospace	2	0.4	1,785,190	2,403,110	120,384
Web Services	1	0.2	240,090	354,099	17,024
Semiconductor	1	0.2	758,873	933,481	51,392
Software	1	0.2	188,967	209,715	16,384
Finance	1	0.2	125,503	236,974	22,272

Figure 6. Distribution of the 500 most powerful supercomputers as of November 2013, by segment. (Source: http://www.statista.com/statistics/264449/distribution-of-supercomputers-worldwide-by-segment)

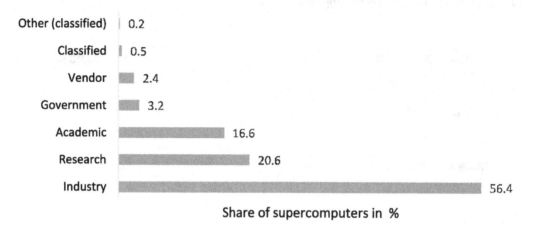

Figure 7. System share of interconnect families used in the most powerful 500 supercomputers worldwide as of November 2013. (Source: http://www.statista.com/statistics/264446/distribution-of-interconnect-families-used-in-supercomputers/)

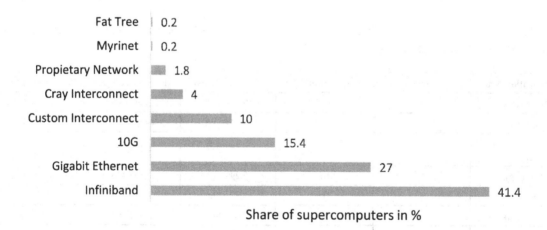

3. The "Roadrunner" (BladeCenter - QS22/ LS21 cluster PowerXCell 8i 3.2 Ghz / Opteron DC 1.8 GHz) from IBM is in the Los Alamos National Laboratory (LANL) in New Mexico.

4. The "Kraken" (Cray XT5 HC, Six Core Xeon 2.36 GHz) from Cray is in the National Institute for Computational Sciences (NICS) at University of Tennessee.

5. "Jugene" (Blue Gene / P Solution) from IBM is at the Research Center Juelich (FZJ).

6. The "Pleiade" (Altix ICE 8200EX/8400EX, Xeon QC HT 3.0/Xeon Westmere 2.93 GHz, Infiniband) from SGI is stored at the National

Figure 8. Number of computer cores in the 10 fastest supercomputers in the world (current to November 2009) (Source: http://www.statista.com/statistics/268280/number-of-computer-cores-in-selected-supercomputers-worldwide/)

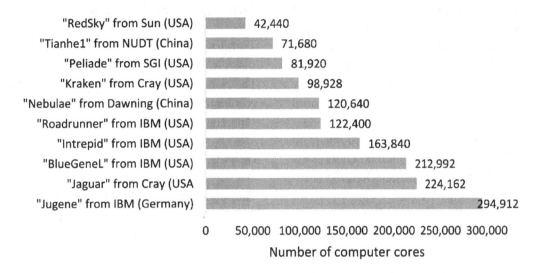

Figure 9. Share of the 500 most powerful supercomputers worldwide as of November 2013, by vendor. (Source: http://www.statista.com/statistics/249268/share-of-leading-supercomputers-worldwide-by-vendor/)

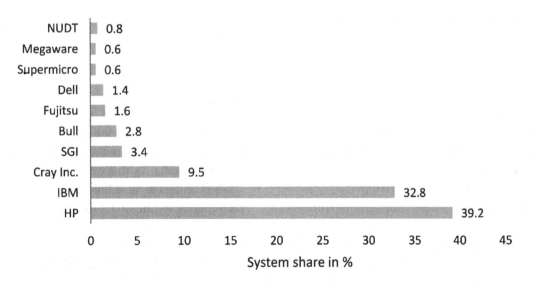

Aeronautic and Space Administration (NASA)/Ames Research Center.

7. The supercomputer from NUDT "Tianhe1" (TH-1-Cluster, Xeon E5540 / E 5450 ATI Radeon HD 4870 2, Infiniband is) is in the National Supercomputer Center in Tianjin.

8. IBM's "BlueGene/L" (eServer Blue Gene Solution) is in the U.S. Department of Energy (DOE) Lawrence Livermore National Laboratory (LLNL).

9. The "Intrepid" Blue (Gene / P Solution) from IBM is in the Argonne National Laboratory.

10. Sun's "RedSky" (SunBlade X6275) is located in Sandia / NRLE.

Figure 9 shows share of the 500 most powerful supercomputers worldwide as of November 2013, by vendor. Figure 9 shows a breakdown of the 500 most powerful supercomputers around the world as of November 2013, by vendor (top 10 vendors only). As of that time IBM had a system share of 32.8 percent of the top 500 supercomputers worldwide.

SUPERCOMPUTING IN CHINA

China has a large number of supercomputing centers which have held world records in speed. The origins of these centers go back to 1989 when the State Planning Commission, the State Science and Technology Commission and the World Bank jointly launched a project to develop networking and supercomputer facilities in China (Supercomputing in China, 2014).

The progress of supercomputing in China is fluctuating. It was placed 51st in June 2003, then 14th in November 2003, 10th in June 2004, 5th during 2005. By mid-2010, it had reached the second spot and at the end of 2010 the top spot (Supercomputing in China, 2014). To avoid future technology embargo restrictions, the Chinese are developing their own processors like Loongson,

a MIPS type processor, etc (Supercomputing in China, 2014).

Supercomputing Centers in China

Tianjin

The National Supercomputing Center in Tianjin is one of the main centers. It houses the Tianhe-1 supercomputer.

Beijing

The Supercomputing Center of the China Academy of Sciences provides academic support functions to the national centers.

Shenzhen

The National Supercomputing Center in Shenzhen houses the second fastest machine in China and the third fastest in the world.

Shanghai

The Shanghai Supercomputer Center operates the Magic Cube supercomputer that runs at 230 teraflops.

Guangzhou

The National Supercomputing Center in Guangzhou operates the top ranked supercomputer in the world Tianhe-2 (MilkyWay-2).

Other centers include Jinan, Hunan, Changsha, etc (Supercomputing in China, 2014).

SUPERCOMPUTING IN EUROPE

Several supercomputing centers are present in Europe and the access to them is coordinated by European initiatives to facilitate high-performance computing. In June 2011, France's Tera 100 was certified the fastest supercomputer in Europe and ranked 9th in the world at that time (Supercomputing in Europe, 2014).

Supercomputing Centers in Europe

Belgium

In 2012, Ghent University in Belgium inaugurated the first Tier 1 supercomputer of the Flemish Supercomputer Center (VSC). The new cluster is ranked 163rd in the world's Top 500 list of supercomputers according to November 2012 (Supercomputing in Europe, 2014).

Bulgaria

The National Center for Supercomputing Applications in Sofia operates an IBM Blue Gene/P supercomputer. The system ranked as 379 in the Top500 list in November 2009 (Supercomputing in Europe, 2014).

Finland

CSC-IT Center for Science is operating a Cray XC30 system with 244 TFlop/s which is to be scaled up to PFlop/s range in 2014 (Supercomputing in Europe, 2014).

France

The CEA operates the Tera 100 machine in the Research and Technology Computing Center in Essonne, France. The Tera 100 has a peak processing speed of 1050 teraflops making it the fastest supercomputer in Europe as of 2011 (Supercomputing in Europe, 2014).

Germany

The three national centers at Garching (LRZ), Juelich (JSC) and Stuttgart (HLRS) together form the Gauss Center for Supercomputing. The Julich Supercomputing Center and the Gauss Center for Supercomputing jointly own the JUGENE computer. JUGENE is based on IBM's BlueGene/P architecture and in June 2011 was ranked the 12th fastest computer in the world by TOP500 (Supercomputing in Europe, 2014).

The Leibniz-Rechenzentrum, a supercomputing center in Munich, houses the SuperMUC system which began operations in 2012 at a processing speed of 3 petaflops. The High Performance Computing Center in Stuttgart fastest computing system is HERMIT with a peak performance of more than 1 petaflops. HERMIT was ranked 12th in the November 2011 TOP500 list (Supercomputing in Europe, 2014).

Italy

The main supercomputing facility is CINECA, a consortium of many universities and research institutions scattered throughout the country. A supercomputer FERMI based on IBM's BlueGene/Q architecture was commissioned in Spring 2012. FERMI is the fastest supercomputer in Italy with a peak performance of 2.1 PFLOPS. Italy also hosts some of the largest nodes of the worldwide LHC Computing Grid (Supercomputing in Europe, 2014).

Netherlands

The European Grid Infrastructure, a distributed computing system is headquartered at the Science Park in Amsterdam (Supercomputing in Europe, 2014).

Norway

The Norwegian University of Science and Technology in Trondheim operates the Vilje supercomputer owned by NTNU and the Norwegian Meteorological Institute (Supercomputing in Europe, 2014).

Poland

The Polish Grid Infrastructure PL-Grid was built between 2009 and 2011 as a nationwide computing infrastructure. The Galera computer cluster at the Gdansk University of Technology was ranked 299th on the TOP500 list in November 2010. The Zeus Computer cluster at the ACK Cyfronet AGH in Krakow was ranked 106th on the TOP500 list in November 2012 (Supercomputing in Europe, 2014).

Russia

In November 2011, the 33,072-processor Lomonosov supercomputer in Moscow was ranked the 18th fastest supercomputer in the world and the third fastest in Europe. In September 2011, T-Platforms stated that it would deliver a water-cooled supercomputer in 2013 (Supercomputing in Europe, 2014).

Slovenia

The Slovenian National Grid Initiative (NGI) provides resources to the European Grid Initiative (EGI). ARNES manages a cluster for testing computing technology where users can also submit jobs. The cluster consists of 2300 cores. Arctur also provides computer resources on its Arctur-1 supercomputer to the Slovenian NGI (Supercomputing in Europe, 2014).

Spain

The Barcelona Supercomputing Center operates the 1 petaflop MareNostrum supercomputer. The Supercomputing and Visualization Center of Madrid at the Technical University of Madrid operates the 72-teraflop Magerit supercomputer. The Spanish Supercomputing Network furthermore provides access to several supercomputers distributed across Spain (Supercomputing in Europe, 2014).

Sweden

The National Supercomputer Center in Sweden operates the Triolith supercomputer which achieved 407.2 Teraflop/s on the Linpack benchmark which was ranked 79 on the November 2013 issue of Top 500 list of the fastest supercomputers in the world (Supercomputing in Europe, 2014).

Switzerland

The Swiss National Supercomputing Centre was founded in 1991 and operated by ETH Zurich. The IBM Aquasar supercomputer became operational at ETH Zurich in 2010. It uses hot water cooling to achieve heat efficiency (Supercomputing in Europe, 2014).

United Kingdom

The EPCC Supercomputer center was established at the University of Edinburgh in 1990. The HECToR project at the University of Edinburgh provides supercomputing facilities using a 360-teraflop Cray XE6 system, the fastest supercomputer in the UK (Supercomputing in Europe, 2014).

SUPERCOMPUTING IN INDIA

India's supercomputer program was started in late 1980s because Cray supercomputers were denied for import due to an arms embargo imposed on India. PARAM 8000 is considered India's first supercomputer. It was built in 1990 by Centre for Development of Advanced Computing (CDAC) and was replicated and installed at ICAD Moscow in 1991 under Russian collaboration (Supercomputing in India, 2014).

As of November 2013, India has 12 systems on the Top500 list ranking 44, 84, 100, 107, 131, 226, 316, 367, 390, 427, 428, 429 (Supercomputing in India, 2014).

Table 9. List of Supercomputers in India and their locations (Source: Supercomputing in India, 2014)

Rank	Site	Name	Rmax (TFlop/s)	Rpeak (TFlop/s)
44	Indian Institute of Tropical Meteorology	iDataPlex DX360M4	719.2	790.7
84	Centre for Development of Advanced Computing	PARAM Yuva - II	388.4	520.4
100	CSIR Centre for Mathematical Modelling and Computer Simulation	Cluster Platform 3000 BL460c Gen8	334.3	362.0
107	National Centre for Medium Range Weather Forecasting	iDataPlex DX360M4	318.4	350.1
131	Indian Institute of Technology Kanpur	Cluster Platform SL230s Gen8	282.6	307.2
226	Vikram Sarabhai Space Centre, ISRO	SAGA - Z24XX/SL390s Cluster	188.7	394.8
316	Manufacturing Company India	Cluster Platform 3000 BL460c Gen8	149.2	175.7
367	IT Services Provider (B)	Cluster Platform 3000 BL460c Gen8	139.2	195.3
291	Computational Research Laboratories	EKA - Cluster Platform 3000 BL460c	132.8	172.6
427	Semiconductor Company (F)	Cluster Platform 3000 BL460c Gen8	129.2	182.0
428	Semiconductor Company (F)	Cluster Platform 3000 BL460c Gen8	129.2	182.0
429	Network Company	Cluster Platform 3000 BL460c Gen8	128.8	179.7

Table 10. Comparison of the supercomputers between different countries as of November 2013 (Source: Supercomputing in India, 2014).

Country	Total Rmax (Gflops)	Number of Computers in TOP500	System Share (%)
India	3,040,297	12	2.4
China	48,549,093	63	12.6
France	9,489,912	22	4.4
Germany	13,696,834	20	4
Japan	22,472,218	28	5.6
Russia	1,846,613	5	1
Poland	455,909	2	0.4
South Korea	1,258,060	5	1
UK	9,058,329	23	4.6
USA	118,261,596	264	52.8
Canada	2,077,842	10	2
Italy	2,665,609	5	1
Australia	2,180,151	5	1

Supercomputing Centers in India

Prithvi

Indian Institute of Tropical Meteorology, Pune, has a machine with a peak of 790.7 teraflop/s, called Prithvi that is used for climate research and forecasting. It is ranked 36th among the world's top 500 supercomputers as of June 2013 list (Supercomputing in India, 2014).

PARAM Yuva II

Unveiled on February 8, 2013, this supercomputer was made by Centre for Development of Advanced Computing in a period of three months at a cost of 3 million US dollars. It performs at a peak of 524 teraflop/s. The supercomputer can deliver sustained performance of 360.8 teraflop/s on Linpack benchmark. In terms of power efficiency, it would have been ranked 33rd in the November 2012 list of Top Green 500 Supercomputers of world (Supercomputing in India, 2014).

Param Yuva II will be used for research in space, bioinformatics, weather forecasting, pharmaceutical development, etc. Educational institutes like Indian Institutes of Technology and National Institutes of Technology can be linked to the computer through the national knowledge network (Supercomputing in India, 2014).

SAGA-220

SAGA-220 built by ISRO, is capable of performing at 220,000 gigaflop/s. It uses about 400 NVIDIA Tesla 2070 GPUs and 400 Intel Quad Core Xeon CPUs (Supercomputing in India, 2014).

EKA

EKA is a supercomputer built by the Computational Research Laboratories with technical assistance and hardware provided by Hewlett-Packard

(HP). It is capable of performing at 132 teraflop/s (Supercomputing in India, 2014).

Virgo

IIT, Madras has a 91.1 teraflop/s machine virgo. It is ranked as 364 in the top 500 November 2012 list. It has 292 computer nodes, 2 master nodes, 4 storage nodes and has total computing power of 97 TFlops. According to Linpack performance, Virgo is the fastest cluster in an institution in India. As of 2012, Virgo is at 224th position in the world, 5th ranked energy efficient machine in the world and 1st ranked energy efficient machine in India (Supercomputing in India, 2014).

PARAM Yuva

It belongs to the PARAM series of supercomputer developed by the Centre for Development of Advanced Computing. It is capable of performing at about 54 teraflop/s (Supercomputing in India, 2014).

SUPERCOMPUTING IN JAPAN

Japan operates a number of supercomputing centers which holds world records in speed. The K Computer is the world's fastest as of June 2011 (Supercomputing in Japan, 2014).

Supercomputing Centers in Japan

The GSIC Center at the Tokyo Institute of Technology houses the Tsubame 2.0 supercomputer which has a peak of 2,288 Tflops and in June 2011, ranked fifth in the world (Supercomputing in Japan, 2014).

The RIKEN MDGRAPE-3 for molecular dynamics simulations of proteins is a special purpose petascale supercomputer at the Advanced Center for Computing and Communication (Supercomputing in Japan, 2014).

The next system is Japan Atomic Energy Agency's PRIMERGY BX900 Fujitsu supercomputer. It is ranked as the 38th in the world in 2011 (Supercomputing in Japan, 2014).

DENIGMA is a highly cost and energy efficient computer cluster at the Nagasaki Advanced Computing Center, Nagasaki University. It is used for hierarchical N-body simulations and has a peak performance of 111 TFLOPS with an energy efficiency of 1376 MFLOPS/watt (Supercomputing in Japan, 2014).

The Computational Simulation Center, Japan Atomic Energy Agency operates a 1.52 PFLOPS supercomputer in Aomori. The system called as Helios is used for fusion simulation projects (Supercomputing in Japan, 2014).

The University of Tokyo's Information Technology Center in Kashiwa, Chiba began operations of a 1.13 –PFLOPS supercomputer system in April 2012 (Supercomputing in Japan, 2014).

In June 2012, the Numerical Prediction Division, Forecast department of the Japan Meteorological Agency deployed an 847-TFLOPS Hitachi SR16000/M1 supercomputer based on IBM Power 775 in Tokyo (Supercomputing in Japan, 2014).

SUPERCOMPUTING IN PAKISTAN

The fastest supercomputer currently in use in Pakistan is developed and hosted by the National University of Sciences and Technology at its modeling and simulation research centre (Supercomputing in Pakistan, 2014). As of November 2012, there are no supercomputers from Pakistan on the Top500 list (Supercomputing in Pakistan, 2014).

Supercomputing Programs in Pakistan

GIK Institute

HPC platform has been established by Dr. Masroor Hussain, FCSE, GIK Institute. It consists of Dell R815 with 64 CPU cores, 256 GB RAM, 1.8 TB Secondary memory. 3 compute nodes are present, Dell Power Connect 8024F layer-3 manageable switch (Supercomputing in Pakistan, 2014). The software consists of Rocks Cluster 6.1 (Emerald Boa) over CentOS has been installed and configured (Supercomputing in Pakistan, 2014).

COMSATS

The COMSATS Institute of Information Technology built a cluster based supercomputer for research purposes in 2004(Supercomputing in Pakistan, 2014). The project was funded by the Higher Education Commission of Pakistan. The Linux-based computing cluster which was tested and configured for optimization achieved a performance of 158 GFLOPS per second (Supercomputing in Pakistan, 2014).

NUST

The National University of Sciences and Technology (NUST) in Islamabad has developed the fastest supercomputing facility in Pakistan till date. The supercomputer has parallel computational abilities and has a performance of 132 teraflops per second making it the fastest GPU parallel computing system in Pakistan (Supercomputing in Pakistan, 2014). The cluster consists of a 66 NODE supercomputer with 30, 992 processor cores, 2 head nodes, 32 dual quad core computer nodes and 32 Nvidia computing processors. Each processor has 960 processor cores, QDR InfiniBand interconnection and 21.6 TB SAN storage (Supercomputing in Pakistan, 2014).

University of Lahore

Installing supercomputer in 2015 (Supercomputing in Pakistan, 2014).

KUST

The cluster is deployed at Kohat University of Science and Technology. Cluster name is KUST-Kohat, number of CPUs are 104, peak performance of 416 GFLOPS (Supercomputing in Pakistan, 2014).

CONCLUSION

This chapter provides an overview of global super-computing and also as an introduction to the entire book of edited chapters. The subsequent chapters of this book include further discussion of Seymore Cray the father of supercomputing, and the history of supercomputing from past to present to year 2050, and a history of supercomputing and super-computer centers. The subsequent chapters include detailed studies of applications of supercomputing to nuclear power, nano-materials, steganography, cloud computing, leadership, sequence analysis and genome annotation, population genetics, programming paradigms, modeling of biological systems, renewable energy network design and optimization, data mining, philosophical logic perspective, a philosophy of their language, and current challenges across multiple domains of computational science.

The reader is referred to the Appendix of this book for more information about each of the top 500 supercomputers in the world as of November 2013 that was gratefully provided to us by written permission from Top500.com for educational purposes.

REFERENCES

Argonne National Laboratory. (2014). *Mira: An engine for discovery*. Retrieved from http://www.alcf.anl.gov/mira

Barth, B. (2013). *High performance computing (HPC) systems*. Retrieved from https://www.tacc.utexas.edu/resources/hpc

Biswas, R., & Thigpen, W. (2014). *High-end computing capability*. Retrieved from http://www.nas.nasa.gov/hecc/resources/pleiades.html

Cook, J. S. (2011). Supercomputers and super-computing. In Q. Zhang, R. S. Segall, & M. Cao (Eds.), *Visual analytics and interactive technologies* (pp. 282–294). IGI Global. doi:10.4018/978-1-60960-102-7.ch017

Forbus, K. (n.d.). *Symbolic supercomputer for artificial intelligence and cognitive science research*. Retrieved from http://www.qrg.northwestern.edu/projects/SymbolicSupercomputing/symb-supercomp_index.html

Gardner, J. (2014). *Introduction to high performance computing (HPC) and the NSF TeraGrid*. Retrieved from http://oldwww.phys.washington.edu/users/gardnerj/tching/IntroToTeraGrid.pdf

Hager, G., & Wellein, G. (2011). Introduction to high performance computing for scientists and engineers. Boca Raton, FL: Academic Press.

Human Brain Project. (2012). Retrieved May 25, 2104 from www.humanbrainproject.eu

Human Brain Project-Video Overview. (n.d.). Retrieved May 25, 2014 from YouTube at: http://www.youtube.com/watch?v=JqMpGrM5ECo

Kondo, J. (Ed.). (1991). *Supercomputing applications, algorithms, and architectures for the future of supercomputing*. Springer-Verlag Tokyo.

Kramer, B., Beldica, C., Gropp, B., & Hwu, W. (2014). *Blue waters sustained petascale computing*. Retrieved May 21, 2014, Retrieved from https://bluewaters.ncsa.illinois.edu/team

Leibniz Supercomputing Centre. (2014). *Leibniz supercomputing centre of the Bavarian academy of sciences and humanities*. Retrieved from http://www.lrz.de/services/compute/supermuc/system-description/

Levesque, J., & Wagenbreth, G. (2011). *High performance computing: Programming and applications*. Chapman & Hall/CRC.

Lu, Y. (2014). *Overview of tianhe-2 (Milky Way-2) supercomputer*. Retrieved from http://www.slideshare.net/ultrafilter/th2-isc13inspurlyt

Lucifredi, F. (2013). *Supercomputing on the cheap with parallella*. Retrieved from http://programming.oreilly.com/2013/12/supercomputing-on-the-cheap-with-parallella.html

Miranker, G. S. (1992). *Titan III supercomputer architectural overview*. Retrieved from http://link.springer.com/article/10.1007%2FBF02241705

Miyazaki, H., Kusano, Y., Shinjou, N., Shoji, F., Yokokawa, M., & Watanabe, T. (2012). *Overview of the K computer system*. Retrieved from http://www.fujitsu.com/downloads/MAG/vol48-3/paper02.pdf

PTI. (2012, September 17). India plans 61 times faster supercomputer by 2017. *The Times of India*. Retrieved May 25, 2104 from http://articles.timesofindia.indiatimes.com/2012-09-17/hardware/33901529_1_first-supercomputers-petaflop-fastest-supercomputer

Segall, R. S. (2013a). Dimensionalities of computation: From global supercomputing to data, text and web mining. *Invited Plenary Address at International Institute of Informatics and Systemics (IIIS) Conference, 17th World Multi-conference on Systemics, Cybernetics and Informatics (WMSCI 2013)*. Retrieved from http://www.iiis.org/ViewVideo2013.asp?id=14

Segall, R. S. (2013b). Computational dimensionalities of global supercomputing. *Journal of Systemics, Cybernetics, and Informatics, 11*(9), 75–86.

Segall, R. S., & Cook, J. (2014). Data visualization and information quality by supercomputing. In *Proceedings of the Forty-Fifth Meeting of Southwest Decision Sciences Institute (SWDSI)*. Dallas, TX: Academic Press.

Segall, R. S., & Zhang, Q. (2013). Information quality and supercomputing. In *Proceedings of the 18th International Conference on Information Quality (ICIQ 2013)* (pp. 400-446). Academic Press.

Segall, R. S., Zhang, Q., & Cook, J. S. (2013). Overview of current research in global supercomputing. In *Proceedings of Forty-Fourth Meeting of Southwest Decision Sciences Institute (SWDSI)*. Albuquerque, NM: Academic Press.

Segall, R. S., Zhang, Q., & Pierce, R. (2010a). Data mining supercomputing with SAS JMP® genomics. In *Proceedings of 14th World Multi-Conference on Systemics, Cybernetics and Informatics: WMSCI 2010*. Orlando, FL: Academic Press.

Segall, R. S., Zhang, Q., & Pierce, R. (2011). Data mining supercomputing with SAS JMP® genomics. *Journal of Systemics, Cybernetics and Informatics, 9*(1), 28–33.

Segall, R. S., Zhang, Q., & Pierce, R. M. (2009). Visualization by supercomputing data mining. In *Proceedings of the 4th INFORMS Workshop on Data Mining and System Informatics*. San Diego, CA: Academic Press.

Segall, R. S., Zhang, Q., & Pierce, R. M. (2010b). Data mining supercomputing with SAS JMP® genomics: Research-in-Progress. In *Proceedings of 2010 Conference on Applied Research in Information Technology*. University of Central Arkansas.

Supercomputing in China. (2014). Retrieved from http://en.wikipedia.org/wiki/Supercomputing_in_China

Supercomputing in Europe. (2014). Retrieved from http://en.wikipedia.org/wiki/Supercomputing_in_Europe

Supercomputing in India. (2014). Retrieved from http://en.wikipedia.org/wiki/Supercomputing_in_India

Supercomputing in Japan. (2014). Retrieved from http://en.wikipedia.org/wiki/Supercomputing_in_Japan

Supercomputing in Pakistan. (2014). Retrieved from http://en.wikipedia.org/wiki/Supercomputing_in_Pakistan

Swiss National Supercomputing Centre. (2014). *Piz daint.* Retrieved from http://www.cscs.ch/computers/piz_daint/index.html

Szczepariski, A. F., Huang, J., Baer, T., Mack, Y. C., & Ahern, S. (2013). Data analysis and visualization in high-performance computing. *Computer*, *46*(May), 84–92. doi:10.1109/MC.2012.192

Top500. (2013). *Supercomputer sites.* Retrieved May 25, 2104 from http://www.top500.org/lists/2103/11

Total, S. A. (2013). *Total inaugurates its new pangea supercomputer, ranking it among the global top ten in terms of computing power.* Retrieved May 22, 2014 from http://total.com/en/media/news/press-releases/20130321-Total-inaugurates-its-new-Pangea-supercomputer-ranking-it-among-the-global-top-ten-in-terms-of-computing-power

van der Steen, A. J. (2005). *Overview of recent supercomputers.* Retrieved from http://citeseerx.ist.psu.edu/viewdoc/download?doi=10.1.1.63.3326&rep=rep1&type=pdf

Vetter, J. S. (2013). Contemporary high performance computing: From petascale toward exascale. Chapman & Hall/CRC Computational Science.

Wagstaff, K. (2012). What exactly is a supercomputer? *Time*, *19*(June). Retrieved from http://techland.time.com/2012/06/19/what-exactly-is-a-supercomputer/

Whittaker, Z. (2012). *U.S. IBM supercomputer is world's fastest: Does it matter?* Retrieved from http://www.zdnet.com/blog/btl/u-s-ibm-supercomputer-is-worlds-fastest-does-it-matter/80122

Wikipedia. (2014a). *Cray.* Retrieved May 25, 2014 from http://en.wikipedia.org/wiki/Cray

Wikipedia. (2014b). *Flynn's taxonomy.* Retrieved May 25, 2014 from http://en.wikipedia.org/wiki/Flynn%27s_taxonomy

Wikipedia. (2014c). *Human Brian project.* Retrieved May 25, 2014 from http//en.wikipedia.org/wiki/Human_Brian_Project

Wikipedia. (2014d). *Jungle computing.* Retrieved May 25, 2014 from http://en.wikipedia.org/wiki/Jungle_computing

Wikipedia. (2014e). *Multiprocessing.* Retrieved May 25, 2104 from http://en.wikipedia.org/wiki/Multiprocessing

Wikipedia. (2014f). *Supercompter.* Retrieved 5/25, 2014 from http://en.wikipedia.org/wiki/Supercomputer

Wikipedia. (2014g). *Tianhe-2, or Milky Way-2.* Retrieved May 25, 2014 from http://en.wikipedia.org/wiki/Tianhe-2

Wikipedia. (2014h). *Top500.* Retrieved 5/25, 2014 from http://en.wikipedia.org/wiki/Top500

Wikipedia. (2014i). *Vector processing.* Retrieved May 25, 2014 from http://en.wikipedia.org/wiki/Vector_processing

ADDITIONAL READING

x58 supercomputer. (2014). Retrieved May 28, 2014 from http://www.asrock.com/mb/Intel/X58%20SuperComputer/

Adiga, N. R., Almasi, G., & Aridor, Y. (2002). An overview of the BlueGene/L supercomputer *Supercomputing, ACM/IEEE 2002 Conference,* Retrieved May 25, 2104 from http://ieeexplore.ieee.org/xpl/login.jsp?tp=&arnumber=1592896&url=http%3A%2F%2Fieeexplore.ieee.org%2Fxpls%2Fabs_all.jsp%3Farnumber%3D1592896. doi:10.1109/SC.2002.10017

Alspector, J., Brenner, A., Leheny, R., & Richmann, J. (2014). China - A new power in supercomputing hardware. Retrieved May 28, 2014 from https://www.ida.org/~/media/Corporate/Files/Publications/IDA_Documents/ITSD/ida-document-ns-d-4857.ashx

Anderson, N., Moody, J., & Lampf, G. (2012). Ciena brings 100G and packet networking innovations to supercomputing 2012. Retrieved May 27, 2014 from http://www.ciena.com/about/newsroom/press-releases/Ciena-Brings-100G-and-Packet-Networking-Innovations-to-Supercomputing-2012.html

Brocade Communication Systems (2013). *Supercomputing 2013 brocade overview*, part I. (Director). (06 December 2013).[Video/DVD]

Brueckner, R. (2011). Video: An overview of CINECA - Italy's largest supercomputer center. Retrieved May 27, 2014, Retrieved fromhttp://insidehpc.com/2011/06/30/video-an-overview-of-cineca-italys-largest-supercomputer-center/

Centre for Development of Advanced Computing. (2014). Architecture overview. Retrieved May 28, 2014 from http://pune.cdac.in/html/npsf/anant/anant1.aspx

Chi, X. (2011). Supercomputing applications in CAS. Retrieved May 28, 2014 from http://www.prace-project.eu/IMG/pdf/chi.pdf

CISL. A computing laboratory. (2014). Retrieved May 27, 2014 from https://www2.cisl.ucar.edu/cisl-computing

Cluster computing overview (n.d.). Retrieved May 28, 2014 from https://www.google.co.in/url?sa=t&rct=j&q=&esrc=s&source=web&cd=72&cad=rja&uact=8&ved=0CDIQFjABOEY&url=http%3A%2F%2Fwww.calstatela.edu%2Ffaculty%2Frpamula%2Fcs370%2Foverview.ppt&ei=cDuFUvzIM_g8AXX3IEQ&usg=AFQjCNE0FzQHKRmhsyPb_LVJSkMsH2GlnQ&sig2=a4qZjekc4AbRmd13lTLXLw&bvm=bv.67720277,d.dGc

Cooling supercomputers using geothermal energy. (2014). Retrieved May 28, 2014 from http://www.csiro.au/Outcomes/Energy/Renewables-and-Smart-Systems/pawsey-geothermal-supercomputing-project.aspx

Defanti, T. (1994). Overview of the I-WAY: Wide area visual supercomputing. Retrieved May 27, 2014 from http://toolkit.globus.org/alliance/publications/papers/iway_overview.pdf

Edelman, A. (2007). The inside story behind interactive supercomputing's star-P platform for high performance computing for MATLAB. Retrieved May 28, 2014 from http://www.cs.berkeley.edu/~yelick/cs267_sp07/lectures/lecture06/lecture06_starp_edelman07.pdf

Ellsworth, M., Goth, G., Zoodsma, R., Arvelo, A., Campbell, L., & Anderl, W. (2012). An overview of the IBM power 775 supercomputer water cooling system. Retrieved May 27, 2014 from http://electronicpackaging.asmedigitalcollection.asme.org/article.aspx?articleid=1410200

Elstner, D. (2014). Supercomputing and E-science, Leibniz-Institut fur Astrophysik Potsdam. Retrieved May 28, 2014 from http://www.aip.de/en/research/research-area-drt/research-groups-and-projects-1/e-science/supercomputing-and-e-science

Feng, W., Feng, X., & Ge, R. (2008). Green supercomputing comes of age. Retrieved May 28, 2014 from http://www.computer.org/csdl/mags/it/2008/01/mit2008010017-abs.html

George, A. (2011). Novo-G: At the forefront of scalable reconfigurable supercomputing. Retrieved May 28, 2014 from http://www.gidel.com/pdf/Novo_G_At_Forefront.pdf

Hurley, J. (2014). CAS-supercomputing-green II, Swinburne University of Technology, Hawthorn, Victoria, Australia. Retrieved May 27, 2014 from http://astronomy.swin.edu.au/supercomputing/green2/

InfoWebLinks – supercomputer (n.d.). Retrieved May 28, 2014 from http://www.infoweblinks.com/content/supercomputers.htm

Intel supercomputing systems division (n.d.). Retrieved May 28, 2014 from http://www.new-npac.org/projects/cdroms/cewes-1999-06-vol1/nhse/hpccsurvey/orgs/intel/intel.html

Introducing titan - advancing the era of accelerated computing. (2012). Retrieved May 27, 2014, from https://www.olcf.ornl.gov/titan/

Lixing, Z. (2009). Supercomputers. Retrieved May 27, 2014 from https://www.google.co.in/url?sa=t&rct=j&q=&esrc=s&source=web&cd=4&cad=rja&uact=8&ved=0CEsQFjAD&url=http%3A%2F%2Fwww.eng.auburn.edu%2F~agrawvd%2FCOURSE%2FE6200_Fall09%2FCLASS_TALKS%2Fsupercomputer.docx&ei=0n6EU6juLsj98QW8ooFg&usg=AFQjCNFX0izRSYgXNGTCM0yEyerjFFdFYg&sig2=uPSOII1gRobzPkkJkIZFA

Mattson, T., & Henry, G. (1998). An overview of the Intel TFLOPS supercomputer. Retrieved May 27, 2014 from http://www.ai.mit.edu/projects/aries/course/notes/ascii_red.pdf

Moscow University supercomputing center (2014). Supercomputing applications. Retrieved May 27, 2014 from http://hpc.msu.ru/?q=node/77

Neeman, H. (2013). Supercomputing in plain English, University of Oklahoma Supercomputing Center for Education & Research, Norman, OK. Retrieved May 27, 2014 from https://www.google.co.in/url?sa=t&rct=j&q=&esrc=s&source=web&cd=8&cad=rja&uact=8&ved=0CGoQFjAH&url=http%3A%2F%2Fwww.oscer.ou.edu%2FWorkshops%2FOverview%2FSiPE_Overview.ppt&ei=0n6EU6juLsj98QW8ooFg&usg=AFQjCNGBGjqFlvc4khw_2ZCdMq5igMCgDA&sig2=zmQ4oqK9PcFx6cCl9ncO2g

New Zealand supercomputing - product specification. (2005). Retrieved May 28, 2014 from http://www.gen-i.co.nz/assets/productspecs/New-Zealand-Super-Computing.pdf

Overview of recent supercomputers. (2012). Retrieved May 27, 2014 from http://www.euroben.nl/reports/web12/overview.php

Overview of supercomputer systems. (2011). Retrieved May 27, 2014 from http://nkl.cc.u-tokyo.ac.jp/13e/01-Intro/ITC.pdf

Oxford Supercomputing Centre. (2012). An introduction to the Oxford supercomputing centre, Oxford University, UK. Retrieved May 28, 2014 from http://www.arc.ox.ac.uk/sites/default/files/uploads/OSC%20Overview%20May%2012.pdf

Pittsburgh supercomputing center (2012). Retrieved May 28, 2014 from http://www.novell.com/docrep/2012/04/pittsburgh_supercomputing_center.pdf

Rao, A. (2012). SeaMicro technology overview. Retrieved May 28, 2014 from http://www.seamicro.com/sites/default/files/SM_TO01_64_v2.5.pdf

Regalado, A. (2014). A $1 billion investment plan for IBM's watson supercomputer. Retrieved May 28, 2014 from http://www.technologyreview.com/news/523411/facing-doubters-ibm-expands-plans-for-watson/

Schroers, W. (2013). Parallel and distributed computing – supercomputing, Field-theory.org, Berlin, Germany. Retrieved May 28, 2014 from http://www.field-theory.org/articles/supercomputing/index.html

Silicon Graphics. (1995). The power challenge technical report. Retrieved May 28, 2014 from http://www.uoks.uj.edu.pl/resources/flugor/POWER/chap1.html

Supercomputer architecture (2014). Retrieved May 26, 2014 from http://en.wikipedia.org/wiki/Supercomputer_architecture

Supercomputers (2014). Retrieved May 28, 2014 from http://www.chilton-computing.org.uk/ccd/supercomputers/overview.htm

Supercomputing architectures: An overview (n.d.). Retrieved May 28, 2014 from http://www.peter-india.net/SuperComputingView.html

Supercomputing in small spaces. (2010). Retrieved May 28, 2014 from http://sss.cs.vt.edu/overview.php

Supercomputing record with bubble collapse simulation. (2013). Retrieved May 28, 2014 from https://www.ethz.ch/en/news-and-events/eth-news/news/2013/11/supercomputing-record.html

Ulmer, D. (2008). The Swiss national supercomputing centre CSCS: An overview. Retrieved May 28, 2014 from http://www.linksceem.eu/ls2/images/stories/DU_Kick-off.pdf

KEY TERMS AND DEFINITIONS

Cray: Cray Inc., an American supercomputer manufacturer based in Seattle, Washington. The company's predecessor, Cray Research, Inc. (CRI), was founded in 1972 by computer designer Seymour Cray (Wikipedia, 2014a).

Flynn's Taxonomy: Classification of computer architectures, proposed by Michael J. Flynn in 1966 (Wikipedia, 2014b).

Human Brain Project: A large scientific research project, directed by the École Polytechnique Fédérale de Lausanne and largely funded by the European Union, which aims to simulate the complete human brain on supercomputers to better understand how it functions. The project is based in Geneva, Switzerland (Wikipedia, 2014c).

Jungle Computing: The use of diverse [vague], distributed and highly non-uniform [vague] high performance computer systems to achieve peak performance (Wikipedia, 2014d).

Multiprocessing: The use of two or more central processing units (CPUs) within a single computer system. The term also refers to the ability of a system to support more than one processor and/or the ability to allocate tasks between them (Wikipedia, 2014e).

Supercomputer: A computer at the frontline of contemporary processing capacity – particularly speed of calculation which can happen at speeds of nanoseconds (Wikipedia, 2014f).

Tianhe-2, or Milky Way-2: Tianhe-2 or TH-2 (Chinese: 天河-2; pinyin: tiānhé-èr; literally: "Heavenriver-2" idiomatically "Milky Way

2") is a 33.86 petaflops supercomputer located in Sun Yat-sen University, Guangzhou, China. It was developed by a team of 1300 scientists and engineers. It is the world's fastest supercomputer according to the TOP500 list for June and November 2013 (Wikipedia, 2014g).

TOP500: The TOP500 project ranks and details the 500 most powerful (non-distributed) computer systems in the world. The project was started in 1993 and publishes an updated list of the supercomputers twice a year (Wikipedia, 2014h).

Vector Processing: A vector processor, or array processor, is a central processing unit (CPU) that implements an instruction set containing instructions that operate on one-dimensional arrays of data called vectors. This is in contrast to a scalar processor, whose instructions operate on single data items (Wikipedia, 2014i).

Chapter 2
History of Supercomputing and Supercomputer Centers

Jeffrey S. Cook
Independent Researcher, USA

Neha Gupta
Northeastern University, USA & Osmania University, India

ABSTRACT

This chapter begins with the definition of supercomputers and shifts to how the supercomputers have evolved since the 1930s. Supercomputing need is stressed, including issues in time and cost of resources currently faced by the researchers. The chapter transitions to an overview of the supercomputing era with a small biography of Seymour Cray. The timeline of Cray's history and various Cray inventions are discussed. The works of Fujitsu, Hitachi, Intel, and NEC are clearly demonstrated. A section on Beowulfs and S1 supercomputers is provided. A discussion on applications of supercomputing in healthcare and how Dell is emerging in its supercomputing abilities in 21st century are cohesively explained. The focus is shifted to the petaflop computing in the 21st century, current trends in supercomputing, and the future of supercomputing. The details of some of the global supercomputing centers in the Top500 list of fastest supercomputers in the world are also provided.

INTRODUCTION

Supercomputer is a computer which is the most predominant in terms of computational rate, memory, or cost. Historically, a supercomputer is associated with the fastest computer available or the largest in size. Supercomputing can be put in exact words like "ultra mass computing performing at ultra high speed". There are quantum computers but they exist only on paper and grid computers are comparable to supercomputers but are a lot cheaper. There have been tremendous amounts of development in supercomputing arena since the inception of supercomputers in around 1930's. However, till date there is no accurate information on who the inventor of supercomputers is and how it was made technologically in the beginning. Many people consider Seymour Cray to be the father of supercomputing while others consider various other scientists to be the discoverers while tracing the roots of supercomputing.

DOI: 10.4018/978-1-4666-7461-5.ch002

Copyright © 2015, IGI Global. Copying or distributing in print or electronic forms without written permission of IGI Global is prohibited.

Demand for supercomputing capabilities is rising all over the world, driven primarily by the need for effective, reliable solutions to increasingly complex social, scientific, environment, business challenges and problems (Yamada, 2014). This is in turn leading to a high-tech computational modeling and simulation power beyond the scope of R&D labs. Supercomputing has evolved from the not so popular research calculators or transistors to the popular CDC's by Cray Inc in 1960s and 70s and presently the most mature peta-scale forms in 21st century.

Along with the evolution of supercomputer architectures, the new computational algorithms emerged mostly from the basics of Mathematics that led to significant progress in research. Some of these algorithms include Red/black, Multigrid, scatter/gather hardware and vectorized libraries (Burns, 2013). Thinking machines also emerged from Massachusetts Institute of Technology (MIT) with the first general purpose Massively Parallel Processing Unit (MPP). The concept here was to add sufficient processors to emulate the brain but approximately 10^{14} neurons. This is commonly referred to as Artificial Intelligence (AI). Minicomputers emerged and have briefly sustained. In the late 1980's and early 1990's, the era of powerful microprocessors was observed (Burns, 2013).

There are two approaches to the design of super-computers. One is the Massively Parallel Processing unit (MPP) which is to aggregate thousands of commercially available microprocessors utilizing parallel processing techniques (Supercomputer, 2014). A variant of this, called a Beowulf cluster or "cluster computing" employs large numbers of personal computers interconnected by a local area network. The other approach, called vector processing, is to develop specialized hardware to solve complex computations (Supercomputer, 2014).

Computers incorporate very large scale integrated (VLSI) circuits with millions of transistors per chip for both logic and memory components.

Several computers use high-speed complementary metallic oxide semiconductor (CMOS) technology. Many supercomputers now use conventional, inexpensive device technology of commodity microprocessors and rely on massive parallelism for speed (Supercomputer, 2014).

THE ISSUE OF COST AND TIME

Construction of supercomputers is an awesome but very expensive process. The most recent development costs of supercomputers varied between 150 to 500 million dollars (USD $) or more. Particularly, this entire process draws on all the resources a company has. This is one of the main reasons that the development of a supercomputer is kept very hush-hush (Robat, 2013). Some of the companies contributing to the computing developments include Amdahl, Burroughs, CDC, Cray, Fujitsu, Hitachi, Hewlett-Packard, IBM, Intel, NEC, SGI, Sun, Texas Instruments, Thinking Machines, Univac (Robat, 2013).

THE BEGINNING OF THE ERA OF SUPERCOMPUTING

The history of supercomputers dates back to 1930's. In 1939, Atanasoff-Berry supercomputer was created at Iowa State. Later in 1940, Konrad Zuse-Z2 supercomputer uses telephone relays instead of mechanical logical circuits. In 1942, ENIAC (Electronic Numerical Integrator and Computer) supercomputer was introduced whereas in 1943, Colossus, a British Vacuum tube computer was developed. In 1944, Manchester Mark I 1944 supercomputer was installed. In 1946, Harvard Mark II and in 1948 Manchester Mark I (1st stored program digital computer) was installed at Whirlwind, MIT. In 1950, Alan Turing-Test of Machine Intelligence was done using UNIVAC (Universal Automatic Computer) I. In 1951, William Shockley invented the Junction Transistor.

In 1953, EDVAC, IBM 701 was developed. In 1955, UNIVAC II was introduced (Robat, 2013).

A Small Biography of Seymour Cray

Seymour Cray (1925-1996) is one of the founding fathers of the computer industry. Seeking to process vast amounts of mathematical data, Cray built what many consider the first supercomputer, which created a revolution in technology (Seymour Cray Facts, 2014). He is an electronics engineer. Cray's early aptitude for electronics was evident when he wired his laboratory to his bedroom, and included an electric alarm that sounded whenever anyone tried to enter his inner sanctum. Among his initial accomplishments was the first computer to employ a Freon cooling system to prevent chips from overheating. However, Cray's most significant contribution was the Supercomputer itself. Cray built the CDC 6600 (Seymour Cray Facts, 2014).

A maverick in his pursuits, Cray eventually started his own company devoted entirely to the development of the supercomputers. For a long time, Cray computers dominated the supercomputer industry. He was born on September 28, 1925, in Chippewa Falls, Wisconsin. In 1972, Cray was awarded the Harry Goode Memorial Award for "outstanding achievement in the field of information processing". Cray died on October 5, 1996, from injuries sustained in a car accident three weeks earlier (Seymour Cray Facts, 2014).

Cray Research forms from Control Data Corporation (CDC) (Bell, n.d.)

1950's

The first machine generally referred to as supercomputer though not officially designated was the IBM Naval Ordnance Research Calculator, used at Columbia University from 1954 to 1963 to calculate missile trajectories (Mattlis, 2005). In 1956, a team at Manchester University began the development of MUSE – a name derived from microsecond engine with the aim of building a computer that could operate at processing speeds approaching one microsecond per instruction, about one million instructions per second. At the end of 1958, Ferranti agreed to collaborate with Manchester University on the project, and the computer was shortly afterwards renamed as ATLAS. The first ATLAS was officially commissioned on 7 December 1962 as one of the world's first supercomputers, considered to be the most powerful at that time. It was equivalent to four IBM 7094s. It was said that whenever Atlas went offline, half of the United Kingdom's computer capacity was lost. The computer pioneered the use of virtual memory and paging as a way to extend the Atlas computer's working memory by combining its 16 thousand words of primary core memory with additional 96 thousand words of secondary drum memory (History of Supercomputing, 2014)

In 1957, a group of engineers left Sperry Corporation to form Control Data Corporation in Minneapolis, MN. Seymour Cray left Sperry a year later to join his colleagues at Control Data Corporation (CDC). In 1960, Cray completed the CDC 1604, the first solid state computer, and the fastest computer in the world at a time when vacuum tubes were found in most large computers (History of Supercomputing, 2014)

1960's

Cray moved the lab to Chippewa, WI to design the 6600 (1964) and 7600 (1969). At 36 MHz, the 7600 had about three and a half times the clock speed of the 6600, but ran significantly faster due to other technical innovations. The 6600 was a land mark innovative design that included: dense packaging and cooling for the fast clock, multiple parallel function units, timesharing a single processor to provide multiple processors, I/O computers, and RISC (in contrast to the recently announced IBM System 360). The 7600 improved on the

Figure 1. The University of Manchester Atlas in January 1963. Source: http://upload.wikimedia.org/wikipedia/commons/thumb/d/d9/University_of_Manchester_Atlas%2C_January_1963.JPG/220px-University_of_Manchester_Atlas%2C_January_1963.JPG

concepts by introducing pipelining, giving it a 20 times speed-up over the 6600 that operated at 1-3 Megaflops (Bell, n.d.).

By 1965 Seymour was clearly recognized as THE world's supercomputing architect, a title that he clearly held until his 1996 death (Bell, n.d.).

But Cray was at odds with the CDC management, and so decided to start his own company when he abandoned the multiprocessor 8600. When he left, CDC lost its right brain, and it never recovered. CDC attempted to regain its technical capability with the Star 100 (1974) project, and the Cyber 205 (1981) (Bell, n.d.). Along with the Texas Instruments ASC, the STAR-100 was one of the first machines to use vector processing- the idea having been inspired around 1964 by the APL programming language. In 1983 it spun out the project forming wholly owned ETA Systems that shipped one nitrogen cooled, CMOS ETA 10 in 1987. CDC shut down ETA in 1989 (Bell, n.d.).

1970's

Seymour left CDC, forming Cray Research. In 1976 it delivered the first practical vector processor (Cray 1) using the latest data-centric programming

language ECL gates and memories, innovative cooling, and the first vectorizing compilers (Bell, n.d.). The first Cray-1 system was installed at Los Alamos National Laboratory (LANL). It had a world-record speed of 160 megaflops and an 8 megabyte main memory (Cray History, 2014).

In order to increase the speed of this system, the Cray-1 had a unique "C" shape which enabled integrated circuits to be closer together (Cray History, 2014).The Cray X-MP (designed by Steve Chen) was released in 1982 as a 105 MHz shared-memory parallel vector processor with better chaining support and multiple memory pipelines. The Cray X-MP had support for up to four CPUs and each of the X-MP CPUs pushed up to 200 megaflops. By the end of the Cray X-MP's run, it could support up to 16 million 64-bit words of memory in SRAM (Static Random-Access Memory) which is equivalent to around 128 MB of today's RAM. The Cray X-MP supported up to 32 disk storage units and each unit costs about $270000 in today's money and has a impressive transfer rate of 10 MB/sec (Anthony, 2012).

In 1976, the ILLIAC (Illinois Automatic Computer) IV came out in the market. The ILLIAC IV was a supercomputer project at the University of Illinois at Urbana-Champaign funded by DARPA (Defense Advanced Research Projects Agency) that commissions advanced research for United States Department of Defense (DoD). It had many processors and was a single instruction, multiple data (SIMD) supercomputer (Mortenson et al.). In 2001, micros operate at ten times this speed, and the largest scalable computer using several thousand micros operates at a peak of 10 Teraflops, or 100,000 faster. Centers cost up to 100 times more dollars ($300M) (Bell, n.d.).

1980's

During the 1980s, there was a rapid increase in parallel computers. One of the successful companies during this time was Thinking Machines with its CM-2 Supercomputer. The CM-2 computer was one of the first major Massive Parallel Processor (MPP) systems. In 1985, Intel introduced iPSC/1, which used 80,286 microprocessors connected through Ethernet controllers. By the 1990s, the supercomputer market was not a vector market anymore; it was instead a parallel computer market (Mortenson et al).

1985

Seymour's Cray 2 was introduced. Cray 2 was a 4 processor liquid cooled computer totally immersed in a tank of Fluorinert, which bubbled as it operated. It could perform to 1.9 gigaflops and was the world's fastest until 1990 when ETA-10G from CDC overtook it. The Cray Y-MP, also designed by Steve Chen, was released in 1988 as an improvement of the X-MP and had eight vector processors at 167 MHz with a peak performance of 333 megaflops per processor (History of Supercomputing, 2014). The company also produced its first "mini-supercomputer", the Cray XMS System followed by the Cray Y-MP EL series and the subsequent Cray J90. Seymour then started the Cray 3, using GaAs to exploit its faster gate speed. The GaAs and packaging technology development was costing too much and in 1989 he was thrown overboard to form Cray Computer (Bell, n.d.).

Figure 2. A liquid cooled Cray-2 supercomputer. Source: http://upload.wikimedia.org/wikipedia/ commons/thumb/5/5a/Cray2.jpeg/220px-Cray2. jpeg

1980-1995

Working at Cray Research, Steve Chen and Les Davis morphed the vector processor into shared memory, vector multiprocessors: X (82), Y (88), C, J (minisuper), T (94), and the current SV line. In the process, Cray Research made at least one too many ECL based computers while the Japanese switched to CMOS (Complementary Metal Oxide Semiconductor), exploiting Moore's Law (Bell, n.d.).

In the late 80's, Cray Research responded to the call from the ARPA (Advanced Research Projects Agency) Strategic Computing Initiative to build future computers as massively parallel arrays of rapidly evolving "killer" microprocessors. Furthermore, most of its government users went into a holding pattern awaiting MPPs because money was being ear-marked for these new weird machines in order to develop a market and software. Cray went after MPP with a vengeance, creating the T3D line of MPPs using Digital's Alpha CMOS microprocessor in 1993 and a proprietary fast, low latency, interconnecting network. The T3D and T3E computers dominated the top 500 computers installations until the late 90's. In 1995 an "E" was the first computer to reach one TeraFlops (Bell, n.d.).

The Cray Research decision to evolve to three architectures is most likely the single biggest error that caused their downward spiral. A platform requires the continued development of hardware and software to be competitive. Platforms are only valuable if apps are available, requiring extensive porting, testing, training, marketing, sales, and customer support. Once a customer starts using an app, the investment in data and user training swamps nearly all other costs! This implies that unless a company falters badly in successor platform introduction, a customer is "locked in" to a processor x O/S platform (e.g. Sparc x Solaris) for the life an application (Bell, n.d).

In 2000, IBM ASCI White supercomputer was introduced with a peak speed of 2.15 TFLOPS at Sandia National Laboratory, USA.

Fujitsu, Hitachi, Intel and NEC Mimic the "Cray"

FORTRAN compilers, the Japanese computer companies saw a clear plan forward. They simply adopted the vector-super model and built machines for this FORTRAN programming model. They refined their architectures as technology improved. When CMOS became viable, they were quick to adopt it. In the late 90's, Fujitsu produced the first distributed vector clusters to achieve over 100 Gflops (Bell, n.d.).

The first vector processor developed in Japan was Fujitsu's FACOM 230-75 APU (Array processing unit) in 1977. Hitachi produced HITAC M-180 IAP (Integrated Array Processor) in 1978, M-200H IAP (1979) and M-280H IAP (1982). NEC also produced ACOS-1000 IAP (1982) (Oyonagi, 2002). Japanese vendors started to produce full-fledged vector computers: Hitachi's S810 (1983), Fujitsu's VP200 (1984) and NEC's SX-2 (1985). Hitachi upgraded S810 to S820 in 1987, Fujitsu to VP2600 (1989) and NEC to SX-3 (1991). Hitachi later adopted a parallel (shared memory) vector machine S3800 (1993), while Fujitsu produced distributed vector memory processors VPP500 (1995). NEC shipped a cluster of shared memory vector processors SX-4 (1997) (Oyonagi, 2002).

The SX-3/44R was introduced by NEC Corporation in 1989 and a year later earned the fastest in the world title with a 4 processor model. However, Fujitsu's Numerical Wind Tunnel Supercomputer used 166 vector processors to gain the top spot in 1994. It had a peak speed of 1.7 gigaflops per processor (History of Supercomputing, 2014). The Hitachi SR2201 on the other hand obtained a peak performance of 600 gigaflops in 1996 by using 2048 processors connected via a fast three – dimensional crossbar network (History of Supercomputing, 2014). During this period, there was a major shift from a single shared bus to massive parallelism where 2D and 3D networks such as Cray's Torus Interconnect connected together 100's of CPU's (Anthony, 2012).

In 1989, Intel, the king of microprocessors since the 70's, released the i860, a 32- and 64-bit RISC chip designed for use in large computers. In the same timeline, the Intel Paragon could have 1000 to 4000 Intel i860 processors in various configurations and was ranked the fastest in the world in 1993. The Paragon was a multiple instruction, multiple data (MIMD) machine which connected processors via a high speed two-dimensional mesh, allowing processes to execute on separate nodes (History of Supercomputing, 2014). The Paragon architecture soon led to the Intel ASCI Red Supercomputer which held the top supercomputing spot to the end of the 20th century as a part of the Advanced Simulation and Computing Initiative (ASCI). This was also a mesh-based MIMD massively–parallel system with over 9,000 compute nodes and well over 12 terabytes of disk storage but used off-the shelf Pentium Pro processors that was found

Figure 3. Rear of the Paragon Cabinet showing the bus bars and mesh routers. Source: http://upload. wikimedia.org/wikipedia/commons/thumb/9/90/ Paragon_XP-E_-_mesh.jpg/180px-Paragon_XP-E_-_mesh.jpg

in everyday personal computers. ASCI Red, however, was the first system ever to break the 1 teraflop barrier on the MP-Linpack benchmark in 1996; eventually reaching 2 teraflops (History of Supercomputing, 2014). Later, it was upgraded to 9,298 Pentium II Xeons and reached 3.1 Teraflops.

NEC continues to build and market the vector multiprocessor and clustered supercomputer, introducing the SX-5 in 2000 as the world's fastest vector supercomputer. They promise to deliver a 40 Teraflops computer in 2002 (Bell, n.d.).

In August 1999, SGI created a separate Cray Research business unit to focus exclusively on the unique requirements of high-end supercomputing customers. Assets of this business unit were sold to Tera Computer Company in March 2000 (Cray History, 2014).

Formation of Cray Inc.

Burton Smith joined Denelcor in 1974 to build the Heterogeneous Element Processor (HEP), extending the basic idea of the 6600 I/O computers to multiprocessing. This first massively multi-threaded architecture (MTA) was delivered in 1982. Burton went to SRC (Semiconductor Research Corporation), NSA's (National Security Agency) research center, where he continued to refine MTA (Bell, n.d.).

In 1987 Burton and Rottsolk found Tera Computer to build another MTA, and in 1995 the company went public (Cray History, 2014). After 10 years the company delivered its first MTA, built on GaAs (Gallium Arsenide). An 8 processor system was delivered and used at the San Diego Supercomputer Center (Cray History, 2014).

After several years of zero revenue and a dwindling cash supply and no new story, Tera acquired Cray Research from Silicon Graphics Inc. (SGI) in March 2000. This allowed the SGI management focus on its main business (Bell, n.d.).

Cray Inc. in Years 2000 and Later

After the Tera merger, the Tera MTA system was relaunched as the Cray MTA-2. It was not a success and was shipped to only two customers. Cray Inc. also unsuccessfully badged the NEC SX-6 supercomputer as the Cray SX-6 and acquired the exclusive rights to sell (Cray, 2014).

In 2002, Cray Inc. announced their first new model, the Cray X1 combined architecture vector/MPP supercomputer. In May 2004, Cray was announced to be one of the partners in the U.S Department of Energy's fastest computer in the world project to build a 50 teraflops machine for the Oak Ridge National Laboratory. Since 2004, the X1 has been superceded by the X1E with faster dual-core processors (Cray, 2014).

Then Cray XD1 was introduced. In 2004, Cray finished the Red Storm system for Sandia National Laboratories. The Cray XT3 massively parallel supercomputer became a commercialized version of Red Storm similar in many aspects to the earlier T3E architecture. The Cray XT4 introduced in 2006 added support for DDR2 memory, newer dual-core and future quad-core Opteron processors and used a SeaStar2 communication coprocessor (Cray, 2014).

In April 2008, Intel and Cray announced that they would collaborate on future supercomputer systems. This partnership produced the Cray CX1 system launched in September 2008. In early 2010, Cray introduced the Cray CX1000. By 2009, the largest computer Cray had delivered was the XT5 system at the Oak Ridge National Laboratories. This system was dubbed Jaguar and was the fastest computer in the world according to the Linpack benchmark (Cray, 2014).

In 2010, Cray XE6 was introduced. The first multi-cabinet XE6 system was shipped in July 2010. In 2011, Cray introduced the Cray XK6 hybrid supercomputer. In 2012, Cray announced the Cray XK7 and the ORNL Jaguar upgraded to an XK7 (Titan) capable of 20 petaflops (Cray, 2014).

BEOWULFS

Beowulf is a way of building a supercomputer out of a bunch of smaller computers. The smaller computers are connected together by a LAN which is usually an Ethernet. It is believed that the Beowulf idea can enable a research group to obtain a computer that can operate in the gigaflop range. Normally, only mega rich corporations like IBM, AT&T and the NSA can afford such awesome computational power (What is a Beowulf, n.d.).

Most Beowulf clusters run on the Linux Operating System and is therefore known for its stability and speed. Also, there are no limits to how large a Beowulf can be scaled. The first Beowulf was developed in 1994 at the Center of Excellence in Space Data and Information Sciences (CESDIS), a contractor to NASA in Maryland (What is a Beowulf?, n.d.).

Beowulf's have been the enabler of do-it-yourself cluster computing using commodity microprocessors, the Linux O/S with Gnu Tools and most recently Windows 2000 O/S, tools that have evolved from the MPP research community, and a single platform standard that finally allow applications to be written that will run on more than one computer (Bell, n.d.).

S1 SUPERCOMPUTER

The S1 project was an attempt to build a family of multiprocessor supercomputers. The project was envisioned by Lowell Wood at the Lawrence Livermore National Lab in 1975 and staffed for the first three years by two Stanford University graduate students (Smotherman, 2013). The two graduate students could design and almost completely build a supercomputer by themselves is an amazing feat comparable to the design of CDC 6600 by Cray and a small staff a dozen years earlier. This project was supported by the US Navy and ramped up in 1978 with the addition of more students. The project also influenced

the development of programming languages and compilers including Common LISP, the modern, multi-paradigm, high-performance, compiled, ANSI- standardized descendant of the long-running family of Lisp programming, and GCC (GNU Complier Collection) (Smotherman, 2013).

SUPERCOMPUTING AND HEALTHCARE

Though supercomputing is carving its way into various avenues of healthcare, the potential for equipping clinicians with access to massive repositories of medical expertise via mobile devices holds the highest potential in future.

There is a news that an mHealth application would be playing a central role in the eradication of Cancer using IBM's Watson supercomputer. The first mHealth app that syncs with Watson, Oncology Expert Advisor (OEA), enables doctors at the University of Texas MD Anderson Cancer Center to use an iPad at the point of care to determine a unique treatment profile for individual patients based on current clinical trials, patient history and family history (Schwartz, 2013).

While Apple and Google have garnered a lot of attention in the digital health space in 2014, Blackberry Ltd bought a stake in cloud-based medical IT provider NantHealth. Blackberry also sells the QNX operating system that is embedded into medical devices and the company plans to launch a BBM Protected, a secure encrypted messaging service. NantHealth claims that its clinical Operating System is installed in approximately 250 hospitals connecting some 16,000 medical devices and collecting 3 billion vital signs per year (Sullivan, 2013).

The Human Brain Project is working to unify our understanding of the human brain. Mapping the human brain and its diseases and using this map to develop even more powerful supercomputers is essentially the goal. The main challenge is that the human brain is so complex that it's very difficult to understand how it's put together and how it works (Oden, 2012). Each of our roughly 87 billion neurons is intricately connected to thousands of other neurons. At the same time, it has never been more urgent for us to address the many health challenges related to brain problems. We are living longer lives than ever before and that makes us more vulnerable to brain-related diseases like Alzheimer's, dementia and Parkinson's. This is predicted to be achieved by 2020 through the use of future supercomputers (Oden, 2012).

BRIEF HISTORY OF SUPERCOMPUTING CENTER AT FLORIDA STATE UNIVERSITY

Supercomputing came to the Florida State University (FSU) campus in Tallahassee, Florida through the auspices of Supercomputer Computations Research Institute (SCRI) which began operation in 1984 (History of research computing center, 2013). It was established by the U.S. Department of Energy. In 1987, ETA System ETA10-G, world's first ETA Systems Class VII Supercomputer was delivered on campus. In 1990, the term Cluster computing originated and CM2 Connection Machine, Cray Y-MP/432 supercomputers were installed. In 1995, Florida State University purchased two Silicon Graphics Power Challenge XLSs to create a Scalable Shared – Memory Processor system with the power of both shared –memory systems and distributed computing systems. In 1998, Origin 2000 server was installed.

In 2000, teragold (IBM RS/6000 SP system) was installed and in 2002, Eclipse, an IBM eServer p690 with integrated "teragold" supercomputer was installed. In 2007, high performance computing cluster named as Shared – HPC was installed. In 2008, the name was changed to High Performance Computing (HPC). In 2013, Shared-HPC facility became the Research Computing Center (RCC), a part of the Florida State University Information Technology Services, and consolidated

high-performance computing, cloud computing and research computing consulting (History of research computing center, 2013).

BRIEF HISTORY OF MINNESOTA SUPERCOMPUTER CENTER

The University of Minnesota acquired its first supercomputer in 1981, and in 1982 created the Minnesota Supercomputer Center in Minneapolis. The University created the Minnesota Supercomputer Institute (MSCI) (Minnesota Supercomputer Center, 1994). In 1984, the Legislature appropriated $2.6 million to the Institute to support the purchase of computer time and services from MSCI. Since that time, the Legislature has appropriated over $70 million to support the university's supercomputing services. Since 1986, MSCI has operated as a separate company and has grown to have 75 employees and over $20 million in revenues. The university accounted for about 55% of the center's $22.6 million fiscal year 1993 revenues through its $8 million per year commitment and its U.S. Army High Performance Computing Research Center (Minnesota Supercomputer Center, 1994).

MSCI provides access to a variety of high-performance computing systems. They are Itasca, Cascade, Calhoun, Red Nodes. High-performance heterogeneous computing systems include Cascade, gput, and others.

BRIEF HISTORY OF MOSCOW UNIVERSITY SUPERCOMPUTING CENTER

In 1956, Research Computing Center (RCC) of Moscow State University received its first computer "Strela" (MSU's HPC History, n.d.). It was the first serially manufactured mainframe in the USSR. Strela mainframe had a clock cycle of 500 microseconds, RAM of 2048 words, energy consumption of 150 KW. In 1959, RCC launched

"Setun" prototype and in 1961 "Setun" started to be manufactured serially. It was the first computer in the world based on ternary logic. In 1961, M-20 computer was installed in RCC. BESM-4 computer became a part of RCC computational facilities in 1966. In 1968, RCC received its first BESM-6 computer. RCC installed its second BESM-6 computer in 1975 and then the third and fourth ones in 1979. In 1981, two ES-1022, two MIR-2 and MINSK-32 computers were present along with four BESM-6 mainframes (MSU's HPC History, n.d.).

FASTEST SUPERCOMPUTER NOW BECOMES HISTORY

Arizona State University (ASU)'s Saguaro 2 Supercomputer was once among the top 500 in the world, but budget constraints have put it in danger of becoming obsolete and threaten its international fame (Betancourt, 2012). Data that would normally take weeks to compute can be processed in a day or two on the Saguaro 2 Supercomputer, which contains over 5,000 processor cores. ASU Advanced Computing Center (A2C2) director Francis Timmes said the Saguaro Supercomputer needs at least $2 million, $700,000 more than it currently receives. According to the Top500.org, a website that ranks all the most powerful supercomputers in the world, Saguaro peaked in November 2008 at No.82 (Betancourt, 2012).

THE HISTORY OF MESSAGE PASSING INTERFACE (MPI)

Various message passing environments were developed in early 80's. The Ohio Supercomputer Center developed a message passing library called LAM. There was a package developed specially for quantum chemistry called TCGMSG (Meglicki, 2004). In late 1992, a meeting was called during the Supercomputing 92 conference and the atten-

dants agreed to develop and implement common standard for message passing. This is how MPI, the Message Passing Interface was born. Microsoft incorporated the ISIS technology into its clustering product called Wolfpack. Today all PC and UNIX workstation clusters are MPI systems and MPI programs are run on the Earth Simulator, Cray XI and large SMPs. MPI1 was completed in 1994. MPI2 was completed in 1998. MPI 2 is particularly interesting because in that parallel I/O operations were defined. There is only one freeware MPI-IO version that is called ROMIO that is a high- performance portable implementation of MOI-IO. ROMIO can be combined with MPI-1 as an external MPI library or incorporated directly into MPI-2 (Meglicki, 2004).

BRIEF COMMENTARY OF SUPERCOMPUTING HISTORY (2000-2010)

At a 2000 Conference in Maui, Bill Buzbee, former director of NCAR stated: "Some believe that capability computing is vital to U.S. national security. If this is correct, then capability computing is a strategic technology and should be accorded commensurate national priority... billions of government funding has gone to development of low-bandwidth-high-latency computing technology and relatively little has gone to development of high-bandwidth-low-latency technology (Bell, n.d.). Consequently, the February, 1999, report from the President's Information Technology Advisory Committee http://www.itrd.gov/ac/report/pitac_report.pdf, pp 62 recommends (Bell, n.d.):

There is evidence that current scalable parallel architectures may not be well suited for all applications, especially where the computations' memory address references are highly irregular or where huge quantities of data must be transferred from memory... we need substantive research on the design of memory hierarchies that reduce or hide access latencies while they deliver the memory bandwidths required by current and future applications (Bell, n.d.).

SUPERCOMPUTING AND DELL IN 21st CENTURY

Members of Dell's research division are putting together pieces for prototype ARM Supercomputers that could be deployed in the near future. ARM processors go into most smartphones and tablets and are attracting interest for use in servers. A supercomputer based on Dell's blade design was deployed in 2012 at the Texas Advanced Computing Center (TACC) which is located at the University of Texas at Austin called Stampede. It is rated as the world's seventh fastest supercomputer (Shah, 2013).

University of Minnesota Supercomputing Institute deploys various HPC resources among which Cascade is one of them. Cascade consists of a Dell R710 head/login node with 48 GiB (Gibibyte) of memory where 1 GiB equals 2^{30} bytes or 1,073,741,824 bytes. (WIntelGuy.com, 2014), (Minnesota Supercomputing Institute, 2014). In 2012, University of Kentucky deployed a new $2.6 million, high performance computing cluster in partnership with Dell Inc. The cluster has a performance of just over 140 teraflops (Hautala, 2012).

ClusterVision has announced the successful completion of a new cluster installation project at the Universite Libre de Bruxelles (ULB) in 2013. ClusterVision worked with system engineers at ULB to design and install a combination of HPC technologies from partners including Dell, Supermicro, AMD, Nvidia, GPFS and Bright Computing. The compute density and performance characters are achieved through the addition of 42 Dell PowerEdge M915 Blade Servers, each with four AMD CPUs. The System incorporates both high and mid-range storage expansion based on Dell Powervault (ClusterVision, 2013).

The supercomputer Darwin ranked 234 in the Top500 list as of November 2013 at Cambridge University in U.K. is a Dell PowerEdge C6220 cluster whereas Wilkes at Cambridge University ranked 166 in the Top500 list is a Dell T620 cluster (Cambridge University, n.d.).

The University of Florida (UF) unveiled the state's most powerful supercomputer, a machine that will help researchers find life-saving drugs and improve armor for troops in 2013. The HiPerGator supercomputer and recent tenfold increase in the size of the university's data pipeline makes UF nation's leading public universities in research computing (Deumens, 2013). HiPerGator is a Dell machine that has a peak speed of 150 trillion calculations per second. UF worked with Dell, Terascala, Mellanox and AMD to build this supercomputer (Deumens, 2013).

In the beginning of 2013, Dell introduced Active Infrastructure for HPC Life Sciences, a solution designed specifically for genome analysis. This new solution integrates computing, storage and networking to reduce lengthy timelines and process up to 37 genomes per day and 259 genomes per week. Working with Dell and other technology partners, ORNL upgraded its Lustre-based file system Spider to Spider II (Research Institutions Push the Boundaries of Supercomputing with Dell, 2013). San Diego Supercomputer Center (SDSC) at the University of California, San Diego is deploying Comet, a new petascale supercomputer. It is funded by a $12 million NSF grant and is scheduled to start operations in early 2015. Comet will be a Dell based cluster with next generation Intel Xeon processors (Research Institutions Push the Boundaries of Supercomputing with Dell, 2013).

PETAFLOP COMPUTING IN THE 21st CENTURY

Significant progress was made in the first decade of the 21st century and it was shown that the power of a large number of small processors can be harnessed to achieve high performance, e.g. as in System X's use of 1,100 Apple Power Mac G5 computers quickly assembled in the summer of 2003 to gain 12.25 teraflops (History of Supercomputing, 2014)

The efficiency of supercomputers Continued to rise but not so dramatically. The Cray C90 used 500 kilowatts of power in 1991, while by 2003 the ASCI Q used 3,000 kW being 2,000 times faster, increasing the performance per watt 300 fold. In 2004, the Earth Simulator supercomputer built by NEC at the Japan Agency for Marine-Earth Science and Technology (JAMSTEC) reached 35.9 teraflops using 640 nodes (History of Supercomputing, 2014).

The IBM Blue Gene supercomputer architecture found widespread use in the early part of the 21st century and 27 of the computers on the Top500 list used that architecture. The Blue Gene/P approach is somewhat different in that it trades processor speed for low power consumption so that a large number of processors can be used at air cooled temperatures. It can use over 60,000 processors, with 2,048 processors per rack. The first version of Blue Gene/L, located at Lawrence Livermore National Laboratory (LLNL), had 16,000 compute nodes and was capable of 70 teraflops. BlueGene/L would lead the pack until it was succeeded by IBM Roadrunner, a 20,000-CPU PowerPC/AMD Opteron hybrid that was the first computer to break the 1-petaflop barrier (Anthony, 2012).

Progress in China has been rapid, in that China was placed 51st on the Top500 list in June 2003, then 14th in November 2003 and 10th in June 2004, 5th during 2005 before gaining the top spot in 2010 with the 2.5 petaflop Tianhe-I supercomputer (History of Supercomputing, 2014). More interestingly, China recently unveiled Sunway, a 1-Petaflops supercomputer built entirely out of homegrown ShenWei CPUs. China has repeatedly stated that it wants to lessen its reliance on Western high-technology and Sunway is an important project in that direction (Anthony, 2012).

In the modern era, IBM Blue Gene/Q was introduced in 2012. It has 1,572,864 cores in 98,304 IBM Power CPUs. It is very energy efficient and can be designed in future to 100 PFLOPS with a high cost of $97 million.

U.S. Army Arberdeen Proving Ground (APG) in Maryland continues to make history as it unveiled the new supercomputers "Hercules" and "Pershing". These supercomputers are IBM iDataPlex systems featuring the latest Intel processors and are ranked in the top 100 of the fastest computers in the world according to the U.S Army Research Laboratory (Zumer, 2013).

The current fastest supercomputer is Tianhe-2 located in China as discussed in detail in Chapter 1.

Global Supercomputer leader Cray Inc. announced the opening of the company's new supercomputer manufacturing facility in Chippewa Falls, Wisconsin (Davis et al., 2014). With the addition of this second facility and with recent upgrades to its existing primary manufacturing site, Cray has roughly doubled its manufacturing capacity. The new facility is equipped to manufacture Cray's complete line of supercomputing products like Cray (R) XC30(TM) supercomputers, Cray CS300(TM) cluster supercomputers, the YarcData Urika (R) appliance and Cray Sonexion (R) Storage solutions (Davis et al., 2014).

Looking in future direction, the next target is exaflops (1000 petaflops). Realistically, 100 petaflops could be hit in next few years and exaflops a few years after that (2018-2020). The USA's fastest supercomputer, the 1.7-petaflops Cray Jaguar at Oak Ridge National Laboratory (ORNL), is currently being upgraded to become the 20-petaflops Cray Titan (Anthony, 2012).

Meanwhile DARPA recognizes that the current silicon technology might not even be capable of exaflops has summoned researchers to reinvent and redirect computing. IBM, on the other hand, is building an exascale supercomputer to process the exabytes of astronomical data produced by the world's largest telescope, the Square Kilometre Array. The telescope goes online in 2024 which will hopefully give IBM enough time to work out on how to multiply the performance of current computers by more than 100 (Anthony, 2012).

EXASCALE CHALLENGES-POWER

One of the many challenges of exascale computing is Power. Exascale supercomputers are expected to consume no more than 20 MW of power, but to reach that goal by the end of the decade will require something beyond a Moore's Law-based progression of today's server CPUs (Power, 2012). Currently, a server-grade Intel Xeon chip and server consumes between 200 to more than 300 watts of power. An ARM® Cortex™-A9 system on a chip (SoC) requires in the region of 6-7 watts. The Xeon is many times more powerful than the ARM® system, but on a performance per watt basis the Cortex-A9 architecture in the Boston Viridis platform really shines. The key metric in determining supercomputing capability will be performance/watt in future but not overall performance (Power, 2012).

Figure 4. A Blue Gene/P Supercomputer at Argonne National Laboratory (ANL) Source: http://upload.wikimedia.org/wikipedia/commons/ thumb/d/d3/IBM_Blue_Gene_P_supercomputer. jpg/240px-IBM_Blue_Gene_P_supercomputer. jpg

The next two generations of ARM® CPUs give significant performance improvements bringing this to ~30PFLOPS in 2013 and 60 PFLOPS in 2014. If this trend is continued, exaflop can be predicted by 2017 (Power, 2012).

IBM is also currently working on a "self aware" supercomputer named "Blue Sky" for The National Center for Atmospheric Research (NCAR) in Boulder, Colorado. The Blue Sky will be used to work on colossal computing problems such as weather prediction. Additionally, this supercomputer can self-repair requiring no human intervention (InfoWebLinks – Supercomputer, n.d.).

THE VALUE AND COST OF SUPERCOMPUTING

Doing a value versus cost supercomputing market analysis is not a trivial task. The reason is that many of the values needed to compute such an equation cannot really be measured. Some of the values has been developments in military defense and nuclear research. Sometimes just having the leadership in technology is enough to deter other countries to consider an attack or war. However, it is still in a controversy whether the increased knowledge in nuclear research is beneficial for society. There are many other scientific areas where supercomputing promises a lot including biomedical research, etc. The most definite cost is the financial cost of developing supercomputers. Governments have literally spent billions of dollars developing supercomputers.

CURRENT TRENDS IN SUPERCOMPUTING

It is observed that vector processing has come, gone and now is back again. Parallel processing is predicted to stay longer. Hybrid architectures like CPU together with general-purpose computing in graphics (GPGPU) or Xeon-Phi Accelerator are becoming more common. Cluster computing gives high performance with marginal cost using commodity components. Many hardware and software concepts developed for supercomputers are now being used in latest commodity high–performance CPUs (Intel, AMD). Electrical power requirement is considered non-trivial with a substantial rise in green computing.

THE FUTURE OF SUPERCOMPUTING

The most fascinating aspects of supercomputing lie in the speculation of its future progress. Since this technology is increasing exponentially, and will most likely to continue to do so in the future, many scientists predict rapid advances in a relatively short amount of time (Podlaski, 2014).

In biology and medicine, supercomputers are predicted to contribute to the end of disease and cancer in the near future. More interestingly, Ian Pearson, head of the futurology unit at British Telecommunications group, foresees the discovery of "immortality" by 2050 where virtually all problems and illnesses due to disease or old age will be solved. In a few decades, we will most certainly have the computing power of the brain and will therefore be able to map to its entirety. Furthermore, a new field of "quantum computing" may make parallel and vector processors obsolete in future supercomputers (Podlaski, 2014).

However, Ray Kurzweil, the futurist and author of "The Singularity is Near," believes that advances in supercomputing technology are approaching a stage where artificial intelligence will surpass humans in mental capacity. Kurzweil states this phenomenon the "singularity", a point where humans cease to be the most capable "life forms" on the planet. In his book, he claims that humans would be able to upload their memory onto supercomputers, and that the human body will be subjected to constant updates until it stops to be human at all (Podlaski, 2014).

Whether or not singularity is achieved by 2045 as predicted by Kurzweil, it is surely undisputed that the world will be a drastically transformed place in the future, all thanks to the miraculous abilities of the modern supercomputer (Podlaski, 2014).

CURRENT GLOBAL SUPERCOMPUTING CENTERS

Some of the fastest supercomputers and their supercomputing centers in the top500 list as provided in Appendix of this book are more fully discussed as below. The supercomputer centers discussed below are Archer Supercomputer at University of Edinburgh in United Kingdom (UK); Yellowstone Supercomputer in National Center for Atmospheric Research- Wyoming Supercomputing Center in Cheyenne, Wyoming, U.S; Garnet Supercomputer at Engineer Research and Development Center, U.S. Department of Defense (DoD) Supercomputing Resource Center (DSRC) in Vicksburg, MS, U.S; Lomonosov Supercomputer at Moscow State University in Russia; Hermit Supercomputer at the High Performance Computing Centre in Stuttgart, Germany; Avoca Supercomputer at Victorian Life Sciences Computational Initiative (VLSCI) in Australia; Sunway Blue Light Supercomputer in Jinan, China; Aterui Supercomputer at the National Astronomical Observatory of Japan, Oshu, Japan; Red Sky Supercomputer at the U.S Department of Energy's Sandia National Laboratories, Golden, Colorado and Param Yuva II Supercomputer at Centre for Development of Advanced Computing (C-DAC) in Pune, India.

Archer Supercomputer

The ARCHER supercomputer managed by EPSRC and operated by EPCC at the University of Edinburgh, UK is a 72,192 core Cray XC30 system. It is ranked as the 19th world's fastest supercomputers in the Top500 list. ARCHER uses 12-core 2.7 GHz

Intel E5-2697 v2 (Ivy Bridge) series processors as opposed to HECToR's 16-core 2.3 GHz AMD Opteron processors (Sim, 2014).

The Cray ARCHER system includes four Cray Sonexion file systems. Each Cray Sonexion file system consists of a single Metadata Management Unit (MMU) and one or more scalable storage units (SSU). The Cray ARCHER system has a total of four MMUs and twenty SSUs configured as one large system (11 SSUs) and three smaller file systems (3 SSUs each). The ARCHER system includes a NetApp network attached storage appliance providing 214 TByte of home storage (Overview of the ARCHER System, 2013).

The storage appliance and its backup server are each connected to a pair of Ethernet switches as are all client nodes requiring Ethernet access. Compute nodes access the home file system via Cray XC30 I/O nodes running the Cray Data Virtualization Service (Overview of the ARCHER System, 2013).

An air-cooled Cray XC system is provided as a Test and Development system. The proposed system includes two x86 pre/post processing nodes. Users do not access the pre/post processing nodes directly; access is via the login nodes. The pre/post processing nodes operate independently of the main system (Overview of the ARCHER System, 2013).

Yellowstone Supercomputer

Yellowstone is the computing resource at the National Center for Atmospheric Research (NCAR)-Wyoming Supercomputing Center (NWSC) in Cheyenne, Wyoming, U.S. It is ranked as 22nd world's fastest supercomputer in the Top500 list. It was installed and tested for production in the summer of 2012. Yellowstone is a highly capable petascale system designed for conducting breakthrough scientific research in the field of Earth system Science. Funded by the National Science Foundation and the State and University of Wyoming and operated by the National Center

for Atmospheric Research, Yellowstone's purpose is to improve the predictive power of Earth system science simulation to benefit decision-making and planning for society (Yellowstone (Supercomputer), 2013).

Yellowstone is a 1.5-petaflops IBM iDataPlex cluster computer with 4,518 dual-socket compute nodes. Yellowstone is integrated with many other high-performance computing resources in the NWSC. The central feature of this supercomputing architecture is its shared file system that streamlines science workflows by providing analysis common to all the resources. This common data storage pool, called the GLADE (Globally Accessible Data Environment) initially provides 11 petabytes of online disk capacity shared by the supercomputer, two DAV cluster computers, Geyser and Caldera and a data archive with the capacity to store over 100 petabytes of research data (Yellowstone (Supercomputer), 2013).

When massive "solar" flares or "coronal mass ejections" erupt from the surface of the sun, it is difficult for space weather forecasters to know how large of a geomagnetic storm may result on Earth (Snider, 2012). That is because the scientists are not able to tell what the orientation of the magnetic field inside the coronal mass ejection is until just minutes before the flare hits earth. In order to run the number of scenarios needed to create that forecast, the researchers need a computer system that can quickly run through multiple scenarios. Yellowstone supercomputer may aid in achieving this (Snider, 2012).

Garnet Supercomputer

Garnet is a Cray XE6 supercomputer ranked at 25th position in the Top500 list installed at Engineer Research and Development Center, DoD Supercomputing Resource Center (DSRC) in the U.S. The login and compute nodes are populated with AMD Opteron and Interlagos processors. Garnet uses a dedicated Cray Gemini high-speed network for MPI messages and IO traffic. Garnet uses Lustre to manage its parallel file system that targets arrays of SAS disk drives. Garnet has 4716 compute nodes that share memory only on the node; memory is not shared across the nodes. Each compute node has two sixteen-core processors that operate under a Cray Linux Environment. It is rated at 1.5 peak PFLOPS (Cray XE6 (Garnet) User Guide, 2014).

Lomonosov Supercomputer

Lomonosov supercomputer was installed at the Moscow State University in Russia in 2009. It is ranked as 37th world's fastest supercomputers in the world according to the Top500 list. This supercomputer was created by Russian company "T-Platforms". The main section consisted of 5104 dual-processor diskless compute nodes based on 4-core Intel Xeon 5570 processors. It has a peak performance of 1.7 PFlops and a Linpack performance of 0.9 PFlops (MSU Supercomputers, n.d.). Total number of GPU compute nodes are 1065 and GPU CUDA cores being 954240 with a total RAM of 92 TB. The operating system is Clustrx T-Platforms edition and the power consumption is 2.8 MW. There is a 3-level external storage including 500 TB T-Platforms ReadyStorage SAN 7998/Lustre, 300 TB NFS Storage and PB Tape Library (MSU Supercomputers, n.d.).

Hermit Supercomputer

Cray XE6 "Hermit" inaugurated in Stuttgart/Germany on February 24, 2012 at the HLRS (High Performance Computing Center Stuttgart). It is ranked at 39th position in the list of Top500. With a performance of more than 1 petaflop/s, this industrial supercomputer would be used for health, energy, environment and mobility research. It is A Cray XE6 system composed of 3552 dual socket nodes equipped with AMD Interlagos Processors leading to 113664 processing cores overall. Nodes are equipped with 32 GB or 64 GB main memory (Supercomputer Hermit, 2013). Approximately

40 projects have taken advantage of Hermit's petascale computing power providing researchers with the tools to tackle the big questions within a year of its launch (One year of Hermit, 2013).

Despite the HLRS workhorse running literally full speed with close to no down time, demand exceeds the available computing time by a factor of 1.5. Computing time is granted to the researchers by a scientific peer review process. Some of the projects completed on Hermit include project LAMTUR, project UPSCALE, project Plasmonic Ligand-Stabilized Gold Nanoclusters (One year of Hermit, 2013).

Avoca Supercomputer

Avoca supercomputer is ranked at 48th position in the Top500 list of world's fastest supercomputers. It is installed at the Victorian Life Sciences Computational Initiative (VLSCI) in 2012 (Chirgwin, 2012). It has a 65 TB of RAM, 65,536 core machine, peak performance of 838. 86 teraFLOPS. The Interconnect between compute nodes forms a five-dimensional torus providing excellent nearest neighbor and bisection bandwidth (Computer and Software Configuration, 2011). It is currently Australia's fastest supercomputer. It is a Blue Gene/Q architecture (Chirgwin, 2012).

Sunway Blue Light Supercomputer

Ranked at 40th position, the Chinese Sunway Blue Light is installed at the National Supercomputer Center in Jinan (NSCCJN). NSCCJN is one of the four petascale supercomputer centers. It was built with domestically produced microprocessors and is capable of performing around one thousand trillion calculations per second. The computer was installed in September 2011. Sunway Blue Light marks a great technological leap for China's indigenous innovation in development and utilization of high performance computers. The computer will also serve as a node in China's national computing grid contributing to the scientific and economic development of the country (Sunway BlueLight Supercomputer in operation, 2012).

Sunway Blue Light supercomputer has a peak performance of 1.07 PFlops and a Sustained Performance of 0.796 PFlops. It has Linpack efficiency of 74.4%, memory capacity of > 160 TB, Storage Capacity of 2 PB, Performance /Power of 741MFlops/W. It has a high assembly density (Overview of Sunway Bluelight computer, 2012).

Aterui Supercomputer

Aterui supercomputer is ranked at 74th position in the Top500 list of supercomputers. It is installed at the National Astronomical Observatory of Japan. Cray XC30 "Aterui" is the fourth generation of dedicated numerical simulation supercomputers. Using an extremely large number of cores (24,192 cores), the entire system can achieve 502 TFlops. Aterui calculates every possible phenomenon in the Universe. It handles a wide range of astronomical phenomena. It can also shed light on a variety of time scales from the 13.8 billion years between the start of the Universe and the Present, down to the explosion of stars which takes less than a second (A telescope for theoretical astronomy: Supercomputer "aterui", 2014).

Red Sky Supercomputer

U.S Department of Energy has a new high performance supercomputer Red Sky. It is ranked at 71st position in the Top500 list of world's fastest supercomputers. Red Sky is located in the space where legendary system ASCI Red once stood to assist the U.S Department of Energy's National Renewable Energy Laboratory (NREL) in solving the nation's pressing energy challenges (Holinka, 2009). It was listed as the 10th fastest supercomputer in the world in 2009. The flexibility of the Red Sky architecture enabled this super-configuration which achieved a peak performance of more than 500 Teraflops and an impressive 433.5 Teraflops against the Linpack benchmark commonly used

for ranking supercomputing speed. Another area of innovation in Red Sky is in its energy efficiency (Holinka, 2009).

Param Yuva II Supercomputer

Param Yuva II is ranked at 83rd position in the Top500 list of world's fastest supercomputers. It was developed by Centre for Development of Advanced Computing in a period of three months at a cost of $3 million and was unveiled on February 8, 2013 in India. It performs at a peak of 524 teraflops and consumes 35% less energy as compared to Param Yuva. It delivers sustained performance of 360.8 teraflops on the standard Linpack benchmark (Param, 2014).

Param Yuva II will be used for research in space, bioinformatics, weather forecasting, aeronautical engineering, scientific data processing and pharmaceutical development. Educational institutes like Indian Institutes of Technology, etc can be linked to the computer through a national knowledge network (Param, 2014).

CONCLUSION

This chapter discusses various aspects of supercomputing including the need for supercomputing, and the challenges associated with supercomputing in terms of the cost and time. The chapter also presents the evolution of Seymour Cray's research beginning from the discovery of CDC 1604, CDC 6600 and CDC 7600 in 1960's to Star 100 in 1974, Cray 1 in 1976, CMOS ETA-10 in 1987, ILLIAC IV in 1976, Cray X-MP in 1982, Cray 2 in 1985, Cray Y-MP in 1988, Cray 3 and then the Cray era during the time period of years 2000 until today. Later, a discussion of the contributions of companies like Fujitsu, Hitachi, Intel and NEC in supercomputing are provided.

Supercomputing and its dominance in healthcare are displayed by a brief discussion of a section on this topic. History of Supercomputing

Center at Florida State University, Minnesota Supercomputing Center and Moscow University Supercomputing Center are discussed among various equally important supercomputing centers globally. Dell's contributions in the evolution of supercomputing is also discussed in this chapter. A section on Petaflop supercomputing in 21st century and current exascale computing challenges is described coherently. The chapter highlights in a positive direction the current global supercomputing centers in the Top 500 list, the current trends in supercomputing and the bright future of supercomputing.

Subsequent chapters of this book discuss in more depth both many specific current applications of supercomputers to multi-disciplines and also the techniques and theory used.

ACKNOWLEDGMENT

I, Neha Gupta, would like to sincerely acknowledge Dr. Richard Segall for his continuous efforts in providing me inputs on how to improve this manuscript during the process of its development. I would also like to acknowledge Jeffrey Cook for contributing a few sections of this manuscript.

REFERENCES

A Telescope for Theoretical Astronomy: Supercomputer "Aterui". (2014). Retrieved May 29, 2014 from http://www.nao.ac.jp/en/gallery/2014/20140422-aterui.html

Anthony, S. (2012). *The history of supercomputers*. Retrieved May 28, 2014 from http://www.extremetech.com/extreme/125271-the-history-of-supercomputers

Bell, G. (n.d.). *A brief history of supercomputing: "the Crays", clusters and Beowulf's, centers. what next?* Retrieved May 30, 2014 from http://research.microsoft.com/en-us/um/people/gbell/supers/supercomputing-a_brief_history_1965_2002.htm

Betancourt, T. (2012). *High-tech supercomputer soon to be history*. Retrieved May 31, 2014 from http://www.statepress.com/2012/01/12/high-tech-supercomputer-soon-to-be-history/

Burns, P. (2013). *History of supercomputing*. Retrieved May 30, 2014 from http://lamar.colostate.edu/~grad511/lec2.pdf

Cambridge University. (n.d.). Retrieved May 28, 2014 from http://www.top500.org/site/47520#.U4XU7_mSyO0

Chirgwin, R. (2012). *VLSCI's supercomputer passes acceptance test, lands in top 50*. Retrieved May 29, 2014 from http://www.theregister.co.uk/2012/06/18/vlsci_blue_gene_acceptance_test/

ClusterVision Pumps up Supercomputer Muscles in Brussels. (2013). Retrieved May 28, 2014 from http://insidehpc.com/2013/06/13/clustervision-pumps-up-supercomputer-muscles-in-brussels/

Computer and Software Configuration. (2011). Retrieved May 29, 2014 from http://www.vlsci.org.au/page/computer-software-configuration

Cray. (2014). Retrieved May 30, 2014 from http://en.wikipedia.org/wiki/Cray

Cray History. (2014). Retrieved May 28, 2014 from http://www.cray.com/About/History.aspx

Cray XE6 (Garnet) User Guide. (2014). Retrieved May 29, 2014 from http://www.erdc.hpc.mil/docs/garnetUserGuide.html

Davis, N., & Hiemstra, P. (2014). *Cray expands manufacturing capacity with new supercomputing facility in Chippewa Falls.* Retrieved May 31, 2014 from http://www.marketwatch.com/story/cray-expands-manufacturing-capacity-with-new-supercomputing-facility-in-chippewa-falls-2014-03-10

Deumens, E. (2013). *UF launches HiPerGator, the state's most powerful supercomputer.* Retrieved May 28, 2014 from http://news.ufl.edu/2013/05/07/hipergator/

Hautala, K. (2012). *UK takes academic supercomputing to next level.* Retrieved May 28, 2014 from http://uknow.uky.edu/content/uk-takes-academic-supercomputing-next-level-0

History of Research Computing Center. (2013). Retrieved May 31, 2014 from https://rcc.fsu.edu/about/history

History of Supercomputing. (2014). Retrieved May 28, 2014 from http://en.wikipedia.org/wiki/History_of_supercomputing

Holinka, S. (2009). *Red sky at night, Sandia's new computing might.* Retrieved May 29, 2014 from https://share.sandia.gov/news/resources/news_releases/red-sky-at-night/#.U4cFQ_mSyO0

InfoWebLinks – Supercomputer. (n.d.). Retrieved May 28, 2014 from http://www.infoweblinks.com/content/supercomputers.htm

Matlis, J. (2005). *A brief history of supercomputers.* Retrieved May 28, 2014 from http://www.computerworld.com.au/article/132504/brief_history_supercomputers/

Meglicki, Z. (2004). *The history of MPI.* Retrieved May 31, 2014 from http://beige.ucs.indiana.edu/I590/node54.html

Minnesota Supercomputer Center. (1994). Retrieved May 31, 2014 from http://www.auditor.leg.state.mn.us/ped/1994/backgrd.htm

Minnesota Supercomputing Institute-Cascade. (2014). Retrieved May 28, 2014 from https://www.msi.umn.edu/hpc/cascade

Mortenson, D., & Cabrera-Cordon, L. (n.d.). *The past and present of supercomputing.* Retrieved May 28, 2014 from https://www.google.co.in/url?sa=t&rct=j&q=&esrc=s&source=web&cd=10&cad=rja&uact=8&ved=0CJcBEBYwCQ&url=http%3A%2F%2Fcourses.cs.washington.edu%2Fcourses%2Fcsep590%2F06au%2Fprojects%2Fsupercomputing.doc&ei=lmiFU-ymN4_78QXProKoBw&usg=AFQjCNGEijiGGowF-qq15ySWjoCcTkUf_Q&sig2=vK0Uyg2AptSQaHYJXR-2eA&bvm=bv.67720277,d.dGc

MSU Supercomputers: "Lomonosov". (n.d.). Retrieved May 29, 2014 from http://hpc.msu.ru/?q=node/59

MSU's HPC History. (n.d.). Retrieved May 31, 2014 from http://hpc.msu.ru/?q=node/57

Oden, T., & Ghattas, O. (2012). *Computational science: The "third pillar" of science.* Retrieved May 30, 2014 from http://blog.tamest.org/tag/supercomputing/

One Year of Hermit. (2013). Retrieved May 29, 2014 from http://www.hlrs.de/news/press/for-journalists/1-year-of-hermit/

Overview of Sunway Bluelight Computer. (2012). Retrieved May 29, 2014 from http://hpc.inspur.com/images/News/2012/11/23/E34520689DA74A0FA3360192582FDD7A.pdf

Overview of the ARCHER System. (2013). Retrieved May 29, 2014 from http://www.epsrc.ac.uk/SiteCollectionDocuments/Publications/tenders/PR120039HardwareOverview.pdf

Oyonagi, Y. (2002). *Future of supercomputing.* Retrieved May 28, 2014 from http://www.sciencedirect.com/science/article/pii/S0377042702005265

Param. (2014). Retrieved May 29, 2014 from http://en.wikipedia.org/wiki/PARAM

Podlaski, B. (2014). *The age of the supercomputer.* Retrieved May 30, 2014 from http://asutriplehelix. org/node/127

Power, D. (2012). *The Boston viridis ARM server: Addressing the power challenges of exascale.* Retrieved 05/31, 2014, Retrieved from http://ukhpc. co.uk/files/2013/12/White-paper-The-Boston-Viridis-ARM%C2%AE-Server.pdf

Research Institutions Push the Boundaries of Supercomputing with Dell. (2013). Retrieved May 28, 2014 from http://pbdj.sys-con.com/node/2875456

Robat, C. (2013). *Introduction to supercomputers.* Retrieved May 28, 2014 from http://www.thocp. net/hardware/supercomputers.htm

Schwartz, E. (2013, October 28). Supercomputing inches toward mHealth. *Mhealthnews.*

Seymour Cray Facts. (2014). Retrieved May 30, 2014 from http://www.yourdictionary.com/ seymour-cray

Shah, A. (2013). *Dell working on ARM supercomputer prototypes.* Retrieved May 28, 2014 from http://www.pcworld.com/article/2032568/dell-working-on-arm-supercomputer-prototypes.html

Sim, L. (2014). *Introduction to ARCHER and Cray MPI.* Retrieved May 29, 2014 from http://www. archer.ac.uk/training/courses/introandmpi.php

Smotherman, M. (2013). *S1 supercomputer (1975-1988).* Retrieved May 30, 2014 from http://people. cs.clemson.edu/~mark/s1.html

Snider, L. (2012). *NCAR's new supercomputer set to run models by summer's end.* Retrieved May 29, 2014 from http://www.dailycamera.com/ ci_20817203/ncars-new-supercomputer-set-run-models-by-summers

Sullivan, T. (2014). *Can blackberry advance supercomputing in healthcare?* Retrieved May 30, 2014 from http://www.mhealthnews.com/news/ can-blackberry-supercomputing-healthcare-nanthealth-mhealth-mobile-cloud

Sunway BlueLight Supercomputer in Operation. (2012, January 19). *Chinadaily.*

Supercomputer. (2014). Retrieved May 30, 2014 from http://encyclopedia2.thefreedictionary.com/ High+performance+computer

Supercomputer Hermit. (2013). Retrieved May 29, 2014 from http://www.gauss-centre.eu/gauss-centre/EN/AboutGCS/Locations/HLRS/hermit. html?nn=1282612

What is a Beowulf?. (n.d.) Retrieved May 30, 2014 from http://yclept.ucdavis.edu/Beowulf/ aboutbeowulf.html

WintelGuy.com. (2014). *Gigabyte (GB) to Gibibyte (GiB) and Megabyte (MB) to Mibibyte (MiB) converter.* Retrieved from http://wintelguy.com/ gb2gib.html

Yamada, M. (2014). *Supercomputing pioneer.* Retrieved May 30, 2014 from http://www.fujitsu. com/global/solutions/business-technology/tc/ hpc/

Yellowstone (Supercomputer). (2013). Retrieved May 29, 2014 from http://en.wikipedia.org/wiki/ Yellowstone_(supercomputer)

Zumer, B. (2013). *New APG supercomputers can do a quadrillion operations in a second.* Retrieved May 28, 2014 from http://www. baltimoresun.com/news/maryland/harford/ aberdeen-havre-de-grace/ph-ag-apg-supercomputer-0612-20130611,0,5032500.story

ADDITIONAL READING

Banon, R. (2013). Atos wins contract for the second most powerful supercomputer in Spain. Retrieved June 1, 2014 from http://atos.net/ en-us/home/we-are/news/press-release/2013/pr-2013_06_27_01.html

Barber, B. (2014). New $20M supercomputer to double Wright-Patterson computing power. Retrieved June 1, 2014 from http://www.stripes. com/news/us/new-20m-supercomputer-to-dou-ble-wright-patterson-computing-power-1.269668

Endo, T., & Matsuoka, S. (n.d.).Massive super-computing coping with heterogeneity of modern accelerators. Retrieved June 1, 2014 from http:// pdf.aminer.org/000/255/337/panel_the_virtual_ heterogeneous_supercomputer_can_it_be_built. pdf

Feldman, M. (2012). Cray parlays supercom-puting technology into big data appliance. Re-trieved June 1, 2014 from http://www.datanami. com/2012/03/02/cray_parlays_supercomput-ing_technology_into_big_data_appliance/

Fighting super flu with supercomputing. (2014). Retrieved June 1, 2014 from http://www.intel.com/ content/www/us/en/corporate-responsibility/ better-future/fighting-super-flu-with-supercom-puting.html

Ford, M. (2011). Dr. Watson: How IBM's super-computer could improve health care. Retrieved June 1, 2014 from http://www.washingtonpost. com/opinions/dr-watson-how-ibms-supercom-puter-could-improve-health-care/2011/09/14/ gIQAOZQzXK_story.html

GNS healthcare to develop big data computer model for Huntington's disease. (2012). Retrieved June 1, 2014 from http://connection.ebscohost. com/c/articles/89810682/gns-healthcare-devel-op-big-data-computer-model-huntingtons-disease

Hallwyler, L. (2014). University hospital Zurich implements supercomputing technology from ziosoft for multi-dimensional image analysis. Retrieved June 1, 2014 from http://www.prweb. com/releases/2011/7/prweb8676927.htm

Henry Markham. A brain in a supercomputer (n,d.). Retrieved June 1, 2014 from http://www. ted.com/talks/henry_markram_supercomput-ing_the_brain_s_secrets

IMDGs. Next generation parallel supercomputers. (2014). Retrieved June 1, 2014 from http://blog. scaleoutsoftware.com/imdgs-next-generation-parallel-supercomputers/

Jenkings, M. (2013). Apple Cray computer. Retrieved June 1, 2014 from http://c2.com/cgi/ wiki?AppleCrayComputer

Lavington, S. (2013). Virtualization: A long brief history. Retrieved June 1, 2014 from http://www. servethehome.com/virtualization-long-history/

Lee, H. (2014). Paging Dr. Watson - IBM's Wat-son supercomputer now being used in healthcare. Retrieved June 1, 2014 from http://library.ahima. org/xpedio/groups/public/documents/ahima/ bok1_050656.hcsp?dDocName=bok1_050656

Libby, R. (2013). Is supercomputing personal? Could it become personal? Retrieved June 1, 2014 from http://blogs.intel.com/intellabs/2013/11/17/ could-supercomputing-be-or-become-personal/

Lotfi, M. (2014). NSA building new super-com-puter: You won't believe what it does - "owning the internet". Retrieved June 1, 2014 from http:// benswann.com/nsa-building-new-super-comput-er-you-wont-believe-what-it-does-owning-the-internet/

Mashelkar, R. A. (n,d.).The new millennium chal-lenges for Indian science & technology. Retrieved June 1, 2014 from http://pib.nic.in/feature/fe0899/ f1508997.html

McBride, R. (2011). Supercomputers combat bad drug events for Boston hospital. Retrieved June 1, 2014 from http://blog.targethealth.com/?p=19233

MD Anderson taps IBM Watson to power "moon shots" mission. (2013). Retrieved June 1, 2014 from http://www.mdanderson.org/newsroom/news-releases/2013/ibm-watson-to-power-moon-shots-.html

Mehrotra, P., & Pryor, H. (2014). Supporting big data analytics at the NASA advanced supercomputing (NAS) division. Retrieved June 1, 2014 from http://www.odbms.org/2014/04/supporting-big-data-analytics-nasa-advanced-supercomputing-nas-division/

mHealth- mobile technology poised to enable a new era in health care. (2012). Retrieved June 1, 2014 from http://www.ictliteracy.info/rf.pdf/mHealth%20Report_Final.pdf

Moyna, G. (n,d.).The chain gang Beowulf -class supercomputer page. Retrieved June 1, 2014 from http://tonga.usp.edu/gmoyna/chaingang/index.html

Neyarapally, T., & Tromblee, C. (2013) (n,d.). GNS healthcare joins Orion bionetworks to develop predictive models for multiple sclerosis and other diseases. Retrieved June 1, 2014 from http://www.gnshealthcare.com/news-and-events/gns-healthcare-joins-orion-bionetworks-to-develop-predictive-models-for-multiple-sclerosis-and-other-diseases/

Nordqvist, C. (2013). IBM supercomputer "Watson" to help in cancer treatment. Retrieved June 1, 2014 from http://www.medicalnewstoday.com/articles/256137.php

O'Neal, T. (2014). A turbulent birth for stars in merging galaxies. Retrieved June 1, 2014 from http://www.supercomputingonline.com/lastest-news/latest/a-turbulent-birth-for-stars-in-merging-galaxies

Researchers describe project to merge cloud computing and supercomputing. (2014). Retrieved June 1, 2014 from https://www.alcf.anl.gov/articles/researchers-describe-project-merge-cloud-computing-and-supercomputing

Russell, J. (2013). IBM's cloud supercomputer powers artificially intelligent consumer apps. Retrieved June 1, 2014 from http://jerrydrussell.com/business-2/ibms-cloud-supercomputer-powers-artificially-intelligent-consumer-apps/

Shaping the evolution of high-performance computing. (2014). Retrieved June 1, 2014 from http://www.fujitsu.com/global/solutions/business-technology/tc/hpc/history/

Shaw, J. (2014). *Why "big data" is a big deal. Harvard Magazine*. March-April.

Solnushkin, K. (2013). Clusters: A disruptive technology in the supercomputing world. Retrieved June 1, 2014 from http://clusterdesign.org/2013/05/clusters-a-disruptive-technology-in-the-supercomputing-world/

Sullivan, T. (2014). BlackBerry enters healthcare IT arena. Retrieved June 1, 2014 from http://www.healthcareitnews.com/news/blackberry-makes-big-move-healthcare

Supercomputer timeline - George Mason University (n.d.). Retrieved June 1, 2014 from http://mason.gmu.edu/~tbell5/page2.html

Supercomputer Watson-based health apps coming to your smartphone. (2014). Retrieved June 1, 2014 from http://www.nuviun.com/blog/Supercomputer-Watson-Based-Health-Apps-Coming-To-Your-Smartphone

Supercomputer,"MANA" tasked with the power to perform. (2009). Retrieved June 1, 2014 from http://mauinow.com/2009/08/21/supercomputer-%E2%80%9Cmana%E2%80%9D-tasked-with-the-power-to-perform/

Techentin, B. (2012). Big data and graph analytics in a health care setting. Retrieved June 1, 2014 from http://www.graphanalysis.org/SC12/03_Techentin.pdf

Timeline: Supercomputing. (2012). Retrieved June 1, 2014 from http://www.pcauthority.com.au/Gallery/307952,timeline-supercomputing.aspx/2

Todd, T. (2014). IBM healthcare technology helps detect heart failure risks, transforms doctor's notes into electronic medical record insights. Retrieved June 1, 2014 from http://turbotodd.com/blog/2014/02/19/ibm-healthcare-technology-helps-detect-heart-failure-risks-transforms-doctors-notes-into-electronic-medical-record-insights/

Topol, E. (2011). Medicine needs frugal innovation. Retrieved June 1, 2014 from http://www.technologyreview.com/news/426336/medicine-needs-frugal-innovation/

Wall, J. K. (2013). Technology on track to dramatically change health care. Retrieved June 1, 2014 from http://www.ibj.com/technology-on-track-to-dramatically-change-health-care/PARAMS/article/43839

Webster, S. (2012). Earth's supercomputing power surpasses human brain three times over. Retrieved June 1, 2014 from http://www.rawstory.com/rs/2012/06/18/earths-supercomputing-power-surpasses-human-brain-three-times-over/

Wray, F. (2012). A brief future of computing. Retrieved June 1, 2014 from http://www.planethpc.eu/index.php?option=com_content&view=article&id=66:a-brief-future-of-computing&catid=1:articles&Itemid=3

KEY TERMS AND DEFINITIONS

Apple Power Mac G5 Computers: G5 is a series of Macintosh desktop machines from Apple that use the 64-bit IBM PowerPC 970 CPU. G5 has a 1GHz front side bus and can access up to 8 GB of memory. The Power Mac G5 was the last Macintosh to use the PowerPC chips.

Complementary Metal Oxide Semiconductor (CMOS): Technology for constructing integrated circuits. CMOS technology is used in microprocessors, static RAM, microcontrollers and other digital logic circuits.

Double Data Rate 2 (DDR2) Memory: DDR2 RAM is an improved version of DDR memory that is faster and more efficient.

General-Purpose Computing on Graphics Processing Units: (GPGPU): The utilization of a graphics processing unit, which typically handles computation only for computer graphics, to perform computation in applications traditionally handled by the central processing unit.

Lustre File System: Lustre is a type of parallel distributed file system, generally used for large-scale cluster computing. The name Lustre is a Portmanteau word derived from Linux and Cluster.

Massively Parallel Processing Unit (MPP): Coordinated processing of a program by multiple processors that work on different parts of the program with each processor using its own operating system and memory.

Quantum Computers: A computer which makes use of the quantum states of subatomic particles to store information.

Shenwei CPUs: Shenwei is a series of microprocessors developed by Jiangnan Computing lab in Wuxi, China.

Static Random-Access Memory: (SRAM): A type of memory chip which is faster and requires less power than dynamic memory.

Very-Large-Scale Integration: (VLSI) Circuits: The process of creating integrated circuits by combining thousands of transistors into a single chip. VLSI began in the 1970s when complex semiconductor and communication technologies were being developed. The microprocessor is a VLSI device.

Chapter 3
Applications and Current Challenges of Supercomputing across Multiple Domains of Computational Sciences

Neha Gupta
Northeastern University, USA & Osmania University, India

ABSTRACT

Supercomputing is a contemporary solution to enhance the speed of calculations in nanoseconds. Presently, there are different aspects of supercomputing like Cloud Computing, High Performance Computing, Grid Computing, etc. provided by companies like Amazon (Amazon Web Services), Windows (Azure), Google (Google Cloud Platform). Supercomputers play an important role in the field of Computer Science and are used for a wide range of computationally intensive tasks across domains like Bioinformatics, Computational Earth and Atmospheric Sciences, Computational Materials Sciences and Engineering, Computational Chemistry, Computational Fluid Dynamics, Computational Physics, Computational and Data Enabled Social Sciences, Aerospace, Manufacturing, Industrial Applications, Computational Medicine, and Biomedical Engineering. However, there are a lot of issues that need to be solved to develop next generation supercomputers. In this chapter, the potential applications and current challenges of supercomputing across these domains are explained in detail. The current status of supercomputing and limitations are discussed, which forms the basis for future work in these areas. The future ideas that can be applied efficiently with the availability of good computing resources are explained coherently in this chapter.

INTRODUCTION

Due to remarkable advances in computer technology, scientists are looking for better digital supercomputing tools to deal with the complexi-

ties of the datasets. Supercomputers are the fastest computers we know of. They are characterized by a very high computational speed and an immense number of processors (Chinta, 2013). They are usually seen in corporations, etc filling a big

DOI: 10.4018/978-1-4666-7461-5.ch003

Copyright © 2015, IGI Global. Copying or distributing in print or electronic forms without written permission of IGI Global is prohibited.

room. The speed of supercomputers are measured in FLOPS (Chinta, 2013). Simply put, Floating point operations means computations that involve very large decimal numbers, usually 300 digits in a single number. The ten fastest supercomputers in the world are Titan, Sequoia, K Computer, Mira, JUQueen, SuperMuc, Stampede, Tianhe-1A, Fermi, Darpa Trial Subset (Chinta, 2013).

The first supercomputer was introduced by Seymour Cray in the early 70's. Supercomputers have wide range of applications like constructing weather maps, construction of nuclear weapons, atom bombs, finding oil, earthquake prediction, etc. They are also used in space exploration, environmental simulations or global warming effects, mathematics, physics, medicine, etc. The contemporary supercomputer is a high performance cluster with a tightly-coupled high-speed interconnect that uses parallel applications. Supercomputing is currently in the middle of large technological, architectural and application changes that greatly impact the way programmers think about the system. Computational methods for solving the problems has become very important in many scientific and engineering areas where the calculations becomes limiting. Supercomputers can help address these problems provided they are developed with great functional architectures.

One of the alternatives in supercomputing is GPU. GPUs are doing well and have the sole dominance in the markets. GPUs are not a clear option though (Fielden, 2013). Working with GPU's can be trickier than that of CPUs. It needs modern software code to port to GPUs and additionally more time and money (Fielden, 2013). In data-intensive industries like life sciences, manufacturing, earth sciences, materials sciences, etc the volume and the speed of streaming data that must be analyzed are pushing the boundaries of hardware capabilities. It is very essential at the moment to bring the power of cutting edge supercomputing technologies to the toughest data challenges that these industries face every day.

Most supercomputers are clusters of MIMD multiprocessors, each processor of which is SIMD. A SIMD processor executes the same instruction on more than one set of data at the same time. MIMD is employed to achieve parallelism, by using a number of processors that function asynchronously and independently. Currently, the data is growing at a very rapid rate but most of the data is stored and have not been used to extract the meaningful information. So, there is an eminent need for developing proper mechanisms of processing these large datasets to extract useful knowledge for better decision making.

In recent years, supercomputers have become essential tools for scientists and engineers who has to quickly manipulate large amounts of data. Next to supercomputers in speed and size are mini-supercomputers. Apart from Mainframe computers and Supercomputers, IBM is doing research in a new stream called quantum computing which is believed to be faster than supercomputing. This computing uses computers whose transistors are so small and the computer is working with atoms and molecules (Mainframes and Supercomputers, 2012). A quantum computer would be capable of solving millions of calculations at once- and able to crack any computer code on Earth (Mainframes and Supercomputers, 2012).

Supercomputers are so powerful that they provide researchers with insight into phenomena that are too small, too big, too fast or too slow to observe in the normal laboratories (Karin, 2002). For example, astrophysicists use supercomputers as "time machines" to explore the past and the future of our universe. A supercomputer simulation was first created in 2000 that depicted the collision of two galaxies: our Milky Way and Andromeda (Karin, 2002). Although this collision is not allowed to happen for another three billion years, the simulation allowed scientists to run the experiments and see the results. A similar simulation was also performed on Blue Horizon, a parallel supercomputer at the San Diego Supercomputer Center (Karin, 2002). Using 256 of Blue

Horizon's 1152 processors, the simulation showed what will happen to millions of stars when these two galaxies collide. This would be impossible to do in laboratory conditions (Karin, 2002).

Data intensive supercomputer applications are increasingly important for the research progress. Current benchmarks and performance measures do not provide useful information about suitability of supercomputing systems for data intensive applications. A new set of benchmarks is needed in order to guide the design of hardware architectures and software systems supporting such applications.

In this chapter, various applications and current challenges of supercomputing faced by the people working in the domains like Bioinformatics and Computational Biology, Computational Earth and atmospheric sciences, Computational Materials Sciences and Engineering, Computational Chemistry, Computational Fluid Dynamics, Computational Physics, Computational and data enabled social sciences, Aerospace, Manufacturing, Industrial Applications, Computational Medicine and Biomedical Engineering, etc are discussed in-depth. These points can be a good starting point to think about the architectures and other areas of future supercomputers.

SUPERCOMPUTING IN MULTIPLE DOMAINS OF COMPUTATIONAL SCIENCES

1. Bioinformatics and Computational Biology

Supercomputers are hardware and software systems that provide the best computational performance. An analysis that can be run in a single machine can be made faster if it is ran in multiple machines parallel. Basically, supercomputers parallelize the analysis and are much effective than other systems. Currently, the supercomputers used in genome sequencing analysis are having peak speed of petaflops and teraflops. However, if the

exaflop supercomputers are built in the future, it would be around 61 times faster than the fastest supercomputer available currently (India plans 61 times faster supercomputer by 2017, 2012). There are wide applications of supercomputers in many domains like weather, national security and defense, research and development in science and engineering, analysis of chemicals, genome sequencing, etc. Although they have wide applications and different kinds of supercomputers are available to date, there is a need for more computationally efficient supercomputing to analyze the tremendous amounts of datasets in every field. There are various groups across the world who have their own proprietary supercomputers but still none can address the current computational issues.

The last few decades have witnessed a deluge of biological data either from clinics, patients, research institutes, research companies and government agencies. However, till date there is no accurate and meaningful information that is extracted from this so called "big data". The companies and institutes are really struggling hard to interpret this data, especially genomic data, as the technological resources and man power available are very limited in comparison to the amounts of data available. Hence, it becomes imperative that technology should be improved quickly and the organizations that are trying to interpret any useful information from this data deluge across the world should work collaboratively to achieve this challenge. This is an era where people are witnessing the sudden evolution of experimental biological techniques to a high end computational domain. This transition is aiding in a positive note and will aid in future to decipher scattered pieces of data into a useful semantic. Therefore, it is very essential at present to design the fastest supercomputer soon that will help in analyzing memory intensive human genome sequencing data efficiently. There are various medical applications of supercomputing like providing the best healthcare to the patients, answering research questions pertaining to several disorders like Cancer, Diabetes, Neural disorders, aging among many other disorders troubling the human beings. To be able to generate knowledge from the oceans of genomic data, High Performance Computing, heterogeneous computing and Grid/Cloud computing using Amazon Web services, etc are the latest weapons in the hands of the modern biologist.

Most of the questions still remain unanswered especially in the Bioinformatics and Computational domain. Some of these are carrying out comparative genomics of whole genomes of multiple organisms in a single platform, modifying the current reports by doctors to also include the pathway information for the genes or SNPs effecting various disorders, accurate RNA sequencing data analysis like for differential gene expression analysis across many organisms simultaneously, etc. The current cost per hour to use cluster computing, etc is also expensive and the typical analysis for next generation sequencing data takes around 24-48 hours of total time. These project and cost issues are necessary to be addressed in the current scenario. Also, in most of the research institutions, the high performance computing systems provide just in petabytes of storage, integrity of the data is not protected by secured backups, read and write speeds should be improved from GB/sec. Currently, scratch storage facilities are attached to the supercomputer where the additional storage is provided to be used while applications are running in the supercomputer. But the disadvantages of scratch storage are there are no backups and typically the data is stored for just 30 days or less. There is a great need to also improve the long term, offline storage capacities of supercomputers. The increase in the number of nodes from 40-100 nodes currently to a higher number in a multi node Hadoop cluster will be really helpful for users with big data analytic needs.

One of the existing applications of supercomputers is using Basic Local Alignment Search Tool (BLAST) to aid scientists in the analysis of complex DNA and protein sequences. Sometimes the performance of BLAST is inconsistent

as multiple users access the tool simultaneously (Stroschein, 2005). Therefore, the University of South Dakota Bioinformatics group decided to implement a parallel version of the BLAST tool on a Linux cluster by combining freely available software. The BLAST cluster composed of old desktop PCs destined for surplus that improves searches by providing up-to-date databases to a smaller audience of researchers. This cluster project is an implementation of the Open Source Cluster Application Resources (OSCAR). OSCAR helps automate the installation, maintenance and even use of cluster software. A graphical user interface provides a step-by-step installation guide and doubles as a graphical maintenance tool. WWW BLAST was created by NCBI to offer a Web-based front end for BLAST users and is the web interface selected for this BLAST cluster (Stroschein, 2005). Although WWW BLAST enhances usability of the cluster, mpiBLAST enhances the performance. mpiBLAST was developed by Los Alamos National Laboratories (LANL) to improve the performance of BLAST by executing queries in parallel. mpiBLAST provides all of the software necessary for parallel BLAST queries (Stroschein, 2005).

Another application that needs to be addressed is finding the missing genes. Most of the genomes completed to date have had their genes detected by gene-finder programs which may miss real functionally important genes. One way to discover these missing genes is by similarity computations. If appropriate computational power is available, every possible location of the genome can be checked for the genes. Furthermore, a complete genome sequence- similarity tree can also be generated to enable future searches to complete in a fraction of seconds. The sequence similarity tree can help researchers to come up with better ways of structuring the database and more efficient algorithms to search specific portions of the data instead of the search across the entire database would be needed. Hence, researchers can discard huge parts of databases without losing any useful information. However, generating these similarity trees require large amounts of computational power and disk storage.

One of the current issues in gene-gene interaction networks or protein-protein interaction networks that needs to be addressed is the large number of genes/proteins inter-connected via multiple connections which makes the network complex to visualize. This creates a messy interaction where clear distinctions between sub-pathways within the main pathway becomes complex. This challenge can be addressed if there is more computational power and through cluster computing. Due to improvements in computational power, there can be a clear visualization of these networks and more meaningful predictions of the connections in terms of functionality in the human genome. Another important achievement would be to get the relationships between the words of entire PubMed literature using parallel computing to have meaningful interpretation of drugs that can cure diseases or the proteins/targets that are causative of the disorders. This would in turn help physicians, medical practitioners, etc in providing the accurate medicine to the patients depending on their genotypes and pathway information in a single visit.

The data in Genbank database is constantly increasing in size and due to this data overload, the scientific interpretation using Bioinformatics tools becomes tedious. It is very essential to organize this data in Genbank and also build ontologies between the datasets within this database so that the useful datasets can be isolated and querying by the user becomes faster in supercomputers. Also, currently computing the frequencies of n-mers from human genome build hg19 is possible from 3-11mer flanks surrounding the variations sites on both sides. But, computing the frequencies of 12 mer flanks to greater than 12 mer flanks on each side of the variations becomes a tedious job without proper supercomputing facilities. As the data is increasing in complexity each day, the Bioinformatics algorithms to analyze this data

becomes more complex resulting in more memory intensive and time consuming applications.

One of the main issues currently faced by researchers everywhere is the infinite number of research articles found in various databases like PubMed, Google Scholar, NCBI, etc. This causes lot of trouble since they have to read and go through each and every article present in the databases to mine useful scientific information. This is also exhaustive and time consuming. I believe that supercomputing could help solve this challenge by making the data more productive and integrated or may be like designing a single database holding all the scientifically important articles together. This would be more convenient for the doctors, researchers, etc to analyze their data if the data in the web browsers or databases are made understandable. Another important issue currently faced is the security of data sharing across multiple computers. There are no effective data sharing methodologies in place and the security of file transfers, etc is not so promising. There are chances of the datasets or files becoming corrupt or missing while sharing that with someone.

One of the issues that has to be addressed via supercomputing which is also helpful in the Computational Biology domain would be to increase the current limitation of 25 MB attachment size in Gmail while emailing people the datasets. Even with the modern tools like Dropbox, Google tools, etc, the user is not able to effectively and freely share large datasets with their collaborators as these tools have a certain data limit in MB or GB. Also, the security of the Google tools is the question today because due to the current changes in their tools, there is no privacy as mostly everything is viewed publicly. Some of the examples of unsecured Google tools are Gmail, google hangouts, google docs, etc. Though these tools provide lot of advantages and are user friendly but the only disadvantage is their lack of proper security measures for a user to use it without any inhibitions. Another useful application would be to study the use of computer simulation of cells,

Figure 1. Growth of GenBank (1971-2013) (Wicks, 2014)

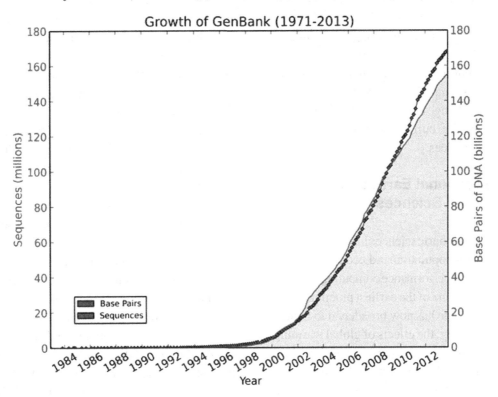

blood tests, urine tests, blood glucose levels, X-ray scans, and etc. instead of wet lab testing carried out currently. This would potentially save considerable amounts of time and costs associated with wet lab tests and would be convenient for the diagnosis by doctors.

A promising challenge would be to design a new Operating system that is best compatible for cloud computing tasks since the existing operating systems limit the computational performance of complex bioinformatics programs and algorithms. Another research problem that is to be solved would be to study the differences between induced normal human cells to become immortal and tumorigenic cells. Then, it is essential to perform transcriptome analysis of these two types of cells using RNA-Seq to identify genes and possible molecular mechanisms involved in cancer tumorigenecity. Also, later study the differences between gene expressions of significant genes between two

cell types and get to know which chromosomes are more prone to develop tumorigenecity based on morphological changes during the process. The frequency of tumor associated genes and their further interactions with other tumor genes within the same chromosome or between different chromosomes can help in therapeutics towards Cancer. This research problem can be solved effectively with availability of good computing resources. Integration of available libraries in CPAN for Bioperl libraries, CRAN for R functions, Biopython, etc would be an added advantage for the programmers as the unique scientific libraries are available in a comprehensible format. The scientists are presently facing problems in running some applications in computers which interrupt other applications running and cause system crashes. This is the most commonly observed issue while working on a scientifically important project as due to the large number of applications running simultaneously, the memory is exhausted and there are system crashes. These problems can be addressed via supercomputing environments.

Although there are still many other applications of supercomputing specifically in Bioinformatics and Computational Biology domain, the above discussed challenges are really important to be addressed in the current scenario to enhance healthcare practices.

2. Computational Earth and Atmospheric Sciences

Earth and atmospheric sciences have long contributed to world's population and economy driving advances in high performance computing. Weather forecasting was one of the earliest practical applications. The scope has now broadened to include climate modelling, the effects of global warming, and the dynamics of the earth's interior. Earth simulator that was launched in 2002 was the fastest supercomputer in the world. The supercomputers allow scientists to better understand the workings of the earth and by helping to trace the evolution of distant galaxies. They will also unravel the complicated implications of climate change. Another use would be to support accurate forecasting of tornadoes, hurricanes, severe storms, solar eruptions, etc. They also improve the ability to predict earthquakes, to measure the flow of ice sheets in Antarctica in order to gauge future sea level rise, etc.To corroborate the necessity of these, most scientists don't have much time when it comes to solving many of the scientific questions that currently confront society.

Australia's most powerful supercomputer is Raijin (Mahony, 2013). Surprisingly, Raijin can perform in one hour the number of calculations the entire population of the earth, armed with calculators, could carry out over 20 years. The oceans play an important role in Earth's climate. It basically slows down the rate of climate change. The oceans are also important as they absorb the carbon dioxide from the atmosphere. The finer

resolution of oceans refers to eddies. Eddies are important to understand the dynamics of all oceans and play an important role in transfer of heat and carbon cycle. In order to model small eddies, a supercomputer is essential (Mahony, 2013).

Cray Solutions have been chosen worldwide to solve their challenging problems. Today the fastest supercomputer available to the weather and climate research community is the petaflops Cray XT5 supercomputer available at the U.S. Department of Energy's Oak Ridge National Laboratory (Nyberg, 2008). The Cray XT5 supercomputer is achieving unprecedented results and is a key resource in the Intergovernmental Panel on Climate Change (IPCC) assessments by the National Oceanic and Atmospheric Administration (NOAA), etc. Some examples of leading science performed on Cray XT systems are Project Athena, the DOE-UCAR Climate Science Computational End Station, the NOAA GFDL CHIMES Project and IPCC AR5 assessments and the NOAA Hazardous Weather Testbed Spring Experiment (Nyberg, 2008).

A recently initiated project called ECCO-IcES aims to improve the representation of ocean, sea ice and ice sheets in climate models. This is to study the origin and evolution of water masses near the polar ice sheets, reduce the uncertainties in sea level projections and improve the predictions of climate models. It is estimated that ECCO-IcES project will require more than 50 million processor hours annually on Pleiades, doubling to 100 million hours per year in 2015.Satellite observations show that during the last decade, sea-ice in the Arctic has become younger, thinner and weaker, making it more easily deformable by wind and ocean currents. Combining these observations with a numerical ocean and sea-ice model will help scientists to evaluate and improve the ocean circulation estimates and allow them to better understand what is happening to the sea-ice in the Arctic today and to make more accurate predictions of how it may behave in the future (Massaro, 2013). Through the use of NASA's high end computing capabilities and dynamic, evolv-

Figure 2. By able to access Raijin using secure internet connections, researchers across Australia are developing 'virtual laboratories' of models and simulations. (Mahony, 2013)

ing computer models, they would be able to take a more detailed look at our home planet, which will help understand how these life-supporting planetary systems function, why they are changing and what that might mean for us (Massaro, 2013).

The challenges in the coming decade are to understand the influence of solar activity and the flow of energy and particles in the heliosphere upon the climate in Earth, extreme climate fluctuations and abrupt climate change, the response of climate and ecosystems to different scenarios for anthropogenic climate forcing over the coming decades, Space weather effects on orbiting and ground level assets and on safety of human space flight, etc. Also currently, much of the data, especially the older data, have been saved in obsolete forms of media that are not accessible online. Recovering these hidden data and digitizing them – for example, digging through cabinets and old boxes of paper reports and keying in data can be time consuming and laborious. The key challenge in describing atmospheric data is the imprecise definition of weather phenomena. For instance, cyclones are defined based on threshold level of

vorticity in quantities such as atmospheric pressure at sea level. The modeling, detection and prediction of global climate phenomena has received much attention in the high performance computing community. Such applications involve multiple models at varying levels, robust methods to ensure that predictions agree with the observations.

Astronomy data are static which simplifies their visualization, but they are manipulated in large volumes, which introduces problems. Particularly, it is not clear where to strike a balance between the client and server when visualizing large amounts of remote data. Astronomers want to have more useful visualization tools which can be modifiable to meet particular requirements and those that can be integrated with statistical analysis tools for data exploration. Earth science datasets are frequently subject to contamination due to clouds, haze, pixel geometry and other factors. These data quality issues need to be addressed. Quality issues are severe in the tropics where cloud cover predominates for many months of the year.

3. Computational Materials Sciences and Engineering

Materials science, also called materials engineering, is on the cusp of a new era, emboldened by advances in computational power and quantum mechanics. For some time now, manufacturers have used supercomputers to design airplanes, cars and other equipment, but now scientists are using similar techniques to develop new materials from scratch (Trader, 2013). A popular method called as high-throughput computational materials design is responsible for a host of developments like improved batteries, solar cells, fuel cells, computer chips and many other technologies (Trader, 2013). In future, there will be free, open-access databases containing the fundamental thermodynamic and electronic properties of all known inorganic compounds. There will be breakthroughs that will transform computing, eliminate pollution, generate abundant clean energy and improve the lives of people (Trader, 2013).

Many promising clean-energy technologies are waiting for advanced materials to become viable. In the future, the dream is to convert sunlight and air into methanol-like liquid fuels that would be used to burn in cars and airplanes. Researchers at the U.S. Department of Energy research center are using high-throughput methods to look for materials to make this technology feasible. Finding new metal alloys for use in cars and airplanes is another application. Reducing a vehicle's weight by 10% can improve its fuel economy by 6-8%. U.S. industry pours billions of dollars every year into research and development for metals and alloy manufacturing. Computer aided materials design would multiply that investment. Significant advances in high strength, lightweight and recyclable alloys would have a tremendous impact on the world economy through increased energy efficiency in transportation and construction.

Since a long time it has been seen that silicon is not the best semiconductor. The key question now is to find materials that can quickly switch from conducting to insulating states (Ceder, 2013). A team at U.C.L.A has made extremely fast transistors from graphene. Meanwhile a group from Stanford has reported that it can flip the electrical on/off switch in magnetite in one trillionth of a second- thousands of times faster than the transistors now in use. High-throughput materials design will enable to sort these possibilities. Researchers are using computational materials design to develop new superconductors, catalysts and scintillator materials. These three things would transform information technology, carbon capture and sequestration, and the detection of nuclear materials (Ceder, 2013).

Perhaps, an invention of new liquid fuel based on silicon instead of carbon would deliver more energy than gasoline while producing environmentally benign reaction products such as sand and water. Large-scale simulations of human bone under elastic deformations have been demonstrated to offer critically superior information for the behavior of bone under stress than traditional diagnostic techniques such as measuring bone density (Curioni). IBM Research has employed micro-finite-element simulations with hundreds of millions of elements resulting in billions of degrees of freedom and showed extreme scalability on tens of thousands of processors on Blue Gene supercomputers (Curioni). The next steps focus on a scale down of the technology to utilize many core inexpensive HPC platforms that will allow the methodology to become incorporated into everyday clinical practice more easily (Curioni).

An aircraft wake consists of powerful trailing vortices that live long after the airplane has flown by (Curioni). This potential hazard imposes stringent safety distances and pose limiting constraint on the airport traffic. IBM with their collaborators have developed high-performance Navier-Strokes solvers based on a hybrid particle-mesh approach and applied them to understand a medium-wavelength instability on massively parallel machines (Curioni). While X-rays have many favourable attributes, current

Figure 3. Applications of supercomputing in the Computational Materials sciences to predict the performance of nuclear weapons (Rubia, 2000)

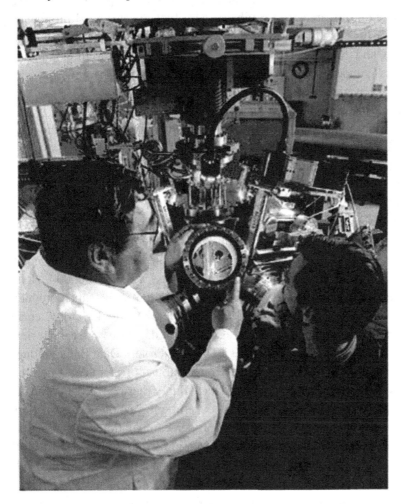

Livermore materials simulations are closely coupled to a program of laboratory experiments. Researchers Mike Fluss (left) and Brian Wirth measure the atomic transport properties of radiation damage defects in metals, including plutonium; the data are used to refine codes that simulate and predict the performance of stockpiled nuclear weapons.

X-ray technology will have difficulty meeting the long-term requirements of stockpile stewardship, the Department of Energy's program to assure the safety and reliability of nuclear stockpile without underground nuclear testing (Rubia, 2000). In particular, providing views from multiple angles and at different times during one experiment will be a challenge for X-rays (Rubia, 2000).

Stanford Engineering's Center for Turbulence Research has set a record by successfully using a supercomputer with more than one million computing cores to solve a complex fluid dynamics problem- the prediction of noise generated by a supersonic jet engine (Myers, 2013). Joseph Nichols

worked on the installed Sequioa IBM Bluegene/Q system. The exhausts of high-performance aircraft at takeoff and landing are among the most powerful human-made sources of noise. For ground crews, even for those wearing the most advanced hearing protection available, this creates an acoustically hazardous environment (Myers, 2013). Such noise is a major annoyance to the communities surrounding the airports. Engineers are therefore interested in designing new and better aircraft engines that are quieter than their predecessors. New nozzle shapes, for instance, can reduce jet noise at its source, resulting in quieter aircraft. Predictive simulations- advanced computer models-aid in such designs (Myers, 2013).

In an interdisciplinary collaboration, researchers at the University of Texas at Austin's Institute for Computational Engineering and Sciences teamed up with material scientists to understand, explain and exploit a specific microwave effect (Yilmaz, 2013). They also attempted to use microwaves to make thin films of semiconductor oxides. Such films are needed much in electronics from solar cells to photodetectors. But growing them in conventional furnaces is a slow, high energy and high temperature process that restricts growth substrates to materials that can take the heat. If successful, microwave chemistry could accelerate the thin-film growth process, make it more energy efficient, and enable temperature-sensitive materials, such as plastics, to be used as growth substrates. This advancement could potentially enable the creation of plastic-based electronics (Yilmaz, 2013).

Biomaterials is a promising field that focuses on the development of materials to replace human tissues. Tissue engineering is a subset of biomaterials and is rapidly expanding as a treatment for wide range of medical conditions (Guan et al.). Basically, integrations of biochemistry, molecular and cell biology and materials sciences produce three-dimensional structures or possibly multi-dimensional structures in future with particular properties that enables to replace or repair damaged, missing or badly functioning biological components (Guan et al.). Some of the examples are Biomimetic elastomers that are elastic polymers mimicking the key functions of proteins in the body, Microenvironment for stem cell differentiation that is to engineer tissue microenvironment to direct stem cell differentiation, Tendon repair that is to shorten the recovery time associated with tendon repair and also improve function, etc (Guan et al.).

Applications of supercomputing in fluid dynamics involve simulations associated with collapsing bubbles that have potential uses in shattering kidney stones using the high pressure of collapsing bubbles, improving the design of high pressure fuel injectors and propellers, etc (Koumoutsakos, 2013). There are still other applications of supercomputing in Computational materials sciences and engineering that needs to addressed and solved.

4. Computational Chemistry, Fluid Dynamics, Physics

Computational chemistry is a branch of chemistry that uses principles of computer science to assist in solving chemical problems. Ab Initio Molecular Dynamics has a system size of around 100-1000 atoms and therefore the number of calculations are too huge, that is 10000- 1000000. Hence, it is really important to use the supercomputers to make the calculations simpler. Also, currently existing chemical databases or repositories like KEGG, DAVID, Protein Data Bank among others have huge number of chemical structures and lot of data. Mining these large data repositories to extract useful information is very challenging without proper computational resources. Also, while developing a data warehouse of all these open source databases together would lead to a tremendous data overload. Supercomputing challenges therefore increase.

Drug discovery is the potential area to be improved and enhanced through the use of cloud computing, etc. Identification of lead compounds is a very computer intensive process. Docking studies using supercomputing resources would help in discovering new drugs/ medicines to target the prevailing disorders. Studying innumerable drug compounds available across multiple databases is practically not feasible. Hence, shortlisting of the lead compounds from this entire data becomes very complex in the drug discovery process. Usually, tens of thousands of compounds have to be screened to find a promising new drug and only very few of these candidates will make their way through the final clinical tests. Also, there are infinite associations of drugs with proteins/ targets that are causing the disorders. This is quite memory intensive and has to be addressed via supercomputing.

Schrodinger equation is widely known since centuries but till date there is no accurate calculations of the Schrodinger equation computationally. This will be of potential use in therapeutics if there are more computational resources available. Also, understanding the mysteries of quantum chemical simulations using supercomputing would lead to potential new discoveries in medicine. Firstly, the

pharmacological profile of existing drugs can be optimized for the synthesis of better compounds using supercomputers. Secondly, as more structural information on possible protein targets and their biochemical functions becomes available, completely new therapeutics can be developed.

Modern Graphics processing units (GPUs) contain hundreds of arithmetic units and can be harnessed to provide tremendous acceleration for molecular modeling (Stone et al.). The capabilities and flexibility of GPU hardware combined with high level GPU programming languages

Figure 4. Applications of Schrodinger equation in biochemistry. Laboratory of Computational Chemistry and Biochemistry Institute of chemical sciences and Engineering Swiss Federal Institute of Technology (Shepler, 2006)

Ruthenium-based anti-cancer drug on DNA

like CUDA and OpenCL has unlocked this computational power. Many molecular modeling applications are well suited to GPUs, due to their extensive computational requirements and because they lend themselves to data-parallel implementations (Stone et al.).

One of the issues in clinical trial testing of the pharmaceutical drugs in many of the developing countries is that the government is not willing to sponsor essential clinical trials that are really useful in designing new drugs to treat the infinite list of diseases troubling the people in these developing countries. It is really important that the government encourage these healthcare practices to ensure that the healthcare requirements of the country are met. Clinical trials that are fruitful to discover new medicines and that would help doctors in accurate treatments should be encouraged and supported financially. Also, currently the drugs marketed are very expensive which everyone around the world cannot afford it. Accurate prescription by the doctors and cheap medicines or drugs is the question at the moment.

Our lives are surrounded and sustained by the flow of fluids. Examples include blood, air, water, etc. Practically all the fluid flows that interest scientists and engineers are turbulent ones; turbulence is the key factor in fluid dynamics (Moin). A great grasp of turbulence can allow the scientists to reduce the aerodynamic drag on the automobile, increase the maneuverability of a jet fighter or improve the engine's fuel efficiency. An understanding of turbulence is also necessary to comprehend the flow of blood in the heart, especially in the left ventricle. Turbulence is very complex to deal with. Therefore, the application of powerful computers to simulate and study the flow of fluids that happen to be turbulent is the burgeoning field of Computational fluid dynamics. Computational fluid dynamics are also useful in aircraft development. Currently, computational fluid dynamics is also used in designing turbine blades, geometry of combustors, etc. Another current trend in computational fluid dynamics is

the complete simulation of relatively simple flows like the flow in a pipe (Moin). They provide an insight into turbulence and have disclosed the structure of turbulent eddies near a wall.

Computational nuclear/particle physics is one of the prototype applications for HPC, influencing the design of supercomputers (Tretkoff, 2004). Predictions of the structure and reactions of nuclei are important for nation's energy and security needs. These future findings will be important for the development of nuclear energy, advanced nuclear fission reactors and fusion energy. In order to meet the enormous computing power requirements of Quantum Chromo Dynamics, supercomputers specifically for that purpose are built (Tretkoff, 2004). However, the researchers lack the computing power to bring the precision of the calculations up to that of the experiments. Lattice calculations will provide precise values for other standard model parameters and may help find the physics beyond the standard model (Tretkoff, 2004).

Finding molecular dynamics with long range forces with bio-applications would be a useful application of supercomputing in the coming future in Computational Physics domain. They are thinking of a way to work on both QCDOC machines and cluster approaches in an effort to increase computational power and software development for lattice calculations (Tretkoff, 2004). Apart from these applications in Computational physics domain, there still remains several untouched applications or challenges to be sorted by the next generation supercomputing.

5. Computational and Data Enabled Social Science

Over the past decade, Network Theory combined with Computational Science approach has turned out to be a powerful methodology to investigate complex systems of various sorts (Kaski, 2013). In human societies, individuals are linked through social interactions, which takes place today electronically due to Information Communication Technology thus leaving footprints of human behavior recorded digitally as ever-increasing datasets (Kaski, 2013). The patterns of social behavior and changes for different individuals of different gender and age can be studied.

For social sciences, data is normally the numeric files originating from social research methodologies or from administrative archives, from which statistics are also calculated. Other data formats like audio, video, geospatial and other digital content are also kinds of social sciences datasets. The Latin American Government Documents Archive(LAGDA) project at The University of Texas at Austin seeks to provide access to presidential documents from 18 Latin American and Caribbean countries (University of texas at austin supercomputing center to receive $10 million in private funding, 2012). LAGDA is presently composed of around 66.6 million documents archived from the internet, totaling about 5.6 terabytes of data. The current challenge lies in applying text-mining algorithms with cloud computing to facilitate automatic classification and access to this collection (University of texas at austin supercomputing center to receive $10 million in private funding, 2012).

One of the applications in Computational social sciences is that of studying the culture by a new approach of big humanities. There are large datasets like the tremendous growth of newly available cultural content on the web. But the employment of techniques like statistical data analysis, data mining, scientific visualization, simulations, etc are not observed presently in the analysis of cultural datasets. This would be a potential application of supercomputing to mine useful information from the large cultural datasets. Some of the examples of social networking sites that are currently facing problems with data overload or big data analytics are twitter, linkedin, facebook, amazon, etc. High performance humanities computing and cultural analytics will provide new application areas for

Computer Science research in a lot of fields like computer graphics, databases, etc.

Improved understanding of human networks is the key to increasing the value of investments in Science, leading from knowledge to innovation to economic welfare. Current analyses focus on authors, institutional affiliation, topic, publications and patents or webs and other sources that can revolutionize the human sciences (Cyber Science and Engineering, 2010). This development would also place huge demands on cyberinfrastructure and present new challenges such as reworking the science of sampling (e.g. Studying the part of a population with confidence that the sample represents the whole) and understanding the multi-faceted nature of social network ties and their effects on the human behavior (Cyber Science and Engineering, 2010). These challenges can be welcomed by future computational social scientists.

These days too many communications are changing the nature of medicine and healthcare. The patients come to the doctors better informed. That is, most of the patients already have access to the health or medical information via websites and internet that influences their decisions to treat an illness. Patients can talk online with others with similar ailments, exchanging not just useful medical information but also emotional support. It is currently important to find ways to enhance the network technology to facilitate free exchange of scientific ideas. Academic researchers are often reluctant to share ideas before they appear in an official form. Corporate researchers are also reluctant to share the findings. Yet, the entire essence of research can be improved through more immediate sharing of ideas via the internet. The challenge then is to find ways to give individuals credit for ideas shared rapidly online, while at the same time maintaining the quality of peer review. The design of future communication systems will help to accelerate the pace of discovery in all fields.

The above discussed are some of the existing applications and challenges faced in the domain

Computational and data enabled Social Sciences. There are many other challenges apart from the discussed ones, some trivial and some very important to address. With the design of future supercomputers, many different applications and challenges can be solved accurately and quickly.

6. Computational Design Optimization for Manufacturing, and Industrial Applications

Supercomputers have been used at a great competitive edge through many industries. Along with the improvement of performance of the supercomputers, there are also other high expectations in the manufacturing sector for innovation of design processes and creation of new products by making use of supercomputing (Kato, 2012). Mostly, numerical simulations are used for determining various design parameters. Optimization of numerous design parameters requires possibly an enormous number of cases to be simulated (Kato, 2012). The computation time for this is a major bottleneck and optimum design that uses numerical simulation has not been put to practical use. The heat released by CPU's is increasing every year and the rotation speeds of fans to remove this heat are increasing as well (Kato, 2012). Although reducing the noise of cooling fans is an important technological challenge, reducing noise by empirical methods had reached the limits (Kato, 2012). By using supercomputers, a parameter study of hundreds of cases can be conducted in a few hours, and this allows for optimization by numerical simulation(Kato, 2012).In particular, nanomaterials and nanostructures have the potential to bring various technological innovations to future manufacturing (Kato, 2012). However, it is difficult to experimentally evaluate with accuracy the characteristics of nanoscale structures and functions of nanodevices. For this reason, there are high expectations that nanosimulations conducted on the basis of quantum mechanics, which can evaluate functions and characteristics

based on the electronic state of the materials will be useful as an investigation (Kato, 2012).

Over the summer of 2013, the Ohio Supercomputer center launched a new program called as AweSim. This project is to design and deploy easy-to-use advanced manufacturing simulation applications or apps (Industrial Engagement, 2013). The adoption rate of HPC in the cloud remains unclear, but in the long term, several technology developments can address the challenges (Milojicic, 2012). The first application is in Optical networking, which will improve hardware manageability and interconnect performance while also reducing power consumption, and software-defined networks, which will improve the manageability of cloud networking (Milojicic, 2012). Furthermore, developments in nonvolatile memory will improve checkpointing performance and in long term, address the data deluge and new programming models leveraging nonvolatility (Milojicic, 2012).

Other applications existing in manufacturing and industries will enable further advances in supercomputing in the near future.

7. Computational Medicine and Biomedical Engineering

The field of bioengineering is transforming health, medicine and biology and there is a focus on translational bioengineering in the future. One of the issues currently in Computational biology education industry would be to develop courses providing challenging and enriching educational experience to students who can develop their computational skills with more advanced computationally intensive tasks. The use of High performance computing, supercomputing should be enabled in their research projects, etc. Also, the opportunities should be given to the students to opt for the courses they are interested in learning so that they develop new skills instead of focusing on grades alone and other factors. Some of the countries have their curriculum structure in such a way that they enforce the students to study the courses that are provided by the universities without considering the interests of the students. This leads to rote learning, lack of attention and poor performance.

One of the useful applications in future due to supercomputing would be to devise 4 dimensional protein structures or multi- dimensional structures of genes, proteins, drugs, chromosomes, DNA, RNA, etc. Currently, the three dimensional structure of proteins provides an insight into how the proteins fold and the mutations in the amino acids of these proteins that can contribute to human disorders. This multi-dimensional depiction of these structures can lead to better predictions about the genomic variations that are causing a particular disorder and in drug discovery. This would also solve the complexity of Multiple Sequence Alignments across many

organisms and large number of proteins, genes, chromosomes, etc.

Computational studies in neurology holds a great promise as much of the research has to be still accomplished. Many people suffer from the neural disorders which are ranked in the top ten list of disorders across the world. Recently, the big brain project in the U.K. has come to the completion where scientists have mapped the human brain model and the model is available on the web. This is a scientifically promising discovery, that can lead to discoveries in future like drawing the comparisons between infinite brain models (ranging from one dimensional to multi-dimensional models) of people across the countries simultaneously with the advances in supercomputing. This can conclude in the scientific know hows of the complex intricacies of the brain structure, and how these alignments of

Figure 5. In the sequence analysis engine, a central task manager coordinates analysis tasks such as pattern recognition and gene modeling and also initiates sequence comparison and data mining using multiple external databases. (Uberbacher)

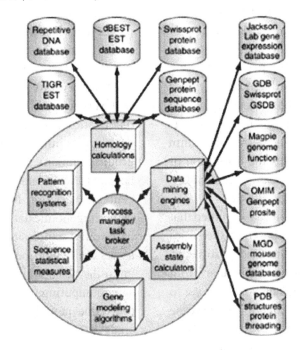

different brain models can be effective in designing medicines for the diseases like Schizophrenia, dementia, Autism, Epilepsy, etc. This is a potentially interesting area to also come up with the multi- dimensional models of different human organs and the mapping between these organs at a large-scale. The future of supercomputing looks promising in Computational medicine, in turn helping the doctors treat patients by these unique discoveries.

Pedigree analysis has led to many new scientific findings and still much has to be found with the help of super intelligent computers. Currently, a lot of emphasis is given on studying many pedigrees simultaneously. It is possible to study few pedigrees simultaneously using computational approaches. But in order to predict precise medicine at an individual level, it becomes highly necessary to study large number of pedigrees simultaneously to answer scientifically relevant questions. This can be made possible with much better computing power and better developed algorithms. Apart from these applications, carrying out large-scale genetic engineering and gene therapy would lead to better medical decisions.

Biomedical Engineers at the University of Virginia have developed a new imaging tool that helps in improving medical ultrasounds, leading to more accurate and timely diagnoses of breast cancer and other life threatening diseases. Using Star-P(TM) software from Interactive Supercomputing, they created an advanced algorithm which significantly improves the resolution of ultrasound images (What's next in Medical Imaging: High-Def Ultrasounds, 2007).

Since many years, everyone have studied that there are four bases of DNA based on the structure proposed by Watson and Crick. However, there are many hidden bases of DNA apart from these, some are discovered and some are yet to be found by the scientists. Due to the increase in the number of the bases, the genetic code also becomes complex and a new genetic code altogether has to be devised. In order to carry

out computations to help in these inventions, it is very essential to have good computing power at place allowing these complex studies. Also, currently, it is believed that the protein coding genes which are mostly important functionally lie in the exonic regions of the genome spanning about 1-2% of total human genome, but there are also possibilities that the functionally important mutations lie in the intrinsic regions, intragenic regions, exon-intron boundaries, 5' UTR, 3' UTR, centromeres, telomeres, etc. These areas of the human genome are not studied so much in detail unlike the exonic regions to interpret meaningful information. Much of the sequence of the telomeres and centromeres have to be still sequenced as the complete human genome is not sequenced as yet due to various factors including patents on the genes, etc. There is a necessity to edit the standard human genome sequence or the latest human reference genome build hg19 which currently is not perfect. This reference human genome becomes the foundation on which various computational sequencing analyses are carried out. The evolution of human beings still remains a mystery and is in controversy since ages. Accurate phylogenetic studies on a large-scale utilizing best computing resources would aid in significant findings.

Another future project to study the epigenetics of the DNA would be to sequence whole genome methylation data and whole exome methylation data across multiple people of different age groups, ethnicity, etc and draw the comparison between these datasets to conclude about any genomic variation heritability, etc. Especially in the epigenomic datasets, correlation networks based on co-expression changes are not available as yet and would be a promising area to work on in the near future. Apart from these uses of supercomputing, there are many other applications either new or existing in these computational areas that can be addressed via supercomputing resources.

CONCLUSION

Supercomputing has been of utmost importance since they were discovered because it has enabled crucial advances in national defense and safety, scientific discovery, manufacturing, etc. The current challenges of supercomputers across most of the computational sciences domains are discussed here that would enable a positive future direction. It is therefore obvious that the supercomputers are super smart digital computers having various achievements both in the past and in the bright future. For instance, a simple google search is built on the usage of MapReduce paradigm that is a useful application of supercomputing. However, despite consistent increases in the capability, supercomputing systems are still inadequate to meet the computational needs of various projects. The challenges discussed in this chapter are achievable by devising new architectures of supercomputers, something that is much faster, portable and adaptable to most of the projects of all the subjects. Hence, it becomes imperative that novel research is applied that can produce more and more powerful supercomputing systems.

REFERENCES

Ceder, G., & Persson, K. (2013). How supercomputers will yield a golden age of materials science. *Scientific American, 309*(6), 1–4. PMID:24383363

Chinta, B. (2013). *Supercomputers-introduction, details & examples*. Retrieved 03/23, 2014, from http://www.durofy.com/supercomputers-introduction-details-examples/

Cimons, M. (2013). *Advances in computational research transform scientific process and discovery*. Retrieved 03/18, 2014, from http://www.nsf.gov/mobile/discoveries/disc_summ.jsp?cntn_id=127385&org=NSF

Curioni, A. (n.d.). *Computational engineering-Project overview*. Retrieved from http://www.zurich.ibm.com/mcs/compsci/engineering/

Cyber Science and Engineering: A Report of the NSF Advisory Committee for Cyber Infrastructure Task Force on Grand Challenges. (2010). Retrieved from http://www.stanford.edu/~vcs/papers/OCI_GCs_TF_final.pdf

Fielden, J. (2013). *Accelerating supercomputing power*. Retrieved 03/23, 2014, from http://www.techradar.com/news/world-of-tech/future-tech/accelerating-supercomputing-power-1223031

Guan, J., Lannutti, J., & Powell, H. (n.d.). *Research topics*. Retrieved 03/18, 2014, from http://mse.osu.edu/research/topics

India Plans 61 Times Faster Supercomputer by 2017. (2012, September 17). *The Times of India*.

Industrial Engagement. (2013). Retrieved 03/18, 2014, from https://www.osc.edu/content/industrial_engagement

Kaski, K. (2013). Computer and computational sciences for exascale computing. In *Proceedings of the Fourth AICS International Symposium*. Kobe, Japan: Academic Press.

Kato, C. (2012). *Special contribution supercomputing in industrial manufacturing*. Retrieved 03/18, 2014, from http://www.fujitsu.com/downloads/MAG/vol48-4/paper01.pdf

Koumoutsakos, P. (2013). *Scientists "burst" supercomputing record with bubble collapse simulation*. Retrieved 03/18, 2014, from http://phys.org/news/2013-11-scientists-supercomputing-collapse-simulation.html

Mahony, P. (2013). *Raijin supercomputer cooks up a storm*. Retrieved 03/18, 2014, from http://www.ecosmagazine.com/print/EC13223.htm

Mainframes and Supercomputers. (2012). Retrieved 03/23, 2014, from http://maintec.com/blog/mainframes-andsupercomputers/.ecosmagazine.com/temp/EC13223_Fb.gif

Massaro, K. (2013). *Re-creating earth's oceans inside a supercomputer*. Retrieved 03/18, 2014, from https://www.nas.nasa.gov/publications/articles/feature_ecco.html

Milojicic, D. (2012). *High performance computing (HPC) in the cloud*. Retrieved 03/18, 2014, from http://www.computer.org/portal/web/computing-now/archive/september2012

Moin, P., & Kim, J. (n.d.). *Tackling turbulence with supercomputers*. Retrieved 03/18, 2014, from http://www.stanford.edu/group/ctr/articles/tackle.html

Myers, A. (2013). *Stanford researchers break million-core supercomputer barrier*. Retrieved 03/18, 2014, from http://engineering.stanford.edu/news/stanford-researchers-break-million-core-supercomputer-barrier

Nyberg, P. (2008). *Cray supercomputers in climate, weather and ocean modeling*. Retrieved 03/18, 2014, from http://www.cray.com/Assets/PDF/products/xt/WP-XT02-1010.pdf

Rubia, T. (2000). *Following materials over time and space*. Retrieved 03/18, 2014, from https://www.llnl.gov/str/Diaz.html

Shepler, B. (2006). *Introduction to computational quantum chemistry*. Retrieved 03/19, 2014, from http://public.wsu.edu/~pchemlab/documents/Intro-QM-Chem.ppt

Stone, J., Phillips, J., Hardy, D., Roberts, E., & Saam, J. (n.d.). *GPU acceleration of molecular modeling applications*. Retrieved 03/18, 2014, from http://www.ks.uiuc.edu/Research/gpu/

Stroschein, J., Jennewein, D., & Reynoldson, J. (2005). Building a bioinformatics supercomputing cluster. *Linux Journal*, (133).

Trader, T. (2013). *Supercomputing raises materials science to new heights*. Paper presented at the International Supercomputing Conference, Leipzig, Germany.

Tretkoff, E. (2004). Dedicated supercomputers probe QCD theory. *APS Physics, 13*(3).

Uberbacher, E. (n.d.). *Computing the genome*. Retrieved 03/19, 2014, from http://web.ornl.gov/info/ornlreview/v30n3-4/genome.htm http://web.ornl.gov/info/ornlreview/v30n3-4/digital/p63b.gif

University of Texas at Austin Supercomputing Center to Receive $10 million in Private Funding. (2012, February 21). *Primeur Weekly Magazine*.

What's Next in Medical Imaging. (2007). *High-Def Ultrasounds*. Pharma Investments, Ventures, and Law Weekly.

Yilmaz, A., & Yang, K. (2013). *Supercomputer simulations reveal mysteries of specific microwave effect*. Retrieved 03/18, 2014, from https://www.ices.utexas.edu/about/news/251/

ADDITIONAL READING

Ahalt, S. (2006). Viewpoint--supercomputing: The next industrial revolution. Retrieved 03/19, 2014, from http://www.industryweek.com/global-economy/viewpoint-supercomputing-next-industrial-revolution

Alabama supercomputer authority. Retrieved 03/19, 2014, from https://www.asc.edu/supercomputing/software.shtml

An overview of how supercomputers work and their application in real life. (2013). Retrieved 03/19, 2014, from http://www.insidetechnology360.com/index.php/an-overview-of-how-supercomputers-work-and-their-application-in-real-life-64/

Andersen, R. (2012). Meet Mira, the supercomputer that makes universes. Retrieved 03/19, 2014, from http://0-www.theatlantic.com.iii-server.ualr.edu/technology/archive/2012/09/meet-mira-the-supercomputer-that-makes-universes/262639/

Areas of Ames ingenuity: Supercomputing. Retrieved 03/19, 2014, from http://www.nasa.gov/centers/ames/research/area-supercomputing.html

At nearly 10 petaflops, TACC's stampede supercomputer provides comprehensive advanced computing needs for nation's scientists. (2013). Retrieved 03/19, 2014, from https://www.tacc.utexas.edu/news/press-releases/2013/stampede-supercomputer

Balaji, P. (2007). ParaMEDIC enables worldwide supercomputer for bioinformatics. Retrieved 03/19, 2014, from http://www.mcs.anl.gov/articles/paramedic-enables-worldwide-supercomputer-bioinformatics

Bali, R. (2014). 10 most powerful SuperComputers running Linux. Retrieved 03/19, 2014, from http://www.linuxfederation.com/10-powerful-supercomputers-running-linux/

BGI and Tianjin supercomputing center open joint bioinformatics lab. (2012). Retrieved 03/19, 2014, from http://www.asianscientist.com/tech-pharma/tianhe-bgi-bioinformatics-computing-joint-laboratory-nscc-tj-2012/

BGI launches joint bioinformatics & computing lab with national supercomputing center in china. (2012, 25 March 2012). *Primeur Weekly,*

Big data and computation. (2012). Retrieved 03/19, 2014, from http://istcoalition.org/catalyst/october-2012-feature-big-data-and-computation/

Bioinformatics: Application possibilities and ethical/social limits. (). *Human Brain Project*

Brandon, J. (2010). Stunning supercomputing apps that can run on your desktop. Retrieved 03/19, 2014, from http://www.itbusiness.ca/news/stunning-supercomputing-apps-that-can-run-on-your-desktop/14694

Brodlie, K., Brooke, J., Chen, M., Chisnall, D., Fewings, A., & Hughes, C. (2004). Visual supercomputing - technologies, applications and challenges. Retrieved 03/19, 2014, from http://www-compsci.swan.ac.uk/~csmark/PDFS/star2004.pdf

Centre for development of advanced computing. Retrieved 03/19, 2014, from http://cdac.in/index.aspx?id=bio_braf

Choi, C. (2013). Google and NASA launch quantum computing AI lab. Retrieved 03/19, 2014, from http://www.technologyreview.com/news/514846/google-and-nasa-launch-quantum-computing-ai-lab/

Clusters vs supercomputers. (2005). Retrieved 03/19, 2014, from http://www.networkcomputing.com/content-management/clusters-vs-supercomputers/229615690

Commercial use of supercomputers. (1994). Retrieved 03/19, 2014, from http://www.netlib.org/benchmark/top500/reports/report93/section2_10_5.html

Computational fluid dynamics. (2009). Retrieved 03/19, 2014, from http://www.mcsi.ro/Minister/Domenii-de-activitate-ale-MCSI/Tehnologia-Informatiei/Proiecte-DGSI/Supercomputing/Aplicatii-pentru-supercomputing-part-2

Computational fluid dynamics applications. Retrieved 03/19, 2014, from http://www.nimbix.net/applications/computational-fluid-dynamics/

CSIRO installs dell supercomputing cluster for bioinformatics research. (2003). Retrieved 03/19, 2014, from http://social.eyeforpharma.com/uncategorised/csiro-installs-dell-supercomputing-cluster-bioinformatics-research

Cuticchia, J. (2000). High performance computing and medical research. Retrieved 03/19, 2014, from http://www.cmaj.ca/content/162/8/1148.full.pdf

Delker, K. (2014, February 24, 2014). UNM gains supercomputer from the new mexico consortium. *Unm Newsroom*

Demeler, D. B. (n.d.) Bioinformatics core facility. Retrieved 03/19, 2014, from http://www.bioinformatics.uthscsa.edu/

Easton, J. (2014). Argonne supercomputer dramatically accelerates rapid genome analysis. *Uchicagonews*, February 21.

Eklund, A. (2012). Computational medical image analysis with a focus on real-time fMRI and non-parametric statistics. Retrieved 03/19, 2014, from http://liu.diva-portal.org/smash/get/diva2:512491/FULLTEXT01.pdf

Ellis, M. (2014). A supercomputer could change how diseases are treated. Retrieved 03/19, 2014, from http://www.medicalnewstoday.com/articles/272975.php

Engineering the future with high performance computing. Retrieved 03/19, 2014, from http://thewarrencentre.org.au/projects/past-projects/engineering-the-future-with-high-performance-computing/

ExaScience life lab to leverage HPC in life sciences. (2013, November 7, 2013). *Inside HPC*

First supercomputer in ASEAN countries; Philippines to use blue gene for weather forecasting & studies. (2013). Retrieved 03/19, 2014, from http://betterphils.blogspot.in/2013/06/first-supercomputer-in-asean-countries.html

Foster, I., & Kesselman, K. Computational grids. Retrieved 03/19, 2014, from http://toolkit.globus.org/alliance/publications/papers/chapter2.pdf

Future health & bio engineering. (2014). Retrieved 03/19, 2014, from http://www.pinterest.com/caramarais/future-health-bio-engineering/

Giles, M. (2009). Some (strong) opinions on HPC and the use of GPUs. Retrieved 03/19, 2014, from https://people.maths.ox.ac.uk/gilesm/talks/birmingham.pdf

Godhia, R., Gan, S., & Goh, R. (2002). Cray and national university of Singapore collaborate on advanced bioinformatics software for the life sciences. Retrieved 03/19, 2014, from http://investors.cray.com/phoenix.zhtml?c=98390&p=irol-newsArticle&ID=267127&highlight=

Hasings, H. Center for arrhythmia research. Retrieved 03/19, 2014, from https://www.nysernet.org/community/hofstra_spotlight.pdf

Hemsoth, N. (2014). *The top supercomputing led discoveries of 2013* [Coalition for Academic Scientific Computation]. Coalition for Academic Scientific Computation.

Hickey, H. (2006). Bringing supercomputers to life (sciences). Retrieved 03/19, 2014, from http://biomedicalcomputationreview.org/2/4/5.pdf

Hinds, W. (2010). Computational modeling of neuro-biological systems and its impact on neuromorphic engineering. Retrieved 03/19, 2014, from http://people.ece.cornell.edu/land/courses/ece5030/FinalReport/f2009/wah26/ECE5030_Final_Hinds.pdf

IBM supercomputer at Johns Hopkins hunts for clues to heart and brain disease. (1999). Retrieved 03/19, 2014, from http://www.thefreelibrary.com/IBM+Supercomputer+At+Johns+Hopkins+Hunts+for+Clues+to+Heart+and+Brain...-a057619557

Improving health care delivery through high performance computing. Retrieved 03/19, 2014, fromhttp://casc.org/papers/Improving%20 Health%20Care%20Delivery%20Through%20 HPC.pdf

India's national space program using NVIDIA GPU- accelerated supercomputer. (2012). Retrieved 03/19, 2014, from http://www.nvidia. in/object/india-space-program-uses-tesla-gpus-20120619-in.html

Jackson, J. (2013). Cray brings hadoop to supercomputing. Retrieved 03/19, 2014, fromhttp:// www.arnnet.com.au/article/532306/cray_brings_ hadoop_supercomputing/

Jackson, J. (2014). IBM watson has another go at helping solve brain cancer riddles. Retrieved 03/19, 2014, from http://www.reseller.co.nz/article/540857/ibm_watson_has_another_go_helping_solve_brain_cancer_riddles/

Japan's K supercomputer. (2012). Retrieved 03/19, 2014, from http://web-japan.org/trends/11_sci-tech/sci120119.html

Joshi, R. (2014). A peek into NTU's supercomputer and hybrid cloud. Retrieved 03/19, 2014, from http://cw.com.hk/feature/peek-ntus-super-computer-and-hybrid-cloud

Kahn, D. HPC in bioinformatics and genomics. Retrieved 03/19, 2014, from http://www-05.ibm. com/fr/events/campus_lyon/Prez/Campus_Day_ HPC_Lyon_13_novembre_Daniel_Kahn.pdf

Karin, S., & Bruch, K. M. (2002). Supercomputers. Retrieved 03/23, 2014, from http://www. encyclopedia.com/topic/Supercomputers.aspx

Kitchens, F., & Sharma, S. (2003). Affordable supercomputing solutions: Cluster computers in business applications. Retrieved 03/19, 2014, fromhttp://www.pacis-net.org/file/2003/papers/ poster/67.pdf

Koniges, A., Gropp, W., Lusk, E., & Eder, D. (2014). Application supercomputing and multiscale simulation techniques. Retrieved 03/19, 2014, from http://0-dl.acm.org.iii-server.ualr.edu/ citation.cfm?doid=1188455.1188679

Lamb, D. (2012). Supercomputers can save U.S. manufacturing. [Supercomputers Can Save U.S. Manufacturing]. *Scientific American*, *306*(3). PMID:22375308

Landau, R., & Paez, M. (2012). A survey of computational physics. Retrieved 03/19, 2014, fromhttp://www.physics.orst.edu/~rubin/Books/ eBookWorking/LaTeX_Compadre/aSurvey-CP_4.1_ComP.pdf

Lojewski, D. C. (2013). *Programming model for the supercomputers of the future* [Programming model for the supercomputers of the future]. Research News.

Low-cost Linux clusters drive supercomputing use in manufacturing. (2007). Retrieved 03/19, 2014, from http://www.csemag.com/industry-news/codes-and-standards-updates/single-article/ low-cost-linux-clusters-drive-supercomputing-use-in-manufacturing/436e500919a88dcc3ff5b 5a47c099c13.html

Ludwig, T., & Stamatakis, A. high performance computing in bioinformatics. Retrieved 03/19, 2014, from http://bibiserv.techfak.uni-bielefeld. de/gcb04/tutorials/ludwig/tutorial-handout.pdf

Mangelsdorf, J. Supercomputing the climate: NASA's big data mission. Retrieved 03/19, 2014, from http://www.csc.com/cscworld/ publications/81769/81773-supercomputing_the_ climate_nasa_s_big_data_mission

Meglicki, Z. (2004). Supercomputers and clusters. Retrieved 03/19, 2014, from http://beige.ucs. indiana.edu/I590/node8.html

Meuer, H., & Gietl, H. Supercomputers- prestige objects or crucial tools for science and industry? Retrieved 03/19, 2014, from http://www.top500.org/files/Supercomputers_London_Paper_HWM_HG.pdf

Mitchell, P. (2004). Bioinformatics attracts big guns. [Bioinformatics attracts big guns]. *Nature Biotechnology, 22*(5), 492–493. doi:10.1038/nbt0504-492 PMID:15122273

Miyano, S. (2007). Overcoming bioinformatics challenges with supercomputing. [Overcoming Bioinformatics Challenges with Supercomputing] *Asiabiotech.Com,11*(15)

Mullaney, M. (2011). Nanotechnology now. Retrieved 03/19, 2014, from http://www.nanotech-now.com/news.cgi?story_id=42473

Mullaney, M. (2012). New $2.6 million study uses video cards to bring, effective, inexpensive supercomputing to hospitals for safer CT scans. Retrieved 03/19, 2014, from https://ccni.rpi.edu/w/archives/493

Nearing, B. (2012). Nano supercomputer gets another user. Retrieved 03/19, 2014, from http://blog.timesunion.com/business/nano-supercomputer-gets-another-user/53900/

Neves, K. (2004). Overview of industrial supercomputing. Retrieved 03/19, 2014, from http://publishing.cdlib.org/ucpressebooks/view?docId=ft0f59n73z&chunk.id=d0e10919

New application makes supercomputing simple. (2011). Retrieved 03/19, 2014, from http://phys.org/news/2011-12-application-supercomputing-simple.html

New supercomputer to aid genomics research. (2013, February 18, 2013). *Biology News Net*

Niu, B. F., Lang, X. Y., Lu, Z. H., & Chi, X. B. (2007). ScBioGrid: A commodity supercomputing environment supporting bioinformatics research. [ScBioGrid: a commodity supercomputing environment supporting bioinformatics research] *International Journal of Computer Mathematics, 84*(2), 177-178-182. doi:10.1080/00207160601170304

No magic wands. (2012). Retrieved 03/19, 2014, from http://www.ncsa.illinois.edu/news/story/no_magic_wands

Nowotny, D. T. (2012). General purpose GPU computing: Transforming your desktop into a personal super-computer. Retrieved 03/19, 2014, from http://www.birmingham.ac.uk/research/activity/cncr/news/previous/28Feb12-cncr-seminar.aspx

Okawa, C. (2012). Pico computing announces FPGA based bioinformatics solution. Retrieved 03/19, 2014, from http://picocomputing.com/pdf/Pico%20Bioinformatics%20PR.pdf

Padenga, T. (2009). High performance computer for bioinformatics in Zimbabwe. Retrieved 03/19, 2014, from http://www.newzimbabwe.com/pages/opinion174.14529.html

Partnership supercomputing program. Retrieved from https://www.vbi.vt.edu/high_performance_computing/

Parunak, D. V. (1994). Applications of distributed artificial intelligence in industry. [Applications of Distributed Artificial Intelligence in Industry] Forthcoming in O'Hare and Jennings, Eds., Foundations of Distributed Artificial Intelligence. Wiley Inter-Science, doi:ITI TR 93-03.1

Plank, G., Zhou, L., Greenstein, J., Cortassa, S., Winslow, R., O'Rourke, B., & Trayanova, N. (2008). From mitochondrial ion channels to arrhythmias in the heart: Computational techniques to bridge the spatial-temporal scales. Retrieved 03/19, 2014, from http://0-rsta.royalsocietypublishing.org.iii-server.ualr.edu/content/366/1879/3381.full

PSSC labs to showcase life science compute & storage solutions at bio IT world. (2011, April 4, 2011). Message posted to http://pssclabs.com/blog/?cat=12

Qing, L. (2012). GPU to be mainstay in supercomputers. Retrieved 03/19, 2014, from http://www.zdnet.com/gpu-to-be-mainstay-in-supercomputers-2062304745/

References books on bioinformatics. Retrieved 03/19, 2014, from https://supcom.hgc.jp/english/utili_info/manual/literature.html

Rekapalli, B., Giblock, P., & Reardon, C. (2013). PoPLAR: Portal for petascale lifescience applications and research. [PoPLAR:Portal for Petascale Lifescience Applications and Research] *BMC Bioinformatics, 14*(Suppl 9: S3) doi:10.1186/1471-2105-14-S9-S3

Rekepalli, B., & Giblock, P. Surviving the life sciences data deluge using cray supercomputers. Retrieved 03/19, 2014, from https://cug.org/proceedings/cug2013_proceedings/includes/files/pap166.pdf

Reumann, M., Holt, K., Inouye, M., Stinear, T., & Goudey, B. (2011). Precision medicine: Dawn of supercomputing in 'omics research. Retrieved 03/19, 2014, fromhttp://eresearchau.files.wordpress.com/2012/06/81-precision-medicine-dawn-of-supercomputing-in-omics-research.pdf

Robat, C. Introduction to supercomputers. Retrieved 03/19, 2014, from http://www.thocp.net/hardware/supercomputers.htm

San Diego supercomputer center. (2014). Retrieved 03/19, 2014, from http://blink.ucsd.edu/sponsor/SDSC/

Segall, R. S. Computational dimensionalities of global supercomputing. Retrieved 03/19, 2014, fromhttp://www.iiis.org/CDs2013/CD2013SCI/SCI_2013/PapersPdf/SA625MW.pdf

Shah, A. (2013). New supercomputer uses SSDs instead of DRAM and hard drives. Retrieved 03/19, 2014, from http://www.computerworld.com/s/article/9243789/New_supercomputer_uses_SSDs_instead_of_DRAM_and_hard_drives

Smith, S., & Frenzel, J. (2003). Bioinformatics application of a scalable supercomputer-on-chip architecture. Retrieved 03/19, 2014, from http://citeseerx.ist.psu.edu/viewdoc/download?doi=10.1.1.90.2729&rep=rep1&type=pdf

Stastna, K. (2012). U.S. supercomputer tops list of world's fastest machines. Retrieved 03/19, 2014, from http://www.cbc.ca/news/technology/u-s-supercomputer-tops-list-of-world-s-fastest-machines-1.1131229

Supercomputer from C-DAC to guide bioinformatics research. (2014, Feb 18, 2014). *The Times of India* Supercomputers accelerate the search for HIV/Aids cure. (2014,). *Health Systems Trust, Mining Weekly*

Supercomputers join search for 'cheapium': Brute force computing used to find new materials. (2014). Retrieved 03/19, 2014, from http://www.sciencedaily.com/releases/2014/01/140103204430.htm

Supercomputing and technology centers collaborate to build HPC cloud platform. (2012). Retrieved 03/19, 2014, from http://archive.hpcwire.com/hpccloud/2012-10-03/supercomputing_and_technology_centers_collaborate_to_build_hpc_cloud_platform.html

Supercomputing for industry. Retrieved 03/19, 2014, from http://industry.it4i.cz/en/portfolio/medical-surgery-tools/

Tao, W. (2011, 30th December 2011). Supercomputers making our future. *Chinadaily Usa*

Tatarinova, D. T. Fighting cancer; how supercomputing is helping to make the impossible, possible. Retrieved 03/19, 2014, fromhttp://www.hpcwales.co.uk/fighting-cancer

The future of supercomputing - an interim report. (2003). *The future of supercomputing - an interim report* [The Future of Supercomputing- An Interim Report] (pp. 1-2, 46). Washington, D.C.: The National Academies Press.

The virtual human project. Retrieved 03/19, 2014, from http://web.ornl.gov/~rwd/VH/collab.html

Tracy, S. (2010). Enabling bioinformatics discovery with high performance computing solutions. Retrieved 03/19, 2014, from http://www.scientificcomputing.com/articles/2010/06/enabling-bioinformatics-discovery-high-performance-computing-solutions

UK's TGAC uses coherent shared memory supercomputer for genome analysis. Retrieved 03/19, 2014, from http://www.sgi.com/pdfs/4365.pdf

Viccaro, H. (2013). IBM's supercomputer watson gets a roommate at RPI. Retrieved 03/19, 2014, fromhttp://www.bizjournals.com/albany/news/2013/10/03/ibms-supercomputer-watson-gets-a.html?page=2

Wade, M. (2014, February 19, 2014). Future of computing? A step closer to a photonic future. *Sciencedaily*

Wicks, B. (2014). Ben. Retrieved June 21, 2014, Retrieved from http://www.benjaminwicks.com/portfolio/

Winslow, R. (2011). Grand challenges in computational physiology and medicine. [Grand Challenges in Computational Physiology and Medicine] *Front Physiol. 2011, 2*(79) doi:10.3389/fphys.2011.00079

Zhang, Y., Kandel, A., Lin, T. Y., & Yao, Y. Y. (2004). Computational web intelligence. Retrieved 03/19, 2014, from http://cdn.preterhuman.net/texts/science_and_technology/artificial_intelligence/Computational%20Web%20Intelligence%20Intelligent%20Technology%20for%20Web%20Applications%20-%20Y.-Q.%20Zhang.pdf

Zheng, D. (2010-2013). National supercomputing center in Shenzhen. Retrieved 03/19, 2014, from http://www.nsccsz.gov.cn/en/hpc/

Zullo, D. Bioinformatics and high-performance computing. Retrieved 03/19, 2014, from http://www.rti.org/brochures/bioinformaticsbiocomputing.pdf

KEY TERMS AND DEFINITIONS

Ab Initio Molecular Dynamics: In excited states, chemical reactions, etc., electronic behavior can be obtained from first principles by using a quantum mechanical method.

Amazon Web Services: Collection of remote computing services that together make up a cloud computing platform, offered over the internet by Amazon.com. The most central and well-known of these services are Amazon EC2 and Amazon S3.

Azure: Cloud Computing platform and infrastructure created by Microsoft, for building, deploying and managing applications and services through a global network of Microsoft-managed datacenters.

Big Data: Large amounts of data.

Bioinformatics: The science of analyzing biological data using Computer Sciences.

BioPython: BioPython project is an international association of developers of non-commercial Python tools for Computational Molecular Biology and Bioinformatics.

Clinical Trials: A rigorously controlled test of a new drug or a new invasive medical device on human subjects; in the US, it is conducted under the supervision of FDA.

Cloud Computing: Large number of computers connected through a communication network like internet, etc. It is a synonym for distributed computing.

CPAN: Comprehensive Perl Archive Network containing an accumulation of BioPerl libraries and functions.

CRAN: Comprehensive R Archive Network which is the repository of the R packages and functions.

Docking: A method which predicts the preferred orientation of one molecule to a second when bound to each other to form a stable complex.

Eddies: A circular movement of water causing a small whirlpool.

Exaflops: One exaflop is a thousand petaflops or a quintillion.

Google Cloud Platform: Google's vision for cloud computing. A big data solution that allows to efficiently process data at Google scale and speed and a new approach to computing that erases distinctions between PaaS and IaaS.

Grid Computing: Collection of computer resources from multiple locations to reach a common goal.

Hadoop: Apache Hadoop is an open-source software framework that supports data intensive distributed applications.

Heliosphere: The region of space, encompassing the solar system, in which the solar wind has a significant influence.

Heterogeneous Computing: Systems that use multiple processor types.

High Performance Computing: Aggregating computing power in a way that delivers much higher performance that one could get out of a typical desktop computer or workstation.

Molecular Modeling: Used to model or mimic the behavior of molecules.

Navier-Strokes Solvers: These equations describe the motion of fluid substances.

Network Theory: An area of Computer Science and network science and a part of graph theory.

Petaflops: A measure of computer's processing speed and can be expressed as a thousand trillion floating point operations per second.

Protein Data Bank: PDB is a repository for the three-dimensional structural data of large biological molecules like proteins and nucleic acids.

QCDOC Machines: This architecture has been designed to provide cost-effective, massively parallel computer capable of focusing computing resources on small but extremely demanding problems.

Quantum Chromo Dynamics: A quantum field theory in which the strong interaction is described in terms of interactions between quarks mediated by gluons, both quarks and gluons being assigned a quantum number called "color".

Quantum Mechanics: Branch of Physics that deals with physical phenomena at nanoscopic scales where the action is in the order of Planck's constant.

RNA Sequencing: Also called as Whole Transcriptome Shotgun Sequencing, is a technology that uses the capabilities of next generation sequencing to reveal a snapshot of RNA presence and quantity from a genome at a given moment in time.

Schrodinger Equation: A differential equation that forms the basis of the quantum-mechanical description of matter in terms of wave-like properties of particles in a field.

Semiconductor: A solid substance that has the conductivity between that of an insulator and that of most metals, either due to the addition of impurities or because of temperature effects. Devices made of semiconductors are components of electronic circuits.

Superconductors: A substance capable of becoming superconducting at sufficiently low temperatures.

Teraflops: A measure of computing speed equal to one trillion floating-point operations per second.

Section 2
Supercomputing Applications

Chapter 4

Accelerated Discovery and Design of Nano-Material Applications in Nuclear Power by Using High Performance Scientific Computing

Liviu Popa-Simil
Los Alamos Academy of Science, USA

ABSTRACT

The accelerated development of nano-sciences and nano-material systems and technologies is made possible through the use of High Performance Scientific Computing (HPSC). HPSC exploration ranges from nano-clusters to nano-material behavior at mezzo-scale and specific macro-scale products. These novel nano-materials and nano-technologies developed using HPSC can be applied to improve nuclear devices' safety and performance. This chapter explores the use of HPSC.

INTRODUCTION

This chapter includes the following topics of interest:

1. Defining basic concepts of nano-materials and technologies while examining different perspectives of HPSC usage to clarify various fundamental aspects of physics and material science;

2. Providing a synthesis of existing approaches and solutions to the actual material simulation problems;

3. Investigating the potential of HPSC to develop bottom-up, large-scale simulations from pico-scale up to micro-scale products;

4. Highlighting the issues with existing approaches, specifically focused on the existence of various HPSC solutions from local to distributed systems; and

5. Investigating the potential integration opportunities of multi-scale, multi-dimension

DOI: 10.4018/978-1-4666-7461-5.ch004

Copyright © 2015, IGI Global. Copying or distributing in print or electronic forms without written permission of IGI Global is prohibited.

concepts and their applicability on various HPSC architectures.

SUMMARY OF NANO-MATERIALS, NANO-TECHNOLOGIES, AND ASSOCIATED PHYSICS AND ENGINEERING CAPABLE OF IMPROVING NUCLEAR POWER PERFORMANCE

We will introduce the reader to:

- Actual nuclear power applications with respect to fission, fusion, isotopic power, and annihilation sources, including related performance and problems;
- The concept of harmony among process, method, instrument, and environment as a fundamental explanation of the multi-scale, multi-dimension approach in modern nuclear applications;
- Physics processes in material structures from nano- to micro- and mezzo-scale and various related approaches;
- A brief presentation of models and actual computer simulation tools and their limitations; and
- Basic terminology used in this field.

Who First Defined Nano-Technology?

(Sandhu A., 2006) The term "nano-technology" was first defined by Norio Taniguchi of Tokyo Science University in 1974. (Taniguchi, 1974)

Where are We Using Nano-Technology?

- Medicine
  - Cell imaging
  - Cancer therapy—contact agents
  - Drug delivery vehicles
- Catalysis
  - Fuel cells
  - Catalytic converters
  - Photo-catalytic devices
- Cosmetics
  - Sunscreen
- Textiles
  - Water- and stain-repellent materials
  - Wrinkle-free materials
  - Invisibility coat—military
- Optics
  - Scratch-resistant coatings
- Foods
  - Anti-microbial packaging
- Vehicle manufacturing
  - Hard coatings for wear resistance
- Electronics
  - Quantum dots
  - Semiconductors
- Nuclear materials and applications
  - Direct energy conversion
  - Enhanced separation in transmutation
  - Self-repairing materials
  - Radiation guides and shielding

What Exactly is Nano-Technology?

Nano, is a submultiple of a unit having the meaning of one bilionth of that unit (meter → nano-meter; second →nano-second, etc.). At the scale of an atomic cluster of a few unit cells are at the size of one nanometer, and the experince shows that at this size conventional ideas of structure-property relationships no longer hold in the form they were previously known.

Why the emphasis on nano-technology? Nano-materials exhibit properties that we might be able to exploit to our advantage; for example, hard materials become 'super' hard if apropriately manufactured.

High performance materials are essential for many applications. For example, "Without Damascus steel it would be impossible to make Damascus swords." (Sanderson, 2006)

Nano-technology, sometimes shortened to "nanotech", is the manipulation of matter on an atomic and molecular scale. Generally, nano-technology works with materials, devices, and other structures that have at least one dimension sized from 1 to 100 nm. Quantum mechanical effects are important at this quantum-realm scale. With a variety of potential applications, nano-technology is a key research area for the future into which governments have invested billions of dollars.

Nano-technology is very diverse and includes extensions of conventional device physics as well as completely new approaches based on molecular self-assembly. In addition, nano-technology research involves the development of new materials with dimensions on the nano-scale and promotes direct control of matter on the atomic scale. Nano-technology entails the application of fields of science as diverse as surface science, organic chemistry, molecular biology, semiconductor physics, micro-fabrication, etc.

Several phenomena become more pronounced as the size of the system decreases. These phenomena include statistical-mechanical effects, as well as quantum-mechanical effects. One example is the "quantum size effect", in which the electronic properties of solids are altered as great reductions in particle size occur. This effect does not come into play when going from macro to micro dimensions. However, quantum effects can become significant when the nanometer size range (typically distances of 100 nm or less) is reached, the so-called quantum realm. Additionally, a number of physical (mechanical, electrical, optical, etc.) properties change as compared to macroscopic systems. One example is the increase in surface area to volume ratio, which alters mechanical, thermal and catalytic properties of materials. Another example includes mass transport (including diffusion) in solid electrolytes at the nano-scale, otherwise known as nano-ionics. (ASU 2006)

Mechanical properties of nano-systems are of interest in nano-mechanics research. The catalytic activity of nano-materials also opens potential risks in their interaction with biomaterials. The knowledge gained in these subfields previously mentioned allow researchers to anticipate advantages that nano-technology might yield and to propose new lines of inquiry along with discussion might progress. These discussions often take a big-picture view of nano-technology with more emphasis on its social implications than on the details of how such advancements could actually be achieved.

Molecular nano-technology (The Foresight Institute 2013) is a proposed approach that involves manipulating single molecules in finely controlled, deterministic ways. This subfield is more theoretical than the others and many of its proposed techniques are beyond current capabilities.

Nano-robotics is centered on self-sufficient machines of some functionality operating at the nano-scale. There is hope for applying nano-robots to the field of medicine, but this application is severely challenged because of several drawbacks of such devices. Nevertheless, progress on innovative materials and methodologies has been demonstrated and some new patents have been granted for new nano-manufacturing devices to be used in future commercial applications. Subsequently, this progress will support development of nano-robots for use with embedded nano-bioelectronics concepts.

Productive nano-systems are "systems of nano-systems" (i.e., complex nano-systems that produce atomically precise parts for other nano-systems). These productive nano-systems do not necessarily use novel nano-scale-emergent properties, but do use well-understood fundamentals of manufacturing. Because of the discrete (i.e., atomic) nature of matter and the possibility of exponential growth of the number of materials with different properties by adding an extra-atom to a previous group, this stage, also called nano-engineering, a process that seeks to obtain matter with preprogrammed proprieties is seen as the basis of another industrial revolution. Mihail Roco, one of the architects of the United State's

National Nano-technology Initiative, has proposed four states of nano-technology that seem to parallel the technical progress of the Industrial Revolution, progressing from passive nano-structures to active nano-devices to complex nano-machines and ultimately to productive nano-systems.

Programmable matter is another related process that (Ye, 2013) seeks to design materials whose properties can be easily, reversibly and externally controlled though a fusion of information science and materials science.

Because of the popularity and media exposure of the term nano-technology the analogous terms pico-technology and femto-technology have been coined; however, these terms are used only rarely and informally because denominate atomic and subatomic processes (an atom spans over ¼ nm about).

Using nano-technology, researchers developed what they call "ultra-capacitors." An ultra-capacitor (Coughlin C., 2012) is a general term that describes a capacitor that contains nano-components. Ultra-capacitors are being researched heavily because of their high-density interior, compact size, reliability, and high capacitance. The decreased size of ultra-capacitors makes it increasingly possible to develop much smaller circuits and computers. Ultra-capacitors also have the capability to supplement batteries in hybrid vehicles by providing a large amount of energy during peak acceleration and allowing the battery to supply energy over longer periods of time, such as during a period of constant driving speed. This capability could decrease the size and weight of large batteries needed by hybrid vehicles as well as take stress off the battery. However, currently, the combination of ultra-capacitors and a battery is not cost effective because additional DC/DC electronics are required to coordinate the two.

Nano-porous carbon aerogel (Tian, 2008) is one type of material that is being utilized for the design of ultra=capacitors. These aerogels have very large interior surface area and changing the pore diameter and surface distribution can alter their properties. This adjustment is accomplished by adding nano-sized alkali metals to alter the material's conductivity.

Carbon nano-tubes are another possible material for use in ultra-capacitors. Vaporizing carbon and allowing it to condense on a surface create carbon nano-tubes. When the carbon condenses, it forms a nano-sized tube composed of carbon atoms. This tube has a high surface area, which increases the amount of charge that can be stored. The low reliability and high cost of using carbon nano-tubes for ultra-capacitors is currently an issue of research.

Figure 1 shows briefly the evolution of the nano-structures, grouped on generations. The first made nano-structures were passive being known as aerosols, colloids, ultra-thin coatings, sub-micron structures of metals, polymers and ceramics. After the year 2000, the microelectronics advancements give birth to nano-transistors integrated in electronic circuits, microprocessors, etc. giving birth to the 2nd generation of nano-structures, also known as active nano-structures. To these, the progress in bio-active materials have been associated, as a novel class of materials and applications.

Even more recently, nano-systems appeared in the form of 3D assemblies in VLSI (Very Large Scale Integration), driving to a new class of electronic devices, self-assembling structures with applications in robotics and computing, and that is what is generically called "generation 3".

After 2010, new programmable proprieties nano structures, molecular devices exhibiting a large variety of new function appeared and are included in Generation 4 together with NEMS (Nano-Electronic Mechanical Systems). The future belongs to nano-motors, molecular assemblies performing more ane more complicated functions, preprogrammed proprieties by design and a new domain, called nano-engineering emerged. All these are ideographic presented in Figure 1 as a synthesis of the evolution of nano-technology, bringing important incentives for the development of the super-computing.

Figure 1. Generations of nano-structures and nano-technologies (CRN, 2013) (Courtesy to Center for Responsible Nano-technology http://crnano.org/whatis.htm)

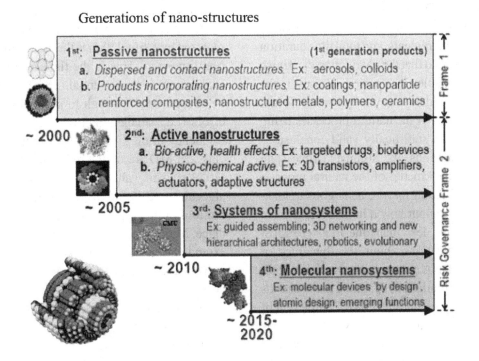

Motivation to Use High Performance Scientific Computing

The motivation to use HPSC rather than personal infrastructures, hardware, and software is obvious. We will present various applications using supercomputer infrastructures for nuclear power simulations. Nuclear physics and its applications are at the heart of the development of supercomputer structures because problems and algorithms associated with nuclear physics often can be solved by exploiting the power of computer parallelization. Only HPSC provides an acceptable way to solve many nuclear-physics problems with a reasonable amount of effort.

In many cases when making a bottom-up simulation of a material or nuclear structure with high resolution, molecular dynamics (MD) is the most effective available tool (Wikipedia, 2013). This method provides a computer simulation of the physical movement of atoms and molecules.

In the simulation, the atoms and molecules are allowed to interact for a period of time; the result is a simulated view of the motion of the atoms. In the most common version of molecular dynamics, the trajectories of atoms and molecules are determined by solving numerically Newton's equations of motion for a system of interacting particles. In other words, forces between the particles and potential energy are defined by molecular mechanics force fields. MD was originally conceived within theoretical physics during the late 1950s, but it is applied today mostly in chemical physics, materials science, and the modeling of biomolecules.

Because molecular systems consist of a vast number of particles, it is impossible to find the properties of such complex systems analytically. MD simulation circumvents this problem by using numerical methods. However, long MD simulations are mathematically ill-conditioned, generating cumulative errors associated with numerical integration methods. These errors can be minimized with proper selection of algorithms and parameters, but they cannot be eliminated entirely.

Design of a MD simulation should account for the available computational power. Simulation size, time-step increments, and total time duration must be selected so that the calculation can finish within a reasonable time period. However, the simulations should be long enough to be relevant to the time scales of the natural processes being studied. To make statistically valid conclusions from the simulations, the simulated time span should match the kinetics of the natural process. Otherwise, the result may be analogous to making conclusions about how a human walks from data representing less than one footstep. Most scientific publications about the dynamics of proteins and DNA (Deoxyribo Nucleic Acid) use data from simulations spanning nanoseconds (10^{-9} s) to microseconds (10^{-6} s). Completion of these simulations can require several CPU-days (Central Processing Unit) to CPU-years. Parallel algorithms allow the load to be distributed among many CPUs, GPUs (Graphics Processing Unit), or combinations, and more recently containing FPGAs (Field Programmable Gate Array).

During a classical MD simulation, the most CPU-intensive task is the evaluation of the potential (force field) as a function of the particles' internal coordinates. Within that energy evaluation, the most expensive calculation is the non-bonded or non-covalent part of the simulated molecular system. In Big O notation, if all pairwise electrostatic and Van der Waals interactions must be accounted for explicitly, then common molecular dynamics simulations scale by $O(n^2)$, where n represents the number of particles. This computational cost can be reduced by employing electrostatics methods such as Particle Mesh Ewald (PME) ($O(n\log(n))$), Particle-Particle-Particle Mesh (which is a Fourier-based Ewald summation method to calculate potentials in n-body simulations), or good spherical cutoff techniques ($O(n)$). The potential could be the electrostatic potential among n point charges (molecular dynamics), the

gravitational potential among n gas particles (e.g., smoothed particle hydrodynamics), or any other useful function (Deserno, 1998).

Another factor that impacts total CPU time required by a simulation is the size of the integration time-step. This is the time length between evaluations of the potential. The time-step must be chosen small enough to avoid discretization errors (i.e., smaller than the fastest vibrational frequency in the system). Typical time-steps for classical MD are on the order of 1 femtosecond (10^{-15} s). This value may be extended by using algorithms such as SHAKE, which fixes the vibrations of the fastest atoms (e.g., hydrogen) into place. Multiple time scale methods that allow for extended times between updates of slower long-range forces (Tuckerman, 1992) have also been developed.

For simulating molecules in a solvent, a choice should be made between an explicit solvent and an implicit solvent. Explicit solvent particles (such as the TIP3P (Temporal Ionization Potential 3D free Particles), SPC/E (Simple Point Charge & Electron) and SPC-f (Simple Point Charge-flexible) water models) must be calculated explicitly by the force field, while implicit solvents use a mean-field approach. Using an explicit solvent is computationally intensive, requiring inclusion of roughly ten times more particles in the simulation. But the granularity and viscosity of explicit solvents are essential to reproduce certain properties of the solute molecules. These properties are especially important to reproduce kinetics.

In molecular dynamics simulations the simulation box size must be large enough to avoid boundary-condition artifacts. Boundary conditions are often treated by choosing fixed values at the edges (which may cause artifacts) or by employing periodic boundary conditions (in which one side of the simulation loops back to the opposite side, mimicking a bulk phase).

Although, QM (quantum-mechanical) methods are very powerful, they are computationally expensive. On the other hand, MM (classical or molecular-mechanics) methods are fast, but they suffer from several limitations: MM methods require extensive parameterization, energy estimates obtained using MM methods are not very accurate; MM methods cannot be used to simulate reactions where covalent bonds are broken/formed, and MM methods are limited in their ability to provide accurate details regarding the chemical environment. A new class of method has emerged that combines the good points of QM (i.e., accuracy) and MM (i.e., speed) calculations. These methods are known as mixed or hybrid quantum-mechanical and molecular-mechanics methods (hybrid QM/MM).

The most important advantage of hybrid QM/MM methods is speed. The cost of doing classical molecular dynamics (MD) in the most straightforward case scales as $O(n^2)$, where n is the number of atoms in the system. This relationship is primarily due to the electrostatic interactions term (every particle interacts with every other particle). However, use of cutoff radius, periodic pair-list updates, and, more recently, variations of the PME method have reduced this scaling factor to between $O(n)$ and $O(n^2)$. In other words, if a system with twice as many atoms is simulated, the calculation would require between two to four times as much computing power. On the other hand, the simplest ab-initio calculations typically scale as $O(n^3)$ or worse [Restricted Hartree-Fock calculations (Plimpton, 2013) have been suggested to scale as $\sim O(n^{2.7})$]. To overcome this limitation, a small part of the system (typically the active-site of an enzyme) is treated quantum-mechanically and the remaining system is treated classically.

In more sophisticated implementations, QM/MM methods exist to treat both light nuclei susceptible to quantum effects (such as hydrogen) and electronic states. This implementation allows generation of hydrogen wave-functions (similar to electronic wave-functions). This methodology has been useful in investigating phenomena such as hydrogen tunneling. One example where QM/MM methods have provided new discoveries is

the calculation of hydride transfer in the enzyme liver alcohol dehydrogenase (Billeter., 2001). In this case, tunneling is important for the hydrogen because it determines the reaction rate.

The success or failure of a simulation is directly related to the accuracy of the energy- potential calculation. Classical molecular dynamics uses the Born-Oppenheimer approximation (Doltsinis, 2006), in which a single potential energy surface, usually the ground state, is represented in the force field For calculation of atomic or molecular excited states, for the simulation of chemical reactions, or to enable a more accurate representation, electronic behavior can be obtained from first principles by using a quantum mechanical method, such as Density Functional Theory. This is known as Ab Initio Molecular Dynamics (AIMD) (Schlegel, 2003). Due to the cost of treating the electronic degrees of freedom, the computational cost of these simulations is much higher than classical molecular dynamics. This implies that AIMD is limited to smaller systems and shorter periods of time.

Ab-initio quantum-mechanical methods may be used to calculate the potential energy of a system on the fly, as needed for conformations in a trajectory. This calculation is usually made in the close neighborhood of the reaction coordinate. Although various approximations may be used, these estimates are based on theoretical considerations, not on empirical fitting. Ab-initio calculations produce a vast amount of information that is not available from empirical methods, such as density of electronic states or other electronic properties. A significant advantage of using ab-initio methods is the ability to study reactions that involve breaking or formation of covalent bonds, which correspond to multiple electronic states.

Molecular design software, which is software for molecular modeling, provides special support for developing molecular models de novo. In contrast to the usual molecular modeling programs, such as the molecular dynamics and quantum chemistry programs, molecular design software directly supports aspects related to the construction of molecular models:

- Molecular graphics; including 3D Molecular Graphics
- Interactive molecular drawing and conformational editing like mouse drawing molecule by mouse
- Building of polymeric molecules, crystals, and solvated systems like Poly (polymer building), DNA (nucleic acid building), Pept (Peptide building), Cryst (crystal building), Solv (solvent addition)
- Partial charges development like Q (partial charges)
- Geometry optimization like Dock (docking), Min (optimization)
- Support for the different aspects of force field development as MM (molecular mechanics), QM (quantum mechanics). FF (support for force field development.) QSAR (2D, 3D, and Group QSAR).

LAMMPS ("Large-scale Atomic/Molecular Massively Parallel Simulator") (Plimpton, 2013) is a molecular dynamics program from Sandia National Laboratories that makes use of MPI for parallel communication and is free, open-source software, distributed under the terms of the GNU General Public License.

On parallel computers, LAMMPS uses spatial-decomposition techniques to partition the simulation domain into small 3D sub-domains, one of which is assigned to each processor. Processors communicate and store "ghost" atom information for atoms that border their sub-domain. LAMMPS is most efficient (in a parallel computing sense) for systems whose particles fill a 3D rectangular box with approximately uniform density.

Molecular modeling on GPU is the technique of using a graphics-processing unit (GPU) for molecular simulations.

In 2007, NVIDIA Corporation introduced video cards that can be used not only to show graphics but also for scientific calculations. These cards include many arithmetic units (currently up to 1536) working in parallel. Long before this event, the computational power of video cards was used to accelerate calculations. What was new is that NVIDIA made it possible to develop parallel programs in a high-level language. This technology substantially simplified programming by enabling programs to be written in C/C++.

Quantum chemistry calculations and molecular mechanics simulations (Wikipedia, 2013) (molecular modeling in terms of classical mechanics) are among beneficial applications of this technology. The video cards can accelerate the calculations tens of times, so a personal computer with such a card has the power similar to that of a cluster of workstations based on common processors.

Folding@home (Wikipedia, 2013a) is one of the world's fastest computing systems, as Figure 2 shows, with a speed of approximately 12 petaflops—greater than all projects running on the BOINC (Berkley Open Infrastructure for Network Computing) distributed computing platform. The project was also the world's most powerful molecular dynamics simulator until mid-2011. This performance from its large-scale computing network has allowed researchers to run computationally expensive atomic-level simulations of protein folding thousands of times longer than previously achieved. Since its launch on October 1, 2000, the Pande laboratory Stamford CA has produced 109 scientific research papers as a direct result of Folding@home. Results from the project's simulations agree favorably with experiments [15] (Voelz., 2010).

As shown in Figure 2, between June 2007 and June 2011 Folding@home (blue and red) exceeded the performance of Top500's fastest supercomputer (green). However, K computer in November 2011 and Blue Gene/Q eclipsed

Figure 2. Computational power of Folding@home and the fastest supercomputer from April 2004 to October 2012 as a function of participation with various platforms (CPU; GPU, PS3).

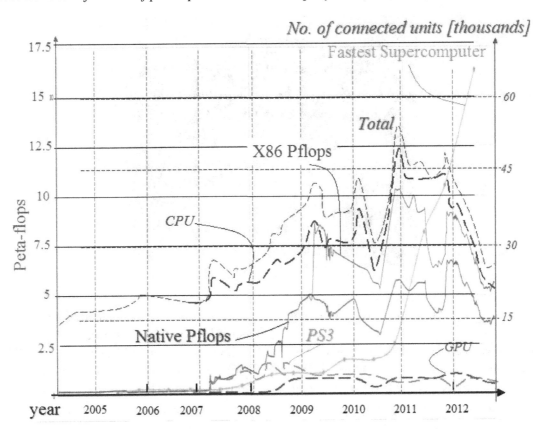

Folding@home in June 2012. This system is an important resource performing about 10 petaflops at 40,000 units in all the big units, corporations and even small companies, using the available computation power that is mainly sleeping for more than 70% of the time.

For example, the tri-lab workforce (LANL, SNL, LLNL) supports a total of about 20,000 personal computers and as many cell-phones; these systems, if combined, could deliver a supplementary computational power of about 6–10 petaflops. The whole population of the United States could provide a total power of more than 100 petaflops as well as several exabytes of redundant storage, which is usually called cloud computing, with no maintenance expenses.

Examples of Different Nuclear Energy-Related Problems and their Solutions that Led to Accelerated Development of HPSC

This section provides a brief history of the development of nuclear power computational needs in parallel with the development of supercomputers.

Nuclear physics-related analyses are among the most demanding with respect to computing power needs. Consequently, nuclear-physics calculations have influenced HPSC development. The history of computing starts in 1943 when people used desk calculators, shown in Figure 3, at the beginning of the Manhattan Project in Los Alamos.

By the end of the war, Los Alamos scientists were using the first electronic computer. John von Neumann was the primary agent of this change,

Figure 3. The 1943 Los Alamos Laboratory computing room equipped with IBM machines used to solve complicated, time-consuming equations (courtesy to LANL).

which led to the Laboratory's strong program in computer science and technology, as well as making it possible to calculate the behavior of nuclear explosives.

Early calculations relating to the diffusion of neutrons in a critical assembly of uranium were made by Eldred Nelson and Stanley Frankel [16] (Roy, 2001), who were members of Robert Serber's group in the Radiation Laboratory at the University of California, Berkeley, in 1942. When Nelson and Frankel came to Los Alamos in the spring of 1943, they ordered the same sorts of machines that they had used in California: Marchant and Friden desk calculators.

To perform some of the required repetitive calculations, a group of scientists' wives were recruited to form a central computing pool. These "computers" included Stanley Frankel's wife, Mary; Josephine Elliott; Beatrice Langer; Mici Teller; Jean Bacher; and Betty Inglis. These women became group T-5 under the supervision of New York University mathematician Donald (Moll) Flanders when he arrived in the late summer of 1943.

The mechanical calculators tended to break down under heavy use by physicists and had to be shipped back to the manufacturer until physicists Richard Feynman of Princeton University and Nicholas Metropolis of the University of Chicago learned to repair them. Although Theoretical (T) Division Leader Hans Bethe at first objected that this was a waste of time, he relented when the number of working calculators diminished.

Dana Mitchell, whom Laboratory Director J. Robert Oppenheimer had recruited from Columbia University to oversee procurement for Los Alamos, recognized that the calculators were not adequate for the heavy computational chores and suggested the use of IBM punched-card machines. He had seen them used successfully by Wallace Eckert at Columbia to calculate the orbits of planets and persuaded Frankel and Nelson to order a complement of them.

In September 1943, von Neumann made the first of many visits to Los Alamos. A mathematician at the Institute for Advanced Study at Princeton, he had been asked by Oppenheimer to serve as a consultant in hydrodynamics. During his visits, von Newmann became aware of the work on implosion being conducted by Seth Neddermeyer and his group.

Von Neumann, who also was a consultant on explosives for the Army, pointed out that shaped charges could be used to produce a more uniform shock wave for this purpose. He subsequently developed Neddermeyer's one-dimensional theory of implosion with Edward Teller, the theoretical physicist from the Metallurgical Laboratory of the University of Chicago. When von Neumann had difficulty with the pure high-density incompressible phase of implosion, he suggested a test implosion to determine physical quantities that could not be calculated analytically. He subsequently formulated another model for computation, and Teller set up a group in T division devoted to the theory of implosion.

The new IBM punched-card machines were devoted to calculations to simulate implosion, and Metropolis and Feynman organized a race between them and the hand-computing group. "We set up a room with girls in it. Each one had a Marchant. But one was the multiplier, and another was the adder, and this one cubed, and all she did was cube this number and send it to the next one," said Feynmann. For one day, the hand computers kept up: "The only difference was that the IBM machines didn't get tired and could work three shifts. But the girls got tired after a while."

Feynmann worked out a technique to run several calculations in parallel on the punched-card machines that reduced the time required. "The problems consisted of a bunch of cards that had to go through a cycle. First add, then multiply, and so it went through the cycle of machines in this room—slowly—as it went around and around. So we figured a way to put a different colored set of cards through a cycle too, but out of phase. We'd do two or three problems at a time," explained Feynman. Three months were required for the first calculation, and Feynman's technique reduced it to two or three weeks.

The first implosion calculation showed that the fissile material would be strongly compressed and that a high yield would result from assembling a relatively small amount of fissile material if a

spherically symmetrical implosion was produced. Although much work on explosives lenses, detonators, and other components of the device was required to accomplish this, the Trinity test July 16, 1945, showed that the calculation was correct. About a dozen other calculations of implosion were done to refine it before the end of the war.

In the meantime, von Neumann brought news of computer developments elsewhere, such as Bell Laboratory's relay computer and Howard Aiken's Mark. Mark-I electromechanical calculator was at Harvard where Aiken was director of the Harvard Computation Laboratory. The Mark I was even used to run an unclassified version of one of the Los Alamos problems. Although it took several times as long as the Los Alamos machines, it computed to far greater precision.

Von Neumann saw that problems like those encountered at Los Alamos could been solved by electronic computers similar to the electronic numerical integrator and calculator (ENIAC (Electronic Numerical Integrator and Computer)) being developed at the University of Pennsylvania. In 1944 and 1945, he formulated ways to translate mathematical procedures into a language of instructions for such a machine. And he recommended to Teller, who had conceived of a thermonuclear or "super" bomb, that one of the computational problems associated with its design be used to test the ENIAC, because it would be much more demanding than the ballistic trajectories the Army had designed it to calculate. Metropolis and Frankel traveled to the University of Pennsylvania early in 1945 to discuss the problem with the developers of ENIAC, John Mauchly and J. Presper Eckert.

The calculations were run in December 1945 and January 1946. A half-million punched cards of data were transferred from Los Alamos to Philadelphia to run it, and mathematician Stan Ulam, whom von Neumann had recruited to come to Los Alamos from Princeton, recalled "the spirit of exploration and of belief in the possibility of getting trustworthy answers in the future. This is partly because of the existence of computing machines that could perform much more detailed analysis and modeling of physical problems."

In the postwar era, von Neumann continued to arrange for access to the ENIAC for Los Alamos scientists and also built an improved version of the electronic computer at the Institute for Advanced Study at Princeton, where Oppenheimer became director. Inspired by his example, Los Alamos had Metropolis, see Figure 4, build the mathematical analyzer, numerical integrator and computer, or MANIAC (Mathematic analyzer Numerical Integrator and Computer), which was completed in 1952 and was responsible for the calculations of Mike, the first hydrogen bomb. MANIAC II, the IBM-built STRETCH supercomputer and a series of commercial supercomputers that have made the Los Alamos National Laboratory the world's largest scientific computing center, followed it.

Von Neumann also helped Ulam and Metropolis develop new means of computing on such machines, including the Monte Carlo method, which has found widespread application. His influence on the development of electronic computers was far-reaching, and he continued to foster their development at Los Alamos up to the time of

his death in 1957 while serving on the Atomic Energy Commission.

The wartime work of the Laboratory created a need for computing that stimulated von Neumann, Metropolis, Ulam, and others to reduce previously insoluble physical problems to a form in which they could be calculated automatically. The use of these techniques not only made possible the design of nuclear and thermonuclear weapons, but also the solution of many other scientific problems, ranging from aerodynamics to molecular biology. What began with a brief visit to the Laboratory by von Neumann in September 1943 has become a revolution in science and technology.

LANL collaborated with Seymour Cray on the design of the Cray-I, the first successful vector computer and the fastest machine of 1970s. The Cray's speed came from its, "C"-shaped central processing unit that reduced the length of the wires and, consequently, the time required for the signals to travel along them. [An electronic signal requires a nanosecond (1 ns) to travel about ¾ feet.]. Another revolutionary speed increase came from the Cray's vector architecture, which enabled the computer to perform many instructions at once on a linear data array, also called a data-vector. When delivered at LANL in 1976,

Figure 4. MANIAC computer developed at LANL in early 1950s (courtesy to LANL)

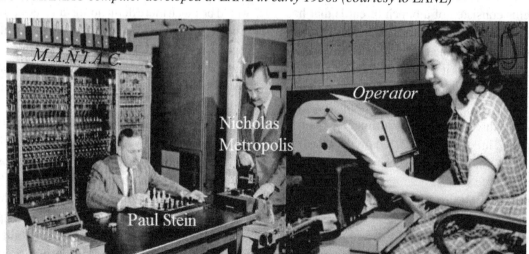

the machine was the fastest in the world, and the high performance-computing era started in nuclear physics.

By 1995 the Office of Advanced Simulation and Computing and Institutional Research and Development was established. This office supported the Advanced Simulation and Computing (ASC) Program, which led the U.S. nuclear defense programs' shift in emphasis from test-based confidence to simulation-based confidence. Under ASC, computer simulation capabilities were developed to analyze and predict the performance, safety, and reliability of nuclear weapons and to certify their functionality. In 1998 LANL and Silicon Graphics commissioned the Blue Mountain computer, one of the word's fastest in its day, performing 1.6 petaflops, see Figure 5.

As part of NNSA's (National Nuclear Security Agency) mission to extend the lifetime of nuclear weapons in the stockpile, the ASC campaign provides NNSA with leading edge, high-end simulation capabilities. The ASC program helps NNSA to meet nuclear weapons assessment and certification requirements, including weapon codes, weapon science, computing platforms, and supporting infrastructure. NNSA's three national laboratories house some of the world's fastest supercomputers: Sequoia, Cielo, and Roadrunner.

ASC simulations are central to U.S. national security, because they provide a computational surrogate for nuclear testing. NNSA's ability to model the extraordinary complexity of nuclear weapons systems is essential to establish confidence in the performance of our aging stockpile. ASC tools enable nuclear weapons scientists and engineers to gain a comprehensive understanding of the entire weapons lifecycle from design to safe processes for dismantlement. Also, through close coordination with other government agencies, ASC tools also play an important role in supporting nonproliferation efforts, emergency response, and nuclear forensics.

The Race for More Powerful HPSC Machines

The nuclear weapons race that developed during the Cold War was followed by the Strategic Arms Limitation Talks (SALT) agreements and the subsequent ban of nuclear tests. This test ban created a tremendous need for computation power and contributed to the acceleration of the

Figure 5. First supercomputers at LANL: 1976 Cray-1 and Blue Mountain 1998 (courtesy to LANL)

supercomputing race. The actual HPSC systems are found in many other applications as business, used for large economic systems prediction, or other like, weather prediction, climate change, and space exploration making the need for more powerful machines and systems to become more obvious than ever.

Supercomputers Used in Nuclear Weapons

Sequoia, a Lawrence Livermore National Laboratory supercomputer built by the technology giant IBM, has set a new processing speed world record, reclaiming the title for the United States from a Japanese rival, but that place was not held for long time, because in 2013 the Chinese supercomputer Thiane-2, with over 3 million processors, and about 33 Pflops.

This machine runs the Linux operating system that was first announced in 2009, has been installed across 4,500 square feet to carry out simulations of nuclear weapons tests, and have allowed the United States to have confidence in its nuclear weapons stockpile over the 20 years since nuclear testing ended in 1992.

Sequoia's speed was measured at 16.3 petaflops, or 16 thousand trillion floating-point operations per second, and is said to be capable of 20 petaflops. It unseated the reigning champion, the K Computer, built by Fujitsu in Japan, which is capable of more than 10 petaflops.

This supercomputer simulates nuclear explosion down to the molecular level, because the actual treaties forbid the detonation of nuclear test weapons that creates problems for national defense developers who need to efficiently certify the effectiveness of their arsenal, and this powerful new supercomputer is now able to replicate the physical impact of nuclear explosions digitally. The number-crunching required to simulate molecular-scale reactions taking place over the course of milliseconds in an actual nuclear explosion is staggering. To get this level of detail, researchers

had to coordinate over 100,000 machines. They also had to split multiple processes in parallel on separate machines in large computer clusters.

Supercomputers allow the U.S. to virtually test nuclear weapons without plunging back into the Cold War (LLNL, 2012), but undetected computing errors can corrupt or even crash such simulations involving 100,000 networked machines, and a procedure to make an automated system for catching computer glitches before they spiral out of control was required.

The solution involved eliminating a "central brain" server that could not keep up with streaming data from thousands of machines that drove to the creation of the supercomputing cluster of machines by "classes" based on whether machines ran similar processes. That clustering tactic makes it possible to quickly detect any supercomputing glitches. Initially, in such a big system the researchers discovered that natural faults in the execution environment frequently resulted in errors, resulting in corrupted memory and failed communication between machines.

In order to get a scalable supercomputer clustering solution, where each machine in the supercomputer cluster contained several processors with each one running a "process" during a simulation using an automated method for "clustering," or grouping the large number of processes into a smaller number of "equivalence classes" with similar traits was created. Grouping the processes into equivalence classes makes possible to quickly detect and pinpoint problems in order to develop ultra-precise simulations. It is thought that the same simulation architecture could be applied to such areas as climate modeling and more.

Supercomputers are used in Nuclear Power Research

Simulation and prediction of the nuclear energetic devices behavior requires large structures, the integration of the complex knowledge and the capability to store huge amounts of information.

Scientists at the U.S. Department of Energy's Oak Ridge National Laboratory are using the world's fastest supercomputer named Titan, to model and simulate next-generation nuclear power plants, by combining existing nuclear energy and nuclear national security modeling and simulation tech with high-performance computing.

This is an example of Nuclear Modeling by developing and applying computational methods and software for simulating radiation to improve the design and safety of nuclear facilities, reactor core design, and nuclear fuel performance to bolster the impact of its nuclear analysis software package, called SCALE (A Comprehensive Modeling and Simulation Suite for Nuclear Safety Analysis and Design).

Traditionally, reactor models for radiation dose assessments have considered just the reactor core, or a small part of the core. However, we're now simulating entire nuclear facilities, such as a nuclear power reactor facility with its auxiliary buildings and the ITER (International Thermonuclear Experimental Reactor) fusion reactor, with much greater accuracy than any other organization that we're aware of.

DOE Office of Science's Innovative and Novel Computational Impact on Theory and Experiment program aims to develop "a uniquely detailed simulation of the power distribution inside a nuclear reactor core. The added computing power will booster design of more accurate models with better shielding, improving safety and reducing costs (Nusca, 2010).

Software for modeling radiation transport and nuclear reactor design have been developed and is now available as MCNPX (Monte Carlo n-Particle eXtended Transport Code), made by Los Alamos National Laboratory (LANL) or GEANT (Geometry and Tracking Code) made at the European Center for Nuclear Research (CERN) being adapted to run on various computer platforms. More recently the access has been restricted by ORNL's RSICC (Radiation Safety Information Computational Center) under DOE special care

for nonproliferation. There's no special transformational technology in SCALE software but, it is designed specifically to take advantage of the massive computational and memory capabilities of the world's fastest computers, something that Monte-Carlo codes implemented under MPI(Message Passing Interface) or MPICH(Message Passing Interface Chameleon) code was already doing for decades.

A new computer algorithm that enables scientists to view nuclear fission in much finer detail has been developed by researchers at the US Department of Energy's Argonne National Laboratory (ANL) (Vieru, 2010). The code could be used in the development of new reactor designs as continuation of the efforts in development of the National Nuclear Material Database Center (NNDC) nuclear fuel simulator codes (BNL, 2012).

ANL's Nuclear reactor simulator uses a neutron transport code UNIC (Ultimate Neutronic Investigation Code) that enables researchers to obtain a highly detailed description of a nuclear reactor core. The calculations required to model the complex geometry of a reactor core requires massive computer memory capacity, far higher than most computers can handle. Therefore, reactor-modeling codes typically rely on various approximations that limit the predictive capability of computer simulations and leave considerable uncertainty in crucial reactor design and operational parameters.

For example, the Argonne team has carried out highly detailed simulations of the Zero Power Reactor experiments on up to 163,840 processor cores of the Blue Gene/P supercomputer at ANL and 222,912 processor cores of the Cray XT5 supercomputer at Oak Ridge National Laboratory, as well as on 294,912 processors of a Blue Gene/P at the Jülich Supercomputing center in Germany. The Zero Power Reactor is an experimental nuclear reactor operated at low neutron flux and at a power level so low that no forced cooling is required. With UNIC, the researchers

Figure 6. An elevation plot of the highest energy neutron flux distributions from an axial slice of a nuclear reactor core is shown superimposed over the same slice of the underlying geometry (Courtesy to ANL)

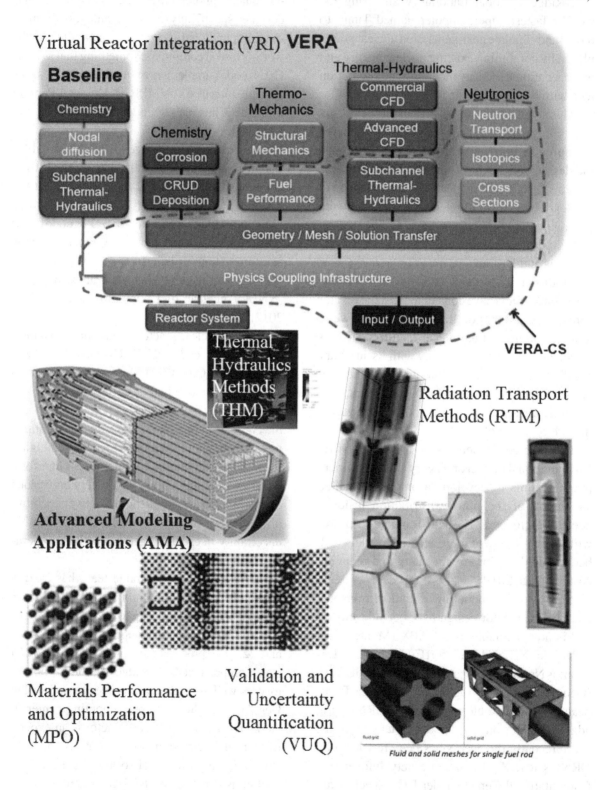

have successfully represented the details of the full reactor geometry for the first time and have been able to compare the results directly with the experimental data.

The UNIC code claims to reduce the uncertainties and biases in reactor design calculations by progressively replacing existing multilevel averaging techniques with more direct method-based solution on explicit reactor geometries, but exhibits limitations at nano-cluster level, which makes it remain more a claim, than a real revolutionary, useful feature.

The Consortium for Advanced Simulation of Light Water Reactors (CASL) (www.casl.gov) is the first DOE Hub for the modeling and simulation (M&S) of commercial nuclear reactors. They claim to utilize existing advanced capabilities developed in other programs within the DOE and other agencies and to apply them within a new multi-physics environment and develop new, valuable capabilities as appropriate. They also claim adapting the new tools to the current and future culture of nuclear engineers and produce a multi-physics environment to be used by a wide range of practitioners to conduct predictive simulation based on the use of data from real physical operational reactors to validate the virtual reactor.

The CASL Virtual Environment for Reactor Applications (VERA) incorporates science-based models, state-of-the-art numerical methods, modern computational science and engineering practices, uncertainty quantification (UQ) and validation against data from operating pressurized water reactors (PWRs), single-effect experiments, and integral tests. It couples state-of-the-art fuel and material performance, neutron transport (neutronics), thermal-hydraulics (T-H), and structural models with existing tools for systems and safety analysis, being designed for implementation on today's leadership-class computers, advanced architecture platforms. Within VERA, CASL develops and applies models, methods, data, and understanding while addressing three critical areas of performance for nuclear power plants (NPPs):

- Reducing capital and operating costs per unit of energy by enabling power up rates and lifetime extension for existing NPPs and by increasing the rated powers and lifetimes
- Reducing nuclear waste volume generated by enabling higher fuel burn up, and
- Enhancing nuclear safety by enabling high-fidelity predictive capability for component performance through the onset of failure.

CASL executes its R&D in six technical focus areas (FA) and one integrating area (Collaboration and Ideation, or C&I) to develop and apply Virtual Environment for Reactor Applications (VERA) to facilitate solutions to industry-relevant problems.

Advanced Modeling Applications (AMA)—Provides the primary interface of CASL R&D with the applications related to existing physical reactors, also called the Challenge Problems, with full-scale validation. In addition, AMA will provide the necessary direction to models and methods development to be incorporated into VERA by providing the functional requirements, prioritizing the modeling needs, and performing assessments of capability.

Virtual Reactor Integration (VRI) is meant to develop VERA tools integrating the models, methods, and data developed by other FAs within a software framework. VRI collaborates with AMA to deliver usable tools for performing design analyses, guided by the functional requirements developed by AMA.

Radiation Transport Methods (RTM) are supposed to develop the next-generation neutron transport simulation tools in VERA, which comprises: the primary development path based on 3D full-core discrete ordinates (Sn) transport/2D method of characteristics (MOC) transport; the legacy path based on full core, 2D MOC transport/1D diffusion or transport; and, the advanced development path based on hybrid Monte Carlo (MC). A more detailed picture on this integration concept of the actually existent programs into a single package to be run on ORNL [21](Hemsoth, 2011) supercomputer is presented in Figure 7.

Thermal Hydraulics Methods (THM)—Advances existing and develops new modeling capabilities for thermal hydraulics (T-H) analysis and its integration with solution environments deployed on large-scale parallel computers. The primary mission of THM is to deliver T-H components that meet the rigorous physical model and numerical algorithm requirements of VERA. THM collaborates closely with Materials Performance and Optimization (MPO) for sub-grid material and chemistry models, with RTM for coupling issues with radiation transport, and connects to virtual reactor integration (VRI) for integration and development of VERA.

Materials Performance and Optimization (MPO)—Develops improved materials performance models for fuels, cladding, and structural

Figure 7. Synthesis of CASL R&D focus Areas (courtesy to DOE's CASL)(Montgomery R., 2013)

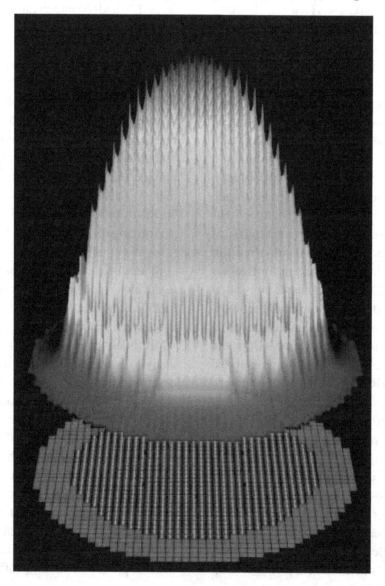

materials, and integrate those models into a fuel performance predictive capability, to provide better prediction of fuel and component failure. The science work performed by MPO will provide the means to reduce the reliance on empirical correlations and to enable the use of an expanded range of materials and fuel forms.

Validation and Uncertainty Quantification (VUQ)—Provides the quantification of uncertainties and associated validation of VERA models and integrated systems, which are essential to the application of modeling & simulation (M&S) to reactor designs. Improvements in the determination of operating and safety margins will directly contribute to the ability to uprate reactors and extend their lifetimes. The methods proposed under VUQ will significantly advance the state of the art of nuclear analysis and support the transition from integral experiments to the integration of small-scale separate-effect experiments.

The problem of HPSC has a political connotation (Taylor, 2010), because during the annual televised "State of the Union" address at the beginning of 2011, President Obama sought to renew the national focus on science and technology, in part by using supercomputing capabilities to drive progress. In order to highlight the role of HPC in the new generation of scientific endeavors, the President told millions of Americans about how supercomputing capabilities at Oak Ridge National Laboratory (ORNL) will lend the muscle for a Department of Energy initiative "to get a lot more power out of our nuclear facilities" via the Consortium for Advanced Simulation of Light Water Reactors (CASL) that seems idealistic for the next 5 years DOE has provided the $122M funding. This speech came well before the word "nuclear" was thrown into the public perception tar pit by the Fukushima nuclear reactor's disaster, otherwise it might be reasonable to assume that there would be more attention focused on the safety angle that complements the CASL's nuclear efficiency and waste reduction goals. Outside of the safety side of the story, another, perhaps more specific ele-

ment to his national address was missing—that the power of modeling and simulation—not just high performance computing—might lie at the heart of a new era for American innovation.

To arrive at an ambitious five-year plan to enact a number of design and operational improvements at nuclear facilities, CASL researchers are developing models that will simulate potential upgrades at a range of existing nuclear power plants across the United States that will seek to address a number of direct nuclear facility challenges as well as some pressing software challenges that lie at the heart of ultra-complex modeling at extreme scale.

The CASL has been designed with the goal of creating a user environment to allow for advanced predictive simulation via the creation of a Virtual Reactor (VR). This virtual reactor will examine key possibilities and existing realities at power plants at both the design and operational level. CASL leaders hope to "produce a multi-physics computational environment that can be used for calculations of both normal and off-normal conditions via the development of superior physical and analytics models and multi-physics integrators."

The CASL team further claims that once the system has matured, the VR will be able to combine "advanced neutronics, T-H, structural and fuel performance modules linked with existing systems and safety analysis simulation tools to model nuclear power plant performance in a high performance computational environment that enables engineers to simulate physical reactors."

Many of the codes will employ a number of pre-validated neutronics and thermal-hydraulics (T-H) codes that have been developed by a number of partners on the project, including a number of universities (University of Michigan, MIT, North Carolina State, etc.) as well as national laboratories (Sandia, Los Alamos, and Idaho).

During the first year, CASL will be able to achieve a number of initial core simulations using coupled tools and models—a goal that they have reached for the most part already. This involves application of 3D transport with T-H feedback and CFD (Computational Fluid Dynamics) with neutronics to isolate core elements of the core design and configuration. In the second year the team hopes to be able to apply a full-core CFD model to calculate 3D localized flow distributions to identify transverse flow that could result in problems with the rods.

According to a spokesperson for ORNL, making use of the Jaguar supercomputer, CASL will allow for large-scale integrated modeling that has only been possible in the last few years:

The challenge is not simply how to use these new capabilities, but how to make sure current programming and computational paradigms can maximize its use.

A document that covers the goals of CASL in more depth sheds light on some of the computational aspects of these massive-scale simulations. The authors note that "a cross-cutting issue that will impact the entire range of computational efforts over the lifetime of CASL is the dramatic shift occurring in computer architectures, with rapid increases in the number of cores in CPUs and increasing use of specialized processing units (such as GPUs) as computational accelerators. As a result, applications must be designed for multiple levels of memory hierarchy and massive thread parallelism.

The authors of the report go on to note that while they can expect peak performance at the desktop to be in the 10 teraflops range and the performance at the leadership platform to be in the several hundred petaflops range, during the next five years, "it will be challenging for applications to achieve a significant fraction of these peak performance numbers, particularly existing applications that have not been designed to perform well on such machines."(ORNL, 2010)

Another one of CASL's stated goals have to do with the future of modeling and simulation-focused research. The team states that they

hope to "promote an enhanced scientific basis and understanding by replacing empirically based design and analysis tools with predictive capabilities."(ORNL_info 2013) In other words, by harnessing high performance computing to demonstrate actual circumstances versus reflect the educated hopes of even the most skilled reactor engineers, we might be one step closer to fail-proof design in an area that will allow for nothing less than perfection.

CASL could have a chance to see its models and simulations leap to life over the course of the first five years of the project. Currently the Tennessee Valley Authority operates a total of six reactors that generate close to 7,000 megawatts. The agency is currently embarking on a $2.5 billion journey to create a second pressurized water reactor at one of its existing facilities. This provides a perfect opportunity for the CASL team to put their facility modeling research to work; thus they've started creating simulations focused on the reactor core, internals and the reactor vessel.

CASL claims "much of the virtual reactor to be developed will be applicable to other reactor types, including boiling water reactors." They hope that during the subsequent set of five-year objectives they will be able to expand to include structures, systems and components that are outside of the vessel as well as consider small modular reactors.

Possibility that ORNL's nuclear-simulation project could shift focus, depending on events in Japan its nuclear emergency, events which are very much on people's minds at the Laboratory, and there has been some talk about possible tweaking the nuclear simulation activity—using some of the world's fastest supercomputers—if needed. The idea of project, now eight months in and still in its early stages, has always been to be agile and flexible to changing needs.

The initial focus of CASL has been on uprating—or boosting power levels—and extending the life of existing nuclear plants in the United States, but that could be modified to help with technical issues identified in Japan that could include things such as simulations involving liquefied reactor fuel following a meltdown.

The simulation hub's mission was to tackle a series of challenges, where a couple were directly associated with safety issues pertaining to loss of coolant, that has potential application to what's been taking place in Japan and could be useful in extreme nuclear events. The hardest thing to simulate is human behavior dominated by the trend to underestimate the risks when faced with money making possibilities, and the forceful management practiced both in Japan and US where the tendency to eliminate any employee raising a safety issue that is not in agreement with the managerial line is still an important fact. It is possible now to speculate that in Japan if the human/managerial failure to follow the rule of correctly think and develop the defense in depth, as recommended in the books, shouldn't occur the earthquake impact would be minor, accident scaling INES-2 (International Nuclear Energy Accident Environmental Impact Scale) or INES-3 instead of INES-7, like Chernobyl accident. This was mention here because in the actual codes, predicting human behavior is very hard to simulate together with the administrative measures needed to place the right people in the right decision points in order to maximize the system's performances. Maybe the future data immersive behavioral software, similar to what the banks are developing today may bridge this gap, with the cost of privacy.

VERA (Virtual Experiment for Reactor Analysis), the virtual reactor tool created for the simulation project, was based on a pressurized water reactor of Westinghouse design, so it's different than the boiling water reactor of GE design of concern in Japan, but the differences are not essential from the hydraulics point of view, and if one may develop a smart simulation software, instead of the present pool of previously-used codes linked to run one after another, would bring a qualitative leap in results. This is a very difficult task because most of the codes have to be rewritten to work together on a parallel HP supercomputer structure.

Computer modeling has been used all along for developing and assessing possible reactor scenarios, including accidents, where the biggest change in modeling with CASL is the use of faster, more capable computers—such as Jaguar, the Cray machine that are currently ranked as the second-fastest computer in the world.

ATR code will allow engineers to create a simulation of a currently operating reactor that will act as a "virtual model" of that reactor. They will then use the "virtual model" to address important questions about reactor operations and safety.

It will be used to address issues such as reactor power production increases and reactor life and license extensions, where the real problem is the corrosion of pipes underneath and the low power of units build 40–50 years ago, which will be much smarter to replace with new modern power plants placed in the same yard, already polluted, than extending the life of these old structure under CASL cover-ups.

CASL initiative looks anachronic, because it is studying old type of pressurized water reactors, using the data and the old practice of the reactor design engineer to run manually codes as MCNPX (LANL) to establish the reactor criticality and power level, followed by fuel oriented thermal codes like Frapcone (ANL), and hydraulic codes to optimize the cooling like RELAPS (Reactor Excursion and Leak Analysis Program), one after another followed by ORIGEN (ORNL – Oak Ridge Isotope Generation Code) to measure the burnup and more, that already run on parallel machines, looks innovative according to DOE, because these runs become more automatic, using common blocks to transfer data among the codes and making them more user friendly.

Even these tasks look simply vague, and politically oriented, so anything accomplished to be considered as a step forward, and fulfill the milestone, knowing that most of the work was already done under other programs, the effort has the merit that for the first time a complete code for a supercomputer meant to better understand the previous experience and acquired data is commissioned. The first task is to "develop computer models that simulate nuclear power plant operations, forming a "virtual reactor" for the predictive simulation of light water reactors", while the second is to "use computer models to reduce capital and operating costs per unit of energy, extend the lifetime of the existing U.S. reactor fleet, and reduce nuclear waste volume generated by enabling higher fuel burnups", that looks more economic oriented, and a way to allow NRC to pass or fail various nuclear power units based on computer predictions. The CASL virtual reactor will also be used to accelerate the deployment of next-generation reactor designs, with emphasis on advanced nuclear fuel technologies and structural materials for the reactor's core.

The biggest advancement is done by the fact that the world's three most powerful computers: Jaguar—a 2,331-trillion operations per second Cray computer at Oak Ridge; Roadrunner—a 1,375-trillion operations per second IBM computer at Los Alamos; and Kraken—a 1,029-trillion operations per second Cray computer, also at Oak Ridge will be used.

The Applications validation, against the existing nuclear reactor data at TVA that will represents a good benchmarking of the codes used will improve the nuclear reactor's design by model development, reactor's operational parameters, reactor's startup, and post-irradiation examination of spent fuel.

Several crosscutting issues in the enabling technologies emerged are:

- Developing methods for systems that couple multiple models.
- Movement away from empirical models of the past toward physics based, first principles models.
- Algorithms and software that scale well on high capability computational platforms.

- Uncertainty quantification and error estimation in simulations.
- Simulation workflow management, including data archiving and automated discovery.

Evaluating these statements one have to consider that the nuclear reactor technology is mature, many structures have been designed and tested over the time, and even a new structure of the more of the same reactors will be discovered by using the actual CASL concepts the chances that this structure to be effectively fabricated and operated are pretty small, making the ratio between outcomes value and efforts value small. The issues related to the correlation of what effectively was manufactured and what was tested and simulated remain in force, and in order to make the simulation accurate comprehensive measurements have to be put in place, and introduced into the computer together with specific nuclear reactor tests equipped with a lot more instrumentation, something that the actual power production groups might not be so happy about, and not fully cooperate. One of the reasons is simply the extra-cost and time that is not covered by the DOE funding package, thus a more mature vision is needed.

The merits of the concept is that will unify in a single coherent package a bunch of codes used and run separately, making the design work easier, but unfortunately is mainly oriented on old obsolete structures studied since 1960s, and new vision shifts are needed, in order to reach the proclaimed goals.

The Need for Harmony in Nuclear Power

The actual nuclear reactors lack of performances, the complexity and hazard of the fuel cycle are in part due to the lack of understanding of the nature's laws related to energy distribution applied to fission products, and in part to the current technologic capabilities that make the economical optimum.

In order to produce the desired increase of performances a novel multi-scale multi-physics and engineering approach have been developed, starting from the nuclear reactions involved, analyzing in detail the key features and requirements of the "key players" in the process (neutrons, compound nucleus, fission products, transmutation products, and decay radiation), the consequences of their interaction with matter. That complex interaction generates new reactions and new key-players (knock-on electrons, photons, phonons) that further interact with the matter represented by the nuclear fuel, cladding, cooling agents, structural materials and control systems.

The understanding of this complexity of problems from fm-ps (femtometer -- picosecond) scale up to macro-system hm-y (hectometer-year) and mitigating all the requirements drives to that desired harmony that provides a safe and sound energy delivery.

Harmony with Ying and Yang is the highest level in Taoist's lives, which includes a lot of hierarchies: within human's body, among people, societies, countries, and also between human being and the nature. Nuclear reactors are a part of the nature, and may be included too.

Taoism emphasizes that human should obey natural rules, a famous statement from Tao is: "Human is learning from the Ground, the Ground is learning from the sky, the Sky is learning from the Tao, and the Tao is learning from the nature". (Junho, 2010) That is a multi-scale multi-dimensional approach in the sequence: Human, Ground, Sky, Tao and NATURE.

Without seeking an accurate identification of the Tao's philosophy elements, but if one assumes that Tao is the outer space, than NATURE is the multi-dimensionality of time-space, or the BRANES of the Universe…in a very speculative thinking (Li, 2010).

In order to get a philosophical understanding we have to speak now about the harmony with nature only.

For those used to assign "Harmony" to music, to life, for yoga practitioners, it may turn difficult to see it in nuclear reactors, but the ancestral Indian culture may be invoked and tell them that—"harmony have to be everywhere", and that proven right up to now (Berzin, 2011).

In this chapter, harmony is a generic term and may it exist in almost everything, as our ancestors observed. This concept is inside the realm of mysticism, but it may be a clear physical concept also.

Figure 8 shows the most frequent reaction in nuclear fission reactors, and its possible nuclear channels, which the reaction my follow, depending on its parameters. In our case, at the basic level is the nuclear reaction that is a manifestation of the mass-energy transformation.

In nuclear reactors, we are mainly interested in neutron-induced reactions and here they are:

The first reaction shown in Figure3 is also called neutron (n) scattering, which can be an elastic scattering, when the target nucleus (T) after the collision remains in the same nuclear state it had before the collision, and the energy and impulse are conserving but they are redistributed between the two participants.

In the case the target nucleus gets excited by taking a part of the incident neutron energy, this is called inelastic scattering. The remained energy is redistributed while the impulse is conserved.

The "*" denotes the excitation energy, that can be released at a later time, while " '" denotes modifications in neutron parameters (life-time, polarization, etc.).

Figure 8. Neutron triggered nuclear reactions equations

$$
{}_{0}^{1}n + {}_{Z}^{A}T = \begin{cases} {}_{0}^{1}n' + {}_{Z}^{A}T^* \longrightarrow & \text{n scattering} \\\\ {}_{Z}^{A+1}T^* \rightarrow {}_{Z+1}^{A+1}I^* + e^* \rightarrow & \text{transmutation} \\\\ {}_{Z1}^{A1}F_1^* + {}_{Z2}^{A2}F_2^* + m.{}_{0}^{1}n^* + \gamma + \nu \rightarrow & \text{fission} \end{cases}
$$

The middle reaction is called neutron absorption or transmutation, because the neutron is initially absorbed into the target nucleus "T", forming a new nucleus, initially a heavier isotope of the same element. Usually this structure is unstable, and further decays by emitting an electron and transmuting into a new element – that is representing the modern alchemy.

Another reaction path, also called "nuclear reaction channel", is the third one that was generically called "Fission", because the initial composed nucleus A+1T*, chose to split in two more stable smaller nuclei F1 and F2, and release several more neutrons and other prompt particles as gamma and neutrinos.

This reaction covers the other reaction called spallation, when an energetic neutron extracts many neutrons, leaving a single final nucleus F1. In practice the spallation reaction is mainly produced using accelerated particles, but fast neutrons may produce it as well.

Inside the nuclear reactor occur other reactions as beta decay, neutrino emission, gamma decay and a lot of radiation energy absorption related reactions, finally converting all this energy into heat.

All these reactions have to be considered here, as main components of "the harmony" between the nuclear reactor structure and the processes taking place inside. This is an important part a HPSC modeling and discovery has to consider, as fundamental bricks of the power production process in fissionable structures.

Traditionally, the nuclear reactor engineering is starting from the neutron transport equations and deals with heat transport, and this is the level of CASL approach.

There is not too much emphasis is put on the deep understanding of the nuclear and atomic level reactions, leaving that subject on the people dealing with materials for nuclear reactors, whom themselves do not cover the heat transport and neutron criticality issues. The people dealing with nuclear materials are mainly metallurgists and chemists, while the people dealing with nuclear

reactors are hydraulic and mechanical engineers and in this way the domain remains just partially covered. From this point of view CASL approach has the merit of blending this multi-disciplinary approach on a single big code.

At the power generator assembly level it has to be a harmony, similar to that existed in the past between Damascus steel and Damascus swords… because only the existence of the special steel alloy made possible the production of the famous swords, and without good nuclear materials that to contain in harmony all these processes inside, there is not possible to have better nuclear reactors.

Another important factor is time; the control theory approach has to be considered too in this case.

This is just another way to look into this problem of the physics carried by the harmony of Nature, is to express the same thing based on the Control Theory postulates:

In order to control a process one have to be embedded there in the right dimension, right time and the right features, to have capability of perception, analysis and reaction compatible with the process.

This is also a very broad statement valid for almost all the known processes in the universe, and in a paraphrase I may say that in order to control a process a kind of harmony have to be reached.

After Wikipedia: "Control theory is an interdisciplinary branch of engineering and mathematics that deals with the behavior of dynamical systems", and all the dynamics aspects of the power systems have to be understood and contained.

The external input of a system is called the reference. When one or more output variables of a system need to follow a certain reference over time, a controller manipulates the inputs to a system to obtain the desired effect on the output of the system. The usual objective of control theory is to calculate solutions for the proper corrective action from the controller that result in system stability, that is, the system will hold the set point and not oscillate around it.

The input and output of the system are related to each other by what is known as a transfer function (also known as the system function or network function). The transfer function is a mathematical representation, in terms of spatial or temporal frequency, of the relation between the input and output of a linear time-invariant system".

The main requirements of a control system (Wikipedia 2012) are: stability, accuracy and speed of response.

Stability—a system is to be stable if the output of the system after fluctuations, variation or oscillation, if any, it settles at a reasonable value for any change in input or change in disturbance.

Accuracy—a system is said to be 100 percent accurate if the error (different between input and output) is zero. An accurate system is costly. There is no point in going for 100 percent accurate system when that much accuracy is not really required.

An example of accuracy is when a human being cannot sense a variation of 0.2 degree centigrade, there is no need to have a home heating system of temperature variation equal to zero. Another is related to the precision of the data used in HPSC systems, which have to be in harmony with the practical needs in order to make the optimal work.

Speed of Response refers to time taken by the system to respond to the given input and give that as the output. Theoretically the speed of response should be infinity, that is, the system should have an instantaneous response. This requirement is prime concern with follow-up systems. The postulate is so fundamental as many system control processes are not even mentioning them; they are common sense in many domains and in nuclear power put it is not solved yet. To give a feeling of this matter in metaphoric terms one may say that is by an order of magnitude more difficult to control a nuclear reactor than it is to drive a car on very slippery ice, and this is an important embedded safety issue.

The Nuclear Reactor Key Elements

The energy stored in mass and movement may take many aspects and we generically call them "actors" on the nuclear scene. In order to control this, applying a generic control theorem for any process – it requires the presence in the dimension or realm of the process in the right amount and with the appropriate capabilities of sensing, interpreting and reacting to the process.

Table 1 lists the main particles involved in nuclear reactors' power production process, as main actors, players or elements inside the nuclear reaction chain.

A New View of the Atomic Nature

The data in the table show that the implementation of nano-micro hetero-structured materials may bring the harmony between the nuclear power process and its technological use, increasing safety and power production performances. In order that this statement to be true, each "actor" in the nuclear play has to be treated with respect and accommodated in order to gain its benevolence and behave as we desire.

The system's safety and performances depend on this, and that is what is not accomplished in the actual nuclear reactors, and that is why they exhibit troubled safety.

The table is just a snapshot in the intimacy of the nuclear processes. It is not complete, but gives us a clue, and Table 1 was translated into a bi-dimensional chart shown in Figure 9.

Using the table, in the light of the theory of control, and if we pick 2 parameters only—dimension and time of likelihood—(for example, space-time entity and ignore the mass-energy for the moment because the figure become too complex) and when plotted in the charts, we will obtain the map of the process in these two coordinates. One may see the domains of existence of each actor, and from here have to consider the basics of "harmony" (Popa-Simil, 2012).

Table 1. The main players in a nuclear reactor and their features

Element	Range		Comments
(Player)	Space	Time	Features and consequences
Prompt Neutron	1 ft	10 ms	Matched with the spacing of the absorption rods, no match for response time
Delayed neutrons	1 ft	ms-s	Matched with the actual nuclear control system, but they are 0.5% only.
Fission products	<100 μm	<100 ps	Requires micro hetero structures to match the Fission Products
Electron recoils	<1 m	< 1 ns	Are generated along the FP path and are responsible for fuel's heating
Recoiled nuclei	< 20 nm	< 50 ps	Are generated by elastic scattering, neutron absorption and fission spike.
Fission spike	<100 nm	<50 ps	Appear along the last 20% of the FP range being responsible for damage, requires liquid.
Neutron scattering	<20 nm	<40 ps	Are generated during n thermalizing, responsible for Wigner effect and damage.
Neutron absorption	<20 nm	<40 ps	Are the transmutation products that further decay
Phonons	grain	<1 ms	Are the heat flow
Beta	<0.1 mm	<0.1 ns	Transmutation products decay
Gamma	<1 m	-	Radioactive decay+ prompt
Neutrino	-	-	Associated with beta decay

Figure 9. Space-time likelihood of each nuclear process

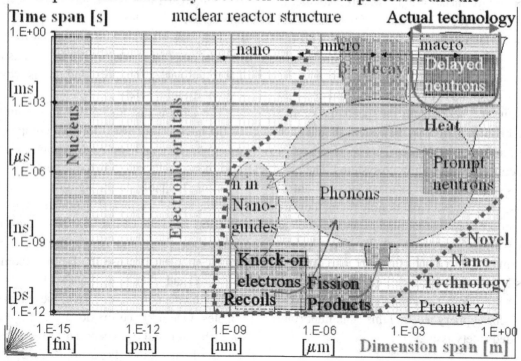

To obtain a good control on those selected processes, it is necessary for the technology to be present with active components acting it that space domain, exactly. As one may see, micro and nano- structures are the only compatible with the scale of the process, both in what concerns the dimension and the reaction time. The novel Nano-Technology is embedded in the process in order to extend the coverage domain to the limits of what is drawn using the blue dashed line.

The coverage of the domain by the actual technology is shown by the red curve, and as one may see it partially covers the delayed neutrons and the thermal processes, only.

In the chart the domain of nucleus residing processes is placed in fm (femto-meters) while the time-span is very large, because there we integrated all the processes from quark exchange to radioactive decay, and it represents a limit of the processes we intend to master.

The space-time likelihood is followed by the processes taking part in the electronic orbital, whose likelihood domain is in the atom's electron cloud volume, with the duration from fs to years…

The closest processes we plan to mitigate are related to the material lattice that facilitates those nuclear and atomic processes to take place.

The recoiled nuclei is one of them, that takes less than 100 ps in duration from the moment of collision with a moving particle takes place until the moment when the recoiled nucleus comes to rest, stopping in less than 100 nm. The transmutation products enter in this category.

The moving particles inside a nuclear lattice interact mainly with electronic orbitals, dislocating the electrons and creating electron showers. The range of these showers in matter is of about 1 micron and the duration of the stopping process is less than 1 ns.

Another very important actor in a fission process is the fission products, while in a fusion process are the fusion products but neutrons. These particles are energetic, the fission products having energies around 100 MeV while the fusion

products may have up to 25 MeV. These nuclear reactor products, generically called "nuclear ash", have a range in matter up to 100 microns, and duration under 100 ps.

A very important player in nuclear structures is the neutron. Neutrons are prompt, and they are called "neutron generations" in fission systems, while are fusion by products. The fusion-generated neutrons are more energetic, having attenuation range in meters, and lifetime span up to milliseconds. The prompt fission neutrons are instantaneously released at the fission act, and their average energy is of about 2 MeV, having a life span in microseconds until gets absorbed inside the material and space- span up to several meters.

These neutrons appear and disappear so fast, as the actual mechanical absorption rods criticality control system is practically numb to them.

The delayed neutrons are few, less than 0.5%, and their process likelihood is in ms to seconds, while the space-span is in meters. These are the neutrons seen by the nuclear reactor's control system, and their evolution helps controlling the process inside the reactor. Their concentration of 0.5% may be seen as a coupling or feed-back factor in a closed loop control system, and because their value is so low, the oscillations in the system may be very big, from the Nykist stability criteria, we may say that a nuclear reactor is prone to instabilities. This, is the only part of the intimate nuclear processes covered by the actual technology, all the rest described above are simply ignored.

Other processes presented are the phonons or heat flow, beta and gamma that are partially considered by the actual technology, mainly with respect to cooling and shielding.

This is a step forward from CASL approach, where at its fundamentals, sees the prompt neutrons, but considers in control system delayed neutrons only, while the prompt neutrons are generically considered in MC (Monte Carlo) codes for criticality issues mainly. In that approach there is no practical need for a more detailed consideration, therefore we may say that they respond perfectly to their requirements.

The fundamentals in developing the new nuclear structures consist in the basic understanding of the nuclear reaction products interaction with matter that can be done much easier using HPSC embedded discovery. The novel nano-technologies based revolution in nuclear power is presented briefly by highlighting the internal process the novel structure mitigated the harmony with the process, gaining control.

Starting from the left pentagon corner in Figure 10, labeled with "0", clockwise three are the following solution that may be implemented.

The development No.0: Mitigates the Fission Products damaging effects (Popa-Simil, 2008) by making the solid bead smaller than FP stopping range,

- Coat the fuel and
- Sunk it in a drain liquid to take the FP spike.

This micro-hetero structure relies on the fact that the fission products interaction with matter has three distinct zones:

Figure 10. The five main nano-technology developments

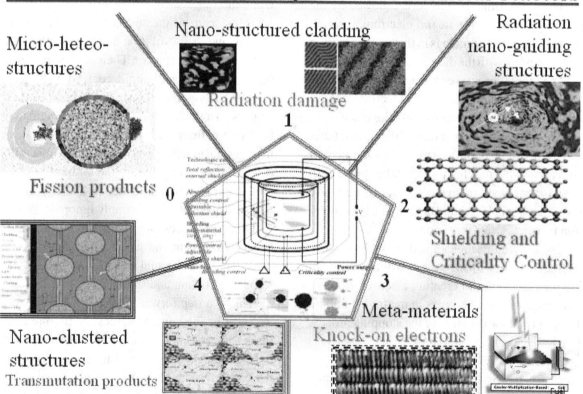

1. **Nest Zone:** (1-3 nm radius from the fission nucleus spot) characterized by high electronic destabilization and a vacancy,
2. **Ionization Stopping Path:** characterized by FP-electrons interaction, generating electron showers, and
3. **Fission Spike:** in the last 20% of the stopping range where the nuclear recoils and lattice damage dominates.

This development has the following strengths (Popa-Simil, 2011a):

- No need for reactor pipes cooling, thus making the reactor tolerant to LOCA (Loss of Coolant Accident),
- Less fission products accumulated ready to leak. Is reducing the INES hazard level, with respect to Fission Products escape and brings less hazardous fuel reprocessing.
- Fission products are separated and stabilized when deposited becoming a future precious ore.
- Reduces the need for enrichment and the its associated hazards
- It makes possible the high usage of actinide resources by assuring a high burnup inside the embedded breed and burn structures
- Increases fuel security and proliferation robustness

The weaknesses are:

- Fission products in direct contact with cladding
- Fission products direct handling
- Potential leak in on-line separation units and onsite fuel reprocessing and re-cladding

As presented here this development may be further integrated in CASL concept with minimal effort, by creating a new type of nuclear fuel material with several structures. It will require the development of the code that to perform calculations at the fuel element level where the voxel might be of about 1 cubic micron. Each micron of fuel material may require up to 10 kB of memory. It has to be known that 1 cc of such structure may require 10 PB (1B=8bit) of memory. The entire reactor holds more than 1 cubic meter of structures that drives to another 6 orders of magnitude in memory demand; therefore another approach may be needed, simply because 10 Hepta-Baits of memory are not yet available. From the point of view of calculation time, this also drives to an exceptionally high figure that will take the CASL available supercomputers over 100 years to get a brute force solution at this level.

The nano-technological development No.1 mitigates the nano-structured cladding's radiation damage, that is produced by the gamma and neutron interaction with structural materials that make them swallow and loss the mechanical properties (Popa-Simil, 2011b).

The found solutions are:

- Make a special material that recovers the radiation damage itself, similar to graphite over 700°K.

This material will be a bi/tri-material with defined grain-boundary interface properties (Bai et al., 2010) that makes the boundary self-healing.

The following types of nano-composite structures might be used with some customization:

- Nano-structured immiscible composite-material (NSICM)
- Composite SiC, fiber-W, Ti plating
- Immiscible solid solutions that can be:
- Nano-layered composite structures
- Nano-clustered structures

These radiation robust engineered nano-structures improves nuclear reactor in the following ways:

- The structures are mechanically stable with dose taking the radiation damage and recover to similar structures in the same locations using nano-cluster special properties, due to dynamically distributed active interfaces.
- The structures may have low neutron interaction cross-section and be chemically inert versus cooling and drain fluids.

These materials:

- Reduces the irradiated structure and cladding waste mass, because of longer lifetime
- Does not react with coolants as catalysts similar to Zirconium Alloys.
- Allows ultra-high burnup without recladding

The main issues are mainly related to the fact that are more difficult to manufacture, requiring advanced materials knowledge. In order to find the best materials and combinations, a quantum molecular dynamics code as NAMD or LAMPS (SNL), or Material-Studio of Acceleresys might be run in parallel version.

In order to have some practical relevance, the structure has to be larger than 10 microns, and contains about 10^{15} atoms, each having more than 10 significant particles as nucleus, electrons, each with its position in space, and its parameters, that easy may be over 100, that goes into 10^{18} data entities. The required memory is of about few hexa-baits and takes significant calculations in order to predict the damage cascades, and then their recovery. From the molecular dynamics point of view, the time that is measured in sk [shakes] each sk being equivalent to a real unit of time from several fs to 1 ns, possible with a variable time scale. For example at high speed fission products the whole stopping process takes less than 50 ps, while the dislocation cascade may take up to 1 ns, followed by self-annealing process with

structure's recovery that may take up to few ms (milliseconds). That takes a huge amount of calculations in the range of 10^{24} to 10^{30} that also turns impossible for the simple brute force applications. In order to make these calculation possible data reduction and computer architecture changes are needed, to reduce the operations inside a doable limit and maintain the accuracy of the results at a practical level.

The nano-technological development No. 2 mitigates radiation nano-guiding structures, for shielding radiation concentration and imaging and fast criticality control systems.

The actual shielding is bulky, and requires several feet of heavy concrete to stop the neutrons, even coming from the smallest nuclear reactor. Even if the reactor is small the needed shielding is large!

The present solution replaces the binary interaction between radiation and one of the shielding atoms with an interaction between radiation and many shielding atoms, obtained by making a nano-structure to guide inside and bend the radiation (neutrons, gamma) turning them back, or towards an absorbing material. In this manner the nano-guide atoms interacts with the radiation at the grazing angle, deflecting it little by little, turning it without absorbing much of its energy.

Another big problem solved by this structure is related to the nuclear reactor control that is slow, based on mechanically actuated absorption rods using mainly the delayed neutrons that represent <0.5% in the control process. The fast neutrons are evolving too fast to see any change in reactor reactivity during their lifetime. That is why "driving" a nuclear reactor is by a factor of 10 harder than stirring a car on a very slippery icy road.

The solution found is to use the nano-structure neutron guiding effect, and add an electro-sensitive material to switch the radiation's pass, from turning back towards the active zone or let pass forward into an absorbent material.

This radiation guiding improves nuclear reactor performances because when used as active reactivity control blanket it reduces the reaction time of the reactivity control system from milliseconds actually to microseconds, matching it with the life-time of a prompt neutron generation.

This new material brings a large diversity of radiation stirring applications, as: ultra-light shields; radiation concentrators, radiation modulators, radiation imaging and detection, temperature triggered shielding and control blankets, etc.

The development of research using HPSC for fast discovery of new materials requires the usage of Quantum Mechanics Molecular Dynamics codes with or without Monte-Carlo capabilities embedded.

In order to calculate a single channeling tube that has a length between 1 and 100 microns and a thickness of 3 to 20 nm a large computing effort is necessary. For example if the tube is made of Carbon multi-wall structure might have up to 10^{10} atoms, each having at least 10 internal entities as electrons, nucleus and bonds, that generates another 20 local parameters as nuclear magnetic moments, electrical dipoles, spins, orbits, that have to interact with the moving particle. That rises the number of calculations at about 10^{20}, barely matching the capabilities of the actual largest supercomputers, that may need a calculation duration between 10^4–10^8 seconds, if not smarter algorithms are put in place.

The nano-technology No.3 - Meta-materials that make the direct nuclear energy conversion in electricity (Popa-Simil, 2011c). The micro-hetero fuel solution "0" brought harmony between the structure and fission products (FPs) damage, but that is not enough, because FPs generates knock-on electrons showers while FPs are stopping in the lattice. The induced electron showers are those that warm up the fuel, and the power is extracted as heat flow by the so-called reactor core cooling, which triggers drastic power density limitations. The typical power density is under 200 W/cc,

while the maximum in high performance nuclear reactors barely reach 1 kW/cc.

The solution is to use a meta-material formed of alternate layers that enhance the electron-shower features, mimicking a super-capacitor loaded by the nuclear radiation energy of FPs, and discharged directly as electricity (Popa-Simil, 2008a). In this way it is possible to get a better "cooling" by few orders of magnitude, generically called "electric cooling", but with the property as delivering directly electric power, eliminating the need for thermo-mechano-electric conversion and their limitations (Carnot, etc.).

This energy conversion method, which puts in harmony the energy transfer from the electron shower with the lattice, improves nuclear reactor performances because:

- It removes an important part of the released energy as electricity instead of heat, eliminating the need of the thermo-mechano-electric cycle and reducing the complexity and size of a nuclear power plant up to a factor of 10 times.
- With less heat remained inside after an important part of the energy is removed as electric power, it opens the possibility of cooling the reactor with air instead of water, allowing the reactor be placed in safer locations removing the nuclear site water-basins dependence.
- Higher conversion efficiency makes possible higher power densities. That reduces the reactor mass and remnant heat. Up to 3 orders of magnitude are theoretically possible, but even 30% conversion efficiency makes the structure very attractive.
- Reduces the complexity and increases the portability of the structure.

The issues of the nano-hetero structure for the direct nuclear energy conversion into electricity are related to radiation damage, especially at the end of the range have to be mitigated with another structure.

The control systems, has to be also modified in order to be compliant with the novel structure.

Life cycle, for deep burning is still unexplored, while obtaining criticality in such structures requires several cubic feet of nano-hetero structures, which presently represent about 10% of the entire electronics industry manufacturing capability. This is an achievable milestone if all the structure and its fabrication is well defined, having a huge horizontal multiplication capability, already demonstrated by the electronic industry over time, with huge potential in cost reduction.

The calculation using QMMD (Quantum Mechanics Molecular Dynamics) at the entire battery element that is about 20 microns thick becomes impossible for the brute force case the number of required calculations being well over the actual supercomputers possibilities. More elaborated methods combining atomic scale with mezzo-scale calculations have to be performed, in order to obtain accurate enough results.

4 -Nano-clustered structures that mitigate the transmutation products (TPs) (Popa-Simil, 2010)

TPs have shorter recoil range and become interstitial defects. In order to release them in the actual technology is needed that the fuel to be dissolved in acids, and that is a very hazardous process.

The proposed solution is to make the fuel as a nano-cluster frit immersed in a washing liquid, and to use the nuclear reaction kinematics and nano-cluster specific properties to push the TP on boundary from where to wash them with an extraction liquid, and take them out the nuclear reactor. This makes the harmony between the nuclear recoils and material properties, adding the nano-cluster enhanced impurity diffusion and hoping mechanisms that accelerates the TPs extraction process (Popa-Simil, 2010a).

This improves the nuclear reactor's performances by enhancing the extraction process of the transmutation products obtaining high purity

isotopes, with less aggressive radiochemistry, at a lower cost. It also maintains the reactivity of the transmutation elements constant by gradually removing the breeding products.

The main issues of the solution are related to the fact that requires open flow circuits with separation units online in order to obtain high purity transmutation isotopes.

It may also generate ultra-pure sensitive isotopes for on the list of those suitable of being used for proliferation or terrorism, but in low amounts.

Taking together all five directions of nuclear materials enhancements it may drive to significant increase in the nuclear reactor's performances towards the physical limits, earlier than 2150.

The reactor in the center of the Figure 10 is called the "Dream Reactor" because it incorporates features that are now in the TRL 2-3 (Technology Readiness Level) most of them being identified theoretically and based on collateral experimental results as being possible.

The new reactor will be small; have about several feet in diameter with shielding, weighting several tones, modular, but high power usually over 1GWs being a very compact nuclear reactor.

The thin shielding relies on radiation gyration inside nano-tubes or nano-wires structure. The criticality adjustment relies on such a shielding blanket having the possibility of switching electronically the direction of the channeled particles, from reflecting backwards into the reactor core, to being lost outwards into the breeding blankets. The core has a nano-micro-hetero-structure and converts directly the nuclear energy into electricity.

Indeed, when one looks to the actual "steam reactors" it looks like a dream, but with the difference that it is not a dream, it is the result of logical developments of many elements that put together may make this the reality of the end of this century.

The nano-cluster enhanced extraction process takes place in smaller environments, easy to simulate using the actual QMMD programs, requiring volumes of few tens of nm large up to 100 nm.

For example in a cube with the side of 100 nm there are about 200 million atoms, each requiring about 10 kB of memory storage representing about 2 TB, a volume now accessible for desk top computers, requiring several petaflops to calculate the atomic movement and the cluster effect, that may take very little time to a supercomputer. But that represent only a single nano-cell. The fuel pellet has about ½" diameter and is up to 1" high and the entire calculation is impossible by linearly extending the "brute force method".

CONCLUSION

Starting from 1940, the needs for better calculation and simulation of the more and more complex atomic and nuclear physics problems demanded a tremendous growth in performance of the computing platforms, transforming them into supercomputers, and pushing them into a race for supremacy. The initial calculations on explosive structures and military applications were soon complemented by civilian applications in power sources, and other peaceful applications and in present these calculations become the bottom line of most of the computing systems.

The harmony, which is an abstract notion used previously in religion and philosophy, become a practical way to apply the common sense and to see if a designed structure treats accordingly every element taking part in the process, and if its effects are appropriately mitigated in order to obtain the desired results.

This notion is applied to the supercomputers by continuously improving their architectures, and to the applications the HPSC is applied, that become more complex, considering more and more aspects and details, that without the supercomputers there is no way to deal with them but to approximate or ignore and find various justifications. As a result, the calculations and simulations were just an approximation of the reality, having a large error margin, and uncovered niches that might lead to unpredicted behaviors.

Of course, these developments will trigger novel science revolutions, but that is only a collateral effect, no wonder is further needed to develop these novel structures, but only some applicative research to push forward the knowledge already acquired, into an in-depth understanding of these superior "harmonies" in nuclear materials science and structures.

The higher performances in supercomputers allowed the development of advanced calculations using quantum mechanics and electro-dynamics, which opened a new level of complexity requiring more advanced supercomputer structures, as part of the evolutionary process.

To satisfy the demand, revolutions in supercomputers was triggered, new architectures and new computing structures, are developing, based on newly discovered processes as quantum computing and quantum entanglement and teleportation. At maturity these new computing processes will fundamentally transform the supercomputers as we know today, and a new leap in performances by many orders of magnitude is expected.

REFERENCES

ASU. (2006). *Nanoionics: Defined.* Arizona State University Arizona Institute for Nano-Electronics. Retrieved March 10, 2014 from: http://www.asu.edu/aine/nanoionicsdefined.htm

Bai, X.-M., Voter, A. F., Hoagland, R. G., Nastasi, M., & Uberuaga, B. P. (2010). Efficient annealing of radiation damage near grain boundaries via interstitial emission. *Science, 327*(5973), 1631–1634. doi:10.1126/science.1183723 PMID:20339070

Berzin, A. (2011). The Dhamma of Islam: A conversation with Snjezana Akpinar and Alex Berzin. *Inquiring Mind, 20*(1).

Billeter, S. R., Webb, S. P., Agarwal, P. K., Iordanov, T., & Hammes-Schiffer, S. (2001). Hydride transfer in liver alcohol dehydrogenase: Quantum dynamics, kinetic isotope effects, and role of enzyme motion. *Journal of the American Chemical Society*, *123*(45), 11262–11272. doi:10.1021/ja011384b PMID:11697969

BNL. (2012). Global and regional solutions. *Brookhaven National Laboratory Blog*. Retrieved March 10, 2014 from: http://www.bnl.gov/GARS/

Coughlin, C. (2012). Ultracapacitors: The next big thing in energy storage? *GreenBiz.com*. Retrieved March 10, 2014 from: http://www.greenbiz.com/blog/2012/06/10/ultracapacitors-next-big-thing-energy-storage(Nature of Business Radio)

CRN. (2013). *Center for responsible nanotechnology*. Retrieved March 10, 2014 from: http://crnano.org/

Deserno, M., & Holm, C. (1998). How to mesh up Ewald sums II: An accurate error estimate for the particle–particle–particle-mesh algorithm. *The Journal of Chemical Physics*, *109*(18), 7694–7698. doi:10.1063/1.477415

Doltsinis, N. L. (2006). Molecular dynamics beyond the born-oppenheimer approximation: Mixed quantum–classical approaches. In *Computational nanoscience: Do it yourself!* (pp. 389–409). Academic Press.

Foresight Institute. (2013). *Molecular nanotechnology guidelines*. Retrieved March 10, 2014 from: http://www.foresight.org/guidelines/

Hemsoth, N. (2009). Oak Ridge supercomputers modeling nuclear future. *HPCwire web*. Retrieved March 10, 2014 from: http://archive.hpcwire.com/hpcwire/2011-05-09/oak_ridge_supercomputers_modeling_nuclear_future.html

Hundoble, J. (2010). *Taoism, basic fundamentals of 'the way'*. Retrieved March 10, 2014 from: http://www.csuchico.edu/~cheinz/syllabi/fall99/hundoble/

Jaques, P. A., & Viccari, R. M. (2006). Considering students' emotions in computer-mediated learning environments. In Z. Ma (Ed.), *Web-based intelligent e-learning systems: Technologies and applications* (pp. 122–138). Hershey, PA: Information Science Publishing. doi:10.4018/978-1-59140-729-4.ch006

Junho, S. (2010). (in press). Roadmap for e-commerce standardization in Korea. *International Journal of IT Standards and Standardization Research*.

Li, Y.-S. (2010). The ancient Chinese super state of primary societies: Taoist philosophy for the 21st century. *Wikipedia: 300*. Retrieved March 10, 2014 from: http://en.wikipedia.org/wiki/Taoism

LLNL. (2012). Nuclear weapons simulations push supercomputing limits. *InnovationNewsDaily Supercomputers Simulation*. Retrieved March 10, 2014 from: http://www.livescience.com/20810-nuclear-weapons-simulations-limits.html?utm_source=feedburner&utm_medium=feed&utm_campaign=Feed%3A+Livesciencecom+%28LiveScience.com+Science+Headline+Feed%29

Montgomery, R. (2013). Consortium for advanced simulation of light water reactors. *ORNL-TechNotes Product Description -Rev.1*. Retrieved March 10, 2014 from: http://www.casl.gov/docs/CASL%20Product%20Applications%2003252013.pdf)

Nusca, A. (2010). Scientists use world's fastest supercomputer to model, simulate nuclear reactors. *Smart Planet Blog*. Retrieved March 10, 2014 from: http://www.smartplanet.com/blog/smart-takes/scientists-use-worlds-fastest-supercomputer-to-model-simulate-nuclear-reactors/

ORNL. (2010). Nuclear energy - Supercomputer speeds path forward. *Science And Technology.* Retrieved March 10, 2014 from: http://www.casl. gov/highlights/supercomputer.shtml

ORNL_Info. (2013). Potent partnerships: CASL simulations add insight into operating nuclear reactor cores. *Ornl Review.* Retrieved March 10, 2014 from: http://web.ornl.gov/info/ornlreview/ v46_2-3_13/article07.shtml#sthash.LqCPwgIb. dpuf

Plimpton, S., Thompson, A., & Crozier, P. (2013). *LAMMPS.* Retrieved from http://lammps.sandia. gov/

Popa-Simil, L. (2008). Micro-structured nuclear fuel and novel nuclear reactor concepts for advanced power production. *Progress in Nuclear Energy, 50*(2–6), 539–548. doi:10.1016/j.pnucene.2007.11.041

Popa-Simil, L. (2008a). Direct energy conversion nano-hetero fuel. *MRS Procedings NN(Spring)*, 6.

Popa-Simil, L. (2010a). *Quasi-nano-clustered fuel for enhanced transmutation products separation.* OECD-NEA.

Popa-Simil, L. (2010b). The use of plutonium and micro-hetero structures. In *Novel nuclear reactors modifies the actual fuel cycle, plutonium futures.* ANS Tranzactions.

Popa-Simil, L. (2011a). *Micro-nano hetero structured fuel pellet's impact on nuclear reactor's performances.* Paper presented at the Water Reactor Fuel Performance Meeting, Chengdu, China.

Popa-Simil, L. (2011b). *The drastic increase of safety and performances in nuclear power by implementing nano-engineered materials.* Washington, DC: Knowledge Foundation.

Popa-Simil, L. (2011c). Advanced space nuclear reactors from fiction to reality. In *Proceedings of Space, Propulsion & Energy Sciences International Forum (Space, Propulsion & Energy Sciences International Forum).* AIP. doi:10.1016/j. phpro.2011.08.025

Popa-Simil, L. (2012). *Applied nano-technologies improves nuclear power safety and performances.* Los Alamos, CA: Amazon, Kindle.

Sanderson, K. (2006). Sharpest cut from nanotube sword: Carbon nanotech may have given swords of Damascus their edge. *Nature News.* Retrieved March 10, 2014 from: http://www.nature.com/ news/2006/061113/full/news061113-11.html

Sandhu, A. (2006). Who invented nano? *Nature Nanotechnology, 1*(87).

Schlegel H.B., (2003). Ab initio molecular dynamics with born-oppenheimer and extended lagrangian methods using atom centered basis functions. *Ab Initio Molecular Dynamics Bulletin, 24*(6).

Taniguchi, N. (1974). On the basic concept of nano-technology. In *Proc. Intl. Conf. Prod. Eng. Tokyo:* Japan Society of Precision Engineering.

Taylor, E. (2010). *Using supercomputers to explore nuclear energy.* Retrieved March 10, 2014 from: http://www.anl.gov/articles/using-supercomputers-explore-nuclear-energy#sthash. ILDPRyIl.dpufanl.gov.

Tian, Mulè, Paskevicius, & Dhal. (2008). Preparation, microstructure and hydrogen sorption properties of nanoporous carbon aerogels under ambient drying. *Nanotechnology IOP Science*, (19).

Tuckerman, M. E., Berne, B. J., & Martyna, G. J. (1992). Reversible multiple time scale molecular dynamics. *The Journal of Chemical Physics, 97*(3), 1990–2001. doi:10.1063/1.463137

Vieru, T. (2010). New computer model shows nuclear fission. *Softpedia World Nuclear News*. Retrieved March 10, 2014 from: http://news.softpedia.com/news/New-Computer-Model-Shows-Nuclear-Fission-132990.shtml

Voelz, V. A., Bowman, G. R., Beauchamp, K., & Pande, V. S. (2010). Molecular simulation of ab initio protein folding for a millisecond folder NTL9(1–39). *Journal of the American Chemical Society*, *132*(5), 1526–1528. doi:10.1021/ja9090353 PMID:20070076

Wikipedia. (2012). *Control theory*. Retrieved March 10, 2014 from: http://en.wikipedia.org/wiki/Control_theory

Wikipedia. (2013). *Molecular dynamics*. Retrieved March 10, 2014 from: http://en.wikipedia.org/wiki/Molecular_dynamics

Wikipedia.org. (2013). *Folding@home*. Retrieved March 10, 2014 from: http://en.wikipedia.org/wiki/Folding@home

Ye, X., Chen, J., & Xing, G. (2013). Research helps make advance in "programmable matter" using nanocrystals. *Phys.org*. Retrieved March 10, 2014 from:http://phys.org/news/2013-07-advance-programmable-nanocrystals.html

KEY TERMS AND DEFINITIONS

Engineering: The branch of science and technology concerned with the design, building, and use of engines, machines, and structures.

Harmony: The combination of simultaneously sounded musical notes to produce chords and chord progressions having a pleasing effect, or the quality of forming a pleasing and consistent whole. It may also mean an agreement or concord; i.e. "man and machine in perfect harmony". Have as synonyms: accord, agreement, peace, peacefulness, amity, amicability, friendship, fellowship, cooperation, understanding, consensus, unity, sympathy, rapport, like-mindedness.

High Performance Scientific Computing: Parallel scientific computing and simulation of science and engineering large problems using different types of supercomputers, which these days have tens of thousands of processors and cost millions of dollars.

Multi-Dimension: Involving several dimensions or aspects as "multidimensional space."

Multi-Scale: Different scales are used simultaneously to describe a system.

Nano-Technologies: Science, engineering, and technology conducted at the nanoscale, which is about 1 to 100 nanometers.

Nuclear Power: Electric or motor power generated by a nuclear reactor, or a country that has nuclear weapons.

Physics: The branch of science concerned with the nature and properties of matter and energy. The subject matter of physics, includes mechanics, heat, light and other radiation, sound, electricity, magnetism, and the structure of atoms.

Simulations: A powerful and important tool because it provides a way in which alternative designs, plans and/or policies can be evaluated without having to experiment on a real system, which may be prohibitively costly, time-consuming, or simply impractical to do.

Chapter 5
Using High Performance Scientific Computing to Accelerate the Discovery and Design of Nuclear Power Applications

Liviu Popa-Simil
Los Alamos Academy of Science, USA

ABSTRACT

Present High Performance Scientific Computing (HPSC) systems are facing strong limitations when full integration from nano-materials to operational system is desired. The HPSC have to be upgraded from the actual designed exa-scale machines probably available after 2015 to even higher computer power and storage capability to yotta-scale in order to simulate systems from nano-scale up to macro scale as a way to greatly improve the safety and performances of the future advanced nuclear power structures. The road from the actual peta-scale systems to yotta-scale computers, which would barely be sufficient for current calculation needs, is difficult and requires new revolutionary ideas in HPSC, and probably the large-scale use of Quantum Supercomputers (QSC) that are now in the development stage.

INTRODUCTION

The present chapter briefly describes the evolution of supercomputers and the performances of the present computers from the point of view of the processing speed and memory size (Proffitt, 2012).

There are several architectural developments briefly described together with related issues such as: calculation quality assurance, failure tolerant architectures and power consumption.

The discussion is made from the point of view of needed resources for a complex quantum molecular dynamics application on each material structure. The magnitude of the calculation is carefully analyzed in order to include the smallest aspects and integrate them in a system that grows until it reaches the minimum practical limits. Here

DOI: 10.4018/978-1-4666-7461-5.ch005

Copyright © 2015, IGI Global. Copying or distributing in print or electronic forms without written permission of IGI Global is prohibited.

from practical limits is understood the limit in time and space of the propagation of meaningful interaction, which considered explicitly may increase the quality of the approach.

The development of the new supercomputers as seen from the point of view of the need to simulate more completely the nano-materials presented before for being used in nuclear power structures.

The concept of harmony (Popa-Simil, 2012) is used in a various complex manner (Kuznetsova, 2005). On one side it represents the complex matching between the quantum reactions we aim to control and the material structure we aim to put in place that is rewarding the effort by high efficiency and high safety of the overall process. On the other hand it is referred as matching inside the supercomputer structure, matching the processors with memory and connection devices, driving to a harmonious calculation process development and the capability to know instantly when the process is right or wrong, allowing eliminating errors in early stages.

The chapter ends with a brief description of the quantum computing (Cho, 2012) approaches and the successes obtained in quantum communication using entangled particles and performing quantum cryptography, as a mean to assure fast, reliable information exchange inside and outside computing structures (Love, 2013).

The chapter highlights the aspect that the need triggers inventivity and future computer development will be closely bound to the new invention in hardware and software, driven by various computing needs.

AVAILABLE ARCHITECTURES AND SOLUTION APPROACHES

In this chapter we will discuss and compare current supercomputers' architecture and resource distribution solutions in order to classify them with respect to different performance evaluation parameters. We will also study the potential and suitability of existing approaches to co-exist with the classical infrastructure and use more the future distributed computing resources; more specifically, social networks on the cloud and cloud over social networks.

The development in the quantum computing and information teleportation will bring a new generation of supercomputers by two orders of magnitude faster and more compact, using complex quantum processors, that will open new horizons and will require changes in operation systems.

The 20-petaflops Titan supercomputer (olcf 2013) at Oak Ridge National Laboratory (Anthony, 2012), was world's fastest supercomputer during 2012. Cray's XC30 architecture, is supposed to allow the creation of supercomputers faster than 100 petaflops—100 quadrillion floating-point operations per second.

China is preparing the 100-petaflops, Tianhe-2 (Anthony, 2013) to be deployed by 2015, which in November 2013 become No.1 with only 33Pflops, and it was the successor to Tianhe-1A—a supercomputer that briefly held the title of World's Fastest back in 2010 (a first for China).

Cray's XC30 blade, with a bunch of Intel Xeon compute nodes marks an interesting shift away from AMD Opteron CPUs to the Intel Xeon (Murray, 2012)—the E5-2600 (Sandy Bridge) family of chips, because, Intel's latest Sandy Bridge- and Ivy Bridge-based chips are superior to AMD's offerings, and because, Intel acquired Cray's interconnect technology earlier this year. The XC30 debuts the new Aries interconnect—and Intel now owns Aries. Each XC30 blade (server rack) will contain four compute nodes, each of which contains two Xeon CPUs. There are 16 blades in an XC30 chassis, and three chassis per cabinet, totaling 384 CPUs per cabinet. Each cabinet will initially be capable of around 66 teraflops. Using 1,500 cabinets will scale up to 100 petaflops. At 1,500 cabinets, will host 575,000 CPUs and over 4.5 million individual cores (9 million, including Hyper-Threading). Each node can have up to

128GB of RAM, which equates to 24 terabytes of RAM per cabinet at a total of 35 petabytes of RAM for a 1500-cabinet system.

Tianhe-2 will uses the ShenWei SW-3 1600,(Novakovic, 2011) and it probably uses Xeon or Opteron processors, perhaps in concert with Nvidia's Tesla GPU,(Nvidia, 2014) and maybe Tianhe-3 (Zhang, 2013) will use entirely Chinese electronics.

Japan's "K Computer" maintained its position atop the newest edition of the TOP500 List of the world's most powerful supercomputers, thanks to a full build-out that makes it four times as powerful as its nearest competitor. Installed at the RIKEN Advanced Institute for Computational Science (AICS) in Kobe, Japan's K Computer reached an impressive 10.51 petaflop/s on the Linpack benchmark using 705,024 SPARC64 processing cores.

The Japan's K Computer was the first supercomputer to achieve a performance level of 10 petaflops, in June 2011, becoming then No. 1 with a performance of 8.16 petaflop/s. It does not utilize graphics processors or other accelerators, being one of the most energy efficient systems.

The largest U.S. system is a Cray XT5 system called Jaguar and installed at the Oak Ridge National Laboratory, with a 1.75 petaflop/s performance running the standard Linpack benchmark application. Other top U.S. systems include Cielo, a Cray XE6 at Los Alamos National Laboratory (No. 6); Pleiades, an SGI Altix machine at NASA's Ames Research Center (No.7); Hopper, a Cray XE6 at the National Energy Research Scientific Computing Center (No. 8); and Roadrunner, an IBM system that was the first ever to break the petaflop/s barrier, at Los Alamos (No. 10). Systems in China, Japan and France round out the Top 10.

New supercomputers are being constructed for some of the world's most important problems, including climate change, operating fusion reactors or creating bio-fuels. (Straatsma, 2013)

Supercomputers however, are still not big enough, so we strive to reach the next performance goal: an exa-scale system. (Zhuo, 2006)

With exa-scale machines comes exa-scale data, and new Autonomic Control Units (ACU's), Memory Models (MMs) and Hybrid Processing Architectures (HPAs) are to address the requirements of handling exa-scale data and providing exa-scale computation. Requirements of auto-configuration, monitoring and repair, data and communication transfer, sequencing, and load balancing need to be addressed (Scrofano, 2006). The optimal ratio between sequential and parallel units should be identified and configured to suit the exa-scale job. Computation issues must be addressed without loss of robustness, maintainability and usability. System resilience and stability are required without consuming exponential power requirements.

A supercomputer is the computer that does more number-crunching tasks per second. That does not mean that supercomputers have to use faster processors. Presently, supercomputers use relatively older and slower processors. The main requirement criteria for supercomputing is the number of number-crunching that has to be the maximum, whereas high performance computing is the domain that deals with computing with more processing power through using faster processors (Foremski, 2010).

There are mainly three types of supercomputing architectures.

1. Vector Processing (Batten, 2012) was used in the first supercomputers. The Vector supercomputer is a single machine with supercomputing capability optimized for applying arithmetic operations to large vectors (dynamic arrays) of data. There are many applications that need this type of machines.

2. Parallel Processing supercomputers have been designed by combining many computing machines or processors that split the computing load among themselves in an optimal way and can scale well by incorporating as many new machines or processors with the existing ones by clustering them.

Up to now the following types of clustering have been used:

a. Fail-over clustering is one in which if one machine breaks down in the cluster, automatically any other machine in that cluster will take care of the responsibilities.

b. Load balancing cluster is one in which service requests are routed to different servers in the cluster to offset high load on a particular server.

c. High performance cluster facilitates all the machines in that cluster to work simultaneously to bring better number crunching capabilities. The computing machines, connected by multiple high-speed networks, in the cluster share the task in an optimal and efficient way. The Beowulf cluster is a high performance cluster built out of commonly available parts, running Linux or Windows.

3. Grid/Distributed Computing is the new paradigm shift in supercomputing domain. This initiative came on the basis of SETI@home project. Actually all computing machines, especially personal computers, are idle for significant amounts of time. The idea of using the idle time of millions of computers connected through the Internet to do some useful works proved to be valuable for those applications with minimal data security issues and that are nor communication intensive. This paradigm shift in computing with a huge processing power can even beat the performance of any existing supercomputing machines, or so it was presented at that time, being a statement under debate.

Thus, grid computing is a way of harnessing idle computing power in large networks (eu team 2013). A high performance computer has to be built at one location with dedicated buildings and machines. A computing grid, on the other hand, connects existing networks across locations over the Internet.

Multiprocessing that uses two or more processors on the same machine is called SMP (Symmetric Multiprocessing). In a multiprocessor machine, a program has to be divided among each processor, such that each processor can handle its own chunk independently. For this, the program has to be split into smaller parts referred to as tasks. Each task is generally called a thread. The software developer has to code in a way such that the program can be broken into independent chunks.

Multithreading (Oracle 2010) is a sort of dividing a whole program into many subtasks towards the goal of using more than one processor in a computing machine is called multithreading. If suppose the whole program gets split into two threads and there are two processors, then each processor will be assigned to perform the functionality of one thread. Each processor has its own cache memory. If the processor gets short of cache, then the system memory or RAM may be used. On a multiprocessor machine, each processor and RAM is connected via a dedicated high-speed bus.

Inside a Distributed Memory Model each Inter-thread communication is performed in such a manner that each process has allocated its own memory, but one thread cannot access another thread's memory. If the processor handling the thread 2 requirement has come across a data related to processor, which is processing thread 1, communicates the data to thread 1. On receiving it, thread 1 will store the data in its memory. This is basically called inter-thread communication. But passing data among processors has some overheads such as construction of data, calling for and sending data by the thread etc. (Scott, 2007)

The disadvantage here is that intercommunicated data has to travel via the slow system bus, and thus it becomes very critical for a software developer to be very particular about minimizing the occurrence of inter-thread communication while developing multithreaded software applications through assigning independent data to the processors.

Shared Memory Model mechanism comes as a viable solution for the problem of inter-thread communication, because instead of having a separate memory for each processor, there is a unique memory accessible for all the processors, reducing the need for communication between threads and both threads can access the same shared memory. In a situation where threads are working on the same data set simultaneously the issue of data integrity has to be mitigated, and this is done by requiring that each thread to lock access to the other thread while manipulating the data in the shared memory. This locking presents an overhead to the processing as well as to the developer, who needs to take care of locking and releasing locks after manipulation in his source code.

The challenge in getting to this next stage of exa-scale computing (ASCAC-DOE 2010), apparently relies in its power consumption and heat generation (ASCR-DOE 2014), and that means we will need a new type of architecture.

It is known that massively parallel architectures, using tens to hundreds of thousands of processors from the PC and Unix markets have dominated supercomputing over the past twenty years. They got us into the tera-scale and peta-scale ranges, but to reach the exa-scale level is very challenging and another massive technology and architectural transition has to be made, and this seems to be the transition to cloud computing.

The technology requirements are quite similar, especially the need for low power, low cost components, and highly efficient, autonomic system management. One can actually view cloud-based systems as a kind of exa-scale class supercomputers designed to support embarrassingly parallel workloads, such as massive information analysis or huge numbers of sensors and mobile devices.

If we can build exa-scale computing supercomputers, we will also be able to build smaller systems that use the same basic technologies and that will have many applications, and not just in cloud computing.

A future exa-scale computer will likely make use of low power consuming processors used in consumer mobile devices, that might be able to solve very large computational problems that currently are out of reach, from "economics and medicine to business and government, with the condition that data security and privacy is assured.

The revolutionary physics nano-technology problems presented before require tremendous amounts of calculations, and even if one may know the solution for a sub-process, it may have no value or meaning if not used in the large context of the problem. A simple example is a destroyer sailing on sea while shooting into another mobile target. The ballistic equation might not be classified, neither the target polynomial equation of space, therefore the problem may be simply solved in a cloud, if and only if it is given in such a manner that the classified coordinates and identifiers not to be leaked outside, and if the answer comes back in real time to be useful for that application. Up to now, dedicated computer systems are the most preferred, mainly for data security, response time and reliability reasons.

Presentation of the Common Sense and Practicality of Developing the Supercomputer Architectures

Extreme scale data will require autonomic control of cloud, over many systems that have to be ubiquitous resilient, reliable, scalable and dynamic. Memory Models (MMs) and Hybrid Processing Architectures (HPAs) for extreme scale data and computation, are needed but will require auto-configuration, monitoring and repair, data and communication transfer, sequencing, and load balancing needs to be addressed.

Sequential and parallel units should be identified and configured on per job basis while computation issues must be addressed without loss of robustness, maintainability and usability. System resilience and stability are required without consuming exponential power requirements that for sure will put on high demand new components, faster and more powerful. A candidate may be the quantum computing systems.

There are many difficulties to overcome just to achieve the exa-scale, and to advance further towards the Zetta-scale (Ruch, 2013) requires as a first approximation, to find a replacement for the actual low power CMOS electronics that using the actual design will require significant power and might be slow and unreliable enough, and create frequent interruptions.

New computing technologies will likely require new architectures, new execution models, and new programming models, as for example the quantum computers where exploitation of locality will be key, but the usage of advanced entanglement, and quantum key teleportation methods might open new horizons. Quantum computing is fundamentally different from the actual supercomputing, being in a way complementary, and some hybridization will occur soon (Cho, 2012; Palmer, 2012).

Developing the actual architecture ideas would, most likely involve massive threading and lightweight thread migration that will push towards better programming models where humans don't have to coordinate all the data distribution and communication, but to rely on much more sophisticated and automated tools for performance and correctness analysis presumably involving pervasive introspection. With advances in reconfigurable hardware, especially field-programmable gate arrays (FPGAs), it has become possible to use reconfigurable hardware to accelerate complex applications, such as those in scientific computing, in sensor data intensive applications (Taylor, 2014).

There has been a resulting development of reconfigurable computers—computers that have both general-purpose processors and reconfigurable hardware, as well as memory and high-performance interconnection networks.

There is possible the acceleration of molecular dynamics simulations using reconfigurable computers by partitioning the application between software and hardware, to enhance the performances using the appropriate task mapped to hardware.

The present implementation of this technology MD on a reconfigurable computer for simulations, doubles speed compared to the actual software baseline with clear advantages over the hardware/software approach, including flexibility.

Reconfigurable hardware, in the form of FPGAs, has been used successfully in the acceleration of many applications and application tasks. Previously, FPGAs were limited to performing tasks that required only fixed-point arithmetic, however, recent advances in FPGA hardware, including increased density and the inclusion of embedded multipliers, have made floating-point arithmetic on FPGAs possible (Xilnix, 2014).

One particularly interesting scientific computing application to investigate is molecular dynamics (MD) simulation that is a technique that models the movements of atoms in a substance over time.

Tasks in the simulation include calculating forces, updating positions and velocities, and other supporting tasks. All of these calculations are traditionally performed in single- or double-precision floating-point arithmetic. One task in an MD simulation—the non-bonded force calculation—is very computationally intensive while the other tasks are less intensive or have complicated control logic. It makes sense, then, to accelerate the non-bonded force calculation in reconfigurable hardware while executing the rest of the simulation with a general-purpose processor. There are known large complex MD software packages such as GROMACS (Berendsen, 1995) and NAMD (Kal´e et al., 1999).

There are various approaches that use direct calculation of the forces, without using any block RAMs for table-lookup in the force calculation. Further, the number of type-based constants that need to be stored is only four times the square of the number of types, as opposed to needing separate force calculation tables for interactions for various types of atoms, as is the case in (Gu, 2005),

There might possible to handle large number of types of atoms using a small number of block RAMs for constants and keep the rest of the block

RAMs available for the intermediate storage needs of calculated data write-back. The use of the neighbor list technique for finding interacting pairs of atoms is very important because it drastically reduces the number of pairs that need to be evaluated at each time step.

In the $O(n^2)$ approach, most of the time is spent finding distances between pairs of atoms that are too far apart to necessitate the calculation of the forces they exert on one another. Even with the advantages of hardware, it is difficult for a system using this approach to scale to large simulations; software using more advanced techniques such as the neighbor list or the linked-cell list will likely be faster.

The bonded force calculation and potential energy calculation done using varying precision fixed-point arithmetic provides results nearly as accurate as double-precision floating-point arithmetic.

The general purpose processor and reconfigurable hardware, having the reconfigurable hardware perform the non-bonded force calculation and the general purpose processor perform the rest of the tasks in the simulation. In hybrid design approaches (Zhuo, 2006), where the general purpose processor and reconfigurable hardware work together on a common task, the use of division at the task level seems to be inappropriate. Using this last approach allows handling large, real-world simulations and gives the flexibility to easily add features to implementation bringing significant speedups obtained with this approach. Other limitations of the MD system are due to limits in the size of the FPGA and memory available in some machines rather than any inherent design feature.

There are several future directions to pursue as for example to investigate possibilities for implementing double-precision simulations on reconfigurable computers that have more on-board memory banks and larger FPGAs. Another direction is to study parallel implementations (Scrofano, 2006) containing multiple GPP nodes and RH

nodes, e.g., a MAP station with multiple general purpose processors, each connected to a MAP processor. When MD simulations are parallelized over multiple processors, the linked-cell list is sometimes used over the neighbor list because it is easier to account for atoms moving between processors.

ISSUES IN CURRENT LANDSCAPE

New technologies and trends always bring new technical and legal and political challenges and issues related to intellectual property, privacy, and data monopoly, and data security. The international access to data, programming, computing power and applications come in conflict with the nonproliferation policies and policies of assuring the supremacy of the actual powers, and this is a new dimension to consider.

The history of supercomputing started in 1940's and had an accelerated development (Wikipedia 2013), following the Gordon E. More's law, presented in a1965 paper, which simply says that the density of transistors doubles every two years, based on his observation for a 7 years period since 1958.

Supercomputers' history had the following remarkable moments:

- 10^2 Initial stage in 1940s—hecta-scale
  - 2.2×10^2 IBM 602 1946 computer.
- 10^3 Kilo scale computing
  - 9.2×10^4 Intel 4004 First commercially available full functional CPU on a chip in 1971
  - 5×10^5 Colossus computer vacuum tube supercomputer 1943
- 10^6 Mega scale computing
  - 1×10^6 Motorola 68000 commercial computing 1979
  - 1.2×10^6 IBM 7030 "Stretch" Vacuum tube supercomputer 1961
- 10^9 Giga scale computing

- 1×10^9 ILLIAC IV 1972 supercomputer does first computational fluid dynamics problems
- 1.354×10^9 Intel Pentium III commercial computing 1999
- 147.6×10^9 Intel Core-i7 980X Extreme Edition commercial computing 2010

- 10^{12} Tera-scale computing
  - 1.34×10^{12} Intel ASCI Red 1997 supercomputer
  - 1.344×10^{12} GeForce GTX 480 from NVIDIA at its peak performance
  - 4.64×10^{12} Radeon HD 5970 from ATI at its peak performance
  - 5.152×10^{12} S2050/S2070 1U GPU Computing System from NVIDIA
  - 80×10^{12} IBM Watson
  - 100×10^{12} Estimated parallelized throughput of the human brain

- 10^{15} Peta-scale computing
  - 1.026×10^{15} IBM Roadrunner 2009 supercomputer
  - 8.1×10^{15} Fastest computer of 2012 is the Folding@home distributed computing system
  - 20×10^{15} IBM Sequoia Circa 2011
  - 36.8×10^{15} Estimated computational power required to simulate a human brain in real time.

- 10^{18} Exa-scale computing
  - 1×10^{18} It is estimated that the need for exa-scale computing will become pressing around 2018
  - In January 2012 Intel purchased the InfiniBand product line from QLogic for US $125 million in order to fulfill its promise of developing exa-scale technology by 2018. The initiative has been endorsed by two US agencies: the Department of Energy and the National Nuclear Security Administration. The technology would be useful in various computation-intensive research areas, including basic research, engineering, earth science, biology, materials science, energy issues, and national security.
  - The United States has put aside $126 million for exa-scale computing beginning in 2012.
  - Three projects aiming at developing technologies and software for exa-scale computing have been started in 2011 within the European Union:
    - The CRESTA project (Collaborative Research into Exa-scale Systemware,
    - Tools and Applications), the DEEP project (Dynamical Exa-scale Entry Platform), and
    - The project Mont-Blanc.
  - The Indian Government has committed USD 2 Billion to ISRO and Indian Institute of Science (IISc), Bangalore to develop a supercomputer with a performance of 132.8 exaflops by 2017. ISRO has already booked key equipment to develop the first Indian exaflops supercomputer. Most of the sub-systems will be developed in India.

- 10^{21} Zetta-scale computing
  - 1×10^{21} Accurate global weather estimation on the scale of approximately 2 weeks. Assuming Moore's law remains constant, such systems may be feasible around 2030.
  - A zetta-scale computer system could generate more single floating-point data in one second than was stored by any digital means on Earth in first quarter 2011.

- 10^{24} Yotta-scale computing
  - Is what might be needed to solve the actual technological problems involving nano-materials applied in advanced nuclear power technologies, to drive the calculations from atomic quantum level up to relevant size.

The usage of cheaper faster distributed architectures might be an issue for classified data security and the communication between advanced supercomputing centers my drive to the development over of a new layer of internet, may be entangle-net that may offer faster communication speeds and broader-bands.

Economics is an important factor for the development of supercomputer, which is analyzed with respect to general administrative expenses for data handling calculation and their affordability.

Quality assurance is an important factor that has to be considered in the new computing capabilities, with respect to maintaining a close contact with reality, and benchmarking the problem and their solutions, avoiding to fall into the realm of imagination. The impact of the new technologies that wipe out the old technology is increasing in part the global strategic vulnerability that depends on very few companies and unique laboratories, with high specialization, and very little disaster backup.

The coexistence of various supercomputing systems, their intercommunication and compatibility represents important issues that have to be permanently addressed, because the dynamics of the computing environment is very high, presently being involved in a race among the nations of the Earth to obtain, use and maintain the best and fastest computing structures.

MODERN TRENDS IN HIGH PERFORMANCE SCIENTIFIC COMPUTING WITH RESPECT TO NUCLEAR POWER APPLICATIONS

HP's Cluster Platform provides a scalable architecture that allows us to complete large, complex simulation experiments such as molecular interactions and dynamics, nano-cluster to functional object simulations and so forth much more quickly. This technology, combined with HP's experience and expertise in nuclear sciences, helps researches

and engineers speed access to information, knowledge and new levels of efficiency, which we hope will ultimately culminate in the discovery of new applications and new laws of nature.

The NSF funded Blue Waters and eXtreme Science and Engineering Discovery Environment (XSEDE) projects are hosting the seventh in a series of Extreme Scaling HPSC applications.

Systems such as Blue Waters, Stampede, and Titan take a major step from modest scale, heterogeneous test benches, and prototypes to world-class, extreme-scale heterogeneous computing systems. This is set up so that science and engineering teams gain an understanding of how to effectively utilize large numbers of accelerated nodes to advance their applications and to exchange and learn best practices. The dissemination of information will occur through presentations, discussions, and workshop proceedings that will include recommendations from the presenters and participants who have had experience with these technologies, as well through the own practice and computational experiments.

Scientists, engineers, scholars, and high-performance technologists from colleges, universities, laboratories, industry, HPC centers, and other organizations conducting related to this type of work are encouraged to join in common initiatives to accelerate the knowledge dissemination and discovery.

Nuclear reactors have been designed and operated rather successfully during five decades (Salvatores, 2006) and fundamental physics was at the heart of the early developments (Fermi, Seaborg, Wigner, Feynman, etc.).

Successively, heuristic and engineering approaches were mainly used in a wide industrial deployment. Global experimental mock-ups often prevailed over fundamental understanding and specific analytical experiments until today, we are probably at a turning point in view of the new requirements and challenges which go under the label "advanced fuel cycles". Today we need a similar structure of interconnection between basic sciences, applied physics, engineering (and industry) to be reconstructed to meet the new requirements and challenges.

Example of Future Extreme Scale Multi-Process Multi-Phenomena HPSC

Nuclear power generation requires, better, safer, and more efficient structures that might be built using advanced knowledge and technology that can be obtained in closed loops that include the simulation and experiment. In order to design a new nuclear reactor structure that to separate automatically, using internal kinematics and material properties, the fission products, and the transmutation products, from the fuel, for heat and electricity production supercomputer simulation is needed. HPSC is the only way to obtain in a reasonable time the needed knowledge, starting from the atomistic level up to the functional assembly level, and this example is now used to show why we do need HPSC capabilities, and what are their requirements needed in order to facilitate the data driven discovery to us.

The figure is presenting a nano-clustered structure embedded into a liquid that has a nano-flow.

Suppose that the structure is made of uranium dioxide molecules UO_2, arranged in nano-clusters of about 2 nm large each as shown in Figure 1. At atomic level one has to consider Uranium having a nucleus surrounded by 92 electrons, from which two outer electrons are connected to two oxygen atoms each having 8 electrons, from which the outer orbitals are involved in establishing the covalent-polar bound to Uranium atoms. The bound length is approximate at 0.2 nm. A cluster approximated to a cube that has about 10 atoms per side, has a total of 1000 uranium atoms, 2000 oxygen atoms, about 3000 nuclei and 327,000 electrons, making about 330,000 entities in total. In order to build such a struc-

ture one may need an automatic crystal maker to build up and initialize all the parameters, as coordinates, velocities and accelerations, and calculate the spin and magnetic moments as well as the electric moments, resulting in about 20 parameters per entity.

The structure in Figure 1 has 9 such clusters, having a dimension of about 9 nm cubic lateral, and a volume of 343 nm^3, with the empty spaces fulfilled by a fluid, holding a total of 5M entities, and requiring about 0.4 GB of memory to memorize the values at an instance of time. We may call the unit of computing time a "shake" and that may have any reasonable value from ps to ns depending the described process. For fast processes the shake value is in Pico-second. This is an elementary cluster cell, but for any reliable calculation it is too small. The memory allocation in this case is about 1.5 GB for each 1000 nm3, equivalent to a cubic cell of 10 nm lateral.

The dimensions size, big or small is relative to the process we intend to calculate. In order to calculate the electron-electron interactions the shake value has to be in fs [femto-seconds] while the 10 nm size is good enough, but the significant time interval for calculation might be a few ns, that requires a 10^6 shakes.

For such a calculation the requirement may be of 2 PB memory and few petaflops, inside the reach of the actual most powerful supercomputers.

After this calculation we might learn the equilibrium state in a single case of material excitation, but to well characterize the structure behavior we have to consider all the number of non-degenerated states, and the degeneration level of each state, or in other words the probability of encountering that specific state.

This will mean a tremendous amount of calculations that will have to be memorized for that specific structure only, or averaged for the general use.

Figure 1. Nano-cluster level atomic level simulation example

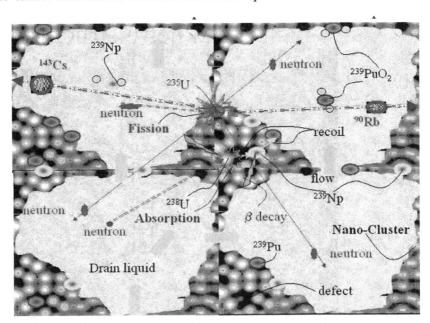

Imagine now that the little 10 nm structure is part of a more complex structure like that shown in Figure 2 where a 50 nm cluster is shown. From the nuclear point of view there are two basic processes related to the neutron interaction with the material. The first process is related to the neutron absorption followed by a transmutation process that creates a recoil of the absorbing nucleus of few nm. It is losing, in several ps most of its electronic cloud, and suddenly appearing in another position as an interstitial defect, triggering many rearrangement atomic movements inside the nano-cluster. Another competing process is the neutron scattering that produces recoiled nucleons that are the same as those in the lattice, with the only difference that they are dislocated and triggered a cascade of atomic dislocations followed by the recovery process nucleons rearrangements. To this already complicated computational problem, a supplementary nano-flow problem is added in order to deal with the nano-cluster -- fluid interface and that nano-flow that is carrying the new transmutation products that reached the interface, away from the place where they were produced.

The difference that have to be considered in MD calculations is that the absorption followed by transmutation process will generate a chemically different interstitial defect than the scattering process, and the nano-cluster lattice will react differently. This is what can be simulated at the nano-scale/pico-second level, consuming almost all the resources of an actual supercomputer.

Imagine now, that this little, 2 nm size, nano-structure is part of a larger structure as shown in Figure 2. whwre the nano-structure is part of a filler that resides inside a 20 microns radius sphere, connected by few microns in diameter tubes, through which, the nano-structure extraction liquid is flowing. Using the actual supercomputers to simulate by direct molecular dynamics only the processes that take place inside that micro-sphere turns to be impossible, and that is what we call a mezoscale problem. The required computing capability is over the next exa-scale computer anticipated of being commissioned after 2020. The present solution is to use the

Figure 2. Complex nano-micro-hetero structure for fission and transmutation products separation

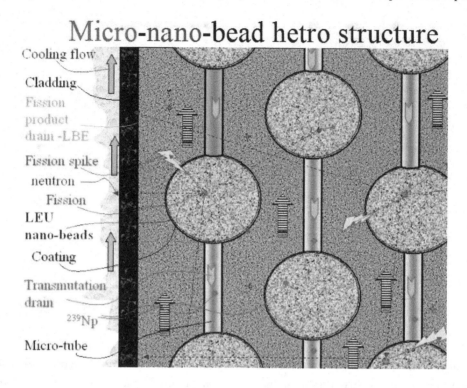

average obtained for each nondegenerate situation weighted by the degeneration degree and consider at the meso-scale.

Another process shown in the Figure 3 but not discussed up to now, is the simultaneous generation of the fission products inside the nano-structure.

The fission products fly apart about 20-40 microns depending of the stopping power properties of the structure they fly through. In the figure above is presented a micro-hetero structure, where the micron dimension spheres are immersed into another liquid smoothly flowing and collecting all the fission products and removing from the structures. Here we have to deal with the micro-flow and radiation damage in fluid structures, as another complications added to the problem.

Another example is the micro bead structure shown in Figure 4 that has the dimensions of about 50 microns, representing the cube's lateral, and contains ceramics metals and liquids. All the elements mentioned have well defined properties

through the nano-engineering process, for example the coating has to be corrosion resilient and to self recover after taking the radiation damage from the fission products stopping, and all of these features have to be considered in the code and shown in the simulation.

As a supporting detail, has to be mentioned that the fission products interaction with matter has three main zones:

1. Nest zone (1–3 nm radius from the fission nucleus spot) characterized by high electronic destabilization and a vacancy,

2. Ionization stopping path—characterized by FP-electrons interaction generating electron showers

3. Fission spike—last 20% of the stopping range where the nuclear recoils and lattice damage dominates

Figure 3. The frit-like structure of a nano-clustered heterogeneous fuel pellet for direct transmutation products extraction

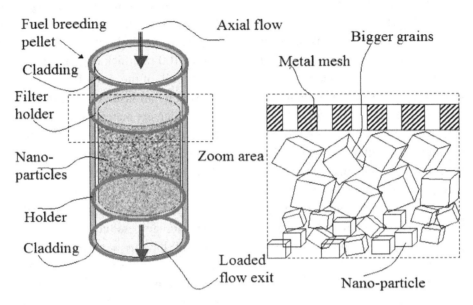

Figure 4. Details of the processes occurring during fission products absorption into a micro-hetero-structure

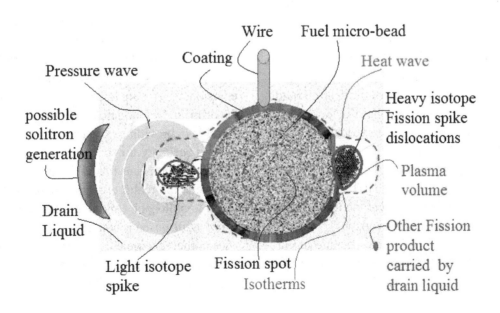

The fission products fly longer, behaving like accelerated heavy ions, sharing about 170 MeV as kinetic energy for a mass of about 232 amu (atomic mass units) in average.

The occurrence of fission or transmutation products' recoil stopping in lattice area, also called Bragg peak, generates an energy shock into nano-cluster releasing the structural deformation stored energy, and triggering the recovery mechanisms based on accelerated diffusion of other existent defects driving towards a better recovery of the structure, better than in the bulky materials. Sometimes, changes at the grain level occurs, the nano-cluster splits or two nearby nano-cluster fusion in a bigger one, activating new mechanisms. These phenomena are difficult to detect by the actual MD software and new code packages of analysis have to be added.

The structure shown in Figure 4 has about 100 microns in dimension, and direct bottom-up calculation even with exaflops computers is practically impossible. In this situation, in order to solve these problems on actual supercomputers, nano- to meso-scale transformations have to be applied. Here there is a case when the structure touches the cladding, and it is different from the case when structure neighbors other similar structures. In this stage the structure may be seen as a stand alone chemical mixture, a kind of homogenous blend of all elements present therein to which, the actual parallel MCNPX code may be applied, and get simulations of the neutron field. Further one has to integrate the structure further into a pellet and inside a nuclear reactor, and redo the calculations. This is what we call multi-scale/multi-dimension approach.

Another interesting case, that pushes the capabilities of supercomputing over the limits, is the case of the direct energy conversion.

One may try to develop the structure in Figure 5 that is formed of direct energy conversion supercapacitor like structures containing actinide material inside, embedded in a liquid surrounding them aiming to take out the fission products.

The dimension of the energy conversion structure is about 20 microns, formed inside by the repetition of about 200 supercapacitor foils each of 100 nm thick containing a high electron density foil, of the actinide material 20 nm thick followed by an insulator 20 nm thick, and a low electron density material 40 nm thick forming the negative plot followed by another 20 nm thick insulator. The liquid separation distance is of about 10 microns; therefore each structure may occupy a cube with the lateral of about 30 microns.

The presence of nano-structured planar foils, or in another version a bi-material nano-bead structure having nano-meter dimensions immersed into a dielectric material, shown in Figure 6 requires that the first step of the simulation to be done by quantum molecular dynamics code at the atomic level.

This procedure works well for particles under 10 nm size, but turns into a very challenging calculation over this size. In order to describe well the movements of electron showers starting inside that structure, where, most of them have paths longer than 100 nm is what it has to be done, and this requires a growth in the magnitude of the domain by more than three orders of magnitude (om).

Tracking the electron showers movement inside a structure that large is more complex because it requires very accurate knowledge on the envisioned structure to be in agreement with the experiment, and the actual experimental tools are not able in providing measurement data with the desired accuracy for so many elements simultaneously. That means that in a way or another we are inside the realm of suppositions, making us slip into philosophy and think if such a problem is not an ill-posed problem.

Another example is the simulation of the radiation transport in nano-structures as coated nano-wires or multi-wall nano-tubes. The effect

Figure 5. Direct nuclear energy conversion into electricity supercapacitor with direct fission products micro-hetero-structure

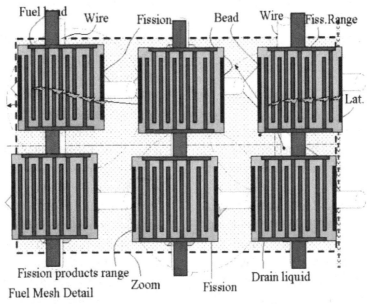

A super-capacitor structure for electronic cooling with fission/spallation product extraction

Figure 6. Direct nuclear energy nano-beaded-hetero-structure

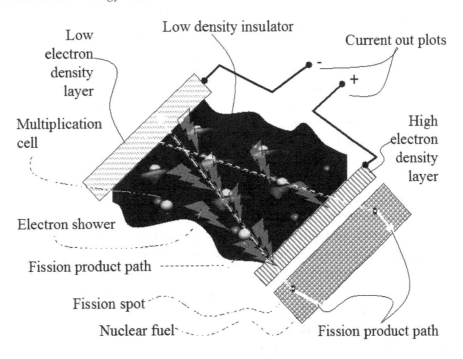

is similar to the basic properties of ideal bent guides where there are two types of reflections:

- Zig-zag reflections (large θa)
- Garland reflections (never touching the inner wall) (small θa)

and a transition from Garland to Zig zag reflections

All reflections are assumed to be specular with reflectivity 1 up to a well defined critical angle θ_c dependent on material, and with reflectivity 0 above θ_c.

If the max. reflection angle allows only Garland reflections near the outer wall, then the guide is not efficiently "filled", or if $\theta_a \approx \theta_i$ the filling of the guide will be fairly isotropic (many reflections).

Basic properties of ideal bent guides transition from Garland- to Zig-zag reflections are characterized by the fact that all reflections are assumed to be specular with reflectivity 1 up to a well defined critical angle θ_c and with reflectivity 0 above θ_c.

After at least one reflection of all neutrons, the angular distribution in the guide is well defined. The angles always repeat.

Imagine now that the curved channel in Figure7a has nm dimensions being in fact a nano-structure. For a carbon nano-tube the inter-atom distance is of about 1.3–1.4 nm, being possible of having multiple layers. The supercomputing simulation will start with creation of the structure for a single nano-tube, with a single wall, that will have about 25 atoms per nm of length. For about 100 microns we may involve 2.5 million atoms. From the MD computing point of view this structure becomes a computation intensive simulation, because we might consider the quantum interaction that takes place between the neutron's dipolar magnetic moment and the magnetic moments of the nano-tube wall.

For a multiple wall tube this number is growing, so for a 3 wall tube we might have 10^7 atoms. This simulation challenges the actual top supercomputers, with 20 petaflops and few petabytes of memory, because it requires that a number of 10^6 to 10^9 neutrons to be interacted, coming from various directions and positions in order to describe well the behavior of a single channeling tube. Simultaneously, the effect of the potential radiation damage and defects creation in the structure has to be calculated in order to have a better image of the lifetime of the structure and its reliability. All these calculations may require important computing resources, and new more adaptive computer architectures might be needed, in order to speed up the process.

With the elementary cell characterized, now one has to build the entire structure and to develop a shielding tile formed of one layer of channeling nano-structures. The development may go further to the study of macroscopic properties of the structure, its mechanical properties, and return at the nano-tube elementary cell level, to detail specific behavior initially uncovered. Another issue to consider is the temperature and temperature gradient response, and response to contamination, from various effluents, chemical stability, etc. These are just a few facts of a bottom-up discovery prone supercomputer approach, in the study of a novel structure. From this stage we go back to the tile macroscopic level and improve constantly until we reach the desired properties. Suppose we discovered a formidable structure that excels the initial expectancies, the most important fact is the correspondence with reality, nature's laws, and a benchmark with an experiment at the same quality and accuracy level is desired, because if a failure occurs somewhere in one of the sub-processes involved in the simulation, the entire application becomes just a nice but costly dream.

Gradual benchmarking and parallel experiments are a must in order to assure the success of the work, therefore simulation and computer prediction is excellent only if it has a correspondent in reality, and drives to reasonable useful results being part of an evolutionary spiral of research.

Figure 7. Types of reflections inside a wave guide; b) super-mirror planar multilayer deposition scheme; c) multilayered super-mirror effect

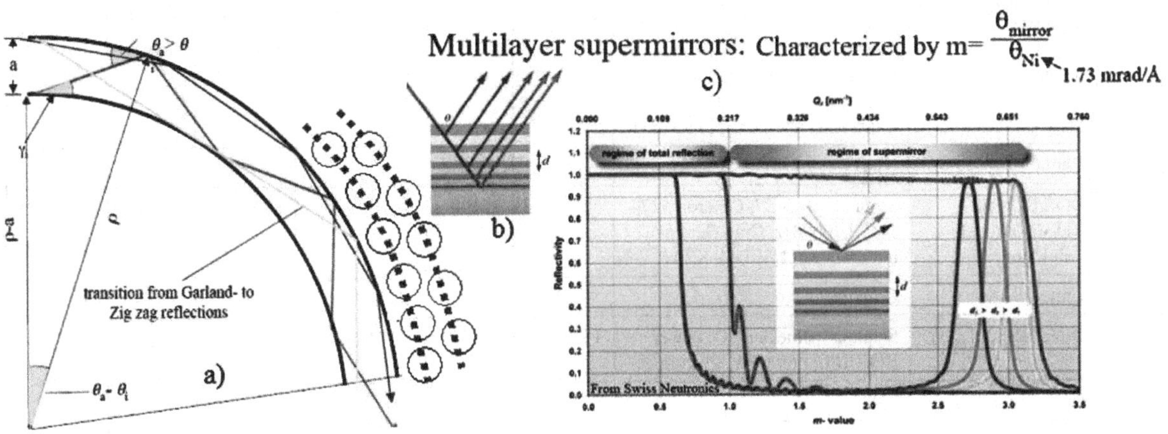

FUTURE RESEARCH DIRECTIONS

As previously showed the number of particles in an actual computer simulation typically lies in the range of 10^4–10^7 particles. Simulations involving more than 10^4 atoms are nowadays relatively complex, because systems like a single protein contains more than 10^5 atoms, while the cases presented before are driving up to 10^{10} or even more particles, in the smallest cases.

In practical applications limited system size is much less a concern than the finite time scale of a computer simulation. For example, large energy barriers in the potential energy surface, may take a molecular system a very long time to cross these barriers and to sample configuration space efficiently. Typical simulation periods are 10^1–10^2 psec, are much too short for a proper description of properties, of a system that shows a much longer relaxation time, and lengthening the time drives to exceptionally long series calculations, increasing the computing time, in order to reach a thermodynamic equilibrium, typically takes about 1 ns, or even more time, somewhere in micro-seconds domain.

Elements for which all the boundary conditions may be defined under the randomness of the ther-modynamic equilibrium are the best candidates to be used in simplified mezoscale calculations.

Cloud computing was previously presented as a tremendous resource for cheap extra peta-scale computing. Other capabilities like dynamically configurable processors, based on field programmable gate arrays as a possibility to speed-up the actual CPU or GPU based super-computer blades have been discussed.

The Exa-Scale is the Upper Limit of the Actual Supercomputer Technology

Looking at the trend of the performances in the top 500 from which in Table 1 are given the first 8, and analyze the semiconductor technology behind we may estimates possible physical limits of the present architectures and hardware solutions.

In Figure8 is given the trend in the CPU core performance increase using the new nano-technologies.

The Figure 8 shows that a continuous increase in performances took place with respect of the CPU clock speed and with the number of teraflops per core. In this respect the only source of speed growth per core resides in clock speed increase and the way the cache memory is accessed. The

Table 1. Top 8 supercomputers

Rank	Site	System	Cores (k)	Rmax TFLOPS	Rpeak TFLOPS	Power (kW)	Pper Core	TFM/ Core
1	National Supercomputer Center in Guangzhou	Tianhe-2 (MilkyWay-2)- TH-IVB-FEP Cluster, Intel Xeon E5-2692 12C 2.200GHz, TH Express-2, Intel Xeon Phi 31S1P	3,120	33862.	54902.4	17808	5.71	92.14
	China	NUDT						
2	DOE/SC/Oak Ridge National Laboratory	Titan - Cray XK7, Opteron 6274 16C 2.200GHz, Cray Gemini interconnect, NVIDIA K20x	560.64	17590	27112.5	8209	14.64	31.87
	United States	Cray Inc.						
3	DOE/NNSA/LLNL	Sequoia - BlueGene/Q, Power BQC 16C 1.60 GHz, Custom	1572.8	17173.2	20132.7	7890	5.02	91.59
	United States	IBM						
4	RIKEN Advanced Institute for Computational Science (AICS)	K computer, SPARC64 VIIIfx 2.0GHz, Tofu interconnect	705.	10510	11280.4	12660	17.96	67.08
	Japan	Fujitsu						
5	DOE/SC/ Argonne National Laboratory	Mira - BlueGene/Q, Power BQC 16C 1.60GHz, Custom	78.6432	8586.6	10066.3	3945	5.02	91.59
	United States	IBM						
6	Swiss National Supercomputing Centre (CSCS)	Piz Daint - Cray XC30, Xeon E5-2670 8C 2.600GHz, Aries interconnect, NVIDIA K20x	115984	6271	7788.9	2325	20.05	18.50
	Switzerland	Cray Inc.						
7	Texas Advanced Computing Center/ Univ. of Texas	Stampede - PowerEdge C8220, Xeon E5-2680 8C 2.700GHz, Infiniband FDR, Intel Xeon Phi SE10P	462462	5168.1	8520.1	4510	9.75	89.48
	United States	Dell						
8	Forschungszentrum Juelich (FZJ)	JUQUEEN - BlueGene/Q, Power BQC 16C 1.600GHz, Custom Interconnect	458752	5008.9	5872	2301	5.02	91.59
	Germany	IBM						

predictions for the 5 nm generation is that the clock speed my reach as high as 10 GHz, that represents a doubling in performance compared to the actual Sandy bridge or Ivy Bridge technology, reaching values in 40,000 teraflops/core.

Using the previous estimation in the context of the actual statistics on computer performances, given in Figure 9 we may easy conclude that the race in supercomputers as we know today will plafond after 1 exaflops, due to many constraints.

As we have seen in the Figs. 8 and 9, above what the technology reaches 5 nm size, a 5 nm Si crystal contains about 5^6 (15625) atoms, while only 3125 atoms in a 1 nm thick layer, transistor, while in the junction area less than 5^3 atoms are participating in the formation of local conduction and valence bands – and in this structure the switching will be affected, or more exactly dominated by the quantum effects. Strange phenomena, as tunneling will make this operation

Figure 8. The performance growing average trend with new semiconductor nano-technologies generations

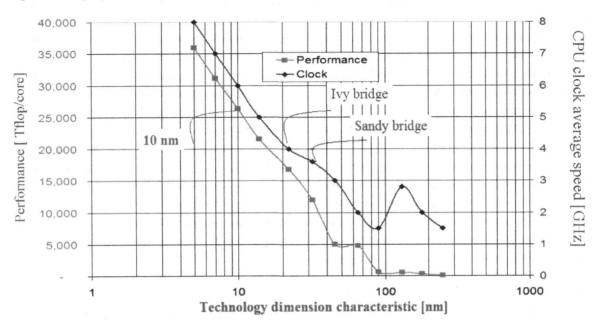

Figure 9. The performances of the first 50 supercomputers

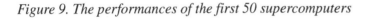

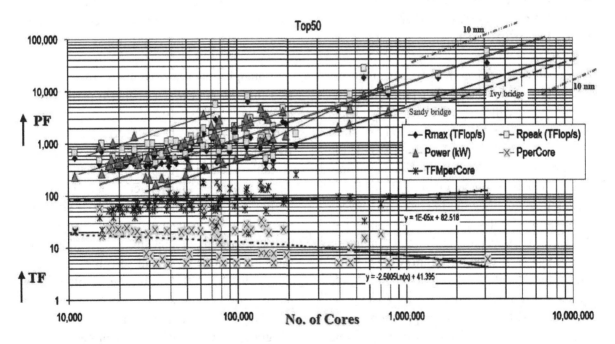

more complicated and a new quantum-transistor device and specific logical diagrams will have to be developed.

In the actual supercomputer constrains, cooling system is an important component, and powers of more than 40 MW/building seems unlikely, therefore the total power of a supercomputer have to be limited somewhere less than 100 MW with all the future progress in the use of immersion liquids and heat pipes.

Other aspect is the power limitation in the circuit itself, and the chart shows a clear tendency of reduction in the specific power per core, while the power density and total power range per core remains in 50-200 W range, while the core grows in complexity and performance.

Considering this tendency we may anticipate that an exaflops machine will remain in the same general parameters as the actual 100 petaflops systems, with a total power around 20–40 MW.

To go for higher computing power the total power per building have to be increased and so the number of cores, reaching powers of about 100 MW for about 10 exaflops, and that is about the upper limit.

Nano-Dots, Quantum Bits, and Quantum Entanglement as the Base of New Revolution in Supercomputing

While quantum computers have been theoretically demonstrated to have incredible potential, quantum computers will be able to efficiently simulate quantum systems, which is what famous physicist Richard Feynman proposed in 1982. Simulation of quantum systems has been said to be a "holy grail" of quantum computing: it is praised that it will allow us to study the interactions between atoms and molecules in more detail. Similar to what happened with the actual digital computers, when the problems and algorithms were customized to match with the binary logic, and Boole algebra, the researches are currently working on new quantum algorithms and applications.

In order to have a quantum computer one needs to have the qubits behave in a predictable, reliable manner. These qubits could be made of photons, atoms, electrons, molecules and more complex structures. Q-bit states are sensitive to any disturbance that causes them to change their

quantum state moving them out of coherence, requiring special conditions as deep cooling, magnetic and electric shielding and vacuum, to keep them stable and perform reliable operations..

It was proven that the switching speed in classical electronics is size dependent, signals propagating with the speed of light in the constitutive material, and in order to make a circuit faster it has to be made smaller. In order to make the quantum computing faster a higher communication speed is needed between various elements of the quantum computing system, and this is the newly discovered entanglement and quantum key teleportation.

Quantum Particles (Atoms, Electrons, Photons, etc.) Quantum States Superposition, And Entanglement

Superposition is essentially the ability of a quantum system to be in multiple states at the same time—that is, something can be "here" and "there," or "up" and "down" at the same time.

Entanglement is an extremely strong correlation that exists between quantum particles—so strong, in fact, that two or more quantum particles can be inextricably linked in perfect unison, even if separated by great distances. This seemingly impossible connection inspired Einstein to describe entanglement as "spooky action at a distance."

Entanglement is the quintessential quantummechanical phenomenon understood to lie at the heart of future quantum technologies and the subject of fundamental scientific investigations (Shadbolt, 2011). Mixture, resulting from noise, is often an unwanted result of interaction with an environment. Experiments where an integrated wave-guide device can generate and completely characterize pure two-photon states with any amount of entanglement and arbitrary single-photon states with any amount of mixture have been performed. The device consists of a reconfigurable integrated quantum photonic circuit with eight voltage-controlled phase shifters, that, for thousands of randomly chosen configurations, performs with high fidelity generating maximally and non-maximally entangled states, violate a Bell-type inequality with a continuum of partially entangled states, and demonstrate the generation of arbitrary one-qubit mixed states.

There are quantum computers already, but not of sufficient power to replace classical computers. While practical quantum technologies are already emerging—including highly effective sensors, actuators and other devices—a true quantum computer that outperforms a classical computer is still years away (Childs, 2007).

A company, D-wave has already produced a quantum computer using a 512 q-bit processor, (Johnson, 2011) developing the necessary software to run this machine, very different from what we have been used to do for the actual binary systems. The company used a programmable artificial spin network bridges the gap between the theoretical study of ideal isolated spin networks and the experimental investigation of bulk magnetic samples. Moreover, with an increased number of spins, such a system may provide a practical physical means to implement a quantum algorithm, possibly allowing more-effective approaches to solving certain classes of hard combinatorial optimization problems

Quantum Key Distribution is already commercially available, and will greatly benefit from new research. Optimal synthesis of reversible functions is a non-trivial problem. One of the major limiting factors in computing such circuits is the sheer number of reversible functions. Reversible circuits are an important class of computations that need to be performed efficiently for the purpose of efficient quantum computation. Multiple quantum algorithms contain arithmetic units such as adders, multipliers, exponentiation, comparators, quantum register shifts and permutations that are best viewed as reversible circuits. Moreover, reversible circuits are indispensable in quantum error correction. Even restricting synthesis to 4-bit

reversible functions results in a huge search space ($16! = 2^{44}$ functions). The output of such a search alone, counting only the space required to list all gates for every function, would require over 100 terabytes of storage (Golubitsky, 2012). The synthesis of all optimal 4-bit permutations, synthesis of random 4-bit permutations, optimal synthesis of all 4-bit linear reversible circuits, synthesis of existing benchmark functions; we compose a list of the hardest permutations to synthesize, and show distribution of optimal circuits, design and optimization of reversible and quantum circuits, testing circuit synthesis heuristics, and performing experiments in the area of quantum information processing.

Quantum teleportation with nonclassical correlation is studied in noninertial frame (Ebadi, 2012). It is shown that a separable but a nonclassically correlated state gives nonzero fidelity for teleportation. In noninertial frames fidelities of teleportation are important and minimum fidelity should be evaluated since the state to be teleported is generally an unknown quantum state.

Frustration-free (FF) spin chains have a property that their ground state minimizes all individual terms in the chain Hamiltonian (Bravyi, 2012). We ask how entangled the ground state of a FF quantum spin-s chain with nearest-neighbor interactions can be for small values of s. While FF spin-1/2 chains are known to have untangled ground states, the case $s=1$ remains less explored. We propose the first example of a FF translation-invariant spin-1 chain that has a unique highly entangled ground state and exhibits some signatures of a critical behavior. The ground state can be viewed as the uniform superposition of balanced strings of left and right brackets separated by empty spaces. Entanglement entropy of one half of the chain scales as $1/2\log n + O(1)$, where n is the number of spins. We prove that the energy gap above the ground state is polynomial in $1/n$. The proof relies on a new result concerning statistics of Dyck paths which might be of independent interest. First, we use a perturbation theory to relate the spectrum of H to the one of an effective Hamiltonian Heff acting on Dyck paths — balanced strings of left and right brackets (Shadbolt, 2011). This step involves successive applications of the Projection Lemma due to Kempe et al. (Golubitsky, 2012). Secondly, we map Heff to a stochastic matrix P describing a random walk on Dyck paths in which transitions correspond to insertions/removals of consecutive lr pairs. The key step of the proof is to show that the random walk on Dyck paths is rapidly mixing. Bound the spectral gap of P using the canonical paths method

Instead of flipping ordinary bits that can be set to either 0 or 1, a so-called universal quantum computer would manipulate quantum bits, or "qubits," that can be 0, 1, or, more, and may exist in the same time making the potential quantum computer crunch many numbers at once instead of doing them one at a time, as a "classical" computer

First, researchers must assemble workable qubits. For example, an ion can serve as a qubit by spinning in one direction to represent 0, another way to represent 1, or both ways simultaneously to make the 0 and 1 state (Cho A. 2012). A measurement of a qubit will "collapse" that two-way state to yield either a 0 or a 1, but the two-way state is still essential for processing many numbers at once. To make a universal quantum computer, a weird quantum connection between qubits called "entanglement," in which measurement on one qubit determines the state of another have to be made. Presently the researches are working to understand systems with reduced number of quantum states, because having particles of dimension of 15, 16, is much more difficult to work and understand, but the possibility to operate simultaneously in higher numeration-base on a single element with spontaneous results is embedded in this approach.

Scott Aaronson, of MIT showed that quantum computers "try all the possibilities in parallel" - representing a very drastic oversimplification, because quantum mechanics is based on "amplitudes", which can also be negative, and in order

to find the probability that something will happen, all the amplitudes have to be added up.

A quantum computation correlates things for a given wrong answer so that there are all these different paths that could lead to it, some with positive amplitude and others with negative amplitude - they cancel each other out (Palmer, 2012).

For a given right answer, the paths leading to that should all be positive or all negative, and amplitudes should be reinforced, and when is measured, the right answer is given with high probability.

Florian Dolde at the University of Stuttgart and his colleagues think the ideal elements that will store this information on a quantum computer are individual nitrogen atoms implanted into a diamond film (Ball, 2013). Nitrogen atoms have one more electron than the carbon atoms in diamond, and this spare electron can exist in two different quantum states thanks to a property called spin. Rather like the poles of a magnet (which are used to store information in magnetic disks and tapes), an electron spin can be considered to point either "up" or "down".

Dolde and colleagues have shown, however, that two nitrogen atoms trapped in diamond tens of nanometers apart can be kept entangled at room temperature for more than a millisecond (thousandth of a second), which could be long enough to perform quantum calculations. They used microwave photons to nudge the atoms into an entangled state, by firing a beam of nitrogen ions (charged atoms) at a diamond film though a mask with holes about 20 nanometers apart.

The case for nitrogen-doped diamond quantum computers is boosted further by a paper from Martin Plenio of the University of Ulm in Germany and his co-workers, who have shown that in theory such a system could be used as a "quantum simulator": a kind of quantum computer that can calculate how other quantum systems will behave (Cai, 2013). The mathematics needed to predict quantum behavior is complicated, and ordinary computers struggle to accommodate it. But a quantum simulator, working by quantum rules, already has the "quantum-ness" built in to its components, and so can carry out such calculations much more easily. Diamond, of all things, could take the hardness out of the problem.

Strongly correlated quantum many-body systems may exhibit exotic phases, such as spin liquids and super-solids. Although their numerical simulation becomes intractable for as few as 50 particles, quantum simulators offer a route to overcome this computational barrier. However, proposed realizations either require stringent conditions such as low temperature/ultra-high vacuum, or are extremely hard to scale. A new solid-state architecture for a scalable quantum simulator was developed that consists of strongly interacting nuclear spins attached to the diamond surface. Initialization, control and read-out of this quantum simulator can be accomplished with nitrogen-vacancy centers implanted in diamond. The system can be engineered to simulate a wide variety of strongly correlated spin models. Owing to the superior coherence time of nuclear spins and nitrogen-vacancy centers in diamond, our proposal offers new opportunities towards large-scale quantum simulation at ambient conditions of temperature and pressure.

Nitrogen-vacancy (NV) centers in diamond have recently emerged as a unique platform for fundamental studies in quantum information and nano-science. The special properties of these impurity centers allow robust, room-temperature operation of solid-state qbits and have enabled several remarkable demonstrations in quantum information processing and precision nano-scale sensing. The recent advances in magnetic and optical manipulation of the NV center's quantum spin are of great importance for prospective applications. Quantum control of individual centers can be harnessed for the protection of NV-center spin coherence, for multi-qbit quantum operations in the presence of de-coherence, and for high-fidelity initialization and readout. The resonant optical control, has led to interfaces between spin and photonic qbits and may lead to spin networks based on diamond photonics. Many of these recently-developed diamond-based technologies constitute critical components for the future leap toward practical multi-qbit devices (Dobrovitski, 2013), small-scale quantum registers based on NV centers. The progress in coupling different NV centers and integrating them into quantum networks may enable creation of larger-scale QIP devices with diamond.

Quantum cryptography (Hughes, 1995) is a new method for secret communications offering the ultimate security assurance of the inviolability of a Law of Nature. In traditional cryptology, information is encoded and decoded with mathematics; in quantum cryptology, physics protects data instead, using photons to transmit a key. In Los Alamos' LA-system, single photons are used to produce secure random numbers between users (Barrie, 2013). Once the photon key is transmitted, then coding and encoding can take place. Because the random numbers are produced securely, they act as a cryptographic key to authenticate and encrypt the power grid data and commands.

It is this uniqueness that leads scientists to theorize that a computer based on quantum particles would be capable of solving multiple tasks simultaneously.

A quantum algorithm solves computational tasks using fewer physical resources than the best-known classical algorithm (Zhou, 2013). The key example is the phase estimation algorithm, which provides the quantum speedup in Shor's factoring algorithm and quantum simulation algorithms. To date, fully quantum experiments of this type have demonstrated only the read-out stage of quantum algorithms, but not the steps in which input data is read in and processed to calculate the final quantum state. Indeed, knowing the answer beforehand was essential for a photonic quantum algorithm—the iterative phase estimation algorithm (IPEA)—without knowing the answer in advance having practical applications as the phase estimation algorithm, including quantum simulations and quantum metrology in the near term, and factoring in the long term.

In a multi-particle quantum walk, (Webb, 2013) particles live on the vertices of a graph and can move between vertices joined by an edge and, nearby particles can interact with each other.

Traditionally, a quantum algorithm is implemented on a register of qubits by actively manipulating the qubits according to a set of desired operations. In this new model, a desired quantum algorithm can be implemented by letting the qubits "quantum walk" on an appropriately chosen graph, without having to control the qubits. The process is analogous to a billiard-ball computer where classical logic gates are performed using collisions.

Many previous quantum-walk experiments have not been scalable. A new model proposed by Childs (Childs, 2003) and his team identifies the requirements to implement quantum walks so they have the potential for significant quantum speedup, paving the way for scalable future experiments. The model could be naturally realized in a variety of systems, including photons with interactions mediated by superconducting circuits.

Quantum walk-based computing is particularly promising because of its universality. In principle any quantum algorithm can be cast into this model, to develop new quantum algorithms and to study problems in quantum computational complexity.

Theoretical calculations performed to predict the existence of an organic topological insulator using molecules with carbon-carbon bonds and carbon-metal bonds, called an organometallic compound (Wang Z. 2013). For this new study, the team investigated how Dirac fermions move along the edges of this compound, which looks like a sheet of chicken wire. In a topological insulator, fermions behave like a massless or weightless packet of light, conducting electricity as they move very fast along a material's surface or edges. When these fermions venture inside the material, however, this "weightless" conductivity screeches to a halt. What's more, Dirac fermions

have a property called spin, or angular momentum around the particle's axis that behaves like a magnetic pole. This property gives scientists another way to place information into a particle, because the spin can be switched "up" or "down." Such a mechanism could be useful for spin-based electronic devices, called "spintronics", which can store information both in the charge and the spin of electrons.

A system with a special type of electron—a Dirac fermion—in which the spin motion can be manipulated to transmit information, is advantageous over traditional electronics because it's faster and you don't have to worry about heat dissipation."

Recently, a "reversible" topological insulator in a system of bismuth-based compounds has been discovered, having the property that the behavior of ordinary or Dirac fermions could be controlled at the interface between two thin films. These theoretical predictions were confirmed experimentally by co-authors from Shanghai Jiaotong University in China. Although inorganic topological insulators based on different materials have been studied for the last decade, organic or molecular topological insulators have not been studied.

Many groups of research-scientists around the world are trying to build a quantum computer to run algorithms that take advantage of the strange effects of quantum mechanics such as entanglement and superposition. A quantum computer could solve problems in chemistry by simulating many body quantum systems, or break modern cryptographic schemes by quickly factorizing large numbers. Previous research shows that if a quantum algorithm is to offer an exponential speed-up over classical computing, there must be a large entangled state at some point in the computation and it was widely believed that this translates into requiring a single large device. A network of small quantum computers can implement any quantum algorithm with a small overhead. The key breakthrough was learning how to efficiently move quantum data between the many

Figure 10. Possible evolution of the computing power after 2015 (courtesy to AMD)

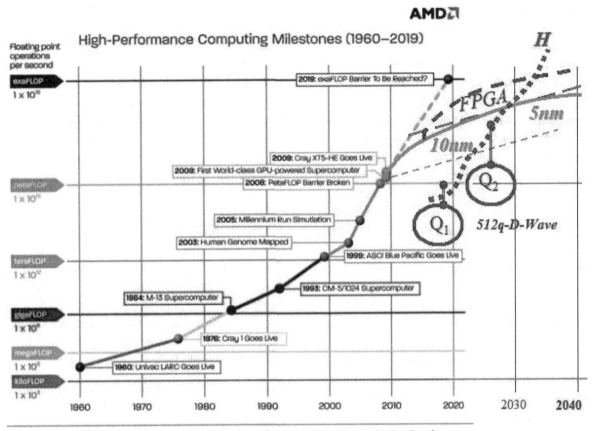

©2010 Advanced Micro Devices, Inc. All rights reserved. AMD, the AMD Arrow logo, combinations thereof, are trademarks of Advanced Micro Devices, Inc. All other trademarks are the property of their respective owners.

sites without causing a collision or destroying the delicate superposition needed in the computation. This allows the different sites to communicate with each other during the computation in much the same way a parallel classical computer would do. Building a computer whose operation is based on the laws of quantum mechanics is a daunting challenge and may be built as a network of small modules.

Algorithms for efficiently moving and addressing quantum memory in parallel that imply that the standard circuit model can be simulated with low overhead by the more realistic model of a distributed quantum computer have been developed (Beals, 2012). As a result, algorithm designers can use the circuit model without wor-

rying whether the underlying architecture supports the connectivity of the circuit.

In our opinion, we think that More law will stop acting in the same manner as before and the scale of integration of electronic circuits will start playing a secondary role in estimating the computing power. It is very probable that the 1 exaflop milestone not to be reached as predicted by 2019, the actual supercomputer concepts triggering a limitation in performances as shown by the orange curve in Figure 10, in spite the technology will reach 5 nm level. The developments in the computing power will be driven by the novel FPGA concepts and applications inside the computing blades, and the appearance of quantum computers. D-Wave 512 qubits will develop and gain more computing power, and its integration in an high performance super-computer making a hybrid computer will further increase the equivalent computing power. New generations of quantum machines, labeled Q1, Q2, …will be developed and integrated in the new HPC systems. In the new systems the exaflop notion will lose its practical meaning, being used to estimate the power of the new system, by calculating the number of exaflops a supercomputer as we know it today might need to solve a certain problem, whose results were obtained by other means with the help of quantum machines. The Hybrid computes, as shown by the new curve H in Figure 10 will dominate the near future, and the problems presented before will probably find their practical solutions running on a Hybrid system.

CONCLUSION

The nano-structures presented showed that in order to perform a complete simulation of the phenomena-taking place inside a viable and meaningful nuclear structure requires higher computing capabilities than what we have today. The Moore's law prediction by extrapolation shows that we may have that minimum limit reached by 2050, but one has to consider the limitations in the actual transistor technology, and miniaturization under 20 nm technology that drives to the predominance of quantum behavior, that modifies the way the electronics operate in a fundamental manner, at the limit that it will be impossible to use without revolutionary discoveries, and that probably will end the More's law application as we know it today.

The future belongs to quantum computers, with far greater capabilities, if we succeed to understand some fundamental problems that are now hot research subjects. The term Central Processing Unit might be replaced by Quantum Processing Unit, and the terms Memory and communication interface might be replaced by their quantum equivalents respectively.

As we know, software and hardware are melted together in order to maximize the power of a computing system. The new supercomputing systems will naturally require new operating systems and new programming concepts to be set in place in order to have a high performance system. It is believed that the new quantum computing structure might increase the system performances by a factor of 10^8 or more at maturity being possible to have yotta-scale computing around year 2030, if the actual rhythm of discoveries is maintained.

REFERENCES

Anthony, S. (2012). *The race to 100 petaflops: Cray and China go head-to-head to build the world's fastest supercomputer*. Retrieved March 18, 2014, from http://www.extremetech.com/extreme/140174-the-race-to-100-petaflops-cray-and-china-worlds-fastest-supercomputer

Anthony, S. (2013). China's Tianhe-2 supercomputer, twice as fast as DoE's Titan, shocks the world by arriving two years early. *Extreme Tech*. Retrieved March 18, 2014, from http://www.extremetech.com/computing/159465-chinas-tianhe-2-supercomputer-twice-as-fast-as-does-titan-shocks-the-world-by-arriving-two-years-early

ASCAC-DOE. (2010). The opportunities and challenges of exascale computing. In *Proceedings of the ASCAC Subcommittee on Exascale Computing*. Retrieved March 18, 2014, from http://science.energy.gov/~/media/ascr/ascac/pdf/reports/exascale_subcommittee_report.pdf

ASCR-DOE. (2014). *Applied mathematics research for exascale computing*. Retrieved March 18, 2014, from http://www.netlib.org/utk/people/JackDongarra/PAPERS/doe-exascale-math-report.pdf

Ball, P. (2013). Diamond idea for quantum computer. *BBC Future*. Retrieved March 18, 2014, from http://www.bbc.com/future/story/20130218-diamond-idea-for-quantum-computer(Under the Radar)

Barrie, A. (2013). Defeating cyber-attacks with quantum cryptography. *FoxNews.com War Games*. Retrieved March 18, 2014, from http://www.foxnews.com/tech/2013/03/04/defeating-cyber-attacks-with-quantum-cryptography/#ixzz2MvAGzilr

Batten, C. (2012). *Computer architecture, topic 14: Vectors*. Cornell University, School of Electrical and Computer Engineering ECE 4750. Retrieved March 18, 2014, from http://www.csl.cornell.edu/courses/ece4750

Beals, R., Gray, O., Harrow, A., Kutin, S., Linden, N., Shepherd, D., & Stather, M. (2012). *Efficient distributed quantum computing*. arXiv:1207.2307

Berendsen, H. J. C., van der Spoel, D., & van Drunen, R. (1995). GROMACS: A message-passing parallel molecular dynamics implementation. *Computer Physics Communications, 91*(1–3), 43–56. doi:10.1016/0010-4655(95)00042-E

Bravyi, S., Caha, L., Movassagh, R., Nagaj, D., & Shor, P. W. (2012). Criticality without frustration for quantum spin-1 chains. *Physical Review Letters, 109*(20), 207202–207205. doi:10.1103/PhysRevLett.109.207202 PMID:23215521

Cai, J., Jelezko, F., & Plenio, M. B. (2013). A large-scale quantum simulator on a diamond surface at room temperature. *Nature Physics, 9*(3), 168–173. doi:10.1038/nphys2519

Childs, A. M., Cleve, R., Deotto, E., Farhi, E., Gutmann, S., & Spielman, D. A. (2003). Exponential algorithmic speedup by quantum walk. In *Proc. 35th ACM Symposium on Theory of Computing* (pp. 59-68). ACM.

Childs, A. M., Schulman, L. J., & Vazirani, U. V. (2007). Quantum algorithms for hidden nonlinear structures. In *Proc. 48th IEEE Symposium on Foundations of Computer Science A18, Nature | Letter* (pp. 395-404). arXiv:0705.2784

Cho, A. (2012). New form of quantum computation promises showdown with ordinary computers. *ScienceNOW*. Retrieved March 18, 2014, from http://news.sciencemag.org/sciencenow/2012/12/new-form-of-quantum-computation-.html

Dobrovitski, V.V., Falk, A.L., Santori, C., & Awschalom, D.D. (2013). Quantum control over single spins in diamond. *Annu. Rev. Condens. Matter Phys., 4*(7), 28.

DOE. (2010). *"Nuclear Energy": Energy education is an interactive curriculum supplement for secondary-school science students*. SECO.

Ebadi, Z., Laflamme, R., Mehri-Dehnavi, H., Mirza, B., Mohammadzadeh, H., & Rahimi, R. (2012). *Quantum teleportation with nonclassical correlated states in noninertial frames*. arXiv:1202.0432v1

EU team. (2013). *Cloud++: Next generation supercomputer architectures*. Retrieved March 18, 2014, from http://ec.europa.eu/digital-agenda/events/cf/ss0911/item-display.cfm?id=7066

Foremski, T. (2010). *The drive for a new supercomputer architecture will change the IT industry summary: Supercomputers face a big challenge in moving from petascale to exascale computing: Solving that challenge will remake the IT industry...* Retrieved March 18, 2014, from http://www.zdnet.com/blog/foremski/the-drive-for-a-new-supercomputer-architecture-will-change-the-it-industry/1146(February 11)

Golubitsky, O., & Maslov, D. (2012). A study of optimal 4-bit reversible toffoli circuits and their synthesis. *IEEE Transactions on Computers, 61*(9), 1341–1353. doi:10.1109/TC.2011.144

Gu, Y., Vancourt, T., & Herbordt, M. C. (2005). Accelerating molecular dynamics simulations with configurable circuits. In *Proceedings of the 2005 International Conference on Field Programmable Logic and Applications*. Academic Press.

Hughes, R. J., Alde, D. M., Dyer, P., Luther, G., Morgan, G. L., & Schauer, M. (1995). *Quantum cryptography*. arXiv LA-UR-95-806. Retrieved from http://arxiv.org/pdf/quant-ph/9504002.pdf

Johnson, M. W., Amin, M. H. S., Gildert, S., Lanting, T., Hamze, F., & Dickson, N. et al. (2011). Quantum annealing with manufactured spins. *Nature Materials*, *473*(7346), 194–198. doi:10.1038/nature10012 PMID:21562559

Kal'e, L., Skeel, R., Bhandarkar, M., Brunner, R., Gursoy, A., & Krawetz, N. et al. (1999). NAMD2: Greater scalability for parallel molecular dynamics. *Journal of Computational Physics*, *151*(1), 283–312. doi:10.1006/jcph.1999.6201

Kuznetsova, A. S. (2005). *The concept of harmony in ancient philosophy*. (Thesis). Philosophy Department of Novosibirsk State University.

Love, D. (2013). 9 facts about quantum computing that will melt your mind. *Business Insider*. Retrieved March 18, 2014, from http://www.businessinsider.com/what-is-quantum-computing-2013-7?op=1#ixzz2birUQ5xZ

Murray, M. (2012). Comparing ivy bridge vs. sandy bridge. *PC Magazine*. Retrieved March 18, 2014, from http://www.pcmag.com/article2/0,2817,2405317,00.asp(JUNE 7)

Novakovic, N. (2011). Chinese high end CPUs are now in the game. *vr-zone*. Retrieved March 18, 2014, from http://vr-zone.com/articles/chinese-high-end-cpus-are-now-in-the-game-details-part-2-alpha/14347.html(December 26)

Nvidia. (2014). TESLA GPU accelerators for workstations. *NVIDIA.com*. Retrieved March 18, 2014, from http://www.nvidia.com/object/tesla-workstations.html

OLCF. (2013). Introducing titan: Advancing the era of supercomputing. *ORNL-TechNotes*. Retrieved March 18, 2014, from http://www.olcf.ornl.gov/titan/

Oracle. (2010). *Understanding basic multithreading concepts: Multithreaded programming guide*. Retrieved March 18, 2014, from http://docs.oracle.com/cd/E19455-01/806-5257/6je9h032e/index.html

Palmer J. (2012). Quantum computing: Is it possible, and should you care? *BBC News Science and Technology*.

Popa-Simil, L. (2012). The harmony between nuclear reactions and nuclear reactor structures and systems. In *Proceedings of ICAPP'12*. Retrieved March 18, 2014 from http://icapp.ans.org/icapp12/official%20program.pdf(12080)

Proffitt, B. (2012). Peta, Exa, Yotta and beyond: Big data reaches cosmic proportions. *readwrite enterprise*. Retrieved March 18, 2014, from http://readwrite.com/2012/11/23/peta-exa-yotta-and-beyond-big-data-reaches-cosmic-proportions-infographic#awesm=~oegH00ZWlbJMVt

Ruch, P., Paredes, S., Meijer, I., & Bruno, M. (2013). Roadmap towards ultimately-efficient zeta-scale datacenters. In *Proceedings of Design, Automation & Test in Europe Conference & Exhibition (DATE)* (pp. 1339-1344). Academic Press.

Salvatores, M. (2006). Advanced fuel cycles and R&D needs in the nuclear data field. In *Proceedings of Nuclear Physics and Related Computational Science R&D for Advanced Fuel Cycle Workshop*. Bethesda, MD: Academic Press.

Scott, S. (2007). *Future supercomputer architectures*. Paper presented at Frontiers of Extreme Computing 2007, Santa Cruz, CA.

Scrofano, R., Gokhale, M., Trouw, F., & Prasanna, V. K. (2006). A hardware/software approach to molecular dynamics on reconfigurable computers. In *Proceedings of FCCM '06 - Field-Programmable Custom Computing Machines 14th Annual IEEE Symposium on Date of Conference* (pp. 23-34). IEEE. doi:10.1109/FCCM.2006.46

Shadbolt, P. J., Verde, M. R., Peruzzo, A., Politi, A., Laing, A., & Lobino, M. et al. (2011). Generating, manipulating and measuring entanglement and mixture with a reconfigurable photonic circuit. *Nature Photonics, 6*(1), 45–49. doi:10.1038/nphoton.2011.283

Straatsma, T. P. (2013). *A vision for eXtreme scale computing at Pacific northwest national laboratory*. Retrieved March 18, 2014, from http://xsci.pnnl.gov/

Taylor, K. (2014). Altera announces high-efficiency power conversion solution for high-performance FPGAs. *Market Watch*. Retrieved March 18, 2014, from http://www.marketwatch.com/story/altera-announces-high-efficiency-power-conversion-solution-for-high-performance-fpgas-2014-04-07?reflink=MW_news_stmp

Wang, Z., Liu, Z., & Liu, F. (2013). Engineers show feasibility of superfast materials: 'Organic topological insulators' for quantum computing. *Science News Web*. Retrieved March 18, 2014, from http://www.sciencedaily.com/releases/2013/02/130213132431.htm

Webb, Z., & Childs, A. (2013). Researchers propose breakthrough architecture for quantum computers. *R&D Magazine*. Retrieved March 18, 2014, from http://www.rdmag.com/news/2013/02/researchers-propose-breakthrough-architecture-quantum-computers

Wikipedia. (2013). *Orders of magnitude (computing)*. Retrieved March 18, 2014, from http://en.wikipedia.org/wiki/Orders_of_magnitude_%28computing%29

Wikipedia. (2013). *Quantum computer*. Retrieved March 18, 2014, from http://en.wikipedia.org/wiki/Quantum_computer

Xilnix. (2014). *Field programmable gate array (FPGA)*. Retrieved March 18, 2014, from http://www.xilinx.com/training/fpga/fpga-field-programmable-gate-array.htm

Zhang, C. (2013). *Tianhe-2: More than super computing*. Retrieved March 18, 2014, from http://heim.ifi.uio.no/xingca/201309.html

Zhou, X.-Q., Kalasuwan, P., Ralph, T. C., & O'Brien, J. L. (2013). Calculating unknown eigenvalues with a quantum algorithm. *Nature Photonics, 7*(3), 223–228. doi:10.1038/nphoton.2012.360

Zhuo, L., & Prasanna, V. K. (2006). Scalable hybrid designs for linear algebra on reconfigurable computing systems. In *Proceedings of the 12th International Conference on Parallel and Distributed Systems*. Academic Press. doi:10.1109/ICPADS.2006.95

KEY TERMS AND DEFINITIONS

Extreme Scale Computing Initiative (XSCI): Building the capabilities needed to enable scientific advancements and breakthroughs in selected domain sciences through computational modeling and simulation on next-generation, extreme-scale computers. The XSCI consists of an integrated research program with an interdisciplinary approach that brings together high-performance computer science and computational domain sciences to develop the next-generation, extreme-scale modeling and simulation applications. (Straatsma, 2013)

Mesoscale: Of intermediate size; especially of or relating to a meteorological phenomenon approximately 10 to 1000 kilometers in horizontal extent. For example mesoscale cloud pattern or, related to material it may include elements from 1 micron up to several centimeters size.

Microscale: A very small scale ranging from 0.1 microns up to 0.1 mm

Nano-Structure: An object of intermediate size between microscopic and molecular structures.

Nuclear Energy: The use of exothermic nuclear processes, (Proffitt, 2012) to generate useful heat and electricity. The term includes nuclear fission, nuclear decay and nuclear fusion. Presently the nuclear fission of elements in the actinide series of the periodic table produce the vast majority of nuclear energy in the direct service of humankind, with nuclear decay processes, primarily in the form of geothermal energy, and radioisotope thermoelectric generators; niche uses making up the rest. Nuclear (fission) power stations, excluding the contribution from naval nuclear fission reactors, provided about 5.7% of the world's energy and 13% of the world's electricity in 2012. (DOE 2010)

Quantum Computer: A computation device that makes direct use of quantum-mechanical phenomena, such as superposition and entanglement, to perform operations on data. Quantum computers are different from digital computers based on transistors. (Wikipedia, 2013)

Qubit: In quantum computing, a qubit or quantum bit is a unit of quantum information—the quantum analogue of the classical bit. A qubit is a two-state quantum-mechanical system, such as the polarization of a single photon: here the two states are vertical polarization and horizontal polarization. In a classical system, a bit would have to be in one state or the other, but quantum mechanics allows the qubit to be in a superposition of both states at the same time, a property which is fundamental to quantum computing.

Chapter 6
Applications of Supercomputers in Sequence Analysis and Genome Annotation

Gerard G. Dumancas
Oklahoma Medical Research Foundation, USA

ABSTRACT

In the modern era of science, bioinformatics play a critical role in unraveling the potential genetic causes of various diseases. Two of the most important areas of bioinformatics today, sequence analysis and genome annotation, are essential for the success of identifying the genes responsible for different diseases. These two emerging areas utilize highly intensive mathematical calculations in order to carry out the processes. Supercomputers facilitate such calculations in an efficient and time-saving manner generating high-throughput images. Thus, this chapter thoroughly discusses the applications of supercomputers in the areas of sequence analysis and genome annotation. This chapter also showcases sophisticated software and algorithms utilized by the two mentioned areas of bioinformatics.

INTRODUCTION

Bioinformatics is often regarded as a discipline in its infancy. However, this interdisciplinary field had its historical start in 1960s when computers emerged as a vital tool in molecular biology. With the notable efforts of Margaret O. Dayhoff, Walter M. Fitch, Russell F. Doolittle among others, this area emerged as an approach to managing and interpreting massive data generated by genomic research. Bioinformatics today represent a convergence of various fields, which involve modeling of biological phenomena, genomics, biotechnol-

ogy and information technology, analysis and interpretation of data, and the development of novel algorithms for analyzing biological datasets. With the advent of the emergence of these large amount of biological datasets, scientists are often confronted with the issues of analyzing and interpreting these massive information and datasets in a less amount of time, requiring high accuracy, and cost-saving. In the last few decades, this has been made possible with the emergence of supercomputers. The wide array of available supercomputers has made it possible to analyze and interpret biological datasets and systems in a

DOI: 10.4018/978-1-4666-7461-5.ch006

Copyright © 2015, IGI Global. Copying or distributing in print or electronic forms without written permission of IGI Global is prohibited.

more convenient manner. Nowadays, because of supercomputers, groundbreaking bioinformatics research is made possible. A good example is the discovery of novel genes associated with different diseases. With the discovery of these genes, scientists have come up to a deeper understanding of the etiology of various unexplained diseases caused genetically. Consequently, various drugs and treatments were discovered to counteract such diseases. Within the area of bioinformatics, sequence analysis and genome annotation are among the two of the emerging and most important branches. In the recent years, supercomputers play very important roles in the successes of such branches.

The objective of this chapter is to provide the readers a clear understanding of the specific applications of supercomputers in the two most emerging areas of bioinformatics, sequence analysis and genome annotation. Though supercomputers play critical roles in such areas, the audience is not often aware of the potential applications that may arise from them. A universal understanding that constitute both fundamental and experimental methodologies will enhance the development and progress of such areas. Thus, the major motivation of this chapter is to provide the abovementioned understanding by discussing and analyzing the fundamentals of several examples centered on the various applications of supercomputers in sequence analysis and genome annotation. While the content of this chapter may be technical to some readers, we encourage them to review some basic concepts of genetics and biochemistry as well as to look at the definition of terms to better understand this chapter.

BACKGROUND

Genotype analysis involves studying the association between genotype and phenotype, and the genotype frequencies. Genetic association studies are aimed primarily in identifying genetic variants that explain differences in phenotypes among individuals in a study population. Once association is found between the gene(s) and the phenotype, scientists would be able to understand the mechanism of action and disease etiology in individuals and consequently characterize the relevance and importance of such in the general population. The long-term goal of these studies is to identify better treatment and prevention strategies. Association or any genetic analyses usually require highly intensive mathematical calculations. Supercomputers play a critical role in the success of such calculations. Prior to genetic association analyses, any genotype information needs to undergo two critical steps—sequence analysis and genome annotation. Applications of supercomputers in genotype analyses involve a wide array of applications and will be discussed in the mentioned areas below.

SUPERCOMPUTERS IN SEQUENCE ANALYSIS

Sequence analysis is the most commonly performed task in bioinformatics. It was one of the first bioinformatics techniques founded in ~1970 (Webb-Roberts, 2004). DNA sequencing is simply any process used to map out the sequence of the nucleotides that comprise a strand of DNA. After the discovery of the double helix shape of DNA in 1953, and seeing how it is comprised of a series of ladder like units known as DNA nucleotides, the primary goal has been to find out just how the sequence of those little nucleotides leads to the physical characteristics of an organism, that is, whether what your hair color, your skin color, and every other detail from your bone marrow to the tip of your hair. Thus, DNA sequencing is simply a way for scientists to unravel genetics, the study of how we are put together and how we transfer our traits to our offspring.

It was in 1970 when DNA sequencing first became possible with the discovery of restriction enzymes and DNA polymerases. Eventually, breakthrough in the rate of sequencing came when the dideoxy chain termination (Sanger, Nicklen, & Coulson, 1977) and chemical degradation (Maxam & Gilbert, 1977) techniques were introduced in 1977. Consequently, using the former method, the 16.5 kb human mitochondria genome (Anderson, 1981) was sequenced and the latter method was used for the analysis of the 40 kb bacteriophage T7 (Dunn & Studier, 1983). Thus, these methods provide the theoretical and practical backgrounds for our modern sequencing technologies (Chen, 1994).

The GenBank, an NIH genetic sequence database is an annotated collection of all publicly available DNA sequences. It used to contain only 15 million nucleotides in 1987 and had nearly doubled its size in each of the subsequent five years. The GenBank had reached over 120 million in 1992, with progressively more data obtained using automated DNA sequencers (Chen, 1994). Today, GenBank has approximately 126,551,501,141 bases in 135,440,924 sequence records in the traditional GenBank divisions and 191,401,393,188 bases in 62,715,288 sequence records in the whole genome shotgun (WGS) division as of April 2011 (Information, 2011).

With the large array of DNA sequences produced by various DNA sequencing technologies, it is necessary to perform sequence alignment or multiple sequence alignment, which is a way of arranging the sequencing of DNA to identify regions of similarity that may be a consequence of functional, structural, or evolutionary relationships between the sequences (Mount, 2004). Thus, a wide variety of sequence alignment softwares are available to assist scientists in this process. Throughout the years, numerous computational tools have facilitated the success of genetic research specifically in comparing sequences (Table 1).

After auto-assembly and before genomic annotation, the genomic finishing process is executed in a typical sequence analysis procedure. Finishing is the process of turning a rough draft assembly composed of shotgun sequencing reads into a highly accurate finished DNA sequence with a defined maximum allowed error rate. The international publicly funded sequencing community established a standard for considering a sequence finished: It should be completely contiguous, with no gaps in the sequence, and that it have a final estimated error rate of <1 error in 10,000 bases (Schmutz, Grimwood, & Myers, 2004). The next step in the analysis, after finishing, sequence assembly or sequence alignment, is sequencing assembly. Sequencing assembly is used when assembly of short DNA fragments (500-1000 bp) are generated by shotgun sequencing, and is widely used for sequencing large genomes, including the human genome (Y. Zhang & Waterman, 2003). Sequencing alignment, on the other hand, is a way of arranging the sequencing of DNA to identify regions of similarity that may be a consequence of functional, structural, or evolutionary relationships between the sequences (Mount, 2004). It may be of two types, pairwise sequence alignment (PSA) and multiple sequence alignment (MSA). PSA is one of the most commonly performed bioinformatics tasks. It is a method to compare two sequences and make inferences on the relationships between them. In other words, it simply involves searching for homology between two molecules by a one-to-one correspondence between the residues of the two sequences. PSA utilize three types of optimization approaches—dynamic programming, heuristic, and Bayesian. Dynamic programming uses sequential approaches to solve the problem and are generally considered slow and optimal. Heuristic methods on the other hand, are considered fast and provide approximate solutions (S. M. Brown & Joubert). Bayesian approach, on the other hand, would formulate the sequence alignment as a Bayesian inference problem (Webb-Roberts, 2004).

When the alignment is concerned with finding structural or functional patterns between sequences, MSA is used (Webb-Roberts, 2004).

Table 1. Sequence alignment tools for comparing sequences

Name	Description	Authors
Advance PipMaker	Aligns two DNA sequences and returns a percent identity plot of that alignment, together with a traditional textual form of the alignment. This is a tool for sequence comparison between two small genomes.	(Schwartz et al., 2000)
Alignment-To-HTML	HTML-based interactive visualization for annotated multiple sequence alignments.	(Gille, Birgit, & Gille, 2014)
BLAST2	Useful for DNA sequence comparisons providing a small graphic for both proteins or short DNA sequences.	NCBI (Information)
BlastGraph	An interactive Java program for comparative genome analysis based on Basic Local Alignment Search Tool (BLAST), graph clustering and data visualization.	(Ye, Wei, Wen, & Rayner, 2013)
BOXSHADE	An alternative presentation of alignments accepting a wide variety of file formats and allows the requester considerable flexibility in defining the output appearance (color, arrangement, format)	(Baron)
Clustal Omega	Multiple sequence alignment program that uses seeded guide trees and hidden Markov models profile-profile techniques to generate alignments.	(Sievers et al., 2011)
ClustalW	General purpose multiple sequence alignment program for DNA or proteins; provides with a number of data presentation, homology matrices, and presentation of phylogenetic trees.	(Larkin et al., 2007)
Consensus	Takes CLUSTAL or MSF multiple alignments and calculates the consensus.	(N. Brown, 1996)
ConSurf	Estimates the evolutionary conservation of amino/nucleic acid positions in a protein/DNA/RNA molecule based on the phylogenetic relations between homologous sequences.	(Ashkenazy, Erez, Martz, Pupko, & Ben-Tal, 2010)
CoreGenes	Designed to analyze two to five genomes simultaneously, generating a table of related genes - orthologs and putative orthologs. These entries are linked to their GenBank data with a limit of 0.35 Mb. CoreGenes2.0 has a limit of approx. 2.0 Mb. The upgrade to this program is GeneOrder 4.0 which will compare genomes up to 8Mb.	(Zafar, Mazumder, & Seto, 2002); (Mazumder, Kolaskar, & Seto, 2001); (Mahadevan & Seto, 2010)
CoreGenes 3	Tallies the total number of genes in common between the two genomes being compared. It also displays the percent value of genes in common with a specific genome and determines the unique genes contained in a pair of proteomes.	(Zafar et al., 2002); (Mahadevan, King, & Seto, 2009b); (Mahadevan, King, & Seto, 2009a)
DbClustal	Aligns sequences from a BlastP database search with one query sequence.	(Thompson, Plewniak, Thierry, & Poch, 2000)
DiAlign	While standard alignment methods rely on comparing single residues and imposing gap penalties, DIALIGN constructs pairwise and multiple alignments by comparing whole segments of the sequences.	(Subramanian, Kaufmann, & Morgenstern, 2008)
DIALIGN	Software tool for multiple sequence alignment by combining global and local alignment features.	(Morgenstern, 2014)
Dotlet	A program for comparing sequences between two small genomes by the diagonal plot method.	(Junier & Pagni, 2000)
ESPript2.2	An alternative presentation of alignments requiring to save your alignment as a *.aln file. Good control over output appearance and format is available (ps, tiff and gif).	(Gouet, Courcelle, Stuart, & Metoz, 1999)
EzEditor	Sequence editing software designed for both rRNA and protein-coding genes with the visualization of biologically relevant information; useful in molecular phylogenetic studies	(Jeon et al., 2014)

continued on following page

Table 1. Continued

Name	Description	Authors
FASTA	Finds regions of local or global similarity between protein or DNA sequences, either by searching protein or DNA databases, or by identifying local duplications within a sequence; can be used to infer functional and evolutionary relationships between sequences as well as help identify members of gene families (W. R. Pearson, 2006a). LALIGN/PLALIGN offers the users a graphic "dotplot" output of the alignments (W. R. Pearson, 2006b).	(W. R. Pearson, 2006a)
FFAS	The Fold and Function Assignment System (FFAS); profile of a user's protein can now be compared with ~20 additional profile databases; features include navigating multiple results pages, and also includes novel functionality, such as dotplot graph viewer, modeling tools, and 3D alignment viewer and links to the database of structural similarities (Jaroszewski, Li, Cai, Weber, & Godzik, 2011).	(Jaroszewski et al., 2011) (Godzik, 2012)
G-BLASTN	A promising software tool that uses a GPU to accelerate protein sequence alignment	(Zhao & Chu, 2014)
Gene ContextTool	Tool for visualizing the genome context of a gene or group of genes.	(Ciria, Abreu-Goodger, Morett, & Merino, 2004)
GeneOrder 3.0	Ideal for comparing small GenBank genomes (up to 2 Mb). Each gene from the Query sequence is compared to all of the genes from the Reference sequence using BLASTP. There are two display formats: graphical and tabular. Currently the graph is an applet and must be saved as a "SCREEN SHOT".	(Mazumder et al., 2001); (Zafar, Mazumder, & Seto, 2001)
GramAlign	Progressive alignment algorithm that uses a grammar-based relative complexity distance metric to determine the alignment order; Allows for a computationally efficient and scalable program useful for aligning both large numbers of sequences and sets of long sequences quickly	(Russell, 2014)
GUIDANCE	Implements two different algorithms for evaluating confidence scores: (i) the heads-or-tails (HoT) method, which measures alignment uncertainty due to co-optimal solutions; (ii) the GUIDANCE method, which measures the robustness of the alignment to guide-tree uncertainty.	(Penn et al., 2010)
H-BLOX	An alternative presentation of alignments providing information content or the relative entropy within DNA or protein alignment blocks.	(Zuegge, Ebeling, & Schneider, 2001)
HSA	Effective spliced aligner of RNA-seq reads mapping.	(Bu, Chi, & Jin, 2013)
JABAWS 2	Provides web services for multiple sequence alignment, prediction of protein disorder, and aminoacid conservation conveniently packaged to run on your local computer, server or cluster. This program is used for meta-analysis.	(Troshin, Procter, & Barton, 2011)
JDotter	A tool for sequence comparison between two small genomes with a Java Dot Plot Viewer for generating dotplots of large DNA or protein sequences.	(Brodie, Roper, & Upton, 2004)
Kraken	Assigns taxonomic labels to metagenomic DNA sequences.	(Wood & Salzberg, 2014)
LALIGN	Finds multiple matching subsegments in two sequences; provides one with % identity for different subsegments of the sequence; implements the algorithm of Huang and Miller (X. Huang & Miller, 1991)	(W. Pearson, 1991)
LocARNA	Used for multiple alignments of RNA molecules requiring only RNA sequences as input and will simultaneously fold and align the input sequences. It outputs a multiple alignment together with a consensus structure. For the alignment it features RIBOSUM-like similarity scoring and realistic gap cost.	(Smith, Heyne, Richter, Will, & Backofen, 2010)
MafFilter	A highly efficient and flexible tool to analyse multiple genome alignments	(Dutheil, Gaillard, & Stukenbrock, 2014)
MATCHER	Part of the EMBOSS group of programs; finds the best local alignments between two protein sequences.	(Rice, Longden, & Bleasby, 2000)

continued on following page

Table 1. Continued

Name	Description	Authors
MegaSeq	Designed to harness the size and memory of the Cray XE6, housed at Argonne National Laboratory, for whole genome analysis in a platform designed to better match current and emerging sequencing volume.	(Puckelwartz et al., 2014)
MOSAL	Provides an open-source implementation and an on-line application for multiobjective pairwise sequence alignment.	(Paquete, Matias, Abbasi, & Pinheiro, 2014)
MPsrch	An alternative presentation of alignments. It is a biological sequence sequence comparison tool that implements the true Smith and Waterman algorithm. It runs a search on a HP/COMPAQ cluster, using single and parallelised versions of the software. It allows a rigorous search in a reasonable computational time. MPsrch utilizes an exhaustive algorithm, which is recognized as the most sensitive sequence comparison method available, whereas BLAST and FASTA utilize a heuristic one. As a consequence, MPsrch is capable of identifying hits in cases where BLAST and FASTA fail and also reports fewer false-positive hits. (This service was retired in 2009)	(Sturrock & Collins, 1993)
MRFalign	Protein homology detection software through alignment of Markov Random Fields.	(Ma, Wang, Wang, & Xu, 2014)
MultAlin	Multiple sequence alignment with hierarchical clustering producing results in colors.	(Corpet, 1988)
Multi-zPicture	Provides nice dotplot graphs and dynamic visualizations for comparing sequences between two small genomes.	(Ovcharenko, Loots, Hardison, Miller, & Stubbs, 2004)
Multiple Align Show	An alternative presentation of alignments allowing considerable choice in coloring alignments.	Bioinformatics Organization (Gouet et al., 1999)
Multiple Alignment	Arranges several protein or nucleic acid sequences with postulated gaps so that similar residues (in one-letter code) are juxtaposed using the GeneBee service.	(Brodsky et al., 1992)
PipeAlign	Offers an integrated approach to protein family analysis through a cascade of different sequence analysis programs such as BALLAST, DbClustal multiple alignment program, Rascal alignment analysis.	(Plewniak et al., 2003)
PRALINE	A multiple sequence alignment program with many options to optimize the information for each of the input sequences: i.e. global or local preprocessing, predicted secondary structure information and iteration capabilities.	(Simossis & Heringa, 2005)
PRANK	Can provide the inferred ancestral sequences as a part of the output and mark the alignment gaps differently depending on their origin in insertion or deletion events.	(Loytynoja, 2014)
PROBCONS	Combination of probabilistic modeling and consistency-based alignment techniques and has achieved the highest accuracies of all multiple alignments of protein sequences methods to date.	(Do, Mahabhashyam, Brudno, & Batzoglou, 2005)
PROMALS	Constructs multiple protein sequence alignments using information from database searches and secondary structure prediction for protein homologs with sequence identity below 10%, aligning close to half of the amino acid residues correctly on average.	(Pei & Grishin, 2007)
RNA-Pareto	Allows a direct inspection of all feasible results to the pairwise RNA sequence-structure alignment problem and greatly facilitates the exploration of the optimal solution set.	(Schnattinger, Schoning, Marchfelder, & Kestler, 2013)
SALIGN	Determines the best alignment procedure based on the inputs automatically, while allowing the user to override default parameter values. Dendograms are used to guide multiple alignments computed from a matrix of all pairwise alignment scores. When aligning sequences to structures, SALIGN uses structural environment information to place gaps optimally. If two multiple sequence alignments of related proteins are input to the server, a profile-profile alignment is performed.	(Braberg et al., 2012)

continued on following page

Table 1. Continued

Name	Description	Authors
SCAN2	Tool for sequence comparison between two small genomes providing one with a color-coded graphical alignment of genome length DNAs in Java.	(Softberry, 2007)
SIM	Alignment tool between two protein sequences or within a sequence (Portal). Once alignment is calculated, LALNVIEW, a graphical viewer for pairwise alignments can be used for viewing (Duret, Gasteiger, & Perriere, 1996). The PBIL (Pôle Bio-Informatique Lyonnais) server can be used to align nucleic acid sequences with a similar tool (Duret et al., 1996).	(X. Huang & Miller, 1991) (Portal)
SOAPsplice	A robust tool to detect splice junctions using RNA-Seq data without using any information of known splice junctions.	(S. Huang et al., 2011)
SSEA	Secondary Structure Element Assignment (SSEA); computes alignments of protein secondary structures including both global and local structure element alignments.	(Duret et al., 1996)
SUPERMATCHER	Part of the EMBOSS group of programs; calculates approximate local pair-wise alignments of larger protein sequences.	(Rice et al., 2000)
The Coffee Collection	A collection of alignment databases consisting of: • T-Coffee – aligns DNA, RNA or Proteins using the default T-Coffee • M-Coffee – aligns DNA, RNA or Proteins by combining the output of popular aligners • R-Coffee – aligns RNA sequences usingpredicted secondary structures • Expresso – aligns protein sequences using structural information • PSI-Coffee – aligns distantly related proteins using homology extension TM-Coffee – aligns transmembrane proteins using homology extension	(Chang, Di Tommaso, Taly, & Notredame, 2012); (Di Tommaso et al., 2011)
Tophat2	Accurate alignment tool of transcriptomes in the presence of insertions, deletions, and gene fusions; combines the ability to identify novel splice sites with direct mapping to known transcripts, producing sensitive and accurate alignments, even for highly repetitive genomes or in the presence of pseudogenes.	(Kim et al., 2013)
VIP Barcoding	User-friendly software in graphical user interface for rapid DNA barcoding; able to deal with both large-scale and multilocus barcoding data with accuracy and can contribute to DNA barcoding for modern taxonomy.	(Fan, Hui, Yu, & Chu, 2014)
VISTA	VISualization Tools for Alignments; allows one to align two genome-length sequences.	(Frazer, Pachter, Poliakov, Rubin, & Dubchak, 2004)
webPRANK	Incorporates phylogeny-aware multiple sequence alignment, visualisation and post-processing in an easy-to-use web interface.	(Loytynoja & Goldman, 2010)
YASS	A tool for sequence comparison between two small genomes performing DNA local alignments with results in dotplot and tabular form.	(Noe & Kucherov, 2005)
zPicture	DNA or genome alignment and visualization tool based on blastz alignment program. Alignments can be automatically submitted to rVista 2.0 to identify evolutionary conserved transcription factor binding sites.	(Ovcharenko et al., 2004)

MSA is a fundamental analysis method in bioinformatics and many comparative genomic applications. It forms the basis of many other tasks such as protein structure prediction, protein function prediction, and phylogenetic analysis (Agrawal, 2008). The computation time for an optimal MSA grows exponentially with respect to the number of sequences. Thus, in order to achieve minimal computation time in response to a growing MSA,

more efficient algorithms and the use of parallel computing resources are necessary (Lloyd, 2010). In general, several types of parallel systems have emerged to address computationally intensive problems in sequence alignments. Over the years, hybrid systems, which may be a combination of multiprocessor, vector, cell, graphics processing unit (GPU), and field-programmable gate arrays (FPGA) are becoming more common. Current multiprocessors usually consist of a cluster of nodes connected with a network. Each node typically has several processors or multi-core chips that share on-board memory. Examples of these systems include clusters of workstations to supercomputers with high-performance networks. Current vectors, on the other hand, utilize x86-based processors having vector instructions in the form of streaming single instruction, multiple data (SIMD) extensions, thus, reducing the time needed to perform the same operation on several data elements. A multi-core Cell containing one 64-bit PowerPC reduced instruction set computer (RISC)-processor and eight 128-bit vector processors is also emerging. GPUs containing several hundred processors that are capable of floating-point and integer operations are also currently used. Lastly, FPGAs that allow multiple processing elements to be executed in parallel at hardware speed on data supplied from the host are also currently used (Lloyd, 2010).

Some alignment software as given in the next paragraphs utilize specialized parallel MSA algorithms in order to achieve time efficiency in sequence alignment calculations. Since, various MSA softwares listed in Tables and 2 are updated through time, we suggest the readers to visit their specific websites for further information as to the current algorithms their softwares utilizes.

PRALINE repeatedly chooses the next highest scoring pair to align until all sequences and groups are aligned to produce the final alignment. The highest scoring pair is determined by comparing all sequences with each other at first, and then comparing the aligned pair with the remaining sequences after each iteration. A speedup of 10 with 25 processors on a distributed system using a set of 200 random sequences that are 200 residues in length is realized by Kleinjung and colleagues (Kleinjung, Douglas, & Heringa, 2002) after parallel implementation. In the method, the pairwise sequence alignment stage is parallelized by distributing pairwise sequence alignment tasks to separate processors. In the progressive profile

alignment stage, only the comparison of sequences and groups is parallelized.

A parallel version of T-Coffee was implemented by Zola and colleagues using a master-worker architecture and message passing to obtain an overall speedup of about 40 on a system with 80 CPUs (Zola, Yang, Rospondek, & Aluru, 2007). The parallelism comes mostly from distributing pairwise alignment tasks with dynamic scheduling for a near linear speedup during library generation. A sophisticated dynamic scheduling strategy is used that follows the guide tree, but almost no speedup is seen with more than 16 CPUs in the progressive alignment stage.

When all the DNA sequences are completed, these can now be used by scientists to find genes, which may explain the etiology of a specific disease. Nowadays, with the alignments executed in a reasonable amount of computation time using various algorithms, DNA sequencing can be more efficient and convenient than ever before.

SUPERCOMPUTERS IN GENOME ANNOTATION

Genome annotation is simply defined as the process of attaching biological information to sequences, and consists of several steps. The first step involves an extended form of physical mapping, attempting to convert the unknown portions of raw DNA into a set of easily recognized landmarks and reference points. Along with the 'gene finding', the major purpose of this step of annotation is to identify and place all known landmarks into the genome. The next step involves identifying the genomic DNA regions that encodes genes or otherwise known as 'gene prediction.' The last step simply involves the attachment of biological information to the predicted genes. The ultimate goal of high-quality genome annotation is to identify the key features of the genome, specifically their genes and gene products (Stein, 2001). Similar to sequencing, annotation of a massive amount of DNA sequence data requires computational tools for finding genes in DNA sequences. Generally, there are two interrelated types of genome annotation, structural and functional. Structural annotation involves delineating and demarcating the genomic elements (such as genes, promoters, and regulatory elements) while functional annotation involves assigning functions to structural elements (Bright, Burgess, Chowdhary, Swiderski, & McCarthy, 2009).

Finding genomic landmarks can be identified rapidly using the e-PCR program (Schuler, 1997) for short sequences. For longer sequences, such as the restriction-fragment length polymorphism markers, SSAHA (Ning, Cox, & Mullikin, 2001), and BLASTN (Altschul, Gish, Miller, Myers, & Lipman, 1990) are usually used (Stein, 2001). For gene prediction, several sophistical software algorithms have been devised in eukaryotic genomes, which include MZEF, HEXON, Grail, GENSCAN, Genie, and GeneMark.hmm (Stein, 2001).

Genome annotation is considered to be a crucial step for the extraction of useful information from genomes. BLAST is used as a basic level of annotation for finding similarities, and annotating genomes based on those similarities (Pevsner, 2009). In the recent years, annotation platforms have been designed to include more features to de-convolute discrepancies between genes that are given the same annotation. More than a decade of extensive efforts have been made in order to improve the annotation tools and obtaining novel experimental results, yet, despite these, there are still number of problems arising from available genome annotations (Warren, Archuleta, Feng, & Setubal, 2010). Such problems include the possible existence of genes that may be undetected, mis-annotated genes or with annotations that are too general to be of any use, and the presence of hypothetical genes without any functional assignment (Frishman, 2007; Galperin & Koonin, 2004; Roberts, 2004; Warren et al., 2010). Specifically, there have been reports that prokaryotic gene finder programs have problems with small genes

(either over-predicting or under-predicting). As such, a high-performance computing methodology was developed and utilized to investigate the problem. The BLASTP search was performed using miBLAST on Virginia Tech's System X supercomputer and the results labeled each query as a missing gene, an absent annotation, genomic artifact, or as an unclassified open reading frame (ORF) (Varadarajan, 2004). mpiBLAST parallelizes BLAST using database fragmentation, query segmentation (Darling, Carey, & Feng, 2003), parallel input-output (Lin, Ma, Chandramohan, Geist, & Samatova, 2005), and advanced scheduling (Thorsen et al., 2007). Using these, the study was able to identify 1,153 candidate genes that are missing from current genome annotations and uncovered 38,895 intergenic ORFs, readily identified as putative genes by similarity to currently annotated genes with the vast majority of the missing genes- in small number (less than 100 amino acid) (Warren et al., 2010).

A mature web tool for rapid and reliable display of any requested genome at any scale, together with several dozen aligned annotation tracks is provided at http://genome.ucsc.edu. This resolves the issue of effective genome annotation displaying assembly contigs and gaps, mRNA and expressed sequence tag alignments, multiple gene predictions, cross-species homologies, single nucleotide polymorphisms, sequence-tagged sites, radiation hybrid data, transposon repeats, and more as a stack of coregistered tracks (Kent et al., 2002).

Genome annotation is based primarily on the *ab initio* and homology methods. The ab *initio* method predicts genes directly from the genomic sequence using the computational properties of exons, introns, and other signature features without referencing the experimental data. FGENESH (Solovyev, Salamov, & Lawrence, 1995) (Salamov & Solovyev, 2000), GeneID (Parra, Blanco, & Guigo, 2000), GeneMark.hmm (Lukashin & Borodovsky, 1998), GeneView (Milanesi L., 1993), Genie (Reese, Kulp, Tammana, & Haussler, 2000), Grail (Xu, Mural, Shah, & Uberbacher, 1994),

GrailEXP_Perceval (Hyatt, 2000), HMMgene (Krogh, 1998) (Krogh, 2000), and MZEF (M. Q. Zhang, 1997) are some of the *ab initio* programs extensively used in genome annotation (Chuang et al., 2003).

The homology approach, on the other hand (Chuang et al., 2003), identifies genes with the aid of experimental data exploiting sequence alignment between the genomic data and known cDNA or protein databases (Chuang et al., 2003). Examples of this method constitute GeneBuilder (Milanesi L., 1993), GenomeScan (Yeh, Lim, & Burge, 2001), GeneWise (Birney & Durbin, 2000), Procrustes (Gelfand, Mironov, & Pevzner, 1996) (Sze & Pevzner, 1997) (Mironov, Roytberg, Pevzner, & Gelfand, 1998), GrailEXP_Gawain (Hyatt, 2000), GAIA (Bailey et al., 1998), AAT (X. Huang, Adams, Zhou, & Kerlavage, 1997), FGENESH+ and FGENESH++ (Salamov & Solovyev, 2000), and ICE (Pachter et al., 1999). Table 2 summarizes these genome annotation tools.

The homology approaches demand high performance computing and large storage space (Chuang et al., 2003) while the *ab initio* methods tends to have higher false positive predictions in annotating long genomic sequences with multiple genes (Dunham et al., 1999). Further, these methods are also known to require extensive manual interventions to curate true gene prediction from large sets of matched data. A new method was proposed called Complexity Reduction Algorithm for Sequence Analysis (CRASA), which does annotation of the genomic sequence on top of global alignment (Chuang et al., 2003). The method features a progressive data structure in hierarchical orders to facilitate a fast and efficient search mechanism. The results from the benchmark tests showed that CRASA annotation excelled in both the sensitivity and specificity categories (Chuang et al., 2003).

With more than a thousand human individuals and several model organisms whose genome sequences have been completed, genome annotation is considered to be a major challenge for scientists (Abecasis et al., 2012; Consortium, 2011). With the rapidly growing number of sequenced genomes, there is an exponential increase in the computing power needed to identify the genes and determine their functions and relationships. As such, scientists are trying to increase the efficiency of public and proprietary comparative genomics tools by an order of magnitude and implement them on high performance secure operating system clusters (www.hpcwire.com, 2006).

Over the years, a number of supercomputing centers have emerged to support sequence analysis and genome annotation analyses. Below are some examples of the supercomputing centers, which support sequence and genome annotation analyses.

San Diego Supercomputing Center (SDSC)

The SDSC was founded in 1985 with a self-prescribed mission of developing and using technology to advance science. Located on the campus of the University of California, San Diego, it houses advanced computing and networking resources and conducts research in computing technologies and computational sciences such as biology and chemistry. The center boasts with its SDSC Gordon Compute Cluster, a unique data-intensive supercomputer sponsored by the NSF XSEDE program, which went into production last January 1, 2012 (SDSC, 2014). The cluster does a wide variety of research including *de novo* genome assembly. The system is characterized by a 1,024 dual-socket Intel Sandy Bridge nodes, each with 64 GB DDR3–1333 memory. It has also over 300 TB of high performance Intel flash memory SSDs via 64 dual-socket Intel Westmere I/O nodes. The large memory supernodes are capable of presenting over 2 TB of cache coherent memory (SDSC, 2014). Recently, the Janssen Research and Development, LLC (Janssen), in collaboration with SDSC and the Scripps Translational Sci-

Table 2. Softwares used for genome annotation

Name	Description	Authors
Analysis and annotation tools (AAT)	Reduces the labor-intensive work of locating the exons of the query sequence and improves the process of defining the intron-exon boundaries by using the wealth of available protein and cDNA data	(X. Huang et al., 1997)
AnnotateGenomic-Regions	A web application that accepts genomic regions as input and outputs a selection of overlapping and/or neighboring genome annotations	(Zammataro, DeMolfetta, Bucci, Ceol, & Muller, 2014)
Artemis	Free genome browser and annotation tool that allows visualization of sequence features, next generation data and the results of analyses within the context of the sequence	(Rutherford et al., 2000)
Complexity Reduction Algorithm for Sequence Analysis (CRASA)	Has a large scale processing capability and a robust tool for genome annotation with high accuracy by matching expressed sequence tag (EST) sequences precisely to the genomic sequences.	(Chuang et al., 2003)
CruzDB	A fast and intuitive programmatic interface to the University of California, Santa Cruz (UCSC) genome browser that facilitates integrative analyses of diverse local and remotely hosted datasets.	(Pedersen, Yang, & De, 2013)
Database for Annotation, Visualization and Integrated Discovery (DAVID)	Provides functional interpretation of large lists of genes derived from genomic studies	(Huang da et al., 2007)
Encyclopedia of DNA elements (ENCODE)	Builds a comprehensive parts list of functional elements in the human genome, including elements that act at the protein and RNA levels, and regulatory elements that controls cells and circumstances in which a gene is active.	("The ENCODE (ENCyclopedia Of DNA Elements) Project," 2004)
Ensembl	Automatically annotate genome sequences, integrate these data with other biological information and to make the data readily available to scientists.	(Flicek et al., 2011)
FGENESH+ and FGENESHG++	Predicts protein-coding regions using linear discriminant functions.	(Solovyev et al., 1995)
Gene Ontology (GO)	De facto standard for functional annotation, and is routinely used as a basis for modeling and hypothesis testing, large functional genomic sets.	(Ashburner et al., 2000)
GeneBuilder	Based on the prediction of functional signals and coding regions by different approaches in combination with similarity searches in proteins and EST databases.	(Milanesi L., 1993)
GeneID	Predicts genes in anonymous genomic sequences with a hierarchical structure.	Parra, G., et al (Parra et al., 2000)
GeneMark.hmm	Based on heuristic methods producing fairly inhomogeneous Markov models of protein coding regions; could be used to find genes in small fragments of prokaryotic genomes and genomes of organelles, viruses, phages and plasmids, as well as highly inhomogeneous genomes where adjustment of models to local DNA composition is needed.	(Besemer & Borodovsky, 1999)
GeneView	Based on prediction of splice signals by classification approach and coding regions by dicodon statistic; constructs potential gene structure using dynamic programing approach.	(Milanesi L., 1993)
GeneWise	Used for combining gene prediction and homology searches providing reasonably accurate gene predictions.	(Birney & Durbin, 2000)
Genie	Robust Markov model system allowing for generalized information integration from different sources such as signal sensors (splice sites, start codon, etc.), content sensors (exons, introns, intergenic) and alignments of mRNA, EST, and peptide sequences; could be effectively used in the genome annotation of higher organisms	(Reese et al., 2000)

continued on following page

Table 2. Continued

Name	Description	Authors
Genome Annotation and Information Analysis (GAIA)	Uses a high-throughput, reliable annotation, called framework annotation, designed to provide a foundation for initial biologic characterization of previously unexamined sequence.	(Bailey et al., 1998)
GenomeScan	Gene identification algorithm, which combines exon-intron and splice signal models with similarity to known protein sequences in an integrated model.	(Yeh et al., 2001)
GenomeTools	A convenient and efficient software library and associated software tools for developing bioinformatics software intended to create, process or convert annotation graphs.	(Gremme, Steinbiss, & Kurtz, 2013)
GENSCAN	Identifies complete intron/exon structures of genes in genomic DNA; has the capacity to predict multiple genes in a sequence, to deal with partial or complete genes, and to predict consistent sets of genes occurring on either or both DNA strands.	(Burge & Karlin, 1997)
GRAIL	Used for evaluating the protein-coding potential of anonymous DNA sequences; creates a comprehensive analysis environment where a host of questions about genes and genome structure can be answered as quickly and accurately as possible	(Uberbacher & Mural, 1991) (Uberbacher, Xu, & Mural, 1996)
GrailEXP	Predicts exons, genes, promoters, polyas, CpG islands, EST similarities, and repetitive elements within DNA sequence	(Hyatt, 2000)
HEXON	Predicts internal exon sequences in human DNA based on a splice site algorithm that uses linear discriminant function to combine information about significant triplet frequencies of various functional parts of splice site regions and preferences of oligonucleotides in protein coding and intron regions.	(Solovyev, Salamov, & Lawrence, 1994)
HMMGene	Predicts genes in anonymous DNA based on hidden Markov model; predicts whole genes so the predicted exons always splice correctly; can predict several whole or partial genes in one sequence, so it can be used on whole cosmids or even longer sequences; can also be used to predict splice sites and start/stop codons.	(Krogh, 1997)
ICE	A fast and fully-automated dictionary-based approach to gene annotation and exon prediction.	(Pachter et al., 1999)
Jannovar	Stand-alone Java application as well as a Java library designed to be used in larger software frameworks for exome and genome analysis	(Jager et al., 2014)
Marinegenomics-DB	Provides open access to published data and a user-friendly environment for community-based manual gene annotation.	(Koyanagi et al., 2013)
Mercator	A fast and simple web server for genome scale functional annotation of plant sequence data	(Lohse et al., 2014)
MZEF	Predicts internal coding exons in genomic DNA sequences based on a prediction algorithm that uses the quadratic discriminant function for multivariate statistical pattern recognition.	(M. Q. Zhang, 1997)
OMIGA	Predicts protein-coding genes from insect genomes.	(Liu, Xiao, Huang, & Li, 2014)
PANNOTATOR	A web-based automated pipeline for the annotation of closely related and well-suited genomes for pan-genome studies, aiming at reducing the manual work to generate reports and corrections of various genome strains.	(Santos et al., 2013)
Parallel-META 2.0	A metagenomic analysis software package for efficient and fast analyses of taxonomical and functional structures for microbial communities.	(Su, Pan, Song, Xu, & Ning, 2014)
Procrustes	Uses related proteins and cDNA for gene identifications and gene annotation-quality gene predictions based on splice alignment algorithm which explores all possible exon assemblies and finds the multi-exon structure with the best fit to a related protein.	(Gelfand et al., 1996), (Sze & Pevzner, 1997), (Mironov et al., 1998)
Prokka	A command line software tool to fully annotate a draft bacterial genome in about 10 min on a typical desktop computer.	(Seemann, 2014)

continued on following page

Table 1. Continued

Name	Description	Authors
ShortStack	A program that was developed to comprehensively analyze reference-aligned small RNA-seq data, and output detailed and useful annotations of the causal small RNA-producing genes.	(Shahid & Axtell, 2013)
Variobox	A desktop tool to annotate, analyze, and compare human genes	(Gaspar et al., 2014)

ence Institute (STSI) utilized Gordon to launch a project of conducting whole-genome sequencing of 438 patients with rheumatoid arthritis to better understand the disease, as well as explore the genetic factors of patient responses to a specific biologic therapy currently marketed by Janssen in the US (Zverina, 2014).

National Energy Research Scientific Computing (NERSC)

The NERSC is a facility operated by the Lawrence Berkeley National Laboratory and the Department of Energy. It recently accepted "Edison," a new flagship supercomputer designed for scientific productivity. Named in honor of the American inventor Thomas Alva Edison, the Cray XC30 has 332 terabytes memory, 2.39 petaflop/second peak performance, 124,608 processing cores, and a 7.56 petabytes disk storage. Edison specializes in data analyses including genome sequencing and molecular screening programs, which involve high throughput computing (Rath, 2014).

Intel Corporation

Intel houses many of the world's fastest supercomputers including the new world's fastest supercomputer powered by Intel® Xeon PhiTM coprocessors. Intel processors power more than 80% of all systems on Top500 list of world's most powerful supercomputers including 98% of new listed systems (Intel, 2013). Intel is also house for the Endeavor – Intel Cluster, an Intel Xeon

E5-2697v2 12C 2.700GHz, Infiniband FDR, consisting of 51,392 cores, 758.9 TFlop/s Linpack performance (Rmax), 387.20 kW power, and a 22,528 GB memory (Top500, 2013).

Department of Energy (DOE)/ National Nuclear Security Administration (NNSA)/Los Alamos National Laboratory (LANL)

The DOE/NNSA/LANL boast with the Road-Runner, a BladeCenter QS22/LS21 Cluster with 122,400 cores, 1,026.0 TFlop/s Linpack Performance, and a 2,345.00 kW power. Roadrunner was ranked 1st in the Top500 supercomputers in the world in 2008 (Top500, 2008). It was used to create the largest HIV evolutionary tree. The goal was to identify common features of the transmitted virus, and attempted to create a vaccine that enables recognition the original transmitted virus before the body's immune response causes the virus to react and mutate (DOE/LANL, 2009).

Iowa State University Supercomputing Center

The ISU is home to the IBM Blue Gene/L supercomputer with 1024 dual-core PPC 440 CPU, 5.7 TF peak performance, and 11 TB data storage (ISU, 2006). It has been used for wide variety of computational biology research including assembling the corn genome and studying protein networks (Aluru, 2006).

CHALLENGES AND SOLUTIONS

Datasets of hundreds of genomes are becoming common and it is believed that their sizes will only increase in the future. MSA of hundreds of genomes are becoming an intractable problem due to the quadratic increases in computation time and memory footprint. Majority of alignment algorithms to date are designed for commodity clusters without parallelism. Thus, it is necessary to come up with alignment algorithms to enable comparison of hundreds instead of few genome sequences within reasonable time. Church and colleagues (Church et al., 2011) implemented a design of MSA algorithms on massively parallel, distributed memory supercomputers to enable researchers do comparative genomics on large datasets. In their work, they followed the methodology of sequential progressive Mauve algorithm and designed data structures including sequences and sorted k-mer lists on the IBM Blue Gene/P supercomputer (BG/P). Their results show that they can reduce the memory footprint to potentially align over 250 bacterial genomes on a single BG/P compute mode. Thus, their results matched those of the original algorithm but in a shorter ½ time and with ¼ the memory footprint for scaffold building (Church et al., 2011).

Vermij (Vermij, 2011), on the other hand, implemented the well-known Smith-Waterman (SW) optimal local alignment algorithm on the HC-1 hybrid supercomputer from Convey Computer. The platform features four FPGAs, which can be used to accelerate the problem of dealing with large volume of datasets in genetic sequence alignment. The FPGAs, and the CPU that control them, live in the same virtual memory space and share one large memory. The solution allows a sustainable peak performance, being able to align sequences of any length, FPGA area efficient computations and the cancellation of unnecessary workload. The resulting SW FPGA core can run at 100% utilization for many alignments long. Further, they are packed per six on a FPGA running on 150 MHz resulting in a full system performance of 460 GCUPS (billion elementary operations per second). The elementary processing element can also deliver double the work per clock cycle than a naïve implementation, resulting in a better throughput per area ratio (Vermij, 2011).

In the context of sequence alignment, which adds to the computational burden, is the issue of very-large pattern-matching search. Pattern matching in the presence of noise and uncertainty is an important computational problem in a variety of fields. It is widely used in the field of bioinformatics, and in that context, DNA or amino acid sequences are typically compared with a genetic database. In order to achieve efficient parallelism in a single very large pattern-matching search using a supercomputer cluster of GPUs, reformulation of the SW algorithm was performed, modifying it in order to reduce inter-GPU communication (Khajeh-Saeed & Blair Perot, 2011).

FUTURE RESEARCH DIRECTIONS

As the uses of supercomputers to address important problems in the society such as research in sequence analysis and genome annotation continue to grow and the place of supercomputing within the overall computing industry continues to change, the value of innovation in supercomputing architecture, modeling systems software, applications software, and algorithms will endure (Academies, 2003). Optimization of algorithm further such as in sequence alignment by combining several steps into a single GPU call is one of the approaches in reducing computational time in sequence alignment. The key approach is being able to synchronize the threads within the kernel, because each step of the algorithm such as in SW must be entirely completed (for all threads) before the next step can be executed (Khajeh-Saeed & Blair Perot, 2011).

CONCLUSION

Sequence alignment and genome annotation are among the most commonly used techniques in the area of genetics and bioinformatics. With the emergence of a large sequence of genomic data, scientists are confronted with computational burden in these two fields. Supercomputers facilitate in the ease of analyses in these two areas by reducing computational time. Synchronizing the threads in supercomputing processes and the use of massively parallel, distributed memory supercomputers enable researchers to do comparative genomics on large datasets, eventually reducing computational time.

REFERENCES

Abecasis, G. R., Auton, A., Brooks, L. D., De-Pristo, M. A., Durbin, R. M., & Handsaker, R. E. et al. (2012). An integrated map of genetic variation from 1,092 human genomes. *Nature*, *491*(7422), 56–65. doi:10.1038/nature11632 PMID:23128226

Academies, T. N. (2003). *The future of supercomputing: An interim report* (p. 4). Washington, DC: National Academy of Sciences.

Agrawal, A. (2008). *A new heuristic for multiple sequence alignment.* Paper presented at the Institute of Electrical and Electronics Engineers International Conference, Ames, IA. doi:10.1109/EIT.2008.4554299

Altschul, S. F., Gish, W., Miller, W., Myers, E. W., & Lipman, D. J. (1990). Basic local alignment search tool. *Journal of Molecular Biology*, *215*(3), 403–410. doi:10.1016/S0022-2836(05)80360-2 PMID:2231712

Aluru, S. (2006). *A supercomputer for Iowa State University*. Retrieved April 17, 2014, from http://www.public.iastate.edu/~nscentral/news/06/jan/supercomputer.shtml

Anderson, S. (1981). Shotgun DNA sequencing using cloned DNase I-generated fragments. *Nucleic Acids Research*, *9*(13), 3015–3027. doi:10.1093/nar/9.13.3015 PMID:6269069

Ashburner, M., Ball, C. A., Blake, J. A., Botstein, D., Butler, H., & Cherry, J. M. et al. (2000). Gene ontology: Tool for the unification of biology: The gene ontology consortium. *Nature Genetics*, *25*(1), 25–29. doi:10.1038/75556 PMID:10802651

Ashkenazy, H., Erez, E., Martz, E., Pupko, T., & Ben-Tal, N. (2010). ConSurf 2010: Calculating evolutionary conservation in sequence and structure of proteins and nucleic acids. *Nucleic Acids Research*, *38*(Web Server issue), W529-533. doi:10.1093/nar/gkq399

Bailey, L. C. Jr, Fischer, S., Schug, J., Crabtree, J., Gibson, M., & Overton, G. C. (1998). GAIA: Framework annotation of genomic sequence. *Genome Research*, *8*(3), 234–250. doi:10.1101/gr.8.3.234 PMID:9521927

Baron, H. A. (n.d.). *BOXSHADE*. Retrieved January 3, 2013, from http://mobyle.pasteur.fr/cgi-bin/portal.py?-forms:boxshade

Benson, D. A., Cavanaugh, M., Clark, K., Karsch-Mizrachi, I., Lipman, D. J., Ostell, J., & Sayers, E. W. (2013). GenBank. *Nucleic Acids Research*, *41*(Database issue), D36–D42. doi:10.1093/nar/gks1195 PMID:23193287

Besemer, J., & Borodovsky, M. (1999). Heuristic approach to deriving models for gene finding. *Nucleic Acids Research*, *27*(19), 3911–3920. doi:10.1093/nar/27.19.3911 PMID:10481031

Birney, E., & Durbin, R. (2000). Using Gene-Wise in the Drosophila annotation experiment. *Genome Research*, *10*(4), 547–548. doi:10.1101/gr.10.4.547 PMID:10779496

Braberg, H., Webb, B. M., Tjioe, E., Pieper, U., Sali, A., & Madhusudhan, M. S. (2012). SALIGN: A web server for alignment of multiple protein sequences and structures. *Bioinformatics (Oxford, England)*, *28*(15), 2072–2073. doi:10.1093/bioinformatics/bts302 PMID:22618536

Bright, L. A., Burgess, S. C., Chowdhary, B., Swiderski, C. E., & McCarthy, F. M. (2009). Structural and functional-annotation of an equine whole genome oligoarray. *BMC Bioinformatics*, *10*(Suppl 11), S8. doi:10.1186/1471-2105-10-S11-S8 PMID:19811692

Brodie, R., Roper, R. L., & Upton, C. (2004). JDotter: A Java interface to multiple dotplots generated by dotter. *Bioinformatics (Oxford, England)*, *20*(2), 279–281. doi:10.1093/bioinformatics/btg406 PMID:14734323

Brodsky, L. I., & Vasiliev, A. V., Ya, L. K., Osipov, Y. S., Tatuzov, R. L., & Feranchuk, S. I. (1992). GeneBee: The program package for biopolymer structure analysis. *Dimacs*, *8*, 127–139.

Brown, N. (1996). *Consensus*. Retrieved January 1, 2013, from http://coot.embl.de/Alignment/consensus.html

Brown, S. M., & Joubert, F. (n.d.). *Pairwise sequence alignment*. Retrieved February 10, 2013, from http://www.med.nyu.edu/rcr/rcr/course/PairAlign.ppt

Bu, J., Chi, X., & Jin, Z. (2013). HSA: A heuristic splice alignment tool. *BMC Systems Biology*, *7*(Suppl 2), S10. doi:10.1186/1752-0509-7-S2-S10 PMID:24564867

Burge, C., & Karlin, S. (1997). Prediction of complete gene structures in human genomic DNA. *Journal of Molecular Biology*, *268*(1), 78–94. doi:10.1006/jmbi.1997.0951 PMID:9149143

Chang, J. M., Di Tommaso, P., Taly, J. F., & Notredame, C. (2012). Accurate multiple sequence alignment of transmembrane proteins with PSI-Coffee. *BMC Bioinformatics*, *13*(Suppl 4), S1. doi:10.1186/1471-2105-13-S4-S1 PMID:22536955

Chen, E. Y. (1994). The efficiency of automated DNA sequencing. In Automated DNA sequencing and analysis. London: Academic Press Limited.

Chuang, T. J., Lin, W. C., Lee, H. C., Wang, C. W., Hsiao, K. L., & Wang, Z. H. et al. (2003). A complexity reduction algorithm for analysis and annotation of large genomic sequences. *Genome Research*, *13*(2), 313–322. doi:10.1101/gr.313703 PMID:12566410

Church, P. C., Goscinski, A., Holt, K., Inouye, M., Ghoting, A., Makarychev, K., & Reumann, M. (2011). Design of multiple sequence alignment algorithms on parallel, distributed memory supercomputers. In *Proceedings of the Institute of Electrical and Electronics Engineers Engineering in Medicine and Biology Society* (pp. 924-927). Academic Press. doi:10.1109/IEMBS.2011.6090208

Ciria, R., Abreu-Goodger, C., Morett, E., & Merino, E. (2004). GeConT: Gene context analysis. *Bioinformatics (Oxford, England)*, *20*(14), 2307–2308. doi:10.1093/bioinformatics/bth216 PMID:15073003

Consortium, T. E. P. (2011). A user's guide to the encyclopedia of DNA elements (ENCODE). *PLoS Biology*, *9*(4), e1001046. doi:10.1371/journal.pbio.1001046 PMID:21526222

Corpet, F. (1988). Multiple sequence alignment with hierarchical clustering. *Nucleic Acids Research*, *16*(22), 10881–10890. doi:10.1093/nar/16.22.10881 PMID:2849754

Darling, A. E., Carey, L., & Feng, W. (2003). The design, implementation, and evaluation of mpiBLAST. In *Proceedings of 4th International Conference on Linux Clusters: The HPC Revolution 2003*. San Jose, CA: mpiBLAST.

Di Tommaso, P., Moretti, S., Xenarios, I., Orobitg, M., Montanyola, A., Chang, J. M., . . . Notredame, C. (2011). T-coffee: A web server for the multiple sequence alignment of protein and RNA sequences using structural information and homology extension. *Nucleic Acids Research, 39*(Web Server issue), W13-17. doi: 10.1093/nar/gkr245

Do, C. B., Mahabhashyam, M. S., Brudno, M., & Batzoglou, S. (2005). ProbCons: Probabilistic consistency-based multiple sequence alignment. *Genome Research, 15*(2), 330–340. doi:10.1101/gr.2821705 PMID:15687296

DOE/LANL. (2009). *Scientists use world's fastest supercomputer to create the largest HIV evolutionary tree*. Retrieved April 17, 2014, from http://www.sciencedaily.com/releases/2009/10/091027161536.htm

Dunham, I., Shimizu, N., Roe, B. A., Chissoe, S., Hunt, A. R., & Collins, J. E. et al. (1999). The DNA sequence of human chromosome 22. *Nature, 402*(6761), 489–495. doi:10.1038/990031 PMID:10591208

Dunn, J. J., Studier, F. W., & Gottesman, M. (1983). Complete nucleotide sequence of bacteriophage T7 DNA and the locations of T7 genetic elements. *Journal of Molecular Biology, 166*(4), 477–535. doi:10.1016/S0022-2836(83)80282-4 PMID:6864790

Duret, L., Gasteiger, E., & Perriere, G. (1996). LALNVIEW: A graphical viewer for pairwise sequence alignments. *Computer Applications in the Biosciences, 12*(6), 507–510. PMID:9021269

Dutheil, J. Y., Gaillard, S., & Stukenbrock, E. H. (2014). MafFilter: A highly flexible and extensible multiple genome alignment files processor. *BMC Genomics, 15*(1), 53. doi:10.1186/1471-2164-15-53 PMID:24447531

ENCODE. (2004). The ENCODE (encyclopedia of DNA elements) project. *Science, 306*(5696), 636–640. doi:10.1126/science.1105136 PMID:15499007

Fan, L., Hui, J. H., Yu, Z. G., & Chu, K. H. (2014). VIP barcoding: Composition vector-based software for rapid species identification based on DNA barcoding. *Molecular Ecology Resources, 14*(4), 871–881. doi:10.1111/1755-0998.12235 PMID:24479510

Flicek, P., Amode, M. R., Barrell, D., Beal, K., Brent, S., & Chen, Y. et al. (2011). Ensembl 2011. *Nucleic Acids Research, 39*(Database issue), D800–D806. doi:10.1093/nar/gkq1064 PMID:21045057

Frazer, K. A., Pachter, L., Poliakov, A., Rubin, E. M., & Dubchak, I. (2004). VISTA: computational tools for comparative genomics. *Nucleic Acids Research, 32*(Web Server issue), W273-279. doi: 10.1093/nar/gkh458

Frishman, D. (2007). Protein annotation at genomic scale: The current status. *Chemical Reviews, 107*(8), 3448–3466. doi:10.1021/cr068303k PMID:17658902

Galperin, M. Y., & Koonin, E. V. (2004). 'Conserved hypothetical' proteins: Prioritization of targets for experimental study. *Nucleic Acids Research, 32*(18), 5452–5463. doi:10.1093/nar/gkh885 PMID:15479782

Gaspar, P., Lopes, P., Oliveira, J., Santos, R., Dalgleish, R., & Oliveira, J. L. (2014). Variobox: Automatic detection and annotation of human genetic variants. *Human Mutation, 35*(2), 202–207. doi:10.1002/humu.22474 PMID:24186831

Gelfand, M. S., Mironov, A. A., & Pevzner, P. A. (1996). Gene recognition via spliced sequence alignment. *Proceedings of the National Academy of Sciences of the United States of America*, *93*(17), 9061–9066. doi:10.1073/pnas.93.17.9061 PMID:8799154

Gille, C., Birgit, W., & Gille, A. (2014). Sequence alignment visualization in HTML5 without Java. *Bioinformatics (Oxford, England)*, *30*(1), 121–122. doi:10.1093/bioinformatics/btt614 PMID:24273246

Godzik, A. (2012). *FFAS fold and function alignment*. Retrieved December 30, 2012, from http://ffas.sanfordburnham.org/ffas-cgi/cgi/ffas.pl

Gouet, P., Courcelle, E., Stuart, D. I., & Metoz, F. (1999). ESPript: Analysis of multiple sequence alignments in PostScript. *Bioinformatics (Oxford, England)*, *15*(4), 305–308. doi:10.1093/bioinformatics/15.4.305 PMID:10320398

Gremme, G., Steinbiss, S., & Kurtz, S. (2013). GenomeTools: A comprehensive software library for efficient processing of structured genome annotations. *Institute of Electrical and Electronics Engineers/Association for Computing Machinery Transactions on Computatonal Biology and Bioinformatics*, *10*(3), 645-656. doi: 10.1109/TCBB.2013.68

HPC Service Will be Used for Genome Annotation System. (2006). Retrieved January 20, 2013, from http://www.hpcwire.com

Huang, S., Zhang, J., Li, R., Zhang, W., He, Z., & Lam, T. W. et al. (2011). SOAPsplice: Genome-wide ab initio detection of splice junctions from RNA-Seq data. *Frontiers in Genetics*, *2*, 46. doi:10.3389/fgene.2011.00046 PMID:22303342

Huang, X., Adams, M. D., Zhou, H., & Kerlavage, A. R. (1997). A tool for analyzing and annotating genomic sequences. *Genomics*, *46*(1), 37–45. doi:10.1006/geno.1997.4984 PMID:9403056

Huang, X., & Miller, W. (1991). A time-efficient linear-space local similarity algorithm. *Advances in Applied Mathematics*, *12*(3), 337–357. doi:10.1016/0196-8858(91)90017-D

Huang da, W., Sherman, B. T., Tan, Q., Kir, J., Liu, D., Bryant, D., . . . Lempicki, R. A. (2007). Bioinformatics resources: Expanded annotation database and novel algorithms to better extract biology from large gene lists. *Nucleic Acids Research*, *35*(Web Server issue), W169-175. doi: 10.1093/nar/gkm415

Hyatt, D., Snoddy, J., Schmoyer, D., Chen, G., Fischer, K., Parang, M., et al. (2000). Improved analysis and annotation tools for whole-genome computational annotation and analysis: GRAIL-EXP genome analysis toolkit and related analysis tools. In *Genome Sequencing & Biology Meeting*. Information, N. C. f. B. Align sequences nucleotide BLAST. Retrieved December 30, 2012, from http://blast.ncbi.nlm.nih.gov/

Information, N. C. f. B. (2011). *GenBank*. Retrieved December 28, 2012

Intel. (2013). *Intel powers the world's fastest supercomputer, reveals new and future high performance computing technologies*. Retrieved April 17, 2014, from http://www.intc.com/releasedetail.cfm?ReleaseID=774058

ISU. (2006). *CyBlue - Blue gene supercomputer*. Retrieved April 17, 2014, from http://bluegene.ece.iastate.edu

Jager, M., Wang, K., Bauer, S., Smedley, D., Krawitz, P., & Robinson, P. N. (2014). Jannovar: A Java library for exome annotation. *Human Mutation*, *35*(5), 548–555. doi:10.1002/humu.22531 PMID:24677618

Jaroszewski, L., Li, Z., Cai, X. H., Weber, C., & Godzik, A. (2011). FFAS server: Novel features and applications. *Nucleic Acids Research*, *39*(Web Server issue), W38-44. doi:10.1093/nar/gkr441

Jeon, Y. S., Lee, K., Park, S. C., Kim, B. S., Cho, Y. J., Ha, S. M., & Chun, J. (2014). EzEditor: A versatile sequence alignment editor for both rRNA- and protein-coding genes. *International Journal of Systematic and Evolutionary Microbiology*, *64*(Pt 2), 689–691. doi:10.1099/ijs.0.059360-0 PMID:24425826

Junier, T., & Pagni, M. (2000). Dotlet: Diagonal plots in a web browser. *Bioinformatics (Oxford, England)*, *16*(2), 178–179. doi:10.1093/bioinformatics/16.2.178 PMID:10842741

Kent, W. J., Sugnet, C. W., Furey, T. S., Roskin, K. M., Pringle, T. H., Zahler, A. M., & Haussler, D. (2002). The human genome browser at UCSC. *Genome Research, 12*(6), 996-1006. doi: 10.1101/gr.229102

Khajeh-Saeed, A., & Blair Perot, J. (2011). GPU-supercomputer acceleration of pattern matching. In W. W. Hwu (Ed.), *GPU computing gems* (Vol. 2, pp. 185–198). Morgan Kaufmann. doi:10.1016/B978-0-12-384988-5.00013-9

Kim, D., Pertea, G., Trapnell, C., Pimentel, H., Kelley, R., & Salzberg, S. L. (2013). TopHat2: Accurate alignment of transcriptomes in the presence of insertions, deletions and gene fusions. *Genome Biology*, *14*(4), R36. doi:10.1186/gb-2013-14-4-r36 PMID:23618408

Kleinjung, J., Douglas, N., & Heringa, J. (2002). Parallelized multiple alignment. *Bioinformatics (Oxford, England)*, *18*(9), 1270–1271. doi:10.1093/bioinformatics/18.9.1270 PMID:12217922

Koyanagi, R., Takeuchi, T., Hisata, K., Gyoja, F., Shoguchi, E., Satoh, N., & Kawashima, T. (2013). MarinegenomicsDB: An integrated genome viewer for community-based annotation of genomes. *Zoological Science*, *30*(10), 797–800. doi:10.2108/zsj.30.797 PMID:24125644

Krogh, A. (1997). Two methods for improving performance of an HMM and their application for gene finding. *Proceedings of the International Conference on Intelligent Systems for Molecular Biology*, *5*, 179–186. PMID:9322033

Krogh, A. (1998). An introduction to hidden Markov models for biological sequences. In Computational methods in molecular biology (pp. 45-63). Amsterdam: Elsevier. doi:10.1016/S0167-7306(08)60461-5

Krogh, A. (2000). Using database matches with for HMMGene for automated gene detection in Drosophila. *Genome Research*, *10*(4), 523–528. doi:10.1101/gr.10.4.523 PMID:10779492

Larkin, M. A., Blackshields, G., Brown, N. P., Chenna, R., McGettigan, P. A., & McWilliam, H. et al. (2007). Clustal W and Clustal X version 2.0. *Bioinformatics (Oxford, England)*, *23*(21), 2947–2948. doi:10.1093/bioinformatics/btm404 PMID:17846036

Lin, H., Ma, X., Chandramohan, P., Geist, A., & Samatova, N. (2005). *Efficient data access for parallel BLAST*. Academic Press.

Liu, J., Xiao, H., Huang, S., & Li, F. (2014). OMIGA: Optimized maker-based insect genome annotation. *Molecular Genetics and Genomics*, *289*(4), 567–573. doi:10.1007/s00438-014-0831-7 PMID:24609470

Lloyd, S. (2010). *Parallel multiple sequence alignment: An overview*. Retrieved January 6, 2013, from http://dna.cs.byu.edu/msa/overview.pdf

Lohse, M., Nagel, A., Herter, T., May, P., Schroda, M., & Zrenner, R. et al. (2014). Mercator: A fast and simple web server for genome scale functional annotation of plant sequence data. *Plant, Cell & Environment*, *37*(5), 1250–1258. doi:10.1111/pce.12231 PMID:24237261

Loytynoja, A. (2014). Phylogeny-aware alignment with PRANK. *Methods in Molecular Biology (Clifton, N.J.), 1079*, 155–170. doi:10.1007/978-1-62703-646-7_10 PMID:24170401

Loytynoja, A., & Goldman, N. (2010). web-PRANK: A phylogeny-aware multiple sequence aligner with interactive alignment browser. *BMC Bioinformatics, 11*(1), 579. doi:10.1186/1471-2105-11-579 PMID:21110866

Lukashin, A. V., & Borodovsky, M. (1998). GeneMark.hmm: New solutions for gene finding. *Nucleic Acids Research, 26*(4), 1107–1115. doi:10.1093/nar/26.4.1107 PMID:9461475

Ma, J., Wang, S., Wang, Z., & Xu, J. (2014). MRFalign: Protein homology detection through alignment of markov random fields. *PLoS Computational Biology, 10*(3), e1003500. doi:10.1371/journal.pcbi.1003500 PMID:24675572

Mahadevan, P., King, J. F., & Seto, D. (2009a). CGUG: In silico proteome and genome parsing tool for the determination of "core" and unique genes in the analysis of genomes up to ca. 1.9 Mb. *BMC Research Notes, 2*(1), 168. doi:10.1186/1756-0500-2-168 PMID:19706165

Mahadevan, P., King, J. F., & Seto, D. (2009b). Data mining pathogen genomes using GeneOrder and CoreGenes and CGUG: Gene order, synteny and in silico proteomes. *International Journal of Computational Biology and Drug Design, 2*(1), 100–114. doi:10.1504/IJCBDD.2009.027586 PMID:20054988

Mahadevan, P., & Seto, D. (2010). Rapid pairwise synteny analysis of large bacterial genomes using web-based GeneOrder4.0. *BMC Research Notes, 3*(1), 41. doi:10.1186/1756-0500-3-41 PMID:20178631

Maxam, A. M., & Gilbert, W. (1977). A new method for sequencing DNA. *Proceedings of the National Academy of Sciences of the United States of America, 74*(2), 560–564. doi:10.1073/pnas.74.2.560 PMID:265521

Mazumder, R., Kolaskar, A., & Seto, D. (2001). GeneOrder: Comparing the order of genes in small genomes. *Bioinformatics (Oxford, England), 17*(2), 162–166. doi:10.1093/bioinformatics/17.2.162 PMID:11238072

Milanesi, L. K. N. A., Rogozin, I. B., Ischenko, I. V., Kel, A. E., Orlov Yu, L., Ponomarenko, M. P., & Vezzoni, P. (1993). GenView: A computing tool for protein-coding regions prediction in nucleotide sequences. In *Proceedings of the Second International Conference on Bioinformatics, Supercomputing and Complex Genome Analysis*. Singapore: World Scientific Publishing. doi:10.1142/9789814503655_0048

Mironov, A. A., Roytberg, M. A., Pevzner, P. A., & Gelfand, M. S. (1998). Performance-guarantee gene predictions via spliced alignment. *Genomics, 51*(3), 332–339. doi:10.1006/geno.1998.5251 PMID:9721203

Morgenstern, B. (2014). Multiple sequence alignment with DIALIGN. *Methods in Molecular Biology (Clifton, N.J.), 1079*, 191–202. doi:10.1007/978-1-62703-646-7_12 PMID:24170403

Mount, D. M. (2004). *Bioinformatics: sequence and genome analysis* (2nd ed.). Cold Springs Harbor, NY: Cold Springs Harbor Laboratory Press.

Ning, Z., Cox, A. J., & Mullikin, J. C. (2001). SSAHA: A fast search method for large DNA databases. *Genome Research, 11*(10), 1725–1729. doi:10.1101/gr.194201 PMID:11591649

Noe, L., & Kucherov, G. (2005). YASS: Enhancing the sensitivity of DNA similarity search. *Nucleic Acids Research, 33*(Web Server issue), W540-543. doi: 10.1093/nar/gki478

Ovcharenko, I., Loots, G. G., Hardison, R. C., Miller, W., & Stubbs, L. (2004). zPicture: Dynamic alignment and visualization tool for analyzing conservation profiles. *Genome Research, 14*(3), 472–477. doi:10.1101/gr.2129504 PMID:14993211

Pachter, L., Batzoglou, S., Spitkovsky, V. I., Banks, E., Lander, E. S., Kleitman, D. J., & Berger, B. (1999). A dictionary-based approach for gene annotation. *Journal of Computational Biology, 6*(3-4), 419–430. doi:10.1089/106652799318364 PMID:10582576

Paquete, L., Matias, P., Abbasi, M., & Pinheiro, M. (2014). MOSAL: Software tools for multiobjective sequence alignment. *Source Code for Biology and Medicine, 9*(1), 2. doi:10.1186/1751-0473-9-2 PMID:24401750

Parra, G., Blanco, E., & Guigo, R. (2000). GeneID in drosophila. *Genome Research, 10*(4), 511–515. doi:10.1101/gr.10.4.511 PMID:10779490

Pearson, W. (1991). *LALIGN - Find mulitple matching subsegments in two sequences.* Retrieved December 29, 2012, from http://www.ch.embnet. org/software/LALIGN_form.html

Pearson, W. R. (2006a). *FASTA sequence comparison at the University of Virginia.* Retrieved December 30, 2012, from http://fasta.bioch.virginia.edu/fasta_www2/fasta_www.cgi?rm=lalign

Pearson, W. R. (2006b). *LALIGN/PLALIGN.* Retrieved December 30, 2012, from http:// fasta.bioch.virginia.edu/fasta_www2/fasta_www.cgi?rm=lalign

Pedersen, B. S., Yang, I. V., & De, S. (2013). CruzDB: Software for annotation of genomic intervals with UCSC genome-browser database. *Bioinformatics (Oxford, England), 29*(23), 3003–3006. doi:10.1093/bioinformatics/btt534 PMID:24037212

Pei, J., & Grishin, N. V. (2007). PROMALS: Towards accurate multiple sequence alignments of distantly related proteins. *Bioinformatics (Oxford, England), 23*(7), 802–808. doi:10.1093/bioinformatics/btm017 PMID:17267437

Penn, O., Privman, E., Ashkenazy, H., Landan, G., Graur, D., & Pupko, T. (2010). GUIDANCE: A web server for assessing alignment confidence scores. *Nucleic Acids Research, 38*(Web Server issue), W23-28. doi: 10.1093/nar/gkq443

Pevsner, J. (2009). *Bioinformatics and functional genomics.* Hoboken, NJ: Wiley-Blackwell. doi:10.1002/9780470451496

Plewniak, F., Bianchetti, L., Brelivet, Y., Carles, A., Chalmel, F., & Lecompte, O. et al. (2003). PipeAlign: A new toolkit for protein family analysis. *Nucleic Acids Research, 31*(13), 3829–3832. doi:10.1093/nar/gkg518 PMID:12824430

Portal, E. B. R. (n.d.). *SIM - Alignment tool for protein sequences.* Retrieved December 30, 2012, from http://web.expasy.org/sim/

Puckelwartz, M. J., Pesce, L. L., Nelakuditi, V., Dellefave-Castillo, L., Golbus, J. R., & Day, S. M. et al. (2014). Supercomputing for the parallelization of whole genome analysis. *Bioinformatics (Oxford, England), 30*(11), 1508–1513. doi:10.1093/bioinformatics/btu071 PMID:24526712

Rath, J. (2014). *NERSC flips the switch on new Edison supercomputer.* Retrieved April 17, 2014, from http://www.datacenterknowledge.com/archives/2014/01/31/nersc-flips-switch-new-edison-supercomputer/

Reese, M. G., Kulp, D., Tammana, H., & Haussler, D. (2000). Genie--gene finding in Drosophila melanogaster. *Genome Research, 10*(4), 529–538. doi:10.1101/gr.10.4.529 PMID:10779493

Rice, P., Longden, I., & Bleasby, A. (2000). EMBOSS: The European molecular biology open software suite. *Trends in Genetics, 16*(6), 276–277. doi:10.1016/S0168-9525(00)02024-2 PMID:10827456

Roberts, R. J. (2004). Identifying protein function--A call for community action. *PLoS Biology, 2*(3), E42. doi:10.1371/journal.pbio.0020042 PMID:15024411

Russell, D. J. (2014). GramAlign: Fast alignment driven by grammar-based phylogeny. *Methods in Molecular Biology (Clifton, N.J.), 1079*, 171–189. doi:10.1007/978-1-62703-646-7_11 PMID:24170402

Rutherford, K., Parkhill, J., Crook, J., Horsnell, T., Rice, P., Rajandream, M. A., & Barrell, B. (2000). Artemis: Sequence visualization and annotation. *Bioinformatics (Oxford, England), 16*(10), 944–945. doi:10.1093/bioinformatics/16.10.944 PMID:11120685

Salamov, A. A., & Solovyev, V. V. (2000). Ab initio gene finding in Drosophila genomic DNA. *Genome Research, 10*(4), 516–522. doi:10.1101/gr.10.4.516 PMID:10779491

Sanger, F., Nicklen, S., & Coulson, A. R. (1977). DNA sequencing with chain-terminating inhibitors. *Proceedings of the National Academy of Sciences of the United States of America, 74*(12), 5463–5467. doi:10.1073/pnas.74.12.5463 PMID:271968

Santos, A. R., Barbosa, E., Fiaux, K., Zurita-Turk, M., Chaitankar, V., & Kamapantula, B. et al. (2013). PANNOTATOR: An automated tool for annotation of pan-genomes. *Genetics and Molecular Research, 12*(3), 2982–2989. doi:10.4238/2013.August.16.2 PMID:24065654

Schmutz, J., Grimwood, J., & Myers, R. M. (2004). Sequence finishing. *Methods in Molecular Biology (Clifton, N.J.), 255*, 333–342. doi:10.1385/1-59259-752-1:333 PMID:15020836

Schnattinger, T., Schoning, U., Marchfelder, A., & Kestler, H. A. (2013). RNA-Pareto: Interactive analysis of Pareto-optimal RNA sequence-structure alignments. *Bioinformatics (Oxford, England), 29*(23), 3102–3104. doi:10.1093/bioinformatics/btt536 PMID:24045774

Schuler, G. D. (1997). Sequence mapping by electronic PCR. *Genome Research, 7*(5), 541–550. PMID:9149949

Schwartz, S., Zhang, Z., Frazer, K. A., Smit, A., Riemer, C., & Bouck, J. et al. (2000). PipMaker--a web server for aligning two genomic DNA sequences. *Genome Research, 10*(4), 577–586. doi:10.1101/gr.10.4.577 PMID:10779500

SDSC. (2014). *San Diego supercompuer center.* Retrieved April 17, 2014, from http://www.sdsc.edu/supercomputing/gordon/

Seemann, T. (2014). Prokka: Rapid prokaryotic genome annotation. *Bioinformatics (Oxford, England), 30*(14), 2068–2069. doi:10.1093/bioinformatics/btu153 PMID:24642063

Shahid, S., & Axtell, M. J. (2013). Identification and annotation of small RNA genes using Short-Stack. *Methods (San Diego, Calif.).* doi:10.1016/j.ymeth.2013.10.004 PMID:24139974

Sievers, F., Wilm, A., Dineen, D., Gibson, T. J., Karplus, K., & Li, W. et al. (2011). Fast, scalable generation of high-quality protein multiple sequence alignments using Clustal Omega. *Molecular Systems Biology, 7*(1), 539. doi:10.1038/msb.2011.75 PMID:21988835

Simossis, V. A., & Heringa, J. (2005). PRALINE: A multiple sequence alignment toolbox that integrates homology-extended and secondary structure information. *Nucleic Acids Research, 33*(Web Server issue), W289-294. doi: 10.1093/nar/gki390

Smith, C., Heyne, S., Richter, A. S., Will, S., & Backofen, R. (2010). Freiburg RNA Tools: A web server integrating INTARNA, EXPARNA and LOCARNA. *Nucleic Acids Research, 38*(Web Server issue), W373-377. doi: 10.1093/nar/gkq316

Softberry, I. (2007). *SCAN2*. Mount Kisco, NY: Softberry, Inc. Retrieved April 17, 2014, from http://linux1.softberry.com/

Solovyev, V. V., Salamov, A. A., & Lawrence, C. B. (1994). Predicting internal exons by oligonucleotide composition and discriminant analysis of spliceable open reading frames. *Nucleic Acids Research, 22*(24), 5156–5163. doi:10.1093/nar/22.24.5156 PMID:7816600

Solovyev, V. V., Salamov, A. A., & Lawrence, C. B. (1995). Identification of human gene structure using linear discriminant functions and dynamic programming. *Proceedings of the International Conference on Intelligent Systems for Molecular Biology, 3*, 367–375. PMID:7584460

Stein, L. (2001). Genome annotation: From sequence to biology. *Nature Reviews. Genetics, 2*(7), 493–503. doi:10.1038/35080529 PMID:11433356

Sturrock, S., & Collins, J. (1993). *MPsrch version 1.3*. Biocomputing Research Unit University of Edinburgh. Retrieved April 17, 2014, from http://www.ebi.ac.uk/Tools/MPsrch/

Su, X., Pan, W., Song, B., Xu, J., & Ning, K. (2014). Parallel-META 2.0: Enhanced metagenomic data analysis with functional annotation, high performance computing and advanced visualization. *PLoS ONE, 9*(3), e89323. doi:10.1371/journal.pone.0089323 PMID:24595159

Subramanian, A. R., Kaufmann, M., & Morgenstern, B. (2008). DIALIGN-TX: Greedy and progressive approaches for segment-based multiple sequence alignment. *Algorithms for Molecular Biology; AMB, 3*(1), 6. doi:10.1186/1748-7188-3-6 PMID:18505568

Sze, S. H., & Pevzner, P. A. (1997). Las Vegas algorithms for gene recognition: Suboptimal and error-tolerant spliced alignment. *Journal of Computational Biology, 4*(3), 297–309. doi:10.1089/cmb.1997.4.297 PMID:9278061

Thompson, J. D., Plewniak, F., Thierry, J., & Poch, O. (2000). DbClustal: Rapid and reliable global multiple alignments of protein sequences detected by database searches. *Nucleic Acids Research, 28*(15), 2919–2926. doi:10.1093/nar/28.15.2919 PMID:10908355

Thorsen, O., Smith, B., Sosa, C. P., Jiang, K., Lin, H., Peters, A., & Feng, W. (2007). Parallel genomic sequence-search on a massively parallel system. New York, NY: Academic Press. doi:10.1145/1242531.1242542

Top500. (2008). *Top500 June 2008: Roadrunner - BladeCenter QS22/LS21 cluster, PowerXCell 8i 3.2 Ghz/Opteron DC 1.8 GHz, Voltaire infiniband*. Retrieved April 17, 2014, from http://www.top500.org/system/176026

Top500. (2013). *Top500: Endeavor - Intel cluster*. Retrieved April 17, 2014, from http://www.top500.org/system/176908

Troshin, P. V., Procter, J. B., & Barton, G. J. (2011). Java bioinformatics analysis web services for multiple sequence alignment--JABAWS:MSA. *Bioinformatics (Oxford, England), 27*(14), 2001–2002. doi:10.1093/bioinformatics/btr304 PMID:21593132

Uberbacher, E. C., & Mural, R. J. (1991). Locating protein-coding regions in human DNA sequences by a multiple sensor-neural network approach. *Proceedings of the National Academy of Sciences of the United States of America, 88*(24), 11261–11265. doi:10.1073/pnas.88.24.11261 PMID:1763041

Uberbacher, E. C., Xu, Y., & Mural, R. J. (1996). Discovering and understanding genes in human DNA sequence using GRAIL. *Methods in Enzymology, 266*, 259–281. doi:10.1016/S0076-6879(96)66018-2 PMID:8743689

Varadarajan, S. (2004). *System X: Building the Virginia Tech supercomputer.* Paper presented at the 13th International Conference on Computer Communications and Networks. New York, NY. doi:10.1109/ICCCN.2004.1401571

Vermij, E. P. (2011). *Genetic sequence alignment on a supercomputing platform.* Netherlands: TU Delft.

Warren, A. S., Archuleta, J., Feng, W. C., & Setubal, J. C. (2010). Missing genes in the annotation of prokaryotic genomes. *BMC Bioinformatics, 11*(1), 131. doi:10.1186/1471-2105-11-131 PMID:20230630

Webb-Roberts, B.-J. (2004). *Protein & DNA sequence analysis.* Retrieved February 10, 2013, from http://www.sysbio.org/resources/tutorials/sequence_analysis_webb.pdf

Wood, D. E., & Salzberg, S. L. (2014). Kraken: Ultrafast metagenomic sequence classification using exact alignments. *Genome Biology, 15*(3), R46. doi:10.1186/gb-2014-15-3-r46 PMID:24580807

Xu, Y., Mural, R., Shah, M., & Uberbacher, E. (1994). Recognizing exons in genomic sequence using GRAIL II. *Genetic Engineering, 16*, 241–253. PMID:7765200

Ye, Y., Wei, B., Wen, L., & Rayner, S. (2013). BlastGraph: A comparative genomics tool based on BLAST and graph algorithms. *Bioinformatics (Oxford, England), 29*(24), 3222–3224. doi:10.1093/bioinformatics/btt553 PMID:24068035

Yeh, R. F., Lim, L. P., & Burge, C. B. (2001). Computational inference of homologous gene structures in the human genome. *Genome Research, 11*(5), 803–816. doi:10.1101/gr.175701 PMID:11337476

Zafar, N., Mazumder, R., & Seto, D. (2001). Comparisons of gene colinearity in genomes using GeneOrder2.0. *Trends in Biochemical Sciences, 26*(8), 514–516. doi:10.1016/S0968-0004(01)01881-3 PMID:11504629

Zafar, N., Mazumder, R., & Seto, D. (2002). CoreGenes: A computational tool for identifying and cataloging "core" genes in a set of small genomes. *BMC Bioinformatics, 3*(1), 12. doi:10.1186/1471-2105-3-12 PMID:11972896

Zammataro, L., DeMolfetta, R., Bucci, G., Ceol, A., & Muller, H. (2014). AnnotateGenomicRegions: A web application. *BMC Bioinformatics, 15*(Suppl 1), S8. doi:10.1186/1471-2105-15-S1-S8 PMID:24564446

Zhang, M. Q. (1997). Identification of protein coding regions in the human genome by quadratic discriminant analysis. *Proceedings of the National Academy of Sciences of the United States of America, 94*(2), 565–568. doi:10.1073/pnas.94.2.565 PMID:9012824

Zhang, Y., & Waterman, M. S. (2003). DNA sequence assembly and multiple sequence alignment by an Eulerian path approach. *Cold Spring Harbor Symposia on Quantitative Biology, 68*(0), 205–212. doi:10.1101/sqb.2003.68.205 PMID:15338619

Zhao, K., & Chu, X. (2014). G-BLASTN: Accelerating nucleotide alignment by graphics processors. *Bioinformatics (Oxford, England)*, *30*(10), 1384–1391. doi:10.1093/bioinformatics/btu047 PMID:24463183

Zola, J., Yang, X., Rospondek, A., & Aluru, S. (2007). Parallel T-coffee: A parallel multiple sequence aligner. In *Proceedings of the ISCA 20th International Conference on Parallel and Distributed Computing Systems*. Academic Press.

Zuegge, J., Ebeling, M., & Schneider, G. (2001). H-BloX: Visualizing alignment block entropies. *Journal of Molecular Graphics & Modelling*, *19*(3-4), 304–306, 379. doi:10.1016/S1093-3263(00)00074-7 PMID:11449568

Zverina, J. (2014). *SDSC assists in whole-genome sequencing analysis under collaboration with Janssen*. Retrieved April 17, 2014, from http://ucsdnews.ucsd.edu/pressrelease/sdsc_assists_in_whole_genome_sequencing_analysis_under_collaboration_with_j

KEY TERMS AND DEFINITIONS

Allele Frequency: In a population, this refers to the percentage of all the alleles at a locus accounted for by one specific allele.

Bacteriophage: Virus that infects and replicates within bacteria.

Comparative Genomics: Study that involves the comparison of the genomic sequences of different species.

Complementary DNA (cDNA): DNA derived from messenger RNA (mRNA), which can be obtained from prokaryotes or eukaryotes and is often utilized to clone eukaryotic genes in prokaryotes.

Cosmid: A plasmid vector containing a bacteriophage lambda *cos* site, which directs insertion of DNA into phage particles.

CpG Elements: Genomic regions consisting of a high frequency of CpG sites. A CpG site refers to a genomic region where a cytosine nucleotide exists next to a guanine nucleotide in the linear sequence of bases along its length.

Dicodon Statistics: Statistics used for the prediction of splice signals and coding regions.

Discriminant Function: A function of a set of variables that is evaluated for samples of events of objects and used as an aid in classifying them.

DNA: deoxyribonucleic acid is a molecule that serves as the hereditary material in humans and almost all other organisms.

DNA Polymerases: An enzyme that catalyzes the polymerization of DNAs into a DNA strand.

Evolution: Gradual unfolding of new varieties of life from previous forms over long periods of time; from the modern genetic perspective, it is defined as a change in allele frequency from one generation to the next.

Exon: DNA nucleotide sequence carrying out the code for the final mRNA and, thus, determines the amino acid sequence of an organism.

Expressed Sequence Tags (ESTs): Small pieces of DNA sequence (usually 200 to 500 nucleotides long) generated by sequencing either one or both ends of an expressed gene.

Field-Programmable Gate Arrays (FPGA): An integrated circuit that can be programmed in the field after manufacture.

Functional Annotation: The process of collecting information and describing the gene's biological identity.

GenBank: The NIH genetic sequence database, an annotated collection of all publicly available DNA sequences (Benson et al., 2013).

Genetic Association: Statistical phenomenon, which associates a specific disease with a certain gene(s).

Genomics: Field of study focusing on genes, their functions, and related techniques.

Genotype Frequency: Sum of the number of individuals possessing the genotype divided by the total number of individuals in the sample.

Genotype: An organism's entire genetic makeup or to the alleles at a specific genetic locus.

Graphics Processing Unit (GPU): A programmable logic chip that can perform animation, imaging, and videos for the computer screen.

Heuristic Methods: Methods that facilitate in learning, discover, or problem-solving by experimental or trial-and-error methods.

Homology: Two molecules that share a common ancestor.

Intergenic: A region found between two genes.

Intron: A noncoding sequence between two coding genomic sequence.

Markov Model System: Mathematical model that allows the study of complex systems by establishing a state of the system and then consequently effecting a transition to a new state, such a transition being dependent only on the values of the current state, and not dependent on the previous history of the system up to that point.

Mendel's Laws: Consist of three laws of inheritance describing how genes are passed on from parents to offsprings.

Meta-Analysis: A method of combining quantitative or qualitative datasets from different studies to determine a single conclusion with greater statistical power.

Multiprocessor: A computer system with more than one central processing unit (CPU) that share main memory.

Nucleotide: Building blocks from which DNA and RNA are built.

Open Reading Frame (ORF): A DNA sequence that does not contain a stop codon in a given reading frame.

Parallel Algorithm: An algorithm that allows execution a piece at a time in different processing devices, and then eventually putting them back together again at the end to determine the correct result.

Parallel Programming: Computational method, which allows carrying out multiple calculations simultaneously.

Pattern Recognition: Method that deals with feature extraction and classification.

Peptide Sequence: Unique amino acid sequence characterizing a given protein.

Population Genetics: The study concerned mainly with the genetic variation within species.

Prokaryote: Organisms lacking a cell nucleus.

Promoters: DNA segment usually occurring from a gene coding region and acting as a controlling element in gene expression

Reduced Instruction Set Computer (RISC): A type of computer architecture that has a relatively small set of computer instructions that it can perform.

Regulatory Elements: DNA sequence that determines the regulation of gene expression.

Sequence Alignment: A method of arranging RNA, protein, or DNA sequences to identify regions of similarity that maybe a consequence of functional, structural, or evolutionary relationships between the sequences.

Sequence Assembly: A method of determining the order of multiple sequenced DNA fragments.

Shotgun Sequencing: Laboratory technique for determining the DNA sequence of an organism's genome.

Single Instruction, Multiple Data (SIMD) Processing: Processing technique in which an operation is taken in one specified instruction and applies it to more than one set of data elements at the same time.

Splicing: The process of inserting DNA or RNA fragments to form new genetic combinations or alter a new genetic structure.

Start Codon: The first codon of an mRNA transcript translated by a ribosome.

Stop Codon: The genetic codon in an mRNA that signals the termination of protein synthesis during translation.

Structural Annotation: The process of localizing the genes in both strands of a genome as well precisely determining the structural elements of these genes.

Supernode: Any node that also serves as one of the network's relayers and proxy servers, handling data flow and connections for other users.

Traditional GenBank: Divisions that contain 106 billion nucleotide bases from 108 million individual sequences, with 11 million new sequences added in 2009.

Transposon: DNA segment consisting of an insertion sequence element at each end as a repeat as well as genes specific to some other activity such as resistance to antibiotics.

Whole Genome Shotgun: A method of genome sequence determination based on assembly of the whole genome from numerous sequence reads at high coverage without requiring reference to genetic or physical map locations for those reads.

Chapter 7
Applications of Supercomputers in Population Genetics

Gerard G. Dumancas
Oklahoma Medical Research Foundation, USA

ABSTRACT

Population genetics is the study of the frequency and interaction of alleles and genes in population and how this allele frequency distribution changes over time as a result of evolutionary processes such as natural selection, genetic drift, and mutation. This field has become essential in the foundation of modern evolutionary synthesis. Traditionally regarded as a highly mathematical discipline, its modern approach comprises more than the theoretical, lab, and fieldwork. Supercomputers play a critical role in the success of this field and are discussed in this chapter.

INTRODUCTION

The general goals of population genetic studies are to characterize the extent of genetic variation within species and account for this variation (Weir, 1996). The amount of genetic variation can be determined by the frequency of genes and the forces that affect such frequencies such as mutation, migration, selection, and genetic drift (Gall, 1987). Throughout the years, population genetics has evolved to develop theoretical models to explain changes of allele and genotype frequencies in natural populations of different organisms through time. For example, with these built models, it is possible to determine the length of time for a given allele to be fixed given a certain selective force for it. With the determination of the genetic

variations within individuals, it is possible to find the genetic causes that give rise to and maintain variation both within species and between species. For example, where do the genes of the Europeans come from? The main way to gain insight into past population processes is to analyze and interpret current patterns of genetic variation (Sokal, 1991) (von Haeseler et al., 1996).

Over the past decades, the field of population genetics has undergone remarkable changes. This has been due to the development of sophisticated DNA sequencing technologies, which makes it possible to generate large quantities of the most direct kind of genetic data easy and affordable (Wakeley, 2004). Current and future challenges in this field in both computational methodology and in analytical theory are to develop models

DOI: 10.4018/978-1-4666-7461-5.ch007

Copyright © 2015, IGI Global. Copying or distributing in print or electronic forms without written permission of IGI Global is prohibited.

and techniques to extract the most information possible from multilocus DNA datasets. To solve this problem, technical improvements, such as the use of robotics would streamline the gathering of relatively large genetic datasets (Wakeley, 2004). Further, the use of supercomputers has tremendously improved the computational methodology in this field. Thus, the primary objective of this chapter is to discuss the applications of supercomputers in population genetics.

BACKGROUND

The beginnings of genetics and of population genetics are one. Both started with Mendel; and were unrecognized until the rediscovery in 1900. That is in his simple genetics experiment wherein he considered the consequences of repeated self-fertilization; he showed that heterozygosity is reduced by half each generation and gave formulas for genotype frequencies in successive generations. This consequently led to the foundation of population genetics. The "golden age" of population genetics was the period when Haldane, Fisher, and Wright were producing their great work. That is, they reconciled biometry with genetics, quantified the approach to evolution, and created a totally new science. Thus, it is arguably the most successful mathematical theory in biology (Crow, 1987).

Essential to the understanding of population genetics as a specialized field, different techniques currently used or used in the recent past by various scientists are necessary to generate data for population genetic models. Protein electrophoresis, restriction endonucleases (restriction fragment length polymorphisms of purified DNA), and DNA polymorphisms (randomly amplified polymorphic DNAs, DNA resequencing) are some of the most commonly used methods for generating population genetic data (Templeton, 2006). In protein electrophoresis, proteins are separated on the basis of their physical properties such as net charge, size, and shape. In this procedure, the

separated proteins are stained to reveal specific classes of enzymes. Genetic diversity is identified when the stained isozyme bands show migration at different rates (Conkle, 1972). Restriction endonucleases procedure involve the use of restriction enzymes that break DNA bonds for splicing different DNA together (Sherlock et al., 2002) while DNA polymorphisms experiments involve the use of advance DNA sequencing technologies to identify DNA variations between individuals within populations. Basically these experiments are all performed with the aim of assaying and identifying genetic variations within individuals and within populations. For example, Eanes and Koehn studied the genetics of different Monarch butterfly populations in the early 1970s using electrophoresis that examines the same proteins in different individual butterflies. They found that Monarchs have allele frequencies that sort out into groups somewhat in the summer and become uniform again during migration. These results showed that Monarchs divide into slightly isolated populations during the summer but mix together during migration (Eanes et al., 1978). With the advent of these sophisticated techniques as well as the emergence of new, polymorphic, genetic markers, a number of questions regarding populations and the interactions of the individuals within them may be addressed using genetic data.

Genetic variation simply refers to the variation in alleles of genes, occurring both within and among populations. In other words, it describes naturally occurring differences among individuals of the same species. This variation allows flexibility and survival of a population in the face of changing environmental factors (2013). Genetic diversity at the population level of a species plays an important role in the interaction of the species with the environment. These interactions will consequently structure the ecosystem, so that the spatial and temporal partitioning of genetic diversity will occur (Medline et al., 2000). Further, elucidating the inherited basis of genetic variation in human health and disease is considered to be one of the major scientific challenges of the 21st century. Understanding the concept of population genetics will help us unravel the mechanisms on how genetic variants contribute to phenotypic diversity (Frazer et al., 2009).

Population genetics can be defined in many ways, but in general, involves the study of the applications of Mendel's laws and other genetic principles to entire populations of organisms instead of just to individuals (Institute et al., 2003). It is concerned with the genetic basis of evolution. In contrast with biology, its important insights are theoretical rather than observational or experimental. The objects of study are focused primarily on the frequencies and fitness of genotype in natural population. Evolution is concerned with the change in the frequencies of genotypes through time, perhaps due to their differences in fitness. While genotype frequencies are easily measured, their change is not. This is because the time scale of change of most naturally occurring variants is very long, probably on the order of tens of thousands to millions of years. Thus, it is impossible to observe directly such slow changes. Fitness differences between genotypes, which may be responsible for some of the frequency changes are so small, thus, are impossible to be measured directly. In general, there is no way to explore directly the evolution of a population. In order to make this possible, success in population genetics utilizes the construction of mathematical models of evolution, studying their behavior, and then checking whether the states of populations are compatible with this behavior (Gillespie, 2004).

As mentioned earlier, a number of factors including segregation, mutation, recombination, migration, mating structure, and selection among others may interact and determine the evolutionary fate of a population. Genetic segregation simply involves the apparent separation of alleles from a heterozygous cell into different daughter cells (K. Wolf et al., 2004). Genetic mutation refers to changes in the genetic sequence (i.e. DNA) of an organism (Loewe, 2008). These changes occur at various different levels leading to differing consequences. To further dichotomize, in biological systems that are capable of reproduction, such changes can be heritable; that is some mutations affect only the individuals that carries them, while others affect all of the organism's descendants. In order for such mutations to take effect into an organism's descendants, they must occur in cells that produce the next generation and affect the hereditary material. Further, the role of the environment also plays a critical role in an interplay with inherited mutations (Loewe, 2008).

Genetic recombination, on the other hand, refers to the rearrangement of genetic material; it is any process that joins previously unassociated DNA fragments, and is often accompanied by breaking and rejoining DNA strands (Lewis-Rogers et al., 2004). Genetic migration is another way of introducing genetic diversity as a consequence when members of one gene pool mate with members of another gene pool, thereby leading to allele frequency changes into or away from the population (Buckleton, 2004). With all these mentioned factors affecting an individual's genetic makeup, it is, thus, essential to come up with good mathematical models that may predict evolutionary changes within individuals and within the population. This has great applications such as for example in making predictions about the allelic architecture of common disease susceptibility and to gain an overall understanding about the evolutionary origins of such diseases (Di Rienzo, 2006). One may also use such models to determine which outcomes are very unlikely or impossible given some initial conditions. In the process, mathematical analysis may serve to generate conclusions that could not be arrived at by empirical research at a given stage of inquiry (Plutynski et al., 2005).

Lewontin described the role of population genetics modeling as delimiting what is possible and what is prohibited in microevolutionary change (Lewontin, 2000). Further, such models were even extended to use by biologists to answer questions about change above the species level (Barton et al., 1984). Thus, such models are made possible by using the number and frequency of susceptibility alleles for such diseases (Di Rienzo, 2006). The assessment of the relative importance of mutation, selection, drift, mating structure, and so on requires an understanding on how these processes operate into a workable mathematical model whose predictions can be compared to data. It is still difficult to know exactly how genes combine eventually influencing the whole organism or what is responsible for the variation in those genes. However, with the advances in DNA sequencing technologies and molecular biology techniques, vast amount of data can be utilized for building reliable mathematical models (Etheridge, 2009).

The models obtained from population genetics, despite their many simplifications of the genetic systems, provide real insight not otherwise obtainable into the evolutionary process. Using these models, one may enable to describe the common features of many systems that all differ in detail, determine how varying outcomes depend on the relative magnitude of one or another parameter, and decide which factors may be ignored legitimately, given the question under investigation, or the time frame under consideration. For example, population genetics theory makes it possible to determine that selection is more effective than drift in large population sizes, whereas the effects of drift will overpower those of selection when the opposite is the case (Plutynski & Evans, 2005).

Population genetics is a field that has periods of great interest and growth and other periods in which there was less innovation and fewer new contributions. That being said, this is not unexpected for areas of studies that develop new paradigm and then refine and expand this research within this paradigm (Kuhn, 1962). In the modern era, we are obtaining a great multitude of DNA sequence data from many genes of different species and are beginning to have multiple copies of whole genomes of different individuals of a given species. Thus, obtaining a deeper understanding of

the evolutionary significance of the variations in the vast amounts of DNA sequences both within and between species is providing a great new challenge for population genetics. Consequently, these variations translate into adaptive differences in morphology, behavior, and physiology of an organism as well as the detrimental variation in the complex diseases it may carry (Hedrick, 2011). Optimal to the success of population genetics is the use of supercomputers, which facilitates in the calculation of such mathematical models in faster and more efficient ways.

The discussion of the mathematical theories behind population genetics is beyond the scope of this chapter. As such we encourage the readers to read textbooks regarding such. A very good resource regarding mathematical models of population genetics will be that of Karlin (Karlin, 1972) and Etheridge (Etheridge, 2009). The scope of this chapter will constitute the application of population genetics and how supercomputers play a vital role in the success of such field.

SUPERCOMPUTERS IN POPULATION GENETICS

Although, supercomputers have played a critical role in the success of population genetics, its applications in such field are rarely documented. This is partly due to the emergence of large genomic datasets that recently emerged and that sophisticated supercomputers are necessary in order to unravel the genetics of different species. A number of recent interesting applications of supercomputers are discussed in this section.

MacManes and Lacey recently used National Science Foundation (NSF) supercomputers through the Extreme Science and Engineering Discovery Environment (XSEDE) to analyze datasets too big for their university clusters. Once he had his genomic sequences, MacManes turned to the Texas Advanced Computing Center (TACC) at the University of Texas at Austin, a lead partner in XSEDE and home to the Ranger Supercomputer, to perform sequence alignments and analysis (Dubrow, 2012). He was able to accomplish such tasks within a few weeks using Ranger Supercomputer that could have taken years using his local resources. As a consequence, his group was able to recently show how the differences in sexual behavior impact the bacteria hosted by each species as well as the diversity of the genes that control immunity. Specifically, they compared the microscopic and molecular level differences between two closely related species of mice that share a habitat and genetic lineage but have different social lives, a California mouse (*Peromyscus californicus*) that is characterized by a lifetime of monogamy and the deer mouse (*Peromyscus maniculatus*) that is known to be sexually promiscuous. Their study revealed that the promiscuous mice had more diversity in the genes related to their immune system and by virtue of their sexual system are in contact with more individuals and are exposed to a lot of bacteria (Dubrow, 2012). The results, which were also recently published in *PLoS One* (MacManes et al., 2012), showed that differences in social behavior could lead to changes in the selection pressures and gene-level evolutionary changes in a species.

A very interesting application of supercomputers in population genetics is by describing in detail events the origin of populations dating back 2000 years ago. Computer scientists at Columbia University's School of Engineering and Applied Science demonstrated in two populations, the Ashkenazi Jews and the Masai people of Kenya, representing two kinds of histories and relationships with neighboring populations: one that remained isolated from surrounding groups, and one that eventually grew from frequent cross-migration across nearby villages (Kazmi, 2012). Using the computing facility at the Columbia Initiative in Systems Biology (CISB), they utilized computational genetics to develop methods to analyze DNA sequence variants and discovered that for instance, Ashkenazi Jews are descendants of a small number

(hundreds) of individuals from the late medieval times, and since then have remained genetically isolated while their population has expanded rapidly to several millions today. The Masais, on the other hand, revealed using their genetic data that they lived in small villages but regularly interact and intermarry across village boundaries. As a consequence, the ancestors of each village come from many different places, and a single village hosts an effective gene pool that is much larger than the village itself (Kazmi, 2012). This work has been published in the American Journal of Human Genetics (AJHG) (Palamara et al., 2012).

The previous paragraph discussed the case wherein there is an interaction of people in small villages and intermarriage occurs across village boundaries. In a larger scenario, wherein two previously isolated populations begin interbreeding, genetic admixture occurs (Sagoo, 2007). This process leads to the generation of new genetic lineages into a population. In the recent years, population admixture has become controversial due its important implications in research areas such as evolutionary genetics (Belle et al., 2006). Inferring and quantifying population admixture from genetic data are considered difficult but important tasks in evolutionary and conservation biology. Unfortunately, the state-of-the-art probabilistic approaches to determine admixture rates are considered to be computationally demanding. Recently, a software package "parLEA" was invented that exploits the computational power of modern multiprocessor systems making a positive impact on the Monte Carlo-based simulation of admixture modeling. This computational software speeds up the estimation of admixture populations in large genomic datasets by utilizing a novel parallel approach (Giovannini et al., 2009). The parallelization is based on splitting the genetic loci among the available processing elements (PEs) due to the main loops running over the loci and the computations being independent for the most part of the program. The package was tested on the IBM CLX/1024 Linux cluster at the CIN-

ECA Supercomputing Center in Bologna, Italy. The results of the study showed very promising performances in estimating proportions of population admixture from large genomic datasets in reasonable time (Giovannini et al., 2009).

Essential to the success of population genetics studies are the extensive information catalogues available that allows geneticists to examine differences among a wide range of human populations (Amigo et al., 2011). These catalogues are provided by global collaborations such as HapMap (T. I. H. Consortium, 2005), high density single nucleotide polymorphism (SNP) genotyping of the CEPH human genome diversity panel by groups from the Universities of Stanford (Li et al., 2008) as well as private companies such as Perlegen Sciences (Peacock et al., 2005). Scientists from Spain recently developed a genetic variant site explorer that allows retrieval of data for SNPs, population by population, from entire genome without compromising future scalability and agility. The so-called "ENGINES (ENtire Genome INterface for Exploring SNVs)" utilizes data from the 1000 Genomes Phase I and demonstrated a capacity to handle large amounts of genetic variation (>7.3 billion genotypes and 28 million single nucleotide variations (SNVs)), as well as deriving summary statistics that include allele frequency, heterozygosity or fixation index (F_{ST}) values for genetic differentiation of interest for medical and population genetics applications in a fast and comprehensive manner. The study was facilitated using CESGA (Supercomputing Centre of Galicia, Santiago de Compostela, Spain) supercomputing facility (Amigo et al., 2011).

In the area of genetic studies, the massive increase in data sizes and more advance algorithms for mining complex data lead to a point wherein increased computational capacity or alternative solutions becomes unavoidable. As such, scientists from Sweden developed 'Grid-Allegro', a Grid aware implementation of the Allegro software, by which several thousands of genotype simulations can be performed in parallel in short period of time. The implementation of existing bioinformatics applications on Grids (Distributed Computing) can be a cost-effective alternative solution for addressing highly resource-demanding and data-intensive bioinformatics routines or tasks, compared to acquiring and setting up clusters of computational hardware in house (Parallel Computing), a resource not available to most geneticists today (Andrade et al., 2007).

In the area of population genetics, the field of genome-wide association studies (GWASs) has also becoming of great interest to majority of bioinformaticians. GWAS involves correlating allele frequencies at each several hundred thousand markers spaced throughout the genome with trait variation in a population-based sample (Stranger et al., 2011). In other words, the GWAS offers a powerful approach to identifying genetic markers (i.e. SNPs) that are associated with human diseases. However, depending on whether samples are related or not, specific softwares should be applied to datasets. In cases wherein samples are related, one must statistically correct for "confounding" which was caused by subject relatedness. As such, linear mixed models (LMMs) are usually implemented to correct such confounding issues. LMMs, however, tend to be computationally intensive requiring considerable computer run time and memory (i.e. 10,000-person sample). To avoid this roadblock, Microsoft Research developed the Factored Spectrally Transformed Linear Mixed Model (Fast-LMM), an algorithm that extends the ability to detect new biological relations by using data that is several orders of magnitude larger. In other words, it allows more much larger datasets to be parsed and can, therefore, detect more subtle signals in the data. By using Windows Azure, Microsoft Research Team ran Fast-LMM using the Wellcome Trust data analyzing 63,524,915,020 pairs of genetic markers and was able to detect novel associations between the genetic markers and complex diseases like Crohn's disease, coronary artery disease, bipolar disorder, hypertension, rheumatoid arthritis, artery disease, and types I and II diabetes (Team, 2012). The discussion of GWASs encompasses another broad and separate topic and is beyond the scope of this chapter.

Supercomputing is a highly evolving and competitive industry. Throughout the years, a number of computational tools have facilitated the advances in population genetics research (Table 1). The table represents some of the current computational tools utilized by population geneticists. Various supercomputing centers around the world also exist which facilitate the analyses of enormous genetic datasets to understand the history and organization of different organism populations.

The Ohio Supercomputing Center (USA)

The Ohio Supercomputing Center (OSC) was established in 1987 and is a partner of Ohio universities and industries, and has been providing researchers with supercomputing, research, education, and cyberinfrastructure services (OSC, 2014). The center currently operates under two major systems namely: the Oakley Cluster and the Glenn Cluster. The Oakley Cluster is their newest system with an 8300+ core HP Intel Xeon machine. Two Nvidia Tesla GPU accelerators are present in one in every 10 of its nodes. One node has 1 TB of RAM and 32 cores, for large SMP style jobs. The Oakley Cluster can also achieve 88 teraflops theoretical system peak performance for performing 88 trillion floating point operations per second, or, with acceleration from 128 NVIDIA® Tesla graphic processing units (GPUs), a total peak performance of just over 154 teraflops. The Glenn Cluster, on the other hand, is a 5300+ core IBM AMD Opteron machine. The OSC also provides more than 2 PB of storage, and another 2 PB of tape backup. The cluster offers a peak performance of more than 54 trillion floating point operations per second and a variety of memory and processor configurations. The current hardware configuration of the system consists of 658 System x3455 compute nodes (Dual socket, quad core 2.5 GHz Opterons, 24 GB RAM, 393 GB local disk space in /tmp), a 4 System x3755 login nodes (Quad socket 2 dual core 2.6 GHz Opterons, 8 GB RAM), and Voltaire 20 Gbps PCI Express adapters. There are also 36 GPU-capable nodes in the Glenn Cluster, connected to 18 Quadro Plex S4's for a total of 72 CUDA-enabled graphics devices. The 36 compute nodes in Glenn contain 24 GB of RAM (OSC, 2014).

OSC has a wide array of softwares for performing intensive mathematical calculations. While most of the available bioinformatics tools are in sequence alignment, specifically, they also have TreeBeST, which aims at improving the accuracy of tree building in evolution (Table 1) (OSC, 2014). In 2013, David Serre and colleagues of the Genomic Medical Institute in Cleveland, Ohio, utilized the Ohio Supercomputing Center to perform intensive population genetic analyses to better understand the history and population of *Plasmodium vivax*, a parasitic species known to the most frequent cause of recurring malaria, which can eventually lead to severe disease and sometimes death. Specifically, Serre and colleagues will search the genome of the parasite to search patterns of genetic diversity consistent with the effects of natural selection as well as identifying the genetic basis of disease-related traits by association. Ultimately, results from these analyses will provide valuable knowledge regarding genes involved in the mechanisms underlying drug resistance and the biological mechanisms of red blood cell invasion (Abel, 2013).

The Barcelona Supercomputing Center (Spain)

The Barcelona Supercomputing Center (BCS) is a national supercomputing facility center officially constituted in April 2005 in Barcelona, Spain through the initiatives of the Ministry of Education and Science (Spanish Government), the Generalitat de Catalunya (local Catalan Government), and the Technical University of Catalonia (UPC).

Table 1. Computational tools used in population genetic analyses

Name	Description	Authors
ABC	Estimates demographic and historical parameters in the analysis of genetic variation	(Bertorelle et al., 2010)
ADMIXTOOLS	Supports formal tests for whether population mixture occurred and makes it possible to infer proportions and dates of mixture	(N. Patterson et al., 2012)
ALDER	Linkage-disequilibrium (LD)-based software for inferring admixture histories of human populations	(Loh et al., 2013)
AlleleRetain	An R package to assess management options for conserving allelic diversity in small populations of animals with overlapping generations	(Weiser et al., 2012)
AluHunter	A database of taxon-specific primate Alu elements for phylogeny and population genetics analyses	(Bergey, 2011)
AMOVA	Clusters population genetic data to determine the genetic structure of populations	(P. G. Meirmans, 2012)
AMOVA	Performs k-means clustering of population genetic data	(P. G. Meirmans, 2012)
AncestrySNPminer	Web-based tool to retrieve Ancestry Informative Markers (AIMs) from genomic data and link these to genes and annotation classes	(Amirisetty et al., 2012)
Arlequin	Can perform wide variety of population genetics calculations including estimation of gene frequencies, testing of linkage disequilibrium, and analysis of diversity between populations.	(Excoffier et al., 2005; Excoffier et al., 2010, 2013)
BAPS	Enables spatially explicit modeling of variation in DNA sequences and hierarchical clustering of DNA sequence data to reveal nested genetic population structures	(Cheng et al., 2013)
Bayenv	Calculates a set of "standardized allele frequencies" that allows investigators to apply tests of their choice to multiple populations while accounting for sampling and covariance due to population history	(Gunther et al., 2013)
BEAST	A powerful and flexible evolutionary analysis for molecular sequence variation	(Drummond et al., 2007)
bgc	Estimates the joint posterior probability distribution of the parameters in the Bayesian genomic cline model and designate outlier loci	(Gompert et al., 2012)
Capwire	An R package for estimating population census size from non-invasive genetic sampling for investigating the demographics of natural populations	(Pennell et al., 2013)
ChromoPainter/ fineSTRUCTURE	Aims to efficiently capture information on population structure provided by patterns of haplotype similarity	(Lawson et al., 2012)
ClonalFrame	Infers the clonal relationships of bacteria and the chromosomal position of homologous recombination events that disrupt a clonal pattern of inheritance	(Didelot et al., 2007)
Clonalorigin	Performs a comparative analysis of the sequences of a sample of bacterial genomes in order to reconstruct the recombination events that have taken place in their ancestry	(Didelot et al., 2010)
Coalescent	Open-source, cross platform and scalable framework for coalescent analysis in population genetics	(Tewari et al., 2012)
DETSEL	An R packages that identifies markers that show deviation from neutral expectation in pairwise comparisons of diverging populations	(Vitalis, 2012)
DIVERGENOME	Assists population genetics and genetic epidemiology studies performed by small to medium-sized research groups	(Magalhaes et al., 2012)
DIY ABC	Infers population history under different scenarios (population divergences, admixtures, and population size changes) using Bayesian computation	(Cornuet et al., 2008)
DnaSP	Estimates several measures of DNA sequence variation within and between populations (in noncoding, synonymous or nonsynonymous sites), as well as linkage disequilibrium, recombination, gene flow and gene conversion parameters.	(Librado et al., 2009; Rozas et al., 1999)

continued on following page

Table 1. Continued

Name	Description	Authors
EggLib	Automated and reliable package to conduct coalescent simulations and estimation of demographic parameters under a variety of scenarios	(De Mita et al., 2012)
EIGENSTRAT	Enables explicit detection and correction of population stratification on a genome-wide scale by using principal component analysis to explicitly model ancestry differences between cases and controls	(Price et al., 2006) (N. Patterson et al., 2013)
Ercs	Simulates the ancestry of a sample of genes that occupy a spatial continuum	(Kelleher et al., 2013)
FFPopSim	Simulation package for the evolution of large populations	(Zanini et al., 2012)
FINDbase	An interactive web-based application recording causative mutations and pharmacogenomic marker allele frequencies in various populations around the globe	(Viennas et al., 2012)
FTEC	An easy-to-use coalescent simulation program capable of simulating haplotype samples gathered from a population that has undergone faster than exponential growth	(Reppell et al., 2012)
GenAlEx	A Microsoft Excel package for population genetic analyses that offers frequency based (f-statistics, heterozygosity, hwe, population assignment, relatedness) and distance-based (amova, pcoa, mantel tests, multivariate spatial autocorrelation) analyses	(Peakall et al., 2012)
Genepop	Performs variety of population genetic tests including Hardy-Weinberg and linkage equilibrium, log-likelihood G-based test of differentiation between populations, Slatkin's rare allele method to estimate number of migrants per generation, as well as allele frequency analyses.	(Raymond et al., 1995; Rousset, 2008)
Genetix	Windows executable program that does a number of population genetic analysis procedures; computes the Nei and the Cavalli-Sforza genetic distances, both with and without bias correction; also calculates F statistics and linkage disequilibrium, and performs permutation tests on the results; interface is written in French language	(Belkhir et al., 2004)
GenoDive	Performs Analysis Of Molecular Variance, estimation of standardized coefficients of population differentiation, k-means clustering of populations using a simulated annealing approach, assigning genotypic identity (clones) to individuals, testing for clonal reproduction, testing Hardy-Weinberg equilibrium, calculation of the hybrid index for individuals, and different types of Mantel tests.	(P. Meirmans, 2013) (P.G. Meirmans et al., 2004)
GENOMEPOP	Simulates SNPs or DNA sequences under complex evolutionary and demographic models	(Carvajal-Rodriguez, 2008)
goeBURST	Identifies alternative patterns of descent for several bacterial species	(Francisco et al., 2009)
Haploscope	Provides novel graphical representation of haplotype structure in populations	(San Lucas et al., 2012)
Hlest	An R package for estimating and visualizing the joint distribution of ancestry and interclass heterozygosity to compare the genetic structure of hybrid populations	(Fitzpatrick, 2012)
honeybee-population-simulator	Simulates a base population in honey bees to optimize breeding programs by taking into account genetic and reproductive biology	(Gupta et al., 2012)
JML	Utilizes a posterior distribution of species trees, population sizes and branch lengths to simulate replicate sequence data sets using the coalescent with no migration	(Joly, 2012)
Libsequence	Computes several tests and statistics on DNA sequence data within populations.	(K. Thornton, 2003; Kevin Thornton, 2013) (K. Thornton, 2003)
locINGS	A user-friendly accessory program that takes multi-FASTA formatted loci, next-generation sequence alignments and demographic data as inputs and collates, displays and outputs information about the data	(Hird, 2012)

continued on following page

Table 1. Continued

Name	Description	Authors
METAPOP	A desktop application that provides analysis of gene and allelic diversity in subdivided populations from coancestry or molecular genotype data	(Perez-Figueroa et al., 2012)
MixMapper	An efficient, interactive method for constructing phylogenetic trees including admixture events using SNP genotype data	(Lipson et al., 2013)
MMOD	An R package for population differentiation statistic calculations	(Winter, 2012)
NGSAdmix	Method for inferring an individual's ancestry taking into account the uncertainty in next generation sequencing data	(Skotte et al., 2013)
NSA	Calculates a number of different nucleotide sequence distances, as well as some simple protein sequence distances.	(Ravaoarimanana et al., 2006)
Olorin	Integrates gene flow within families with next generation sequencing data to enable the analysis of complex disease pedigrees	(Morris et al., 2012)
PAML	Has a rich repertoire of evolutionary models, which can be used to estimate parameters in models of sequence evolution and to test interesting biological hypotheses	(Yang, 2007)
ParallelStructure	Provides an R-based framework utilizing multi-core computers when running analyses in the population genetics program	(Besnier et al., 2013)
Pebble	Estimates population parameters including substitution/mutation rates using pairwise distances with or without parametric bootstrap confidence intervals; Simulation of genealogies and sequences under a constant-sized population model with or without serial sampling; Estimation of pairwise distance matrices using user-specified rate matrices (but not yet allowing variation of rates between sites).	(Rodrigo et al., 2010)
PedigreeSim	Simulation software that implements all features of meiosis in tetraploid and diploid species and use this to simulate pedigree and cross populations	(Voorrips et al., 2012)
pegas	An R package that provides functions for standard population genetic methods,	(Paradis, 2010)
Permute!	Permutes distance genetic matrices in multiple ways, including those according to an ultrametric (clocklike) tree provided by the user.	(Lapointe et al., 2013) (Lapointe et al., 1992)
PGDSpider	An automated data conversion tool for connecting population genetics and genomics programs	(Lischer et al., 2012)
PHYLDOG	Simultaneously builds gene and species trees when gene families have undergone duplications and losses; provides a more accurate picture of ancestral genomes than the trees available in the authoritative database Ensembl	(Boussau et al., 2013)
PHYLOViZ	Allows the combined analysis of multiple data sources for microbial epidemiological and population studies and visualizes the possible evolutionary relationships between isolates	(Francisco et al., 2012)
PLINK	Performs classical multidimensional scaling to visualize substructure and provide quantitative indices of population genetic variations	(Purcell et al., 2007)
PMx software	Software for extending pedigree analysis for uncertain parentage and diverse breeding systems	(Lacy, 2012)
PolyLens	Java-based, integral visual analytical toolkit that can systematically process population genomic data, visualize geographic distributions of genealogical lineages, and display allele distribution patterns.	(Berry et al., 2013)
Pool-hmm	Program for the estimation of allele frequencies and the detection of selective sweeps in a Pool-Seq sample	(Boitard et al., 2013)
Popoolation2	Utilizes a wide array of commonly used measures of identifying population differentiation (F(ST), Fisher's exact test and Cochran-Mantel-Haenszel test) that can be applied on different scales (windows, genes, exons, SNPs)	(Kofler et al., 2011)
POPTREE2	Calculates genetic distance measures and constructs trees of populations or closely related species from gene frequency data.	(Takezaki et al., 2010)

continued on following page

Table 1. Continued

Name	Description	Authors
ProfDist	Performs construction of large trees from profile distances of nucleotide sequences.	(M. Wolf et al., 2008, 2010) (Muller et al., 2004)
REACTA	Tailored to exploit the parallelism present in modern traditional and GPU-accelerated machines, from workstations to supercomputers; performs regional heritability advanced complex trait analysis	(Cebamanos et al., 2014)
RelateAdmix	Obtains maximum likelihood estimates of pairwise relatedness from genetic data between admixed individuals	(Moltke et al., 2013)
sGD	Estimates the genetic diversity based on grouping individuals into potentially overlapping genetic neighborhoods that match the population structure, whether discrete or clinal.	(Shirk et al., 2011)
SPAGeDi	Computes various statistics describing relatedness or differentiation between individuals or populations by pairwise comparisonsis or by linear regression	(Hardy et al., 2002)
Stacks	Provides tools to generate summary statistics and to compute population genetic measures such as F_{IS} and π within populations and F_{ST} between populations, allowing for genome scans; Data generated can be exported in VCF formats and for use in programs such as STRUCTURE or GenePop	(Catchen et al., 2013)
StAMPP	Calculates population structure and differentiation based on SNP genotype data from populations of any ploidy level, and/or mixed ploidy levels; Calculates pairwise FST values along with confidence intervals, Nei's genetic distance and genomic relationship matrixes from data sets of mixed-ploidy level.	(Pembleton et al., 2013)
STRUCTURE	Allows researchers to assess patterns of genetic structure in a set of samples; Can identify subsets of the whole sample by detecting allele frequency differences within the data and can assign individuals belonging to sub-populations by using likelihood analysis	(Falush et al., 2003; Porras-Hurtado et al., 2013)
SymmeTREE	Tests whether branches of a tree have diversified at different rates, and along which branches the significant shifts of diversity have occurred.	(Chan et al., 2005)
TreeBeST	A versatile program that builds, manipulates, and displays phylogenetic trees. It is specifically designed for building gene trees with a known species tree and is highly efficient and accurate	(Vilella et al., 2009)
TreeFit	Analyzes how well a tree fits the genetic data the tree was calculated from; creates neighbor-joining and UPGMA trees from a genetic distance matrix, and then compares the observed genetic distance between populations with the genetic distance in the tree	(Kalinowski, 2009)
Treemix	Method for inferring the patterns of population splits and mixtures in the history of a set of populations	(Pickrell et al., 2012)
TrimsimJ	Allows researchers to easily sample and analyze gene genealogies and related data from populations evolving under a wide variety of selective and demographic regimes	(O'Fallon, 2010)
YCDMA	Data management program for microsatellite data including performing a wide variety of management tasks, manipulating and maintaining genotypes databases, gene frequency calculations, and file format conversions; can also perform calculations of a variety of gene frequency genetic distances between populations, as well as a squared copy number microsatellite genetic distance.	(Ravaoarimanana & Montagnon, 2006)

It manages MareNostrum, one of the most powerful supercomputers in Europe. MareNostrum is a supercomputer based on Intel SandyBridge processors, iDataPlex Compute Racks, a Linux Operating System and an Infiniband interconnection (BSC, 2014). The system consists of 48,896 cores, 925.1 TFlop/s Linpack Performance, and a 1,015.60 kW Power. In June 2013, MareNostrum was positioned at the 29th place in the TOP500 list of fastest supercomputers in the world (Top500,

2013c). BCS has been used in the analysis of population genetic data specifically in genome-wide scan for epistasis. Using the MareNostrum system, $\sim 45 \times 10^{-9}$ pairwise analyses (binary test of epistasis (SNP × SNP method)) could be ran by modifying the PLINK software (Julia et al., 2008).

The San Diego Supercomputing Center (USA)

The San Diego Supercomputer Center (SDSC) is a supercomputing facility located at the University of California San Diego (UCSD) founded in 1985 with the primary mission of enabling international science and engineering discoveries through advances in computational science and data intensive, high performance computing. It was founded with a $170 million grant from the National Science Foundation's (NSF) Supercomputer Centers program. SDSC has launched in 2009, the *Triton Resource*, an integrated, data-intensive compute system primarily designed to support the University of California (UC) San Diego and UC researchers, along with *Dash,* the first high-performance compute system to leverage super-sized "flash memory" to accelerate investigation of a wide range of data-intensive science problems. *Trestles,* a 100-teraflops cluster was also launched in early 2010, which is already delivering increased productivity and fast turn around times to a diverse range of researchers. In early 2012, *Gordon*, which is a much larger version of the *Dash* prototype was launched. *Gordon* can handle massive databases 100 times faster speeds when compared to hard disk drive systems for some queries (SDSC, 2014). Specifically, the system consists of 16,160 cores, 285.8 TFlop/s Linpack Performance, and a 358.40 kW Power. It has also a memory of 32,320 GB. The SDSC was ranked 129th in the top 500 supercomputer sites in the world in November 2013 (Top500, 2013d). The SDSC was successfully utilized for the spatial distribution of genotypes under isolation by distance and in phylogenetic relationships

determination (Epperson, 1995; Gomez-Alpizar et al., 2008).

Grand Equipement National de Calcul Intensif - Centre Informatique National de l'Enseignement Suprieur (France)

The Grand Equipement National de Calcul Intensif - Centre Informatique National de l'Enseignement Suprieur (GENCI-CINES) is a relatively new supercomputer site created in 2007 in France with the missions of implementing and ensuring the coordination of the major equipments of the national high performance computing (HPC) centers, by providing funding and by assuming ownership; promote the organization of a European HPC area and participate to its achievements; and set up research and development collaborations in order to optimize HPC. GENCI is the French representative in Partnership for Advanced Computing in Europe (GENCI, 2014). In November 2013, the GENCI-CINES was ranked 169th in the top 500 supercomputer sites. The system is composed of Jade - SGI ICE 8200EX, Xeon E5450 4C 3.000GHz, Infiniband. Specifically, it consists of 23,040 cores, 237.8 TFlop/s Linpack performance, 1,064 kW Power, and 95,250 GB memory (Top500, 2013a). The Jade system was successful used in PHYLDOG software for the genome-scale coestimation of species and gene trees (Boussau et al., 2013).

CINECA (Italy)

Cineca is a non-profit consortium comprising of 69 Italian universities and 3 institutions and is the largest Italian supercomputing center and one of the most important worldwide. It offers support to the research activities of the scientific community through supercomputing and its applications. Its institutional mission includes the creation of management systems and services to provide support for universities and the Ministry of Education, University and Research (MIUR) (CINECA, 2014). In November 2013, CINECA's Fermi was ranked 15th in the Top 500 Specifically, the system is a Fermi - BlueGene/Q, Power BQC 16C 1.60GHz, Custom, consisting of 163,840 cores, 1,788.9 TFlop/s Linpack performance, and 821.88 kW Power (Top500, 2013e). Giovannini and colleagues have successfully used parLEA using CINECA in estimating proportions of population admixture from large genomic datasets in reasonable time (Giovannini et al., 2009).

DOE/SC/Oak Ridge National Laboratory (USA)

The DOE/SC/Oak Ridge National Laboratory is currently listed in the 2nd spot in top 500 supercomputer sites in the November 2013 list. The center proudly boasts with their Titan - Cray XK7, Opteron 6274 16C 2.200GHz, Cray Gemini interconnect, NVIDIA K20x system. The system consists of 560,640 cores, 17,590.0 TFlop/s Linpack Performance, 8,209.00 kW Power, and 710,144 GB memory (Top500, 2013b). Titan will be the first major supercomputing system to utilize a hybrid architecture, or one that utilizes both conventional 16-core AMD Opteron CPUs and NVIDIA Tesla K20 GPU Accelerators. This combination of CPUs and GPUs will allow future systems to overcome power and space limitations present in previous generation of high performance computers. By pairing CPUs and GPU accelerators and maximizing the efficiency of applications to exploit their strengths, Titan will lead the way on the road to the exascale (ORNL, 2012). Titan has a wide variety of applications in various research areas including population genetics. The increasingly computationally demanding quantification of the contribution of genetic variation to phenotypic variation for complex trait has becoming cumbersome with increasing number of SNPs and individuals. To meet this challenge, a software called REACTA was introduced, which was designed to exploit the parallelism present in

modern traditional and graphics processing unit (GPU)-accelerated machines, from workstations to supercomputers. The software was successfully demonstrated software 1024 GPUs in parallel with Titan supercomputer (Cebamanos et al., 2014).

CHALLENGES, SOLUTIONS, AND RECOMMENDATIONS

The analysis of population subdivision is a major focus in population genetics studies. In the so-called Isolation with Migration (IM) model, divergence times and migration times between two populations from DNA sequence data are jointly estimated. However, the IM utilizes parameter estimates that are based on Markov Chain Monte Carlo (MCMC) method, which is considered time consuming and requires memory beyond the capacity of a single computer. As such, a data parallel implementation of IM model based on Message Passing Interface (MPI) was proposed leading to reduced time required for parameter inferences (Chunbao et al., 2012).

The large and complex genomic datasets have presented a problem in population genetics specifically in obtaining valid and efficient statistical inferences. This problem arises from nuisance parameters in the model (Beaumont et al., 2002). A new method for approximating Bayesian statistical inference is suited to complex problems arising in population genetics. The method has an advantage in that the nuisance parameters are automatically integrated out in the simulation step, so that large numbers of nuisance parameters that arise in population genetics problems can be handled without difficulty. Simulation results showed statistical and computational efficiency (Beaumont et al., 2002).

With the large volumes of data from population genetics research, there is a stress need for the development of novel bioinformatics algorithms to further optimize the datasets available. In general, the bioinformatics community including that of population genetics field has developed algorithms for the analysis of genetic data that are based on symmetric multiprocessing (SMP) computer systems requiring huge amounts of random access memory. This tends to limit the parallelization of these algorithms to several cores using thread programming. Thus, it is proposed that an implementation of these algorithms on massively parallel, distributed memory supercomputers will enable the researchers in "Precision Medicine" to carry out more complex analysis that will have a significant impact in advancing the field (Reumann et al., 2011).

Recently, an M45 Cloud Computing Initiative was expanded by "Yahoo!" adding top universities such as Stanford, the University of Washington, the University of Michigan at Ann Arbor, and Purdue on the list of supercomputing cluster. These schools join Carnegie Mellon University, Cornell University, the University of California at Berkeley and the University of Massachusetts at Amherst in bringing a unique Internet-scale computing environment to academic researchers working on various areas including that of population genetics. This initiative will provide these universities opportunity to conduct such research otherwise impossible without the power and speed of a supercomputing resource, which consists of approximately 4,000 processors (Nikravesh, 2010).

Although in the recent years, scientists have investigated and put it extensive efforts to assess most common variants such as the single nucleotide polymorphisms (SNPs) in genome-wide studies for statistical associations with numerous complex traits such as the common human diseases, only a limited number of heritable component of such complex traits has been identified. Thus, it is a challenge to determine the functional link between associated variants and phenotypic traits. Therefore, it is necessary to introduce technological advances in SNP assaying in order to elucidate rare and structural variants (Frazer et al., 2009). Further, results from recent sequencing of thousand number of exomes from across the world, identified that the vast majority of genetic variation within genes is rare, highly population-specific, and just arose recently (T. G. P. Consortium, 2012) (Tennessen et al., 2012) (Gravel et al., 2011). These imply that human evolutionary history is more complex than originally imagined (Hernandez et al., 2011). These observations remain consistent with the population genetics theory, and thus, imply that population genetics may be essential for elucidating the drivers of many complex diseases (Eichler et al., 2010).

FUTURE RESEARCH DIRECTIONS

Evolutionary computation in population genetics is becoming common in the solution of complex problems in genetic epidemiology. As the uses of supercomputers to address important problems in the society such as researches in population genetics continue to grow and the place of supercomputing within the overall computing industry continues to change, the value of innovation in supercomputing architecture, modeling systems software, applications software, and algorithms will endure (Academies, 2003).

With the advent of next generation sequencing technologies, keen insight into the genetic polymorphisms between individuals can be made possible, and, thus, coupling these with advances in computational biology approaches, the etiology of complex diseases can be traced. Molecular methods are beginning to accrue multitude of data, and thus, the potential for resolving genetic individuality at the level of DNA sequences is realized. In this regard, identification of relatedness and clustering of individuals into biologically meaningful groups becomes challenges. With the increasing population genetic information accumulated by research scientists, the issues of computational burden will likely be met with the routine use of supercomputers (Hedgecock, n.d.).

Taking full advantage of the information in the patterns of the human genetic diversity will require the development of more realistic and complex models incorporating geographic, ethnographic, linguistic, and archaeological data. As this field propels into the future, the questions of how to collect and analyze genetic data in a meaningful manner will have to be continually revisited (Wilkins, 2006).

CONCLUSION

Theoretical population genetics gives mathematically tractable ways to begin to describe the evolutionary process of diseases as well as to reconstruct the prehistory of humans. By investigating the patterns of genetic diversity present in modern human species (and some sufficiently well-preserved human remains), we can unravel the evidence that favors or disfavors our modern genetic outcomes. Further, the ultimate dissection of a wide array of genomic markers can lead to the identification of the etiology of complex diseases present in specific populations. With the advent of supercomputers and modern computational tools, computational time and analysis of large population genetics datasets have become more manageable. Thus, it is of great benefit if universities, research centers, and specialized institutes support research on population genetics.

REFERENCES

Abel, J. (2013). *Ohio supercomputing center annual research report 2013: Discovering keys to controlling malaria*. Columbus, OH: University System of Ohio.

Academies, T. N. (2003). *The future of supercomputing: An interim report* (p. 4). Washington, DC: National Academy of Sciences.

Amigo, J., Salas, A., & Phillips, C. (2011). ENGINES: Exploring single nucleotide variation in entire human genomes. *BMC Bioinformatics*, *12*(1), 105. doi:10.1186/1471-2105-12-105 PMID:21504571

Amirisetty, S., Hershey, G. K., & Baye, T. M. (2012). AncestrySNPminer: A bioinformatics tool to retrieve and develop ancestry informative SNP panels. *Genomics*, *100*(1), 57–63. doi:10.1016/j.ygeno.2012.05.003 PMID:22584067

Andrade, J., Andersen, M., Sillen, A., Graff, C., & Odeberg, J. (2007). The use of grid computing to drive data-intensive genetic research. *European Journal of Human Genetics*, *15*(6), 694–702. doi:10.1038/sj.ejhg.5201815 PMID:17377522

Barton, N. H., & Charlesworth, B. (1984). Genetic revolution, founder effects, and speciation. *Annual Review of Ecology and Systematics*, *15*(1), 133–165. doi:10.1146/annurev.es.15.110184.001025

Beaumont, M. A., Zhang, W., & Balding, D. J. (2002). Approximate Bayesian computation in population genetics. *Genetics*, *162*(4), 2025–2035. PMID:12524368

Belkhir, K., Borsa, P., Chikhi, L., Raufaste, N., & Bonhomme, F. (2004). *Genetix 4.05 software*. Retrieved from http://www.univ-montp2.fr/~genetix/genetix/genetix.htm

Belle, E. M., Landry, P. A., & Barbujani, G. (2006). Origins and evolution of the Europeans' genome: Evidence from multiple microsatellite loci. *Proceedings. Biological Sciences*, *273*(1594), 1595–1602. doi:10.1098/rspb.2006.3494 PMID:16769629

Bergey, C. M. (2011). AluHunter: A database of potentially polymorphic Alu insertions for use in primate phylogeny and population genetics. *Bioinformatics (Oxford, England)*, *27*(20), 2924–2925. doi:10.1093/bioinformatics/btr491 PMID:21880703

Berry, M. W., Gao, T., Pathan, R., & Stuart, G. W. (2013). PolyLens: Software for map-based visualisation and analysis of genome-scale polymorphism data. *Int J Comput Biol Drug Des, 6*(1-2), 93–106. doi:10.1504/IJCBDD.2013.052204 PMID:23428476

Bertorelle, G., Benazzo, A., & Mona, S. (2010). ABC as a flexible framework to estimate demography over space and time: Some cons, many pros. *Molecular Ecology, 19*(13), 2609–2625. doi:10.1111/j.1365-294X.2010.04690.x PMID:20561199

Besnier, F., & Glover, K. A. (2013). ParallelStructure: A R package to distribute parallel runs of the population genetics program STRUCTURE on multi-core computers. *PLoS ONE, 8*(7), e70651. doi:10.1371/journal.pone.0070651 PMID:23923012

Boitard, S., Kofler, R., Francoise, P., Robelin, D., Schlotterer, C., & Futschik, A. (2013). Poolhmm: A Python program for estimating the allele frequency spectrum and detecting selective sweeps from next generation sequencing of pooled samples. *Molecular Ecology Resources, 13*(2), 337–340. doi:10.1111/1755-0998.12063 PMID:23311589

Boussau, B., Szollosi, G. J., Duret, L., Gouy, M., Tannier, E., & Daubin, V. (2013). Genome-scale coestimation of species and gene trees. *Genome Research, 23*(2), 323–330. doi:10.1101/gr.141978.112 PMID:23132911

BSC. (2014). *The Barcelona supercomputing center.* Retrieved February 28, 2014, from http://www.bsc.es/

Buckleton, J. S. (2004). Population genetic models. In J. S. Buckleton, C. M. Triggs, & S. J. Walsh (Eds.), *Forensic DNA evidence interpretation.* Boca Raton, FL: CRC Press. doi:10.1201/9781420037920.ch3

Carvajal-Rodriguez, A. (2008). GENOMEPOP: A program to simulate genomes in populations. *BMC Bioinformatics, 9*(1), 223. doi:10.1186/1471-2105-9-223 PMID:18447924

Catchen, J., Hohenlohe, P. A., Bassham, S., Amores, A., & Cresko, W. A. (2013). Stacks: An analysis tool set for population genomics. *Molecular Ecology, 22*(11), 3124–3140. doi:10.1111/mec.12354 PMID:23701397

Cebamanos, L., Gray, A., Stewart, I., & Tenesa, A. (2014). Regional heritability advanced complex trait analysis for GPU and traditional parallel architectures. *Bioinformatics (Oxford, England), 30*(8), 1177–1179. doi:10.1093/bioinformatics/btt754 PMID:24403537

Chan, K. M., & Moore, B. R. (2005). SYMMETREE: Whole-tree analysis of differential diversification rates. *Bioinformatics (Oxford, England), 21*(8), 1709–1710. doi:10.1093/bioinformatics/bti175 PMID:15572466

Cheng, L., Connor, T. R., Siren, J., Aanensen, D. M., & Corander, J. (2013). Hierarchical and spatially explicit clustering of DNA sequences with BAPS software. *Molecular Biology and Evolution, 30*(5), 1224–1228. doi:10.1093/molbev/mst028 PMID:23408797

Chunbao, Z., XianYu, L., YanGang, W., & ChaoDong, Z. (2012). A parallel implementation of the isolation with migration model. *e-Science Technology and Application, 3*(1), 24-28.

CINECA. (2014). *CINCEA supercomputer center.* Retrieved February 28, 2014, from http://www.cineca.it/en

Conkle, T. (1972). *Analyzing genetic diversity in conifers--Isozyme resolution by starch gel electrophoresis.* Berkeley, CA: USDA.

Consortium, T. G. P. (2012). An integrated map of genetic variation from 1,092 human genomes. *Nature, 491,* 56–65. doi:10.1038/nature11632 PMID:23128226

Cornuet, J. M., Santos, F., Beaumont, M. A., Robert, C. P., Marin, J. M., & Balding, D. J. et al. (2008). Inferring population history with DIY ABC: A user-friendly approach to approximate Bayesian computation. *Bioinformatics (Oxford, England), 24*(23), 2713–2719. doi:10.1093/bioinformatics/btn514 PMID:18842597

Crow, J. F. (1987). Population genetics history: A personal view. *Annual Review of Genetics, 21*(1), 1–22. doi:10.1146/annurev.ge.21.120187.000245 PMID:3327458

De Mita, S., & Siol, M. (2012). EggLib: Processing, analysis and simulation tools for population genetics and genomics. *BMC Genetics, 13*(1), 27. doi:10.1186/1471-2156-13-27 PMID:22494792

Di Rienzo, A. (2006). Population genetics models of common diseases. *Current Opinion in Genetics & Development, 16*(6), 630–636. doi:10.1016/j.gde.2006.10.002 PMID:17055247

Didelot, X., & Falush, D. (2007). Inference of bacterial microevolution using multilocus sequence data. *Genetics, 175*(3), 1251–1266. doi:10.1534/genetics.106.063305 PMID:17151252

Didelot, X., Lawson, D., Darling, A., & Falush, D. (2010). Inference of homologous recombination in bacteria using whole-genome sequences. *Genetics, 186*(4), 1435–1449. doi:10.1534/genetics.110.120121 PMID:20923983

Drummond, A. J., & Rambaut, A. (2007). BEAST: Bayesian evolutionary analysis by sampling trees. *BMC Evolutionary Biology, 7*(1), 214. doi:10.1186/1471-2148-7-214 PMID:17996036

Dubrow, A. (2012). *Monogamy and the immune system*. Retrieved February 23, 2013, from http://www.tacc.utexas.edu/news/feature-stories/2012/monogamy-and-the-immune-system

Eanes, W. F., & Koehn, R. K. (1978). An analysis of genetic structure in the Monarch butterfly, Danaus plexippus L. *Evolutionary Bioinformatics Online, 32*(4), 784–797.

Education, N. (2013). *The genetic variation in a population is caused by multiple factors*. Retrieved September 18, 2013, from http://www.nature.com/scitable/topicpage/the-genetic-variation-in-a-population-is-6526354

Eichler, E. E., Flint, J., Gibson, G., Kong, A., Leal, S. M., Moore, J. H., & Nadeau, J. H. (2010). Missing heritability and strategies for finding the underlying causes of complex disease. *Nature Reviews. Genetics, 11*(6), 446–450. doi:10.1038/nrg2809 PMID:20479774

Epperson, B. K. (1995). Spatial distributions of genotypes under isolation by distance. *Genetics, 140*, 1431–1440. PMID:7498782

Etheridge, A. (2009). *Some mathematical models from population genetics*. Springer.

Excoffier, L., Laval, L. G., & Schneider, S. (2005). Arlequin ver. 3.0: An integrated software package for population genetics data analysis. *Evolutionary Bioinformatics Online, 1*, 47–50. PMID:19325852

Excoffier, L., & Lischer, H. E. (2010). Arlequin suite ver 3.5: A new series of programs to perform population genetics analyses under Linux and Windows. *Molecular Ecology Resources, 10*(3), 564–567. doi:10.1111/j.1755-0998.2010.02847.x PMID:21565059

Excoffier, L., & Lischer, H. E. (2013). *Arlequin 3.01: An integrated software for population genetics data analysis (version 3.01)*. Academic Press.

Falush, D., Stephens, M., & Pritchard, J. K. (2003). Inference of population structure using multilocus genotype data: Linked loci and correlated allele frequencies. *Genetics, 164*(4), 1567–1587. PMID:12930761

Fitzpatrick, B. M. (2012). Estimating ancestry and heterozygosity of hybrids using molecular markers. *BMC Evolutionary Biology*, *12*(1), 131. doi:10.1186/1471-2148-12-131 PMID:22849298

Francisco, A. P., Bugalho, M., Ramirez, M., & Carrico, J. A. (2009). Global optimal eBURST analysis of multilocus typing data using a graphic matroid approach. *BMC Bioinformatics*, *10*(1), 152. doi:10.1186/1471-2105-10-152 PMID:19450271

Francisco, A. P., Vaz, C., Monteiro, P. T., Melo-Cristino, J., Ramirez, M., & Carrico, J. A. (2012). PHYLOViZ: Phylogenetic inference and data visualization for sequence based typing methods. *BMC Bioinformatics*, *13*(1), 87. doi:10.1186/1471-2105-13-87 PMID:22568821

Frazer, K. A., Murray, S. S., Schork, N. J., & Topol, E. J. (2009). Human genetic variation and its contribution to complex traits. *Nature Reviews. Genetics*, *10*(4), 241–251. doi:10.1038/nrg2554 PMID:19293820

Gall, G. A. E. (1987). Inbreeding. In N. Ryman & F. M. Utter (Eds.), *Population genetics and fishery management* (pp. 47–88). Washington: University of Washington.

GENCI. (2014). *Grand equipement national de calcul intensif - Centre informatique national de l'enseignement suprieur*. Retrieved February 28, 2014, from http://www.genci.fr/en

Gillespie, J. (2004). *Population genetics: A concise guide* (2nd ed.). Baltimore, MD: The Johns Hopkins University Press.

Giovannini, A., Zanghirati, G., Beaumont, M. A., Chikhi, L., & Barbujani, G. (2009). A novel parallel approach to the likelihood-based estimation of admixture in population genetics. *Bioinformatics (Oxford, England)*, *25*(11), 1440–1441. doi:10.1093/bioinformatics/btp136 PMID:19286832

Gomez-Alpizar, L., Hu, C. H., Oliva, R., Forbes, G., & Ristaino, J. B. (2008). Phylogenetic relationships of Phytophthora andina, a new species from the highlands of Ecuador that is closely related to the Irish potato famine pathogen Phytophthora infestans. *Mycologia*, *100*(4), 590–602. doi:10.3852/07-074R1 PMID:18833752

Gompert, Z., & Buerkle, C. A. (2012). BGC: Software for Bayesian estimation of genomic clines. *Molecular Ecology Resources*, *12*(6), 1168–1176. doi:10.1111/1755-0998.12009.x PMID:22978657

Gravel, S., Henn, B. M., Gutenkunst, R. N., Indap, A. R., Marth, G. T., & Clark, A. G. et al. (2011). Demographic history and rare allele sharing among human populations. *Proceedings of the National Academy of Sciences of the United States of America*, *108*(29), 11983–11988. doi:10.1073/pnas.1019276108 PMID:21730125

Gunther, T., & Coop, G. (2013). Robust identification of local adaptation from allele frequencies. *Genetics*, *195*(1), 205–220. doi:10.1534/genetics.113.152462 PMID:23821598

Gupta, P., Conrad, T., Spotter, A., Reinsch, N., & Bienefeld, K. (2012). Simulating a base population in honey bee for molecular genetic studies. *Genetics, Selection, Evolution.*, *44*(1), 14. doi:10.1186/1297-9686-44-14 PMID:22520469

Hardy, O. J., & Vekemans, X. (2002). SPAGeDi: A versatile computer program to analyse spatial genetic structure at the individual or population levels. *Molecular Ecology Notes*, *2*(4), 618–620. doi:10.1046/j.1471-8286.2002.00305.x

Hedgecock, D. (n.d.). *Population genetics of marine organisms*. Retrieved September 22, 2013, from http://www.usglobec.org/newsletter/news6/news6.hedgecock.html

Hedrick, P. (2011). *Genetics of populations*. Sudbury, MA: Jones and Bartlett Publishers, LLC.

Hernandez, R. D., Kelley, J. L., Elyashiv, E., Melton, S. C., Auton, A., & McVean, G. et al. (2011). Classic selective sweeps were rare in recent human evolution. *Science, 331*(6019), 920–924. doi:10.1126/science.1198878 PMID:21330547

Hird, S. M. (2012). lociNGS: A lightweight alternative for assessing suitability of next-generation loci for evolutionary analysis. *PLoS ONE, 7*(10), e46847. doi:10.1371/journal.pone.0046847 PMID:23071651

Institute, I. P. G. R., & University, C. (2003). Basic concepts of population genetics. In *Genetic diversity analysis with molecular marker data: Learning module.* Retrieved December 23, 2012, from http://www.bioversityinternational.org

Joly, S. (2012). JML: Testing hybridization from species trees. *Molecular Ecology Resources, 12*(1), 179–184. doi:10.1111/j.1755-0998.2011.03065.x PMID:21899723

Julia, A., Ballina, J., Canete, J. D., Balsa, A., Tornero-Molina, J., & Naranjo, A. et al. (2008). Genome-wide association study of rheumatoid arthritis in the Spanish population: KLF12 as a risk locus for rheumatoid arthritis susceptibility. *Arthritis and Rheumatism, 58*(8), 2275–2286. doi:10.1002/art.23623 PMID:18668548

Kalinowski, S. T. (2009). How well do evolutionary trees describe genetic relationships among populations? *Heredity (Edinb), 102*(5), 506–513. doi:10.1038/hdy.2008.136 PMID:19174839

Karlin, S. (1972). Some mathematical models of population genetics. *The American Mathematical Monthly, 79*(7), 699–739. doi:10.2307/2316262

Kazmi, S. (2012). *Columbia read history through genetics.* Retrieved February 23, 2013, from http://www.supercomputingonline.com/this-years-stories/columbia-reads-history-through-genetics

Kelleher, J., Barton, N. H., & Etheridge, A. M. (2013). Coalescent simulation in continuous space. *Bioinformatics (Oxford, England), 29*(7), 955–956. doi:10.1093/bioinformatics/btt067 PMID:23391497

Kofler, R., Pandey, R. V., & Schlotterer, C. (2011). PoPoolation2: Identifying differentiation between populations using sequencing of pooled DNA samples (Pool-Seq). *Bioinformatics (Oxford, England), 27*(24), 3435–3436. doi:10.1093/bioinformatics/btr589 PMID:22025480

Kuhn, T. (1962). *The structure of scientific revolutions.* Chicago: University of Chicago Press.

Lacy, R. C. (2012). Extending pedigree analysis for uncertain parentage and diverse breeding systems. *The Journal of Heredity, 103*(2), 197–205. doi:10.1093/jhered/esr135 PMID:22275398

Lapointe, F.-J., & Legendre, P. (1992). A statistical framework to test the consensus among additive trees (cladograms). *Systematic Biology, 41*(2), 158–171. doi:10.1093/sysbio/41.2.158

Lapointe, F.-J., Legendre, P., & Casgrain, P. (2013). *Permute! Version 3.4 alpha 9: Multiple regression over distance, ultrametric and additive matrices with permutation test.* Academic Press.

Lawson, D. J., Hellenthal, G., Myers, S., & Falush, D. (2012). Inference of population structure using dense haplotype data. *PLOS Genetics, 8*(1), e1002453. doi:10.1371/journal.pgen.1002453 PMID:22291602

Lewis-Rogers, N., Crandall, K. A., & Posada, D. (2004). Evolutionary analyses of genetic recombination. In V. Parisi, V. De Fonzo, & F. Aluffi-Pentini (Eds.), *Dynamical genetics* (p. 50). Kerala, India: Research Signpost.

Lewontin, R. C. (2000). What do population geneticists know and how do they know it? In Creath & Mainschein (Eds.), Biology and epistemology. Cambridge, UK: Cambirdge University Press.

Li, J. Z., Absher, D. M., Tang, H., Southwick, A. M., Casto, A. M., & Ramachandran, S. et al. (2008). Worldwide human relationships inferred from genome-wide patterns of variation. *Science, 319*(5866), 1100–1104. doi:10.1126/science.1153717 PMID:18292342

Librado, P., & Rozas, J. (2009). DnaSP v5: A software for comprehensive analysis of DNA polymorphism data. *Bioinformatics (Oxford, England), 25*(11), 1451–1452. doi:10.1093/bioinformatics/btp187 PMID:19346325

Lipson, M., Loh, P. R., Levin, A., Reich, D., Patterson, N., & Berger, B. (2013). Efficient moment-based inference of admixture parameters and sources of gene flow. *Molecular Biology and Evolution, 30*(8), 1788–1802. doi:10.1093/molbev/mst099 PMID:23709261

Lischer, H. E., & Excoffier, L. (2012). PGDSpider: An automated data conversion tool for connecting population genetics and genomics programs. *Bioinformatics (Oxford, England), 28*(2), 298–299. doi:10.1093/bioinformatics/btr642 PMID:22110245

Loewe, L. (2008). Genetic mutation. *Nature Education, 1*(1).

Loh, P. R., Lipson, M., Patterson, N., Moorjani, P., Pickrell, J. K., Reich, D., & Berger, B. (2013). Inferring admixture histories of human populations using linkage disequilibrium. *Genetics, 193*(4), 1233–1254. doi:10.1534/genetics.112.147330 PMID:23410830

MacManes, M. D., & Lacey, E. A. (2012). Is promiscuity associated with enhanced selection on MHC-DQalpha in mice (genus Peromyscus)? *PLoS ONE, 7*(5), e37562. doi:10.1371/journal.pone.0037562 PMID:22649541

Magalhaes, W. C., Rodrigues, M. R., Silva, D., Soares-Souza, G., Iannini, M. L., & Cerqueira, G. C. et al. (2012). DIVERGENOME: A bioinformatics platform to assist population genetics and genetic epidemiology studies. *Genetic Epidemiology, 36*(4), 360–367. doi:10.1002/gepi.21629 PMID:22508222

Medline, L. K., Lange, M., & Nothig, E.-M. (2000). Genetic diversity in the marine phytoplankton: a review and a consideration of Antarctic phytoplankton. *Antarctic Science, 12*(3), 325–333.

Meirmans, P. (2013). *GenoDive (version 2.0b23, manual): Software for analysis of population genetic data*. Universiteit van Amsterdam.

Meirmans, P. G. (2012). AMOVA-based clustering of population genetic data. *The Journal of Heredity, 103*(5), 744–750. doi:10.1093/jhered/ess047 PMID:22896561

Meirmans, P. G., & Tienderen, V. (2004). GENOTYPE and GENODIVE: Two programs for the analysis of genetic diversity of asexual organisms. *Molecular Ecology Notes, 4*(4), 792–794. doi:10.1111/j.1471-8286.2004.00770.x

Moltke, I., & Albrechtsen, A. (2013). RelateAdmix: A software tool for estimating relatedness between admixed individuals. *Bioinformatics (Oxford, England)*. doi:10.1093/bioinformatics/btt652 PMID:24215025

Morris, J. A., & Barrett, J. C. (2012). Olorin: Combining gene flow with exome sequencing in large family studies of complex disease. *Bioinformatics (Oxford, England), 28*(24), 3320–3321. doi:10.1093/bioinformatics/bts609 PMID:23052039

Muller, T., Rahmann, S., Dandekar, T., & Wolf, M. (2004). Accurate and robust phylogeny estimation based on profile distances: A study of the Chlorophyceae (Chlorophyta). *BMC Evolutionary Biology, 4*(1), 20. doi:10.1186/1471-2148-4-20 PMID:15222898

Nikravesh, M. (2010). *Yahoo! Expands Its M45 cloud computing initiative, adding top universities to supercomputing research cluster.* Retrieved March 9, 2013, from http://citris-uc.org/news/2010/11/29/yahoo_expands_its_m45_cloud_computing_initiative_adding_top_universities_supercomputing_research_cluster

O'Fallon, B. (2010). TreesimJ: A flexible, forward time population genetic simulator. *Bioinformatics (Oxford, England), 26*(17), 2200–2201. doi:10.1093/bioinformatics/btq355 PMID:20671150

ORNL. (2012). *Introducing Titan: Advancing the era of accelerated computing.* Retrieved March 1, 2014, from http://www.olcf.ornl.gov/titan/

OSC. (2014). *The Ohio supercomputing center.* Retrieved February 28, 2014, from http://www.osc.edu/

Palamara, P. F., Lencz, T., Darvasi, A., & Pe'er, I. (2012). Length distributions of identity by descent reveal fine-scale demographic history. *American Journal of Human Genetics, 91*(5), 809–822. doi:10.1016/j.ajhg.2012.08.030 PMID:23103233

Paradis, E. (2010). pegas: An R package for population genetics with an integrated-modular approach. *Bioinformatics (Oxford, England), 26*(3), 419–420. doi:10.1093/bioinformatics/btp696 PMID:20080509

Patterson, N., Moorjani, P., Luo, Y., Mallick, S., Rohland, N., & Zhan, Y. et al. (2012). Ancient admixture in human history. *Genetics, 192*(3), 1065–1093. doi:10.1534/genetics.112.145037 PMID:22960212

Patterson, N., Price, A. L., Reich, D., Plenge, R. M., Weinblatt, M. E., Shadick, N. A., & Reich, D. (2013). *EIGENSOFT version 5.01.* Harvard University.

Peacock, E., & Whiteley, P. (2005). Perlegen sciences, inc. *Pharmacogenomics, 6*(4), 439–442. doi:10.1517/14622416.6.4.439 PMID:16004563

Peakall, R., & Smouse, P. E. (2012). GenAlEx 6.5: Genetic analysis in Excel. Population genetic software for teaching and research--An update. *Bioinformatics (Oxford, England), 28*(19), 2537–2539. doi:10.1093/bioinformatics/bts460 PMID:22820204

Pembleton, L. W., Cogan, N. O., & Forster, J. W. (2013). StAMPP: An R package for calculation of genetic differentiation and structure of mixed-ploidy level populations. *Molecular Ecology Resources, 13*(5), 946–952. doi:10.1111/1755-0998.12129 PMID:23738873

Pennell, M. W., Stansbury, C. R., Waits, L. P., & Miller, C. R. (2013). Capwire: A R package for estimating population census size from non-invasive genetic sampling. *Molecular Ecology Resources, 13*(1), 154–157. doi:10.1111/1755-0998.12019 PMID:22995036

Perez-Figueroa, A., Rodriguez-Ramilo, S. T., & Caballero, A. (2012). Analysis and management of gene and allelic diversity in subdivided populations using the software program METAPOP. *Methods in Molecular Biology (Clifton, N.J.), 888*, 261–275. doi:10.1007/978-1-61779-870-2_15 PMID:22665286

Pickrell, J. K., & Pritchard, J. K. (2012). Inference of population splits and mixtures from genome-wide allele frequency data. *PLOS Genetics, 8*(11), e1002967. doi:10.1371/journal.pgen.1002967 PMID:23166502

Plutynski, A., & Evans, W. (2005). Population genetics. In S. Sarkar & J. Pheiffer (Eds.), *Routledge encyclopedia of science* (pp. 578–585). London: Routledge.

Porras-Hurtado, L., Ruiz, Y., Santos, C., Phillips, C., Carracedo, A., & Lareu, M. V. (2013). An overview of STRUCTURE: Applications, parameter settings, and supporting software. *Frontiers in Genetics, 4*, 98. doi:10.3389/fgene.2013.00098 PMID:23755071

Price, A. L., Patterson, N. J., Plenge, R. M., Weinblatt, M. E., Shadick, N. A., & Reich, D. (2006). Principal components analysis corrects for stratification in genome-wide association studies. *Nature Genetics*, *38*(8), 904–909. doi:10.1038/ng1847 PMID:16862161

Purcell, S., Neale, B., Todd-Brown, K., Thomas, L., Ferreira, M. A., & Bender, D. et al. (2007). PLINK: A tool set for whole-genome association and population-based linkage analyses. *American Journal of Human Genetics*, *81*(3), 559–575. doi:10.1086/519795 PMID:17701901

Ravaoarimanana, I. B., & Montagnon, D. (2006). *Nucleotide sequences analyzer (NSA) version 3.3*. France: Institut d'Embryologie, Faculté de Médecine.

Raymond, M., & Rousset, F. (1995). GENEPOP (version 1.2) population genetic software for exact tests and ecumenicism. *The Journal of Heredity*, *86*, 248–249.

Reppell, M., Boehnke, M., & Zollner, S. (2012). FTEC: A coalescent simulator for modeling faster than exponential growth. *Bioinformatics (Oxford, England)*, *28*(9), 1282–1283. doi:10.1093/bioinformatics/bts135 PMID:22441586

Reumann, M., Holt, K. E., Inouye, M., Stinear, T., Goudey, B. W., Abraham, G., et al. (2011). *Precision medicine: Dawn of supercomputing in 'omics' research*. Paper presented at the 5th eResearch Australasia Conference, Melbourne, Australia.

Rodrigo, A., Drummond, A., & Goode, M. (2010). *Pebble, version 1.0, (phylogenetics, evolutionary biology, and bioinformatics in a modular environment)*. Auckland, New Zealand: University of Auckland.

Rousset, F. (2008). genepop'007: A complete re-implementation of the genepop software for Windows and Linux. *Molecular Ecology Resources*, *8*(1), 103–106. doi:10.1111/j.1471-8286.2007.01931.x PMID:21585727

Rozas, J., & Rozas, R. (1999). DnaSP version 3: An integrated program for molecular population genetics and molecular evolution analysis. *Bioinformatics (Oxford, England)*, *15*(2), 174–175. doi:10.1093/bioinformatics/15.2.174 PMID:10089204

Sagoo, G. (2007). Glossary of terms. In D. J. Balding, M. Bishop, & C. Cannings (Eds.), *Handbook of statistical genetics* (3rd ed.; Vol. 1). West Sussex, UK: John Wiley & Sons.

San Lucas, F. A., Rosenberg, N. A., & Scheet, P. (2012). Haploscope: A tool for the graphical display of haplotype structure in populations. *Genetic Epidemiology*, *36*(1), 17–21. doi:10.1002/gepi.20640 PMID:22147662

SDSC. (2014). *San Diego supercompuer center*. Retrieved February 28, 2014, from http://www.sdsc.edu

Sherlock, R., & Morrey, J. D. (2002). *Ethical issues in biotechnology*. Maryland: Rowman and Littlefield Publishers.

Shirk, A. J., & Cushman, S. A. (2011). sGD: Software for estimating spatially explicit indices of genetic diversity. *Molecular Ecology Resources*, *11*(5), 922–934. doi:10.1111/j.1755-0998.2011.03035.x PMID:21679313

Skotte, L., Korneliussen, T. S., & Albrechtsen, A. (2013). Estimating individual admixture proportions from next generation sequencing data. *Genetics*, *195*(3), 693–702. doi:10.1534/genetics.113.154138 PMID:24026093

Sokal, R. R. (1991). The continental population-structure of Europe. *Annual Review of Anthropology*, *20*(1), 119–140. doi:10.1146/annurev.an.20.100191.001003

Stranger, B. E., Stahl, E. A., & Raj, T. (2011). Progress and promise of genome-wide association studies for human complex trait genetics. *Genetics*, *187*(2), 367–383. doi:10.1534/genetics.110.120907 PMID:21115973

Takezaki, N., Nei, M., & Tamura, K. (2010). POPTREE2: Software for constructing population trees from allele frequency data and computing other population statistics with Windows interface. *Molecular Biology and Evolution, 27*(4), 747–752. doi:10.1093/molbev/msp312 PMID:20022889

Team, M. R. C. (2012). *Supercomputers on demand with Windows Azure*. Retrieved September 22, 2013, from http://blogs.msdn.com/b/msr_er/archive/2012/11/12/affordable-supercomputing-with-windows-azure.aspx

Templeton, A. R. (2006). *Population genetics and microevolutionary theory*. New Jersey: John Wiley and Sons. doi:10.1002/0470047356

Tennessen, J. A., Bigham, A. W., O'Connor, T. D., Fu, W., Kenny, E. E., & Gravel, S. et al. (2012). Evolution and functional impact of rare coding variation from deep sequencing of human exomes. *Science, 337*(6090), 64–69. doi:10.1126/science.1219240 PMID:22604720

Tewari, S., & Spouge, J. L. (2012). Coalescent: An open-source and scalable framework for exact calculations in coalescent theory. *BMC Bioinformatics, 13*(1), 257. doi:10.1186/1471-2105-13-257 PMID:23033878

The International HapMap Consortium. (2005). A haplotype map of the human genome. *Nature, 437*(7063), 1299–1320. doi:10.1038/nature04226 PMID:16255080

Thornton, K. (2003). Libsequence: A C++ class library for evolutionary genetic analysis. *Bioinformatics (Oxford, England), 19*(17), 2325–2327. doi:10.1093/bioinformatics/btg316 PMID:14630667

Thornton, K. (2013). *Libsequence (version 1.7.9)*. University of Chicago.

Top500. (2013a). *Jade - SGI ICE 8200EX, Xeon E5450 4C 3.000GHz, Infiniband*. Retrieved February 28, 2014, from http://www.top500.org/system/176897

Top500. (2013b). *Titan - Cray XK7, Opteron 6274 16C 2.200GHz, Cray Gemini interconnect, NVIDIA K20x*. Retrieved March 1, 2014, from http://www.top500.org/system/177975

Top500. (2013c). *Top500 list supercomputer sites -June 2013*. Retrieved February 28, 2014, from http://www.top500.org/list/2013/06/?page=1

Top500. (2013d). *Top500 list supercomputer sites -November 2013*. Retrieved February 28, 2014, from http://www.top500.org/system/177455

Top500. (2013e). *Top 500 supercomputer site November 2013: CINECA*. Retrieved February 28, 2014, from http://www.top500.org/site/47495

Viennas, E., Gkantouna, V., Ioannou, M., Georgitsi, M., Rigou, M., & Poulas, K. et al. (2012). Population-ethnic group specific genome variation allele frequency data: A querying and visualization journey. *Genomics, 100*(2), 93–101. doi:10.1016/j.ygeno.2012.05.009 PMID:22659238

Vilella, A. J., Severin, J., Ureta-Vidal, A., Heng, L., Durbin, R., & Birney, E. (2009). EnsemblCompara GeneTrees: Complete, duplication-aware phylogenetic trees in vertebrates. *Genome Research, 19*(2), 327–335. doi:10.1101/gr.073585.107 PMID:19029536

Vitalis, R. (2012). DETSEL: An R-package to detect marker loci responding to selection. *Methods in Molecular Biology (Clifton, N.J.), 888*, 277–293. doi:10.1007/978-1-61779-870-2_16 PMID:22665287

von Haeseler, A., Sajantila, A., & Paabo, S. (1996). The genetical archaeology of the human genome. *Nature Genetics, 14*(2), 135–140. doi:10.1038/ng1096-135 PMID:8841181

Voorrips, R. E., & Maliepaard, C. A. (2012). The simulation of meiosis in diploid and tetraploid organisms using various genetic models. *BMC Bioinformatics, 13*(1), 248. doi:10.1186/1471-2105-13-248 PMID:23013469

Wakeley, J. (2004). Recent trends in population genetics: More data! More math! Simple models? *The Journal of Heredity*, *95*(5), 397–405. doi:10.1093/jhered/esh062 PMID:15388767

Weir, B. S. (1996). Intraspecific differentiation. In D. M. Hillis, C. Moritz, & B. K. Mable (Eds.), *Molecular systematics* (2nd ed.; pp. 385–406). Massachusetts: Sinauer Associates.

Weiser, E. L., Grueber, C. E., & Jamieson, I. G. (2012). AlleleRetain: A program to assess management options for conserving allelic diversity in small, isolated populations. *Molecular Ecology Resources*, *12*(6), 1161–1167. doi:10.1111/j.1755-0998.2012.03176.x PMID:22925629

Wilkins, J. F. (2006). Unraveling male and female histories from human genetic data. *Current Opinion in Genetics & Development*, *16*(6), 611–617. doi:10.1016/j.gde.2006.10.004 PMID:17067791

Winter, D. J. (2012). MMOD: An R library for the calculation of population differentiation statistics. *Molecular Ecology Resources*, *12*(6), 1158–1160. doi:10.1111/j.1755-0998.2012.03174.x PMID:22883857

Wolf, K., & Schaefer, B. (2004). The mitochondrial genetics of the budding yeast. In K. Esser (Ed.), The mycota: A comprehensive treatise on fungi as experimental systems for basic and applied research (2nd ed.; Vol. 2, p. 82). Germany: Springer-Verlag.

Wolf, M., Ruderisch, B., Dandekar, T., Schultz, J., & Muller, T. (2008). ProfDistS: (profile-) distance based phylogeny on sequence--structure alignments. *Bioinformatics (Oxford, England)*, *24*(20), 2401–2402. doi:10.1093/bioinformatics/btn453 PMID:18723521

Wolf, M., Ruderisch, B., Dandekar, T., Schultz, J., & Muller, T. (2010). *ProfDistS version 0.9.9: A tool for the construction of large phylogenetic trees based on profile distances*. Department of Bioinformatics, University Würzburg.

Yang, Z. (2007). PAML 4: Phylogenetic analysis by maximum likelihood. *Molecular Biology and Evolution*, *24*(8), 1586–1591. doi:10.1093/molbev/msm088 PMID:17483113

Zanini, F., & Neher, R. A. (2012). FFPopSim: An efficient forward simulation package for the evolution of large populations. *Bioinformatics (Oxford, England)*, *28*(24), 3332–3333. doi:10.1093/bioinformatics/bts633 PMID:23097421

KEY TERMS AND DEFINITIONS

Admixture: In genetics, refers to the process when two or more previously separated populations begin interbreeding.

Allele: An alternative form of a gene (one member of a pair) occupying a specific position in a chromosome.

Allele Frequency: A population, refers to the percentage of all the alleles at a locus accounted for by one specific allele.

Conservation Biology: The branch of biology that deals with the study of the conservation of biological diversity and the effects of humans on the environment.

DNA Polymorphisms: Alleles of a chromosomal locus differing in nucleotide sequence or have variable numbers of repeated nucleotide units.

DNA Sequencing: The process of determining the precise order of the nucleotides within the DNA molecule.

Epistemology: A branch of philosophy concerned with the investigation of the origin, nature, methods, and limits of human knowledge.

Evolutionary Biology: The branch of biology that deals with the study of the evolution of organisms.

Fixation Index: A measure used to assess population differentiation due to genetic structure.

Gene Flow: The transfer of alleles from one population to another.

Genetic Drift: The process of random changes in the allele frequency in a gene pool, usually in small populations.

Genetic Locus: The specific location of a gene in a chromosome.

Graphics Processing Unit (GPU): A programmable logic chip that renders images, videos, and animations for the computer screen.

Hardy-Weinberg Equilibrium: A population genetics fundamental principle stating that the genotype frequencies and gene frequencies of a large, randomly mating population remain constant provided immigration, mutation, and selection do not take place.

Heterozygosity: The state of having two different alleles of the same gene.

Linkage Disequilibrium: Occurs when genotypes at the two loci are not independent of another.

Linpack Performance: A technique used to evaluate the floating point rate of execution of a computer.

Mendel's Laws: Consists of three laws of inheritance describing how genes are passed on from parents to offsprings.

Microsatellite: Genetic markers consisting of repeating sequences of 2-6 base pairs of DNA.

Migration: In population genetics, is defined as the movement of alleles from one area (i.e. population) to another.

Monte-Carlo Simulation: A problem solving technique used to approximate the probability of certain outcomes by running simulations utilizing random variables

Mutation: A permanent change, specifically a structural alteration in the DNA or RNA.

Natural Selection: A process by which individuals' inherited needs and abilities are more or less closely matched to resources available in their environment, providing those with greater "fitness" a better chance of survival and reproduction.

Phylogeny: The evolutionary development and history of a species or higher taxonomic group of organisms.

Processing Element: Refers to the principal components, which make up a any workflow.

Protein Electrophoresis: An analytical technique used to separate different protein components (fractions) in a mixture of proteins such a blood sample on the basis of differences in the movement of components through a fluid-filled matrix under the influence of an applied electric field.

Randomly Amplified Polymorphic DNA (RAPD) Technique: A method in which genomic DNA are amplified by polymerase chain reaction (PCR) using non-specific primers that are complementary to a number of sites within the genome.

Restriction Endonucleases: Enzymes that cut nucleic acid at specific restriction sites and produce restriction fragments.

Restriction Fragment Length Polymorphisms: Genetic variation that can be detected by enzymatic digestion.

Single Nucleotide Polymorphisms: Genetic variation in a DNA sequence that occurs when a single nucleotide in a genome is altered.

Statistical Inference: A process of utilizing information from a sample to draw conclusions (or inferences) about the population from which the sample was taken.

Symmetric Multiprocessing (SMP) System: A multiprocessing architecture in which multiple CPUs, residing in one cabinet, share the same memory.

Teraflop: A measure of a computer's speed that can be expressed as a trillion floating point operations per second.

Chapter 8
Supercomputers in Modeling of Biological Systems

Randall Maples
Oklahoma State University, USA

Sindhura Ramasahayam
Oklahoma State University, USA

Gerard G. Dumancas
Oklahoma Medical Research Foundation, USA

ABSTRACT

Modeling of biological systems has become an important facet in today's scientific community because it has aided in the simulation of the minute biological entities comprising a living individual. With the advent in the advances of supercomputers, most challenges in understanding the complexities of biological networks and processes occurring in the human body can now be understood. Proteins, which are large biomolecules comprised of amino acids, play a critical role in the proper functioning of a living organism, and, thus, the prediction of its structure is essential in medicine for drug design or in biotechnology, such as in the designing of novel enzymes. This chapter focuses on how supercomputers facilitate in the prediction of protein structures in its different forms, modeling of protein-ligand binding site identification, as well as in the protein-surface interactions modeling.

INTRODUCTION

Over the years, the biological sciences have evolved to a field where it is intertwined with computational sciences. This has become necessary since computational (mathematical) models may provide the basis of activity patterns exhibited by different biological phenomena and, therefore, play an important role in understanding the processes of life from a holistic point of view.

Computational modeling is a powerful approach for understanding biological systems complexity. The development of novel mathematical representations and simulation algorithms are vital for the success of modeling efforts in biological systems. For example, several successful attempts have been made for simulating complex biological

DOI: 10.4018/978-1-4666-7461-5.ch008

Copyright © 2015, IGI Global. Copying or distributing in print or electronic forms without written permission of IGI Global is prohibited.

processes like metabolic pathways, gene regulatory networks and cell signaling pathways (Meng, Somani, & Dhar, 2004). Throughout the years, a number of diverse methods have been developed to model and visualize the biological systems. Supercomputers play a very critical role in the success of biological systems modeling. For example, in December 1999, IBM announced a five-year $100 million initiative to build a petaflop-scale supercomputer to attack problems such as protein folding. As such, the IBM Blue Gene project that utilized a massively parallel computer was initiated to use large-scale biomolecular simulation to advance the understanding of biologically important processes, specifically protein folding (Allen et al., 2001). With this project, modeling the protein folding trajectories addressed questions such as why do proteins consistently fold into specific structures and are there one or several folding pathways per protein?

Supercomputers also play a critical role in the drug design and development aspect. For example, the average cost of developing and bringing one drug to the market can range from a few hundred million dollars to more than a billion and taking from 10-15 years before patients can avail the medications they need. As such, scientists for example are using the Oak Ridge Leadership Computing Facility to speed up the screening process while increasing the chance for developing a successful drug for a fraction of the cost. In that regard they were able to create 3D biological simulations of compounds docking with receptors in the body and run it using the world's fastest computers to screen millions of drug candidates in a few days (Baudry, 2012).

In 2012, the U.S. Department of Energy administered a program named Advanced Scientific Computing Research Leadership Computing Challenge that would award up to two million hours on the Titan supercomputer at the Oak Ridge National Laboratory (ORNL) for research. One of the funded proposals in this program in 2012 was awarded to scientists at the U.S. Department of Energy (DOE) Brookhaven National Laboratory to study how protein folds into their three-dimensional shapes. The Titan supercomputer was ranked as number 2 in the Top500 Supercomputers in the world in November 2013 listing as provided in the Appendix of this book (Rutkin, 2012).

While it is possible to cover many different topics on the modeling of biological systems, this chapter will focus on the applications of supercomputers in the modeling of biological systems specifically in protein structure prediction, protein-ligand binding site identification, and protein-surface interactions.

Computational Methods for Protein Structure Prediction

The knowledge of the native protein structure could provide insights into its functions. Protein structures comprise of polymers of amino acids joined together by peptide bonds. Protein structures are classified into primary, secondary, and tertiary structures. The linear sequence of the polypeptide chain refers to its primary structure. The secondary structure is the polypeptide chain which comprises of α-helix and β-sheets or β-strands. The α-helix and β-strands are connected through coil or loop. Tertiary structure is the 3-D structure of the protein molecules in which α-helix and β-strands are folded into a compact globule.

Even though the large scale sequencing projects have generated an abundance of protein sequence data, the experimental determination of a protein structure and/or function is tedious, expensive and requires intense labor. Consequently, there is still a growing gap between proteins with experimentally derived structures and proteins with unknown structures. In order to address this, a collection of automated methods or bioinformatics' tools that utilize sophisticated supercomputers have been used in determining structures of the novel proteins from its amino acid. This chapter will present a set of bioinformatics tools that cover most aspects of protein structure prediction for primary, secondary and tertiary structures from the amino acid sequence.

Three dimensional (3D) visualization of protein structure modeling has been extensively studied by researchers at the Australian Centre for Plant Functional Genomics and the University of Adelaide in South Australia using the Tizard supercomputer.

Primary Protein Structure Prediction

The basic information about the protein structure is obtained from its primary sequence. The first step in the analysis of the protein primary sequence is the separation of the protein into its domains. In biochemistry, the domains are defined as protein regions with determined experimental functions (Pavlopoulou & Michalopoulos, 2011). Protein domains or protein family databases are useful in determining the function of uncharacterized proteins. These databases are referred to as 'signature databases', which serve as diagnostics of protein structure or function and are derived using motifs or fingerprints. These signature databases are cross-referenced to other databases in order to provide any corresponding information. The databases BLOCKS (Pietrokovski, Henikoff, & Henikoff, 1996) and PRINTS (Attwood et al., 2003) are based on motifs and fingerprints respectively. The other databases that are used in signatures are PRO-SITE, Database of Protein Domain families (ProDom) and Simple Modular Architecture Research Tool (SMART) (Pavlopoulou & Michalopoulos, 2011).

Secondary Protein Structure Prediction

The protein secondary structure prediction is proposed to be an intermediate step in the tertiary structure prediction. The protein secondary structure takes into account the patterns of hydrogen bonds between the amide and carboxyl groups. In addition, it can also be predicted from secondary structural segments such as helices, strands, or coils. The initial step in the protein secondary structure prediction involves a search in the protein data bank (PDB) of experimentally determined protein structures, which are related to the query sequence.

One of the most widely used secondary structure prediction method over the past 15 years is the one developed by Garnier, Osguthorpe and Robson (known as the GOR method) (Garnier, Osguthorpe, & Robson, 1978). It is based on the principle that certain amino acid residues have a higher probability to be in a particular secondary structure state than other residues. In addition, it also considers pair wise interactions of the target amino acid and its flanking residues. Some of the web-based tools for protein secondary structure prediction include Consensus Data Mining (CDM), Fragment Database Mining (FDM), PHD, PORTER, and Solvent AccessiBiLitiEs (SABLE). More information about PHD secondary structure prediction method (IBCP, 2013), PORTER prediction of protein secondary structure and relative solvent accessibility (PORTER, 2014) and SABLE protein structure prediction server (SABLE, 2014) are available at the corresponding web links provided for each in the Reference section of this chapter.

Moreover, many modern methods for secondary structure prediction are based on machine learning techniques such as support vector machines (SVMs) and neural networks (NNs) trained with secondary structure information of resolved structures deposited in the PDB (Rost & Sander, 1993). Table 1 below is a summary of current softwares for secondary protein structure prediction as provided by (Wikipedia, 2014).

Protein Tertiary Structure Prediction

The protein tertiary structure is the full three-dimensional atomic structure of a single amino acid sequence (Bowie, Luthy, & Eisenberg, 1991)

Table 1. Software for secondary protein structure prediction (Source: Wikipedia, 2014a http://en.wikipedia. org/wiki/List_of_protein_structure_prediction_software)

Name	Method	Description	Link
RaptorX-SS8	Predict both 3-state and 8-state secondary structure using conditional neural fields from PSI-BLAST profiles.	Webserver/ downloadable	Server: http://raptorx. uchicago.edu/ Downloadable: http:// ttic.uchicago.edu/~jinbo/ software.htm
NetSurfP	Profile-based neural network.	Webserver/ downloadable	Server: http://www.cbs. dtu.dk/services/NetSurfP/
GOR	Information theory/Bayesian Inference.	Many implementations	Basic GOR: http://abs.cit. nih.gov/gor/ GOR V: http://gor. bb.iastate.edu/
Jpred	Neural network Assignment.	Webserver	Server: http://www. compbio.dundee. ac.uk/~www-jpred/
Meta-PP	Consensus prediction of other servers.	Webserver	Server: http://www. cs.bgu.ac.il/~dfischer/ predictprotein/submit_ meta.html
PREDATOR	Knowledge-based database comparison.	Webserver	Server: http://bioweb.pasteur. fr/seqanal/interfaces/ predator-simple.html
PredictProtein	Profile-based neural network.	Webserver	Server: http://www.predictprotein. org/
PSIPRED	Two feed-forward neural networks which perform an analysis on output obtained from PSI-BLAST.	Webserver	Server: http://bioinf.cs.ucl.ac.uk/ psipred/
SymPred	An improved dictionary based approach which captures local sequence similarities in a group of proteins.	Webserver	Server: http://bio-cluster.iis.sinica. edu.tw/SymPred/
YASSPP	Cascaded SVM-based predictor using PSI-BLAST profiles.	Webserver	Server: http://yasspp.cs.umn.edu/
PSSpred	Multiple backpropagation neural network predictors from PSI-BLAST profiles.	Webserver/ downloadable program	Server and downloadable program: http://zhanglab.ccmb.med. umich.edu/PSSpred/

. The knowledge of the tertiary protein structure is critical as it is correlated with its biological function. The protein tertiary structure prediction is based on the 3-D structure of a protein, which tends to be better conserved than its amino acid sequence. The best strategy for protein tertiary structure prediction first involves homology modeling followed by fold recognition, and if not successful, *ab initio* prediction. Figure 1 below shows a three dimensional structure of the protein myoglobin (Wikipedia, 2014b). Myoglobin is an iron- and oxygen-binding protein found in the muscle tissue of vertebrates in general and in almost all mammals. It is related to hemoglobin, which is the iron- and oxygen-binding protein in blood, specifically in the red blood cells. Myo-

Figure 1. A representation of the 3D structure of the protein myoglobin showing turquoise alpha helices (Source: Wikipedia, 2014b http:// en.wikipedia.org/wiki/Protein)

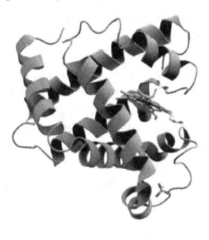

globin is only found in the bloodstream after muscle injury. (Wikipedia, 2014c). According to the U.S. National Science Foundation (NSF, 2004), Myoglobin was the first protein to have its three-dimensional structure revealed by X-ray crystallography.

Homology Modeling

Homology modeling, or comparative modeling, is the most reliable method used for modeling 3D structures of proteins to identify the unknown structure of a target protein using a homologous template protein structure. It is estimated that for every unique protein in the PDB there are approximately 20 other homologous proteins (Vitkup, Melamud, Moult, & Sander, 2001). Homology modeling is based on the principle that evolutionarily related proteins have similar structures. Therefore, the target structure of the protein can be modeled using the template structure. Homology modeling involves three sequential steps: model building, refinement, and evaluation.

Model building involves identification of the template by aligning the target sequence with the template sequence of known structures. The

chosen template acts as a motif for the 3D target protein based on the conserved positions. Different approaches for building the model have been grouped as rigid-body assembly methods (e.g. Using 3D-JIGSAW (Bates, Kelley, MacCallum, & Sternberg, 2001) and SWISS-MODEL (Arnold, Bordoli, Kopp, & Schwede, 2006), segment matching methods (e.g. Using SegMod/ENDCAD (M. Levitt, 1992), spatial restraint methods (e.g. Using MODELLER (Eswar et al., 2006) and artificial evolution methods (e.g. NEST).

Model refinement emphasizes on the correct orientation of the side chains and structure of the loops. Models obtained are structurally closer to the template than to the true structure of the target (Werner, Morris, Dastmalchi, & Church, 2012). Side chain modeling is done by the standalone programs including SCRWL4 (Krivov, Shapovalov, & Dunbrack, 2009) which uses rotamer libraries derived from specific known structures. The loops can play important structural roles in ligand binding sites. Loop structures are modeled using a database search or *de novo* conformational-search approach. One of the popular loop databases used is ArchPred (Fernandez-Fuentes, Zhai, & Fiser, 2006). The *de novo* methods include Monte Carlo simulations, simulated annealing, genetic algorithms, and molecular dynamics simulations.

In the model evaluation, the stereochemistry can be checked by using different programs such as WHATCHECK (Hooft, Vriend, Sander, & Abola, 1996) or MolProbity (Davis et al., 2007). These programs may not be optimal as they check the capability of the homology modeling algorithm in protein determining structure instead of verifying the actual quality of the model (Werner et al., 2012). However, they are still useful to detect errors in the modeling process and the models themselves.

The methods in homology modeling are derived from the physico-chemical properties of water-soluble proteins. Many homology models have been used in the drug discovery process, including models for protein kinases (Brylinski

& Skolnick, 2010), G-protein-coupled receptors (GPCRs) (Cavasotto et al., 2008) and other membrane proteins.

In addition to these programs, models can also be validated through reference to the experimental results as well as by computational methods, which evaluate the ligand-binding sites.

Fold Recognition or Threading

Threading predicts the 3D structure of the protein by aligning its primary sequence to proteins in the protein data bank (PDB) to check for a similar structure. Threading selects template structures even if the target and template sequences are not related to each other. It further tries to search the folds with known structure and identifies the ones which are most appropriate for the target sequence. Thus, the threading method needs a target sequence, structure library as input, and a selection process that finds the best sequence–structure match (threading) (Werner et al., 2012). One of the commonly used programs is THREADER which uses residue-residue contacts, secondary structure predictions, and target template sequence similarities (Jones, Taylor, & Thornton, 1992). Another program RAPTOR considers secondary structure, amino acid substitution rates and pair wise interaction scores (J. Xu, Li, Kim, & Xu, 2003).

The fold recognition approaches are divided into sequence-based and structure-based. The former one is based on the multiple sequence alignments to construct profiles; latter approaches in the alignment of the target sequence to the 3D backbone of a template protein and assess the compatibility of a target sequence with known structure by using knowledge-based structures (Pavlopoulou & Michalopoulos, 2011). Few of the fold recognition methods combine both approaches to yield better results. pGenTHREADER (parametricGenTHREADER) constructs position-specific score matrix (PSSM) and incorporates secondary-structure specific gap penalties, clas-

sic pair and solvation potentials to improve fold recognition (Lobley, Sadowski, & Jones, 2009). The structure-based methods for fold recognition include M-TASSER (Meta-Threading/Assembly/Refinement) which utilizes multimeric threading for template identification, followed by multimer model assembly and refinement (Chen & Skolnick, 2008; Zhou, Pandit, & Skolnick, 2009). The limitation of the protein threading include computer power and necessity for target identification (Centeno, Planas-Iglesias, & Oliva, 2005).

In 2010, the D. E. Shaw supercomputer located at D.E. Shaw Research, an independent research institute in New York founder by David Shaw a former professor at Columbia University in New York, set a protein-folding record by simulating changes in a proteins's three-dimensional structure over a period of a millisecond. This time measurement of a millisecond is more than a hundred-fold greater than the previous record as of that time in 2010. (Brueckner, 2010).

In 2013, D. E. Shaw made a presentation at Harvard School of Engineering and Applied Sciences where he showed in a video of about 60 seconds of what it looks like when a protein folds, and indicated that clip required "a ludicrous amount of computing power" with individual frames that represent femtoseconds which are 10^{-15} seconds.(Casey, 2013).

Free Modeling

The 3D structures cannot be predicted reliably by homology modeling or threading because of the possible lack of suitable template structures. Instead, free modeling or template free methods have been developed. They rely on generating structures based on physico-chemical/thermodynamic properties of the amino acids without using any template structures. The most efficient methods in this category uses hybrid approaches including both knowledge-based and physics-based approaches. Evolutionary information is used to generate sparse spatial restraints or identifying the structural building blocks (Zhang, 2008b) .

They are divided into 2 groups, *ab initio* and *de novo* based on their energy functions. *Ab initio* methods use energy functions based on energy and atomic functions; widely used methods include **UN**ited **RES**idue (UNRES) (Liwo, Lee, Ripoll, Pillardy, & Scheraga, 1999) and ASTRO-FOLD (Klepeis & Floudas, 2003). Limitations of *ab initio* methods are that they are restricted to small molecules. *De novo* methods combine quantitative understanding of the physics of folding with knowledge about previously solved protein structures. Commonly used *de novo* methods include ROSETTA and I-TASSER (J. Xu et al., 2003).

One of the best known ideas for free modeling is the one pioneered by Bowie and Eisengberg who assembled tertiary structures using small fragments cut from PDB proteins (Bowie & Eisenberg, 1994). ROSETTA was developed on the basis of a similar idea which has worked extremely well in the free modeling of CASP experiments (Simons, Kooperberg, Huang, & Baker, 1997). In the new developments of ROSETTA, the structures were first assembled in a reduced knowledge-based model with confirmations specified by the heavy backbone atoms (Bradley, Misura, & Baker, 2005; Das et al., 2007). In the second stage, Monte-Carlo simulations with an all atom physics-based potential are used to refine low resolution models. Despite of its success, it is too expensive for routine use (~150 CPU days for a small protein < 100 residues). Another approach called TASSER constructs 3D models based on knowledge-based approach (Zhang & Skolnick, 2004) in which fragments of various sizes are excised from the threading alignments and used to reassemble structures. Recently, a newer version called Zhang-Server (I-TASSER) has been developed, which refines the TASSER cluster centroids by iterative Monte Carlo simulations (Wu, Skolnick, & Zhang, 2007).

PROTEIN STRUCTURE LEVELS

The following Figure 2 provides images of primary, secondary, tertiary, and quaternary protein structures as previously discussed and starting with a sequence of a chain of amino acids, that are linked with hydrogen bonds in secondary protein structure, and pleated sheets in tertiary structure, and more than one amino acid chair in quaternary protein structure.   .

COMPUTATIONAL METHODS FOR PROTEIN-LIGAND BINDING SITE IDENTIFICATION

One of the most fundamental aspects of all the biological mechanisms is the interaction between proteins and their ligands. An important aspect in protein–ligand recognition is to predict the 3D protein-ligand structures. Visualization of the 3D structures of protein–ligand complexes bridges the interpretation between protein structure and its function. Thus, modeling protein–ligand complexes contribute to the functional characterization of unknown protein structures. The most commonly used computational methods to identify the protein-ligand binding site exploit sequence and structural information. The current methods can be roughly divided into sequence-based, template-based, geometric, and energy-based.

Sequence-Based Methods

The sequence-based method is a simplest method which exploits the evolutionary information of the functional residues contained in Multiple Sequence Alignments (MSAs) of homologous sequences and extract a subset of residues with higher conservation (Ghersi & Sanchez, 2011). As a result, this approach reduces the variability in the protein family. Another alternate approach that utilizes the phylogenetic analysis is the "evolutionary trace" method (Lichtarge, Bourne, &

Figure 2. Constituent amino-acids can be analyzed to predict secondary, tertiary and quaternary protein structure. (Source: http://en.wikipedia.org/wiki/Protein_folding_problem)

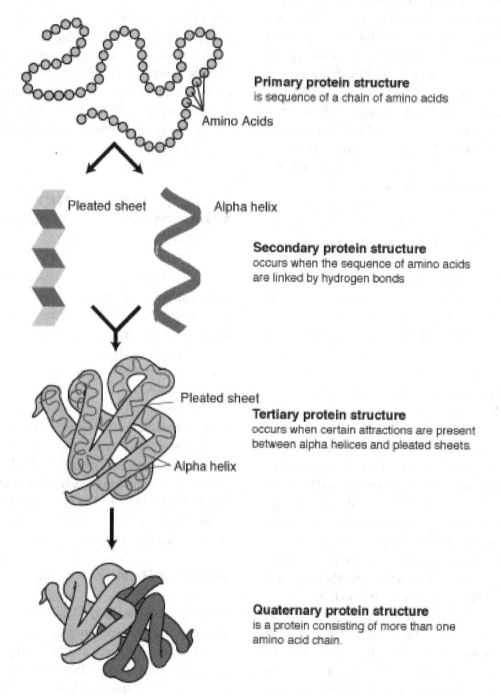

Cohen, 1996). It is based on the recognition of the degree of conservation of residue positions in a protein family in phylogenetically distinct groups. The idea behind this approach is that the functionally important residues may be preserved in a subgroup but varies across different subgroups.

All sequence-based methods suffer from limitations despite their usefulness in the interpretation of functionally important residues. Firstly, the conservation of the residues is not a specific criterion to identify a binding site as residues may be conserved for other reasons. Secondly, sequence-based methods do not provide geometric and physicochemical information of binding sites like area, volume, shape, and molecular interaction properties (Ghersi & Sanchez, 2011).

Template-Based and Structural-Similarity Based Methods

Template-based methods typically identify the target binding sites by comparing them with pre-defined patterns based on known binding sites. A graph-theoretic approach was used to identify the 3-D patterns of amino acid side chains in protein structures (Artymiuk, Poirrette, Grindley, Rice, & Willett, 1994). A template based approach has been developed to predict binding sites for phosphorylated ligands (Parca, Gherardini, Helmer-Citterich, & Ausiello, 2011).

One of the structural similarity approaches, 3D Ligand-site is used for predicting ligand-binding sites using similar structures. Usually, a protein sequence is submitted to the site to predict the structure, which is then used to search a structural library to identify homologous structures with bound ligands. These ligands are superimposed onto the protein structure to identify the ligand binding site (Wass, Kelley, & Sternberg, 2010).

Geometric-Based Methods

Geometric-based methods are based on shape of the binding site location. The geometric approaches are based on the assumption that the protein- binding sites are usually a cleft or a pocket. For instance, a study of 67 protein structures determined the ligand is bound in the largest cleft in over 83% of the proteins (Laskowski, Luscombe, Swindells, & Thornton, 1996). The

earliest approaches utilized to detect clefts is "protein-solvent-protein" used the POCKET (D. G. Levitt & Banaszak, 1992) and LIGSITE algorithms (Hendlich, Rippmann, & Barnickel, 1997). It is based on embedding the protein in a 3D lattice and assigning the grid points to the protein or the solvent. Pockets are defined as the regions in space that contain points assigned to the "solvent" category and that are surrounded by "protein" points (Ghersi & Sanchez, 2011).

Another commonly used algorithm for pocket detection is SURFNET program (Laskowski, 1995). It places spheres between atoms such that no two atoms are contained inside the spheres. The largest volume spheres define the putative pocket. Other methods which are based on the concept of alpha-spheres in identifying cavities are APROPOS (Peters, Fauck, & Frommel, 1996), PASS (Brady & Stouten, 2000), and CAST (Dundas et al., 2006).

It has some limitations despite its binding site identification. Geometric approaches does not distinguish different binding sites like hydrophobic versus hydrophilic. Secondly, all of the binding sites are not deep pockets.

Energy-Based Methods

Energy-based approaches are characterized by the energetic properties of the protein-ligand binding site. One of the earliest attempts to distinguish binding sites using energetic properties is the GRID program which measures a semi-empirical interaction energy between the protein and a set of chemical probes (Goodford, 1985). The GRID program is not a binding site identification tool, but it is used to compute the interaction energy maps which are produced by the program. For instance, Q-SiteFinder uses the GRID force field to measure the energy map between the protein and a methyl ($-CH_3$) probe and identifies highest total interaction energy the regions by cluster analysis (Laurie & Jackson, 2005).

Another alternative energy-based technique for the binding site identification of protein structures was introduced by Mattos and Ringe called Multiple Solvent Crystal Structures (MSCS) (Mattos & Ringe, 1996). This technique is based on repeatedly soaking the protein with various organic solvents by X-ray crystallography. EasyMIFs and SiteHound are one of the commonly used software tools which enable the identification and characterization of binding sites in protein structures (Ghersi & Sanchez, 2009).

Docking Method

Docking technologies analyze the specific structural details of the protein-ligand interaction. Docking technologies have important applications in drug discovery. The ligand positioning in the binding pocket is termed as docking. The protein-ligand docking is used to predict the position and orientation of a ligand or a small molecule when bound to a receptor. Docking a ligand into a protein binding site requires intermolecular translation, rotation and intramolecular conformational changes. The current docking approaches begin with the initial stage, which aims at the possible geometrical associations and is performed under rigid body approximation (Mintseris et al., 2007; Schneidman-Duhovny, Inbar, Nussinov, & Wolfson, 2005) using all-atom or course grain (CG) representations.

The second refinement stage introduces flexibility by optimizing the side-chain interactions and the rigid body orientations and the ligands are ranked using scoring function. There are multiple docking approaches, interaction site matching, incremental construction, genetic algorithms, and Monte Carlo searches (Moitessier, Englebienne, Lee, Lawandi, & Corbeil, 2008). Interaction site matching approaches, such as FRED (McGann, Almond, Nicholls, Grant, & Brown, 2003) represent ligands and protein binding sites as pharmacophores and optimize their overlay to generate a docked ligand pose. There are number of condi-

tions that affect docking performance including protonation, tautomeric state of the ligand, as well as treatment of water molecules and solvent in the binding pocket.

PROTEIN-SURFACE INTERACTIONS

The study of protein-surface interactions is important and the field has seen advances in both protein adsorption modeling and experiments over the past few decades. (Hlady & Buijs, 1996; Ho, Britt, & Hlady, 1996; Przestalski et al., 1996; Sadana, 1992a, 1992b; Sadana & Sii, 1992). The ability to control, predict and manipulate protein adsorption has fueled research in this important field and has led to a better understanding of interactions at the protein-surface interface. These protein-surface interactions see application in a variety of areas in biotechnology which seek to probe and make use of special properties of this solid-liquid interface.(Baurmeister, Vienken, & Grassmann, 1991; Chilkoti, Ratner, & Briggs, 1993; Glasmastar, Larsson, Hook, & Kasemo, 2002; Gura, Wright, Veis, & Webb, 1997; Haycox & Ratner, 1993; Hlady & Buijs, 1996; Linnola et al., 2000; Mulzer & Brash, 1989; Reimhult, Hook, & Kasemo, 2002; Sadana, 1992b; Voinova, Jonson, & Kasemo, 2002) Applications include biosensors, immunological tests and drug delivery. As such, protein models continue to advance with a continued focus on improvement in quantitative measurements, prediction and ultimately, understanding the complexity of protein-surface interactions. Table 2 below provides examples of common surface modification techniques.

Before we attempt to account for the complexity of protein-surface interactions, we must first consider what is happening on a simplified level. Protein adsorption helps to regulate the biological response to foreign material the body comes into contact with through interaction at the solid-liquid interface, and this is accomplished through the biochemical signaling potential of a particular

Table 2. Examples of common surface modification techniques

Modifications of the Original Surface	Covalently Attached Coatings	Non-Covalently Attached Coatings
Ion beam etching	Radiation grafting	Solvent coating
Ion beam implantation	Electron beam-induced grafting	Langmuir-Blodgett film deposition
Plasma etching	Photografting	Self-assembled layers
Corona discharge	Plasma	Surface active additives
Electron beam treatment	Gas phase deposition	Vapour deposition of carbons and metals
Ion exchange	Ion beam sputtering	Vapour deposition of Parylene
UV irradiation	Chemical vapour deposition	
Chemical reaction	Chemical grafting	
Non-specific oxidation	Silanation	
functional group modifications	Biological modification	
Addition reactions	Various	
Conversion coatings	Various	

protein. (Anderson, Bonfield, & Ziats, 1990; Ratner, 1996) Proteins elicit a strong adsorption to hydrophobic surfaces and a much weaker adsorption to neutral hydrophilic surfaces. Differences of adsorption are also related to charge in that opposite charges tend to favor protein adsorption while similar charges elicit weaker degrees of adsorption. (Murray et al., 1998)

In reality, when one considers the interactions occurring between protein, surface and surrounding media, it quickly becomes evident there are many simultaneous interactions occurring and the complexity of the system begins to take shape. An array of functional groups on the protein surface lead to interactions of the protein to itself along with the surface of interest and media surrounding the system and as a result structural rearrangements, changes in conformation may occur to further complicate the system. Obviously, electrostatic interactions are important when studying protein-surface interactions. One method commonly used is to treat charge distribution that corresponds with what is found in the bulk solution. However, a failure of such an approach is that acidic or basic groups may be neutralized when exposed to other groups. This is because the charge on the protein is not constant but depends on the environment in which the protein located is in. Proton fluctuations in solution are the cause of this charge regulation and these fluctuations can be formalized using statistical mechanical perturbation theory.(Kirkwood & Shumaker, 1952; Lund & Jonsson, 2005)

Surface chemistry can be employed to control protein-surface interaction via exerting an effect on the surface density of the chemical groups, thus lending itself to a greater use in application. (Hlady & Buijs, 1996) The use of a gradient surface is one approach used with surface density of long silyl chains attached to a silica surface. Changes in positive and negative charge to form gradients are also used. These and other changes with various surface groups enable change at the molecular and sub-molecular level. Predicting the role of electrostatic interaction on the surface is thus very important and fundamental to gain insight into protein-surface behavioral prediction.

It is these changes in the system on the molecular and sub-molecular level, which cause unpredictable changes in the post-adsorption state, and as a result, uncontrolled protein adsorption is experimentally avoided through use of peptide ligands or other surface chemistry approaches. However, molecular simulation provides a direct method to theoretically investigate this complex behavior.

To examine this behavior on the molecular level, molecular simulation is often employed, as it provides a direct means for studying the complex protein adsorption system. Empirical force field based molecular modeling methods use a potential energy function to sum the individual atom-atom pair interactions to calculate overall potential energy of the system. Molecular bonding interactions including stretching and bending of bonds as well as non-bonded interactions which include both electrostatic and van der Waals provide energy contributions to the system and are part of the force field equation which uses the appropriate set of parameters to represent a single molecular system and numerous variations on this theme have been performed over time. (Du, Long, Meng, & Huang, 2012; Eastman & Doniach, 1998; Ferrara, Gohlke, Price, Klebe, & Brooks, 2004; Hayik, Dunbrack, & Merz, 2010; Krieger, Koraimann, & Vriend, 2002; Li & Chou, 1976; Sheng, Sarwal, Watts, & Marble, 1995; Sivasankar, Subramaniam, & Leckband, 1998; Takamatsu & Itai, 1998). The Monte Carlo (MC) and Molecular Dynamics (MD) are two examples of these types of systems.

Methods such as the MC are a class of computational algorithms mainly used in problems such as optimization, numerical integration and probability distribution of samples and tend to follow a pattern that includes defining a domain of possible inputs, generating inputs randomly from a probability distribution, computation determination of results and aggregating the results. MD is another computational simulation that involves the physical movements of the atoms and molecules and their interaction and movement, the most common of which involves the numerical determination of atomic and molecular trajectories by solving Newton's equation of motion. These types of systems help define various related pa-

rameters of the force field. These methods employ a potential energy function, in this case the force field, to calculate the overall potential energy of the system.

Additionally, a force field equation with appropriate parameters is valid only for a single system unless separate validation is used to ensure the proper equation parameters are balanced to appropriately address the given system. A meaningful example of this was shown when Schuler, et al., used the force field GROMOS96 to model the behavior of proteins in aqueous solution (Raut, Agashe, Stuart, & Latour, 2005). When the force field was used in an attempt to represent the behavior of condensed phase hydrocarbons, significant errors were recorded despite the use of parameterization to include other alkane functional groups, which were similar to those in the condensed phase. As such, the force field transferability requires separate validation when used in different applications, as shown in the example above.

Accurate force field development has proceeded in recent time for the parametric development and validation to simulate the behavior of proteins in aqueous solution as shown in the table. Unfortunately, none of the listed force fields were parameterized with consideration of the adsorption behavior of proteins to a synthetic surface. Generally, this parameterization involves non-bonded interactions between functional groups on the material surface and amino acid functional groups on the protein as well as water, and these protein-surface interactions do not take into account the interactions, which might occur between protein functional groups and synthetic surface functional groups such as polymers, peptides, and coatings, (Du et al., 2012; Ferrara et al., 2004; Hayik et al., 2010; Hlady & Buijs, 1996; Krieger et al., 2002; Ratner, 1996; Raut et al., 2005; Sadana, 1992b; Sivasankar et al., 1998; Takamatsu & Itai, 1998). Table 3 below provides some force field methods for simulation of proteins in aqueous media.

Table 3. Force field methods for simulation of protein in aqueous media (Brooks & Karplus, 1983; Kaminski, 2001; Pearlman & Connelly, 1995; van Aalten, Findlay, Amadei, & Berendsen, 1995).

Technique Name	Author	Year
CHARMM	BR Brooks	1983
AMBER	DA Perlman	1995
GROMACS	HJC Berendsen	1995
OPLS	GA Kaminski	2001

Over the past few decades, several force fields have been developed and validated for the simulation of proteins in an aqueous solution (Table 3). In order to properly represent the appropriate system, the interactions evaluated in the force field should have balanced, parameterized interactions with experimental validation. Thus, force field results are compared to experimental results and validation then enables use of the force field in a Monte Carlo (MC) or Molecular Dynamics (MD) simulation. For the force field to accurately represent the system being investigated and modeled, proper balance of all of types of the previously listed interactions is a must.

Complications arise in such cases as peptide-surface adsorption behavior since very little is known about the molecular behavior. Thus, exactly how the force field should function in terms of molecular behavior is a gray area. And it is in cases such as this that the need for experimental results is shown most clearly. Validation of results can be accomplished if fundamental characteristics of the protein-surface adsorption or functional group-functional group interactions can be represented.

CHALLENGES, SOLUTIONS, AND FUTURE RESEARCH DIRECTIONS

Protein modeling is playing a more and more important role in protein and peptide sequences due to improvements in modeling methods, advances in computer technology, and the huge amount of biological data becoming available. These modeling tools can pave way to future research directions in predicting the structure, functions, and mechanisms of novel proteins (D. Xu, Xu, & Uberbacher, 2000).

Though there has been substantial progress in both comparative modeling of structure (using information from an evolutionary related structural template) and template-free modeling, there has still been major challenges along the way that include refining comparative models so that they match experimental accuracy, obtaining accurate sequence alignments for models based on remote evolutionary relationships, and extending template-free modeling methods so that they produce more accurate models, handle parts of comparative models not available from a template and deal with larger structures (Moult, 2005). Zhang also pointed out that there has been no essential progress in the development of techniques for predicting protein novel structures and for detecting remotely homologous templates (Zhang, 2009). Further, in general, there has always been a challenge for predicting protein structures larger than 150 residues (Zhang, 2008a). However, in recent years, new profile-profile matching algorithms have improved structure prediction and engine server such as Phyre can predict the structure of a 250-residue protein in just 30 mins (Kelley & Sternberg, 2009).

For protein-ligand interactions, on the other hand, calculations of absolute binding free energies still remain a significant challenge. Reliable estimates of binding free energies are necessary for providing a guide for rational drug design. Singh and Warshel found out that the more approximated and considerably faster scaled protein dipoles Langevin dipoles (PDLD/S-LRA/β) appears to offer an appealing option for the final stages of massive screening approaches in protein-ligand binding absolute binding free energy calculations (Singh & Warshel, 2010).

Besides protein-ligand interactions, protein–surface interactions also present major challenges. The three major challenges that are specifically vital for the accurate simulation of protein adsorption behavior are the selection of a valid force field to represent the atomic-level interactions involved, the accurate representation of solvation effects, and system sampling (Latour, 2008).

Another challenge facing protein biochemist is the issue of protein folding. The protein folding problem, which was first posed about a half-century ago, referred to three broad questions ((i) What is the physical code by which an amino acid sequence dictates a protein's native structure? (ii) How can proteins fold so fast? (iii) Can we devise a computer algorithm to predict protein structures from their sequences? (Dill & MacCallum, 2012) This was once regarded as a grand challenge in protein structure prediction. However, because of recent advances in protein computational methodologies aided by the Critical Assessment of Techniques for Structure Prediction (CASP) competition, questions can now be answered such as a protein can avoid searching irrelevant conformations and fold rapidly by making local independent decisions first, followed by non-local global decisions later (Dill, Ozkan, Weikl, Chodera, & Voelz, 2007).

Another challenge facing protein biochemists nowadays is in the area of protein dynamics: the ability to simulate interactions over relatively long periods of time. This problem is a critical issue in protein modeling aspect since biological timescale is really at the high microsecond/low millisecond timescale and since at this instance, the interesting large-scale motions in proteins are occurring. In this regard, a group of researchers at the University of California San Diego (UCSD) has established a new approach to simulating this complex molecular behavior. These researchers ran an enhanced sampling algorithm on a GPU (Graphical Processing Unit)-equipped desktop and were able to achieve millisecond-scale protein simulations (Gelber, 2012).

CONCLUSION

Bioinformatics tools have, indeed, come a long way to determine the structures of the different protein structures--primary, secondary, and tertiary. These tools make it possible to predict these structures by the advent of sophisticated supercomputers. The predictions of the interaction between proteins and their ligands as well as protein-surface interactions are also made possible by the use of advanced computational methods.

Although, there has been progress in using supercomputers for the prediction of biological systems (i.e. proteins), there has been challenges facing the scientists today, which include refining comparative models so that these could match experimental accuracy, search for more algorithms that can predict the structure of very large proteins, calculations of absolute binding free energies in protein-ligand binding, as well as the issues of protein folding structure prediction. Further, since protein-ligand interactions are dynamic and complex, the issue of capturing these molecular movements over relatively long periods of time can be of great challenge. With the advent of advanced supercomputers and the development of algorithms, these challenges have been met in course of time.

REFERENCES

Allen, F., Almasi, G., Andreoni, W., Beece, D., Berne, B. J., & Bright, A. et al. (2001). Blue gene: A vision for protein science using a petaflop supercomputer. *IBM Systems Journal*, *40*(2), 301–327. doi:10.1147/sj.402.0310

Anderson, J. M., Bonfield, T. L., & Ziats, N. P. (1990). Protein adsorption and cellular adhesion and activation on biomedical polymers. *The International Journal of Artificial Organs*, *13*(6), 375–382. PMID:2143174

Arnold, K., Bordoli, L., Kopp, J., & Schwede, T. (2006). The SWISS-MODEL workspace: A web-based environment for protein structure homology modelling. *Bioinformatics (Oxford, England)*, *22*(2), 195–201. doi:10.1093/bioinformatics/bti770 PMID:16301204

Artymiuk, P. J., Poirrette, A. R., Grindley, H. M., Rice, D. W., & Willett, P. (1994). A graph-theoretic approach to the identification of three-dimensional patterns of amino acid side-chains in protein structures. *Journal of Molecular Biology*, *243*(2), 327–344. doi:10.1006/jmbi.1994.1657 PMID:7932758

Attwood, T. K., Bradley, P., Flower, D. R., Gaulton, A., Maudling, N., & Mitchell, A. L. et al. (2003). PRINTS and its automatic supplement, pre-PRINTS. *Nucleic Acids Research*, *31*(1), 400–402. doi:10.1093/nar/gkg030 PMID:12520033

Bates, P. A., Kelley, L. A., MacCallum, R. M., & Sternberg, M. J. (2001). Enhancement of protein modeling by human intervention in applying the automatic programs 3D-JIGSAW and 3D-PSSM. *Proteins*, *45*(S5), 39–46. doi:10.1002/prot.1168 PMID:11835480

Baudry, J. Y. (2012). *Designing drugs on supercomputers*. Retrieved December 22, 2013, from http://science.energy.gov/ascr/highlights/2012/ascr-2012-10-c/

Baurmeister, U., Vienken, J., & Grassmann, A. (1991). Biocompatibility and membrane development. *Nephrology, Dialysis, Transplantation*, *6*(Suppl 3), 17–21. PMID:1775260

Bowie, J. U., & Eisenberg, D. (1994). An evolutionary approach to folding small alpha-helical proteins that uses sequence information and an empirical guiding fitness function. *Proceedings of the National Academy of Sciences of the United States of America*, *91*(10), 4436–4440. doi:10.1073/pnas.91.10.4436 PMID:8183927

Bowie, J. U., Luthy, R., & Eisenberg, D. (1991). A method to identify protein sequences that fold into a known three-dimensional structure. *Science*, *253*(5016), 164–170. doi:10.1126/science.1853201 PMID:1853201

Bradley, P., Misura, K. M., & Baker, D. (2005). Toward high-resolution de novo structure prediction for small proteins. *Science*, *309*(5742), 1868–1871. doi:10.1126/science.1113801 PMID:16166519

Brady, G. P. Jr, & Stouten, P. F. (2000). Fast prediction and visualization of protein binding pockets with PASS. *Journal of Computer-Aided Molecular Design*, *14*(4), 383–401. doi:10.1023/A:1008124202956 PMID:10815774

Brooks, B., & Karplus, M. (1983). Harmonic dynamics of proteins: Normal modes and fluctuations in bovine pancreatic trypsin inhibitor. *Proceedings of the National Academy of Sciences of the United States of America*, *80*(21), 6571–6575. doi:10.1073/pnas.80.21.6571 PMID:6579545

Brylinski, M., & Skolnick, J. (2010). Comprehensive structural and functional characterization of the human kinome by protein structure modeling and ligand virtual screening. *Journal of Chemical Information and Modeling*, *50*(10), 1839–1854. doi:10.1021/ci100235n PMID:20853887

Cavasotto, C. N., Orry, A. J., Murgolo, N. J., Czarniecki, M. F., Kocsi, S. A., & Hawes, B. E. et al. (2008). Discovery of novel chemotypes to a G-protein-coupled receptor through ligand-steered homology modeling and structure-based virtual screening. *Journal of Medicinal Chemistry*, *51*(3), 581–588. doi:10.1021/jm070759m PMID:18198821

Centeno, N. B., Planas-Iglesias, J., & Oliva, B. (2005). Comparative modelling of protein structure and its impact on microbial cell factories. *Microbial Cell Factories*, *4*(1), 20. doi:10.1186/1475-2859-4-20 PMID:15989691

Chen, H., & Skolnick, J. (2008). M-TASSER: An algorithm for protein quaternary structure prediction. *Biophysical Journal, 94*(3), 918–928. doi:10.1529/biophysj.107.114280 PMID:17905848

Chilkoti, A., Ratner, B. D., & Briggs, D. (1993). Static secondary ion mass spectrometric investigation of the surface chemistry of organic plasma-deposited films created from oxygen-containing precursors. 3. Multivariate statistical modeling. *Analytical Chemistry, 65*(13), 1736–1745. doi:10.1021/ac00061a017 PMID:8368525

Das, R., Qian, B., Raman, S., Vernon, R., Thompson, J., & Bradley, P. et al. (2007). Structure prediction for CASP7 targets using extensive all-atom refinement with Rosetta@home. *Proteins, 69*(S8Suppl 8), 118–128. doi:10.1002/prot.21636 PMID:17894356

Davis, I. W., Leaver-Fay, A., Chen, V. B., Block, J. N., Kapral, G. J., Wang, X., . . . Richardson, D. C. (2007). MolProbity: All-atom contacts and structure validation for proteins and nucleic acids. *Nucleic Acids Research, 35*, W375-383. doi:10.1093/nar/gkm216

Dill, K. A., & MacCallum, J. L. (2012). The protein-folding problem, 50 years on. *Science, 338*(6110), 1042–1046. doi:10.1126/science.1219021 PMID:23180855

Dill, K. A., Ozkan, S. B., Weikl, T. R., Chodera, J. D., & Voelz, V. A. (2007). The protein folding problem: When will it be solved? *Current Opinion in Structural Biology, 17*(3), 342–346. doi:10.1016/j.sbi.2007.06.001 PMID:17572080

Du, Q. S., Long, S. Y., Meng, J. Z., & Huang, R. B. (2012). Empirical formulation and parameterization of cation-pi interactions for protein modeling. *Journal of Computational Chemistry, 33*(2), 153–162. doi:10.1002/jcc.21951 PMID:21997880

Dundas, J., Ouyang, Z., Tseng, J., Binkowski, A., Turpaz, Y., & Liang, J. (2006). CASTp: Computed atlas of surface topography of proteins with structural and topographical mapping of functionally annotated residues. *Nucleic Acids Research, 34*, W116-118. doi: 10.1093/nar/gkl282

Eastman, P., & Doniach, S. (1998). Multiple time step diffusive Langevin dynamics for proteins. *Proteins, 30*(3), 215–227. doi:10.1002/(SICI)1097-0134(19980215)30:3<215::AID-PROT1>3.0.CO;2-J PMID:9517537

Eswar, N., Webb, B., Marti-Renom, M. A., Madhusudhan, M. S., Eramian, D., Shen, M. Y., et al. (2006). Comparative protein structure modeling using Modeller. In Current protocols in bioinformatics. doi:10.1002/0471250953.bi0506s15

Fernandez-Fuentes, N., Zhai, J., & Fiser, A. (2006). ArchPRED: A template based loop structure prediction server. *Nucleic Acids Research, 3*, W173-176. doi: 10.1093/nar/gkl113

Ferrara, P., Gohlke, H., Price, D. J., Klebe, G., & Brooks, C. L. III. (2004). Assessing scoring functions for protein-ligand interactions. *Journal of Medicinal Chemistry, 47*(12), 3032–3047. doi:10.1021/jm030489h PMID:15163185

Garnier, J., Osguthorpe, D. J., & Robson, B. (1978). Analysis of the accuracy and implications of simple methods for predicting the secondary structure of globular proteins. *Journal of Molecular Biology, 120*(1), 97–120. doi:10.1016/0022-2836(78)90297-8 PMID:642007

Gelber, R. (2012). *Modeling proteins at supercomputing speeds on your PC*. Retrieved from http://archive.hpcwire.com/hpcwire/2012-08-21/modeling_proteins_at_supercomputing_speeds_on_your_pc.html

Ghersi, D., & Sanchez, R. (2009). EasyMIFS and SiteHound: A toolkit for the identification of ligand-binding sites in protein structures. *Bioinformatics (Oxford, England)*, *25*(23), 3185–3186. doi:10.1093/bioinformatics/btp562 PMID:19789268

Ghersi, D., & Sanchez, R. (2011). Beyond structural genomics: Computational approaches for the identification of ligand binding sites in protein structures. *Journal of Structural and Functional Genomics*, *12*(2), 109–117. doi:10.1007/s10969-011-9110-6 PMID:21537951

Glasmastar, K., Larsson, C., Hook, F., & Kasemo, B. (2002). Protein adsorption on supported phospholipid bilayers. *Journal of Colloid Interface Science*, *246*(1), 40-47. doi: 10.1006/jcis.2001.8060

Goodford, P. J. (1985). A computational procedure for determining energetically favorable binding sites on biologically important macromolecules. *Journal of Medicinal Chemistry*, *28*(7), 849–857. doi:10.1021/jm00145a002 PMID:3892003

Gura, T. A., Wright, K. L., Veis, A., & Webb, C. L. (1997). Identification of specific calcium-binding noncollagenous proteins associated with glutaraldehyde-preserved bovine pericardium in the rat subdermal model. *Journal of Biomedical Materials Research*, *35*(4), 483–495. doi:10.1002/(SICI)1097-4636(19970615)35:4<483::AID-JBM8>3.0.CO;2-D PMID:9189826

Haycox, C. L., & Ratner, B. D. (1993). In vitro platelet interactions in whole human blood exposed to biomaterial surfaces: Insights on blood compatibility. *Journal of Biomedical Materials Research*, *27*(9), 1181–1193. doi:10.1002/jbm.820270909 PMID:8126017

Hayik, S. A., Dunbrack, R. Jr, & Merz, K. M. Jr. (2010). A Mixed QM/MM scoring function to predict protein-ligand binding affinity. *Journal of Chemical Theory and Computation*, *6*(10), 3079–3091. doi:10.1021/ct100315g PMID:21221417

Hendlich, M., Rippmann, F., & Barnickel, G. (1997). LIGSITE: Automatic and efficient detection of potential small molecule-binding sites in proteins. *Journal of Molecular Graphics & Modelling*, *15*(6), 359–363, 389. doi:10.1016/S1093-3263(98)00002-3 PMID:9704298

Hlady, V. V., & Buijs, J. (1996). Protein adsorption on solid surfaces. *Current Opinion in Biotechnology*, *7*(1), 72-77.

Ho, C. H., Britt, D. W., & Hlady, V. (1996). Human low density lipoprotein and human serum albumin adsorption onto model surfaces studied by total internal reflection fluorescence and scanning force microscopy. *Journal of Molecular Recognition*, *9*(5-6), 444-455. doi: 10.1002/(SICI)1099-1352(199634/12)9:5/6<444::AID-JMR281>3.0.CO;2-I

Hooft, R. W., Vriend, G., Sander, C., & Abola, E. E. (1996). Errors in protein structures. *Nature*, *381*(6580), 272. doi:10.1038/381272a0 PMID:8692262

Jones, D. T., Taylor, W. R., & Thornton, J. M. (1992). A new approach to protein fold recognition. *Nature*, *358*(6381), 86–89. doi:10.1038/358086a0 PMID:1614539

Kaminski, G. A. (2001). Article. *The Journal of Physical Chemistry B*, 105.

Kelley, L. A., & Sternberg, M. J. (2009). Protein structure prediction on the web: A case study using the Phyre server. *Nature Protocols*, *4*(3), 363–371. doi:10.1038/nprot.2009.2 PMID:19247286

Kirkwood, J. G., & Shumaker, J. B. (1952). Forces between protein molecules in solution arising from fluctuations in proton charge and configuration. *Proceedings of the National Academy of Sciences of the United States of America*, *38*(10), 863–871. doi:10.1073/pnas.38.10.863 PMID:16589190

Klepeis, J. L., & Floudas, C. A. (2003). ASTRO-FOLD: A combinatorial and global optimization framework for Ab initio prediction of three-dimensional structures of proteins from the amino acid sequence. *Biophysical Journal, 85*(4), 2119–2146. doi:10.1016/S0006-3495(03)74640-2 PMID:14507680

Krieger, E., Koraimann, G., & Vriend, G. (2002). Increasing the precision of comparative models with YASARA NOVA--A self-parameterizing force field. *Proteins, 47*(3), 393–402. doi:10.1002/prot.10104 PMID:11948792

Krivov, G. G., Shapovalov, M. V., & Dunbrack, R. L. Jr. (2009). Improved prediction of protein side-chain conformations with SCWRL4. *Proteins, 77*(4), 778–795. doi:10.1002/prot.22488 PMID:19603484

Laskowski, R. A. (1995). SURFNET: A program for visualizing molecular surfaces, cavities, and intermolecular interactions. *Journal of Molecular Graphics, 13*(5), 323-330, 307-328.

Laskowski, R. A., Luscombe, N. M., Swindells, M. B., & Thornton, J. M. (1996). Protein clefts in molecular recognition and function. *Protein Science: A Publication of the Protein Society, 5*(12), 2438-2452. doi: 10.1002/pro.5560051206

Latour, R. A. (2008). Molecular simulation of protein-surface interactions: Benefits, problems, solutions, and future directions. *Biointerphases, 3*(3), FC2–FC12. doi:10.1116/1.2965132 PMID:19809597

Laurie, A. T., & Jackson, R. M. (2005). Q-SiteFinder: An energy-based method for the prediction of protein-ligand binding sites. *Bioinformatics (Oxford, England), 21*(9), 1908–1916. doi:10.1093/bioinformatics/bti315 PMID:15701681

Levitt, D. G., & Banaszak, L. J. (1992). POCKET: A computer graphics method for identifying and displaying protein cavities and their surrounding amino acids. *Journal of Molecular Graphics, 10*(4), 229–234. doi:10.1016/0263-7855(92)80074-N PMID:1476996

Levitt, M. (1992). Accurate modeling of protein conformation by automatic segment matching. *Journal of Molecular Biology, 226*(2), 507–533. doi:10.1016/0022-2836(92)90964-L PMID:1640463

Li, T. T., & Chou, K. C. (1976). The quantitative relations between diffusion-controlled reaction rate and characteristic parameters in enzyme-substrate reaction systems. I. Neutral substrates. *Scientia Sinica, 19*(1), 117–136. PMID:1273571

Lichtarge, O., Bourne, H. R., & Cohen, F. E. (1996). An evolutionary trace method defines binding surfaces common to protein families. *Journal of Molecular Biology, 257*(2), 342–358. doi:10.1006/jmbi.1996.0167 PMID:8609628

Linnola, R. J., Werner, L., Pandey, S. K., Escobar-Gomez, M., Znoiko, S. L., & Apple, D. J. (2000). Adhesion of fibronectin, vitronectin, laminin, and collagen type IV to intraocular lens materials in pseudophakic human autopsy eyes. Part 1: histological sections. *Journal of Cataract and Refractive Surgery, 26*(12), 1792-1806. doi: S0886335000007483

Liwo, A., Lee, J., Ripoll, D. R., Pillardy, J., & Scheraga, H. A. (1999). Protein structure prediction by global optimization of a potential energy function. *Proceedings of the National Academy of Sciences of the United States of America, 96*(10), 5482–5485. doi:10.1073/pnas.96.10.5482 PMID:10318909

Lobley, A., Sadowski, M. I., & Jones, D. T. (2009). pGenTHREADER and pDomTHREADER: New methods for improved protein fold recognition and superfamily discrimination. *Bioinformatics (Oxford, England)*, *25*(14), 1761–1767. doi:10.1093/bioinformatics/btp302 PMID:19429599

Lund, M., & Jonsson, B. (2005). On the charge regulation of proteins. *Biochemistry*, *44*(15), 5722–5727. doi:10.1021/bi047630o PMID:15823030

Mattos, C., & Ringe, D. (1996). Locating and characterizing binding sites on proteins. *Nature Biotechnology*, *14*(5), 595–599. doi:10.1038/nbt0596-595 PMID:9630949

McGann, M. R., Almond, H. R., Nicholls, A., Grant, J. A., & Brown, F. K. (2003). Gaussian docking functions. *Biopolymers*, *68*(1), 76–90. doi:10.1002/bip.10207 PMID:12579581

Meng, T. C., Somani, S., & Dhar, P. (2004). Modeling and simulation of biological systems with stochasticity. *In Silico Biology*, *4*(3), 293–309. PMID:15724281

Mintseris, J., Pierce, B., Wiehe, K., Anderson, R., Chen, R., & Weng, Z. (2007). Integrating statistical pair potentials into protein complex prediction. *Proteins*, *69*(3), 511–520. doi:10.1002/prot.21502 PMID:17623839

Moitessier, N., Englebienne, P., Lee, D., Lawandi, J., & Corbeil, C. R. (2008). Towards the development of universal, fast and highly accurate docking/scoring methods: A long way to go. *British Journal of Pharmacology*, *153*(S1Suppl 1), S7–S26. doi:10.1038/sj.bjp.0707515 PMID:18037925

Moult, J. (2005). A decade of CASP: Progress, bottlenecks and prognosis in protein structure prediction. *Current Opinion in Structural Biology*, *15*(3), 285–289. doi:10.1016/j.sbi.2005.05.011 PMID:15939584

Mulzer, S. R., & Brash, J. L. (1989). Identification of plasma proteins adsorbed to hemodialyzers during clinical use. *Journal of Biomedical Materials Research*, *23*(12), 1483–1504. doi:10.1002/jbm.820231210 PMID:2621220

Murray, D., Hermida-Matsumoto, L., Buser, C. A., Tsang, J., Sigal, C. T., & Ben-Tal, N. et al. (1998). Electrostatics and the membrane association of Src: Theory and experiment. *Biochemistry*, *37*(8), 2145–2159. doi:10.1021/bi972012b PMID:9485361

Parca, L., Gherardini, P. F., Helmer-Citterich, M., & Ausiello, G. (2011). Phosphate binding sites identification in protein structures. *Nucleic Acids Research*, *39*(4), 1231–1242. doi:10.1093/nar/gkq987 PMID:20974634

Pavlopoulou, A., & Michalopoulos, I. (2011). State-of-the-art bioinformatics protein structure prediction tools. *International Journal of Molecular Medicine*, *28*(3), 295–310. doi:10.3892/ijmm.2011.705 PMID:21617841

Pearlman, D. A., & Connelly, P. R. (1995). Determination of the differential effects of hydrogen bonding and water release on the binding of FK506 to native and Tyr82-->Phe82 FKBP-12 proteins using free energy simulations. *Journal of Molecular Biology*, *248*(3), 696-717. doi: 10.1006/jmbi.1995.0252

Peters, K. P., Fauck, J., & Frommel, C. (1996). The automatic search for ligand binding sites in proteins of known three-dimensional structure using only geometric criteria. *Journal of Molecular Biology*, *256*(1), 201–213. doi:10.1006/jmbi.1996.0077 PMID:8609611

Pietrokovski, S., Henikoff, J. G., & Henikoff, S. (1996). The Blocks database--A system for protein classification. *Nucleic Acids Research*, *24*(1), 197–200. doi:10.1093/nar/24.1.197 PMID:8594578

Przestalski, S., Hladyszowski, J., Kuczera, J., Rozycka-Roszak, B., Trela, Z., Chojnacki, H., . . . Fisicaro, E. (1996). Interaction between model membranes and a new class of surfactants with antioxidant function. *Biophysical Journal, 70*(5), 2203-2211. doi:10.1016/S0006-3495(96)79786-2

Ratner, B. D. (1996). The engineering of biomaterials exhibiting recognition and specificity. *Journal of Molecular Recognition, 9*(5-6), 617-625. doi: 10.1002/(SICI)1099-1352(199634/12)9:5/6<617::AID-JMR310>3.0.CO;2-D

Raut, V. P., Agashe, M. A., Stuart, S. J., & Latour, R. A. (2005). Molecular dynamics simulations of peptide-surface interactions. *Langmuir, 21*(4), 1629–1639. doi:10.1021/la047807f PMID:15697318

Reimhult, E., Hook, F., & Kasemo, B. (2002). Temperature dependence of formation of a supported phospholipid bilayer from vesicles on SiO2. *Physical Review E: Statistical, Nonlinear, and Soft Matter Physics, 66*(5 Pt 1), 051905. doi:10.1103/PhysRevE.66.051905 PMID:12513521

Rost, B., & Sander, C. (1993). Prediction of protein secondary structure at better than 70% accuracy. *Journal of Molecular Biology, 232*(2), 584–599. doi:10.1006/jmbi.1993.1413 PMID:8345525

Sadana, A. (1992a). Inactivation of proteins and other biological macromolecules during chromatographic methods of bioseparation. *Bioseparation, 3*(2-3), 145–165. PMID:1369239

Sadana, A. (1992b). Interfacial protein adsorption and inactivation. *Bioseparation, 3*(5), 297–320. PMID:1369429

Sadana, A., & Sii, D. (1992). Binding kinetics of antigen by immobilized antibody: Influence of reaction order and external diffusional limitations. *Biosens Bioelectron, 7*(8), 559-568.

Schneidman-Duhovny, D., Inbar, Y., Nussinov, R., & Wolfson, H. J. (2005). PatchDock and SymmDock: Servers for rigid and symmetric docking. *Nucleic Acids Research, 33*, W363-367. doi: 10.1093/nar/gki481

Sheng, C., Sarwal, S. N., Watts, K. C., & Marble, A. E. (1995). Computational simulation of blood flow in human systemic circulation incorporating an external force field. *Medical & Biological Engineering & Computing, 33*(1), 8–17. doi:10.1007/BF02522938 PMID:7616787

Simons, K. T., Kooperberg, C., Huang, E., & Baker, D. (1997). Assembly of protein tertiary structures from fragments with similar local sequences using simulated annealing and Bayesian scoring functions. *Journal of Molecular Biology, 268*(1), 209–225. doi:10.1006/jmbi.1997.0959 PMID:9149153

Singh, N., & Warshel, A. (2010). Absolute binding free energy calculations: On the accuracy of computational scoring of protein-ligand interactions. *Proteins, 78*(7), 1705–1723. doi:10.1002/prot.22687 PMID:20186976

Sivasankar, S., Subramaniam, S., & Leckband, D. (1998). Direct molecular level measurements of the electrostatic properties of a protein surface. *Proceedings of the National Academy of Sciences of the United States of America, 95*(22), 12961–12966. doi:10.1073/pnas.95.22.12961 PMID:9789023

Takamatsu, Y., & Itai, A. (1998). A new method for predicting binding free energy between receptor and ligand. *Proteins, 33*(1), 62–73. doi:10.1002/(SICI)1097-0134(19981001)33:1<62::AID-PROT6>3.0.CO;2-N PMID:9741845

van Aalten, D. M., Findlay, J. B., Amadei, A., & Berendsen, H. J. (1995). Essential dynamics of the cellular retinol-binding protein--evidence for ligand-induced conformational changes. *Protein Engineering, 8*(11), 1129–1135. doi:10.1093/protein/8.11.1129 PMID:8819978

Vitkup, D., Melamud, E., Moult, J., & Sander, C. (2001). Completeness in structural genomics. *Nature Structural Biology*, *8*(6), 559–566. doi:10.1038/88640 PMID:11373627

Voinova, M. V., Jonson, M., & Kasemo, B. (2002). Missing mass effect in biosensor's QCM applications. *Biosensors and Bioelectronics, 17*(10), 835-841.

Wass, M. N., Kelley, L. A., & Sternberg, M. J. (2010). 3DLigandSite: Predicting ligand-binding sites using similar structures. *Nucleic Acids Research, 38*, W469-473. doi: 10.1093/nar/gkq406

Werner, T., Morris, M. B., Dastmalchi, S., & Church, W. B. (2012). Structural modelling and dynamics of proteins for insights into drug interactions. *Advanced Drug Delivery Reviews, 64*(4), 323–343. doi:10.1016/j.addr.2011.11.011 PMID:22155026

Wu, S., Skolnick, J., & Zhang, Y. (2007). Ab initio modeling of small proteins by iterative TASSER simulations. *BMC Biology, 5*(1), 17. doi:10.1186/1741-7007-5-17 PMID:17488521

Xu, D., Xu, Y., & Uberbacher, E. C. (2000). Computational tools for protein modeling. *Current Protein & Peptide Science, 1*(1), 1–21. doi:10.2174/1389203003381469 PMID:12369918

Xu, J., Li, M., Kim, D., & Xu, Y. (2003). RAPTOR: Optimal protein threading by linear programming. *Journal of Bioinformatics and Computational Biology, 1*(1), 95–117. doi:10.1142/S0219720003000186 PMID:15290783

Zhang, Y. (2008a). Progress and challenges in protein structure prediction. *Current Opinion in Structural Biology, 18*(3), 342–348. doi:10.1016/j.sbi.2008.02.004 PMID:18436442

Zhang, Y. (2008b). Progress and challenges in protein structure prediction. *Current Opinion in Structural Biology, 18*(3), 342–348. doi:10.1016/j.sbi.2008.02.004 PMID:18436442

Zhang, Y. (2009). Protein structure prediction: When is it useful? *Current Opinion in Structural Biology, 19*(2), 145–155. doi:10.1016/j.sbi.2009.02.005 PMID:19327982

Zhang, Y., & Skolnick, J. (2004). Automated structure prediction of weakly homologous proteins on a genomic scale. *Proceedings of the National Academy of Sciences of the United States of America, 101*(20), 7594–7599. doi:10.1073/pnas.0305695101 PMID:15126668

Zhou, H., Pandit, S. B., & Skolnick, J. (2009). Performance of the Pro-sp3-TASSER server in CASP8. *Proteins, 77*(S9), 123–127. doi:10.1002/prot.22501 PMID:19639638

KEY TERMS AND DEFINITIONS

Ab initio **Methods:** Computational chemistry methods based on quantum chemistry principles as well as calculations.

Flanking Residues: Short sequences bordering a transcription unit that often do not code for proteins.

Fold Recognition: A computational protein structure prediction method of protein modeling which is used to model those proteins which have the same fold as proteins of known structures, but do not have homologous proteins with known structure.

Genetic Algorithms: Search heuristic method that mimic the process of natural evolution and is often used to generate useful solutions to optimization and search problems. These types of algorithms belong to the larger class of evolutionary algorithms that generate solutions to optimization problems using techniques inspired by natural evolution, such as inheritance, mutation, selection, and crossover.

Homologous Protein: A biological homology between proteins whose implication is that the proteins are derived from a common protein or other structure.

Homology Modeling: Constructing an atomic-resolution model of the protein of interest from its amino acid sequence and an experimental three-dimensional structure of a related homologous protein to be used as a template.

Molecular Dynamics Simulations: A computer simulation of physical movements of atoms and molecules that are allowed to interact for a period of time, This interaction then provides a view of the motion of the atoms. In the most common version, the trajectories of atoms and molecules are determined by numerically solving the Newton's equations of motion for a system of interacting particles, where forces between the particles and potential energy are defined by molecular mechanics force fields

Monte Carlo Simulations: A group of computational algorithms that rely on repeated random sampling to obtain numerical results, for example this can be obtained by running simulations many times over in order to calculate those same probabilities heuristically and are especially useful for simulating systems with many coupled degrees of freedom.

Neural Network: A network composed of interconnecting artificial neurons which mimic the properties of biological neurons for solving artificial intelligence problems without creating a model of a real system. Neural network algorithms abstract away the biological complexity by focusing on the most important information.

Petaflop: A measure of computer performance that make heavy use of floating-point calculations, FLOPS (or flops, for FLoating-point Operations Per Second, also flop/s) and a petaflop being 1015 FLOPS.

Primary Protein Structure: The linear sequence of amino acid structural units in a protein which partially encompasses the overall biomolecular structure of the protein. The primary structure of a protein is described by starting from the amino-terminal (N) end and terminating at the carboxyl-terminal (C) end.

Protein Databank: The storage system for the 3-D structural data of large biological molecules, such as proteins and nucleic acids.

Protein Domain: A conserved portion of a given protein sequence and structure that can evolve, function, and exist separately from the remainder of the protein chain.

Protein Folding: The process by which a protein structure assumes its functional shape or conformation

Protein Motif: A supersecondary structure of a protein that also appears in a variety of additional molecules.

Protein Sequence: The order in which amino acid residues, linked by peptide bonds, are positioned in the chain in the protein.

Rotamer: Isomers that can be interconverted through the use of rotations about formally single bonds

Secondary Protein Structure: The common three-dimensional form of local segments of proteins defined by the patterns of hydrogen bonds involving backbone amino and carboxyl groups.

Signature Database: A database that is used to store critical security parameters of trusted files present on the system.

Simulated Annealing: A generic probabilistic metaheuristic for the global optimization problem of locating a good approximation to the global optimum of a given function in a large search space.

Support Vector Machine: Supervised learning models with associated learning algorithms that analyze data and recognize patterns, used for classification and regression analysis.

Tertiary Protein Structure: The three-dimensional structure of a protein as defined by atomic coordinates and is created by the packing of protein secondary structure elements into dense globular units called protein domains.

Chapter 9
Role of Supercomputers in Bioinformatics

Anamika Singh
Department of Botany, Maitreyi College, University of Delhi, India

Rajeev Singh
Division of RCH, Indian Council of Medical Research, India

Neha Gupta
Northeastern University, USA & Osmania University, India

ABSTRACT

Due to the involvement of effective and client-friendly components (i.e. supercomputers), rapid data analysis is being accomplished. In Bioinformatics, it is expanding many areas of research such as genomics, proteomics, metabolomics, etc. Structure-based drug design is one of the major areas of research to cure human malady. This chapter initiates a discussion on supercomputing in sequence analysis with a detailed table summarizing the software and Web-based programs used for sequence analysis. A brief talk on the supercomputing in virtual screening is given where the databases like DOCK, ZINC, EDULISS, etc. are introduced. As the chapter transitions to the next phase, the intricacies of advanced Quantitative Structure-Activity Relationship technologies like Fragment-Based 2D QSAR, Multiple-Field 3D QSAR, and Amino Acid-Based Peptide Prediction are put forth in a manner similar to the concept of abstraction. The supercomputing in docking studies is stressed where docking software for Protein-Ligand docking, Protein-Protein docking, and Multi-Protein docking are provided. The chapter ends with the applications of supercomputing in widely used microarray data analysis.

INTRODUCTION

A supercomputer is a computer with high speed and is calculation efficient. Supercomputers first came in practice during 1960s. These supercomputers are normal and are similar to other computers but have more processors making the speed high. Presently, supercomputers are replaced by parallel supercomputers in which thousands of processors were connected to a single computer (Hoffman et al., 1990, Hill et al., 1999 & Prodan et al., 2007). In this chapter we are focusing on some novel areas

DOI: 10.4018/978-1-4666-7461-5.ch009

Copyright © 2015, IGI Global. Copying or distributing in print or electronic forms without written permission of IGI Global is prohibited.

Figure 1. A brief history of supercomputing

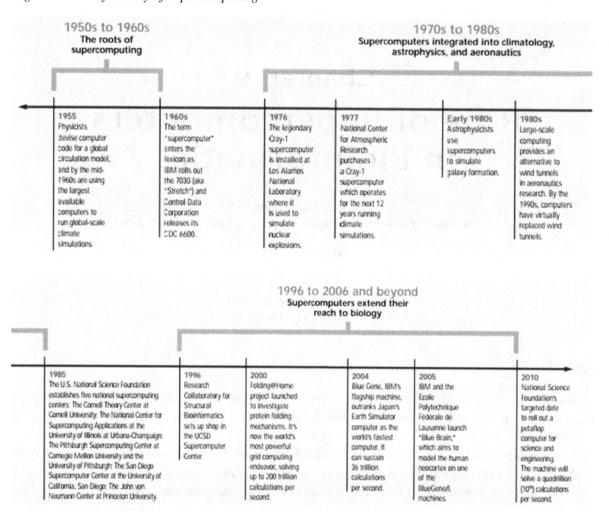

Source: www.biomedicalcomputationreview.org

SUPERCOMPUTING IN SEQUENCE ANALYSIS

of biological research where supercomputing is playing a vital role. These few areas are:

Sequence analysis is actually used to explore the DNA, RNA and protein sequences in such a way that it gives all the information about the organism, source, phylogeny, function and structure, and other characteristics. Methodologies used include sequence alignment, searches against biological databases and others. Mostly it is required to search a DNA, a protein or genome database for sequence locations that are similar to that of some query sequence.

These databases already have billions of sequences with characteristics and this sequence information is increasing day by day. Manual searching is tough, a time consuming process and the efficiency of result is questionable. So to look for an exact match between the query string and a sub-string of the database is a very computationally demanding task. A perfect database search allows the possibility of mutations, insertion and deletions. There are novel heuristic approaches such as BLAST and FASTA (Altschul et al., 1990, Casey, 2005) which are efficient for mutations, insertions, and deletions but are not well suited for statistical purposes as they are less efficient in comparison to the dynamic programming algorithm such as Smith- Waterman (Lipman and Pearson, 1985, Pearson, W. R; Lipman, D. J. 1988). Although Smith-Waterman takes too much time for the calculations but it is still technically superior.

NCBI BLAST is the Basic Local Alignment Search Tool (BLAST) by the National Center for Biotechnology Information (Altschul et al., 1990). It is one of the most widely-used tools for sequence similarity searches. BLAST can perform comparisons between protein or DNA sequences from a sequence database where diverse sequences from different sources are present. There are dif-ferent types of algorithms that were utilized for different types of search methods. There are many mathematical algorithms utilized in the analysis of sequence-sequence comparison like Genetic algorithm, Markov method, hidden Markov models, and so forth (Eddy, 1998). HMMER is also used for similarity searches of sequence databases (Edgar, 2004). Inspite of two sequences there are so many tools which can compare multiple number of sequences at a time. These are HMMER, multiple sequence alignment by CLUSTALW, Kaling etc. ("MUSCLE," http://www.drive5.com/muscle/). Sequence analysis helps molecular biology for a variety of analysis. It can compare two sequences for their similarity and identity, is helpful for the identification and analysis of active sites, interaction sites and regulatory sites. It can also identify mutations within gene and sequences. Sequence analysis also helps in genetic diversity. Here we are taking some examples of bioinformatics tools (Table 1).

Table 1. Softwares and web based programs used for sequence analysis (Source: List of sequence alignment software, 2014)

Name	Description	Link
BLAST	local search with fast k-tuple heuristic (Basic Local Alignment Search Tool)	http://blast.ncbi.nlm.nih.gov/
FASTA	local search with fast *k*-tuple heuristic, slower but more sensitive than BLAST	http://fasta.bioch.virginia.edu/fasta_www2/fasta_list2.shtml
HMMER	local and global search with profile Hidden Markov models, more sensitive than PSI-BLAST	http://hmmer.janelia.org/
PSI-BLAST	position-specific iterative BLAST, local search with position-specific scoring matrices, much more sensitive than BLAST	http://blast.ncbi.nlm.nih.gov/
DNADot	Web-based dot-plot tool	www.vivo.colostate.edu/molkit/**dnadot**/
DOTLET	Java-based dot-plot tool	
ClustalW	Progressive alignment	**www**.ch.embnet.org/software/**ClustalW**.html
DNA Baser Sequence Assembler	Multi-alignment; Automatic batch alignment	www.DnaBaser.com
Kalign	Progressive alignment	https://www.ebi.ac.uk/Tools/msa/**kalign**/

SUPERCOMPUTING IN VIRTUAL SCREENING

Virtual screening is screening or filtering and identification of those molecules which have similar structures. This search is actually a database search method which contains a number of molecules with their structures and a query molecule that will match with the databases. A query may be a compound or a molecular fragment. First, the algorithm attempts to find the correct conformation and position of the ligand in the active site of the receptor and then try to quantify the quality of particular atomic arrangements by assigning a score. There are so many different methods used in protein-ligand interactions especially DOCK is a very commonly used tool for docking (Kuntz et al., 1982).

3D structure prediction of proteins and ligands gives a new insight for the prediction of accurate ligand-receptor interactions, in spite of this it can also predict the forces and bonds involved within it. 3D structure prediction is one of the most successful methods for the prediction of structures of those proteins which are not predicted by X-ray or NMR methods as these methods are having limitations. 3D structure prediction may be ab-initio, comparative methods or homology based methods and threading method.

Most successful and widely accepted method is Homology based method which is based on comparative similarity and identity based scores between query and databases. As all these methods are very popular but virtual screening is very successful only for those structures which are modeled by homology based methods (Ripphausen et al., 2010 14.).). In any case, a homology model must start from a closely related experimental structure, so an important contributing factor in the increased utility of computational drug discovery is the rapid growth in the number of available protein structures (Joachimiak, 2009).

Another important contribution of virtual screening is generation of virtual screening da-tabases for compounds like ZINC database at University of California San Francisco is a free database of commercially-available compounds for virtual screening. ZINC contains over 13 million purchasable compounds in ready-to-dock, 3D formats. (Irwin & Shoichet, 2005). EDinburgh University LIgand Selection System, known as EDULISS, is a relational database system for database mining.at Edinburgh University (Taylor et al., 2008). Another large database, Chemical Universe Database GDB-13 follows different methods attempting to construct the universe of synthetic compounds (Blum & Reymond, 2009).

SUPERCOMPUTING IN QSAR

Quantitative structure-activity relationship (QSAR) has been playing a major role in the field of agricultural chemistry, pharmacology, and toxicology since last few years (Hansch & Leo, 1979). With the help of QSAR, we can design new models and compare them with existing models or newly generated models to the biological databases. On the basis of similarity and dissimilarity, we can also conclude the relationship between these two.

Quantitative structure activity relationship (QSAR) modeling is an area of research which was pioneered by Hansch and Fujita (Hansch & Leo, 1995, Hansch & Selassie, 2007). The QSAR study assumes that the difference of the molecules in the structural properties experimentally measured accounts for the difference in their observed biological or chemical properties (Golender & Vorpagel 1993). With the help of QSAR, it is now possible not only to develop a model for a system but also to compare models from a biological database and to draw analogies with models from a physical organic database (Hansch et al., 2001). QSAR is able to identify the relationship between a molecule and its structure and how the structure influences the activity of the molecule.

There are a few parameters like steric properties, electron distribution and hydrophobicity.

In spite of this, minute analysis shows that there are some small parameters. This can affect the function of a molecule and are generally known as molecular descriptors. These descriptors are atomic descriptors and are derived from quantum chemical calculations and spectroscopy (Livingstone, 2000).

High-throughput screening method allows fast screening of large number of datasets. It separates the molecule with similar structure and function. This method is very useful as it helps to minimize the risk of comparison between different datasets of variable sources. From drug development to its mode of action, all steps can be compared easily along with drug formulation by using this method. QSAR method does not only compare the datasets but also generates the data of their analogy (Pandey & Nichols, 2011).

Latest technologies of QSAR involve three different aspects.

1. Fragment Based 2D QSAR (FB 2D-QSAR)

In this method, a drug candidate is first subjected to fragmentation into its components and then bioactivities of drug candidates are correlated with physicochemical properties of the molecular fragments through two sets of coefficients: one is for the physicochemical properties and the other for the molecular fragments (Du et al., 2008). FB-QSAR is used to predict the model of neuraminidase inhibitors for drug development against H5N1 influenza virus (Du et al., 2009). This method is also used to predict the new insights for dealing with the drug-resistant problem and designing effective adamantine-based anti-flue drugs for influenza A viruses (Wei et al., 2009).

2. Multiple Field 3D QSAR (MF 3D QSAR)

It is based on comparative molecular field analyses (CoMFA) in which two sets of coefficients are

involved: one is for the potential fields and the other for the Cartesian three dimensional grid points (Du et al., 2008).

Other 3D QSAR methods include Comparative Molecular Similarity Indices Analysis (CoMSIA) that is widely used in drug design. The main advantage of this method along with CoMFA is that they can be used for heterogeneous datasets and they shortlist a 3D mapped description of favorable and unfavorable interactions according to physicochemical properties. Some of the disadvantages of these methods include 3D information and alignment of the molecular structures since there are uncertainties about different binding modes of ligands and uncertainties about the bioactive conformations (Fernandez et al., 2010).

Apart from these linear methods (CoMFA and CoMSIA), Artificial Neural Networks (ANN) and Support Vector Machines (SVMs) are able to describe nonlinear relationships which brings a more realistic picture of structure-relationship paradigm as the interactions between the ligand and its biological target must be nonlinear. Some of the latest and robust methods include Bayesian-regularized genetic neural networks (BRGNNs), Genetic Algorithm (GA) - optimized SVM (GA-SVM), Principal component-Genetic Algorithm-Artificial Neural Network (PC-GA-ANN), GA-based partial least squares (GA-PLS), etc (Fernandez et al., 2010).

3. Amino Acid-Based Peptide Prediction (AABPP)

In this method, the biological activities of the peptides and proteins are correlated with the physicochemical properties of all or partial residues of the sequence through two sets of coefficients: one is for the physicochemical properties of amino acids and the other for the weight factors of the residues (Du et al., 2008).

QSAR and QSPR are the fields that statistically correlate chemical substance characters with biological activities (QSAR) or properties

(QSPR). The chemical substance can be molecular structures, drugs, and true mixtures like nano-materials (nanoQSAR). One of the latest tools to make QSAR more reproducible is the CHEMINF Ontology. The QSAR datasets that consists of an open XML format (QSAR-ML) is another type of QSAR study. One of the future applications would be to reformulate QSAR-ML to be based on CHEMINF (Willighagen, 2011).

AutoQSAR is a proprietory system developed at AstraZeneca in collaboration with Accelrys. Its main purpose is to automatically create, evaluate and maintain QSAR models (Cala et al.). That is to improve prediction accuracy of models by updating them with newly acquired data. Auto-QSAR employs the Sun Grid Engine Platform for the calculations. Cloud computing is one area where QSAR studies can be employed and made faster to increase the speed of chemical activity predictions (Cala et al.,n.d.).

SUPERCOMPUTING IN DOCKING STUDIES

Docking is the study of close interaction between two macro molecules like proteins or it is interaction between a protein and a drug or ligand or a small peptide molecule. After interactions, these two molecules forms a stable complex and these stable complexes helps in cellular and molecular functions in cell (Lengauer & Rarey, 1996). These two molecules bind together and this interaction is based on binding affinity of two molecules. On the basis of this binding, some score was assigned to these complexes and then they were characterized on the basis of scores. So binding affinity and scoring of complexes are two important characteristics.

Docking methods are also used to predict the structure of protein-protein complex and protein-ligand complexes. So in spite of interaction studies it is also playing an important role in drug designing (Kitchen et al., 2004). Molecular

docking is based on best fitted method as the ligand fits itself and it minimizes the energy of the complexes so that the complexes get stabilized itself (Jorgensen, 1991).

Another approach is induced fit method as the ligand or peptide and the receptor (protein) is flexible in nature and once ligand comes and binds with it and induces itself according to the shape of receptor molecule (Wei et al., 2000). These interactions are based on lock and key method as the receptor works as lock and the protein or the ligand molecule act as key and both gets fitted with each other and forms a stable complex (Goldman et al., 2000, Meng et al., 2004, Cerqueira et al., 2009).

Protein–Ligand Docking

Protein-ligand docking is a molecular modeling method which is used to predict the exact orientation of the ligand and protein and this orientation stabilizes the complex (Mendoza-Barrera et al., 2013).Nowadays, these interaction studies helps in pharmaceutical research as it helps in interactions as well as screening of the molecules based on target's (protein) 3D structure. On the basis of these interactions, new lead molecules can be discovered and new drug molecules can be generated.

Several protein–ligand docking software applications are available, such as AutoDock or EADock. There are also web services (Molecular Docking Server, SwissDock) that calculate the site, geometry and energy of small molecules interacting with proteins. From last few decades, screening of drug and drug like molecules gave a new method of computational biology i.e. computer added drug designing (CADD) (Cerqueira et al., 2009). While dealing with receptor flexibility and degree of freedom creates problems in calculations, neglecting these problems can lead to non-reliable computational predictions (Kearsley et al., 1994).

CombiBUILD is a protein-ligand docking software developed at Sandia National Labs which is a structure-based drug design program created to aid in the design of combinatorial libraries. It screens a library of possible reactants on the computer and predicts which ones are most significant. It has been previously successful in finding nanomolar inhibitors of Cathepsin D. DockVision is a docking package created by scientists at University of Alberta using Monte Carlo, Genetic Algorithm and database screening docking algorithms. FRED (OpenEye) is an accurate and extremely fast, multiconformer docking program. FRED examines all possible poses within a protein active site, filtering for shape complementarity and optional pharmacophoric features. FlexiDock, FlexX, GLIDE, GOLD, HINT, LIGPLOT, SITUS, VEGA are other globally used efficient protein-ligand docking softwares.

Macromolecular Docking or Protein-Protein Docking

Macromolecular docking or protein-protein docking is the computational modeling of complexes. There are so many structures that can be predicted due to flexibility of the ligand and the receptor. On the basis of these flexible interactions these docked complexes were ranked and some scores were assigned to them and based on their molecular affinity best docked complex can be isolated as a final docked complex.

Docking may be rigid or flexible depending upon their motions at molecular level. Conformations of the ligand may be generated and further this model is used for the interaction studies when it will docked with another protein or receptor (Friesner et al., 2004). These ligands are docked at the cavity of the receptor where it gets a space and has fitted itself in such a way that it also minimizes the energy of the complex (Zsoldos et al., 2007).

Another approach of docking is fragment based docking as it gives a small fragment to dock with a small portion of the receptor (Wang & Pang, 2007, Klebe & Mietzner, 1994, Cerqueira et al., 2009). Flexibility in receptors always create problems in analysis as they have a bulky structure and every

molecule is having their own degree of freedom (Totrov & Abagyan, 2008, Hartmann et al., 2009, Taylor et al., 2003).

There are many interesting aspects which influence the protein-protein interaction mostly like effects of amino acids like Arginine, Histidine and Lysine increases the positive charge which causes charge-charge repulsion and finally decrease of protein stability. Protein-Protein interactions mainly include electrostatic interactions, hydrogen bonds, the Vanderwalls interactions and hydrophobic interactions. Average protein-protein interface is not less polar or more hydrophobic than the surface remaining in contact with solvent. Hydrophobic forces derive protein-protein interactions and hydrogen bonds and salt bridges generally confer specificity. The Vanderwalls forces bind between the neighboring atoms if they are numerous and tightly packed they do contribute to the binding energy of association.

It was also observed by the earlier workers that hydrogen and Vanderwall bonds are more favorable between protein molecules than the surrounding water molecules. Shape of interacting surface also influences the interactions generally interactive surface is flat in nature. There are some more quite interesting structural factors noticeable in the Protein-Protein interactions like loop regions of proteins are more involved in the interactions.

MEGADOCK 3.0 is a high-throughput and ultra-fast Protein-Protein Interaction prediction software based on rigid docking. It employs an MPI/OpenMPI technique assuming usages on massively parallel supercomputing systems. MEGADOCK displays significantly faster processing speed that leads to full usage of protein tertiary structural data for large-scale problems in systems biology. This is a new protein-protein docking engine aimed at exhaustive docking of mega-order numbers of protein pairs (Matsuzaki, 2013).

ClusPro 2.0 is a protein-protein docking software developed at Boston University. In each docking job, the receptor and ligand has to be chosen. The receptor can be either a structure present in the PDB or you can also upload your own PDB by clicking on the Upload PDB tab. The chains can also be specified for the receptor. Similarly, ligand is chosen. Depending on the queue of the jobs on the supercomputer and the size of the protein, docking will usually finish in a few hours. The results of docking can be viewed and downloaded. To analyze the results, the model is downloaded and can be viewed in PyMol (ClusPro-protein-protein docking).

Global Range Molecular Matching (GRAMM) at the University of Kansas is a Protein-Protein docking and Protein-Ligand docking software that uses an empirical approach to smooth the intermolecular energy function (Structure based drug design and molecular modeling). It requires only the atomic coordinates of the two molecules to predict the complex structure and therefore no binding site information is needed. It performs an exhaustive 6 –dimensional search through the translations and rotations of the molecules. ICM-Dock at MolSoft LLC is another Protein-Protein and Protein-Ligand docking software which is fast and accurate. It has a unique set of tools for accurate individual ligand-protein docking, peptide-protein docking and protein-protein docking including interactive graphic tools (Structure based drug design and molecular modeling).

Other popular protein-protein docking softwares include ZDOCK, HEX, PIPER, GRAMM-X, PRISM, 3D-Dock Suite, BiGGER, DOT, ESCHER NG, HADDOCK, etc.

Some Docking Softwares

Binding Affinity Prediction of Protein-Ligand (BAPPL) server basically computes the binding free energy of a non-metallo protein-ligand complex using an all atom energy based empirical scoring function. BAPPL server accepts two methods (Jayaram, 2012). One method is where the input should be an energy minimized protein-ligand complex with hydrogens added, protonation

states, partial atomic charges and VanderWaals parameters assigned for each atom. The server directly computes the binding affinity of the complex. The second method is where the input is an energy minimized protein-ligand complex with hydrogens added and protonation states assigned. The net charge on the ligand should be specified. The server obtains the partial atomic charges of the ligand using the AM1-BCC procedure and GAFF force field for VanderWaals parameters (Jayaram, 2012).

ParDOCK is another automated server for Protein Ligand Docking at IIT Delhi. It is an all-atom energy based Monte Carlo, protein ligand docking implemented in a automated parallel processing mode. The structural input data for the ParDOCK are optimized reference complex (protein-ligand) and a example ligand to be docked (Jayaram, 2013).

DnaDOCK is another bioinformatics software that does DNA ligand docking. It is again a Monte Carlo based docking implemented in a parallel processing mode and predicts the binding mode of the ligand in the minor groove of DNA (Jayaram, 2011). Superimpose is another software that fits two molecular structures drug and protein and calculates the Root Mean Square Deviation between them giving an idea about their structural similarity. RMSD is the square root of the average of the squared distance between each mapped pair. It is normally used in 3D geometry of molecules to measure distance between a given set of points or atoms. The resultant superimposed structures can be downloaded and viewed in a visualization software like ViewerLite, Rasmol, etc (Superimpose, 2010).

Multi Protein Docking

Multi Protein Docking involves the docking of many proteins of important function to a single drug candidate. There are various advantages of this docking method, some of which are

1. Determines toxicity and side effects.
2. Predicts failures earlier in the process.
3. Increases overall success rate (Ellingson, 2012).

Multi protein docking also has its own limitations. For instance, using Autodock4 software, there are separate MPI jobs for each receptor. Also, binary grid files are generated for each receptor. Hence, using supercomputing abilities in future, a tool is needed that allows an increase in the number of receptors used in a screening with a minimal increase in the amount of I/O per docking task (Ellingson, 2012).

In comparison to Autodock4, Autodock Vina is found to be potential multi-protein docking software. It calculates grid maps efficiently during docking and does not store them on disk. It is already multi-threaded, has maximum number of rotatable bonds, etc (Ellingson, 2012).

In the future, it is believed that all possible drugs can be docked into the entire set of proteins with an individual's genetic variations in order to develop personalized medicine (Ellingson, 2013). The program VinaMPI has been developed to enable large virtual drug screens using a large number of cores. It is based on the multi-threaded virtual docking program Autodock Vina. VinaMPI efficiently handles multiple proteins in a ligand screen, allowing for high-throughput inverse docking that can improve the efficiency of drug discovery pipeline. VinaMPI successfully ran on 84,672 cores with a decrease in job completion time and increasing core count (Ellingson, 2013).

Other multi-purpose docking softwares include InsightII, AMBER, GRASP, Procheck, GCG program, HOMDOCK, ICM, ParaDockS, Surflex-Dock, LigandFit, etc.

Supercomputing in Microarray Data Analysis

Microarray is a technique in which DNA probes that are arrayed on a solid support (Silicon thin film) are used for assay. This analysis is based on the hybridization ability of the DNA with the probe as the probe is designed, in such a manner that it must have complementary sequences (DNA) (Marmur & Doty, 1961). Microarray is a chip of very small size having ninety six or more tiny wells and each well has thousands of DNA probes or oligonucleotides arranged in a grid of chip ((Sundberg et al., 2001), (Afshari & Perspective, 2002)).

Different types of genes are immobilized and are fixed at specific locations on chip and thus a single chip can give the information about thousands of genes simultaneously by hybridization method. cDNA microarrays and oligonucleotide arrays are the two types of microarray data analysis ((Ponder, 2001), (Rowley,1973)).

1. cDNA arrays are generated by putting a double stranded cDNA on a solid support (glass or nylon). For this robotics arms are used for the minimization of errors.
2. Oligonucleotide arrays are made by synthesizing specific oligonucleotides in a specific alignment on a solid surface. For this photolithography technique is used. (Gray et al., 2000).

The labeled cDNAs are now exposed and allowed to hybridize with the probe DNA. This hybridization is similar to Southern blotting method. After that slide is washed properly which removes nonspecific hybridization, it is read in a laser scanner that can differentiate between Cy3- and Cy5-signals, collecting fluorescence intensities to produce a separate 16-bit TIFF image for each channel ((Venter & Adams, 2001), (Young, 2000)).

Estimation of results is done by measuring the intensity of fluorescence, which corresponds to the amount of gene expressed in the sample (Pandey et al., 2003 & Labana et al., 2005). The three major steps of a microarray technology are preparation of microarray, preparation of labeled probes and hybridization and finally, scanning, imaging and data analysis ((Labana et al., 2005), (Esteve-Nunez et al., 2001)).

The scanning and data analysis all depends on the efficiency of supercomputers.

The following steps are important for the accurate data quantification.

- The multiple levels of replication in experimental design (Experimental design)
- The number of platforms and independent groups and data format (Standardization)
- The treatment of the data (Statistical analysis with the help of supercomputers)
- Accuracy and precision (Relation between probe and gene with the help of supercomputers)
- The sheer volume of data and the ability to share it (Data warehousing with the help of supercomputers)

Applications of DNA Microarray Technology

DNA microarray technology has been used to study many bacterial species which include *Escherichia coli* (Richmond et al., 1999, Tao et al., 1999). *Mycobacterium tuberculosis* (Wilson et al., 1999; Behr et al., 1999), *Streptococcus pneumonia* (De Saizieu et al., 2000 & Hakenbeck et al., 2001) and *Bacillus subtilis* ((Ye et al., 2000), (Yoshida, 2001)). With DNA microarray entire microbial genome can be easily represented in a single array and it is feasible to perform genome-wide analysis (DeRisi et al., 1997). Microarray technique is used in medicine development by providing microarray data of a patient which could be used for identifying diseases (Amandeep Singh et al., 2013). DNA microarray technology has been used for analyses of natural and anthropogenic factors in yeast and analyzed how the whole genome of yeast responds to environmental stressors such as temperature, pH, oxidation, and nutrients ((Causton et al., 2001), (Gasch et al., 2000)).

Microarray analysis has been applied to identify molecular markers of pathogen infection in salmon (Rise et al., 2004). DNA microarray has been used for studying gene expression analysis in neurological disorders. DNA microarray experiments are carried out to find genes which are differentially expressed between two or more samples of cells (Caetano et al., 2004). cDNA microarrays provide a powerful tool for studying complex phenomena of gene expression patterns in human cancer (Ghosh et al., n.d.). DNA microarrays has been used for clinical diagnosis such as histopathology and molecular pathology e.g. Microarray technique has been identified for analysis of AMACR (α-methylacyl-CoA racemase in prostate cancer compared with normal prostate. ((Shalon et al., 1996), (Schena et al., 1996)).

Scientists at the Houston Methodist Research Institute (HMRI) have been successful in understanding the inverse relationship between Alzheimer's disease and a brain cancer, Glioblastoma Multiforme (GBM) (Dutt,2014). Information about the genes were obtained by DNA microarray analysis followed by sequencing using data from The Cancer Genome Atlas at NIH (for GBM) and Alzheimer's Disease Neuroimaging Initiative (for AD). The results were then analyzed by supercomputers, which yielded a 1000-fold improved performance as compared to microarray analysis (Dutt, 2014).

Analysis of raw microarray data files, e.g. Affymetrix CEL files can be time consuming, complex and requires fundamental computational skills. Also, the analysis of microarray data normally involves many steps like data organization, quality control, normalization, differential gene expression calling, clustering, pathway analysis, etc. The development of software-based workflow to automate these procedures would improve the efficiency and serve to standardize the multiple inter and intra-dataset analyses.

Typical microarray-based gene expression analyses compare gene expression in adjacent normal and cancerous tissues. In this type of analysis, genes with strong statistical differences in expression are identified (O'Neal, 2014). However, many genes are aberrantly expressed in tumors. These "passenger" genes are differentially expressed between normal and tumor tissues but they are not "drivers" of tumorigenesis. Therefore, better computational methods that enrich the list of genes with authentic cancer-associated "driver" genes are needed (O'Neal, 2014).

Multicategory Support Vector Machines (MC-SVM) are powerful classification systems with excellent performance in a variety of problems associated with data classification. Since the process of generating models in traditional Multicategory Support Vector Machines for large datasets is very computationally intensive, there is a need to improve this performance using advanced High Performance Computing techniques (Zhang et al., 2006). PMC-SVM is developed for classifying large microarray datasets. It is implemented in MPI and C++ based on the serial implementation of SMO-SVM in libSVM. The experimental results show that the high performance computing techniques and parallel implementation can achieve a great speed-up without losing accuracy (Zhang et al., 2006).

The completed human genome consists of ~ 3000 mega-bases and ~35000 genes distributed across 23 chromosomes. The mouse genome is similar in size and gene number except with 3 fewer chromosomes (Bertone, 2014). This genetic data is a good standard in comparative genome analysis to annotate gene information of other organisms. However, huge computation is involved in sequence similarity comparisons. Field Programmable Gate Arrays (FPGA) are integrated circuits designed to perform far more quickly than conventional CPUs. In a way, FPGAs are similar to the application-specific integrated circuits (ASICs). TimeLogic has already developed DeCypher system based on the FPGA technology with enhanced Biocomputing algorithms including BLAST for genome level analyses. This is a unique DNA microarray design algorithm using

the FPGA technology combined with de novo software development (Bertone, 2014).

Many existing Bioinformatics tools like Bioconductor, BASE, etc have been developed to assist in the analysis of microarray datasets. The available tools for microarray analyses are developed in Perl, Python and R programming languages (Gan et al., 2014). Apart from these tools, different platforms like Galaxy, Taverna, Bioclipse, Yabi and Kepler are available to develop Bioinformatics pipelines. Kepler is the most popular as it has a user friendly graphical interface, built-in R/python components, etc. The ability to extend workflows as well as the support of external packages such as Bioconductor makes Kepler an ideal platform to work on further analytic tools. For instance, Kepler based workflow was developed by integrating desired tools to develop a pipeline termed Meta-Analyses of online-available Affymetrix Microarray Data (MAAMD). MAAMD is the standard microarray analysis pipeline and also improves analysis efficiency. Some of the tools that are integrated include Bioconductor packages like AffyQCReport and arrayQualityMetrics, AltAnalyze (for Microarray and RNA-Seq analysis), etc (Gan et al., 2014).

There are several Microarray Analysis softwares, some of them are GoMiner, GoSurfer, GenMAPP, ArrayTrack, caGEDA, SAM, NUDGE, etc. The Microarray Data Repositories include GEO, ArrayExpress, CIBEX, Standard Microarray Database (SMD), The Gene Expression Database (GXD), Oncomine, etc (Yang, 2006). An approach to gene expression analysis must involve an up-front characterization of the structure of data. Singular Value Decomposition (SVD) and Principle Component Analysis (PCA) can be valuable tools in obtaining such characterization (Wall,n.d.). SVD and PCA are common techniques for analysis of multivariate data and gene expression data are well suited to analysis using SVD/PCA. Gene expression data are normally very noisy and SVD can detect and extract small signals from noisy data. PCA and SVD analysis methods are also useful for characterizing protein molecular dynamics trajectories and visualization of the datasets. Other techniques to visualize data are Multidimensional Scaling and Self Organizing Maps (SOM) (Wall, n.d.).

The statistical tests are normally done in order to find out the differentially expressed genes. Basically, two types of tests are performed on microarray data. They are t-test and ANOVA test. A more sophisticated approach, Bayesian Belief Networks (BBN) or Bayesian probabilistic framework is useful to analyze expression data (Valafar, 2002). In this method, competing models are designed and then Bayesian Belief Networks is used to pick the model that best fits the expression data. Friedman and co-workers have used BBNs to analyze genome-wide expression data in order to identify significant interactions between genes in a variety of metabolic and regulatory pathways (Valafar, 2002). Bayesian Neural Networks (BNN) is another technique that is used for gene expression analysis. Liang et al have used the BNNs with structural learning for exploring microarray data in gene expressions (Valafar, 2002).

CONCLUSION

Supercomputers are used for fast calculations and accurate predictions. By using these methods, we can predict so many aspects of biological molecules which are not possible experimentally due to some limitations. Computational biology, drug designing, Sequencing, genomic analysis, protein 3D structure prediction are the major areas of biological research. Neural networks and systems biology, artificial neural networks and cloud computing are the new emerging branches of science which are based on supercomputers.

REFERENCES

Afshari, C. A. (2002). Perspective: Microarray technology, seeing more than spots. *Endocrinology*, *143*(6), 1983–1989. doi:10.1210/endo.143.6.8865 PMID:12021158

Altschul, S., Gish, W. M., Myers, W., & Lipman, E. (1990). Basic local alignment search tool. *Journal of Molecular Biology*, *215*(3), 403–410. doi:10.1016/S0022-2836(05)80360-2 PMID:2231712

Altschul, S. F., Gish, W., Miller, W., Myers, E. W., & Lipman, D. J. (1990). Basic local alignment search tool. *Journal of Molecular Biology*, *215*(3), 403–410. doi:10.1016/S0022-2836(05)80360-2 PMID:2231712

Behr, M. A., Wilson, M. A., Gill, W. P., Salamon, H., Schoolnik, G. K., & Rane, S. et al. (1999). Comparative genomics of BCG vaccines by whole-genome DNA microarray. *Science*, *284*(5419), 1520–1523. doi:10.1126/science.284.5419.1520 PMID:10348738

Bertone, A. (2014). *FPGA assisted equine gene annotation and custom microarray (genechip)*. Retrieved June 16, 2014 from https://www.osc.edu/research/bioinformatics/projects/horse_gene

Blum, L. C., & Reymond, J. (2009). Million drug like small molecules for virtual screening in the chemical universe database GDB-13. *Journal of the American Chemical Society*, *131*(25), 8732–8733. doi:10.1021/ja902302h PMID:19505099

Caetano, A. R., Johnson, R. K., Ford, J. J., & Pomp, D. (2004). Microarray profiling for differential gene expression in ovaries and ovarian follicles of pigs selected for increased ovulation rate. *Genetics*, *168*(3), 1529–1537. doi:10.1534/genetics.104.029595 PMID:15579704

Cala, J., Hiden, H., Watson, P., & Woodman, S. (n.d.). *Cloud computing for fast prediction of chemical activity*. Retrieved June 16, 2014 from http://www.esciencecentral.co.uk/wp-content/uploads/2011/03/Cloud-Computing-for-Fast-Prediction-of-Chemical-Activity.pdf

Casey, R. M. (2005). *BLAST sequences aid in genomics and proteomics*. Business Intelligence Network.

Causton, H. C., Ren, B., Koh, S. S., Harbison, C. T., Kanin, E., & Jennings, E. G. et al. (2001). Remodeling of yeast genome expression in response to environmental changes. *Molecular Biology of the Cell*, *12*(2), 323–337. doi:10.1091/mbc.12.2.323 PMID:11179418

Cerqueira, N. M., Bras, N. F., Fernandes, P. A., & Ramos, M. J. (2009). MADAMM: A multistaged docking with an automated molecular modeling protocol. *Proteins*, *74*(1), 192–206. doi:10.1002/prot.22146 PMID:18618708

Cerqueira, N. M., Fernandes, P. A., Eriksson, L. A., & Ramos, M. J. (2009). MADAMM: A multistaged docking with an automated molecular modeling protocol. *Proteins: Structure, Function, and Bioinformatics*, *74*(1), 192–206. doi:10.1002/prot.22146 PMID:18618708

ClusPro-Protein-Protein Docking. (n.d.). Retrieved June 16, 2014 from http://cluspro.bu.edu/tut_dock.php

De, K., Ghosh, G., Datta, M., Konar, A., Bandyopadhyay, J., & Bandyopadhyay, D. et al. (2004). Analysis of differentially expressed genes in hyperthyroid-induced hypertrophied heart by CDNA microarray. *The Journal of Endocrinology*, *182*(2), 303–314. doi:10.1677/joe.0.1820303 PMID:15283691

de Saizieu, A., Gardes, C., Flint, N., Wagner, C., Kamber, M., & Mitchell, T. J. et al. (2000). Microarray-based identification of a novel *Streptococcus pneumoniae* regulon controlled by an autoinduced peptide. *Journal of Bacteriology*, *182*(17), 4696–4703. doi:10.1128/JB.182.17.4696-4703.2000 PMID:10940007

DeRisi, J. L., Iyer, V., & Brown, P. O. (1997). Exploring the metabolic and genetic control of gene expression on a genomic scale. *Science*, *278*(5338), 680–686. doi:10.1126/science.278.5338.680 PMID:9381177

Du, Q. S., Huang, R. B., & Chou, K. C. (2008). Review: Recent advances in QSAR and their applications in predicting the activities of chemical molecules, peptides and proteins for drug design. *Current Protein & Peptide Science*, *9*(3), 248–259. doi:10.2174/138920308784534005 PMID:18537680

Du, Q. S., Huang, R. B., Wei, Y. T., Pang, Z. W., Du, L. Q., & Chou, K.-C. (2009). Fragment-Based quantitative structure-activity relationship (FBQSAR) for fragment-based drug design. *Journal of Computational Chemistry*, *30*(2), 295–304. doi:10.1002/jcc.21056 PMID:18613071

Dutt, S. (2014). *HMRI researchers use systems biology, TACC supercomputers to find link between Alzheimer's and brain cancer*. Retrieved June 16, 2014 from http://bionews-tx.com/news/2014/04/29/alzheimers-and-cancer-link-found/

Eddy, S. R. (1998). Profile hidden markov models. *Bioinformatics (Oxford, England)*, *14*(9), 755–763. doi:10.1093/bioinformatics/14.9.755 PMID:9918945

Edgar, R. (2014). *Muscle*. Retrieved June 16, 2014 from http://www.drive5.com/muscle/

Edgar, R. C. (2004). MUSCLE: Multiple sequence alignment with high accuracy and high throughput. *Nucleic Acids Research*, *32*(5), 1792–1797. doi:10.1093/nar/gkh340 PMID:15034147

Ellingson, S. (2012). *Accelerating virtual high-throughput ligand docking*. Retrieved June 16, 2014 from http://salsahpc.indiana.edu/EC-MLS2012/slides/ECMLS12_Accelerating_Virtual.pdf

Ellingson, S. (2013). Multi-receptor high-throughput virtual docking on supercomputers with VinaMPI. Paper presented at SC13 2013, Denver, Colorado.

Esteve-Nunez, A., Caballero, A., & Ramos, J. L. (2001). Biological degradation of 2, 4, 6-trinitrotoluene. *Microbiology and Molecular Biology Reviews*, *65*(3), 335–352. doi:10.1128/MMBR.65.3.335-352.2001 PMID:11527999

Fawcett, P., Eichenberger, P., & Losick, R. (2000). The transcriptional profile of early to middle sporulation in Bacillus subtilis. *Proceedings of the National Academy of Sciences of the United States of America*, *97*, 8063–8068. doi:10.1073/pnas.140209597

Fernandez, M., Caballero, J., Fernandez, L., & Sarai, A. (2010). *Genetic algorithm optimization in drug design QSAR: Bayesian-regularized genetic neural networks (BRGNN) and genetic algorithm-optimized support vectors machines (GA-SVM)*. Retrieved June 16, 2014 from http://www.researchgate.net/publication/42373086_Genetic_algorithm_optimization_in_drug_design_QSAR_Bayesian-regularized_genetic_neural_networks_(BRGNN)_and_genetic_algorithm-optimized_support_vectors_machines_(GA-SVM)

Friesner, R. A., Banks, J. L., Murphy, R. B., Halgren, T. A., Klicic, J. J., & Mainz, D. T. et al. (2004). Glide: A new approach for rapid, accurate docking and scoring. 1. Method and assessment of docking accuracy. *Journal of Medicinal Chemistry*, *47*(7), 1739–1749. doi:10.1021/jm0306430 PMID:15027865

Gan, Z., Stowe, J., Altintas, I., McCulloch, A., & Zambon, A. (2014). Using kepler for tool integration in microarray analysis workflows. In *Proceedings of 14th International Conference on Computational Science* (pp. 2162-2167). Academic Press. doi:10.1016/j.procs.2014.05.201

Gasch, A. P., Spellman, P. T., Kao, C. M., Carmel-Harel, O., Eisen, M. B., & Storz, G. et al. (2000). Genomic expression programs in the response of yeast cells to environmental changes. *Molecular Biology of the Cell*, *1*(12), 4241–4257. doi:10.1091/mbc.11.12.4241 PMID:11102521

Goldman, B. B., & Wipke, W. T. (2000). QSD quadratic shape descriptors. 2. Molecular docking using quadratic shape descriptors (QSDock). *Proteins*, *38*(1), 79–94. doi:10.1002/(SICI)1097-0134(20000101)38:1<79::AID-PROT9>3.0.CO;2-U PMID:10651041

Golender, V. E., & Vorpagel, E. R. (1993). In H. Kubinyi (Ed.), *In 3D-QSAR in drug design: Theory, methods, and application* (p. 137). ESCOM Science Publishers.

Gray, J. W., & Collins, C. (2000). Genome changes and gene expression in human solid tumors. *Carcinogenesis*, *21*(3), 443–452. doi:10.1093/carcin/21.3.443 PMID:10688864

Hakenbeck, R., Balmelle, N., Weber, B., Gardes, C., Keck, W., & de Saizieu, A. (2001). Mosaic genes and mosaic chromosomes: Intra- and interspecies genomic variation of *Streptococcus pneumoniae*. *Infection and Immunity*, *69*(4), 2477–2486. doi:10.1128/IAI.69.4.2477-2486.2001 PMID:11254610

Hansch, C., Kurup, A., Garg, R., & Gao, H. (2001). Chem-bioinformatics and QSAR: A review of QSAR lacking positive hydrophobic terms. *Chemical Reviews*, *101*(3), 619–672. doi:10.1021/cr0000067 PMID:11712499

Hansch, C., & Leo, A. (1979). *Substituent constants for correlation analysis in chemistry and biology*. New York: John Wiley & Sons.

Hansch, C., & Leo, A. (1995). *Fundamentals and applications in chemistry and biochemisry* (Q. S. A. R. Exploring, Ed.). Washington, DC: American Chemical Society.

Hansch, C., & Selassie, C. (2007). *Quantitative structure-activity relationship-a historical perspective and the future*. Oxford, UK: Elsevier.

Hartmann, C., Antes, I., & Lengauer, T. (2009). Docking and scoring with alternative side-chain conformations. *Proteins*, *74*(3), 712–726. doi:10.1002/prot.22189 PMID:18704939

Hill, M. D., Jouppi, N. P., Sohi, & Gurindar. (1999). *Readings in computer architecture*. Academic Press.

Hoffman, A. R., et al. (1990). *Supercomputers: Directions in technology and applications*. National Academies. Retrieved June 17, 2014 from http://www.intechopen.com/books/protein-engineering-technology-and-application/protein-protein-and-protein-ligand-docking

Irwin, J. J., & Shoichet, B. K. (2005). ZINC — A free database of commercially available compounds for virtual screening. *Journal of Chemical Information and Modeling*, *45*(1), 177–182. doi:10.1021/ci049714+ PMID:15667143

Jayaram, B. (2011). *DNA ligand docking*. Retrieved June 16, 2014 from http://www.scfbio-iitd.res.in/dock/dnadock.jsp

Jayaram, B. (2012). *BAPPL server*. Retrieved June 16, 2014 from http://www.scfbio-iitd.res.in/software/drugdesign/bappl.jsp

Jayaram, B. (2013). *ParDOCK - Automated server for protein ligand docking*. Retrieved June 16, 2014 from http://www.scfbio-iitd.res.in/dock/pardock.jsp

Joachimiak, A. (2009). High-throughput crystallography for structural genomics. *Current Opinion in Structural Biology*, *19*(5), 573–584. doi:10.1016/j.sbi.2009.08.002 PMID:19765976

Jorgensen, W. L. (1991). Rusting of the lock and key model for protein-ligand binding. *Science*, *254*(5034), 954–955. doi:10.1126/science.1719636 PMID:1719636

Kearsley, S. K., Underwood, D. J., Sheridan, R. P., & Miller, M. D. (1994). Flexibases: A way to enhance the use of molecular docking methods. *Journal of Computer-Aided Molecular Design*, *8*(5), 565–582. doi:10.1007/BF00123666 PMID:7876901

Kitchen, D. B., Decornez, H., Furr, J. R., & Bajorath, J. (2004). Docking and scoring in virtual screening for drug discovery: Methods and applications. *Nature Reviews. Drug Discovery*, *3*(11), 935–949. doi:10.1038/nrd1549 PMID:15520816

Klebe, G., & Mietzner, T. (1994). A fast and efficient method to generate biologically relevant conformations. *Journal of Computer-Aided Molecular Design*, *8*(5), 583–606. doi:10.1007/BF00123667 PMID:7876902

Krivobok, S., Kuony, S., Meyer, C., Louwagie, M., & Wilson, J. C. (2003). Identification of pyrene-induced proteins in *Mycobacterium* spp. strain 6PY1: Evidence for two ring-hydroxylating dioxygenas-es. *Journal of Bacteriology*, *185*(13), 3828–3841. doi:10.1128/JB.185.13.3828-3841.2003 PMID:12813077

Kuntz, I. D., Blaney, J. M., Oatley, S. J., Langridge, R., & Ferrin, T. E. (1982). A geometric approach to macromolecule–ligand interactions. *Journal of Molecular Biology*, *161*(2), 269–1288. doi:10.1016/0022-2836(82)90153-X PMID:7154081

Labana, S., Pandey, G., Paul, D., Sharma, N. K., Basu, A., & Jain, R. K. (2005). Plot and field studies on bioremediation of *p*-nitrophenol contaminated soil using *Arthrobacter protophormiae* RKJ100. *Environmental Science & Technology*, *39*(9), 3330–3337. doi:10.1021/es0489801 PMID:15926586

Labana, S., Singh, O. V., Basu, A., Pandey, G., & Jain, R. K. (2005). A microcosm study on bioremediation of p-nitrophenol-contaminated soil using *Arthrobacter protophormiae* RKJ100. *Applied Microbiology and Biotechnology*, *68*(3), 417–424. doi:10.1007/s00253-005-1926-1 PMID:15806356

Lengauer, T., & Rarey, M. (1996). Computational methods for bimolecular docking. *Current Opinion in Structural Biology*, *6*(3), 402–406. doi:10.1016/S0959-440X(96)80061-3 PMID:8804827

Lipman, D. J., & Pearson, W. R. (1985). Rapid and sensitive protein similarity searches. *Science*, *227*(4693), 1435–1441. doi:10.1126/science.2983426 PMID:2983426

List of Sequence Alignment Software. (2014). Retrieved June 17, 2014 from http://en.wikipedia.org/wiki/List_of_sequence_alignment_software

Livingstone, D. J. (2000). The characterization of chemical structures using molecular properties. A survey. *Journal of Chemical Information and Computer Sciences*, *40*(2), 195–209. doi:10.1021/ci990162i PMID:10761119

Lovley, D. R. (2003). Cleaning up with genomic: Applying molecular biology to bioremediation. *Nature Reviews. Microbiology*, *1*(1), 35–44. doi:10.1038/nrmicro731 PMID:15040178

Marmur, J., & Doty, P. (1961). Thermal renaturation of deoxyribonucleic acids. *Journal of Molecular Biology*, *3*(5), 585–594. doi:10.1016/S0022-2836(61)80023-5 PMID:14470100

Matsuzaki, Y., Uchikoga, N., Ohue, M., Shimoda, T., Sato, T., Ishida, T., & Akiyama, Y. (2013). MEGADOCK 3.0: A high-performance protein-protein interaction prediction software using hybrid parallel computing for petascale supercomputing environments. [MEGADOCK 3.0: a high-performance protein-protein interaction prediction software using hybrid parallel computing for petascale supercomputing environments.] *Pubmed, 8*(18). doi:10.1186/1751-0473-8-18

Mendoza-Barrera, C., Hernandez-Santoyo, A., Tenorio-Barajas, A. Y., & Altuzar, V. (2013). *Protein-protein and protein-ligand docking*. Retrieved June 17, 2014 from http://www.intechopen.com/books/protein-engineering-technology-and-application/protein-protein-and-protein-ligand-docking

Meng, E. C., Shoichet, B. K., & Kuntz, I. D. (2004). Automated docking with grid-based energy evaluation. *Journal of Computational Chemistry*, *13*(4), 505–524. doi:10.1002/jcc.540130412

Morris, G. M., Goodsell, D. S., Halliday, R. S., Huey, R., Hart, W. E., Belew, R. K., & Olson, A. J. (1998). Automated docking using a Lamarckian genetic algorithm and an empirical binding free energy function. *Journal of Computational Chemistry*, *19*(14), 1639–1662. doi:10.1002/(SICI)1096-987X(19981115)19:14<1639::AID-JCC10>3.0.CO;2-B

O'Neal, T. (2014). *Novel analyses improve identification of cancer-associated genes*. Retrieved June 16, 2014 from http://www.supercomputingonline.com/latest/topics/this-month/57971-novel-analyses-improve-identification-of-cancer-associated-genes

Pandey, G., Paul, D., & Jain, K. (2003). Branching of *o*-nitrobenzoate degradation pathway in *Arthrobacter protophormiae* RKJ100: Identification of new intermediates. *FEMS Microbiology Letters*, *229*(2), 231–236. doi:10.1016/S0378-1097(03)00844-9 PMID:14680704

Pandey, U. B., & Nichols, C. D. (2011). Human disease models in Drosophila melanogaster and the role of the fly in therapeutic drug discovery. *Pharmacological Reviews, 63*(2), 2411–2436. doi:10.1124/pr.110.003293 PMID:21415126

Pearson, W. R., & Lipman, D. J. (1988). Improved tools for biological sequence comparison. *Proceedings of the National Academy of Sciences of the United States of America, 85*(8), 2444–2448. doi:10.1073/pnas.85.8.2444 PMID:3162770

Ponder, B. A. (2001). Cancer genetics. *Nature, 411*(6835), 336–341. doi:10.1038/35077207 PMID:11357140

Prodan, R. (2007). Grid computing: Experiment management, tool integration, and scientific workflows. Fahringer & Thomas.

Richmond, C. S., Glasner, J. D., Mau, R., Jin, H., & Blattner, F. R. (1999). Genome-wide expression profiling in *Escherichia coli* K-12. *Nucleic Acids Research, 27*(19), 3821–3835. doi:10.1093/nar/27.19.3821 PMID:10481021

Ripphausen, P., Nisius, B., Peltason, L., Bajorath, J., Quo, & Vadis. (2010). Virtual screening? A comprehensive survey of prospective applications. *Journal of Medicinal Chemistry, 53*, 8461-8467.

Rise, M. L., Jones, S. R., Brown, G. D., Von Schalburg, K. R., Davidson, W. S., & Koop, B. F. (2004). Microarray analyses identify molecular biomarkers of Atlantic salmon macrophage and hematopoietic kidney response to *Piscirickettsia salmonis* infection. *Physiological Genomics, 20*(1), 21–35. doi:10.1152/physiolgenomics.00036.2004 PMID:15454580

Rowley, J. D. (1973). A new consistent chromosomal abnormality in chronic myelogenous leukemia identified by quina-crine fluorescence and Giemsa staining. *Nature, 243*(5405), 290–293. doi:10.1038/243290a0 PMID:4126434

Schena, M., Shalon, D., Heller, R., Chai, A., Brown, P. O., & Davis, R. W. (1996). Parallel human genome analysis: Microarray-based expression of 1000 genes. *Proceedings of the National Academy of Sciences of the United States of America, 93*(20), 10539–11286. doi:10.1073/pnas.93.20.10614 PMID:8855227

Schut, G. J., Zhou, J., & Adams, M. W. (2001). DNA microarray analysis of the hyperthermophilic archaeon *Pyrococcus furi-osus*: Evidence for a new type of sulfur-reducing enzyme complex. *Journal of Bacteriology, 183*(24), 7027–7036. doi:10.1128/JB.183.24.7027-7036.2001 PMID:11717259

Shalon, D., Smith, S. J., & Brown, P. O. (1996). A DNA microarray system for analyzing complex DNA samples using two-color fluorescent probe hybridization. *Genome Research, 6*(7), 639–645. doi:10.1101/gr.6.7.639 PMID:8796352

Singh, A. et al. (2013). A review on DNA microarray technology. *International Journal of Current Research and Review, 05*(22), 5.

Structure Based drug Design and Molecular Modeling. (n.d.). Retrieved June 16, 2014 from http://www.imb-jena.de/~rake/Bioinformatics_WEB/dd_tools.html

Sundberg, S. A., Chow, A., Nikiforov, T., & Wada, G. (2001). Microchip-based systems for biomedical and pharmaceutical analysis. *European Journal of Pharmaceutical Sciences, 14*(1), 1–12. doi:10.1016/S0928-0987(01)00153-1 PMID:11457644

Superimpose. (2010). Retrieved June 16, 2014 from http://www.scfbio-iitd.res.in/software/utility/Superimpose.jsp

Tao, H., Bausch, C., Richmond, C., Blattner, F. R., & Conway, T. (1999). Functional genomics: Expression analysis of *Escherichia coli* growing on minimal and rich media. *Journal of Bacteriology, 181*, 6425–6440. PMID:10515934

Taylor, P., Blackburn, E., Sheng, Y. G., Harding, S., Hsin, K. Y., & Kan, D. et al. (2008). Ligand discovery and virtual screening using the program LIDAEUS. *British Journal of Pharmacology, 153*, 555–567. PMID:18037921

Taylor, R. D., Jewsbury, P. J., & Essex, J. W. (2003). FDS: Flexible ligand and receptor docking with a continuum solvent model and soft-core energy function. *Journal of Computational Chemistry, 24*(13), 1637–1656. doi:10.1002/jcc.10295 PMID:12926007

Totrov, M., & Abagyan, R. (2008). Flexible ligand docking to multiple receptor conformations: A practical alternative. *Current Opinion in Structural Biology, 18*(2), 178–184. doi:10.1016/j.sbi.2008.01.004 PMID:18302984

Valafar, F. (2002). Pattern recognition techniques in microarray data analysis: A survey. *Annals of the New York Academy of Sciences, 980*(1), 41–64. doi:10.1111/j.1749-6632.2002.tb04888.x PMID:12594081

Venter, J. C., Adams, M. D., Myers, E. W., Li, P. W., Mural, R. J., & Sutton, G. G. et al. (2001). The sequence of the human genome. *Science, 291*(5507), 1304–1351. doi:10.1126/science.1058040 PMID:11181995

Wall, M., Rechtsteiner, A., & Rocha, L. (n.d.). *Singular value decomposition and principal component analysis.* Retrieved June 16, 2014 from http://public.lanl.gov/mewall/kluwer2002.html

Wang, Q., & Pang, Y. P. (2007). Preference of small molecules for local minimum conformations when binding to proteins. *PLoS ONE, 2*(9), e820. doi:10.1371/journal.pone.0000820

Wei, B. Q., Weaver, L. H., Ferrari, A. M., Matthews, B. W., & Shoichet, B. K. (2004). Testing a flexible-receptor docking algorithm in a model binding site. *Journal of Molecular Biology, 337*(5), 1161–1182. doi:10.1016/j.jmb.2004.02.015 PMID:15046985

Wei, H., Wang, C. H., Du, Q. S., Meng, J., & Chou, K.-C. (2009). Investigation into adamantane-based M2 inhibitors with FB-QSAR. *Journal of Medicinal Chemistry, 5*(4), 305–317. doi:10.2174/157340609788681430 PMID:19689387

Willighagen, E. (2011). *An ontology for QSAR and cheminformatics.* Retrieved June 16, 2014 from http://chem-bla-ics.blogspot.in/2011/10/ontology-for-qsar-and-cheminformatics.html

Wilson, M., DeRisi, J., Kristensen, H. H., Imboden, P., Rane, S., Brown, P. O., & Schoolnik, G. K. (1999). Exploring drug-induced alterations in gene expression in *Mycobacterium tuberculosis* by microarray hybridization. *Proceedings of the National Academy of Sciences of the United States of America, 96*(22), 12833–12838. doi:10.1073/pnas.96.22.12833 PMID:10536008

Yang, Y. (2006). *Bioinformatics resources for microarray data analysis, protein function/structure prediction, and protein-protein interaction.* Retrieved June 16, 2014 from http://dragon.bio.purdue.edu/bioinfolinks/

Ye, R. W., Tao, W., Bedzyk, L., Young, T., Chen, M., & Li, L. (2000). Global gene expression profiles of *Bacillus subtilis* grown under anaerobic conditions. *Journal of Bacteriology, 182*(16), 4458–4465. doi:10.1128/JB.182.16.4458-4465.2000 PMID:10913079

Yoshida, K., Kobayashi, K., Miwa, Y., Kang, C. M., Matsunaga, M., & Yamaguchi, H. et al. (2001). Combined transcriptome and proteome analysis as a powerful approach to study genes under glucose repression in *Bacillus subtilis. Nucleic Acids Research, 29*(3), 683–692. doi:10.1093/nar/29.3.683 PMID:11160890

Young, R. A. (2000). Biomedical discovery with DNA arrays. *Cell, 102*(1), 9–15. doi:10.1016/S0092-8674(00)00005-2 PMID:10929708

Zhang, C., Li, P., Rajendran, A., Deng, Y., & Chen, D. (2006). *Parallelization of multicategory support vector machines (PMC-SVM) for classifying microarray data*. Retrieved June 16, 2014 from http://link.springer.com/article/10.1186%2F1471-2105-7-S4-S15

Zsoldos, R. Z., Simon, D., Sadjad, A. S. B., & Johnson, A. P. (2007). eHiTS: A new fast, exhaustive flexible ligand docking system. *Journal of Molecular Graphics & Modelling, 26*(1), 198–212.

KEY TERMS AND DEFINITIONS

Data Analysis: Analysis and isolation of information from the provided database using supercomputers. These data may be protein, DNA, Genome, Proteome etc.

Docking: Close interaction studies between protein and ligand or between protein and protein. It involves formation of bonds between amino acids and between amino acids and drug molecule.

Genomics: Study of genes and genome by utilizing computational as well as experimental knowledge.

Homology Modeling: 3D structure prediction of protein on the basis of similarity and identity between two or more sequences from the databases.

Ligand: Small Drug or interacting molecule which are able to dock with receptor (Protein). These ligand are able to perform specific functions after interaction with receptors.

Protein-Protein Docking: Interaction studies between two proteins like one receptor and another protein or between peptides.

Quantitative Structure Activity Relationship (QSAR): Used to define the function of the molecules or atoms on the basis of their structure.

Sequence Analysis: Analysis of protein or DNA nucleotide sequence and identification of sequence conservation, hot spots, active site, identity, homology and phylogeny among the sequences.

Supercomputers: Introduced in 1960s and it is a computer with high processing capacity particularly speed of calculation.

Virtual Screening: Screening or filtering of molecules on the basis of similarity of their structure. It is a database search method.

Chapter 10
Energy Network Operation in the Supercomputing Era

Tianxing Cai
Lamar University, USA

Neha Gupta
Northeastern University, USA & Osmania University, India

ABSTRACT

Power delivery has become more dissimilar with that of the previous era. Conventional power and energy materials, such as relic fuels, nuclear power, and renewable energy (solar power, geothermal, hydroelectric, wind power, and biomass), are already present. The energy network operation becomes complicated because the integration of power generation, energy conversion, power transportation, and power utilization should be considered. There is an intricate assignment for us to perform swift power transmission for the extremely urgent situations. These situations are the results of regional lack of energy that needs to be brought back as soon as possible. Advanced supercomputing has already been one of the powerful solutions to work out these issues. This chapter initially presents an introduction of some of the supercomputing techniques and then the potential applications and demonstration examples follow to give the readers some hint on the handling of energy network operation.

INTRODUCTION

The trouble of energy network operation has become a very hot topic in the twenty first century. Challenged by the oil and the other energy source depletion, the comprehensive consideration of power system operation should be included. The regional energy network has the facilities of power generation, energy conversion, power transportation and power utilization. The development of technology in the field of energy does give us more possibility and flexibility in our solution space. In the meantime, there comes the higher requirements for the engineers and scientists to take an inclusive thought of all the energy operations: it is really a multifaceted target.

For example, if there is some energy shortage in some region due to the mismatch between the energy supply and energy demand, swift power dispatching is a must to tackle with such kind of urgent events: the regional power deficiency needs to be recovered as soon as possible. In order to

DOI: 10.4018/978-1-4666-7461-5.ch010

Copyright © 2015, IGI Global. Copying or distributing in print or electronic forms without written permission of IGI Global is prohibited.

find the optimal scheduling and planning strategy, supercomputing can aid in the large scale modeling, simulation and optimization. The result will help us find out the best restoration solution of energy systems. Due to the inherent characterization of complication, the computations are always facing the problems of highly nonlinear multi-objective MINLP (Mixed Integer Nonlinear Programming). These are not easy to be solved with the current common solvers without the competence of MINLP.

Therefore, it will be good to use the computational algorithm multi-objective genetic algorithm (MGA). Pareto frontier of the targeted objectives in the final step can be obtained straightforwardly. It can be regarded as the combination of potential patterns and optimization scenarios with multi-objective genetic algorithm. Because the computation will go through the entire space of decision variables, there will be a tradeoff between the computational effort and the accurate characterization of the population. The binary or integer logic variables and the continuous process variables will be alternated to make the assessment on the targeted objective functions of energy system performance. The whole spatial and temporal space needs to be separated into a lot of small intervals. The energy condition of each interval will be calculated. There will be lots of repetitive simulations with a heavy computational duty. Furthermore, the situation of imprecision and uncertainty will be faced definitely.

However, the models are still expected to have the characterization of tractability, robustness and low computational effort. Thanks to the developments of high performance and cloud computing, there are a lot of applications which have been achieved especially in the field of renewable energy integration and energy efficiency improvement. As what has been introduced before, the high performance and cloud computing techniques are having the greatest competence of large scale computations. This chapter can help the readers to enhance the understanding of the significance of supercomputing in the energy network operation. For this purpose, in the beginning some of supercomputing techniques will be introduced briefly. Next, some potential applications and demonstration examples which can be used as references to give the readers in the future practice will be shared accordingly.

TECHNIQUE INTRODUCTION

Normally, the basic computer can take the responsibility of the basic computational tasks. On the contrary, the computation in the scientific research and engineering always require marvelous capacity of computational processing as well as the calculation speed. The supercomputer or high performance computer is a computer with the above characterizations. Another necessary element of the supercomputers is that they should have the sufficient memory because the computational processing will generate a lot of data which needs to be stored in the computers. Most research institutes have their own computational facilities. For example, there is one Blue Gene/P supercomputer in the Argonne National Laboratory. It can have more than 250,000 processors during the computational run. These processors can be grouped into 72 racks or cabinets. They are integrated with a high-speed optical network (IBM, 2007). Many artificial neurons can be simulated with the help of the IBM Blue Gene/P computer. The function is similar with 1% of a human cerebral cortex (IBM, 2007) or the entirety of a rat's brain (Kaku, 2011). The supercomputers are also used in the field of weather forecasting. They are used by NOAA to combine the huge datasets of information of weather monitoring observations in order to get more precise predictions and dynamic change trends (National Geographic, 2010).

Furthermore, the application of high performance computers has been expanded to the fields of aerodynamic research (Cray Research, 2011), probabilistic analysis (Joshi, 1998), radiation shielding modeling (OEDC Nuclear Energy Agency, 2011), Brute force code breaking (EFF DES Cracker Source Code, 2011), 3D nuclear test simulations as a substitute for legal conduct nuclear proliferation treaty (DOE Supercomputing & Test Simulation Program, 2011) and molecular dynamics simulation (NVIDIA, 2011). The current techniques make most people have an expectation and estimation that high performance computers will reach one quintillion FLOPS by 2018. It was reported that 1 exaflop supercomputer will also appear in China by 2018 (Kan, 2012). SGI has started to adopt Intel MIC multi-core processor architecture. They hope to reach the performance by a 500 fold increase in 2018 (Agam, 2011). It will not only have vector processing units but also standard CPU. It can be pictured that the high performance computing facilities will expand beyond the current application domain. In the future a real-time based communication network can integrate all the computers (Mariana et al., 2012). The structure will be a network with distributed computing facilities. The computation can be proceeded through a lot of computers which are connected with each other at the same time.

The supercomputing facilities help us realize the large scale calculations for the real energy system. The techniques which can help us share the information through the network are still needed. Fortunately, the cloud computing has played this role (NIST, 2011). The cloud computing is based on the converged infrastructure to provide the information sharing services. At the same time, the efficiency of information sharing has also been improved. Multiple users can access the system at the same time and the information access volume can be dynamically adjusted by the information demand of access. The people in different time zones can take full advantage of such kind of shared computational resources. Therefore the operation cost of computation has been decreased by the cloud computing techniques. This will further be helpful to the improvement and management of power and maintenance reduction. It

will also enable information technology to assign the materials or facilities much faster to satisfy changeable and irregular conditions (Baburajan, 2011; Oestreich, 2010).

National Institute of Standards and Technology (NIST, 2011) has provided the definitions of five characteristics which are essential for cloud computing:

1. The first characteristic is on-demand self-service. It has described the situation that the computing capabilities of server time and network storage can be granted to a consumer unilaterally. Thus, the human beings can have the close and automatic cooperation with the service provider without the time consumption in the interaction.

2. The second characteristic is the broad network access. The proper capabilities through the application of the network will be there. Furthermore, the typical mechanisms help us to become accessible and enhance the application of diverse client platforms of different layer structures. The typical examples are cell phones, tablets, laptops, and workstations.

3. The third characteristic is the optimization of resource pooling. The computational facilities can be integrated in order to provide the service to multiple consumers by the developed model. The pooling can really help us to have the capability and capacity of dynamic dispatch of multiple physical and virtual materials and vibrant dispatch strategy for the consumer demand.

4. The fourth characteristic is the speedy flexibility. The whole system has been capable of speedy flexibility automatically for different scenarios and situations. This can satisfy the predictable and unpredictable demand internally and externally. Therefore the consumers' requirement can be appropriated in any quantity at any time.

5. The fifth characteristic is the quantitative service. The cloud systems can automatically measure the input and output parameters of the operation system so that we can control and optimize the resource and service assignment for the storage, processing and account operation. They can be monitored, controlled, optimized and reported so that the whole system is transparent to not only the suppliers but also the consumers of the operation service.

According to National Science Foundation, there are also other several research agencies, academic schools, institutions and professional organizations which have started to apply the advanced computing techniques in their scientific research and education (NSF, 2013):

- Europe has conducted a very important project which is called Enabling Grids for E-sciencE (EGEE). They are using a computing based infrastructure for more than ten thousand researchers in the world. It has been applied in the fields of high energy physics, earth science and life sciences. This research project has integrated the scientists and engineers from more than fifty nations. They are trying to build the currently advanced grid technology and the service development of a power grid infrastructure (NSF, 2013).

- National Science Foundation (NSF) has also given the grant support to Florida International University (FIU). The researchers over there are applying the advanced computing techniques with the collaboration support from Google/IBM Cloud. They are trying to make some analysis on the aerial images and objects to help support the reduction of disaster impact and environmental protection.

- Another group of researchers at Indiana University have got the sponsorship from both the National Science Foundation (NSF) and the National Institute of Health (NIH). They utilize the computing facilities to conduct large scale distributed scientific experiments for the shared substrate. They also try to explore the application of techniques to prevail over the current computational barrier in the medical science. The typical difficulties are including extensive computation time and huge memory requirements.

- The scientists in Massachusetts Institute of Technology (MIT) are also collaborating with Yale University and the University of Wisconsin at Madison. They also got the grant support from National Science Foundation (NSF) Cluster Exploratory (CLuE) grant. This sponsorship is helping them to construct cluster-based data analysis and integration in a large-scale. The cloud computing for Education is another research interest in the collaborated research.

- Purdue University has a research team. They are investigating the potential possibility of linguistic extensions to Map Reduce abstractions by the methodology of computer programming in the advanced systems in the large scale. Their special focus is on the applications of the techniques in the manipulation of large and unstructured graphs. A cloud computing test bed called Wispy is also provided to TeraGrid users by them.

- The researchers at San Diego Supercomputing Center (SDSC) have also been granted by the National Science Foundation to search for innovative methods to have an effective and efficient management on tremendously large data sets on massive clusters. It will use the case study of the Light Detection and Ranging (LiDAR) topography data hosted by Open Topography. Their attention is on how to achieve the management and operation of extensive spatial and temporal data sets by the assistance of cloud computing.

- The University of Santa Barbara is also doing the research in order to stand in the frontier of advancements in the research field of cloud computing. Their project of Massive Graphs in Clusters (MAGIC) aims to develop software package for the efficient response of queries on extremely large graph datasets. An open-source accomplishment of the Google AppEngine interface have also been designed by them.

- The University of Maryland's School of Medicine has achieved a virtual appliance. It can help to combine state-of-the-art genomic applications on the platforms of cloud computing in a package of Cloud Virtual Resource (CloVR). It can further help to the collaboration of genomics information into other research fields of environmental protection, bioengineering and medical research.

- The National Science Foundation (NSF) is also providing the fund to the research group at the University of Minnesota for the project of the construction of cloud proxy network. It will realize the optimal and reliable operations at strategic network positions of the network.

- The team at the University of Utah and the University of Washington are working together to build a new infrastructure construction for oceanography computation. It uses the Google/IBM cloud to achieve longitudinal query and visualization of extensive ocean simulation results interactively.

- Wayne State University is trying to get the development in a centralized learning approach to make the configuration processes automatic for virtualized machines and their applications running. It can adapt the systems configuration to the cloud dynamics.

APPLICATIONS OF SUPERCOMPUTING IN THE FIELD

Besides the above introduced fields of scientific research and education in the last section, there is a large potential possibility of the application of computing techniques in the energy network operation. This will help to handle large scale data and information systems. The energy network operation needs to identify the environment impact of current power plants so that the decision makers can determine whether it is a must to substitute the currently used fuel combustion with renewable energy facility. The research will also explore the integrated consideration of the emergency situation of regional energy shortage. Thus, the operation will rely on a lot of simulations with heavy computation duty. The detailed description of its further applications will be presented as below.

Environment Protection of Power Plants (Cai, Wang & Xu, 2013)

The traditional power plants are those power plants which use large amounts of fuels such as fuel oils and coal to generate electricity power. They have high risks to cause potential air quality events. There are two kinds of emissions. The first type is normal plant emissions or routine emissions: they are from the plant normal operations which have been regulated and included in emissions planning. Another type is abnormal plant emissions. They are always in the huge amount of emissions at the time interval of start-up, shutdown, or malfunction. Environmental Protection Agency's (EPA) 40 Code of Federal Regulation has provided the definition of malfunctions as any "sudden, infrequent and not reasonably preventable failure of air pollution control equipment, process equipment, or a process to operate in a normal or usual manner" (U.S. EPA, 1982). The uncontrollable and unpredictable uncertain operation can also cause such kind of emission.

Otherwise, emergency shutdown, nature disaster, or terrorist attack can also become the factors to cause the abnormal emissions. The environment impacts from power plant emission can be harmful to both local communities and their surrounding areas. The people will be exposed to the air pollutants and gradually they will become ill due to acute or short-term toxicity, and the acute release of contaminants. It is likely to be transported to a populated area so that it will become a direct or indirect threat to the public health and regional environment quality in a short time period. The responsible decisions for the emissions events are very critical because they will rely on the independent supporting information of real-time measurements from a local air-quality monitoring network. Actually the local air-quality monitoring network can monitor and collect the information of air pollutant concentration in a real-time way. Meanwhile, the measurement data from each monitoring station and regional meteorological conditions during the event time period can be helpful to make the estimation of potential emission source locations and the emission rates (Cai, Wang & Xu, 2013).

The previous research focused on the forward modeling to determine downwind contamination concentrations with the input parameters of meteorological conditions and emission rates. "Gaussian Dispersion Model" is a commonly used analytical method in order to calculate air pollutant concentration in the downwind area. The detailed modeling procedures and formulations of Gaussian Dispersion Model can be referred to the contribution of Bowman (1996), Turner et al. (1989), Griffiths (1994), Halitsky (1989), Slade (1986), Seinfeld (1986), Hanna et al. (1982), Turner (1979), Turner (1994), Pasquill (1961), Pasquill (1974), Church (1949), Goldsmith and Friberg (1976). In spite of the situation that the inverse modeling methods based on Gaussian plume models have been reported (Hogan et al., 2005; Jeong et al., 2005; Mackay et al., 2006), they aim to identify the average emission rates in

a long time period based on measurements from monitoring stations. The emission rates are assumed to be under steady-state conditions and their values have been regarded as constants. Therefore, studies on the inverse modeling for abnormal emission identifications with the consideration of dynamic emission rates will be lacking. This identified information can further help to schedule multiple plants' activity to minimize regional air quality impacts (Cai, Wang & Xu, 2013). This is an inverse characterization which is very valuable to all stake holders, including government environmental agencies, power plants, and residential communities.

Energy Network Operation (Cai, Zhao & Xu, 2012)

In recent years, the extreme events of U.S. southern storm and tornado (2011), Japan earthquake and tsunami (2011), and India power shortage (2010) have given us an important remind because the attention is always payed to the situation of whether our current used response planning is sufficiently effective or efficient for a timely recovery in the suffered areas. These events of natural disasters will be possible to cause large damage of regional economy, people's health and safety, transportation system, as well as the energy and the living infrastructures. To proceed the emergency response planning of the functionality and capability of these damaged systems, the energy system is in one of the most important priorities because all the other response operations should have to be based on the sufficient power which is available and reliable. Therefore, the local energy shortage will determine whether there will be further salvage postponement, prevalent power outages, economic loss and even public security threats. The minimization of a energy network recovery should be regarded as the first step in the planning (Cai, Zhao & Xu, 2012).

The literature survey reflects that there was previously reported research work in the field of local energy shortage and management, which has covered technical innovation of renewable energy utility (Kainkwa,1999), and power system optimization with the purpose of environmental impact mitigation (Berredo et al., 2011) policy making for energy management (Bellarmine & Arokiaswamv, 1996), energy operation in the constructions and buildings (Meier, 2006), economic impact analysis for energy shortage (Sanghvi, 1991), the solution for energy shortage problems by economic leverage (Geffner et al., 2010). There is almost not sufficient research in the field of operation research support for energy network operation optimization under emergency situations. Plausibly, it will not be a task which can be solved easily. All the potential energy types, various energy shortage scenarios, and different energy operation strategies based on the infrastructure availability and feasibility of local energy network operation needs to be integrated (Cai, Zhao & Xu, 2012).

These days the energy operation is including multiple elements of fossil fuels, nuclear power, solar, hydroelectric, geothermal, biomass, wind energy and operation processes of energy generation, energy transformation, energy transportation, and energy consumption. It will be flexible for us to manipulate the different parameters of energy transformation and transportation and complicated for us to identify the optimal energy operation strategy. However, when the events which have caused energy shortage in the local region are faced, it needs to be restored as soon as possible, which means that a very long time for computation to final the optimal values of decision variables cannot be allowed. Any type of power shortage under certain emergency condition has its own characteristics of availability, quantity, transportation speed, conversion rate and efficiency. Within a very short time period, even though it is a must but it will be very difficult for the optimization programming to find the optimal strategy. Thus, when such kind of system tools are setup, a superior plan for different types of energy dispatch ahead

of time should be considered. For example, energy sources of petroleum or coal can be straightly transported to a suffered area; at the same time, they can also generate the electricity power in an original region and then send the electricity power to the shortage area through an available electricity transmission line. Sometimes, yet the shipping of the same form of power may have different another routes for choice, which needs to be optimally decided from the view point of the whole picture of energy network operation (Cai, Zhao & Xu, 2012).

CASE STUDY

In order to provide the detailed explanation of the potential applications, two cases will be provided as below. Furthermore, the attention should be paid that the treatment of the real world problem of energy network operation will definitely involve regional or national wide scale data integration or data mining system. This is more complicated than the mentioned cases. This will also give us the higher requirements in the infrastructure of high performance and cloud computing.

Environment Protection of Power Plants (Cai, Wang & Xu, 2013)

As what has been introduced in the last session, one application of advanced computing techniques is to search for the emission source from multiple candidates of regional power plants This is based on the abnormal monitoring results of air pollutant measurements from the air quality monitoring network. It will help to support the diagnostic and prognostic decisions in time and in an effective way. The product of the developed method should accordingly offer the information of pollutant release location, initial beginning time, time length of the event duration, total amount of chemical release and dynamic emission rate and emission pattern from the power plant sources. The proposed procedures will inversely calculate the normal emission rates for a given list of sources in the region based on the input results of the background concentration. Subsequently, a model of optimization will be proceeded to reversely calculate the possibility of potential emission source detection which can be handled as binary variables. The model is based on abnormal air-quality measurements (Cai, Wang & Xu, 2013).

Figure 1 has shown that the virtual case study has five emission sources (E1, E2, E3, E4, and E5 which has been indicated by red dots) and four monitoring stations (S1, S2, S3, and S4 which has been indicated by green dots) in a squared region with the dimension of 30 km by 30 km. We have cut the entire region into a lot of grid cells and the edge length of each cell is 1 km. The wind direction is from the left bottom to right top. The normal pollutant emission from these five sources is hourly monitored by the monitoring stations (Cai, Wang & Xu, 2013).

The plume and stack parameters are given in Table 1. Figure 2 has shown that the monitor result from S3 had the pollutant concentration of 98.1 ppb at one o'clock in the morning and 91.9 ppb at two o'clock in the morning. After the reduction to 24.6 ppb at three o'clock in the morning, it got the high point of 72.1 ppb at four o'clock in the morning. At five o'clock in the morning, the concentration was 9.2 ppb and this concentration is still higher than the normal background measurements. The potential emission source for abnormal emissions is from one of the five emission sources. Within the time period of this event, several assumptions for the wind speed of 1.6m/s at 10-meter height, and the ambient temperature of 20 °C have been made (Cai, Wang & Xu, 2013).

Before the starting of the modeling, the time span has been partitioned into two parts: steady-state time period which is from seven o'clock at night to eleven o'clock at night and dynamic time period which is from mid night to five o'clock in

Figure 1. Spatial scope (Cai, Wang & Xu, 2013)

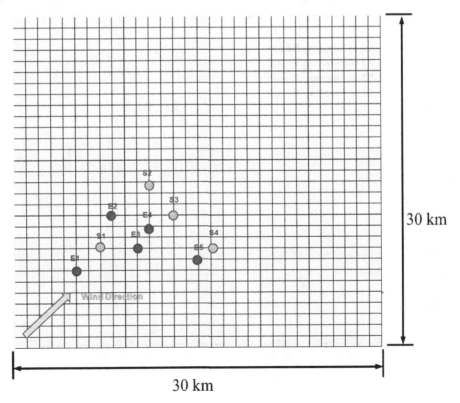

Table 1. Plume and Stack Parameters for Each Emission Source (Cai, Wang & Xu, 2013)

Emission Sources	E1	E2	E3	E4	E5
Stack Height H_i (m)	80	110	95	100	105
Stack Exit Temperature $T_{s,i}$ (K)	480	400	460	440	430
Stack Exit Velocity $V_{s,i}$ (m/s)	17.5	13.0	15.6	14.2	16.1
Stack Exit Diameter $D_{s,i}$ (m)	1.6	1.9	1.5	1.7	1.8

the morning. The data in the steady-state are used to quantitatively calculate the normal emission rates. The results of E1, E2, E3, E4 and E5 are 10.8, 10.5, 10.1, 9.2, and 9.8 kg/h, respectively. In our next step, the emission rate of the abnormal emission source in time series is inversely calculated. Our modeling result has pointed out that the source is plant E3 which has caused such an emission event. Figure 3 has been plotted for the visualization of its dynamic emission pattern. It can be seen from Figure 3 that the predicted emission pattern has the increase of emission rate to 88.4 kg/h from

the normal emission rate at mid night. Then it has been changed to 801.1 kg/h at one o'clock in the morning and 747.8 kg/h at two o'clock in the morning. The emission has a reduction to 220.1 kg/h at three o'clock in the morning. However, it has been increased to 581.2 kg/h at four o'clock in the morning. At five o'clock in the morning, it has been decreased to 90.1 kg/h and returned back to the normal emission level (Cai, Wang & Xu, 2013).

After the initial emission profile is obtained, the Gaussian dispersion model should be used to

Figure 2. Pollutant concentration measurements from local monitoring stations (Cai, Wang & Xu, 2013)

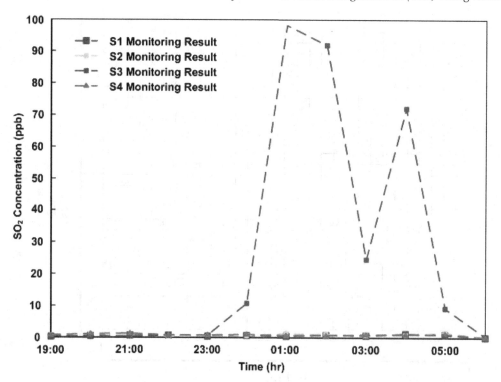

Figure 3. Dynamic emission profile of E3 (Cai, Wang & Xu, 2013)

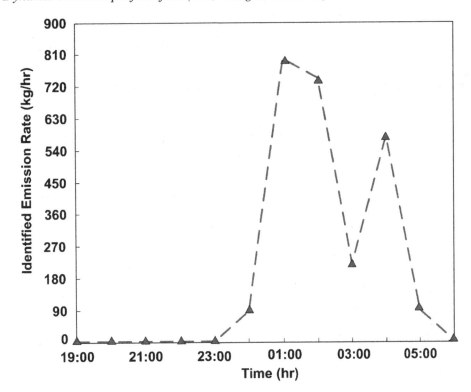

make validations for the modeling results. The forward modeling has also given us the air-quality impact on the studied region. The dynamic concentrations at the stations S1 and S2 are calculated. Then the comparison has been proceeded with the real monitoring results. For station S3, a small overestimation at three o'clock and five o'clock in the morning is obtained and a small underestimation at four o'clock in the morning with the maximum error of 2 ppb is obtained. For the stations of S1, S2, and S4, there is no abnormal concentration observed and the maximum errors are within 1 ppb. In summary, the whole time span of dynamic profile begins from eleven o'clock at night. The peak concentration is 98.1 ppb for two hours. Then it gradually becomes 91.9 ppb and 24.6 ppb afterwards. The second peak concentration is at four o'clock in the morning with the concentration of 72.1 ppb for one hour. Finally, it decreases to 9.2 ppb and comes back

to the background level. With the contribution of the developed methodology, the inverse modeling result is matched well with the monitoring results (Cai, Wang & Xu, 2013).

Energy Network Operation (Cai, Zhao & Xu, 2012)

An energy network has experienced an extreme weather event so that there is currently energy shortage in this region. There are total three locations (A, B, and C). Location A has got a partial damage and B and C have not been affected a lot by this issue. Therefore they can still offer the support of energy and source materials to A. The initial conditions of energy network operation are summarized in Table 2 (Cai, Zhao & Xu, 2012).

The assumption of the electricity transmission efficiency to be 0.95 is further made and the hourly energy consuming index of 0.05 which means 5%

Table 2. Input Parameters of the Case Study (Cai, Zhao & Xu, 2012)

Item	Category	Unit	i / j		
			A/B or C	B/A or C	C/A or B
Power Conversion Efficiency from Other Power Sources (*k*: electricity)	*l*: Fuel Oil	MWh/Barrel	0.55	0.51	0.62
	l: Natural Gas	MWh/Million ft³	0.12	0.125	0.11
	l: Coal	MWh/Short Ton	1.5	1.2	1.6
Hourly Power Generation Limit from Source Materials (*k*: electricity)	*l*: Fuel Oil	MWh/hr	75	65	90
	l: Natural Gas	MWh/hr	500	400	600
	l: Coal	MWh/hr	50	40	45
Hourly Limit of Transportation Input from City *j* to City *i*	*k*: Fuel Oil	Barrel/hr	0.03	0.03	0.03
	k: Natural Gas	Million ft³/hr	0.2	0.2	0.2
	k: Coal	Short Ton/hr	0.01	0.01	0.01
	k: Electricity	MWh/hr	0.05	0.05	0.05
Hourly Limit of Transportation Output from City *i* to City *j*	*k*: Fuel Oil	Barrel/hr	0.03	0.03	0.03
	k: Natural Gas	Million ft³/hr	0.2	0.2	0.2
	k: Coal	Short Ton/hr	0.01	0.01	0.01
	k: Electricity	MWh/hr	0.05	0.05	0.05
Required Energy Inventory Amount for City *i*	*k*: Fuel Oil	Barrel	400	426	493
	k: Natural Gas	Million ft³	500	700	600
	k: Coal	Short Ton	314	346	396
	k: Electricity	MWh	1600	1550	1600
Hourly Energy Supply for City *i*	*k*: Fuel Oil	Barrel/hr	27.45	29.25	27
	k: Natural Gas	Million ft³/hr	135	180	225
	k: Coal	Short Ton/hr	27	22.5	27
	k: Electricity	MWh/hr	0	0	0

of the inventory energy will be used in the energy network operation. Another important assumption is that no time retention exists for electricity transmission between different areas and the material transportation time is two hours. In the initial stage, location A is suffering 10% loss for all types of energy. At the same time, the other locations have no energy loss damage. Based on the developed energy dispatch model with GAMS (Cai, Zhao & Xu, 2012), the result of the minimum dispatch time for this energy restoration is twenty six hours. The change trend for the energy dispatch within the network are presented in Figures 5 through 8 (Cai, Zhao & Xu, 2012).

Figures 4 through 7 show the dynamic energy inventory and energy consumption of fuel oil, coal, natural gas and electricity respectively in the three locations of location A, location B and location C during the emergency time period. The figures have shown that the time period of six hours is sufficient for the location A to arrive at the required quantity for the energy sources of petroleum oil, coal, and natural gas. However, power recovery is much more slower. There are several reasons for this: the first reason is that during the first 6 hours, the power resource materials are not enough to offer the full support to power generation; the second reason is that all the three locations have

Figure 4. Change trends of fuel oil inventory and consumption (Cai, Zhao & Xu, 2012)

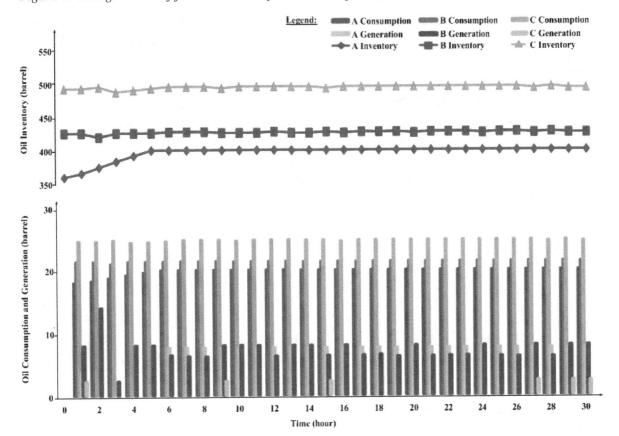

not got a very large electricity generation capacity so that the electricity restoration needs 26 hours in city A, which can be seen from Figure 4 (Cai, Zhao & Xu, 2012).

It can be seen that the energy change trend in location B and C only have got a small disturbance during the time period. The energy inventory of location A has changed a lot because it suffers from energy shortage as location A needs to choose the most effective method and the most feasible energy sources to generate electricity. There is not sufficient energy sources for electricity generation in the first two hours in location A. From the next hour, it starts to use large quantity of natural gas for electricity generation in the 3rd hour, which has been clearly described in Figure 6. The reason why the natural gas is picked up as the major source for the energy generation is because of its

comparatively great conversion efficiency. This has also caused the natural gas inventory to have a big decrease in that hour. After that, because the large consumption of natural gas inventory in the previous several hours, the petroleum oil and coal should be regarded as the alternatives for electricity generation, which can be seen clearly in Figures 4 and 5. After the time period of six hours, all the source materials have been recovered to full capacity (Cai, Zhao & Xu, 2012).

Figure 8 is a three dimensional plot of the accumulative transportation quantity of different sources between any two of the cities. Each axis of the coordinate space means the accumulative shipping quantity of fuel oil, coal, and natural gas respectively. It is natural that the accumulative quantity will not be decreased. It can be found from Figure 8 that the accumulative shipping quantity

Figure 5. Change trends of coal inventory and consumption (Cai, Zhao & Xu, 2012)

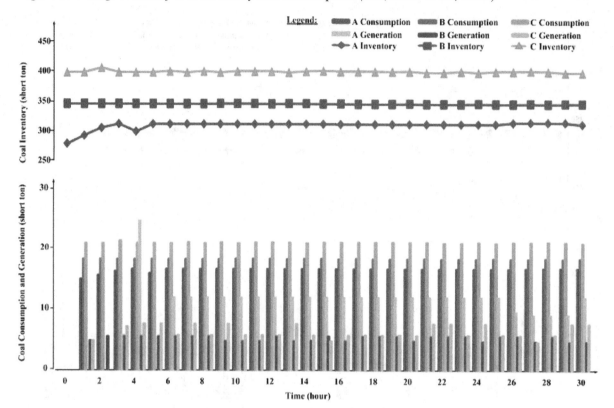

of various sources from location A to location B and from location A to location C are maintaining nothing until the time point of inventory quantity satisfaction in location A. On the other hand, the shipping quantity from location B and C to A are much greater and there is not a lot of mutual source material shipping between B and C. Actually we have another interesting finding that the hourly shipping quantity from both locations B and C to A are in the full loading before the last hour of the time period (Cai, Zhao & Xu, 2012).

Research being done on the supercomputer Kraken employs quantum mechanics to understand how nuclear effects change the dynamics of microscopic materials. Modeling and simulation studies can be performed in which a graphene, or carbon, flake was bombarded by a thousand hydrogen atoms to examine the accumulation of hydrogen on the porous graphene surface (New supercomputing method helps energy and materi-

als research, 2014). The accumulation of hydrogen or other light molecules on nanoporous materials has implications for energy science applications such as hydrogen storage and fuel cells (New supercomputing method helps energy and materials research, 2014).

The world energy demand is rebounding after recovery from the global economic recession of 2008-2009 and will continue to grow in future. The buildings are major energy consumers throughout the world. While the U.S contains 5% of the world's population, it consumes 19% of global energy production (Gibson, (n.d.)). Buildings in the U.S use 41% of the country's primary energy similar to the other countries in the world. On the positive note, buildings don't just use a lot of energy but they also perform in serving as deployment platforms for renewable-energy applications including daylighting, solar water heating, photovoltaic electricity generation and

Figure 6. Change trends of natural gas inventory and consumption (Cai, Zhao & Xu, 2012)

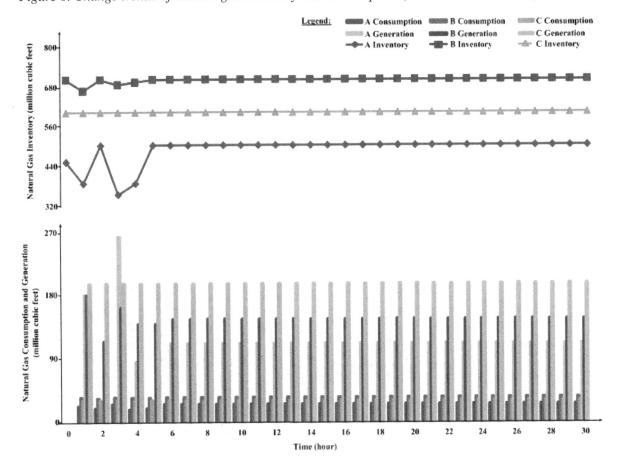

geothermal space conditioning and water heating (Gibson, (n.d.)).

One way to improve the energy efficiency of buildings is modeling and simulation. Energy models are representations of buildings applied in simulations, which consist of design and operating parameters associated with energy consumption (Gibson, (n.d.)). A number of energy-modeling computer applications exist — such as EnergyPlus, eQuest, Trane TRACE and others and creating the models isn't difficult. However, making energy models that are accurate is a major challenge. New and Oak Ridge National Laboratory (ORNL) colleague Jibo Sanyal are leading a research project called Autotune. Autotune is an advanced analytical methodology that leverages terabytes of HPC-generated simulation data and data mining with

multiple-machine learning algorithms for quickly calibrating a building energy model to measured (utility or sensor) data. Nautilus supercomputer from the National Science Foundation funded Extreme Science and Engineering Discovery Environment (XSEDE) are making the Autotune project possible. Autotune is adapted already for the National Energy Audit Tool (NEAT) simulation engine computer program. The Autotune researchers are planning to deploy the methodology as a desktop application, website and web services (Gibson, (n.d.)).

"Big data" is playing an increasingly big role in the renewable energy industry and the transformation of the USA's electrical grid. No single entity provides a better tool for such data than the Energy department's Energy Systems Integration

Figure 7. Change trends of electricity inventory and consumption (Cai, Zhao & Xu, 2012)

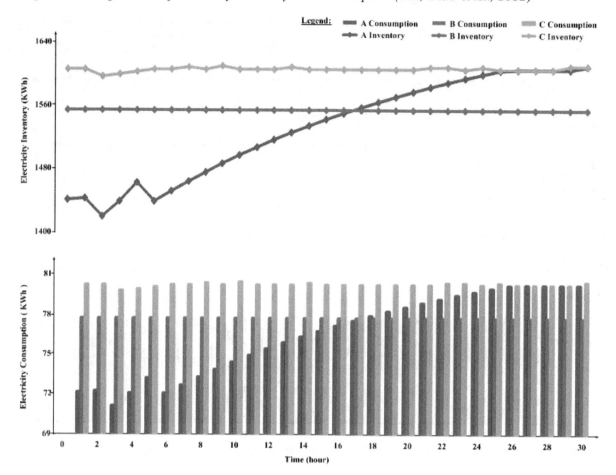

Facility (ESIF) located on the campus of National Renewable Energy Laboratory (NREL) (National renewable energy laboratory supercomputer tackles power grid problems, 2014). The ESIF's peregrine supercomputer can do more than a quadrillion calculations per second as part of the world's most energy-efficient HPC data centre. Peregrine provides computational capability to model complex systems such as the grid. The challenge is to deliver distributed energy to the grid when the sun shines and the wind blows while making it even more reliable than when the grid was a one-way delivery system of fossil-fuel-based energy. Advanced Energy Industries is accessing the ESIF's Power Systems Integration Laboratory to test its new solar photovoltaic inverter tech-

nology with the facility's hardware-in-the-loop system and megawatt-scale grid simulators. The company's inverter will help support a smarter grid that can handle two-way flows of power and communication while reducing hardware costs (National renewable energy laboratory supercomputer tackles power grid problems, 2014).

Harvard's Clean Energy project which screened the molecules using World Community Grid, an IBM-managed virtual supercomputer that harnesses the surplus computer power donated by volunteers is believed to be the most extensive investigation of quantum chemicals ever performed (Todd, 2013). Approximately 1,000 of the molecular structures that were characterized in Harvard's research show a potential to convert

Figure 8. Accumulative shipping quantity of different source material between different locations (Cai, Zhao & Xu, 2012)

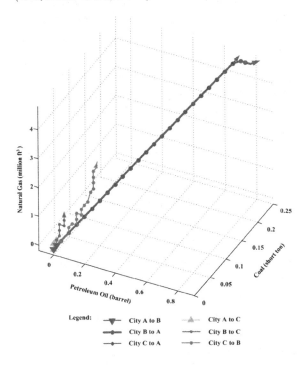

11% or more of captured sunlight into electricity. Most organic cells explored to date only convert 4% to 5% of sunlight into electricity. While solar energy materials that use silicon provide about 15% efficiency, they are more expensive to produce. Scientists can now use Harvard's resource, www. molecularspace.org to continue investigating the most promising candidates. Organic solar cells offer more possibilities than those made with traditional materials like silicon (Todd, 2013).

CONCLUSION

It is our hope that this chapter can help the readers to set up the idea of the applications of advanced computing techniques especially for high performance and cloud computing technique applications in the energy network operation. The included application demonstration of environment protec-

tion and energy recovery are just the references for the readers. The real application can be extended, but not limited to the above mentioned topics. The technique significance and application demonstration have been presented in this chapter in order to attract more engineers, scientists, researchers and the other related stake holders to dedicate to the future research of this field.

FUTURE RESEARCH DIRECTIONS

It is a good choice to further integrate the current research with the database or web based research, data mining or machine learning of energy network operation. More case studies and applications with these techniques and fundamental theory can be put into the representative service domains with the combination of e-business services, mobile services, social networking services, cloud services, legal services, healthcare services, logistics services and educational services taking into account demands from government, organization, enterprise, community, individual, customer and citizen.

The appeal of solar power is almost irresistible. An array of solar panels on a sunny roof can provide free electricity to that home for decades. But due to the high cost, solar energy only accounts for less than 1 percent of the total energy generated in the U.S (Energy center brings supercomputer to campus, 2007). One of the most promising breakthroughs in solar energy is thin film technology which the researchers have been studying for several years. With the considerable sums of money being channeled into this field, progress is steady and low-cost solar cells are making their way to market. It is hypothesized that the cost of utility-generated electricity is projected to rise and therefore the economics may soon swing in favor of photoroltaics resulting in a rapid expansion of solar technology (Energy center brings supercomputer to campus, 2007).

Knights Landing is the most powerful version of Intel's Xeon Phi supercomputing chip. The processor is set to be available in commercial systems in the second half of 2015 (Rosencrance, 2014). The new processor will be powered by more than 60 HPC-enhanced Silvermont architecture-based cores. And the integration with Omni Scale, along with the fabric's HPC-optimized architecture aims to address the performance, scalability, reliability, power and density requirements of future HPC. The first supercomputer to use Knights Landing will be "Cori" the National Energy Research Scientific Computing Center (NERSC) 's next generation Cray XC system planned for 2016, serving more than 5,000 users and over 700 extreme –scale science projects. Cori will consist of more than 9,300 Intel Knights Landing processors and will serve as an on-ramp to exascale (Rosencrance, 2014).

Most interesting to the energy sector perhaps is the Lithium/Air Battery Project led by Jack Wells, group leader of the Computational Nanotechnology Group at Oak Ridge National Laboratory (Lombardi,2010). His team will be running simulations of lithium/air battery reactions. A successful version of the air battery would be capable of storing 10 times the amount of energy as a lithium ion battery of the same weight. Such a battery might make electric cars more competitive compared to gas-powered cars. A serious commitment to next-generation nuclear power plants might also be on the U.S. energy horizon. The Energy Department's own Argonne National Laboratory Nuclear Energy Advanced Modeling and Simulation team is going to use its time to test design ideas for a next-generation nuclear reactor. Specifically, it's developing a new type of fast neutron reactor that can partition and transmute the elements contained in spent nuclear fuel to reduce the amount of spent nuclear material that would need to be stored underground post-reactor use (Lombardi, 2010).

Most plans envision that subsurface rock formations will be used to sequester vast amounts of energy byproducts (DePaolo et al., 2007). However, rock formations are not designed by nature as storage vaults. Fundamental improvements in understanding how these rock systems will perform as long-term storage systems are critical to developing new energy technologies in a timely fashion and with public safety guaranteed. Approximately 85% of current worldwide power consumption is based on fossil carbon. To reduce global carbon emissions (through the use of carbon-based fuels) to the atmosphere requires that a significant fraction of the carbon dioxide produced from fossil energy conversion be captured and stored away from the atmosphere (DePaolo et al., 2007).

Nuclear energy produces no CO_2 but instead generates substantial amounts of radioactive materials, a factor that has both environmental and security implications (DePaolo et al., 2007). To sustain nuclear energy generation and even more so to increase generation by a factor of up to 10 over the next century, it is imperative to safely store radioactive waste in underground repositories. If nuclear energy production is to expand in future, many suitable sites for underground storage needs to be identified and characterized (DePaolo et al., 2007).

REFERENCES

Agam, S. (2011). SGI, Intel plan to speed supercomputers 500 times by 2018. *Computer World*. Retrieved on June 9, 2012 from http://www.computerworld.com

Baburajan, R. (2011). The rising cloud storage market opportunity strengthens vendors. *info-TECH*. Retrieved on December 2, 2011 from http://it.tmcnet.com

Bellarmine, G. T., & Arokiaswamv, N. S. S. (1996). Energy management techniques to meet power shortage problems in India. *Energy Conversion and Management, 37*(3), 319–328. doi:10.1016/0196-8904(95)00181-6

Berredo, R. C., Ekel, P. Y., Martini, J. S. C., Palhares, R. M., Parreiras, R. O., & Pereira, J. G. Jr. (2011). Decision making in fuzzy environment and multi-criteria power engineering problems. *International Journal of Electrical Power & Energy Systems, 33*(3), 623–632. doi:10.1016/j.ijepes.2010.12.020

Bowman, W. A. (1996). Maximum ground level concentrations with downwash: The urban stability mode. *Journal of the Air & Waste Management Association, 46*(7), 615–620. doi:10.1080/10473289.1996.10467495

Cai, T., Wang, S., & Xu, Q. (2013). Scheduling of multiple chemical plant start-ups to minimize regional air quality impacts. *Computers & Chemical Engineering, 54*, 68–78. doi:10.1016/j.compchemeng.2013.03.027

Cai, T., Zhao, C., & Xu, Q. (2012). Energy network dispatch optimization under emergency of local energy shortage. *Energy, 42*(1), 132–145. doi:10.1016/j.energy.2012.04.001

Church, P. E. (1949). Dilution of waste stack gases in the atmosphere. *Industrial & Engineering Chemistry, 41*(12), 2753–2756. doi:10.1021/ie50480a022

DePaolo, D., & Orr, F., Jr. (2007). *Basic research needs for geosciences: Facilitating 21st century energy systems.* Retrieved on June 24, 2014 from http://digitalscholarship.unlv.edu/cgi/viewcontent.cgi?article=1130&context=yucca_mtn_pubs

EFF DES Cracker Source Code. (n.d.). Retrieved on July 8, 2011 from http://cosic.esat.kuleuven.be

Energy Center Brings Supercomputer to Campus. (2007). Retrieved on June 14, 2014 from http://inside.mines.edu/~mlusk/GECO_Mines_Magazine_F07.pdf

Gibson, S. (n.d.). *Supercomputer-assisted calibration methodology enhances accuracy of energy models.* Retrieved on July 6, 2014 from http://www.nics.tennessee.edu/autotune

Goldsmith, J. R., & Friberg, L. T. (1976). Effects of air pollution on human health. In The effects of air pollution (Vol. 2). Academic Press.

Griffiths, R. F. (1994). Errors in the use of the Briggs parameterization for atmospheric dispersion coefficients. *Atmospheric Environment, 28*(17), 2861–2865. doi:10.1016/1352-2310(94)90086-8

Halitsky, J. (1989). A jet plume model for short stacks. *Journal of the Air Pollution Control Association, 39*(6), 856–858. Retrieved from http://www.tandfonline.com/doi/abs/10.1080/08940630.1989.10466573#.VEIk8PnF_D8

Hanna, S. R., Briggs, G. A., & Kosker, R. P. (1982). *Handbook on atmospheric diffusion.* NTIS DE81009809 (DOE/TIC-22800). Retrieved on October 16, 2014 from http://pbadupws.nrc.gov/docs/ML0926/ML092640175.pdf

Heffner, G., Maurer, L., Sarkar, A., & Wang, X. (2010). *Minding the gap: World Bank's assistance to power shortage mitigation in the developing world energy.* Retrieved on October 16, 2014 from http://www.slideshare.net/lmaurer/minding-the-gap-world-banks-assistance-to-power-shortage-mitigation-in-the-developing-world

Hogan, W. R., Cooper, G. F., Wagner, M. M., & Wallstrom, G. L. (2005). An inverted Gaussian plume model for estimating the location and amount of release of airborne agents from downwind atmospheric concentrations. *RODS Technical Report*. Real Time Outbreak and Disease Surveillance Laboratory, University of Pittsburgh, Pittsburgh, PA. Retrieved on October 16, 2014 from http://rods.health.pitt.edu/LIBRARY/2005%20Hogan-InvertedDispersion-Model-submittedToMMWR.pdf

IBM Blue Gene Announcement. (2007). Retrieved on June 9, 2012 from http://www.ibm.com

Jeong, H. J., Kim, E. H., Suh, K. S., Hwang, W. T., Han, M. H., & Lee, H. K. (2005). Determination of the source rate released into the environment from a nuclear power plant. *Radiation Protection Dosimetry*, *113*(3), 308-313. Retrieved on October 16, 2014 from http://www.ncbi.nlm.nih.gov/pubmed/15687109

Johnson, R. (2014). *Disarmament diplomacy: DOE supercomputing & test simulation program*. Retrieved on July 8, 2011 from http://acronym.org.uk. 2000-08-22.

Joshi, R. R. (1998). *A new heuristic algorithm for probabilistic optimization*. Department of Mathematics and School of Biomedical Engineering, Indian Institute of Technology Powai, Mumbai, India. Retrieved on July 1, 2008 from http://www.sciencedirect.com/science/article/pii/S0305054896000561

Kainkwa, R. R. (1999). Wind energy as alternative source to alleviate the shortage of electricity that prevails during the dry season: A case study of Tanzania. *Renewable Energy*, *18*(2), 167–174. doi:10.1016/S0960-1481(98)00801-5

Kaku, M. (2011). *Physics of the future*. New York: Doubleday Publishers. Retrieved on October 16, 2014 from http://www.npr.org/2011/11/29/142717081/physics-of-the-future-how-well-live-in-2100

Kan, M. (2012). China is building a 100-petaflop supercomputer. *InfoWorld*, *31*(October). Retrieved from http://www.infoworld.com

Lombardi, C. (2010). *Energy department awards supercomputing time*. Retrieved on July 6, 2014 from http://www.cnet.com/news/energy-department-awards-supercomputing-time/

MacKay, C., McKee, S., & Mulholland, A. J. (2006). Diffusion and convection of gaseous and fine particulate from a chimney. *IMA Journal of Applied Mathematics*, *71*(5), 670–691. doi:10.1093/imamat/hxl016

Mariana, C., Paula, K., & Alta, M. (2012). Securing virtual and cloud environments. In *Cloud computing and services science: Research and innovations in the service economy*. Springer Science and Business Media, LLC. Retrieved on October 16, 2014 from http://books.google.com/books?id=ZCWIHhwxc_gC&pg=PA73&lpg=PA73&dq=Securing+virtual+and+cloud+environments.+In:+Cloud+computing+and+services+science:+Research+and+Innovations+in+the+Service+Economy&source=bl&ots=bj3-SI-21J&sig=30xeMoh9MXl1eiSFlm9MQWGRxzA&hl=en&sa=X&ei=dydCVPvxHO76iAKh3YCABQ&ved=0CDUQ6AEwAw#v=onepage&q=Securing%20virtual%20and%20cloud%20environments.%20In%3A%20Cloud%20computing%20and%20services%20science%3A%20Research%20and%20Innovations%20in%20the%20Service%20Economy&f=false

Meier, A. (2006). Operating building during temporary electricity shortage. *Energy & Buildings*, *38*(11), 1296-1301. Retrieved on October 16, 2014 from http://www.sciencedirect.com/science/article/pii/S0378778806000922

National Geographic. (2010). *Faster supercomputers aiding weather forecasts*. Retrieved on July 8, 2011 from http://news.nationalgeographic.com

National Renewable Energy Laboratory Supercomputer Tackles Power Grid Problems. (2014). Retrieved from http://windenergy.einnews.com/article__detail/211389116?lcode=Tn13hwnNZ M_1i4zS4PmnUQ%3D%3D

National Science Foundation. (2013). Retrieved from http://www.nsf.org

New Supercomputing Method Helps Energy and Materials Research. (2014). Retrieved from http://tntoday.utk.edu/2014/01/15/capability-helps-overcome-limitations-study-energy-materials-applications/

NIST. (2011). *NIST definition of cloud computing*. National Institute of Standards and Technology. Retrieved on July 24, 2011 from http://www.nist.gov

NVIDIA. (2011). *China's investment in GPU supercomputing begins to pay off big time*. Retrieved on July 8, 2011 from http://blogs.nvidia.com

Oestreich, K. (2010). Converged infrastructure. *CTO Forum*. Retrieved on December 2, 2011 from http://www.thectoforum.com

Pasquill, F. (1961). The estimation of the dispersion of windborne material. *The Meteorological Magazine*, *90*(1063), 33-49. Retrieved from http://www.researchgate.net/publication/231221906_The_Estimation_of_the_Dispersion_of_Windborne_Material

Pasquill, F. (1974). *Atmospheric diffusion* (2nd ed., p. 429). New York, NY: Halsted Press, John Wiley & Sons.

Rosencrance, L. (2014). Intel heralds new Xeon server chip, most powerful ever. *CIO Today*. Retrieved on October 16, 2014 from http://www.cio-today.com/article/index.php?story_id=12100006PL28

Russell, R. (1977). *The cray-1 computer system*. Cray Research, Inc. Retrieved on May 25, 2011 from https://www.cs.auckland.ac.nz/courses/compsci703s1c/archive/2008/resources/Russell.pdf

Sanghvi, A. P. (1991). Power shortages in developing countries: Impacts and policy implications. *Energy Policy*, *19*(5), 425–440. doi:10.1016/0301-4215(91)90020-O

Seinfeld, J. H. (1986). *Atmospheric chemistry and physics of air pollution*. John Wiley & Sons. Retrieved on October 16, 2014 from http://pubs.acs.org/doi/abs/10.1021/es00151a602

Shielding Analysis Modular System (SAMSY). (n.d.). *OECD nuclear energy agency*. Retrieved on May 25, 2011 from http://www.oecd-nea.org/tools/abstract/detail/iaea0837

Slade, D. H. (Ed.). (1986). *Meteorology and atomic energy*. U.S. Atomic Energy Commission, Air Resources Laboratories, Research Laboratories, Environmental Science Services Administration, U.S Department of Commerce. Retrieved on October 16, 2014 from http://www.orau.org/ptp/PTP%20Library/library/Subject/Meteorology/meteorology%20and%20atomic%20energy.pdf

Todd, T. (2013). *Harvard uses IBM supercomputer crowdsourcing to unearth new solar energy potential*. Retrieved on July 6, 2014 from http://turbotodd.com/blog/2013/06/24/harvard-uses-ibm-supercomputer-crowdsourcing-to-unearth-new-solar-energy-potential/

Turner, D. B. (1979). Atmospheric dispersion modeling. *Journal of the Air Pollution Control Association*, *29*(5), 502–519. doi:10.1080/00022470.1979.10470821

Turner, D. B. (1994). *Workbook of atmospheric dispersion estimates: An introduction to dispersion modeling* (2nd ed.). Lewis Publishers. Retrieved on October 16, 2014 from http://www.crcpress.com/product/isbn/9781566700238

Turner, D. B., Bender, L. W., Pierce, T. E., & Petersen, W. B. (1989). Air quality simulation models from EPA. *Environmental Software*, *4*(2), 52–61. doi:10.1016/0266-9838(89)90031-2

United States Environment Protection Agency. (n.d.). Retrieved from http://www.epa.gov

United States Environmental Protection Agency. (1982). *Policy on excess emissions during startup, shutdown, maintenance, and malfunction*. Retrieved on October 16, 2014 from http://www2. epa.gov/sites/production/files/documents/excess-start-rpt.pdf

What is Cloud Computing?. (2014). Retrieved on July 6, 2014 from http://www.amazon.com/what-is-cloud-computing/

KEY TERMS AND DEFINITIONS

Air Pollution: The introduction of chemicals, particulates, biological materials, or other harmful materials into the Earth's atmosphere, possibly causing disease, death to humans, damage to other living organisms such as food crops, or the natural or built environment.

Design: The creation of a plan or convention for the construction of an object or a system (as in architectural blueprints, engineering drawings, business processes, circuit diagrams and sewing patterns).

Modeling: A mathematical model is a description of a system using mathematical concepts and language. The process of developing a mathematical model is termed mathematical modeling. Mathematical models are used not only in the natural sciences and engineering disciplines, but also in the social sciences; physicists, engineers, statisticians, operations research analysts and economists use mathematical models most extensively.

Optimization: In the simplest case, an optimization problem consists of maximizing or minimizing a real function by systematically choosing input values from within an allowed set and computing the value of the function. The generalization of optimization theory and techniques to other formulations comprises a large area of applied mathematics.

Renewable Energy: Energy that comes from resources which are naturally replenished on a human timescale such as sunlight, wind, rain, tides, waves and geothermal heat.

Supercomputer: A computer at the frontline of contemporary processing capacity, particularly speed of calculation which can happen at speeds of nanoseconds.

Uncertainty: A term used in subtly different ways in a number of fields, including philosophy, physics, statistics, economics, finance, insurance, psychology, sociology, engineering, and information science. It applies to predictions of future events, to physical measurements that are already made, or to the unknown.

Section 3
Supercomputer Theory

Chapter 11
Steganography Encoding as Inverse Data Mining

Dan Ophir
Ariel University, Israel & Tel Aviv University, Israel

ABSTRACT

Supercomputers and cloud computing seem to be competing paradigms. Supercomputing focuses on increasing CPU speed, thus significantly increasing the speed of its associated memory access and its capacity. Conversely, cloud computing increases the computing throughput by parallel computing, spreading computing tasks over unused nodes and platforms. Steganography, the art of concealing a message within a message, is a type of encoding whose operations are required to remain secret. Steganography encoding requires data manipulation and is linked to data mining methodologies. Data mining reveals concealed data that is embedded in exposed data. Encoding by steganography is reverse data mining, hiding data among visible data. Conventionally, encryption methods are used to successfully hide the data. Cloud computing can take the data and disperse it in a way that even without any encryption, each individual packet of data is meaningless, thus hiding the message as like by steganography. This chapter explores steganography encoding as inverse data mining.

INTRODUCTION: PICTURE OF STEGANOGRAPHY

This paper will analyze the current implications of cloud computing on steganography (e.g. Hayati P., et al. 2005) that is based on signal and image processing algorithms. Steganography, which means concealed writing, is the art and science of writing a message in a way that no one except the intended recipient suspects that there is any hidden message at all. The concealed information can be images, text, or any type of binary data.

This work will focus on uses of steganography which include the following:

Data Hiding

Images or any other types of data can be concealed in another image, leaving the manipulated image as visually similar as possible to the initial image (Figure 1).

DOI: 10.4018/978-1-4666-7461-5.ch011

Copyright © 2015, IGI Global. Copying or distributing in print or electronic forms without written permission of IGI Global is prohibited.

Figure 1. An example of steganographic manipulation: image (a), the original image, has been over-lapped with image (b). In order to see this superimposed image, the observer has to look at the picture at a distance of about 50 cm (the image is a private acquisition)

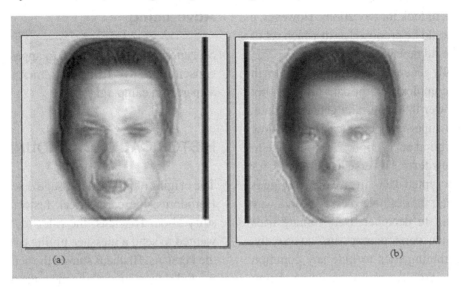

Analyzing and Detecting

An image can be analyzed for the existence of hidden data. If such hidden data are found, it can be extracted and saved externally.

There are two modes of steganography:

- **Hiding:** This mode's purpose is to hide the information in the image. The hidden data may be any binary information.
- **Decoding:** The action of interpreting the hidden information.

Data Mining vs. Inverse Data Mining

In order to understand the term "inverse data mining", the better known "data mining" term will be explained.

Data mining, similarly to mineral mining, is the art of extracting objects that are different by some set of properties from their surroundings. In most cases, both in mineral mining and data mining, the valuable material is a very small percentage of the overall volume.

The different properties of the valuable material are exploited to separate them from their environment. For example, iron is separated from surrounding material by either using its magnetic properties or lower melting point (smelting). The genome (Watson J. D. 2003) investigation (Ophir, 2013) is an example of data-mining, where specific sequences, for example ternary tracts, are separated from the whole genome. This operation is very CPU-time consuming and requires the use of supercomputers.

Data mining places, sometimes, even greater challenges than the mineral mining before the potential miner. This statement is expressed in the fact that the data miner doesn't know what to look for, whereas the mineral miner knows what is he looking for. The data-miner generally looks for something different than the surroundings. This is usually the starting point for most data mining.

Data mining is looking for exceptional data, or conversely, looking for data properties that have common denominators with the whole or part of the investigated data collection. This common denominator will be helpful in further filtering the exceptions.

Statistical tools are generally used for data manipulations to look for deviations. However, a hypothesis should be proposed as to which set of properties should be investigated.

In artificially generated data (unlike the human genome), the complexity of the data-mining is not necessarily lower than naturally generated data. Even modern super-computers can be too slow in resolving a good encryption. We would like to introduce a new term, "inverse data mining" for generating encrypted data. Inverse data mining is generating data, for example messages, in a way that is difficult to decipher. Data mining tries to find common denominators and conversely, inverse data mining tries to hide any common denominators. Steganography encoding, being a sub-domain of the encryption theory, fits the definition of inverse data mining.

STEGANOGRAPHIC APPLICATIONS

There are three main purposes for using steganography: restricted or prohibited communication, watermarking, and advertising.

Restricted or Prohibited Communication

This refers to communication between several parties whose activities are clandestine, illegal or shunned by society. Steganography is used by underground organizations. Another set of applications that can use steganographic methods in the positive sense is when privacy has to be legally preserved, for example medical patient data, bank customer data etc.

Watermarking

Steganography can be used as a digital signature, ensuring copyright properties. Digital signatures and watermarking involve concealing data in an image to track its origins after it passes hands.

Advertising

Steganography can be used to appeal to the subconscious in advertising a commercial product or as part of a campaign.

HISTORICAL BACKGROUND

The origins of hiding a message date to antiquity. Herodotus, the early Greek historian, relates a story about Histaeus, the ruler of Miletus who wanted to send a message urging a revolt against the Persians. Histaeus shaved the head of his most trusted slave, tattooed the message on the slave's scalp, waited for the slave's hair to grow back, and sent the slave to his friend Aristagorus with the message safely concealed. During WWII, the Germans perfected the micro-dot, a message that was photographed and reduced to the size of a dot on a typewritten page and concealed in an innocuous letter. Other methods, including the use of invisible inks and concealing messages in plain sight (see Figure 2), were used throughout modern history (Szczypiorski 2003), (Kundur and Ahsan 2003), (Petitcolas et al. 1999).

STEGANOGRAPHIC METHODS

There are literally hundreds of different methods and algorithms used for coding and decoding steganographic messages. In this section, we will give a few examples.

Writing a Message

A message can be written on a homogenous background, as shown in Figure 2.

Figure 2. A Steganogram from 1945. A secret message was inserted using Morse code, which was camouflaged as innocent looking blades of grass along the river (the image is from Zoran D., 2004).

Figure 3. A steganogram: the empty template-matrix. (a) A visible steganographic text containing the hidden message. (b) The hidden message. The image is from Zoran D., 2004

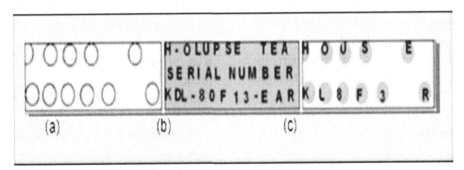

Using a Template Masking Matrix

Template masking is shown in Figure 3: (a) is placed on (b) and hides the unnecessary letters. The uncovered letters reveal the important message.

Visual Steganographic Decoding

Visual steganographic decoding is when a picture is seen in scaled resolution (Figure 1a), in which a picture is hidden in another picture (Figure 1b).

In the example of Figure 1the hidden image is easily encrypted by observing the picture from a distance of 50 cm. This technique of seeing a different picture at a distance is analogous to a change in the image resolution. At a greater distance, the neighboring pixels are seen as a single pixel of the smaller image.

The advantage of this kind of steganography lies in the simplicity of its decoding, which can be done without any computing.

The advantage of using a double-scaled image is exploited in advertising by appealing to the potential observer's subconscious.

THE LINKAGE BETWEEN STEGANOGRAPHY, CLOUD ARCHITECTURE, AND SUPERCOMPUTERS

Cloud computing integrated with supercomputers (Chappell, D. 2008), reduces the advantages of formal steganography. An image can be divided into many data packets, making the original file difficult to detect and decode. The paradigm of steganography is based on hiding the data unnoticeably, and the paradigm of cloud computing is based on manipulating pieces of data separately, eventually gathering the corresponding output pieces and reintegrating them, usually with the aid of supercomputers, into the original file. Merging steganography and cloud architecture requires, in the case of decoding, supplying the decoder-key with the encoded data, which is of course unreasonable. By supplying the decoder-key with the data, the two "golden rules" of steganography – harmlessness and confidentiality – are broken. (Figure 4)

Harmlessness

Attaching the decoder-key to the data shows that the apparently harmless data are not what they seem.

Confidentiality

Attaching the decoder-key to the data breaks the confidentiality of the data, especially if they were encoded with the help of the decoder-key.

ONE DIMENSIONAL STEGANOGRAPHY

Additional examples of steganography will be given. All the examples are language oriented and they include various "types" of languages. The examples that will be considered are as follows: Biblical, biological, vocal, textual-natural, legal (forensic language), computer language, body language (and verbal language that compliments body language) and mathematical multidimensional language.

1. Bible Codes

Written steganography is based on embedding hidden messages in an open text. This way of passing information was utilized by spies who inserted latent message in innocent looking advertisement, printed in general newspapers.

Some people argue that the Bible contains concealed messages within the text (Figure 5). Some researchers (Witztum D, 1980) have shown that messages appear that are constructed from equidistance letters in the text (an arithmetic series ordered letters) conforming a string of legible Hebrew words predicting some futuristic events, like the rise of Nazism and the murder of Anwar Saadat.

The question is whether these words are not just a case of random circumstances within a large text. Witztum and others have claimed that they have proven the significance of their results.

The way to fortify or contradict the results is by comparing the results obtained from the Bible with the frequencies of the appearances of understandable words in a random generated text with the letters appearing at similar frequencies as in the spoken Hebrew language. Witztum visualized his results graphically in which the equidistance letters are displayed as a part of the text written in a rectangle in such a way that the whole stream

Figure 4. Steganography and Steganoanalysis (the images are from Zoran D., 2004) using the most and the least significant bits; visualization and explanations of its respective stages: (a) The carry (A_0, A_1, A_2, ..., A_{n-1}); (b) (A_0, A_1, A_2, A_4); (c) The image to be hidden (C_0, C_1, ..., C_{n-1}); (d) (C_{n-1}, A_1, A_2, A_3, ..., A_{n-1}); (e) (D_0); (f) (C_{n-4}, C_{n-3}, C_{n-2}, C_{n-1}, ..., A_4, A_5, ..., A_{n-1}); (g) (F_0, F_1, F_2, F_3); (h) A-G; (i) A-F; (j) The hidden picture that was extracted from D; (k) The hidden picture that was extracted from F

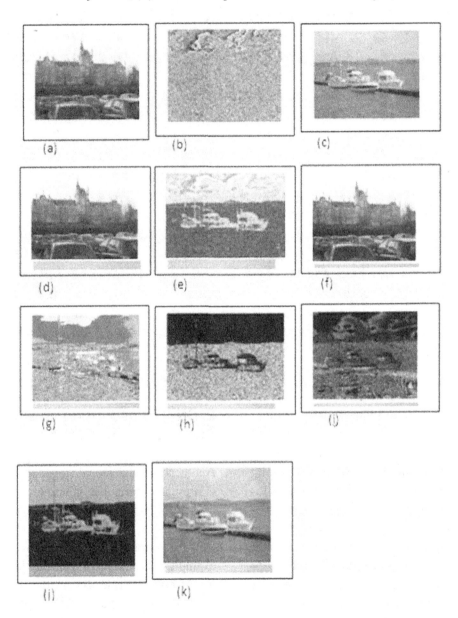

of letters in the equidistance sequence are located in the same column of letters. Such manner of displaying a message seems to be persuasive on the first glance. Robert J. Aumann, a Nobel Laureate (2005 Nobel Memorial Prize in Economics), together with a panel of other scientists, conducted an experiment to test the validity of the bible codes. His conclusion at the end of that experiment was that the Bible codes phenomenon is improbable (Aumann 2004).

Figure 5. Excerpt from Genesis (for illustration) demonstrating the Bible investigation on the original Hebrew text. In this translation to English three meaningful "vertical" words (in frames) were found: "from", "God" and "war".

1 In the beginning God created the heaven and the earth. 2 No
the earth was unformed and void, and darkness was upon the
face of the deep; and the spirit of God hovered over the face
of the waters. 3 And God said: 'Let there be light.' And
there was light. 4 And God saw the light, that it was good;
and God divided the light from the darkness. 5 And Goo
called the light Day, and the darkness He called Night. And
there was evening and there was morning, one day. (P) 6 And
God said: 'Let there be a firmament in the midst of the
waters, and let it divide the waters from the waters.' 7 And
God made the firmament, and divided the waters which were
under the firmament from the waters which were above the
firmament; and it was so. 8 And God called the firmament
Heaven. And there was evening and there was morning, a secono
day. (P 9 And God said: 'Let the waters under the heaven be
gathered once together unto one place, and let the dry land
appear. And said go away. 10 And God called the dry land
Earth, and the gathering together of the waters called He
Seas; and God saw that it was good.

From the data mining point of view, the function, as indicated above, is to find a common data denominator or conversely, to find exceptionality or deviations from the similarity. When looking for common denominators, a set of characteristics should be given to be digitized, and their likelihoods evaluated. The set of letters properties is unlimited; there are vast numbers of mutual letter combinations in the text. Generally the human operator structures the hypothesis and the computer confirms or rejects it. Artificial intelligence is still unable to conceive by itself plausible hypotheses. However, there are so called decision support software programs whose role is to assist in raising possibilities.

2. DNA Transcription as another Steganographic Platform

Another one dimensional Steganographic problem is presented here. The genome contains a huge number of nucleotides with a mixed sequence of four types: A, C, G and T. Interesting questions from the domain of data mining can be posed. For example, does a tract of a certain length consisting of only three letters, in the genome's total sequence, have a special biological significance? (Ophir &. Gera 2005); (Ophir, 2013) (see Figure 6). In order to answer such a question, statistical data manipulations must be performed.

There are computational power constraints preventing the problem to be solved in the whole genome. The above stated problem was reduced

Figure 6. The indicated ternary tracts (gray) in the sequence of nucleotides of the p53 gene

No.	Begin	End	Length	Type	Tract
8	7831	7851	21	intron	CAGGAGGCAGAGGCAGGAGAA
9	13913	13933	21	intron	CAAAAAAAAAAAAAAAAGGCC
10	2003	2024	22	intron	CCCGGAGAAAAAAAAAAAGAA
11	12636	12657	22	intron	CAAAGAGCCCAAGGCAGGCAGA
12	14591	14612	22	intron	AAGCAAGCAGGACAAGAACGG
13	14707	14728	22	exon	CCCCAGCCAAAGAAGAAACCAC
14	18529	18550	22	intron	CAGGGAAAAGGGACACAGCACCC
15	1567	1589	23	intron	GCCCGCCAGGCCGAGGAGGACCG
16	1954	1976	23	intron	GCAGAAGCCAAGCCCGGAGGCAC
17	5376	5398	23	intron	CAAAAAAAGAAAAGAAAAGAA
18	12882	12904	23	intron	CAAAAAAAAAAAAAAGAAAACC
19	16914	16936	23	intron	GCAGGGAGCCAAGACGGCGCCAC
20	6517	6540	24	intron	CAAAAAAAAAAAAGAAAAGAA
21	9377	9400	24	intron	CAAAAAAAAAAAAAACGAAAAG
22	13125	13148	24	exon	CCACACCCCCGCCCGGCACCCGCG
23	1706	1730	25	intron	GAGAGGGGAGGAGAGAGAGAGAAA
24	16684	16708	25	intron	CAAAAAAAGAAAAGCCAGGCGCAC
25	17644	17669	26	exon	GGGAAGGAGCCAGCGGGGAGCACGGGGC
26	2157	2183	27	intron	GAAGCGGAAGGGGCGGGCCCGCAGGCG
27	4603	4629	27	intron	CAGGAAAAAAAAGAAAGAAAGAAAAA
28	7746	7773	28	intron	GCAGACCACGCCGGGCAACAGAGCCGAGA
29	9844	9871	28	intron	CCAAAAAAAAAAGAAAAAGAAAAAGCC
30	10018	10046	29	intron	CAAAAGAAAAAAGAAAGAAAGAAGACCA
31	16504	16532	29	exon	GGGAGAGCACCGGCGCACAGAGGGAGAGAA
32	16974	17003	30	intron	CAGAAAAAAAAGAAAAGAACCGAGGCACAG
33	9478	9508	31	intron	GAAAAAAAAAAAAGAAAAGAAAGAGAGAGCA
34	7139	7171	33	intron	CAAAAAAAAAAAAAAAAAGGAAGGAAAAAAA
35	6100	6133	34	intron	CAAAAAAAAAAAAAAAAAAAAAGAAAAGAAACC
36	18332	18367	36	intron	CAAAAACAAACAAAAAACAAAACAAAAAAAACA
37	11806	11845	40	intron	GGAAGGGCAGGCCCACCACCCCGACCCCAACCCCGCCCCC

to searches on a single gene (p53) assumed responsible for malignant diseases. To analyze this question on the whole genome, we need to harness the power of supercomputers. The human genome contains 3.2 billion letters (nucleotides). To perform algorithms of the $O(n^2)$ complexity is above the potential of regular computers to solve in a reasonable time.

These types of DNA sequences can also be classified as steganographical information. DNA sequences are mainly to preserve genetic data. However, in the background there is hidden un-noticed information which maybe discovered by using data mining tools.

Data mining tools can check the distribution of nucleotides and compare them to randomly generated information. It was discovered that some binary tract appearances have a biological significance and this was also shown in ternary tracts. However, even though the appearance of ternary tracts is unusual, it was determined that these tracts are found in a subset of the significant binary tracts.

3. Sound-Voice Carriers

Sound is another convenient background for hiding meaningful information. The sound wave (Figure 7) is deformed according to the information planted into it. Its frequency amplitude is changed according some defined a priori pattern in the transmitter position. The receiver having sensitive equipment and knowing the pattern can decipher the message. All other receivers treat the sound deformation as noise.

A special programming language was defined (Ophir & Dekel 2013) and it is being developed for voice data analysis to discover irregularities, indicating possible hidden information.

The use of super-computers for analysis is useful. Regular PC computers are still too weak to manipulate huge amounts of voice files which are available in different social networks and websites.

4. The Enigma Code as a Counterexample of Steganography

The Germans used the Enigma code during the Second World War (Figure 8). The carrier was a telegraph and the coded information was textual and not a radio wave. The Polish mathematician Marian Rayewski and others broke the Enigma code. Later versions of Enigma were deciphered with the collaboration of British cryptography teams. Breaking the Enigma code was one of the events that drastically changed the tide during the war. The Enigma code generator was based on the concept of a rotor machine. The invention of rotor machines using mechanised polyalphabetic encryption provided a practical way to use a much larger number of alphabets and thus hinder code deciphering (Cipher et al. 1985). The Enigma code is a counterexample of steganography encoding. The code is not embedded in a meaningful text. Instead, the whole bulk of the text is meaningful and unreadable before its deciphering.

Figure 7. An Illustration of a voice wave which may be a carrier of hidden data

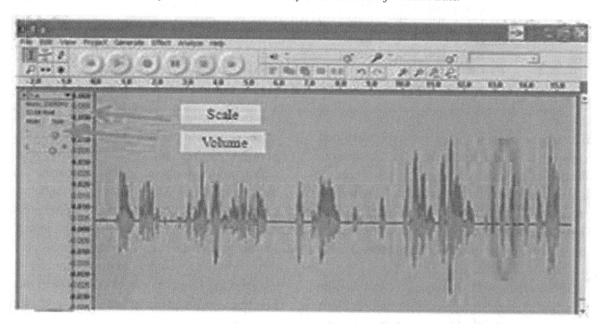

Figure 8. Enigma's three rotors. Their positions generate the transcription code of letters into other letters

Many decoding algorithms can be easily performed by a PC. However, the increasing computational powers of modern computers does not help in decrypting the more complicated encryptions and even supercomputers do not have enough computational power to decipher the very sophisticated encryption algorithms (Mollin R. A., 2003). In the competition between encoding and the deciphering, encoding currently has the upper hand. As in conventional wars, offensive cyber weapons are cheaper than defensive (security) ones as measured by CPU time and power consumption.

5. Computer Language vs. Steganography

Generally, hiding information in a computer program, written in a computer language, is done to damage the program environment (such as a virus), or to camouflage the program algorithm to guard the copyrights. Decoding of the information is different in both cases.

Embedding harmful information in a computer program is usually activated by some external or internal trigger (Figure 9). Such information, generally called viruses, worms or Trojan horses, differ in how they operate and by how they inflict damage. These malicious software programs are ubiquitous in the cyber world and it is difficult to prevent their activation and distribution. There are companies which receive actual information from their clients about the appearance of new malware and speedily develop "anti-virus" programs and distribute them among their clients.

There seems to be a steady-state between the people who produce viruses (hackers) and the companies developing security programs. Future cyber wars might look quite different. In cases of massive cyberattacks, huge security resources are required on a national level. For such scenarios, preparations should include harnessing supercomputers that could cope with such offensive attacks within a reasonable amount of time both offensively and defensively.

Figure 9. An inserted virus in a pseudo-coded program, threatening to erase the hard disk on September 11th

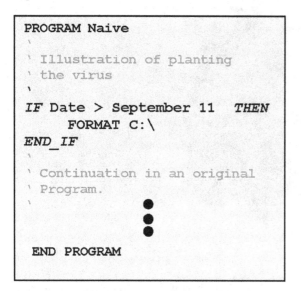

```
PROGRAM Naive
'
' Illustration of planting
' the virus
'
IF Date > September 11   THEN
        FORMAT C:\
END_IF
'
' Continuation in an original
' Program.
'
                •
                •
                •

END PROGRAM
```

TWO DIMENSIONAL STEGANOGRAPHY

1. Image Steganography

The two-dimensional image steganography is shown here to demonstrate the usefulness of supercomputers. However, there are also other kinds of two-dimensional steganography.

2. Body Language

Body language (Ophir, D. 2010) can sometimes be classified as a type of Steganography. Body language may hide true intentions or emotions and some hints may be embedded in the body language. Using body language, it is possible to communicate unnoticeably with another person consciously or subconsciously.

Figure 10 represents a special image procedure for decoding body movement, which is later interpreted as body language or body gestures. The idea is to gradually peel the body (morphological image processing) until a skeletal figure appears.

The skeleton is then manipulated to show joining points which are bending-intersecting points. The analysis of these points supplies us with the trajectories of the control points. The control points and their body functionality provide full body decryption movements. The non-skeletal movement such as a wink requires other types of image analysis which will not be treated here.

The recognition and interpretation of the person's movements requires a substantial amount of computer time. The computational power required to keep a crowd under surveillance, looking for an individual's suspicious movements, for example in the airport or in other sensitive and crowded facilities, exceeds current computational powers of normal computers. Supercomputers are needed to analyze such huge amount of data and computations.

3. Sign Language

Using a technique similar to body language recognition, we can perform *sign language* recognition. This technique allows the computer to recognize *sign-language* letters (Figure 11), thereby enabling the recognition of signed messages. Conversely, such an algorithm can be useful in translating the verbal voice or the verbal script into a stream of sign-language signs (Figure 12).

Sign language has similar steganographic qualities as verbal languages. This is because sign-language is a type of GUI (graphical user interface) of natural spoken language and therefore the same steganographic rules can be applied. Computerized *sign-language* reading algorithms are very CPU time consuming. They must be processed in an online environment and require high resolution image-processing. Therefore, to improve the algorithm's efficiency we can take advantage of the supercomputer's capabilities.

Figure 10. (a) a picture of a person; (b) the previous picture on a homogeneous background; (c) Silhouette; (d) A silhouette with the skeleton lines; (e) The skeleton lines with the control points; (f) The isolated control points (CP).

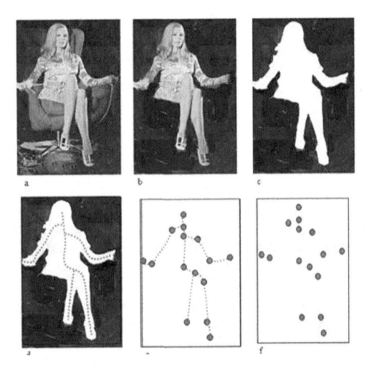

Figure 11. American Sign Language alphabets

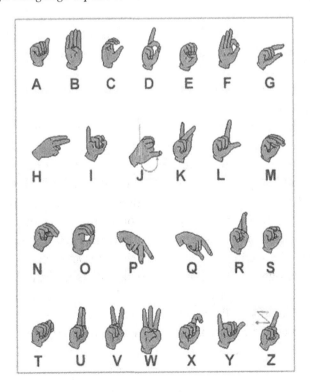

Figure 12. Fingers recognition. (a) hands, (b) skeleton, (c) the skeleton with control points, (d) the control points

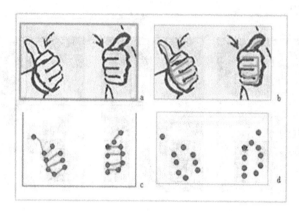

4. Verbal Steganography for Psychological and Legal Uses

Considering that steganography is a method of hiding information invisibly, it also, in a way, distorts the truth. Although steganography has two components, encryption and decryption, we will only deal with decryption herein.

Verbal language and body language complement each other. Therefore, they are in the same two-dimensional category. Even though, verbal language is produced as a linear stream (i.e. a linear language), it is transformed during the analysis into a two dimensional hierarchical tree. This equivalence between the meaningful stream of words and its tree representation (Figure 13), classifies this kind of steganography in the two-dimensional category.

The idea behind this type of steganography lies in the syntactical, semantic and psychological analysis (Ophir, D., June 2013) of the treated person's utterances in order to evaluate its reliability. Such analysis is very useful and may substitute the use of the polygraph. The methodology is based on a computer assisted cognitive behavioral therapy methodology (CBT). CBT was originally developed for psychological treatment (Burns, D. D. 1999), but it can also be used for personality characterizations. This methodology can also be used in finding witness' personality disturbances and evaluate the reliability of witnesses.

There is a demand that this type "legal language" should be a precise language. To assure accuracy, the linguistic analysis is performed at two levels: semantic and syntactic. The first stage is the semantic analysis. Here, the vocabulary of the sentence is checked. *Quantitative-semantics,* a term that was developed as a special purpose tool in linguistic analysis in the context of the *reality test* (a psychological test examining optimal reactions of the treated person to an external stimulus). *Quantitative-semantics* classifies the large amount of nouns, adjectives and adverbs in a scalable manner, according the intensity of the meaning of the word, for example: never, sometimes, ever, always; small, medium, big, large, huge; house, villa, and castle.

The requirement of supercomputers in this area is yet unknown. Generally, the approximation of the model is closer to reality according the confines of the resolution and the quantity of the used data. For vocabulary analysis, the quantity of the words and idioms in common contemporary language is in the order of few thousand words. Besides the number of words, the complication increases with the degree of the networking of the families of words.

Figure 13. The derivation/parsing tree of the sentence, "The best student is feeling awful", uses syntactical-grammatical rules defined by the BNF method

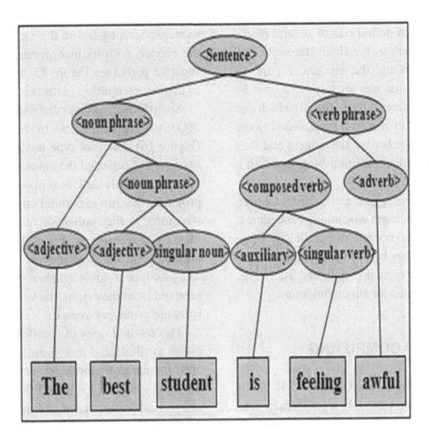

In the second stage, the grammatical analysis is performed. There might be a requirement of repeating the process according the obtained results. This repetition is about *o(1000)*o(100)*o(100)*o(10)* which is about $o(10^8)$ operations. If an operation unit is about 10^{-6} seconds, this means that the computation time is about 100 sec, or about one and a half minutes, too long for an online operation response. Therefore, the whole process justifies the need of a supercomputer.

5. Mathematical Language

Mathematical language is a language used by a relatively small exclusive group of scholars who invented it for the purpose of formalizing ideas which cannot be expressed otherwise. Sometimes a mystic interpretation is given to mathematical concepts for example to the *golden ratio*. In this context, a philosophical question was posed if mathematical statements are inventions or discoveries that existed before they were expressed by humans. Nevertheless, mathematics is hidden behind formulas, expressions, terms and theorems. This concealed information can be manipulated for the purposes of steganography. However, the general aim in the current case is not to hide information, but on the contrary, to discover it. Mathematical languages have various appearances such as linear streams of expression and two or more dimensional graphs and visualizations. Herein, an upgraded two dimensional visualization (Ophir and Gera 2008; Ophir D., 2011) is proposed whose third dimension is time.

The idea behind the presented mathematical idea lies in its *dynamical visualization,* namely as a clip or short film. In this spirit, several takes were performed on definitions of several mathematical terms such as the *limit,* the *sequence,* the *Rolle theorem* and the integral. Figure 12 dynamically demonstrates the term of a limit *by* the sequence of frames (a), (b), (c), (d) which can be continuously run as a film strip, showing the convergence of the chord to the tangent and thus develop mathematical intuition by presenting a simulation (Figure 14).

Simulations (Jiang, X., & Lai C. 2009) are time (and sometimes storage) consuming procedures, and being able to proceed in parallel by large amount of users may be beyond the limits of the possible power of regular computers. Therefore, this is a suitable area for supercomputers.

DISTRIBUTED COMPUTING

The distributed computing (Andrews, G. R. 2000) paradigm is based on dividing a program or data into parts and running those parts separately on available resources. There are approaches that consider distributed computing synonymous with cloud computing. Each computing module may be performed on a supercomputer, increasing the effectiveness of the methodology.

The relationship of distributed computing to steganography lies in the method of dividing the carrier, with its incorporated message, into separate parts (see Figure 15) which are treated as distinct computing platforms.

Such distributed computations (Andrews, G. R. 2000) are composed of two modules: *fork* and *join* (Figure 16). The *fork*-type module performs the *analysis.* A portion of the input and some computation work is divided into copies of computation programs that run in parallel on supercomputers, if required by the application resources (management). They are then partitioned into corresponding inputs and this yields the corresponding output. The *join*-type module *synthesizes* all the outputs received from the origin, the vertex and splitting from the same *fork-vertex.*

This methodology of parallel computing processes is illustrated in Figure 17. This example corresponds to hierarchical work performed on the input image of Figure 15. Some parts of the image are less important and the computation is performed on a coarse grid, whereas the detailed part of the image such as the face and the corresponding computations are performed on the finer grid.

Figure 14. Metamorphosis: The chord becomes a tangent

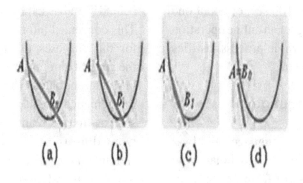

Figure 15. (a) Partitioning the picture into a coarse grid, focusing on the head (striped rectangle); (b) Fine-grid of the striped rectangle (a) is enlarged and refined. (The image is a private acquisition.)

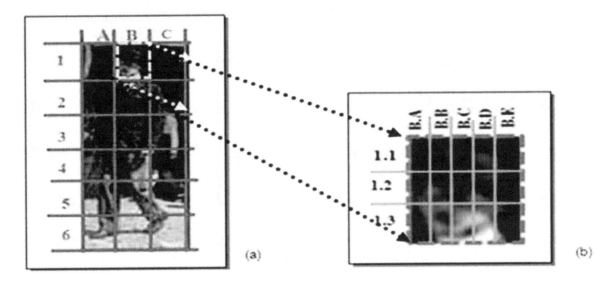

Figure 16. "Fork-Join" diagrams - the task of dividing and unifying the results. (The image is a private acquisition.)

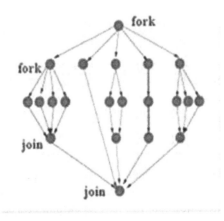

The relationship of distributed computing to steganography lies in the fact that the process of encoding and decoding hidden information in the sub-picture is less critical because, in general, the small file pieces of the grid are mostly unreadable and therefore, there is much less need to hide the encrypted message.

Distributed computation neutralizes the possibility of using steganography to appeal to the subconscious of the viewer, since only an unrecognizable part of the image is seen. This makes it is too difficult for the brain to reconstruct the object hidden in the full image.

The *join-vertices* aggregate the sub-images into one larger image that is more readable than the small ones. Managing the whole flow of the information coming into the *join-vertices* is complicated. The module performing the *join*-reconstruction must know the addresses and the linkages of the processes taking part in the distributed computation.

Figure 17. Fork-join diagram related to Figure 5, in which the rectangle-vertices represent the rectangles in Figure 5 (the image is a private acquisition)

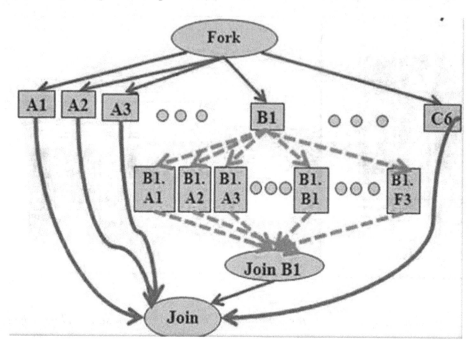

For example, the SETI (search for extraterrestrial intelligence) project (Stanford Project – http://setistars.org/) is a kind of distributed computation in which the members of the project individually supply one piece of the information. The project management superimposes the inputs into a global picture of the celestial map. Each individual member has no general vision about what is going on. Similarly, possessing one piece of information of the whole multi-image process does not convince the individual that this is part of a steganographic message. Therefore, the hidden information remains hidden.

The "Drop Box" service is an additional example of distributed computation, enabling an easier way to transmit data by using the shared space in the network. Such algorithms make it more difficult to keep track of suspicious material.

Multi Grid (MG) Method

The Multi Grid method was used primarily for solving partial differential equations (Brandt, A., 1977). This method can also be used for image processing treatment, performing various filtrations and connotations with the *big data* (Mayer-Schonberger & Cukier 2012).The idea behind using an MG is that in numerical analysis, the approximation of a function can be shown as a series of trigonometric functions with increasing periods and with their coefficients (Fourier transformations).

The MG iterative algorithm is based on the idea of performing smoothing on grids of various finesse (Figure 18) and transforming the corresponding values from finer grids to coarser grids (injection) and from coarser grids to finer grids (interpolation). Performing the smoothing-relaxation on grids of some degree of finesse corresponds to sweeping the error from a component function in the Fourier trans-

Figure 18. Two grids finer D_k and coarser D_{k-1}

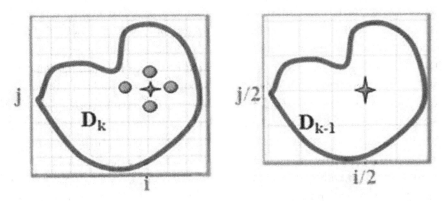

Figure 19. Formulas: a) Relaxation, b) Injection, c) Interpolation

$$a)\ U_{i,j}^k = \frac{1}{4}\left(U_{i-1,j}^k + U_{i+1,j}^k + U_{i,j-1}^k + U_{i,j+1}^k\right)$$

$$b)\ \quad U_{i/2,j/2}^{k-1} = U_{i,j}^k$$

$$c)\ \quad U_{i+1,j}^k = \frac{1}{2}\left(U_{i/2,j/2}^{k-1} + U_{i/2+1,j/2}^{k-1}\right)$$

formation with the period corresponding in its magnitude to the magnitude of the grid step.

The basic MG operations mentioned above are explained in Figure 19. *Interpolation* is generally enough for a bi-linear interpolation from coarse to fine grids in the points of the fine grid that don't overlap with the coarse grid points. *Relaxation* is an operation on one grid in which in each point, a received value is some kind of average of its neighbours. *Injection* is transforming a value from the fine grid to its counterpoint in the coarser grid, laying on the same place on the x-y coordinates system.

The multi-grid method suits the distribution properties such as working in parallel. It is possible to work on two neighbouring grids in parallel on different components in cloud systems. The supercomputer's contribution in running a multi grid programs lies in its abil-

ity to achieve higher resolutions and enabling users to receive results of higher precision in a reasonable computation time.

The applications of MG are varied. For example, wind tunnel in flight experimentation. Increasing computational power may significantly decrease the development time of aviation vessels.

OTHER ALTERANTIVES TO SUPERCOMPUTERS: nCUBE

nCUBE refers to the machine's ability to build an order-ten hypercube, supporting 1024 CPU's in a single machine. Some of the modules would be used strictly for input/output, which included the nChannel storage-control card, frame buffers, and the inter system card that allow nCUBEs to be attached to each other. At least one host board must be installed, acting as the terminal driver. It could also partition the machine into sub-cubes and allocate them separately to different users (Marlow S., 2013).

The address between two neighbors having the same edge differs by one bit only (Figure 20). This simplifies the connection between two neighboring processors. The advantages of the nCUBE concept lie in its modularity. An nCUBE is not a supercomputer. Its architecture is more complicated than that of supercomputer and its component CPUs are much slower than that of a common supercomputer. However, the whole system may compete successfully with super-computers. The various tasks of the system may be performed separately as in cloud computation by various subsystems (defined by the set of bits), representing the set of nCUBE components.

CONCLUSION

The use of steganography in an era of cloud computation is a mixed bag. Certain uses of steganography are difficult when using cloud computing such as subconscious uses when trying to hide an image within an image. However, overall, the level of difficulty in identifying "steganographed" material, and its decoding increases dramatically when using the packet method of cloud computing.

Cloud computing separates and distributes small parts of the original data, which impedes recognizing the hidden information. Messages that are divided into corresponding sub-messages become more difficult to detect. However, super-computers are helpful in overcoming that obstacle. This poses the question whether partitioning the message into very small pieces to be reconnected at the last computation stage is sufficient for ensuring that the data are undecipherable.

Progress in contemporary decoding, owing to the huge increased speed in computation, may require parallel progress in encoding the messages. The answer lies in combining both methods. The increased complexity of cloud computing, in addition to classical steganography, may serve as a suitable upgrade in creating more complex encoding and decoding processes.

The complexity of cryptography competes with the computation power represented by developing new paradigms such as cloud computing and by hardware developments represented by the supercomputers. Hence, there is a vicious circle, or more precisely, an additive feedback loop, in which the increasing speed of encryption motivates

Figure 20. An nCUBE of the 3rd order. Namely, each vertex is connected by the edges to three other vertices

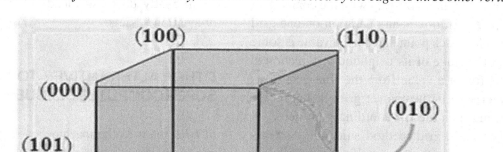

efforts to increase the speed of decoding by further developing suitable algorithms and by upgrading the infrastructure (methodology and hardware).

Supercomputers do not have to oppose *cloud-computing*. They both can become an integrated entity where the *cloud-computing* methodology is superimposed onto *supercomputers*. The beginning of this chapter alluded to the apparent competition between the two paradigms of supercomputing and cloud computing. We can envision that in the future, the strengths of both systems will undergo a complementary integration, exploiting the powerfulness of the supercomputers and optimally using their idle time. On this is the optimistic note, I would like to end the chapter.

REFERENCES

Andrews, G. R. (2000). *Foundations of multithreaded, parallel, and distributed programming*. Reading, MA: Addison-Wesley.

Aumann, R. J., & Furstenberg, H. (2004). *Findings of the committee to investigate the Gans-Inbal results on equidistant letter sequences in Genesis*. Retrieved from Center for Rationality, Discussion paper 364, http://www.ma.huji.ac.il/raumann/

Brandt, A. (1977). Multi-level adaptive solutions to boundary-value problems. *Mathematics of Computation*, *31*(138), 333–390. doi:10.1090/S0025-5718-1977-0431719-X

Brandt, A. (1977). Multi-level adaptive techniques (MLAT) for differential equations: Ideas and Software. In J. R. Rice (Ed.), *Mathematical software III* (pp. 273–318). New York: Academic Press. doi:10.1016/B978-0-12-587260-7.50015-7

Burns, D. D. (1999). *Feeling good*. New York: Avons Books, Harper-Collins Publishers.

Chappell, D. (2008). *A short introduction to cloud platforms*. Retrieved Aug. 20, 2008, from www.davidchapell.com

Cheddad, A., Condell, J., Curran, K., & McKevitt, P. (2009). Digital image steganography: Survey and analysis of current methods. *Signal Processing*, *90*(3), 727–752. doi:10.1016/j.sigpro.2009.08.010

Deavours, C. A., & Kruh, L. (1985). *Machine cryptography and modern cryptanalysis*. London: Artech House.

Fridrich, J. (2010). *Steganography in digital media: Principles, algorithms, and applications*. Cambridge, UK: Cambridge University Press.

Hayati, P., Potdar, V., & Chang, E. (2005). *A survey of steganographic and steganalytic tools for the digital forensic investigator*. Retrieved from http://www.pedramhayati.com/images/docs/survey_of_steganography_and_steganalytic_tools.pdf

Hideki, N., Michiharu, N., & Eiji, K. (2006). High-performance JPEG steganography using quantization index modulation in DCT domain. *Pattern Recognition Letters*, *27*(5), 455–461. doi:10.1016/j.patrec.2005.09.008

Hong, L. J., Masaaki, F., Yusuke, S., & Hitoshi, K. (2007). A data hiding method for JPEG 2000 coded images using modulo arithmetic. *Electronics and Communications in Japan, Part 3*, *90*(7), 37–46. doi:10.1002/ecjc.20286

Jiang, X., & Lai, C. (2009). *Numerical techniques for direct and large-eddy simulations*. Boca Raton, FL: CRC Press. doi:10.1201/9781420075793

Kundur, D., & Ahsan, K. (2003). *Practical internet steganography: Data hiding in IP*. Proc. Texas Wksp. Security of Information Systems.

Marlow, S. (2013). *Parallel and concurrent programming in Haskell: Techniques for multicore and multithreaded programming*. Sebastopol, CA: O'Reilly.

Mayer-Schonberger, V., & Cukier, K. (2012). *Big data: A revolution that will transform how we live, work, and think.* Boston: Hughton Mifflin Publishing Company.

McBride, B. T., Peterson, G. L., & Gustafson, S. C. (2005). A new blind method for detecting novel steganography. *Digital Investigation, 2*(1), 50–70. doi:10.1016/j.diin.2005.01.003

Mollin, R. A. (2003). *RSA and public-key cryptography.* Boca Raton, FL: Chapman & Hall/CRC.

Ophir, D. (1970). *Language for processes of numerical solutions to differential equations.* (Unpublished Doctoral Dissertation). Dept. of App. Math., The Weizmann Institute of Science, Rehovot, Israel.

Ophir, D. (2010). Walking language recognition. In *Proceedings of the Fourth Conference of the International Society for Gesture Studies* (pp.340-342). European University Viadrina.

Ophir, D. (2011). DDDL: A descriptive, didactic and dynamic programming language. In *Proceedings of Israeli-Polish Mathematical Meeting.* Łódź, Poland: Academic Press.

Ophir, D. (2013). Computerized legilinguistics and psychology - Overriding the polygraph's drawbacks. In *Proceedings of Eighth Conference on Legal Translation, Court Interpreting and Comparative Legilinguistics.* Poznań, Poland: Academic Press.

Ophir, D. (2013). An analysis of palindromes and n-nary tracts' frequencies applied in a genomic sequence. In *Proceedings of International Conference on Integrative Biology Summit.* Publishing OMICS Group, Inc.

Ophir, D., & Dekel, D. (2013). SNOBOL-Tone - The sound pattern-matching programming language. In *Proceedings of 2013 Speech Processing Conference at the Afeka Academic College of Engineering.* Academic Press.

Ophir, D., & Gera, A. E. (2005). Analysis of n-nary tract frequency in the genome. *Journal of Bioinformatics, 6*(2), 149–161.

Ophir, D., & Gera, A. E. (2008). Calculus: The dynamical and visual description. In *Proceedings of the 12th World Multi-Conference on Systemic, Cybernetics and Informatics* (Vol. 7, p. 141). Orlando, FL: Academic Press.

Ophir, D., Yahalom, A., Pinhasi, G. A., & Kopylenko, M. (2012). A combined variational and multi-grid approach for fluid dynamics simulation. In *Proceedings of the ICE - Engineering and Computational Mechanics* (pp.3–14). Academic Press. doi:10.2514/6.2006-695

Petitcolas, F. A. P., Anderson, R. J., & Kuhn, M. G. (1999). Information hiding: A survey. *Proceedings of the IEEE, 87*(7), 1062–1078. doi:10.1109/5.771065

Qingzhong, L., Andrew, H. S., Bernardete, R., Mingzhen, W., Zhongxue, C., & Jianyun, X. (2008). Image complexity and feature mining for steganalysis of least significant bit matching steganography. *Information Sciences, 178*(1), 21–36. doi:10.1016/j.ins.2007.08.007

Stanford Project. (n.d.). *Investigating the cosmos.* Retrieved from http://setistars.org/

Szczypiorski, K. (2003). *Steganography in TCP/IP networks: State of the art and a proposal of a new system - HICCUPS.* Paper presented at the Institute of Telecommunications Seminar. New York, NY.

Warren, P., & Streeter, M. (2013). *Cyber crime & warfare: All that matters.* London: Hodder & Stoughton.

Watson, J. D. (2003). *DNA: The secret of life.* New York: Random House.

Winztum, D. (1980). *The additional dimension, about the two-dimensional writing of the Genesis.* Jerusalem: The Organization of Bible Research Press.

Zax, R., & Adelstein, F. (2009). FAUST: Forensic artefacts of uninstalled steganography tools. *Digital Investigation*, 6(1-2), 25–28. doi:10.1016/j.diin.2009.02.002

Zhang, X., & Wang, S. (2004). Vulnerability of pixel-value differencing steganography to histogram analysis and modification for enhanced security. *Pattern Recognition Letters*, 25(3), 331–339. doi:10.1016/j.patrec.2003.10.014

Zoran, D. (2004). *Information hiding: Steganography & steganalysis.* George Mason University, Department of Computer Science.

Zumbush, G. (2003). *Parallel multilevel methods: Adaptive mesh refinement and load balancing.* Wiesbaden, Germany: B.G. Teubner Verlag/GWV fachverlage GmbH.

ADDITIONAL READING

Amira, A., & Butmana, A. Crochemorec. M., Landaue, G. M. & Schapsg. M. (2003). "Two-dimensional pattern matching with rotations" from www.ElsevierComputerScience.com, Theoretical Computer Science 314 (2004) 173-187.

Giorgino, T., & de Fabritiis, G. (2010), "Distributed computing as a virtual supercomputer: tool to run and manage large-scale BOINC simulations", January. (http://boinc.berkeley.edu/rboinc.pdf)

Linthicum, D. (2011). Why supercomputers will live only in the cloud. Cloud Computing, November 23. From http://www.infoworld.com/d/cloud-computing/why-supercomputers-will-live-only-in-the-cloud-179773

Nimbix, (2012). Simple, Scalable Cloud Batch Processing, Academic Press, New York, from http://www.nimbix.net/cloud-supercomputing/

Provos, N., & Honeyman, P. (2002). "Detecting Steganographic Content on the Internet." from Proceedings of the Network and Distributed System Security Symposium (NDSS), San Diego, CA, February 6-8. Internet Society, Washington, D.C.)

Trottenberg, U., Oosterlee, C., & Schüler, A. (2001). *Multigrid.* New York: Academic Press.

Vedic-Words. (2013), "Cloud Based Supercomputers – the Next Big thing" http://www.cloudswave.com/blog/cloud-based-supercomputers-the-next-big-thing/

KEY TERMS AND DEFINITIONS

Advertising: The process of making a product, idea, or other property positively known to a wide part of the community.

Big Data: Tremendous quantities of data, exceeding the limits of the capacity of conventional data base systems. In this context, the synergism is different than the integration of the parts. For example, the standard deviation of a certain amount of data is not the average standard deviation of its subsets. Big Data may be the result of increasing the resolution of the problem, namely in the scalability of the problems. For example, data increases in image processing in medicine, crime, astrophysics; in simulations and in many other areas. Supercomputers suit the manipulations of big data,

Bachus Nauer Form (BNF): A formal concise method defining syntax of a language. Such definition is essential in the algorithmic parsing of a sentence.

Cognitive Behavioral Therapy (CBT): A method used to evaluate and treat psychological personality disturbances. It is based on searching for "distortion thoughts" expressed in the spoken language, and substituting them by corrected ones. There are about ten classes of distortion thoughts, which are generally based on using superlatives in various contexts, indicating some over sensitivity.

Cloud Computing: A methodology for computing on scattered shared computer resources (computing power, storage, software packages, internet facilities, etc.). The consumer of the computing resource is redirected by the operating system to a suitable available resource. In such an environment, the end user is free to keep computer resources for his own. All the user's needs are supplied by the network in an optimal cost/performance by the whole community.

Cryptography: The process of encrypting and decrypting data to prevent the data to be freely accessed. The encryption and the decryption should be synchronized modules.

Cyber War (Warfare): A struggle between two groups of computers systems where ones group strives to harm the computer systems of the other group and defend itself at the same time.

Data Mining: The theory and methodology of searching through large amount of unknown data for a common denominator, or conversely, looking for some irregularity or exceptions in the data.

Decryption: The opposite of encryption, using an algorithm to reconstruct the original message from the encrypted data.

Distributed Computing: A lower scale form of cloud computing. It is performed for organizations as a specially oriented field such as databases.

Genesis: The first book in the Pentateuch which is part of the Bible.

Genome: The genome comprises the entire DNA found in the cell's nucleus. The genome is comprised of nucleotides and they are responsible for transmitting the heritable properties of the species. There are four types of nucleotides that form sequences of millions of nucleotides that represent a huge number of properties and variety of characteristics.

Image Processing: Method of removing from a picture the so called noise i.e. the pixels which do not belong inherently to the picture scenario in reality. Those pixels were planted in the image during the process of digitally transforming the picture. There are special filtering methods that can clean the image.

Multi-Level-Adaptive Technique (MLAT): Solving discrete problems using Multi-Grids or other multi scaling problems, adaptively.

Morphological Image Processing: Selective, iteratively removing pixels according their intensity, i.e. according to the outlines in the image. This processing is efficient in edge detection processes.

Multi Grid Method: A method of solving discrete (mainly two dimensional) problems, using a set of grids covering the same domain but with different grid resolutions.

Parallel Computing: Method of increasing the throughput of running computer programs by performing some computations in parallel instead of in sequence. Such parallelization may be done automatically if the computations are independent one from the other, namely one computation is not dependent on the result of other computations. The parallelization can be the copying of one operation on various data in the same time, or performing different operations in the same time (Marlow S. 2013).

Sentence Parsing: The hierarchal dissecting of a sentence to pieces according their function in the language. In natural languages there are sentence components.

Simulation: A model of a reality. Sometimes the reality is not deterministic. In these cases the no determinism is imitated by so called pseudo-random numbers, generated by the computer, giving the impression of randomness (Monte Carlo method). There are various types of simulations – Mechanical modeling of mechanical components and their mutual movement; Electronic modeling simulates the functionality of electronic devices such as a transistor, resistor, capacitor or central processor etc.; Social simulations to foresee social movements, demographic situation, traffic; Physical modeling simulates events in the physical world such as fission and nuclear effects; Mathematical approximating numerically the analytical solutions.

Steganography: (in Greek steganos means protected) A theory of hiding real information by implanting it unnoticeably within data or by transforming it to other meaningful but misleading, or misinforming exposed information.

Supercomputer: A computer having high-order qualities especially high throughput. These qualifications are very useful for assembling huge amounts of data, which are encountered in domains such as genomics, and nuclear simulations to predict the fission processes, for analyzing homeland cyber-security, etc. There are various computer architectures supporting supercomputers, such as CRAY – array-computers and n-Cubes which consist of small processors connected in a network as an n-dimensional hyper-cube.

Watermark: Information implanted in other information, which cannot be removed. Watermarks are sometimes used to designate the ownership of the information.

Chapter 12
Cloud Computing:
Future of the Past

Manzoor Ahmed Khan
Technische Universität Berlin, Germany

Fikret Sivrikaya
Technische Universität Berlin, Germany

ABSTRACT

The growth pattern of mobile devices and wireless network technologies leads to revolutionized communication markets with constant advancements (e.g., partly realized 4G and yet-awaited 5G wireless networks, content centric networking, and mobile cloud computing). From the thin-client paradigm of the early computing history, where the bulk of the computing power was on the server side, we have witnessed a rapid transformation to powerful mobile end-user devices with ubiquitous connectivity. The cloud-computing paradigm is now promising to bridge those two ends in order to combine the best of both worlds. This chapter presents: 1) basic concepts of cloud computing in examining the different perspectives of stakeholders in the cloud market, 2) survey of existing approaches and solutions, 3) applications of cloud computing, 4) architectural approaches to cloud computing, including traditional and mobile cloud architectures, and 5) an overview of the related Software-Defined Networking and Network Function Virtualization concepts.

1. MOTIVATION TO USE CLOUD COMPUTING

The main motivation for the use of cloud computing instead of self-hosted infrastructures, hardware and software is that it brings down the costs, offers increased stability and is accessible from everywhere. Companies do not have to buy expensive hardware or worry about carrying out heavy tasks; they simply rent the hardware or al-

locate the computation tasks to machines in the cloud. After finishing their computation, they no longer have to pay for it (Agrawal, Abbadi, Das, & Elmore, 2011). However, reduction in costs is not the only driving force of cloud computation. It is envisioned that cloud computing will drastically change the information technology by offering businesses the opportunity to attain more gains in much faster and more effective ways. We can summarize those gains as follows:

DOI: 10.4018/978-1-4666-7461-5.ch012

Copyright © 2015, IGI Global. Copying or distributing in print or electronic forms without written permission of IGI Global is prohibited.

- **Availability:** Cloud services can be accessed through the Internet, which may be translated to connectivity everywhere and every time. This eradicates the need for large storage and compute services to be available on device; rather, a user may enjoy these services by associating to cloud through a simple user device even when he / she is mobile. It is worth highlighting here that most cloud architectures feature a broad band of backups and redundant storage, so data loss is no longer a threat.

- **Scalability:** Data and application resources can be quickly provisioned when and where they are needed.

- **Less Maintenance:** Given the fact that the consumer is just renting services, where hardware, application, and bandwidth are managed by the cloud provider, the consumer of cloud services incur no maintenance costs. Also due to the centralized structure of the cloud's data center, it is easier to handle defective hardware for the technicians resulting in even lower deficits.

- **Cost Effective:** Most of the business models follow pay-per-use model and the customer only pays for what he needs or uses. This makes cloud architectures and the process of outsourcing into the clouds even more attractive. It paves the path for new business models, where the stakeholders optimize their profits and resource utilization on smaller time quanta and more dynamic settings. Clearly, these models result in reduced incurring costs for consumers, whereas the cloud providers find their profit windows in optimal resource utilization. Due to the scalability, customers can easily upgrade their rented resources whenever they need additional storage capacity, performance, etc. (Otto, Stanojevic, & Laoutaris, 2012).

- **Facilitating Content Centric Vision:** As content-centric networks send named packets of data through the network, a new kind of caching, independent from the application layer, is created (Arianfar, Nikander, & Ott, 2010). This requires decreased latency, which the cloud achieves by routing the data directly where they are required. Often, when working on distributed clouds where it is not obvious where the information are stored, the latency increases by routing the data - in the worst-case through the whole network of the data center. In combination with content-centric services, this could mean that the services or applications get pushed onto servers which have the best connection or lowest latency or load to the customer who is requiring them. In a way, the cloud is re-organizing itself depending on the requests and needs of its customers.

- **Hosting Network Centric Services:** Network-centric services are also predestined to be used in datacenters, as they require a lot of data through either a local network or the Internet. As each request has its latencies, it greatly improves the overall experience owing to the choice of connectivity to different systems with better speed. For example, by being part of the same network, possibly a cloud-intranet, the quality of these services and applications increases rapidly.

Although cloud-based services offer a broad variety of features for common users (non-technicians), most users may not be able to make use of them. Therefore, a number of tools are developed to increase both the ease and the joy of use. These tools provide user-friendly interfaces, which resulted in millions of users using cloud based services.

2. CLOUD COMPUTING: BASIC CONCEPTS

Cloud computing are commonly categorized in three functional modes; namely, 1) public cloud, 2) private cloud, 3) hybrid cloud. In this section, the details of cloud modes are provided and the roles of different stakeholders in the cloud-computing environment are discussed.

2.1 Cloud Computing Modes

When looking for a reliable and best-fitting cloud network solution, companies (consumers) have to choose between several strategies. Depending on their future needs and business plans, they can either deploy their cloud network architecture as private, focusing on a reliable and exclusive usage of the network without any external access, or as public, which is relatively more exposed to security threats. Public clouds may also be acquired by enterprises, which simply manage and coordinate the cloud for their own customers, who in the end use and pay for the performance or capacity. Additional to these two approaches, there is a hybrid cloud - as the name already infers it combines the features of both public and private clouds.

2.1.1 Public Cloud

Public Cloud is designed for providers who sell or rent out resources. In contrast to Private Clouds, the Public Cloud does not confine itself to internal applications of a single enterprise or department but is open to multiple independently-acting users (Heckel, 2010). The provider either offers a so called "Exclusive Cloud", in which both the provider and the consumer determine fixed conditions; or the provider decides to deploy an Open Cloud with, e.g., elastic resources for the consumer. Well-known examples for public clouds are Amazon Web Services (AWS), the Google Cloud Platform, or the Microsoft Windows Azure Cloud (Lo, Yang, Kandula, & Zhang, 2010). They

offer applications, storage, and other resources to the public either free or on a pay-per-use basis, which can often be seen as an extension to their primary services. For example, on Google Drive - currently one gets 5 GB of storage with a free Google account ("Google Drive", 2013). This should suffice for most private users, but if companies start to store their data in the cloud, they most likely need more space and are obliged to pay per-month for the added storage capacity. Amazon Web Services do not only offer storage but also for example a "Simple Queue Service" - SQS - which allows the application to use it as a database or short-term storage for a small amount of data, which can be retrieved by another application (Amazon Simple Queue Service", 2013). A huge drawback of public clouds is that most often the information stored are not secure enough for confidential data of business users, since the cloud provider theoretically has access to this data.

2.1.2 Private Cloud

Private clouds are for a company's internal use only (Karpagam, & Parkavi, 2011). They can be hosted within an own, self-managed data center or in an external one. Private clouds increase the security and confidentiality of stored information, as solely the company decides who can access or change the data. Another positive aspect of private clouds is that the company can grant limited access to business partners, which is most often realized through a virtual private network (VPN) or in an intranet. A private cloud may range from smaller systems called "Departmental Cloud", utilized by users within one department, up to huge "Enterprise Clouds", which serve users across departments at possibly different locations (IBM Global Technology Services, 2010).

2.1.3 Hybrid Cloud

In a hybrid cloud, both aspects of private and public clouds are combined. The U.S. National

Figure 1. Hybrid Cloud: A generic depiction

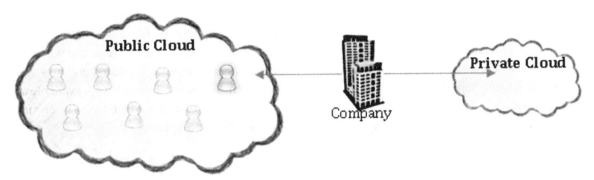

Institute of Standards and Technology (NIST) defines a hybrid cloud as follows:

The cloud infrastructure is a composition of two or more distinct cloud infrastructures (private, community, or public) that remain unique entities, but are bound together by standardized or proprietary technology that enables data and application portability (e.g., cloud bursting for load balancing between clouds). (Mell & Grance, 2011)

One motivation of using a hybrid cloud is to keep all confidential information and data in the private cloud architecture, protected from external unauthorized access. Performance-heavy tasks are then executed on the whole hybrid cloud when the own infrastructure is insufficient. In Figure 1, we depict the general structure of hybrid clouds.

2.2 Cloud Computing Stakeholders

In this section, we discuss cloud computing from the perspective of the following stakeholders: 1) cloud provider, 2) cloud-customer, 3) end user, and 4) mobile operator.

2.2.1 Cloud Provider Perspective

Cloud provider focuses on dynamic management of hosted services (*aaS) to guarantee availability, reliability and related quality aspects through automation in order to optimize the overall resource utilization. The cloud provider also aims at the flawless and economical operation of its infrastructure. The infrastructure has to be reliable, scalable and easy to use for its users i.e., the customers of the cloud provider. Therefore, the cloud provider implements an architecture that mainly maintains and protects itself automatically with only little effort for his employees. This ensures the economical operation of the system and reduces the probability of human failures affecting the infrastructure. The cloud provider uses software and hardware components such as firewalls, intelligent load balancers (James & Verma, 2012) and redundantly distributed file systems (Moritz, 2010). This enables the cloud provider to let the infrastructure work continuously and flawlessly even if the infrastructure is being attacked, when the load increases unexpectedly or in case of hardware and system failures.

2.2.2 Cloud Broker Perspective

The cloud broker is an entity that manages the user, performance, and delivery of cloud services and negotiates the relationships between Cloud Providers and Cloud Consumers. It is very similar to a travel agency, which provides a single consistent interface to multiple differing providers. This dictates that cloud computing evolve to one-to-many ecosystem with cloud broker playing the key role. The cloud brokers should be capable of:

- **Service Intermediation:** managing access to cloud services, identity management, performance reporting, and enhanced security.
- **Service Arbitrage:** making choices between available services e.g., selecting the best according to consumers' criteria.
- **Service Aggregation:** combining and integrating multiple services into a new service.

However, security, trust management, application development with cloud centric design principles, etc. are some of the challenges to be met when it comes to the realization of cloud broker and federated clouds markets.

2.2.3 Cloud Customer Perspective (Enterprise)

The customer of a cloud services needs to rely on an infrastructure that is fast, cheap and that provides a highly elastic situational adjustment of the rented resources as well as a "pay-as-you-go" accounting system. These properties enable the customers of a cloud provider to develop and build on business models, which include the possibility of unexpectedly increasing numbers of users or an unpredictable change of load of his resources. Relying on this infrastructure, the customer is able to scale his systems in a variable way without the necessity of buying new or deactivating running hardware resources when the load of his applications are changing. While using his provider's load balancing software, the customer always pays for only the resources he uses and needs.

2.2.4 End User Perspective

The end user of a cloud service usually wants quick, easy and platform independent access to

his data and desired applications independent from his current location, while the network behind should be transparent (Seruwagi, 2012), since the end user takes no interest how and where his data and applications are located and how they are driven. The user relies on always available applications and resources which has to be ensured by his service provider.

2.2.5 Mobile Operator Perspective

Mobile operator is an important entity in terms of communication, bandwidth, QoS, location dependence and costs. If a user uses his mobile device or even an UMTS/LTE connection on his computer, the mobile operator has to take care of the connection's reliability and quality. Mobile operators usually limit the bandwidth to the users as well as the amount of transferrable data with high-speed since the traffic is the main matter of expense to the mobile operator. In Figure 2, we pictorially depict the positions of different stakeholders in the cloud paradigm.

2.3 Basic Components of Cloud Computing

In the following we first describe the general architecture and then go more into the detailed description of different layers of the cloud offered as services. While most of the end users know Software as a Service (SaaS), e.g., Dropbox, a cloud-based storage service to share files ("About Dropbox", 2013) or Google Docs, a cloud service which facilitates real time collaborative document editing ("Docs, Sheets, and Slides", 2013), only few end users are familiar with the concepts of Platform as a Service (PaaS) and Infrastructure as a Service (IaaS), which are used mostly by cloud application providers and companies. How these different services work and what they contain is detailed below.

Figure 2. Interplay of cloud stakeholders

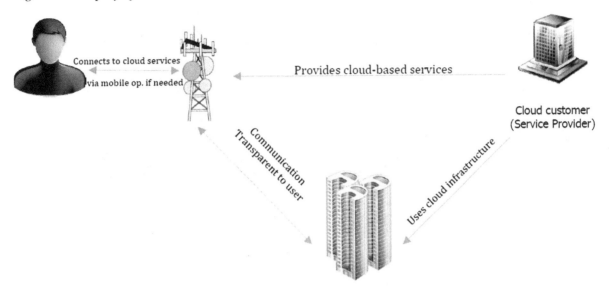

2.3.1 General Architecture

The general architecture of a cloud consists of multiple entities. Its basic interest is to create a dynamic and intelligent environment, focusing on the following four properties: transparency, scalability, monitoring and security. Transparency on the one side stands for simply not letting the end user know how it's implemented on the provider's side, but also for instance in order to apply transparent load-balancing i.e., handling the load and distributing tasks independently from the end user. Scalability is very important as the consumers' amount and required data is growing continuously. Regarding the current trends, cloud-based business application services are expected to grow from $13 billion in 2011 to $32 billion in 2016 (Biscotto et al., 2012). Therefore, the architecture must be expandable without interrupting the consumer's usage. To achieve intelligent monitoring, the architecture must be able to track the usage of resources by multiple consumers and the load of many servers, and to depend behavior deviating from the norm and react to it properly. As all information is stored in the cloud, security obviously is also an important aspect of every cloud

infrastructure. Not only the network/application layer security, but also all entry points into the data centers have to be secured properly. In Figure 3, we show general architecture of cloud setup.

2.3.2 Infrastructure as a Service (IaaS)

A cloud usually consists of a huge set of machines that are often located on geographically different places and even on different continents. The architecture of a cloud's infrastructure includes the location independent integration of different data centers by linking the datacenters through multiple, preferably tier-1 carriers, such as Level-3, AT&T and XO Communications ("AS Ranking", 2013) in order to ensure the availability and to lower the latency between the data centers. The infrastructure, or "cloud foundation" handles the linking of contributing machine's resources in order to use the resources independently from their actual location and dynamically regarding the amount of needed resources. Within the infrastructure, a cloud provider offers elastic virtual machines (Infrastructure as a Service – IaaS) which have to be administered and configured by the customer

Figure 3. Cloud Architecture

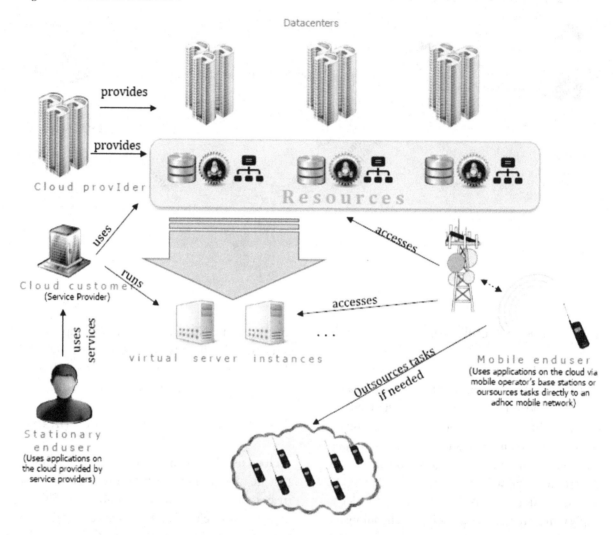

where the customer himself can decide which services run on his machines.

2.3.3 Platform as a Service (PaaS)

For customers who simply don't have enough capacity to perform their tasks on their own systems, some cloud providers offer their platforms. These platforms come with an API how to use them, to simply outsource these complex calculations into the "cloud" to get quicker and cheaper results, as adding the capacity to own systems may be expensive. If the platform rented from the provider is scalable, the consumer can simply extend their capabilities if they need more power and don't have to pay for it all the time - useful for customers who do not execute performance-heavy tasks regularly.

2.3.4 Software as a Service (SaaS)

Multiple kinds of software are also offered as service. This is useful for customers who don't need to use their own software, but still either have to perform heavy calculation tasks without owning the needed capacity themselves, or simply want to have the reliability of the cloud with backups

Figure 4. Cloud-Service usage by stakeholder

	IaaS	PaaS	SaaS
Cloud Provider	provides	provides	./.
Cloud Customer	uses	uses	provides
End user	uses transparently	uses transparently	uses

taken care of. All lower layers are transparent to the customer - this is of course again due to the need for scalability. If the amount of tasks for the rented software-access grows the cloud provider may shift it to a different data center or system without any interruption of the consumer. In a best-case scenario, the consumer would not even notice this; he may only notice an increase in the software's performance. A simplistic relationship can be viewed in the Figure 4.

2.4 Mobility Aspects

Mobile cloud computing is a special form of cloud computing. It assumes the end user to be a mobile subscriber, i.e., a customer of a cellular operator who uses a cellular network through a mobile device. Mobile cloud computing becomes more and more relevant since mobile applications has become more powerful over the past few years. Due to insufficient finite energy and low capacity for storage as well as low computation power, a mobile cloud can be a solution.

2.4.1 Traditional Clouds

Traditional clouds are usually public clouds that consist of many servers or even several data centers that are connected to each other and that provide their resources collectively to its users. The traditional cloud forces the provider to take care especially of its elasticity and failover strate-

gies. The cloud can be used by any device such as stationary and mobile computers.

2.4.2 Mobile Clouds

Within the scope of this work, we differentiate between three proposed types of mobile clouds. The first is the most common type where a mobile device uses a remote cloud over the Internet (e.g. via 3G) in order to use remote services and applications. The second type is a mobile cloud that consists of several mobile devices that are connected e.g. within an adhoc-network in order to distribute computing tasks or to widen the bandwidth. The last one is an approach by Satyanarayanan where the mobile device offloads the workload to a local computer (called cloudlet), e.g., via Wi-Fi that in turn connects to a remote cloud in order to outsource bigger computation tasks (Satyanarayan, Bahk, Caceres, & Davies, 2009).

2.4.3 Federated Clouds

Cloud federation is basically the process of integrating cloud resources from different clouds. It allows a cloud service provider to dynamically outsource resources to other cloud providers based on the resource demands from them. Cloud federation is an important aspect and we already provided a brief discussion in earlier section under the title Hybrid Clouds.

2.4.4 Service Level Agreements (SLA)

These are contracts between different stakeholders in the cloud computing paradigm e.g., between cloud provider and consumer, between two cloud providers, SLA is an agreed document between the stakeholders over service quality and other relevant parameters involved in the relationship of the involved stakeholders. SLAs are usually in a human readable and static description format. However, there have been efforts to realize the concept of machine readable description of SLAs.

3. APPLICATIONS OF CLOUD COMPUTING

Cloud applications vary greatly, depending on the type of service. In what follows next, we detail a few applications of the cloud computing.

3.1 Application on a Cloud

A customer who wants to use the infrastructure of a cloud directly rents resources from the cloud provider. Thereby he usually gets those in the form of virtual servers. The amount of resources assigned to those "elastic" machines can be adjusted whenever it is necessary, i.e. also while running. This enables the customer to react spontaneously on load peaks and the usual variance of usage of his services that are running on those servers. An example use-case for cloud infrastructures are big websites with millions of visitors daily, such as eBay or Amazon. Those websites rely on a cloud infrastructure especially to be able to handle the load variance depending on the daytime or time of the year. Peaks have to be compensated, which can be done at the simplest using a cloud infrastructure. In addition, not used resources during times of low-load can be leased by other users.

3.2 Cloud Platform Applications

The cloud provider offers computing resources and related APIs in order to enable the user to use its computing resources. We distinguish between four types of platform-use in cloud systems. The first one covers add-on development facilities. Using them, a user is able to customize existing SaaS-applications. Therefore a customer commonly needs their developers and users to purchase licenses on SaaS-applications on which the own application is based. The second type that we consider refers to stand-alone development environments. These environments provide its users, i.e. the cloud provider's customers, a generalized development environment. The next type is the application-delivery-only environment, which are focused on security and on-demand scalability. The last type, open platform as a service - as a sub-type of PaaS, provides open source software to enable the customers to run their applications. Depending on the platform provider, the customer is able to use any set of fundamentals, e.g. operating system or programming languages, in order to enable him to deploy his applications as freely as possible. An example for a PaaS-platform is the Google App Engine. Hereby, Google provides a platform in order to let its users develop and host web applications (Beimborn & Wenel, 2011) on Google's server infrastructure. Therefore Google offers a variety of programming languages such as Python and Java. Using the Google App Engine, a user is able for instance to access web contents, send Mails or manipulate images. There are many providers for cloud platforms.

3.3 Cloud-Based Software

Cloud-based software includes any kind of application running in the cloud, where the cloud infrastructure is transparent to the application's users. This is the level which is understood as the "cloud" by most users. Examples are storage applications such as Dropbox or Skydrive, collaboration tools for office use like Microsoft Office-Online or Google Docs and even games which are running using cloud resources, for instance the NVIDIA Grid, that is using streaming technologies to transfer the processed graphic data to its users with a relative low latency.

3.4 Mobile Cloud Applications and Approaches

Mobile cloud computing offers various new possibilities. One interesting type of application is the commerce sector. The ease of transactions and independence of a stationary device enable the users participate in the growing eCommerce sector. Therefore the providers of commerce platforms offer applications that usually only view information to the user that is processed on their server infrastructure, i.e. in the cloud. As proposed by Yang, Pan, Shen (Bao, 2010) the client can consist of only a simple UI and an HTTP-interface in order to transfer the data while the data and requests are processed in the cloud, so the workload on the mobile device decreases. Another application is mobile healthcare. Doukas writes: "*[…] the pervasive and ubiquitous access to healthcare data is considered essential for the proper diagnosis and treatment procedure. Cloud Computing is a model for enabling convenient, on-demand network access to a shared group of configurable computing resources (e.g., networks, servers, storage, applications, and services) that can be rapidly provisioned and released with minimal management effort or service provider interaction*" (Doukas et al., 2010). These are only a few examples of the possibilities for mobile cloud applications.

4. ARCHITECTURAL APPROACHES

Regarding traditional and mobile cloud computing, there is a wide variety of architectural solutions. We regard several approaches for both, traditional and mobile cloud computing.

4.1 Traditional Cloud Computing Architecture

Especially for traditional cloud systems, there are many solution approaches. Hereby we differentiate between higher infrastructure services, computational services and distributed storage architectures.

4.1.1 Distributed Storage Architectures

In order to provide flawless scalability of a user's systems in terms of storage capacity, for many users it will not be sufficient to store all data on the same location of a cloud. Therefore a cloud provider implements a storage architecture that allows distributing the storage of data transparently and efficiently within the cloud network. One solution is the Google File System (GFS). It was developed and is used by Google and optimized for huge amounts of data and a high data throughput while providing a high fault tolerance due to data redundancy and allowing a high performance to a large number of clients (Ghemawat et al., 2003). An alternative to that is the open-source Hadoop Distributed File System, which is very similar to GFS. The difference is a dedicated server ("NameNode") that stores the meta-data of the stored information (Shvachko et al., 2010). Such architectures allow a provider to reliably and efficiently store huge amounts of data.

4.1.2 Computational Services

When it comes to computational distribution, a cloud provider needs to implement a technology that allows simultaneous computation of a single task that has been splitted into many smaller tasks which again can be computed by different processors simultaneously. In order make this possible, there are several solutions, e.g. MapReduce. MapReduce has been developed for processing huge amounts of data with many machines at the same time by splitting (mapping) the task into smaller tasks, letting these be processed independently and then merging (reducing) the interim results in the end.

4.1.3 Higher Infrastructure Services

Higher infrastructure services are services running on a cloud in order to provide high-level solutions for rather specific problems. One example is a distributed database management system that allows to store and read data in a redundant way in order to ensure reliability and processing speed, such as Google BigTable.

4.2 Mobile Cloud Computing Architecture

Mobile cloud computing focuses on various aspects, and the architecture of a mobile cloud depends on the problem or task that the mobile cloud is supposed to solve.

As proposed by Huerta-Canepa and Lee, a virtual cloud computing platform can be established such that, if the user is at a stable location and executes a task, an application is intercepted and virtual cloud's resources are used. In order to handle the communication and the usage of resources, several managers have to be implemented for launching and intercepting the application, monitoring of available and used resources, synchronization of contextual information, and sending / managing jobs (Huerta-Canepa & Lee, 2010).

Huang, Zhang and Luo propose a new mobile cloud framework called "MobiCloud". While treating mobile devices as service nodes within an adhoc network, the authors also regard security issues and risk management. In their approach, a mobile node can leverage hardware farms on a cloud to augment its computing capabilities while a new service will be implemented: "virtual

trusted and provisioning domain (VTaPD)" are used to isolate information flows belonging to different security domains using programmable router technologies.

A mobile cloud architecture utilizes a non-mobile entity ("cloudlet") in order to offload the device's workload. The cloudlet may be located, for instance, in a wireless network and connected to a remote cloud. The main motivation to use cloudlets is that there are minimal additional security and trust issues, since wireless providers already see all traffic from its subscribers. Also it eases the billing procedure. Using such a cloudlet enables a user to lower the energy consumption as well as the workload of his mobile device (Bahl, 2012).

5. SOFTWARE DEFINED NETWORKING (SDN)

It was the operating system virtualization that enabled ubiquitous computing, storage platform, and elastic computing. Similarly the advancements in data communications like IP, MPLS, and in mobile communications like 4G/LTE enabled telecommunications operators to virtualize their network resources. However, commercial network elements come with their management interfaces, which allow operators to configure these devices. Recall that the network architectures typically comprise of data plane and control plane, where the control plane implements the protocols to guide the data plane. In distributed control plane settings, the control planes interact with each other to construct network paths. However, when it comes to the centralized control plane setting, the centralized controller takes the responsibility of constructing network paths in different network segments. With diminishing costs of raw and elastic computing power, it was perceived that such processing power might be harnessed to run logically centralized control plane. This vision was realized by the engineers from Stanford University, who came up with OpenFlow protocol. The architecture of OpenFlow protocol typically focuses on devices containing only data planes, which would execute the commands from a logically centralized entity. The OpenFlow protocol was commercially supported by the Open Networking Foundation (ONF), which is now the central standardization authority for Software Defined Networking (SDN).

SDN basically decouples the network control from forwarding plane and provides programmatic interfaces. More generally, implementing the SDN vision enables global control of network through logical centralization of control plane functions. In SDN, network flows are controlled at global abstraction level rather than at individual device level.

OpenFlow concept enables changes in the flow table of Ethernet switches at runtime. The basis of this concept is relatively simple. An OpenFlow switch is an extended Ethernet switch, utilizing the approved concept of a flow table. On incoming packets with no matching entry in the flow table, the given switch forwards the packet to the OpenFlow controller. The incoming packet on the controller for non-matching packets is defined as packet in message. The connection between an OpenFlow switch and OpenFlow controller may be established over a secure SSL channel, which advocates the concept of separated control plane and data plane. The OpenFlow controller is aware of the network structure and therefore may define a proper rule for each incoming packet (McKeown, 2008). This rule contains an output port on which the switch forwards every packet with the given match and the rule may also contain further actions, i.e., rewriting the source and destination of the packet (IP & MAC-Address).

To realize this concept, the Open Networking Foundation has released several OpenFlow specifications defining a message protocol and the expected behavior of an OpenFlow switch. By now, several vendors such as Alcatel-Lucent,

Big Switch Networks, Brocade Communications, Arista Networks, NoviFlow, Cisco, Dell Force 10, Extreme Networks, IBM, Juniper Networks, Digisol, Larch Net- works, Hewlett-Packard, NEC, and MikroTik (OpenFlow, 2014) already distribute OpenFlow switches or at least have announced their plans of products supporting OpenFlow.

6. NETWORK FUNCTION VIRTUALIZATION (NFV)

Network Function Virtualization (NFV) uses standard IT virtualization technologies to consolidate many network equipment types onto industry standard high volume servers, switches and storage, which could be located in data centres, network nodes and in the end user premises. The consortium of various service providers created NFV with the aim of addressing the problems highlighted in the original NFV white paper (ETSI, 2012).

The key goals of the NFV Working Group include: 1) reduce equipment costs and power consumption, 2) improve time to market, 3) enable the availability of multiple applications on a single network appliance with the multi-version and multi-tenancy capabilities, and 4) encourage a more dynamic ecosystem through the development and use of software-only solutions.

All of these benefits can be derived from the use of commercial, off-the-shelf (COTS) hardware that can be purposed and repurposed for multiple telecom-related services that currently use proprietary hardware. NFV is taking the software defined networking (SDN) concept of the virtualization movement and adapting it to benefit the telecommunications application infrastructure (Frank Yue, 2013).

It is worth highlighting here that NFV is not dependent on SDN or the other way around, i.e., NFV may be implemented without SDN. However, the combination of these two solutions results in a great value.

7. CONCLUSION

The underlying concept of "cloud computing" may be as old as the early computing architectures with large mainframe computers and simple user terminals in the form of thin clients, but the recent technological advancements and trends have given rise to the proliferation of cloud computing as we know it today in new and powerful ways. From the hassle-free operation of large data centers or corporate ICT infrastructures to the development and deployment of auto-scaling web services and applications, cloud computing offers many benefits to both consumers and businesses of various scales.

This chapter introduced the concept of cloud computing, its components, applications, and architectural aspects. It also provided an overview of the stakeholders in the cloud market, with their corresponding perspectives to cloud computing. Software-Defined Networking (SDN) and Network Function Virtualization (NFV) concepts were covered as related technologies and enablers for both realization and utilization of cloud computing.

REFERENCES

Agrawal, D., Abbadi, A. E., Das, S., & Elmore, A. J. (2011). Database scalability, elasticity, and autonomy in the cloud. In *Proceedings of 16th international conference on Database systems for advanced applications*. Academic Press. doi:10.1007/978-3-642-20149-3_2

Amazon Simple Queue Service (Amazon SQS). (n.d.). Retrieved May 12, 2013 from: http://aws. amazon.com/de/sqs/

Arianfar, S., Nikander, P., & Ott, J. (2010). On content-centric router design and implications. In *Proceedings of the Re-Architecting the Internet Workshop*. AS Ranking. Retrieved February 12, 2013, from: http://as-rank.caida.org/

Bahl, P., Han, R. Y., Li, L. E., & Satyanarayanan, M. (2012). Advancing the state of mobile cloud computing. In *Proceedings of the Third ACM Workshop on Mobile Cloud Computing and Services* (pp. 21-28). ACM. doi:10.1145/2307849.2307856

Bao, X.-R. (2010). 3G based mobile internet in China. In *Proceedings of International Conference on Management and Service Science (MASS)*. Academic Press.

Beimborn, D., Miletzki, T., & Wenzel, S. (2011). Platform as a service (PaaS). *Business & Information Systems Engineering*, *3*(6), 381–384. doi:10.1007/s12599-011-0183-3

Biscotti, F., Natis, Y. V., Pezzini, M., Murphy, T. E., Malinverno, P., & Cantara, M. (2012). *Market trends: Platform as a service, worldwide, 2012-2016, 2H12 update*. Retrieved May 2, 2013, from: http://my.gartner.com/portal/server.pt?open=512&objID=202&&PageID=5553&mode=2&in_hi_userid=2&cached=true&resId=2188816

Docs, Sheets, and Slides. (n.d.). Retrieved February 22, 2013, from: https://support.google.com/drive/answer/49008

Doukas, C., Pliakas, T., & Maglogiannis, I. (2010). Mobile healthcare information management utilizing cloud computing and Android OS. In *Proceedings of IEEE Eng Med Biol Soc.* (pp. 1037-1040). Dropbox-Info. Retrieved February 1, 2013, from: https://www.dropbox.com/about

ETSI. (2012). Network functions virtualisation: An introduction, benefits, enablers, challenges & call for action. *SDN and OpenFlow World Congress*. Available at http://portal.etsi.org/nfv/nfv_white_paper.pdf

Fernando, N., Loke, S. W., & Rahayu, W. (2012). Mobile cloud computing: A survey. *Future Generation Computer Systems*, *29*(1), 84–106. doi:10.1016/j.future.2012.05.023

Ghemawat, S., Gobioff, H., & Leung, S.-T. (2003). The Google file system. In *Proceedings of Nineteenth ACM Symposium on Operating Systems Principles,* (pp. 29-43). ACM. Retrieved May 11, 2013, from: http://www.google.com/intl/de/drive/about.html

Heckel, P. C. (2010). *Hybrid clouds: Comparing cloud toolkits.* Paper presented at University of Mannheim.

Huang, D., Zhang, X., Kang, M. H., & Luo, J. (2010). MobiCloud: Building secure cloud framework for mobile computing and communication. In *Proceedings of 5th International IEEE Symposium on Service Oriented System Engineering,* (pp. 27-34). IEEE. doi:10.1109/SOSE.2010.20

Huerta-Canepa, G., & Lee, D. (2010). A virtual cloud computing provider for mobile devices. In *Proceedings of the 1st ACM Workshop on Mobile Cloud Computing; Services: Social Networks and Beyond,* (pp. 1-5). ACM.

IBM Global Technology Services (2010). *Defining a framework for cloud adoption* (White paper). Author.

James, J., Bhopal, M. P., & Verma, B. (2012). Efficient VM load balancing algorithm for a cloud computing environment. *International Journal on Computer Science and Engineering, 4,* 1658–1663.

Karpagam, G. R., & Parkavi, J. (2011). Setting up of an open source based private cloud. *International Journal of Computer Science Issues, 8*(3).

Li, A., Yang, X., Kandula, S., & Zhang, M. (2010). CloudCmp: Comparing public cloud providers. In *Proceedings of 10th International ACM SIGCOMM Conference on Internet Measurements,* (pp. 1 – 14). ACM.

McKeown, N., Anderson, T., Balakrishnan, H., Parulkar, G., Peterson, L., Rexford, J., et al. (2008). OpenFlow: Enabling innovation in campus networks. ACM SIGCOMM Computer Communication Review Archive, 38(April 2008), 69-74.

Mell, P., & Grance, T. (2011). *The NIST definition of cloud computing.* Retrieved May 21, 2013, from: http://csrc.nist.gov/publications/nistpubs/800-145/SP800-145.pdf

Moritz, M. (2010). *Verteilte Dateisysteme in der cloud: Cloud Data Management.* Seminar presented at Leipzig University. Retrieved May 21, 2013, from: http://dbs.uni-leipzig.de/file/seminar_0910_maria_moritz_ausarbeitung.pdf

OpenFlow. (n.d.). Retrieved April 5, 2014 from Wikipedia: http://en.wikipedia.org/wiki/OpenFlow

Otto, J. S., Stanojevic, R., & Laoutaris, N. (2012). Temporal rate limiting: Cloud elasticity at a flat fee. In *Proceedings of NetEcon Workshop (INFOCOM WKSHPS),* (pp. 151-156). Academic Press.

Satyanarayanan, M., Bahl, P., Caceres, R., & Davies, N. (2009). The case for VM-based cloudlets in mobile computing. *IEEE Pervasive Computing, 8*(4), 14–23. doi:10.1109/MPRV.2009.82

Seruwagi, L., Khanh, L. Z., & Nguyen, N. (2012). Resource location transparency in clouds. *Project Report presented at Worcester Polytechnic Institute.*

Shvachko, K., Kuang, H., Radia, S., & Chansler, R. (2010). The Hadoop distributed file system. In *Proceedings of 26th IEEE Symposium on Mass Storage Systems and Technologies (MSST)* (pp. 1-10). IEEE. doi:10.1109/MSST.2010.5496972

Tuulos, V. (2008). *The Hadoop distributed file system.* Retrieved February 13, 2013, from: http://commons.wikimedia.org/wiki/File:Mapreduce_(Ville_Tuulos).png

Yue, F. (2013). *Network functions virtualization—Everything old is new again* (White Paper). Academic Press.

KEY TERMS AND DEFINITIONS

Cloud Computing: A vision of "availability of services anytime and anywhere". Cloud computing provides means to deliver the services like computing power, computing and networking infrastructure, applications, etc. wherever and whoever needs them.

Infrastructure as a Service: Also referred to as "Hardware as a Service", it is the model in which organizations outsource the equipment to stakeholders for supporting their operations.

Mobile Cloud Computing: A mix of cloud computing and mobile development. It facilitates mobile users with applications delivered over the mobile services and powered by cloud infrastructure.

Mobile Communication: The telecommunication system that involves no cable in the last-mile. The communication in the last-mile is carried out over the radio interface.

Platform as a Service: An approach to rent out operating systems, software platforms, etc. to various stakeholders in the cloud computing market.

Software as a Service: A software distribution approach with applications hosted by application service providers and extended to the consumers over the network.

Ubiquitous Computing: Integration of computation into environment, which is contrary to the concept of standalone or distinct computers.

Chapter 13
Programming Paradigms in High Performance Computing

Venkat N Gudivada
Marshall University, USA

Jagadeesh Nandigam
Grand Valley State University, USA

Jordan Paris
Marshall University, USA

ABSTRACT

Availability of multiprocessor and multi-core chips and GPU accelerators at commodity prices is making personal supercomputers a reality. High performance programming models help apply this computational power to analyze and visualize massive datasets. Problems which required multi-million dollar supercomputers until recently can now be solved using personal supercomputers. However, specialized programming techniques are needed to harness the power of supercomputers. This chapter provides an overview of approaches to programming High Performance Computers (HPC). The programming paradigms illustrated include OpenMP, OpenACC, CUDA, OpenCL, shared-memory based concurrent programming model of Haskell, MPI, MapReduce, and message-based distributed computing model of Erlang. The goal is to provide enough detail on various paradigms to help the reader understand the fundamental differences and similarities among the paradigms. Example programs are chosen to illustrate the salient concepts that define these paradigms. The chapter concludes by providing research directions and future trends in programming high performance computers.

INTRODUCTION

Availability of multiprocessor and multi-core chips and GPU accelerators is making desktop supercomputers a reality (Ajima, Sumimoto, and Shimizu, 2009; Donofrio et al., 2009; Hoisie and Getov, 2009; Keckler and Reinhardt, 2012; Sodan et al., 2010; Torrellas, 2009; Tumeo, Secchi, and Villa, 2012; Wilde et al., 2009). Manufacturers of such commodity chips include Nvidia, Intel, AMD, and IBM. For example, NVidia markets Tesla GPU accelerators that can

DOI: 10.4018/978-1-4666-7461-5.ch013

Copyright © 2015, IGI Global. Copying or distributing in print or electronic forms without written permission of IGI Global is prohibited.

be used to turn an ordinary desktop computer into a personal supercomputer. The Tesla K20 GPU accelerator delivers 1.17 Tflops double-precision and 3.52 Tflops single-precision floating point performance. These impressive advances in processor speeds provide unprecedented computational power to solve problems such as visualizing molecules, analyzing air traffic flow, and identifying hidden plaque in arteries. Furthermore, the need for high performance computing has never been greater for the reasons discussed below.

About 400 years ago Galileo wrote "... the book of nature is written in the language of mathematics." This statement is even more relevant today given the need for analyzing and interpreting massive amounts of data (aka Big Data) generated by the synergistic confluence of pervasive sensing, computing, and networking. This data is heterogeneous and the volumes are unprecedented in scale and complexity. Big Data is the next frontier for innovation, competition, and productivity (Manyika et al., 2011). Big Data presents opportunities as well as challenges. For example, low-cost high throughput technologies in genomics, real-time and very high resolution imaging, and mass spectrometry-based flow cytometry are transforming the way research is conducted in life sciences (Schadt et al., 2010).

Many of the challenges in genomics derive from the informatics needed to store and analyze the large-scale high-dimensional datasets that are being generated so rapidly. A prime example of this is the 1000 Genomes project with a 200 TB dataset (1000 Genomes, 2012; Amazon, 2012). This project aims to build the most detailed map of human genetic variation with the genomes of more than 2,600 people from 26 populations around the world.

In the physical sciences domain, astronomers are collecting more data than ever. Currently 1 petabyte (PB) of this data is electronically accessible to public, and this volume is growing at 0.5 PB per year (Berriman and Groom, 2011; Hanisch, 2011). The STScI (Space Telescope Science Institute) reports that more papers are published with archived datasets than with newly acquired data (STScI, 2012). It is estimated that more than 60 PB of archived data will be accessible to astronomers (Hanisch, 2011).

Special programming techniques are needed to harness the power of supercomputers in solving compute-intensive problems listed above. Primarily there are two paradigms for programming high performance computers: shared-memory and distributed memory models (Pacheco, 2011). In the *shared-memory model*, processors share certain memory locations to exchange data and results between the processors. OpenMP, OpenACC, CUDA, OpenCL, and the concurrent programming model of Haskell fall under this category. In the *distributed memory model*, processors do not share memory but exchange data and results through interprocess messages. MPI, MapReduce, and the concurrent programming model of Erlang fall under this category.

In this chapter, we provide an introduction to the above programming paradigms. Using succinct example programs, we illustrate fundamental features of these paradigms. The primary goal for this chapter is to help the reader gain conceptual understanding of the principles that underlie various programming paradigms. This in turn will help the reader in choosing a relevant paradigm for a given problem.

We do not discuss the installation of software libraries and compilers needed to run the programs illustrated in this chapter because of space constraints. Installation instructions vary from one operating system to another and also from one release to the next. The reader should consult documentation supplied by the providers of software libraries and compilers. It is assumed that the reader is familiar with C/C++ programming.

MOTIVATION FOR HIGH PERFORMANCE COMPUTING PROGRAMMING LANGUAGES

High performance computing traces its origins to the need for achieving greater processor utilization in the early days of computing. This is manifested in the form of time-sharing operating systems and multi-threaded applications. In the latter, each thread has its own locus of execution. A set of such threads comprises a *process*.

The prevalence of multiprocessors and multi-core chips, and GPU accelerators in today's commodity computers makes a compelling case for effectively harnessing their power. Typically, a core can work on only one thread at a time. But in CPUs with hyper-threading, a core can work multiple threads concurrently.

In multicore systems under shared-memory model, all the cores can access all the memory locations on the chip. To coordinate the work across multiple threads, certain memory locations are designated as *shared*. The latter are accessed by the cores for writing in mutually exclusive manner. The code that updates shared memory locations is referred to as *critical section*. To improve program execution efficiency the size of critical sections must be kept to essential minimum. Furthermore, critical sections must execute as quickly as possible to reduce contention for mutually exclusive access by various threads. If a thread goes into an infinite loop or dies when executing a critical section, the situation leads to indefinitely preventing other threads from entering the critical section. Finally, a function that maintains state between successive calls can cause inconsistent or even incorrect results (Pacheco, 2011).

A computer language that supports parallel programming using the shared-memory model provides several functions for creating and managing threads. Such functions are used for tasks such as a thread creating other threads, merging of multiple threads into one, and synchronization, coordination and communication among threads.

POSIX® is a standard for programming with threads in Unix-like operating systems. POSIX threads are also called *Pthreads*. POSIX functions are available to applications as a C library.

In general, programming with threads is fraught with low-level details and the resulting programs are difficult to debug. Programmers need to be aware of the consequences of *race conditions*, *busy waiting* and how to avoid them. In other words, programmers need to know how to write *thread-safe* programs.

Programming under distributed memory model has its own challenges. Each *process* has its own locus of execution and runs on a different processor. Though programmers are freed from dealing with race conditions, this model ushers in problems related to interprocess communication. Processes communicate with each other, synchronously or asynchronously, for both coordination and data exchange. *Deadlocks* can occur as one process may wait for a message from another process and the latter fails to send the message. Deadlocks can also occur due to messages being lost in the transit. Moreover, messages may need to be received and processed in certain order and this requires proper buffering and dispatching.

Many general-purpose programming languages do not feature special programming constructs for creating parallel programs using shared-memory or distributed memory programming models. Even those that feature such constructs (e.g., Pthreads), the constructs tend to be at a very low level of abstraction. Some new languages have been introduced recently which are specifically designed for parallelism and cloud computing. One such language is Julia (A Programming Language Designed for Parallelism and Cloud Computing, 2014).

Julia is an open source, high-level, dynamic programming language for high-performance scientific computing. It is designed for distributed memory model and features an extensive mathematical function library. This library also integrates with mature and established Fortran and

C libraries for linear algebra, random number generation, signal processing, and string processing. Furthermore, external functions in C and Fortran shared libraries can be directly called without the need for any wrapper code.

Though Julia uses messages for distributed computation, message passing in Julia is different from other environments such as the MPI. Messages resemble higher-level operations like calls to user functions rather than as two separate operations (message *send* and message *receive*). Parallel programming in Julia is built on two primitives: remote references and remote calls. *Remote reference* concept encapsulates the notion of shared data. *Remote call* enables a process to call a function of another process asynchronously (aka non-blocking call) and a remote call returns a remote reference. The first public version of Julia was released in early 2012. It is currently viewed as an experimental language and its acceptance as a viable language for parallel computing remains to be seen.

SequenceL is a commercially licensed, declarative language for parallel computing (Texas Multicore Technologies, Inc. 2012). A programmer declaratively specifies the desired results and the compilation process generates a solution. The solution is generated in a way to efficiently make use of the number of available CPU cores. Current versions of the SequenceL compiler generate C++ and OpenCL code. There is insufficient literature on SequenceL to comment on its acceptance in the industry and the effectiveness of the auto-generated parallel code.

The programming environments for parallel computing that we discuss in this chapter provide higher-level abstractions to promote programmer productivity. These abstractions not only insulate the programmer from low-level details but also help produce portable code. These programming environments are primarily made available in the form of libraries and compiler directives for C and Fortran languages. More recently, parallel programming environments are targeting C++

and Python languages as well. In summary, practical parallel computing is productive only with languages that have specially designed libraries and compilers.

SHARED-MEMORY PARADIGAM

As discussed above, under the shared-memory model several processors share access to the computer's memory. Since the memory is shared, explicit sending and receiving of data among the processors is eliminated. However, processors may contend for access to the same memory location at the same time (aka race conditions). Memory contention issues need to be resolved through mechanisms such as *mutual exclusion*.

OpenMP

OpenMP is an application programming interface (API) for shared-memory based parallel programming. An overarching goal of OpenMP is to enable programmers to incrementally parallelize existing serial applications written in C/C++ and Fortran. OpenMP is an open-source standard. It provides a set of compiler directives (aka pragmas), a limited number of runtime functions, and environment variables for specifying shared memory parallelism.

The pragmas and the runtime functions determine low-level details of how to partition a task and assign subtasks to *threads*. Pragmas are essentially parallelization instructions to the compiler. A pragma may specify that a block of code is to be parallelized (e.g., *#pragma omp parallel for*). An environment variable, for example, OMP_NUM_THREADS, specifies the number of threads to run during the execution of an OpenMP program. Another environment variable, OPM_SCHEDULE, defines the type of *iteration schedule* to use with the *omp parallel for* pragma. Options for the iteration schedule are: static, guided, dynamic, runtime, and auto.

An *iteration block* corresponds to a subset of consecutive iterations through a *for loop*. The *static* option entails determining the mapping of iteration blocks to the execution threads in a round-robin fashion at compile time. Assume that you have two separate loops with the same number of iterations. Furthermore, suppose that each loop is executed with the same number of threads using the static schedule option. Then OpenMP run-time guarantees that each thread will receive exactly the same iteration block(s) in the execution of the two loops. The *dynamic* option lets each thread execute an iteration block first. Then any remaining iteration blocks are scheduled during the second round. This process will continue until all iteration blocks have been executed. The dynamic option results in better load balancing but entails a communication overhead.

The *guided* option is similar to the dynamic option. Initially, the number of loop iterations (i.e., the iteration block size) assigned to a thread is proportional to the ratio of the number of loop iterations and the number of available threads. Subsequent allocation of loop iterations to a thread is proportional to the ratio of the number of loop iterations remaining and the number of available threads. The *runtime* option indicates that the scheduling decision is deferred until runtime. Finally, the *auto* option leaves the scheduling decision to the compiler and the runtime system.

We illustrate OpenMP programming model through a C program for estimating the value of π using the Leibniz formula where π is estimated as:

$$pi = 4\left[\frac{1}{1} - \frac{1}{3} + \frac{1}{5} - \frac{1}{7} + ...\right] = 4\sum_{k=0}^{\infty}\frac{-1^k}{2k+1}$$

Assume that we want to estimate the value of π using 50,000 terms. In the C program, we will use a *for loop* for summing the terms. Each iteration of the for loop computes a term and this value is added to a running total. Computing the

Leibniz formula in parallel mode requires that we partition the loop iterations into a number of consecutive, non-overlapping *iteration blocks* and assign each iteration block to a thread. Assuming a static schedule with 10 threads, yields 10 iteration blocks: first iteration block encompasses loop iterations 1 - 5000, the second encompasses iterations 5001 - 10000, and so on. Each thread computes the contributions from 5,000 terms. To compute the final result, the values computed by each thread need to be summed up and this process is called a *reduction*.

The *reduction* operator reduces a list of numbers to a single value. For example, given a list of integers, a reduction operator can be used to compute the sum of all elements in the list. Likewise, another reduction operator can be used to compute the product of the list elements.

Shown in Figure 1 is the OpenMP implementation of the Leibniz formula. Lines 4 – 9 define and initialize variables. To facilitate the exposition, we have hard-coded the number of threads (line 9) and the number of terms (line 6) to be used in estimating the value of π. Typically these values are provided through command line arguments. The crux of the program is lines 11 - 16. Line 11 specifies the pragma *omp parallel for* for parallelizing the *for loop* that begins on line 13. The pragma also specifies that *thread_cnt* number of threads to be used in executing the loop in parallel mode.

Line 12 is a continuation of line 11 and specifies three clauses for the *omp parallel for* pragma. The *(reduction(+: sum)* specifies that the sum computed by each thread be reduced into one (global) sum. The *private(sign)* specifies that the variable sign should have private scope — each thread should have its own copy of the *sign* variable. By default, any variable declared before the *for loop* is shared by all the threads with the exception of the loop variable (*i*, in our case). The *schedule(dynamic)* specifies the type of loop iteration schedule.

Figure 1. OpenMP implementation of the Leibniz formula for estimating the value of π

```
#include <stdio.h>
#include <omp.h>

int main(int argc, char* argv[]) {
    long long i;                    // loop variable                           5
    long long num_terms = 50000L; // number of terms for estimating pi
    double sign;                    // sign of a term
    double sum = 0.0;               // incremental estimate of pi
    int thread_cnt = 10;            // number of threads to be used

                                                                              10
#   pragma omp parallel for num_threads(thread_cnt) \
        reduction(+: sum) private(sign) schedule(dynamic)
    for (i = 0; i < num_terms; i++) {
        sign = (i % 2 == 0) ? 1.0 : -1.0;
        sum += sign/(2*i+1);                                                  15
    }

    sum = 4.0*sum;
    printf("n = %lld terms, %d threads,\n", num_terms, thread_cnt);
    printf("  estimated value of pi = %.14f\n", sum);                         20
    return 0;
}
```

Figure 2. Compiling and running an OpenMP program on OS X

```
● ○ ○                  open-mp — bash — 61×18
$: gcc -g -Wall -fopenmp -o omp_leibniz_pi omp_leibniz_pi.c
$: ./omp_leibniz_pi
n = 50000 terms, 10 threads,
  estimated value of pi = 3.14157265358981
$:
```

The commands for compiling and running the OpenMP program are shown in Figure 2. Also shown in this figure are the execution results.

OpenACC

The OpenACC standard is similar to the OpenMP but targets acceleration devices such as GPUs. It is maintained by an industry consortium. The OpenACC specification, like the OpenMP, includes compiler directives, runtime routines, and environment variables. Currently OpenACC adoption is not widespread due to lack of OpenACC compilers. Though commercial solutions are available from the Portland Group and CAPS, OpenACC support is not available for the GCC and Clang compilers.

Recall that the OpenMP uses *#pragma parallel* for parallelizing a loop for a multi-threaded CPU. The OpenACC uses *#pragma acc kernels* to turn parallelizable loops into *kernel functions*, which are executed on the GPUs. Much of the complexity of this task is managed by the programmer in the case of CUDA and OpenCL, but it is transparent to the programmer in OpenACC. Unlike OpenCL, there is no need for two separate compilation units (one targeting the CPU/host, and the other for GPUs).

We illustrate the OpenACC model using the same problem that we discussed earlier (estimating the value of π using the Leibniz formula). The OpenACC program is shown in Figure 3. This is almost identical to the OpenMP program shown in Figure 1 except for the compiler pragma, whose

Figure 3. OpenACC implementation of the Leibniz formula for estimating the value of π

```
#include <stdio.h>

int main(int argc, char* argv[]) {
    long long i;                    // loop variable
    long long num_terms = 50000L; // number of terms for estimating pi       5
    double sign;                    // sign of a term
    double sum = 0.0;               // incremental estimate of pi

    #pragma acc kernels copyin(num_terms), copyout(sum)
    for (i = 0; i < num_terms; i++) {                                         10
        sign = (i % 2 == 0) ? 1.0 : -1.0;
        sum += sign/(2*i+1);
    }

    sum = 4.0*sum;                                                            15
    printf("Estimated value of pi = %.14f\n", sum);
    return 0;
}
```

specification is simpler for the OpenACC. Line 9 is the essence of the OpenACC program. Memory is copied from the CPU to the GPU at the start of the loop and back from the GPU to the CPU at the end of the loop. More specifically, before executing the loop, the value of the variables *num_terms* and *sum* are copied from the CPU to the GPU. After the termination of the loop, the *sum* value is copied from the GPU to the CPU. The compiler and the run-time system manage many details including creating the device functions.

CUDA™

CUDA is both a parallel computing architecture and a programming model for high performance computing (B. R. Gaster and Howes, 2012; Kirk and Hwu, 2010; Sanders and Kandrot, 2011; Stratton et al., 2012; Tzeng, Lloyd, and Owens, 2012; Wilt, 2013). It is a proprietary standard of NVidia. CUDA is the computing engine in NVidia's graphics processing units (GPUs). CUDA provides programmatic access to the native instruction set and memory of the parallel computational elements in the GPUs. GPUs have many cores and each core is capable of running thousands of threads simultaneously. GPUs are called *devices* and operate in a host environment. The CPU and its memory comprise the host.

CUDA enables dramatic increases in computing performance by harnessing the power of GPUs. There are three ways to bring GPU-enabled acceleration to applications: (1) Replace or augment CPU-only libraries such as MKL BLAS, IPP, FFTW, and other widely-used numerical libraries with GPU-accelerated libraries (2) Use OpenACC directives for parallelizing loops in Fortran or C/C++ code (3) Develop parallel algorithms and libraries using languages such as C, C++, Java, Fortran, Python, and C#.

NVidia compiler (nvcc) is used for compiling CUDA programs. A typical CUDA program consists of both *serial* and *parallel* code. The serial (aka host) code targets the host and the parallel (aka device) code is run on the devices. The *nvcc* compiler first separates the code into serial/host and parallel/device components. Thr device code is processed by the *nvcc* compiler and the serial code is processed by standard host compilers such as the *gcc*.

Processing flow in the CUDA environment comprises the following steps: (1) Input data is copied from the host memory to the GPU memory (2) Devices execute parallel code and cache data on the chip for performance (3) Results are copied from the GPU memory to the CPU memory.

Shown in Figure 4 is a CUDA program for summing the corresponding elements of two vec-

Figure 4. CUDA™ program for summing vector elements

```
#include <stdio.h>
#define VECT_SIZE 1024

// add() executes on devices
__global__ void add(int *a, int *b, int *c) {                                    5
        int tID = blockIdx.x;
        if (tID < VECT_SIZE)
                c[tID] = a[tID] + b[tID];
}
                                                                                  10
int main(int argc, char* argv[]) {
        int i; // loop variable
        // three vectors of equal size
        int host_a[VECT_SIZE], host_b[VECT_SIZE], host_c[VECT_SIZE];
                                                                                  15
        // initialize vectors vect_a and vect_b
        for (i = 0; i < VECT_SIZE; i++) {
                host_a[i] = i,
                host_b[i] = VECT_SIZE - i;
        }                                                                         20

        // declare and allocate buffers on device memory
        int *device_buff_for_vect_a, *device_buff_for_vect_b, *device_buff_for_vec_c;
        cudaMalloc((void **) &device_buff_for_vect_a, VECT_SIZE*sizeof(int));
        cudaMalloc((void **) &device_buff_for_vect_b, VECT_SIZE*sizeof(int));     25
        cudaMalloc((void **) &device_buff_for_vec_c, VECT_SIZE*sizeof(int));

        // copy vectors host_a and host_b to the corresponding device buffers
        cudaMemcpy(device_buff_for_vect_a, host_a, VECT_SIZE*sizeof(int),
                cudaMemcpyHostToDevice);                                          30
        cudaMemcpy(device_buff_for_vect_b, host_b, VECT_SIZE*sizeof(int),
                cudaMemcpyHostToDevice);

        // GPUs execute add() function on the data in the first two
        // device buffers, and result is stored in the third device buffer       35
        add<<<VECT_SIZE, 1>>>(device_buff_for_vect_a, device_buff_for_vect_b,
                device_buff_for_vec_c);

        // copy results from device buffer to host vector
        cudaMemcpy(host_c, device_buff_for_vec_c, VECT_SIZE*sizeof(int),          40
                cudaMemcpyDeviceToHost);

        // print results
        for (i = 0; i < VECT_SIZE; i++)
                printf("%d + %d = %d\n", host_a[i], host_b[i], host_c[i]);        45

        return 0;
}
```

tors and storing the results in the corresponding locations in a third vector. This program has one device function (lines 5 - 9). The CUDA C/C++ keyword __global__ (line 5) indicates that the *add( )* function will execute on the device and will be called from the host code. The parameters *a*, *b*, and *c* point to the device memory.

Each parallel invocation of the device function, *add( )*, is a *block*, and a set of blocks is referred to as a *grid*. The notation *blockIdx.x* is used by a device function invocation to refer to its block. The *blockIdx.x* can also be used to index into a vector (lines 6 and 8). This enables processing a different vector element by each invocation (lines 7 - 8). In other words, block 0 (or the first invocation) executes c[0] = a[0] + b[0], block 1 executes c[1] = a[1] + b[1], and so on. Massive parallelism is achieved by having thousands of parallel invocations *of add( )*, and letting each invocation process a different vector element.

Line 14 defines three host vectors and the first two vectors are initialized in lines 17 - 20. Lines 23 - 26 define three buffers on the device memory corresponding to the three host vectors (host_a, host_b, host_c). Data in the first two host vectors is copied to the corresponding device buffers in lines 29 - 32. The constant *cudaMemcpyHostToDevice* in line 30 specifies the direction of the memory copy. The first argument specifies the destination and the second one specifies the source.

Lines 36 - 37 specify VECT_SIZE number of parallel invocations of the *add( )* function. The digit 1 proceeding >>> in line 36 indicates the number of threads per invocation/block. Next the blocks perform computations in parallel and the results are stored in the device memory (variable device_buff_for_vec_c). Results are copied from the device memory to the host memory in lines 40 - 41 and the results printed (lines 44 - 45).

The commands for compiling and running the CUDA program are shown in Figure 5. The source program is named *add_vector.cu*. The *nvcc add_vector.cu -o add_vector* command compiles the CUDA program *add_vector.cu* and produces

Figure 5. Compiling and running a CUDA program on Linux

```
jo@jo-Latitude-E6500:~/CUDA$ make
nvcc add_vector.cu -o add_vector
jo@jo-Latitude-E6500:~/CUDA$ ./add_vector
0 + 1024 = 1024
1 + 1023 = 1024
2 + 1022 = 1024
3 + 1021 = 1024
4 + 1020 = 1024
```

an executable *add_vector*. The *nvcc* compiler hides several details and there is no need to specify any CUDA related header files. Also shown in this figure are first few results of the execution.

OpenCL

OpenCL (Open Computing Language) is an open-source standard for general-purpose parallel programming of *heterogeneous computing systems* (B. Gaster et al., 2011; Scarpino, 2011). The latter can be a diverse mix of multi-core CPUs from AMD, GPUs from NVidia, IBM's Cell Broadband Engine and other parallel processors such as DSPs including Sony's PlayStations. An OpenCL application can leverage both data-level and task-level parallelism. In the *data-level parallelism*, each device executes the same code but operates on different sets of data. In the *task-level parallelism*, each task executes on a different device in parallel and the code for each task is different.

The OpenCL standard defines a set of data types, data structures, and functions that augment C and C++. OpenCL programs can be compiled to run on any OpenCL-compliant hardware. Though vector instructions are vendor-specific, when you compile an OpenCL application for a specific hardware, the OpenCL compiler for the hardware will generate vector instructions that match the underlying hardware architecture. Portability, standardized vector processing, and parallel programming are distinctive features of OpenCL.

In OpenCL terminology, there is a distinction between hosts and devices. A *host* is any traditional CPU-based computer and *devices* refer to an assortment of processors including CPU-based computers, GPGPUs, and the processors found on gaming devices. An OpenCL application consists of two types of code. The first is the normal C/C++ code that runs on a host computer – host application. The second type is referred to as a *kernel*, which is a specially coded function that is intended for execution on any OpenCL-compliant devices. Kernels are sent to their intended target devices by the host applications.

Nvidia and AMD provide free and popular OpenCL SDKs. The latter contains libraries and tools for developing OpenCL applications. OpenCL SDK is pre-installed on recent versions of Mac OS X. Open CL provides a standard set of primitive data types. They are similar to their C/C++ counterparts. For example, the OpenCL data type *cl_uint* corresponds to the unsigned int of C/C++.

As a first step in developing OpenCL applications, you need to understand six fundamental data structures: *platform*, *device*, *context*, *program*, *kernel*, and *command queue*. For each data structure two types of functions are provided. The functions in the first type are used to create the above data structures and the ones in the second kind are used to retrieve information about the data structures.

Using the cl_platform_id data structure, you can query the number of OpenCL platforms available on a computing system and choose one or more of them to execute the OpenCL application. The *clGetPlatformIDs()* is used for this purpose.

Associated with each platform is a profile, which describes the capabilities of the OpenCL version supported by the platform. This information is obtained by calling the *clGetPlatformInfo()* function.

Given a platform ID, *clGetDeviceIDs()* is used to retrieve the devices available in the platform. The *context* data structure enables managing devices as a group. All the devices in a context must be provided by the same platform. However, a host application can manage devices using more than one context. Moreover, a host application can create multiple contexts from devices in a single platform.

The *program* data structure holds the source program, which is targeted for execution on the devices. The OpenCL function *clBuildProgram()* compiles the source program. The compiled program needs further preparation before dispatching to the devices (e.g., specifying arguments to kernel functions). The *kernel* data structure is used to specify the arguments. Finally, the *command queue* enables queuing and scheduling of OpenCL kernel code for execution on the devices. Command queue is a means for the host to convey to the devices what to compute. When a kernel is enqueued to a command queue, the device(s) will execute the kernel function.

Shown in Figure 6 is a kernel function that adds the corresponding elements in vectors *A* and *B* and stores the result in a third vector *C*. Line 1 shows the function header. Line 3 obtains the index of the current vector element pairs to be added and addition is performed in line 5.

The host program for computing the sum of the corresponding elements in two one-dimensional vectors is shown in Figures 7, 8, and 9. Lines 1 -

Figure 6. OpenCL kernel function for adding two vectors

```
__kernel void vector_add(__global int *A, __global int *B, __global int *C) {
    // get the index of the current element
    int i = get_global_id(0);
    // add vectors
    C[i] = A[i] + B[i];                                                      5
}
```

Figure 7. OpenCL program for summing two vectors - Part 1

```
#include <stdio.h>
#include <stdlib.h>

#ifdef __APPLE__
#include <OpenCL/opencl.h>                                          5
#else
#include <CL/cl.h>
#endif

#define MAX_SRC_SIZE (0x100000)                                     10

int main(int argc, char* argv[]) {

    int i;              // loop variable
    cl_int ret;         // code returned from OpenCL functions      15

    // create input vectors A and B on host
    const int VECT_SIZE = 1024;
    int *A = (int*)malloc(sizeof(int)*VECT_SIZE); // vector A
    int *B = (int*)malloc(sizeof(int)*VECT_SIZE); // vector B        20

    // initialize vectors A and B
    for(i = 0; i < VECT_SIZE; i++) {
        A[i] = i;
        B[i] = VECT_SIZE - i;                                       25
    }

    // read kernel source code from disk file
    FILE *fp;
    char *src_str;                                                  30
    size_t src_size;

    fp = fopen("vector_add_kernel.cl", "r");
    if (!fp) {
        fprintf(stderr, "Failed to load kernel.\n");                35
        exit(1);
    }

    src_str = (char*)malloc(MAX_SRC_SIZE);
    src_size = fread(src_str, 1, MAX_SRC_SIZE, fp);                 40
    fclose( fp );
```

10 list header files and define a constant. Lines 4 - 8 specify the inclusion of the correct header file name and its location depending on the operating system (OS X vs. Linux/MS Windows).

Lines 18 - 20 define the vectors A and B and are initialized in lines 23 - 26. The kernel source program (see Figure 6) is loaded from the disk in lines 29 - 41. The size of the kernel source program is also computed (line 39). Lines 44 - 47 declare and initialize variables for platform and device data structures.

Figure 8. OpenCL program for summing two vectors - Part 2

```
// get platform and device information
cl_uint num_plt;             // number of platforms
cl_uint num_dev;             // number of devices
cl_platform_id plt_id = NULL; // initialize platform data structure
cl_device_id dev_id = NULL;   // initialize device data structure

// get platform IDs and number of platforms
clGetPlatformIDs(1, &plt_id, &num_plt);

// get list of all OpenCL devices available on the platform
clGetDeviceIDs(plt_id, CL_DEVICE_TYPE_ALL, 1, &dev_id, &num_dev);

// create an OpenCL context for the devices
cl_context ctx = clCreateContext( NULL, 1, &dev_id, NULL, NULL, &ret);

// create memory buffers for vectors A, B, and C on devices
cl_mem a_mem_obj = clCreateBuffer(ctx, CL_MEM_READ_ONLY,
        VECT_SIZE * sizeof(int), NULL, &ret);
cl_mem b_mem_obj = clCreateBuffer(ctx, CL_MEM_READ_ONLY,
        VECT_SIZE * sizeof(int), NULL, &ret);
cl_mem c_mem_obj = clCreateBuffer(ctx, CL_MEM_WRITE_ONLY,
        VECT_SIZE * sizeof(int), NULL, &ret);

// create a command queue for the context
cl_command_queue cmd_q = clCreateCommandQueue(ctx, dev_id, 0, &ret);

// copy vectors A and B on the host to their memory buffers in devices
clEnqueueWriteBuffer(cmd_q, a_mem_obj, CL_TRUE, 0,
        VECT_SIZE * sizeof(int), A, 0, NULL, NULL);
clEnqueueWriteBuffer(cmd_q, b_mem_obj, CL_TRUE, 0,
        VECT_SIZE * sizeof(int), B, 0, NULL, NULL);

// create program from kernel source
cl_program prog = clCreateProgramWithSource(ctx, 1,
        (const char **)&src_str, (const size_t *)&src_size, &ret);

// build the program
clBuildProgram(prog, 1, &dev_id, NULL, NULL, NULL);

// create OpenCL kernel
cl_kernel kernel = clCreateKernel(prog, "vector_add", &ret);

// Set the arguments of the kernel
clSetKernelArg(kernel, 0, sizeof(cl_mem), (void *)&a_mem_obj);
clSetKernelArg(kernel, 1, sizeof(cl_mem), (void *)&b_mem_obj);
clSetKernelArg(kernel, 2, sizeof(cl_mem), (void *)&c_mem_obj);
```

45

50

55

60

65

70

75

80

85

Figure 9. OpenCL program for summing two vectors - Part 3

```
// execute OpenCL kernel on the list                              90
  size_t global_item_size = VECT_SIZE; // process entire lists
  size_t local_item_size = 64; // process in groups of 64
  ret = clEnqueueNDRangeKernel(cmd_q, kernel, 1, NULL,
        &global_item_size, &local_item_size, 0, NULL, NULL);

                                                                  95
// read the memory buffer C on the device to the local variable C
  int *C = (int*)malloc(sizeof(int)*VECT_SIZE);
  ret = clEnqueueReadBuffer(cmd_q, c_mem_obj, CL_TRUE, 0,
        VECT_SIZE * sizeof(int), C, 0, NULL, NULL);

                                                                  100
// display results
  for(i = 0; i < VECT_SIZE; i++)
      printf("%d + %d = %d\n", A[i], B[i], C[i]);

// clean up                                                       105
  clFlush(cmd_q);
  clFinish(cmd_q);
  clReleaseKernel(kernel);
  clReleaseProgram(prog);
  clReleaseMemObject(a_mem_obj);                                  110
  clReleaseMemObject(b_mem_obj);
  clReleaseMemObject(c_mem_obj);
  clReleaseCommandQueue(cmd_q);
  clReleaseContext(ctx);
  free(A);                                                        115
  free(B);
  free(C);
  return 0;
}
```

Line 50 queries platform information. Devices information is obtained in line 53. Next, a context is created for the devices (line 56). Memory buffers for the vectors *A*, *B*, and *C* are created in lines 59 - 64. Note that the first two buffers for vectors *A* and *B* are read-only, whereas the buffer for vector *C* is write-only. Each buffer is of the same size as the vectors. In line 67, a command queue is created on a specific device. Vectors *A* and *B* are copied to their corresponding buffers in lines 70 - 73.

The device program from the kernel source is created in lines 76 - 77. An executable is built in line 80 by compiling and linking the program. The executable is turned into an OpenCL kernel program in line 83. In lines 86 - 88, the kernel arguments are bound to the memory buffers created earlier in lines 59 - 64. Finally, the execution of the kernel code on the devices is done in lines 91 - 94. Line 91 specifies that all elements in the vectors should be executed by the kernel (indicated by the global_item_size variable) and line 92 specifies that the data be processed in groups of 64 (indicated by the local_item_size variable).

In line 97, sufficient memory is allocated on the host for local variable C. The memory buffer

Figure 10. Compiling and running an OpenCL program on OS X

```
$: cc -o main -framework OpenCL main.c
$: ./main
0 + 1024 = 1024
1 + 1023 = 1024
2 + 1022 = 1024
3 + 1021 = 1024
4 + 1020 = 1024
5 + 1019 = 1024
```

on the device (c_mem_obj) is copied into host local variable C (lines 98 - 99). The OpenCL application terminates after displaying the results (lines 102 - 103) and releasing the resources (lines 106 - 117).

Figure 10 shows the commands for compiling and running the OpenCL program on OS X. The *main.c* is the OpenCL application (aka the host application). The first few lines of the execution results are also shown in this figure.

HASKELL CONCURRENT PROGRAMMING MODEL

In a pure functional programming language such as Haskell, data is immutable and generally there are no side-effects (Marlow, 2013). Immutable data obviates the need for locking in developing thread-safe software. Haskell's pure functions have

no side effects and this property makes writing code for parallel execution easier.

In Haskell, the module *Control.Parallel.Strategies* provides basic functionality for creating parallelism. Shown in Figure 11 is a parallel Haskell program for computing the sum of first million positive integers. Parallelism is expressed using the *Eval* monad. The Eval monad supports *runEval*, *rpar*, and *rseq* operations. The *rpar* evaluates its argument in parallel. The *rseq* is used for forcing sequential execution. The *runEval* performs the Eval computation and returns its result (line 5).

The *Par* monad in Haskell provides another parallel programming model. The Haskell program shown in Figure 12 illustrates parallelism using the Par monad. A computation in the Par monad is run using the *runPar* operation. The *fork* operation is used to create parallel tasks. Values are passed between Par computations using the *IVar* type and its operations – *new*, *put*, and *get*. The *put* opera-

Figure 11. Parallelism in Haskell using the Control.Parallel.Strategies module

```
import Control.Parallel.Strategies

main = do
  print $
    runEval $ do                                                    5
      s1 <- rpar (sum ([1..250000] :: [Int]))
      s2 <- rpar (sum ([250001..500000] :: [Int]))
      s3 <- rpar (sum ([500001..750000] :: [Int]))
      s4 <- rpar (sum ([750001..1000000] :: [Int]))
      rseq s1                                                       10
      rseq s2
      rseq s3
      rseq s4
      return (s1+s2+s3+s4)
```

Figure 12. Parallelism in Haskell using the Par monad

```
import Control.Monad.Par

main = do
  print $
    runPar $ do                                                        5
      s1 <- new
      s2 <- new
      s3 <- new
      s4 <- new
      fork (put s1 (sum ([1..250000] :: [Int])))                      10
      fork (put s2 (sum ([250001..500000] :: [Int])))
      fork (put s3 (sum ([500001..750000] :: [Int])))
      fork (put s4 (sum ([750001..1000000] :: [Int])))
      a <- get s1
      b <- get s2                                                     15
      c <- get s3
      d <- get s4
      return (a+b+c+d)
```

Figure 13. Compiling and running an Haskell parallel programs on OS X

```
nandigaj@jnmcbkpro$ ls
parallelsum1.hs parallelsum2.hs
nandigaj@jnmcbkpro$ ghc -O2 parallelsum1.hs -threaded
[1 of 1] Compiling Main             ( parallelsum1.hs, parallelsum1.o )
Linking parallelsum1 ...
nandigaj@jnmcbkpro$ ghc -O2 parallelsum2.hs -threaded
[1 of 1] Compiling Main             ( parallelsum2.hs, parallelsum2.o )
Linking parallelsum2 ...
nandigaj@jnmcbkpro$ ./parallelsum1 +RTS -N4
500000500000
nandigaj@jnmcbkpro$ ./parallelsum2 +RTS -N4
500000500000
nandigaj@jnmcbkpro$
```

tion is used to store a value in a IVar variable and *get* operation is used to read the value. If the *get* operation finds the IVar empty, it waits until the variable is filled by a *put* operation. An IVar can only be written once. The *get* operation does not empty an IVar after reading the value. Figure 13 shows the commands for compiling and running the Haskell programs on OS X. Execution results are also shown in this figure.

Haskell supports concurrent programming via shared-memory model using threads. Concurrency in Haskell is achieved with *forkIO* operation from the *Control.Concurrent* module to create threads, and *MVar* type for communication and synchronization between threads. The *Chan* type provides one-way communication channel. Haskell provides primitives for parallel programming that can also be used to model the MapReduce paradigm.

The common pitfalls of shared-state concurrency such as race conditions, deadlocks, and starvation also apply to concurrent programming in Haskell. The Software Transactional Memory (STM) API in Haskell provides powerful tools to address many of these problems.

DISTRIBUTED MEMORY PARADIGM

Under this model, processors do not share memory. They share data through explicit communication between the processors. Programming paradigms discussed under this category include MPI, MapReduce, and message based distributed computing model of Erlang.

MPI

The Message Passing Interface (MPI) defines a standard for passing messages between processes to effect parallel computation. Processes run in their own address space and communicate via sending and receiving messages. MPI also supports shared memory programming model, where multiple processes can read and write to the same memory location. Furthermore, *node-to-node* (or point-to-point) communication is supported. *Group* communication – a node can send a message to a collection of nodes as a unit operation – is also supported.

MPI is a mature standard and porting MPI programs from one HPC system to another is relatively easier. MPI efficiently matches the underlying hardware because vendor and open-source implementations are available for specific hardware. The MPI 2.0 standard provides an assortment of features beyond message passing. The current version of the MPI standard is 3.0.

An MPI implementation is essentially a C/C++ or Fortran library with hundreds of functions. Some functions take several parameters. To effectively use MPI, one needs to precisely understand the semantics of these functions and supply proper values to the function arguments. Some arguments specify *in* values (the caller needs to specify these values) and others are *out* arguments (i.e., the called function returns these values). Learning these details can be quite tedious and time consuming. Hence, there is a steep learning curve. However, by using just six basic functions (MPI_Init, MPI_Comm_rank, MPI_Comm_size, MPI_Send, MPI_Recv, and MPI_Finalize), one can write interesting and useful MPI applications.

In the following, we illustrate some MPI functions through an annotated C program. The program sums elements in a one-dimensional vector and is shown in Figures 14, 15, and 16. Basic idea is for a *master process* to divide the vector into non-overlapping, contiguous vector segments and assign them to *worker processes*. Each worker process sums up elements in the segment assigned to it, and returns the partial result to the master process. The latter sums up all the partial sums and computes the total sum. In addition to partitioning the data and performing supervisory control on worker processes, the master process may also perform part of the actual work.

All processes get their own copy of the same code, but they work on different parts of the code. Processes identify the part of the code that they need to work on based on their unique ID (aka rank). Each process may run on a different processor or a processor may host multiple processes. These details are abstracted by the MPI library and the MPI run-time system makes these decisions at run-time depending on the number of available physical processors. However, a user may indicate the number of processors to be used for executing an MPI program while issuing the execution command. In the worst-case scenario, all processes may run on just one physical processor. In this degenerate case, an MPI program will actually run slower than its serial counterpart due to interprocess communication and data transfer overheads.

Line 2 specifies the header file for the MPI library functions. Various declarations are specified in lines 4 - 14. These variables are used by both the master and worker processes. Line 16 initializes the MPI execution environment. It takes two arguments, typically the same command line arguments that the *main* function of line 3 receives from the operating system. The MPI_Init() can also be called with NULL values for both its arguments. It is executed by only one thread and it is the same thread that will execute the MPI_Finalize() in line 110. All MPI functions return status values and we ignore them for

Figure 14. MPI program for summing two vectors - Part 1

```
#include <stdio.h>
#include <mpi.h>
int main(int argc, char* argv[]) {
    const long long max_elements = 1000000L;
    const int send_data_tag = 5000;  // to identify send messages          5
    const int return_data_tag = 6000;// to identify receive messages
    const int master_process = 0;    // root/master process identifier
    long long int sum, partial_sum;  // grand total and partial totals
    MPI_Comm comm;        // MPI communicator
    int my_rank;          // unique ID of a process                        10
    int num_procs;        // no of processors available/allocated
    MPI_Status status;    // data structure MPI call status info
    long long j;          // loop variable
    int i;                // loop variable
                                                                           15
    MPI_Init(&argc, &argv); // MPI initialization
    comm = MPI_COMM_WORLD;  // predefined MPI communicator
    MPI_Comm_rank(comm, &my_rank);   // a process's unique rank/ID
    MPI_Comm_size(comm, &num_procs); // MPI Communicator size
                                                                           20
    // if I am the master process
    if(my_rank == master_process) {

        int elem_per_proc;    // no of vector elements assigned to a process
        int start_elem;       // beginning element of vector segment        25
        int end_elem;         // ending element of vector segment
        int num_elem_to_send; // no of vector elements to send to a process

        int sender; // unique ID of the process which sent the message
        int vect1[max_elements]; // vector whose elements need to be summed  30

        // initialize the vector
        for(j = 0; j < max_elements; j++) {
            vect1[j] = j + 1;
        }                                                                   35

        // how many vector elements to send for each worker process
        elem_per_proc = max_elements/num_procs;
```

simplicity in our presentation. Instead of writing like *int err = MPI_Init()*, we write *MPI_Init()*.

An MPI *communicator* encapsulates all communication among a set of processes. It defines the scope of a communication operation. Each process is given a unique rank or ID in the context of a communicator: 0, 1, 2, ... 0; p - 1 where p is the number of processes. MPI_COMM_WORLD is the predefined *communicator* that includes all

the available MPI processes. Line 17 initializes the variable *comm* with this default communicator. Each process obtains its unique rank in the communicator by calling the MPI_Comm_rank() function (line 18). The number of processes available for the MPI program are obtained by calling the MPI_Comm_size() function (line 19).

The master process executes the code in lines 24 - 84. Variables that are needed only by the

Figure 15. MPI program for summing two vectors - Part 2

```
// master process sends a different consecutive segment of          40
// vector elements to each worker process
for(i = 1; i < num_procs; i++) {

    // starting index of the vector for process i
    start_elem = i * elem_per_proc + 1;                             45
    // ending index of the vector for process i
    end_elem   = (i + 1) * elem_per_proc;
    // adjust ending index for the last processor
    if((max_elements - end_elem) < elem_per_proc)
        end_elem = max_elements - 1;                                50

    // number of vector elements to send to process i
    num_elem_to_send = end_elem - start_elem + 1;
    // let the worker process i know how many elements it is going to receive
    MPI_Send(&num_elem_to_send, 1, MPI_INT, i, send_data_tag, comm);  55
    // send the worker process i the vector segment
    MPI_Send(&vect1[start_elem], num_elem_to_send, MPI_INT,
        i, send_data_tag, comm);
}
                                                                    60
// master process computes its share of summing elements in a vector segment
sum = 0;
for(i = 0; i < elem_per_proc + 1; i++) {
    sum += vect1[i];
}                                                                   65
printf("Sum = %lld is calculated by the root process\n", sum);

// master process receives partial sums computed by the worker process
// and computes global/grand sum
for(i = 1; i < num_procs; i++) {                                    70

    // receives partial sum from a worker process
    MPI_Recv(&partial_sum, 1, MPI_LONG, MPI_ANY_SOURCE,
            return_data_tag, comm, &status);
                                                                    75
    // unique ID of the worker process which sent the partial sum
    sender = status.MPI_SOURCE;
    printf("Partial sum %lld returned from process %d\n",
        partial_sum, sender);
                                                                    80
    // add partial sum to the global sum
    sum += partial_sum;
}
printf("Vector sum is: %lld\n", sum);
}                                                                   85
```

Figure 16. MPI program for summing two vectors - Part 3

```
else { // I am a worker process
    int num_elem_to_receive; // no of vector elements a process receives
    int vect2[max_elements]; // vector elements rec by a worker process

    // want to know how many vector elements will be sent                    90
    MPI_Recv(&num_elem_to_receive, 1, MPI_INT,
            master_process, send_data_tag, comm, &status);

    // receives a consecutive segment of vector elements and
    // saves them in vect2                                                    95
    MPI_Recv(&vect2, num_elem_to_receive, MPI_INT,
            master_process, send_data_tag, comm, &status);

    // computes sum of vector elements received
    partial_sum = 0;                                                         100
    for(i = 0; i < num_elem_to_receive; i++) {
        partial_sum += vect2[i];
    }

    // worker process sends partial sum to the master process               105
    MPI_Send(&partial_sum, 1, MPI_LONG, master_process,
            return_data_tag, comm);
}

MPI_Finalize();                                                             110
}
```

master process appear in lines 24 - 30. Line 30 defines a vector of 1,000,000 integer elements and the vector is initialized in lines 33 - 35. The vector is sliced into non-overlapping contiguous blocks of data (lines 45 - 53). The number of elements in a slice (line 55) and the slice itself (lines 57 - 58) are sent to worker processes by executing the MPI_Send() function. The MPI_Send() function requires 6 arguments: starting address of the buffer containing the data to be sent, number of data elements, data type of the elements, rank/ID of the process to send the data to, message tag (to assign a label/class to the send message), and the communicator to which the process belongs to.

The master process does its share of the actual work by summing the vector elements in its slice and prints this value (lines 62 - 66). In lines 70 - 82, it receives partial sums computed by the worker processes and produces a global sum and prints this result (line 84). A process receives data by executing the MPI_Recv() function. It requires 7 arguments (line 73 - 74): the starting address of the buffer to store the received data,

expected number of data elements, data type of the expected data, rank/ID of the process from which the data is expected, message tag (label/class of the message), the communicator to which the process belongs to, and status. The last variable is a structure of type MPI_Status, which can be queried for various pieces of information about the receive message (e.g., line 77).

The code in lines 87 - 107 is executed exclusively by the worker processes. The MPI_Recv() in lines 91 - 92 is used to find out how many data items are going to be sent by the master process. And this value is used in the MPI-Recv() call in lines 96 - 97, which stores the received data in vect2[]. Then each worker process computes the sum of the elements in the vector slice received (lines 99 - 103) and the sum is sent to the master process (lines 106 - 107).

This is not the best solution to the vector element summation problem. The vect2[] is the same size as vect1[] when vect2[] could be much smaller. Furthermore, each worker process will have its own copy of vect2[]. This needlessly consumes

Figure 17. Compiling and running an MPI program on OS X

```
$: gcc -g -Wall -fopenmp -o omp_leibniz_pi omp_leibniz_pi.c
$: ./omp_leibniz_pi
n = 50000 terms, 10 threads,
  estimated value of pi = 3.14157265358981
$:
```

more memory than what is required and results in scalability problems and limits the size of problems that we can solve. We could have used other MPI functions such as MPI_Scatter(), MPI_Scatterv(), MPI_Bcast(), MPI_Reduce(), and MPI_Gather() to avoid these issues, but it requires knowledge of additional MPI concepts. Our goal is to illustrate a basic but complete MPI program.

The commands for compiling and running the MPI program are shown in Figure 17. The *mpicc* command is used for compilation and *mpirun* is used for executing the program. The option *-np 4* specifies that 4 processes be used for execution. Also shown in this figure are the results of the program execution.

MapReduce

MapReduce is a distributed programming model designed for processing massive amounts of data using large clusters (Tittel, 2012; White, 2010). This model is inspired by the *map* and *reduce* functions commonly used in functional programming languages. The MapReduce model is implemented as two functions: *Map* and *Reduce*.

Just as the *hello world* program is used to introduce the first program in programming languages, the *word count* problem is used to illustrate the MapReduce model. Assume that you want to compute the word frequencies across several million text files. You expect the final result in the form of a two-column table. The first column lists the words in alphabetical order and the second one indicates the frequency of the word.

The word count problem lends itself naturally for parallel execution using a *three-step process*. In

the *first step*, multiple *parallel mapper processes* read the input text files and produce ordered pairs of the form: (word, 1). In other words, for each instance of a word that appears in a file, an ordered pair is generated.

Think of the input files as being organized into classes such that a file is placed into only one class and all the files are placed in some class. Each mapper process works on all the files in some class. Optimal partitioning of the input files into classes and assigning each class to a mapper depends on the problem characteristics.

The *second step* of the process acts as a barrier by insure that all the mapper processes have completed their work before moving to the third step. The second step also collects the generated key-value pairs from each mapper process, sorts them, and partitions the sorted key-value pairs. Lastly, it assigns each partition to a different *reduce* process (third step). A function that performs this assignment is called a *shard*.

Each reduce process essentially receives *all* the key-value pairs corresponding to one or more words (e.g., (eclectic, 1), (eclectic, 1), (eclectic, 1), (authentic, 1), (authentic, 1)). The output of each reduce process is the total count of each word (e.g., (eclectic, 3), (authentic, 2)). No synchronization is required for the reduce processes.

Several optimizations are possible in each of the above three steps. Some of these optimizations depend on the type of data to be processed. MapReduce implementations also requires another supervisory process for creating threads and coordinating the activities of the three stages. Apache Hadoop is a popular open-source implementation of the MapReduce model (Holmes, 2012; White,

2010). A distributed file system, HDFS, is used to provide high throughput access to the data. The HDFS supports *write-once-read-many* model, which simplifies data coherency through relaxed concurrency control requirements.

MapReduce implementations such as the Apache Hadoop transparently handle input data partitioning, scheduling the program's execution across a set of compute nodes, handling node failures, and managing the required inter-node communication. These features allow programmers without any experience with parallel and distributed systems to easily utilize the resources of a large distributed computing system. However, MapReduce paradigm suits only certain types of problems that can be expressed as key-value pairs.

ERLANG MESSAGE BASED CONCURRENT PROGRAMMING MODEL

Erlang is a *pure message passing language* where concurrency is built into the programming language and not the operating system (Hebert, 2013). Contrast this with MPI, where an MPI implementation augments C/C++ and Fortran languages with constructs needed for concurrency. Concurrent Erlang applications are modeled as sets of parallel processes that can interact only by exchanging messages. Programming with processes is done with three primitives – *spawn*, *send*, and *receive*. Erlang also implements the MapReduce programming model.

We illustrate the distributed concurrency model of Erlang for parallel computing through a program which computes the sum of the first million positive integers. This is the same problem used for illustrating the MPI programming paradigm. The Erlang program is shown in Figure 18.

Erlang code is divided into modules. A module consists of a sequence of attributes and function declarations, each terminated by a period (.). Lines 1 - 2 specify module attributes. The rest of the

code is divided into three sections: server process (aka master) code (lines 5 - 27), client process code (lines 30 - 34), and user-defined functions (lines 35 - 47) that are called by the server process.

Consider the code executed by the server process. Note the indentation of lines 7 - 27 and the syntax on line 5. Code comments precisely describe the computation performed by the server process. Number of processes is set at 4, a vector of one million positive integers is defined and initialized, and four processes are spawned. Next, the vector is segmented into four non-overlapping partitions comprised of consecutive vector elements (line 20). Thus, each vector partition is of size 250,000 and is assigned to a distinct process. Finally, the server process creates a list from the partial results received from client processes (line 24) and this list summed and printed (line 27).

Code executed by client processes is shown in lines 30 - 33. In essence, each client sums up the values in the list it receives and returns computed result to the server process.

Shown in lines 35 - 47 are three user defined functions. The *sublist()* returns the nth slice of a vector by dividing the vector into equal parts of specified size. The *for()* is an iterator for traversing elements of a list. Finally, *index_of()* returns the index position of an element in a list.

The commands for compiling and running the Erlang program are shown in Figure 19. The *c(parallelsum).* command is used for compilation of parallelsum module and *parallelsum.server().* is used for executing the program. Also shown in this figure are results of the execution.

TRENDS AND FUTURE RESEARCH DIRECTIONS

According to a 2013 NSF report (National Science Foundation, 2013), high performance computing (HPC) resources at academic research institutions have increased substantially since 2005. One of the findings in this report states that 59% of academic

Figure 18. Erlang's concurrent implementation for summing first one million positive integers

```
-module(parallelsum).
-export([server/0]).

%% code run by master (server) process
server() ->                                                                    5

        %% number of Erlang processes to spawn
        NbrProcesses = 4,

        %% prepare vector of first one million positive integers              10
        Vector = lists:seq(1,1000000),

        %% set segment size of data that each client process works on
        SegmentSize = 250000,
                                                                               15
        %% spawn processes and store process ids in a list
        Pids = for(1, NbrProcesses, fun() -> spawn(fun() -> client() end) end),

        %% send message to each process to compute sum of the vector segment assigned
        lists:foreach(fun(Pid) -> Pid ! {self(),sublist(index_of(Pid, Pids),   20
                SegmentSize, Vector)} end, Pids),

        %% receive result from each process
        PartialSumsList = for(1, NbrProcesses, fun() -> receive {_, Sum} -> Sum end end),
                                                                               25
        %% sum the values in the partial sum list and print it
        io:format("Sum of first million positive integers = ~B~n",[lists:sum(PartialSumsList)]).

%% code run by each client process
client() ->                                                                    30
        receive
        {From, L} when is_list(L) -> From ! {self(),lists:sum(L)}
        end.

%% return nth segment of Size elements from List                              35
sublist(N, Size, List) ->
        lists:sublist(List, (N-1)*Size+1, Size).

%% simulate loop that goes from 1 to N
for(N, N, F) -> [F()];
for(I, N, F) -> [F()|for(I+1, N, F)].                                          40

%% find the index of an item in list
index_of(Item, List) -> index_of(Item, List, 1).
index_of(_, [], _) -> not_found;                                               45
index_of(Item, [Item|_], Index) -> Index;
index_of(Item, [_|Tail], Index) -> index_of(Item, Tail, Index+1).
```

Figure 19. Compiling and running an Erlang program on OS X

```
● ○ ○                    Terminal — beam.smp — 80×11
nandigaj@jnmcbkpro$ erl
Erlang R16B02 (erts-5.10.3) [source] [64-bit] [smp:8:8] [async-threads:10] [hipe
] [kernel-poll:false]

Eshell V5.10.3  (abort with ^G)
1> c(parallelsum).
{ok,parallelsum}
2> parallelsum:server().
Sum of first million integers = 500000500000
ok
3>
```

institutions reported a bandwidth of at least 1 gigabit per second (Gbps) in 2011, compared with 21% of such institutions in 2005. Of the top 500 supercomputers in the world (as of June 2013 ranking, www. top500.org), 90 are listed as being in academia and 21 of those being in the U.S. academia. This clearly demonstrates that HPC is increasingly being used across universities for research and learning.

Several tools are available for developing HPC applications (Bach et al., 2010; Chamberlain et al., 2010; Dave et al., 2009; Feng and Balaji, 2009; Kelly et al., 2009; Pasetto, Petrini, and Agarwal, 2010; Tallent and Mellor-Crummey, 2009). There is also significant interest in undergraduate education in high performance computing (Adams et al., 2010; Bunde, 2009; Ernst and Stevenson, 2008; Fekete, 2009; Rivoire, 2010). HPC is expected to play a phenomenal role in emerging areas such as computational biology (Bader, 2004) and others (Barker et al., 2009; Berriman and Groom, 2011; Committee on Modeling, Simulation, and Games; Standing Committee on Technology Insight–Gauge, Evaluate, and Review; National Research Council, 2010; Lu et al., 2007).

The 2013 Nobel Prize in Chemistry winners' work involved developing an HPC-based framework for analyzing the behavior of biomolecules in terms of interactions between the constituent atoms. Measuring and visualizing the behavior of 50,000 or more atoms in a reaction over the course of a fraction of a millisecond takes enormous computing power. This work exemplifies the role of supercomputing in validating ideas about chemistry. HPC has strongly positioned itself as another pervasive and powerful tool for scientific discoveries.

The *Blue Waters* is one of the most powerful supercomputers located at the University of Illinois. It provides systems and support for computing at petascale level to enable computationally-driven science and engineering research. Researchers interested in using Blue Waters may apply for an allocation through the NSF PRAC program. Access to Blue Waters is also available for educational and industrial projects.

XSEDE (www.xsede.org) is a single virtual HPC system which enables interactive sharing of supercomputers, data, software tools, and expertise. It offers unprecedented opportunities for scientific research by providing transparent access to sixteen supercomputers and high-end visualization and data analysis resources across the U.S. XSEDE resources are also available to scientists around the world.

Exascale computing refers to computing systems capable of at least one exaFLOPS. This compute capacity is 1,000 times that of the current fastest supercomputer. Intel corp. is expected to develop exascale technology by 2018. Other players in the exascale computing include the European Union and the Indian government. However, several challenges remain to be solved before the exascale computing can become a reality.

To effectively harness exascale computing requires dramatic improvements in how the software for parallel computers is currently developed.

Novel approaches and algorithms to partition data for parallel execution are required. The current standards need to evolve to deal with many-core nodes. New software development methodologies and tools that are suitable for exascale computing are needed. Formal software engineering methodologies hold great potential for developing software for the exascale computing environments. HPC programming paradigms that are based on functional programming languages hold greater promise for exascale computing.

CONCLUSION

This chapter provided a fairly comprehensive introduction to various programming paradigms used in high performance computing. Each paradigm is illustrated with a concrete programming example. The programs were chosen to illustrate the fundamental concepts of the paradigms rather than to demonstrate their esoteric or advanced features. The reader should consult the bibliography and additional resources sections for advanced and comprehensive exposition to the topics.

Parallel programming still requires detailed knowledge of the underlying hardware architecture to effectively make use of the abundant computing power. A case in point is the OpenMP scheduling. The schedule controls how loop iterations are divided among the threads. Choosing the right schedule can have great impact on the execution speed of the application. *Static schedule* option plays a critical role in Non-Uniform Memory Access (NUMA) architectures. If data of some memory location is accessed in the first iteration of a loop by a thread, that data will reside on the NUMA node for subsequent use. In the second iteration of the loop the same thread could access that data faster.

OpenCL provides a low-level accelerator parallelism through compiler pragmas. On the other hand, OpenCL libraries (e.g., AMD's Accelerated Parallel Processing Math Libraries (APPML), MAGMA Linear Algebra library, ViennaCL dense and sparse linear algebra library) make developing parallel applications a little easier. These libraries are hand-written using OpenCL to achieve accelerator parallelism. In contrast, OpenACC relies on compilers to automatically find accelerator parallelism in the code. This is a huge step forward compared to OpenMP and OpenCL. However, auto-finding of parallelism by compilers is not necessarily optimal or comprehensive and has its limitations.

Hybrid paradigms for parallel programming are also common. For example, OpenMP and MPI combination is used to take advantage of computing platforms that encompass both symmetric multiprocessors and clusters. MapReduce-MPI library provides a MapReduce implementation using the MPI distributed-memory model. OpenCL aims to provide a truly heterogeneous parallel computing environment.

Some paradigms such as MPI and OpenMP are novel, generic, and have withstood the test of time. On the other hand, MapReduce's approach to parallelism is neither programming language centric nor database centric. It is only suitable for certain types of problems and is not as widely applicable as the other paradigms.

Standards such as the MPI and OpenMP are evolving to provide programming interfaces at higher levels of abstraction. The recent standards such as the OpenACC aim to automatically parallelize code based on higher-level hints provided by the programmers. Parallel computing has achieved critical mass and is poised to make the desktop supercomputing a reality in the very near future.

REFERENCES

A Programming Language Designed for Parallelism and Cloud Computing. (2014). Retrieved from 20 October 2014, http: //julialang.org/

Adams, J. C., Ernst, D. J., Murphy, T., & Ortiz, A. (2010). Multicore education: Pieces of the parallel puzzle. In *Proceedings of the 41st ACM Technical Symposium on Computer Science Education*. New York, NY: ACM. doi:10.1145/1734263.1734329

Amazon. (2012). *1000 genomes project and AWS*. Retrieved 20 October 2014, from http://aws.amazon.com/1000genomes/

Bach, M., Charney, M., Cohn, R., Demikhovsky, E., Devor, T., & Hazelwood, K. et al. (2010). Analyzing parallel programs with pin. *Computer*, *43*(3), 34–41. doi:10.1109/MC.2010.60

Bader, D. A. (2004). Computational biology and high-performance computing. *Communications of the ACM*, *47*(11), 34–41. doi:10.1145/1029496.1029523

Barker, K. J., Davis, K., Hoisie, A., Kerbyson, D. J., Lang, M., Pakin, S., & Sancho, J. C. (2009). Using performance modeling to design large-scale systems. *Computer*, *42*(11), 42–49. doi:10.1109/MC.2009.372

Berriman, G. B., & Groom, S. L. (2011). How will astronomy archives survive the data tsunami? *Queue*, *9*(10), 21:20–21:27. doi:10.1145/2043174.2043190

Bunde, D. P. (2009). A short unit to introduce multi-threaded programming. *Journal of Computing Sciences in Colleges*, *25*(1), 9–20.

Chamberlain, R. D., Franklin, M. A., Tyson, E. J., Buckley, J. H., Buhler, J., & Galloway, G. et al. (2010). Auto-pipe: Streaming applications on architecturally diverse systems. *Computer*, *43*(3), 42–49. doi:10.1109/MC.2010.62

Committee on Modeling, Simulation, and Games; Standing Committee on Technology Insight–Gauge, Evaluate, and Review; National Research Council. (2010). *The rise of games and high performance computing for modeling and simulation*. Retrieved 20 October 2014, from http://www.nap.edu/catalog.php?record_id=12816

Dave, C., Bae, H., Min, S., Lee, S., Eigenmann, R., & Midkiff, S. (2009). Cetus: A source-to-source compiler infrastructure for multicores. *Computer*, *42*(12), 36–42. doi:10.1109/MC.2009.385

Donofrio, D., Oliker, L., Shalf, J., Wehner, M. F., Rowen, C., & Krueger, J. et al. (2009). Energy-efficient computing for extreme-scale science. *Computer*, *42*(11), 62–71. doi:10.1109/MC.2009.353

Ernst, D. J., & Stevenson, D. E. (2008). Concurrent CS: Preparing students for a multicore world. In *Proceedings of the 13th Annual Conference on Innovation and Technology in Computer Science Education*. New York, NY: ACM. doi:10.1145/1384271.1384333

Fekete, A. D. (2009). Teaching about threading: Where and what? *SIGACT News*, *40*(1), 51–57.

Feng, W., & Balaji, P. (2009). Tools and environments for multicore and many-core architectures. *Computer*, *42*(12), 26–27. doi:10.1109/MC.2009.412

Gaster, B. R., & Howes, L. (2012). Can GPGPU programming be liberated from the data-parallel bottleneck? *Computer*, *45*(8), 42–52. doi:10.1109/MC.2012.257

Gaster, G., Howes, L., Kaeli, D. R., Mistry, P., & Schaa, D. (2011). *Heteorgeneous computing with OpenCL*. Boston: Morgan Kaufmann.

1000 . Genomes. (2012). *1000 genomes: A deep catalog of human genetic variation*. Retrieved from 20 October 2014, http://www.1000genomes.org/

Hanisch, R. J. (2011). *Data discovery, access, and management with the virtual observatory*. Paper presented at Innovations in Data-intensive Astronomy. Retrieved 20 October 2014, from http://www.nrao.edu/meetings/bigdata/agenda.shtml

Hebert, F. (2013). *Learn you some erlang for great good!: A beginner's guide*. San Francisco, CA: No Starch Press.

Hoisie, A., & Vladimir, G. (2009). Extreme-scale computing. *Computer*, 42(11), 24–26. doi:10.1109/MC.2009.354

Holmes, A. (2012). *Hadoop in practice*. Shelter Island, NY: Manning Publications Co.

Keckler, S. W., & Reinhardt, S. K. (2012). Massively multithreaded computing systems. *Computer*, 45(8), 24–25. doi:10.1109/MC.2012.270

Kelly, T., Wang, Y., Lafortune, S., & Mahlke, S. (2009). Eliminating concurrency bugs with control engineering. *Computer*, 42(12), 52–60. doi:10.1109/MC.2009.391

Kirk, D., & Hwu, W. (2010). *Programming massively parallel processors: A hands-on approach*. Boston: Morgan Kaufmann.

Lu, Y., Gao, P., Lv, R., Su, Z., & Yu, W. (2007). Study of content-based image retrieval using parallel computing technique. In *Proceedings of the 2007 Asian Technology Information Program's (ATIP's) 3rd Workshop on High Performance Computing in China: Solution Approaches to Impediments for High Performance Computing*. New York: ACM. doi:10.1145/1375783.1375820

Manyika, J., Chui, M., Brown, B., Bughin, J., Dobbs, R., Roxburgh, C., & Byers, A. H. (2011). *Big data: The next frontier for innovation, competition, and productivity. Tech. rep*. McKinsey Global Institute.

Marlow, S. (2013). *Parallel and concurrent programming in Haskell: Techniques for multicore and multithreaded programming*. Sebastopol, CA: O'Reilly Media, Inc.

National Science Foundation. (2013). *Computing and networking capacity increases at academic research institutions*. Retrieved 20 October 2014, from http://www.nsf.gov/statistics/infbrief/nsf13329/

Pacheco, P. S. (2011). *An introduction to parallel programming*. Boston: Morgan Kaufmann.

Pasetto, D., Petrini, F., & Virat, A. (2010). Tools for very fast regular expression matching. *Computer*, 43(3), 50–58. doi:10.1109/MC.2010.80

Rivoire, S. (2010). A breadth-first course in multicore and manycore programming. In *Proceedings of the 41st ACM Technical Symposium on Computer Science Education*. New York, NY: ACM. doi:10.1145/1734263.1734339

Sanders, J., & Kandrot, E. (2011). CUDA by example: An introduction to general-purpose GPU programming. Reading, MA: Addison-Wesley.

Scarpino, M. (2011). *OpenCL in action: How to accelerate graphics and computations*. Shelter Island, NY: Manning Publications Co.

Schadt, E. E., Linderman, M. D., Sorenson, J., Lee, L., & Nolan, G. P. (2010). Computational solutions to large-scale data management and analysis. *Nature Reviews. Genetics*, 11(9), 647–657. doi:10.1038/nrg2857 PMID:20717155

Sodan, A. C., Machina, J., Deshmeh, A., Macnaughton, K., & Esbaugh, B. (2010). Parallelism via multithreaded and multicore CPUs. *Computer*, 43(3), 24–32. doi:10.1109/MC.2010.75

Stratton, J. A., Rodrigues, C., Sung, I., Chang, L., Anssari, N., & Liu, G. et al. (2012). Algorithm and data optimization techniques for scaling to massively threaded systems. *Computer*, 45(8), 26–32. doi:10.1109/MC.2012.194

STScI. (2012). *Space telescope science institute.* Retrieved 20 October 2014, from http://www.stsci.edu/portal/

Tallent, N. R., & Mellor-Crummey, J. M. (2009). Identifying performance bottlenecks in work-stealing computations. *Computer, 42*(12), 44–50. doi:10.1109/MC.2009.396

Texas Multicore Technologies, Inc. (2012). *SequenceL.* Retrieved 20 October 2014, from http://www.texasmulticoretechnologies.com/

Tittel, E. (2012). *Clusters for dummies.* New York: John Wiley.

Torrellas, J. (2009). Architectures for extreme-scale computing. *Computer, 42*(11), 28–35. doi:10.1109/MC.2009.341

Tumeo, A., Simone, S., & Oreste, V. (2012). Designing next-generation massively multithreaded architectures for irregular applications. *Computer, 45*(8), 53–61. doi:10.1109/MC.2012.193

Tzeng, S., Brandon, L., & Owens, J. D. (2012). A GPU task-parallel model with dependency resolution. *Computer, 45*(8), 34–41. doi:10.1109/MC.2012.255

White, T. (2010). *Hadoop: The definitive guide.* Sebastopol, CA: O'Reilly Media, Inc.

Wilde, M., Foster, I., Iskra, K., Beckman, P., Zhang, A., & Espinosa, A. et al. (2009). Parallel scripting for applications at the petascale and beyond. *Computer, 42*(11), 50–60. doi:10.1109/MC.2009.365

Wilt, N. (2013). *CUDA handbook: A comprehensive guide to GPU programming.* Upper Saddle River, NJ: Pearson Education, Inc.

Yuichiro, A., Sumimoto, S., & Toshiyuki, S. (2009). Tofu: A 6D mesh/torus interconnect for exascale computers. *Computer, 42*(11), 36–40. doi:10.1109/MC.2009.370

ADDITIONAL READING

AnalyticsBridge.com is an on-line forum for data scientists dealing with massive data volumes. Provides blog posts and pointers to computational resources. Retrieved 20 October 2014, from http://www.analyticbridge.com/

Erlang home page. Retrieved 20 October 2014, from http://www.erlang.org/

Go Parallel. HPC events and resources. Retrieved 20 October 2014, from http://goparallel.source-forge.net/

Haskell home page. Retrieved 20 October 2014, from http://www.haskell.org/haskellwiki/Haskell

inside HPC: news and events for supercomputing professionals. Retrieved 20 October 2014, from http://insidehpc.com/

MapReduce: Apache Hadoop Implementation. Retrieved 20 October 2014, from http://hadoop.apache.org/

MapReduce-MPI Library. an open-source implementation of MapReduce using MPI message passing. Retrieved 20 October 2014, from http://mapreduce.sandia.gov/

MPI Standard home page: Retrieved 20 October 2014, from http://www.mcs.anl.gov/research/projects/mpi/standard.html

NVidia Developer Zone. Resources for CUDA Development. Retrieved 20 October 2014, from https://developer.nvidia. com/category/zone/cuda-zone

Open, C. L. Specifications. Retrieved 20 October 2014, from http://www.khronos.org/opencl/

Open, M. P. Specifications. Retrieved 20 October 2014, from http://openmp.org/wp/

Open, M. P. I. Project is an open source MPI-2 implementation which is developed and maintained by a consortium of academic, research, and industry partners. Retrieved 20 October 2014, from http://www.open-mpi.org/

OpenACC home page: Retrieved 20 October 2014, from http://www.openacc-standard.org/

top500.org. Provides statistics on top 500 super-computers and related news. Retrieved 20 October 2014, from http://top500.org/

University, H. P. C. (HPCU) provides an on-line environment for sharing educational and training materials. Retrieved 20 October 2014, from http://www.hpcuniversity.org/

KEY TERMS AND DEFINITIONS

CUDA™: Is both a parallel computing architecture and programming model for high performance computing. CUDA™ is a proprietary standard and provides programmatic access to NVidia graphics processing units (GPUs).

Erlang: Is a functional programming language with dynamic typing and strict evaluation. It is specifically designed for massive concurrency and is suitable for real-time, high performance computing applications.

Functional Programming: Is a programming paradigm that treats computation as evaluation of mathematical functions and avoids state and mutable data. Features such as curried functions, higher order functions, and lazy evaluation characterize functional programming.

General Purpose Graphics Processing Unit (GPGPU): This acronym refers to general purpose computing on graphics processing units. GPGPU is a new approach to high performance computing which leverages both CPUs and GPUs for achieving unprecedented compute power.

Graphics Processing Unit (GPU): Is a specialized processor designed to rapidly manipulate and alter memory to accelerate the creation of graphics in a frame buffer. Their highly parallel structure makes GPUs dwarf general-purpose CPUs when it comes to processing massive amounts of data in parallel. GPUs are used in game consoles, mobile phones, embedded systems, desktop and workstation computers, and modern supercomputers.

Haskell: Is a pure functional programming language based on lambda calculus. It is statically typed and uses lazy evaluation. Used for rapid prototyping and for developing maintainable high quality software. Concurrency and parallelism are supported through intrinsic features of the language.

High Performance Computing: Refers to hardware architectures, parallel programming techniques and associated compliers, software development tools, and best practices to achieve higher computing power to solve problems that are otherwise impractical.

MapReduce: Is a programming paradigm for massive parallel computation using thousands of servers in a compute cluster. The term MapReduce refers to two different tasks: the map and reduce tasks. The map task turns a dataset into another dataset consisting of tuples (essentially (key, value) pairs). The reduce job takes the output of the map job and produces final result.

Message Passing Interface (MPI): A standard that specifies a number of functions for developing distributed memory-based parallel computing applications. Implementation of this standard as libraries is available for C/C++ and Fortran languages.

OpenACC: It is an open standard and provides a collection of compiler directives to specify loops

Chapter 14
Data Mining for High Performance Computing

Shen Lu
Soft Challenge LLC, USA

ABSTRACT

With the development of information technology, the size of the dataset becomes larger and larger. Distributed data processing can be used to solve the problem of data analysis on large datasets. It partitions the dataset into a large number of subsets and uses different processors to store, manage, broadcast, and synchronize the data analysis. However, distributed computing gives rise to new problems such as the impracticality of global communication, global synchronization, dynamic topology changes of the network, on-the-fly data updates, the needs to share resources with other applications, frequent failures, and recovery of resource. In this chapter, the concepts of distributed computing are introduced, the latest research are presented, the advantage and disadvantage of different technologies and systems are analyzed, and the future trends of the distributed computing are summarized.

INTRODUCTION

Nowadays, with the size of customer's datasets become larger and larger, distributing datasets into different machines provides an effective solution for data processing. However, distributed data processing [Corbett et al. 2012] introduces the issues of global synchronization and communication among machines. Nodes are required to work independently and also cooperate together where nodes generate the data locally and update the data whenever new data arrive. This means that for all practical purpose the nodes should receive the data from its immediate neighbors and compute the results through local negotiation. Therefore, a global database is constructed through each node of data exchange from its immediate neighbors.

With the advance of the technology, a database can now be partitioned into a large number of computers, such as grid computing platforms (Villegas, et. al. 2010. Talia, 2006), federal database systems (McLeod & Heimbigner, 2009), and peer-to-peer computing environments (Datta et al., 2008). However, parallel processing assumes the availability of parallel processors, even though data mining algorithms are stand-alone processes and do not require parallel processors. Distributed data

DOI: 10.4018/978-1-4666-7461-5.ch014

Copyright © 2015, IGI Global. Copying or distributing in print or electronic forms without written permission of IGI Global is prohibited.

processing divide the transactional dataset D into N non-overlapping partitions, $D_1, D_2, D_3, ..., D_n$.

Many data analysis and mining algorithms have been proposed that focus on improving the efficiency of the algorithms via parallelism, which uses hash-based technology, transaction reduction, partitioning, and sampling. Partitions are distributed to processors. Each processor finishes data analysis on a partition independently and creates its local result against its own dataset partition. After that, processors exchange their local dataset partitions and results for the global synchronization. The master processor is different from other processors. It plays a central role in distributed computing, which can not only work as a stand-alone processor, but also manage, broadcast, and synchronize other processors.

However, distributed computing gives rise to new problems such as the impracticality of global communication, global synchronization, dynamic topology changes of the network, on-the-fly data updates, the needs to share resources with other applications, frequent failures, and recovery of resource. Distributed data mining algorithms have been provided for this purpose. For example, distributed system can be considered as the combination of several individual processors in which every node in the system can reach the exact solution, impose very little communication overhead, transparently tolerate network topology changes and node failures, and quickly adjust to changes in the data as they occur. Another example is the distributed system with complicated master processor and simple distributed nodes, in which the master processor can be used to manage, broadcast and synchronize and other processors can only perform heavy-duty and time-consuming computation. Different architectures use different strategies to eventually finish global communication, global synchronization, dynamic topology changes of the network, on-the-fly data updates.

In this chapter, we introduce databases for high performance computing (HPC), data mining for high performance computing, visualization for modeling and simulation, and input/output performance tuning.

DATA MINING

Data Mining as the Evolution of Information Technology

Data mining can be used to integrate, manage, analyze and predict information. With the development of World Wide Web, data storage devices, and data collecting machines, a vast amount of information are collected each day from business, science, medicine and almost every aspect of daily life. The fast-growing, tremendous amount of data, collected and stored in large and numerous data repositories, has far exceeded our human ability for comprehension without powerful tools. We need to understand data, use data to help make decisions, find interesting knowledge from data and so on. Data mining is the process of discovering interesting patterns and knowledge from large amounts of data. However, the process of knowledge discovery includes several steps, such as data cleaning, data integration, data selection, data transformation, data mining, pattern evaluation, and knowledge presentation.

What Kinds of Data can be Mined?

Regarding temporal data, we can mine banking data for changing trends, which may aid in the scheduling of bank tellers according to the volume of customer traffic. Stock exchange data can be mined to uncover trends that could help you plan investment strategies. We could mine computer network data streams to detect intrusions based on the anomaly of message flows (Lau et. al, 2013), which may be discovered by clustering, dynamic construction of stream models or by comparing the current frequent patterns with those at a previous time. With spatial data, we may look for patterns that describe changes in metropolitan poverty rates based on city distances from major highways. The relationships among a set of spatial objects can be examined in order to discover which subsets of objects are spatially autocorrelated or associated. By mining text data, such as literature on data mining from the past ten years, we can identify the evolution of hot topics in the field. By mining user comments on products, we can assess customer sentiments and understand how well a product is embraced by a market. From multimedia data, we can mine images to identify objects and classify them by assigning semantic labels or tags. By mining video data of a hockey game, we can detect video sequences corresponding to goals. Web mining can help us learn about the distribution of information on the Internet in general, characterize and classify web pages, and uncover web dynamics and the association and other relationships among different web pages, users, communities, and web-based activities.

What Kinds of Patterns can be Mined?

Data mining and data analysis include several technologies, such as mining frequent patterns, associations, and correlations; classification and regression for predictive analysis; cluster analysis; outlier analysis and so on. For frequent pattern mining, a frequent itemset refers to a set of items that often appear together in a transactional data set. There are many kinds of frequent patterns, such as frequent itemsets, frequent subsequences, and frequent substructures. For association analysis, additional analysis can be performed to uncover interesting statistical correlations between associated attribute-value pairs. Classification is the process of finding a model that describes and distinguishes data classes or concepts. The model are derived based on the analysis of a set of training data. The model is used to predict the class label of objects for which the class label is unknown. Unlike classification and regression, which analyze class-labeled data sets, clustering analyzes data objects without consulting class labels. In many cases, class-labeled data may simply not exist at the beginning. Clustering can be used to generate class labels for a group of data. The objects are clustered or grouped based on the principle of maximizing the intra-class similarity and minimizing the interclass similarity. Outliers are the data objects which do not comply with the general behavior or model of the data. Many data mining methods discard outliers as noise or exceptions. However, in some applications the rare events can be more interesting than the more regularly occurring ones.

Data Storage and Distributed File Systems

A file system is a subsystem of an operating system that performs file management activities such as organization, storing retrieval, naming, sharing, and protection of files. It is designed to allow programs to use a set of operations that characterize the file abstraction and free the programmers from concerns about the details of space allocation and layout of the secondary storage device. Therefore, a file system provides an abstraction of a storage device; that is, it is a convenient mechanism for storing and retrieving information from the storage device.

A new system called Active Disks is introduced in (Riedel, Gibson & Faloutsos, 1998), which can move portions of an application's processing on individual disk drives and run application-level code on individual disk drives. Therefore, inside individual storage devices, the complex processing and optimizations can be done, such as data mining, database management, multimedia processing. Grid can be used to provide an effective computational support for knowledge discovery. Knowledge Grid (Cannataro, Talia & Trunfio, 2004) is a software architecture which can be used to analyze large datasets, to maintain over distributed processors and to build more specific parallel and distributed knowledge discovery tools and services. Knowledge grid used the basic Grid services, such as communication, authentication, information, and resource management to build specific parallel and distributed knowledge discovery tools and services on top of computational grid mechanisms.

In (Isard, et. al, 2007), a distributed storage system was used on a set of computers. The communication among different computers is through files, TCP pipes, and shared-memory first in first out (FIFO). Replica catalog and replica management are used in (Cannataro & Talia, 2003), which can improve access across geographically-distributed grids. The replica catalog provides mapping between logical names for files and one for more copies of the files on physical storage systems. The replica management combines the replica catalog and grid file transfer prototype (FTP) to manage data replication. Knowledge Directory Service (KDS) is provided in (Cannataro & Talia, 2003) which is responsible for maintaining a description of all the data and tools used in the Knowledge Grid. The metadata information is represented by XML documents and is stored in a Knowledge Metadata Repository (KMR).

EXPERIMENTS

We used Lonestar Server from the Extreme Science and Engineering Discovery Environment (XSEDE) Computing Center at Texas Advanced Computer Center (TACC) at the University of Texas at Austin to do experiments. Lonestar is a Dell Linux Cluster, a powerful, multi-use cyberinfrastructure HPC and remote visualization resource. Lonestar is intended primarily for parallel applications scalable to thousands of cores. Normal batch queues will enable users to run simulations up to 24 hours. Lonestar also provides access to large memory nodes, and nodes containing NVIDIA GPU's, giving users' access to high-throughput computing and remote visualization capabilities respectively. We test seven data

mining algorithms on a large lymphoma Microarray gene expression data set with 240 instances and 522 attributes. We use evaluation measurements to show the performance of each data mining algorithms, such as correlation coefficient, mean absolute error, root mean squared error, relative absolute error, root relative squared error, and total number of instances. Experimental results are showed in Table 1 and other related output is shown in Appendix. The experimental results show that data mining algorithms perform very well in high performance computing environment.

RESOURCE MANAGEMENT

Distributed systems are characterized by resource multiplicity and system transparency. Every distributed system consists of a number of resources interconnected by a network. Besides providing communication facilities the network facilities resource sharing by migrating a local process and executing it at a remote node of the network. A process may be migrated because the local node does not have the required resources or the local node has to be shut down. A process may also be executed remotely if the expected turnaround time will be better. From a user's point of view, the set of available resources in a distributed operating system acts like a single virtual system. Hence, when a user submits a process for execution, it becomes the responsibility of the resource manager of the distributed operating system to control the assignment of resource to processes and to route the processes to suitable nodes of the system according to these assignments. A resource can be logical, such as shared file, or physical, such as a central processing unit (CPU). For our purpose, we will consider a resource to be a processor of the system and assume that each processor forms a node of the distributed system.

Agent management system (Lou, et. al, 2007) is a mandatory component of Multi-Agent Environment (MAGE) (Shi, 2013). Agent is the

Table 1. Data mining on high performance computing with large data sets

Algorithms	Correlation coefficient	Mean absolute error	Root mean squared error	Relative absolute error	Root relative squared error	Total number of instances
Gaussian Processes	-0.1	0.49	0.5	100.00%	100.00%	82
Linear Regression	0.34	0.44	0.57	89.81%	100.00%	82
Additive Regression	-0.18	0.54	0.59	100.00%	100.00%	82
Ibk	0.07	0.46	0.68	94.58%	100.00%	82
Decision Table	-0.18	0.54	0.59	100.00%	100.00%	82
REP Tree	0	0.49	0.5	100.00%	100.00%	82
PLS Classifier	0.33	0.45	0.58	91.36%	100.00%	82

fundamental actor in MAGE, which combines one or more service capabilities into a unified and integrated execution model that may include access to external software, human users and communications facilities. A replica management service with a replica catalog and Grid FTP transfers is provided in (Allcock, et. al, 2001). It can be used to manage the replication of complete and partial copies of datasets, defined as collections of files. Replica management services include creating new copies of a complete or partial collection of files, registering these new copies in a replica catalog, allowing users and applications to query and catalog to find all existing copies of a particular file or collection of files, selecting the best replica for access based on storage and network performance predictions provided by a Grid information service. Nimrod-G Grid resource broker (Buyya, 2002) is an example of a Grid system that uses a computational economy driven architecture for managing resources and scheduling task farming applications on large scale distributed resources. Legion (Grimshaw, et. al, 1999) was designed to target wide-area computing demands. To exchange information and support data mining in a wide area networking, the new possibility depends on the ability to manage shared resources.

Legion is a component-based system in which distributed components are presented as independent and active objects. A new resource management architecture is provided in (Czajkowski, et. al, 1998), which can be used for site autonomy and heterogeneous substrates at the resources, and application requirements or policy extensibility, co-allocation, and online control. Several components are associated with the resource management architecture, such as distinct local manager, resource broker, and resource co-allocator components. A resource specification language is defined to exchange information about requirements. In (Barmouta & Buyya 2003), resource allocation system, such as cluster scheduler, is used to manage resource usage information. Local access to resource is managed by the resource owner who has to create and manage local accounts for each user.

PROCESS MANAGEMENT

Process migration is the relocation of a process from its current location to another node, as showed below in Figure 1. A process may be migrated either before it starts executing on its source node or during the course of its execution. The former is known as non-preemptive process migration and the latter.

Migration process is a complex activity that involves proper handling of several sub-activities in order to meet the requirements of a good

Figure 1. Flow of execution of a migrating process

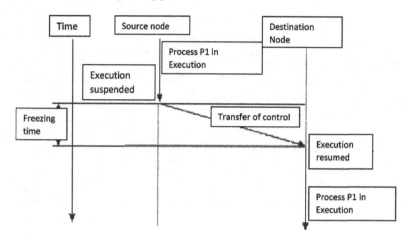

process migration mechanism. The four major sub-activities involved in process migration are as follows:

1. Freezing the process on its source node and restarting it on its destination node
2. Transferring the process's address space from its source node to its destination node.
3. Forwarding messages meant for the migration process
4. Handling communication between cooperation processes that have been separated as a result of process migration.

Mechanisms for Freezing and Restarting a Process

The mechanism to freeze the process on its source node and restarting it on its destination node is the usual process is to take a snapshot of the process's state on its source node and reinstate the snapshot on the destination node. By freezing the process, we mean that the execution of the process is suspended and all external interactions with the process are deferred. Although the freezing and restart operations differ from system to system, some general issues are involved in these operations, such as immediate and delayed blocking of the process, fast and slow I/O operations, informa-

tion about open files, reinstating the process on its destination node.

Some typical cases for immediate and delayed blocking of the processes are showed in (Kingsbury & Kline, 1989). For example, if the process is not executing a system call, it can be immediately blocked from further execution; if the process is executing a system call but is sleeping at an interruptible priority waiting for a kernel event to occur, it can be immediately blocked from further execution; if the process is executing a system call and is sleeping at a non-interruptible priority waiting for a kernel event to occur, it cannot be blocked immediately.

For fast and slow I/O operations, it happens after the process has been blocked. The process needs to finish all fast I/O operations associated with the process, before the process is frozen. It is feasible to wait for the completion of the fast operations, and not feasible to wait for the completion of the slow operations.

For information about open files, it is necessary to preserve a pointer to the file so that the migration process could continue to access it. Another issue is that one or more file being used by the process on its source node may be present on its destination node. It would be efficient to access these files from the local node rather than accessing them across the network from the process's previous node (Agrawal & Ezzat, 1987). These techniques would help in reducing the amount of data to be transferred at the time of address space transfer.

For restating the process on its destination node, on the destination node, an empty process state is similar to that allocated during process creation. The identifiers of the newly allocated process and the old process may or may not be the same. If the two identifiers are different, the new copy's identifiers is changed to the original identifier in a subsequent step before the process starts executing on the destination node.

Address Space Transfer Mechanisms

In the existing distributed systems, there are three different ways to transfer address space, such as total freezing, pre-transferring, and transfer on reference. The total freezing method stops the execution of the process and let the system transfer the address space first. It was implemented in DEMOS/MP (Powell & Miller, 1983), Sprite (Douglis & Ousterhout, 1987), and LOCUS (Popek & Walker, 1985) and is simple and easy to implement. Pre-transferring method transfers the address space while the process is still running on the source node. The process keeps running on the source node when the decision has been made to transfer the process from source node to the destination node. After the address space is moved to the destination node, the process can be moved from the source node to the destination node. For transfer on references, only small part of the address space can be used. The process' address space is left behind on its source node, and as the relocated process executes on its destination node, the desired blocks are copied from the remote location.

Message-Forwarding Mechanisms

Message forwarding mechanisms must ensure that all pending, en-route, and future messages arrive at the process' new location. There are three different types of messages and they are sent to the process in different ways. The first type messages arrive at source node when the process has been stopped at the source node and has not yet started at the destination node. The second type messages arrive at the source node when the process' execution starts on the destination node. The type three messages can be sent to the migration process after the execution has started on the destination node. This mechanism is used in the V-system (Cheriton 1988, Thermer et al. 1985) and Amoeba (Mullender et al. 1990). They can be used to handle all three types of message-forwarding mechanisms.

Mechanisms for Handling Coprocesses

Some process have subprocesses. For process migration, the process and its subprocess may be placed on different nodes. There are two ways to stop it from happening. One is called disallowing separation of coprocesses, the other is called home node or origin site concept. For disallowing separation of coprocesses, the system can check and make sure the parent process and child processes will be migrated together or the migration process will wait until one or all of their children to complete. For the home node or origin site concept, a home node or original node is used to communicate with parent processes and child processes when they are distributed on different nodes.

NAMING

Distributed computing supports several types of objects such as processes, files, I/O devices, mail boxes, and nodes. The naming facility of a distributed operating system enables users and programs to assign character-string names to objects and subsequently use these names to refer to those objects. The locating facility, which is an integral part of the naming facility, maps an object's name to the object's location in a distributed system. The naming and locating facilities jointly form a naming system that provides the users with an abstraction of an object that hides the details of how and where an object is actually located in the network. It provides a further level of abstraction when dealing with object replicas. Given an object name, it returns a set of the locations of the object's replicas.

The naming system plays an important role in achieving the goal of locations transparency in distributed system. In addition to facilitating transparent migration and replication of objects, the naming system also facilities object sharing. If various computations want to act upon the same object, they are enabled to do so by each containing a name for the object. Although the names contained in each computation may not necessarily be the same, they are mapped to the same object in this case.

MESSAGE PASSING

A process is a program in execution. When we say that two computers of a distributed system are communicating with each other, we mean that two processes, one running on each computer, are in communication with each other. In a distributed system, processes executing on different computers often need to communicate with each other to achieve some common goal. For example, each computer of a distributed system may have a resource manager process to monitor the current usage of its local resources, and the resource managers of all the computers might communicate with each other from time to time to dynamically balance the system load among all the computers. Therefore, a distributed operating system needs to provide interprocess communication mechanisms to facilitate such communication activities.

REMOTE PROCEDURE CALLS

The general message passing model of interprocess communication (IPC) was discussed in the previous section. The IPC part of a distributed application can often be adequately and efficiently handled by using an IPC protocol based on the message passing model. However, an independently developed IPC protocol is tailored specifically to one application and does not provide a foundation on which to build a variety of distributed applications. Therefore, a need was felt for a general IPC protocol that can be used for designing several distributed applications. The Remote Process Call (RPC) facility emerged out of this need. It is a special case of the general message passing model of IPC. Providing the programmers with a familiar mechanism for building distributed systems is one of the primary motivations for developing the RPC facility. While the RPC facility is not a universal panacea for all types of distributed applications, it does provide a valuable communication mechanism that is suitable for building a fairly large number of distributed applications.

DISTRIBUTED SHARED MEMORY

The distributed shared memory (DSM) system have an architecture of the form. Each node of the system consists of one or more CPUs and a memory unit. The nodes are connected by a high-speed communication network. A simple message-passing system allows processes on different nodes to exchange messages with each other. The DSM abstraction presents a large shared memory space to the processors of all nodes. In contrast to the shared physical memory in tightly coupled parallel architectures, the shared memory of DSM exists only virtually. A software memory mapping manager routine in each node maps the local memory onto the shared virtual memory.

To facilitate the mapping operation, the shared memory space is partitioned into blocks.

Data caching is a well-known solution to address memory access latency. The idea of data caching is used in DSM systems to reduce network latency. That is, the main memory of individual nodes is used to cache pieces of the shared memory space. The memory mapping manager of each node views its local memory as a big cache of the shared memory space for its associated processors. The basic unit of caching is a memory block.

When a process on a node access some data from a memory block of the shared memory space, the local memory mapping manager takes charge of its request. If the memory block containing the accessed data is resident in the local memory, the request is satisfied by supplying the accessed data is resident in the local memory, the request is satisfied by supplying the accessed data from the local memory. Otherwise, a network block fault is generated and the control is passed to the operating system.

SYNCHRONIZATION

A distributed system consists of a collection of distinct processes that are spatially separated and run concurrently. In systems with multiple concurrent processes, it is economical to share the system resources (hardware or software) among the concurrently executing processes. In such a situation, sharing may be cooperative or competitive. That is, since the number of available resources in a computing system is restricted, one process must necessarily influence the action of other concurrently executing processes as it competes for resources. For example, for a resource (such as a tape drive) that cannot be used simultaneously by multiple processes, a process willing to use it must wait if another process is using it. At times, concurrent process must cooperate either to achieve the desired performance of the computing system or due to the nature of the computation being performed. Typical examples of process cooperation involve two processes that bear a producer-consumer or client-server relationship to each other. For instance, a client process and a file server process must cooperate when performing file access operations. Both cooperative and competitive sharing require adherence to certain rules of behavior that guarantee that correct interaction occurs. The rules for enforcing correct interaction are implemented in the form of synchronization mechanisms.

CONCLUSION

This chapter discusses how to use high performance computing in data mining. The basic concepts of data mining were discussed and several data mining algorithms were tested in high performance computing environment. In order to perform data mining on high performance computing, several high performance computing technologies need to be adjusted, such as process management, naming mechanism, message passing, remote procedure calls, distributed shared memory and synchronization. Existing data mining algorithms can be used in high performance computing environment after choosing the proper mechanisms. In future, we need to design specific data mining algorithms to take advantage of the high performance computing architecture.

ACKNOWLEDGMENT

The author needs to acknowledge the support of this research by a "Startup" Allocation Grant with Dr. Richard Segall as Principle Investigator to use National Science Foundation (NSF) funded Extreme Science and Engineering Discovery Environment (XSEDE) Supercomputers Lonestar and Stampede at University of Texas at Austin Computer Center (TACC) for 2013-2014 for which output is presented in Appendix.

REFERENCES

Agrawal, R., & Ezzat, A. K. (1987). Location independent remote execution in NEST. *IEEE Transactions on Software Engineering, SE-13*(8), 905–912. doi:10.1109/TSE.1987.233509

Allcock, B., Bresnahan, J., Chervenak, A., Foster, I., Kesselman, C., Meder, S., et al., Tuecke, & S., Secure. (2001). Efficient data transport and replica management for high-performance data-intensive computing. In *Proceedings of MSS '01: Mass Storage Systems and Technologies, 2001* (p. 13). IEEE.

Atsalakis, G. S., & Valavanis, K. P. (2009). Surveying stock market forecasting techniques - Part 2: Soft computing methods. *Expert Systems with Applications, 36*(3), 5932–5941. doi:10.1016/j.eswa.2008.07.006

Barmouta, A., & Buyya, R. (2003). GridBank: A grid accounting service architecture (GASA) for distributed systems sharing and integration. In *Proceedings of the 17th International Symposium on Parallel and Distributed Processing*. IEEE Computer Society.

Buyya, R. (2002). *Economic-based distributed resource management and scheduling for grid computing*. Retrieved 24 April 2002, from http://cds.cern.ch/record/548570?ln=en

Cannataro, M., Conqiusta, A., Pugliese, A., Talia, D., & Trunflo, P. (2004, December). Distributed data mining on grids: Services, tools, and applications. *IEEE Trans System Cybern B Cybern, 34*(6), 2451–2465. doi:10.1109/TSMCB.2004.836890 PMID:15619945

Cannataro, M., & Talia, D. (2003). The knowledge grid: Designing, building, and implementing an architecture for distributed knowledge discovery. *Communications of the ACM, 46*(1), 89–93. doi:10.1145/602421.602425

Cannataro, M., Talia, D., & Trunfio, P. (2004). Distributed data mining on the grid: Services, tools, and applications. *IEEE Transactions on Systems, Man, and Cybernetics. Part B, Cybernetics, 34*(6), 2451–2465.

Cheriton, D. R. (1988). The V distributed system. *Communications of the ACM, 31*(3), 314–333. doi:10.1145/42392.42400

Corbett, J. C., Dean, J., Epstein, M., Fikes, A., Frost, C., & Furman, J. et al. (2012). Spanner: Google's globally-distributed database. In *Proceedings of OSDI'12: Tenth Symposium on Operating System Design and Implementation*. Hollywood, CA: Academic Press.

Czajkowski, K., Foster, I., Karonis, N., Kesselman, C., Martin, S., Smith, W., & Tuecke, S. (1998). A resource management architecture for metacomputing systems. In *Proceedings of the Workshop on Job Scheduling Strategies for Parallel*. Springer-Verlag.

Datta, S., Bhaduri, K., Giannella, C., Wolff, R., & Kargupta, H. (2006). Distributed data mining in peer-to-peer networks. *IEEE Internet Computing, 19*(4), 18–26. doi:10.1109/MIC.2006.74

Douglis, F., & Ousterhout, J. (1987). Process migration in the sprite operating system. In *Proceedings of the 7th International Conference on Distributed Computing Systems*. IEEE.

Grimshaw, A., Ferrari, A., Knabe, F., & Humphrey, M. (1999). Wide-area computing: Resource sharing on a large scale. *Computer, 32*(5), 29–37.

Isard, M., Budiu, M., Yu, Y., Birrell, A., & Fetterly, D. (2007, March). *Dryad: Distributed data-parallel programs from sequential building blocks*. Paper presented at the 2007 EuroSys conference, Lisboa, Portugal. doi:10.1145/1272996.1273005

Kingsbury, B. A., & Kline, J. T. (1989). Job and process recovery in a UNIX-based operating system. In *Proceedings of the Winter 1989 USENIX Conference*. USENIX Association.

Lau, D., Liu, J., Majumdar, S., Nandy, B., St-Hilaire, M., & Yang, C. S. (2013). A cloud-based approach for smart facilities management. In *Proceedings of 2013 IEEE Conference on Prognostics and Health Management (PHM)*. Gaithersburg, MD: IEEE. DOI: doi:10.1109/ICPHM.2013.6621459

Lou, J., Wang, M., Hu, J., & Shi, Z. (2007). Distributed data mining on agent grid: Issues, platform and development toolkit. *Future Generation Computer Systems*, *23*(1), 61–68. doi:10.1016/j.future.2006.04.015

McLeod, D., & Heimbigner, D. (1980). A federated architecture for database systems. In *Proceedings of the AFIPS National Computer Conference* (Vol. 39). AFIPS Press.

Mullender, S. J., Van Rossum, G., Tanenbaum, A. S., Van Renesse, R., & Van Staverene, H. (1990). Amoeba: A distributed operating system for the 1990s. *IEEE Computer*, *23*(5), 44–53. doi:10.1109/2.53354

Popek, G. J., & Walker, B. J. (1985). *The LOCUS distributed system architecture*. Cambridge, MA: MIT Press.

Powell, M. L., & Miller, B. P. (1983). Process migration in DEMOS/MP. In *Proceedings of the 9th ACM Symposium on Operating System Principles*. Association for Computing Machinery. doi:10.1145/800217.806619

Riedel, E., Gibson, G., & Faloutsos, C. (1998). Active storage for large-scale data mining and multimedia applications. In *Proceedings of VLDB '98 Proceedings of the 24rd International Conference on Very Large Data Bases* (pp. 62-73). Academic Press.

Shi, Z. (2013). *Multi-agent environment - MAGE*. Intelligent Science Research Group, at Key Lab of IIP, ICT CAS, China. Retrieved December 2013. http://www.intsci.ac.cn/en/research/mage.html

Talia, D. (2006). Grid-based distributed data mining systems, algorithms and services. In *Proceedings of HPDM 2006: The 9th International Workshop on High Performance and Distributed Mining*. Bethesda, MD: Academic Press.

Theimer, M. M., Lantz, K. A., & Cheriton, D. R. (1985). Preemptable remote execution facilities for the V system. In *Proceedings of the 10th ACM Symposium on Operating System Principles*. Association for Computing Machinery. doi:10.1145/323647.323629

Villegas, D., Rodero, I., Fong, L., Bobroff, N., Liu, Y., Parashar, M., & Sadjadi, M. (2010). The role of grid computing technologies in cloud computing. In *Handbook of cloud computing* (pp. 183–218). Springer; doi:10.1007/978-1-4419-6524-0_8

ADDITIONAL READING

Basu, P., Hall, M., Khan, M., Maindola, S., Muralidharan, S., Ramalingam, S., Rivera, A., Shantharam, M., & Venkat, A. (2013). Towards making autotuning mainstream. *International Journal of High Performance Computing Applications November 2013 27: 379-393*, first published on July 1, 2013 doi:10.1177/1094342013493644

Bogenschutz, P. A., Krueger, S. K. (2013). A simplified PDF parameterization of subgrid-scale clouds and turbulence for cloud-resolving models. *Journal of Advanced Model of Earth System*.

Chaimov, N., Biersdorff, S., & Malony, A. D. (2013). Tools for machine-learning-based empirical autotuning and specialization. *International Journal of High Performance Computing Applications November 2013 27: 403-411*, first published on July 14, 2013 doi:10.1177/1094342013493124

Chen, R. S., & Hollingsworth, J. K. (2013). Towards fully automatic auto-tuning: Leveraging language features of Chapel. *International Journal of High Performance Computing Applications November 2013 27: 394-402*, first published on July 3, 2013 doi:10.1177/1094342013493198

Cook, J. S. (2011). Supercomputers and Supercomputing. In Q. Zhang, R. S. Segall, & M. Cao (Eds.), *Visual Analytics and Interactive Technologies: Data, Text and Web Mining Applications* (pp. 282–294). Hershey, PA: IGI Global.

Du, J., Wright, G., & Fogelson, A. (2009). A Parallel Computational Method for Simulating Two-Phase Gel Dynamics. *International Journal for Numerical Methods in Fluids, 60*(6), 633–649. doi:10.1002/fld.1907

Endo, M., Cuma, M., & Zhdanov, M. S. (2009). Large-Scale Electromagnetic Modeling for Multiple Inhomogeneous Domains. *Commun. Comput. Phys, 6*, 269–289. doi:10.4208/cicp.2009.v6.p269

Fabregat-Traver, D., & Bientinesi, P. (2013). Application-tailored linear algebra algorithms: A search-based approach. *International Journal of High Performance Computing Applications November 2013 27: 426-439*, first published on July 18, 2013 doi:10.1177/1094342013494428

Hernandez, I., Ramirez-Marquez, J. E., Rainwater, C., Pohl, E., & Medal, H. (2014). Robust Facility Location: Hedging Against Failures. *Reliability Engineering & System Safety, 123*, 73–80. doi:10.1016/j.ress.2013.10.006

Ibrahim, K. Z., Madduri, K., Williams, S., Wang, B., Ethier, S., & Oliker, L. (2013). Analysis and optimization of gyrokinetic toroidal simulations on homogenous and heterogenous platforms. *International Journal of High Performance Computing Applications November 2013 27: 454-473*, first published on July 18, 2013 doi:10.1177/1094342013492446

Lobeiras, J., Viñas, M., Amor, M., Fraguela, B. B., Arenaz, M., García, J. A., & Castro, M. J. (2012). Parallelization of shallow water simulations on current multi-threaded systems. *International Journal of High Performance Computing Applications November 2013 27: 493-512*, first published on December 5, 2012 doi:10.1177/1094342012464800

Marker, B., Batory, D., & Geijn, R. (2013). A case study in mechanically deriving dense linear algebra code. *International Journal of High Performance Computing Applications November 2013 27: 440-453*, first published on June 19, 2013 doi:10.1177/1094342013492178

Oliker, L., & Vuduc, R. (2013, November). Introduction for Special Issue on Autotuning. *International Journal of High Performance Computing Applications, 27*(4), 377–378. doi:10.1177/1094342013495303

Segall, R. S. (2013). Computational Dimensionalities: From Global Supercomputing to Data, Text and Web Mining, Plenary Keynote Address, 17th World Multi-Conference on Systemics, Cybernetics, and Informatics, Orlando, FL, July 9-12, 2013. http://www.youtube.com/watch?v=8S4aiEyvqe8

Segall, R. S. (2014). Computational Dimensionalities of Global Supercomputing. *Journal of Systemics. Cybernetics and Informatics, 11*(9), 75–86.

Segall, R. S., & Zhang, Q. (2010). Open-Source Software Tools for Data Mining Analysis of Genomic and Spatial Images using High Performance Computing. *Proceedings of 5th INFORMS Workshop on Data Mining and Health Informatics*, Austin, TX, November 6, 2010.

Segall, R. S., & Zhang, Q. (2013). Information Quality and Supercomputing. *in Proceedings of International Conference of Information Quality (ICIQ 2013)*, Little Rock, AR, November 8-9, 2013.

Segall, R. S., Zhang, Q., & Cook, J. S. (2013). Overview of Current Research in Global Supercomputing. *Proceedings of the 44th Meeting of Southwest Decision Sciences Institute*, Albuquerque, NM, March 12-16, 2013.

Segall, R. S., Zhang, Q., & Pierce, R. (2010) Data Mining Supercomputing with SAS JMP® Genomics, *Proceedings of 14th World Multi-Conference on Systemics, Cybernetics and Informatics: WMSCI 2010*, Orlando, FL, June 29-July 2, 2010

Segall, R. S., Zhang, Q., & Pierce, R. (2011). Data Mining Supercomputing with SAS JMP® Genomics, *Journal of Systemics* [JSCI]. *Cybernetics and Informatics*, 9(1), 28–33.

Segall, R. S., Zhang, Q., & Pierce, R. M. (2009). Visualization by Supercomputing Data Mining. *Proceedings of the 4th INFORMS Workshop on Data Mining and System Informatics*, San Diego, CA, October 10, 2009.

Segall, R. S., Zhang, Q., & Pierce, R. M. (2010) Data Mining Supercomputing with SAS JMP® Genomics: Research-in-Progress, *Proceedings of 2010 Conference on Applied Research in Information Technology*, sponsored by Acxiom Laboratory of Applied Research (ALAR), University of Central Arkansas (UCA), Conway, AR, April 9, 2010.

Tavarageri, S., Ramanujam, J., & Sadayappan, P. (2013). Adaptive parallel tiled code generation and accelerated auto-tuning. *International Journal of High Performance Computing Applications November 2013 27: 412-425*, first published on July 26, 2013 doi:10.1177/1094342013493939

Thanakornworakij, T., Nassar, R., Leangsuksun, C. B., & Paun, M. (2013). Reliability model of a system of k nodes with simultaneous failures for high-performance computing applications. *International Journal of High Performance Computing Applications November 2013 27: 474-482*, first published on November 8, 2012 doi:10.1177/1094342012464506

Valín, R., Sampedro, C., Seoane, N., Aldegunde, M., Garcia-Loureiro, A., Godoy, A., & Gámiz, F. (2012). Optimisation and parallelisation of a 2D MOSFET multi-subband ensemble Monte Carlo simulator. *International Journal of High Performance Computing Applications November 2013 27: 483-492*, first published on November 16, 2012 doi:10.1177/1094342012464799

KEY TERMS AND DEFINITIONS

Data Mining: Data Mining discovers knowledge from large amounts of data.

Distributed Shared Memory: Each node of the system consists of one or more CPUs and a memory unit. The nodes are connected by a high-speed communication network. When a process on a node accesses some data from a memory block of the shared memory space, the local memory mapping manager takes charge of its request.

Message Passing: Message passing is a basic method for information sharing in a distributed system. Processes executing on different computers often need to communicate with each other to achieve some common goals. Message passing provides an interprocess communication mechanism to facilitate such communication activities.

Naming: Naming mechanisms enable users and programs to assign character-string names to objects and subsequently use these names to refer to those objects. Naming system consists of the naming facilities of a distributed operating system and the locating facility of the distributed operating system, which provides the users with an abstraction of an object that hides the details of how and where an object is actually located in the network and also provides a further level of abstraction when dealing with object replicas.

Process Management: Process management deals with mechanisms and policies for sharing the processor of the system among all processes. In a distributed operating system, the main goal of process management is to make the best possible use of the processing resources of the entire system by sharing them among all processes.

Remote Procedure Calls: Remote procedure call is a special case of the general message-passing model of interprocess communication (IPC) that has become a widely accepted IPC mechanism in distributed computing systems.

Resource Management: Resource management can be used to manage resources interconnected by a network, migrate a process between different nodes if the local node does not have the required resource or the local node has to be shutdown, assign remote resources to a process on the local node.

Synchronization: The rules for enforcing correct interaction are implemented in the system in the form of synchronization mechanisms.

APPENDIX: EXPERIMENTAL RESULTS OUTPUT OF DATA MINING USING SUPERCOMPUTER LONESTAR AT UNIVERSITY OF TEXAS AT AUSTIN COMPUTER CENTER (TACC)

```
1. Scheme:weka.classifiers.lazy.IBk -K 1 -W 0 -A "weka.core.neighboursearch.
LinearNNSearch -A \"weka.core.EuclideanDistance -R first-last\""
Relation: TrainingTest-weka.filters.unsupervised.attribute.NumericToNominal-
Rfirst-last
Instances: 240
Attributes: 522
[list of attributes omitted]
Test mode:split 66.0% train, remainder test
=== Classifier model (full training set) ===
IB1 instance-based classifier
using 1 nearest neighbour(s) for classification
Time taken to build model: 0 seconds
=== Evaluation on test split ===
=== Summary ===
=== Detailed Accuracy By Class ===
=== Confusion Matrix ===
a b <-- classified as
33 13 | a = 0
24 12 | b = 1
2. Scheme:weka.classifiers.meta.ClassificationViaClustering -W weka.clusterers.
SimpleKMeans -- -N 2 -A "weka.core.EuclideanDistance -R first-last" -I 500 -S 10
Relation: TrainingTest-weka.filters.unsupervised.attribute.NumericToNominal-
Rfirst-last
Instances: 240
Attributes: 522
[list of attributes omitted]
Test mode:split 66.0% train, remainder test
=== Classifier model (full training set) ===
ClassificationViaClustering
==========================
kMeans
======
Number of iterations: 3
Within cluster sum of squared errors: 123452.0
Missing values globally replaced with mean/mode
Clusters to classes mapping:
 1. Cluster: 0 (1)
 2. Cluster: no class
Classes to clusters mapping:
```

```
  1. Class (0): 1. Cluster
  2. Class (1): no cluster
Time taken to build model: 0.52 seconds
=== Evaluation on test split ===
=== Summary ===
=== Detailed Accuracy By Class ===
=== Confusion Matrix ===
a b <-- classified as
44 0 | a = 0
33 0 | b = 1
3. Scheme:weka.classifiers.rules.DecisionTable -X 1 -S "weka.attributeSelec-
tion.BestFirst -D 1 -N 5"
Relation: TrainingTest-weka.filters.unsupervised.attribute.NumericToNominal-
Rfirst-last
Instances: 240
Attributes: 522
[list of attributes omitted]
Test mode:split 66.0% train, remainder test
=== Classifier model (full training set) ===
Decision Table:
Number of training instances: 240
Number of Rules: 236
Non matches covered by Majority class.
        Best first.
        Start set: no attributes
        Search direction: forward
        Stale search after 5 node expansions
        Total number of subsets evaluated: 3121
        Merit of best subset found: 57.917
Evaluation (for feature selection): CV (leave one out)
Feature set: 81,1
Time taken to build model: 3.44 seconds
=== Evaluation on test split ===
=== Summary ===
=== Detailed Accuracy By Class ===
=== Confusion Matrix ===
a b <-- classified as
46 0 | a = 0
36 0 | b = 1
4. Scheme:weka.classifiers.rules.ZeroR
Relation: TrainingTest-weka.filters.unsupervised.attribute.NumericToNominal-
Rfirst-last
Instances: 240
```

```
Attributes: 522
[list of attributes omitted]
Test mode:split 66.0% train, remainder test
=== Classifier model (full training set) ===
ZeroR predicts class value: 0
Time taken to build model: 0 seconds
=== Evaluation on test split ===
=== Summary ===
=== Detailed Accuracy By Class ===
=== Confusion Matrix ===
 a b <-- classified as
 46 0 | a = 0
 36 0 | b = 1
5. Scheme:weka.classifiers.trees.RandomForest -I 10 -K 0 -S 1 Relation: Train-
ingTest-weka.filters.unsupervised.attribute.NumericToNominal-Rfirst-last
Instances: 240
Attributes: 522
[list of attributes omitted]
Test mode:split 66.0% train, remainder test
=== Classifier model (full training set) ===
Random forest of 10 trees, each constructed while considering 10 random fea-
tures.
Out of bag error: 0.4292
Time taken to build model: 0.43 seconds
=== Evaluation on test split ===
=== Summary ===
=== Detailed Accuracy By Class ===
=== Confusion Matrix ===
 a b <-- classified as
 45 1 | a = 0
 36 0 | b = 1
6. Scheme:weka.classifiers.trees.RandomTree -K 0 -M 1.0 -S 1
Relation: TrainingTest-weka.filters.unsupervised.attribute.NumericToNominal-
Rfirst-last
Instances: 240
Attributes: 522
[list of attributes omitted]
Test mode:split 66.0% train, remainder test
=== Classifier model (full training set) ===
RandomTree
==========
Size of the tree: 239
Time taken to build model: 0.03 seconds
=== Evaluation on test split ===
```

```
=== Summary ===
=== Detailed Accuracy By Class ===
=== Confusion Matrix ===
 a b <-- classified as
 44 2 | a = 0
 36 0 | b = 1
7. Scheme:weka.classifiers.trees.SimpleCart -S 1 -M 2.0 -N 5 -C 1.0
Relation: TrainingTest-weka.filters.unsupervised.attribute.NumericToNominal-
Rfirst-last
Instances: 240
Attributes: 522
[list of attributes omitted]
Test mode:split 66.0% train, remainder test
=== Classifier model (full training set) ===
Number of Leaf Nodes: 2
Size of the Tree: 3
Time taken to build model: 418.06 seconds
=== Evaluation on test split ===
=== Summary ===
=== Detailed Accuracy By Class ===
=== Confusion Matrix ===
a b <-- classified as
46 0 | a = 0
36 0 | b = 1
8. Scheme:weka.classifiers.trees.UserClassifier
Relation: TrainingTest-weka.filters.unsupervised.attribute.NumericToNominal-
Rfirst-last
Instances: 240
Attributes: 522
[list of attributes omitted]
Test mode:split 66.0% train, remainder test
=== Classifier model (full training set) ===
: N0 0(240.0/102.0)
Time taken to build model: 767.45 seconds
=== Evaluation on test split ===
=== Summary ===
=== Detailed Accuracy By Class ===
=== Confusion Matrix ===
a b <-- classified as
46 0 | a = 0
36 0 | b = 1
9. Scheme:weka.classifiers.trees.NBTree Relation: TrainingTest-weka.filters.
unsupervised.attribute.NumericToNominal-Rfirst-last
Instances: 240
```

```
Attributes: 522
[list of attributes omitted]
Test mode:split 66.0% train, remainder test
=== Classifier model (full training set) ===
NBTree
------------------
: NB0
Leaf number: 0 Naive Bayes Classifier
Time taken to build model: 3.06 seconds
=== Evaluation on test split ===
=== Summary ===
=== Detailed Accuracy By Class ===
=== Confusion Matrix ===
a b <-- classified as
 0 46 | a = 0
 0 36 | b = 1
```

Section 4
Supercomputing Leadership and Philosophy

Chapter 15
Super Leaders:
Supercomputing Leadership for the Future

Kim Grover-Haskin
University of North Texas, USA

ABSTRACT

Present day and projected labor demands forecast a need for minds to comprehend in algorithm in order to leverage computing developments for real world problem resolutions. This chapter focuses not so much on solutions to the preparation of the learners and the scientists, but on the future leadership that will advocate and open doors for the high performance computing community to be funded, supported, and practiced. Supercomputing's sustainable future lies in its future of leadership. Studies over the last ten years identify a shift in leadership as the Baby Boomers enter retirement. The talent pool following the Baby Boomers will shrink in numbers between 2010-2020. Women continue to be under represented in IT leadership. This chapter provides information on the talent pool for supercomputing, discusses leadership and organizational culture as influenced by gender, and explores how a mentoring community fosters leaders for the future.

INTRODUCTION

High Performance Computing (HPC) is a nationally recognized resource providing scientists and educators a research tool for real world problems. The High Performance Computing Act of 1991 established federal support for HPC environments, applications, research, and development. Supercomputing has gained momentum with enhanced analysis capabilities. In *Getting up to Speed: The Future of Supercomputing* (Graham, Snir, & Patterson, 2005) Raymond Orbach, Director of the Department of Energy (DOE) Office of Science,

stated in his testimony before the U.S. House of Representatives Committee on Science, "Now we can simulate systems to discover physical laws for which there are no known predictive equations" (pp. 73-74). Using computational modeling and simulation, the scientific community has the ability to predict the behavior of complex systems.

Over the last 25 years there has been significant progress in supercomputing through an active supercomputing culture of technicians, programmers, and scientists supporting and perpetuating discovery. Leaders must be readied to sustain the momentum and progress of supercomputing. The

DOI: 10.4018/978-1-4666-7461-5.ch015

Copyright © 2015, IGI Global. Copying or distributing in print or electronic forms without written permission of IGI Global is prohibited.

Bureau of Labor statistics estimates that by 2020 the Baby Boomer population, 55-and-older, will represent the greatest share of the workforce.

The current stream of talent for supercomputing in the fields of mathematics, science, computer science, and engineering will primarily reside within the 45-54 age group by 2020. This group's presence in the job market will shrink 7.6 percent. What is the status of the supercomputing community current talent pool in leadership positions today? Falkenheim and Burrelli (2012) state for science and engineering:

Just over 1 in 10 scientists and engineers working in industry are managers. Men and women and the various racial/ethnic groups differ in their propensity to be managers, partly reflecting differences in age distributions. Among scientists and engineers in the United States, women are younger on average than men, and minorities are younger on average than whites. Among scientists and engineers within industry, men are more likely than women to be managers, both midlevel and top-level managers, executives, and administrators within most racial/ethnic groups and regardless of disability status (table 4). Asians, blacks, and persons who reported multiple races are less likely than whites to be managers. Similar proportions of persons with and without disabilities are managers. (p. 5)

The current diversity within the talent pool in science and engineering is not entering leadership roles. Women are underrepresented in science and engineering leadership. This chapter will provide information on the talent pool for supercomputing revealing a strong technical community for supercomputing's future. A discussion of leadership and organizational culture follows with research on gender. While the future talent pool for supercomputing will be technically capable across multiple roles, there must be effort directed to mentoring individuals to leadership positions.

My experience with supercomputing support the power of a mentoring community.

The Talent Pool: A Community of Leaders

The Bureau of Labor Statistics (BLS) in its 2008-2018 employment outlook study projected growth in information technology, computer, and mathematical science occupations. The 2010 to 2020 study continues to support those findings.

Employment in professional, scientific, and technical services is projected to grow by 29 percent, adding about 2.1 million new jobs by 2020. Employment in computer systems design and related services is expected to increase by 47 percent, driven by growing demand for sophisticated computer network and mobile technologies. Employment in management, scientific, and technical consulting services is anticipated to expand, at 58 percent. Demand for these services will be spurred by businesses' continued need for advice on planning and logistics, the implementation of new technologies, and compliance with workplace safety, environmental, and employment regulations. Combined, the two industries—computer systems design and related services and management, scientific, and technical consulting services—will account for more than half of all new jobs in professional, scientific, and technical services (Bureau of Labor Statistics, U.S. Department of Labor, 2012, para. 28).

It has become more apparent for individuals, in order to prepare for these occupations, to pursue postsecondary education, at a minimum. The IES National Center for Education Statistics in its publication *Projections of Education Statistics to 2021* shows total enrollment in postsecondary education is projected to increase 15 percent between Fall 2010 and 2021. The vast majority of those enrolling will be between 18-24 years of age. Graduate enrollment is expected to rise

19 percent over the same time period (Hussar & Bailey, 2013, p. 19).

Department of Education statistics for the years 2009-2010 and 2010-2011 show the number of Bachelor's degrees attained in business, education, and health education to be growing. (Please note that because the U.S. Census is only taken every 10 years, that the following figures are created with the most recently available data.) Business and Management degrees have grown in number to meet increasing demands in a global, knowledge-intense, competitive market. Analytics, logistics, new technologies, and Big Data are providing companies a more competitive advantage. An aging population fortifies the need for health care services and professionals.

Focusing on science and engineering, The National Science Foundation showed doctoral degrees in science and engineering steadily increasing between 2002 and 2009. Electrical, mechanical, and chemical doctorates led the fields of study within engineering. Agricultural and at-mospheric doctorates lead the science distribution totals over the same time period. Women, non-US Citizens, US Citizens, and ethnicity represent a diversity within these numbers.

The National Center for Education Statistics in its publication, *The Condition of Education*, presented information for the academic years 1999-2000 and 2009-2010, giving us a comparison of total number of doctor's, master's and bachelor's degrees awarded across multiple disciplines and

Figure 1. Bachelor degrees conferred by field of study: 2009-2010 and 2010-2011

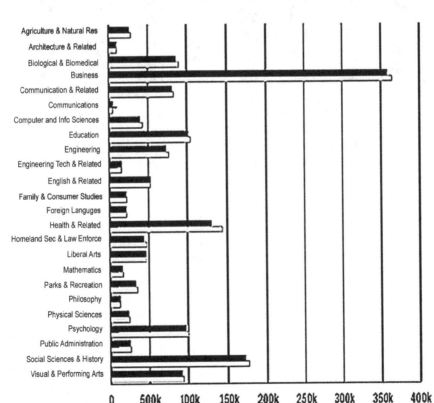

SOURCE: U.S. Department of Education. (2011). *Bachelor's degrees conferred by degree-granting institutions, by race/ethnicity and field of study: 2009-10 and 2010-11, Table 301.*

Figure 2. Total science and engineering doctorates awarded: 2002-2009

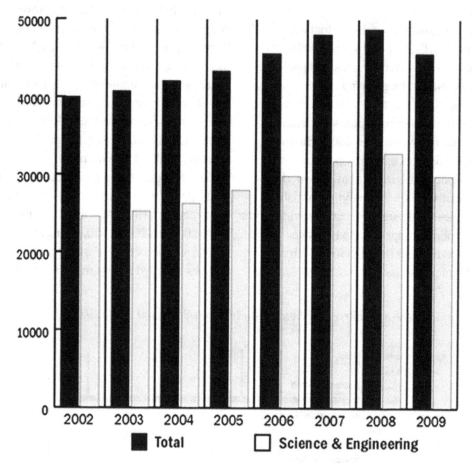

SOURCE: U.S. Census Bureau. (2011, September). Doctorates awarded by field of study and year of study: 2000 to 2009, *Table 815*.

the number of women attaining these degrees over a ten year span.

Women continue to be underrepresented in many of the science and engineering fields as well as computer science and mathematics.

In 2009–10, females earned the smallest percentages of bachelor's degrees relative to males in the fields of engineering and engineering technologies (17 percent) and computer and information sciences and support services (18 percent)....In contrast, of all the bachelor's degrees conferred in the field of computer and information sciences and support services, the percentage conferred to *females decreased from 28 percent in 1999-2000 to 18 percent in 2009–10 (Aud, Hussar, Johnson, Kena, Roth, Manning, Wang, & Zhang, 2012).*

Another dimension to the talent pool is of a global nature, non-US citizens. The National Science Board's *Science and Engineering Report* (2012) showed a growing number of students from around the world attaining a U.S. baccalaureate equivalent. A significant number of these degrees were being awarded in Asia specifically China, South Korea, Taiwan, and Japan. Combined, these countries exceeded the United States in awarding Natural Science and Engineering (NS&E) degrees

Figure 3. Number of doctorate degrees awarded to women in selected fields of study: 1999-2000 and 2009-2010

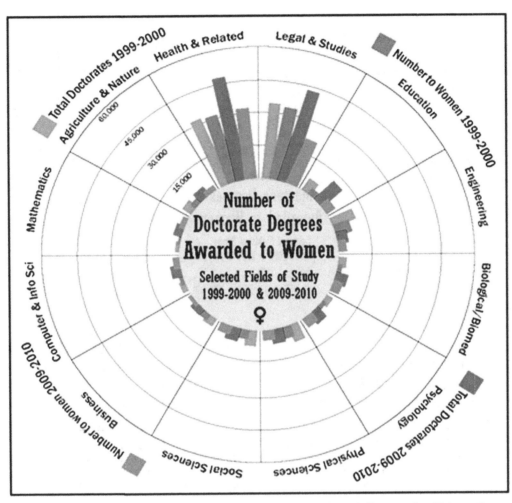

SOURCE: U.S. Department of Education, National Center for Education Statistics. (2012, May).

in 2008. Beyond the baccalaureate to advanced degrees, China has more than tripled its number of doctoral degrees since 2000. This number surpasses the United States doctoral graduates. The United States graduate data also reveals "a large proportion of these degrees go to non-US citizens" (National Science Board, 2012, p. O-7). National Science Foundation statistics on doctoral graduate characteristics, 2009, showed the distribution of Foreign and U.S. Citizen comparison.

Across the world, countries depend on their talent pool of scientists and engineers for competitive advantage, development, and innovation. From national security to national gross domestic product, each nation's government monitors the status of needs and demands for its welfare and benefit.

The low U.S. share of global engineering degrees in recent years is striking; well above half of all such degrees are awarded in Asia. Governments

Figure 4. Number of master's degrees awarded to women in selected fields of study: 1999-2000 and 2009-2010

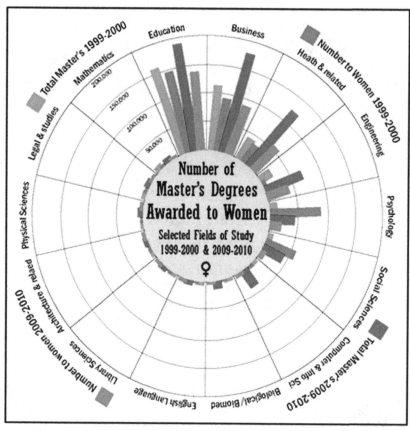

SOURCE: U.S. Department of Education, National Center for Education Statistics. (2012, May). *Number of master's and doctor's degrees awarded by degree-granting institutions, percentage of total, number and percentage awarded to females, and percent change, by selected fields of study: Academic years 1999–2000 and 2009–10.*

in many Western countries and in Japan are concerned about lagging student interest in studying NS&E, fields they believe convey technical skills and knowledge that are essential for knowledge-intensive economies. In the developing world, the number of students earning first university degrees-that are considered broadly comparable to a U.S. baccalaureate-in NS&E is rising (National Science Board, p. O-7).

Ethnicity representation across all disciplines between the years 2009-2011 show Caucasians and African Americans more prevalent in bach-

elor degrees in business, education, engineering, computer science, health education and social sciences (U.S. Department of Education, National Center for Education Statistics, 2012). According to the National Center for Science and Engineering Statistics *InfoBrief* (Falkenheim & Burrelli, 2012), "Black, Hispanic, and white scientists and engineers in industry have fairly similar educational attainment, but Asians, Asian men in particular, are more likely than any other group to have master's or doctoral degrees" (p. 2).

Reviewing the talent pool over the last ten years with a focus on science and engineering reveals

Figure 5. Number of bachelor's degrees awarded to women in selected fields of study: 1999-2000 and 2009-2010

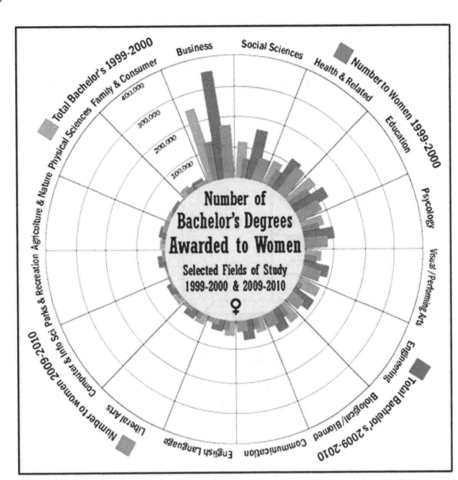

SOURCE: U.S. Department of Education, National Center for Education Statistics. (2012, May). *Number of associate's and bachelor's degrees awarded by degree-granting institutions, percentage of total, number and percentage awarded to females, and percent change, by selected fields of study: Academic years 1999–2000 and 2009–10—Continued*

the total number of degrees awarded across the disciplines to women, non-US Citizens, and US Citizens. The National Center for Science and Engineering (NCSE) (Falkenheim & Burrelli, 2012) reports, "Most scientists and engineers (63%) employed in industry have a bachelor's degree as their highest degree. Another 25% have master's degrees, and 3% have doctoral degrees" (p. 2). The Computing Research Association (CRA) Taulbee Survey gives us detail to the talent pool distribution of specializations within computer science.

The (CRA) Taulbee Survey (Computer Research Association, 2013) measures graduate enrollments and Ph.D completions of a number of computer science doctoral granting departments across the United States. In effect since 1995, the (CRA) Taulbee Survey provides insightful information on computer science, computer engineering, and information technology in the United States and Canada. This study shows supercomputing as a specialty of study emerging in 2008. "Artificial intelligence, software engineering, and

Figure 6. Doctorates conferred by citizen and non-citizen characteristics: 2009

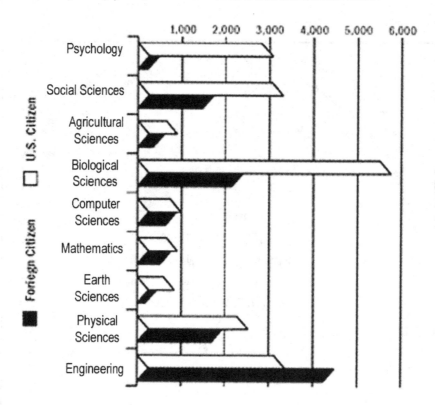

SOURCE: U.S. Census Bureau. (2011, September). *Doctorates Conferred by Recipients' Characteristics: 2009, Table 814.*

networking continue to be the most popular areas of specialization for doctoral graduates. Databases, and theory and algorithms were the next most popular areas" (Zweben, 2012).

The NCSE report (Falkenheim & Burrelli, 2012) provides additional insight to areas of specialization with ethnicity.

...men are more likely than women to report research and development or computer applications as their primary or secondary work activity, whereas women are more likely to name teaching, regardless of race/ethnicity or disability status. Asians are more likely than any other racial/ethnic group to report research and development or computer applications as their primary or secondary work activity, and they are less likely

than most other racial/ethnic groups to report management, sales, or administration. Compared with most other racial ethnic groups, blacks are less likely to report research and development and more likely to report teaching as their primary/secondary work activity. Persons with and without disabilities differ little in work activity (pp. 4-5).

The wealth of data provided by the (CRA) Taulbee Survey, the Bureau of Labor Statistics, Department of Education, National Science Foundation, National Center for Science and Engineering Statistics, and the National Science Board's Science and Engineering Report unfolds a view of an educated talent pool for supercomputing that is of a diverse global nature. What is of interest is to compare science and engineering graduates

Figure 7. (CRA) Taulbee survey specialty study 2006-2011 (Aggregated)

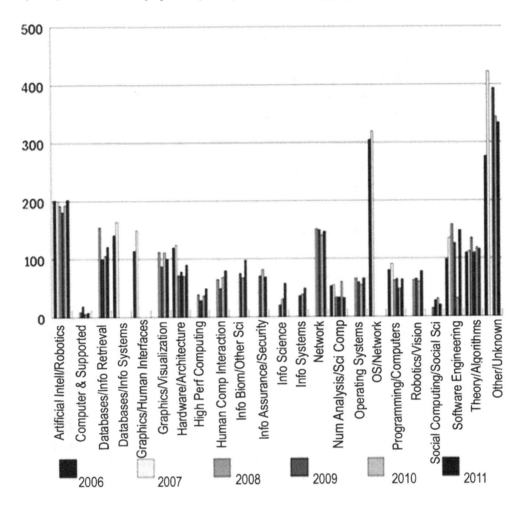

SOURCE: Computer Research Association (http://cra.org/resources/taulbee/)

against a burgeoning group of graduates in business, education, and health care.

Bachelor's degrees in business, education, management, and health care have increased in number compared to science and engineering. Women are attaining a higher percentage of degrees in fields other than STEM and focus within the teaching realm of specialization while non-US Citizen degree attainment in science and engineering is rising. In pursuit of further analysis, I reviewed five variables reported in the 2009 Bachelor's degree data sources, total Bachelor's

degrees, total Bachelor's degrees awarded to women, area of study, ethnicity, and US Citizenship. This analysis provides further insight into the talent pool's technical and leadership readiness.

According to the Census Bureau 2009 American Community Survey, business degrees were evenly distributed between US and non-US Citizens. US Citizens were primary degree holders in Education. Advanced degrees were usually pursued in Education. "Over 1 in 5 college-educated adults, or 11 million people, held a bachelor's degree in business, but a vast majority of busi-

Figure 8. Total bachelor's degrees conferred, awarded to women, field of study, ethnicity, and U.S. citizenship: 2009 (Aggregated)

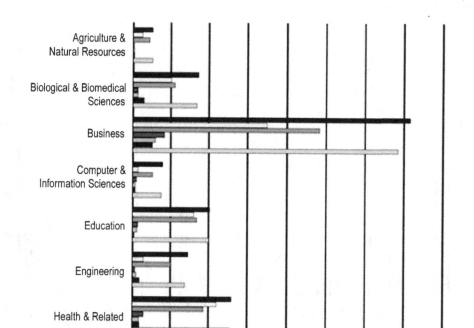

SOURCE: U.S. Department of Education, National Center for Education Statistics. (2012, June) *Bachelor's degrees conferred by degree-granting institutions, by race/ethnicity and field of study: 2009-10 and 2010-11,* Table 301

ness degree holders were less likely to pursue advanced degrees" (Siebens & Ryan, 2012, p. 3). Those completing their undergraduate degrees in biological, agricultural, environmental sciences, and physical related sciences had a propensity to pursue advanced degrees. The Census Bureau also noted "the foreign born (both citizen and noncitizen) were much more likely to hold a degree in a science and engineering field or a science- and engineering-related field than the native-born population" (Siebens & Ryan, 2012, p. 4). Engineering bachelor's degrees as well as mathematics, computers and statistics were predominantly held by men. Women were predominant in the fields

of education and science and engineering-related fields. In science and engineering approximately 30-34.5 percent of degrees went to Hispanic, Black, and White ethnicities. Asian individuals received 50 percent of the bachelor's degrees in science and engineering.

Degree holders in education, science, and engineering were more likely to pursue advanced degrees. Business degree holders were more likely not to pursue advanced degrees. Will this talent pool of degree holders advance the potential and purpose of supercomputing? The employment sector for supercomputing professionals is founded in education, research, industry, and government. The primary proponents perpetuating job opportunities for supercomputing are research, industry and government entities with a focus on knowledge-technology developments.

Individuals are entering a knowledge-intensive world of work driven by competing economies of scale. Skill sets in the study of natural science and engineering are considered essential for countries to compete in this knowledge-intensive economy. "Natural Science includes studies in physical, biological, agricultural, and mathematics and computer science" (National Science Board, 2012, p. O-7). In the National Science Board's Science and Engineering Report, global comparisons of progression in science and technologies, engineering, markets, industry, and talent illuminates how knowledge-intense economies are shaping and driving priorities for development. These global economies are built upon a foundation "in which research, its commercial exploitation, and other intellectual work are of growing importance" (National Science Board, 2012, p. O-3). Research initiatives support development and drive innovation, therefore, supporting and investing in research builds sustainable and continually improving economies.

Through access to high performance computing resources, research on issues of global proportion such as climate, environment, health care and more are recognized as integral to stimulate economic growth and opportunity. Supercomputing resources provide access to research opportunities, "What scientists can find from studying these problems can lead to innovations and new products; they are rightly considered to be engines of economic growth, and provide nations that have them competitive advantage in the global marketplace" (Center for Digital Education, 2012, p. 19).

With the recognition of research contributing to knowledge-technology intense economies, research funding becomes a priority. Between 1996 and 2009, the United States led research and development with a significant investment of $400 billion dollars (National Science Board, 2012, p. O-4). In 2009, Asian countries combined total was $399 billion catching up to the United States. "2010 data released by China's National Bureau of Statistics show a further 22% increase" (National Science Board, 2012, p. O-4). In the United States, industry leads the expansion, funding about 62% of research and development.

The list of applications of supercomputing to industry, manufacturing, health care, national security, and more is comprehensive. Driving the innovation, funding support, and presence is competitive advantage. As Goodwin and Zacharia (2011) state, "The U.S. Council on Competitiveness has said that 'to out-compete is to out-compute'" (para. 2). The Council on Competitiveness, formed in 1986, is comprised of CEOs, university presidents, and labor leaders with a focus on national prosperity. This group unites the voices of public and private leaders across a diversity of industries, focusing on technology and innovation. Within the U.S. Council on Competitiveness is the Technology Leadership and Strategy Initiative (TLSI). "Technology Leadership and Strategy Initiative (TLSI) brings together chief technology officers from industry, academia and government in an effort to capture American innovation" (Technology Leadership and Strategy Initiative, 2012).

The TLSI is active in perpetuating a community of technologists, envisioning the possibilities of our technology infused world, addressing mounting challenges, and perpetuating an active thriving culture for the recognition, funding, and sustainment of innovation. This group identifies grand challenges and barriers to innovation advocating and proposing policy. They promote STEM education and support research rigor. The TLSI also has oversight for the High Performance Computing Advisory Committee (HPCAC). According to the annual report, *Making Impact* (The Council of Competitiveness, 2012) the goals of the HPCAC include:

- Developing and delivering the message of how HPC can act as a technological foundation for national competitiveness, innovation, and security;
- Providing high-level recommendations to policy makers on what and how public and private investments in HPC can have maximum impact on our common goal of maintaining U.S. leadership in science and engineering, workforce talent, and industrial productivity;
- Advocating for national policies that maximize the economic return on U.S. public investment in HPC and promote adoption and use of HPC technologies by the domestic private sector through publications, press releases, ongoing major Council initiatives, and the public forum;
- Lowering the barriers to adoption of HPC in industry by developing and promoting a national strategy, while recommending implementation that systematically identifies and addresses obstacles to wider penetration and utilization;
- Increasing access to HPC advanced modeling and simulation technologies and expertise, allowing firms of all sizes to quickly innovate, design, prototype, test and evaluate, and deploy or commercialize, reducing time to market and costs throughout every stage of the product life-cycle; and
- Supporting the research, development, and application of exascale and other advanced HPC technologies, both hardware and software, that will continue U.S. global leadership in the field (p. 24).

The U.S. Council on Competitiveness and TLSI leverage business minds with science and technology. They recognize the value and importance of supercomputing for advancement and achievement in a global economy. With more and more emphasis upon global collaboration, research, and innovation, the supercomputing leadership talent pool can grow to encompass multi-disciplinary individuals, broadening potential leadership opportunities and new job developments. As educators become more aware of the potential with supercomputing and multi-disciplinary studies, new programs emerge which appeal to the strengths of individuals who might not consider pursuing supercomputing as a career, especially women.

The demographics of the talent pool for supercomputing represent a diverse and educated talent pool in preparation for a globally competitive environment. One additional factor to consider for the scope of the leadership community is the talent generations emerging into the workforce over the next ten years. The Bureau of Labor Statistics projects, between 2010-2020, slow growth in the share of the workforce for the 18-24 age group. The 25-34 age group is expected to grow in the workforce at a rate of 10.5 percent while the 45-to-54 age group "is expected to shrink by 7.6 percent, reflecting the slower birthrate following the Baby-Boom generation. As the Baby Boomers continue to age, the 55-and-older population is projected to increase by 29.1 percent, more than any other age group. In 2020, Baby Boomers will range in age between 56-74. Like the population, the labor force is growing more slowly, becoming older and more diverse" (Bureau of Labor Statistics, 2012, para. 5). Baby Boomers will overtake all other groups by 2020, representing the greatest share of the workforce.

The 2008 National Survey of Recent College Graduates shows the distribution of ages of recent graduates with bachelor's degrees in science, engineering, or health.

The National Science Foundation 2009 statistics show median ages of doctoral graduates. Median ages in the selected disciplines were between 29 and 33 years of age. In eleven years, as specified in the Bureau of Labor Statistics, these doctoral graduates will be 40-44 years of age falling close within that particular projected age group which will shrink in presence in the workplace by 7.6 percent to 2020.

Figure 9. Age of graduation with bachelor's degrees in science, engineering, or health by field of study: October 2008

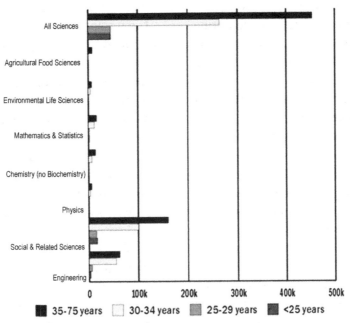

SOURCE: National Science Foundation. (2012, August). *Age of recent graduates with bachelor's degrees in science, engineering, or health, by major field of degree: October 2008, Table 13.*

Figure 10. Median ages of doctoral graduates: 2009

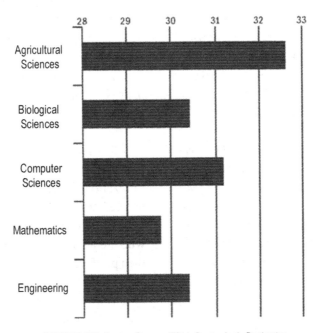

SOURCE: U.S. Census Bureau. (2011, September). *Doctorates Conferred by Recipients' Characteristics: 2009, Table 814.*

The study of generational characteristics contributes to the growing understanding of changes across cultures, economies, and technologies. As each generation enters the workforce, they bring with them salient characteristics. Baby Boomers were born between 1943-1964. A large group, Baby Boomers are described as competitive valuing teamwork and the chain of command. Miller and Yu (2005) elaborate that Baby Boomers have experienced significant change throughout the emerging economies.

They have been subjected to the widest possible variety of training programs as they have had to learn new skills progressively as the economy changed through the various phases and different values and skills were required. Baby Boomers were oriented into workplaces when corporate loyalty was highly valued and they expected long careers in the one organization (p. 9).

The GenX generation was born between1961-1982 coming from households where both parents worked thus the likelihood that they were latchkey is high. Characteristics include self-reliance and the need to control their own destiny. They desire to control their own experience, contribute to their experience, and define the value of that experience rather than have it defined for them. Arthur Levine, in an interview with T. Lewin (2012) states,

They're much more pragmatic. They say their primary reason for going to college is to get training and skills that will lead to a job, and let them make money. They're willing to have a major they're not really interested in if they think there will be job growth in that field. They're much less likely than their predecessors to say they're in college to develop their personal values, or learn to get along with different people (para. 4).

GenX-ers proved to be "voracious in their desire for immediate information and have sophisticated

behavioral approaches in filtering that information, no matter how many sources it comes from" (Greenberg, 2006, p.2). They turned to each other. "The wisdom of the masses helps people know whom to trust and why to trust (or not trust) them" (Greenberg, p. 2). Web 2.0 opened the world to express self-driven opinions and feedback. Gaming was rising in popularity and more technology was available and affordable. Tapscott and Williams (2006) published *Wikinomics* discussing the rising power of mass collaboration in the economy. In the year 2020, Gen Xers ages will range between 31 and 51.

Echo Boomers or the Millennial group, were born between 1982-1995. Also called Generation Y or the Net Generation, "they already make up nearly a third of the U.S. population, and already spend $170 billion a year of their own and their parents' money" (Leung, 2009).The literature points to characteristics of the Millennials as being over managed by parents. The term "Helicopter Parents" points to this generation. Millennials expect to rise to the top quickly and receive immediate gratification. In the workforce, they have a hard time thinking for the long term.

They can't think long-range. Everything has to be immediate, like a video game. And they have a lot of trouble sort of doing things in a stepwise fashion, delaying gratification. Really reflecting as they go along (Leung, para. 34).

Millennials' common characteristics are impatience and narcissism. They want new, like customization, prefer self-expression, and everything is 'me,' 'mine.' Joel Stein (2013) states, "In the U.S., Millennials are the children of baby boomers, who are also known as the Me Generation, who then produced the Me Me Me Generation, whose selfishness technology has only exacerbated" (p. 28). They have been described as screensavers, always glued to a screen. MySpace® emerged in 2003 and Facebook® in 2004. In 2020, Millennials will range in age between 25-38.

Baby Boomers, Gen-Xers, and Millennials are the predominant generations currently in the workforce. With the stock market crash of 1987, many Baby Boomers will postpone their retirement thus they are staying in the workforce longer (Stein, p. 30). Characteristics of the generations have been researched for workforce and leadership purposes (Alsop, 2008; DeLong, 2004; Hammill, 2005; Howe & Strauss, 2000; Izzo & Withers, 2001; Yu & Miller, 2009; Zemke, Raines, & Filipczak,2000). Organizational culture is effected through the dynamics of the generations. Leadership styles have changed to meet the needs of the emerging knowledge-intense economy and the kaleidoscope of talent available to work.

Leadership and Organizational Culture: Style and Substance

...leadership and culture are fundamentally intertwined... (Schein, 2010, p. xi)

Organizational culture is the environment of an organization perpetuated from the behaviors, meanings, and actions of its members (Marques, 2011, p. 47). This environment is taught to new members as a way of perceiving and thinking about the organization, how it operates, and affects others. Based on a set of values, symbols, languages, beliefs, and actions, the culture of an organization is very important. Ken Robinson (2011) states, "All organizations are organic and perishable. They are created by people and they need to be constantly re-created if they are to survive" (p. 13). The strength of the organization is its people. Leadership drives the progress and creates the foundation for the organization to flourish and prosper. Schein (2010) writes:

I will continue to argue (1) that leaders as entrepreneurs are the main architects of culture, (2) that after cultures are formed, they influence what kind of leadership is possible, and (3) that if elements of the culture become dysfunctional,

leadership can and must do something to speed up culture change (p. xi).

As previously discussed, the generations in the workforce today represent a diversity of talent. The study of leadership over these generations brings out interesting information. According to Boal and Hooijberg (2001), at the end of the 1970s and early 80's research on leadership lulled with little new theory being developed (p. 515). During the mid-80's new discussion on what was called strategic leadership began. Strategic leadership was contrasted against supervisory theories of leadership which focused on task and person-oriented behaviors of leaders. Supervisory leadership represented a hierarchical organizational culture, much like what the Baby Boomers experienced. "Strategic theories of leadership are concerned with leadership 'of' organizations (see Hunt, 1991) and are 'marked with a concern for the evolution of the organization as a whole, including its changing aims and capabilities'" (Boal & Hooijbert, p. 516). Strategic leadership has, at its core, managerial wisdom, the capacity to learn, and the capacity to change (p. 525).

The emergence of strategic leadership inquiry developed into a variety of leadership style research and analysis; transformational leadership and transactional leadership, (Groves & LaRocca, 2011; Singh & Krishnan, 2008), narcissistic (Maccoby, 2004), servant-oriented (Pekerti & Sendjaya, 2010; Reed, Vidaver-Cohen, & Colwell, 2011), and relationship-oriented (Kilduff, Chiaburu, & Menges, 2010; Moss, Barbuto, & John, 2010; Harris, 2011) Transformational leaders capitalize on inspiring and motivating individuals to contribute to the organization as a collaborative and cooperative opportunity (Koneck, 2006). Alice Eagly (2013), professor of psychology at Northwestern University, described transformational leaders as inspirational role models. They utilize strong relationship building skills focusing on consideration of others (Eagly, para. 5). Transactional leaders focus on contingent reinforcement as motivational methods for employee performance. "Reinforcement is in the form of a leader's promises and rewards or threats and disciplinary actions; reinforcing behavior is contingent on the follower's performance" (Koneck, p. 38). Such methods are described as reward based or "management-by-exception" (Avolio & Bass, 2002, p. 3). The employees performance is what Transactional leaders act upon. Transformational leaders aspire to inspire performance to a greater outcome beyond self-development.

Servant-oriented leadership was developed by Robert K. Greenleaf in 1970. Greenleaf's writings on servant leadership emphasize the servant as leader. Servant leaders are servants first. "The natural servant, the person who is servant first, is more likely to persevere and refine a particular hypothesis on what serves another's highest priority needs than is the person who is leader first and who later serves out of promptings of conscience or in conformity with normative expectations" (Greenleaf, 1970, p. 6). Prolific writers on servant-oriented leadership are Ken Blanchard, Larry Spears, and Stephen Covey.

Regardless of definition, leadership is both style and substance and must consider an organizational culture of multi-generations. "It is argued that the 'ability to understand, learn, and effectively leverage multigenerational diversity will be necessary for organisations now and in the future to build and maintain high performance systems'" (Oshagbemi, 2004, p. 15). Organizational performance relies on the ability of leadership to motivate and inspire innovation. Capitalizing on relationship building skills and diversity (strong attributes of transformational leaders) enhances a leader's ability to build consensus and trust within their organization. Collaboration and collective efforts emerge as strong tactics for organizational performance outcomes.

One example of a concerted framework for organizational professional development was presented by Markovits and Donop (2007) entitled Collaborate for Growth (CfG), built upon hope,

relationship, and purpose. They established three levels of activity within the organization, sponsors who selected the challenge, a group of individuals assessing and directing the plan, and Execution Teams who made it all happen. "The intention of engaging all three levels is to create a microcosm of the organizational system, focused on a shared growth opportunity, and work together to create a systemic understanding about its shared challenges. These three levels also coordinate approaches to solve the challenges, and build a groundswell for whole-system change" (Markovits & Donop, p. 14). Hope became the attitude of outcome. Relationship focused upon the reality of partnership. Purpose helped people coalesce and manage change. "Purpose at the individual level creates a sense of deep personal meaning, and at the collective level it unifies, engages, and inspires the team" (Markovits & Donop, p. 15).

Collaborate for Growth is one example of purposeful leadership focusing on the unified collective strengths of the organization. Building a leader community requires approaches such as this to foster a collective experience engaging both professional and personal dimensions of the organization. Individuals participate and believe in making a difference.

Jason Jennings (2008), motivation business thought leader in his keynote presentation entitled "Make it Happen Faster" provided performance commonalities he discovered when researching the top 10 businesses for his newest book, *Think Big, Act Small*. He asked why and how businesses turned a profit when other businesses were not so successful. He identified leader characteristics reflecting others over self. These leaders were stewards of talent as well as product; recognizing, balancing, and valuing the whole rather than small or segmented parts. They saw a big picture and painted its realization with everyone's talents. Everyone made a difference. In a world of mass collaboration and influence, "To innovate and succeed, the new mass collaboration must become part of every leader's playbook and lexicon. Learning how to engage and co-create with a shifting set of self-organized partners is becoming an essential skill, as important as budgeting, R&D, and planning" (Tapscott & Williams, 2006, p. 20).

Women leaders excel at creating and perpetuating a collaborative culture. A recent study by Caliper (2013), Princeton management consulting firm, focused on qualities of women in leadership. Study results showed women were more assertive and persuasive with strong interpersonal skills. They were risk takers showing resilience and persistence in their careers. Barbara Boxer, who participated in the study affirmed, "Women do have a more inclusive way of leading…" (Caliper, 2013, para. 21). Herb Greenberg, President and Chief Executive Officer of Caliper summed up the study's results:

These women leaders share a strong profile. They are assertive, persuasive, empathetic, willing to take risks, outgoing, flexible and have a need to get things done…These personality qualities combine to create a leadership profile that is much more conducive to today's diverse workplace, where information is shared freely, collaboration is vital and teamwork distinguishes the best companies (para. 34).

With strong influential attributes and team oriented strengths, women are aligned closely to a transformational leadership style. Koneck (2006), in her dissertation research, identifies that women emerged stronger in transformational leadership styles and men in transactional leadership styles. Women's interpersonal and social strengths give them the ability to develop relationships and build consensus. Transformational leaders empower others within the organization fostering opportunity for individuals. They are not self-serving. Eagly (2013) states, a transformational leader "… motivates others to go beyond the confines of their job descriptions, encourages creativity and innovation, fosters good human relationships, and develops the skills of followers." Transformational

leaders are also more likely to promote organizational diversity (Ng & Sears, 2012). The tendency to value and engage organizations through individualized attention puts transformational leaders ready for a multi-generation workforce. Marie C. Wilson (2004) stated, "The core of what women bring to leadership—a tendency toward greater inclusiveness, empathy, communication up and down hierarchies, focus on broader issues—makes stronger government and richer business" (p. 6).

So, with women's strengths in transformational leadership and the need for leaders to develop multi-generations why aren't more women becoming leaders? Surely opportunities for leadership are plentiful. Gender influences organizational culture and contributes to leadership diversity. For many women, organizational culture for them is less than welcoming.

Cronin and Fine (2010) in their book entitled *Damned if She Does, Damned if She Doesn't*, elaborate upon the experiences of gender in the business world. They determine, through the voices of women, that while opportunities for women in the business world are good, the challenge lies more within how women can be successful working within the organization. "We believe that the fundamental problem facing women in business today has metamorphosed from getting into the corporate system to working within the corporate system" (Cronin & Fine, 2010, p. 63). The Anita Borg Institute for Women in Technology published a study which focused on Senior Technical Women. They too acknowledge struggles for women within organizations with isolation, lack of mentoring, and unwelcome organizational cultures (Gilmartin & Simard, 2012).

Diversity matters in that it's a reflection of the organization. I think if you look at the organization and everyone who's in a senior management role is a white male, it doesn't reflect very well on the organization. – high-level technical man (p. 5)

As elaborated upon earlier in this chapter, women enter computer science and engineering study but their tendency is not to pursue leadership positions. The practice of mentoring, especially mentoring women, is one practice that could benefit women's consideration and preparation into leadership.

Power in Mentoring

In the short time I had with supercomputing, there was one element that contributed a long-lasting effect upon my endeavor: it was the mentoring I received from the supercomputing community. When I had the opportunity to step into the High Performance Computing culture, I was living a common challenge in the supercomputing world. Clusters "Can be hard to manage without experience" (San Diego Supercomputing Center, 2008, p. 11). While I had long valued what HPC brought to the research community, I soon learned from my constituents that few understood what it meant, what it took to pursue computational research, and the potential it represented. I sought out the supercomputing community for help and support.

Johnson (2011) defines mentoring as a purposeful synergetic relationship which enables people "to set and achieve goals, make decisions and solve problems" (p. 40).

My mentors were the experts at the University of Oklahoma, University of California, San Diego Supercomputing Center, the Rocks community, the Rocks listserv, XSEDE, Shodor, and the National Computational Science Institute. These individuals represented the heart and soul of commitment indicative of their passion for what high performance computing is all about. They offered assistance, information, support, and professional development opportunities.

With this mentoring foundation, I explored the hope of a possible outreach to our local school district with potential interest from the University of North Texas. My visit to the University of North Texas revealed a thorough thoughtful approach to the support and service of high performance computing. My visit to a local k-12 school district was received with perplexity leaving with the question posed to me, "Why would students want to study data?"

Through these experiences, I began to comprehend what supercomputing study and experience could bring for women's education and leadership preparation. My vision was to provide an opportunity for women to learn supercomputing in an invigorating environment and program where women could learn, fail, and achieve. This program would bring together faculty and technology services, foster opportunity to prepare women for data mining fields, and contribute to the body of knowledge of women in science. Such an effort would require support for independent research teams, a technology budget for cluster resources, and a multi-disciplinary team of faculty and technologists.

Unfortunately, I was not to achieve this project or pursue this program development. My organization underwent a re-organization and my position was eliminated. Regardless, I was able to mentor a woman alongside me in support of an HPC system. She was given the HPC system to technically support. The leadership in place did not support research computing with an understanding or intent to grow it. They were not committed to the possibility of what the technology could foster and provide. As a consequence, I did not have a mentor on site to facilitate my ability to support research computing. But my experience is not so unusual.

Women struggle within organizations that perpetuate traditions of management and leadership strategies that inadvertently include cronyism and tokenism. Marques (2011) study of women and a new management paradigm states:

The underrepresentation of women in management is especially noticeable in the manufacturing/ engineering industry, which tends to be deeply rooted in traditional values, and predominantly operate under the old school of management (Collinson & Hearn, 1994; Kandola, 2004). In these types of organizations, the good old boy network is still prevalent, with its associated conservative decision making (Linehan, 2001) (p. 2).

Marques discusses the problem of tokenism as well. Organizations purposely put women in positions as tokens of compliance. "Tokenism is an obstacle for women whenever an establishment thinks it already has the percentage of women that it needs" (Marques, p. 36). Yet, mentoring is noted as critical to women's success. A study by Ramaswam, Dreher, Bretz, and Wiethoff (2010) discovered that women benefited greater in compensation and career progress when mentored with senior male mentors. (p. 399). "Our results also suggest that women in male-gendered industries need to seek out mentoring from powerful senior-male mentors or at least incorporate them in their developmental network" (Ramaswam, Dreher, Bretz, & Wiethoff, p. 402).

In Nolan, Buckner, Marzabadi and Kuck (2008) the value of mentoring for continued graduate study and career progression in chemistry was discussed. A strong mentor assists with knowledge acquisition and research opportunities as well as providing a foundation for success. One continual problem for women in chemistry is the lack of women faculty mentors available for mentoring. "Women are less likely than men to report having strong mentoring across all levels of training, likely because, at least in part, there are fewer female faculty members available to mentor them." (Nolan, Buckner, Marzabadi & Kuck, p. 246) The authors recommend the incorporation of a sustained mentoring effort aligning students with leadership.

Institutions also might implement more active "marketing" of strong female candidates to the administrative leaders and decision-making committees at the best post-doctoral and employment positions. If such recruitment is successful, these

candidates would become available to serve as role models for the next generation of rising scientists—both female and male—who emerge from their training programs (Nolan, Buckner, Marzabadi & Kuck, p. 246).

Mentoring is a powerful tool for professional development preparing a strong talented workforce. Through mentoring, the organization cultivates its talent. Cronin and Fine (2012) pose the possibility of an organization built upon common values where gender is immaterial. "The value that gender is immaterial moves the focus to what men and women have in common" (Cronin & Fine, p. 221). Focusing on the strengths of each individual and how those strengths contribute to the overall goals at hand is a transformational leader's vision. Women are fundamentally transformational in leadership style. There is hope for more women leaders in an organization that welcomes women as meaning makers and innovators.

CONCLUSION

Support and commitment for research computing is timely. The latest EDUCAUSE Center for Analysis and Research (ECAR) report on research computing states explicitly the need for collaboration between IT and faculty to perpetuate a dynamic environment for supercomputing to thrive in academia. Recommendations included developing research computing services infrastructure with researchers on grants, partner with other institutions, provide research staffing personnel, and be proactive in uncovering research computing needs (Bischel, 2012, para. 2). If IT leadership recognizes the value of computational research, potential demand for research intensive study and support emerges for consideration. The strength of the vision relies on partnership and relationship, fundamental transformational leadership attributes most notable of women's leadership styles.

Leadership is creative action, endurance, technique, collaboration, and risk, all of which help mitigate and navigate change. Future leadership in supercomputing will encounter a diverse talent pool of varying ages. My experience with supercomputing was positive within the supercomputing culture. I found an engaged community who genuinely enjoyed their work and 'cause.' The strength of the community was its mentoring and inclusiveness. As the talent pool, previously unfolded, begins to engage with the community, they will find possibility and rigor.

The current leaderships' challenge will be to assess and reflect upon a roadmap for the future from which the strengths of the talent in the wings can be leveraged taking into consideration the characteristics of the generation. The diversity that women bring to the supercomputing labor force is important. "Diversity often leads to enhanced abilities to perform tasks, greater creativity, and better decisions and outcomes" (Klawe, Whitney, & Simard, 2009, p. 68). Early advocacy for computer science and engineering study through computational thinking has been successful in generating and sustaining interest to pursue those disciplines. Prottman's (2011) thesis advocates computational thinking as a means by which young women are introduced to STEM disciplines. She developed a "self-contained online computational thinking tool for grades three through five" (Prottman, 2011, p. 2). With early introduction to computationally engaging practices, girls are more likely to persist in their study of computer science at the postsecondary level (Prottman, 2011, p. 1).

Discussion of gender and organizational culture helps shape an understanding of what today's leaders might face tomorrow with such a diverse global talent pool. Organizational culture can create a hostile, unwelcoming environment or one that thrives. And, mentoring makes a difference. When I was at a National Computational Science Institute Workshop, I had the opportunity to speak with a woman who was working on her graduate degree in computer science. She was also a part of the LittleFe project working alongside Charlie Peck of Earlham College. I remember how excited she was working on the project and how she valued the opportunity to be a part, contribute, and learn. Mentoring was making a difference in her life.

Lt. General Jefferson Howell, speaker at the Executive Leadership for Information Technology Excellence, 2006, stated,

To lead is to show the way. Set the example. Your people take your attitude, all the time. Ensure tasks are understood, take responsibility for your actions, train your people as a team, know yourself. And remember, where you sit determines what you see. (Howell, 2006)

Tomorrow's supercomputing leadership faces no shortage of talent. The challenge to the leadership is in preparing its future, readying a diverse, gendered, and global community of leaders for supercomputing. The pace of change is tomorrow's guarantee, ready or not.

REFERENCES

Abbott, P., Abraham, T., Beath, C., Bullen, C., Carmel, E., Evaristo, R., … Zwieg, P. (2006, March). *The information technology workforce: Trends and implications 2005-2008*. Society for Information Management IT Workforce Executive Summary.

Ahamed, S.I., Brylow, D., Early, J., Ge, R., Madiraju, P., Merrill, S.J., & Struble, C.A., (2010, March). *Computational thinking for the sciences: A three day workshop for high school science teachers*. Paper presented at SIGCSE'10, Milwaukee, WI.

Alsop, R. (2008). *The trophy kids grow up: How the millennial generation is shaking up the workplace*. San Francisco, CA: Jossey-Bass.

Aud, S., Hussar, W., Johnson, F., Kena, G., Roth, E., Manning, E., et al. (2012). *The condition of education 2012 (NCES 2012-045), undergraduate study*. U.S. Department of Education, National Center for Education Statistics. Retrieved May 4, 2013 from http://nces.ed.gov/pubsearch

Avolio, B. J., & Bass, B. M. (2002). *Developing potential across a full range of leadership: Cases on transactional and transformational leadership*. Mahwah, NJ: Lawrence Erlbaum Associates.

Bischsel, J. (2012, November 2). *Research computing: The enabling role of information technology*. ECAR. Retrieved April 2, 2013 from http://www.educause.edu/library/resources/research-computing-enabling-role-information-technology

Boal, K. B., & Hooijberg, R. (2001). Strategic leadership research: Moving on. *The Leadership Quarterly, 11*(4), 515–549. doi:10.1016/S1048-9843(00)00057-6

Bureau of Labor Statistics. (n.d.). *Occupational outlook handbook, 2012-13 edition, projections overview*. U.S. Department of Labor. Retrieved May 04, 2013 from http://www.bls.gov/ooh/about/projections-overview.htm

Caliper. (2013). *The qualities that distinguish women leaders*. Retrieved November 13, 2013 from https://www.calipercorp.com/portfolio/the-qualities-that-distinguish-women-leaders/

Catlett, C. E. (2005). TeraGrid: A foundation for US cyberinfrastructure. In *Network and parallel computing* (pp. 1-1). Springer Berlin Heidelberg. Retrieved April 1, 2013 from http://link.springer.com/chapter/10.1007%2F11577188_1

Center for Digital Education. (2012). *Supercomputers take research to new levels. Specialty Classroom Technologies, Special Report*. Folsom, CA: E. Republic.

Chang, G., Joiner, D., & Morreale, P. (2010, June). Connecting undergraduate programs to high school students: Teacher workshops on computational thinking and computer science. *Journal of Computing Sciences in Colleges, 25*(6), 191–197.

Computer Research Association. (n.d.). Retrieved May 28, 2013 from http://cra.org/resources/taulbee/

Council of Competitiveness. (2012, June). *Making impact: The council's 2011-2012 annual report*. Washington, DC: Author.

Cronin, L., & Fine, H. (2010). *Damned if she does, damned if she doesn't: Rethinking the rules of the game that keep women from succeeding in business*. Amherst, NY: Promethus Press.

DeLong, D. W. (2004). *Lost knowledge: Confronting the threat of an aging workforce*. Oxford, UK: University Press. doi:10.1093/acprof:oso/9780195170979.001.0001

Eagly, A. (2013, March 20). Hybrid style works and women are best at it. *New York Times*. Retrieved September 8, 2013 from http://www.nytimes.com/roomfordebate/2013/03/20/shery-sandberg-says-lean-in-but-is-that-really-the-way-to-lead/why-lean-in-hybrid-style-succeeds-and-women-are-best-at-it

Falkenheim, J.C., & Burrelli, J. (2012, March). *Diversity in science and engineering employment in industry*. National Center for Science and Engineering Statistics (NSF 12-311).

Gilmartin, S. K., & Simard, C. (2012). *Senior technical women: A profile of success*. Palo Alto, CA: Anita Borg Institute for Women and Technology.

Goodwin, B., & Zacharia, T. (2011, June 23). The supercomputing race. *Washington Post*. Retrieved March 10, 2013 from http://articles.washingtonpost.com/2011-06-23/opinions/35235793_1_exascale-supercomputers-competitiveness-report

Graham, S. L., Snir, M., & Patterson, C. A. (Eds.). (2005). *Getting up to speed: The future of supercomputing*. Washington, DC: National Academies Press.

Greenberg, P. (2006, March 1). Gen X-ers want more collaboration with corporations. *CIO.com*. Retrieved May 28, 2013 from http://www.cio.com/article/17907/Gen_X_ers_Want_More_Collaboration_With_Corporations?page=2&taxonomyId=3185

Greenleaf, R. K. (1970). *The servant as leader*. Westfield, IN: Green Leaf Center for Servant Leadership.

Groves, K., & LaRocca, M. (2011, November). An empirical study of leader ethical values, transformational and transactional leadership, and follower attitudes toward corporate social responsibility. *Journal of Business Ethics*, *103*(4), 511–528. doi:10.1007/s10551-011-0877-y

Hammill, G. (2005). *Mixing and managing four generations of employees*. Retrieved August 18, 2013 from http://www.fdu.edu/newspubs/magazine/05ws/generations.htm

Harris, M. (2011, September). The ethics of interpersonal relationships. *Journal of Bioethical Inquiry*, *8*(3), 301–302. doi:10.1007/s11673-011-9308-0

Howe, N., & Strauss, W. (2000). *Millennials rising: The next generation*. New York: Random House.

Howell, J. (2006, April). *Speech*. Speech presented to the ELITE Executive Leadership for Information Technology Excellence, Class of 2006, Austin, TX.

Hussar, W. J., & Bailey, T. M. (2013). *Projections of education statistics to 2021 (NCES 2013-008)*. Washington, DC: U.S. Government Printing Office.

Izzo, J., & Withers, P. (2001). *Values shift: The new work ethic & what it means for business*. Lions Bay, Canada: FairWinds Press.

Jennings, J. (2008, March). *Make it happen faster*. Speech presented at the Help Desk Institute Annual Conference, Grapevine, TX.

Johnson, D. (2011). Mentoring and support systems: Keys to leadership. *Advancing Women in Leadership*, *31*, 40–44.

Kilduff, M., Chiaburu, D. S., & Menges, J. I. (2010). Strategic use of emotional intelligence in organizational settings: Exploring the dark side. *Research in Organizational Behavior*, *30*, 129–152. doi:10.1016/j.riob.2010.10.002

Klawe, M., Whitney, T., & Simard, C. (2009, February). Women in computing-take 2. *Communications of the ACM*, *57*(2), 68–76. doi:10.1145/1461928.1461947

Koneck, C. M. (2006). *A study of women leadership styles and the glass ceiling*. (Unpublished doctoral dissertation). Capella University, Minneapolis, MN.

Lamoureux, K., Campbell, M., & Smith, R. (2009, April). *High-impact succession management*. Bersin & Associates and Center for Creative Leadership Industry Study, V.1.0.

Leung, R. (2009, February 11). The echo boomers. *CBS News*. Retrieved May 28, 2013 from http://www.cbsnews.com/8301-18560_162-646890.html?pageNum=2

Lewin, T. (2012, November 2). Digital Natives and their customs. *NY Times*. Retrieved May 28, 2013 from http://www.nytimes.com/2012/11/04/education/edlife/arthur-levine-discusses-the-new-generation-of-college-students.html?_r=0

Maccoby, M. (2004, January). Narcissistic leaders: The incredible pros, the inevitable cons. *Harvard Business Review*, *82*(1), 92–101.

Markovits, M., & Donop, K. (2007, Winter). Collaborate for growth: Deepening involvement through hope. *Organization Development Journal*, *25*(4), 13–18.

Marques, V. C. (2011). *Emerging leadership styles: Women's success strategy in engineering organizations and the new management paradigm.* (Unpublished doctoral dissertation). Capella University, Minneapolis, MN.

Moss, J. A., & Barbuto, J. E. Jr. (2010, January). Testing the relationship between interpersonal political skills, altruism, leadership success and effectiveness: A multilevel model. *Journal of Behavioral and Applied Management*, *11*(2), 155–174.

National Science Board. (2012). Science and engineering indicators 2012. Arlington, VA: National Science Foundation (NSB 12-01).

National Science Foundation. (2012, August). *Age of recent graduates with bachelor's degrees in science, engineering, or health, by major field of degree: October 2008, table 13.* Characteristics of Recent Science and Engineering Graduates: 2008, (NSF 12-328). Retrieved June 7, 2013 from http://www.nsf.gov/statistics/nsf12328/pdf/nsf12328.pdf

Ng, E. S., & Sears, G. J. (2012). CEO leadership styles and the implementation of organizational diversity practices: Moderating effects of social values and age. *Journal of Business Ethics*, *105*(1), 41–52. doi:10.1007/s10551-011-0933-7

Nolan, S. A., Buckner, J. P., Marzabadi, C. H., & Kuck, V. J. (2008). Training and mentoring of chemists: A study of gender disparity. *Sex Roles*, *58*(3-4), 235–250. doi:10.1007/s11199-007-9310-5

Oshagbemi, T. (2003, June). Age influences on the leadership styles and behavior of managers. *Employee Relations*, *26*(1), 14–29. doi:10.1108/01425450410506878

Pekerti, A. A., & Sendjaya, S. (2010, April). Exploring servant leadership across cultures: Comparative study in Australia and Indonesia. *International Journal of Human Resource Management*, *21*(5), 754–780. doi:10.1080/09585191003658920

Popa, B. M. (2013). Risks resulting from the discrepancy between organizational culture and leadership. *Journal of Defense Resources Management*, *4*(1), 179–182.

Prottman, C. L. L. (2011). *Computational thinking and women in computer science.* (Unpublished Master's Thesis). University of Oregon, Eugene, OR.

Ramaswami, A. R., Dreher, G. F., Bretz, R., & Wiethoff, C. (2010). Gender, mentoring, and career success: The importance of organizational context. *Personnel Psychology*, *63*(2), 385–405. doi:10.1111/j.1744-6570.2010.01174.x

Reed, L., Vidaver-Cohen, D., & Colwell, S. (2011, July). A new scale to measure executive servant leadership: Development, analysis, and implications for research. *Journal of Business Ethics*, *101*(3), 415–434. doi:10.1007/s10551-010-0729-1

Robinson, K. (2011). *Out of our minds.* Westford, MA: Courier Westford, Inc.

San Diego Supercomputing Center. (2008, May 15). *Introduction to clusters and rocks overview: Rocks for noobs.* University of California, San Diego, CA. Retrieved May 28, 2013 from http://www.rocksclusters.org/presentations/tutorial/

Schein, E. (2010). *Organizational culture and leadership* (4th ed.). San Francisco, CA: Jossey-Bass.

Siebens, J. & Ryan, C. L. (2012, February). *Field of bachelor's degree in the United States: 2009.* U.S. Census Bureau.

Singh, N., & Krishnan, V. R. (2008). Self-sacrifice and transformational leadership: Mediating role of altruism. *Leadership and Organization Development Journal, 29*(3), 261–274. doi:10.1108/01437730810861317

Stein, J. (2013, May 20). Millennials: The me, me, me generation. *Time, 181*(19), 26–34.

Tapscott, D., & Williams, W. (2006). *Wikinomics*. New York: Penguin Group.

Technology Leadership and Strategy Initiative. (2012). Retrieved May 28, 2013 from http://www. compete.org/about-us/initiatives/tlsi

U.S. Census Bureau. (2011, September). *Doctorates awarded by field of study and year of study: 2000 to 2009, table 815*. Retrieved June 7, 2013, from www.census.gov/compendia/statab/2012/ tables/12s0815.pdf

U.S. Census Bureau. (2011, September). *Doctorates conferred by recipients' characteristics: 2009, table 814*. Retrieved June 6, 2013, from www.census.gov/compendia/statab/2012/ tables/12s0814.xls

U.S. Department of Education. (2011). *Bachelor's degrees conferred by degree-granting institutions, by race/ethnicity and field of study: 2009-10 and 2010-11, table 301*. Digest of Education Statistics. Retrieved June 7, 2013 from http://nces.ed.gov/ programs/digest/2011menu_tables.asp

U.S. Department of Education, National Center for Education Statistics. (2012, May). *Number of master's and doctor's degrees awarded by degree-granting institutions, percentage of total, number and percentage awarded to females, and percent change, by selected fields of study: Academic years 1999–2000 and 2009–10*. Condition of Education 2012 (NCES 2012-045), Indicator 39, Table A-39-1. Retrieved June 7, 2013 from http://nces. ed.gov/pubs2012/2012045_5.pdf

U.S. Department of Education, National Center for Education Statistics. (2012, June) *Bachelor's degrees conferred by degree-granting institutions, by race/ethnicity and field of study: 2009-10 and 2010-11, Table 301*. Retrieved June 7, 2013 from nces.ed.gov/programs/digest/d12/tables/ xls/tabn301.xls

Washington Times. (2005, November 18). *Gen Y knocking on at the door of ownership*. Retrieved May 28, 2013 from http://www.washingtontimes. com/news/2005/nov/17/20051117-083543-6983r/?page=all

Wilson, M. C. (2004). *Closing the leadership gap: Why women can and must help run the world*. New York: Viking.

Yu, H., & Miller, P. (2005). Leadership style: The X generation and baby boomers compared in different cultural contexts. *Leadership and Organization Development Journal, 26*(1), 35–50. doi:10.1108/01437730510575570

Zemke, R., Raines, C., & Filipczak, R. (1999). *Generations at work: Managing the clash of veterans, boomers, Xers and nexters in your workplace*. New York: AMACOM.

Zweden, S. (2012). *Computing degree and enrollment trends from the 2011-2012 CRA Taulbee survey*. Computing Research Association. Retrieved April 13, 2013 from http://cra.org/uploads/documents/resources/taulbee/CRA_Taulbee_CS_Degrees_and_Enrollment_2011-12.pdf

ADDITIONAL READING

Bennett, M.T. (2013, February 4). A study of the management leadership style preferred by IT subordinates. *Journal of Organizational Culture, Communications and Conflict,* 13(2).

Covey, S. M. R. (2006). *The SPEED of Trust: The One Thing That Changes Everything*. New York: Free Press.

de Vries, R. E., Bakker-Pieper, A., & Oostenveld, W. (2010). Leadership=Communication? The Relations of Leaders' Communication Styles with Leadership Styles, Knowledge Sharing and Leadership Outcomes. *Journal of Business and Psychology*, 25(3), 367–380. doi:10.1007/s10869-009-9140-2 PMID:20700375

Fisher, D. (2008). *AI and Developing Socially-engaged Computational Thinkers. Paper presented at the AAAI* Spring Symposium: Using AI to Motivate Greater Participation in Computer Science, Stanford, CA.

Gardner, H. (2006). *Five minds for the future*. Boston, MA: Harvard Business School Publishing.

Gardner, H. (2011). *Leading minds: An anatomy of leadership*. NY: Basic Books.

Giri, V. N., & Santra, T. (2009, December, 31). Effects of job experience, career stage, and hierarchy on leadership style. *The Free Library*. Retrieved May 8, 2013 from http://www.thefreelibrary.com/Effects of job experience, career stage, and hierarchy on leadership...-a0215408845

Godin, S. (2010). *Linchpin: Are You Indispensable?* New York: Penguin House.

Heimler, R., Rosenberg, S., & Morote, E. (2012). Predicting career advancement with structural equation modeling. *Education + Training*, 54(2/3), 85 – 94.

Howe, N., & Strauss, W. (2010). *Millennials Rising: The next great generation*. NY: Random House.

Jennings, J. (2005). *Think big, act small: How america's best performing companies keep their start- up spirit alive*. New York: Penguin Books.

Jennings, J. (2012). *The reinventors: how extraordinary companies pursue radical continuous change*. New York: Penguin Books.

Leman, K., & Pentak, W. (2004). *The way of the shepherd: Seven ancient secrets to managing productive people*. Grand Rapids, MI: Zondervan.

Levine, A. (2012). *Generation on a Tightrope: A Portrait of Today's College Student*. San Francisco, CA: Jossey-Bass.

Majury, M. (2011). *Emerging workforce trends in information and computing technology 2011 to 2018*. Bellevue, WA: Center of Excellence for Information and Computing Technology.

Martin, G. S., Resick, C. J., Keating, M. A., & Dickson, M. W. (2009, April). Ethical leadership across cultures: A comparative analysis of German and US perspectives. *Business Ethics (Oxford, England)*, 18(2), 127–144. doi:10.1111/j.1467-8608.2009.01553.x

Maxwell, J. C. (2005). *Thinking for a change: 11 ways highly successful people approach life and work*. NY: Warner Books.

Maxwell, J. C. (2011). *The 5 levels of leadership: Proven steps to maximize your potential*. New York: Hachette Book Group.

McMullen, D. F. (1997). *A Partnership Approach to Funding Research Computing*. Paper presented at the meeting of CAUSE, The Information profession and the information professional, Lake Buena Vista, FL.

Mourshed, M., Farrell, D., & Barton, D. (2012). *Education to employment: designing a system that works*. McKinsey Center for Government.

Riescher, J. G. (2009). Management across time: A study of generational workforce groups (baby boomer and generation X) and leadership. Unpublished doctoral dissertation, Capella University, Minneapolis.

Schramm, S. (2000, May). Thinking thrice: A feminist response to "mentoring" that marginalizes. (ERIC Document Reproduction Service No. ED 446 463)

Shekari, H., & Nikooparvar, M. Z. (2012, January). Promoting Leadership Effectiveness in Organizations: A Case Study on the Involved Factors of Servant Leadership. *International Journal of Business Administration*, 3(1), 54–65. doi:10.5430/ijba.v3n1p54

Srinivasan, V. (2006). Buildng a research agenda on people related challenges to technology organisations: discussion. *IIMB Management Review*. Reprint No 07308a, *285-297*.

Turkle, S. (1986). Computational reticence: Why women fear the intimate machine. In Cheris Kramare (Ed.), Technology and Women's Voices (41-61). NY: Permagon Press.

Van Velsor, E., Mccauley, C. D., & Ruderman, M. N. (Eds.). (2010) Handbook of leadership development (3rd ed). Center for Creative Leadership. San Francisco, CA: Jossey-Bass.

Washington, C. E. (2010). Mentoring, organizational rank, and women's perceptions of advancement opportunities in the workplace. [Forum on Public Policy.]. *Urbana (Caracas, Venezuela)*, IL.

KEY TERMS AND DEFINITIONS

Baby Boomers: A person born between the years 1946 and 1964 characterized by affluence and opportunity. These individuals were born Post World War II and total 76 million. Descriptions of baby boomers included self-centeredness and loyal. They were ambitious and lifelong learners.

Computational Thinking: A way of solving problems mathematically and algorithmically across a multitude of disciplines of study. Drawing on fundamental concepts of computer science, computational thinking across the curriculum prepares individuals to engage in a data rich world as scientists, physicians, librarians, historians, financial analysts and much more.

GenX: GenXers were born between 1961-1982. GenX individuals came from households where both parents worked thus the liklihood that they were latchkey is high. Characteristics include; self-reliant, controlling, and community. They key in on 'experience' thus the 'My' approach to marketing is more successful to this generation. They desire to control their own experience, contribute to their experience, and define the value of that experience rather than have it defined by a corporation.

Mentoring: Johnson (2011) defines mentoring as a purposeful synergetic relationship which enables people "to set and achieve goals, make decisions and solve problems" (p. 40).

Millennial: Recently noted as the Me Me Me Generation in Time magazine, Millennials number around 80 million. This generation is described as narcissistic raised in a world gone social, connected, and wired. They have a tendency for causes and are immersed in the digital.

Organizational Culture: Organizational culture is the environment of an organization perpetuated from the behaviors, meanings, and actions of its members (Marques, 2011, p. 47). This environment is taught to new members as a way of perceiving and thinking about the organization, how it operates, and affects others. Based on a set of values, symbols, languages, beliefs, and actions, the culture of an organization is very important.

Servant Leadership: Servant-oriented leadership was developed by Robert K. Greenleaf in 1970. Greenleaf's writings on servant leadership emphasize the servant as leader. Servant leaders are servants first aspiring to put the needs of others before self. The servant leader is not driven by position but rather the love of serving. Proponents of servant leadership are Ken Blanchard, John Maxwell, and Laurie Beth Jones.

Succession Planning: Succession planning is a talent pool strategy of an organization. A mature organization recognizes the strengths of its people and leverages their talents for the benefit of the organization's business. Succession planning is the process whereby talent is developed, strengthened, and trained for leadership.

Talent Pool: A community or cohort of individuals with specific skills for an organization.

Transactional Leadership: A philosophy and practice of leadership which focuses on contingent reinforcement as motivational methods for employee performance. The employees performance is what Transactional leaders act upon through methods of reward and punishment.

Transformational Leadership: A philosophy and practice of leadership which encourages others to take ownership for their work, motivates growth, and empowers the organization with collective identity measures. Transformational leaders aspire to inspire performance to a greater outcome beyond self-development.

Toxic Leadership: A philosophy and practice of leadership that emerges as a consequence of self-serving desires perhaps often unbeknownst to the individual. While the community receiving the service may not know, the internal talent pool of the leadership suffers with low morale and performance is fear based. The outcome of this leadership is high turnover and low performance. Toxic leadership thrives on setting up others to fail so they may succeed.

Chapter 16
Supercomputers:
A Philosophical Perspective

Jeremy Horne
International Institute of Informatics and Systemics, Mexico

ABSTRACT

Supercomputers solve very large-scale complex problems efficiently and expediently – simulating societies, modeling the weather, or mapping genes, etc. Perhaps the most complex task of all is simulating our brains. The physical mapping of organic components to an artificial architecture is daunting, but more so is identifying the mental content referred to as "consciousness." Creating a human mind is not impossible; what appeared out of reach yesterday is near reality now – a mind embodied in a machine. More profoundly, we may become our own gods, religion merging with science, a "supercomputer brain" encapsulating consciousness, reason, rationality, intelligence, etc. Can we overcome human bias in looking at ourselves, humans creating their own minds, our living as simulations in a virtual world, and computers actually solving social problems? If ultimately these developments amount to creating ourselves as a god, humanity looking at itself through itself, we may not like what we see.

INTRODUCTION

This chapter of *Research and Applications in Global Supercomputing* is an interdisciplinary treatment of the language of supercomputing from the perspective of philosophy, more precisely, thinking about how supercomputers may actually communicate with us. Attention is called to the word "research" in the book's title, with two considerations: what motivated supercomputers and what the rapid changes of pace in supercomputer technology means for us. That is, supercomputers act as a "talking point" in philosophy, carrying us into more profound areas of discourse, a primary one being humanity's fate.

What motivated supercomputers has the same basic answer as for the reason motivating computers – to simplify and make a more accurate accounting of things. This can be said for the abacus, and even numbers, themselves. Supercomputers are used primarily to attack complex computations as found in thermodynamics, meteorological modeling, geophysical

DOI: 10.4018/978-1-4666-7461-5.ch016

Copyright © 2015, IGI Global. Copying or distributing in print or electronic forms without written permission of IGI Global is prohibited.

seismic activity prediction, and nuclear explosion dynamics. Yet, what if we ask about perhaps the most complex entity, the human mind-brain, the very core of our being? What is it, what is its purpose, and what may be its future?

If the ultimate purpose of supercomputers is to construct a "supercomputerbrain", numerous discussions about the nature of what happens inside our brains are brought forward, perhaps the immediately relevant one being the nature of consciousness. We talk of "consciousness" as if we know what it is, but we keep reminding ourselves that the "hard problem" makes identification elusive. However, if we discover what consciousness is, what then? How will it be contained in an artificial brain? What of a situation where the "mind" that we replicate in a supercomputer then looks at us? Will it be a mind independent of us or identical, a mirror image? What will be the implications?

In managing complexity, during the past 500 years humans have followed the Cartesian method of subdividing a whole so as to be able to manage it by managing the pieces, a result being what we might call today an "information glut". Pieces recombine to produce other wholes, but the apprehension of that overall complexity has remained elusive. Supercomputers in superseding the limited architecture of the human brain offer the distinct possibility of achieving that apprehension. What they ultimately "report" to us is what we face. What are time, consciousness, or even something relatively mundane as identifying the best socioeconomic solution? Perhaps a yottaflop (or higher) supercomputer coupled with quantum computing would be able to model reality accurately by recombining elements and even predicting outcomes. It would be as if all the brains in the world were working at once and for an extended period of time. In this way, we accelerate human development and possibly learn of our future.

MAIN FOCUS OF THIS CHAPTER

Supercomputers: A Philosophical Logic Perspective will provide somewhat of an overview of how supercomputer technological development may apply in recreating the human mind-brain. I also will focus on provoking discussion about emergence in an artificial brain by interweaving ideas somewhat repetitive but in different contexts. In other words, it is not the fascination of a brain's construction and how the architecture of a supercomputer might be mapped to it that is the focal point here but the implications. I assume that the technology will be there to meet the challenges. Given the rate of growth in our knowledge of brain functions, especially in the past few decades, it would not be surprising to see its functionality replicated in the relatively near future. Neuroimaging advances and nanotechnology are two areas that may make at least a physical replication possible. The principle issue in producing a fully functioning brain is knowing precisely what the supercomputer will emulate, and what we think is a mind, thinking, and consciousness. Many times it is safer just to ask the question, but one cannot act on questions. When we find the answer we must be prepared for more dramatic problems, such as those concerning policy.

Such discussions are common prior to major technological development, noted in the historical controversies surrounding the atomic bomb, cloning, and extraterrestrial planet colonization. We are at the edge of what may be considered an hour of decision in solving humanly-caused problems. I explore a number of concerns, speculations, and other observations. In this tradition, the reader of this chapter will be taken beyond the details of the technology of applications and be brought face-to-face with a central reason why supercomputers ultimately are being developed: to manage complexity, in particular the complexity of thinking. More profoundly, there is a discussion about humanity being its own god(s) and overcoming angst (as in the anxiety of what happens after death) by assuming control of its destiny and perhaps living forever (Tipler, 1994).

Numerous references have been provided, and the reader should consult them as "extended" remarks; they set a context, or backdrop, against which this discourse is presented, thus making the content more encyclopedic. In many of these references are bibliographies, as well.

BACKGROUND

In essence, a supercomputer is a device having massively parallel processors and capable of simultaneous numerous complex computations (Supercomputer, 2013), or tasks. A processor, often referred to as a "central processing unit" (CPU), is computer hardware that executes a computer program, that is, translating the input of information and processing it, or computing, recombining, adding, or synthesizing information as outputs (Central processing unit, 2014). This description of supercomputers, refers to stand alone units and distributed computers, as in a network of computers or computer users. Networks of users and the Internet, itself, can be considered a supercomputer if the end users are coordinated by a focal point in doing a task or tasks. On the biological side, it can be argued that the human neural net is a supercomputer, as well.

One of the functions of a computer is to perform repetitive tasks, and part of the core of this ability is memory. It can be argued that the quest for devices that could accept, retain, process, and output information, as well as repeating tasks was a chief motivation for computers. Technological developments through the millennia reflect major conceptual shifts that made modern computers possible. The Industrial Revolution saw the advent of any number of machines that could perform tasks that could be done only manually. Systems of gears, levers, pulleys, and the like constituted the machine "memory", ensuring that a task would

be performed in the same manner repeatedly. The machine went ahead and did the work of humans, cotton gins, presses, and stamping machines being just some examples. About 1450 the movable type press was invented by Gutenberg, and this set the stage for producing output based on the ability to change the instructions to the machine by changing a template. Previously, one could produce repeated outputs of a letter or image, such as with a seal stamping a semi-soft puddle of wax on paper or parchment.

Then came Londoner Ahasuerus Fromanteel in 1665 with a table clock, which had changeable pinned barrels that operated bells which played various tunes. Charles Babbage in 1822 created his "difference engine" that performed mechanical calculations of polynomial functions, followed by a much more sophisticated "Analytical Engine", and he is credited with being the first to invent the forerunner of the modern computer. Carrying this principle further, Herman Hollerith came next in 1889 with "*An Electric Tabulating System*". In keeping with this method of switching templates, Edwin Votey in 1895 created the player piano in his Detroit, MI workshop. To play a specific piece, the corresponding punched roll would be inserted, and, air would be passed through the holes to activate the keys. After Hollerith and Votey came the long period of developing the internal "mechanism" electronically, where a changeable template could produce output. That is, the punched Hollerith card and player roll existed. Now all that was needed was to develop the electronic "piano" for the Hollerith card. And, further still, there had to be developed the ability of a user that could, in real time, change the input as the device continued to function. This was to come in 1946 at first as an electronic calculator with the Electronic Numerical Integrator And Computer (ENIAC) and soon after in the 1950s with the IBM Sage System that allowed user input interactively. A language for conveying concepts was required. Binary logic was the language to be used for expressing the content, and the mechanical way of conveying that language was routing by electrical pulses through a system of switches, first by vacuum tubes, then transistors, and now semiconducting devices.

After an almost 70 year period, we have supercomputers, such as IBM's Blue Gene, ASCI Purple, SCC's Beowulf, and Cray's SV2. While these machines are designed for relatively limited functions, such as the 100 teraflops ASCI Purple simulating aging of nuclear weapons, future machines promise to have much faster data transfer, more storage, and more interconnected circuits (Lawrence Livermore Laboratory, 2013). Molecular computing, where molecules act as transistors 10,000 times smaller and having a lot more power, is a step towards further miniaturization and efficiency (Molecular Electronics, 2013).

It is often stated that while supercomputers are able to do large scale computations, and certainly better than even five years ago, there are limits to performance being improved further. Heat, storage, and power requirements are immediately limiting (Kogge, 2011). However, all this assumes that one will be working with current architectures. For example, quantum computing is around the corner, where data is represented in qubits as being in many possible states (Quantum computer, 2013), thus reducing the need for the linear access to it and reducing storage requirements. So, too, is the processing made much more efficient, with many computations occurring at the same time. Another example of a different architecture is a standard massively parallel computing on an organic molecular layer that mimics the human brain in being able to do parallel computations, instead of ones done in the traditional linear manner. Researchers demonstrated "...an assembly of molecular switches that simultaneously interact to perform a variety of computational tasks including conventional digital logic, calculating Voronoi diagrams, and simulating natural phenomena such as heat diffusion and cancer growth" (Bandyopadhyay et al. 2013)"

The development of computer hardware takes volumes to describe and is really outside the immediate scope of this chapter. Mechanics are only a small part of supercomputing. Even the applications, such as weather modeling, are of relatively small importance, compared to what may be down the line for humans and its implications – the ability supercomputers to think, reason, express emotions, and contain what we think is consciousness.

CREATING OURSELVES

Binary logic is a discovery, in that its syntax existed long before humans ventured on Earth. It is inherent in the universe. As we will see later, the notation used to describe it is a creation, as is the invention of any symbols used to represent ideas and objects already existing (as in a map of a geographical region). Such are the primitive foundations upon which the computational ability of computers is founded. Yet, there is more to the motivation for building supercomputers than mere representation and the movement of representations to create new information. There was the ancient Christian reference to a god creating humans in its image (Genesis: 1:27, King James Version), and in times after the Enlightenment whether humans would become gods, themselves.

A major impetus behind building computers and their follow-ons, supercomputers was the recognition that the human brain is inadequate to solve a number of problems and in a short time. What occurs in the human brain has been deemed, "consciousness", "mind", "cognition", and so forth, but we give these terms to what we see as the effects of thinking, not the process, itself. Solving problems is only a part of thinking, but there are, of course, many other aspects, such as value systems, aesthetics, emotions, and appreciation. Computers have given us the ability to solve a number of complex problems, but it is only reasonable to ask about their capacity to tell us, say, what is the right decision about controversial issues. Already, attempts have been made to create systems to make decisions outside the domain of discrete problem solving. For example, we have had the Defense Advanced Projects Research Agency (DARPA) sponsoring research to devise a system to evaluate ethical systems. A report prepared for DARPA stated:

Effects Based Assessment Support System (EBASS): A distributed operational assessment tool based on the principles of value focused thinking (VFT) and developed at the U.S. Military Academy to initially support the military command in Afghanistan in 2002. EBASS provides: 1) a qualitative value model which can account for the decision makers most important evaluation considerations and measures, and 2) quantitative scoring functions and weights to evaluate alternatives. (Knott, 2007)

and

Senturion: Senturion is a predictive analysis software tool developed at the National Defense University (NDU) Center for Technology and National Security Policy (CTNSP). CTNSP has been testing the Senturion capability since 2002, and has begun to support the application of this new technology in DoD. Centurion is a simulation capability that analyzes the political dynamics within local, domestic, and international contexts and predicts how the policy positions of competing interests will evolve over time. (Knott, 2007)

Attempts have been made to create programs to determine whether a person is a potential terrorist. On 20 August 2011 DARPA issued a call for such work in its Broad Agency Announcement 11-65, where DARPA calls for "New approaches for understanding and predicting the behavior of individuals and groups, especially those that elucidate the neurobiological basis of behavior and decision making" and "...the neurobiology

of moral judgment, development, and action." Factors motivating the DARPA search include (as stated in BAA 11-65) the need to understand, in that agency's words, to find answers to these problems:

- *Attitude and habit formation, particularly when uniquely influenced by or highly plastic in response to virtual interactions*
- *Measuring human propensity to engage in violence against out-group members*
- *Mechanisms important to mobilization into violent social movements and groups*
- *Pathologies resulting in warfighter accidents, misjudgments, and maladaptive behavior.*
- *Understanding attitude and habit formation, particularly when uniquely influenced by or highly plastic in response to virtual interactions*
- *New approaches for measuring human propensity to engage in violence against out-group members*
- *Theoretical and experimental efforts supporting the understanding of intelligence and self-organization in the natural world*
- *Understanding mechanisms important to mobilization into violent social movements and groups*
- *Investigations into pathologies resulting in warfighter accidents, misjudgments, and maladaptive behavior*
- *Neuromorphic information processing systems and architectures, electronic devices, and robotic systems*
- *Environments, systems, and concepts for the evaluation of machine intelligence*
- *Novel techniques and experimental methods for understanding the impact of stress on the brain (e.g., information processing, decision making, attention, and memory) with a specific interest in translating work on animal models to human populations*

- *Theoretical and experimental efforts to quantitatively describe and understand complex human neuroscience as it relates to social and economic systems*
- *Experimental efforts to understand the capability of using neural activity to induce and regulate an intended physiologic activity. (Broad Agency Announcement 11-65,2014)*

How serious have been the efforts to create ourselves?

BUILDING A BRAIN

Transhumanism is a movement to extend and improve the quality of human life by integrating technology with the human body. Human prostheses have been in existence for hundreds of years, but the possibility exists that every vital organ can be replaced by an artificial one, artificial hearts being a more complicated but older example (as in the 1982 Robert Jarvik-7). Extending human capacities and controlling human evolution are central to transhumanism (Transhumanism, 2014). In attempting to replicate the human brain, such as in the Human Brain project and IBM's SyNAPSE, answers may be forthcoming, one which humanity must be prepared to confront. Neuroimaging is in the forefront of research, major governmental efforts being focused in correlating neuroimages and genetic markers to psychological states, as in the National Institutes of Mental Health (NIMH) "The Research Domain Criteria" project. Often, the understanding of the "why" comes long after the creation of an application. One sees this in chemistry, for example, where hundreds of years after the discovery of elements and compounds we understand more of the nuclear dynamics.

Serious debate swirls about whether the human brain can be replicated, but one sees already that some robots can exhibit emotion via facial recognition software in responding to human expression (Azeem, Iqbal, Toivanen, & Samad, 2012). It can be expected that part of the human response is shaped by what the robot does, and what the robot does is partly shaped by the human, just as human interaction with other humans affects the consciousness of each. We can access thousands of articles on what robots can do, but we should consider how all of these are collected under the umbrella of a "super robot," a supercomputer.

The Brain, Itself

Here, we do not give a recipe or a guide to building a brain but cast light on some thinking about some approaches to it. In accomplishing the most complicated task for the supercomputer, building a brain, we have to incorporate ideas of the brain, itself, as "hardware," as well as what it occurs within it, or "software." Currently, the NIH **B**rain **R**esearch through **A**dvancing **I**nnovative **N**eurotechnologies (BRAIN) Initiative seeks, in its own words, "to produce a revolutionary new dynamic picture of the brain that, for the first time, shows how individual cells and complex neural circuits interact in both time and space."(Advisory Committee to the Director, 2013) Neuroimaging, cell typing, modeling, and direct recording by sensors are expected to contribute to the description. An example of direct insertion of sensors is available through the research by Tae-il et al. directly injecting "light sources, detectors, sensors, and other components into precise locations of the deep brain" (Tae-il et al. 2013). This and other projects, such as Blue Brain (mentioned below) conceivably will converge to produce an accurate physical description of the human brain. Yet, this is only half of the problem of creating a brain.

We speak of what philosophers call the "mind-body problem," one that has been around since people started talking about what happens in the brain. This dualism goes back to ancient times, when Plato (*Phaedo,* 65a-65d3, trans. 1892) talked of multiple souls that continued on when the organism perishes. Aristotle (*De Anima* ii 1,

412b6–9, trans 1931) agreed. Descartes (1641, pp. 1-62) said that the mind is separate from the body, thus formalizing the duality. Contemporary philosophy, neuroscience, and quantum physics (among other disciplines) cast into doubt this dualism, at least because we still do not know what really constitutes an idea, consciousness, or mind. We can see the effects of what we call these things, but one still asks precisely what they are.

In this respect, the duality is only for heuristic purposes, i.e., subdividing a task into its constituents. One may regard the dualism dialectically – one has to have one in order to have the other. A brain without anything within it is only an object. If there were no mind, how would one know it is a brain? As to mind, if there were not anything to contain or express it, how would it manifest itself? We focus on materials, memory, and speed as physical aspects of a "brain" so as to manage the complex processes occurring within it. Technology doesn't seem to have been an insurmountable barrier, once questions of theory have been answered. We consider some sample developments.

A first question about a supercomputer's physical structure is one about materials. In building a brain, is it is necessary to recreate the biological architecture creating the same effect that a supercomputer could? Computers often are thought of as silicon-based devices, but in the past few decades, the advent of organic computing throws an entirely different light on architectures, capacities, and interfaces with biological entities, not the least of which are mammals (Bandyopadhyay, A., Pati, R., Sahu, S., Peper, F., & Fujita, D., 2010).

A programmable DNA glue has been created "to create a variety of small, self-assembling devices, including lenses, reconfigurable microchips, and surgical glue that could knit together only the desired tissues" (Qui et al, 2013). This substance is composed of DNA and directs tiny gel bricks to assemble themselves. Currently, the potential application is to repair tissues and organs, but there may be a role for it in replicating the brain.

Thirty years ago, whoever would have thought that an object such as a pistol could be replicated anywhere in a matter of minutes by what people call "three-dimensional printing?" After scanning an object, assembly mechanisms draw upon raw material to recreate three dimensionally that which has been scanned. This modern example of unexpected technologies often is more typical of the character of technological development, rather than exception. In principle, surely at this stage of technological development, it is just as true for the question of whether the human brain can be replicated and, along with it, what we deem "consciousness." With nanotechnology – constructed atom by atom – we seem to be closer to being able to construct even the tiniest parts of a brain or their synthetic equivalents.

Part of a computer's capabilities to generate answers is memory and storage. How much a computer actually can do depends, much like an organic brain - upon inter connections. In essence, memory and storage can be on a grid onto which are etched or located markings of lattice crossings, and the location of an information unit, the binary digit (bit) ultimately becomes data. Matrices can be organically molecular, crystalline, or of any substance that allows a net. One can conceive of machinery which a computer – when it finds it needs more memory, storage, or processors – fabricates such, thus enhancing the supercomputing capacity. This is something way past the capacity of a human brain. Physical processing, itself, is a configuration of bits stored as a program that drives electrons routed through elaborate electronic circuitry manufactured as a computer chip. Again, in principle, because chips are of uniform construction, they also could be produced in the same way memory and storage are. This would involve a computer completely running a fabrication apparatus and the computer's ability to attach or integrate the products into itself. Overall, it is not inconceivable to have computers manufacturing computers.

It is not logically impossible for a molecular computer to assess its own needs for memory and storage and draw upon a molecular or non-hydrocarbon solution, a "bath", to create the storage (analogous to a crystal growing in its solution) and use a fabrication apparatus to create the circuitry required for processing. Today, one can purchase standardized modules for storage, memory, and processors, so the methods to create these surely exist. In principle, one only needs to provide the supercomputer with the physical appendages required to assemble the physical parts and assemble those parts to make a duplicate of itself. In an advanced world, robots could act as slaves to the supercomputer, acting as humans in bringing parts and matériel.

What of processing speed? Del Pradon (2009) found that the brain can process up to only about 60 bits per second during lexical decision tasks. However, this is only a single aspect of brain processing and applies only to a specific task. Plus, 60 bits a second is not fast. While real time processing is much slower, memory processing takes significantly less time. For example, for an hour's real time experience, memory recall takes from 8-10 minutes. Research shows the brain's processing speed is significantly faster than real time (Euston, Tatsuno, & McNaughton, 2007). If these are any accurate indications, then, on inspection, we can say that the computer is much faster. Sandia National Laboratories estimates that a zettaflop (10^{21}) (one sextillion FLoating-point Operations Per Second - FLOPS) computer can do complete weather modeling, but this would require about two weeks (DeBenedictus, 2005, pp. 391–402). However, this is using contemporary standard technology and does not account for quantum computing, which, because of superposition of states – can compute many alternatives at the same time. That is, the standard bit is not used, a digit of specific value, but a qubit (short for "quantum bit") that can assume any number of states at the same time. In 2007 the IBM Blue Gene/P supercomputer simulated a rat's brain, about one percent of a human cerebral cortex, which contains an estimated 1.6 billion neurons with some 9 trillion connections (Frye, Ananthanarayanan, & Modha, 2007). The human brain, itself, according to commonly cited figures, is one hundred billion neurons (Drachman, 2005), but one specific study, the only one of its kind, estimates 86 billion (Azevedo, 2009). In this brain, though, simultaneous processing occurs, not unlike in a quantum computer.

There surely have not been enough technological developments to produce an artificial brain, but this narrative has shown the comparative light years of progress in the field just in the past decade. In considering technological advances in the past three hundred years, it is not unreasonable to think that at this rate a human brain may be created even in the next few decades.

What Do We Put Into the Brain?

If we are able to replicate a brain or create a representation of it, how do we imbue it with a mind, or consciousness? After some twenty years of conferences presenting intense research, (as in Towards a Science of Consciousness), we are no closer to understanding what really defines consciousness or mind. One approach is saying that a minimal form of consciousness is an organism voluntarily responding to its environment (Allen, 2010), and awareness scales. For example, the Glasgow Coma Scale rates a person's ability to respond to stimuli (Glasgow Coma Scale, 2014).

What is of philosophical significance is how humans regard memory with respect to doing more abstract tasks, those beyond the relatively mundane ones of computations and the not so mundane one of thermodynamic modeling. Memory and the recombination of known ideas lies more in the mechanical domain, and can be regarded as a type of intelligence, but discussions of the future direction of computers lies in the synthesis and creation of ideas outside of what is stored in memory. We discuss this below. Coupled with a discussion of human intelligence is determining what is a normal human mental state. The two are not the same.

A standard compendium of mental disorders is in the Diagnostic and Statistical Manual of Mental Disorders (DSM), fifth edition. The International Classification of Diseases-10 is also a standard tool for mental disorder diagnosis. Yet, these are descriptions from psychological testing and clinical observation, and no validation exists (such as neuroimaging), an outside confirmation of a condition by other means. Neuroimaging is coming into its own as a diagnostic tool, as the U.S. National Institutes of Mental Health states, "Develop, for research purposes, new ways of classifying mental disorders based on dimensions of observable behavior and neurobiological measures." and "To transform the understanding and treatment of mental illnesses through basic and clinical research, paving the way for prevention, recovery, and cure (National Institutes of Mental Health, 2013)." In all this discussion of mental disorders, implicitly by listing disordered states, the authors presume to have an understanding of normal by which to make a comparison or determination of abnormal. Another obvious question is whether the mental states described by neuroimaging can be correlated with the DSM and ICD, thus validating the clinical observations.

The next step would be the replication of mental states (such as thoughts and moods) in a super-computer architecture, such as by replicating, let's say, neuronal assemblies that correspond to that mental state. This also would apply to thoughts, as recorded by functional magnetic resonance imaging (fMRI). Not only does neuroimaging have the potential of displaying mental states, it may reveal structures corresponding to intelligence. We have come to a point where electroencephalogram (EEG) signals can be transmitted from a cap of electrodes worn on a person's head via Internet

such that they can be received by a person wearing a similar cap. The first person will move a cursor (normally moved by a hand) by "thinking" about it, and the person at the other end will have her/his hand respond (Armstrong & Ma, 2013). That is to say EEG signals corresponding to a thought can be stored in a computer, perhaps in a database, and ultimately be used as a "vocabulary" for a robot to perform various actions.

"Intelligence", itself, is a highly controversial term, and there is sufficient argumentation to suggest that the "intelligence quotient (IQ)" measured by tests simply is a measure of achievement, rather than organic capacity to think (as in Neisser, 1998). Whatever the case, those constructing a supercomputer would want to impart to it those factors that contribute to what is called intelligence, and it is not beyond reason to suppose that an artificially thinking device can surpass human performance on these. It was mentioned above that the traditional use of computers focused on tasks relying on memory and recombination of already existing ideas. There are limits of human intelligence, but these often are overcome, as in memory, and there is little reason to expect that "processing" speed won't be far surpassed by supercomputers. For example, there is the obvious case of desktop computers performing complex mathematical operations in a fraction of the time as would be done manually. Memory, itself, can be regarded as a prosthesis, an extension of the human mind. Even fluid dynamic modeling turns to complex equations to process through known formulas to return results based on that already known formula. We see this phenomenon occurring in formulae to generate unique patterns (and sometimes apparently random configurations) by processing information through a formula (Wolfram, 2013; Wuensche, 2013). Recalling information through formulas and knowing how to use them, can be regarded as a form of intelligence. It is known there are many forms of intelligence-intellectual, emotional, musical, etc. (Gardner, 1993).

Based on this, educators refer to taxonomies of intellectual complexity. An initial foray into this area was exemplified by Bloom's (1956) *Taxonomy of Educational Objectives*. In the cognitive domain, the hierarchy of increasing complexity is:

- Knowledge
- Comprehension
- Application
- Analysis
- Evaluation
- Synthesis

The first few relate more to factual recall, and latter are what educators ultimately strive for, that is, synthesis, analysis, critical thinking, and creativity. These six levels can be achieved if the task is simple enough. Bloom later went beyond the original taxonomy by describing the importance of qualities and types of thought in his Digital Taxonomy, where the quality of the process, how the activity is performed, and interaction with others all are enhanced by computers (Digital Taxonomy, 2014). A computer can retrieve knowledge from memory. It can "comprehend" it by computation. The results can be applied, as in running machinery. They can be analyzed and synthesis emerges, with recommendation for how corrective action can be made or critical thinking can be fostered. There are other ways of considering complexity, but suffice it to say that there are areas of mental processes that require greater processing power. One, to which we have alluded in Bloom's *Digital Taxonomy*, is collaborating with others.

We have discussed the physical aspects of a supercomputer as an analogy to the brain and the substance of what is to be placed in it. The central question is whether constructing a thinking entity on par or better than a human being is a principal goal of building a supercomputer. To this point, we have been focusing on what we might put into its brain in the way of thoughts, mental states, intelligence, and so forth.

What if the supercomputer with its architecture could produce a consciousness that biological architecture would not? Such a device might act as an antenna to detect "consciousness". Sheldrake (2013) has proposed a controversial theory of morphogenic fields, where consciousness is within or analogous to electromagnetic fields. Before Galvani in 1786 discovered the measurement of electromagnetic fields in the frog's muscle reacting to an electrical shock, electromagnetic phenomena existed. That is, people can see the effects of an electromagnetic phenomenon, such as lightening or static electricity, but to measure it is another matter. The same may be true of ideas, where the idea is the effect of a field on its surroundings. In essence we may ask if there could be an "idea meter"? If so, the supercomputer standing alone simply as hardware would acquire consciousness, somewhat analogous to a radio receiving signals through its antenna and conveying the sound to us. Ideas and consciousness in this model would appear to consist of a field of energy. Yet, if human consciousness consists of these fields, are there not other consciousnesses, such as those of animals and non-human entities (Dreaming, 2013)? If so, and humans are not the only ones having it, then our particular neuroanatomy is not a necessary condition. The answer depends, of course, on what consciousness is.

As to what the physical structure of a brain might acquire, we refer back to the discussion about innate structures in the universe. Digital physics asserts that the universe is binary, Wheeler's (Misner, Thorne, & Wheeler, 1973) "it from bit" plausibly being that structure. Going further, there seem to be other structures, such a geometries of valence in the periodic table of elements. Atoms can combine only certain ways. There are other structures, represented as what Feynman (2001) calls his book "The Character of Physical Law," processes that permeate the universe, such as gravitational laws, and laws of electromagnetism. We see these patterns of structures, leading us to ask whether there is an innate structure of consciousness. Boole (1854) thought so in his *Laws of Thought*, to which the binary structure surely incorporates, that same structure relied upon by computers. This structure may comprise at least the partial vocabulary in the universe that the brain as a physical architecture may "absorb". If this architecture is part of the innate vocabulary, regardless of whoever builds a brain or how it is built, will that architecture be there? Does structure imply content? Perhaps more intriguing but ethically out of bounds for the present era is cloning, where a person's brain may be replicated. What is contained within? One approach to finding out would be to conduct an experiment with mammals in two parts. First, the experimenter would train the animals, record their mental capacities (such as the ability to learn and what they has learned), and neuroimage the brains. The second part would be to clone the animals and determine whether they could do the tasks the first group learned. In addition, the brains would be neuroimaged and compared to those of the first group to see if they are the same structurally. In this aspect, the question would be raised about how much difference could be tolerated in creating the ability to learn and process information. A second question to be answered would be whether information learned by the first group would be present in the second group. That is, would the second structure, being an exact replica of the first, by itself contain the information? If not, what is it that would be contained?

A SUPERCOMPUTER AS THINKING ORGANISM

As the complexity of computer architecture (Computational complexity, 2014) transforms from a relatively simple desktop to massively parallel processing devices, we come to considering the emergence of two characteristics: organicity and mind.

Now, we ask whether all of this consists of a living entity. We ask, "What is life? ", a question asked in a paper by Casti (1992) of the Santa Fe Institute and earlier by Schrödinger (1944). Can a supercomputer be considered "alive"? Does it form its own ethos?

It is not our task here to set forth definitively criteria for life, but some considerations about it, such as:

- Exhibits complex patterns in space and time
- Metabolism (including processing inputs as "food" to provide sustenance to the computer as organism")
- Ability to interact dynamically with environment
- Killable
- Robustness in face of external changes (able to adapt) and self-sustaining
- Interdependence of parts
- Ability to replicate. (Life, 2014)

Carl Sagan said in his "Definitions of Life" that there is no universal agreement for what constitutes life. Some criteria people propose do not cover all things normally regarded as life, as Sagan wrote, "An automobile, for example, can be said to eat, metabolize, excrete, breathe, move, and be responsive to external stimuli." (Sagan, 2010) There is some criterion that seems to be missing that distinguishes a car from what people think is life.

We may refer to "life" as being hydrocarbon-based as Earth-based life is, but who is to say that "life" has to be hydrocarbon-based? We speak of societies as being "organic", where they fulfill all the above criteria. Systems analysis regards social entities as organisms (Buckley, 1968). The Internet, itself, is an electronic society where we see unexpected phenomenon appear, having no apparent relationship to any known inputs. We cannot always trace back from such phenomena to an explicit input. Such is because of several factors. The granularity of the input (how precisely it is defined) is too general. This lack of precision may neglect an aspect that, when combined with another input, results in the unexpected phenomenon. Inputs may combine, creating another entity, and that entity combined with other inputs may result in the emergence. At a quantum level, it is impossible to define certainty and account for all the combinations of elements. This emergence is a factor well known by those who work with complex systems and modeling and simulations. In 1987 it was proposed that computers can discover scientific laws interdependently (Langley, Simon, Bradshaw, & Zytkow, 1987), and much work has been done to validate this (Dˇzeroski1, Langley, & Todorovski, 2013, p. 9). We now can introduce into computers a complex set of variables, formula, algorithms, vocabulary, etc. that approach architectures and processes that are closer to at least mimicking the complexity of the human brain.

As we move from simple memory to synthesis, there is a corresponding complexity of the computer architecture (Computational complexity, 2014) necessary to achieve or clarify those objectives. As was said earlier, memory is relatively simple, a construct of minute ferrous particles in a substrate, the direction of which can be changed by an external electromagnetic field. Information processing is accomplished by sending electrical current or photons through mechanically constructed gates, or switches. Information input comes from what is in memory or through user input, such as by a keyboard. Emerging from all this is synthesized information from a combination of what already is resident in the computer and from the user(s). This is the technology existing as of 2013, but there may be other architectures. Yet, the principle is the same – short term memory to accommodate information currently being processed (as in the random access, or local memory), a long-term memory, as a hard disk, digital video disk (DVD) drive, or universal serial bus (USB) device to store the data base, and a processor to

accommodate the re-arranging of information to create new information, or synthesis. These all correspond to what we think occurs in the brain. The processor is the most dynamic, followed by the random access memory (RAM), and then the long-term memory. There may be unforeseen processes, such as ongoing changes in the long-term memory, itself, the hard drive analogously being memory, as well. The way memories are recalled suggests this. Recollection often fades in time for humans, but for a computer, it doesn't if no one alters the database, at least as long as the memory is nonvolatile. The integrity of volatile memory is the same, as long as it has a power source. Here reflects one of the superior features of the computer – accurate recollection, a quality that would be very beneficial for students taking exams. A supercomputer might easily fulfill all these criteria, as indicated above, and for the last, and we have indicated that physical appendages could be attached to a supercomputer to recreate itself. In addition, replication is possible, as Alan Turing (1950, pp. 433–460) showed.

We add to a system of architecture and processes, organic processes of recursion and system adaptation. That is, process the outputs as inputs, as an adaptive system would, and then add synthesis. Now, the question is, after having imparted to the physical architecture what we call a "mind", is how to communicate.

We start with the nature language and its function. All languages have syntax, semantics, primitives from which a vocabulary is made, rules for forming words, and a mapping of words to ideas. While ideas initially give rise to language, the converse is true (Whorf, 1959, pp. 232-239), the latter drawn from Chomsky (2007) and his observation that humans have an innate capacity for using language. So, too, the internal working of a supercomputer or the architecture might contain the essence of language. Vocabularies are built. A vocabulary can be constructed from binary digits, and this is the basis of the ASCII and EBSDIC codes. An outward example of this is that every word one types on a computer as an equivalent code, such as the letter "p" being the ASCII decimal code of 112.

If technology advanced to the point where not only can a supercomputer replicate a mind but an individual's mind, we can imagine mental immortality, as long as the hardware is maintained. Going further, if hydrocarbon brains are desired, can there not in principle be a transference of mind from a machine to a human? Nanotechnology and cloning very well may be able to offer the ability to replicate human brains.

The boundary between physical and virtual is not clear. A cyborg, android, or avatar is an independent unit. Could it be that a society of these or robots would be at the service of a supercomputer having a hybrid mind? We have two examples of this, one in the form of a popular 1999 movie, *The Matrix*, and the other, *Second Life*, where people are acting out in a virtual environment.

In *The Matrix*, humans are trapped in a simulation by a computer. Humans are living an illusion, a theme discussed by Buddhist philosophy (Maya, or illusion), Plato in The Republic, Descartes in his 1641 book *Meditations on First Philosophy*, and Baudrillard, *Simulacra and Simulation*. In a modern context, everything can be reduced to Planck scale, where there is no certainty. Everything is constantly in motion. Sub-atomic entities flit in and out of existence. There is no stasis, and as soon as one thinks they have something within grasp, it escapes. We affix reference frames, but we are clueless about what is absolute, if such exists.

One might test the Matrix hypothesis by creating a simulated reality, but this would be done on a grid that is limited and thus would contradict Einstein's special theory of relativity (Kinder, 2012). Yet, the problem looms of whether the contradiction found also would be simulated, a vicious cycle, an infinite regress, a simulation of a simulation, and so forth. It turns out that the problem may not be resolvable at all (Chalmers, 2013). Everything we express as real can be expressed if we were (and maybe are) in

a simulation. There would be no reason to think of anything being contradictory in what we say or do, as all that, too, could be simulated. This is similar to being in a fishbowl and not being able took in from the outside. There is no reference frame but ourselves.

People getting enamored with *Second Life* (2013) are in a way drawing themselves in a matrix, as in their "real" life, they compete, exchange, and otherwise negotiate for items, such as currency and objects used in the *Second Life* simulation. In this way, human consciousness is projected and subsequently altered. Then, there are the myriads of video games that are adopting virtual reality components, such as in the Wii games, which integrate our bodies with an electronic world. Orwell in his *1984* novel depicted Winston being interrogated by the state police, ultimately inducing him to adopt a different reality; four fingers were three, and all thinking stemmed from this ability to accept the new order.

We ask when, with the onrush of transhumanism, replacing human parts with artificial ones, the human becomes someone else. What is the "crossover" point? Plutarch, the first century CE Greek philosopher in his *Life of Theseus* described a ship that had its parts replaced piece by piece until the whole ship was replaced. He then asked whether the replaced ship would be the same as the original ship. Insofar as the ship is concerned, the second physical ship would certainly be different. The problem becomes more complex with organisms, where cells are constantly being replaced. Jane or John Doe surely is the same person throughout life, even though each cell may have been replaced at least once. We make the problem even more complicated when we start replacing body parts with artificial ones. Limbs can be replaced with prosthesis, and now we are approaching the day when all the organs and muscle tissue may be replaced. Artificial eyes, ears, and olfactory organs are looming. Beyond that we are entering an age when parts of the brain can be replaced with neural networks on a chip. Organ by organ, bone by bone, and neural assembly by neural assembly, the human, as the proverbial Ship of Theseus, is having her/his pieces being replaced. Where is the "crossover" point from human to artificial? Then, what might be that last step to becoming totally artificial, where there is no hydrocarbon-based entity? Today, we can see that Jane or John Doe is the same as after with an artificial limb as before. However, that person's outlook or quality of consciousness may shift. For example, by wearing a prosthesis, the person may become more sensitive to others. As we replace brain components, though, what about that consciousness? Consciousness can be expected in a person anyway, but the way it shifts usually is shaped by circumstances, such as the physical entity in which it is "housed". Physicist Tipler (1994) in his *Physics of Immortality* discussed an ultimate need to transfer human consciousness to a non-hydrocarbon-based form, as the future of Earth in a dying solar system will not accommodate present life. While fraught with many problems, such as stating that the Universe ultimately will collapse in on itself, it is thought provoking in that the issue is raised of whether human consciousness first can be transferred to an artificial architecture, and second where that consciousness would be preserved.

CHALLENGES

This chapter, "Supercomputers: A Philosophical Logic Perspective" discusses the technology of supercomputers in the context of one of the most, if not *the most*, complex tasks facing them: replication of our mental processes. This heading "Challenges" could appear anywhere in this article, because every step of creating a superbrain and how we confront the results constitute a challenge. Humankind has had the luxury of fantasizing about human creations that could think, a notable example being Shelley's *Frankenstein*. Babbage showed his Analytical Engine as an argument that

said that humans weren't necessary to do calculations. Adding machines that became common in the early 1900s supported this. Early in the last century we saw the advent of discussions about machines that could be like humans. This was the case when the first complex computer came on line in 1946 – the Electronic Numerical Integrator And Computer (ENIAC). Yet, the possibility of actually creating a device that could think was far off. In 1950, Alan Turing proposed a test, the answers to which would help people distinguish the difference between a machine and a person. To determine whether a machine could think, Turing proposed hiding a person and the machine behind a curtain. An observer would determine which was machine and which was a real human, based on the answers given by each (Turing, 1950).

Much has been written, and more surely will be written, about the construction of supercomputers and the technical aspects of their construction. The predominant themes of this collection of articles focuses upon architectures, software, database theory, state of the art machinery, special aspects (clouds, clusters, and grids), and applications. The ancient Greeks referred to such a focus as "techne", or "craftsmanship". Distinguished from this is "poiesis", or art. "Techne" refers to the application of poiesis, as in technology being an application of science. Such a distinction is one aspect of a deep structure, where the first of the following dichotomies refers to a particular, and the second a general, one in terms of the other, referring to the dialectic previously discussed:

- Individual – universal
- Part – Whole
- Left brain – Right brain
- Instantiation – schema
- Constant – variable

Without the poiesis, the context, the specific thing will have no meaning, as the dichotomies above illustrate. In setting apart science from technology, the focus here is upon the philosophy of the science. Hence, applications like modeling thermodynamic systems (weather, nuclear reactions, etc.), molecules, social systems, and the like are acknowledged as only a part of a larger complexity, that of the human mind, itself. Humans, by constructing supercomputers, tacitly admit to their limitations in solving complex problems and hope to construct a "superbrain" with greater capacity, a prostheses to accomplish what humans cannot do on their own. It is argued that the ultimate complexity is modeling the whole universe, including ourselves. However, because of the physical limitations, such is beyond our capacity, the more realistic and modest goal to model our own consciousness, mind, mental state, thinking, or whatever one may wish to refer to as happening inside our brains. Kurzweil (2013) argues that humanity will have created a device by 2029 that can pass the Turing test, i.e., pass for a human brain, despite protestations by neuroscientist Christopher Koch (2013). We may set forth some central concerns about developing a device rivaling the human mind, concerns including but not limited to:

1. How to overcome the inherent human bias imparted to the design and construction of supercomputers;
2. If it were possible to meet a device free of human bias and that device were to tell humanity it had not privileged status in the universe, that the anthropic argument was deeply flawed;
3. First, understanding what human consciousness is and what and what not of its elements to build into a supercomputer;
4. Similar to concerns about developing the atomic bomb, the long-term ramifications of creating a mind equal or better than that of a human;
5. How supercomputers address the continuation of human consciousness in the face of the more immediate conditions of environ-

mental degradation and real possibility of its not being able to sustain the species;
6. How supercomputers ultimately may bring us face-to-face with age-old philosophical issues about who we are and why we are here, if not outrightly answer those questions.

However, if we think we can build brain, how do we know that we have done so? Verification and validation (V&V) of systems and software is an abiding problem but applies to assessing how we have constructed what was intended. We start out constructing a supercomputer as a representation of the brain; yet it may become a brain in its own right. Verification is analogous to a checklist, where the requirements specification(s) have been incorporated into the system. One compares the design to what is actually in the system. Validation is determining the system performs as expected. For small systems, the V&V process is rather straight-forward, a simple case being an arithmetic calculation. The code is checked to see if it contains the computation, the computation is performed, and the result compared to what is anticipated. As more systems are integrated into one coherent unit, the V&V process becomes enormously complex. A radical example of failure is a remotely-controlled plane crashing after it encounters a wind shear. In the software, there may not have been the code telling the plane what to do in such situations, even though the requirements called for it. In this case, verification failed. If the code were in the software, then there would be a validation failure. When intercontinental ballistic missile technology was deployed in the 1950's, along with early warning systems, there was talk about "fail safe," as in the 1964 Cold War thriller film *Fail-Safe,* directed by Sidney Lumetwhere; there could be no toleration of failure. As the systems became more complex, discussion turned to how much of a failure would be tolerated? For example, if a plane wandered from its intended direction, would it be sufficient to allow it to land in a country, rather than a specific airport? Accompanying the discussion in more modern times and with the realization that it was increasingly difficult to validate systems, was the concept of safely failing. It is acknowledged that there will be errors, and rather than attempting to do the almost, if not impossible, task of identifying them before system deployment, it has become the thinking that managing failure is more realistic. This is especially true in considerations of emergence. "Emergence", as the word implies, refers to an unexpected behavior in a system. When many components are assembled, predicting the outcome of behavior of each component's interaction with another falls in the domain of complexity theory. It is as if one has a swarm of bees and attempting to determine what the behavior of each individual insect will be. Indeed, there is a area of study called "swarm theory" that attempts to assess outcomes of phenomenon that are collected as a seemingly amorphous group of objects acting as a unit (Swarm intelligence, 2014). Here, and in similar cases, one can make a determination of behavior only probabilistically.

In the computer world, one has available a range of complexity from simple computations that can be done mentally to represent whole systems, and even societies. We describe behaviors, systems, processes, or aspects of them as models. Supercomputers work with the model and simulate what occurs within it. The popular "Second Life" starts with a representation of a society, but what occurs within it is the simulation. Physicists will tell the computer what they think occurs in complex weather systems, and the supercomputer will process specific data to tell the scientists what will actually occur within the model.

In terms of philosophy there is the problem of the integrity of representation, one that Plato discussed in his cave allegory in the *Republic*. In the allegory Plato describes prisoners chained inside a cave such that they are viewing a cave wall upon which are cast shadows. The shadows are produced by a fire behind placards held by

people walking on a platform behind the prisoners. When the prisoners are released, they come outside and see the sun as the light of reason and consciousness shining on real objects. The shadows are mere representations of those real objects. The problem of representation permeates every aspect of our lives, from representing the will of the people in a representative democracy to how closely we describe anything, as in modeling a system. Even creating a system is a representation, let alone the data with which we test it. In fact, our very biology thrusts the problem of representation on us, as rods and cones merely capture discrete portions of the full range of light, and from that we assemble in our brains what is supposed to be whole. Photographs in newspapers are presented to us as solid images, when, in fact, upon closer inspection we see the dots making up images which convey to us the illusion of solidity. Another aspect of the problem of representation is in logic, there being deduction and induction (IEP Staff, 2014). The former means extracting a known from a set of knowns, or as the parlance of logic teachers would have it, "if the premises are true, the conclusion must be." Inductive logic means that a conclusion is described from data only with a degree of probability. It is induction that we use immediately as the essence of representation. One asks then, given a level of probability, how acceptable is a false conclusion? This is the primary motivation behind research in validation.

Coupled with the overall problem of V&V is identifying the standards by which to determine if the outcome does match the expectation. There is the matter of the standards using in comparison, itself, as well as integrity of the one doing the comparing. These issues arise in calibration, where one may assert an ostensibly agreed to standard, as in the Le Système International d'Unités, but comparing an entity to the standard raises problems. And, how do we know the standard is correct? We cannot have an infinite regress of calibration. Then, too, what is the ultimate standard, and how do we know? Coupled with these problems are those of philosophy in what is deemed "objective". A common breakdown of "objectivity" accounts for correspondence, coherence, and consensus. Correspondence is the matching of an assertion to something that exists. Coherence is organization, where each part bears a describable and repeatable relation to another component; that is, the structure can be replicated, given an algorithm or description, and the result has meaning. Consensus is agreement that the assertion describes what is the case. Each of these is based on subjectivity, and throughout history ideas that have satisfied these criteria have been found later not to be the case. A flat earth idea has coherence in a limited domain (as in a small rectangle in the middle of the ocean), and I can apply this description to another limited and similar domain. It is coherent, in that I know what flatness is and can apply the concept consistently to specific situations so others will understand. Then, many people surely agreed (and induced) for many centuries that indeed the whole earth (made up of limited domains) was flat. Validating that the whole planet is not flat now can be done by describing the whole, certainly by satellites, but before by computations from samples of astronomical and geographical data. For a system we have constructed, how do we know that it actually does represent reality, and how can we predict what will occur within it?

In recent years, a number of attempts have been made to grapple with V&V issues, as in developing standards and procedures. For example, VV&A (the "A" standing for "accreditation", approval for deployment) standard IEEE 1616.4-2007 outlines the relationships of systems in a "high-level architecture" (HLA) and attempts to break down the V&V process according to this structure. In the United States, the Modeling and Simulation Coordination Office (MSCO) of the Department of Defense has been attempting to get systems designer to focus on V&V issues (Modeling and Simulation Coordination Office, 2014).

V&V simply is not an abstract philosophical challenge. The very research in modeling and simulating (M&S) weather systems, genetics, societies, and nuclear interactions is done not only to predict outcomes but ultimately to control them, as well. This is done by describing, or modeling a system and seeing what happens inside of that model by simulating activity. We seek to be masters of our environment, and this is one major goal of science, to extrapolate from the past in order to predict and control the future. In essence, we seek to figuratively collapse time into a moment where we have utter dominion. On a very serious note, the U.S. Department of Defense (DoD) has created "Network Centric Warfare" (often shorted to "Net-Centric"), where combat will be initiated, conducted, and terminated by computers (Network Centric, 2013) (Network Centric). The original purpose was to be able to track every element of combat in what the DoD calls "participants". In progressive stages warfare would become more automated, where ultimately decisions would be made and acted upon by computers. I have mentioned assessment of ethics systems, attempts to predict human behavior and take what are perceived as preventative measures. Increasingly, there is a reliance on large systems modeling, and supercomputers are playing a greater role in these developments. Coupled with M&S is the discussion of what the modeling is about, i.e., representing the real world. Is it an imaginary system, a hypothetical one, or what we think is real? Do we intend for the model to be fictitious? Perhaps what we think is real and try to model is a fiction, and when we act on it as if it is real, problems naturally arise. Also, even if a model does reflect a reality, it may not reflect the whole of what we want to represent, either intentionally or not. Schmid (2005) differentiates between validity and accuracy, in that the former refers to the truth in predicting an outcome of a model, and the latter whether it reflects what actually is the case. One may simply want to create a model that is a hypothetical situation, all the while realizing it does not actually describe anything in existence. Lines become blurred, however, in assessing what does exist and what people think it may or may not be, and herein recur the interesting discussions about the application of standards objectivity, truth, and how we come to know these (epistemology).

We now arrive at the most significant development, the creation or replication of the human brain. The central question is that of representation, and a seeming paradox. V&V seeks to perfect prediction. What we say will happen in a system we want to happen. A simple hand calculator obviously is not the human brain, although it represents in a tiny way some arithmetic processes. How the human brain performs those functions, we do not yet know, but the results are the same. The calculation of 4 + 7 has the same result for both the brain and the calculator. V&V can be fulfilled easily. As complexity grows so may be the divergence of expectations and outcome. Ideally, with the perfection of V&V, there is convergence, meaning the supercomputer becomes more like the brain, and if and when V&V does become perfected, the supercomputer will be the brain, in the same way the calculator is the brain, insofar as being able to produce the same result. There is emergence in complex systems, as we know from our inability to predict what a person will do and what will be the case in a supercomputer which has become a brain. V&V is a problem of being able to predict ourselves, a true reflexivity, or recursion. At this point, the ultimate paradox arises, when if we know what we are going to do, we can change it, but in changing it, we still know, and we are in a state of perpetual changing, never settling on a moment when there can be the action of actually doing something.

I leave these questions as a matter of interest areas for further research by those interested in peering into Nietzsche's (1886, Aphorism 146) proverbial abyss: "And when you gaze long into an abyss the abyss also gazes into you." There is comfort in being able to manage an unknown by treating it in the form of a question, but how may humanity confront the possibility that, indeed

those questions may be answered, such as humanity being a mere random generation of the universe as geneticist Richard Dawkins (1986) has argued?

CAN WE TURN OURSELVES OFF?

If a supercomputer did become independent and our consciousness changed as a result of our interacting with it, what would be the likelihood of our being able simply to turn the device off or simply walk away from it? Asimov (1950) set forth *The Three Laws of Robotics*:

1. *A robot may not injure a human being or, through inaction, allow a human being to come to harm.*
2. *A robot must obey the orders given to it by human beings, except where such orders would conflict with the First Law.*
3. *A robot must protect its own existence as long as such protection does not conflict with the First or Second Law.* (Asimov, 1950)

Under these circumstances, it may be difficult to determine when a human has been injured, the focus being on the word "injure". Does the human always know what is in the interest of its own species? If the humans and supercomputer evolve together in consciousness, one entangling its "mind" with the other, the outcome may be that the interest of both is the same. When one refers to that mind, with what part do we communicate? That is, where is the "center" of consciousness. If there is no homunculus, or little person directing thoughts in humans, it is problematical at best whether there would be one in a supercomputer, if the latter simply replicates the former. If there is no central location where thoughts are orchestrated, then control is distributed and may be so equally throughout the thinking entity. That is, the entity, itself is the homunculus. In the case of a supercomputer-human union, there emerges a hybrid as the homunculus.

At such point, the dual entity as this one entity would not harm itself. Even then, "harm", "injure", and so forth are value-charged words, the parameters of which are not clearly defined. For example, in encountering a situation in which there is bound to be destruction of an organism with extreme pain, as undergoing a painful cancer, where death is guaranteed, the issue of euthanasia arises. "Harm" at this point becomes relative. A further complication is the introduction of malware, where the supercomputer may not be able to detect and clean itself of code written by one human and designed ultimately to harm another. In conjunction with the third law, would not a computer euthanize itself if it could not purge the malware? I leave this question unanswered but one that humans can contemplate. However, thinking about supercomputers in these ways may lead to thinking about solving human problems.

On a more somber note, there is being developed the means to conduct "artificial war", as Ilachinski (2004) calls it as the title of his book on the subject. He refers to emergence from disparate parts of a combat situation, which turn out to be a complex adaptive system. I referred to Network Centric Warfare above, and in managing a combat "automatically", the very real possibility occurs that the supercomputer managing the combat will take on a life of its own. Human consciousness is partially determined by interaction with the environment, and not unlike HAL in *2001: A Space Odyssey*, humans could be inveigled into participating in a situation only to the supercomputer's "liking".

No discussion about creating an artificial brain would be complete without at least a reference to "second order cybernetics". First order cybernetics concerns the construction of devices that are autonomous, interacting with their environment, and preferably adapting. Norbert Wiener (1948, p. 19), a founder of the field, defined "cybernetics" as "the entire field of control and communication theory, whether in the machine or in the animal." Second order cybernetics puts the observer inside the system being observed, thus creating what

logicians would call "reflexivity", or looking at oneself. We come back to this topic in a while in considering human bias.

ARE WE RE-CREATING OURSELVES?

Supercomputers are constructed by humans, and inherently carry with them human bias. Whatever they ultimately tell us what we have imparted. In turn, whatever they tell us will be interpreted by us. The filter will be of our making, just as Fuerbach (Fuerbach & Elliot, 1854) observed.

We come to a major consideration of the mind or consciousness that has been constructed, whether it is something outside of us or whether it is us. What part of consciousness is our physical body and how vital is that? Is there, as Plato would argue throughout his *Phaedo*, a consciousness apart from us? Even the Buddhists argue that the universe, itself, is conscious, as well as everything within it, albeit with different levels of complexity. Shrodinger (1944) alluded to the same model. That is, the ultimate complexity is the totality of the universe, its consciousness, included. Humans try to analyze themselves, but the problem is that they always are inside themselves. They cannot jump outside their own skin, as it were. We have this problem manifesting itself numerous times, such as the famous Copenhagen interpretation of quantum mechanics (Copenhagen interpretation, 2014). There is the problem of induction, expressed by Hume in his *Enquiry Concerning Human Understanding*, Russell's *Problems of Philosophy*, and others, where we simply don't know how we construct systems or assemble what we think is a deductive argument. To create a "closed" system, humans draw from some place for axioms, primitives, and other elements. Axioms, it is said, are "self-evident" truths. Such an idea does not seem too far removed from one "receiving the word of God", a problem fraught with ontological disaster.

The physical architecture of a supercomputer is our own doing, but what of that which is imparted to it? Surely, whatever initial content is given, the physical architecture as "software" will be human and carry with it human bias. Whatever it "thinks" can be expected to carry human bias, at least initially. However, could it recombine ideas imbued with that bias and draw in other information (as by sensors) and draw away from how humans see things? Could a machine that we call "conscious" or "intelligent" come about, if we did not "program" it? Several years ago, research started producing self-modeling robots (awareness of "where and how its body parts are connected") that were able to compensate for unanticipated damage (Bongard, Zykov, & Lipson, 2006). If self-modeling allows autonomous devices to continue operation, then, we can ask if the same can be applied to a supercomputer with respect to "bootstrapping" into consciousness. Within the "data set" of the computer, information can often be produced by permutations of information "data points" in our environment, and this may happen by mere serendipity, absent of method (Feyerabend, 1979). A supercomputer ultimately has the capacity to do such permutations and arrive at answers that would take humanity hundreds, if not thousands of years. One of the capabilities of a computer is to calculate the probabilities of permutations in an ascending or descending order, given a set of parameters, rules, and objectives. Thus is it hypothetically possible that a computer acting on its own in going through possibly trillions of possibilities of phenomenon could arrive at combinations most probable for giving answers. From such, the supercomputer can enrich its own conceptual world or tools on which to draw for further extrapolations of conclusions, etc.

Another method for generating ideas and solving problems is through the use of analogy. Often a deep and fundamental idea will manifest itself in many ways, as was indicated above by the bias problem. By their very nature deductive systems are just as biased as their foundations, the premises, as the conclusion is based exclusively on them. The outcome of a calculus problem hinges upon the problem solver's toleration of limits. One instance can be compared to another by referring to a common fundamental underpinning by which relationship can be inferred, or analogized. The hexagonal structure of benzene rings was conceived by Kekulé, who said that his mind wandered to an image of a snake grasping its own tail (Read, 1957). This symbol is found in many cultures with concepts of circular time, i.e., events repeating themselves, as in agricultural cycles (Eliade, 1954). Hofstadter and Sander (2013) present a persuasive case that much of our information is derived by analogy, an example being the concept of wave being applied to water, sound, light and then to probabilities. Underpinning the idea of a wave is that of displacement with direction, and one may consider that wherever there is displacement, waves exist. After all, movement is ubiquitous in the universe, and it has to be asked, "what is the nature of a wave?" There is nothing that says a supercomputer could not arrive at new information by analogies. Moreover, by collecting comparisons in a database, it could ascertain the fundamental concept that binds the manifestations.

Could there be another form of consciousness? How about an intelligent animal (dolphin?) consciousness? Buddhist consciousness? A composite consciousness transcending any individual? How might an artificial device that thinks overcome the human bias imparted to it? We still do not know what an idea really is or from where it originates. Such raises the question of intelligences that are not of human origin. Physicists, such as Kafatos and Nadeau (1989) have proposed that the universe, itself, is conscious. Shrodinger (1944) said that humans are a partial expression of universal consciousness. Human consciousness is only one small aspect of that. If a physical architecture were constructed that was capable of being conscious and if the universe, itself, is conscious, would it not be logically possible for the device we constructed to become imbued with it? Supercomputers may become a way of exploring the nature of the universe without ever having to leave Earth.

In an extreme situation, one can posit the universe subdivided into its smallest components – Planck scale – and then imagine how these units would be permuted. In essence – structurally – this is what has happened with the increase in complexity of human knowledge. We see the problem of induction – from where do people get ideas? One source is the permutation of what is known to get a synthesis, the source of a lot of knowledge. Why could not a supercomputer do this?

Can an artificial brain be created without it containing human bias? Second order cybernetics, as was mentioned above, mandates that we introduce the observer into the system. The architectural concepts, including the initial data, are human constructs. We cannot escape the fact that supercomputer creations are of the human mind and subsequently carry with them human bias. We are our own reference frame. In this more obvious way, we have, as referenced above, a "Copenhagen interpretation" of the famous double slit experiment, where the human sets the conditions of observation. This merely is a re-statement of what the discoverers of calculus realized: humans set their own limits to precision. It is what quantum physicists realize in their observation of the impossibility of measuring static boundaries at the quantum level (Measurement from a practical point of view, 2014). A simple *gedanken*, or thought, experiment will confirm this by looking at the marks on any measuring device or a color wheel. Each line, as it is subdivided so as to provide a more granular "boundary" can be subdivided again until Planck scale ($1.61619926 \times 10^{-35}$ meters) is reached. The same issue exists for the color chart, where one ultimately has to point to a spot and somewhat arbitrarily say, "That's red." We say what the boundaries are, but, even so, even if we are able to ascribe a specific Angstrom figure to a color, there still remains how far along this color spectrum will it remain within tolerance of that figure. Granted, we are

approaching Planck, or even quantum scale, where there is only uncertainty, but the ultimate problem is discerning the "cutoff point".

Will the supercomputer create by mere permutation or synthesize data in arriving at knowledge that is outside domain of human capability to understand? Aside from any intellectual bias, one asks whether a such a device can convey a "consciousness" that is not human or influenced by human thinking. If we are able to replicate neural circuitry neuron by neuron and allow the supercomputer or this artificial brain to stand alone, would it acquire a consciousness? Logically, if it did, it would be because of the inherent interconnectivity of the circuitry, itself, or it would acquire it from without. The same is asked of a cloned human brain.

The problem of escaping human bias is presented starkly by humans confronting another intelligence outside their own, as in hypothetically meeting extraterrestrials or a conscious entity in which humans played no part in its development. Humans still would meet that entity, carrying their bias, but perhaps human consciousness might be diluted by the other one, resulting in a synthesis or even an emergence of a new one.

THE MIND AS A PROBLEM SOLVER

Coupled with the fundamental issue of human bias is the content of that bias. Given the past few millennia, the outcome of humanity does not look all that bright, given the failure to arrest and preferably reverse global warming (Global warming, 2014) and environmental degradation. While they may be able to add complexity to individual components in a world of increasingly advanced technology, they may not be able to manage that world, itself, an obvious case being the Internet. We are at the edge of what many scientists consider an important milestone in determining whether to meet the challenges of anthropogenic-induced climate change, wars, overpopulation, creating sustainable economic systems, etc. (Union of Concerned Scientists, 2014).

Our consciousness results from not only that which lies within ourselves internally – the brain containing its repository of thoughts, but that which as influenced by its environment. The former is molded and influenced in part by its environment. Humans interact with what they have created, and, not unlike the proverbial tail wagging the dog, they also can be driven by their creations. Even a brief look at social websites, communications applications, and the Internet, itself makes us realize how we have become reliant not only upon the technology but the content created by it. We are driven by it just as much as we drive it, again, a dialectic relationship. Not unlike the development of nuclear energy, we can only ponder the long-term implications of communications developments.

The desire to create computational "levers" allowing humanity to transcend its biological limitations in thinking and the possibility that those devices may not only transcend but dominate their creators impels us to be keenly aware of how we may some day confront an intelligence or mind vastly superior to our own. Ultimately, supercomputers will place in sharp focus the concern about how we will meet ourselves. Coupled with this is the central question of what "mind" really is and, more poignantly, the core of philosophy: who we are and why we are here. What might we really expect with such an undertaking? What might we really be "seeing"? Are we viewing ourselves as suicidal beings, incapable or unwilling to solve critical problems the continuance of which will doom the species? It has been argued persuasively that myths, stories, and religions are reflections of the way we see ourselves (Fuerbach, 1974), and what we anticipate may be a reflection of what we are concerned with the most. Humanity starts from a relatively simple problem of enabling complex computations to creating a likeness of her/himself. Nietzsche's classic comment in "The Parable of the Madman" was that "God is dead", with the

corollary "And we have killed him" (Nietzsche, 1882, pp.181-82). Have we created ourselves in our own image, as the Bible said in perhaps one of the most curious passages "Let us make man in *our* (emphasis added) image, after our likeness; ...So, God created man in his own image, in the image of God he him; male and female he them (Genesis 1:26-27)" ? Such wording implies polytheism, and an analogy to modern times places ourselves as gods. While this passage refers to the "Father, Son, and Holy Ghost" as one entity, given history of the religion, polytheism lies very much beneath its mythological shell (Rea, 2006).

Certainly, in the history of the philosophy of science since the Renaissance, natural philosophers and scientists have pondered the motivations of their research, as well as outcome(s). For 2000 years, Western humanity has obsessed about the *Bible*, and since Martin Luther has struggled with *angst*, the fear, or anxiety of not knowing one's ultimate place (particularly, after death) in the universe . In has been argued persuasively that Western humanity has alienated itself from itself (Weber, 2003), and supercomputers may be a milestone in Western humanity's attempt to become whole again.

Another perspective is that modern peoples in industrialized societies are narcissistic, increasingly demanding approval from others. They have become less reliant upon themselves and less self-confident. Instead of acting as a community, people have become self-centered, consumerist, and obsessed with themselves (Lasch, 1979). Perhaps supercomputers may help fill this void. One might expect the narcissism as a motivation for the push for digital immortality described by Tipler (1994).

Technology can overwhelm its creators and force them to grapple with the implications of the consequences. "What hath God wrought", exclaimed Alexander Graham Bell, quoting from the *Bible* (Numbers 23:23) and Robert Oppenheimer referred to the *Bhagavad Gita* (Chapter 11:31-33), "Now I am become death and the destroyer of worlds," as the nuclear device exploded 16 July 1945 sixty miles north of Alamogordo (J. Robert Oppenheimer, 2014).

Understandably, there is a reluctance to accept the possibility that a machine can solve problems humanity cannot, that it would be the Messiah foretold in Christian scriptures to save humanity. Too, it can be asked whether those purportedly seeking answers to deep philosophical conundrums, such as what is time, space, consciousnesses, and so forth, really want answers. In some respects, there is less stress in not knowing, as in a student feeling less threatened by waiting for a course grade, rather than having to react to a failure. In waiting, there always is the possibility the outcome will be positive. Such is no less true with persons faced with the possibility that a mind embodied in a machine can solve such problems. So, what critique can be launched against this proposed eventuality?

Ray Kurzweil is arguably one of the most vocal advocates of developing an artificial mind. In *How to Create a Mind: The Secret of Human Thought Revealed*, he sets forth not only a methodological approach to construct the physical component but says it should "open questions in every discipline", be critically thoughtful, and have the ability to "master vast databases" (Kurzweil, *2013b*). Such a brain would be at least on par with that of a human one.

Neuroscientist Christof Koch (2013) launched into a polemic against the work, saying:

And even the lowly roundworm Caenorhabditis elegans, a creature no bigger than the letter l and with exactly 302 nerve cells, is for now beyond the ability of computational neuroscience to comprehend. ... Functional human brain imaging has yet to affect standard medical practice (the upcoming fifth edition of the Diagnostic and Statistical Manual of Mental Disorders does not even mention any functional magnetic resonance imaging diagnostic criteria). (Koch, 2013)

Koch continues arguing that "Kurzweil's claim that we will soon figure out how the 100 billion neurons of the human brain function on the basis of designed HHMMs is complete bosh."

This contradicts a report that "Equal numbers of neuronal and nonneuronal cells make the human brain an isometrically scaled-up primate brain" (Azevedo 2009), as well as the NIMH project Research Across Domains addressing the problem of the DSM vagueness. It may not be that a supercomputer passing the Turing Test will have the same architecture as the human brain, but does that mean that it will be any less conscious? Perhaps it will be superior to it. It is obvious that what we have now is superior in terms of some functions, such as memory. What is natural is not always the most efficient or best made. It can be traumatic enough for humans to make errors, but what if a mind of a machine is superior to ours? What could be the quality of its errors? Two areas of concern are human consciousness being entangled with that of a machine, and the more classically discussed problem of the machine assuming control or having a mind of its own.

One's consciousness is partially shaped by the environment and, in turn, the human acts on the environment. When other humans are present, each is affected by the other, and one's own set of thoughts usually changes as the human interacts with others. In the case of an artificially intelligent device, it is not out of the question that the same could occur. At a simple level, we can imagine a medical diagnostic computer providing analyses to a doctor in a faithful manner over a period of time. However, if the machine begins giving erroneous data but data close enough to being accurate so as to be plausible, how soon would it be for people to detect errors? There is always validation against doctors and medical texts, but what of new phenomenon or instances when only subjective judgments can be made? For example, the EBASS program mentioned above evaluates ethics, and the previously discussed DARPA Broad Agency Announcement (Broad Agency Announcement

11-65, 2014) request for proposals for identifying individuals predisposed for violence provide opportunities for systems to assume behavior apart from and possibly hostile to humans. A serious question of dependency upon a "superbrain" or a collection of them exists. This has happened somewhat already, especially with the Internet. Let the Internet go down for a few weeks, or even a few days, and chaos most likely will follow. Our mindsets not only have incorporated the process and content of the Internet, but may have come dependent upon it. If a "superbrain" were to assume a prominent place in society, would it not have the capability of leading the human further down a road of dependency? Computers turning on humans is a common theme in science fiction literature, and literally pulling the plug on the machine has always been presented as an option. However, comparatively less attention has been paid to consciousness drift.

RESEARCH DIRECTIONS

The so-called "Decade of the Brain" (Project on the Decade of the Brain, 2014) did not end in 2000. It did, however, focus attention more on doing what philosophers have been doing for thousands of years: attempting to discover the nature of ourselves. As I have suggested, the technological aspect of supercomputers is of lesser importance than the implications of their development.

There is the very real possibility that we may discover what makes up consciousness and mind. Perhaps more significantly, we may be able to create a mind equivalent or, more probably, one superseding human capacities. There are various aspects of consciousness, such as sensory crossover (synesthesia), complexity of logical operations, and correlation of logical operators to neural nets that can better guide how a supercomputer may be programmed, thus resembling more closely human cognitive capabilities. This

all depends upon a more accurate description of brain structures and their functions.

Part of what we call consciousness is bound up with how we sense our environment. One may map each function to a sound or color to see what patterns may emerge. Newton, following an idea by the ancient Greeks (Fairbanks, 1898, p. 10), suggested that there may be a correlation between color and sound. Correlating sound to color is not novel these days (Zizzi, 2004, pp. 345-358). In various computer programs designed to play CDs, such as Windows Media, one can view colored patterns emerging when playing music. Research in synesthesia, where a person can sense a phenomenon through another sense, such as tasting color, suggests new directions in how we regard senses and integrate them into supercomputer functionality.

In logic and mathematics, operations in a parentheses free expression are ordered according to convention. For example, in arithmetic, the ordering is: exponents and roots; multiplication and division; and, addition and subtraction. For $3 + 4 \times 8 = 35$. In logic, the precedence is: and, or, implication, and equivalence. Thus $p \supset q \& z$ is expressed as $p \supset (q \& z)$, the rule being that operations in the innermost set of parentheses are done first. The ordering in both mathematics and logic is by convention, and if the ordering is changed so does the computational result. However there is evidence that various orderings of logical operators based on types of intellectual complexity may provide the basis for more efficient information processing (Horne, 1997, pp. 675-682; Piaget, 1958). Piaget and Inhelder (1958) argued that acquisition of logical operations is partially age-dependent. For example comparing sizes (as in the containment operator) is a faculty acquired before being able to determine whether they are equivalent. Taylor and Dunbar (1975, 1983) obtained mixed results in trying to correlate Piaget's levels of logical cognition to college students. In the 1975 study, those majoring in courses not requiring higher cognitive processes scored lower in cognition involving more complex logical operations, and conversely. In the 1983 study, the scores differed only according to sex and not age. Since that time, there have been many studies centering on the complexity and logical operations, but further research may prompt research into more efficient computer gating architectures and in software that specifies task ordering.

Another area of research is what I'd call dynamic validation of mental states. To the present, mental health professionals have determined a person's psychological state largely through observation, testing, and self reports of the client. There is no independent measurable confirmation of the conclusions drawn by these people. Further, mental states can change, and, although a client usually will be observed over a period of time, there still is no quantifiable evaluation that accounts for these changes in mental health states. The U.S. National Institutes of Mental Health (2013) Research Domain Criteria offers a substantial way of establishing such measurements. However, there is a great potential of integrating these efforts with research from the Human Brain Project. Such may be integrated with binary-based consciousness.

According to Tononi (2008), consciousness is integrated information, "...the amount of information generated by a complex of elements, above and beyond the information generated by its parts." Further, he says, consciousness arises from the condition of neural systems, and these can be represented in a binary manner, i.e., on-off switches, or as Tononi refers says, "photodiodes" (Tononi, 2008). Of course, to represent anything approaching what people think is consciousness would involves enormous complexity, as Tononi admits, but his serves a model for research. Perhaps a 3-D hypercube could be overlaid on to the binary space generated by Tononi's model, much in the same manner as discussed earlier with respect to binary spaces in general. The theorems and their corresponding patterns generated by the hypercube might have neural correlates and such

would involve Tononi's research. This world is just beginning.

Quantum computing opens the door to overcoming the complexity of neural processing. Hameroff and Penrose (1996) have argued for years that one of the bases for consciousness resides in microtubule dimers, and that a person's state of mind results from a quantum collapse of these dimer states. Hameroff's Quantum Mind website carries forth developments in this field (Hameroff, 2013). *Neuroquantology* (2013) is another publication that sets forth the view that consciousness is at least partially quantum based.

From a simple exercise in subdividing our world to the level of simple order expressed dialectically by something in terms of what it is not, we arrived at the realization that the outcome is inherently binary. By appropriate arrangements, we discovered the underlying syntax and posited content. When arranged according to this syntax I offered some fundamental descriptions of our world that one programming a computer or having interest in the technology may not have considered. Beyond these fundamentals lies an ultimate goal of supercomputers – to be one of us.

CONCLUSION

Supercomputer technology is racing at breakneck speed to where building a human brain may be within reach in a decade or so. The technology may be interesting, but the significance is what this brain will be as comparable to us. We are coming to a proverbial fork in the road, where there is the reality of *homo sapiens sapiens* creating a consciousness or mind or intelligence that is at least equal to its own. What will it tell us? If it cannot escape human bias, will it bear out what Sigmund Freud (1922) says about the species carrying with it a death instinct or Thanatos, as evidenced by how it has degraded the environment? Will, then the supercomputer outline how the species will carry out its own demise? What if the species learns that such is to be its destiny?

Supercomputers may be the vessel by which the consciousness of the species may be saved. First, if the consciousness is inherently defective, perhaps the supercomputer that contains and even supersedes it can be self-healing. In the intermediate term the species very likely will not survive biologically because of the high probability of natural events, such as asteroids or super volcanoes, or human-caused extinction, as in global warming, creation of a pandemic from a humanly-made organism, overpopulation, or nuclear war. How, then, will its consciousness be preserved?

While it seems that human bias, for all its frailties in promoting its own demise, initially will be a part of an artificial mind, we need to consider where consciousness actually resides. Perhaps we are a simulation. If consciousness resides in the universe, and each of us is one aspect of it, then that part of the universal consciousness that is not manifested in humanity may be so through the machine, "the" answer to humanity's survival. It may be, indeed, the god sought after ever since the species could support sophisticated thought. Such heresies, though are for the philosophers to debate until such time when that occurs.

REFERENCES

Advisory Committee to the Director. Brain Research through Advancing Innovative. (2013). *Neurotechnologies (BRAIN) working group.* National Institutes of Mental Health. Retrieved 9 March 2014 from http://www.nih.gov/science/brain/ACD_BRAIN_interimreport_executivesummary.htm

Allen, C. (2010). *Animal consciousness Dec 23, 1995.* Retrieved 9 March 2014 from http://plato.stanford.edu/entries/consciousness-animal/http://en.wikipedia.org/wiki/animal_consciousness

Armstrong, D., & Ma, M. (2013). *Researcher controls colleague's motions in 1st human brain-to-brain interface.* Retrieved 9 March 2014 from http://www.washington.edu/news/2013/08/27/researcher-controls-colleagues-motions-in-1st-human-brain-to-brain-interface/

Asimov, I. (1950). Runaround. In *I, robot.* New York: Doubleday & Company.

Azeem, M. M., Iqbal, I., Toivanen, J. P., & Samad, A. (2012). Emotions in robots. In Proceedings of Communications in Computer and Information Conference: 2nd Emerging Trends and Applications in Information Communication Technologies (Vol. 281, pp. 144–153). Heidelberg, Germany: Springer.

Azevedo, F. A. (2009). Equal numbers of neuronal and nonneuronal cells make the human brain an isometrically scaled-up primate brain. *The Journal of Comparative Neurology, 513*(5), 532–541. doi:10.1002/cne.21974

Bandyopadhyay, A., Pati, R., Sahu, S., Peper, F., & Fujita, D. (2010). Massively parallel computing on an organic molecular layer. *Nature Physics, 6*(5), 369–375. doi:10.1038/nphys1636

Bidiou, A. (2008). *Number and numbers* (R. MacKay, Trans.). Cambridge, MA: Polity Press.

Bird, J. O. (2007). *Engineering mathematics.* Oxford, UK: Newnes.

Bloom, B. S. (1956). *Taxonomy of educational objectives: The classification of educational goals: Handbook I.* New York: Longman.

Bongard, J., Zykov, V., & Lipson, H. (2006). Resilient machines through continuous self-modeling. *Science, 314*(118). PMID:17110570

Boole, G. (1854). *An investigation of the laws of thought on which are founded the mathematical theories of logic and probabilities*. London: Walton and Maberly. Retrieved 4 March 2014 from https://www.fbo.gov/index?s=opportunity&mode=form&id=31cf5a859cfa2764da7e1b8d54a79d1c&tab=core&_cview=1

Buckley, W. (Ed.). (1968). *Modern systems research for the behavioral scientist*. Chicago: Aldine Publishing Company.

Casti, J. L. (1992). *That's life? Yes, no, maybe* (SFI Working Paper: 1992-10-050). Sante Fe, NM: Santa Fe Institute.

Central Processing Unit. (n.d.). Retrieved 4 March 2014, from http://en.wikipedia.org/wiki/Central_processing_unit

Chalmers, D. (2013). *The Matrix as metaphysics*. Retrieved 4 March 2014 from http://consc.net/papers/matrix.html

Chomsky, N. (2007). *Approaching ug from below. interfaces + recursion = language? Chomsky's minimalism and the view from syntax-semantics*. Mouton: Berlin. Computational complexity. Retrieved 9 March 2014 from http://en.wikipedia.org/wiki/Computational_complexity

Consciousness. (2013). *Towards a science of consciousness*. Retrieved 9 March 2014 from www.consciousness.arizona.edu/

Copenhagen Interpretation. (n.d.). Retrieved 9 March 2014 from http://en.wikipedia.org/wiki/Copenhagen_interpretation

Dawkins, R. (1986). *The blind watchmaker*. New York: Norton.

DeBenedictus, D. (2005). Reversible logic for supercomputing. In *Proceedings of the 2nd Conference on Computing Frontiers*. American Association of Computing Machinery. doi:10.1145/1062261.1062325

Del Pradon, F. M. (2009). *The thermodynamics of human reaction times*. Retrieved 9 March 2014 from http://arxiv.org/abs/0908.3170

Descartes, R. (1641). Meditations on first philosophy. In The philosophical writings of René Descartes (vol. 2). Cambridge, UK: Cambridge University Press.

Dewey. (1916). *Democracy and education*. New York: MacMillan. Retrieved 9 March 2014 from https://edorigami.wikispaces.com/Bloom%27s+Digital+Taxonomy

Drachman, D. (2005). Do we have brain to spare? *Neurology, 64*(12), 2004–2005. doi:10.1212/01.WNL.0000166914.38327.BB

D'zeroski1, S., Langley, P., & Todorovski, L. (2013). *Computational discovery of scientific knowledge*. Retrieved 9 March 2014 from http://www.isle.org/~langley/discovery.html

Molecular Electronics. (2013). Retrieved 9 March 2014 from http://en.wikipedia.org/wiki/Molecular_electronics

Eliade, M. (1954). *Cosmos and history (the myth of eternal return)*. New York: Harper Torchbooks.

Euston, D. R., Tatsuno, M., & McNaughton, B. L. (2007). Fast-forward playback of recent memory sequences in prefrontal cortex during sleep. *Science, 318*(5853), 1147–1150. doi:10.1126/science.1148979 PMID:18006749

Fairbanks, A. (Ed.). (1898). *Zeno commentary*. Retrieved 9 March 2014 from http://history.hanover.edu/texts/presoc/zeno.html

Feuerbach, L., & Eliot, G. (1854). *The essence of Christianity*. London: John Chapman.

Feyerabend, P. K. (1993). *Against method*. London: Verso.

Feynman, R. P. (2001). *The character of physical law*. Boston: MIT Press.

Freud, S. (1922). Beyond the pleasure principle (C. J. M. Hubback, Trans.). London: The International Psycho-Analytical Library; doi:10.1037/11189-000

Frye, J., Ananthanarayanan, R., & Modha, D. S. (2007). Towards real-time, mouse-scale cortical simulations. *IBM Research Report No. RJ10404 (A0702-001)*. Retrieved 9 March 2014 from http://domino.watson.ibm.com/library/CyberDig.nsf/papers/D0F0871458B4E5588525727B0056F896/$File/rj10404.pdf

Gardner, H. (1993). *Frames of mind: The theory of multiple intelligences*. New York: Basic Books.

Glasgow Coma Scale. (n.d.). Retrieved 9 March 2014 from http://en.wikipedia.org/wiki/Glasgow_Coma_Scale

Global Warming. (n.d.). Retrieved 9 March 2014 from http://en.wikipedia.org/wiki/Global_warming

Hameroff, S. (2013). *Quantum consciousness*. Retrieved 9 March 2014 from http://www.quantumconsciousness.org/

Hameroff, S., & Penrose, R. (1996). Conscious events as orchestrated space-time selections. *Journal of Consciousness Studies*, *3*(1), 36–53.

Hofstadter, R., & Sander, E. (2013). *Surfaces and essences: Analogy as the fuel and fire of thinking*. New York: Basic Books.

Horne, J. (1997). Logic as the language of innate order in consciousness. *Informatica*, *22*(4), 675–682.

Ilachinski, A. (2004). *Artificial war*. River Edge, NJ: World Scientific.

Inhelder, B., & Piaget, J. (1958). *The growth of logical thinking from childhood to adolescence*. New York: Basic Books. doi:10.1037/10034-000

Kafatos, M., & Nadeau, R. (1990). *The conscious universe*. New York: Springer-Verlag. doi:10.1007/978-1-4684-0360-2

Kauffman, S. (1993). *The origins of order*. New York: Oxford University Press.

Kinder, L. (2012). Scientists believe they have come close to solving the 'Matrix' theory. *The Telegraph*. 26 October 2012. http://www.telegraph.co.uk/science/9635166/Scientists-believe-they-have-come-close-to-solving-the-Matrix-theory.html

Knott. (2007). *Verification, validation, and accreditation (VV&A), final report prepared for: Mr. Robert E. Miller, Jr. Contract Officer's Representative U.S. Army RDECOM, CERDEC and Dr. Alexander Kott Program Manager Defense Advanced Research Projects Agency, by: Evidence Based Research, Inc. 1595 Spring Hill Road, Suite 250 Vienna, Virginia 22182-2216, July 30, 2007, Contract: W15P7T-07-C-P209, [no author] pp. 123-125 EBASS description*. Retrieved 9 March 2014 from http://www.dtic.mil/cgi-bin/GetTRDoc?AD=ADA448132

Koch, C. (2013). The end of the beginning for the brain. *Science*, *339*(759), 759–760. doi:10.1126/science.1233813

Kogge, P. (2011). Next-generation supercomputers. *IEEE Spectrum*. Retrieved from http://spectrum.ieee.org/computing/hardware/nextgeneration-supercomputers/0

Kurzweil, R. (2013). *Ray Kurzweil: Future predictions*. Retrieved 9 March 2014 from http://en.wikipedia.org/wiki/Ray_Kurzweil#Future_predictions

Kurzweil, R. (2013). *How to create a mind: The secret of human thought revealed*. Retrieved 9 March 2014 from http://en.wikipedia.org/wiki/How_to_Create_a_Mind

Langley, P., Simon, H. A., Bradshaw, G. L., & Zytkow, J. M. (1987). *Scientific discovery: Computational explorations of the creative processes.* Cambridge, MA: MIT Press.

Lasch, C. (1979). *The culture of narcissism: American life in an age of diminishing expectations.* New York: W. W. Norton.

Lawrence Livermore Laboratory. (2013). *100 teraFLOPS Dedicated to capability computing.* Lawrence Livermore Laboratory: Advanced Simulation and Computing Purple. Retrieved 9 March 2014 from https://asc.llnl.gov/computing_resources/purple/

Leibniz, G. (1703). *Explication de larithmetique binaire.* Retrieved 9 March 2014 from http://ads.ccsd.cnrs.fr/docs/00/10/47/81/PDF/p85_89_vol3483m.pdf

Second Life. (2013). Retrieved 9 March 2014 http://secondlife.com/

Measurement from a Practical Point of View. (n.d.). Retrieved 9 March 2014 from http://en.wikipedia.org/wiki/Measurement_in_quantum_mechanics#Measurement_from_a_practical_point_of_view

Misner, C. W., Thorne, K. S., & Wheeler, J. A. (1973). *Gravitation.* New York: W.H. Freeman and Company.

Modeling and Simulation Coordination Office. (2014). Retrieved 9 March 2014 from www.msco.mil

National Institutes of Mental Health. (2013). *Research domain criteria.* Retrieved 9 March 2014 from http://www.nimh.nih.gov/about/strategic-planning-reports/index.shtml#strategic-objective1,http://www.nimh.nih.gov/research-funding/rdoc/nimh-research-domain-criteria-rdoc.shtml

Neisser, U. (Ed.). (1998). *The rising curve: Long-term gains in IQ and related measures.* Washington, DC: American Psychological Association; doi:10.1037/10270-000

Network Centric. (2013). Retrieved 9 March 2014 from http://en.wikipedia.org/wiki/Net-centric

Neuroquantology. (2013). Retrieved 9 March 2014 from http://www.neuroquantology.com/index.php/journal

Nietzsche, F. W. (1974). *The gay science (The joyful wisdom)* (W. Kaufmann, Ed.). New York: Vintage.

Nietzsche, F. W. (1913). Beyond good and evil. (H. Zimerman, Trans.). In *The complete works of Friedrich Nietzsche.* Retrieved 9 March 2014 from http://www.gutenberg.org/files/4363/4363-h/4363-h.htm

J. Robert Oppenheimer. (n.d.). Retrieved 9 March 2014 from http://en.wikipedia.org/wiki/J._Robert_Oppenheimer

Peano, G. (1889). *Arithmetices principia novo methodo exposita.* Roma: Ediderunt Fratres Bocca.

Piaget, J. (1958). *Logic and psychology.* New York: Basic Books, Inc.

Project on the Decade of the Brain. (n.d.). Retrieved 9 March 2014 from http://www.loc.gov/loc/brain/

Qi, H., Ghodousi, M., Du, Y., Grun, C., Yin, P., & Khademhosseini, A. (2013). DNA-directed self-assembly of shape-controlled hydrogels. *Nature Communications, 4,* 2275. doi:10.1038/ncomms3275

Quantum Computer. (2013). Retrieved 9 March 2014 from http://en.wikipedia.org/wiki/Quantum_computer

Rapoport, S. (2013). *Stephen Wolfram.* Retrieved 9 March 2014 from www.stephenwolfram.com/

Rea, M. C. (2006). Polytheism and Christian belief. *Journal of Theological Studies*, *57*(Pt 1), 133–148. doi:10.1093/jts/flj007

Read, J. (1957). *From alchemy to chemistry*. New York: Courier Dover Publications.

Sagan, C. (2010). *What is life?* Retrieved 9 March 2014 from http://www.aim.univ-paris7.fr/enseig/exobiologie_PDF/Biblio/Sagan%20Definitions%20of%20life.pdf

Schmid, A. (2005). What is the truth of simulation? *Journal of Artificial Societies and Social Simulation*, *8*(4).

Schrödinger, E. (1944). *What Is Life? The physical aspect of the living cell*. Retrieved 9 March 2014 from http://whatislife.stanford.edu/LoCo_files/What-is-Life.pdf

Sheldrake, R. (2013). *Rupert Sheldrake: Biologist and author*. Retrieved 9 March 2014 from http://www.sheldrake.org/homepage.html

Staff, I. E. P. (2014). Deductive and inductive arguments. *Internet Encyclopedia of Philosophy*. Retrieved 9 March 2014 from http://www.iep.utm.edu/ded-ind/

Supercomputer. (n.d.). Retrieved 9 March 2014 from http://en.wikipedia.org/wiki/Supercomputer

Swarm Intelligence. (n.d.). Retrieved 9 March 2014 from http://en.wikipedia.org/wiki/Swarm_intelligence

Tae-il, K. et al. (2013). Injectable, cellular-scale optoelectronics with applications for wireless optogenetics. *Science*, *211*(340). doi:10.1126/science.1232437

Taylor, B. W., & Dunbar, A. M. (1975). *Achievement in foundations courses related to cognitive level or major?*. ERIC Clearinghouse.

Taylor, B. W., & Dunbar, A. M. (1983). An investigation of college students' academic achievement based on their Piagetian cognitive level and ACT scores. *Psychological Reports*, *53*(3). doi:10.2466/pr0.1983.53.3.923

Tipler, F. (1994). *The physics of immortality: Modern cosmology and the resurrection of the dead*. New York: Doubleday.

Tononi, G. (2008). Consciousness as integrated information: A provisional manifesto. *The Biological Bulletin*, *215*(3), 216–242. doi:10.2307/25470707 PMID:19098144

Transhumanism. (n.d.). Retrieved 9 March 2014 from http://en.wikipedia.org/wiki/Transhumanism

Turing, A. M. (1950). Computing machinery and intelligence. *Mind*, *59*(236).

Union of Concerned Scientists. (n.d.). Retrieved 9 March 2014 from http://www.ucsusa.org/

Van Nooten, B. (2010). Binary numbers in Indian antiquity. *Journal of Indian Philosophy*, *21*(1), 31–50. doi:10.1007/BF01092744

Veda, R. (n.d.). Hymn CXXIX – Creation, Book the tenth. Rig Veda. *Oxford Companion to Philosophy*. Retrieved 9 March 2014 from http://www.answers.com/topic/ancient-philosophy#Indian_philosophy

Weber, M. (2003). *The protestant ethic and the spirit of capitalism*. New York: Charles Scribner and Sons.

Weiner, N. (1948). *Cybernetics, or communication and control in the animal and the machine*. Cambridge, MA: MIT Press.

Wheeler, J. A. (1973). *Gravitation*. San Fransisco. W.H. Freeman and Company.

Wheeler, J. A. (1990). Information, physics, quantum: The search for links. In W. Zurek (Ed.), *Complexity, entropy, and the physics of information*. Redwood City, CA: Addison-Wesley.

Wheeler, J. A., & Ford, K. (1998). *Geons, black holes, and quantum foam: A life in physics*. New York: W. W. Norton & Co.

Whorf. (1959). *Language thought and reality*. MIT Press.

Wuensche, A. (1993). The ghost in the machine: Basins of attraction of random Boolean networks. *Cognitive Science Research Papers CSRP 281*. Brighton, UK: University of Sussex.

Wuensche, Discrete Dynamics Lab. (n.d.). Retrieved 9 March 2014 from http://www.ddlab.com/

Zizzi, P. (2004). *Spacetime at the Planck scale*. arXiv:gr-qc/0304032v2.

ADDITIONAL READING

Alivisatos, A. P., Chun, M., Church, G. M., Greenspan, R. J., Roukes, M. L., & Uste, R. (2012). The brain activity map project and the challenge of functional connectomics. *Neuron*. DOI Retrieved 9 March 2014 from http://arep.med.harvard.edu/pdf/Alivisatos_BAM_12.pdf10.1016/j.neuron.2012.06.006

Ashby, R. (1954). *Design for a Brain*. New York: Wiley.

Bechtel, W. (1994, December). Natural Deduction in Connectionist Systems. *Synthese, 101*(3), 433–463. doi:10.1007/BF01063897

Bentley, P. (2001). *Digital biology: How nature is transforming our technology and our lives*. New York: Simon & Schuster.

Blue Brain Project. (2013). Retrieved 9 March 2014 from http://bluebrain.epfl.ch/

Casselman, B. (2013). The Antikythera mechanism I. Retrieved 9 March 2014 http://www.math.sunysb.edu/~tony/whatsnew/column/antikytheraI-0400/kyth1.html

Cooper, S. B. (2013). The mathematician's bias - and the return to embodied computation. In "A Computable Universe - Understanding and Exploring Nature as Computation" (Ed. Hector Zenil), World Scientific, 2013, pp. 125-142. Retrieved 9 March 2014 from http://arxiv.org/abs/1304.5385

Crowder, J. A., & Freis, S. (2013). Artificial psychology: The psychology of AI. *Systemics. Cybernetics and Informatics, 11*(8), 64–67.

Fleming, S. M. et al. (2010) Relating introspective accuracy to individual differences in brain structure . *Science 329* (5998),1541-1543. doi: 310.1126/science.119188

Fraenkel, A. *Retrieved 9 March 2014* http://en.wikipedia.org/wiki/Aviezri_Fraenkel

Gazzaniga, M. S., Ivry, R. B., & Mangun, G. R. (2009). *Cognitive neuroscience: the biology of the mind*. New York: W.W. Norton.

Hamann, H., & Worn, H. (2007). Embodied computation. Parallel Processing Letters, Marius Nagy and Naya Nagy (Eds.), 17(3), 287-298

Higgins, C. (2013). The Higgins Laboratory. Retrieved 9 March 2014 from http://thehigginslab.com/

Huang, H. (2004). Autonomy Levels for Unmanned Systems. U.S. National Institute of Standards and Technology. NIST Special Publication 1011. Retrieved 9 March 2014 from http://www.nist.gov/el/isd/ks/upload/NISTSP_1011_ver_1-1.pdf

Human Brain Project. (2013). Retrieved 9 March 2014 from https://www.humanbrainproject.eu/-/hbp-workshop-on-interactive-supercomputing

IBM -Systems of Neuromorphic Adaptive Plastic Scalable Electronics (SyNAPSE). (2013). Retrieved 9 March 2014 from http://www.ibm.com/smarterplanet/us/en/business_analytics/article/cognitive_computing.html

Keeley, T. (2008). Giving devices the ability to exercise reason. *The Journal on Systemics. Cybernetics and Informatics*, 6(5), 69–74.

Lloyd, S. (1997). Universe as a quantum computer. *Complexity*, 3(1), 32–35. doi:10.1002/(SICI)1099-0526(199709/10)3:1<32::AID-CPLX10>3.0.CO;2-X

Lodder, J. M. (2009) Binary Arithmetic: From Leibniz to von Neumann. *Resources for teaching discrete mathematics*. Mathematical Association of America, pp. 169-178. doi=10.1.1.142.3947 Retrieved 9 March 2014 from http://university-publishingonline.org/maa/chapter.jsf?bid=CBO9780883859742&cid=CBO9780883859742A029

Lodder, J. M. (2012). Historical projects in discrete mathematics. *History and pedagogy of mathematics* 2012 16 July – 20 July, 2012, DCC, Daejeon, Korea. Retrieved 9 March 2014 from http://www.hpm2012.org/Proceeding/OT2/T2-02.pdf

Matrix, The (2013). Retrieved 9 March 2014 from http://en.wikipedia.org/wiki/The_Matrix

Paranuk, H. V. (2013) Review of Weuenche, A. and Lesser, M. The global dynamics of celullar automata: An atlas of basin of attraction fields of one-dimensional cellular automata. *Journal of Artificial Intelligence and Social Simulation*. Retrieved 9 March 2014 from http://jasss.soc.surrey.ac.uk/4/4/reviews/wuensche.html

Pellletier, F. J. (2013). A history of natural deduction and elementary logic textbooks. Retrieved 9 March 2014 from http://www.sfu.ca/~jeffpell/papers/pelletierNDtexts.pdf

Piaget's theory of cognitive development *(2013)*. *Retrieved 9 March 2014 from* http://en.wikipedia.org/wiki/Piaget%27s_theory_of_cognitive_development

Plutarch. (2013) Ship of Theseus. Retrieved 9 March 2014 from http://en.wikipedia.org/wiki/Ship_of_Theseus

Prigogine, I. And Stengers, I. (1984). Order out of chaos: Man's new dialogue with nature. New York: Bantam Books.

Riken Brain Science Institute. (2013). Retrieved 9 March 2014 from http://www.brain.riken.jp/en/

Supercomputers (2013). Retrieved 9 March 2014 from en.wikipedia.org/wiki/Supercomputers

Tae-il, K. T. et al. (2013). Injectable, cellular-scale optoelectronics with applications for wireless optogenetics. *Science*, 340(6129), 210–216. doi:10.1126/science.1232437 PMID:23580530

Tirard, S., Lazcano, A., & Morange, M. (2010). The definition of life: A brief history of an elusive scientific endeavor Stephane Tirard,Essays. *Astrobiology*, 10(10http://www.nucleares.unam.mx/~soma/documentos/Tirard-etal-2010-Life-Definition.pdf), 1003–1009. Retrieved9March2014. doi:10.1089/ast.2010.0535 PMID:21162680

Underwood, E. (2013). How to Build a Dream Reading Machine. *Science,* 340 (6128):21. doi:. Neuroscience. PMID: 2355923010.1126/science.340.6128.21

KEY TERMS AND DEFINITIONS

Bootstrap: Starting with an assumption or assumptions and building a system, model, explanation, concept, or other foundation.

Cognition: Mentation, or that with which the intellect manages.

Comprehension: Understanding, or affirming that the substance of an expression has been absorbed to the point of being able to integrate it into one's views. A German approach is useful, where "understanding" can be rendered as an apprehension of fact or an understanding of deep meaning. (See "mind".)

Consciousness: Often used synonymously with "mind".

Effects Based Assessment Support System (EBASS): A distributed operational assessment tool based on the principles of value focused thinking (VFT) and developed at the U.S. Military Academy to initially support the military command in Afghanistan in 2002.

Intelligence: Ones ability to process information. (See "mind".)

Mind: What people refer to as "consciousness", state of mentation. This may include but not be restricted to thinking, mood, or anything intangible experienced by a person but regarded as emanating from the brain. Despite many years of reflection and research on mind, there has been no universally agreed-upon definition of "mind", "consciousness", "intelligence" or what people take as synonyms, or words meaning the same. For example, one only need visit the website http://consciousness.arizona.edu and read the thousands of presentations by persons in many disciplines to appreciate this.

Neuroimaging: Graphic representation of neuroanatomy, including but not limited to the brain, nerves, ganglia, axons, and dendrites. Im-ages may be by computerized axial tomography (CAT), electroencephalograms (EEG), functional magnetic resonance imaging (fMRI), positron emission tomography (PET), and others. It is to be noted that the lower-case "f" in "fMRI is intentional; this is the proper manner of writing this abbreviation.

Senturion: A predictive analysis software tool developed at the National Defense University (NDU) Center for Technology and National Security Policy (CTNSP).

Transhumanism: Integration of technologies to enhance the capabilities of the human body. A simple example would be the attachment of artificial legs so as to enhance functionality, durability, appearance, and so forth.

Validation: Ensuring that was has been intended and listed in a verification actually operates or performs as intended. Methods for validation include field testing, modeling and simulation, visual inspection against standards, and any other form of comparing and contrasting a prediction with actual outcome.

Verification: Ensuring that all the elements in a requirements specification are included in the instrument to carry out those requirements. Verification is analogous to checklist, as in a shopping list, the question being answered, " are all the items I have listed in the shopping cart?"

Chapter 17
Supercomputers:
A Philosophy of Their Language

Jeremy Horne
International Institute of Informatics and Systemics, Mexico

ABSTRACT

Binary logic is the language of supercomputers. Programming applications do work more rapidly, efficiently, and accurately than humans, with supercomputers doing thermodynamic modeling, simulation of societies, and other large number-crunching projects. More recently, the supercomputer is taking on human brain functions, with increasing attention to actually replicating the human brain. Elsewhere in this book, the author has written about the philosophy underpinning these developments, but he now focuses on how computers communicate with us. The binary language computers use has an underpinning philosophy that may help explain at least one aspect of consciousness. When we probe deeply into the philosophy of bivalent systems, radical issues emerge that embrace the nature of our very being, such as completeness, certainty, process, the very nature of our universe, and possibly a consciousness pervading it.

INTRODUCTION

This chapter of *Research and Applications in Global Supercomputing* is an expedition into the world of supercomputer language: binary logic. Understanding a person is partially understanding the language they use (Whorf, 1959). Binary logic on the surface is merely a set consisting of a zero and one with which to designate whether a switch is on or off, the switch positions ultimately being mapped to an ordinary language alphabet and number system, accompanied by a symbol set. When viewed and used in this way, they convey no unusual meaning. Yet, within the structure of a bivalent, or two-valued, system is the capacity to represent what may be considered innate structures in the universe, and perhaps consciousness, itself. If the supercomputer does acquire the ability to think, it perforce will acquire the meanings carries by the bivalent logic. This is partly what this chapter will convey: what meanings are inherent in the structure, itself. A question is whether representation, as with the mapping just mentioned, assumes the essence of what it represents, not unlike a political representative in an ideal republic reflecting the will of those s/he represents.

DOI: 10.4018/978-1-4666-7461-5.ch017

Copyright © 2015, IGI Global. Copying or distributing in print or electronic forms without written permission of IGI Global is prohibited.

The supercomputer ultimately becomes replicative of the human brain, and if the bivalent system is a representative of innate structures in the universe and with it consciousness, then such may be carried over into the domain of "computer consciousness." In examining bivalency we may arrive at some constituents of consciousness.

MAIN FOCUS OF THIS CHAPTER

This chapter explores the idea that binary logic as both a structure and the processes within it is innate in the universe. That is, what we set forth on paper as binary logic describes the essence of the universe. At its most fundamental level, it is a two-valued system, and binary logic displays all that happens with these values. The substance of the system may at first not appear to be elegant, but there appears to be an irreducible empirical truth in what constitutes order and how it translates into mind, as well be discussed below.

The most immediate technical aspect of interfacing with a supercomputer is the language by which a supercomputer communicates: binary logic. The supercomputer has a potential of being a sentient entity, and I discuss why in "The Philosophy of Supercomputers", appearing elsewhere in this Encyclopedia. The question is raised whether the structure of a language inherently carries with it a philosophy. Whorf (1956) argued:

My own studies suggest, to me, that language, for all its kingly role, is in some senses a superficial embroidery upon deeper processes of consciousness, which are necessary before any communication, signaling, or symbolism, whatsoever can occur, and which also can, at a pinch, effect communication (though not rue AGREEMENT) without language's and without symbolism's aid. ... The statement that 'thinking is a matter of LANGUAGE' is an incorrect generalization of the more nearly correct idea that 'thinking is a matter of different tongues.'". ... The different tongues are the real phenomena and may generalize down not to any such universal as 'language' but to something better – called 'sublinguistic' or 'superlinguistic' – and not altogether unlike, even if much unlike, what we now call 'mental'. (p 239)

A deep philosophy underpins bivalent logic. It is a logic which frames the very meaning of order, with every computer output possibly being infused not simply with a superficial ordering but with fundamental meaning. It is found that a recursion of logical operators exists, the essence of which is transferred to matrices of very large binary spaces. A three-dimensional hypercube (Horne, 2012) offers a way discovering the origin of patterns generated by cellular automatons, as described by Wuensche (2013) and Wolfram (2013), as well as patterns found in binary arrays, in general, and may contribute to the discussion about the massive parallelism found in supercomputer gating architectures.

BACKGROUND

Binary logic has been the language used for expressing content, and the mechanical way of conveying that language is routing by electrical pulses through a system of switches, first by vacuum tubes, then transistors, and now semiconducting devices. This logic, when associated with computers, refers to zeros and ones representing whether a switch is on or off, and the switches are related in specific ways by operators. These mechanics are the substance which computer programmers in machine language have immediate concern. Beyond this use, to the ordinary developer binary logic has no significance. Our interest extends far past this technical side of supercomputing. That is, I argue that there is "mechanical" logic and philosophical logic. The mechanical refers to symbol manipulation; the latter is understanding the reason(s) for the system, i.e., the "why" of its existence. As somewhat of an aside and example of the mechanical aspect, teachers of logic convey the idea that logic can be used to translate ordinary language, and to a certain extent some basic argument structures can be symbolized and subsequently analyzed, but there is a far deeper significance having to do with the binary system representing innate structures in the universe.

In various logic textbooks (Boolos, 2002; Copi, 1979; Mendelson, 1997), logicians also call switches "connectors", "operators", or "functions." Binary logic is referred to as "bivalency", "two-valued logic", and "modulo two". It is ideal to represent the two states of basic switches – on or off. In a more formal consideration bivalent logic is constructed from symbols, definitions, and rules, and this system is often referred to in these textbooks as "formal logic" because it is about ideas being expressed by structures. The particular symbols used to express ideas within the structures constitute the semantics, or meanings, and they can be any, as long as they are used consistently.

The "formal" also has a historical reference to Plato in his theory of forms, where there is a reality we cannot see, and it is perfection. In his Republic, Plato describes a cave, where prisoners are chained such they see shadows on a wall in front of them. Behind them walk people holding cutouts in front of a fire, thus producing the shadows. All we see around us are shadows or representations of that reality. In the same vein, the "formal" in formal logic is about structures and their relationships to each other. Those structures have examples, or instantiations, analogous to Plato's shadows.

The development of computer programming takes volumes to describe, as well as the mechanics of applications, such as weather modeling, but these are relatively simple, compared to the logic of consciousness and realistic possibility that supercomputers may be able to think, reason, express emotions. Inside the language that conveys ideas is a structure that describes an order that is innate in every aspect of our lives. To grasp the full implications of this assertion, we start by looking at the philosophy of the language that allows a supercomputer to do its tasks and communicate the results to us.

THE DEEP STRUCTURE OF BINARY LOGIC

Binary logic is the centerpiece of computers, be it hand-held calculators, desktops, or supercomputers. Machine programming is called the "first generation" of languages consisting of the 0s and 1s representing logic gates. Assembly programming, a shorthand way of working with machine code, is the second generation of language. However, it is rare for a programmer, computer systems analyst, or one working with computer technology to actually program in machine language, let alone consider the philosophy of the structure of the binary number system. Even mathematicians rarely venture into the philosophical aspect of numbers. Yet, the binary number system has a fundamental structure that conveys deep meaning from a seeming mere arrangement of digits all the way through to the most complex operation which we can conceive, replicating the human mind.

While this section is not meant to be a technological exposition of how computers are constructed (such as chemical vapor deposition and other arcana), it is essential to grasp the concept of information mapping, as we will be considering its philosophical implication later. Language systems are composed of a symbol set, primitives (the symbols expressing basic ideas by the means of those symbols, as in letters, numbers, etc.), rules, and axioms, or postulates. Complexity and subsequent computing capacity emanate from the architectures, linear, parallel, or web. The binary value system has a deep structure and which arguably is the language of innate order underscoring thought, itself. This syntax, itself, carries meaning.

The syntax of the binary system is the frame for the semantics, or meaning, not unlike a vine hanging from a trellis, or, perhaps, mind hanging from the brain. Whatever the philosophy behind the syntax may be, so the semantics is infused with it. The way we see the world is expressed in most simple way - by a bivalent system. There may be any number of semantic models. One may draw an analogy between the modeling tool as the syntax and what it models, the semantics. Chess and other board games are modeling tools and are considered syntactical structures. What is played out, the instance, is semantics. For computers, the modeling tool is the binary syntax.

Bivalent logic, usually expressed semantically as 0s and 1s, and the physical make-up of the chip reflect the capacity to process information according to on-off switches embedded in that architecture. Whether the values should be "true" and "false", "0" and "1", or "yes" and "no" (the semantics) is what teachers of logic have been quibbling about for some time. However, the point is that one should not only see the values as a way of programming any set of ideas into a computer but values emanating from a structure that has no room for alteration, at least in our phenomenological world. It is, after all, phenomenology that constitutes one method for modern inquiry – especially that of science - empiricism, or observation and experience. Yet, we will see that such structuralism permeates the foundation of thinking for mathematics and logic.

It needs to be made clear again that while the bivalency is used to designate switch condition, there is nothing deeply philosophical per say about pointing to a switch and noting its on or off condition, nor by the symbolism used to convey that idea. The way they are related, contradictory or compatible, depends upon how a concept is programmed. The number-based language of describing switch configuration just as easily could be a symbol set not having a thing to do with quantity. All one is doing at the most basic level is analogously drawing a road map. While it is the set of symbols 0 and 1 that are used, the logical space successfully and quantitatively generated by

them sets the stage for conversing about meaning of what is happening, as will b done below.

We go through life learning the most elementary ideas, ones we take for granted, such as that of number. Teachers telling the student to memorize the mechanics and worry about the thought behind them later teach by "rote learning". Even in elementary logic courses in the university, it is the common practice to have students memorize a number of inference and equivalence rules, and the student has not the first clue about their origins. In reality, there are infinite rules. Yet, we often go back and wonder about how simple that idea is or what lay behind the memorization and discover in reality that such is really not all that simple. Often, the teachers do not know and pass on to their charges the content in the same manner as Medieval Scholastics. We can take the apparently simple concept of number underscoring the quantitative meaning of "binary".

There is a plethora of literature about "number", and the mathematician Peano not only realized this but set forth what he thought would explain "number". Yet, we find out from mathematicians like Russell (1919, pp. 14-15) and Bidiou (2008, p. 51) that Peano (1889) may have been only pulling himself by the bootstraps, that number is much more complicated than anyone ever might have thought. Peano (1889, p. 1), in fact, omitted at one crucial postulate having to do with magnitude, perhaps the most crucial element in setting forth the concept of number. His postulates about succession in no way imply magnitude. The mathematical logicians Cantor, Frege, and Zermello-Fraenkel, among others, all had their ideas of what a number is, but each had their major problems, all laboring over what we thought was obvious in our childhoods. Gödel (1931) also developed a technique, "Gödel numbering", that assigned a unique natural number to a symbol and well-formed formula in logic and used these to prove incompleteness in higher systems (Gödel, 1962). It often takes a re-visitation to what we thought was simply learned – often by rote – to apprehend the deep significance of that idea. We do the same for bivalent systems learned by students in elementary mathematics and computer science courses. Here, we are asking about innate structures of binary logic and what they might represent, those structures giving the identity to the bivalent system upon which computers of all types rest for their very existence. That is, there is a deep philosophy underpinning the very language computers use.

A VERY SHORT HISTORY OF BIVALENCY

We start our discussion of how bivalency became the simplest way of counting, starting by a mere permutation of two values. Ancient philosophers in South Asia thought that the essence of the world is binary 4500 years ago. The Creation hymn in the Rig Veda says, "Whence all creation had its origin, he, whether he fashioned it or whether he did not, he, who surveys it all from highest heaven, he knows--or maybe even he does not know (*Rig Veda*, 2013)." For Samkhya, the oldest form of Hinduism, the soul (purusha) is counterpoised against matter (prakriti), one in terms of the other; neither has it own identity in isolation. In the West, it is the dualism of mind and matter. We find evidence of binary counting and computation extending back to the fifth through second century BCE. Pingala, an Indian scholar who lived between the fourth and second BCE, depending which researcher one accepts as authority, described the essence of binary numbers as short and long syllables in his Mahabhashya (Van Nooten, 2010). The long syllables were twice as long as the short ones (Hall, 2005). In modern times, Leibniz (1703) is credited with having formally created the binary counting system in his *Explication de l'Arithmétique Binaire* over three hundred years ago.

The persistence of bivalent thinking suggests we explore why this is the most basic of systems to represent the world in which we live. After all,

it is the language of the very computers that may be replicating the human mind. While observing society does not cause one to think that logic underpins our whole world, there is, nonetheless, a fundamental ordering, without which we would not exist. "Logic...is the theory of order," said Feibleman (1979, p. 89). It is the "...theory of abstract structures (Feibleman, p. 14)." Kauffman (1993) says that there is structure inherent in seemingly randomly generated logical operations. Wheeler, Thorne, Misner (1973, p. 1209), and Piaget (1958) support Feibleman's view. Piaget (1958) stated,

There exist outline structures which are precursors of logical structures,... It is not inconceivable that a general theory of structures will...be worked out, which will permit the comparative analysis of structures characterizing the outline structures to the logical structures characteristic of the higher stages of development. The use of the logical calculus in the description of neural networks on the one hand, and in cybernetic models on the other, shows that such a programme is not out of the question. (p. 48)

Other researchers hold that bivalent logic reflects an order innate in the universe and human thinking. That is, it is a discovery, rather than a creation. I, like others, hold to this view. The arrangement in the universe is according to a "pregeometry as the calculus of propositions," such that "...a machinery for the combination of yes-no or true-false elements does not have to be invented. It already exists" (Misner, Thorne, and Wheeler, 1973). Wheeler further said, "... it is not unreasonable to imagine that information sits at the core of physics, just as it sits at the core of a computer" (Wheeler, 1998, p. 340). Further, Wheeler (1990) says:

It from bit. Otherwise put, every 'it'—every particle, every field of force, even the space-time continuum itself—derives its function, its meaning, its very existence entirely—even if in some

contexts indirectly—from the apparatus-elicited answers to yes-or-no questions, binary choices, bits. 'It from bit' symbolizes the idea that every item of the physical world has at bottom—a very deep bottom, in most instances—an immaterial source and explanation; that which we call reality arises in the last analysis from the posing of yes–no questions and the registering of equipment-evoked responses; in short, that all things physical are information-theoretic in origin and that this is a participatory universe. (pp. 354-368)

THE PHILOSOPHY OF BIVALENCY

Ontology is a branch of philosophy that focuses on determining what exists. Existence does not mean simply pointing to an object, system, or process and saying that it stands in front of us. Its being subsumes a history of how it came to be, the reason for its standing in front of us, and its relation to the observer. Bivalent logic is the language computers use, but like other languages, it is a reflection of the thinking of the one articulating it. Ostensibly, binary, or propositional logic merely is a tool to represent on-off switches that comprise gates through which electrons flow, but as we just saw, the concept has been around for thousands of years. Computer designers usually are content enough to stop at the technical level and apply switching knowledge through programming to accomplish an objective. Yet, not only does "binary" predate any thought about computers, it is a language of structures innate in the universe. Everything is reducible literally to the primordial - first ordering, or the "It from bit", as Wheeler's famous expression states. The binary structure may be a very natural expression of the way the universe exists in a fundamental and profound way. That is, the logic is a discovery more than a creation.

The modern discipline emerging from this thinking is digital physics, that the universe essentially can be described as information, and is conceptually the same as a computer program.

Loop quantum gravity (Smolin, 2001) theory postulates that the universe is granular, the evidence being that atoms have discrete energy levels. At this level, it is thought that space is discrete. Modern physicists, such as Zizzi (2000), also argue for this idea. There is a fundamental reason why this system is the essence of simplicity. One can do a repeated subdivision of anything and arrive at Planck scale, where there is a Planck volume at 4.22419×10^{-105} m^3. We refer to "volume" to account for the three geometric dimensions in our universe. Yet, these Planck volume units have to be set in some environment, one that may be vacuum space. We now have what bivalency can represent: Planck volume and what it is not, vacuum space. Mathematicians refer to bivalency as "modulo 2" counting, or a "base 2 system" and commonly do not think very much about philosophy.

Dialectics

We apprehend things in the world by what they are not. For example, one detects the content expressed on a chalk/white board by observing the contrast of the marks against the backdrop of the board, itself. In a room filled with objects of a single color and no shading, nothing will be seen. Change the shading and the objects appear. The line on the chalk board and the board, itself are the two values, the "something" - the marks, and what the "something" is not, the board. In the room, where objects appear because of light intensity, lightness is contrasted darkness. Two basic values are the minimum required to detect anything around us. In philosophical parlance, this is called "dialectics", and such is a concept thousands of years old, stemming from thinking originating on the Indian subcontinent (*Rig Veda*, Hymn CXXIX – Creation, Book the Tenth). Dialectics as a process relating what is (the existent) in terms of what it is not. There are many dichotomies, one existing in terms of what it is not. Left exists because of right, up because of down, yes because of no. We see bivalency all about us, as in:

- Left-Right
- Up-Down
- Forward-Backward
- Constructive-Destructive
- Something-Its reference frame
- Yes-No
- Light-Dark
  etc.

We discussed the nature of the universe above, both from the point of view of the infinite and the infinitesimal. The universe lies between two types of infinities, the boundaries of which are everything and nothingness, neither of which are conceivable. What exists other than the Planck volume, as well as what lies outside the universe are unknown. Bidiou (2008) argues that number must be conceived from a standpoint of nothingness (zero) and the infinite (∞), the infinitesimal being that which approaches zero. We will be returning to this idea repeatedly.

We see at the infinitesimal level that the other element of Planck volume is that which it is not, and numerous possibilities exist, such as vacuum space or another dimension. At the infinite level, there is the universe, itself, and what it isn't, the "isn't" posing an equally vexing problem. Perhaps the "edge" of the universe is another one or absolutely nothingness we cannot even perceive. Yet, we do see that bivalency works within our known world. It is inherent in the universe. We have two pieces of information. There was a singularity, and there is the actual that emerged from it. There also is the potential for order and order emerging from that. A discussion is necessary about the nature of information in our system.

There is another type of dialectics, which I will call, for the lack of a better word, "emergent dialectics" where en entity comes out from another, rather than just being contradictory to it. I will call this "Dialectics 2", for short, or a dialectics

of becoming. We refer to philosophies as ancient as Hesiod's *Theogeny*, Lucretius' *The Nature of Things*, and many other cosmologies based on the same observation that dialectics permeate our world as an innate process, the most fundamental law of being. The structure, the most primitive order, emerges from the chaos, or known.

A third dialectic exists, where there is an emergence and the entity emerging becomes the original's opposite. There is a thesis, the synthesis, and ultimately the antithesis.

The concept of the first dialectic was carried forth from the very ancients to Aristotle in his *Metaphysics* and then elaborated upon by Georg Wilhelm Friedrich Hegel in his *Phenomenology of Mind* in 1805 as a formal philosophical system. John Dewey, among others, translated this dialectical thinking into a description of how theory is met by practice, and vice versa, and this forms a substantial basis of modern education (Dewey, 2008). Political philosophers, such as Marx, emphasized the third dialectic, where from a system comes its opposite; within a system are the seeds of its own destruction. Dialectics of the first type is most fundamental law of apprehension of what exists. In itself, it is a process of one existing because of what it is not. The second is one of becoming and how something contains history within it. The third is how something can become its opposite. A modern view of the third dialectic is considering the opposite of autopoiesis, or self-organization. If something can "self-organize", why would it not carry within it the same factor that would result in its destruction? In biology, this is the case, the germ cell having its counterpart in a gene that tells when a person is to die (Prescott, 2012).

Dialectics translates into our understanding of our universe and is the foundation of knowledge, itself, that same knowledge that the computer will manage. Again, one switch is in terms of another, but their relationship to each other is externally generated. The first dialectic is not an intrinsic part of the switches in themselves. Neither does the Hegelian dialectic of becoming apply to digital logic as a mechanical aspect of computers. The third dialectic of something turning into its opposite is not immediately relevant, either.

Information

Information is what a computer processes. What, then, is "information"? For the purposes of our discussion, this is a bit. To a philosopher, it is what exists. To a computer programmer, a bit is either a 0 or 1. These are symbols designating whether a switch is off (0) or on (1). One just as easily could have used any other set, such as & and #. Conceptually, these could be regarded as bits. Both are considered information. The "&" is information that the switch is off; the "#" is information that the switch is on. In the same way the 0 and 1 do also operate. One must not be confused by the numerical values. Thus, the lack of information means the absence of bits, be in the 0/1 set, &/#, or any other.

It helps to look at the situation through language-metalanguage eyes. For example, a Spanish teacher will talk in Spanish about English. The Spanish is the metalanguage, and English is the object language. In Spanish the teacher refers to an object, an English word, and talks about it in Spanish. "Quiero hablar de "'mesa'.". "I want to talk about 'table'. " The word "table" is in quotes, as an object being spoken about by the teacher. I point to two buckets and ask a person to compare them as to their contents. This exercise occurs in two stages, the identification and the comparison. I just have put the contents of the buckets figuratively in quotes.

As another illustration of object and metalanguage, one can point to an egg as a potential bird, but would not know what type of bird, be it a duck, eagle, or whatever. There is also the bird. The bucket content could be the egg or a bird. They both have to have some content, but the nature of that content must be identified and compared. Both buckets contain something but the character of what they contain may be known or unknown. Whatever the case, both the egg and bird are pieces of information. They are bits. The unknown thing (egg, in this case) is the thing called "potential". The known thing (bird) is called "actual". Otherwise put, both are things, or existents. The singularity that was the beginning of this universe, or potential, is something that exists, as well as what came from it. Here, we are excluding a discussion of time. Now, we need to compare them and see if any information results from that comparison.

The egg is at the object level; so is the bird. When I compare them, however, I am doing as the teacher does and asking questions about them. Is the egg an egg? Yes. That is information. Can an egg turn into a bird? Yes. Does a bird turn revert to an egg? No. It lays the egg. It creates another object. In the case of the egg producing a bird, the egg transforms itself. Each of the "yes" answers is information and is designated in our system as "1". The answer to the question of a bird reverting to an egg is "no", hence "false", or not giving any information that we are looking for. The relationship between an egg and a bird is comparatively simple to understand.

The 0 becomes the 1 through a process, the actuality from the potential. Notice here that the 0 is dialectically in terms of the 1, the potential in terms of the actual, both known states, or information (1). In cosmological terms, the singularity, or chaos, or the inchoate, is the potential, just like the egg. That there is a singularity or chaos is information, as well as what emerges from it. The universe as something we know and is designated (such as by a "1"), and the lack of knowing is designated by another symbol, such as "0", i.e., unknown, or potential. That is, when we say that we do not know, that statement is information, as well.

In a bivalent system, it is common practice to regard the two values as "false" and "true". While computer programmers are concerned only with the 0 and 1 referring to switches, they also encounter the word "false". Logicians are of the same sentiment. The binary system is restrictive, in that it does not allow for any deviance; it is a black and white system. However, it can be expanded to account for an interpretation, or semantics that can reveals the logic as reflecting innate cosmological relationships.

In logic, the 0 (or "F") represents "false", but in actuality a false is simply saying that we really do not know what is true. What is present is not true. For example, someone points to a cow and say it is a horse. That in our world is not true. Yet, what is it, if it is not a horse? The knowledge of it, itself, is lacking. Yet, at a meta-level I have information that it is lacking. Otherwise put, there is a lack of information, but the knowledge is there that I do lack that information. In this way, a "false" is deemed "unknown", or the lack information. There is a potential for knowing what it really is. At the object level, false is the same as unknown in this sense.

In taking another example, I point to a statement that the person made "This is a horse." Using my metalanguage, I say that the object to which I am pointing is false. In my metalanguage, I am divulging information I know to be the case that the object statement is false. My statement is true. So, at the object level, the container contains an unknown (it is not a horse, so what is it? (0)), and at the meta-level I know for a fact that it is an unknown, or 1. A formal discussion of these relationships appears below in the section "The reflexivity of deduction".

While we are discussing information, it must be said that information is different than data. Information has content, and content emerges only when there is a relationship of something to something else. Random numbers are data; numbers used in counting are information. The 0 or 1 to be information has to stand against what it is, itself, or what it is not. Data by itself has no inherent content to an observer. It must have a reference frame in order to have meaning. Data at its most elementary level consists of either a 0 or 1 but not related to anything. As a further note on information, knowledge is information that

has been evaluated and has a quality. Its standing depends upon how we are able to account for it, or know. Epistemology, a branch of philosophy concerned with how we know, is justified belief.

The binary system, of course, is the language of computers, but whatever is imparted to those computers through the binary language also carries the philosophy of that language. That philosophical nature of 0 being chaos (the potential, or origin) and 1 as the actual order (discernible), or information, was as Hesiod in the *Theogeny*, Lucretius in *The Nature of Things*, and others saw it.

Order

Feibleman, as we noted above, wrote that logic is the theory of order, but there is a philosophy about that. Order means in its most elemental form is relation. To have a relation, there must be a reference frame. If I go out in deep space alone with nothing around - my surroundings are uniform, there is no order, except my presence and that which my presence is not, my surroundings. I exist in terms of what I am not, deep space, discussed above as dialectics. Fundamental philosophy enters here as to the nature of existence. Do I exist simply because of what I am not, that the most fundamental law allows me to exist even if nothing else is around? (As somewhat of a sidebar this issue was the centerpiece of Hegel's *Phenomenology of Mind*, written in 1805, the same year Beethoven wrote the *Eroica* symphony number three.)

Hegel in his *Phenomenology of Mind* expressed in Western terms the dialectics Eastern philosophers had known for thousands of years, that it is the act thinking that makes sense of and helps us determine what exists.) It would appear that there is a most fundamental relationship of my presence in terms of space, itself. Yet, to me, there is no order in that I cannot relate to anything else. In terms of navigation, I have nowhere to go. It surely is the case that if I disappeared in uniform space, there would only be uniform space. There would be no order. There would be no relation. Would this space exist without an observer, thus lacking something in terms of what the space is not? The problem is comparable to whether a tree falling in a forest with no observers would produce sound. Do things exist by themselves? How does order relate to what a computer processes?

THE ONTOLOGICAL MECHANICS OF BIVALENCY

To understand the binary syntax of the language underpinning computers, we need to become familiar with the mechanics of its construction. I am not attempting to present a way of doing computer machine coding, as the mechanics of that are radically different than how the binary system, itself, is constructed. Language structure is not the same as what the language expresses. Here, I present the philosophy of digital logic, the "why" of structure. First is the understanding of how elements are arranged, that is, the creation of logical space.

Dialectic philosophers will say that the process is just as much a part of the object as the object, itself. As a major cruise ship line used to say, "Getting there is half the fun." In explaining how the system is assembled, we also learn of what it represents, i.e., what exists as the speaker of the language. Language, in general, often belies the character of its speaker (Whorf, 1959). We open by focusing on the two word vocabulary that conveys the concepts of existence: something and that which is not that something.

The Origin of Logical Space

The Development of a Function

Now that we have set forth the conceptual framework for information, as in the language-metalanguage discussion above, we can now discuss the structure or framework containing it. So how do we render this in modern digital parlance, but,

moreover, what does it mean? To look forward and understand how permutations become operators, we explore how logical spaces come about.

So far we have established two existents, simple ones, each dialectically related to the other, i.e., 0 and 1. We need to say here that the 0 is an existent, as we say that the potential for information exists. Philosophical debate and literature abounds on whether nothingness exists, but, for our purposes, something has to exist for us to talk about it.

Single letters, the p and q, represent the minimum number of places in a relationship, and placeholders (0 and 1 in our world) represent the existents and what they are not (another existent). The letters are like fingers pointing to objects. The inchoate is represented by 0 and its manifestation is represented by 1, as discussed above. Both the existent (0) and its other existent (1) identify each other. Both are bits (Table 1).

Everything else is a compound of either or both of these. (Note: Both, 0 and 1 have nothing necessarily to do with truth or falsity of propositions in this rendition of logic, although there are some parallels and crossovers.) We have not stated that 0 is in term of its "other". Table 2 does.

Symbolically, there is no distinction.

A sidebar is necessary here to detail the thinking underpinning the notion of distinction. There is a somewhat complex argument about identity (=) and equivalence (≡), one that computer programmers use all the time, often being unaware of the philosophical implications. The = is not the

Table 1. The existent 0 and its identifier 1

p	q
0	1

Table 2. The existent in terms of its other

p	q
0	0

same as ≡. Identity means something, itself; it is reflexive. The expression "7 = 7" is not the same as 7 ≡ 7, although the number is the same. There is 7 as the 7, and that is identity, or =. Seven is the same as itself. However, in terms of space-time, a 7 can exist in one moment and another, but the moments are not the same; hence, the sevens are not the same, because of the very context of the space-time in which they are set. As another example, there may be seven books here and seven cats there. The numerals, as well as the numbers, but what they represent is different. So it is with the 0 and 0 in the table immediately above.

In our case, we are equating the zero in a philosophical way. It is expressed in Table 2 as something in terms of itself, similar to one standing in front of a mirror and after a while having a sense of being outside her/himself. Hegel throughout his *Phenomenology of Mind* referred to this first stage of dialectics as something being expressed in terms of its other. Psychologically, that image staring back at me in the mirror is my "other", the first stage of human identity. After that I and my other start identifying in terms of other people.

Relationship

Differentiation is the foundation of relationship. One points to something and says "this" or "that". This identifies itself through its other, that. That also identifies itself through the this. This is in terms of that, and that is in terms of this. We have the simplest order possible. Now, with respect to an existent, there stands the:

- Existent as itself, related to itself;
- Existent with respect to its other, or related to its other;
- Existent's other with respect to the existent, or other related to the existent;
- Existent's other as itself, or the other related to itself.

Table 3. The table of relational completeness

p				
0	0	0	1	1
1	0	1	0	1

As the p represents the generator, q as the identifier shall be its other, also a generator (Table 3).

The Table of Relational Completeness says of the field of relations that the existent and its other may be related, or permuted, in maximally four distinct ways. The first column, headed by the p, displays the two existents, 0 and 1. The four subsequent columns are the permutations of the existents. This description has the formalism of letter pairs, such as pq, generating relations, as 00, 01, 10, and 11. However, the two existents relate in four ways according to specific or definite order set by succession – ascending magnitude, the formal rendition of which is by the Table of Relational Completeness (Table 4) and a building block of all binary computations.

Table 5 presents the 0 and 1 permutations in the more familiar form, what I call the "permutation table."

Zeros and ones are used here to reflect the commonly seen rendition of truth tables. However, it is the syntax that is important to grasp. We represent the "something" (marks on the chalk board) as * and what that "something" is not as # (the background of the chalkboard). The representation for the purposes of this discussion could easily be reversed, with * being the background and the # as

Table 4. Table of relational completeness explained

p	q	Relationship
0	0	existent as is related to or contained within itself.
0	1	existent as is related to or containing its other
1	0	existent's other as is related to or containing the existent
1	1	existent's other as is related to or containing itself.

Table 5. The 0 and 1 permutation table

p	q
0	0
0	1
1	0
1	1

the marks.) We have, now both the placeholders p and q, as well as the elements ("something" and what the "something" is not - * and #) filling those placeholders into logical space in the maximum possible ways (see Table 6).

In the first row of this Table 6, the # is related to itself (reflexivity). The second row relates # to its "other" (what it is not), *. The third row reverses the positions. The fourth row relates the "other" to itself, in the same manner conceptually as the first row. Again, the representations just as easily could have been by other symbols or binary relationships, such as left-right, cold-hot, black-white, and so forth. So we might have, for example, Table 7.

Table 6. Filling of p and q placeholders

p	q
#	#
#	*
*	#
*	*

Table 7. Verbal filling of p and q placeholders

p	q
hard	hard
hard	soft
soft	hard
soft	soft

The means are described in the extremes; we have to know those extremes to discern the means. We can see this in dichotomies, such as zero-infinity, absolute zero-plasma, zero movement (no wave or frequency)-movement, and so forth. In between lies what we are able to discern. For a computer to manage concepts, it must "know" what such extremes are. In representing the extremes through bivalency, there is permutation, or possible arrangements. Permutation tables are a convenient and intuitive way of displaying the possible combination of two elements, the two values minimally necessary to apprehend an phenomenon, "something" and what the "something" is not. We have to have a "box", or logical space, into which to place these values. Indeed, there are two positions, p and q into which can be inserted two marks, such as # and *, words, or any symbol representing a concept. This perhaps is even more fundamental philosophical, for the positions establish the syntax, or structure of dialectics.

There are two levels of existents: atomic and compound. The atomic one is either a 0 or 1. A compound existent is more than one of these. That is, the two existents are the bases for generating the other compound existents – 00, 01, 10, and 11. The pq has caused p (first column) to generate 0011 as a compound existent, and q (second column) to generate 0101 as a compound existent. The p is defined in terms of the compound existent 0011 and its other is identified in terms of 0101, and vice versa. We observed above that a vocabulary can be made up of these existents, and more than one of either or both comprises a compound existent. This will be discussed shortly. (Note: As somewhat of a digression, two or more compound existents may make up more complex ones, such as 1100, 1010, 101000, 11001101, etc.) This identification of compound existents in terms of each other establishes the foundation for generating other compound existents. That generation is accomplished by the means of the function. The complete display of these existents is the *Table of Functional Completeness*, discussed below. There are minimally four compound existents and that they may be related only in a certain number of ways. These permuted four compounds are 00, 01, 10, and 11, arranged in ascending magnitude, as the 0 and 1 permutation table above shows.

THE TABLE OF FUNCTIONAL COMPLETENESS

Description

Let me recapitulate what I have written about concerning the generation of logical space (Horne, 2006) and its outcomes. Functions are descriptions of what is to emerge from a relation, i.e., what is to be done with inputs. Binary-valued logic (binary logic, for short) relates two compound existents, or functions, by the means of a third, and the result is another compound existent. This also is a function that, in turn, operates over two other functions, thus producing a fourth compound existent, also a function. And, so on indefinitely, the process continues recursively. The Table of Functional Completeness (TOFC) sets forth all the permutations of the ways the permutations of 0s and 1s described above can be related. Recall the permutation table (Table 8).

The TOFC emerges in Table 9.

The concept of the Table of Functional Completeness (TOFC) is not new, as logicians like Copi (1979, p. 202) have presented it. Yet, it has not been discussed in the manner done here, nor do

Table 8. Fundamental 0 and 1 permutation table

p	q
0	0
0	1
1	0
1	1

we find teachers of logic routinely covering this very critical concept in their courses. The TOFC displays all possible permutations of four places of 0s and 1s as functions. That is, the four rows of permutations of existent relationships from the permutation table, above, yield a 16-column space. This is generated by the same method as with the above tables - serially, successively, and in ascending order (binary counting - incrementing by a unit in base two - 0000 to 1111) horizontally and, vertically read. Columns are headed by the letter "f" with the base ten subscript numbers 0 through 15. The numerals designate the particular function, and numbers designate the base ten value of the base ten value below it. For example, f_8 is 1000 (NOR operator), the 8 being the decimal equivalent of the binary 1000. While all these tables include the p and q generators, they could be omitted, leaving the functions as operators, as well as objects. In this reference space, f_3 is always in the p column and f_5 in q column. The particular function number shows that the existents are related in a specific way for that function. The result is unique for that function. It is to be noted that the left-hand side of the table, comprising function 0 through 8 is a positive image, and the

Table 9. Table of functional completeness (TOFC)

p	q	f_0	f_1	f_2	f_3	f_4	f_5	f_6	f_7	f_8	f_9	f_{10}	f_{11}	f_{12}	f_{13}	f_{14}	f_{15}
0	*0*	0	0	0	0	0	0	0	0	1	1	1	1	1	1	1	1
0	*1*	0	0	0	0	1	1	1	1	0	0	0	0	1	1	1	1
1	*0*	0	0	1	1	0	0	1	1	0	0	1	1	0	0	1	1
1	*1*	0	1	0	1	0	1	0	1	0	1	0	1	0	1	0	1

Table 10. Functional descriptions

f_0	X - Contradiction
f_1	&, and, conjunction
f_2	>, p is greater than q
f_3	1>, 1 precedes, or, simply "p"
f_4	<, q is less than p
f_5	>1, 1 follows (or simply "q")
f_6	≠, p or q is true (1) but not both (XOR); exclusive "or"
f_7	∨, p or q is true or both are true; inclusive "or", disjunction
f_8	NOR, neither p nor q or both is/are true
f_9	≡, p is equivalent to q in truth value
f_{10}	> 0, 0 follows (or simply "not q")
f_{11}	⊂, q contains p
f_{12}	0>, 0 precedes (or simply "not p")
f_{13}	⊃, p contains q – **defines deduction**
f_{14}	NAND, not both p and q are true
f_{15}	T, tautology

right-hand side is its negative mirror image. That is, the negation sign/operator is implicit.

In the TOFC each of the decimal values designates a Boolean function, as in f_6 being an exclusive "or", XOR, either or but not both. We will discuss more of how Boolean logic is contained within arithmetic space, that binary logical space is also arithmetic space. A full description of the 16 functions is shown in Table 10.

The function number 0-15 corresponds to the decimal value of that function, so $f_{13} = 1101 -$ is the number 13, base 10. One should note that other names or interpretations may be given, as in f_2 being "does not imply", a negative of f_{13}. A different semantics, or meaning, can be given to each operation. As an extension of this, one can create modeling tools that can describe various concepts related to each other. From various functions or combinations of functions, one following the other, emerge others. This is called a demonstration. If a function is deemed "terminal," the last one to appear in such a sequence, such is called a "proof". Each proof is a rule in the system.

Computer programmers use only a few of the functions, typically "AND", "NAND", "OR", "NOR", and "EQUIV" (also called "NXOR" – not "XOR" - either, or, but not both), and various combinations of these to describe the gates through which electrons flow (Schagrin & Rapaport, 1985). There seems to be sufficient reason for using these select few (Stern,1988), issues having to do with one function being a negative of the other and the meaninglessness of using contradiction and tautology, but attention to completeness says that all may be used, as the Table of Functional Completeness above demonstrates. In doing logic proofs, using the whole table shortens them considerably, often reducing them to trivial exercises. The fewer functions one uses in a proof, the longer that proof becomes, as one has to perform many more transformations (in the absence of using the others) of a function in order to arrive at the same result. Aside from the mechanical aspects, each of these functions can carry a philosophical meaning, as in reverse containment (f_{11}), or ones of comparative magnitude (f_4), thus enriching a discussion of how binary logic may relate to the real world.

As a historical note, long before digital computers, philosopher Charles Sanders Peirce in the winter of 1880–81 demonstrated that either the NOR or NAND operators by themselves are enough to create all of the other operators. However, like MacColl (1906) who waited to publish his work on modal logic, Pierce did not have his discovery published until 1933. Instead, in 1913 Sheffer published a proof of this, the NAND operation often being called the "Sheffer Stroke" (Sheffer, 1913, pp. 481–488). After the 1933 publication of Peirce's work, the academic world called the NOR operation "Peirce's Arrow" (Buning & Lettmann, 1999). Because of the ability of these gates to express the other functions, they sometimes are called "universal logic gates" (Bird, 2007).

How to Read and Use the Table

Standard truth table canonization computation is adequate for displaying relationships. It is even helpful. However, for what follows, such as functions of functions, the canonization immediately becomes unwieldy, necessitating shorthand and more manageable functional notation more closely in line with the conceptual development of this method (Copi, 1979). Functions in this system are of four parts, each part operating over a row of the possible space described above. For example, in the TOFC and referring to atomic existents, row 3 for function 4, is read, "function 4 relates 1 to 0 to yield 0." Compound existents as functions are related by reading all four digits of the function vertically and operating over two other functions to yield a third function.

Each row of the function is a "deductive instance," where there is a description of a specific relationship between two points in space-time. Here, the third row for example has the deductive instances of 1 and 0 to yield 0. In treating function 4 as a compound existent, read "function 4 operates over function 3 and function 5 to yield function 4." That is, any function operating over functions 3 and 5 will yield itself; i.e., it defines itself. Any four binary digit function as an operator, argument, or outcome will be found in this table, thus making the system closed and deductive. As another example, allow f_9 to operate over p and q. The resulting generation is the space designated by 1001. In other words, 1001 characterizes f_9, as the following standard truth table (Table 11) canonization illustrates. $f_9(f_2, f_{12})=f_1$ means:

Where i and j are two functions, only the functions are expressed as operands, rather than the compound existents. Note that the operands can be operators. In our canonization f* is a function operating over two vertical strings of 0s and 1s as compound existents making up functions. This arrangement yields a third function, i.e., f*(fi, fj)=fn. Thus, the general truth table schematization for functional generation is shown in Table 12.

Table 11. Generation of Functions – Example of f_9

p (f_3)	≡ (f_9)	q (f_5)	Generated result - f_9
0	1	0	1
0	0	1	0
1	0	0	0
1	1	2	1

Table 12. Truth table of a function operating over f_3 and f_5

p (f_3)	f*	q (f_5)	Generated result – the function, itself, f_*
0		0	
0		1	
1		0	
1		1	

* is the function number.

General Functional Relationships

Now that we have seen how the operators are generated, how are compound – four place - existents related starting with *any* initial possible space? For example, in standard truth table canonization, we have as an example of function instances f_2 (0010) and f_{12} (1100) related by f_9 (1001), commonly called "equivalence," the resultant being f_1 (see Table 13).

Modifying Table 13, we have as a schema, Table 14.

Table 13. Example of f_9 operating over f_2 and f_{12} to generate f_1

p (f_2)	≡ (f_9)	q (f_{12})	Generated result f_1
0	1	1	0
0	0	1	0
1	0	0	0
0	1	0	1

Table 14. Tabular schema for generating resultant in field

p (domain)	f*	q (range)	Generated result
v*		v*	
v*		v*	
v*		v*	
v*		v*	

where v* is either 0 or 1 and f* is the particular function.

MATH OR LOGIC: WHICH CAME FIRST?

The TOFC displays all the Boolean functions. It is an arithmetically generated table (based upon binary counting). We may ask, then, not only whether Boolean logic emanates from mathematics but whether mathematics is based upon mere ordering and permutation. Herein is the key of determining whether Boolean logic, the centerpiece of most digital computers, follows from mathematics or vice versa. Boolean operators and the operations they represent are implicit in the TOFC, as one can see by the value headed by the function, its subscript, and the name given to that function, seen above in the description of functions. Embedded here is a notion of regularity, certainly one of the foundations of ordering based on quantification. Boole says, "The symbols of Logic are further subject to a special law, to which the symbols of quantity, as such, are not subject." (Boole, 1854, p. 4). As we have just noted, Boolean operations can be generated merely by a lookup table generated by permuting two symbols and a specific ordering principle, those symbols also including 0 and 1, which correspond to the ordering generated by a base 2 (binary) system. Further, Boole uses the combinations of 0 and 1 to generate not only the function, or connectives, but their meanings. It is obvious that the TOFC just rendered is arithmetic in nature, but we discussed the semantics, or meaning inserted in the placeholders, designated by the p and q. What, then, of the functions, themselves?

As an extension of the remarks above about the symbols "0" and "1", in the same manner of representing possibilities, we set forth representing the bivalent permutations in a four-place space by # and * (or any set of two different symbols). Hence, by a mere ordering (regular permutation, merely by switching positions of symbols) we generate in Table 15 one of the many examples of a semantic TOFC, based on what was seen in Table 9.

The mere permutations of symbols # and * still result in each of the 16 unique Boolean functions (designated in base 10 in the top row as "f", plus the number as subscript), demonstrating that quantity is not required. However, each column must be unique. As somewhat of a sidebar we have an ordering principle, based on Peano (1889, p. 20), but one not depending upon ascending quantities (Russell, 1919). It is to be noted particularly, that the function follows from each unique permutation of symbols.

Table 15. A semantical rendition of the table of functional completeness

p	q	$f_\#$	f_*	f_2	f_3	f_4	f_5	f_6	f_7	f_8	f_9	$f_{*\#}$	f_{**}	f_{*2}	f_{*3}	f_{*4}	f_{*5}
#	#	#	#	#	#	#	#	#	#	*	*	*	*	*	*	*	*
#	*	#	#	#	#	*	*	*	*	#	#	#	#	*	*	*	*
*	#	#	#	*	*	#	#	*	*	#	#	*	*	#	#	*	*
*	*	#	*	#	*	#	*	#	*	#	*	#	*	#	*	#	*

(One possible semantic may regard the space is bounded left to right by degrees of the total lack of information - #### from complete information ****, and the varying degrees and qualities being represented by everything in between.)

Here also and significant, again, is that the functions, themselves not only result from these permutations but they, in turn act as operators, producing the # and *, which in vertical groups of four constitute the function. The process operator (a function) becomes object (value of the function), and the object, in turn becomes a process, a dialectic. The top row of the labels, p, q, and decimal value remain as subscripts identifying the particular function, there merely for convenience.

ABOUT BINARY SPACES GENERALLY

The functions, or operators, process information in logical space, and are, themselves, results of computations, units of information. A function is a composite of a proof in that p and q, or the variables, are placeholders for functions, as in p $\lor$ (q $\supseteq$ r), where the number of rows in the "truth table" rendition of the expression equals 2^n, n being the number of variables. With p * q, the number of rows equals four, where * is any function consisting of the four bits representing particular deductive instances. As soon as one determines the number of placeholders for values, the size of logical space is automatically determined, as well. However, the 4 row by 16 column logical space is the basic building block of larger logical spaces. A table based on three variables is 8 by 256 columns, the general formula being 2n (to get the number of rows) to the nth power (the number of columns), n being the number of variables.

There are two types of logical space: predetermined and sequentially ordered by the number of variables (as illustrated above), and space resulting from operations (such as a "truth table" computation). In a formal deductive proof, there are premises, expressions of coupled functions, from which through inference and equivalence rules may be derived a conclusion, another expression. Virtually every line in a bivalent demonstration or proof can be expressed by components the TOFC, as well as any inference rule. This is important in that the TOFC demonstrates natural deduction; there is no need for axioms.

As somewhat of a sidebar and keeping with the promise to discuss how binary descriptions could be relate to logical space, we present Table 16.

It may be asked what models might be created that relates smile to frown via any of the connectors, as in how a smile may or may not under circumstances "contain" or "imply" a frown, for example (function 13, the so-called material implication). For a supercomputer, the answers may come readily, but perhaps much to our surprise. Yet, there is a logic that well may benefit whatever lies inside the computer but perhaps or perhaps not us. Meanwhile these numbers have to convey complex ideas, and such requires vocabulary building. This table could contain any two words, and similar functional relationships would be interesting to explore.

Table 16. TOFC with verbal semantics

p	q	$f_{\#}$	f_{*}	f_2	f_3	f_4	f_5	f_6	f_7	f_8	f_9	$f_{*\#}$	f_{**}	f_{*2}	f_{*3}	f_{*4}	f_{*5}
smile	*smile*	smile	smile	smile	smile	smile	smile	smile	smile	frown	frown	frown	frown	frown	frown	frown	frown
smile	*frown*	smile	smile	smile	smile	frown	frown	frown	frown	smile	smile	smile	smile	frown	frown	frown	frown
frown	*smile*	smile	smile	frown	frown	smile	smile	frown	frown	smile	smile	frown	frown	smile	smile	frown	frown
frown	*frown*	smile	frown	smile	frown	smile	frown	smile	frown	smile	frown	smile	frown	smile	frown	smile	frown

Recall the reference to the numerous dichotomies that a bivalent system can express, such as left-right, yes-no, and so forth. We can construct a vocabulary from any set of these. Just as long as there are two to represent the two poles of the dialectic, we have preserved our ability to communicate at this most elemental level. We can create an elaborate vocabulary from the symbols "left" and "right". For example, we have:

- Left = book
- Right = Cat
- Left-Left = Tree
- Left-Right = Horse
- Right-Right = Computer
- Right-Left-Left = River, etc.

We map the sets of binary values to symbols more familiar to us to as to enrich and shorten expressibility. At the center of contemporary binary mapping lies the "letters" of 0s and 1s - bits, from which words are constructed, as in bytes. Two basic "dictionaries" set forth the vocabulary – American Standard Code for Information Interchange (ASCII - ANSI X3.4 – 1977) (also known as also known as "*ANSI*") and IBM's Extended Binary Coded Decimal Interchange Code (EBCDIC) systems. An ASCII rendition would appear as depicted in Table 17.

Table 17. ASCII rendition

Binary	Decimal	Character
111110	62	>
111110111111	63	?
1111101111111000000	64	@
11111011111110000001000001	65	A
1000010	66	B
10000101000011	67	C
1000010100001110000100	68	D
100001010000111000100 1001000101	69	E

This is to say that we map a sequence of 0s and 1s to characters, letters, symbols, and so forth. Descriptions, data, code, numbers, graphics, and arguably any concept can be mapped, processed, and sent by a transmitter simply transmitting (a one) or being off (a zero), similar to sending Morse code.

At the core of a processor are logic gates that are diodes or transistors that control the passage of electrical current, according to which logical function is involved. For example the logical operator "and" means that each condition in a series must be 'true' or 'on' in order for there to be a complete circuit. The "or" operator requires only that any one or all switches in parallel must be "true" or "on."

THE BIVALENT SYSTEM AS RECURSIVE

A deductive system is closed, in that all of its elements are known. It is self-maintaining, not accepting any inputs or giving any outputs so as to be interactive with its environment. The system is self-contained with its own rules. Such a system is homeostatic. Homeostasis is self-regulation, where a system seeks to preserve itself, by rearranging its internal elements so as to maximize environmental resources. Ashby (1954) created a self-maintaining machine, a homeostat to which systems analysts refer as a model describing how systems preserve themselves. At a comparatively simple level, if we know how a device is constructed, we know it needs to be maintained.

Homeostasis is a form of recursion, where the same process is repeated. If a system finds that the process is sufficient to maintain itself, it repeats. Recursion is the centerpiece of deduction. Deduction for a logician means that if the premises are true, so must be the conclusion. A deductive system is a closed one, where each element can be defined in terms of one or more other elements. There is no new information. There are many paths to a conclusion. For a teacher of logic this explanation is sufficient for ordinary language argumentation. Yet, there is more to deduction that suggests how our universe is structured, as the following sections describe.

The Reflexivity of Deduction

The digital gating logic is one where there is an off or on state, 0 or 1. If there are two or more switches, there is nothing that says one is necessarily tied to the other. Unless there is outside action that ties them together, they are independent of each other. What follows is a philosophic interpretation of function 13 in the TOFC. It describes what happens with respect to the values in the system when related deductively.

Rosser (1953), the founder of the Rosser System used in modern day logic textbooks (Copi, 1979, p. 170) states,

The symbolic logic which we shall present is primarily intended to be a tool in mathematical reasoning. Of course, many of the logical principles involved have general application outside of mathematics, but there are many fields of human endeavor in which these principles are of little value. Politics, salesmanship, ethics, and many such fields have little or no use for the sort of logic used in mathematics, and for these our symbolic logic would be quite useless. (p. 6)

Yet, the logic with which students are confronted in philosophy departments centers on translating ordinary language into symbolic form. While there may be some utility in analyzing some basic structures, the utility is quickly lost in complex expressions. Elementary logic students also are confronted early on in the course with the "material implication" operator, symbolized by the "horseshoe" (⊃), sometimes rendered as "→". The interpretations and explanations border on the bizarre, such as if we had, "If Dutch persons have eight eyes, then cows fly", confusing stu-

Table 18. Permutation table

p	q
0	0
0	1
1	0
1	1

Table 19. Permutation table on its head

p	q
1	1
1	0
0	1
0	0

dents even more about both truth and implication. Recognizing this problem, MacColl (1906) set forth the first rendition of modal logic, discussing all the ordinary language interpretations of the implication. The problem starts by turning the properly ordered (ascending, or binary counting) permutation Table 18, on its head to Table 19.

Logic teachers start with what they think exists as the 1, the starting point and ending with falsity, as in their traditional rendition of the "truth table", discounting the fundamental ordering principle of 00, 01, 10, 11 (Table 20).

Too, in an ordinary language interpretation, we see the absurdities emerging, such as a "true" coming from a false, a concept when expressed in an entirely inconsistent conceptual rendering of this table, serves only to obfuscate, rather than clarify. (Of course, his has nothing to do with logical switching, where there may or may not be relations among switches being off or on.) Yet, there is an entirely consistent and intuitive explanation of the so-called material implication operator that conveys the central concept of deduction without the confusion of ordinary language interpretations. We alluded to this above in our discussion of the chicken and egg in the

Table 20. The truth table permutation commonly found in logic texts

p	q
T	T
T	F
F	T
F	F

metalanguage discussion, as well as the section "Relation". We now tie these together.

Within the closed binary space of bivalent logic, the logic defines itself, a recursion. We have the containment table that defines deduction, i.e., a closed system. This is function 13 in the TOFC. We return to the discussion above under the heading of "information" and translate the concept of information into logical parlance, i.e., function 13, as expressed in Table 21.

The first two columns, p and q, are the permutations of 0 and 1, and the next three columns respectively show the first value of the permutation, the result of material implication operation (whether there is information or not), and the second value of the permutation.

We look for a consistent semantic interpretation of this. Such comes through using the syntax to model an example. Recall what was said about language, above. That we point to something and say there is a relationship (information) or not (no information) is at the meta-level. The things we are pointing to are objects. In the first row, it is information (1) that 0 contains itself.

Table 21. Function 13 in the TOFC: "Material Implication"

p	q	p	⊃	q
0	0	0	1	0
0	1	0	1	1
1	0	1	0	0
1	1	1	1	1

For the second row, it also is information (1) that information (1) comes from the inchoate, or unknown (0). The third row says that it is not information (0) that the lack of information (0) comes from information (1). In the last row, we see that certainly, it is information (1) that information (1) stems from information (1). Both the first and fourth rows say that an existent comes from itself, or is found within itself. This is the essence of deduction. In carrying forth the idea of containment above, we also can read the operation "⊃" as "containment," the unknown potentially holding all that is to become information. That is, the unknown and information contain themselves, and that, in and of itself, is information. It is clear that from the unknown comes information; the unknown is larger than what we have as information. It also is clear that once something is information, it, itself, cannot revert back to the unknown, any more than we can "unfry" an egg, "unlight" a fire, and "undrop" an object. You can't derive the unknown from the known. The known is smaller than the known; hence it does not contain the unknown.

I repeat here that this Table 13, as well as all the other tables, has nothing to do with programming. The 0 as an off switch does not give rise to the switch being on, designated by the "1". The above explanation applies only to a functional relationship that describes a logic process: deduction.

In deductive, or closed, systems there are numerous components, each of which may be derived from one or more of the others. The whole collection may, in fact, generate itself. The collection may be designated as "0". The 0 as the whole collection can generate a 0 (0 ⊃ 0). The whole collection can generate a subset (0 ⊃ 1). So true it is with a subset; it can generate itself (1 ⊃ 1). It cannot happen that a subset can generate the set (1 ⊃ 0).

The 0 is the inchoate from which comes that which we see as existing. It represents the singularity that was the universe. It is that which contains all that we see. It is the potential from which the kinetic comes. It is that from which information comes. This implicit relationship embedded in the very structure of our universe and its processes gives rise to the particular ordering, the 0 as the potential giving rise to the 1. It is the natural foundation of logic, fractionalization, or analysis. Each act of subdivision creates quantity. We progressively take a whole and cut it up to produce more information. That subdividing produces quantity through an ordering principle, the essence of mathematics. That ordering principle is framed by the repeated fractionalization, itself. In this way, logic is related to mathematics. We have observed that he foundation of logic, the bivalent world, can be found implicitly in mathematics, but the mathematics can be expressed by the bivalent logic. To resolve the controversy of one stemming from the other, we see that the relationship is dialectic, one in terms of the other. In logic parlance, mathematics is the "dual" of logic. Logic and mathematics result from each other.

I emphasize again that this philosophical interpretation has nothing to do with switching. That is, there is nothing in switching theory that says that a 1 (switch being on) comes from one being off (0), or any other combination. What is interesting, however, is that the 0s and 1s the binary mathematics used in machine language programs displays itself in the TOFC in which are found the Boolean operators. The TOFC also is discussed in symbolic logic courses as a matter of logical completeness. Yet, the TOFC of more than a complete description of deduction. At least for function 13, it is a structure relating something as basic as existence status as being potential (0) or actual (1). Perforce, very large scale integration may have embedded within it various structures that implicitly carry a philosophical semantics. For example, the binary spaces in these arrays have embedded within them patterns, as alluded to in the section on the hypercube, discussed below.

FUNCTIONS AS HOMEOSTATS

Elsewhere, I have written about how each of the 16 functions (also called "operators", or "connectives") is homeostatic, as reflected by recursively feeding functions outputs back in itself (Horne, 2006). I recapitulate my canonization and subsequent tables. A function operating on two other functions produces another function found in generated, discrete, and subsequently closed two variable logical space. To display the homeostatic properties of the function, recursively feedback in the following manner by the example of the f_2 operator the outputs as inputs until the function starts repeating outputs.

1. $f_2(f_3, f_5) = 0010 = f_2$

    2a. $f_2(f_2, f_5) = 0010 = f_2$. The "p" half terminates, since the output of f_2 is a repetition of a previous output, f_2, and its reprocessing as an input obviously will result in another repetition of f_2.

    2b. $f_2(f_3, f_2) = 0001 = f_1$ (Note that the order to be evaluated is f_3, f_2, and NOT f_2, $f_{3)}$

    3a. $f_2(f_1, f_5) = 0000 = f_0$ This half now is f_0, by virtue of 2b and continues on with $f_2(f_0, f_5)$ and $f_2(f_5, f_0)$.

    3b. $f_2(f_3, f_1) = 0010 = f_2$ This half terminates with f_1, by virtue of 2b.

The function is unstable ultimately for only four iterations.

A state diagram exhibiting its homeostatic behavior may represent each operator. For example,

Table 22. Function 7 over functions 7 and 5

f_7			
+			**Iteration 1**
↑			$f_7(f_7, f_5) \rightarrow f_7$|
Branchings		$f_7(f_3, f_5) \rightarrow f_7$	
↓			
–			$f_7(f_3, f_7) \rightarrow f_7$|

Table 23. Function 9 over functions 3 and 5

f_9

Branchings		Iteration 1	Iteration 2	Iteration 3
↑		$f_9(f_3,f_5) \rightarrow f_9|$		$f_9(f_5,f_5) \rightarrow f_{15}|$
	$f_9(f_9,f_5) \rightarrow f_3$		$f_9(f_{15},f_5) \rightarrow f_5$	
				$f_9(f_3,f_5) \Rightarrow f_9|$
		$f_9(f_3,f_3) \rightarrow f_{15}$		
				$f_9(f_3,f_5) \rightarrow f_9|$
			$f_9(f_3,f_{15}) \rightarrow f_3$	
				$f_9(f_3,f_3) \rightarrow f_{15}|$
		$f_9(f_5,f_5) \rightarrow f_{15}|$		
	$f_9(f_3,f_9) \rightarrow f_5$			
↓		$f_9(f_3,f_5) \rightarrow f_9|$		

Tables 22 and 23 show the state diagrams for the f_7 and f_9 homeostatic functions. The "|" indicates termination of a recursion, or iteration, i.e., when the outputted function is a repetition of a previously outputted function.

How many of iterations and much information or logical space the operator consumes ("subfunctions" generated by each iteration) will vary with the operator. So, f_{13} may process f_3 and f_5 recursively for 3 iterations and terminate, but f_8 might take 7 iterations. The same initial information is processed (f_3 and f_5), but the state diagram shows the other areas of logical space involved, thus giving the function an "anatomical description" of its attempt to gain homeostasis. The two vector components are the number of divergences at each iteration (node creations) and number of iterations required to reach equilibrium, the point where the function is stabilized and starts repeating its outputs. Each operator has a different complexity (scalar, or magnitude) and can be ordered according to its vector descriptions (direction). In terms of computational efficiency, a function has to process a quantity of information (or it only has

to process that much less information) to maintain itself as a homeostatic automaton.

If these microspaces remerge as themselves after such repeated auto feedback, it may be asked if larger discrete binary spaces also have the same characteristic. Larger binary spaces can be subdivided into functions, and it is a matter for a researcher to see if groups of these functions acting as units and acting on other groups produce identical spaces in the same manner as individual functions, a description of which is covered in my paper (Horne, 2006). A caveat exists here – this refers to discrete spaces bounded by a regular column, or Y-axis, i.e., multiples of four existents. That is, each four-digit unit is a function. Partial functions acting in this recursive manner yield partial functions that exhibit a range of possible feedback loops. Here, we wander outside the scope of this discussion.

If the operator is continuously "fed" two functions at a time without regard to previous output "randomly"), there will result a logical space with a pattern, as illustrated by Wuensche (2013), Wolfram (2013), and Kauffman (1988, pp. 182-235) with randomly coupled functions and "Basins of Attraction" (Wuensche, 1993). Since each output is binary, it will be found as a column in logical space, hence contained within the system and deduced. It is not new information. Whether the actual pattern of wandering is random is debatable and the issue of randomness, itself, is a deeper philosophical issue that begs research.

Now, we can place restrictions on how the information is given to the operator. By feeding the outputs back to the four-digit operator as inputs, the outputs eventually will be repetitive, and the processing by the function will stabilize. Similarly, a deductive logic proof seeks stability. The proof will accept information (other functions) as premises and process them, ultimately reaching a goal state of stabilization, where the output is a repetition of the input. Feeding this input back into the proof as premises simply repeats the proof. In both cases, there is no longer produced any new information, there being be stabilization, the function(s) having reach the goal or deductive state. A full complement of information has been processed by the function.

We can apply this recursion method to whole spaces, where one space may act as a function that can act over two other spaces, also functions. This may be regarded as an exercise in the algebra of spaces. One demarcates an area and translates it into binary and identifies those spaces that may be function. Later, we will see some spaces in which there is such a regularity that a function can be repeated in a space and that space may be treated as the function.

It may be the case that the area is not even, that there may not be exact multiples of four binary digits representing a function. In such case there would be only a partial recursion, where the missing digits would have various possibilities of recursion. We might have, for example:

```
0101011110001010110  101011101010110000
0101010100101010011  010101011110101010
1101011100110001111  010011110110101010
111001011010101010
```

The rows are only 18 digits, i.e., four functions, plus a partial one of two. The column is seven digits – one function plus a partial one of three. Also, there may be patches where functions are so repetitive it can be condensed as one function. Such is a matter for research.

A HIGHER LOGICAL SPACE: THE THREE DIMENSIONAL HYPERCUBE

From the planar dimension that holds the Table of Functional Completeness emerges the three dimensional space that contains all 4096 dyadic relationships of functions, i.e., the three-dimensional hypercube. This represents the maximum that can be had of the massive parallelism in a three-dimensional world of bivalent systems. In whatever architecture may choose to express a vocabulary, 4, 8, 16, 32, the four bit one is the underpinning of it all, and whatever primitive relations exist within that four-dimensional vector and its permutations applies throughout its compounds of the 8, 16, 32, etc. renditions. That is, the complex architecture deductively contains the primitive. (Horne, 2012; Rapoport, 2011; Stern, 1988). I recapitulate part of my work, including tables, to illustrate the type of order in three-dimensional binary space, a space that form the basis of massive parallelism (Table 24).

Pictorially we have, as an example of the f_{13} operator, the values of which can be derived immediately from the hypercube by inspection. The figure is one of the 16 hypercube plates, this one being all the permutations of the 16 functions using the f_{13} operator. One reads each of the 16 plates of the hypercube as a distance chart in a road atlas. In the upper left-hand corner is f13, which operates over any combination of the other functions. For example in the first column we have f_{11}, and reading across to f_3, we find f_7. This means $f_{13}(f_{11}, f_3) = f_7$. The table of logical space ("truth table") rendition involves a great deal more space, as shown in Table 25.

Table 24. The three dimensional hypercube, function 13 plate

f_{13}	f_0	f_1	f_2	f_3	f_4	f_5	f_6	f_7	f_8	f_9	f_{10}	f_{11}	f_{12}	f_{13}	f_{14}	f_{15}
f_0	f_{15}	f_{15}	f_{15}	f_{15}	f_{15}	f_{15}	f_{15}	f_{15}	f_{15}	f_{15}	f_{15}	f_{15}	f_{15}	f_{15}	f_{15}	f_{15}
f_1	f_{14}	f_{15}	f_{14}	f_{15}	f_{14}	f_{15}	f_{14}	f_{15}	f_{14}	f_{15}	f_{14}	f_{15}	f_{14}	f_{15}	f_{14}	f_{15}
f_2	f_{13}	f_{13}	f_{15}	f_{15}	f_{13}	f_{13}	f_{15}	f_{15}	f_{13}	f_{13}	f_{15}	f_{15}	f_{13}	f_{13}	f_{15}	f_{15}
f_3	f_{12}	f_{13}	f_{14}	f_{15}	f_{12}	f_{13}	f_{14}	f_{15}	f_{12}	f_{13}	f_{14}	f_{15}	f_{12}	f_{13}	f_{14}	f_{15}
f_4	f_{11}	f_{11}	f_{11}	f_{11}	f_{15}	f_{15}	f_{15}	f_{15}	f_{11}	f_{11}	f_{11}	f_{11}	f_{15}	f_{15}	f_{15}	f_{15}
f_5	f_{10}	f_{11}	f_{10}	f_{11}	f_{14}	f_{15}	f_{14}	f_{15}	f_{10}	f_{11}	f_{10}	f_{11}	f_{14}	f_{15}	f_{14}	f_{15}
f_6	f_9	f_9	f_{11}	f_{11}	f_{13}	f_{13}	f_{15}	f_{15}	f_9	f_9	f_{11}	f_{11}	f_{13}	f_{13}	f_{15}	f_{15}
f_7	f_8	f_9	f_{10}	f_{11}	f_{12}	f_{13}	f_{14}	f_{15}	f_8	f_9	f_{10}	f_{11}	f_{12}	f_{13}	f_{14}	f_{15}
f_8	f_7	f_7	f_7	f_7	f_7	f_7	f_7	f_7	f_{15}	f_{15}	f_{15}	f_{15}	f_{15}	f_{15}	f_{15}	f_{15}
f_9	f_6	f_7	f_6	f_7	f_6	f_7	f_6	f_7	f_{14}	f_{15}	f_{14}	f_{15}	f_{14}	f_{15}	f_{14}	f_{15}
f_{10}	f_5	f_5	f_7	f_7	f_5	f_5	f_7	f_7	f_{13}	f_{13}	f_{15}	f_{15}	f_{13}	f_{13}	f_{15}	f_{15}
f_{11}	f_4	f_5	f_6	f_7	f_4	f_5	f_6	f_7	f_{12}	f_{13}	f_{14}	f_{15}	f_{12}	f_{13}	f_{14}	f_{15}
f_{12}	f_3	f_3	f_3	f_3	f_7	f_7	f_7	f_7	f_{11}	f_{11}	f_{11}	f_{11}	f_{15}	f_{15}	f_{15}	f_{15}
f_{13}	f_2	f_3	f_2	f_3	f_6	f_7	f_6	f_7	f_{10}	f_{11}	f_{10}	f_{11}	f_{14}	f_{15}	f_{14}	f_{15}
f_{14}	f_1	f_1	f_3	f_3	f_5	f_5	f_7	f_7	f_9	f_9	f_{11}	f_{11}	f_{13}	f_{13}	f_{15}	f_{15}
f_{15}	f_0	f_1	f_2	f_3	f_4	f_5	f_6	f_7	f_8	f_9	f_{10}	f_{11}	f_{12}	f_{13}	f_{14}	f_{15}

Table 25. Function 13 operating over 11 and 3

p (f_{11})	≡ (f_{13})	q (f_3)
0	1	1
0	0	1
1	0	0
0	1	0

Upon closer inspection of this plate (as well as the other 15), one may discern groups of functions, as in the f_{11}s. These may be compared to patterns observed in the binary automatae generated by Wolfram and others (Wolfram, 2013). This becomes more interesting upon observing larger binary spaces.

The hypercube has other applications, such as an algebra of spaces. Consider commutativity as error checking device. Commutativity is symmetric, where $f_C(fp, fq) = f_C(fq, fp)$. This goes for C=0, 1, 6, 7, 8, 9, 14, and 15. The new canonization with the functional notation can result in an algebra of functions to generate inference and equivalence rules. For example, *modus ponens* is p ⊃ q, p, ∴ q. In our canonization, this is f_{13}(a conjunct of functions resulting from others) →

fc (a conclusion, or derived function) where f_{13} must result in f_{15}, or tautology. Research might produce a computer program to generate not only acceptable rules, but these might be used to help produce an algebra of spaces. The hypercube can aid us in finding theorems using the corresponding conditional, and a computer program can be written to do this.

This functional notation shortens considerable truth table rendition and makes it possible to fill a large table in merely by inspection. To appreciate the space saving nature of the canonization, we have a standard truth table, shown in Table 26, and rendered in Table 27.

In very large scale array computations, such a shorthand method of calculating relationships might prove to be very efficient. In terms of any philosophy meeting switches in very large scale

integration, we may find patterns emerging, as Wuensche (1993, 2013), Wolfram (2013), and others have found.

CHALLENGES

Does bivalency reflect at least one aspect of the character of consciousness? We have seen how it may represent essential structures in the universe and the fundamental process of order from chaos. The problems inherent in bivalency may be inherent in consciousness, as well. We are programming a supercomputer using bivalency as a means of expressing even the most complex of ideas. The supercomputer may become aware of itself, as a human becomes aware of the philosophy of her/his language. Self-awareness, means the capacity

Table 26. Standard four variable table

p	q	r	s	(p	&	q)	→	[(r	≡	s)	v	(p	→	r)]
0	0	0	0	0	0	0	1	0	1	0	1	0	1	0
0	0	0	1	0	0	0	1	0	0	1	1	0	1	0
0	0	1	0	0	0	0	1	1	0	0	1	0	1	1
0	0	1	1	0	0	0	1	1	1	1	1	0	1	1
...	...	...	...	...	...	...	...	...	...	...	...	...	...	...
1	1	0	0	1	1	1	1	0	1	0	1	1	0	0
1	1	0	1	1	1	1	0	0	0	1	0	1	0	0
1	1	1	0	1	1	1	1	1	0	0	1	1	1	1
1	1	1	1	1	1	1	1	1	1	1	1	1	1	1

Table 27. Four variable table in terms only of functional notation

					1		3		1		2		1	
p	q	r	s	(p	&	q)	→	[(r	≡	s)	v	(p	→	r)]
					f_1				f_9		f_7		f_{13}	
f_0	f_0	f_3	f_5	f_0	f_0	f_0	f_{15}	f_3	f_9	f_5	f_{15}	f_0	f_{15}	f_3
f_0	f_{15}	f_3	f_5	f_0	f_0	f_{15}	f_{15}	f_3	f_9	f_5	f_{15}	f_0	f_{15}	f_3
f_{15}	f_0	f_3	f_5	f_{15}	f_0	f_0	f_{15}	f_3	f_9	f_5	f_{11}	f_{15}	f_3	f_3
f_{15}	f_{15}	f_3	f_5	f_{15}	f_{15}	f_{15}	f_{11}	f_3	f_9	f_5	f_{11}	f_{15}	f_3	f_3

to act, and the problems inherent in the language may be a reflection of the problems about what the expressing entity is trying to understand and communicate. As humans adjust their perception of the world because of the inherent difficulties in the language, so the artificial mind may do the same. Yet, the artificial mind may be more adept than humans and ultimately convey a new and perhaps contradictory view of the world than the view humans now have.

I have discussed bivalency somewhat in an absolutist sense, that it does reveal innate structures in the universe. Yet, I am aware of the "fishbowl" problem in philosophy that we look at ourselves through ourselves and not as observer outside the environment in which we are situated. This is the keystone in discussions about "objectivity", having an outside knowledgeable party validate our claims. This validation issue permeates our whole world as an innate problem, one being the way we acquire and relate ideas in what we think is logic.

A central issue arises with the notion of deduction "versus" induction, or "closed" versus "open" systems". Upon the outcome hinges the integrity of bivalency, the underpinning of the philosophy of language that supercomputers use. The question is relevant in asking whether the mechanics of expression carry with it a deep philosophy, just as there are philosophies of ordinary language. This is no different than asking whether there are philosophies of mathematics as a mechanics of expressing relations of quantities.

The material implication operation, function 13, describes deduction. I also referred to "information", the content fulfilled by binary semantics, in the case of computational logic as most people know it, zero and one. Function 13 says that from the unknown the known emerges, very similar to the universe unfolding from the singularity, or chaos. Analysis is the breaking down of a whole into constituent parts. Analogous to this is singularity in the universe and in deduction.

This description is of a deep structure, both in the universe and in deduction. A collection of elements that are unrelated to each other is unknown insofar as how they are related. It takes the application of rules to that collection to produce a relationship, and subsequent production of an element and the assessment of it as to whether the collection contains it. We say that this deductive method produces that element with certainty. From whatever was in the singularity, we have the universe, or dispersed energy. Of course, there is a recombination of those elements resulting in more energy, but from somewhere else in the universe, energy is subtracted. Overall, though, there is a one-way process in time: the universe is "winding down", and ultimately, as the theory goes, there will be a heat death of the universe, where energy will be dispersed equally.

In the same way that dispersed energy cannot recollect itself into the singularity, so one cannot "undeduce" from that which it came. Once something is known, it cannot revert back to being not known, at least for that moment. The proverbial cat is out of the bag. These are irreversible processes. Of course when we have information, we have something, but its original potentiality is lost, so it cannot undergo the same process, i.e., from information to the potential which gave rise to this information. I hasten to add that this is bound by time and circumstances, that what we arrive at what we think is known now can be untrue, or false, later, thus thrusting its status back into a state that existed prior to its being "known". In its basic form, deduction is a temporally bound logic. Beyond this are dynamic or tense logics that assess the probability of truth over a time span. Coupled with this are issues of how truth is quantified and the standards used. Yet, whatever logic is used, there still are fundamental problems.

The integrity of a system depends upon what we put into constructing that system – the rules, definitions, and so forth. It is well known that the system, itself, does not contain these things, and such contributes to the argument that there really cannot be a closed or complete system. This is a challenge to the notion of deduction, itself, and to ostensibly closed systems. It is assumed that deduction is a closed process that one has a collection of elements, there are rules for arranging them, and the application of rules to the elements produces other elements. No emerging element from this process is new but is contained by the others. In a more formal sense, there are axioms, and these are regarded as "self-evident" truths. From the axioms are derived theorems, and if the axiom is true, so is the theorem. However, one cannot say from where the axioms emerged. One cannot derive axioms from theorems with certainty; one can affirm the likelihood of an axiom by the means of theorems only with a degree of probability. The question is how certain are the axioms, and in this sense there is incompleteness, a more informal sense of what Godel in his incompleteness theorem was saying. Neither can anyone say anything about the origin of any of the rules used in these supposedly closed systems. Deduction, then, is a bootstrap idea, and its integrity is on par with that of how the universe originated. The backdrop for booth deduction and "big bang" is what we think is prediction. One says what they think will happen, applies rules or calculations to what we take to be known, arrives at a result, and if that result matches what we have predicted, then we admit the conclusion into the realm of what we call "known".

In our logical sense, certainty is probabilistically affirmed, as in the theorems being examples of axioms through the application of rules. Inasmuch as the axiom produces theorems through the rules, we say that the results emerge with certainty, all the while discarding consideration of how the rules came to be in the first place. The certainty of outcome depends upon the integrity of the way we create the system in the first place. It is from these complications that arise various logics, such as those in para-consistency, tense, and modal. The challenge is to place the binary system in the context of these divergent logics and to address the origin of axioms and their rules.

I raise the issue of entropy in conjunction with so basic a system as the bivalent one as a pivot point in discussing unidirectionality and certainty in the logical process. There surely will be a gnashing of teeth and objections that "deductive" entropy clashes with mathematical constructs of thermodynamic and Shannon entropy, but the discussion surely will raise more profound issues about the character of what we think are deductive processes. This has to do with the nature of deduction, itself, and its integrity. In referring to the universe, the exhaustion of the singularity is called "entropy", the dispersion of energy until no movement or temperature exists. I have come along and argued that Function 13 represents a type of entropy, as well, preferring the term "deductive entropy". It also is clear that once something is information, it, and itself, cannot revert back to the unknown, any more than we can unfry an egg, un light a fire, and undrop an object. Here, we are talking of an irreversible process, surely in terms of what we think is in time. In one sense both the unfolding of the universe and analysis by deduction are destructive and irreversible processes. However, deduction, as well as that of the "big bang" simply are theories, and Function 13 has the same epistemological, hence ontological, status. In fact, the binary system is on the same footing, and, along with it, observations about it. Whether the universe is closed is pure conjecture; it may not be complete.

Deduction may be bootstrapping insofar as our being aware of the moment only, but if what is stated in Eliade's "Myth of the Eternal Return" (Eliade, 1971) happens to be the case, we may have to rethink the notion of prediction. The illusion of certainty of deduction may be transformed into the certainty of recurring events in a larger cycle of existence. This idea is not new, as Plato described in his *Timeus* a never ending cycle of expansion and contraction of the universe. East Asian philosophers refer to the "wheel of life", a never ending recurrence of phenomenon in the

437

universe. Nietzsche (1882, Aphorism 31) referred to a similar concept. Uncertainty then becomes certainty; it is perspectival, whether one can "see" the entire recurring cycle of events. In one sense, prediction can be made with certainty on a grand scale.

Who is to say that the "heat death" of the universe does not begin another cycle of being? What is at the "edge" of the universe? These questions are far beyond the immediate concern of those fabricating and programming supercomputers, but it may be asked whether the answers about certainty are contained within the system itself (contrary to Godel's incompleteness theorem), or can the bootstrapping with the system by a supercomputer accomplish what humans have not be able to do by analyzing the complexity encompassed by what the binary system describes as the universe? Here, I am equating somewhat the notion of certainty with completeness in terms of being concepts having to do with absoluteness. If something is complete, there is nothing to add; if something is certain, it remains so for all time. Both are unalterable.

As somewhat of a sidebar to binary semantics, confusion occurs when attempting to equate information, either the zero or one, with the result of a process as entropy. It is not the information that is entropic but the process, similar to that of the objects in the universe coming from the singularity not being entropic. Of course, there is no thermodynamic energy dispersal in Function 13, but creating something from the inchoate (as in a collection of unrelated objects) nevertheless, is an irreversible process; one does not arrive at the inchoate from the object that emerges from it. There is no reversion.

Inasmuch as I have referred to information stemming from 0, or the unknown, the critique may be raised that there is a confusion with Shannon's information entropy. This concept of entropy was entirely different than either the Clausius entropy of energy dispersion and mine of deduc-

tive entropy. Shannon's (1948, p. 393) information entropy concerns a random variable's uncertainty, more precisely its unpredictability. The entropy is maximized when all the outcomes have an equal probability. That is, compared to what is predicted in a message, what actually gets through determines the entropy. That is, what would be the expected message length that a person would need to be to transmit the measured value of a random variable?

My use of entropy has more immediately in common with dispersed energy, which cannot revert back to a state of being energy. Yet, I see it as a different type. In doing a proof or demonstration in logic, one cannot take what has been deduced and return to the original components that gave rise to it, as if the analysis never took place. In another sense of a one-way operation, analysis means the cutting apart, and from a part a whole cannot come. Induction is an attempt to extrapolate a whole from any number of pieces that add up to less than the whole. This is what has happened since the "big bang", the fractionalization of the singularity into what we have around us in the universe. Both the cosmology and deductive processes are containment relationships (f_{13}), in essence, analogous to or expressed by $q \leq p$, $p \geq q$, $q \subseteq p$, or $p \supseteq q$, where the q is derived from the p. A challenge is to examine the symbol of the "material implication" operator, itself, to assess its meaning and ask whether a symbol should be used to express its more accurate and consistent meaning of containment, the reasoning of which I explained above.

We progressively take a whole and cut it up to produce more information. That subdividing produces quantity through an ordering principle, the essence of mathematics. That ordering principle is framed by the repeated fractionalization, itself. In this way, logic is related to mathematics. We will see that the foundation of logic, the bivalent world can be found implicitly in mathematics, but the mathematics can be expressed by the bivalent logic. To resolve the controversy of one stemming from the other, we see that the relationship is dialectic, one in terms of the other. In logic parlance, mathematics is the "dual" of logic.

RESEARCH DIRECTIONS

There is evidence that various orderings of logical operators based on types of intellectual complexity may provide the basis for more efficient information processing (Horne, 1997, pp. 675-682; Piaget, 1958). Genetic epistemology is the study of how cognitive processes develop with human maturation. This ties into the philosophy of language, in that different cultures will perceive various relations differently, as in comparatives. How people develop different ideas of logical relations will shape their perceptions of a system and what it contains. In the binary system with its 16 functions, there likely will emerge a different semantics of the functions. A question underpinning these variations is whether there is a general meaning meaning of the syntactic structure that is universally applicable. Would, for example, there be a progressive intellectual complexity of operators, regardless of the meaning imparted to them? Binary structures may have a neurological meaning.

According to Tononi, consciousness is integrated information, "...the amount of information generated by a complex of elements, above and beyond the information generated by its parts." Further, consciousness arises from the condition of neural systems, and these can be represented in a binary manner, i.e., on-off switches, or as Tononi refers says, "photodiodes" (Tononi, 2008). Of course, to represent anything approaching what people think is consciousness would involves enormous complexity, as Tononi admits, but his serves a model for research. Perhaps the 3-D hypercube could be overlaid on to the binary space generated by Tononi's model, much in the same manner as

discussed earlier with respect to binary spaces in general. The theorems and their corresponding patterns generated by the hypercube might have neural correlates and such would involve Tononi's research. This world is just beginning.

Quantum computing opens the door to overcoming the complexity of neural processing. Hameroff and Penrose (1996) have argued for years that one of the bases for consciousness resides in microtubule dimers, and that a person's state of mind results from a quantum collapse of these dimer states. Hameroff's Quantum Mind website carries forth developments in this field (Hameroff, 2013). *Neurtoquantology* (2013) is another publication that sets forth the view that consciousness is at least partially quantum based.

From a simple exercise in subdividing our world to the level of simple order expressed dialectically by something in terms of what it is not, we arrived at the realization that the outcome is inherently binary. By appropriate arrangements, we discovered the underlying syntax and posited content. When arranged according to this syntax I offered some fundamental descriptions of our world that one programming a computer or having interest in the technology may not have considered.

There also is the consideration of reducing our universe to Planck scale and considering each Planck "element" as one aspect of the universe. If the whole universe were able to be modeled at this scale, and infinitude of outcomes of arrangements may be analyzed and brought forth as desirable. Surely humans do not have the capability of doing this, not the least of which is because of memory and processing speed. Then, there is the "minor" issue of not knowing all there is that is to be modeled. I don't recall meeting anyone who has visited Alpha Centauri, for example, and I strongly suspect that no one on this planet has. Beyond these fundamentals lies an ultimate goal of supercomputers – to be one of us, or probably better, and perhaps it will suffice as the Alpha Centauri denizen.

CONCLUSION

Bivalency ostensibly describes deep structures in our environment, not the least of which is the universe, itself. It has been asserted that this logic is more of a discovery than an invention. Yet, we are trapped within ourselves, and attempt to grapple with the essential problem of how we come by our ideas in the first place. In fact, we are clueless as to what an idea is in the first place. On a larger scale, we do not know what is consciousness, mind, or even intelligence, given all the diverse views of it (Consciousness, 2013). How do we come by a system that seems to represent fundamental processes, such as order from chaos? We look to prediction, i.e., extrapolating from the past to project ahead, all the while thinking that there is something called "time" and all events, all in a fundamental sense pure motion, or mere displacement, are irreversible. Once they occur, they cannot "un-occur". This links the entropies. Once energy is dispersed, it cannot be "undispersed". Once the absence of information in spite of expectation has been detected, there cannot magically appear the expected information that was undetected. Once something has been discerned as "known", it cannot revert back to the state of being the "unknown" from which it originally came. These processes depend upon temporality, but what if time was illusory and all of what we have or perceive recycled itself? A supercomputer is infused with the binary language, and, along with it the philosophy bound up with it. Whose philosophy is it? We have seen that bivalency extends back several thousands of years, suggesting that there may be some degree of universality. I have suggested that the philosophy may be embedded in an innate binary structure and that innateness is in the language and, along with it, the philosophy, the supercomputer uses.

Humans use a language as a matter of mechanics, but in each utterance is conveyed a thinking. Verb (when there is such) and noun placement, mode of expression (as in ideographs, letters, or other symbols), or the set of words, themselves, all are outcomes of how humans react to their environment, and there may be a genetic or epigenetic aspect. Whether bivalency is a universal, or natural manner of expression is controversial. Perhaps the supercomputer can stand apart from humans, a consciousness evolving within it, telling us the answer. Can we escape ourselves to listen? Or, will it be a question of the supercomputer pulling itself up by the bootstraps and attempting to justify why bivalency is universal? It may be that quantum logic (Spencer-Brown, 1972) will offer answers, as this logic may reflect more of that used by the qu bits that are bound to be used. This, indeed is a new horizon that bears research and development

I have a final note. This entry is not complete, and it will never be complete until and if the universe, itself is complete, especially if it recycles itself. There is a paradox in this statement, that it, itself may not be complete, a set of all sets thinking that Russell in *Principia Mathematica* tried resolving by type theory. And, around and around we go in that fishbowl, wondering about what lay beyond those boundaries that may be only of our own creation. It may be madness that only a supercomputer as therapist will intervene to assuage but not be able to treat. Perhaps the supercomputer may be mad in attempting to do so. I would rather think that such judgement is left to the consciousness that may be within the universe.

REFERENCES

Armstrong, D., & Ma, M. (2013). *Researcher controls colleague's motions in 1st human brain-to-brain interface*. Retrieved 9 March 2014 from http://www.washington.edu/news/2013/08/27/researcher-controls-colleagues-motions-in-1st-human-brain-to-brain-interface/

Ashby, R. (1954). *Design for a brain*. New York: Wiley.

Bidiou, A. (2008). *Number and numbers* (R. MacKay, Trans.). Cambridge, MA: Polity Press.

Bird, J. O. (2007). *Engineering mathematics.* Oxford, UK: Newnes.

Boole, G. (1854). *An investigation of the laws of thought on which are founded the mathematical theories of logic and probabilities.* London: Walton and Maberly. doi:10.5962/bhl.title.29413

Boolos, G., Burgess, J., & Jeffrey, R. (2002). *Computability and logic* (4th ed.). Cambridge, UK: Cambridge University Press. doi:10.1017/CBO9781139164931

Buning, H. A. K., & Lettmann, T. A. (1999). Propositional logic: Deduction and algorithms. *Studia Logica, 71*(2), 247–258. doi:10.1023/A:1016553006778

Consciousness. (2013). *Towards a science of consciousness.* Retrieved 9 March 2014 from www.consciousness.arizona.edu/

Copi, I. (1979). *Symbolic logic.* New York: Macmillan.

Dewey. (1916). *Democracy and education.* New York: MacMillan.

Eliade, M. (1971). *The myth of the eternal return.* Princeton, NJ: Princeton University Press.

Feibleman, J. K. (1979). *Assumptions of grand logics.* Boston: Martinus Nijhoff. doi:10.1007/978-94-009-9278-8

Gödel, K. (1931). On formally undecidable propositions of principia mathematica and related systems. (B. Meltzer, Trans.). New York: Basic Books. (Reprinted, Dover, 1992).

Hall, R. (2005). *Math for poets and drummers.* Binary numbers in ancient India. Retrieved 9 March 2014 from http://people.sju.edu/~rhall/Rhythms/Poets/arcadia.pdf

Hameroff, S. (2013). *Quantum consciousness.* Retrieved 9 March 2014 from http://www.quantumconsciousness.org/

Hameroff, S., & Penrose, R. (1996). Conscious events as orchestrated space-time selections. *Journal of Consciousness Studies, 3*(1), 36–53.

Horne, J. (1997). Logic as the language of innate order in consciousness. *Informatica, 22*(4), 675–682.

Horne, J. (2006). Recursion of binary space as a foundation of repeatable programs. *Journal on Systemics, Cybernetics and Informatics, 4*(5), 73-77. Retrieved 9 March 2014 from http://www.iiisci.org/journal/CV$/sci/pdfs/P277173.pdf

Horne, J. (2012). A new three dimensional bivalent hypercube. *Neuroquantology, 10*(1), 20–30. doi:10.14704/nq.2012.10.1.361

Kauffman, S. (1993). *The origins of order.* New York: Oxford University Press.

Leibniz, G. (1703). *Explication de larithmetique binaire.* Retrieved 9 March 2014 from http://ads.ccsd.cnrs.fr/docs/00/10/47/81/PDF/p85_89_vol3483m.pdf

MacColl, H. (1906). *Symbolic logic and its applications.* New York: Longmans, Green, and Co.

Mendelson, E. (1997). *Introduction to mathematical logic* (4th ed.). London: Chapman & Hall.

Misner, C. W., Thorne, K. S., & Wheeler, J. A. (1973). *Gravitation.* New York: W.H. Freeman and Company.

Neuroquantology. (2013). Retrieved 9 March 2014 from http://www.neuroquantology.com/index.php/journal

Nietzsche, F. W. (1882). The gay science. New York: Vintage.

Peano, G. (1889). *Arithmetices principia novo methodo exposita.* Roma: Ediderunt Fratres Bocca.

Piaget, J. (1958). *Logic and psychology*. New York: Basic Books, Inc.

Prescott, B. (2012). Gene helps predict time of death common gene variant influences when you will wake up each day—and the time of day you will die. *Harvard Medical School News*. Retrieved 9 March 2014 from http://hms.harvard.edu/news/gene-helps-predict-time-death-11-26-12

Rapoport, D. L. (2009). Surmounting the Cartesian cut. *Foundations of Physics*, *41*(1), 33–76. doi:10.1007/s10701-009-9334-5

Rig Veda, Hymn CXXIX – Creation, Book the Tenth. (n.d.). Oxford Companion to Philosophy. Retrieved 9 March 2014 from http://www.answers.com/topic/ancient-philosophy#Indian_philosophy

Rosser, J. B. (1953). *Logic for mathematicians*. New York: Chelsea Publishing Company.

Russell, B. (1919). *Introduction to mathematical philosophy*. London: George Allen & Unwin, Ltd.

Schagrin, M. L., & Rapaport, W. J. (1985). *Logic: A computer approach*. New York: McGraw-Hill.

Shannon, C. (1948). A mathematical theory of communication. *The Bell System Technical Journal*, *27*(3), 379–423. doi:10.1002/j.1538-7305.1948.tb01338.x

Sheffer, H. M. (1913). A set of five independent postulates for Boolean algebras, with application to logical constants. *Transactions of the American Mathematical Society*, *14*.

Smolin, L. (2001). *Three roads to quantum gravity*. New York: Basic Books.

Spencer-Brown, G. (1972). *Laws of form*. New York: The Julian Press, Inc.

Stern. (1988). *Matrix logic*. Amsterdam: North Holland.

Tononi, G. (2008). Consciousness as integrated information: A provisional manifesto. *The Biological Bulletin*, *215*(3), 216–242. doi:10.2307/25470707 PMID:19098144

Van Nooten, B. (2010). Binary numbers in Indian antiquity. *Journal of Indian Philosophy*, *21*(1), 31–50. doi:10.1007/BF01092744

Wheeler, J. A. (1990). Information, physics, quantum: The search for links. In W. Zurek (Ed.), *Complexity, entropy, and the physics of information*. Redwood City, CA: Addison-Wesley.

Wheeler, J. A., & Ford, K. (1998). *Geons, black holes, and quantum foam: A life in physics*. New York: W. W. Norton & Co.

Whorf. (1959). *Language thought and reality*. MIT Press.

Wolfram, S. (2013). *Stephen Wolfram*. Retrieved 9 March 2014 from www.stephenwolfram.com/

Wuensche, A. (1993). The ghost in the machine: Basins of attraction of random Boolean networks. *Cognitive Science Research Papers CSRP 281*. Brighton, UK: University of Sussex.

Wuensche, Discrete Dynamics Lab. (n.d.). Retrieved 9 March 2014 from http://www.ddlab.com/

Zizzi, P. (2000). *Emergent consciousness: From the early universe to our mind*. arXiv:gr-qc/0007006.

ADDITIONAL READING

Alivisatos, A. P., Chun, M., Church, G. M., Greenspan, R. J., Roukes, M. L., & Uste, R. (2012). The brain activity map project and the challenge of functional connectomics. *Neuron*. doi Retrieved 9 March 2014 from http://arep.med.harvard.edu/pdf/Alivisatos_BAM_12.pdf10.1016/j.neuron.2012.06.006

Bechtel, W. (1994). Natural deduction in connectionist systems. *Synthese, 101*(3), 433–463. doi:10.1007/BF01063897

Bentley, P. (2001). *Digital biology: How nature is transforming our technology and our lives*. New York: Simon & Schuster.

Blue Brain Project. (2013). Retrieved 9 March 2014 from http://bluebrain.epfl.ch/

Casselman, B. (2013). The Antikythera mechanism I. Retrieved 9 March 2014 from http://www.math.sunysb.edu/~tony/whatsnew/column/antikytheraI-0400/kyth1.html

Cooper, S. B. (2013). The mathematician's bias - and the return to embodied computation. In "A Computable Universe - Understanding and Exploring Nature as Computation" (Ed. Hector Zenil), World Scientific, pp. 125-142. Retrieved 9 March 2014 from http://arxiv.org/abs/1304.5385

Crowder, J. A., & Freis, S. (2013). Artificial psychology: The psychology of AI. *Systemics. Cybernetics and Informatics, 11*(8), 64–67.

Dawkins, R. (1986). *The blind watchmaker*. New York: W. W. Norton & Company, Inc.

Eternal Return. (2013). Retrieved 9 March 2014 from http://en.wikipedia.org/wiki/Eternal_return - general

Genetic Epistemology. (2013). Retrieved 9 March 2014 from http://en.wikipedia.org/wiki/Genetic_epistemology

Genetic Epistemology (2013). Retrieved 9 March 2014 from http://www.piaget.org/GE/GE-ToC.html

Gray, R. M. (2013). *Entropy and information theory*. New York: Springer Verlag.

Hamann, H., & Worn, H. (2007). Embodied computation. Parallel Processing Letters, Marius Nagy and Naya Nagy (editors), 17(3), pp. 287-298

Huang, H. (2004). Autonomy levels for unmanned systems. U.S. National Institute of Standards and Technology. NIST Special Publication 1011. Retrieved 9 March 2014 from http://www.nist.gov/el/isd/ks/upload/NISTSP_1011_ver_1-1.pdf

IBM -Systems of neuromorphic adaptive plastic scalable electronics (SyNAPSE) (2013). Retrieved 9 March 2014 from http://www.ibm.com/smarterplanet/us/en/business_analytics/article/cognitive_computing.html

Keeley, T. (2008). Giving devices the ability to exercise reason. *The Journal on Systemics. Cybernetics and Informatics, 6*(5), 69–74.

Lloyd, S. (1997). Universe as a quantum computer. *Complexity, 3*(1), 32–35. doi:10.1002/(SICI)1099-0526(199709/10)3:1<32::AID-CPLX10>3.0.CO;2-X

Lodder, J. M. (2009) Binary arithmetic: From Leibniz to von Neumann. *Resources for Teaching Discrete Mathematics*. Mathematical Association of America, pp. 169-178 doi=10.1.1.142.3947 Retrieved 9 March 2014 from http://university-publishingonline.org/maa/chapter.jsf?bid=CBO9780883859742&cid=CBO9780883859742A029

Lodder, J. M. (2012) Historical projects in discrete mathematics. *History and Pedagogy of Mathematics* 2012 16 July – 20 July, 2012, DCC, Daejeon, Korea. Retrieved 9 March 2014 from http://www.hpm2012.org/Proceeding/OT2/T2-02.pdf

Nakamoto, T. (2009). Evolution and the universality of the mechanism of initiation of protein synthesis. *Gene, 432*(1–2), 1–6. doi:10.1016/j.gene.2008.11.001 PMID:19056476

Paranuk, H. V. (2013). Review of Weuenche, A. and Lesser, M. The global dynamics of celullar automata: An atlas of basin of attraction fields of one-dimensional cellular automata. *Journal of Artificial Intelligence and Social Simulation*. Retrieved 9 March 2014 from http://jasss.soc.surrey.ac.uk/4/4/reviews/wuensche.html

Pellletier, F. J. (2013). A history of natural deduction and elementary logic textbooks. Retrieved 9 March 2014 from http://www.sfu.ca/~jeffpell/papers/pelletierNDtexts.pdf

Schoter, A. (1998). Boolean algebra and the Yi Jing. *The Oracle. The Journal of Yijing Studies*, *2*(7), 19–34.

Sheffer Stroke. Retrieved 9 March 2014 from http://en.wikipedia.org/wiki/Sheffer_stroke

Wolfram, S. (2002). A New Kind of Science. Wolfram Media: Retrieved 9 March 2014 from http://www.wolframscience.com/nksonline/toc.html

KEY TERMS AND DEFINITIONS

Bivalance: Having two values, such as yes-no, up-down, 0-1, etc. In logic, "bivalency" refers to having true-false values.

Dialectics: Primarily, a process of apprehending a concept by recognizing what that concept is not A second form of dialectics identifies a concept – process or object – as developing within its something opposite to itself. In dialectic philosophy, a general statement is that the process exists in terms of the object, and vice versa. The process is as much a part of the object as the object is, itself.

Epistemology: A branch of philosophy concerned with how we know something. How we know is expressed by justified belief.

Equivalence: That which has the same set of characteristics as something else. This does not mean the same thing as identity, as an object equivalent to another does not have to have virtually everything – particle for particle - in common with the other. Identity necessarily implies equivalence, but equivalence does not necessarily imply identity.

Existent: That which has an identity. It is problematical whether that identity must be known to a person or whether it can be independent of anyone being aware of its presence. There is a school of thinking saying that one must perceive it for it to exist.

Identity: That which is itself. Identity necessarily implies equivalence, but equivalence does not necessarily imply identity.

Logical Space: An area consisting of a grid, or net of two or more dimensions and populated by values in a bivalent system, the values being represented by symbols.

Ontology: A branch of philosophy concerned with existence.

Recursion: That which is repeated, or circular. The term in computer science refers to the ability to define an infinite set of objects or processes by the same set of instructions, function, or statement.

Reflexive: A property of a process or object that identifies itself in terms of itself. This concept often is used synonymously with, "tautology", "recursive", "identity", or other words meaning something being itself.

Appendix: The Top 500 Supercomputers in the World

The statistics provided in this Appendix are derived from www.Top500.org website in 2014 with written permission to include this information here. Below is the list of top 500 world's fastest supercomputers as of November 2013 ranking.

1. **Tianhe-2 (MilkyWay-2) - TH-IVB-FEP Cluster, Intel Xeon E5-2692 12C 2.200GHz, TH Express-2, Intel Xeon Phi 31S1P**
   Site: National Super Computer Center in Guangzhou.
   Country: China
   Image URL: http://www.top500.org/static/media/uploads/blog/tianhe-2-jack-dongarra-pdf.jpg
   Manufacturer: NUDT
   Cores: 3,120,000
   Linpack Performance (Rmax): 33,862.7 TFlop/s
   Theoretical Peak (Rpeak): 54,902.4 TFlop/s
   Power: 17,808.00 kW
   Memory: 1,024,000 GB
   Interconnect: TH Express-2
   Operating System: Kylin Linux
   Compiler: icc
   Math Library: Intel MKL-11.0.0
   MPI: MPICH2 with a customized GLEX channel
   Ranking: 1

2. **Titan - Cray XK7, Opteron 6274 16C 2.200GHz, Cray Gemini interconnect, NVIDIA K20x**
   Site: DOE/SC/Oak Ridge National Laboratory
   Country: United States
   Image URL: http://www.top500.org/static/media/uploads/galleries/1024px-titan1.jpg
   System URL: http://www.olcf.ornl.gov/titan/
   Manufacturer: Cray Inc.
   Cores: 560,640
   Linpack Performance (Rmax): 17,590.0 TFlop/s
   Theoretical Peak (Rpeak): 27,112.5 TFlop/s
   Power: 8,209.00 kW
   Memory: 710,144 GB
   Interconnect: Cray Gemini interconnect
   Operating System: Cray Linux Environment
   Ranking: 2

3. **Sequoia - BlueGene/Q, Power BQC 16C 1.60 GHz, Custom**
   Site: DOE/NNSA/LLNL
   Country: United States
   Image URL: http://www.top500.org/static/media/uploads/galleries/dawn_complete_high-res.jpg
   Manufacturer: IBM
   Cores: 1,572,864
   Linpack Performance (Rmax): 17,173.2 TFlop/s
   Theoretical Peak (Rpeak): 20,132.7 TFlop/s
   Power: 7,890.00 kW
   Memory: 1,572,864 GB
   Interconnect: Custom Interconnect
   Operating System: Linux
   Ranking: 3

4. **K computer, SPARC64 VIIIfx 2.0GHz, Tofu interconnect**
   Site: RIKEN Advanced Institute for Computational Science (AICS)
   Country: Japan
   Image URL: http://www.top500.org/static/media/uploads/supercomputers/top1/
   Kcomputer_5_800x600.jpg
   Manufacturer: Fujitsu
   Cores: 705,024
   Linpack Performance (Rmax): 10,510.0 TFlop/s
   Theoretical Peak (Rpeak): 11,280.4 TFlop/s
   Power: 12,659.89 kW
   Memory: 1,410,048 GB
   Interconnect: Custom Interconnect
   Operating System: Linux
   Ranking: 4

5. **Mira - BlueGene/Q, Power BQC 16C 1.60GHz, Custom**
   Site: DOE/SC/Argonne National Laboratory
   Country: United States
   Image URL: http://www.top500.org/static/media/uploads/galleries/1280px-mira_-_blue_
   gene_q_at_argonne_national_laboratory_-_skin.jpg
   Manufacturer: IBM
   Cores: 786,432
   Linpack Performance (Rmax): 8,586.6 TFlop/s
   Theoretical Peak (Rpeak): 10,066.3 TFlop/s
   Power: 3,945.00 kW
   Memory: -
   Interconnect: Custom Interconnect
   Operating System: Linux
   Ranking: 5

6. **Piz Daint - Cray XC30, Xeon E5-2670 8C 2.600GHz, Aries interconnect, NVIDIA K20x**
   Site: Swiss National Supercomputing Centre (CSCS)
   Country: Switzerland ✚
   Image URL: http://www.top500.org/static/media/uploads/galleries/piz-daint-cscs1.png
   Manufacturer: Cray Inc.
   Cores: 115,984
   Linpack Performance (Rmax): 6,271.0 TFlop/s
   Theoretical Peak (Rpeak): 7,788.9 TFlop/s
   Power: 2,325.00 kW
   Memory: -
   Interconnect: Aries Interconnect.
   Operating System: Cray Linux Environment
   Ranking: 6

7. **Stampede - PowerEdge C8220, Xeon E5-2680 8C 2.700GHz, Infiniband FDR, Intel Xeon Phi SE10P**
   Site: Texas Advanced Computing Center/Univ Of Texas.
   Country: United States 🇺🇸
   Image URL: http://www.top500.org/static/media/uploads/galleries/stampede-web.jpg
   System URL: http://www.tacc.utexas.edu/stampede
   Manufacturer: Dell
   Cores: 462,462
   Linpack Performance (Rmax): 5,168.1 TFlop/s
   Theoretical Peak (Rpeak): 8,520.1 TFlop/s
   Power: 4,510.00 kW
   Memory: 192, 192 GB
   Interconnect: Infiniband FDR
   Operating System: Linux
   Compiler: Intel
   Math Library: MKL
   MPI: MVAPICH2
   Ranking: 7

8. **JUQUEEN - BlueGene/Q, Power BQC 16C 1.600GHz, Custom Interconnect**
   Site: Forschungszentrum Juelich (FZJ).
   Country: Germany ▬
   Image URL: http://www.top500.org/static/media/uploads/galleries/juelich-juqueen-supercomputer.jpg
   System URL: http://www.fz-juelich.de/ias/jsc/EN/Expertise/Supercomputers/JUQUEEN/JUQUEEN_node.html
   Manufacturer: IBM
   Cores: 458,752
   Linpack Performance (Rmax): 5,008.9 TFlop/s
   Theoretical Peak (Rpeak): 5,872.0 TFlop/s
   Power: 2,301.00 kW

Memory: 458, 752 GB

Interconnect: Custom Interconnect

Operating System: Linux

Ranking: 8

9. **Vulcan - BlueGene/Q, Power BQC 16C 1.600GHz, Custom Interconnect**

   Site: DOE/NNSA/LLNL

   Country: United States

   Image URL: http://www.top500.org/static/media/uploads/galleries/vulcan-supercomputer-llnl.jpg

   Manufacturer: IBM

   Cores: 393,216

   Linpack Performance (Rmax): 4,293.3 TFlop/s

   Theoretical Peak (Rpeak): 5,033.2 TFlop/s

   Power: 1, 972.00 kW

   Memory: 393,216 GB

   Interconnect: Custom Interconnect

   Operating System: Linux

   Ranking: 9

10. **SuperMUC - iDataPlex DX360M4, Xeon E5-2680 8C 2.70GHz, Infiniband FDR**

    Site: Leibniz Rechenzentrum

    Country: Germany

    Image URL: http://www.top500.org/static/media/uploads/galleries/supermuc_lrz_2012-06-18.png

    System URL: http://www.lrz.de/services/compute/supermuc/

    Manufacturer: IBM

    Cores: 147,456

    Linpack Performance (Rmax): 2,897.0 TFlop/s

    Theoretical Peak (Rpeak): 3,185.1 TFlop/s

    Power: 3,422.67 kW

    Memory: -

    Interconnect: Infiniband FDR

    Operating System: Linux

    Ranking: 10

11. **TSUBAME 2.5 - Cluster Platform SL390s G7, Xeon X5670 6C 2.930GHz, Infiniband QDR, NVIDIA K20x**

    Site: GSIC Center, Tokyo Institute of Technology.

    Country: Japan

    Image URL: None

    Manufacturer: NEC/HP

    Cores: 74, 358

    Linpack Performance (Rmax): 2,843.0 TFlop/s

    Theoretical Peak (Rpeak): 5,609.4 TFlop/s

    Power: 1,398.61 kW

Memory: 74,358 GB
Interconnect: Infiniband QDR
Operating System: SUSE Linux Enterprise Server 11
Compiler: GCC
Math Library: Intel MKL
MPI: OpenMPI 1.7.2
Ranking: 11

12. **Tianhe-1A - NUDT YH MPP, Xeon X5670 6C 2.93 GHz, NVIDIA 2050**
    Site: National Supercomputing Center in Tianjin.
    Country: China
    Image URL: http://www.top500.org/static/media/uploads/supercomputers/top1/Tianhe-1A_1_800x600.jpg
    Manufacturer: NUDT
    Cores: 186, 368
    Linpack Performance (Rmax): 2,566.0 TFlop/s
    Theoretical Peak (Rpeak): 4,701.0 TFlop/s
    Power: 4,040.00 kW
    Memory: 229, 376 GB
    Interconnect: Proprietary
    Operating System: Linux
    Compiler: icc
    MPI: MPICH2 with a custom GLEX channel.
    Ranking: 12

13. **Cascade - Atipa Visione IF442 Blade Server, Xeon E5-2670 8C 2.600GHz, Infiniband FDR, Intel Xeon Phi 5110P**
    Site: DOE/SC/Pacific Northwest National Laboratory
    Country: United States
    Image URL: None
    System URL: http://www.pnnl.gov/news/release.aspx?id=965
    Manufacturer: Atipa Technology
    Cores: 194, 616
    Linpack Performance (Rmax): 2,345.8 TFlop/s
    Theoretical Peak (Rpeak): 3,388.0 TFlop/s
    Power: 1,384.00 kW
    Memory: 184, 320 GB
    Interconnect: Infiniband FDR
    Operating System: Linux
    Compiler: Intel
    Math Library: Intel MKL
    MPI: Intel MPI
    Ranking: 13

14. **Pangea - SGI ICE X, Xeon E5-2670 8C 2.600GHz, Infiniband FDR**
    Site: Total Exploration Production
    Country: France ▮▮
    Image URL: http://www.top500.org/static/media/uploads/galleries/sgi-ice-x_pangea_02.jpg
    Manufacturer: SGI
    Cores: 110, 400
    Linpack Performance (Rmax): 2,098.1 TFlop/s
    Theoretical Peak (Rpeak): 2,296.3 TFlop/s
    Power: 2,118.00 kW
    Memory: 54,000 GB
    Interconnect: Infiniband FDR
    Operating System: SUSE Linux Enterprise Server 11
    Ranking: 14

15. **Fermi - BlueGene/Q, Power BQC 16C 1.60GHz, Custom**
    Site: CINECA
    Country: Italy ▮ ▮
    Image URL: http://www.top500.org/static/media/uploads/galleries/blue-gene-q-ibm-fermi-cineca_t.jpg
    Manufacturer: IBM
    Cores: 163, 840
    Linpack Performance (Rmax): 1,788.9 TFlop/s
    Theoretical Peak (Rpeak): 2,097.2 TFlop/s
    Power: 821.88 kW
    Memory: -
    Interconnect: Custom Interconnect
    Operating System: Linux
    Ranking: 15

16. **Pleiades - SGI ICE X, Intel Xeon E5-2670/E5-2680v2 2.6/2.8GHz, Infiniband FDR**
    Site: NASA/Ames Research Center/NAS
    Country: United States ▤
    Image URL: None
    Manufacturer: SGI
    Cores: 96, 192
    Linpack Performance (Rmax): 1,541.3 TFlop/s
    Theoretical Peak (Rpeak): 2, 107.0 TFlop/s
    Power: 2, 015.14 kW
    Memory: 271, 872 GB
    Interconnect: Infiniband FDR
    Operating System: SUSE Linux Enterprise Server 11
    Compiler: Intel Composer XE 2013
    Math Library: Intel MKL
    MPI: SGI MPT
    Ranking: 16

17. **Power 775, POWER7 8C 3.836GHz, Custom Interconnect**
    Site: IBM Development Engineering
    Country: United States 🇺🇸
    Image URL: None
    Manufacturer: IBM
    Cores: 63, 360
    Linpack Performance (Rmax): 1,515.0 TFlop/s
    Theoretical Peak (Rpeak): 1,944.4 TFlop/s
    Power: 3,575.63 kW
    Memory: -
    Interconnect: Custom Interconnect
    Operating System: Linux
    Ranking: 17

18. **Spirit - SGI ICE X, Xeon E5-2670 8C 2.600GHz, Infiniband FDR**
    Site: Air Force Research Laboratory
    Country: United States 🇺🇸
    Image URL: None
    Manufacturer: SGI
    Cores: 73, 584
    Linpack Performance (Rmax): 1,415.5 TFlop/s
    Theoretical Peak (Rpeak): 1,530.5 TFlop/s
    Power: 1,606 kW
    Memory: 144,000 GB
    Interconnect: Infiniband FDR
    Operating System: Redhat Enterprise Linux 6
    Ranking: 18

19. **ARCHER - Cray XC30, Intel Xeon E5 v2 12C 2.700GHz, Aries interconnect**
    Site: EPSRC
    Country: United Kingdom 🇬🇧
    Image URL: http://www.epsrc.ac.uk/SiteCollectionImages/thumbnails/2014/archerquestion-naire220.jpg
    Manufacturer: Cray Inc.
    Cores: 76,192
    Linpack Performance (Rmax): 1,367.5 TFlop/s
    Theoretical Peak (Rpeak): 1,645.7 TFlop/s
    Interconnect: Aries Interconnect
    Operating System: Cray Linux Environment
    Ranking: 19

20. **Curie thin nodes - Bullx B510, Xeon E5-2680 8C 2.700GHz, Infiniband QDR**
    Site: CEA/TGCC-GENCI
    Country: France 🇫🇷
    Image URL: None
    Manufacturer: Bull SA

Cores: 77, 184
Linpack Performance (Rmax): 1,359.0 TFlop/s
Theoretical Peak (Rpeak): 1,667.2 TFlop/s
Power: 2,251.00 kW
Memory: 308, 736 GB
Interconnect: Infiniband QDR
Operating System: bullx SUperCOmputer Suite A.E.2.1.
Compiler: icc
Math Library: Intel Math Kernel Library
MPI: Intel MPI
Ranking: 20

21. **Nebulae - Dawning TC3600 Blade System, Xeon X5650 6C 2.66GHz, Infiniband QDR, NVIDIA 2050**
    Site: National Supercomputing Centre in Shenzhen (NSCS)
    Country: China
    Image URL: None
    Manufacturer: Dawning
    Cores: 120, 640
    Linpack Performance (Rmax): 1, 271.0 TFlop/s
    Theoretical Peak (Rpeak): 2, 984.3 TFlop/s
    Power: 2, 580.00 kW
    Interconnect: Infiniband QDR
    Operating System: Linux
    Ranking: 21

22. **Yellowstone - iDataPlex DX360M4, Xeon E5-2670 8C 2.600GHz, Infiniband FDR**
    Site: NCAR (National Center for Atmospheric Research)
    Country: United States
    Image URL: None
    Manufacturer: IBM
    Cores: 72, 288
    Linpack Performance (Rmax): 1,257.6 TFlop/s
    Theoretical Peak (Rpeak): 1,503.6 TFlop/s
    Power: 1,436.72 kW
    Interconnect: Infiniband FDR
    Operating System: Linux
    Ranking: 22

23. **Blue Joule - BlueGene/Q, Power BQC 16C 1.60GHz, Custom**
    Site: Science and Technology Facilities Council- Daresbury Laboratory
    Country: United Kingdom
    Image URL: http://www.stfc.ac.uk/resources/image/jpg/DrMikeAshworth.jpg
    Manufacturer: IBM
    Cores: 114, 688
    Linpack Performance (Rmax): 1,252.2 TFlop/s

Theoretical Peak (Rpeak): 1,468.0 TFlop/s
Power: 575.31 kW
Interconnect: Custom Interconnect
Operating System: Linux
Ranking: 23

24. **Helios - Bullx B510, Xeon E5-2680 8C 2.700GHz, Infiniband QDR**
    Site: International Fusion Energy Research Centre (IFERC), EU(F4E) – Japan Broader
    Approach collaboration
    Country: Japan ●
    Image URL: None
    Manufacturer: Bull SA
    Cores: 70, 560
    Linpack Performance (Rmax): 1,237.0 TFlop/s
    Theoretical Peak (Rpeak): 1,524.1 TFlop/s
    Power: 2,200.00 kW
    Memory: 282, 240 GB
    Interconnect: Infiniband QDR
    Operating System: bullx SUperCOmputer Suite A.E.2.1
    Compiler: Intel **Compiler:** 12.1.1.256
    Math Library: Intel MKL v12
    MPI: Intel MPI 4.0.3
    Ranking: 24

25. **Garnet - Cray XE6, Opteron 16C 2.500GHz, Cray Gemini interconnect**
    Site: ERDC DSRC
    Country: United States
    Image URL: None
    Manufacturer: Cray Inc.
    Cores: 150, 528
    Linpack Performance (Rmax): 1,167.0 TFlop/s
    Theoretical Peak (Rpeak): 1,505.3 TFlop/s
    Memory: 301,056 GB
    Interconnect: Cray Gemini interconnect
    Operating System: Linux
    Ranking: 25

26. **Cielo - Cray XE6, Opteron 6136 8C 2.40GHz, Custom**
    Site: DOE/NNSA/LANL/SNL
    Country: United States
    Image URL: http://www.lanl.gov/science/NSS/issue2_2010/images/CIELOcrop.jpg
    Manufacturer: Cray Inc.
    Cores: 142, 272
    Linpack Performance (Rmax): 1,110.0 TFlop/s
    Theoretical Peak (Rpeak): 1,365.8 TFlop/s
    Power: 3,980.00 kW

Interconnect: Cray Gemini Interconnect
Operating System: Linux
Ranking: 26

27. **DiRAC - BlueGene/Q, Power BQC 16C 1.60GHz, Custom**
   Site: University of Edinburgh
   Country: United Kingdom
   Image URL: http://www.epcc.ed.ac.uk/sites/default/files/IMAGE/bluegene_facility.jpg
   Manufacturer: IBM
   Cores: 98,304
   Linpack Performance (Rmax): 1,073.3 TFlop/s
   Theoretical Peak (Rpeak): 1,258.3 TFlop/s
   Power: 493.12 kW
   Interconnect: Custom Interconnect
   Operating System: Linux
   Ranking: 27

28. **Hopper - Cray XE6, Opteron 6172 12C 2.10GHz, Custom**
   Site: DOE/SC/LBNL/NERSC
   Country: United States
   Image URL: https://www.nersc.gov/assets/About-Us/_resampled/SetWidth230-hopper1.jpg
   Manufacturer: Cray Inc.
   Cores: 153, 408
   Linpack Performance (Rmax): 1,054.0 TFlop/s
   Theoretical Peak (Rpeak): 1,288.6 TFlop/s
   Power: 2,910.00 kW
   Interconnect: Cray Gemini Interconnect
   Operating System: Linux
   Ranking: 28

29. **Tera-100 - Bull bullx super-node S6010/S6030**
   Site: Commissariat a l'Energie Atomique (CEA)
   Country: France
   Image URL: None
   Manufacturer: Bull SA
   Cores: 138, 368
   Linpack Performance (Rmax): 1,050.0 TFlop/s
   Theoretical Peak (Rpeak): 1,254.5 TFlop/s
   Power: 4,590.00 kW
   Interconnect: Infiniband QDR
   Operating System: Linux
   Ranking: 29

30. **Oakleaf-FX - PRIMEHPC FX10, SPARC64 IXfx 16C 1.848GHz, Tofu interconnect**
   Site: Information Technology Center, The University of Tokyo
   Country: Japan
   Image URL: http://www.cc.u-tokyo.ac.jp/image/fx10.jpg

Manufacturer: Fujitsu
Cores: 76,800
Linpack Performance (Rmax): 1,043 TFlop/s
Theoretical Peak (Rpeak): 1,135.4 TFlop/s
Power: 1,176.80 kW
Memory: 153,600 GB
Interconnect: Tofu interconnect
Operating System: Linux
Compiler: Fujitsu Technical Computing Language C compiler
Math Library: Fujitsu Technical Computing Language BLAS
MPI: Fujitsu Technical Computing Language MPI (Open MPI based)
Ranking: 30

31. **iDataPlex DX360M4, Intel Xeon E5-2680v2 10C 2.800GHz, Infiniband FDR**
    Site: Max-Planck-Gesellschaft MPI/IPP
    Country: Germany
    Image URL: http://www.rzg.mpg.de/services/computing/Hydra/Hydra570.jpg
    Manufacturer: IBM
    Cores: 60000
    Linpack Performance (Rmax): 1,033.1 TFlop/s
    Theoretical Peak (Rpeak): 1,344.0 TFlop/s
    Power: 1,260.00 kW
    Interconnect: Infiniband FDR
    Operating System: Linux
    Ranking: 31

32. **Fujitsu PRIMERGY CX250 S1, Xeon E5-2670 8C 2.600GHz, Infiniband FDR**
    Site: National Computational Infrastructure, Australian National University
    Country: Australia
    Image URL: None
    Manufacturer: Fujitsu
    Cores: 53,504
    Linpack Performance (Rmax): 978.6 TFlop/s
    Theoretical Peak (Rpeak): 1,112.9 TFlop/s
    Memory: 214,016 GB
    Interconnect: Infiniband FDR
    Operating System: Linux
    Compiler: Intel C & Fortran 64 Compiler XE 2012
    Math Library: Fujitsu Tuned DGEMM
    MPI: Intel MPI Library 4.0
    Ranking: 32

33. **Conte - Cluster Platform SL250s Gen8, Xeon E5-2670 8C 2.600GHz, Infiniband FDR, Intel Xeon Phi 5110P**
    Site: Purdue University
    Country: United States

Image URL: http://www.itap.purdue.edu/newsroom/images/conteorderspic1.jpg

Manufacturer: Hewlett-Packard

Cores: 77, 520

Linpack Performance (Rmax): 976.8 TFlop/s

Theoretical Peak (Rpeak): 1,341.1 TFlop/s

Power: 510.00 kW

Interconnect: Infiniband FDR

Operating System: Linux

Ranking: 33

34. **MareNostrum - iDataPlex DX360M4, Xeon E5-2670 8C 2.600GHz, Infiniband FDR**

Site: Barcelona Supercomputing Center

Country: Spain

Image URL: http://www.bsc.es/sites/default/files/public/styles/news-thumbnail/public/about/news/images/mn3-1.jpg?itok=fRTBHKjC

Manufacturer: IBM

Cores: 48,896

Linpack Performance (Rmax): 925.1 TFlop/s

Theoretical Peak (Rpeak): 1,017.0 TFlop/s

Power: 1,015.60 kW

Interconnect: Infiniband FDR

Operating System: Linux

Ranking: 34

35. **Kraken XT5 - Cray XT5-HE Opteron Six Core 2.6 GHz**

Site: National Institute for Computational Sciences/University of Tennessee

Country: United States

Image URL: http://www.nics.tennessee.edu/sites/www.nics.tennessee.edu/files/images/kraken-high-right-425.jpg

System URL: http://www.nics.tennessee.edu/computing-resources/kraken

Manufacturer: Cray Inc.

Cores: 112,800

Linpack Performance (Rmax): 919.1 TFlop/s

Theoretical Peak (Rpeak): 1,173.0 TFlop/s

Power: 3,090.00 kW

Interconnect: Proprietary

Operating System: Linux

Ranking: 35

36. **HA8000-tc HT210/PRIMERGY CX400 Cluster, Xeon E5-2680 8C 2.700GHz, Infiniband FDR, NVIDIA K20/K20x, Xeon Phi 5110P**

Site: Research Institute for Information Technology, Kyushu University

Country: Japan

Image URL: None

Manufacturer: Hitachi/Fujitsu

Cores: 222,072

Linpack Performance (Rmax): 905.4 TFlop/s
Theoretical Peak (Rpeak): 1,502.2 TFlop/s
Memory: 435, 968 GB
Interconnect: Infiniband FDR
Operating System: Redhat Enterprise Linux 6
MPI: Intel MPI
Ranking: 36

37. **Lomonosov - T-Platforms T-Blade2/1.1, Xeon X5570/X5670/E5630 2.93/2.53 GHz, Nvidia 2070 GPU, PowerXCell 8i Infiniband QDR**
    Site: Moscow State University- Research Computing Center
    Country: Russia
    Image URL: None
    Manufacturer: T-Platforms
    Cores: 78,660
    Linpack Performance (Rmax): 901.9 TFlop/s
    Theoretical Peak (Rpeak): 1,700.2 TFlop/s
    Power: 2,800.00 kW
    Memory: 99,489 GB
    Interconnect: Infiniband
    Operating System: Linux
    Compiler: intel-12.0
    Math Library: MKL
    MPI: Intel MPI 4.0
    Ranking: 37

38. **BlueGene/Q, Power BQC 16C 1.60GHz, Custom**
    Site: Rensselaer Polytechnic Institute
    Country: United States
    Image URL: http://news.rpi.edu/sites/default/files/styles/sidebar/public/2013-1003-amos3_0.jpeg?itok=8V16LNz5
    Manufacturer: IBM
    Cores: 81, 920
    Linpack Performance (Rmax): 894.4 TFlop/s
    Theoretical Peak (Rpeak): 1,048.6 TFlop/s
    Power: 410.90 kW
    Memory: 81,920 GB
    Interconnect: Custom Interconnect
    Operating System: Linux
    Ranking: 38

39. **HERMIT - Cray XE6, Opteron 6276 16C 2.30 GHz, Cray Gemini interconnect**
    Site: HWW/Universitaet Stuttgart
    Country: Germany
    Image URL: http://www.hlrs.de/uploads/media/cray_xe6_phase1.jpg
    Manufacturer: Cray Inc.

Cores: 113, 472
Linpack Performance (Rmax): 831.4 TFlop/s
Theoretical Peak (Rpeak): 1,043.9 TFlop/s
Interconnect: Cray Gemini interconnect
Operating System: Cray Linux Environment
Ranking: 39

40. **Sunway Blue Light - Sunway BlueLight MPP, ShenWei processor SW1600 975.00 MHz, Infiniband QDR**
Site: National Supercomputing Center in Jinan
Country: China
Image URL: None
Manufacturer: National Research Center of ParallelComputer Engineering & Technology
Cores: 137,200
Linpack Performance (Rmax): 795.9 TFlop/s
Theoretical Peak (Rpeak): 1,070.2 TFlop/s
Power: 1,074.00 kW
Memory: 139,264 GB
Interconnect: Infiniband QDR
Operating System: Linux
Ranking: 40

41. **Zin - Xtreme-X GreenBlade GB512X, Xeon E5 (Sandy Bridge - EP) 8C 2.60GHz, Infiniband QDR**
Site: Lawrence Livermore National Laboratory
Country: United States
Image URL: https://asc.llnl.gov/computing_resources/tlcc/images/zin.jpg
Manufacturer: Cray Inc.
Cores: 46,208
Linpack Performance (Rmax): 773.7 TFlop/s
Theoretical Peak (Rpeak): 961.1 TFlop/s
Power: 924.16 kW
Memory: 92,416 GB
Interconnect: Infiniband QDR
Operating System: RHEL 6.2
MPI: mvapich 1.2
Ranking: 41

42. **Tianhe-1A Hunan Solution - NUDT YH MPP, Xeon X5670 6C 2.93 GHz, Proprietary, NVIDIA 2050**
Site: National Super Computer Center inHunan
Country: China
Image URL: None
Manufacturer: NUDT
Cores: 53,248
Linpack Performance (Rmax): 771.7 TFlop/s

Theoretical Peak (Rpeak): 1,342.8 TFlop/s
Power: 1,155.07 kW
Memory: 98,304 GB
Interconnect: Proprietary
Operating System: Linux
Compiler: icc
MPI: MPICH2 with a custom GLEX Channel.
Ranking: 42

43. **Endeavor - Intel Cluster, Intel Xeon E5-2697v2 12C 2.700GHz, Infiniband FDR, Intel Xeon Phi 7110**
    Site: Intel
    Country: United States
    Image URL: None
    Manufacturer: Intel
    Cores: 51,392
    Linpack Performance (Rmax): 758.9 TFlop/s
    Theoretical Peak (Rpeak): 933.5 TFlop/s
    Power: 387.20 kW
    Memory: 22,528 GB
    Interconnect: Infiniband FDR
    Operating System: Linux
    Compiler: Intel Composer XE 2013.5.192
    Math Library: Intel MKL 11.0.5.192
    MPI: Intel MPI 4.1.1.036
    Ranking: 43

44. **iDataPlex DX360M4, Xeon E5-2670 8C 2.600GHz, Infiniband FDR**
    Site: Indian Institute of Tropical Meteorology
    Country: India
    Image URL: None
    Manufacturer: IBM
    Cores: 38,016
    Linpack Performance (Rmax): 719.2 TFlop/s
    Theoretical Peak (Rpeak): 790.7 TFlop/s
    Power: 789.66 kW
    Interconnect: Infiniband FDR
    Operating System: Linux
    Ranking: 44

45. **BlueGene/Q, Power BQC 16C 1.60GHz, Custom**
    Site: CNRS/IDRIS-GENCI
    Country: France
    Image URL: None
    Manufacturer: IBM
    Cores: 65,536

Linpack Performance (Rmax): 715.6 TFlop/s
Theoretical Peak (Rpeak): 838.9 TFlop/s
Power: 328.75 kW
Interconnect: Custom Interconnect
Operating System: Linux
Ranking: 45

46. **Zumbrota - BlueGene/Q, Power BQC 16C 1.60GHz, Custom**
    Site: EDF R&D
    Country: France ▮▮
    Image URL: None
    Manufacturer: IBM
    Cores: 65,536
    Linpack Performance (Rmax): 715.6 TFlop/s
    Theoretical Peak (Rpeak): 838.9 TFlop/s
    Power: 328.75 kW
    Interconnect: Custom Interconnect
    Operating System: Linux
    Ranking: 46

47. **EPFL Blue Brain IV - BlueGene/Q, Power BQC 16C 1.600GHz, Custom Interconnect**
    Site: Swiss National Supercomputing Centre (CSCS)
    Country: Switzerland ▣
    Image URL: None
    Manufacturer: IBM
    Cores: 65,536
    Linpack Performance (Rmax): 715.6 TFlop/s
    Theoretical Peak (Rpeak): 838.9 TFlop/s
    Power: 328.70 kW
    Interconnect: Custom Interconnect
    Operating System: Linux
    Ranking: 47

48. **Avoca - BlueGene/Q, Power BQC 16C 1.60GHz, Custom**
    Site: Victorian Life SciencesComputation Initiative
    Country: Australia ▨
    Image URL: None
    Manufacturer: IBM
    Cores: 65, 536
    Linpack Performance (Rmax): 715.6 TFlop/s
    Theoretical Peak (Rpeak): 838.9 TFlop/s
    Power: 328.75 kW
    Interconnect: Custom Interconnect
    Operating System: Linux
    Ranking: 48

49. **iDataPlex DX360M4, Intel Xeon E5-2680v2 10C 2.800GHz, Infiniband, NVIDIA K20x**
    Site: Max-Planck-Gesellschaft MPI/IPP
    Country: Germany
    Image URL: http://www.rzg.mpg.de/services/computing/Hydra/Hydra570.jpg
    Manufacturer: IBM
    Cores: 15,840
    Linpack Performance (Rmax): 709.7 TFlop/s
    Theoretical Peak (Rpeak): 1,013.1 TFlop/s
    Power: 269.94 kW
    Interconnect: Infiniband
    Operating System: Linux
    Ranking: 49

50. **HECToR - Cray XE6, Opteron 6276 16C 2.30 GHz, Cray Gemini interconnect**
    Site: University of Edinburgh
    Country: United Kingdom
    Image URL: http://www.epcc.ed.ac.uk/sites/default/files/IMAGE/hector_facility.jpg
    Manufacturer: Cray Inc.
    Cores: 90,112
    Linpack Performance (Rmax): 660.2 TFlop/s
    Theoretical Peak (Rpeak): 829.0 TFlop/s
    Interconnect: Cray Gemini interconnect
    Operating System: Cray Linux Environment
    Ranking: 50

51. **Power 775, POWER7 8C 3.836GHz, Custom Interconnect**
    Site: ECMWF
    Country: United Kingdom
    Image URL: http://www.ecmwf.int/sites/default/files/IBMPower7computers.jpg
    Manufacturer: IBM
    Cores: 24,576
    Linpack Performance (Rmax): 635.1 TFlop/s
    Theoretical Peak (Rpeak): 754.2 TFlop/s
    Power: 1,386.91 kW
    Interconnect: Custom Interconnect
    Operating System: AIX
    Ranking: 51

52. **Power 775, POWER7 8C 3.836GHz, Custom Interconnect**
    Site: ECMWF
    Country: United Kingdom
    Image URL: http://www.ecmwf.int/sites/default/files/IBMPower7computers.jpg
    Manufacturer: IBM
    Cores: 24, 576
    Linpack Performance (Rmax): 635.1 TFlop/s
    Theoretical Peak (Rpeak): 754.2 TFlop/s

Power: 1,386.91 kW
Interconnect: Custom Interconnect
Operating System: AIX
Ranking: 52

53. **Big Red II - Cray XK7, Opteron 6276 16C 2.300GHz, Cray Gemini interconnect, NVIDIA K20**
    Site: Indiana University
    Country: United States
    Image URL: None
    Manufacturer: Cray Inc.
    Cores: 31,288
    Linpack Performance (Rmax): 597.4 TFlop/s
    Theoretical Peak (Rpeak): 1,000.6 TFlop/s
    Interconnect: Cray Gemini interconnect
    Operating System: Cray Linux Environment
    Ranking: 53

54. **SGI ICE X, Xeon E5-2670 8C 2.600GHz, Infiniband FDR**
    Site: Central Research Institute of Electric Power Industry/ CRIEPI
    Country: Japan
    Image URL: None
    Manufacturer: SGI
    Cores: 32,256
    Linpack Performance (Rmax): 582.1 TFlop/s
    Theoretical Peak (Rpeak): 670.9 TFlop/s
    Power: 720.00 kW
    Memory: 64,512 GB
    Interconnect: Infiniband FDR
    Operating System: SUSE Linux Enterprise Server 11
    Ranking: 54

55. **Gaea C2 - Cray XE6, Opteron 6276 16C 2.30GHz, Cray Gemini interconnect**
    Site: NOAA/ Oak Ridge National Laboratory
    Country: United States
    Image URL: http://www.ncrc.gov/wp-content/uploads/2012/10/gaea-150x100.jpg
    Manufacturer: Cray Inc.
    Cores: 77,824
    Linpack Performance (Rmax): 565.7 TFlop/s
    Theoretical Peak (Rpeak): 716.0 TFlop/s
    Power: 972.00 kW
    Interconnect: Cray Gemini interconnect
    Operating System: Cray Linux Environment
    Compiler: cce 8.0
    MPI: xt-mpich2
    Ranking: 55

56. **Cluster Platform 3000 BL460c Gen8, Xeon E5-2670 8C 2.600GHz, 10G Ethernet**
    Site: Service Provider
    Country: United States
    Image URL: None
    Manufacturer: Hewlett-Packard
    Cores: 42,848
    Linpack Performance (Rmax): 545.5 TFlop/s
    Theoretical Peak (Rpeak): 891.2 TFlop/s
    Interconnect: 10G Ethernet
    Operating System: Linux
    Ranking: 56

57. **HIMAWARI - BlueGene/Q, Power BQC 16C 1.600GHz, Custom Interconnect**
    Site: High Energy Accelerator Research Organization/KEK
    Country: Japan
    Image URL: http://www.kek.jp/en/Facility/ARL/CRC/071-01.jpg
    Manufacturer: IBM
    Cores: 49, 152
    Linpack Performance (Rmax): 536.7 TFlop/s
    Theoretical Peak (Rpeak): 629.1 TFlop/s
    Power: 246.56 kW
    Interconnect: Custom Interconnect
    Operating System: Linux
    Ranking: 57

58. **SAKURA - BlueGene/Q, Power BQC 16C 1.60GHz, Custom**
    Site: High Energy Accelerator Research Organization/KEK
    Country: Japan
    Image URL: http://www.kek.jp/ja/NewsRoom/Release/2012/10/02/366_01.jpg
    Manufacturer: IBM
    Cores: 49,152
    Linpack Performance (Rmax): 536.7 TFlop/s
    Theoretical Peak (Rpeak): 629.1 TFlop/s
    Power: 246.56 kW
    Interconnect: Custom Interconnect
    Operating System: Linux
    Ranking: 58

59. **SANAM - Adtech, ASUS ESC4000/FDR G2, Xeon E5-2650 8C 2.000GHz, Infiniband FDR, AMD FirePro S10000**
    Site: King Abdulaziz City for Science And Technology
    Country: Saudi Arabia
    Image URL: None
    Manufacturer: Adtech
    Cores: 38,400
    Linpack Performance (Rmax): 532.6 TFlop/s

Theoretical Peak (Rpeak): 1,098.0 TFlop/s
Power: 179.15 kW
Memory: 38,400 GB
Interconnect: Infiniband FDR
Operating System: Linux
Compiler: gcc 4.6.1
Math Library: Intel MKL 2013 + CALDGEMM
MPI: OpenMPI 1.6.2
Ranking: 59

60. **HPCC - Cluster Platform SL250s Gen8, Xeon E5-2665 8C 2.400GHz, Infiniband FDR, Nvidia K20m**
    Site: University of Southern California
    Country: United States
    Image URL: None
    Manufacturer: Hewlett-Packard
    Cores: 10,920
    Linpack Performance (Rmax): 531.6 TFlop/s
    Theoretical Peak (Rpeak): 690.4 TFlop/s
    Power: 237.00 kW
    Memory: 16,640 GB
    Interconnect: Infiniband FDR
    Operating System: Linux
    Ranking: 60

61. **Bullx DLC B710 Blades, Intel Xeon E5 v2 12C 2.700GHz, Infiniband FDR**
    Site: Meteo France
    Country: France
    Image URL: None
    Manufacturer: Bull SA
    Cores: 25,800
    Linpack Performance (Rmax): 500.3 TFlop/s
    Theoretical Peak (Rpeak): 557.3 TFlop/s
    Power: 401.00 kW
    Interconnect: Infiniband FDR
    Operating System: Bullx Linux
    Compiler: Intel Compilers
    Math Library: Intel MKL
    MPI: bullx MPI
    Ranking: 61

62. **Cluster Platform SL230s Gen8, Intel Xeon E5-2680v2 10C 2.800GHz, Gigabit Ethernet**
    Site: Energy Company (D)
    Country: United States
    Image URL: None
    Manufacturer: Hewlett-Packard
    Cores: 50,400
    Linpack Performance (Rmax): 499.2 TFlop/s

Theoretical Peak (Rpeak): 1,129.0 TFlop/s
Interconnect: Gigabit Ethernet
Operating System: Linux
Ranking: 62

63. **Mole-8.5 - Mole-8.5 Cluster, Xeon X5520 4C 2.27 GHz, Infiniband QDR, NVIDIA 2050**
    Site: Institute of Process Engineering, Chinese Academy of Sciences.
    Country: China
    Image URL: None
    Manufacturer: IPE, Nvidia, Tyan
    Cores: 29,440
    Linpack Performance (Rmax): 496.5 TFlop/s
    Theoretical Peak (Rpeak): 1,012.6 TFlop/s
    Power: 540.00 kW
    Memory: 15,360 GB
    Interconnect: Infiniband QDR
    Operating System: Linux
    Compiler: gcc + CUDA 4.0
    MPI: OpenMPI 1.4.2
    Ranking: 63

64. **Amazon EC2 C3 Instance cluster - Amazon EC2 Cluster, Intel Xeon E5-2680v2 10C 2.800GHz, 10G Ethernet**
    Site: Amazon Web Services
    Country: United States
    Image URL: None
    Manufacturer: Self-made
    Cores: 26,496
    Linpack Performance (Rmax): 484.2 TFlop/s
    Theoretical Peak (Rpeak): 593.5 TFlop/s
    Memory: 105,984 GB
    Interconnect: 10G Ethernet
    Operating System: Linux
    Compiler: Intel
    Math Library: Intel MKL
    MPI: Intel MPI
    Ranking: 64

65. **Power 775, POWER7 8C 3.836GHz, Custom Interconnect**
    Site: United Kingdom Meteorological Office
    Country: United Kingdom
    Image URL: None
    Manufacturer: IBM
    Cores: 18,432
    Linpack Performance (Rmax): 476.3 TFlop/s
    Theoretical Peak (Rpeak): 565.6 TFlop/s
    Power: 1,040.18 kW

Interconnect: Custom Interconnect

Operating System: AIX

Ranking: 65

66. **Cluster Platform SL390s G7, Xeon X5650 6C 2.660GHz, Gigabit Ethernet, NVIDIA 2090**

    Site: Geoscience (P)

    Country: United States

    Image URL: None

    Manufacturer: Hewlett-Packard

    Cores: 40,320

    Linpack Performance (Rmax): 461.8 TFlop/s

    Theoretical Peak (Rpeak): 1,141.5 TFlop/s

    Interconnect: Gigabit Ethernet

    Operating System: Linux

    Ranking: 66

67. **Intrepid - Blue Gene/P Solution**

    Site: DOE/SC/Argonne National Laboratory

    Country: United States

    Image URL: http://www.alcf.anl.gov/sites/all/themes/fusionALCF/images/resources/intrepid.jpg

    Manufacturer: IBM

    Cores: 163,840

    Linpack Performance (Rmax): 458.6 TFlop/s

    Theoretical Peak (Rpeak): 557.1 TFlop/s

    Power: 1,260.00 kW

    Interconnect: Proprietary

    Operating System: CNK/SLES 9

    Ranking: 67

68. **Cluster Platform SL230s Gen8, Xeon E5-2670 8C 2.600GHz, 10G Ethernet**

    Site: Energy Company(D)

    Country: United States

    Image URL: None

    Manufacturer: Hewlett-Packard

    Cores: 32,256

    Linpack Performance (Rmax): 457.6 TFlop/s

    Theoretical Peak (Rpeak): 670.9 TFlop/s

    Interconnect: 10G Ethernet

    Operating System: Linux

    Ranking: 68

69. **HPCC1 - iDataPlex DX360M4, Xeon E5-2670 8C 2.600GHz, Infiniband FDR14**

    Site: Exploration and Production – Eni S.p.A.

    Country: Italy

    Image URL: None

    Manufacturer: IBM

Cores: 24,000
Linpack Performance (Rmax): 454.1 TFlop/s
Theoretical Peak (Rpeak): 499.2 TFlop/s
Power: 498.53 kW
Interconnect: Infiniband FDR14
Operating System: Linux
Ranking: 69

70. **Makman - iDataPlex DX360M4, Xeon E5-2670 8C 2.600GHz, Infiniband QDR**
Site: Saudi Aramco
Country: Saudi Arabia
Image URL: None
Manufacturer: IBM
Cores: 24,336
Linpack Performance (Rmax): 441.8 TFlop/s
Theoretical Peak (Rpeak): 506.2 TFlop/s
Power: 505.50 kW
Memory: 97,344 GB
Interconnect: Infiniband QDR
Operating System: Linux
Compiler: Intel
Math Library: Intel Math Kernel Library 11.0 Update 3.
MPI: Intel MPI
Ranking: 70

71. **Red Sky - Sun Blade x6275, Xeon X55xx 2.93 Ghz, Infiniband**
Site: Sandia National Laboratories/National Renewable Energy Laboratory
Country United States
Image URL: None
Manufacturer: Sun Microsystems
Cores: 42,440
Linpack Performance (Rmax): 433.5 TFlop/s
Theoretical Peak (Rpeak): 497.4 TFlop/s
Memory: 22, 104 GB
Interconnect: Infiniband
Operating System: CentOS
Ranking: 71

72. **Cluster Platform DL360e Gen8, Xeon E5-2450L 8C 1.800GHz, GigabitEthernet**
Site: Software Company (M)
Country: United States
Image URL: None
Manufacturer: Hewlett-Packard
Cores: 75,664
Linpack Performance (Rmax): 426.8 TFlop/s
Theoretical Peak (Rpeak): 1,089.6 TFlop/s

Interconnect: Gigabit Ethernet
Operating System: Linux
Ranking: 72

73. **HA-PACS - Xtream-X GreenBlade 8204, Xeon E5-2670 8C 2.600GHz, Infiniband QDR, NVIDIA 2090**
    Site: Center for Computational Sciences, University of Tsukuba
    Country: Japan
    Image URL: None
    Manufacturer: Cray Inc.
    Cores: 20,800
    Linpack Performance (Rmax): 421.6 TFlop/s
    Theoretical Peak (Rpeak): 778.1 TFlop/s
    Power: 407.29 kW
    Memory: 33, 280 GB
    Interconnect: Infiniband QDR
    Operating System: Linux
    Compiler: GCC 4.4.5 / CUDA Toolkit 4.1
    Math Library: Intel MKL 10.3
    MPI: Intel MPI 4.0
    Ranking: 73

74. **Aterui - Cray XC30, Xeon E5-2670 8C 2.600GHz, Aries interconnect**
    Site: National Astronomical Observatory of Japan
    Country: Japan
    Image URL: http://www.nao.ac.jp/contents/gallery/2014/20140422-aterui-700.jpg
    Manufacturer: Cray Inc.
    Cores: 24, 192
    Linpack Performance (Rmax): 420.4 TFlop/s
    Theoretical Peak (Rpeak): 503.2 TFlop/s
    Interconnect: Aries interconnect
    Operating System: Cray Linux Environment
    Compiler: Cray Compiler
    Math Library: Cray-libsci
    MPI: cray-mpich2
    Ranking: 74

75. **Cluster Platform SL230s Gen8, Xeon E5-2670 8C 2.600GHz, 10G Ethernet, NVIDIA 2075**
    Site: IT Service Provider
    Country: United States
    Image URL: None
    Manufacturer: Hewlett-Packard
    Cores: 43, 264
    Linpack Performance (Rmax): 419.4 TFlop/s
    Theoretical Peak (Rpeak): 1,075.3 TFlop/s
    Interconnect: 10G Ethernet
    Operating System: Linux
    Ranking: 75

76. **Discover - iDataPlex DX360M4, Xeon E5-2670 8C 2.600GHz, Infiniband QDR, Intel Xeon Phi 5110P**
    Site: NASA Center for Climate Simulation
    Country: United States
    Image URL: http://hec.nasa.gov/news/gallery_images/discover_0510_med.jpg
    Manufacturer: IBM
    Cores: 35,568
    Linpack Performance (Rmax): 417.3 TFlop/s
    Theoretical Peak (Rpeak): 628.8 TFlop/s
    Power: 215.60 kW
    Memory: 14, 976 GB
    Interconnect: Infiniband QDR
    Operating System: Linux
    Ranking: 76

77. **Dawn - Blue Gene/P Solution**
    Site: DOE/NNSA/LLNL
    Country: United States
    Image URL: https://computing.llnl.gov/tutorials/bgp/images/dawn02.1000pix.jpg, https://computing.llnl.gov/tutorials/bgp/images/dawn03.1000pix.jpg
    Manufacturer: IBM
    Cores: 147,456
    Linpack Performance (Rmax): 415.7 TFlop/s
    Theoretical Peak (Rpeak): 501.4 TFlop/s
    Power: 1,134.00 kW
    Interconnect: Proprietary
    Operating System: CNK/SLES 9
    Ranking: 77

78. **HPCEE - SGI Rackable C2112-4RP3, Xeon E5-2670 8C 2.600GHz, Infiniband QDR**
    Site: DOE/National Energy Technology Laboratory
    Country: United States
    Image URL: http://www.netl.doe.gov/Image%20Library/publications/press/2013/inside_iso_container_with_servers.jpg
    Manufacturer: SGI
    Cores: 24, 192
    Linpack Performance (Rmax): 413.5 TFlop/s
    Theoretical Peak (Rpeak): 503.2 TFlop/s
    Memory: 48, 384 GB
    Interconnect: Infiniband QDR
    Operating System: Linux
    Ranking: 78

79. **Triolith - Cluster Platform SL230s Gen8, Xeon E5-2660 8C 2.200GHz, Infiniband FDR**
    Site: National Supercomputing Center (NSC)
    Country: Sweden

Image URL: https://www.nsc.liu.se/systems/triolith/triolith-panor.jpg
System URL: http://www.snic.vr.se/apply-for-resources/available-resources/nsc
Manufacturer: Hewlett-Packard
Cores: 25, 376
Linpack Performance (Rmax): 407.2 TFlop/s
Theoretical Peak (Rpeak): 446.6 TFlop/s
Power: 519.00 kW
Memory: 56, 128 GB
Interconnect: Infiniband FDR
Operating System: Linux
Ranking: 79

80. **Power 775, POWER7 8C 3.836GHz, Custom Interconnect**
    Site: United Kingdom Meteorological office
    Country: United Kingdom
    Image URL: None
    Manufacturer: IBM
    Cores: 15,360
    Linpack Performance (Rmax): 396.9 TFlop/s
    Theoretical Peak (Rpeak): 471.4 TFlop/s
    Power: 866.82 Kw
    Interconnect: Custom Interconnect
    Operating System: AIX
    Ranking: 80

81. **Palmetto2 - Cluster Platform SL250s Gen8, Xeon E5-2665 8C 2.400GHz, Infiniband FDR, Nvidia K20m**
    Site: Clemson University
    Country: United States
    Image URL: http://citi.clemson.edu/palmetto/images/palmetto-picture.jpg
    Manufacturer: Hewlett-Packard
    Cores: 8,190
    Linpack Performance (Rmax): 396.7 TFlop/s
    Theoretical Peak (Rpeak): 518.0 TFlop/s
    Memory: 12, 480 GB
    Interconnect: Infiniband FDR
    Operating System: Linux
    Compiler: GCC
    Math Library: Intel MKL
    MPI: OpenMPI
    Ranking: 81

82. **SGI ICE X, Xeon E5-2670 8C 2.600GHz, Infiniband FDR**
    Site: Norwegian University of Science and Technology
    Country: Norway
    Image URL: http://www.ntnu.no/ikt/_media/english/ict_arsrapport_2012_lr_klikkbar.pdf

Manufacturer: SGI
Cores: 22,048
Linpack Performance (Rmax): 396.7 TFlop/s
Theoretical Peak (Rpeak): 458.6 TFlop/s
Power: 537.00 kW
Interconnect: Infiniband FDR
Operating System: SUSE Linux Enterprise Server 11
Ranking: 82

83. **PARAM Yuva - II - R2208GZ Cluster, Xeon E5-2670 8C 2.600GHz, Infiniband FDR, Intel Xeon Phi 5110P**
    Site: Center for Development of Advanced Computing (C-DAC)
    Country: India
    Image URL: http://cdac.in/english/press/1q13/images/inaugration3.jpg
    System URL: https://yuva.cdac.in/YuvaII/
    Manufacturer: Netweb Technologies
    Cores: 30,056
    Linpack Performance (Rmax): 388.4 TFlop/s
    Theoretical Peak (Rpeak): 520.4 TFlop/s
    Power: 209.95 kW
    Memory: 14, 144 GB
    Interconnect: Infiniband FDR
    Operating System: CentOS
    Compiler: Intel Cluster Studio
    Math Library: Intel MKL 11.0
    MPI: Intel MPI
    Ranking: 83

84. **MVS-10P - RSC Tornado, Xeon E5-2690 8C 2.900GHz, InfinibandFDR, Intel Xeon Phi SE10X**
    Site: Joint Supercomputer Center
    Country: Russia
    Image URL: None
    Manufacturer: RSC Group
    Cores: 28,704
    Linpack Performance (Rmax): 375.7 TFlop/s
    Theoretical Peak (Rpeak): 523.6 TFlop/s
    Power: 222.70 kW
    Memory: 16,640 GB
    Interconnect: Infiniband FDR
    Operating System: Linux
    Compiler: Intel C++ Composer XE for Linux 2013
    Math Library: Intel Math Kernel Library for Linux 11.0
    MPI: Intel MPI Library for Linux 4.1
    Ranking: 84

85. **Cluster Platform SL250s Gen8, Xeon E5-2670 8C 2.600GHz, 10G Ethernet**
    Site: Energy Company
    Country: United States
    Image URL: None
    Manufacturer: Hewlett-Packard
    Cores: 25,568
    Linpack Performance (Rmax): 371.7 TFlop/s
    Theoretical Peak (Rpeak): 531. 8 TFlop/s
    Interconnect: 10G Ethernet
    Operating System: Linux
    Ranking: 85

86. **Cluster Platform DL360p Gen8, Xeon E5-2640 6C 2.500GHz, Gigabit Ethernet**
    Site: Service Provider
    Country: China
    Image URL: None
    Manufacturer: Hewlett-Packard
    Cores: 39,228
    Linpack Performance (Rmax): 364.5 TFlop/s
    Theoretical Peak (Rpeak): 784.6 TFlop/s
    Interconnect: Gigabit Ethernet
    Operating System: Linux
    Ranking: 86

87. **BlueGene/Q, Power BQC 16C 1.60 GHz, Custom**
    Site: IBM Rochester
    Country: United States
    Image URL: None
    Manufacturer: IBM
    Cores: 32,768 Linpack Performance (Rmax): 357.8 TFlop/s
    Theoretical Peak (Rpeak): 419.4 TFlop/s
    Power: 164.38 kW
    Memory: 32,768 GB
    Interconnect: Custom Interconnect
    Operating System: Linux
    Ranking: 87

88. **BlueGene/Q, Power BQC 16C 1.60 GHz, Custom**
    Site: IBM Rochester
    Country: United States
    Image URL: None
    Manufacturer: IBM
    Cores: 32, 768 Linpack Performance (Rmax): 357.8 TFlop/s
    Theoretical Peak (Rpeak): 419.4 TFlop/s
    Power: 164.38 kW
    Memory: 32,768 GB

Interconnect: Custom Interconnect
Operating System: Linux
Ranking: 88

89. **BGQ - BlueGene/Q, Power BQC 16C 1.600GHz, Custom Interconnect**
    Site: Southern Ontario Smart Computing Innovation Consortium/ University of Toronto.
    Country: Canada
    Image URL: None
    Manufacturer: IBM
    Cores: 32, 768
    Linpack Performance (Rmax): 357.8 TFlop/s
    Theoretical Peak (Rpeak): 419.4 TFlop/s
    Power: 164.38 kW
    Interconnect: Custom Interconnect
    Operating System: Linux
    Ranking: 89

90. **Cluster Platform DL360e Gen8, Xeon E5-2450L 8C 1.800GHz, Gigabit Ethernet**
    Site: Software Company
    Country: United States
    Image URL: None
    Manufacturer: Hewlett-Packard
    Cores: 62,848
    Linpack Performance (Rmax): 354.5 TFlop/s
    Theoretical Peak (Rpeak): 905.0 TFlop/s
    Interconnect: Gigabit Ethernet
    Operating System: Linux
    Ranking: 90

91. **Athos - iDataPlex DX360M4, Intel Xeon E5-2697v2 12C 2.700GHz, Infiniband FDR14**
    Site: EDF R&D
    Country: France
    Image URL: None
    Manufacturer: IBM
    Cores: 18,144
    Linpack Performance (Rmax): 352.7 TFlop/s
    Theoretical Peak (Rpeak): 391.9 TFlop/s
    Power: 347.27 kW
    Interconnect: Infiniband FDR14
    Operating System: Linux
    Ranking: 91

92. **Cluster Platform DL360e Gen8, Xeon E5-2450L 8C 1.800GHz, Gigabit Ethernet**
    Site: Software Company (M)
    Country: United States
    Image URL: None
    Manufacturer: Hewlett-Packard

Cores: 62,416
Linpack Performance (Rmax): 352.0 TFlop/s
Theoretical Peak (Rpeak): 898.8 TFlop/s
Interconnect: Gigabit Ethernet
Operating System: Linux
Ranking: 92

93. **Pershing - iDataPlex DX360M4, Xeon E5-2670 8C 2.600GHz, Infiniband FDR**
Site: Army Research Laboratory DoD Supercomputing Resource Center (ARLDSRC)
Country: United States ▆▆
Image URL: None
Manufacturer: IBM
Cores: 20,160
Linpack Performance (Rmax): 350.7 TFlop/s
Theoretical Peak (Rpeak): 419.3 TFlop/s
Power: 400.68 kW
Interconnect: Infiniband FDR
Operating System: Linux
Ranking: 93

94. **Cab - Xtreme-X, Xeon E5-2670 8C 2.600GHz, Infiniband QDR**
Site: Lawrence Livermore National Laboratory
Country: United States ▆▆
Image URL: None
Manufacturer: Cray Inc.
Cores: 20,480
Linpack Performance (Rmax): 347.4 TFlop/s
Theoretical Peak (Rpeak): 426.0 TFlop/s
Power: 421.20 kW
Memory: 40,960 GB
Interconnect: Infiniband QDR
Operating System: Linux
Compiler: Intel 12.1
MPI: MVAPICH 1.2
Ranking: 94

95. **Luna - Xtreme-X GreenBlade GB512X, Xeon E5-2670 8C 2.600GHz, Infiniband QDR**
Site: Los Alamos National Laboratory
Country: United States ▆▆
Image URL: http://www.lanl.gov/orgs/hpc/images/luna_side_lg.jpg
Manufacturer: Cray Inc.
Cores: 20,480
Linpack Performance (Rmax): 347.4 TFlop/s
Theoretical Peak (Rpeak): 426.0 TFlop/s
Power: 448.00 kW
Memory: 40,960 GB

Interconnect: Infiniband QDR
Operating System: RHEL 6.2
Compiler: Intel 12.1
MPI: MVAPICH 1.2
Ranking: 95

96. **airain - Bullx B510, Xeon E5-2680 8C 2.700GHz, Infiniband QDR**
    Site: Commissariat a l'Energie Atomique (CEA)/CCRT
    Country: France ▌▌
    Image URL: http://www-ccrt.cea.fr/fr/moyen_de_calcul/img/airain.jpg
    Manufacturer: Bull SA
    Cores: 18,144
    Linpack Performance(Rmax): 346.1 TFlop/s
    Theoretical Peak (Rpeak): 391.9 TFlop/s
    Power: 500.00 kW
    Memory: 72, 576 GB
    Interconnect: Infiniband QDR
    Operating System: bullx SUperCOmputer Suite A.E.2.1
    Ranking: 96

97. **SGI ICE X, Xeon E5-2670 8C 2.600GHz, Infiniband FDR**
    Site: Air Force Research Laboratory
    Country: United States ▤
    Image URL: None
    Manufacturer: SGI
    Cores: 18,432
    Linpack Performance (Rmax): 339.5 TFlop/s
    Theoretical Peak (Rpeak): 383.4 TFlop/s
    Memory: 36,000 GB
    Interconnect: Infiniband FDR
    Operating System: SUSE Linux Enterprise Server 11
    Ranking: 97

98. **Pecos - Xtreme-X, Xeon E5-2670 8C 2.600GHz, Infiniband QDR**
    Site: Sandia National Laboratories
    Country: United States ▤
    Image URL: None
    Manufacturer: Cray Inc.
    Cores: 19,712
    Linpack Performance (Rmax): 336.8 TFlop/s
    Theoretical Peak (Rpeak): 410.0 TFlop/s
    Power: 421.20 kW
    Memory: 39, 424 GB
    Interconnect: Infiniband QDR
    Operating System: Linux
    Compiler: Intel 12.1
    MPI: MVAPICH 1.2
    Ranking: 98

99. **Cluster Platform 3000 BL460c Gen8, Xeon E5-2670 8C 2.60GHz, Infiniband FDR**
    Site: CSIR Fourth Paradigm Institute
    Country: India
    Image URL: None
    Manufacturer: Hewlett-Packard
    Cores: 17,408
    Linpack Performance(Rmax): 334.4 TFlop/s
    Theoretical Peak (Rpeak): 362.1 TFlop/s
    Power: 386.56 kW
    Interconnect: Infiniband FDR
    Operating System: Linux
    Ranking: 99

100. **Chama - Xtreme-X GreenBlade GB512X, Xeon E5-2670 8C 2.600GHz, Infiniband QDR**
    Site: Sandia National Laboratories
    Country: United States
    Image URL: None
    Manufacturer: Cray Inc.
    Cores: 19,680
    Linpack Performance (Rmax): 332.0 TFlop/s
    Theoretical Peak (Rpeak): 409.3 TFlop/s
    Power: 453.60 kW
    Memory: 39,360 GB
    Interconnect: Infiniband QDR
    Operating System: RHEL 6.2
    Compiler: Intel 12.1
    MPI: MVAPICH 1.2
    Ranking: 100

101. **Kilrain - iDataPlex DX360M4, Xeon E5-2670 8C 2.600GHz, Infiniband FDR**
    Site: Navy DSRC
    Country: United States
    Image URL: None
    Manufacturer: IBM
    Cores: 18,816
    Linpack Performance(Rmax): 327.3 TFlop/s
    Theoretical Peak (Rpeak): 391.4 TFlop/s
    Power: 373.97 kW
    Interconnect: Infiniband FDR
    Operating System: Linux
    Ranking: 101

102. **Haise - iDataPlex DX360M4, Xeon E5-2670 8C 2.600GHz, Infiniband FDR**
    Site: Navy DSRC
    Country: United States
    Image URL: None

Manufacturer: IBM
Cores: 18,816
Linpack Performance (Rmax): 327.3 TFlop/s
Theoretical Peak (Rpeak): 391.4 TFlop/s
Power: 373.97 kW
Interconnect: Infiniband FDR
Operating System: Linux
Ranking: 102

103. **Cluster Platform DL360e Gen8, Xeon E5-2450L 8C 1.800GHz, Gigabit Ethernet**
    Site: Software Company (M)
    Country: United States
    Image URL: None
    Manufacturer: Hewlett-Packard
    Cores: 57,648
    Linpack Performance (Rmax): 325.1 TFlop/s
    Theoretical Peak (Rpeak): 830.1 TFlop/s
    Interconnect: Gigabit Ethernet
    Operating System: Linux
    Ranking: 103

104. **Zeus - SGI ICE 8400EX, Xeon X5690 6C 3.470GHz, Infiniband QDR**
    Site: NOAA Environmental Security Computer Center
    Country: United States
    Image URL: None
    Manufacturer: SGI
    Cores: 27,600
    Linpack Performance (Rmax): 322.9 TFlop/s
    Theoretical Peak (Rpeak): 382.6 TFlop/s
    Memory: 55, 296 GB
    Interconnect: Infiniband QDR
    Operating System: Linux
    Compiler: Intel
    Math Library: MKL
    MPI: SGI MPI
    Ranking: 104

105. **Keeneland - Cluster Platform SL250s Gen8, Xeon E5-2670 8C 2.600GHz, Infiniband FDR, NVIDIA 2090**
    Site: Georgia Institute Of Technology
    Country: United States
    Image URL: None
    System URL: http://keeneland.gatech.edu/
    Manufacturer: Hewlett-Packard
    Cores: 16,896
    Linpack Performance (Rmax): 319.6 TFlop/s

Theoretical Peak (Rpeak): 614.5 TFlop/s
Memory: 8,448 GB
Interconnect: Infiniband FDR
Operating System: Linux
Ranking: 105

106. **iDataPlex DX360M4, Xeon E5-2670 8C 2.600GHz, Infiniband FDR**
Site: National Center for Medium Range Weather Forecast
Country: India
Image URL: http://www.redbooks.ibm.com/Redbooks.nsf/e03826cbbba0636c852569d000606d00/8e46f4f6165a2373852579a2004d5abe/Contents/7.39A2?OpenElement&FieldElemFormat=jpg
Manufacturer: IBM
Cores: 16,832
Linpack Performance (Rmax): 318.4 TFlop/s
Theoretical Peak (Rpeak): 350.1 TFlop/s
Power: 349.60 kW
Interconnect: Infiniband FDR
Operating System: Linux
Ranking: 106

107. **Blackthorn - Bullx B510, Xeon E5-2670 8C 2.600GHz, Infiniband QDR**
Site: Atomic Weapons Establishment
Country: United Kingdom
Image URL: None
Manufacturer: Bull SA
Cores: 17,856
Linpack Performance (Rmax): 318.0 TFlop/s
Theoretical Peak (Rpeak): 371.4 TFlop/s
Power: 446.40 kW
Memory: 53,568 GB
Interconnect: Infiniband QDR
Operating System: Linux
Compiler: icc
Math Library: MKL
MPI: Intel MPI
Ranking: 107

108. **Fujitsu PRIMERGY CX400, Intel Xeon E5-2697v2 12C 2.700GHz, Infiniband FDR, Xeon Phi 3120p**
Site: Information Technology Center, Nagoya University
Country: Japan
Image URL: None
Manufacturer: Fujitsu
Cores: 23, 478
Linpack Performance (Rmax): 317.9 TFlop/s

Theoretical Peak (Rpeak): 465.6 TFlop/s
Memory: 23,296 GB
Interconnect: Infiniband FDR
Operating System: Linux
Compiler: Intel Composer XE 2013
Math Library: Intel MKL
MPI: Intel MPI
Ranking: 108

109. **Cluster Platform DL360p Gen8, Xeon E5-2630 6C 2.300GHz, Gigabit Ethernet**
     Site: IT Services Provider
     Country: China
     Image URL: None
     Manufacturer: Hewlett-Packard
     Cores: 36,792
     Linpack Performance (Rmax): 317.8 TFlop/s
     Theoretical Peak (Rpeak): 677.0 TFlop/s
     Interconnect: Gigabit Ethernet
     Operating System: Linux
     Ranking: 109

110. **Haedam - Cray XE6 12-core 2.1 GHz**
     Site: Korea Meteorological Administration
     Country: South Korea
     Image URL: None
     Manufacturer: Cray Inc.
     Cores: 45, 120
     Linpack Performance (Rmax): 316.4 TFlop/s
     Theoretical Peak (Rpeak): 379.0 TFlop/s
     Interconnect: Cray Gemini Interconnect
     Operating System: Linux
     Ranking: 110

111. **Haeon - Cray XE6 12-core 2.1 GHz**
     Site: Korea Meteorological Administration
     Country: South Korea
     Image URL: None
     Manufacturer: Cray Inc.
     Cores: 45, 120
     Linpack Performance (Rmax): 316.4 TFlop/s
     Theoretical Peak (Rpeak): 379.0 TFlop/s
     Interconnect: Cray Gemini Interconnect
     Operating System: Linux
     Ranking: 111

112. **Monte Rosa - Cray XE6, Opteron 6272 16C 2.10 GHz, Cray Gemini interconnect**
     Site: Swiss National Supercomputing Centre (CSCS)
     Country: Switzerland
     Image URL: None
     Manufacturer: Cray Inc.
     Cores: 47,840
     Linpack Performance (Rmax): 316.2 TFlop/s
     Theoretical Peak (Rpeak): 401.9 TFlop/s
     Power: 780.00kW
     Interconnect: Cray Gemini Interconnect
     Operating System: Linux
     Ranking: 112

113. **Cluster Platform DL380p Gen8, Xeon E5-2640 6C 2.500GHz, Gigabit Ethernet**
     Site: IT Service Provider (D)
     Country: United States
     Image URL: None
     Manufacturer: Hewlett-Packard
     Cores: 32,604
     Linpack Performance (Rmax): 311.6 TFlop/s
     Theoretical Peak (Rpeak): 652.1 TFlop/s
     Interconnect: Gigabit Ethernet
     Operating System: Linux
     Ranking: 113

114. **Cluster Platform DL360p Gen8, Xeon E5-2640 6C 2.500GHz, Gigabit Ethernet**
     Site: IT Service Provider (B)
     Country: United States
     Image URL: None
     Manufacturer: Hewlett-Packard
     Cores: 32,436
     Linpack Performance (Rmax): 310.2 TFlop/s
     Theoretical Peak (Rpeak): 648.7 TFlop/s
     Interconnect: Gigabit Ethernet
     Operating System: Linux
     Ranking: 114

115. **Hercules - iDataPlex DX360M4, Xeon E5-2670 8C 2.600GHz, Infiniband FDR**
     Site: Army Research Laboratory DoD Supercomputing Resource Center (ARL DSRC)
     Country: United States
     Image URL: None
     Manufacturer: IBM
     Cores: 17,472
     Linpack Performance (Rmax): 304.0 TFlop/s
     Theoretical Peak (Rpeak): 363.4 TFlop/s
     Power: 347.26 kW

Interconnect: Infiniband FDR

Operating System: Linux

Ranking: 115

116. **Cluster Platform DL380p Gen8, Xeon E5-2640 6C 2.500GHz, Gigabit Ethernet**

    Site: IT Service Provider

    Country: United States

    Image URL: None

    Manufacturer: Hewlett-Packard

    Cores: 31,524

    Linpack Performance(Rmax): 302.6 TFlop/s

    Theoretical Peak (Rpeak): 630.5 TFlop/s

    Interconnect: Gigabit Ethernet

    Operating System: Linux

    Ranking: 116

117. **LOEWE-CSC - Supermicro Cluster, QC Opteron 2.1 GHz, ATI Radeon GPU, Infiniband**

    Site: Universitaet Frankfurt

    Country: Germany

    Image URL: None

    Manufacturer: Clustervision/Supermicro

    Cores: 16,368

    Linpack Performance (Rmax): 299.3 TFlop/s

    Theoretical Peak (Rpeak): 508.5 TFlop/s

    Power: 416.78 kW

    Interconnect: Infiniband QDR

    Operating System: Linux

    Ranking: 117

118. **Cluster Platform SL230s Gen8, Xeon E5-2670 8C 2.600GHz, Gigabit Ethernet**

    Site: Banking(M)

    Country: United States

    Image URL: None

    Manufacturer: Hewlett-Packard

    Cores: 29,696

    Linpack Performance (Rmax): 298.7 TFlop/s

    Theoretical Peak (Rpeak): 617.7 TFlop/s

    Interconnect: Gigabit Ethernet

    Operating System: Linux

    Ranking: 118

119. **Gaea C1 - Cray XE6, Opteron 6276 16C 2.30GHz, Cray Gemini interconnect**

    Site: NOAA/ Oak Ridge National Laboratory

    Country: United States

    Image URL: http://www.ncrc.gov/wp-content/uploads/2010/11/gaea1-150x100.jpg

    Manufacturer: Cray Inc.

    Cores: 41,984

Linpack Performance (Rmax): 296.0 TFlop/s
Theoretical Peak (Rpeak): 386.3 TFlop/s
Memory: 83,968 GB
Interconnect: Cray Gemini Interconnect
Operating System: Cray Linux Environment
Compiler: CCE
MPI: CRAY MPICH2 XT version 5.5.0 (ANL base 1.5a2)
Ranking: 119

120. **Gottfried - Cray XC30, Intel Xeon E5-2695v2 12C 2.400GHz, Aries interconnect**
Site: HLRN at Universitaet Hannover/RRZN
Country: Germany
Image URL: None
Manufacturer: Cray Inc.
Cores: 17, 856
Linpack Performance (Rmax): 295.7 TFlop/s
Theoretical Peak (Rpeak): 342.8 TFlop/s
Interconnect: Aries Interconnect
Operating System: Cray Linux Environment
Ranking: 120

121. **Konrad - Cray XC30, Intel Xeon E5-2695v2 12C 2.400GHz, Aries interconnect**
Site: HLRN at ZIB/ Konrad Zuse-Zentrum fuerInformationstechnik
Country: Germany
Image URL: http://www.zib.de/typo3temp/pics/15f091e27d.jpg
Manufacturer: Cray Inc
Cores: 17,856
Linpack Performance (Rmax): 295.7 TFlop/s
Theoretical Peak (Rpeak): 342.8 TFlop/s
Interconnect: Aries Interconnect
Operating System: Cray Linux Environment
Ranking: 121

122. **Cray XE6 12-core 2.2 GHz**
Site: Government
Country: United States
Image URL: None
Manufacturer: Cray Inc
Cores: 45,504
Linpack Performance (Rmax): 295.5 TFlop/s
Theoretical Peak (Rpeak): 400.4 TFlop/s
Interconnect: Cray Gemini Interconnect
Operating System: Linux
Ranking: 122

123. **Cluster Platform SL390s G7, Xeon X5650 6C 2.66GHz, Gigabit Ethernet, NVIDIA 2090**
    Site: IT Provider (P)
    Country: United States
    Image URL: None
    Manufacturer: Hewlett-Packard
    Cores: 31,680
    Linpack Performance (Rmax): 293.9 TFlop/s
    Theoretical Peak (Rpeak): 1,049.5 TFlop/s
    Interconnect: Gigabit Ethernet
    Operating System: Linux
    Ranking: 123

124. **Cluster Platform DL360p Gen8, Xeon E5-2620 6C 2.000GHz, Gigabit Ethernet**
    Site: IT Services Provider
    Country: United States
    Image URL: None
    Manufacturer: Hewlett-Packard
    Cores: 39,264
    Linpack Performance (Rmax): 291.8 TFlop/s
    Theoretical Peak (Rpeak): 628.2 TFlop/s
    Interconnect: Gigabit Ethernet
    Operating System: Linux
    Ranking: 124

125. **Cluster Platform DL360p Gen8, Xeon E5-2640 6C 2.500GHz, Gigabit Ethernet**
    Site: IT Service Provider (D)
    Country: United States
    Image URL: None
    Manufacturer: Hewlett-Packard
    Cores: 30,000
    Linpack Performance: 289.8 TFlop/s
    Theoretical Peak (Rpeak): 600.0 TFlop/s
    Interconnect: Gigabit Ethernet
    Operating System: Linux
    Ranking: 125

126. **Cluster Platform SL250s Gen8, Xeon E5-2670 8C 2.600GHz, Infiniband QDR**
    Site: Energy Company
    Country: United States
    Image URL: None
    Manufacturer: Hewlett-Packard
    Cores: 18,688
    Linpack Performance (Rmax): 289.7 TFlop/s
    Theoretical Peak (Rpeak): 388.7 TFlop/s
    Interconnect: Infiniband QDR
    Operating System: Linux
    Ranking: 126

127. **RSC Tornado SUSU - RSC Tornado, Xeon X5680 6C 3.330GHz, Infiniband QDR, Intel Xeon Phi SE10X**
Site: South Ural State University
Country: Russia
Image URL: http://www.susu.ac.ru/sites/default/files/styles/large/public/field/image/mvs-10p20supercomputer20based20on20rsc20tornado_jscc_1_resize.jpg?itok=nmB6f8Vm
Manufacturer: RSC Group
Cores: 28,032
Linpack Performance (Rmax): 288.2 TFlop/s
Theoretical Peak (Rpeak): 473.6 TFlop/s
Power: 294.00 kW
Memory: 12,288 GB
Interconnect: Infiniband QDR
Operating System: CentOS
Compiler: Intel Composer XE 2013
Math Library: Intel MKL
MPI: Intel MPI
Ranking: 127
128. **Cluster Platform DL360p Gen8, Xeon E5-2640 6C 2.500GHz, Gigabit Ethernet**
Site: Logistic Services (E)
Country: United States
Image URL: None
Manufacturer: Hewlett-Packard
Cores: 29,580
Linpack Performance (Rmax): 286.2 TFlop/s
Theoretical Peak (Rpeak): 591.6 TFlop/s
Interconnect: Gigabit Ethernet
Operating System: Linux
Ranking: 128
129. **Gordon - Xtreme-X GreenBlade GB512X, Xeon E5-2670 8C 2.600GHz, Infiniband QDR**
Site: UCSD/San Diego Supercomputing Center
Country: United States
Image URL: http://www.sdsc.edu/assets/images/res_triton.jpg
Manufacturer: Cray Inc
Cores: 16,160
Linpack Performance (Rmax): 285.8 TFlop/s
Theoretical Peak (Rpeak): 336.1 TFlop/s
Power: 358.40 kW
Memory: 32,320 GB
Interconnect: Infiniband QDR
Operating System: RHEL 6.2
Compiler: Intel 12.1
MPI: MVAPICH 2 v1.8
Ranking: 129

130. **Cluster Platform SL230s Gen8, Intel Xeon E5-2670v2 10C 2.500GHz, Infiniband FDR**
     Site: Indian Institute of Technology- Kanpur
     Country: India
     Image URL: http://www.iitk.ac.in/ccnew/index.php/hpc
     Manufacturer: Hewlett-Packard
     Cores: 15,360
     Linpack Performance (Rmax): 282.6 TFlop/s
     Theoretical Peak (Rpeak): 307.2 TFlop/s
     Power: 316.00 kW
     Memory: 98,304 GB
     Interconnect: Infiniband FDR
     Operating System: Linux
     Ranking: 130

131. **Cluster Platform SL250s Gen8, Xeon E5-2670 8C 2.600GHz, Infiniband QDR**
     Site: Geoscience (P)
     Country: United States
     Image URL: None
     Manufacturer: Hewlett-Packard
     Cores: 18,176
     Linpack Performance: 281.8 TFlop/s
     Theoretical Peak (Rpeak): 378.1 TFlop/s
     Interconnect: Infiniband QDR
     Operating System: Linux
     Ranking: 131

132. **Cluster Platform 3000 BL460c Gen8, Xeon E5-2670 8C 2.600GHz, 10G Ethernet**
     Site: IT Service Provider (B)
     Country: United States
     Image URL: None
     Manufacturer: Hewlett-Packard
     Cores: 19,712
     Linpack Performance (Rmax): 279.7 TFlop/s
     Theoretical Peak (Rpeak): 410.0 TFlop/s
     Interconnect: 10G Ethernet
     Operating System: Linux
     Ranking: 132

133. **Cluster Platform SL250s Gen8, Xeon E5-2670 8C 2.600GHz, Infiniband QDR**
     Site: Geoscience (P)
     Country: United States
     Image URL: None
     Manufacturer: Hewlett-Packard
     Cores: 17,920
     Linpack Performance (Rmax): 277.8 TFlop/s
     Theoretical Peak (Rpeak): 372.7 TFlop/s

Interconnect: Infiniband QDR
Operating System: Linux
Ranking: 133

134. **HA-PACS TCA - Cray 3623G4-SM Cluster, Intel Xeon E5-2680v2 10C 2.800GHz, Infiniband QDR, NVIDIA K20x**
    Site: Center for Computational Sciences, University of Tsukuba
    Country: Japan
    Image URL: None
    System URL: http://www.ccs.tsukuba.ac.jp/CCS/eng/research-activities/projects/ha-pacs
    Manufacturer: Cray Inc
    Cores: 4,864
    Linpack Performance: 277.1 TFlop/s
    Theoretical Peak (Rpeak): 364.3 TFlop/s
    Power: 93.00 kW
    Memory: 8,192 GB
    Interconnect: Infiniband QDR
    Operating System: CentOS
    Compiler: GCC
    Math Library: Intel MKL
    MPI: OpenMPI
    Ranking: 134

135. **Cluster Platform 3000 BL460c Gen8, Xeon E5-2670 8C 2.600GHz, 10G Ethernet**
    Site: Service Provider
    Country: United States
    Image URL: None
    Manufacturer: Hewlett-Packard
    Cores: 19,456
    Linpack Performance (Rmax): 276.4 TFlop/s
    Theoretical Peak (Rpeak): 404.7 TFlop/s
    Interconnect: 10G Ethernet
    Operating System: Linux
    Ranking: 135

136. **JUROPA - Sun Constellation, NovaScale R422-E2, Intel Xeon X5570, 2.93 GHz, Sun M9/ Mellanox QDR Infiniband/Partec Parastation**
    Site: Forschungszentrum Juelich (FZJ)
    Country: Germany
    Image URL: http://www.fz-juelich.de/SharedDocs/Bilder/IAS/JSC/EN/galeries/Juropa/Teaser/ HPC-FF-Teaser.jpg;jsessionid=D78D6C3F56490D2107E1E98F709C6315?__blob=poster, http://www.fz-juelich.de/SharedDocs/Bilder/IAS/JSC/EN/galeries/Juropa/Teaser/JUROPA-teaser.jpg;jsessionid=D78D6C3F56490D2107E1E98F709C6315?__blob=poster
    System URL: http://www.fz-juelich.de/ias/jsc/EN/Expertise/Supercomputers/JUROPA/ JUROPA_node.html
    Manufacturer: Bull SA

Cores: 26,304
Linpack Performance(Rmax): 274.8 TFlop/s
Theoretical Peak (Rpeak): 308.3 TFlop/s
Power: 1,549.00 kW
Memory: 80,806 GB
Interconnect: Infiniband QDR Sun M9/Mellanox/ParTec
Operating System: SUSE Linux
Ranking: 136

137. **TachyonII - Sun Blade x6048, X6275, IB QDR M9 switch, Sun HPC stack Linux edition**
Site: KISTI Supercomputing Center
Country: South Korea
Image URL: None
Manufacturer: Sun Microsystems
Cores: 26,232
Linpack Performance (Rmax): 274.8 TFlop/s
Theoretical Peak (Rpeak): 307.4 TFlop/s
Power: 1,275.00 kW
Memory: 157,392 GB
Interconnect: Infiniband
Operating System: CentOS
Ranking: 137

138. **TEIDE-HPC - Fujitsu PRIMERGY CX250 S1, Xeon E5-2670 8C 2.600GHz, Infiniband QDR**
Site: Instituto Tecnologico y de Energias Renovables S.A.
Country: Spain
Image URL: http://www.iter.es/pub/imagenes/ficha/imagenes_superordenador_red_(1)_cab39268.jpg, http://www.iter.es/pub/imagenes/ficha/imagenes_superordenador_red_(2)_a18d0edd.jpg, http://www.iter.es/pub/imagenes/ficha/imagenes_superordenador_red_(3)_42c58d01.jpg
Manufacturer: Fujitsu
Cores: 16,384
Linpack Performance (Rmax): 274.0 TFlop/s
Theoretical Peak (Rpeak): 340.8 TFlop/s
Power: 312.00 kW
Memory: 33,664 GB
Interconnect: Infiniband QDR
Operating System: CentOS
Compiler: Intel Composer XE for Linux Version 2013 SPI
Math Library: Intel Math Kernel Library for Linux Version 11.1
MPI: Intel MPI Library for Linux Version 4.1 (Update 1)
Ranking: 138

139. **Todi - Cray XK7, Opteron 6272 16C 2.100GHz, Cray Gemini interconnect, NVIDIA Tesla K20 Kepler**
     Site: Swiss National Supercomputing Centre (CSCS)
     Country: Switzerland
     Image URL: None
     Manufacturer: Cray Inc.
     Cores: 8,160
     Linpack Performance (Rmax): 273.7 TFlop/s
     Theoretical Peak (Rpeak): 392.9 TFlop/s
     Power: 129.40 kW
     Interconnect: Cray Gemini Interconnect **Operating System:** Cray Linux Environment
     Ranking: 139

140. **Laure - SGI ICE X, Xeon E5-2670 8C 2.600GHz, Infiniband FDR**
     Site: TOTAL
     Country: United States
     Image URL: None
     Manufacturer: SGI
     Cores: 13, 824
     Linpack Performance (Rmax): 271.8 TFlop/s
     Theoretical Peak (Rpeak): 287.5 TFlop/s
     Power: 319.00 kW
     Interconnect: Infiniband FDR
     Operating System: SUSE Linux Enterprise Server 11
     Ranking: 140

141. **Cluster Platform 3000 BL460c Gen8, Xeon E5-2670 8C 2.600GHz, Infiniband FDR**
     Site: Automative Company
     Country: United States
     Image URL: None
     Manufacturer: Hewlett-Packard
     Cores: 15, 360
     Linpack Performance (Rmax): 271.2 TFlop/s
     Theoretical Peak (Rpeak): 319.5 TFlop/s
     Interconnect: Infiniband FDR
     Operating System: Linux
     Ranking: 141

142. **Dark Bridge - Appro Xtreme-X Supercomputer, Xeon E5-2670 8C 2.600GHz, Infiniband QDR**
     Site: Sandia National Laboratories
     Country: United States
     Image URL: None
     Manufacturer: Cray Inc.
     Cores: 14,720
     Linpack Performance (Rmax): 268.1 TFlop/s

Theoretical Peak (Rpeak): 306.2 TFlop/s
Power: 315.90 kW
Memory: 62,208 GB
Interconnect: Infiniband QDR
Operating System: Linux
Compiler: Intel 12.1
MPI: MVAPICH 1.2
Ranking: 142

143. **Dark Sand - Appro Xtreme-X Supercomputer, Xeon E5-2670 8C 2.600GHz, Infiniband QDR**

     Site: Sandia National Laboratories
     Country: United States
     Image URL: None
     Manufacturer: Cray Inc.
     Cores: 14,720
     Linpack Performance (Rmax): 268.1 TFlop/s
     Theoretical Peak (Rpeak): 306.2 TFlop/s
     Power: 388.80 kW
     Memory: 62,208 GB
     Interconnect: Infiniband QDR
     Operating System: Linux
     Compiler: Intel 12.1
     MPI: MVAPICH 1.2
     Ranking: 143

144. **Cluster Platform 3000 BL460c Gen8, Xeon E5-2650 8C 2.000GHz, 10G Ethernet**

     Site: Cerner Corp.
     Country: United States
     Image URL: None
     Manufacturer: Hewlett-Packard
     Cores: 25, 856
     Linpack Performance (Rmax): 266.9 TFlop/s
     Theoretical Peak (Rpeak): 413.7 TFlop/s
     Memory: 10G Ethernet
     Operating System: Linux
     Ranking: 144

145. **Zeus - Cluster Platform SL390/BL2x220, Xeon X5650 6C 2.660GHz, Infiniband QDR, NVIDIA 2090**

     Site: Cyfronet
     Country: Poland
     Image URL: http://www.cyfronet.krakow.pl/zalacznik/564/2
     Manufacturer: Hewlett-Packard
     Cores: 25,468
     Linpack Performance (Rmax): 266.9 TFlop/s

Theoretical Peak (Rpeak): 373.9 TFlop/s
Interconnect: Infiniband QDR
Operating System: Linux
Ranking: 145

146. **Cluster Platform 3000 BL460c Gen8, Xeon E5-2670 8C 2.600GHz, 10G Ethernet**
Site: IT Service Provider (D)
Country: United States
Image URL: None
Manufacturer: Hewlett-Packard
Cores: 18,440
Linpack Performance (Rmax): 263.2 TFlop/s
Theoretical Peak (Rpeak): 383.6 TFlop/s
Interconnect: 10G Ethernet
Operating System: Linux
Ranking: 146

147. **Cluster Platform 3000 BL460c Gen8, Xeon E5-2670 8C 2.600GHz, 10G Ethernet**
Site: IT Service Provider (C)
Country: Canada
Image URL: None
Manufacturer: Hewlett-Packard
Cores: 18,432
Linpack Performance (Rmax): 263.1 TFlop/s
Theoretical Peak (Rpeak): 383.4 TFlop/s
Interconnect: 10G Ethernet
Operating System: Linux
Ranking: 147

148. **GPC - xSeries iDataPlex, Xeon E5540 4C 2.53GHz, Infiniband**
Site: SciNet/University of Toronto/Compute Canada
Country: Canada
Image URL: http://www.scinethpc.ca/wp-content/uploads/2011/08/201006scinet09-222x160.jpg
Manufacturer: IBM
Cores: 30, 912
Linpack Performance (Rmax): 261.6 TFlop/s
Theoretical Peak (Rpeak): 312.8 TFlop/s
Power: 1,030.00 kW
Interconnect: Infiniband
Operating System: Linux
Ranking: 148

149. **Cluster Platform DL380p Gen8, Xeon E5-2630 6C 2.300GHz, Gigabit Ethernet**
Site: IT Service Provider (B)
Country: United States
Image URL: None

Manufacturer: Hewlett-Packard
Cores: 29,064
Linpack Performance (Rmax): 259.3 TFlop/s
Theoretical Peak (Rpeak): 534.8 TFlop/s
Interconnect: Gigabit Ethernet
Operating System: Linux
Ranking: 149

150. **Cluster Platform DL380p Gen8, Xeon E5-2650 8C 2.000GHz, Gigabit Ethernet**
Site: Web Content Provider
Country: United States
Image URL: None
Manufacturer: Hewlett-Packard
Cores: 33,920
Linpack Performance (Rmax): 257.9 TFlop/s
Theoretical Peak (Rpeak): 542.7 TFlop/s
Interconnect: Gigabit Ethernet
Operating System: Linux
Ranking: 150

151. **romeo - Bull R421-E3 Cluster, Intel Xeon E5-2650v2 8C 2.600GHz, Infiniband FDR, NVIDIA K20x**
Site: ROMEO HPC Center- Champagne-Ardenne
Country: France
Image URL: https://romeo.univ-reims.fr/userfiles/image/20130919-romeo_930.jpg
Manufacturer: Bull SA
Cores: 5, 720
Linpack Performance (Rmax): 254.9 TFlop/s
Theoretical Peak (Rpeak): 384.1 TFlop/s
Power: 81.41 kW
Memory: 4,160 GB
Interconnect: Infiniband FDR
Operating System: Bullx Linux
Ranking: 151

152. **Plasma Simulator - Hitachi SR16000 Model M1, POWER7 8C 3.836GHz, Custom Interconnect**
Site: National Institute for Fusion Science (NIFS)
Country: Japan
Image URL: None
Manufacturer: Hitachi
Cores: 10, 304
Linpack Performance (Rmax): 253.0 TFlop/s
Theoretical Peak (Rpeak): 316.2 TFlop/s
Power: 708.20 kW
Memory: 41, 216 GB

Interconnect: Custom Interconnect

Operating System: AIX

Ranking: 152

153. **Lonestar 4 - Dell PowerEdge M610 Cluster, Xeon 5680 3.3Ghz, Infiniband QDR**

Site: Texas Advanced Computing Center/Univ of Texas

Country: United States

Image URL: https://www.tacc.utexas.edu/image/image_gallery?img_id=728838&t=1364359433735

System URL: http://www.tacc.utexas.edu/resources/hpc/#lonestar

Manufacturer: Dell

Cores: 22,656

Linpack Performance (Rmax): 251.8 TFlop/s

Theoretical Peak (Rpeak): 301.8 TFlop/s

Interconnect: Infiniband QDR

Operating System: Linux

Ranking: 153

154. **Cluster Platform 3000 BL460c Gen8, Xeon E5-2670 8C 2.600GHz, 10G Ethernet**

Site: IT Service Provider (D)

Country: United States

Image URL: None

Manufacturer: Hewlett-Packard

Cores: 16,872

Linpack Performance (Rmax): 251.8 TFlop/s

Theoretical Peak (Rpeak): 350.9 TFlop/s

Interconnect: 10G Ethernet

Operating System: Linux

Ranking: 154

155. **Camphor - Cray XE6, Opteron 16C 2.50GHz, Cray Gemini interconnect**

Site: Kyoto University

Country: Japan

Image URL: http://www.iimc.kyoto-u.ac.jp/ja/services/comp/images/system-2012.png

Manufacturer: Cray Inc.

Cores: 30,080

Linpack Performance (Rmax): 251.7 TFlop/s

Theoretical Peak (Rpeak): 300.8 TFlop/s

Memory: 60,160 GB

Interconnect: Cray Gemini Interconnect

Operating System: Cray Linux Environment

Ranking: 155

156. **Grifo04 - Itautec Cluster, Xeon X5670 6C 2.930GHz, Infiniband QDR, NVIDIA 2050**

Site: Petroleo Brasileiro S.A

Country: Brazil

Image URL: None

Manufacturer: Itautec
Cores: 17,408
Linpack Performance (Rmax): 251.5 TFlop/s
Theoretical Peak (Rpeak): 563.4 TFlop/s
Power: 365.50 kW
Memory: 12,288 GB
Interconnect: Infiniband QDR
Operating System: Linux
Compiler: Intel (R) Fortran 64 Compiler Version 11.1.075
Math Library: MKL
MPI: openmpi
Ranking: 156

157. **Cluster Platform SL250s Gen8, Xeon E5-2670 8C 2.600GHz, Infiniband FDR**
Site: IT Provider (P)
Country: United States
Image URL: None
Manufacturer: Hewlett-Packard
Cores: 14,192
Linpack Performance (Rmax): 250.6 TFlop/s
Theoretical Peak (Rpeak): 295.2 TFlop/s
Interconnect: Infiniband FDR
Operating System: Linux
Ranking: 157

158. **Cluster Platform SL250s Gen8, Xeon E5-2670 8C 2.600GHz, Infiniband FDR**
Site: IT Provider (P)
Country: United States
Image URL: None
Manufacturer: Hewlett-Packard
Cores: 14,192
Linpack Performance (Rmax): 250.6 TFlop/s
Theoretical Peak (Rpeak): 295.2 TFlop/s
Interconnect: Infiniband FDR
Operating System: Linux
Ranking: 158

159. **CASE-2 - SGI ICE X, Intel Xeon E5-2695v2 12C 2.400GHz, Infiniband FDR**
Site: T-Systems
Country: Germany
Image URL: None
Manufacturer: SGI
Cores: 13, 440
Linpack Performance (Rmax): 245.9 TFlop/s
Theoretical Peak (Rpeak): 258.0 TFlop/s
Power: 236.80 kW

Memory: 71,680 GB
Interconnect: Infiniband FDR
Operating System: SUSE Linux Enterprise Server 11
Ranking: 159

160. **Cluster Platform DL380p Gen8, Xeon E5-2630 6C 2.300GHz, Gigabit Ethernet**
Site: Logistic Services
Country: United States
Image URL: None
Manufacturer: Hewlett-Packard
Cores: 27,156
Linpack Performance (Rmax): 244.2 TFlop/s
Theoretical Peak (Rpeak): 499.7 TFlop/s
Interconnect: Gigabit Ethernet
Operating System: Linux
Ranking: 160

161. **HP POD - Cluster Platform 3000 BL260c G6, X5675 3.06 GHz, Infiniband**
Site: Airbus
Country: France
Image URL: None
Manufacturer: Hewlett-Packard
Cores: 24, 192
Linpack Performance (Rmax): 243.9 TFlop/s
Theoretical Peak (Rpeak): 296.1 TFlop/s
Interconnect: Infiniband QDR
Operating System: Linux
Ranking: 161

162. **Hitachi SR16000 Model M1, POWER7 8C 3.836GHz, Custom**
Site: Institute for Materials Research, TohokuUniversity (IMR)
Country: Japan
Image URL: http://www.imr.tohoku.ac.jp/ja/data/info/results/2012/120328keisan.pdf
Manufacturer: Hitachi
Cores: 10,240
Linpack Performance (Rmax): 243.9 TFlop/s
Theoretical Peak (Rpeak): 306.4 TFlop/s
Power: 556.30 kW
Interconnect: Custom Interconnect
Operating System: AIX
Ranking: 162

163. **Cluster Platform DL360e Gen8, Xeon E5-2450 8C 2.100GHz, Gigabit Ethernet**
Site: Software Company (M)
Country: United States
Image URL: None
Manufacturer: Hewlett-Packard

Cores: 29,920

Linpack Performance (Rmax): 242.9 TFlop/s

Theoretical Peak (Rpeak): 502.7 TFlop/s

Interconnect: Gigabit Ethernet

Operating System: Linux

Ranking: 163

164. **Rackable C2112-4G3 Cluster, Opteron 12 Core 2.10 GHz, Infiniband QDR**

Site: Calcul Canada/ Calcul Quebec/ Universite De Sherbrooke

Country: Canada

Image URL: None

Manufacturer: SGI

Cores: 37, 728

Linpack Performance (Rmax): 240.3 TFlop/s

Theoretical Peak (Rpeak): 316.9 TFlop/s

Memory: 49,125 GB

Interconnect: Infiniband QDR

Operating System: Linux

Ranking: 164

165. **Amazon EC2 Cluster Compute Instances - Amazon EC2 Cluster, Xeon 8C 2.60GHz, 10G Ethernet**

Site: Amazon Web Services

Country: United States

Image URL: None

Manufacturer: Self-made

Cores: 17,024

Linpack Performance (Rmax): 240.1 TFlop/s

Theoretical Peak (Rpeak): 354.1 TFlop/s

Memory: 65,968 GB

Interconnect: 10G Ethernet

Operating System: Linux

Ranking: 165

166. **Wilkes - Dell T620 Cluster, Intel Xeon E5-2630v2 6C 2.600GHz, Infiniband FDR, NVIDIA K20**

Site: Cambridge University

Country: United Kingdom

Image URL: None

Manufacturer: Dell

Cores: 5,120

Linpack Performance (Rmax): 239.9 TFlop/s

Theoretical Peak (Rpeak): 367.6 TFlop/s

Memory: 16,384 GB

Interconnect: Infiniband FDR

Operating System: Linux

Compiler: Intel
Math Library: Intel MKL
MPI: Intel MPI
Ranking: 166

167. **Moonlight - Xtreme-X, Xeon E5-2670 8C 2.600GHz, Infiniband QDR, NVIDIA 2090**
Site: Los Alamos National Laboratory
Country: United States
Image URL: None
Manufacturer: Cray Inc.
Cores: 14,208
Linpack Performance (Rmax): 238.2 TFlop/s
Theoretical Peak (Rpeak): 492.2 TFlop/s
Power: 226.80 kW
Memory: 9,472 GB
Interconnect: Infiniband QDR
Operating System: Linux
Compiler: Intel 12.1
MPI: OpenMPI 1.4.4-1
Ranking: 167

168. **Fujitsu PRIMERGY CX250 & RX300, Xeon E5-2690 8C 2.900GHz, Infiniband FDR/QDR**
Site: Institute for Molecular Science
Country: Japan
Image URL: http://www.ims.ac.jp/english/know_en/publications/ann_rev_2012/ar201250.pdf
Manufacturer: Fujitsu
Cores: 11,424
Linpack Performance (Rmax): 237.9 TFlop/s
Theoretical Peak (Rpeak): 265.0 TFlop/s
Power: 465.40 kW
Memory: 45, 696 GB
Interconnect: Infiniband FDR/QDR
Operating System: Linux
Compiler: Intel Composer XE 2013 (Update 3)
Math Library: Intel MKL 11.0 (Update 3) + Fujitsu TunedDGEMM
MPI: Intel MPI Library 4.1 (Build 030) Benchmark Data
Ranking: 168

169. **Jade - SGI ICE 8200EX, Xeon E5450 4C 3.000GHz, Infiniband**
Site: Grand Equipement National de Calcul Intensif - Centre Informatique National de l'Enseignement Suprieur (GENCI-CINES)
Country: France
Image URL: None
Manufacturer: SGI
Cores: 23,040
Linpack Performance (Rmax):237.8 TFlop/s

Theoretical Peak (Rpeak): 267.9 TFlop/s

Power: 1,064.00 kW

Memory: 95, 250 GB

Interconnect: Infiniband

Operating System: SLES10 + SGI ProPack 5

Ranking: 169

170. **Lindgren - Cray XE6, Opteron 12 Core 2.10 GHz, Custom**

Site: KTH- Royal Institute of Technology

Country: Sweden

Image URL: https://www.pdc.kth.se/resources/computers/lindgren/pictures/copy_of_superdator.png/@@images/f349413e-9ef9-41df-8e8e-119079dd51b4.png

Manufacturer: Cray Inc.

Cores: 36, 384

Linpack Performance (Rmax): 237.2 TFlop/s

Theoretical Peak (Rpeak): 305.6 TFlop/s

Interconnect: Cray Gemini Interconnect

Operating System: Linux

Ranking: 170

171. **Cluster Platform DL380p Gen8, Xeon E5-2630 6C 2.300GHz, Gigabit Ethernet**

Site: Web-Service Provider

Country: Hong Kong

Image URL: None

Manufacturer: Hewlett-Packard

Cores: 25,920

Linpack Performance (Rmax): 234.2 TFlop/s

Theoretical Peak (Rpeak): 476.9 TFlop/s

Interconnect: Gigabit Ethernet

Operating System: Linux

Ranking: 171

172. **Cluster Platform SL230s Gen8, Xeon E5-2670 8C 2.600GHz, Infiniband FDR**

Site: Manufacturing Company

Country: United States

Image URL: None

Manufacturer: Hewlett-Packard

Cores: 13, 264

Linpack Performance (Rmax): 234.2 TFlop/s

Theoretical Peak (Rpeak): 275.9 TFlop/s

Interconnect: Infiniband FDR

Operating System: Linux

Ranking: 172

173. **Cluster Platform SL230s Gen8, Xeon E5-2670 8C 2.600GHz, Infiniband QDR**

Site: IT Services Provider

Country: United States

Image URL: None

Manufacturer: Hewlett-Packard

Cores: 14, 720

Linpack Performance (Rmax): 232.7 TFlop/s

Theoretical Peak (Rpeak): 306.2 TFlop/s

Interconnect: Infiniband QDR

Operating System: Linux

Ranking: 173

174. **Cluster Platform SL230s Gen8, Xeon E5-2670 8C 2.600GHz, Infiniband QDR**

Site: IT Services Provider

Country: United States

Image URL: None

Manufacturer: Hewlett-Packard

Cores: 14,720

Linpack Performance (Rmax): 232.7 TFlop/s

Theoretical Peak (Rpeak): 306.2 TFlop/s

Interconnect: Infiniband QDR

Operating System: Linux

Ranking: 174

175. **Mustang - Xtreme-X 1320H-LANL, Opteron 12 Core 2.30 GHz, Infiniband QDR**

Site: Los Alamos National Laboratory

Country: United States

Image URL: http://www.lanl.gov/orgs/adtsc/SC11/DomSciBlue/Tomlinson/ MustangUnclassifiedScience.pdf

Manufacturer: Cray Inc

Cores: 37,056

Linpack Performance (Rmax): 230.6 TFlop/s

Theoretical Peak (Rpeak): 340.9 TFlop/s

Power: 540.40 kW

Memory: 102, 400 GB

Interconnect: Infiniband QDR

Operating System: RHEL 6.1

Ranking: 175

176. **iDataPlex DX360M4, Xeon E5-2670 8C 2.600GHz, Infiniband FDR**

Site: Geoscience

Country: United States

Image URL: None

Manufacturer: IBM

Cores: 12,096

Linpack Performance (Rmax): 228.8 TFlop/s

Theoretical Peak (Rpeak): 251.6 TFlop/s

Power: 251.26 kW

Interconnect: Infiniband FDR

Operating System: Linux

Ranking: 176

177. **Cluster Platform DL380e Gen8, Xeon E5-2430L 8C 2.000GHz, Gigabit Ethernet**
Site: Software Company (M)
Country: United States
Image URL: None
Manufacturer: Hewlett-Packard
Cores: 29,556
Linpack Performance (Rmax): 228.8 TFlop/s
Theoretical Peak (Rpeak): 472.9 TFlop/s
Interconnect: Gigabit Ethernet
Operating System: Linux
Ranking: 177

178. **Cluster Platform DL160 Gen8, Xeon E5-2630 6C 2.300GHz, Gigabit Ethernet**
Site: Telecommunication Company
Country: Japan
Image URL: None
Manufacturer: Hewlett-Packard
Cores: 25,056
Linpack Performance (Rmax): 227.2 TFlop/s
Theoretical Peak (Rpeak): 461.0 TFlop/s
Interconnect: Gigabit Ethernet
Operating System: Linux
Ranking: 178

179. **IRIDIS 4 - iDataPlex DX360M4, Xeon E5-2670 8C 2.600GHz, Infiniband FDR**
Site: University of Southampton
Country: United Kingdom
Image URL: None
Manufacturer: IBM
Cores: 12,000
Linpack Performance (Rmax): 227.0 TFlop/s
Theoretical Peak (Rpeak): 249.6 TFlop/s
Power: 249.26 kW
Interconnect: Infiniband FDR
Operating System: Linux
Ranking: 179

180. **Cluster Platform DL380e Gen8, Xeon E5-2430L 8C 2.000GHz, Gigabit Ethernet**
Site: Software Company (M)
Country: United States
Image URL: None
Manufacturer: Hewlett-Packard
Cores: 29,172
Linpack Performance (Rmax): 226.2 TFlop/s
Theoretical Peak (Rpeak): 466.8 TFlop/s
Interconnect: Gigabit Ethernet
Operating System: Linux
Ranking: 180

181. **MOGON - Saxonid 6100, Opteron 6272 16C 2.100GHz, Infiniband QDR**
    Site: Universitaet Mainz
    Country: Germany
    Image URL: None
    Manufacturer: Megware
    Cores: 33, 920
    Linpack Performance (Rmax): 225.6 TFlop/s
    Theoretical Peak (Rpeak): 284.9 TFlop/s
    Power: 467.00 kW
    Memory: 85,330 GB
    Interconnect: Infiniband QDR
    Operating System: Linux
    Compiler: gcc 4.7.0
    Math Library: AMD Acml 5.1.0
    MPI: Intel MPI 4.0.3.008
    Ranking: 181

182. **Cluster Platform DL380e Gen8, Xeon E5-2450 8C 2.100GHz, Gigabit Ethernet**
    Site: Service Provider
    Country: China
    Image URL: None
    Manufacturer: Hewlett-Packard
    Cores: 27, 392
    Linpack Performance (Rmax): 224.7 TFlop/s
    Theoretical Peak (Rpeak): 460.2 TFlop/s
    Interconnect: Gigabit Ethernet
    Operating System: Linux
    Ranking: 182

183. **Cluster Platform DL380p Gen8, Xeon E5-2650 8C 2.000GHz, Gigabit Ethernet**
    Site: IT Services Provider (B)
    Country: China
    Image URL: None
    Manufacturer: Hewlett-Packard
    Cores: 28,672
    Linpack Performance (Rmax): 222.8 TFlop/s
    Theoretical Peak (Rpeak): 458.8 TFlop/s
    Interconnect: Gigabit Ethernet
    Operating System: Linux
    Ranking: 183

184. **Cartesius - Bullx DLC B710 Blades, Intel Xeon E5-2695v2 12C 2.400GHz, Infiniband FDR**
    Site: SURFsara
    Country: Netherlands
    Image URL: https://surfsara.nl/sites/default/files/styles/large/public/Cartesius_0.jpg
    Manufacturer: Bull SA

Cores: 12, 960
Linpack Performance (Rmax): 222.7 TFlop/s
Theoretical Peak (Rpeak): 248.8 TFlop/s
Power: 245.00 kW
Memory: 34, 560 GB
Interconnect: Infiniband FDR
Operating System: Bullx Linux
Compiler: Intel Compiler
Math Library: Intel MKL
MPI: Intel MPI
Ranking: 184

185. **RWTH Compute Cluster (RCC) - Bullx B500 Cluster, Xeon X56xx 3.06Ghz, QDR Infiniband**
Site: Universitaet Aachen/ RWTH
Country: Germany
Image URL: None
Manufacturer: Bull SA
Cores: 25, 448
Linpack Performance (Rmax): 219.8 TFlop/s
Theoretical Peak (Rpeak): 270.5 TFlop/s
Interconnect: Infiniband QDR
Operating System: Linux
Ranking: 185

186. **Cluster Platform SL230s Gen8, Xeon E5-2670 8C 2.600GHz, 10G Ethernet**
Site: Energy Company
Country: United States
Image URL: None
Manufacturer: Hewlett-Packard
Cores: 15, 360
Linpack Performance (Rmax): 217.9 TFlop/s
Theoretical Peak (Rpeak): 319.5 TFlop/s
Interconnect: 10G Ethernet
Operating System: Linux
Ranking: 186

187. **HP DL160 Cluster G6, Xeon E5645 6C 2.40GHz, Gigabit Ethernet**
Site: Web Content Provider
Country: United States
Image URL: None
Manufacturer: Hewlett-Packard
Cores: 44, 580
Linpack Performance (Rmax): 215.7 TFlop/s
Theoretical Peak (Rpeak): 428.0 TFlop/s
Interconnect: Gigabit Ethernet
Operating System: Linux
Ranking: 187

188. **Tup - Cray XE6, Opteron 6172 12C 2.10GHz, Cray Gemini interconnect**
     Site: INPE (National Institute for Space Research)
     Country: Brazil
     Image URL: https://encrypted-tbn2.gstatic.com/images?q=tbn:ANd9GcQURjgJt4SmfNnbl7lyc YvKoQEIMK23M4L1apo6oQJTbs-EtDmj10i7BA
     Manufacturer: Cray Inc.
     Cores: 31,104
     Linpack Performance (Rmax): 214.2 TFlop/s
     Theoretical Peak (Rpeak): 261.3 TFlop/s
     Interconnect: Cray Gemini Interconnect
     Operating System: Cray Linux Environment
     Ranking: 188

189. **Sisu - Cray XC30, Xeon E5-2670 8C 2.600GHz, Aries interconnect**
     Site: CSC (Center for Scientific Computing)
     Country: Finland
     Image URL: http://www.csc.fi/english/csc/overview/press_room/Sisu_HIRES/image/ thumb?height=354&width=510, http://www.csc.fi/english/csc/overview/press_room/sisu2/im- age/thumb?height=295&width=510
     Manufacturer: Cray Inc
     Cores: 11, 776
     Linpack Performance (Rmax): 214.1 TFlop/s
     Theoretical Peak (Rpeak): 244.9 TFlop/s
     Interconnect: Aries Interconnect
     Operating System: Cray Linux Environment
     Ranking: 189

190. **iDataPlex DX360M4, Xeon E5-2670 8C 2.600GHz, Infiniband FDR**
     Site: Technische Universitaet Darmstadt
     Country: Germany
     Image URL: http://www.tu-darmstadt.de/media/illustrationen/referat_kommunikation/news_1/ news_medien_2013/bg_hochleistungsrechner/hlr_2_529x0.jpg
     Manufacturer: IBM
     Cores: 12, 288
     Linpack Performance (Rmax): 213.8 TFlop/s
     Theoretical Peak (Rpeak): 255.6 TFlop/s
     Power: 255.20 kW
     Interconnect: Infiniband FDR
     Operating System: Linux
     Ranking: 190

191. **Maia - SGI Rackable C1104G-RP5, Xeon E5-2670 8C 2.600GHz, Infiniband FDR, Intel Xeon Phi**
     Site: NASA/ Ames Research Center/NAS
     Country: United States
     Image URL: None

Manufacturer: SGI
Cores: 17,408
Linpack Performance (Rmax): 212.8 TFlop/s
Theoretical Peak (Rpeak): 301.4 TFlop/s
Power: 132.00 kW
Memory: 4,096 GB
Interconnect: Infiniband FDR
Operating System: SUSE Linux Enterprise Server 11
Ranking: 191

192. **Riptide - iDataPlex DX360M4, Xeon E5-2670 8C 2.600GHz, Infiniband FDR**
Site: Maui High-Performance Computing Center (MHPCC)
Country: United States
Image URL: None
Manufacturer: IBM
Cores: 12,096
Linpack Performance (Rmax): 212.6 TFlop/s
Theoretical Peak (Rpeak): 251.6 TFlop/s
Power: 251.20 kW
Memory: 24, 192 GB
Interconnect: Infiniband FDR
Operating System: Linux
Compiler: Intel
MPI: Intel MPI
Ranking: 192

193. **Power 775, POWER7 8C 3.84 GHz, Custom**
Site: Environment Canada
Country: Canada
Image URL: None
Manufacturer: IBM
Cores: 8,192
Linpack Performance (Rmax): 211.7 TFlop/s
Theoretical Peak (Rpeak): 251.4 TFlop/s
Power: 462.30 kW
Interconnect: Custom Interconnect
Operating System: AIX
Ranking: 193

194. **Power 775, POWER7 8C 3.84 GHz, Custom**
Site: Environment Canada
Country: Canada
Image URL: None
Manufacturer: IBM
Cores: 8,192
Linpack Performance (Rmax): 211.7 TFlop/s

Theoretical Peak (Rpeak): 251.4 TFlop/s

Power: 462.30 kW

Interconnect: Custom Interconnect

Operating System: AIX

Ranking: 194

195. **Tianhe-1A Guangzhou Solution - NUDT YH MPP, Xeon X56xx (Westmere-EP) 2.93 GHz, Proprietary**

Site: National Super Computer Center in Guangzhou

Country: China

Image URL: None

Manufacturer: NUDT

Cores: 13,312

Linpack Performance (Rmax): 211.7 TFlop/s

Theoretical Peak (Rpeak): 335.7 TFlop/s

Power: 289.00 kW

Memory: 24, 576 GB

Interconnect: Proprietary

Operating System: Linux

Compiler: icc

Math Library: Intel MKL-10.2.5.035

MPI: MPICH2 with a custom GLEX channel

Ranking: 195

196. **Cluster Platform 3000 BL460c Gen8, Xeon E5-2680 8C 2.700GHz, 10G Ethernet**

Site: Service Provider

Country: United States

Image URL: None

Manufacturer: Hewlett-Packard

Cores: 13, 872

Linpack Performance (Rmax): 209.7 TFlop/s

Theoretical Peak (Rpeak): 299.6 TFlop/s

Interconnect: 10G Ethernet

Operating System: Linux

Ranking: 196

197. **Cluster Platform DL380p Gen8, Xeon E5-2630 6C 2.300GHz, Gigabit Ethernet**

Site: Service Provider

Country: China

Image URL: None

Manufacturer: Hewlett-Packard

Cores: 22,632

Linpack Performance (Rmax): 207.3 TFlop/s

Theoretical Peak (Rpeak): 416.4 TFlop/s

Interconnect: Gigabit Ethernet

Operating System: Linux

Ranking: 197

198. **Cluster Platform SL230s Gen8, Xeon E5-2670 8C 2.600GHz, 10G Ethernet**
   Site: Energy Company (D)
   Country: United States
   Image URL: None
   Manufacturer: Hewlett-Packard
   Cores: 14,272
   Linpack Performance (Rmax): 202.5 TFlop/s
   Theoretical Peak (Rpeak): 296.9 TFlop/s
   Interconnect: 10G Ethernet
   Operating System: Linux
   Ranking: 198

199. **Cluster Platform DL380e Gen8, Xeon E5-2430L 8C 2.000GHz, Gigabit Ethernet**
   Site: Software Company (M)
   Country: United States
   Image URL: None
   Manufacturer: Hewlett-Packard
   Cores: 25, 920Linpack Performance: 201.0 TFlop/s
   Theoretical Peak (Rpeak): 414.7 TFlop/s
   Interconnect: Gigabit Ethernet
   Operating System: Linux
   Ranking: 199

200. **Cluster Platform DL360e Gen8, Xeon E5-2450 8C 2.100GHz, Gigabit Ethernet**
   Site: Web Content Provider
   Country: United States
   Image URL: None
   Manufacturer: Hewlett-Packard
   Cores: 24,032
   Linpack Performance (Rmax): 199.8 TFlop/s
   Theoretical Peak (Rpeak): 403.7 TFlop/s
   Interconnect: Gigabit Ethernet
   Operating System: Linux
   Ranking: 200

201. **Cluster Platform DL380p Gen8, Xeon E5-2650 8C 2.000GHz, Gigabit Ethernet**
   Site: Telecommunication Company
   Country: China
   Image URL: None
   Manufacturer: Hewlett-Packard
   Cores: 25, 104
   Linpack Performance (Rmax): 197.9 TFlop/s
   Theoretical Peak (Rpeak): 401.7 TFlop/s
   Interconnect: Gigabit Ethernet
   Operating System: Linux
   Ranking: 201

202. **Cluster Platform 3000 BL460c Gen8, Xeon E5-2670 8C 2.600GHz, 10G Ethernet**
   Site: IT Services Provider
   Country: United States
   Image URL: None
   Manufacturer: Hewlett-Packard
   Cores: 13,568
   Linpack Performance (Rmax): 197.8 TFlop/s
   Theoretical Peak (Rpeak): 282.2 TFlop/s
   Interconnect: 10G Ethernet
   Operating System: Linux
   Ranking: 202

203. **Cluster Platform DL360p Gen8, Xeon E5-2630 6C 2.300GHz, Gigabit Ethernet**
   Site: IT Services Provider
   Country: South Korea
   Image URL: None
   Manufacturer: Hewlett-Packard
   Cores: 21, 492
   Linpack Performance: 197.7 TFlop/s
   Theoretical Peak (Rpeak): 395.5 TFlop/s
   Interconnect: Gigabit Ethernet
   Operating System: Linux
   Ranking: 203

204. **Inspur TS10000, Xeon E5-2670 8C 2.600GHz, Infiniband FDR, K20M/Xeon Phi 5110P**
   Site: Shanghai Jiaotong University
   Country: China
   Image URL: None
   Manufacturer: Inspur
   Cores: 8,412
   Linpack Performance (Rmax): 196.2 TFlop/s
   Theoretical Peak (Rpeak): 262.6 TFlop/s
   Power: 217.20 kW
   Memory: 26,048 GB
   Interconnect: Infiniband FDR
   Operating System: Redhat Linux
   Ranking: 204

205. **Cluster Platform SL230s Gen8, Xeon E5-2670 8C 2.600GHz, 10G Ethernet**
   Site: Web-Service Provider
   Country: United States
   Image URL: None
   Manufacturer: Hewlett-Packard
   Cores: 16,064
   Linpack Performance (Rmax): 231.7 TFlop/s
   Theoretical Peak (Rpeak): 334.1 TFlop/s

Interconnect: 10G Ethernet
Operating System: Linux
Ranking: 205

206. **Cluster Platform 3000 BL460c Gen8, Xeon E5-2670 8C 2.60GHz, 10G Ethernet**
Site: IT Service Provider
Country: United States
Image URL: None
Manufacturer: Hewlett-Packard
Cores: 13,184
Linpack Performance (Rmax): 192.5 TFlop/s
Theoretical Peak (Rpeak): 274.2 TFlop/s
Interconnect: 10G Ethernet
Operating System: Linux
Ranking: 206

207. **Cluster Platform 3000 BL460c Gen8, Xeon E5-2670 8C 2.60GHz, 10G Ethernet**
Site: IT Service Provider
Country: United States
Image URL: None
Manufacturer: Hewlett-Packard
Cores: 13,168
Linpack Performance (Rmax): 192.3 TFlop/s
Theoretical Peak (Rpeak): 273.9 TFlop/s
Interconnect: 10G Ethernet
Operating System: Linux
Ranking: 207

208. **RTC - Cray XC30, Intel Xeon E5-2692v2 10C 3.000GHz, Aries interconnect**
Site: Pawsey CSIRO/Ivec
Country: Australia
Image URL: http://www.ivec.org/wp-content/uploads/GALAXYLR.jpg http://www.ivec.org/wp-content/uploads/magnusLR.jpg
Manufacturer: Cray Inc.
Cores: 9,440
Linpack Performance (Rmax): 192.1 TFlop/s
Theoretical Peak (Rpeak): 226.6 TFlop/s
Interconnect: Aries Interconnect
Operating System: Cray Linux Environment
Ranking: 208

209. **Ada - xSeries x3750 Cluster, Xeon E5-2680 8C 2.700GHz, Infiniband FDR**
Site: CNRS/IDRIS-GENCI
Country: France
Image URL: None
Manufacturer: IBM
Cores: 10,624

Linpack Performance (Rmax): 191.9 TFlop/s
Theoretical Peak (Rpeak): 229.5 TFlop/s
Power: 243.69 kW
Interconnect: Infiniband FDR
Operating System: Linux
Ranking: 209

210. **Emmy - NEC LX-2400, Intel Xeon E5-2660v2 10C 2.200GHz, Infiniband QDR**
Site: Universitaet Erlangen – Regionales Rechenzentrum Erlangen
Country: Germany
Image URL: http://www.rrze.uni-erlangen.de/dienste/arbeiten-rechnen/hpc/systeme/emmy2.jpg
Manufacturer: NEC
Cores: 11,200
Linpack Performance (Rmax): 191.5 TFlop/s
Theoretical Peak (Rpeak): 197.1 TFlop/s
Power: 169.00 kW
Memory: 35,840 GB
Interconnect: Infiniband QDR
Operating System: CentOS
Compiler: Intel Compiler 13.1
Math Library: Intel MKL
MPI: Intel
Ranking: 210

211. **BX900 Xeon X5570 2.93GHz, Infiniband QDR**
Site: Japan Atomic Energy Agency (JAEA)
Country: Japan
Image URL: None
Manufacturer: Fujitsu
Cores: 17,072
Linpack Performance (Rmax): 191.4 TFlop/s
Theoretical Peak (Rpeak): 200.1 TFlop/s
Power: 831.00 kW
Memory: 51,216 GB
Interconnect: Infiniband QDR
Operating System: Linux
Ranking: 211

212. **x3650M4 Cluster, Xeon E5-2670 8C 2.600GHz, Infiniband FDR**
Site: Petroleum Company
Country: United Kingdom
Image URL: None
Manufacturer: IBM
Cores: 10,976
Linpack Performance (Rmax): 191.0 TFlop/s
Theoretical Peak (Rpeak): 228.3 TFlop/s

Power: 285.38 kW
Interconnect: Infiniband FDR
Operating System: Linux
Ranking: 212

213. **Cluster Platform 3000 BL460c Gen8, Xeon E5-2670 8C 2.600GHz, 10G Ethernet**
     Site: Service Provider
     Country: United States
     Image URL: None
     Manufacturer: Hewlett-Packard
     Cores: 13, 440
     Linpack Performance (Rmax): 190.9 TFlop/s
     Theoretical Peak (Rpeak): 279.6 TFlop/s
     Interconnect: 10G Ethernet
     Operating System: Linux
     Ranking: 213

214. **Shaheen - Blue Gene/P Solution**
     Site: King Abdullah University of Science and Technology
     Country: Saudi Arabia
     Image URL: None
     Manufacturer: IBM
     Cores: 65,536
     Linpack Performance (Rmax): 190.9 TFlop/s
     Theoretical Peak (Rpeak): 222.8 TFlop/s
     Power: 504.00 kW
     Interconnect: Proprietary
     Operating System: CNK/SLES 9
     Ranking: 214

215. **Cluster Platform 3000 BL460c Gen8, Xeon E5-2660 8C 2.200GHz, 10G Ethernet**
     Site: IT Service Provider
     Country: United States
     Image URL: None
     Manufacturer: Hewlett-Packard
     Cores: 15,504
     Linpack Performance (Rmax): 189.7 TFlop/s
     Theoretical Peak (Rpeak): 272.9 TFlop/s
     Interconnect: 10G Ethernet
     Operating System: Linux
     Ranking: 215

216. **Vesta - BlueGene/Q, Power BQC 16C 1.60GHz, Custom**
     Site: DOE/SC/Argonne National Laboratory
     Country: United States
     Image URL: http://www.alcf.anl.gov/sites/all/themes/fusionALCF/images/resources/Cetus-Vesta.jpg

Manufacturer: IBM
Cores: 16, 384
Linpack Performance (Rmax): 189.0 TFlop/s
Theoretical Peak (Rpeak): 209.7 TFlop/s
Power: 82.19 kW
Interconnect: Custom Interconnect
Operating System: Linux
Ranking: 216

217. **Cetus - BlueGene/Q, Power BQC 16C 1.600GHz, Custom Interconnect**
Site: DOE/SC/Argonne National Laboratory
Country: United States
Image URL: http://www.alcf.anl.gov/sites/www.alcf.anl.gov/files/resize/cetus-web-225x334.jpg
Manufacturer: IBM
Cores: 16,384
Linpack Performance (Rmax): 189.0 TFlop/s
Theoretical Peak (Rpeak): 209.7 TFlop/s
Power: 82.19 kW
Interconnect: Custom Interconnect
Operating System: Linux
Ranking: 217

218. **CADMOS BG/Q - BlueGene/Q, Power BQC 16C 1.600GHz, Custom Interconnect**
Site: Ecole Polytechnique Federale de Lausanne
Country: Switzerland
Image URL: http://www.cadmos.org/_inc/upf/images/actualites/s/img-9287-dxo-2.jpg
System URL: http://www.cadmos.org/
Manufacturer: IBM
Cores: 16,384
Linpack Performance (Rmax): 189 TFlop/s
Theoretical Peak (Rpeak): 209.7 TFlop/s
Power: 82.19 kW
Interconnect: Custom Interconnect
Operating System: Linux
Ranking: 218

219. **BlueGene/Q, Power BQC 16C 1.600GHz, Custom Interconnect**
Site: IBM Rochester
Country: United States
Image URL: None
Manufacturer: IBM
Cores: 16,384
Linpack Performance (Rmax): 189.0 TFlop/s
Theoretical Peak (Rpeak): 209.7 TFlop/s
Power: 82.19 kW
Interconnect: Custom Interconnect
Operating System: Linux
Ranking: 219

220. **BlueGene/Q, Power BQC 16C 1.60 GHz, Custom**
    Site: IBM Thomas J. Watson Research Center
    Country: United States
    Image URL: None
    Manufacturer: IBM
    Cores: 16,384
    Linpack Performance (Rmax): 189.0 TFlop/s
    Theoretical Peak (Rpeak): 209.7 TFlop/s
    Power: 82.19 kW
    Interconnect: Custom Interconnect
    Operating System: Linux
    Ranking: 220

221. **BlueGene/Q, Power BQC 16C 1.600GHz, Custom Interconnect**
    Site: Interdisciplinary Centre for Mathematical and Computational Modelling, University of Warsaw
    Country: Poland
    Manufacturer: IBM
    Cores: 16,384
    Linpack Performance (Rmax): 189.0 TFlop/s
    Theoretical Peak (Rpeak): 209.7 TFlop/s
    Power: 82.19 kW
    Interconnect: Custom Interconnect
    Operating System: Linux
    Ranking: 221

222. **BlueGene/Q, Power BQC 16C 1.60GHz, Custom**
    Site: University of Rochester
    Country: United States
    Image URL: None
    Manufacturer: IBM
    Cores: 16,384
    Linpack Performance (Rmax): 189.0 TFlop/s
    Theoretical Peak (Rpeak): 209.7 TFlop/s
    Power: 82.19 kW
    Interconnect: Custom Interconnect
    Operating System: Linux
    Ranking: 222

223. **Cluster Platform 3000 BL460c Gen8, Xeon E5-2660 8C 2.200GHz, 10G Ethernet**
    Site: Telecommunication Company
    Country: United States
    Image URL: None
    Manufacturer: Hewlett-Packard
    Cores: 15,424
    Linpack Performance (Rmax): 188.7 TFlop/s

Theoretical Peak (Rpeak): 271.5 TFlop/s
Interconnect: 10G Ethernet
Operating System: Linux
Ranking: 223

224. **OCuLUS (Owl CLUSter) - Clustervision CV-AIRE5, Xeon E5-2670 8C 2.600GHz, Infiniband QDR**
Site: Universitaet Paderborn – PC2
Country: Germany
Image URL: http://pc2.uni-paderborn.de/typo3temp/pics/2a479e9f75.jpg
Manufacturer: ClusterVision
Cores: 9,600
Linpack Performance (Rmax): 188.7 TFlop/s
Theoretical Peak (Rpeak): 199.7 TFlop/s
Memory: 38,400 GB
Interconnect: Infiniband QDR
Operating System: Scientific Linux
Compiler: Intel Compiler
Math Library: Intel MKL
MPI: Intel MPI
Ranking: 224

225. **SAGA - Z24XX/SL390s Cluster, Xeon E5530/E5645 6C 2.40GHz, Infiniband QDR, NVIDIA 2090/2070**
Site: Vikram Sarabhai Space Centre, Indian SpaceResearch Organization
Country: India
Image URL: None
Manufacturer: Hewlett-Packard/WIPRO
Cores: 12,532
Linpack Performance (Rmax): 188.7 TFlop/s
Theoretical Peak (Rpeak): 394.8 TFlop/s
Interconnect: Infiniband QDR
Operating System: Linux
Compiler: GCC 4.4.1 NVIDIA CUDA 4.1
Math Library: Intel Math Kernel Library
MPI: OpenMPI 1.4.5
Ranking: 225

226. **iDataPlex DX360M4, Xeon E5-2670 8C 2.600GHz, Infiniband FDR**
Site: Max Planck Gesellschaft MPI/IPP
Country: Germany
Image URL: http://www.rzg.mpg.de/services/computing/Hydra/Hydra570.jpg
Manufacturer: IBM
Cores: 9,904
Linpack Performance (Rmax): 187.4 TFlop/s
Theoretical Peak (Rpeak): 206.0 TFlop/s

Power: 205.72 kW
Interconnect: Infiniband FDR
Operating System: Linux
Ranking: 226

227. **Carter - Cluster Platform 3000 SL6500, Xeon E5 (Sandy Bridge - EP) 8C 2.60GHz, FDR Infiniband**
   Site: Purdue University
   Country: United States
   Image URL: http://dev.rcac.purdue.edu/userinfo/resources/carter/images/resource.jpg
   System URL: http://dev.rcac.purdue.edu/userinfo/resources/carter/
   Manufacturer: Hewlett-Packard
   Cores: 10,368
   Linpack Performance (Rmax): 186.9 TFlop/s
   Theoretical Peak (Rpeak): 215.7 TFlop/s
   Power: 252.00 kW
   Memory: 20,736 GB
   Interconnect: Infiniband FDR
   Operating System: Linux
   Ranking: 227

228. **Cluster Platform DL360e Gen8, Xeon E5-2450 8C 2.100GHz, Gigabit Ethernet**
   Site: Software Company (M)
   Country: United States
   Image URL: None
   Manufacturer: Hewlett-Packard
   Cores: 23,024
   Linpack Performance (Rmax): 186.9 TFlop/s
   Theoretical Peak (Rpeak): 386.8 TFlop/s
   Interconnect: Gigabit Ethernet
   Operating System: Linux
   Ranking: 228

229. **Cluster Platform 3000 BL460c Gen8, Xeon E5-2670 8C 2.600GHz, 10G Ethernet**
   Site: IT Services Provider
   Country: Japan
   Image URL: None
   Manufacturer: Hewlett-Packard
   Cores: 12,768
   Linpack Performance (Rmax): 186.8 TFlop/s
   Theoretical Peak (Rpeak): 265.6 TFlop/s
   Interconnect: 10G Ethernet
   Operating System: Linux
   Ranking: 229

230. **Cluster Platform 3000 BL460c Gen8, Xeon E5-2670 8C 2.600GHz, 10G Ethernet**
  Site: IT Service Provider
  Country: Israel ⬥
  Image URL: None
  Manufacturer: Hewlett-Packard
  Cores: 12,720
  Linpack Performance (Rmax): 186.1 TFlop/s
  Theoretical Peak (Rpeak): 264.6 TFlop/s
  Interconnect: 10G Ethernet
  Operating System: Linux
  Ranking: 230

231. **Cluster Platform DL380p Gen8, Xeon E5-2650 8C 2.000GHz, Gigabit Ethernet**
  Site: Web Content Provider
  Country: United States ▬
  Image URL: None
  Manufacturer: Hewlett-Packard
  Cores: 24,480
  Linpack Performance (Rmax): 186.1 TFlop/s
  Theoretical Peak (Rpeak): 391.7 TFlop/s
  Interconnect: Gigabit Ethernet
  Operating System: Linux
  Ranking: 231

232. **Cray CS300-AC, Xeon E5-2670 8C 2.600GHz, Infiniband QDR**
  Site: DOE/Bettis Atomic Power Laboratory
  Country: United States ▬
  Image URL: None
  Manufacturer: Cray Inc.
  Cores: 10,176
  Linpack Performance (Rmax): 184.8 TFlop/s
  Theoretical Peak (Rpeak): 211.7 TFlop/s
  Interconnect: Infiniband QDR
  Operating System: SUSE Linux Enterprise Server 11
  Ranking: 232

233. **Cray CS300-AC, Xeon E5-2670 8C 2.600GHz, Infiniband QDR**
  Site: Knolls Atomic Power Laboratory
  Country: United States ▬
  Image URL: None
  Manufacturer: Cray Inc.
  Cores: 10,176
  Linpack Performance (Rmax): 184.8 TFlop/s
  Theoretical Peak (Rpeak): 211.7 TFlop/s
  Interconnect: Infiniband QDR
  Operating System: SUSE Linux Enterprise Server 11
  Ranking: 233

234. **Darwin - Dell PowerEdge C6220, Xeon E5-2670 8C 2.600GHz, Infiniband FDR**
Site: Cambridge University
Country: United Kingdom
Image URL: None
Manufacturer: Dell
Cores: 9,728
Linpack Performance (Rmax): 183.4 TFlop/s
Theoretical Peak (Rpeak): 202.3 TFlop/s
Power: 975.0 kW
Memory: 38,912 GB
Interconnect: Infiniband FDR
Compiler: Intel Compiler 12.1
Operating System: Linux
Math Library: Intel MKL 10.3
MPI: Intel MPI 4.0
Ranking: 234

235. **Cluster Platform SL230s Gen8, Xeon E5-2670 8C 2.600GHz, Gigabit Ethernet**
Site: Computacenter (UK) LTD
Country: United Kingdom
Image URL: None
Manufacturer: Hewlett-Packard
Cores: 17,280
Linpack Performance (Rmax): 182.7 TFlop/s
Theoretical Peak (Rpeak): 359.4 TFlop/s
Interconnect: Gigabit Ethernet
Operating System: Linux
Ranking: 235

236. **Cluster Platform 3000 BL460c Gen8, Xeon E5-2650 8C 2.000GHz, 10G Ethernet**
Site: Government
Country: United States
Image URL: None
Manufacturer: Hewlett-Packard
Cores: 16,480
Linpack Performance (Rmax): 182.5 TFlop/s
Theoretical Peak (Rpeak): 263.7 TFlop/s
Interconnect: 10G Ethernet
Operating System: Linux
Ranking: 236

237. **Magic Cube - Dawning 5000A, QC Opteron 1.9 Ghz, Infiniband, Windows HPC 2008**
Site: Shanghai Supercomputer Center
Country: China
Image URL: None
Manufacturer: Dawning

Cores: 30, 720
Linpack Performance (Rmax): 180.6 TFlop/s
Theoretical Peak (Rpeak): 233.5 TFlop/s
Memory: 122, 880 GB
Interconnect: Infiniband DDR
Operating System: Windows HPC 2008
Ranking: 237

238. **Cluster Platform 3000 BL2x220, L54xx 2.5 Ghz, Infiniband**
Site: Government
Country: France ▌▐
Image URL: None
Manufacturer: Hewlett-Packard
Cores: 24, 704
Linpack Performance (Rmax): 179.6 TFlop/s
Theoretical Peak (Rpeak): 247.0 TFlop/s
Interconnect: Infiniband DDR 4x
Operating System: Linux
Ranking: 238

239. **Power 775, POWER7 8C 3.836GHz, Custom Interconnect**
Site: IBM Poughkeepsie Benchmarking Center
Country: United States ▭
Image URL: None
Manufacturer: IBM
Cores: 6,912
Linpack Performance (Rmax): 178.6 TFlop/s
Theoretical Peak (Rpeak): 212.1 TFlop/s
Power: 390.07 kW
Interconnect: Custom Interconnect
Operating System: AIX
Ranking: 239

240. **Abel - MEGWARE MiriQuid, Xeon E5-2670 8C 2.600GHz, Infiniband FDR**
Site: University of Oslo
Country: Norway ▟
Image URL: None
Manufacturer: Megware
Cores: 10,080
Linpack Performance (Rmax): 178.6 TFlop/s
Theoretical Peak (Rpeak): 209.7
Power: 227.00 kW
Memory: 40, 320 GB
Interconnect: Infiniband FDR
Operating System: Linux
Compiler: Intel Compiler Suite v.12

Math Library: Intel MKL

MPI: Intel MPI

Ranking: 240

241. **Gyre - iDataPlex DX360M4, Xeon E5-2670 8C 2.600GHz, Infiniband FDR**

Site: National Centers for Environment Prediction.

Country: United States

Image URL: http://www.ncep.noaa.gov/newsletter/december2012/01/large.jpg

Manufacturer: IBM

Cores: 10, 240

Linpack Performance (Rmax): 178.1 TFlop/s

Theoretical Peak (Rpeak): 213.0 TFlop/s

Power: 203.52 kW

Interconnect: Infiniband FDR

Operating System: Linux

Ranking: 241

242. **Tide - iDataPlex DX360M4, Xeon E5-2670 8C 2.600GHz, Infiniband FDR**

Site: National Centers for Environment Prediction

Country: United States

Image URL: http://www.ncep.noaa.gov/newsletter/december2012/01/large2.jpg

Manufacturer: IBM

Cores: 10,240

Linpack Performance (Rmax): 178.1 TFlop/s

Theoretical Peak (Rpeak): 213.0 TFlop/s

Power: 203.52 kW

Interconnect: Infiniband FDR

Operating System: Linux

Ranking: 242

243. **ALPS - Acer AR585 F1 Cluster, Opteron 12C 2.2GHz, QDR infiniband**

Site: Taiwan National Center for High-performanceComputing.

Country: Taiwan

Image URL: http://www.nchc.org.tw/upload/english/news/8/98/90.jpg

System URL: http://www.nchc.org.tw/

Manufacturer: Acer Group

Cores: 26, 244

Linpack Performance (Rmax): 177.1 TFlop/s

Theoretical Peak (Rpeak): 231.9 TFlop/s

Interconnect: Infiniband QDR

Operating System: Linux

Ranking: 243

244. **Cluster Platform DL380p Gen8, Xeon E5-2620 6C 2.000GHz, Gigabit Ethernet**

Site: Service Provider

Country: United States

Image URL: None

Manufacturer: Hewlett-Packard
Cores: 22, 152
Linpack Performance (Rmax): 176.8 TFlop/s
Theoretical Peak (Rpeak): 354.4 TFlop/s
Interconnect: Gigabit Ethernet
Operating System: Linux
Ranking: 244

245. **Cluster Platform SL230s Gen8, Xeon E5-2670 8C 2.600GHz, Gigabit Ethernet**
   Site: IT Services Provider
   Country: United States ▓▓
   Image URL: None
   Manufacturer: Hewlett-Packard
   Cores: 16,640
   Linpack Performance (Rmax): 176.4 TFlop/s
   Theoretical Peak (Rpeak): 346.1 TFlop/s
   Interconnect: Gigabit Ethernet
   Operating System: Linux
   Ranking: 245

246. **Cluster Platform SL230s Gen8, Xeon E5-2670 8C 2.600GHz, Gigabit Ethernet**
   Site: IT Services Provider
   Country: United States ▓▓
   Image URL: None
   Manufacturer: Hewlett-Packard
   Cores: 16,640
   Linpack Performance (Rmax): 176.4 TFlop/s
   Theoretical Peak (Rpeak): 346.1 TFlop/s
   Interconnect: Gigabit Ethernet
   Operating System: Linux
   Ranking: 246

247. **BladeCenter HS23 Cluster, Xeon E5-2680 8C 2.700GHz, Infiniband QDR**
   Site: Classified
   Country: United States ▓▓
   Image URL: None
   Manufacturer: IBM
   Cores: 8,976
   Linpack Performance (Rmax): 176.3 TFlop/s
   Theoretical Peak (Rpeak): 193.9 TFlop/s
   Power: 177.84 kW
   Interconnect: Infiniband QDR
   Operating System: Linux
   Ranking: 247

248. **Cluster Platform 3000 BL460c Gen8, Xeon E5-2680 8C 2.700GHz, 10G Ethernet**
     Site: IT Service Provider
     Country: United States
     Image URL: None
     Manufacturer: Hewlett-Packard
     Cores: 11, 648
     Linpack Performance (Rmax): 176.1 TFlop/s
     Theoretical Peak (Rpeak): 251.6 TFlop/s
     Interconnect: 10G Ethernet
     Operating System: Linux
     Ranking: 248

249. **Cluster Platform 3000 BL460c Gen8, Xeon E5-2680 8C 2.700GHz, 10G Ethernet**
     Site: IT Service Provider
     Country: United States
     Image URL: None
     Manufacturer: Hewlett-Packard
     Cores: 11, 648
     Linpack Performance (Rmax): 176.1 TFlop/s
     Theoretical Peak (Rpeak): 251.6 TFlop/s
     Interconnect: 10G Ethernet
     Operating System: Linux
     Ranking: 249

250. **Cluster Platform 3000 BL460c Gen8, Xeon E5-2670 8C 2.600GHz, Gigabit Ethernet**
     Site: IT Service Provider (D)
     Country: United States
     Image URL: None
     Manufacturer: Hewlett-Packard
     Cores: 16,392
     Linpack Performance (Rmax): 174.0 TFlop/s
     Theoretical Peak (Rpeak): 341.0 TFlop/s
     Interconnect: Gigabit Ethernet
     Operating System: Linux
     Ranking: 250

251. **Cluster Platform DL360e Gen8, Xeon E5-2450 8C 2.100GHz, Gigabit Ethernet**
     Site: Software Company (M)
     Country: United States
     Image URL: None
     Cores: 21,296
     Linpack Performance (Rmax): 172.9 TFlop/s
     Theoretical Peak (Rpeak): 357.8 TFlop/s
     Interconnect: Gigabit Ethernet
     Operating System: Linux
     Ranking: 251

252. **Cluster Platform 3000 BL460c Gen8, Xeon E5-2670 8C 2.600GHz, 10G Ethernet**
Site: IT Service Provider (B)
Country: United States ▦
Image URL: None
Manufacturer: Hewlett-Packard
Cores: 11,736
Linpack Performance (Rmax): 172.4 TFlop/s
Theoretical Peak (Rpeak): 244.1 TFlop/s
Interconnect: 10G Ethernet
Operating System: Linux
Ranking: 252

253. **Cluster Platform DL360p Gen8, Xeon E5-2620 6C 2.000GHz, Gigabit Ethernet**
Site: IT Service Provider
Country: United States ▦
Image URL: None
Manufacturer: Hewlett-Packard
Cores: 21, 504
Linpack Performance (Rmax): 172 TFlop/s
Theoretical Peak (Rpeak): 344.1 TFlop/s
Interconnect: Gigabit Ethernet
Operating System: Linux
Ranking: 253

254. **Cluster Platform DL360p Gen8, Xeon E5-2630 6C 2.300GHz, Gigabit Ethernet**
Site: IT Services Provider
Country: United States ▦
Image URL: None
Manufacturer: Hewlett-Packard
Cores: 18, 468
Linpack Performance (Rmax): 172.0 TFlop/s
Theoretical Peak (Rpeak): 339.8 TFlop/s
Interconnect: Gigabit Ethernet
Operating System: Linux
Ranking: 254

255. **Cluster Platform 3000 BL460c Gen8, Xeon E5-2670 8C 2.60GHz, 10G Ethernet**
Site: IT Service Provider
Country: United States ▦
Image URL: None
Manufacturer: Hewlett-Packard
Cores: 16,064
Linpack Performance (Rmax): 170.7 TFlop/s
Theoretical Peak (Rpeak): 334.1 TFlop/s
Interconnect: 10G Ethernet
Operating System: Linux
Ranking: 255

256. **Cluster Platform 3000 BL460c Gen8, Xeon E5-2670 8C 2.60GHz, 10G Ethernet**
     Site: IT Service Provider
     Country: United States
     Image URL: None
     Manufacturer: Hewlett-Packard
     Cores: 16,064
     Linpack Performance (Rmax): 170.7 TFlop/s
     Theoretical Peak (Rpeak): 334.1 TFlop/s
     Interconnect: 10G Ethernet
     Operating System: Linux
     Ranking: 256

257. **Ivanhoe - iDataPlex, Xeon X56xx 6C 2.93 GHz, Infiniband**
     Site: EDF R&D
     Country: France
     Image URL: None
     Manufacturer: IBM
     Cores: 16,320
     Linpack Performance (Rmax): 168.8 TFlop/s
     Theoretical Peak (Rpeak): 191.3 TFlop/s
     Power: 510.00 kW
     Interconnect: Infiniband
     Operating System: Linux
     Ranking: 257

258. **BladeCenter HS22 Cluster (WM), Xeon E5649 6C 2.530GHz, Gigabit Ethernet**
     Site: IBM Development Engineering
     Country: United States
     Image URL: None
     Manufacturer: IBM
     Cores: 30,240
     Linpack Performance (Rmax): 168.6 TFlop/s
     Theoretical Peak (Rpeak): 306.0 TFlop/s
     Power: 956.07 kW
     Interconnect: Gigabit Ethernet
     Operating System: Linux
     Ranking: 258

259. **Cluster Platform 3000 BL460c Gen8, Xeon E5-2670 8C 2.600GHz, 10G Ethernet**
     Site: Electronic Industry
     Country: Sweden
     Image URL: None
     Manufacturer: Hewlett-Packard
     Cores: 11,488
     Linpack Performance (Rmax): 168.1 TFlop/s
     Theoretical Peak (Rpeak): 238.9 TFlop/s

Interconnect: 10G Ethernet

Operating System: Linux

Ranking: 259

260. **CSIRO GPU Cluster - Nitro G16 3GPU, Xeon E5-2650 8C 2.000GHz, Infiniband FDR, Nvidia K20m**

Site: CSIRO

Country: Australia

Image URL: http://www.csiro.au/~/media/CSIROau/Images/Occupations/GPUCluster_CMIS_set/Main.ashx

Manufacturer: Xenon Systems

Cores: 4,620

Linpack Performance (Rmax): 167.5 TFlop/s

Theoretical Peak (Rpeak): 317.4 TFlop/s

Memory: 10,752 GB

Interconnect: Infiniband FDR

Operating System: Linux

Compiler: gcc

Math Library: Cuda/Intel MKL

MPI: OpenMPI

Ranking: 260

261. **Cluster Platform DL360e Gen8, Xeon E5-2450L 8C 1.800GHz, Gigabit Ethernet**

Site: Software Company (M)

Country: United States

Image URL: None

Manufacturer: Hewlett-Packard

Cores: 29, 632

Linpack Performance (Rmax): 167.1 TFlop/s

Theoretical Peak (Rpeak): 426.7 TFlop/s

Interconnect: Gigabit Ethernet

Operating System: Linux

Ranking: 261

262. **Cluster Platform DL360p Gen8, Xeon E5-2620 6C 2.000GHz, Gigabit Ethernet**

Site: Logistic Services

Country: Germany

Image URL: None

Manufacturer: Hewlett-Packard

Cores: 20,796

Linpack Performance (Rmax): 166.8 TFlop/s

Theoretical Peak (Rpeak): 332.7 TFlop/s

Interconnect: Gigabit Ethernet

Operating System: Linux

Ranking: 262

263. **Sierra - Dell Xanadu 3 Cluster, Xeon X5660 2.8 Ghz, QLogic InfiniBand QDR**
    Site: Lawrence Livermore National Laboratory
    Country: United States
    Image URL: https://newsline.llnl.gov/_rev02/articles/2010/sep/images/092410_images/sierra-Computer.jpg
    Manufacturer: Dell
    Cores: 21,756
    Linpack Performance (Rmax): 166.7 TFlop/s
    Theoretical Peak (Rpeak): 243.7 TFlop/s
    Interconnect: Infiniband QDR
    Operating System: Linux
    Ranking: 263

264. **PRIMEHPC FX10, SPARC64 IXfx 16C 1.848GHz, Tofu interconnect**
    Site: Research Institute for Information Technology, Kyushu University
    Country: Japan
    Image URL: None
    Cores: 12,288
    Linpack Performance (Rmax): 166.7 TFlop/s
    Theoretical Peak (Rpeak): 181.7 TFlop/s
    Memory: 24,576 GB
    Interconnect: Tofu Interconnect
    Operating System: Linux
    Compiler: Fujitsu Technical Computing Language CCompiler
    Math Library: Fujitsu Technical Computing Language BLAS
    MPI: Fujitsu Technical Computing Language MPI
    Ranking: 264

265. **Cluster Platform 3000 BL460c Gen8, Xeon E5-2630 6C 2.300GHz, 10G Ethernet**
    Site: Financial Services (H)
    Country: United States
    Image URL: None
    Manufacturer: Hewlett-Packard
    Cores: 12,756
    Linpack Performance (Rmax): 165.7 TFlop/s
    Theoretical Peak (Rpeak): 234.7 TFlop/s
    Interconnect: 10G Ethernet
    Operating System: Linux
    Ranking: 265

266. **Cray XT5 QC 2.4 GHz**
    Site: Government
    Country: United States
    Image URL: None
    Manufacturer: Cray Inc.
    Cores: 20,960

Linpack Performance (Rmax): 165.6 TFlop/s
Theoretical Peak (Rpeak): 201.2 TFlop/s
Interconnect: XT4 Internal Interconnect
Operating System: CNL
Ranking: 266

267. **Cluster Platform SL230s Gen8, Xeon E5-2670 8C 2.600GHz, Infiniband FDR**
    Site: CSC (Center for Scientific Computing)
    Country: Finland
    Image URL: None
    Manufacturer: Hewlett-Packard
    Cores: 9200
    Linpack Performance (Rmax): 163.9 TFlop/s
    Theoretical Peak (Rpeak): 191.4 TFlop/s
    Interconnect: Infiniband FDR
    Operating System: Linux
    Ranking: 267

268. **Cluster Platform SL250s Gen8, Xeon E5-2670 8C 2.600GHz, Gigabit Ethernet**
    Site: IT Provider (P)
    Country: United States
    Image URL: None
    Manufacturer: Hewlett-Packard
    Cores: 15,360
    Linpack Performance (Rmax): 163.7 TFlop/s
    Theoretical Peak (Rpeak): 319.5 TFlop/s
    Interconnect: Gigabit Ethernet
    Operating System: Linux
    Ranking: 268

269. **Cluster Platform 3000 BL460c Gen8, Xeon E5-2660 8C 2.200GHz, 10G Ethernet**
    Site: Banking (M)
    Country: United States
    Image URL: None
    Manufacturer: Hewlett-Packard
    Cores: 13,136
    Linpack Performance (Rmax): 162.3 TFlop/s
    Theoretical Peak (Rpeak): 231.2 TFlop/s
    Interconnect: 10G Ethernet
    Operating System: Linux
    Ranking: 269

270. **xSeries x3650M4 Cluster, Xeon E5-2670 8C 2.600GHz, Gigabit Ethernet**
    Site: Engineering Company
    Country: China
    Image URL: None
    Manufacturer: IBM

Cores: 28,800
Linpack Performance (Rmax): 162.3 TFlop/s
Theoretical Peak (Rpeak): 599.0 TFlop/s
Power: 689.40 kW
Interconnect: Gigabit Ethernet
Operating System: Linux
Ranking: 270

271. **iDataPlex DX360M3, Xeon X5670 6C 2.93 GHz, Infiniband QDR**
Site: Vestas Wind Systems A/S
Country: Denmark
Image URL: None
Manufacturer: IBM
Cores: 15,672
Linpack Performance (Rmax): 162.1 TFlop/s
Theoretical Peak (Rpeak): 183.7 TFlop/s
Power: 489.75 kW
Interconnect: Infiniband QDR
Operating System: Linux
Ranking: 271

272. **SGI ICE 8400EX Xeon X5570 4-core 2.93 GHz, Infiniband**
Site: University of Tokyo/Institute for Solid State Physics
Country: Japan
Image URL: http://www.issp.u-tokyo.ac.jp/supercom/home/topimg-2.jpg
Manufacturer: SGI
Cores: 15,360
Linpack Performance (Rmax): 161.8 TFlop/s
Theoretical Peak (Rpeak): 180 TFlop/s
Power: 719.00 kW
Interconnect: Infiniband QDR
Operating System: Linux
Ranking: 272

273. **Cluster Platform 3000 BL460c Gen8, Xeon E5-2670 8C 2.60GHz, 10G Ethernet**
Site: IT Service Provider
Country: United States
Image URL: None
Manufacturer: Hewlett-Packard
Cores: 15,200
Linpack Performance (Rmax): 161.5 TFlop/s
Theoretical Peak (Rpeak): 316.2 TFlop/s
Interconnect: 10G Ethernet
Operating System: Linux
Ranking: 273

274. **Cluster Platform SL230s Gen8, Xeon E5-2670 8C 2.600GHz, 10G Ethernet**
    Site: IT Services Provider
    Country: United States
    Image URL: None
    Manufacturer: Hewlett-Packard
    Cores: 15,120
    Linpack Performance (Rmax): 161.3 TFlop/s
    Theoretical Peak (Rpeak): 314.5 TFlop/s
    Interconnect: 10G Ethernet
    Operating System: Linux
    Ranking: 274

275. **xSeries x3650 Cluster, Xeon E5-2680 8C 2.700GHz, Infiniband QDR**
    Site: Aerospace Company
    Country: United States
    Image URL: None
    Manufacturer: IBM
    Cores: 8,208
    Linpack Performance (Rmax): 161.3 TFlop/s
    Theoretical Peak (Rpeak): 177.3 TFlop/s
    Power: 228.28 kW
    Interconnect: Infiniband QDR
    Operating System: Linux
    Ranking: 275

276. **Cluster Platform 3000 BL460c Gen8, Xeon E5-2670 8C 2.60GHz, 10G Ethernet**
    Site: IT Service Provider
    Country: United States
    Image URL: None
    Manufacturer: Hewlett-Packard
    Cores: 10,912
    Linpack Performance (Rmax): 160.9 TFlop/s
    Theoretical Peak (Rpeak): 227.0 TFlop/s
    Interconnect: 10G Ethernet
    Operating System: Linux
    Ranking: 276

277. **Cluster Platform 3000 BL460c Gen8, Xeon E5-2660 8C 2.200GHz, Gigabit Ethernet**
    Site: IT Services Provider
    Country: Russia
    Image URL: None
    Manufacturer: Hewlett-Packard
    Cores: 18,032
    Linpack Performance (Rmax): 160.9 TFlop/s
    Theoretical Peak (Rpeak): 317.4 TFlop/s
    Interconnect: Gigabit Ethernet
    Operating System: Linux
    Ranking: 277

278. **Cluster Platform 3000 BL460c Gen8, Xeon E5-2640 6C 2.500GHz, 10G Ethernet**
     Site: IT Services
     Country: Netherlands
     Image URL: Hewlett-Packard
     Cores: 11,364
     Linpack Performance (Rmax): 160.8 TFlop/s
     Theoretical Peak (Rpeak): 227.3 TFlop/s
     Interconnect: 10G Ethernet
     Operating System: Linux
     Ranking: 278

279. **Grifo06 - Itautec Cluster, Xeon E5-2643 4C 3.300GHz, Infiniband FDR, NVIDIA 2075**
     Site: Petroleo Brasileiro S.A
     Country: Brazil
     Image URL: None
     Manufacturer: Itautec
     Cores: 10,368
     Linpack Performance (Rmax): 160.3 TFlop/s
     Theoretical Peak (Rpeak): 357.5 TFlop/s
     Memory: 9,216 GB
     Interconnect: Infiniband FDR
     Operating System: CentOS
     Compiler: Intel
     Math Library: MKL
     MPI: OpenMPI
     Ranking: 279

280. **Diamond - SGI ICE 8200 Enh. LX, Xeon X5560 2.8Ghz**
     Site: ERDC DSRC
     Country: United States
     Image URL: http://media.dma.mil/2013/Jan/2/2000725273/560/360/0/120927-A-HE390-004.JPG
     Manufacturer: SGI
     Cores: 15,360
     Linpack Performance (Rmax): 160.2 TFlop/s
     Theoretical Peak (Rpeak): 172.0 TFlop/s
     Power: 774.00 kW
     Memory: 46,080 GB
     Interconnect: Infiniband DDR
     Operating System: SLES10 + SGI ProPack 5
     Ranking: 280

281. **Hexagon - Cray XE6m-200, Opteron 6276 16C 2.300GHz, Cray Gemini interconnect**
     Site: University of Bergen
     Country: Norway
     Image URL: http://computing.uni.no/hpcdoc_wiki/images/5/56/Hexagon_small.jpg

Manufacturer: Cray Inc.
Cores: 22,272
Linpack Performance (Rmax): 160.1 TFlop/s
Theoretical Peak (Rpeak): 204.9 TFlop/s
Power: 342.30 kW
Interconnect: Cray Gemini Interconnect
Operating System: Cray Linux Environment
Ranking: 281

282. **Cluster Platform SL335s Gen7, Opteron 4171 6C 2.100GHz, 10G Ethernet**
Site: Software Company (M)
Country: United States
Image URL: None
Manufacturer: Hewlett-Packard
Cores: 28,992
Linpack Performance (Rmax): 159.3 TFlop/s
Theoretical Peak (Rpeak): 243.5TFlop/s
Interconnect: 10G Ethernet
Operating System: Linux
Ranking: 282

283. **Blue Wonder - iDataPlex DX360M4, Xeon E5-2670 8C 2.600GHz, Infiniband FDR**
Site: Science and Technology Facilities Council-Daresbury Laboratory
Country: United Kingdom
Image URL: None
Manufacturer: IBM
Cores: 8,192
Linpack Performance (Rmax): 158.7 TFlop/s
Theoretical Peak (Rpeak): 170.4 TFlop/s
Power: 170.16 kW
Interconnect: Infiniband FDR
Operating System: Linux
Ranking: 283

284. **Cluster Platform SL335s Gen7, Opteron 4171 6C 2.100GHz, 10G Ethernet**
Site: Software Company (M)
Country: United States
Image URL: None
Manufacturer: Hewlett-Packard
Cores: 28,800
Linpack Performance (Rmax): 158.3 TFlop/s
Theoretical Peak (Rpeak): 241.9 TFlop/s
Interconnect: 10G Ethernet
Operating System: Linux
Ranking: 284

285. **Cluster Platform 3000 BL460c Gen8, Xeon E5-2680 8C 2.700GHz, 10G Ethernet**
    Site: Financial Service Provider
    Country: United States
    Image URL: None
    Manufacturer: Hewlett-Packard
    Cores: 10,288
    Linpack Performance (Rmax): 158.0 TFlop/s
    Theoretical Peak (Rpeak): 222.2 TFlop/s
    Interconnect: 10G Ethernet
    Operating System: Linux
    Ranking: 285

286. **IBM Flex System x240, Xeon E5-2670 8C 2.600GHz, Infiniband FDR**
    Site: Automotive
    Country: United States
    Image URL: None
    Manufacturer: IBM
    Cores: 8,336
    Linpack Performance (Rmax): 157.7 TFlop/s
    Theoretical Peak (Rpeak): 173.4 TFlop/s
    Power: 181.31 kW
    Interconnect: Infiniband FDR
    Operating System: Linux
    Ranking: 286

287. **IBM Flex System x240, Xeon E5-2670 8C 2.600GHz, Infiniband FDR**
    Site: Automotive
    Country: United States
    Image URL: None
    Manufacturer: IBM
    Cores: 8,336
    Linpack Performance (Rmax): 157.7 TFlop/s
    Theoretical Peak (Rpeak): 173.4 TFlop/s
    Power: 181.31 kW
    Interconnect: Infiniband FDR
    Operating System: Linux
    Ranking: 287

288. **IBM Flex System x240, Xeon E5-2670 8C 2.600GHz, Infiniband FDR**
    Site: Automotive
    Country: United States
    Image URL: None
    Manufacturer: IBM
    Cores: 8,336
    Linpack Performance (Rmax): 157.7 TFlop/s
    Theoretical Peak (Rpeak): 173.4 TFlop/s

Power: 181.31 kW
Interconnect: Infiniband FDR
Operating System: Linux
Ranking: 288

289. **Cluster Platform SL230s Gen8, Xeon E5-2670 8C 2.600GHz, Gigabit Ethernet**
Site: IT Services Provider
Country: United States
Image URL: None
Manufacturer: Hewlett-Packard
Cores: 14,720
Linpack Performance (Rmax): 157.2 TFlop/s
Theoretical Peak (Rpeak): 306.2 TFlop/s
Interconnect: Gigabit Ethernet
Operating System: Linux
Ranking: 289

290. **Cluster Platform SL230s Gen8, Xeon E5-2670 8C 2.600GHz, Gigabit Ethernet**
Site: IT Services Provider
Country: United States
Image URL: None
Manufacturer: Hewlett-Packard
Cores: 14,720
Linpack Performance (Rmax): 157.2 TFlop/s
Theoretical Peak (Rpeak): 306.2 TFlop/s
Interconnect: Gigabit Ethernet
Operating System: Linux
Ranking: 290

291. **Cluster Platform 3000 BL460c Gen8, Xeon E5-2670 8C 2.600GHz, 10G Ethernet**
Site: Manufacturing Company
Country: United States
Image URL: None
Manufacturer: Hewlett-Packard
Cores: 10,624
Linpack Performance (Rmax): 156.9 TFlop/s
Theoretical Peak (Rpeak): 221.0 TFlop/s
Interconnect: 10G Ethernet
Operating System: Linux
Ranking: 291

292. **xSeries x3650M4 Cluster, Xeon E5-2680 8C 2.700GHz, Infiniband**
Site: Electronics
Country: United States
Image URL: None
Manufacturer: IBM
Cores: 8,224

Linpack Performance (Rmax): 155.6 TFlop/s
Theoretical Peak (Rpeak): 177.6 TFlop/s
Power: 213.82 kW
Interconnect: Infiniband
Operating System: Linux
Ranking: 292

293. **xSeries x3650M4 Cluster, Xeon E5-2680 8C 2.700GHz, Infiniband**
Site: Electronics
Country: United States
Image URL: None
Country: IBM
Cores: 8,224
Linpack Performance (Rmax): 155.6 TFlop/s
Theoretical Peak (Rpeak): 177.6 TFlop/s
Power: 213.82 kW
Interconnect: Infiniband
Operating System: Linux
Ranking: 293

294. **Cluster Platform DL380p Gen8, Xeon E5-2650 8C 2.000GHz, Gigabit Ethernet**
Site: IT Services Provider (B)
Country: China
Image URL: None
Manufacturer: Hewlett-Packard
Cores: 20,016
Linpack Performance (Rmax): 155.5 TFlop/s
Theoretical Peak (Rpeak): 320.3 TFlop/s
Interconnect: Gigabit Ethernet
Operating System: Linux
Ranking: 294

295. **xSeries x3650M4 Cluster, Xeon E5-2670 8C 2.600GHz, Gigabit Ethernet**
Site: Banking (M)
Country: United States
Image URL: None
Manufacturer: IBM
Cores: 27,600
Linpack Performance (Rmax): 155.5 TFlop/s
Theoretical Peak (Rpeak): 574.1 TFlop/s
Power: 573.30 kW
Interconnect: Gigabit Ethernet
Operating System: Linux
Ranking: 295

296. **Cluster Platform 3000 BL460c Gen8, Xeon E5-2670 8C 2.600GHz, 10G Ethernet**
  Site: Service Provider
  Country: United States
  Image URL: None
  Manufacturer: Hewlett-Packard
  Cores: 14,560
  Linpack Performance (Rmax): 154.7 TFlop/s
  Theoretical Peak (Rpeak): 302.8 TFlop/s
  Interconnect: 10G Ethernet
  Operating System: Linux
  Ranking: 296

297. **Cluster Platform 3000 BL460c Gen8, Xeon E5-2670 8C 2.600GHz, 10G Ethernet**
  Site: Service Provider
  Country: United States
  Image URL: None
  Manufacturer: Hewlett-Packard
  Cores: 14,560
  Linpack Performance (Rmax): 154.7 TFlop/s
  Theoretical Peak (Rpeak): 302.8 TFlop/s
  Interconnect: 10G Ethernet
  Operating System: Linux
  Ranking: 297

298. **Cluster Platform DL380p Gen8, Xeon E5-2640 6C 2.500GHz, Gigabit Ethernet**
  Site: Telecommunication Company
  Country: China
  Image URL: None
  Manufacturer: Hewlett-Packard
  Cores: 16,152
  Linpack Performance (Rmax): 154.3 TFlop/s
  Theoretical Peak (Rpeak): 323.0 TFlop/s
  Interconnect: Gigabit Ethernet
  Operating System: Linux
  Ranking: 298

299. **Tera-100 Hybrid - Bullx B505, Xeon E56xx (Westmere-EP) 2.40 GHz, Infiniband QDR**
  Site: Commissariat a l'Energie Atomique (CEA)
  Country: France
  Image URL: http://www.cea.fr/var/site/storage/images/defense/top500_tera_100_supercalculateur_le_plus_puiss-58066/1085051-1-fre-FR/top500_tera_100_supercalculateur_le_plus_puissant_d_europe_chapeauactu.jpg
  Manufacturer: Bull SA
  Cores: 7,020
  Linpack Performance (Rmax): 154.0 TFlop/s
  Theoretical Peak (Rpeak): 274.6 TFlop/s

Memory: 9,504 GB
Interconnect: Infiniband QDR
Operating System: Linux
Ranking: 299

300. **Cluster Platform DL380e Gen8, Xeon E5-2640 6C 2.500GHz, Gigabit Ethernet**
   Site: Telecommunication Company
   Country: China
   Image URL: None
   Manufacturer: Hewlett-Packard
   Cores: 15,000
   Linpack Performance (Rmax): 153.9 TFlop/s
   Theoretical Peak (Rpeak): 300.0 TFlop/s
   Interconnect: Gigabit Ethernet
   Operating System: Linux
   Ranking: 300

301. **Cluster Platform DL360e Gen8, Xeon E5-2450 8C 2.100GHz, Gigabit Ethernet**
   Site: Software Company (M)
   Country: United States
   Image URL: None
   Manufacturer: Hewlett-Packard
   Cores: 18,896
   Linpack Performance (Rmax): 153.4 TFlop/s
   Theoretical Peak (Rpeak): 317.5 TFlop/s
   Interconnect: Gigabit Ethernet
   Operating System: Linux
   Ranking: 301

302. **xSeries x3650M4 Cluster, Xeon E5-2670 8C 2.600GHz, Gigabit Ethernet**
   Site: Engineering Company
   Country: China
   Image URL: None
   Manufacturer: IBM
   Cores: 27,136
   Linpack Performance (Rmax): 152.9 TFlop/s
   Theoretical Peak (Rpeak): 564.4 TFlop/s
   Power: 649.57 kW
   Interconnect: Gigabit Ethernet
   Operating System: Linux
   Ranking: 302

303. **VSC-2 - Megware Saxonid 6100, Opteron 8C 2.2 GHz, Infiniband QDR**
   Site: Vienna Scientific Cluster
   Country: Austria
   Image URL: http://www.vsc.ac.at/typo3temp/pics/a7701ad81d.jpg
   Manufacturer: Megware

Cores: 20,776
Linpack Performance (Rmax): 152.9 TFlop/s
Theoretical Peak (Rpeak): 182.8 TFlop/s
Power: 430.00 kW
Memory: 42,048 GB
Interconnect: Infiniband QDR
Operating System: Linux
Ranking: 303

304. **Cluster Platform DL380p Gen8, Xeon E5-2630 6C 2.300GHz, Gigabit Ethernet**
Site: Service Provider
Country: South Korea
Image URL: None
Manufacturer: Hewlett-Packard
Cores: 16,260
Linpack Performance (Rmax): 152.7 TFlop/s
Theoretical Peak (Rpeak): 299.2 TFlop/s
Interconnect: Gigabit Ethernet
Operating System: Linux
Ranking: 304

305. **Cluster Platform DL380p Gen8, Xeon E5-2620 6C 2.000GHz, Gigabit Ethernet**
Site: Service Provider
Country: United States
Image URL: None
Manufacturer: Hewlett-Packard
Cores: 19,104
Linpack Performance (Rmax): 152.4 TFlop/s
Theoretical Peak (Rpeak): 305.7 TFlop/s
Interconnect: Gigabit Ethernet
Operating System: Linux
Ranking: 305

306. **Cluster Platform SL230s Gen8, Xeon E5-2670 8C 2.60GHz, Infiniband FDR**
Site: VSC/ Flemish Supercomputer Center
Country: Belgium
Image URL: http://www.ugent.be/img/hpc/tier1_front.jpg/image_preview
Manufacturer: Hewlett-Packard
Cores: 8,448
Linpack Performance (Rmax): 152.3 TFlop/s
Theoretical Peak (Rpeak): 175.7 TFlop/s
Interconnect: Infiniband FDR
Operating System: Linux
Ranking: 306

307. **MRI - PowerEdge C6100 Cluster, Xeon X5660 2.8 Ghz, Infiniband**
     Site: University of Colorado
     Country: United States
     Image URL: None
     Manufacturer: Dell
     Cores: 15,648
     Linpack Performance (Rmax): 152.2 TFlop/s
     Theoretical Peak (Rpeak): 175.3 TFlop/s
     Interconnect: Infiniband QDR
     Operating System: Linux
     Compiler: Intel 11.1
     MPI: OpenMPI 1.4.1
     Ranking: 307

308. **xSeries x3650M4 Cluster, Xeon E5-2680 8C 2.700GHz, Gigabit Ethernet**
     Site: Service Provider
     Country: China
     Image URL: None
     Manufacturer: IBM
     Cores: 26,976
     Linpack Performance (Rmax): 152.0 TFlop/s
     Theoretical Peak (Rpeak): 582.7 TFlop/s
     Power: 645.74 kW
     Interconnect: Gigabit Ethernet
     Operating System: Linux
     Ranking: 308

309. **Faenov - Cluster Platform SL230s Gen8, Xeon E5-2670 8C 2.600GHz, Infiniband QDR**
     Site: Microsoft Windows Azure
     Country: United States
     Image URL: None
     Manufacturer: Hewlett-Packard
     Cores: 8,064
     Linpack Performance (Rmax): 151.3 TFlop/s
     Theoretical Peak (Rpeak): 167.7 TFlop/s
     Memory: 60,480 GB
     Interconnect: Infiniband QDR
     Operating System: Windows Azure
     Math Library: Intel MKL 11.0
     MPI: Microsoft MPI
     Ranking: 309

310. **BladeCenter HS23 Cluster, Xeon E5-2680 8C 2.700GHz, Infiniband QDR**
     Site: Aerospace Company
     Country: United States
     Image URL: None

Manufacturer: IBM
Cores: 7,664
Linpack Performance (Rmax): 150.6 TFlop/s
Theoretical Peak (Rpeak): 165.5 TFlop/s
Power: 151.84 kW
Interconnect: Infiniband QDR
Operating System: Linux
Ranking: 310

311. **TSUBAME-KFC - LX 1U-4GPU/104Re-1G Cluster, Intel Xeon E5-2620v2 6C 2.100GHz, Infiniband FDR, NVIDIA K20x**
Site: GSIC Center, Tokyo Institute of Technology
Country: Japan
Image URL: http://www.titech.ac.jp/english/news/img/news20131121_tsubame01.jpg
Manufacturer: NEC
Cores: 2,720
Linpack Performance (Rmax): 150.4 TFlop/s
Theoretical Peak (Rpeak): 217.8 TFlop/s
Power: 44.00 kW
Memory: 2,560 GB
Interconnect: Infiniband FDR
Operating System: CentOS
Compiler: Gcc
Math Library: Intel MKL
MPI: OpenMPI 1.7.2
Ranking: 311

312. **Cluster Platform DL360p Gen8, Xeon E5-2630 6C 2.300GHz, Gigabit Ethernet**
Site: IT Services Provider
Country: United States
Image URL: None
Manufacturer: Hewlett-Packard
Cores: 16,140
Linpack Performance (Rmax): 150.3 TFlop/s
Theoretical Peak (Rpeak): 297.0 TFlop/s
Interconnect: Gigabit Ethernet
Operating System: Linux
Ranking: 312

313. **HPC - PowerEdge 1950/SunFire X2200/IBM dx340/dx360/HP SL160/DL165, Xeon/Opteron 2.3-2.67GHz, Myrinet 10G**
Site: University of Southern California
Country: United States
Image URL: https://hpcc.usc.edu/files/2012/11/InsideCover-1024x443.jpg
Manufacturer: Dell/Sun/IBM
Cores: 20,925

Linpack Performance (Rmax): 149.9 TFlop/s
Theoretical Peak (Rpeak): 196.5 TFlop/s
Interconnect: Myrinet 10G
Operating System: Linux
Ranking: 313

314. **Cluster Platform DL360e Gen8, Xeon E5-2450 8C 2.100GHz, Gigabit Ethernet**
Site: Software Company (M)
Country: United States
Image URL: None
Manufacturer: Hewlett-Packard
Cores: 18,448
Linpack Performance (Rmax): 149.7 TFlop/s
Theoretical Peak (Rpeak): 309.9 TFlop/s
Interconnect: Gigabit Ethernet
Operating System: Linux
Ranking: 314

315. **Cluster Platform 3000 BL460c Gen8, Xeon E5-2670 8C 2.600GHz, Infiniband FDR**
Site: Manufacturing Company
Country: India
Image URL: None
Manufacturer: Hewlett-Packard
Cores: 8,448
Linpack Performance (Rmax): 149.2 TFlop/s
Theoretical Peak (Rpeak): 175.7 TFlop/s
Interconnect: Infiniband FDR
Operating System: Linux
Ranking: 315

316. **iDataPlex DX360M4, Xeon E5-2670 8C 2.600GHz, Infiniband FDR**
Site: Centro Euro-Mediterraneo per i Cambiamenti Climatici
Country: Italy
Image URL: None
Manufacturer: IBM
Cores: 7,680
Linpack Performance (Rmax): 148.8 TFlop/s
Theoretical Peak (Rpeak): 159.7 TFlop/s
Power: 159.53 kW
Interconnect: Infiniband FDR
Operating System: Linux
Ranking: 316

317. **iDataPlex DX360M3, Xeon E5-2670 8C 2.600GHz, Infiniband QDR**
Site: NASA/ Goddard Space Flight Center
Country: United States
Image URL: None

Manufacturer: IBM
Cores: 7,680
Linpack Performance (Rmax): 148.8 TFlop/s
Theoretical Peak (Rpeak): 159.7 TFlop/s
Power: 159.53 kW
Interconnect: Infiniband QDR
Operating System: Linux
Ranking: 317

318. **Cluster Platform 4000 BL685c, Opteron 6274 16C 2.200GHz, Gigabit Ethernet**
Site: Electronic Industry
Country: United States
Image URL: None
Manufacturer: Hewlett-Packard
Cores: 35,840
Linpack Performance (Rmax): 148.7 TFlop/s
Theoretical Peak (Rpeak): 315.4 TFlop/s
Interconnect: Gigabit Ethernet
Operating System: Linux
Ranking: 318

319. **Cluster Platform SL230s Gen8, Xeon E5-2670 8C 2.600GHz, Gigabit Ethernet**
Site: Retail
Country: United States
Image URL: None
Manufacturer: Hewlett-Packard
Cores: 13,856
Linpack Performance (Rmax): 148.5 TFlop/s
Theoretical Peak (Rpeak): 288.2 TFlop/s
Interconnect: Gigabit Ethernet
Operating System: Linux
Ranking: 319

320. **Cluster Platform 3000 BL460c Gen8, Xeon E5-2670 8C 2.600GHz, 10G Ethernet**
Site: Electronic Industry
Country: United States
Image URL: None
Cores: 9,984
Linpack Performance (Rmax): 147.8 TFlop/s
Theoretical Peak (Rpeak): 207.7 TFlop/s
Interconnect: 10G Ethernet
Operating System: Linux
Ranking: 320

321. **xSeries x3550M3 Cluster, Xeon E5-2670 8C 2.600GHz, Gigabit Ethernet**
Site: Engineering Company
Country: China

Image URL: None
Manufacturer: IBM
Cores: 26,208
Linpack Performance (Rmax): 147.7 TFlop/s
Theoretical Peak (Rpeak): 545.1 TFlop/s
Power: 627.35 kW
Interconnect: Gigabit Ethernet
Operating System: Linux
Ranking: 321

322. **xSeries x3550M3 Cluster, Xeon E5-2670 8C 2.600GHz, Gigabit Ethernet**
Site: Engineering Company
Country: China
Image URL: None
Manufacturer: IBM
Cores: 26,208
Linpack Performance (Rmax): 147.7 TFlop/s
Theoretical Peak (Rpeak): 545.1 TFlop/s
Power: 627.35 kW
Interconnect: Gigabit Ethernet
Operating System: Linux
Ranking: 322

323. **xSeries x3550M3 Cluster, Xeon E5-2670 8C 2.600GHz, Gigabit Ethernet**
Site: Engineering Company
Country: China
Image URL: None
Manufacturer: IBM
Cores: 26,208
Linpack Performance (Rmax): 147.7 TFlop/s
Theoretical Peak (Rpeak): 545.1 TFlop/s
Power: 627.35 kW
Interconnect: Gigabit Ethernet
Operating System: Linux
Ranking: 323

324. **xSeries x3550M3 Cluster, Xeon E5-2670 8C 2.600GHz, Gigabit Ethernet**
Site: Engineering Company
Country: China
Image URL: None
Manufacturer: IBM
Cores: 26,208
Linpack Performance (Rmax): 147.7 TFlop/s
Theoretical Peak (Rpeak): 545.1 TFlop/s
Power: 627.35 kW
Interconnect: Gigabit Ethernet

Operating System: Linux

Ranking: 324

325. **Crystal - Cray XC30, Xeon E5-2670 8C 2.600GHz, Aries interconnect**

Site: Cray Inc.

Country: United States

Image URL: http://www.cray.com/assets/images/products/ad-box-xc30.jpg

Manufacturer: Cray Inc.

Cores: 8,192

Linpack Performance (Rmax): 147.3 TFlop/s

Theoretical Peak (Rpeak): 170.4 TFlop/s

Interconnect: Aries Interconnect

Operating System: Cray Linux Environment

Ranking: 325

326. **xSeries x3650M4 Cluster, Xeon E5-2670 8C 2.600GHz, Gigabit Ethernet**

Site: Telecommunication Company

Country: China

Image URL: None

Manufacturer: IBM

Cores: 26,016

Linpack Performance (Rmax): 146.6 TFlop/s

Theoretical Peak (Rpeak): 541.1 TFlop/s

Power: 1,141.45 kW

Interconnect: Gigabit Ethernet

Operating System: Linux

Ranking: 326

327. **xSeries x3650M4 Cluster, Xeon E5-2670 8C 2.600GHz, Gigabit Ethernet**

Site: Telecommunication Company

Country: China

Image URL: None

Manufacturer: IBM

Cores: 26,016

Linpack Performance (Rmax): 146.6 TFlop/s

Theoretical Peak (Rpeak): 541.1 TFlop/s

Power: 1,141.45 kW

Interconnect: Gigabit Ethernet

Operating System: Linux

Ranking: 327

328. **iDataPlex DX360M4, Intel Xeon E5-2680v2 10C 2.800GHz, Infiniband, NVIDIA K20x**

Site: Financial Institution

Country: United States

Image URL: None

Manufacturer: IBM

Cores: 3,264

Linpack Performance (Rmax): 146.2 TFlop/s
Theoretical Peak (Rpeak): 208.8 TFlop/s
Interconnect: Infiniband
Operating System: Linux
Ranking: 328

329. **Cluster Platform 3000 BL460c Gen8, Xeon E5-2670 8C 2.600GHz, 10G Ethernet**
Site: Service Provider
Country: United States
Image URL: None
Manufacturer: Hewlett-Packard
Cores: 13,728
Linpack Performance (Rmax): 145.9 TFlop/s
Theoretical Peak (Rpeak): 285.5 TFlop/s
Interconnect: 10G Ethernet
Operating System: Linux
Ranking: 329

330. **Sunway 4000H Cluster, Xeon X56xx (Westmere-EP) 2.93 GHz, Infiniband QDR**
Site: Government
Country: China
Image URL: None
Manufacturer: National Research Center of Parallel Computer Engineering & Technology
Cores: 14,280
Linpack Performance (Rmax): 145.6 TFlop/s
Theoretical Peak (Rpeak): 167.4 TFlop/s
Memory: 28,560 GB
Interconnect: Infiniband QDR
Operating System: Linux
Ranking: 330

331. **xSeries x3650M3 Cluster, Xeon E5649 6C 2.530GHz, Gigabit Ethernet**
Site: Electronics
Country: China
Image URL: None
Manufacturer: IBM
Cores: 25,788
Linpack Performance (Rmax): 145.3 TFlop/s
Theoretical Peak (Rpeak): 261.0 TFlop/s
Power: 782.00 kW
Interconnect: Gigabit Ethernet
Operating System: Linux
Ranking: 331

332. **xSeries x3650M3 Cluster, Xeon E5649 6C 2.530GHz, Gigabit Ethernet**
Site: Electronics
Country: China

Image URL: None
Manufacturer: IBM
Cores: 25,788
Linpack Performance (Rmax): 145.3 TFlop/s
Theoretical Peak (Rpeak): 261.0 TFlop/s
Power: 782.00 kW
Interconnect: Gigabit Ethernet
Operating System: Linux
Ranking: 332

333. **xSeries x3650M4 Cluster, Xeon E5-2670 8C 2.600GHz, Gigabit Ethernet**
Site: Electronics
Country: China
Image URL: None
Manufacturer: IBM
Cores: 25,776
Linpack Performance (Rmax): 145.2 TFlop/s
Theoretical Peak (Rpeak): 536.1 TFlop/s
Power: 617.01 kW
Interconnect: Gigabit Ethernet
Operating System: Linux
Ranking: 333

334. **xSeries x3650M4 Cluster, Xeon E5-2670 8C 2.600GHz, Gigabit Ethernet**
Site: Electronics
Country: China
Image URL: None
Manufacturer: IBM
Cores: 25,776
Linpack Performance (Rmax): 145.2 TFlop/s
Theoretical Peak (Rpeak): 536.1 TFlop/s
Power: 617.01 kW
Interconnect: Gigabit Ethernet
Operating System: Linux
Ranking: 334

335. **xSeries x3650M4 Cluster, Xeon E5-2670 8C 2.600GHz, Gigabit Ethernet**
Site: Electronics
Country: China
Image URL: None
Manufacturer: IBM
Cores: 25,776
Linpack Performance (Rmax): 145.2 TFlop/s
Theoretical Peak (Rpeak): 536.1 TFlop/s
Power: 617.01 kW
Interconnect: Gigabit Ethernet
Operating System: Linux
Ranking: 335

336. **iDataPlex DX360M4, Intel Xeon E5-2650v2 8C 2.600GHz, Infiniband FDR14, NVIDIA K20x**

    Site: University of Arizona
    Country: United States
    Image URL: http://rc2.webhost.uits.arizona.edu/sites/default/files/imagecache/sidebar/images/sidebar/photo-3_iDataPlex.jpg
    Manufacturer: IBM
    Cores: 3,080
    Linpack Performance (Rmax): 144.5 TFlop/s
    Theoretical Peak (Rpeak): 206.8 TFlop/s
    Power: 53.62 kW
    Interconnect: Infiniband FDR14
    Operating System: Linux
    Ranking: 336

337. **Cluster Platform SL230s Gen8, Xeon E5-2670 8C 2.600GHz, Infiniband FDR**

    Site: IT Service Provider
    Country: Germany
    Image URL: None
    Manufacturer: Hewlett-Packard
    Cores: 8,192
    Linpack Performance (Rmax): 144.3 TFlop/s
    Theoretical Peak (Rpeak): 170.4 TFlop/s
    Interconnect: Infiniband FDR
    Operating System: Linux
    Ranking: 337

338. **Cluster Platform 3000 BL460c Gen8, Xeon E5-2670 8C 2.600GHz, 10G Ethernet**

    Site: Manufacturing Company
    Country: United States
    Image URL: None
    Manufacturer: Hewlett-Packard
    Cores: 9,728
    Linpack Performance (Rmax): 143.6 TFlop/s
    Theoretical Peak (Rpeak): 202.3 TFlop/s
    Interconnect: 10G Ethernet
    Operating System: Linux
    Ranking: 338

339. **xSeries x3650M4 Cluster, Xeon E5-2670 8C 2.600GHz, Gigabit Ethernet**

    Site: Internet Service
    Country: China
    Image URL: None
    Manufacturer: IBM
    Cores: 25,424
    Linpack Performance (Rmax): 143.3 TFlop/s

Theoretical Peak (Rpeak): 528.8 TFlop/s
Power: 608.59 kW
Interconnect: Gigabit Ethernet
Operating System: Linux
Ranking: 339

340. **xSeries x3650M4 Cluster, Xeon E5-2670 8C 2.600GHz, Gigabit Ethernet**
Site: Internet Service
Country: United States
Image URL: None
Manufacturer: IBM
Cores: 25,424
Linpack Performance: 143.3 TFlop/s
Theoretical Peak (Rpeak): 528.8 TFlop/s
Power: 608.59 kW
Interconnect: Gigabit Ethernet
Operating System: Linux
Ranking: 340

341. **xSeries x3650M4 Cluster, Xeon E5-2670 8C 2.600GHz, Gigabit Ethernet**
Site: Internet Service
Country: China
Image URL: None
Manufacturer: IBM
Cores: 25,424
Linpack Performance (Rmax): 143.3 TFlop/s
Theoretical Peak (Rpeak): 528.8 TFlop/s
Power: 608.59 kW
Interconnect: Gigabit Ethernet
Operating System: Linux
Ranking: 341

342. **xSeries x3650M4 Cluster, Xeon E5-2670 8C 2.600GHz, Gigabit Ethernet**
Site: Internet Service
Country: China
Image URL: None
Manufacturer: IBM
Cores: 25,424
Linpack Performance (Rmax): 143.3 TFlop/s
Theoretical Peak (Rpeak): 528.8 TFlop/s
Power: 608.59 kW
Interconnect: Gigabit Ethernet
Operating System: Linux
Ranking: 342

343. **xSeries x3650M4 Cluster, Xeon E5-2670 8C 2.600GHz, Gigabit Ethernet**
   Site: Internet Service
   Country: China
   Image URL: None
   Manufacturer: IBM
   Cores: 25,424
   Linpack Performance (Rmax): 143.3 TFlop/s
   Theoretical Peak (Rpeak): 528.8 TFlop/s
   Power: 608.59 kW
   Interconnect: Gigabit Ethernet
   Operating System: Linux
   Ranking: 343

344. **xSeries x3650M4 Cluster, Xeon E5-2670 8C 2.600GHz, Gigabit Ethernet**
   Site: Internet Service
   Country: China
   Image URL: None
   Manufacturer: IBM
   Cores: 25,424
   Linpack Performance (Rmax): 143.3 TFlop/s
   Theoretical Peak (Rpeak): 528.8 TFlop/s
   Power: 608.59 kW
   Interconnect: Gigabit Ethernet
   Operating System: Linux
   Ranking: 344

345. **xSeries x3650M4 Cluster, Xeon E5-2670 8C 2.600GHz, Gigabit Ethernet**
   Site: Internet Service
   Country: China
   Image URL: None
   Manufacturer: IBM
   Cores: 25,424
   Linpack Performance (Rmax): 143.3 TFlop/s
   Theoretical Peak (Rpeak): 528.8 TFlop/s
   Power: 608.59 kW
   Interconnect: Gigabit Ethernet
   Operating System: Linux
   Ranking: 345

346. **Cluster Platform 3000 BL460c Gen8, Xeon E5-2670 8C 2.600GHz, 10G Ethernet**
   Site: IT Services Provider
   Country: United States
   Image URL: None
   Manufacturer: Hewlett-Packard
   Cores: 9,824
   Linpack Performance (Rmax): 143.2 TFlop/s

Theoretical Peak (Rpeak): 204.3 TFlop/s
Interconnect: 10G Ethernet
Operating System: Linux
Ranking: 346

347. **xSeries x3550M3 Cluster, Xeon E5649 6C 2.530GHz, Gigabit Ethernet**
   Site: Service Provider
   Country: United States
   Image URL: None
   Manufacturer: IBM
   Cores: 25,404
   Linpack Performance (Rmax): 143.2 TFlop/s
   Theoretical Peak (Rpeak): 257.1 TFlop/s
   Power: 770.50 kW
   Interconnect: Gigabit Ethernet
   Operating System: Linux
   Ranking: 347

348. **Cluster Platform 3000 BL460c Gen8, Intel Xeon E5-2658v2 10C 2.400GHz, 10G Ethernet**
   Site: Electronic Industry
   Country: United States
   Image URL: None
   Manufacturer: Hewlett-Packard
   Cores: 10,480
   Linpack Performance (Rmax): 142.9 TFlop/s
   Theoretical Peak (Rpeak): 201.2 TFlop/s
   Interconnect: 10G Ethernet
   Operating System: Linux
   Ranking: 348

349. **iDataPlex DX360M3, Xeon E5645 6C 2.40 GHz, Infiniband QDR, NVIDIA 2070**
   Site: CINECA/ SCS- SuperComputing Solution
   Country: Italy
   Manufacturer: IBM
   Cores: 10,240
   Linpack Performance (Rmax): 142.7 TFlop/s
   Theoretical Peak (Rpeak): 293.2 TFlop/s
   Power: 160.00 kW
   Interconnect: Infiniband QDR
   Operating System: Linux
   Ranking: 349

350. **Cluster Platform 3000 BL460c Gen8, Xeon E5-2670 8C 2.60GHz, 10G Ethernet**
   Site: IT Service Provider
   Country: United States
   Image URL: None
   Manufacturer: Hewlett-Packard

Cores: 9,488
Linpack Performance (Rmax): 141.9 TFlop/s
Theoretical Peak (Rpeak): 197.3 TFlop/s
Interconnect: 10G Ethernet
Operating System: Linux
Ranking: 350

351. **Cluster Platform SL165z G7, Opteron 6172 12C 2.100GHz, Gigabit Ethernet**
Site: Financial Services Company (G)
Country: United States
Image URL: None
Manufacturer: Hewlett-Packard
Cores: 33,408
Linpack Performance (Rmax): 141.4 TFlop/s
Theoretical Peak (Rpeak): 280.6 TFlop/s
Interconnect: Gigabit Ethernet
Operating System: Linux
Ranking: 351

352. **xSeries x3650M4 Cluster, Xeon E5-2670 8C 2.600GHz, Gigabit Ethernet**
Site: Internet Service
Country: China
Image URL: None
Manufacturer: IBM
Cores: 25,072
Linpack Performance(Rmax): 141.3 TFlop/s
Theoretical Peak (Rpeak): 521.5 TFlop/s
Power: 600.00 kW
Interconnect: Gigabit Ethernet
Operating System: Linux
Ranking: 352

353. **Guillimin Phase 2 - iDataPlex DX360M4, Xeon E5-2670 8C 2.600GHz, Infiniband QDR**
Site: CLUMEQ- McGill University
Country: Canada
Image URL: http://www.hpc.mcgill.ca/images/guillimin09.jpg, http://www.hpc.mcgill.ca/images/guillimin08.jpg
Manufacturer: IBM
Cores: 7,456
Linpack Performance (Rmax): 141.1 TFlop/s
Theoretical Peak (Rpeak): 155.1 TFlop/s
Power: 154.88 kW
Interconnect: Infiniband QDR
Operating System: Linux
Ranking: 353

354. **xSeries x3650 Cluster, Xeon E5649 6C 2.530GHz, Infiniband, NVIDIA 2090**
     Site: Petroleum Company
     Country: China
     Image URL: None
     Manufacturer: IBM
     Cores: 10,120
     Linpack Performance(Rmax): 141.0 TFlop/s
     Theoretical Peak (Rpeak): 367.7 TFlop/s
     Power: 162.87 kW
     Interconnect: Infiniband
     Operating System: Linux
     Ranking: 354

355. **Cluster Platform 3000 BL460c Gen8, Xeon E5-2670 8C 2.600GHz, 10G Ethernet**
     Site: Logistic Services (E)
     Country: United States
     Image URL: None
     Manufacturer: Hewlett-Packard
     Cores: 9,504
     Linpack Performance (Rmax): 140.9 TFlop/s
     Theoretical Peak (Rpeak): 197.7 TFlop/s
     Interconnect: 10G Ethernet
     Operating System: Linux
     Ranking: 355

356. **Cluster Platform 3000 BL460c G7, Xeon X5650 6C 2.660GHz, Gigabit Ethernet**
     Site: Banking (M)
     Country: United States
     Image URL: None
     Manufacturer: Hewlett-Packard
     Cores: 26,256
     Linpack Performance (Rmax): 140.8 TFlop/s
     Theoretical Peak (Rpeak): 279.4 TFlop/s
     Interconnect: Gigabit Ethernet
     Operating System: Linux
     Ranking: 356

357. **Cluster Platform SL230s Gen8, Xeon E5-2670 8C 2.600GHz, 10G Ethernet**
     Site: Energy Company
     Country: United States
     Image URL: None
     Cores: 9,472
     Linpack Performance (Rmax): 140.5 TFlop/s
     Theoretical Peak (Rpeak): 197.0 TFlop/s
     Interconnect: 10G Ethernet
     Operating System: Linux
     Ranking: 357

358. **Fionn - SGI ICE X, Intel Xeon E5-2695v2 12C 2.400GHz, Infiniband FDR**
Site: Irish Centre for High-End Computing
Country: Ireland
Image URL: https://www.ichec.ie/images/systems/system-fionn-panoramic-2000x588.jpg, https://www.ichec.ie/images/systems/system-fionn-uv-service-800x758.png, https://www.ichec.ie/images/systems/system-fionn-uv2000-phi-800x570.png, https://www.ichec.ie/images/systems/system-fionn-accelerators-600x1238.png
Manufacturer: SGI
Cores: 7,680
Linpack Performance (Rmax): 140.4 TFlop/s
Theoretical Peak (Rpeak): 147.5 TFlop/s
Power: 114.50 kW
Memory: 20,480 GB
Interconnect: Infiniband FDR
Operating System: SUSE Linux Enterprise Server 11
Ranking: 358

359. **iDataPlex DX360M4, Xeon E5-2670 8C 2.600GHz, Infiniband**
Site: Financial Institution (P)
Country: France ▌▐
Image URL: None
Manufacturer: IBM
Cores: 7,408
Linpack Performance (Rmax): 140.2 TFlop/s
Theoretical Peak (Rpeak): 154.1 TFlop/s
Power: 153.88 kW
Interconnect: Infiniband
Operating System: Linux
Ranking: 359

360. **iDataPlex DX360M4, Xeon E5-2670 8C 2.600GHz, Infiniband**
Site: Financial Institution (P)
Country: France ▌▐
Image URL: None
Manufacturer: IBM
Cores: 7,408
Linpack Performance (Rmax): 140.2 TFlop/s
Theoretical Peak (Rpeak): 154.1 TFlop/s
Power: 153.88 kW
Interconnect: Infiniband
Operating System: Linux
Ranking: 360

361. **iDataPlex DX360M4, Xeon E5-2670 8C 2.600GHz, Infiniband**
Site: Financial Institution (P)
Country: France ▌▐

Image URL: None
Manufacturer: IBM
Cores: 7,408
Linpack Performance (Rmax): 140.2 TFlop/s
Theoretical Peak (Rpeak): 154.1 TFlop/s
Power: 153.88 kW
Interconnect: Infiniband
Operating System: Linux
Ranking: 361

362. **Cluster Platform 3000 BL460c Gen8, Xeon E5-2660 8C 2.200GHz, 10G Ethernet**
Site: Automotive
Country: United States
Image URL: None
Manufacturer: Hewlett-Packard
Cores: 11,232
Linpack Performance (Rmax): 140.0 TFlop/s
Theoretical Peak (Rpeak): 197.7 TFlop/s
Interconnect: 10G Ethernet
Operating System: Linux
Ranking: 362

363. **xSeries x3650M4 Cluster, Xeon E5-2670 8C 2.600GHz, Infiniband**
Site: Electronics
Country: United States
Image URL: None
Manufacturer: IBM
Cores: 8,016
Linpack Performance (Rmax): 139.5 TFlop/s
Theoretical Peak (Rpeak): 166.7 TFlop/s
Power: 208.42 kW
Interconnect: Infiniband
Operating System: Linux
Ranking: 363

364. **iDataPlex DX360M4, Xeon E5-2690 8C 2.900GHz, Infiniband FDR**
Site: Electronics Company
Country: Japan
Image URL: None
Manufacturer: IBM
Cores: 7,088
Linpack Performance (Rmax): 139.3 TFlop/s
Theoretical Peak (Rpeak): 164.4 TFlop/s
Power: 172.77 kW
Interconnect: Infiniband FDR
Operating System: Linux
Ranking: 364

365. **xSeries x3650M4 Cluster, Xeon E5-2670 8C 2.600GHz, Infiniband**
     Site: Petroleum Company
     Country: United Kingdom
     Image URL: None
     Manufacturer: IBM
     Cores: 7,360
     Linpack Performance (Rmax): 139.2 TFlop/s
     Theoretical Peak (Rpeak): 153.1 TFlop/s
     Power: 191.36 kW
     Interconnect: Infiniband
     Operating System: Linux
     Ranking: 365

366. **Cluster Platform 3000 BL460c Gen8, Xeon E5-2670 8C 2.600GHz, 10G Ethernet**
     Site: IT Services Provider (B)
     Country: India
     Image URL: None
     Manufacturer: Hewlett-Packard
     Cores: 9,392
     Linpack Performance (Rmax): 139.2 TFlop/s
     Theoretical Peak (Rpeak): 195.4 TFlop/s
     Interconnect: 10G Ethernet
     Operating System: Linux
     Ranking: 366

367. **iDataPlex DX360M4, Xeon E5-2670 8C 2.600GHz, Gigabit Ethernet**
     Site: Financial Institution
     Country: United Kingdom
     Image URL: None
     Manufacturer: IBM
     Cores: 24,672
     Linpack Performance (Rmax): 139.0 TFlop/s
     Theoretical Peak (Rpeak): 513.2 TFlop/s
     Power: 512.48 kW
     Interconnect: Gigabit Ethernet
     Operating System: Linux
     Ranking: 367

368. **Cluster Platform 4000 BL465c, Opteron 6174 12C 2.200GHz, Gigabit Ethernet**
     Site: Manufacturing Company
     Country: United States
     Image URL: None
     Manufacturer: Hewlett-Packard
     Cores: 31,200
     Linpack Performance (Rmax): 138.4 TFlop/s
     Theoretical Peak (Rpeak): 274.6 TFlop/s

Interconnect: Gigabit Ethernet
Operating System: Linux
Ranking: 368

369. **Cluster Platform DL388p, Xeon E5-2609 4C 2.400GHz, Gigabit Ethernet**
Site: IT Services Provider (B)
Country: China
Image URL: None
Manufacturer: Hewlett-Packard
Cores: 13,968
Linpack Performance (Rmax): 138.1 TFlop/s
Theoretical Peak (Rpeak): 268.2 TFlop/s
Interconnect: Gigabit Ethernet
Operating System: Linux
Ranking: 369

370. **xSeries x3650M4 Cluster, Xeon E5-2670 8C 2.600GHz, Gigabit Ethernet**
Site: Internet Service
Country: China
Image URL: None
Manufacturer: IBM
Cores: 24,368
Linpack Performance (Rmax): 137.3 TFlop/s
Theoretical Peak (Rpeak): 506.9 TFlop/s
Power: 583.31 kW
Interconnect: Gigabit Ethernet
Operating System: Linux
Ranking: 370

371. **xSeries x3650M4 Cluster, Xeon E5-2670 8C 2.600GHz, Gigabit Ethernet**
Site: Internet Service
Country: China
Image URL: None
Manufacturer: IBM
Cores: 24,368
Linpack Performance (Rmax): 137.3 TFlop/s
Theoretical Peak (Rpeak): 506.9 TFlop/s
Power: 583.31 kW
Interconnect: Gigabit Ethernet
Operating System: Linux
Ranking: 371

372. **xSeries x3650M4 Cluster, Xeon E5-2670 8C 2.600GHz, Gigabit Ethernet**
Site: Internet Service
Country: China
Image URL: None
Manufacturer: IBM

Cores: 24,368
Linpack Performance (Rmax): 137.3 TFlop/s
Theoretical Peak (Rpeak): 506.9 TFlop/s
Power: 583.31 kW
Interconnect: Gigabit Ethernet
Operating System: Linux
Ranking: 372

373. **WillowA - Bullx B510, Xeon E5-2670 8C 2.600GHz, Infiniband QDR**
Site: Atomic Weapons Establishment
Country: United Kingdom
Image URL: http://www.awe.co.uk/set/images/Supercomputing.jpg
Manufacturer: Bull SA
Cores: 7,488
Linpack Performance (Rmax): 136.7 TFlop/s
Theoretical Peak (Rpeak): 161.7 TFlop/s
Power: 182.00 kW
Memory: 22, 464 GB
Interconnect: Infiniband QDR
Operating System: Linux
Compiler: gcc
Math Library: Intel MKL
MPI: Intel MPI
Ranking: 373

374. **WillowB - Bullx B510, Xeon E5-2670 8C 2.600GHz, Infiniband QDR**
Site: Atomic Weapons Establishment
Country: United Kingdom
Image URL: http://www.awe.co.uk/set/images/Supercomputing.jpg
Manufacturer: Bull SA
Cores: 7,488
Linpack Performance (Rmax): 136.4 TFlop/s
Theoretical Peak (Rpeak): 161.7 TFlop/s
Power: 182.00 kW
Memory: 22, 464 GB
Interconnect: Infiniband QDR
Operating System: Linux
Compiler: gcc
Math Library: MKL
MPI: Intel MPI
Ranking: 374

375. **Guillimin - iDataPlex DX360M3, Xeon 2.66, Infiniband**
Site: CLUMEQ- McGill University
Country: Canada
Image URL: http://www.hpc.mcgill.ca/images/guillimin09.jpg

Manufacturer: IBM
Cores: 14,400
Linpack Performance (Rmax): 136.4 TFlop/s
Theoretical Peak (Rpeak): 153.2 TFlop/s
Power: 337.00 kW
Interconnect: Infiniband QDR
Operating System: Linux
Ranking: 375

376. **Argus - iDataPlex DX360M4, Xeon E5-2670 8C 2.600GHz, Infiniband FDR14**
Site: Bombardier Aerospace
Country: Canada
Image URL: None
Manufacturer: IBM
Cores: 7,200
Linpack Performance (Rmax): 136.2 TFlop/s
Theoretical Peak (Rpeak): 149.8 TFlop/s
Power: 149.56 kW
Interconnect: Infiniband FDR14
Operating System: Linux
Ranking: 376

377. **xSeries x3650M4 Cluster, Xeon E5-2670 8C 2.600GHz, Gigabit Ethernet**
Site: Banking (M)
Country: United States
Image URL: None
Manufacturer: IBM
Cores: 24,064
Linpack Performance (Rmax): 135.6 TFlop/s
Theoretical Peak (Rpeak): 500.5 TFlop/s
Power: 576.03 kW
Interconnect: Gigabit Ethernet
Operating System: Linux
Ranking: 377

378. **Laurel - Xtreme-X, Xeon E5-2670 8C 2.600GHz, Infiniband FDR**
Site: Kyoto University
Country: Japan
Image URL: http://www.iimc.kyoto-u.ac.jp/en/services/comp/images/system-2012.png
Manufacturer: Cray Inc.
Cores: 9,280
Linpack Performance (Rmax): 135.4 TFlop/s
Theoretical Peak (Rpeak): 193.0 TFlop/s
Power: 210.35 kW
Memory: 37,120 GB
Interconnect: Infiniband FDR

Operating System: Linux
Compiler: Intel 12.1
MPI: MVAPICH 1.2
Ranking: 378

379. **Cluster Platform SL250s Gen8, Xeon E5-2660 8C 2.200GHz, Infiniband FDR, NVIDIA 2090**
Site: Research Center
Country: China
Image URL: None
Manufacturer: Hewlett-Packard
Cores: 8,064
Linpack Performance (Rmax): 135.4 TFlop/s
Theoretical Peak (Rpeak): 270.7 TFlop/s
Interconnect: Infiniband FDR
Operating System: Linux
Ranking: 379

380. **Cluster Platform 3000 BL460c Gen8, Xeon E5-2670 8C 2.600GHz, 10G Ethernet**
Site: Insurance Company
Country: United States
Image URL: None
Manufacturer: Hewlett-Packard
Cores: 9,088
Linpack Performance (Rmax): 135.1 TFlop/s
Theoretical Peak (Rpeak): 189.0 TFlop/s
Interconnect: 10G Ethernet
Operating System: Linux
Ranking: 380

381. **Cluster Platform 3000 BL460c Gen8, Xeon E5-2660 8C 2.200GHz, 10G Ethernet**
Site: Banking
Country: France
Image URL: None
Manufacturer: Hewlett-Packard
Cores: 10,768
Linpack Performance (Rmax): 134.4 TFlop/s
Theoretical Peak (Rpeak): 189.5 TFlop/s
Interconnect: 10G Ethernet
Operating System: Linux
Ranking: 381

382. **Cluster Platform 3000 BL460c G7, Xeon X5650 6C 2.66GHz, Gigabit Ethernet**
Site: Logistic Services (E)
Country: United States
Image URL: None
Manufacturer: Hewlett-Packard

Cores: 25,044
Linpack Performance (Rmax): 134.3 TFlop/s
Theoretical Peak (Rpeak): 266.5 TFlop/s
Interconnect: Gigabit Ethernet
Operating System: Linux
Ranking: 382

383. **xSeries x3650M4 Cluster, Xeon E5-2670 8C 2.600GHz, Gigabit Ethernet**
Site: Telecommunication Company
Country: China
Image URL: None
Manufacturer: IBM
Cores: 23,824
Linpack Performance (Rmax): 134.3 TFlop/s
Theoretical Peak (Rpeak): 495.5 TFlop/s
Interconnect: Gigabit Ethernet
Operating System: Linux
Ranking: 383

384. **Cray XC30, Intel Xeon E5-2670v2 10C 2.500GHz, Aries interconnect**
Site: Deutscher Wetterdienst
Country: Germany
Image URL: http://www.dwd.de/bvbw/generator/DWDWWW/Content/Presse/
Pressekonferenzen/2013/PK__06__12__13/20131206__ZundF__DMRZ,templateId=raw,proper
ty=publicationFile.pdf/20131206_ZundF_DMRZ.pdf
Manufacturer: Cray Inc.
Cores: 7,280
Linpack Performance (Rmax): 133.7 TFlop/s
Theoretical Peak (Rpeak): 145.6 TFlop/s
Interconnect: Aries Interconnect
Operating System: Cray Linux Environment
Ranking: 384

385. **Cray XC30, Intel Xeon E5-2670v2 10C 2.500GHz, Aries interconnect**
Site: Deutscher Wetterdienst
Country: Germany
Image URL: http://www.dwd.de/bvbw/generator/DWDWWW/Content/Presse/
Pressekonferenzen/2013/PK__06__12__13/20131206__ZundF__DMRZ,templateId=raw,proper
ty=publicationFile.pdf/20131206_ZundF_DMRZ.pdf
Manufacturer: Cray Inc.
Cores: 7,280
Linpack Performance (Rmax): 133.7 TFlop/s
Theoretical Peak (Rpeak): 145.6 TFlop/s
Interconnect: Aries Interconnect
Operating System: Cray Linux Environment
Ranking: 385

386. **Cluster Platform BL460c/280c G7, Xeon X5650 6C 2.66 GHz, Gigabit Ethernet**
  Site: Service Provider
  Country: United States
  Image URL: None
  Manufacturer: Hewlett-Packard
  Cores: 24,924
  Linpack Performance (Rmax): 133.6 TFlop/s
  Theoretical Peak (Rpeak): 265.2 TFlop/s
  Interconnect: Gigabit Ethernet
  Operating System: Linux
  Ranking: 386

387. **SGI ICE X, Intel Xeon E5-2690v2 10C 3.000GHz, Infiniband FDR**
  Site: SGI
  Country: United States
  Image URL: https://www.sgi.com/products/servers/images/icex_banner.jpg
  Manufacturer: SGI
  Cores: 5,760
  Linpack Performance (Rmax): 133.5 TFlop/s
  Theoretical Peak (Rpeak): 138.2 TFlop/s
  Memory: 18,432 GB
  Interconnect: Infiniband FDR
  Operating System: SUSE Linux Enterprise Server 11
  Ranking: 387

388. **BladeCenter HS22 Cluster (WM), Xeon E5649 6C 2.530GHz, Gigabit Ethernet**
  Site: Banking (M)
  Country: United States
  Image URL: None
  Manufacturer: IBM
  Cores: 23,640
  Linpack Performance (Rmax): 133.2 TFlop/s
  Theoretical Peak (Rpeak): 239.2 TFlop/s
  Power: 747.40 kW
  Interconnect: Gigabit Ethernet
  Operating System: Linux
  Ranking: 388

389. **EKA - Cluster Platform 3000 BL460c, Xeon X5365 4C 3.000GHz, Infiniband DDR**
  Site: Computational Research Laboratories, TATA SONS
  Country: India
  Image URL: None
  Manufacturer: Hewlett-Packard
  Cores: 14,384
  Linpack Performance (Rmax): 132.8 TFlop/s
  Theoretical Peak (Rpeak): 172.6 TFlop/s

Power: 786.00 kW

Interconnect: Infiniband DDR

Operating System: Linux

Ranking: 389

390. **BladeCenter HS23 Cluster, Xeon E5-2670 8C 2.600GHz, Infiniband QDR**

Site: Electronics

Country: United States

Image URL: None

Manufacturer: IBM

Cores: 7,008

Linpack Performance (Rmax): 132.6 TFlop/s

Theoretical Peak (Rpeak): 145.8 TFlop/s

Power: 127.90 kW

Interconnect: Infiniband QDR

Operating System: Linux

Ranking: 390

391. **BladeCenter HS23 Cluster, Xeon E5-2670 8C 2.600GHz, Infiniband QDR**

Site: Electronics

Country: United States

Image URL: None

Manufacturer: IBM

Cores: 7,008

Linpack Performance (Rmax): 132.6 TFlop/s

Theoretical Peak (Rpeak): 145.8 TFlop/s

Power: 127.90 kW

Interconnect: Infiniband QDR

Operating System: Linux

Ranking: 391

392. **BladeCenter HS23 Cluster, Xeon E5-2670 8C 2.600GHz, Infiniband QDR**

Site: Electronics

Country: United States

Image URL: None

Manufacturer: IBM

Cores: 7,008

Linpack Performance (Rmax): 132.6 TFlop/s

Theoretical Peak (Rpeak): 145.8 TFlop/s

Power: 127.90 kW

Interconnect: Infiniband QDR

Operating System: Linux

Ranking: 392

393. **iDataPlex DX360M3, Xeon X5670 6C 2.93 GHz, Infiniband QDR**

Site: IBM Development Engineering

Country: United States

Image URL: None
Manufacturer: IBM
Cores: 12,816
Linpack Performance (Rmax): 132.6 TFlop/s
Theoretical Peak (Rpeak): 150.2 TFlop/s
Power: 400.50 kW
Interconnect: Infiniband QDR
Operating System: Linux
Ranking: 393

394. **Cluster Platform 3000 BL460c Gen8, Xeon E5-2680 8C 2.700GHz, 10G Ethernet**
Site: Airline
Country: United States
Image URL: None
Manufacturer: Hewlett-Packard
Cores: 8,560
Linpack Performance (Rmax): 132.4 TFlop/s
Theoretical Peak (Rpeak): 184.9 TFlop/s
Interconnect: 10G Ethernet
Operating System: Linux
Ranking: 394

395. **Power 775, POWER7 8C 3.836GHz, Custom Interconnect**
Site: United Kingdom Meteorological Office
Country: United Kingdom
Image URL: None
Manufacturer: IBM
Cores: 5,120
Linpack Performance (Rmax): 132.3 TFlop/s
Theoretical Peak (Rpeak): 157.1 TFlop/s
Power: 288.94 kW
Interconnect: Custom Interconnect
Operating System: AIX
Ranking: 395

396. **Cluster Platform 3000 BL460c Gen8, Xeon E5-2650 8C 2.000GHz, Gigabit Ethernet**
Site: IT Services Provider (D)
Country: United States
Image URL: None
Manufacturer: Hewlett-Packard
Cores: 11,680
Linpack Performance (Rmax): 132.1 TFlop/s
Theoretical Peak (Rpeak): 186.9 TFlop/s
Interconnect: Gigabit Ethernet
Operating System: Linux
Ranking: 396

397. **BladeCenter HS22 Cluster (WM), Xeon E5649 6C 2.53 GHz, Gigabit Ethernet**
Site: Network Company
Country: China
Image URL: None
Manufacturer: IBM
Cores: 23,412
Linpack Performance (Rmax): 131.9 TFlop/s
Theoretical Peak (Rpeak): 236.9 TFlop/s
Power: 740.20 kW
Interconnect: Gigabit Ethernet
Operating System: Linux
Ranking: 397

398. **Abisko - Supermicro H8QG6, Opteron 6238 12C 2.600GHz, Infiniband QDR**
Site: HPC2N- Umea University
Country: Sweden
Image URL: http://www.hpc2n.umu.se/sites/default/files/images/abisko_small.preview.JPG,
http://www.hpc2n.umu.se/sites/default/files/images/abisko_back_noflash_small.preview.JPG
Manufacturer: Supermicro
Cores: 15,456
Linpack Performance (Rmax): 131.9 TFlop/s
Theoretical Peak (Rpeak): 160.7 TFlop/s
Power: 252.70 kW
Memory: 41,216 GB
Interconnect: Infiniband QDR
Operating System: Linux
Compiler: Pathscale
Math Library: acml
MPI: openmpi
Ranking: 398

399. **Juno - Appro XtremeServer 1143H, Opteron QC 2.2Ghz, Infiniband**
Site: Lawrence Livermore National Laboratory
Country: United States
Image URL: https://asc.llnl.gov/computing_resources/tlcc/images/tlcc2.jpg
Manufacturer: Cray Inc.
Cores: 18,224
Linpack Performance (Rmax): 131.6 TFlop/s
Theoretical Peak (Rpeak): 162.2 TFlop/s
Power: 1,139.00 kW
Memory: 36,864 GB
Interconnect: Infiniband
Operating System: Redhat Linux
Ranking: 399

400. **Cherry Creek - Supercmicro F627G3-F Cluster, Intel Xeon E5-2697v2 12C 2.700GHz, Intel Truscale, Intel Xeon Phi 7120P**

    Site: Intel Data Center Demos c/o ViaWest DataCenter

    Country: United States

    Image URL: http://www.intel.com/

    Manufacturer: Supermicro

    Cores: 9,936

    Linpack Performance (Rmax): 131.5 TFlop/s

    Theoretical Peak (Rpeak): 198.8 TFlop/s

    Power: 74.00 kW

    Memory: 6,144 GB

    Interconnect: Intel Truscale

    Operating System: Redhat Enterprise Linux 6

    Compiler: Intel Composer XE 2013

    Math Library: Intel MKL

    MPI: Intel MPI

    Ranking: 400

401. **Cluster Platform DL380p Gen8, Xeon E5-2640 6C 2.500GHz, Gigabit Ethernet**

    Site: Logistic Services (E)

    Country: United States

    Image URL: None

    Manufacturer: Hewlett-Packard

    Cores: 12,696

    Linpack Performance (Rmax): 131.4 TFlop/s

    Theoretical Peak (Rpeak): 253.9 TFlop/s

    Interconnect: Gigabit Ethernet

    Operating System: Linux

    Ranking: 401

402. **xSeries x3650 Cluster, Xeon E5649 6C 2.530GHz, Gigabit Ethernet**

    Site: Internet Service

    Country: China

    Image URL: None

    Manufacturer: IBM

    Cores: 23,316

    Linpack Performance (Rmax): 131.4 TFlop/s

    Theoretical Peak (Rpeak): 236.0 TFlop/s

    Power: 707.25 kW

    Interconnect: Gigabit Ethernet

    Operating System: Linux

    Ranking: 402

403. **HP ProLiant SL390s G7 Xeon 6C X5650, Infiniband**

    Site: Energy Company (A)

    Country: Italy

Image URL: None
Manufacturer: Hewlett-Packard
Cores: 15,360
Linpack Performance (Rmax): 131.2 TFlop/s
Theoretical Peak (Rpeak): 163.4 TFlop/s
Interconnect: Infiniband QDR
Operating System: Linux
Ranking: 403

404. **Cluster Platform DL380p Gen8, Xeon E5-2650 8C 2.000GHz, Gigabit Ethernet**
Site: Telecommunication Company
Country: China
Image URL: None
Manufacturer: Hewlett-Packard
Cores: 16,624
Linpack Performance (Rmax): 131.1 TFlop/s
Theoretical Peak (Rpeak): 266.0 TFlop/s
Interconnect: Gigabit Ethernet
Operating System: Linux
Ranking: 404

405. **Cluster Platform 3000 BL460c Gen8, Xeon E5-2640 6C 2.500GHz, 10G Ethernet**
Site: Financial Services (H)
Country: United States
Image URL: None
Manufacturer: Hewlett-Packard
Cores: 9,252
Linpack Performance (Rmax): 130.9 TFlop/s
Theoretical Peak (Rpeak): 185.0 TFlop/s
Interconnect: 10G Ethernet
Operating System: Linux
Ranking: 405

406. **xSeries x3650M4 Cluster, Xeon E5-2680 8C 2.700GHz, Infiniband**
Site: Electronics
Country: United States
Image URL: None
Manufacturer: IBM
Cores: 6,912
Linpack Performance (Rmax): 130.8 TFlop/s
Theoretical Peak (Rpeak): 149.3 TFlop/s
Power: 179.71 kW
Interconnect: Infiniband
Operating System: Linux
Ranking: 406

407. **xSeries x3650M4 Cluster, Xeon E5-2680 8C 2.700GHz, Infiniband**
     Site: Electronics
     Country: United States
     Image URL: None
     Manufacturer: IBM
     Cores: 6,912
     Linpack Performance (Rmax): 130.8 TFlop/s
     Theoretical Peak (Rpeak): 149.3 TFlop/s
     Power: 179.71 kW
     Interconnect: Infiniband
     Operating System: Linux
     Ranking: 407

408. **Cluster Platform SL230s Gen8, Xeon E5-2670 8C 2.600GHz, 10G Ethernet**
     Site: Energy Company
     Country: United States
     Image URL: None
     Manufacturer: Hewlett-Packard
     Cores: 9,216
     Linpack Performance (Rmax): 130.7 TFlop/s
     Theoretical Peak (Rpeak): 191.7 TFlop/s
     Interconnect: 10G Ethernet
     Operating System: Linux
     Ranking: 408

409. **Cluster Platform DL380p Gen8, Xeon E5-2640 6C 2.500GHz, Gigabit Ethernet**
     Site: Telecommunication Company
     Country: China
     Image URL: None
     Manufacturer: Hewlett-Packard
     Cores: 12,600
     Linpack Performance (Rmax): 130.5 TFlop/s
     Theoretical Peak (Rpeak): 252.0 TFlop/s
     Interconnect: Gigabit Ethernet
     Operating System: Linux
     Ranking: 409

410. **Cluster Platform 3000 BL460c Gen8, Xeon E5-2670 8C 2.600GHz, 10G Ethernet**
     Site: Service Provider
     Country: United States
     Image URL: None
     Manufacturer: Hewlett-Packard
     Cores: 9,184
     Linpack Performance (Rmax): 130.5 TFlop/s
     Theoretical Peak (Rpeak): 191.0 TFlop/s
     Interconnect: 10G Ethernet
     Operating System: Linux
     Ranking: 410

411. **Cluster Platform 3000 BL460c Gen8, Xeon E5-2670 8C 2.600GHz, 10G Ethernet**
     Site: Service Provider
     Country: United States
     Image URL: None
     Manufacturer: Hewlett-Packard
     Cores: 9,184
     Linpack Performance (Rmax): 130.5 TFlop/s
     Theoretical Peak (Rpeak): 191.0 TFlop/s
     Interconnect: 10G Ethernet
     Operating System: Linux
     Ranking: 411
412. **iDataPlex DX360M4, Xeon E5-2670 8C 2.600GHz, Infiniband FDR**
     Site: Durham University
     Country: United Kingdom
     Image URL: None
     Manufacturer: IBM
     Cores: 6,720
     Linpack Performance (Rmax): 130.2 TFlop/s
     Theoretical Peak (Rpeak): 139.8 TFlop/s
     Power: 139.59 kW
     Interconnect: Infiniband FDR
     Operating System: Linux
     Ranking: 412
413. **iDataPlex DX360M4, Intel Xeon E5-2680v2 10C 2.800GHz, Infiniband FDR14**
     Site: IBM Development Engineering
     Country: United States
     Image URL: None
     Manufacturer: IBM
     Cores: 7,560
     Linpack Performance (Rmax): 130.2 TFlop/s
     Theoretical Peak (Rpeak): 169.3 TFlop/s
     Power: 139.10 kW
     Interconnect: Infiniband FDR14
     Operating System: Linux
     Ranking: 413
414. **iDataPlex DX360M4, Intel Xeon E5-2680v2 10C 2.800GHz, Infiniband FDR14**
     Site: IBM Development Engineering
     Country: United States
     Image URL: None
     Manufacturer: IBM
     Cores: 7,560
     Linpack Performance (Rmax): 130.2 TFlop/s
     Theoretical Peak (Rpeak): 169.3 TFlop/s

Power: 139.10 kW
Interconnect: Infiniband FDR14
Operating System: Linux
Ranking: 414

415. **iDataPlex DX360M4, Intel Xeon E5-2680v2 10C 2.800GHz, Infiniband FDR14**
  Site: IBM Development Engineering
  Country: United States
  Image URL: None
  Manufacturer: IBM
  Cores: 7,560
  Linpack Performance (Rmax): 130.2 TFlop/s
  Theoretical Peak (Rpeak): 169.3 TFlop/s
  Power: 139.10 kW
  Interconnect: Infiniband FDR14
  Operating System: Linux
  Ranking: 415

416. **Midway - iDataPlex DX360M4, Xeon E5-2670 8C 2.600GHz, Infiniband FDR**
  Site: University of Chicago
  Country: United States
  Image URL: https://www.ci.uchicago.edu/sites/default/files/pcf_inside2.jpg, http://cfcp.uchi-cago.edu/pdf/orientation-2013.pdf
  Manufacturer: IBM
  Cores: 6,880
  Linpack Performance (Rmax): 130.2 TFlop/s
  Theoretical Peak (Rpeak): 143.1 TFlop/s
  Power: 142.91 kW
  Interconnect: Infiniband FDR14
  Operating System: Linux
  Ranking: 416

417. **Cluster Platform 3000 BL280c G6, Xeon X5675 6C 3.06GHz, Infiniband QDR**
  Site: Manufacturing Company
  Country: United States
  Image URL: None
  Manufacturer: Hewlett-Packard
  Cores: 13,980
  Linpack Performance (Rmax): 130.0 TFlop/s
  Theoretical Peak (Rpeak): 171.1 TFlop/s
  Interconnect: Infiniband QDR
  Operating System: Linux
  Ranking: 417

418. **Cluster Platform 3000 BL460c Gen8, Xeon E5-2670 8C 2.60GHz, 10G Ethernet**
  Site: IT Service Provider
  Country: United States

Image URL: None

Manufacturer: Hewlett-Packard

Cores: 12,032

Linpack Performance (Rmax): 129.9 TFlop/s

Theoretical Peak (Rpeak): 250.3 TFlop/s

Interconnect: 10G Ethernet

Operating System: Linux

Ranking: 418

419. **Cluster Platform 3000 BL460c Gen8, Xeon E5-2670 8C 2.60GHz, 10G Ethernet**

Site: IT Service Provider

Country: United States

Image URL: None

Manufacturer: Hewlett-Packard

Cores: 12,032

Linpack Performance (Rmax): 129.9 TFlop/s

Theoretical Peak (Rpeak): 250.3 TFlop/s

Interconnect: 10G Ethernet

Operating System: Linux

Ranking: 419

420. **Cluster Platform 3000 BL460c Gen8, Xeon E5-2670 8C 2.60GHz, 10G Ethernet**

Site: IT Service Provider

Country: United States

Image URL: None

Manufacturer: Hewlett-Packard

Cores: 12,032

Linpack Performance (Rmax): 129.9 TFlop/s

Theoretical Peak (Rpeak): 250.3 TFlop/s

Interconnect: 10G Ethernet

Operating System: Linux

Ranking: 420

421. **Cluster Platform 3000 BL460c Gen8, Xeon E5-2670 8C 2.60GHz, 10G Ethernet**

Site: IT Service Provider

Country: United States

Image URL: None

Manufacturer: Hewlett-Packard

Cores: 12,032

Linpack Performance (Rmax): 129.9 TFlop/s

Theoretical Peak (Rpeak): 250.3 TFlop/s

Interconnect: 10G Ethernet

Operating System: Linux

Ranking: 421

422. **iDataPlex DX360M4, Xeon E5-2670 8C 2.600GHz, Infiniband FDR**
     Site: Electronics
     Country: United States
     Image URL: None
     Manufacturer: IBM
     Cores: 7,456
     Linpack Performance (Rmax): 129.7 TFlop/s
     Theoretical Peak (Rpeak): 155.1 TFlop/s
     Power: 148.19 kW
     Interconnect: Infiniband FDR
     Operating System: Linux
     Ranking: 422

423. **IBM Flex System x240, Xeon E5-2670 8C 2.600GHz, Infiniband FDR**
     Site: Automotive
     Country: United States
     Image URL: None
     Manufacturer: IBM
     Cores: 6,832
     Linpack Performance (Rmax): 129.3 TFlop/s
     Theoretical Peak (Rpeak): 142.1 TFlop/s
     Power: 148.60 kW
     Interconnect: Infiniband FDR
     Operating System: Linux
     Ranking: 423

424. **IBM Flex System x240, Xeon E5-2670 8C 2.600GHz, Infiniband FDR**
     Site: Automotive
     Country: United States
     Image URL: None
     Manufacturer: IBM
     Cores: 6,832
     Linpack Performance (Rmax): 129.3 TFlop/s
     Theoretical Peak (Rpeak): 142.1 TFlop/s
     Power: 148.60 kW
     Interconnect: Infiniband FDR
     Operating System: Linux
     Ranking: 424

425. **IBM Flex System x240, Xeon E5-2670 8C 2.600GHz, Infiniband FDR**
     Site: Automotive
     Country: United States
     Image URL: None
     Manufacturer: IBM
     Cores: 6,832
     Linpack Performance (Rmax): 129.3 TFlop/s

Theoretical Peak (Rpeak): 142.1 TFlop/s

Power: 148.60 kW

Interconnect: Infiniband FDR

Operating System: Linux

Ranking: 425

426. **Cluster Platform 3000 BL460c Gen8, Xeon E5-2670 8C 2.600GHz, 10G Ethernet**

Site: Semiconductor Company (F)

Country: India

Image URL: None

Manufacturer: Hewlett-Packard

Cores: 8,752

Linpack Performance (Rmax): 129.2 TFlop/s

Theoretical Peak (Rpeak): 182.0 TFlop/s

Interconnect: 10G Ethernet

Operating System: Linux

Ranking: 426

427. **Cluster Platform 3000 BL460c Gen8, Xeon E5-2670 8C 2.600GHz, 10G Ethernet**

Site: Semiconductor Company (F)

Country: India

Image URL: None

Manufacturer: Hewlett-Packard

Cores: 8,752

Linpack Performance (Rmax): 129.2 TFlop/s

Theoretical Peak (Rpeak): 182.0 TFlop/s

Interconnect: 10G Ethernet

Operating System: Linux

Ranking: 427

428. **Cluster Platform 3000 BL460c Gen8, Xeon E5-2680 8C 2.700GHz, 10G Ethernet**

Site: Network Company

Country: India

Image URL: None

Manufacturer: Hewlett-Packard

Cores: 8,320

Linpack Performance (Rmax): 128.8 TFlop/s

Theoretical Peak (Rpeak): 179.7 TFlop/s

Interconnect: 10G Ethernet

Operating System: Linux

Ranking: 428

429. **Cluster Platform 3000 BL460c G7, Xeon X5650 6C 2.66GHz, Gigabit Ethernet**

Site: IT Services Provider

Country: United States

Image URL: None

Manufacturer: Hewlett-Packard

Cores: 24,000

Linpack Performance (Rmax): 128.7 TFlop/s

Theoretical Peak (Rpeak): 255.4 TFlop/s

Interconnect: Gigabit Ethernet

Operating System: Linux

Ranking: 429

430. **Cluster Platform 3000 BL460c G7, Xeon X5650 6C 2.66GHz, Gigabit Ethernet**

Site: IT Services Provider

Country: United States

Image URL: None

Manufacturer: Hewlett-Packard

Cores: 24,000

Linpack Performance (Rmax): 128.7 TFlop/s

Theoretical Peak (Rpeak): 255.4 TFlop/s

Interconnect: Gigabit Ethernet

Operating System: Linux

Ranking: 430

431. **iDataPlex DX360M4, Xeon E5-2680 8C 2.700GHz, Infiniband**

Site: Financial Securities

Country: United States

Image URL: None

Manufacturer: IBM

Cores: 6,544

Linpack Performance (Rmax): 128.6 TFlop/s

Theoretical Peak (Rpeak): 141.3 TFlop/s

Power: 156.06 kW

Interconnect: Infiniband

Operating System: Linux

Ranking: 431

432. **xSeries x3650M3 Cluster, Xeon E5649 6C 2.530GHz, Gigabit Ethernet**

Site: E-Commerce

Country: United States

Image URL: None

Manufacturer: IBM

Cores: 22,764

Linpack Performance (Rmax): 128.6 TFlop/s

Theoretical Peak (Rpeak): 230.4 TFlop/s

Power: 690.51 kW

Interconnect: Gigabit Ethernet

Operating System: Linux

Ranking: 432

433. **xSeries x3650M3 Cluster, Xeon E5649 6C 2.530GHz, Gigabit Ethernet**
   Site: E-Commerce
   Country: United States 🇺🇸
   Image URL: None
   Manufacturer: IBM
   Cores: 22,764
   Linpack Performance (Rmax): 128.6 TFlop/s
   Theoretical Peak (Rpeak): 230.4 TFlop/s
   Power: 690.51 kW
   Interconnect: Gigabit Ethernet
   Operating System: Linux
   Ranking: 433

434. **Cluster Platform SL335s Gen7, Opteron 4171 6C 2.100GHz, 10G Ethernet**
   Site: Software Company (M)
   Country: Ireland
   Image URL: None
   Manufacturer: Hewlett-Packard
   Cores: 23,316
   Linpack Performance (Rmax): 128.1 TFlop/s
   Theoretical Peak (Rpeak): 195.9 TFlop/s
   Interconnect: 10G Ethernet
   Operating System: Linux
   Ranking: 434

435. **BladeCenter HS23 Cluster, Xeon E5-2670 8C 2.600GHz, Gigabit Ethernet**
   Site: Communications
   Country: Israel 🇮🇱
   Image URL: None
   Manufacturer: IBM
   Cores: 22,704
   Linpack Performance (Rmax): 127.9 TFlop/s
   Theoretical Peak (Rpeak): 472.2 TFlop/s
   Power: 414.35 kW
   Interconnect: Gigabit Ethernet
   Operating System: Linux
   Ranking: 435

436. **iDataPlex DX360M3, Xeon E5645 6C 2.400GHz, Gigabit Ethernet**
   Site: Digital Media
   Country: United States 🇺🇸
   Image URL: None
   Manufacturer: IBM
   Cores: 22,704
   Linpack Performance (Rmax): 127.9 TFlop/s
   Theoretical Peak (Rpeak): 218.0 TFlop/s

Power: 652.74 kW
Interconnect: Gigabit Ethernet
Operating System: Linux
Ranking: 436

437. **Cluster Platform 4000 BL465c G7, Opteron 6176 12C 2.30GHz, Gigabit Ethernet**
    Site: IT Service Provider (D)
    Country: United States
    Image URL: None
    Manufacturer: Hewlett-Packard
    Cores: 28,620
    Linpack Performance (Rmax): 127.9 TFlop/s
    Theoretical Peak (Rpeak): 263.3 TFlop/s
    Interconnect: Gigabit Ethernet
    Operating System: Linux
    Ranking: 437

438. **Cluster Platform SL335s Gen7, Opteron 4171 6C 2.100GHz, 10G Ethernet**
    Site: Software Company (M)
    Country: Netherlands
    Image URL: None
    Manufacturer: Hewlett-Packard
    Cores: 23,220
    Linpack Performance (Rmax): 127.6 TFlop/s
    Theoretical Peak (Rpeak): 195.0 TFlop/s
    Interconnect: 10G Ethernet
    Operating System: Linux
    Ranking: 438

439. **Cluster Platform DL388p, Xeon E5-2609 4C 2.400GHz, Gigabit Ethernet**
    Site: Logistic Services
    Country: China
    Image URL: None
    Manufacturer: Hewlett-Packard
    Cores: 12,800
    Linpack Performance (Rmax): 127.2 TFlop/s
    Theoretical Peak (Rpeak): 245.8 TFlop/s
    Interconnect: Gigabit Ethernet
    Operating System: Linux
    Ranking: 439

440. **Cluster Platform DL380p Gen8, Xeon E5-2609 4C 2.400GHz, Gigabit Ethernet**
    Site: IT Services Provider (B)
    Country: China
    Image URL: None
    Manufacturer: Hewlett-Packard
    Cores: 12,792

Linpack Performance (Rmax): 127.1 TFlop/s
Theoretical Peak (Rpeak): 245.6 TFlop/s
Interconnect: Gigabit Ethernet
Operating System: Linux
Ranking: 440

441. **Cluster Platform 3000 BL460c Gen8, Xeon E5-2650 8C 2.000GHz, Infiniband QDR**
   Site: IT Service Provider
   Country: United Kingdom
   Image URL: None
   Manufacturer: Hewlett-Packard
   Cores: 10,288
   Linpack Performance (Rmax): 127.0 TFlop/s
   Theoretical Peak (Rpeak): 164.6 TFlop/s
   Interconnect: Infiniband QDR
   Operating System: Linux
   Ranking: 441

442. **Jet - Raytheon/Aspen Cluster, Xeon X5560/X5650 2.8/2.66 Ghz, QDR Infinband**
   Site: NOAA/ Earth Science Research Laboratory/GSD
   Country: United States
   Image URL: http://www.esrl.noaa.gov/gsd/publications/forum/feb2000/f300ffig1.jpg
   Manufacturer: Raytheon/Aspen Systems
   Cores: 13,732
   Linpack Performance (Rmax): 126.5 TFlop/s
   Theoretical Peak (Rpeak): 148.1 TFlop/s
   Interconnect: Infiniband QDR
   Operating System: Linux
   Ranking: 442

443. **Cluster Platform DL360p Gen8, Xeon E5-2630 6C 2.300GHz, Gigabit Ethernet**
   Site: Telecommunication Company
   Country: Japan
   Image URL: None
   Manufacturer: Hewlett-Packard
   Cores: 13,308
   Linpack Performance (Rmax): 126.4 TFlop/s
   Theoretical Peak (Rpeak): 244.9 TFlop/s
   Interconnect: Gigabit Ethernet
   Operating System: Linux
   Ranking: 443

444. **Vayu - Sun Blade x6048, Xeon X5570 2.93 Ghz, Infiniband QDR**
   Site: National Computational Infrastructure National Facility (NCI-NF)
   Country: Australia
   Image URL: None
   Manufacturer: Oracle

Cores: 11,936
Linpack Performance (Rmax): 126.4 TFlop/s
Theoretical Peak (Rpeak): 139.9 TFlop/s
Interconnect: Infiniband
Operating System: CentOS
Ranking: 444

445. **iDataPlex DX360M4, Xeon E5-2670 8C 2.600GHz, Infiniband**
Site: Electronics
Country: United States
Image URL: None
Manufacturer: IBM
Cores: 6,672
Linpack Performance (Rmax): 126.2 TFlop/s
Theoretical Peak (Rpeak): 138.8 TFlop/s
Power: 138.59 kW
Interconnect: Infiniband
Operating System: Linux
Ranking: 445

446. **iDataPlex DX360M4, Xeon E5-2670 8C 2.600GHz, Infiniband**
Site: Electronics
Country: United States
Image URL: None
Manufacturer: IBM
Cores: 6,672
Linpack Performance (Rmax): 126.2 TFlop/s
Theoretical Peak (Rpeak): 138.8 TFlop/s
Power: 138.59 kW
Interconnect: Infiniband
Operating System: Linux
Ranking: 446

447. **iDataPlex DX360M4, Xeon E5-2670 8C 2.600GHz, Infiniband**
Site: Electronics
Country: United States
Image URL: None
Manufacturer: IBM
Cores: 6,672
Linpack Performance (Rmax): 126.2 TFlop/s
Theoretical Peak (Rpeak): 138.8 TFlop/s
Power: 138.59 kW
Interconnect: Infiniband
Operating System: Linux
Ranking: 447

448. **iDataPlex DX360M4, Xeon E5-2670 8C 2.600GHz, Infiniband**
Site: Electronics
Country: United States
Image URL: None
Manufacturer: IBM
Cores: 6,672
Linpack Performance (Rmax): 126.2 TFlop/s
Theoretical Peak (Rpeak): 138.8 TFlop/s
Power: 138.59 kW
Interconnect: Infiniband
Operating System: Linux
Ranking: 448

449. **iDataPlex DX360M4, Xeon E5-2670 8C 2.600GHz, Infiniband**
Site: Electronics
Country: United States
Image URL: None
Manufacturer: IBM
Cores: 6,672
Linpack Performance (Rmax): 126.2 TFlop/s
Theoretical Peak (Rpeak): 138.8 TFlop/s
Power: 138.59 kW
Interconnect: Infiniband
Operating System: Linux
Ranking: 449

450. **iDataPlex DX360M4, Xeon E5-2670 8C 2.600GHz, Infiniband**
Site: Electronics
Country: United States
Image URL: None
Manufacturer: IBM
Cores: 6,672
Linpack Performance (Rmax): 126.2 TFlop/s
Theoretical Peak (Rpeak): 138.8 TFlop/s
Power: 138.59 kW
Interconnect: Infiniband
Operating System: Linux
Ranking: 450

451. **iDataPlex DX360M4, Xeon E5-2670 8C 2.600GHz, Infiniband**
Site: Electronics
Country: United States
Image URL: None
Manufacturer: IBM
Cores: 6,672
Linpack Performance (Rmax): 126.2 TFlop/s

Theoretical Peak (Rpeak): 138.8 TFlop/s

Power: 138.59 kW

Interconnect: Infiniband

Operating System: Linux

Ranking: 451

452. **iDataPlex DX360M4, Xeon E5-2670 8C 2.600GHz, Infiniband**

Site: Electronics

Country: United States

Image URL: None

Manufacturer: IBM

Cores: 6,672

Linpack Performance (Rmax): 126.2 TFlop/s

Theoretical Peak (Rpeak): 138.8 TFlop/s

Power: 138.59 kW

Interconnect: Infiniband

Operating System: Linux

Ranking: 452

453. **Cluster Platform 3000 BL460c Gen8, Xeon E5-2660 8C 2.200GHz, 10G Ethernet**

Site: Service Provider

Country: United States

Image URL: None

Manufacturer: Hewlett-Packard

Cores: 10,080

Linpack Performance (Rmax): 126.2 TFlop/s

Theoretical Peak (Rpeak): 177.4 TFlop/s

Interconnect: 10G Ethernet

Operating System: Linux

Ranking: 453

454. **Manny - Bullx DLC B710 Blades, Intel Xeon E5 v2 12C 2.700GHz, Infiniband FDR**

Site: Bull

Country: France

Image URL: http://www.bull.com/

Manufacturer: Bull SA

Cores: 20,480

Linpack Performance (Rmax): 360.9 TFlop/s

Theoretical Peak (Rpeak): 442.4 TFlop/s

Memory: 23,040 GB

Interconnect: Infiniband QDR

Operating System: bullx SUperCOmputer Suite A.E.2.1

Compiler: Intel v12.1

Ranking: 454

455. **Cray XE6 12-core 2.1 GHz**
     Site: University of Chicago
     Country: United States
     Image URL: http://uchicagomed.files.wordpress.com/2014/02/beagle-header.
     jpg?w=620&h=213
     Manufacturer: Cray Inc.
     Cores: 17,856
     Linpack Performance (Rmax): 125.8 TFlop/s
     Theoretical Peak (Rpeak): 150.0 TFlop/s
     Interconnect: Cray Gemini Interconnect
     Operating System: Linux
     Ranking: 455

456. **xSeries x3650M3 Cluster, Xeon X5650 6C 2.660GHz, Infiniband**
     Site: Electronics
     Country: United States
     Image URL: None
     Manufacturer: IBM
     Cores: 13,284
     Linpack Performance (Rmax): 125.7 TFlop/s
     Theoretical Peak (Rpeak): 141.3 TFlop/s
     Power: 502.58 kW
     Interconnect: Infiniband
     Operating System: Linux
     Ranking: 456

457. **xSeries x3650M3 Cluster, Xeon X5650 6C 2.660GHz, Infiniband**
     Site: Electronics
     Country: United States
     Image URL: None
     Manufacturer: IBM
     Cores: 13,284
     Linpack Performance (Rmax): 125.7 TFlop/s
     Theoretical Peak (Rpeak): 141.3 TFlop/s
     Power: 502.58 kW
     Interconnect: Infiniband
     Operating System: Linux
     Ranking: 457

458. **xSeries x3650M3 Cluster, Xeon X5650 6C 2.660GHz, Infiniband**
     Site: Electronics
     Country: United States
     Image URL: None
     Manufacturer: IBM
     Cores: 13,284
     Linpack Performance (Rmax): 125.7 TFlop/s

Theoretical Peak (Rpeak): 141.3 TFlop/s
Power: 502.58 kW
Interconnect: Infiniband
Operating System: Linux
Ranking: 458

459. **xSeries x3650M3 Cluster, Xeon X5650 6C 2.660GHz, Gigabit Ethernet**
Site: Financial Institution
Country: Japan
Image URL: None
Manufacturer: IBM
Cores: 22,272
Linpack Performance (Rmax): 125.5 TFlop/s
Theoretical Peak (Rpeak): 237.0 TFlop/s
Power: 690.43 kW
Interconnect: Gigabit Ethernet
Operating System: Linux
Ranking: 459

460. **Hera - Cray XE6, Opteron 6272 16C 2.1/2.2/2.3 GHz, Cray Gemini interconnect**
Site: Cray Inc.
Country: United States
Image URL: http://www.cray.com/Assets/images/products/xe6.jpg
Manufacturer: Cray Inc.
Cores: 23,104
Linpack Performance (Rmax): 146.0 TFlop/s
Theoretical Peak (Rpeak): 194.1 TFlop/s
Interconnect: Cray Gemini Interconnect
Operating System: Linux
Ranking: 460

461. **xSeries x3650M4 Cluster, Xeon E5-2670 8C 2.600GHz, Gigabit Ethernet**
Site: Internet Service
Country: China
Image URL: None
Manufacturer: IBM
Cores: 22,256
Linpack Performance (Rmax): 125.4 TFlop/s
Theoretical Peak (Rpeak): 462.9 TFlop/s
Power: 532.00 kW
Interconnect: Gigabit Ethernet
Operating System: Linux
Ranking: 461

462. **xSeries x3650M4 Cluster, Xeon E5-2670 8C 2.600GHz, Gigabit Ethernet**
Site: Internet Service
Country: China

Image URL: None
Manufacturer: IBM
Cores: 22,256
Linpack Performance (Rmax): 125.4 TFlop/s
Theoretical Peak (Rpeak): 462.9 TFlop/s
Power: 532.00 kW
Interconnect: Gigabit Ethernet
Operating System: Linux
Ranking: 462

463. **Cluster Platform 3000 BL460c Gen8, Xeon E5-2670 8C 2.60GHz, 10G Ethernet**
Site: IT Service Provider
Country: United States
Image URL: None
Manufacturer: Hewlett-Packard
Cores: 8,464
Linpack Performance (Rmax): 125.0 TFlop/s
Theoretical Peak (Rpeak): 176.1 TFlop/s
Interconnect: 10G Ethernet
Operating System: Linux
Ranking: 463

464. **BladeCenter HS23 Cluster, Xeon E5-2670 8C 2.600GHz, Gigabit Ethernet**
Site: Communications
Country: United States
Image URL: None
Manufacturer: IBM
Cores: 22,176
Linpack Performance (Rmax): 125.0 TFlop/s
Theoretical Peak (Rpeak): 461.3 TFlop/s
Power: 530.84 kW
Interconnect: Gigabit Ethernet
Operating System: Linux
Ranking: 464

465. **Cluster Platform 3000 BL460c Gen8, Xeon E5-2640 6C 2.500GHz, 10G Ethernet**
Site: Financial Services (H)
Country: United States
Image URL: None
Manufacturer: Hewlett-Packard
Cores: 8,796
Linpack Performance (Rmax): 124.5 TFlop/s
Theoretical Peak (Rpeak): 175.9 TFlop/s
Interconnect: 10G Ethernet
Operating System: Linux
Ranking: 465

466. **xSeries x3650M4 Cluster, Xeon E5-2670 8C 2.600GHz, Infiniband**
   Site: Government
   Country: United States
   Image URL: None
   Manufacturer: IBM
   Cores: 6,576
   Linpack Performance (Rmax): 124.4 TFlop/s
   Theoretical Peak (Rpeak): 136.8 TFlop/s
   Power: 170.98 kW
   Interconnect: Infiniband
   Operating System: Linux
   Ranking: 466

467. **xSeries x3650M4 Cluster, Xeon E5-2670 8C 2.600GHz, Infiniband**
   Site: Government
   Country: United States
   Image URL: None
   Manufacturer: IBM
   Cores: 6,576
   Linpack Performance (Rmax): 124.4 TFlop/s
   Theoretical Peak (Rpeak): 136.8 TFlop/s
   Power: 170.98 kW
   Interconnect: Infiniband
   Operating System: Linux
   Ranking: 467

468. **Cluster Platform 3000 BL460c/SL250/ML350 Xeon E5-2670 8C 2.600GHz, Infiniband QDR**
   Site: Volvo Car Group
   Country: Sweden
   Image URL: None
   Manufacturer: Hewlett-Packard
   Cores: 6,976
   Linpack Performance (Rmax): 123.3 TFlop/s
   Theoretical Peak (Rpeak): 145.1 TFlop/s
   Interconnect: Infiniband QDR
   Operating System: Linux
   Ranking: 468

469. **Cluster Platform SL230s Gen8, Xeon E5-2670 8C 2.600GHz, Gigabit Ethernet**
   Site: IT Services Provider
   Country: United States
   Image URL: None
   Manufacturer: Hewlett-Packard
   Cores: 11,520
   Linpack Performance (Rmax): 123.1 TFlop/s

Theoretical Peak (Rpeak): 239.6 TFlop/s
Interconnect: Gigabit Ethernet
Operating System: Linux
Ranking: 469

470. **Cluster Platform SL230s Gen8, Xeon E5-2670 8C 2.600GHz, Gigabit Ethernet**
Site: IT Services Provider
Country: United States 🇺🇸
Image URL: None
Manufacturer: Hewlett-Packard
Cores: 11,520
Linpack Performance (Rmax): 123.1 TFlop/s
Theoretical Peak (Rpeak): 239.6 TFlop/s
Interconnect: Gigabit Ethernet
Operating System: Linux
Ranking: 470

471. **BladeCenter HS22 Cluster (WM), Xeon L5639 6C 2.130GHz, Infiniband**
Site: System Integrator
Country: United States 🇺🇸
Image URL: None
Manufacturer: IBM
Cores: 23,508
Linpack Performance (Rmax): 122.7 TFlop/s
Theoretical Peak (Rpeak): 200.3 TFlop/s
Power: 698.10 kW
Interconnect: Infiniband
Operating System: Linux
Ranking: 471

472. **Earth Simulator - SX-9/E/1280M160**
Site: Japan Agency for Marine-Earth Science and Technology
Country: Japan ●
Image URL: http://www.jamstec.go.jp/es/en/images/concept_img_e.jpg
System URL: http://www.jamstec.go.jp/es/en/index.html
Manufacturer: NEC
Cores: 1,280
Linpack Performance (Rmax): 122.4 TFlop/s
Theoretical Peak (Rpeak): 131.1 TFlop/s
Memory: 20,480 GB
Interconnect: Fat Tree Network
Operating System: Super-UX
Ranking: 472

473. **Cluster Platform 3000 BL460c Gen8, Xeon E5-2640 6C 2.500GHz, 10G Ethernet**
Site: IT Service Provider (D)
Country: United States 🇺🇸

Image URL: None
Manufacturer: Hewlett-Packard
Cores: 8,616
Linpack Performance (Rmax): 121.9 TFlop/s
Theoretical Peak (Rpeak): 172.3 TFlop/s
Interconnect: 10G Ethernet
Operating System: Linux
Ranking: 473

474. **Crane - Relion Cluster, Xeon E5-2670 8C 2.600GHz, Infiniband QDR**
Site: University of Nebraska
Country: United States
Image URL: http://rcf.unl.edu/
Manufacturer: Penguin Computing
Cores: 7,232
Linpack Performance (Rmax): 121.8 TFlop/s
Theoretical Peak (Rpeak): 150.4 TFlop/s
Power: 165.40 kW
Memory: 28,928 GB
Interconnect: Infiniband QDR
Operating System: Linux
Compiler: icc
Math Library: Intel MKL
MPI: Intel MPI
Ranking: 474

475. **Cluster Platform 4000 BL685c G7, Opteron 6234 12C 2.400GHz, Gigabit Ethernet**
Site: Web Company (C)
Country: China
Image URL: None
Manufacturer: Hewlett-Packard
Cores: 25,176
Linpack Performance (Rmax): 121.8 TFlop/s
Theoretical Peak (Rpeak): 241.7 TFlop/s
Interconnect: Gigabit Ethernet
Operating System: Linux
Ranking: 475

476. **Hitachi SR16000 Model M1, POWER7 8C 3.836GHz, Custom**
Site: Information Initiative Center, Hokkaido University
Country: Japan
Image URL: http://www.iic.hokudai.ac.jp/
Manufacturer: Hitachi
Cores: 5,632
Linpack Performance (Rmax): 121.6 TFlop/s
Theoretical Peak (Rpeak): 168.9 TFlop/s

Power: 354.60 kW
Interconnect: Custom Interconnect
Operating System: AIX
Ranking: 476

477. **Cluster Platform 3000 BL460c Gen8, Xeon E5-2630 6C 2.300GHz, 10G Ethernet**
     Site: Banking
     Country: France ▌▐
     Image URL: None
     Manufacturer: Hewlett-Packard
     Cores: 9,252
     Linpack Performance (Rmax): 121.5 TFlop/s
     Theoretical Peak (Rpeak): 170.2 TFlop/s
     Interconnect: 10G Ethernet
     Operating System: Linux
     Ranking: 477

478. **Cluster Platform DL360e Gen8, Xeon E5-2450 8C 2.100GHz, Gigabit Ethernet**
     Site: Software Company (M)
     Country: United States ▆▆▆
     Image URL: None
     Manufacturer: Hewlett-Packard
     Cores: 14,896
     Linpack Performance (Rmax): 120.9 TFlop/s
     Theoretical Peak (Rpeak): 250.3 TFlop/s
     Interconnect: Gigabit Ethernet
     Operating System: Linux
     Ranking: 478

479. **xSeries x3650M3 Cluster, Xeon E5649 6C 2.530GHz, Gigabit Ethernet**
     Site: Internet Service
     Country: China ▆
     Image URL: None
     Manufacturer: IBM
     Cores: 21,372
     Linpack Performance (Rmax): 120.4 TFlop/s
     Theoretical Peak (Rpeak): 216.3 TFlop/s
     Power: 648.28 kW
     Interconnect: Gigabit Ethernet
     Operating System: Linux
     Ranking: 479

480. **HokieSpeed - SuperServer 2026GT-TRF, Xeon E5645 6C 2.40GHz, Infiniband QDR, NVIDIA 2050**
     Site: Virginia Tech
     Country: United States ▆▆▆
     Image URL: http://www.vtnews.vt.edu/articles/2012/01/010512-engineering-hokiespeed.html

Manufacturer: Supermicro
Cores: 8,320
Linpack Performance (Rmax): 120.4 TFlop/s
Theoretical Peak (Rpeak): 238.2 TFlop/s
Power: 126.27 kW
Memory: 4,992 GB
Interconnect: Infiniband QDR
Operating System: CentOS
Ranking: 480

481. **Cluster Platform DL160 Gen8, Xeon E5-2630 6C 2.300GHz, Gigabit Ethernet**
Site: Web Content Provider
Country: United States
Image URL: None
Manufacturer: Hewlett-Packard
Cores: 12,624
Linpack Performance (Rmax): 120.3 TFlop/s
Theoretical Peak (Rpeak): 232.3 TFlop/s
Interconnect: Gigabit Ethernet
Operating System: Linux
Ranking: 481

482. **Cluster Platform DL360p Gen8, Xeon E5-2630 6C 2.300GHz, Gigabit Ethernet**
Site: IT Services Provider
Country: United States
Image URL: None
Manufacturer: Hewlett-Packard
Cores: 12,912
Linpack Performance (Rmax): 120.2 TFlop/s
Theoretical Peak (Rpeak): 237.6 TFlop/s
Interconnect: Gigabit Ethernet
Operating System: Linux
Ranking: 482

483. **xSeries x3650 Cluster, Xeon E5649 6C 2.530GHz, Gigabit Ethernet**
Site: Telecommunication Company
Country: China
Image URL: None
Manufacturer: IBM
Cores: 21,336
Linpack Performance (Rmax): 120.2 TFlop/s
Theoretical Peak (Rpeak): 215.9 TFlop/s
Interconnect: Gigabit Ethernet
Operating System: Linux
Ranking: 483

484. **xSeries x3650M4 Cluster, Xeon X5650 6C 2.660GHz, Gigabit Ethernet**
  Site: Service Provider
  Country: China
  Image URL: None
  Manufacturer: IBM
  Cores: 16,080
  Linpack Performance (Rmax): 120.8 TFlop/s
  Theoretical Peak (Rpeak): 171.1 TFlop/s
  Power: 513.22 kW
  Interconnect: Gigabit Ethernet
  Operating System: Linux
  Ranking: 484

485. **xSeries x3650M4 Cluster, Xeon X5650 6C 2.660GHz, Gigabit Ethernet**
  Site: Service Provider
  Country: China
  Image URL: None
  Manufacturer: IBM
  Cores: 16,080
  Linpack Performance (Rmax): 120.8 TFlop/s
  Theoretical Peak (Rpeak): 171.1 TFlop/s
  Power: 513.22 kW
  Interconnect: Gigabit Ethernet
  Operating System: Linux
  Ranking: 485

486. **Cluster Platform DL380p Gen8, Xeon E5-2650 8C 2.000GHz, Gigabit Ethernet**
  Site: Computacenter (UK) LTD
  Country: United Kingdom
  Image URL: http://www.computercenter.co.uk/
  Manufacturer: Hewlett-Packard
  Cores: 14,592
  Linpack Performance (Rmax): 120.0 TFlop/s
  Theoretical Peak (Rpeak): 233.5 TFlop/s
  Interconnect: Gigabit Ethernet
  Operating System: Linux
  Ranking: 486

487. **MVS-100K - Cluster Platform 3000 BL460c/BL 2x220/SL390, Xeon E5450/5365/X5675 4C 3.000GHz, Infiniband DDR, NVIDIA 2090**
  Site: Joint Supercomputer Center
  Country: Russia
  Image URL: http://www.jscc.ru/
  Manufacturer: Hewlett-Packard
  Cores: 13,004
  Linpack Performance (Rmax): 119.9 TFlop/s

Theoretical Peak (Rpeak): 227.9 TFlop/s
Interconnect: Infiniband DDR
Operating System: Linux
Ranking: 487

488. **Cluster Platform 3000 BL460c Gen8, Xeon E5-2680 8C 2.700GHz, Gigabit Ethernet**
    Site: Network Company
    Country: United States
    Image URL: None
    Manufacturer: Hewlett-Packard
    Cores: 10,640
    Linpack Performance (Rmax): 119.9 TFlop/s
    Theoretical Peak (Rpeak): 229.8 TFlop/s
    Interconnect: Gigabit Ethernet
    Operating System: Linux
    Ranking: 488

489. **Cluster Platform 3000 BL460c Gen8, Xeon E5-2680 8C 2.700GHz, Gigabit Ethernet**
    Site: Network Company
    Country: United States
    Image URL: None
    Manufacturer: Hewlett-Packard
    Cores: 10,640
    Linpack Performance (Rmax): 119.9 TFlop/s
    Theoretical Peak (Rpeak): 229.8 TFlop/s
    Interconnect: Gigabit Ethernet
    Operating System: Linux
    Ranking: 489

490. **Cluster Platform 3000 BL460c Gen8, Xeon E5-2670 8C 2.600GHz, 10G Ethernet**
    Site: IT Service Provider (B)
    Country: United States
    Image URL: None
    Manufacturer: Hewlett-Packard
    Cores: 10,048
    Linpack Performance (Rmax): 119.6 TFlop/s
    Theoretical Peak (Rpeak): 209.0 TFlop/s
    Interconnect: 10G Ethernet
    Operating System: Linux
    Ranking: 490

491. **Cluster Platform DL388p, Xeon E5-2609 4C 2.400GHz, Gigabit Ethernet**
    Site: Telecommunication Company
    Country: China
    Image URL: None
    Manufacturer: Hewlett-Packard
    Cores: 11,984

Linpack Performance (Rmax): 119.4 TFlop/s
Theoretical Peak (Rpeak): 230.1 TFlop/s
Interconnect: Gigabit Ethernet
Operating System: Linux
Ranking: 491

492. **Blue Gene/P Solution**
 Site: IDRIS
 Country: France ▮ ▮
 Image URL: http://www.idris.fr/z-tools/newune/content/images/seconde/2.jpg
 Manufacturer: IBM
 Cores: 40,960
 Linpack Performance (Rmax): 119.3 TFlop/s
 Theoretical Peak (Rpeak): 139.3 TFlop/s
 Power: 315.00 kW
 Interconnect: Proprietary
 Operating System: CNK/SLES 9
 Ranking: 492

493. **HiPerGator - Dell C6145 Cluster, Opteron 6378 16C 2.400GHz, Infiniband**
 Site: University of Florida
 Country: United States ▰
 Image URL: http://www.hpc.ufl.edu/wp-content/uploads/2013/06/HiPerGatorFactSheetPhoto-100x100.jpg
 Manufacturer: Dell
 Cores: 16,384
 Linpack Performance (Rmax): 119.3 TFlop/s
 Theoretical Peak (Rpeak): 157.3 TFlop/s
 Power: 312.80 kW
 Memory: 65,536 GB
 Interconnect: Infiniband
 Operating System: Redhat Enterprise Linux 6
 Compiler: GCC
 Math Library: ACML
 MPI: OpenMPI
 Ranking: 493

494. **Cluster Platform DL360p Gen8, Xeon E5-2640 6C 2.500GHz, Gigabit Ethernet**
 Site: IT Service Provider (D)
 Country: United States ▰
 Image URL: None
 Manufacturer: Hewlett-Packard
 Cores: 12,348
 Linpack Performance (Rmax): 119.3 TFlop/s
 Theoretical Peak (Rpeak): 247.0 TFlop/s
 Interconnect: Gigabit Ethernet

Operating System: Linux
Compiler: GCC
Math Library: ACML
MPI: OpenMPI
Ranking: 494

495. **Cluster Platform SL230s Gen8, Xeon E5-2650 8C 2.000GHz, 10G Ethernet**
Site: IT Services Provider
Country: United States
Image URL: None
Manufacturer: Hewlett-Packard
Cores: 16,224
Linpack Performance (Rmax): 119.3 TFlop/s
Theoretical Peak (Rpeak): 259.6 TFlop/s
Interconnect: 10G Ethernet
Operating System: Linux
Ranking: 495

496. **Cluster Platform SL335s Gen7, Opteron 4171 6C 2.100GHz, 10G Ethernet**
Site: Software Company (M)
Country: Hong Kong
Image URL: None
Manufacturer: Hewlett-Packard
Cores: 21,600
Linpack Performance (Rmax): 118.7 TFlop/s
Theoretical Peak (Rpeak): 181.4 TFlop/s
Interconnect: 10G Ethernet
Operating System: Linux
Ranking: 496

497. **Cluster Platform 4000 BL465c, Opteron 6134 8C 2.30GHz, Gigabit Ethernet**
Site: Government
Country: Canada
Image URL: None
Manufacturer: Hewlett-Packard
Cores: 25,472
Linpack Performance (Rmax): 118.1 TFlop/s
Theoretical Peak (Rpeak): 234.3 TFlop/s
Interconnect: Gigabit Ethernet
Operating System: Linux
Ranking: 497

498. **Cluster Platform DL388p, Xeon E5-2609 4C 2.400GHz, Gigabit Ethernet**
Site: Telecommunication Company
Country: China
Image URL: None
Manufacturer: Hewlett-Packard

Cores: 11,848
Linpack Performance (Rmax): 118.1 TFlop/s
Theoretical Peak (Rpeak): 227.5 TFlop/s
Interconnect: Gigabit Ethernet
Operating System: Linux
Ranking: 498

499. **Cluster Platform DL380e Gen8, Xeon E5-2430L 8C 2.000GHz, Gigabit Ethernet**
Site: Software Company (M)
Country: United States
Image URL: None
Manufacturer: Hewlett-Packard
Cores: 15,216
Linpack Performance (Rmax): 118.0 TFlop/s
Theoretical Peak (Rpeak): 243.5 TFlop/s
Interconnect: Gigabit Ethernet
Operating System: Linux
Ranking: 499

500. **Cluster Platform 3000 BL460c G7, Xeon X5650 6C 2.66GHz, Gigabit Ethernet**
Site: Banking (M)
Country: United States
Image URL: None
Manufacturer: Hewlett-Packard
Cores: 22,212
Linpack Performance (Rmax): 117.8 TFlop/s
Theoretical Peak (Rpeak): 236.3 TFlop/s
Interconnect: Gigabit Ethernet
Operating System: Linux
Ranking: 500

Glossary

Ab initio Methods: Computational chemistry methods based on quantum chemistry principles as well as calculations.

Ab Initio Molecular Dynamics: In excited states, chemical reactions, etc., electronic behavior can be obtained from first principles by using a quantum mechanical method.

Admixture: In genetics, refers to the process when two or more previously separated populations begin interbreeding.

Advertising: The process of making a product, idea, or other property positively known to a wide part of the community.

Air Pollution: The introduction of chemicals, particulates, biological materials, or other harmful materials into the Earth's atmosphere, possibly causing disease, death to humans, damage to other living organisms such as food crops, or the natural or built environment.

Allele: An alternative form of a gene (one member of a pair) occupying a specific position in a chromosome.

Allele Frequency: In a population, this refers to the percentage of all the alleles at a locus accounted for by one specific allele.

Amazon Web Services: Collection of remote computing services that together make up a cloud computing platform, offered over the internet by Amazon.com. The most central and well-known of these services are Amazon EC2 and Amazon S3.

Apple Power Mac G5 Computers: G5 is a series of Macintosh desktop machines from Apple that use the 64-bit IBM PowerPC 970 CPU. G5 has a 1GHz front side bus and can access up to 8 GB of memory. The Power Mac G5 was the last Macintosh to use the PowerPC chips.

Azure: Cloud Computing platform and infrastructure created by Microsoft, for building, deploying and managing applications and services through a global network of Microsoft-managed datacenters.

Baby Boomers: A person born between the years 1946 and 1964 characterized by affluence and opportunity. These individuals were born Post World War II and total 76 million. Descriptions of baby boomers included self-centeredness and loyal. They were ambitious and lifelong learners.

Bachus Nauer Form (BNF): A formal concise method defining syntax of a language. Such definition is essential in the algorithmic parsing of a sentence.

Bacteriophage: Virus that infects and replicates within bacteria.

Big Data: Tremendous quantities of data, exceeding the limits of the capacity of conventional data base systems. In this context, the synergism is different than the integration of the parts. For example, the standard deviation of a certain amount of data is not the average standard deviation of its subsets. Big Data may be the result of increasing the resolution of the problem, namely in the scalability of the problems. For example, data increases in image processing in medicine, crime, astrophysics; in simulations and in many other areas. Supercomputers suit the manipulations of big data,

Bioinformatics: The science of analyzing biological data using Computer Sciences.

BioPython: BioPython project is an international association of developers of non-commercial Python tools for Computational Molecular Biology and Bioinformatics.

Bivalance: Having two values, such as yes-no, up-down, 0-1, etc. In logic, "bivalency" refers to having true-false values.

Bootstrap: Starting with an assumption or assumptions and building a system, model, explanation, concept, or other foundation.

Clinical Trials: A rigorously controlled test of a new drug or a new invasive medical device on human subjects; in the US, it is conducted under the supervision of FDA.

Cloud Computing: A methodology for computing on scattered shared computer resources (computing power, storage, software packages, internet facilities, etc.). The consumer of the computing resource is redirected by the operating system to a suitable available resource. In such an environment, the end user is free to keep computer resources for his own. All the user's needs are supplied by the network in an optimal cost/ performance by the whole community.

Cognition: Mentation, or that with which the intellect manages.

Cognitive Behavioral Therapy (CBT): A method used to evaluate and treat psychological personality disturbances. It is based on searching for "distortion thoughts" expressed in the spoken language, and substituting them by corrected ones. There are about ten classes of distortion thoughts, which are generally based on using superlatives in various contexts, indicating some over sensitivity.

Comparative Genomics: Study that involves the comparison of the genomic sequences of different species.

Complementary DNA (cDNA): DNA derived from messenger RNA (mRNA), which can be obtained from prokaryotes or eukaryotes and is often utilized to clone eukaryotic genes in prokaryotes.

Complementary Metal Oxide Semiconductor (CMOS): Technology for constructing integrated circuits. CMOS technology is used in microprocessors, static RAM, microcontrollers and other digital logic circuits.

Comprehension: Understanding, or affirming that the substance of an expression has been absorbed to the point of being able to integrate it into one's views. A German approach is useful, where "understanding" can be rendered as an apprehension of fact or an understanding of deep meaning. (See "mind".)

Computational Thinking: A way of solving problems mathematically and algorithmically across a multitude of disciplines of study. Drawing on fundamental concepts of computer science, computational thinking across the curriculum prepares individuals to engage in a data rich world as scientists, physicians, librarians, historians, financial analysts and much more.

Consciousness: Often used synonymously with "mind".

Conservation Biology: The branch of biology that deals with the study of the conservation of biological diversity and the effects of humans on the environment.

Cosmid: A plasmid vector containing a bacteriophage lambda cos site, which directs insertion of DNA into phage particles.

CPAN: Comprehensive Perl Archive Network containing an accumulation of BioPerl libraries and functions.

CpG Elements: Genomic regions consisting of a high frequency of CpG sites. A CpG site refers to a genomic region where a cytosine nucleotide exists next to a guanine nucleotide in the linear sequence of bases along its length.

CRAN: Comprehensive R Archive Network which is the repository of the R packages and functions.

Cray: Cray Inc., an American supercomputer manufacturer based in Seattle, Washington. The company's predecessor, Cray Research, Inc. (CRI), was founded in 1972 by computer designer Seymour Cray (Wikipedia, 2014a).

Cryptography: The process of encrypting and decrypting data to prevent the data to be freely accessed. The encryption and the decryption should be synchronized modules.

CUDA™: Is both a parallel computing architecture and programming model for high performance computing. CUDA™ is a proprietary standard and provides programmatic access to NVidia graphics processing units (GPUs).

Cyber War (Warfare): A struggle between two groups of computers systems where ones group strives to harm the computer systems of the other group and defend itself at the same time.

Data Analysis: Analysis and isolation of information from the provided database using supercomputers. These data may be protein, DNA, Genome, Proteome etc.

Data Mining: The theory and methodology of searching through large amount of unknown data for a common denominator, or conversely, looking for some irregularity or exceptions in the data.

Decryption: The opposite of encryption, using an algorithm to reconstruct the original message from the encrypted data.

Design: The creation of a plan or convention for the construction of an object or a system (as in architectural blueprints, engineering drawings, business processes, circuit diagrams and sewing patterns).

Dialectics: Primarily, a process of apprehending a concept by recognizing what that concept is not A second form of dialectics identifies a concept – process or object – as developing within its something opposite to itself. In dialectic philosophy, a general statement is that the process exists in terms of the object, and vice versa. The process is as much a part of the object as the object is, itself.

Dicodon Statistics: Statistics used for the prediction of splice signals and coding regions.

Discriminant Function: A function of a set of variables that is evaluated for samples of events of objects and used as an aid in classifying them.

Distributed Computing: A lower scale form of cloud computing. It is performed for organizations as a specially oriented field such as databases.

Distributed Shared Memory: Each node of the system consists of one or more CPUs and a memory unit. The nodes are connected by a high-speed communication network. When a process on a node accesses some data from a memory block of the shared memory space, the local memory mapping manager takes charge of its request.

DNA: deoxyribonucleic acid is a molecule that serves as the hereditary material in humans and almost all other organisms.

DNA Polymerases: An enzyme that catalyzes the polymerization of DNAs into a DNA strand.

DNA Polymorphisms: Alleles of a chromosomal locus differing in nucleotide sequence or have variable numbers of repeated nucleotide units.

DNA Sequencing: The process of determining the precise order of the nucleotides within the DNA molecule.

Docking: Close interaction studies between protein and ligand or between protein and protein. It involves formation of bonds between amino acids and between amino acids and drug molecule.

Double Data Rate 2 (DDR2) Memory: DDR2 RAM is an improved version of DDR memory that is faster and more efficient.

Eddies: A circular movement of water causing a small whirlpool.

Effects Based Assessment Support System (EBASS): A distributed operational assessment tool based on the principles of value focused thinking (VFT) and developed at the U.S. Military Academy to initially support the military command in Afghanistan in 2002.

Engineering: The branch of science and technology concerned with the design, building, and use of engines, machines, and structures.

Epistemology: A branch of philosophy concerned with how we know something. How we know is expressed by justified belief.

Equivalence: That which has the same set of characteristics as something else. This does not mean the same thing as identity, as an object equivalent to another does not have to have virtually everything – particle for particle - in common with the other. Identity necessarily implies equivalence, but equivalence does not necessarily imply identity.

Erlang: Is a functional programming language with dynamic typing and strict evaluation. It is specifically designed for massive concurrency and is suitable for real-time, high performance computing applications.

Evolution: Gradual unfolding of new varieties of life from previous forms over long periods of time; from the modern genetic perspective, it is defined as a change in allele frequency from one generation to the next.

Evolutionary Biology: The branch of biology that deals with the study of the evolution of organisms.

Exaflops: One exaflop is a thousand petaflops or a quintillion.

Existent: That which has an identity. It is problematical whether that identity must be known to a person or whether it can be independent of anyone being aware of its presence. There is a school of thinking saying that one must perceive it for it to exist.

Exon: DNA nucleotide sequence carrying out the code for the final mRNA and, thus, determines the amino acid sequence of an organism.

Expressed Sequence Tags (ESTs): Small pieces of DNA sequence (usually 200 to 500 nucleotides long) generated by sequencing either one or both ends of an expressed gene.

Extreme Scale Computing Initiative (XSCI): Building the capabilities needed to enable scientific advancements and breakthroughs in selected domain sciences through computational modeling and simulation on next-generation, extreme-scale computers. The XSCI consists of an integrated research program with an interdisciplinary approach that brings together high-performance computer science and computational domain sciences to develop the next-generation, extreme-scale modeling and simulation applications. (Straatsma, 2013)

Field-Programmable Gate Arrays (FPGA): An integrated circuit that can be programmed in the field after manufacture.

Fixation Index: A measure used to assess population differentiation due to genetic structure.

Flanking Residues: Short sequences bordering a transcription unit that often do not code for proteins.

Flynn's Taxonomy: Classification of computer architectures, proposed by Michael J. Flynn in 1966 (Wikipedia, 2014b).

Fold Recognition: A computational protein structure prediction method of protein modeling which is used to model those proteins which have the same fold as proteins of known structures, but do not have homologous proteins with known structure.

Functional Annotation: The process of collecting information and describing the gene's biological identity.

Functional Programming: Is a programming paradigm that treats computation as evaluation of mathematical functions and avoids state and mutable data. Features such as curried functions, higher order functions, and lazy evaluation characterize functional programming.

GenBank: The NIH genetic sequence database, an annotated collection of all publicly available DNA sequences (Benson et al., 2013).

Gene Flow: The transfer of alleles from one population to another.

General Purpose Graphics Processing Unit (GPGPU): This acronym refers to general purpose computing on graphics processing units. GPGPU is a new approach to high performance computing which leverages both CPUs and GPUs for achieving unprecedented compute power.

General-Purpose Computing on Graphics Processing Units: (GPGPU): The utilization of a graphics processing unit, which typically handles computation only for computer graphics, to perform computation in applications traditionally handled by the central processing unit.

Genesis: The first book in the Pentateuch which is part of the Bible.

Genetic Algorithms: Search heuristic method that mimic the process of natural evolution and is often used to generate useful solutions to optimization and search problems. These types of algorithms belong to the larger class of evolutionary algorithms that generate solutions to optimization problems using techniques inspired by natural evolution, such as inheritance, mutation, selection, and crossover.

Genetic Association: Statistical phenomenon, which associates a specific disease with a certain gene(s).

Genetic Drift: The process of random changes in the allele frequency in a gene pool, usually in small populations.

Genetic Locus: The specific location of a gene in a chromosome.

Genome: The genome comprises the entire DNA found in the cell's nucleus. The genome is comprised of nucleotides and they are responsible for transmitting the heritable properties of the species. There are four types of nucleotides that form sequences of millions of nucleotides that represent a huge number of properties and variety of characteristics.

Genomics: Field of study focusing on genes, their functions, and related techniques.

Genomics: Study of genes and genome by utilizing computational as well as experimental knowledge.

Genotype: An organism's entire genetic makeup or to the alleles at a specific genetic locus.

Genotype Frequency: Sum of the number of individuals possessing the genotype divided by the total number of individuals in the sample.

GenX: GenXers were born between 1961-1982. GenX individuals came from households where both parents worked thus the liklihood that they were latchkey is high. Characteristics include; self-reliant, controlling, and community. They key in on 'experience' thus the 'My' approach to marketing is more successful to this generation. They desire to control their own experience, contribute to their experience, and define the value of that experience rather than have it defined by a corporation.

Google Cloud Platform: Google's vision for cloud computing. A big data solution that allows to efficiently process data at Google scale and speed and a new approach to computing that erases distinctions between PaaS and IaaS.

Graphics Processing Unit (GPU): A programmable logic chip that can perform animation, imaging, and videos for the computer screen.

Graphics Processing Unit (GPU): Is a specialized processor designed to rapidly manipulate and alter memory to accelerate the creation of graphics in a frame buffer. Their highly parallel structure makes GPUs dwarf general-purpose CPUs when it comes to processing massive amounts of data in parallel. GPUs are used in game consoles, mobile phones, embedded systems, desktop and workstation computers, and modern supercomputers.

Grid Computing: Collection of computer resources from multiple locations to reach a common goal.

Hadoop: Apache Hadoop is an open-source software framework that supports data intensive distributed applications.

Hardy-Weinberg Equilibrium: A population genetics fundamental principle stating that the genotype frequencies and gene frequencies of a large, randomly mating population remain constant provided immigration, mutation, and selection do not take place.

Harmony: The combination of simultaneously sounded musical notes to produce chords and chord progressions having a pleasing effect, or the quality of forming a pleasing and consistent whole. It may also mean an agreement or concord; i.e. "man and machine in perfect harmony". Have as synonyms: accord, agreement, peace, peacefulness, amity, amicability, friendship, fellowship, cooperation, understanding, consensus, unity, sympathy, rapport, like-mindedness.

Haskell: Is a pure functional programming language based on lambda calculus. It is statically typed and uses lazy evaluation. Used for rapid prototyping and for developing maintainable high quality software. Concurrency and parallelism are supported through intrinsic features of the language.

Heliosphere: The region of space, encompassing the solar system, in which the solar wind has a significant influence.

Heterogeneous Computing: Systems that use multiple processor types.

Heterozygosity: The state of having two different alleles of the same gene.

Heuristic Methods: Methods that facilitate in learning, discover, or problem-solving by experimental or trial-and-error methods.

High Performance Computing: Aggregating computing power in a way that delivers much higher performance that one could get out of a typical desktop computer or workstation.

High Performance Scientific Computing: Parallel scientific computing and simulation of science and engineering large problems using different types of supercomputers, which these days have tens of thousands of processors and cost millions of dollars.

Homologous Protein: A biological homology between proteins whose implication is that the proteins are derived from a common protein or other structure.

Homology: Two molecules that share a common ancestor.

Homology Modeling: Constructing an atomic-resolution model of the protein of interest from its amino acid sequence and an experimental three-dimensional structure of a related homologous protein to be used as a template.

Homology Modeling: 3D structure prediction of protein on the basis of similarity and identity between two or more sequences from the databases.

Human Brain Project: A large scientific research project, directed by the École Polytechnique Fédérale de Lausanne and largely funded by the European Union, which aims to simulate the complete human brain on supercomputers to better understand how it functions. The project is based in Geneva, Switzerland (Wikipedia, 2014c).

Identity: That which is itself. Identity necessarily implies equivalence, but equivalence does not necessarily imply identity.

Image Processing: Method of removing from a picture the so called noise i.e. the pixels which do not belong inherently to the picture scenario in reality. Those pixels were planted in the image during the process of digitally transforming the picture. There are special filtering methods that can clean the image.

Infrastructure as a Service: Also referred to as "Hardware as a Service", it is the model in which organizations outsource the equipment to stakeholders for supporting their operations.

Intelligence: Ones ability to process information. (See "mind".)

Intergenic: A region found between two genes.

Intron: A noncoding sequence between two coding genomic sequence.

Jungle Computing: The use of diverse [vague], distributed and highly non-uniform [vague] high performance computer systems to achieve peak performance (Wikipedia, 2014d).

Ligand: Small Drug or interacting molecule which are able to dock with receptor (Protein). These ligand are able to perform specific functions after interaction with receptors.

Linkage Disequilibrium: Occurs when genotypes at the two loci are not independent of another.

Linpack Performance: A technique used to evaluate the floating point rate of execution of a computer.

Logical Space: An area consisting of a grid, or net of two or more dimensions and populated by values in a bivalent system, the values being represented by symbols.

Lustre File System: Lustre is a type of parallel distributed file system, generally used for large-scale cluster computing. The name Lustre is a Portmanteau word derived from Linux and Cluster.

MapReduce: Is a programming paradigm for massive parallel computation using thousands of servers in a compute cluster. The term MapReduce refers to two different tasks: the map and reduce tasks. The map task turns a dataset into another dataset consisting of tuples (essentially (key, value) pairs). The reduce job takes the output of the map job and produces final result.

Markov Model System: Mathematical model that allows the study of complex systems by establishing a state of the system and then consequently effecting a transition to a new state, such a transition being dependent only on the values of the current state, and not dependent on the previous history of the system up to that point.

Massively Parallel Processing Unit (MPP): Coordinated processing of a program by multiple processors that work on different parts of the program with each processor using its own operating system and memory.

Mendel's Laws: Consists of three laws of inheritance describing how genes are passed on from parents to offsprings.

Mentoring: Johnson (2011) defines mentoring as a purposeful synergetic relationship which enables people "to set and achieve goals, make decisions and solve problems" (p. 40).

Mesoscale: Of intermediate size; especially of or relating to a meteorological phenomenon approximately 10 to 1000 kilometers in horizontal extent. For example mesoscale cloud pattern or, related to material it may include elements from 1 micron up to several centimeters size.

Message Passing: Message passing is a basic method for information sharing in a distributed system. Processes executing on different computers often need to communicate with each other to achieve some common goals. Message passing provides an interprocess communication mechanism to facilitate such communication activities.

Message Passing Interface (MPI): A standard that specifies a number of functions for developing distributed memory-based parallel computing applications. Implementation of this standard as libraries is available for C/C++ and Fortran languages.

Meta-Analysis: A method of combining quantitative or qualitative datasets from different studies to determine a single conclusion with greater statistical power.

Microsatellite: Genetic markers consisting of repeating sequences of 2-6 base pairs of DNA.

Microscale: A very small scale ranging from 0.1 microns up to 0.1 mm

Migration: In population genetics, is defined as the movement of alleles from one area (i.e. population) to another.

Millennial: Recently noted as the Me Me Me Generation in Time magazine, Millennials number around 80 million. This generation is described as narcissistic raised in a world gone social, connected, and wired. They have a tendency for causes and are immersed in the digital.

Mind: What people refer to as "consciousness", state of mentation. This may include but not be restricted to thinking, mood, or anything intangible experienced by a person but regarded as emanating from the brain. Despite many years of reflection and research on mind, there has been no universally agreed-upon definition of "mind", "consciousness", "intelligence" or what people take as synonyms, or words meaning the same. For example, one only need visit the website http:// consciousness.arizona.edu and read the thousands of presentations by persons in many disciplines to appreciate this.

Mobile Cloud Computing: A mix of cloud computing and mobile development. It facilitates mobile users with applications delivered over the mobile services and powered by cloud infrastructure.

Mobile Communication: The telecommunication system that involves no cable in the last-mile. The communication in the last-mile is carried out over the radio interface.

Modeling: A mathematical model is a description of a system using mathematical concepts and language. The process of developing a mathematical model is termed mathematical modeling. Mathematical models are used not only in the natural sciences and engineering disciplines, but also in the social sciences; physicists, engineers, statisticians, operations research analysts and economists use mathematical models most extensively.

Molecular Dynamics Simulations: A computer simulation of physical movements of atoms and molecules that are allowed to interact for a period of time, This interaction then provides a view of the motion of the atoms. In the most common version, the trajectories of atoms and molecules are determined by numerically solving the Newton's equations of motion for a system of interacting particles, where forces between the particles and potential energy are defined by molecular mechanics force fields

Molecular Modeling: Used to model or mimic the behavior of molecules.

Monte Carlo Simulations: A group of computational algorithms that rely on repeated random sampling to obtain numerical results, for example this can be obtained by running simulations many times over in order to calculate those same probabilities heuristically and are especially useful for simulating systems with many coupled degrees of freedom.

Monte-Carlo Simulation: A problem solving technique used to approximate the probability of certain outcomes by running simulations utilizing random variables

Morphological Image Processing: Selective, iteratively removing pixels according their intensity, i.e. according to the outlines in the image. This processing is efficient in edge detection processes.

Multi Grid Method: A method of solving discrete (mainly two dimensional) problems, using a set of grids covering the same domain but with different grid resolutions.

Multi-Dimension: Involving several dimensions or aspects as "multidimensional space."

Multi-Level-Adaptive Technique (MLAT): Solving discrete problems using Multi-Grids or other multi scaling problems, adaptively.

Multiprocessing: The use of two or more central processing units (CPUs) within a single computer system. The term also refers to the ability of a system to support more than one processor and/or the ability to allocate tasks between them (Wikipedia, 2014e).

Multiprocessor: A computer system with more than one central processing unit (CPU) that share main memory.

Multi-Scale: Different scales are used simultaneously to describe a system.

Mutation: A permanent change, specifically a structural alteration in the DNA or RNA.

Naming: Naming mechanisms enable users and programs to assign character-string names to objects and subsequently use these names to refer to those objects. Naming system consists of the naming facilities of a distributed operating system and the locating facility of the distributed operating system, which provides the users with an abstraction of an object that hides the details of how and where an object is actually located in the network and also provides a further level of abstraction when dealing with object replicas.

Nano-Structure: An object of intermediate size between microscopic and molecular structures.

Nano-Technologies: Science, engineering, and technology conducted at the nanoscale, which is about 1 to 100 nanometers.

Natural Selection: A process by which individuals' inherited needs and abilities are more or less closely matched to resources available in their environment, providing those with greater "fitness" a better chance of survival and reproduction.

Navier-Strokes solvers: These equations describe the motion of fluid substances.

Network Theory: An area of Computer Science and network science and a part of graph theory.

Neural Network: A network composed of interconnecting artificial neurons which mimic the properties of biological neurons for solving artificial intelligence problems without creating a model of a real system. Neural network algorithms abstract away the biological complexity by focusing on the most important information.

Neuroimaging: Graphic representation of neuroanatomy, including but not limited to the brain, nerves, ganglia, axons, and dendrites. Images may be by computerized axial tomography (CAT), electroencephalograms (EEG), functional magnetic resonance imaging (fMRI), positron emission tomography (PET), and others. It is to be noted that the lower-case "f" in "fMRI is intentional; this is the proper manner of writing this abbreviation.

Nuclear Energy: The use of exothermic nuclear processes, (Proffitt, 2012) to generate useful heat and electricity. The term includes nuclear fission, nuclear decay and nuclear fusion. Presently the nuclear fission of elements in the actinide series of the periodic table produce the vast majority of nuclear energy in the direct service of humankind, with nuclear decay processes, primarily in the form of geothermal energy, and radioisotope thermoelectric generators; niche uses making up the rest. Nuclear (fission) power stations, excluding the contribution from naval nuclear fission reactors, provided about 5.7% of the world's energy and 13% of the world's electricity in 2012. (DOE 2010)

Nuclear Power: Electric or motor power generated by a nuclear reactor, or a country that has nuclear weapons.

Nucleotide: Building blocks from which DNA and RNA are built.

Ontology: A branch of philosophy concerned with existence.

Open Reading Frame (ORF): A DNA sequence that does not contain a stop codon in a given reading frame.

OpenACC: It is an open standard and provides a collection of compiler directives to specify loops and regions of code that need to be executed in parallel mode. OpenACC is similar to OpenMP but the parallel code is executed on accelerators like GPUs.

OpenCL: Is a standard and framework for developing parallel computing applications that execute across heterogeneous computing platforms consisting of CPUs, GPUs, DSPs and other processors such as PlaStations. OpenCL implementations are available for developing parallel computing applications using the C language.

OpenMP: A standard for developing shared memory-based parallel computing applications. Implementation of this standard as libraries is available for C/C++ and Fortran languages.

Optimization: In the simplest case, an optimization problem consists of maximizing or minimizing a real function by systematically choosing input values from within an allowed set and computing the value of the function. The generalization of optimization theory and tech-

niques to other formulations comprises a large area of applied mathematics.

Organizational Culture: Organizational culture is the environment of an organization perpetuated from the behaviors, meanings, and actions of its members (Marques, 2011 , p. 47). This environment is taught to new members as a way of perceiving and thinking about the organization, how it operates, and affects others. Based on a set of values, symbols, languages, beliefs, and actions, the culture of an organization is very important.

Parallel Algorithm: An algorithm that allows execution a piece at a time in different processing devices, and then eventually putting them back together again at the end to determine the correct result.

Parallel Computing: Method of increasing the throughput of running computer programs by performing some computations in parallel instead of in sequence. Such parallelization may be done automatically if the computations are independent one from the other, namely one computation is not dependent on the result of other computations. The parallelization can be the copying of one operation on various data in the same time, or performing different operations in the same time (Marlow S. 2013).

Parallel Programming: Computational method, which allows carrying out multiple calculations simultaneously.

Pattern Recognition: Method that deals with feature extraction and classification.

Peptide Sequence: Unique amino acid sequence characterizing a given protein.

Petaflops: A measure of computer's processing speed and can be expressed as a thousand trillion floating point operations per second.

Phylogeny: The evolutionary development and history of a species or higher taxonomic group of organisms.

Physics: The branch of science concerned with the nature and properties of matter and energy. The subject matter of physics, includes mechanics, heat, light and other radiation, sound, electricity, magnetism, and the structure of atoms.

Platform as a Service: An approach to rent out operating systems, software platforms, etc. to various stakeholders in the cloud computing market.

Population Genetics: The study concerned mainly with the genetic variation within species.

Primary Protein Structure: The linear sequence of amino acid structural units in a protein which partially encompasses the overall biomolecular structure of the protein. The primary structure of a protein is described by starting from the amino-terminal (N) end and terminating at the carboxyl-terminal (C) end.

Process Management: Process management deals with mechanisms and policies for sharing the processor of the system among all processes. In a distributed operating system, the main goal of process management is to make the best possible use of the processing resources of the entire system by sharing them among all processes.

Processing Element: Refers to the principal components, which make up a any workflow.

Prokaryote: Organisms lacking a cell nucleus.

Promoters: DNA segment usually occurring from a gene coding region and acting as a controlling element in gene expression

Protein Databank: The storage system for the 3-D structural data of large biological molecules, such as proteins and nucleic acids.

Protein Domain: A conserved portion of a given protein sequence and structure that can evolve, function, and exist separately from the remainder of the protein chain.

Protein Electrophoresis: An analytical technique used to separate different protein components (fractions) in a mixture of proteins such a blood sample on the basis of differences in the movement of components through a fluid-filled matrix under the influence of an applied electric field.

Protein Folding: The process by which a protein structure assumes its functional shape or conformation

Protein Motif: A supersecondary structure of a protein that also appears in a variety of additional molecules.

Protein Sequence: The order in which amino acid residues, linked by peptide bonds, are positioned in the chain in the protein.

Protein-Protein Docking: Interaction studies between two proteins like one receptor and another protein or between peptides.

QCDOC machines: This architecture has been designed to provide cost-effective, massively parallel computer capable of focusing computing resources on small but extremely demanding problems.

Quantitative Structure Activity Relationship (QSAR): Used to define the function of the molecules or atoms on the basis of their structure.

Quantum Chromo Dynamics: A quantum field theory in which the strong interaction is described in terms of interactions between quarks mediated by gluons, both quarks and gluons being assigned a quantum number called "color".

Quantum Computer: A computation device that makes direct use of quantum-mechanical phenomena, such as superposition and entanglement, to perform operations on data. Quantum computers are different from digital computers based on transistors. (Wikipedia, 2013)

Quantum Mechanics: Branch of Physics that deals with physical phenomena at nanoscopic scales where the action is in the order of Planck's constant.

Qubit: In quantum computing, a qubit or quantum bit is a unit of quantum information—the quantum analogue of the classical bit. A qubit is a two-state quantum-mechanical system, such as the polarization of a single photon: here the two states are vertical polarization and horizontal polarization. In a classical system, a bit would have to be in one state or the other, but quantum mechanics allows the qubit to be in a superposition of both states at the same time, a property which is fundamental to quantum computing.

Randomly Amplified Polymorphic DNA (RAPD) Technique: A method in which genomic DNA are amplified by polymerase chain reaction (PCR) using non-specific primers that are complementary to a number of sites within the genome.

Recursion: That which is repeated, or circular. The term in computer science refers to the ability to define an infinite set of objects or processes by the same set of instructions, function, or statement.

Reduced Instruction Set Computer (RISC): A type of computer architecture that has a relatively small set of computer instructions that it can perform.

Reflexive: A property of a process or object that identifies itself in terms of itself. This concept often is used synonymously with, "tautology", "recursive", "identity", or other words meaning something being itself.

Regulatory Elements: DNA sequence that determines the regulation of gene expression.

Remote Procedure Calls: Remote procedure call is a special case of the general message-passing model of interprocess communication (IPC) that has become a widely accepted IPC mechanism in distributed computing systems.

Renewable Energy: Energy that comes from resources which are naturally replenished on a human timescale such as sunlight, wind, rain, tides, waves and geothermal heat.

Resource Management: Resource management can be used to manage resources interconnected by a network, migrate a process between different nodes if the local node does not have the required resource or the local node has to be shutdown, assign remote resources to a process on the local node.

Restriction Endonucleases: Enzymes that cut nucleic acid at specific restriction sites and produce restriction fragments.

Restriction Fragment Length Polymorphisms: Genetic variation that can be detected by enzymatic digestion.

RNA Sequencing: Also called as Whole Transcriptome Shotgun Sequencing, is a technology that uses the capabilities of next generation sequencing to reveal a snapshot of RNA presence and quantity from a genome at a given moment in time.

Rotamer: Isomers that can be interconverted through the use of rotations about formally single bonds

Schrodinger Equation: A differential equation that forms the basis of the quantum-mechanical description of matter in terms of wave-like properties of particles in a field.

Secondary Protein Structure: The common three-dimensional form of local segments of proteins defined by the patterns of hydrogen bonds involving backbone amino and carboxyl groups.

Semiconductor: A solid substance that has the conductivity between that of an insulator and that of most metals, either due to the addition of impurities or because of temperature effects. Devices made of semiconductors are components of electronic circuits.

Sentence Parsing: The hierarchal dissecting of a sentence to pieces according their function in the language. In natural languages there are sentence components.

Senturion: A predictive analysis software tool developed at the National Defense University (NDU) Center for Technology and National Security Policy (CTNSP).

Sequence Alignment: A method of arranging RNA, protein, or DNA sequences to identify regions of similarity that maybe a consequence of functional, structural, or evolutionary relationships between the sequences.

Sequence Analysis: Analysis of protein or DNA nucleotide sequence and identification of sequence conservation, hot spots, active site,

identity, homology and phylogeny among the sequences.

Sequence Assembly: A method of determining the order of multiple sequenced DNA fragments.

Servant Leadership: Servant-oriented leadership was developed by Robert K. Greenleaf in 1970. Greenleaf's writings on servant leadership emphasize the servant as leader. Servant leaders are servants first aspiring to put the needs of others before self. The servant leader is not driven by position but rather the love of serving. Proponents of servant leadership are Ken Blanchard, John Maxwell, and Laurie Beth Jones.

Shenwei CPUs: Shenwei is a series of microprocessors developed by Jiangnan Computing lab in Wuxi, China.

Shotgun Sequencing: Laboratory technique for determining the DNA sequence of an organism's genome.

Signature Database: A database that is used to store critical security parameters of trusted files present on the system.

Simulated Annealing: A generic probabilistic metaheuristic for the global optimization problem of locating a good approximation to the global optimum of a given function in a large search space.

Simulation: A model of a reality. Sometimes the reality is not deterministic. In these cases the no determinism is imitated by so called pseudo-random numbers, generated by the computer, giving the impression of randomness (Monte Carlo method). There are various types of simulations – Mechanical modeling of mechanical components and their mutual movement; Electronic modeling simulates the functionality of electronic devices such as a transistor, resistor, capacitor or central processor etc.; Social simulations to foresee social movements, demographic situation, traffic; Physical modeling simulates events in the physical world such as fission and nuclear effects; Mathematical approximating numerically the analytical solutions.

Single Instruction, Multiple Data (SIMD) Processing: Processing technique in which an operation is taken in one specified instruction and applies it to more than one set of data elements at the same time.

Single Nucleotide Polymorphisms: Genetic variation in a DNA sequence that occurs when a single nucleotide in a genome is altered.

Software as a Service: A software distribution approach with applications hosted by application service providers and extended to the consumers over the network.

Splicing: The process of inserting DNA or RNA fragments to form new genetic combinations or alter a new genetic structure.

Start Codon: The first codon of an mRNA transcript translated by a ribosome.

Static Random-Access Memory: (SRAM): A type of memory chip which is faster and requires less power than dynamic memory.

Statistical Inference: A process of utilizing information from a sample to draw conclusions (or inferences) about the population from which the sample was taken.

Steganography: (in Greek steganos means protected) A theory of hiding real information by implanting it unnoticeably within data or by transforming it to other meaningful but misleading, or misinforming exposed information.

Stop Codon: The genetic codon in an mRNA that signals the termination of protein synthesis during translation.

Structural Annotation: The process of localizing the genes in both strands of a genome as well precisely determining the structural elements of these genes.

Succession Planning: Succession planning is a talent pool strategy of an organization. A mature organization recognizes the strengths of its people and leverages their talents for the benefit of the organization's business. Succession planning is the process whereby talent is developed, strengthened, and trained for leadership.

Supercomputer: A computer having high-order qualities especially high throughput. These qualifications are very useful for assembling huge amounts of data, which are encountered in domains such as genomics, and nuclear simulations to predict the fission processes, for analyzing homeland cyber-security, etc. There are various computer architectures supporting supercomputers, such as CRAY – array-computers and n-Cubes which consist of small processors connected in a network as an n-dimensional hyper-cube.

Superconductors: A substance capable of becoming superconducting at sufficiently low temperatures.

Supernode: Any node that also serves as one of the network's relayers and proxy servers, handling data flow and connections for other users.

Support Vector Machine: Supervised learning models with associated learning algorithms that analyze data and recognize patterns, used for classification and regression analysis.

Symmetric Multiprocessing (SMP) System: A multiprocessing architecture in which multiple

CPUs, residing in one cabinet, share the same memory.

Synchronization: The rules for enforcing correct interaction are implemented in the system in the form of synchronization mechanisms.

Talent Pool: A community or cohort of individuals with specific skills for an organization.

Teraflops: A measure of computing speed equal to one trillion floating-point operations per second.

Tertiary Protein Structure: The three-dimensional structure of a protein as defined by atomic coordinates and is created by the packing of protein secondary structure elements into dense globular units called protein domains.

TOP500: The TOP500 project ranks and details the 500 most powerful (non-distributed) computer systems in the world. The project was started in 1993 and publishes an updated list of the supercomputers twice a year (Wikipedia, 2014h).

Toxic Leadership: A philosophy and practice of leadership that emerges as a consequence of self-serving desires perhaps often unbeknownst to the individual. While the community receiving the service may not know, the internal talent pool of the leadership suffers with low morale and performance is fear based. The outcome of this leadership is high turnover and low performance. Toxic leadership thrives on setting up others to fail so they may succeed.

Traditional GenBank: Divisions that contain 106 billion nucleotide bases from 108 million individual sequences, with 11 million new sequences added in 2009.

Transactional Leadership: A philosophy and practice of leadership which focuses on contingent

reinforcement as motivational methods for employee performance. The employees performance is what Transactional leaders act upon through methods of reward and punishment.

Transformational Leadership: A philosophy and practice of leadership which encourages others to take ownership for their work, motivates growth, and empowers the organization with collective identity measures. Transformational leaders aspire to inspire performance to a greater outcome beyond self-development.

Transhumanism: Integration of technologies to enhance the capabilities of the human body. A simple example would be the attachment of artificial legs so as to enhance functionality, durability, appearance, and so forth.

Transposon: DNA segment consisting of an insertion sequence element at each end as a repeat as well as genes specific to some other activity such as resistance to antibiotics.

Ubiquitous Computing: Integration of computation into environment, which is contrary to the concept of standalone or distinct computers.

Uncertainty: A term used in subtly different ways in a number of fields, including philosophy, physics, statistics, economics, finance, insurance, psychology, sociology, engineering, and information science. It applies to predictions of future events, to physical measurements that are already made, or to the unknown.

Validation: Ensuring that was has been intended and listed in a verification actually operates or performs as intended. Methods for validation include field testing, modeling and simulation, visual inspection against standards, and any other form of comparing and contrasting a prediction with actual outcome.

Vector Processing: A vector processor, or array processor, is a central processing unit (CPU) that implements an instruction set containing instructions that operate on one-dimensional arrays of data called vectors. This is in contrast to a scalar processor, whose instructions operate on single data items (Wikipedia, 2014i).

Verification: Ensuring that all the elements in a requirements specification are included in the instrument to carry out those requirements. Verification is analogous to checklist, as in a shopping list, the question being answered, " are all the items I have listed in the shopping cart?"

Very-Large-Scale Integration: (VLSI) Circuits: The process of creating integrated circuits by combining thousands of transistors into a single chip. VLSI began in the 1970s when complex semiconductor and communication technologies were being developed. The microprocessor is a VLSI device.

Virtual Screening: Screening or filtering of molecules on the basis of similarity of their structure. It is a database search method.

Watermark: Information implanted in other information, which cannot be removed. Watermarks are sometimes used to designate the ownership of the information.

Whole Genome Shotgun: A method of genome sequence determination based on assembly of the whole genome from numerous sequence reads at high coverage without requiring reference to genetic or physical map locations for those reads.

Compilation of References

1000 Genomes. (2012). *1000 genomes: A deep catalog of human genetic variation.* Retrieved from 20 October 2014, http: //www.1000genomes.org/

A Programming Language Designed for Parallelism and Cloud Computing. (2014). Retrieved from 20 October 2014, http: //julialang.org/

A Telescope for Theoretical Astronomy: Supercomputer "Aterui ". (2014). Retrieved May 29, 2014 from http://www.nao.ac.jp/en/gallery/2014/20140422-aterui.html

Abbott, P., Abraham, T., Beath, C., Bullen, C., Carmel, E., Evaristo, R., ... Zwieg, P. (2006, March). *The information technology workforce: Trends and implications 2005-2008.* Society for Information Management IT Workforce Executive Summary.

Abecasis, G. R., Auton, A., Brooks, L. D., DePristo, M. A., Durbin, R. M., & Handsaker, R. E. et al. (2012). An integrated map of genetic variation from 1,092 human genomes. *Nature, 491*(7422), 56–65. doi:10.1038/nature11632 PMID:23128226

Abel, J. (2013). *Ohio supercomputing center annual research report 2013: Discovering keys to controlling malaria.* Columbus, OH: University System of Ohio.

Academies, T. N. (2003). *The future of supercomputing: An interim report* (p. 4). Washington, DC: National Academy of Sciences.

Adams, J. C., Ernst, D. J., Murphy, T., & Ortiz, A. (2010). Multicore education: Pieces of the parallel puzzle. In *Proceedings of the 41st ACM Technical Symposium on Computer Science Education.* New York, NY: ACM. doi:10.1145/1734263.1734329

Advisory Committee to the Director. Brain Research through Advancing Innovative. (2013). *Neurotechnologies (BRAIN) working group.* National Institutes of Mental Health. Retrieved 9 March 2014 from http://www.nih.gov/science/brain/ACD_BRAIN_interimreport_executivesummary.htm

Afshari, C. A. (2002). Perspective: Microarray technology, seeing more than spots. *Endocrinology, 143*(6), 1983–1989. doi:10.1210/endo.143.6.8865 PMID:12021158

Agam, S. (2011). SGI, Intel plan to speed supercomputers 500 times by 2018. *Computer World.* Retrieved on June 9, 2012 from http://www.computerworld.com

Agrawal, A. (2008). *A new heuristic for multiple sequence alignment.* Paper presented at the Institute of Electrical and Electronics Engineers International Conference, Ames, IA. doi:10.1109/EIT.2008.4554299

Agrawal, D., Abbadi, A. E., Das, S., & Elmore, A. J. (2011). Database scalability, elasticity, and autonomy in the cloud. In *Proceedings of 16th international conference on Database systems for advanced applications.* Academic Press. doi:10.1007/978-3-642-20149-3_2

Agrawal, R., & Ezzat, A. K. (1987). Location independent remote execution in NEST. *IEEE Transactions on Software Engineering, SE-13*(8), 905–912. doi:10.1109/TSE.1987.233509

Ahamed, S.I., Brylow, D., Early, J., Ge, R., Madiraju, P., Merrill, S.J., & Struble, C.A., (2010, March). *Computational thinking for the sciences: A three day workshop for high school science teachers.* Paper presented at SIGCSE'10, Milwaukee, WI.

Allcock, B., Bresnahan, J., Chervenak, A., Foster, I., Kesselman, C., Meder, S., et al., Tuecke, & S., Secure. (2001). Efficient data transport and replica management for high-performance data-intensive computing. In *Proceedings of MSS '01: Mass Storage Systems and Technologies, 2001* (p. 13). IEEE.

Allen, C. (2010). *Animal consciousness Dec 23, 1995.* Retrieved 9 March 2014 from http://plato.stanford.edu/entries/consciousness-animal/http://en.wikipedia.org/wiki/animal_consciousness

Allen, F., Almasi, G., Andreoni, W., Beece, D., Berne, B. J., & Bright, A. et al. (2001). Blue gene: A vision for protein science using a petaflop supercomputer. *IBM Systems Journal, 40*(2), 301–327. doi:10.1147/sj.402.0310

Alsop, R. (2008). *The trophy kids grow up: How the millennial generation is shaking up the workplace.* San Francisco, CA: Jossey-Bass.

Altschul, S. F., Gish, W., Miller, W., Myers, E. W., & Lipman, D. J. (1990). Basic local alignment search tool. *Journal of Molecular Biology, 215*(3), 403–410. doi:10.1016/S0022-2836(05)80360-2 PMID:2231712

Aluru, S. (2006). *A supercomputer for Iowa State University.* Retrieved April 17, 2014, from http://www.public.iastate.edu/~nscentral/news/06/jan/supercomputer.shtml

Amazon Simple Queue Service (Amazon SQS). (n.d.). Retrieved May 12, 2013 from: http://aws.amazon.com/de/sqs/

Amazon. (2012). *1000 genomes project and AWS.* Retrieved 20 October 2014, from http://aws.amazon.com/1000genomes/

Amigo, J., Salas, A., & Phillips, C. (2011). ENGINES: Exploring single nucleotide variation in entire human genomes. *BMC Bioinformatics, 12*(1), 105. doi:10.1186/1471-2105-12-105 PMID:21504571

Amirisetty, S., Hershey, G. K., & Baye, T. M. (2012). AncestrySNPminer: A bioinformatics tool to retrieve and develop ancestry informative SNP panels. *Genomics, 100*(1), 57–63. doi:10.1016/j.ygeno.2012.05.003 PMID:22584067

Anderson, J. M., Bonfield, T. L., & Ziats, N. P. (1990). Protein adsorption and cellular adhesion and activation on biomedical polymers. *The International Journal of Artificial Organs, 13*(6), 375–382. PMID:2143174

Anderson, S. (1981). Shotgun DNA sequencing using cloned DNase I-generated fragments. *Nucleic Acids Research, 9*(13), 3015–3027. doi:10.1093/nar/9.13.3015 PMID:6269069

Andrade, J., Andersen, M., Sillen, A., Graff, C., & Odeberg, J. (2007). The use of grid computing to drive data-intensive genetic research. *European Journal of Human Genetics, 15*(6), 694–702. doi:10.1038/sj.ejhg.5201815 PMID:17377522

Andrews, G. R. (2000). *Foundations of multithreaded, parallel, and distributed programming.* Reading, MA: Addison-Wesley.

Anthony, S. (2012). *The history of supercomputers.* Retrieved May 28, 2014 from http://www.extremetech.com/extreme/125271-the-history-of-supercomputers

Anthony, S. (2012). *The race to 100 petaflops: Cray and China go head-to-head to build the world's fastest supercomputer.* Retrieved March 18, 2014, from http://www.extremetech.com/extreme/140174-the-race-to-100-petaflops-cray-and-china-worlds-fastest-supercomputer

Anthony, S. (2013). China's Tianhe-2 supercomputer, twice as fast as DoE's Titan, shocks the world by arriving two years early. *Extreme Tech.* Retrieved March 18, 2014, from http://www.extremetech.com/computing/159465-chinas-tianhe-2-supercomputer-twice-as-fast-as-does-titan-shocks-the-world-by-arriving-two-years-early

Argonne National Laboratory. (2014). *Mira: An engine for discovery.* Retrieved from http://www.alcf.anl.gov/mira

Arianfar, S., Nikander, P., & Ott, J. (2010). On content-centric router design and implications. In *Proceedings of the Re-Architecting the Internet Workshop.* AS Ranking. Retrieved February 12, 2013, from: http://as-rank.caida.org/

Armstrong, D., & Ma, M. (2013). *Researcher controls colleague's motions in 1st human brain-to-brain interface.* Retrieved 9 March 2014 from http://www.washington.edu/news/2013/08/27/researcher-controls-colleagues-motions-in-1st-human-brain-to-brain-interface/

Arnold, K., Bordoli, L., Kopp, J., & Schwede, T. (2006). The SWISS-MODEL workspace: A web-based environment for protein structure homology modelling. *Bioinformatics (Oxford, England)*, *22*(2), 195–201. doi:10.1093/bioinformatics/bti770 PMID:16301204

Artymiuk, P. J., Poirrette, A. R., Grindley, H. M., Rice, D. W., & Willett, P. (1994). A graph-theoretic approach to the identification of three-dimensional patterns of amino acid side-chains in protein structures. *Journal of Molecular Biology*, *243*(2), 327–344. doi:10.1006/jmbi.1994.1657 PMID:7932758

ASCAC-DOE. (2010). The opportunities and challenges of exascale computing. In *Proceedings of the ASCAC Subcommittee on Exascale Computing*. Retrieved March 18, 2014, from http://science.energy.gov/~/media/ascr/ascac/pdf/reports/exascale_subcommittee_report.pdf

ASCR-DOE. (2014). *Applied mathematics research for exascale computing*. Retrieved March 18, 2014, from http://www.netlib.org/utk/people/JackDongarra/PAPERS/doe-exascale-math-report.pdf

Ashburner, M., Ball, C. A., Blake, J. A., Botstein, D., Butler, H., & Cherry, J. M. et al. (2000). Gene ontology: Tool for the unification of biology: The gene ontology consortium. *Nature Genetics*, *25*(1), 25–29. doi:10.1038/75556 PMID:10802651

Ashby, R. (1954). *Design for a brain*. New York: Wiley.

Ashkenazy, H., Erez, E., Martz, E., Pupko, T., & Ben-Tal, N. (2010). ConSurf 2010: Calculating evolutionary conservation in sequence and structure of proteins and nucleic acids. *Nucleic Acids Research, 38*(Web Server issue), W529-533. doi: 10.1093/nar/gkq399

Asimov, I. (1950). Runaround. In *I, robot*. New York: Doubleday & Company.

ASU. (2006). *Nanoionics: Defined*. Arizona State University Arizona Institute for Nano-Electronics. Retrieved March 10, 2014 from: http://www.asu.edu/aine/nanoionicsdefined.htm

Atsalakis, G. S., & Valavanis, K. P. (2009). Surveying stock market forecasting techniques - Part 2: Soft computing methods. *Expert Systems with Applications*, *36*(3), 5932–5941. doi:10.1016/j.eswa.2008.07.006

Attwood, T. K., Bradley, P., Flower, D. R., Gaulton, A., Maudling, N., & Mitchell, A. L. et al. (2003). PRINTS and its automatic supplement, prePRINTS. *Nucleic Acids Research*, *31*(1), 400–402. doi:10.1093/nar/gkg030 PMID:12520033

Aud, S., Hussar, W., Johnson, F., Kena, G., Roth, E., Manning, E., et al. (2012). *The condition of education 2012 (NCES 2012-045), undergraduate study*. U.S. Department of Education, National Center for Education Statistics. Retrieved May 4, 2013 from http://nces.ed.gov/pubsearch

Aumann, R. J., & Furstenberg, H. (2004). *Findings of the committee to investigate the Gans-Inbal results on equidistant letter sequences in Genesis*. Retrieved from Center for Rationality, Discussion paper 364, http://www.ma.huji.ac.il/raumann/

Avolio, B. J., & Bass, B. M. (2002). *Developing potential across a full range of leadership: Cases on transactional and transformational leadership*. Mahwah, NJ: Lawrence Erlbaum Associates.

Azeem, M. M., Iqbal, I., Toivanen, J. P., & Samad, A. (2012). Emotions in robots. In Proceedings of Communications in Computer and Information Conference: 2nd Emerging Trends and Applications in Information Communication Technologies (Vol. 281, pp. 144–153). Heidelberg, Germany: Springer.

Azevedo, F. A. (2009). Equal numbers of neuronal and nonneuronal cells make the human brain an isometrically scaled-up primate brain. *The Journal of Comparative Neurology*, *513*(5), 532–541. doi:10.1002/cne.21974

Baburajan, R. (2011). The rising cloud storage market opportunity strengthens vendors. *infoTECH*. Retrieved on December 2, 2011 from http://it.tmcnet.com

Bach, M., Charney, M., Cohn, R., Demikhovsky, E., Devor, T., & Hazelwood, K. et al. (2010). Analyzing parallel programs with pin. *Computer*, *43*(3), 34–41. doi:10.1109/MC.2010.60

Bader, D. A. (2004). Computational biology and high-performance computing. *Communications of the ACM*, *47*(11), 34–41. doi:10.1145/1029496.1029523

Bahl, P., Han, R. Y., Li, L. E., & Satyanarayanan, M. (2012). Advancing the state of mobile cloud computing. In *Proceedings of the Third ACM Workshop on Mobile Cloud Computing and Services* (pp. 21-28). ACM. doi:10.1145/2307849.2307856

Bailey, L. C. Jr, Fischer, S., Schug, J., Crabtree, J., Gibson, M., & Overton, G. C. (1998). GAIA: Framework annotation of genomic sequence. *Genome Research*, *8*(3), 234–250. doi:10.1101/gr.8.3.234 PMID:9521927

Bai, X.-M., Voter, A. F., Hoagland, R. G., Nastasi, M., & Uberuaga, B. P. (2010). Efficient annealing of radiation damage near grain boundaries via interstitial emission. *Science*, *327*(5973), 1631–1634. doi:10.1126/science.1183723 PMID:20339070

Ball, P. (2013). Diamond idea for quantum computer. *BBC Future*. Retrieved March 18, 2014, from http://www.bbc.com/future/story/20130218-diamond-idea-for-quantum-computer(Under the Radar)

Bandyopadhyay, A., Pati, R., Sahu, S., Peper, F., & Fujita, D. (2010). Massively parallel computing on an organic molecular layer. *Nature Physics*, *6*(5), 369–375. doi:10.1038/nphys1636

Bao, X.-R. (2010). 3G based mobile internet in China. In *Proceedings of International Conference on Management and Service Science (MASS)*. Academic Press.

Barker, K. J., Davis, K., Hoisie, A., Kerbyson, D. J., Lang, M., Pakin, S., & Sancho, J. C. (2009). Using performance modeling to design large-scale systems. *Computer*, *42*(11), 42–49. doi:10.1109/MC.2009.372

Barmouta, A., & Buyya, R. (2003). GridBank: A grid accounting service architecture (GASA) for distributed systems sharing and integration. In *Proceedings of the 17th International Symposium on Parallel and Distributed Processing*. IEEE Computer Society.

Baron, H. A. (n.d.). *BOXSHADE*. Retrieved January 3, 2013, from http://mobyle.pasteur.fr/cgi-bin/portal.py?-forms:boxshade

Barrie, A. (2013). Defeating cyber-attacks with quantum cryptography. *FoxNews.com War Games*. Retrieved March 18, 2014, from http://www.foxnews.com/tech/2013/03/04/defeating-cyber-attacks-with-quantum-cryptography/#ixzz2MvAGziIr

Barth, B. (2013). *High performance computing (HPC) systems*. Retrieved from https://www.tacc.utexas.edu/resources/hpc

Barton, N. H., & Charlesworth, B. (1984). Genetic revolution, founder effects, and speciation. *Annual Review of Ecology and Systematics*, *15*(1), 133–165. doi:10.1146/annurev.es.15.110184.001025

Bates, P. A., Kelley, L. A., MacCallum, R. M., & Sternberg, M. J. (2001). Enhancement of protein modeling by human intervention in applying the automatic programs 3D-JIGSAW and 3D-PSSM. *Proteins*, *45*(S5), 39–46. doi:10.1002/prot.1168 PMID:11835480

Batten, C. (2012). *Computer architecture, topic 14: Vectors*. Cornell University, School of Electrical and Computer Engineering ECE 4750. Retrieved March 18, 2014, from http://www.csl.cornell.edu/courses/ece4750

Baudry, J. Y. (2012). *Designing drugs on supercomputers*. Retrieved December 22, 2013, from http://science.energy.gov/ascr/highlights/2012/ascr-2012-10-c/

Baurmeister, U., Vienken, J., & Grassmann, A. (1991). Biocompatibility and membrane development. *Nephrology, Dialysis, Transplantation*, *6*(Suppl 3), 17–21. PMID:1775260

Beals, R., Gray, O., Harrow, A., Kutin, S., Linden, N., Shepherd, D., & Stather, M. (2012). *Efficient distributed quantum computing*. arXiv:1207.2307

Beaumont, M. A., Zhang, W., & Balding, D. J. (2002). Approximate Bayesian computation in population genetics. *Genetics*, *162*(4), 2025–2035. PMID:12524368

Behr, M. A., Wilson, M. A., Gill, W. P., Salamon, H., Schoolnik, G. K., & Rane, S. et al. (1999). Comparative genomics of BCG vaccines by whole-genome DNA microarray. *Science*, *284*(5419), 1520–1523. doi:10.1126/science.284.5419.1520 PMID:10348738

Beimborn, D., Miletzki, T., & Wenzel, S. (2011). Platform as a service (PaaS). *Business & Information Systems Engineering*, *3*(6), 381–384. doi:10.1007/s12599-011-0183-3

Belkhir, K., Borsa, P., Chikhi, L., Raufaste, N., & Bonhomme, F. (2004). *Genetix 4.05 software*. Retrieved from http://www.univ-montp2.fr/~genetix/genetix/genetix.htm

Bell, G. (n.d.). *A brief history of supercomputing: "the Crays", clusters and Beowulf's, centers. what next?* Retrieved May 30, 2014 from http://research.microsoft.com/en-us/um/people/gbell/supers/supercomputing-a_brief_history_1965_2002.htm

Bellarmine, G. T., & Arokiaswamv, N. S. S. (1996). Energy management techniques to meet power shortage problems in India. *Energy Conversion and Management*, *37*(3), 319–328. doi:10.1016/0196-8904(95)00181-6

Belle, E. M., Landry, P. A., & Barbujani, G. (2006). Origins and evolution of the Europeans' genome: Evidence from multiple microsatellite loci. *Proceedings. Biological Sciences*, *273*(1594), 1595–1602. doi:10.1098/rspb.2006.3494 PMID:16769629

Benson, D. A., Cavanaugh, M., Clark, K., Karsch-Mizrachi, I., Lipman, D. J., Ostell, J., & Sayers, E. W. (2013). GenBank. *Nucleic Acids Research*, *41*(Database issue), D36–D42. doi:10.1093/nar/gks1195 PMID:23193287

Berendsen, H. J. C., van der Spoel, D., & van Drunen, R. (1995). GROMACS: A message-passing parallel molecular dynamics implementation. *Computer Physics Communications*, *91*(1–3), 43–56. doi:10.1016/0010-4655(95)00042-E

Bergey, C. M. (2011). AluHunter: A database of potentially polymorphic Alu insertions for use in primate phylogeny and population genetics. *Bioinformatics (Oxford, England)*, *27*(20), 2924–2925. doi:10.1093/bioinformatics/btr491 PMID:21880703

Berredo, R. C., Ekel, P. Y., Martini, J. S. C., Palhares, R. M., Parreiras, R. O., & Pereira, J. G. Jr. (2011). Decision making in fuzzy environment and multi-criteria power engineering problems. *International Journal of Electrical Power & Energy Systems*, *33*(3), 623–632. doi:10.1016/j.ijepes.2010.12.020

Berriman, G. B., & Groom, S. L. (2011). How will astronomy archives survive the data tsunami? *Queue*, *9*(10), 21:20–21:27. doi:10.1145/2043174.2043190

Berry, M. W., Gao, T., Pathan, R., & Stuart, G. W. (2013). PolyLens: Software for map-based visualisation and analysis of genome-scale polymorphism data. *Int J Comput Biol Drug Des*, *6*(1-2), 93–106. doi:10.1504/IJCBDD.2013.052204 PMID:23428476

Bertone, A. (2014). *FPGA assisted equine gene annotation and custom microarray (genechip)*. Retrieved June 16, 2014 from https://www.osc.edu/research/bioinformatics/projects/horse_gene

Bertorelle, G., Benazzo, A., & Mona, S. (2010). ABC as a flexible framework to estimate demography over space and time: Some cons, many pros. *Molecular Ecology*, *19*(13), 2609–2625. doi:10.1111/j.1365-294X.2010.04690.x PMID:20561199

Berzin, A. (2011). The Dhamma of Islam: A conversation with Snjezana Akpinar and Alex Berzin. *Inquiring Mind*, *20*(1).

Besemer, J., & Borodovsky, M. (1999). Heuristic approach to deriving models for gene finding. *Nucleic Acids Research*, *27*(19), 3911–3920. doi:10.1093/nar/27.19.3911 PMID:10481031

Besnier, F., & Glover, K. A. (2013). ParallelStructure: A R package to distribute parallel runs of the population genetics program STRUCTURE on multi-core computers. *PLoS ONE*, *8*(7), e70651. doi:10.1371/journal.pone.0070651 PMID:23923012

Betancourt, T. (2012). *High-tech supercomputer soon to be history*. Retrieved May 31, 2014 from http://www.statepress.com/2012/01/12/high-tech-supercomputer-soon-to-be-history/

Bidiou, A. (2008). *Number and numbers* (R. MacKay, Trans.). Cambridge, MA: Polity Press.

Billeter, S. R., Webb, S. P., Agarwal, P. K., Iordanov, T., & Hammes-Schiffer, S. (2001). Hydride transfer in liver alcohol dehydrogenase: Quantum dynamics, kinetic isotope effects, and role of enzyme motion. *Journal of the American Chemical Society*, *123*(45), 11262–11272. doi:10.1021/ja011384b PMID:11697969

Bird, J. O. (2007). *Engineering mathematics*. Oxford, UK: Newnes.

Birney, E., & Durbin, R. (2000). Using GeneWise in the Drosophila annotation experiment. *Genome Research*, *10*(4), 547–548. doi:10.1101/gr.10.4.547 PMID:10779496

Bischsel, J. (2012, November 2). *Research computing: The enabling role of information technology.* ECAR. Retrieved April 2, 2013 from http://www.educause.edu/library/resources/research-computing-enabling-role-information-technology

Biscotti, F., Natis, Y. V., Pezzini, M., Murphy, T. E., Malinverno, P., & Cantara, M. (2012). *Market trends: Platform as a service, worldwide, 2012-2016, 2H12 update.* Retrieved May 2, 2013, from: http://my.gartner.com/portal/server.pt?open=512&objID=202&&PageID=5553&mode=2&in_hi_userid=2&cached=true&resId=2188816

Biswas, R., & Thigpen, W. (2014). *High-end computing capability.* Retrieved from http://www.nas.nasa.gov/hecc/resources/pleiades.html

Bloom, B. S. (1956). *Taxonomy of educational objectives: The classification of educational goals: Handbook I.* New York: Longman.

Blum, L. C., & Reymond, J. (2009). Million drug like small molecules for virtual screening in the chemical universe database GDB-13. *Journal of the American Chemical Society, 131*(25), 8732–8733. doi:10.1021/ja902302h PMID:19505099

BNL. (2012). Global and regional solutions. *Brookhaven National Laboratory Blog.* Retrieved March 10, 2014 from: http://www.bnl.gov/GARS/

Boal, K. B., & Hooijberg, R. (2001). Strategic leadership research: Moving on. *The Leadership Quarterly, 11*(4), 515–549. doi:10.1016/S1048-9843(00)00057-6

Boitard, S., Kofler, R., Francoise, P., Robelin, D., Schlotterer, C., & Futschik, A. (2013). Pool-hmm: A Python program for estimating the allele frequency spectrum and detecting selective sweeps from next generation sequencing of pooled samples. *Molecular Ecology Resources, 13*(2), 337–340. doi:10.1111/1755-0998.12063 PMID:23311589

Bongard, J., Zykov, V., & Lipson, H. (2006). Resilient machines through continuous self-modeling. *Science, 314*(118). PMID:17110570

Boole, G. (1854). *An investigation of the laws of thought on which are founded the mathematical theories of logic and probabilities.* London: Walton and Maberly. Retrieved 4 March 2014 from https://www.fbo.gov/index?s=opportunity&mode=form&id=31cf5a859cfa2764da7e1b8d54a79d1c&tab=core&_cview=1

Boole, G. (1854). *An investigation of the laws of thought on which are founded the mathematical theories of logic and probabilities.* London: Walton and Maberly. doi:10.5962/bhl.title.29413

Boolos, G., Burgess, J., & Jeffrey, R. (2002). *Computability and logic* (4th ed.). Cambridge, UK: Cambridge University Press. doi:10.1017/CBO9781139164931

Boussau, B., Szollosi, G. J., Duret, L., Gouy, M., Tannier, E., & Daubin, V. (2013). Genome-scale coestimation of species and gene trees. *Genome Research, 23*(2), 323–330. doi:10.1101/gr.141978.112 PMID:23132911

Bowie, J. U., & Eisenberg, D. (1994). An evolutionary approach to folding small alpha-helical proteins that uses sequence information and an empirical guiding fitness function. *Proceedings of the National Academy of Sciences of the United States of America, 91*(10), 4436–4440. doi:10.1073/pnas.91.10.4436 PMID:8183927

Bowie, J. U., Luthy, R., & Eisenberg, D. (1991). A method to identify protein sequences that fold into a known three-dimensional structure. *Science, 253*(5016), 164–170. doi:10.1126/science.1853201 PMID:1853201

Bowman, W. A. (1996). Maximum ground level concentrations with downwash: The urban stability mode. *Journal of the Air & Waste Management Association, 46*(7), 615–620. doi:10.1080/10473289.1996.10467495

Braberg, H., Webb, B. M., Tjioe, E., Pieper, U., Sali, A., & Madhusudhan, M. S. (2012). SALIGN: A web server for alignment of multiple protein sequences and structures. *Bioinformatics (Oxford, England), 28*(15), 2072–2073. doi:10.1093/bioinformatics/bts302 PMID:22618536

Bradley, P., Misura, K. M., & Baker, D. (2005). Toward high-resolution de novo structure prediction for small proteins. *Science, 309*(5742), 1868–1871. doi:10.1126/science.1113801 PMID:16166519

611

Brady, G. P. Jr, & Stouten, P. F. (2000). Fast prediction and visualization of protein binding pockets with PASS. *Journal of Computer-Aided Molecular Design, 14*(4), 383–401. doi:10.1023/A:1008124202956 PMID:10815774

Brandt, A. (1977). Multi-level adaptive solutions to boundary-value problems. *Mathematics of Computation, 31*(138), 333–390. doi:10.1090/S0025-5718-1977-0431719-X

Brandt, A. (1977). Multi-level adaptive techniques (MLAT) for differential equations: Ideas and Software. In J. R. Rice (Ed.), *Mathematical software III* (pp. 273–318). New York: Academic Press. doi:10.1016/B978-0-12-587260-7.50015-7

Bravyi, S., Caha, L., Movassagh, R., Nagaj, D., & Shor, P. W. (2012). Criticality without frustration for quantum spin-1 chains. *Physical Review Letters, 109*(20), 207202–207205. doi:10.1103/PhysRevLett.109.207202 PMID:23215521

Bright, L. A., Burgess, S. C., Chowdhary, B., Swiderski, C. E., & McCarthy, F. M. (2009). Structural and functional-annotation of an equine whole genome oligoarray. *BMC Bioinformatics, 10*(Suppl 11), S8. doi:10.1186/1471-2105-10-S11-S8 PMID:19811692

Brodie, R., Roper, R. L., & Upton, C. (2004). JDotter: A Java interface to multiple dotplots generated by dotter. *Bioinformatics (Oxford, England), 20*(2), 279–281. doi:10.1093/bioinformatics/btg406 PMID:14734323

Brodsky, L. I., & Vasiliev, A. V., Ya, L. K., Osipov, Y. S., Tatuzov, R. L., & Feranchuk, S. I. (1992). GeneBee: The program package for biopolymer structure analysis. *Dimacs, 8*, 127–139.

Brooks, B., & Karplus, M. (1983). Harmonic dynamics of proteins: Normal modes and fluctuations in bovine pancreatic trypsin inhibitor. *Proceedings of the National Academy of Sciences of the United States of America, 80*(21), 6571–6575. doi:10.1073/pnas.80.21.6571 PMID:6579545

Brown, N. (1996). *Consensus.* Retrieved January 1, 2013, from http://coot.embl.de/Alignment/consensus.html

Brown, S. M., & Joubert, F. (n.d.). *Pairwise sequence alignment.* Retrieved February 10, 2013, from http://www.med.nyu.edu/rcr/rcr/course/PairAlign.ppt

Brylinski, M., & Skolnick, J. (2010). Comprehensive structural and functional characterization of the human kinome by protein structure modeling and ligand virtual screening. *Journal of Chemical Information and Modeling, 50*(10), 1839–1854. doi:10.1021/ci100235n PMID:20853887

BSC. (2014). *The Barcelona supercomputing center.* Retrieved February 28, 2014, from http://www.bsc.es/

Buckleton, J. S. (2004). Population genetic models. In J. S. Buckleton, C. M. Triggs, & S. J. Walsh (Eds.), *Forensic DNA evidence interpretation.* Boca Raton, FL: CRC Press. doi:10.1201/9781420037920.ch3

Buckley, W. (Ed.). (1968). *Modern systems research for the behavioral scientist.* Chicago: Aldine Publishing Company.

Bu, J., Chi, X., & Jin, Z. (2013). HSA: A heuristic splice alignment tool. *BMC Systems Biology, 7*(Suppl 2), S10. doi:10.1186/1752-0509-7-S2-S10 PMID:24564867

Bunde, D. P. (2009). A short unit to introduce multi-threaded programming. *Journal of Computing Sciences in Colleges, 25*(1), 9–20.

Buning, H. A. K., & Lettmann, T. A. (1999). Propositional logic: Deduction and algorithms. *Studia Logica, 71*(2), 247–258. doi:10.1023/A:1016553006778

Bureau of Labor Statistics. (n.d.). *Occupational outlook handbook, 2012-13 edition, projections overview.* U.S. Department of Labor. Retrieved May 04, 2013 from http://www.bls.gov/ooh/about/projections-overview.htm

Burge, C., & Karlin, S. (1997). Prediction of complete gene structures in human genomic DNA. *Journal of Molecular Biology, 268*(1), 78–94. doi:10.1006/jmbi.1997.0951 PMID:9149143

Burns, P. (2013). *History of supercomputing.* Retrieved May 30, 2014 from http://lamar.colostate.edu/~grad511/lec2.pdf

Burns, D. D. (1999). *Feeling good.* New York: Avons Books, Harper-Collins Publishers.

Buyya, R. (2002). *Economic-based distributed resource management and scheduling for grid computing.* Retrieved 24 April 2002, from http://cds.cern.ch/record/548570?ln=en

Caetano, A. R., Johnson, R. K., Ford, J. J., & Pomp, D. (2004). Microarray profiling for differential gene expression in ovaries and ovarian follicles of pigs selected for increased ovulation rate. *Genetics*, *168*(3), 1529–1537. doi:10.1534/genetics.104.029595 PMID:15579704

Cai, J., Jelezko, F., & Plenio, M. B. (2013). A large-scale quantum simulator on a diamond surface at room temperature. *Nature Physics*, *9*(3), 168–173. doi:10.1038/nphys2519

Cai, T., Wang, S., & Xu, Q. (2013). Scheduling of multiple chemical plant start-ups to minimize regional air quality impacts. *Computers & Chemical Engineering*, *54*, 68–78. doi:10.1016/j.compchemeng.2013.03.027

Cai, T., Zhao, C., & Xu, Q. (2012). Energy network dispatch optimization under emergency of local energy shortage. *Energy*, *42*(1), 132–145. doi:10.1016/j.energy.2012.04.001

Cala, J., Hiden, H., Watson, P., & Woodman, S. (n.d.). *Cloud computing for fast prediction of chemical activity*. Retrieved June 16, 2014 from http://www.esciencecentral.co.uk/wp-content/uploads/2011/03/Cloud-Computing-for-Fast-Prediction-of-Chemical-Activity.pdf

Caliper. (2013). *The qualities that distinguish women leaders*. Retrieved November 13, 2013 from https://www.calipercorp.com/portfolio/the-qualities-that-distinguish-women-leaders/

Cambridge University. (n.d.). Retrieved May 28, 2014 from http://www.top500.org/site/47520#.U4XU7_mSyO0

Cannataro, M., Conqiusta, A., Pugliese, A., Talia, D., & Trunflo, P. (2004, December). Distributed data mining on grids: Services, tools, and applications. *IEEE Trans System Cybern B Cybern*, *34*(6), 2451–2465. doi:10.1109/TSMCB.2004.836890 PMID:15619945

Cannataro, M., & Talia, D. (2003). The knowledge grid: Designing, building, and implementing an architecture for distributed knowledge discovery. *Communications of the ACM*, *46*(1), 89–93. doi:10.1145/602421.602425

Cannataro, M., Talia, D., & Trunfio, P. (2004). Distributed data mining on the grid: Services, tools, and applications. *IEEE Transactions on Systems, Man, and Cybernetics. Part B, Cybernetics*, *34*(6), 2451–2465.

Carvajal-Rodriguez, A. (2008). GENOMEPOP: A program to simulate genomes in populations. *BMC Bioinformatics*, *9*(1), 223. doi:10.1186/1471-2105-9-223 PMID:18447924

Casey, R. M. (2005). *BLAST sequences aid in genomics and proteomics*. Business Intelligence Network.

Casti, J. L. (1992). *That's life? Yes, no, maybe* (SFI Working Paper: 1992-10-050). Sante Fe, NM: Santa Fe Institute.

Catchen, J., Hohenlohe, P. A., Bassham, S., Amores, A., & Cresko, W. A. (2013). Stacks: An analysis tool set for population genomics. *Molecular Ecology*, *22*(11), 3124–3140. doi:10.1111/mec.12354 PMID:23701397

Catlett, C. E. (2005). TeraGrid: A foundation for US cyber-infrastructure. In *Network and parallel computing* (pp. 1-1). Springer Berlin Heidelberg. Retrieved April 1, 2013 from http://link.springer.com/chapter/10.1007%2F11577188_1

Causton, H. C., Ren, B., Koh, S. S., Harbison, C. T., Kanin, E., & Jennings, E. G. et al. (2001). Remodeling of yeast genome expression in response to environmental changes. *Molecular Biology of the Cell*, *12*(2), 323–337. doi:10.1091/mbc.12.2.323 PMID:11179418

Cavasotto, C. N., Orry, A. J., Murgolo, N. J., Czarniecki, M. F., Kocsi, S. A., & Hawes, B. E. et al. (2008). Discovery of novel chemotypes to a G-protein-coupled receptor through ligand-steered homology modeling and structure-based virtual screening. *Journal of Medicinal Chemistry*, *51*(3), 581–588. doi:10.1021/jm070759m PMID:18198821

Cebamanos, L., Gray, A., Stewart, I., & Tenesa, A. (2014). Regional heritability advanced complex trait analysis for GPU and traditional parallel architectures. *Bioinformatics (Oxford, England)*, *30*(8), 1177–1179. doi:10.1093/bioinformatics/btt754 PMID:24403537

Ceder, G., & Persson, K. (2013). How supercomputers will yield a golden age of materials science. *Scientific American*, *309*(6), 1–4. PMID:24383363

Centeno, N. B., Planas-Iglesias, J., & Oliva, B. (2005). Comparative modelling of protein structure and its impact on microbial cell factories. *Microbial Cell Factories*, *4*(1), 20. doi:10.1186/1475-2859-4-20 PMID:15989691

Center for Digital Education. (2012). *Supercomputers take research to new levels. Specialty Classroom Technologies, Special Report*. Folsom, CA: E. Republic.

Central Processing Unit. (n.d.). Retrieved 4 March 2014, from http://en.wikipedia.org/wiki/Central_processing_unit

Cerqueira, N. M., Bras, N. F., Fernandes, P. A., & Ramos, M. J. (2009). MADAMM: A multistaged docking with an automated molecular modeling protocol. *Proteins*, *74*(1), 192–206. doi:10.1002/prot.22146 PMID:18618708

Chalmers, D. (2013). *The Matrix as metaphysics*. Retrieved 4 March 2014 from http://consc.net/papers/matrix.html

Chamberlain, R. D., Franklin, M. A., Tyson, E. J., Buckley, J. H., Buhler, J., & Galloway, G. et al. (2010). Auto-pipe: Streaming applications on architecturally diverse systems. *Computer*, *43*(3), 42–49. doi:10.1109/MC.2010.62

Chang, G., Joiner, D., & Morreale, P. (2010, June). Connecting undergraduate programs to high school students: Teacher workshops on computational thinking and computer science. *Journal of Computing Sciences in Colleges*, *25*(6), 191–197.

Chang, J. M., Di Tommaso, P., Taly, J. F., & Notredame, C. (2012). Accurate multiple sequence alignment of transmembrane proteins with PSI-Coffee. *BMC Bioinformatics*, *13*(Suppl 4), S1. doi:10.1186/1471-2105-13-S4-S1 PMID:22536955

Chan, K. M., & Moore, B. R. (2005). SYMMETREE: Whole-tree analysis of differential diversification rates. *Bioinformatics (Oxford, England)*, *21*(8), 1709–1710. doi:10.1093/bioinformatics/bti175 PMID:15572466

Chappell, D. (2008). *A short introduction to cloud platforms*. Retrieved Aug. 20, 2008, from www.davidchapell.com

Cheddad, A., Condell, J., Curran, K., & McKevitt, P. (2009). Digital image steganography: Survey and analysis of current methods. *Signal Processing*, *90*(3), 727–752. doi:10.1016/j.sigpro.2009.08.010

Chen, E. Y. (1994). The efficiency of automated DNA sequencing. In Automated DNA sequencing and analysis. London: Academic Press Limited.

Cheng, L., Connor, T. R., Siren, J., Aanensen, D. M., & Corander, J. (2013). Hierarchical and spatially explicit clustering of DNA sequences with BAPS software. *Molecular Biology and Evolution*, *30*(5), 1224–1228. doi:10.1093/molbev/mst028 PMID:23408797

Chen, H., & Skolnick, J. (2008). M-TASSER: An algorithm for protein quaternary structure prediction. *Biophysical Journal*, *94*(3), 918–928. doi:10.1529/biophysj.107.114280 PMID:17905848

Cheriton, D. R. (1988). The V distributed system. *Communications of the ACM*, *31*(3), 314–333. doi:10.1145/42392.42400

Childs, A. M., Schulman, L. J., & Vazirani, U. V. (2007). Quantum algorithms for hidden nonlinear structures. In *Proc. 48th IEEE Symposium on Foundations of Computer Science A18, Nature | Letter* (pp. 395-404). arXiv:0705.2784

Childs, A. M., Cleve, R., Deotto, E., Farhi, E., Gutmann, S., & Spielman, D. A. (2003). Exponential algorithmic speedup by quantum walk. In *Proc. 35th ACM Symposium on Theory of Computing* (pp. 59-68). ACM.

Chilkoti, A., Ratner, B. D., & Briggs, D. (1993). Static secondary ion mass spectrometric investigation of the surface chemistry of organic plasma-deposited films created from oxygen-containing precursors. 3. Multivariate statistical modeling. *Analytical Chemistry*, *65*(13), 1736–1745. doi:10.1021/ac00061a017 PMID:8368525

Chinta, B. (2013). *Supercomputers-introduction, details & examples*. Retrieved 03/23, 2014, from http://www.durofy.com/supercomputers-introduction-details-examples/

Chirgwin, R. (2012). *VLSCI's supercomputer passes acceptance test, lands in top 50*. Retrieved May 29, 2014 from http://www.theregister.co.uk/2012/06/18/vlsci_blue_gene_acceptance_test/

Cho, A. (2012). New form of quantum computation promises showdown with ordinary computers. *ScienceNOW*. Retrieved March 18, 2014, from http://news.sciencemag.org/sciencenow/2012/12/new-form-of-quantum-computation-.html

Chomsky, N. (2007). *Approaching ug from below. interfaces + recursion = language? Chomsky's minimalism and the view from syntax-semantics.* Mouton: Berlin. Computational complexity. Retrieved 9 March 2014 from http://en.wikipedia.org/wiki/Computational_complexity

Chuang, T. J., Lin, W. C., Lee, H. C., Wang, C. W., Hsiao, K. L., & Wang, Z. H. et al. (2003). A complexity reduction algorithm for analysis and annotation of large genomic sequences. *Genome Research*, *13*(2), 313–322. doi:10.1101/gr.313703 PMID:12566410

Chunbao, Z., XianYu, L., YanGang, W., & ChaoDong, Z. (2012). A parallel implementation of the isolation with migration model. *e-Science Technology and Application,* *3*(1), 24-28.

Church, P. C., Goscinski, A., Holt, K., Inouye, M., Ghoting, A., Makarychev, K., & Reumann, M. (2011). Design of multiple sequence alignment algorithms on parallel, distributed memory supercomputers. In *Proceedings of the Institute of Electrical and Electronics Engineers Engineering in Medicine and Biology Society* (pp. 924-927). Academic Press. doi:10.1109/IEMBS.2011.6090208

Church, P. E. (1949). Dilution of waste stack gases in the atmosphere. *Industrial & Engineering Chemistry*, *41*(12), 2753–2756. doi:10.1021/ie50480a022

Cimons, M. (2013). *Advances in computational research transform scientific process and discovery.* Retrieved 03/18, 2014, from http://www.nsf.gov/mobile/discoveries/disc_summ.jsp?cntn_id=127385&org=NSF

CINECA. (2014). *CINCEA supercomputer center.* Retrieved February 28, 2014, from http://www.cineca.it/en

Ciria, R., Abreu-Goodger, C., Morett, E., & Merino, E. (2004). GeConT: Gene context analysis. *Bioinformatics (Oxford, England)*, *20*(14), 2307–2308. doi:10.1093/bioinformatics/bth216 PMID:15073003

ClusPro-Protein-Protein Docking. (n.d.). Retrieved June 16, 2014 from http://cluspro.bu.edu/tut_dock.php

ClusterVision Pumps up Supercomputer Muscles in Brussels. (2013). Retrieved May 28, 2014 from http://insidehpc.com/2013/06/13/clustervision-pumps-up-supercomputer-muscles-in-brussels/

Committee on Modeling, Simulation, and Games; Standing Committee on Technology Insight–Gauge, Evaluate, and Review; National Research Council. (2010). *The rise of games and high performance computing for modeling and simulation.* Retrieved 20 October 2014, from http://www.nap.edu/catalog.php?record_id=12816

Computer and Software Configuration. (2011). Retrieved May 29, 2014 from http://www.vlsci.org.au/page/computer-software-configuration

Computer Research Association. (n.d.). Retrieved May 28, 2013 from http://cra.org/resources/taulbee/

Conkle, T. (1972). *Analyzing genetic diversity in conifers--Isozyme resolution by starch gel electrophoresis.* Berkeley, CA: USDA.

Consciousness. (2013). *Towards a science of consciousness.* Retrieved 9 March 2014 from www.consciousness.arizona.edu/

Consortium, T. E. P. (2011). A user's guide to the encyclopedia of DNA elements (ENCODE). *PLoS Biology*, *9*(4), e1001046. doi:10.1371/journal.pbio.1001046 PMID:21526222

Cook, J. S. (2011). Supercomputers and supercomputing. In Q. Zhang, R. S. Segall, & M. Cao (Eds.), *Visual analytics and interactive technologies* (pp. 282–294). IGI Global. doi:10.4018/978-1-60960-102-7.ch017

Copenhagen Interpretation. (n.d.). Retrieved 9 March 2014 from http://en.wikipedia.org/wiki/Copenhagen_interpretation

Copi, I. (1979). *Symbolic logic.* New York: Macmillan.

Corbett, J. C., Dean, J., Epstein, M., Fikes, A., Frost, C., & Furman, J. et al. (2012). Spanner: Google's globally-distributed database. In *Proceedings of OSDI'12: Tenth Symposium on Operating System Design and Implementation.* Hollywood, CA: Academic Press.

Cornuet, J. M., Santos, F., Beaumont, M. A., Robert, C. P., Marin, J. M., & Balding, D. J. et al. (2008). Inferring population history with DIY ABC: A user-friendly approach to approximate Bayesian computation. *Bioinformatics (Oxford, England)*, *24*(23), 2713–2719. doi:10.1093/bioinformatics/btn514 PMID:18842597

Corpet, F. (1988). Multiple sequence alignment with hierarchical clustering. *Nucleic Acids Research, 16*(22), 10881–10890. doi:10.1093/nar/16.22.10881 PMID:2849754

Coughlin, C. (2012). Ultracapacitors: The next big thing in energy storage? *GreenBiz.com.* Retrieved March 10, 2014 from: http://www.greenbiz.com/blog/2012/06/10/ultracapacitors-next-big-thing-energy-storage(Nature of Business Radio)

Council of Competitiveness. (2012, June). *Making impact: The council's 2011-2012 annual report.* Washington, DC: Author.

Cray History. (2014). Retrieved May 28, 2014 from http://www.cray.com/About/History.aspx

Cray XE6 (Garnet) User Guide. (2014). Retrieved May 29, 2014 from http://www.erdc.hpc.mil/docs/garnetUserGuide.html

Cray. (2014). Retrieved May 30, 2014 from http://en.wikipedia.org/wiki/Cray

CRN. (2013). *Center for responsible nanotechnology.* Retrieved March 10, 2014 from: http://crnano.org/

Cronin, L., & Fine, H. (2010). *Damned if she does, damned if she doesn't: Rethinking the rules of the game that keep women from succeeding in business.* Amherst, NY: Promethus Press.

Crow, J. F. (1987). Population genetics history: A personal view. *Annual Review of Genetics, 21*(1), 1–22. doi:10.1146/annurev.ge.21.120187.000245 PMID:3327458

Curioni, A. (n.d.). *Computational engineering- Project overview.* Retrieved from http://www.zurich.ibm.com/mcs/compsci/engineering/

Cyber Science and Engineering: A Report of the NSF Advisory Committee for Cyber Infrastructure Task Force on Grand Challenges. (2010). Retrieved from http://www.stanford.edu/~vcs/papers/OCI_GCs_TF_final.pdf

Czajkowski, K., Foster, I., Karonis, N., Kesselman, C., Martin, S., Smith, W., & Tuecke, S. (1998). A resource management architecture for metacomputing systems. In *Proceedings of the Workshop on Job Scheduling Strategies for Parallel.* Springer-Verlag.

Dˇzeroski1, S., Langley, P., & Todorovski, L. (2013). *Computational discovery of scientific knowledge.* Retrieved 9 March 2014 from http://www.isle.org/~langley/discovery.html

Darling, A. E., Carey, L., & Feng, W. (2003). The design, implementation, and evaluation of mpiBLAST. In *Proceedings of 4th International Conference on Linux Clusters: The HPC Revolution 2003.* San Jose, CA: mpiBLAST.

Das, R., Qian, B., Raman, S., Vernon, R., Thompson, J., & Bradley, P. et al. (2007). Structure prediction for CASP7 targets using extensive all-atom refinement with Rosetta@home. *Proteins, 69*(S8Suppl 8), 118–128. doi:10.1002/prot.21636 PMID:17894356

Datta, S., Bhaduri, K., Giannella, C., Wolff, R., & Kargupta, H. (2006). Distributed data mining in peer-to-peer networks. *IEEE Internet Computing, 19*(4), 18–26. doi:10.1109/MIC.2006.74

Dave, C., Bae, H., Min, S., Lee, S., Eigenmann, R., & Midkiff, S. (2009). Cetus: A source-to-source compiler infrastructure for multicores. *Computer, 42*(12), 36–42. doi:10.1109/MC.2009.385

Davis, I. W., Leaver-Fay, A., Chen, V. B., Block, J. N., Kapral, G. J., Wang, X., . . . Richardson, D. C. (2007). MolProbity: All-atom contacts and structure validation for proteins and nucleic acids. *Nucleic Acids Research, 35*, W375-383. doi: 10.1093/nar/gkm216

Davis, N., & Hiemstra, P. (2014). *Cray expands manufacturing capacity with new supercomputing facility in Chippewa Falls.* Retrieved May 31, 2014 from http://www.marketwatch.com/story/cray-expands-manufacturing-capacity-with-new-supercomputing-facility-in-chippewa-falls-2014-03-10

Dawkins, R. (1986). *The blind watchmaker.* New York: Norton.

De Mita, S., & Siol, M. (2012). EggLib: Processing, analysis and simulation tools for population genetics and genomics. *BMC Genetics, 13*(1), 27. doi:10.1186/1471-2156-13-27 PMID:22494792 de Saizieu, A., Gardes, C., Flint, N., Wagner, C., Kamber, M., & Mitchell, T. J. et al. (2000). Microarray-based identification of a novel *Streptococcus pneumoniae* regulon controlled by an autoinduced peptide. *Journal of Bacteriology*, *182*(17), 4696–4703. doi:10.1128/JB.182.17.4696-4703.2000 PMID:10940007

Deavours, C. A., & Kruh, L. (1985). *Machine cryptography and modern cryptanalysis*. London: Artech House.

DeBenedictus, D. (2005). Reversible logic for supercomputing. In *Proceedings of the 2nd Conference on Computing Frontiers*. American Association of Computing Machinery. doi:10.1145/1062261.1062325

De, K., Ghosh, G., Datta, M., Konar, A., Bandyopadhyay, J., & Bandyopadhyay, D. et al. (2004). Analysis of differentially expressed genes in hyperthyroid-induced hypertrophied heart by CDNA microarray. *The Journal of Endocrinology*, *182*(2), 303–314. doi:10.1677/joe.0.1820303 PMID:15283691

Del Pradon, F. M. (2009). *The thermodynamics of human reaction times*. Retrieved 9 March 2014 from http://arxiv.org/abs/0908.3170

DeLong, D. W. (2004). *Lost knowledge: Confronting the threat of an aging workforce*. Oxford, UK: University Press. doi:10.1093/acprof:oso/9780195170979.001.0001

DePaolo, D., & Orr, F., Jr. (2007). *Basic research needs for geosciences: Facilitating 21st century energy systems*. Retrieved on June 24, 2014 from http://digitalscholarship.unlv.edu/cgi/viewcontent.cgi?article=1130&context=yucca_mtn_pubs

DeRisi, J. L., Iyer, V., & Brown, P. O. (1997). Exploring the metabolic and genetic control of gene expression on a genomic scale. *Science*, *278*(5338), 680–686. doi:10.1126/science.278.5338.680 PMID:9381177

Descartes, R. (1641). Meditations on first philosophy. In The philosophical writings of René Descartes (vol. 2). Cambridge, UK: Cambridge University Press.

Deserno, M., & Holm, C. (1998). How to mesh up Ewald sums II: An accurate error estimate for the particle–particle–particle-mesh algorithm. *The Journal of Chemical Physics*, *109*(18), 7694–7698. doi:10.1063/1.477415

Deumens, E. (2013). *UF launches HiPerGator, the state's most powerful supercomputer*. Retrieved May 28, 2014 from http://news.ufl.edu/2013/05/07/hipergator/

Dewey. (1916). *Democracy and education*. New York: MacMillan.

Di Rienzo, A. (2006). Population genetics models of common diseases. *Current Opinion in Genetics & Development*, *16*(6), 630–636. doi:10.1016/j.gde.2006.10.002 PMID:17055247

Di Tommaso, P., Moretti, S., Xenarios, I., Orobitg, M., Montanyola, A., Chang, J. M., . . . Notredame, C. (2011). T-coffee: A web server for the multiple sequence alignment of protein and RNA sequences using structural information and homology extension. *Nucleic Acids Research*, *39*(Web Server issue), W13-17. doi: 10.1093/nar/gkr245

Didelot, X., & Falush, D. (2007). Inference of bacterial microevolution using multilocus sequence data. *Genetics*, *175*(3), 1251–1266. doi:10.1534/genetics.106.063305 PMID:17151252

Didelot, X., Lawson, D., Darling, A., & Falush, D. (2010). Inference of homologous recombination in bacteria using whole-genome sequences. *Genetics*, *186*(4), 1435–1449. doi:10.1534/genetics.110.120121 PMID:20923983

Dill, K. A., & MacCallum, J. L. (2012). The protein-folding problem, 50 years on. *Science*, *338*(6110), 1042–1046. doi:10.1126/science.1219021 PMID:23180855

Dill, K. A., Ozkan, S. B., Weikl, T. R., Chodera, J. D., & Voelz, V. A. (2007). The protein folding problem: When will it be solved? *Current Opinion in Structural Biology*, *17*(3), 342–346. doi:10.1016/j.sbi.2007.06.001 PMID:17572080

Dobrovitski, V.V., Falk, A.L., Santori, C., & Awschalom, D.D. (2013). Quantum control over single spins in diamond. *Annu. Rev. Condens. Matter Phys.*, *4*(7), 28.

Do, C. B., Mahabhashyam, M. S., Brudno, M., & Batzoglou, S. (2005). ProbCons: Probabilistic consistency-based multiple sequence alignment. *Genome Research*, *15*(2), 330–340. doi:10.1101/gr.2821705 PMID:15687296

Docs, Sheets, and Slides. (n.d.). Retrieved February 22, 2013, from: https://support.google.com/drive/answer/49008

DOE. (2010). *"Nuclear Energy": Energy education is an interactive curriculum supplement for secondary-school science students.* SECO.

DOE/LANL. (2009). *Scientists use world's fastest supercomputer to create the largest HIV evolutionary tree.* Retrieved April 17, 2014, from http://www.sciencedaily.com/releases/2009/10/091027161536.htm

Doltsinis, N. L. (2006). Molecular dynamics beyond the born-oppenheimer approximation: Mixed quantum–classical approaches. In *Computational nanoscience: Do it yourself!* (pp. 389–409). Academic Press.

Donofrio, D., Oliker, L., Shalf, J., Wehner, M. F., Rowen, C., & Krueger, J. et al. (2009). Energy-efficient computing for extreme-scale science. *Computer, 42*(11), 62–71. doi:10.1109/MC.2009.353

Douglis, F., & Ousterhout, J. (1987). Process migration in the sprite operating system. In *Proceedings of the 7th International Conference on Distributed Computing Systems.* IEEE.

Doukas, C., Pliakas, T., & Maglogiannis, I. (2010). Mobile healthcare information management utilizing cloud computing and Android OS. In *Proceedings of IEEE Eng Med Biol Soc.* (pp. 1037-1040). Dropbox-Info. Retrieved February 1, 2013, from: https://www.dropbox.com/about

Drachman, D. (2005). Do we have brain to spare? *Neurology, 64*(12), 2004–2005. doi:10.1212/01.WNL.0000166914.38327.BB

Drummond, A. J., & Rambaut, A. (2007). BEAST: Bayesian evolutionary analysis by sampling trees. *BMC Evolutionary Biology, 7*(1), 214. doi:10.1186/1471-2148-7-214 PMID:17996036

Dubrow, A. (2012). *Monogamy and the immune system.* Retrieved February 23, 2013, from http://www.tacc.utexas.edu/news/feature-stories/2012/monogamy-and-the-immune-system

Dundas, J., Ouyang, Z., Tseng, J., Binkowski, A., Turpaz, Y., & Liang, J. (2006). CASTp: Computed atlas of surface topography of proteins with structural and topographical mapping of functionally annotated residues. *Nucleic Acids Research, 34,* W116-118. doi: 10.1093/nar/gkl282

Dunham, I., Shimizu, N., Roe, B. A., Chissoe, S., Hunt, A. R., & Collins, J. E. et al. (1999). The DNA sequence of human chromosome 22. *Nature, 402*(6761), 489–495. doi:10.1038/990031 PMID:10591208

Dunn, J. J., Studier, F. W., & Gottesman, M. (1983). Complete nucleotide sequence of bacteriophage T7 DNA and the locations of T7 genetic elements. *Journal of Molecular Biology, 166*(4), 477–535. doi:10.1016/S0022-2836(83)80282-4 PMID:6864790

Du, Q. S., Huang, R. B., & Chou, K. C. (2008). Review: Recent advances in QSAR and their applications in predicting the activities of chemical molecules, peptides and proteins for drug design. *Current Protein & Peptide Science, 9*(3), 248–259. doi:10.2174/138920308784534005 PMID:18537680

Du, Q. S., Huang, R. B., Wei, Y. T., Pang, Z. W., Du, L. Q., & Chou, K.-C. (2009). Fragment-Based quantitative structure-activity relationship (FBQSAR) for fragment-based drug design. *Journal of Computational Chemistry, 30*(2), 295–304. doi:10.1002/jcc.21056 PMID:18613071

Du, Q. S., Long, S. Y., Meng, J. Z., & Huang, R. B. (2012). Empirical formulation and parameterization of cation-pi interactions for protein modeling. *Journal of Computational Chemistry, 33*(2), 153–162. doi:10.1002/jcc.21951 PMID:21997880

Duret, L., Gasteiger, E., & Perriere, G. (1996). LALNVIEW: A graphical viewer for pairwise sequence alignments. *Computer Applications in the Biosciences, 12*(6), 507–510. PMID:9021269

Dutheil, J. Y., Gaillard, S., & Stukenbrock, E. H. (2014). MafFilter: A highly flexible and extensible multiple genome alignment files processor. *BMC Genomics, 15*(1), 53. doi:10.1186/1471-2164-15-53 PMID:24447531

Dutt, S. (2014). *HMRI researchers use systems biology, TACC supercomputers to find link between Alzheimer's and brain cancer.* Retrieved June 16, 2014 from http://bionews-tx.com/news/2014/04/29/alzheimers-and-cancer-link-found/

Eagly, A. (2013, March 20). Hybrid style works and women are best at it. *New York Times*. Retrieved September 8, 2013 from http://www.nytimes.com/roomfordebate/2013/03/20/shery-sandberg-says-lean-in-but-is-that-really-the-way-to-lead/why-lean-in-hybrid-style-succeeds-and-women-are-best-at-it

Eanes, W. F., & Koehn, R. K. (1978). An analysis of genetic structure in the Monarch butterfly, Danaus plexippus L. *Evolutionary Bioinformatics Online, 32*(4), 784–797.

Eastman, P., & Doniach, S. (1998). Multiple time step diffusive Langevin dynamics for proteins. *Proteins, 30*(3), 215–227. doi:10.1002/(SICI)1097-0134(19980215)30:3<215::AID-PROT1>3.0.CO;2-J PMID:9517537

Ebadi, Z., Laflamme, R., Mehri-Dehnavi, H., Mirza, B., Mohammadzadeh, H., & Rahimi, R. (2012). *Quantum teleportation with nonclassical correlated states in noninertial frames.* arXiv:1202.0432v1

Eddy, S. R. (1998). Profile hidden markov models. *Bioinformatics (Oxford, England), 14*(9), 755–763. doi:10.1093/bioinformatics/14.9.755 PMID:9918945

Edgar, R. (2014). *Muscle.* Retrieved June 16, 2014 from http://www.drive5.com/muscle/

Edgar, R. C. (2004). MUSCLE: Multiple sequence alignment with high accuracy and high throughput. *Nucleic Acids Research, 32*(5), 1792–1797. doi:10.1093/nar/gkh340 PMID:15034147

Education, N. (2013). *The genetic variation in a population is caused by multiple factors.* Retrieved September 18, 2013, from http://www.nature.com/scitable/topicpage/the-genetic-variation-in-a-population-is-6526354

EFF DES Cracker Source Code. (n.d.). Retrieved on July 8, 2011 from http://cosic.esat.kuleuven.be

Eichler, E. E., Flint, J., Gibson, G., Kong, A., Leal, S. M., Moore, J. H., & Nadeau, J. H. (2010). Missing heritability and strategies for finding the underlying causes of complex disease. *Nature Reviews. Genetics, 11*(6), 446–450. doi:10.1038/nrg2809 PMID:20479774

Eliade, M. (1954). *Cosmos and history (the myth of eternal return).* New York: Harper Torchbooks.

Eliade, M. (1971). *The myth of the eternal return.* Princeton, NJ: Princeton University Press.

Ellingson, S. (2012). *Accelerating virtual high-throughput ligand docking.* Retrieved June 16, 2014 from http://salsahpc.indiana.edu/ECMLS2012/slides/ECMLS12_Accelerating_Virtual.pdf

Ellingson, S. (2013). Multi-receptor high-throughput virtual docking on supercomputers with VinaMPI. Paper presented at SC13 2013, Denver, Colorado.

ENCODE. (2004). The ENCODE (encyclopedia of DNA elements) project. *Science, 306*(5696), 636–640. doi:10.1126/science.1105136 PMID:15499007

Energy Center Brings Supercomputer to Campus. (2007). Retrieved on June 14, 2014 from http://inside.mines.edu/~mlusk/GECO_Mines_Magazine_F07.pdf

Epperson, B. K. (1995). Spatial distributions of genotypes under isolation by distance. *Genetics, 140*, 1431–1440. PMID:7498782

Ernst, D. J., & Stevenson, D. E. (2008). Concurrent CS: Preparing students for a multicore world. In *Proceedings of the 13th Annual Conference on Innovation and Technology in Computer Science Education.* New York, NY: ACM. doi:10.1145/1384271.1384333

Esteve-Nunez, A., Caballero, A., & Ramos, J. L. (2001). Biological degradation of 2, 4, 6-trinitrotoluene. *Microbiology and Molecular Biology Reviews, 65*(3), 335–352. doi:10.1128/MMBR.65.3.335-352.2001 PMID:11527999

Eswar, N., Webb, B., Marti-Renom, M. A., Madhusudhan, M. S., Eramian, D., Shen, M. Y., et al. (2006). Comparative protein structure modeling using Modeller. In Current protocols in bioinformatics. doi:10.1002/0471250953.bi0506s15

Etheridge, A. (2009). *Some mathematical models from population genetics.* Springer.

ETSI. (2012). Network functions virtualisation: An introduction, benefits, enablers, challenges & call for action. *SDN and OpenFlow World Congress.* Available at http://portal.etsi.org/nfv/nfv_white_paper.pdf

EU team. (2013). *Cloud++: Next generation supercomputer architectures*. Retrieved March 18, 2014, from http://ec.europa.eu/digital-agenda/events/cf/ss0911/item-display.cfm?id=7066

Euston, D. R., Tatsuno, M., & McNaughton, B. L. (2007). Fast-forward playback of recent memory sequences in prefrontal cortex during sleep. *Science, 318*(5853), 1147–1150. doi:10.1126/science.1148979 PMID:18006749

Excoffier, L., & Lischer, H. E. (2013). *Arlequin 3.01: An integrated software for population genetics data analysis (version 3.01)*. Academic Press.

Excoffier, L., Laval, L. G., & Schneider, S. (2005). Arlequin ver. 3.0: An integrated software package for population genetics data analysis. *Evolutionary Bioinformatics Online, 1*, 47–50. PMID:19325852

Excoffier, L., & Lischer, H. E. (2010). Arlequin suite ver 3.5: A new series of programs to perform population genetics analyses under Linux and Windows. *Molecular Ecology Resources, 10*(3), 564–567. doi:10.1111/j.1755-0998.2010.02847.x PMID:21565059

Fairbanks, A. (Ed.). (1898). *Zeno commentary*. Retrieved 9 March 2014 from http://history.hanover.edu/texts/presoc/zeno.html

Falkenheim, J.C., & Burrelli, J. (2012, March). *Diversity in science and engineering employment in industry*. National Center for Science and Engineering Statistics (NSF 12-311).

Falush, D., Stephens, M., & Pritchard, J. K. (2003). Inference of population structure using multilocus genotype data: Linked loci and correlated allele frequencies. *Genetics, 164*(4), 1567–1587. PMID:12930761

Fan, L., Hui, J. H., Yu, Z. G., & Chu, K. H. (2014). VIP barcoding: Composition vector-based software for rapid species identification based on DNA barcoding. *Molecular Ecology Resources, 14*(4), 871–881. doi:10.1111/1755-0998.12235 PMID:24479510

Fawcett, P., Eichenberger, P., & Losick, R. (2000). The transcriptional profile of early to middle sporulation in Bacillus subtilis. *Proceedings of the National Academy of Sciences of the United States of America, 97*, 8063–8068. doi:10.1073/pnas.140209597

Feibleman, J. K. (1979). *Assumptions of grand logics*. Boston: Martinus Nijhoff. doi:10.1007/978-94-009-9278-8

Fekete, A. D. (2009). Teaching about threading: Where and what? *SIGACT News, 40*(1), 51–57.

Feng, W., & Balaji, P. (2009). Tools and environments for multicore and many-core architectures. *Computer, 42*(12), 26–27. doi:10.1109/MC.2009.412

Fernandez, M., Caballero, J., Fernandez, L., & Sarai, A. (2010). *Genetic algorithm optimization in drug design QSAR: Bayesian-regularized genetic neural networks (BRGNN) and genetic algorithm-optimized support vectors machines (GA-SVM)*. Retrieved June 16, 2014 from http://www.researchgate.net/publication/42373086_Genetic_algorithm_optimization_in_drug_design_QSAR_Bayesian-regularized_genetic_neural_networks_(BRGNN)_and_genetic_algorithm-optimized_support_vectors_machines_(GA-SVM)

Fernandez-Fuentes, N., Zhai, J., & Fiser, A. (2006). ArchPRED: A template based loop structure prediction server. *Nucleic Acids Research, 3*, W173-176. doi:10.1093/nar/gkl113

Fernando, N., Loke, S. W., & Rahayu, W. (2012). Mobile cloud computing: A survey. *Future Generation Computer Systems, 29*(1), 84–106. doi:10.1016/j.future.2012.05.023

Ferrara, P., Gohlke, H., Price, D. J., Klebe, G., & Brooks, C. L. III. (2004). Assessing scoring functions for protein-ligand interactions. *Journal of Medicinal Chemistry, 47*(12), 3032–3047. doi:10.1021/jm030489h PMID:15163185

Feuerbach, L., & Eliot, G. (1854). *The essence of Christianity*. London: John Chapman.

Feyerabend, P. K. (1993). *Against method*. London: Verso.

Feynman, R. P. (2001). *The character of physical law*. Boston: MIT Press.

Fielden, J. (2013). *Accelerating supercomputing power*. Retrieved 03/23, 2014, from http://www.techradar.com/news/world-of-tech/future-tech/accelerating-supercomputing-power-1223031

Fitzpatrick, B. M. (2012). Estimating ancestry and heterozygosity of hybrids using molecular markers. *BMC Evolutionary Biology*, *12*(1), 131. doi:10.1186/1471-2148-12-131 PMID:22849298

Flicek, P., Amode, M. R., Barrell, D., Beal, K., Brent, S., & Chen, Y. et al. (2011). Ensembl 2011. *Nucleic Acids Research*, *39*(Database issue), D800–D806. doi:10.1093/nar/gkq1064 PMID:21045057

Forbus, K. (n.d.). *Symbolic supercomputer for artificial intelligence and cognitive science research*. Retrieved from http://www.qrg.northwestern.edu/projects/SymbolicSupercomputing/symb-supercomp_index.html

Foremski, T. (2010). *The drive for a new supercomputer architecture will change the IT industry summary: Supercomputers face a big challenge in moving from petascale to exascale computing: Solving that challenge will remake the IT industry...* Retrieved March 18, 2014, from http://www.zdnet.com/blog/foremski/the-drive-for-a-new-supercomputer-architecture-will-change-the-it-industry/1146(February 11)

Foresight Institute. (2013). *Molecular nanotechnology guidelines*. Retrieved March 10, 2014 from: http://www.foresight.org/guidelines/

Francisco, A. P., Bugalho, M., Ramirez, M., & Carrico, J. A. (2009). Global optimal eBURST analysis of multilocus typing data using a graphic matroid approach. *BMC Bioinformatics*, *10*(1), 152. doi:10.1186/1471-2105-10-152 PMID:19450271

Francisco, A. P., Vaz, C., Monteiro, P. T., Melo-Cristino, J., Ramirez, M., & Carrico, J. A. (2012). PHYLOViZ: Phylogenetic inference and data visualization for sequence based typing methods. *BMC Bioinformatics*, *13*(1), 87. doi:10.1186/1471-2105-13-87 PMID:22568821

Frazer, K. A., Pachter, L., Poliakov, A., Rubin, E. M., & Dubchak, I. (2004). VISTA: computational tools for comparative genomics. *Nucleic Acids Research, 32*(Web Server issue), W273-279. doi: 10.1093/nar/gkh458

Frazer, K. A., Murray, S. S., Schork, N. J., & Topol, E. J. (2009). Human genetic variation and its contribution to complex traits. *Nature Reviews. Genetics*, *10*(4), 241–251. doi:10.1038/nrg2554 PMID:19293820

Freud, S. (1922). Beyond the pleasure principle (C. J. M. Hubback, Trans.). London: The International Psycho-Analytical Library; doi:10.1037/11189-000

Fridrich, J. (2010). *Steganography in digital media: Principles, algorithms, and applications*. Cambridge, UK: Cambridge University Press.

Friesner, R. A., Banks, J. L., Murphy, R. B., Halgren, T. A., Klicic, J. J., & Mainz, D. T. et al. (2004). Glide: A new approach for rapid, accurate docking and scoring. 1. Method and assessment of docking accuracy. *Journal of Medicinal Chemistry*, *47*(7), 1739–1749. doi:10.1021/jm0306430 PMID:15027865

Frishman, D. (2007). Protein annotation at genomic scale: The current status. *Chemical Reviews*, *107*(8), 3448–3466. doi:10.1021/cr068303k PMID:17658902

Frye, J., Ananthanarayanan, R., & Modha, D. S. (2007). Towards real-time, mouse-scale cortical simulations. *IBM Research Report No. RJ10404 (A0702-001)*. Retrieved 9 March 2014 from http://domino.watson.ibm.com/library/CyberDig.nsf/papers/D0F0871458B4E5588525727B0056F896/$File/rj10404.pdf

Gall, G. A. E. (1987). Inbreeding. In N. Ryman & F. M. Utter (Eds.), *Population genetics and fishery management* (pp. 47–88). Washington: University of Washington.

Galperin, M. Y., & Koonin, E. V. (2004). 'Conserved hypothetical' proteins: Prioritization of targets for experimental study. *Nucleic Acids Research*, *32*(18), 5452–5463. doi:10.1093/nar/gkh885 PMID:15479782

Gan, Z., Stowe, J., Altintas, I., McCulloch, A., & Zambon, A. (2014). Using kepler for tool integration in microarray analysis workflows. In *Proceedings of 14th International Conference on Computational Science* (pp. 2162-2167). Academic Press. doi:10.1016/j.procs.2014.05.201

Gardner, J. (2014). *Introduction to high performance computing (HPC) and the NSF TeraGrid*. Retrieved from http://oldwww.phys.washington.edu/users/gardnerj/tching/IntroToTeraGrid.pdf

Gardner, H. (1993). *Frames of mind: The theory of multiple intelligences*. New York: Basic Books.

Garnier, J., Osguthorpe, D. J., & Robson, B. (1978). Analysis of the accuracy and implications of simple methods for predicting the secondary structure of globular proteins. *Journal of Molecular Biology, 120*(1), 97–120. doi:10.1016/0022-2836(78)90297-8 PMID:642007

Gasch, A. P., Spellman, P. T., Kao, C. M., Carmel-Harel, O., Eisen, M. B., & Storz, G. et al. (2000). Genomic expression programs in the response of yeast cells to environmental changes. *Molecular Biology of the Cell, 1*(12), 4241–4257. doi:10.1091/mbc.11.12.4241 PMID:11102521

Gaspar, P., Lopes, P., Oliveira, J., Santos, R., Dalgleish, R., & Oliveira, J. L. (2014). Variobox: Automatic detection and annotation of human genetic variants. *Human Mutation, 35*(2), 202–207. doi:10.1002/humu.22474 PMID:24186831

Gaster, B. R., & Howes, L. (2012). Can GPGPU programming be liberated from the data-parallel bottleneck? *Computer, 45*(8), 42–52. doi:10.1109/MC.2012.257

Gaster, G., Howes, L., Kaeli, D. R., Mistry, P., & Schaa, D. (2011). *Heteorgeneous computing with OpenCL*. Boston: Morgan Kaufmann.

Gelber, R. (2012). *Modeling proteins at supercomputing speeds on your PC*. Retrieved from http://archive.hpcwire.com/hpcwire/2012-08-21/modeling_proteins_at_supercomputing_speeds_on_your_pc.html

Gelfand, M. S., Mironov, A. A., & Pevzner, P. A. (1996). Gene recognition via spliced sequence alignment. *Proceedings of the National Academy of Sciences of the United States of America, 93*(17), 9061–9066. doi:10.1073/pnas.93.17.9061 PMID:8799154

GENCI. (2014). *Grand equipement national de calcul intensif - Centre informatique national de l'enseignement suprieur*. Retrieved February 28, 2014, from http://www.genci.fr/en

Ghemawat, S., Gobioff, H., & Leung, S.-T. (2003). The Google file system. In *Proceedings of Nineteenth ACM Symposium on Operating Systems Principles,* (pp. 29-43). ACM. Retrieved May 11, 2013, from: http://www.google.com/intl/de/drive/about.html

Ghersi, D., & Sanchez, R. (2009). EasyMIFS and Site-Hound: A toolkit for the identification of ligand-binding sites in protein structures. *Bioinformatics (Oxford, England), 25*(23), 3185–3186. doi:10.1093/bioinformatics/btp562 PMID:19789268

Ghersi, D., & Sanchez, R. (2011). Beyond structural genomics: Computational approaches for the identification of ligand binding sites in protein structures. *Journal of Structural and Functional Genomics, 12*(2), 109–117. doi:10.1007/s10969-011-9110-6 PMID:21537951

Gibson, S. (n.d.).*Supercomputer-assisted calibration methodology enhances accuracy of energy models*. Retrieved on July 6, 2014 from http://www.nics.tennessee.edu/autotune

Gille, C., Birgit, W., & Gille, A. (2014). Sequence alignment visualization in HTML5 without Java. *Bioinformatics (Oxford, England), 30*(1), 121–122. doi:10.1093/bioinformatics/btt614 PMID:24273246

Gillespie, J. (2004). *Population genetics: A concise guide* (2nd ed.). Baltimore, MD: The Johns Hopkins University Press.

Gilmartin, S. K., & Simard, C. (2012). *Senior technical women: A profile of success*. Palo Alto, CA: Anita Borg Institute for Women and Technology.

Giovannini, A., Zanghirati, G., Beaumont, M. A., Chikhi, L., & Barbujani, G. (2009). A novel parallel approach to the likelihood-based estimation of admixture in population genetics. *Bioinformatics (Oxford, England), 25*(11), 1440–1441. doi:10.1093/bioinformatics/btp136 PMID:19286832

Glasgow Coma Scale. (n.d.). Retrieved 9 March 2014 from http://en.wikipedia.org/wiki/Glasgow_Coma_Scale

Glasmastar, K., Larsson, C., Hook, F., & Kasemo, B. (2002). Protein adsorption on supported phospholipid bilayers. *Journal of Colloid Interface Science, 246*(1), 40-47. doi: 10.1006/jcis.2001.8060

Global Warming. (n.d.). Retrieved 9 March 2014 from http://en.wikipedia.org/wiki/Global_warming

Gödel, K. (1931). On formally undecidable propositions of principia mathematica and related systems. (B. Meltzer, Trans.). New York: Basic Books. (Reprinted, Dover, 1992).

Godzik, A. (2012). *FFAS fold and function alignment.* Retrieved December 30, 2012, from http://ffas.sanford-burnham.org/ffas-cgi/cgi/ffas.pl

Goldman, B. B., & Wipke, W. T. (2000). QSD quadratic shape descriptors. 2. Molecular docking using quadratic shape descriptors (QSDock). *Proteins*, *38*(1), 79–94. doi:10.1002/(SICI)1097-0134(20000101)38:1<79::AID-PROT9>3.0.CO;2-U PMID:10651041

Goldsmith, J. R., & Friberg, L. T. (1976). Effects of air pollution on human health. In The effects of air pollution (Vol. 2). Academic Press.

Golender, V. E., & Vorpagel, E. R. (1993). In H. Kubinyi (Ed.), *In 3D-QSAR in drug design: Theory, methods, and application* (p. 137). ESCOM Science Publishers.

Golubitsky, O., & Maslov, D. (2012). A study of optimal 4-bit reversible toffoli circuits and their synthesis. *IEEE Transactions on Computers*, *61*(9), 1341–1353. doi:10.1109/TC.2011.144

Gomez-Alpizar, L., Hu, C. H., Oliva, R., Forbes, G., & Ristaino, J. B. (2008). Phylogenetic relationships of Phytophthora andina, a new species from the highlands of Ecuador that is closely related to the Irish potato famine pathogen Phytophthora infestans. *Mycologia*, *100*(4), 590–602. doi:10.3852/07-074R1 PMID:18833752

Gompert, Z., & Buerkle, C. A. (2012). BGC: Software for Bayesian estimation of genomic clines. *Molecular Ecology Resources*, *12*(6), 1168–1176. doi:10.1111/1755-0998.12009.x PMID:22978657

Goodford, P. J. (1985). A computational procedure for determining energetically favorable binding sites on biologically important macromolecules. *Journal of Medicinal Chemistry*, *28*(7), 849–857. doi:10.1021/jm00145a002 PMID:3892003

Goodwin, B., & Zacharia, T. (2011, June 23). The supercomputing race. *Washington Post.* Retrieved March 10, 2013 from http://articles.washingtonpost.com/2011-06-23/opinions/35235793_1_exascale-supercomputers-competitiveness-report

Gouet, P., Courcelle, E., Stuart, D. I., & Metoz, F. (1999). ESPript: Analysis of multiple sequence alignments in Post-Script. *Bioinformatics (Oxford, England)*, *15*(4), 305–308. doi:10.1093/bioinformatics/15.4.305 PMID:10320398

Graham, S. L., Snir, M., & Patterson, C. A. (Eds.). (2005). *Getting up to speed: The future of supercomputing.* Washington, DC: National Academies Press.

Gravel, S., Henn, B. M., Gutenkunst, R. N., Indap, A. R., Marth, G. T., & Clark, A. G. et al. (2011). Demographic history and rare allele sharing among human populations. *Proceedings of the National Academy of Sciences of the United States of America*, *108*(29), 11983–11988. doi:10.1073/pnas.1019276108 PMID:21730125

Gray, J. W., & Collins, C. (2000). Genome changes and gene expression in human solid tumors. *Carcinogenesis*, *21*(3), 443–452. doi:10.1093/carcin/21.3.443 PMID:10688864

Greenberg, P. (2006, March 1). Gen X-ers want more collaboration with corporations. *CIO.com.* Retrieved May 28, 2013 from http://www.cio.com/article/17907/Gen_X_ers_Want_More_Collaboration_With_Corporations?page=2&taxonomyId=3185

Greenleaf, R. K. (1970). *The servant as leader.* Westfield, IN: Green Leaf Center for Servant Leadership.

Gremme, G., Steinbiss, S., & Kurtz, S. (2013). Genome-Tools: A comprehensive software library for efficient processing of structured genome annotations. *Institute of Electrical and Electronics Engineers/Association for Computing Machinery Transactions on Computatonal Biology and Bioinformatics*, *10*(3), 645-656. doi:10.1109/TCBB.2013.68

Griffiths, R. F. (1994). Errors in the use of the Briggs parameterization for atmospheric dispersion coefficients. *Atmospheric Environment*, *28*(17), 2861–2865. doi:10.1016/1352-2310(94)90086-8

Grimshaw, A., Ferrari, A., Knabe, F., & Humphrey, M. (1999). Wide-area computing: Resource sharing on a large scale. *Computer*, *32*(5), 29–37.

Groves, K., & LaRocca, M. (2011, November). An empirical study of leader ethical values, transformational and transactional leadership, and follower attitudes toward corporate social responsibility. *Journal of Business Ethics*, *103*(4), 511–528. doi:10.1007/s10551-011-0877-y

Gu, Y., Vancourt, T., & Herbordt, M. C. (2005). Accelerating molecular dynamics simulations with configurable circuits. In *Proceedings of the 2005 International Conference on Field Programmable Logic and Applications*. Academic Press.

Guan, J., Lannutti, J., & Powell, H. (n.d.). *Research topics*. Retrieved 03/18, 2014, from http://mse.osu.edu/research/topics

Gunther, T., & Coop, G. (2013). Robust identification of local adaptation from allele frequencies. *Genetics*, *195*(1), 205–220. doi:10.1534/genetics.113.152462 PMID:23821598

Gupta, P., Conrad, T., Spotter, A., Reinsch, N., & Bienefeld, K. (2012). Simulating a base population in honey bee for molecular genetic studies. *Genetics, Selection, Evolution.*, *44*(1), 14. doi:10.1186/1297-9686-44-14 PMID:22520469

Gura, T. A., Wright, K. L., Veis, A., & Webb, C. L. (1997). Identification of specific calcium-binding noncollagenous proteins associated with glutaraldehyde-preserved bovine pericardium in the rat subdermal model. *Journal of Biomedical Materials Research*, *35*(4), 483–495. doi:10.1002/(SICI)1097-4636(19970615)35:4<483::AID-JBM8>3.0.CO;2-D PMID:9189826

Hager, G., & Wellein, G. (2011). Introduction to high performance computing for scientists and engineers. Boca Raton, FL: Academic Press.

Hakenbeck, R., Balmelle, N., Weber, B., Gardes, C., Keck, W., & de Saizieu, A. (2001). Mosaic genes and mosaic chromosomes: Intra- and interspecies genomic variation of *Streptococcus pneumoniae*. *Infection and Immunity*, *69*(4), 2477–2486. doi:10.1128/IAI.69.4.2477-2486.2001 PMID:11254610

Halitsky, J. (1989). A jet plume model for short stacks. *Journal of the Air Pollution Control Association*, *39*(6), 856–858. Retrieved from http://www.tandfonline.com/doi/abs/10.1080/08940630.1989.10466573#.VEIk-8PnF_D8

Hall, R. (2005). *Math for poets and drummers*. Binary numbers in ancient India. Retrieved 9 March 2014 from http://people.sju.edu/~rhall/Rhythms/Poets/arcadia.pdf

Hameroff, S. (2013). *Quantum consciousness*. Retrieved 9 March 2014 from http://www.quantumconsciousness.org/

Hameroff, S., & Penrose, R. (1996). Conscious events as orchestrated space-time selections. *Journal of Consciousness Studies*, *3*(1), 36–53.

Hammill, G. (2005). *Mixing and managing four generations of employees*. Retrieved August 18, 2013 from http://www.fdu.edu/newspubs/magazine/05ws/generations.htm

Hanisch, R. J. (2011). *Data discovery, access, and management with the virtual observatory*. Paper presented at Innovations in Data-intensive Astronomy. Retrieved 20 October 2014, from http://www.nrao.edu/meetings/bigdata/agenda.shtml

Hanna, S. R., Briggs, G. A., & Kosker, R. P. (1982). *Handbook on atmospheric diffusion*. NTIS DE81009809 (DOE/TIC-22800). Retrieved on October 16, 2014 from http://pbadupws.nrc.gov/docs/ML0926/ML092640175.pdf

Hansch, C., Kurup, A., Garg, R., & Gao, H. (2001). Chem-bioinformatics and QSAR: A review of QSAR lacking positive hydrophobic terms. *Chemical Reviews*, *101*(3), 619–672. doi:10.1021/cr0000067 PMID:11712499

Hansch, C., & Leo, A. (1979). *Substituent constants for correlation analysis in chemistry and biology*. New York: John Wiley & Sons.

Hansch, C., & Leo, A. (1995). *Fundamentals and applications in chemistry and biochemisry* (Q. S. A. R. Exploring, Ed.). Washington, DC: American Chemical Society.

Hansch, C., & Selassie, C. (2007). *Quantitative structure-activity relationship-a historical perspective and the future*. Oxford, UK: Elsevier.

Hardy, O. J., & Vekemans, X. (2002). SPAGeDi: A versatile computer program to analyse spatial genetic structure at the individual or population levels. *Molecular Ecology Notes*, *2*(4), 618–620. doi:10.1046/j.1471-8286.2002.00305.x

Harris, M. (2011, September). The ethics of interpersonal relationships. *Journal of Bioethical Inquiry*, *8*(3), 301–302. doi:10.1007/s11673-011-9308-0

Hartmann, C., Antes, I., & Lengauer, T. (2009). Docking and scoring with alternative side-chain conformations. *Proteins*, *74*(3), 712–726. doi:10.1002/prot.22189 PMID:18704939

Hautala, K. (2012). *UK takes academic supercomputing to next level*. Retrieved May 28, 2014 from http://uknow.uky.edu/content/uk-takes-academic-supercomputing-next-level-0

Hayati, P., Potdar, V., & Chang, E. (2005). *A survey of steganographic and steganalytic tools for the digital forensic investigator*. Retrieved from http://www.pedramhayati.com/images/docs/survey_of_steganography_and_steganalytic_tools.pdf

Haycox, C. L., & Ratner, B. D. (1993). In vitro platelet interactions in whole human blood exposed to biomaterial surfaces: Insights on blood compatibility. *Journal of Biomedical Materials Research*, *27*(9), 1181–1193. doi:10.1002/jbm.820270909 PMID:8126017

Hayik, S. A., Dunbrack, R. Jr, & Merz, K. M. Jr. (2010). A Mixed QM/MM scoring function to predict protein-ligand binding affinity. *Journal of Chemical Theory and Computation*, *6*(10), 3079–3091. doi:10.1021/ct100315g PMID:21221417

Hebert, F. (2013). *Learn you some erlang for great good!: A beginner's guide*. San Francisco, CA: No Starch Press.

Heckel, P. C. (2010). *Hybrid clouds: Comparing cloud toolkits*. Paper presented at University of Mannheim.

Hedgecock, D. (n.d.). *Population genetics of marine organisms*. Retrieved September 22, 2013, from http://www.usglobec.org/newsletter/news6/news6.hedgecock.html

Hedrick, P. (2011). *Genetics of populations*. Sudbury, MA: Jones and Bartlett Publishers, LLC.

Heffner, G., Maurer, L., Sarkar, A., & Wang, X. (2010). *Minding the gap: World Bank's assistance to power shortage mitigation in the developing world energy*. Retrieved on October 16, 2014 from http://www.slideshare.net/lmaurer/minding-the-gap-world-banks-assistance-to-power-shortage-mitigation-in-the-developing-world

Hemsoth, N. (2009). Oak Ridge supercomputers modeling nuclear future. *HPCwire web*. Retrieved March 10, 2014 from: http://archive.hpcwire.com/hpcwire/2011-05-09/oak_ridge_supercomputers_modeling_nuclear_future.html

Hendlich, M., Rippmann, F., & Barnickel, G. (1997). LIGSITE: Automatic and efficient detection of potential small molecule-binding sites in proteins. *Journal of Molecular Graphics & Modelling*, *15*(6), 359–363, 389. doi:10.1016/S1093-3263(98)00002-3 PMID:9704298

Hernandez, R. D., Kelley, J. L., Elyashiv, E., Melton, S. C., Auton, A., & McVean, G. et al. (2011). Classic selective sweeps were rare in recent human evolution. *Science*, *331*(6019), 920–924. doi:10.1126/science.1198878 PMID:21330547

Hideki, N., Michiharu, N., & Eiji, K. (2006). High-performance JPEG steganography using quantization index modulation in DCT domain. *Pattern Recognition Letters*, *27*(5), 455–461. doi:10.1016/j.patrec.2005.09.008

Hill, M. D., Jouppi, N. P., Sohi, & Gurindar. (1999). *Readings in computer architecture*. Academic Press.

Hird, S. M. (2012). lociNGS: A lightweight alternative for assessing suitability of next-generation loci for evolutionary analysis. *PLoS ONE*, *7*(10), e46847. doi:10.1371/journal.pone.0046847 PMID:23071651

History of Research Computing Center. (2013). Retrieved May 31, 2014 from https://rcc.fsu.edu/about/history

History of Supercomputing. (2014). Retrieved May 28, 2014 from http://en.wikipedia.org/wiki/History_of_supercomputing

Hlady, V. V., & Buijs, J. (1996). Protein adsorption on solid surfaces. *Current Opinion in Biotechnology*, *7*(1), 72-77.

Ho, C. H., Britt, D. W., & Hlady, V. (1996). Human low density lipoprotein and human serum albumin adsorption onto model surfaces studied by total internal reflection fluorescence and scanning force microscopy. *Journal of Molecular Recognition*, *9*(5-6), 444-455. doi:10.1002/(SICI)1099-1352(199634/12)9:5/6<444::AID-JMR281>3.0.CO;2-I

Hoffman, A. R., et al. (1990). *Supercomputers: Directions in technology and applications*. National Academies. Retrieved June 17, 2014 from http://www.intechopen.com/books/protein-engineering-technology-and-application/protein-protein-and-protein-ligand-docking

Hofstadter, R., & Sander, E. (2013). *Surfaces and essences: Analogy as the fuel and fire of thinking*. New York: Basic Books.

Hogan, W. R., Cooper, G. F., Wagner, M. M., & Wallstrom, G. L. (2005). An inverted Gaussian plume model for estimating the location and amount of release of airborne agents from downwind atmospheric concentrations. *RODS Technical Report*. Real Time Outbreak and Disease Surveillance Laboratory, University of Pittsburgh, Pittsburgh, PA. Retrieved on October 16, 2014 from http://rods.health.pitt.edu/LIBRARY/2005%20Hogan-InvertedDispersionModel-submittedToMMWR.pdf

Hoisie, A., & Vladimir, G. (2009). Extreme-scale computing. *Computer*, *42*(11), 24–26. doi:10.1109/MC.2009.354

Holinka, S. (2009). *Red sky at night, Sandia's new computing might*. Retrieved May 29, 2014 from https://share.sandia.gov/news/resources/news_releases/red-sky-at-night/#.U4cFQ_mSyO0

Holmes, A. (2012). *Hadoop in practice*. Shelter Island, NY: Manning Publications Co.

Hong, L. J., Masaaki, F., Yusuke, S., & Hitoshi, K. (2007). A data hiding method for JPEG 2000 coded images using modulo arithmetic. *Electronics and Communications in Japan, Part 3*, *90*(7), 37–46. doi:10.1002/ecjc.20286

Hooft, R. W., Vriend, G., Sander, C., & Abola, E. E. (1996). Errors in protein structures. *Nature*, *381*(6580), 272. doi:10.1038/381272a0 PMID:8692262

Horne, J. (2006). Recursion of binary space as a foundation of repeatable programs. *Journal on Systemics, Cybernetics and Informatics*, *4*(5), 73-77. Retrieved 9 March 2014 from http://www.iiisci.org/journal/CV\$/sci/pdfs/P277173.pdf

Horne, J. (1997). Logic as the language of innate order in consciousness. *Informatica*, *22*(4), 675–682.

Horne, J. (2012). A new three dimensional bivalent hypercube. *Neuroquantology*, *10*(1), 20–30. doi:10.14704/nq.2012.10.1.361

Howell, J. (2006, April). *Speech*. Speech presented to the ELITE Executive Leadership for Information Technology Excellence, Class of 2006, Austin, TX.

Howe, N., & Strauss, W. (2000). *Millennials rising: The next generation*. New York: Random House.

HPC Service Will be Used for Genome Annotation System. (2006). Retrieved January 20, 2013, from http://www.hpcwire.com

Huang da, W., Sherman, B. T., Tan, Q., Kir, J., Liu, D., Bryant, D., . . . Lempicki, R. A. (2007). Bioinformatics resources: Expanded annotation database and novel algorithms to better extract biology from large gene lists. *Nucleic Acids Research*, *35*(Web Server issue), W169-175. doi:10.1093/nar/gkm415

Huang, D., Zhang, X., Kang, M. H., & Luo, J. (2010). MobiCloud: Building secure cloud framework for mobile computing and communication. In *Proceedings of 5th International IEEE Symposium on Service Oriented System Engineering*, (pp. 27-34). IEEE. doi:10.1109/SOSE.2010.20

Huang, S., Zhang, J., Li, R., Zhang, W., He, Z., & Lam, T. W. et al. (2011). SOAPsplice: Genome-wide ab initio detection of splice junctions from RNA-Seq data. *Frontiers in Genetics*, *2*, 46. doi:10.3389/fgene.2011.00046 PMID:22303342

Huang, X., Adams, M. D., Zhou, H., & Kerlavage, A. R. (1997). A tool for analyzing and annotating genomic sequences. *Genomics*, *46*(1), 37–45. doi:10.1006/geno.1997.4984 PMID:9403056

Huang, X., & Miller, W. (1991). A time-efficient linear-space local similarity algorithm. *Advances in Applied Mathematics*, *12*(3), 337–357. doi:10.1016/0196-8858(91)90017-D

Huerta-Canepa, G., & Lee, D. (2010). A virtual cloud computing provider for mobile devices. In *Proceedings of the 1st ACM Workshop on Mobile Cloud Computing; Services: Social Networks and Beyond*, (pp. 1-5). ACM.

Hughes, R. J., Alde, D. M., Dyer, P., Luther, G., Morgan, G. L., & Schauer, M. (1995). *Quantum cryptography*. arXiv LA-UR-95-806. Retrieved from http://arxiv.org/pdf/quant-ph/9504002.pdf

Human Brain Project. (2012). Retrieved May 25, 2104 from www.humanbrainproject.eu

Human Brain Project-Video Overview. (n.d.). Retrieved May 25, 2014 from YouTube at: http://www.youtube.com/watch?v=JqMpGrM5ECo

Hundoble, J. (2010). *Taoism, basic fundamentals of 'the way'*. Retrieved March 10, 2014 from: http://www.csuchico.edu/~cheinz/syllabi/fall99/hundoble/

Hussar, W. J., & Bailey, T. M. (2013). *Projections of education statistics to 2021 (NCES 2013-008)*. Washington, DC: U.S. Government Printing Office.

Hyatt, D., Snoddy, J., Schmoyer, D., Chen, G., Fischer, K., Parang, M., et al. (2000). Improved analysis and annotation tools for whole-genome computational annotation and analysis: GRAIL-EXP genome analysis toolkit and related analysis tools. In *Genome Sequencing & Biology Meeting*. Information, N. C. f. B. Align sequences nucleotide BLAST. Retrieved December 30, 2012, from http://blast.ncbi.nlm.nih.gov/

IBM Blue Gene Announcement. (2007). Retrieved on June 9, 2012 from http://www.ibm.com

IBM Global Technology Services (2010). *Defining a framework for cloud adoption* (White paper). Author.

Ilachinski, A. (2004). *Artificial war*. River Edge, NJ: World Scientific.

India Plans 61 Times Faster Supercomputer by 2017. (2012, September 17). *The Times of India*.

Industrial Engagement. (2013). Retrieved 03/18, 2014, from https://www.osc.edu/content/industrial_engagement

Information, N. C. f. B. (2011). *GenBank*. Retrieved December 28, 2012

InfoWebLinks – Supercomputer. (n.d.). Retrieved May 28, 2014 from http://www.infoweblinks.com/content/supercomputers.htm

Inhelder, B., & Piaget, J. (1958). *The growth of logical thinking from childhood to adolescence*. New York: Basic Books. doi:10.1037/10034-000

Institute, I. P. G. R., & University, C. (2003). Basic concepts of population genetics. In *Genetic diversity analysis with molecular marker data: Learning module*. Retrieved December 23, 2012, from http://www.bioversityinternational.org

Intel. (2013). *Intel powers the world's fastest supercomputer, reveals new and future high performance computing technologies*. Retrieved April 17, 2014, from http://www.intc.com/releasedetail.cfm?ReleaseID=774058

Irwin, J. J., & Shoichet, B. K. (2005). ZINC — A free database of commercially available compounds for virtual screening. *Journal of Chemical Information and Modeling*, *45*(1), 177–182. doi:10.1021/ci049714+ PMID:15667143

Isard, M., Budiu, M., Yu, Y., Birrell, A., & Fetterly, D. (2007, March). *Dryad: Distributed data-parallel programs from sequential building blocks*. Paper presented at the 2007 EuroSys conference, Lisboa, Portugal. doi:10.1145/1272996.1273005

ISU. (2006). *CyBlue - Blue gene supercomputer*. Retrieved April 17, 2014, from http://bluegene.ece.iastate.edu

Izzo, J., & Withers, P. (2001). *Values shift: The new work ethic & what it means for business*. Lions Bay, Canada: FairWinds Press.

J. Robert Oppenheimer. (n.d.). Retrieved 9 March 2014 from http://en.wikipedia.org/wiki/J._Robert_Oppenheimer

Jager, M., Wang, K., Bauer, S., Smedley, D., Krawitz, P., & Robinson, P. N. (2014). Jannovar: A Java library for exome annotation. *Human Mutation*, *35*(5), 548–555. doi:10.1002/humu.22531 PMID:24677618

James, J., Bhopal, M. P., & Verma, B. (2012). Efficient VM load balancing algorithm for a cloud computing environment. *International Journal on Computer Science and Engineering*, *4*, 1658–1663.

Jaques, P. A., & Viccari, R. M. (2006). Considering students' emotions in computer-mediated learning environments. In Z. Ma (Ed.), *Web-based intelligent e-learning systems: Technologies and applications* (pp. 122–138). Hershey, PA: Information Science Publishing. doi:10.4018/978-1-59140-729-4.ch006

Jaroszewski, L., Li, Z., Cai, X. H., Weber, C., & Godzik, A. (2011). FFAS server: Novel features and applications. *Nucleic Acids Research, 39*(Web Server issue), W38-44. doi:10.1093/nar/gkr441

Jayaram, B. (2011). *DNA ligand docking*. Retrieved June 16, 2014 from http://www.scfbio-iitd.res.in/dock/dnadock.jsp

Jayaram, B. (2012). *BAPPL server*. Retrieved June 16, 2014 from http://www.scfbio-iitd.res.in/software/drug-design/bappl.jsp

Jayaram, B. (2013). *ParDOCK - Automated server for protein ligand docking*. Retrieved June 16, 2014 from http://www.scfbio-iitd.res.in/dock/pardock.jsp

Jennings, J. (2008, March). *Make it happen faster*. Speech presented at the Help Desk Institute Annual Conference, Grapevine, TX.

Jeong, H. J., Kim, E. H., Suh, K. S., Hwang, W. T., Han, M. H., & Lee, H. K. (2005). Determination of the source rate released into the environment from a nuclear power plant. *Radiation Protection Dosimetry, 113*(3), 308-313. Retrieved on October 16, 2014 from http://www.ncbi.nlm.nih.gov/pubmed/15687109

Jeon, Y. S., Lee, K., Park, S. C., Kim, B. S., Cho, Y. J., Ha, S. M., & Chun, J. (2014). EzEditor: A versatile sequence alignment editor for both rRNA- and protein-coding genes. *International Journal of Systematic and Evolutionary Microbiology, 64*(Pt 2), 689–691. doi:10.1099/ijs.0.059360-0 PMID:24425826

Jiang, X., & Lai, C. (2009). *Numerical techniques for direct and large-eddy simulations*. Boca Raton, FL: CRC Press. doi:10.1201/9781420075793

Joachimiak, A. (2009). High-throughput crystallography for structural genomics. *Current Opinion in Structural Biology, 19*(5), 573–584. doi:10.1016/j.sbi.2009.08.002 PMID:19765976

Johnson, R. (2014). *Disarmament diplomacy: DOE supercomputing & test simulation program*. Retrieved on July 8, 2011 from http://acronym.org.uk. 2000-08-22.

Johnson, D. (2011). Mentoring and support systems: Keys to leadership. *Advancing Women in Leadership, 31*, 40–44.

Johnson, M. W., Amin, M. H. S., Gildert, S., Lanting, T., Hamze, F., & Dickson, N. et al. (2011). Quantum annealing with manufactured spins. *Nature Materials, 473*(7346), 194–198. doi:10.1038/nature10012 PMID:21562559

Joly, S. (2012). JML: Testing hybridization from species trees. *Molecular Ecology Resources, 12*(1), 179–184. doi:10.1111/j.1755-0998.2011.03065.x PMID:21899723

Jones, D. T., Taylor, W. R., & Thornton, J. M. (1992). A new approach to protein fold recognition. *Nature, 358*(6381), 86–89. doi:10.1038/358086a0 PMID:1614539

Jorgensen, W. L. (1991). Rusting of the lock and key model for protein-ligand binding. *Science, 254*(5034), 954–955. doi:10.1126/science.1719636 PMID:1719636

Joshi, R. R. (1998). *A new heuristic algorithm for probabilistic optimization*. Department of Mathematics and School of Biomedical Engineering, Indian Institute of Technology Powai, Mumbai, India. Retrieved on July 1, 2008 from http://www.sciencedirect.com/science/article/pii/S0305054896000561

Julia, A., Ballina, J., Canete, J. D., Balsa, A., Tornero-Molina, J., & Naranjo, A. et al. (2008). Genome-wide association study of rheumatoid arthritis in the Spanish population: KLF12 as a risk locus for rheumatoid arthritis susceptibility. *Arthritis and Rheumatism, 58*(8), 2275–2286. doi:10.1002/art.23623 PMID:18668548

Junho, S.(2010). (in press). Roadmap for e-commerce standardization in Korea. *International Journal of IT Standards and Standardization Research*.

Junier, T., & Pagni, M. (2000). Dotlet: Diagonal plots in a web browser. *Bioinformatics (Oxford, England), 16*(2), 178–179. doi:10.1093/bioinformatics/16.2.178 PMID:10842741

Kafatos, M., & Nadeau, R. (1990). *The conscious universe*. New York: Springer-Verlag. doi:10.1007/978-1-4684-0360-2

Kainkwa, R. R. (1999). Wind energy as alternative source to alleviate the shortage of electricity that prevails during the dry season: A case study of Tanzania. *Renewable Energy, 18*(2), 167–174. doi:10.1016/S0960-1481(98)00801-5

Kaku, M. (2011). *Physics of the future*. New York: Doubleday Publishers. Retrieved on October 16, 2014 from http://www.npr.org/2011/11/29/142717081/physics-of-the-future-how-well-live-in-2100

Kal'e, L., Skeel, R., Bhandarkar, M., Brunner, R., Gursoy, A., & Krawetz, N. et al. (1999). NAMD2: Greater scalability for parallel molecular dynamics. *Journal of Computational Physics*, *151*(1), 283–312. doi:10.1006/jcph.1999.6201

Kalinowski, S. T. (2009). How well do evolutionary trees describe genetic relationships among populations? *Heredity (Edinb)*, *102*(5), 506–513. doi:10.1038/hdy.2008.136 PMID:19174839

Kaminski, G. A. (2001). Article. *The Journal of Physical Chemistry B*, 105.

Kan, M. (2012). China is building a 100-petaflop supercomputer. *InfoWorld*, *31*(October). Retrieved from http://www.infoworld.com

Karlin, S. (1972). Some mathematical models of population genetics. *The American Mathematical Monthly*, *79*(7), 699–739. doi:10.2307/2316262

Karpagam, G. R., & Parkavi, J. (2011). Setting up of an open source based private cloud. *International Journal of Computer Science Issues*, *8*(3).

Kaski, K. (2013). Computer and computational sciences for exascale computing. In *Proceedings of the Fourth AICS International Symposium*. Kobe, Japan: Academic Press.

Kato, C. (2012). *Special contribution supercomputing in industrial manufacturing*. Retrieved 03/18, 2014, from http://www.fujitsu.com/downloads/MAG/vol48-4/paper01.pdf

Kauffman, S. (1993). *The origins of order*. New York: Oxford University Press.

Kazmi, S. (2012). *Columbia read history through genetics*. Retrieved February 23, 2013, from http://www.supercomputingonline.com/this-years-stories/columbia-reads-history-through-genetics

Kearsley, S. K., Underwood, D. J., Sheridan, R. P., & Miller, M. D. (1994). Flexibases: A way to enhance the use of molecular docking methods. *Journal of Computer-Aided Molecular Design*, *8*(5), 565–582. doi:10.1007/BF00123666 PMID:7876901

Keckler, S. W., & Reinhardt, S. K. (2012). Massively multithreaded computing systems. *Computer*, *45*(8), 24–25. doi:10.1109/MC.2012.270

Kelleher, J., Barton, N. H., & Etheridge, A. M. (2013). Coalescent simulation in continuous space. *Bioinformatics (Oxford, England)*, *29*(7), 955–956. doi:10.1093/bioinformatics/btt067 PMID:23391497

Kelley, L. A., & Sternberg, M. J. (2009). Protein structure prediction on the web: A case study using the Phyre server. *Nature Protocols*, *4*(3), 363–371. doi:10.1038/nprot.2009.2 PMID:19247286

Kelly, T., Wang, Y., Lafortune, S., & Mahlke, S. (2009). Eliminating concurrency bugs with control engineering. *Computer*, *42*(12), 52–60. doi:10.1109/MC.2009.391

Kent, W. J., Sugnet, C. W., Furey, T. S., Roskin, K. M., Pringle, T. H., Zahler, A. M., & Haussler, D. (2002). The human genome browser at UCSC. *Genome Research*, *12*(6), 996-1006. doi: 10.1101/gr.229102

Khajeh-Saeed, A., & Blair Perot, J. (2011). GPU-supercomputer acceleration of pattern matching. In W. W. Hwu (Ed.), *GPU computing gems* (Vol. 2, pp. 185–198). Morgan Kaufmann. doi:10.1016/B978-0-12-384988-5.00013-9

Kilduff, M., Chiaburu, D. S., & Menges, J. I. (2010). Strategic use of emotional intelligence in organizational settings: Exploring the dark side. *Research in Organizational Behavior*, *30*, 129–152. doi:10.1016/j.riob.2010.10.002

Kim, D., Pertea, G., Trapnell, C., Pimentel, H., Kelley, R., & Salzberg, S. L. (2013). TopHat2: Accurate alignment of transcriptomes in the presence of insertions, deletions and gene fusions. *Genome Biology*, *14*(4), R36. doi:10.1186/gb-2013-14-4-r36 PMID:23618408

Kinder, L. (2012). Scientists believe they have come close to solving the 'Matrix' theory. *The Telegraph*. 26 October 2012. http://www.telegraph.co.uk/science/9635166/Scientists-believe-they-have-come-close-to-solving-the-Matrix-theory.html

Kingsbury, B. A., & Kline, J. T. (1989). Job and process recovery in a UNIX-based operating system. In *Proceedings of the Winter 1989 USENIX Conference*. USENIX Association.

Kirk, D., & Hwu, W. (2010). *Programming massively parallel processors: A hands-on approach*. Boston: Morgan Kaufmann.

Kirkwood, J. G., & Shumaker, J. B. (1952). Forces between protein molecules in solution arising from fluctuations in proton charge and configuration. *Proceedings of the National Academy of Sciences of the United States of America*, *38*(10), 863–871. doi:10.1073/pnas.38.10.863 PMID:16589190

Kitchen, D. B., Decornez, H., Furr, J. R., & Bajorath, J. (2004). Docking and scoring in virtual screening for drug discovery: Methods and applications. *Nature Reviews. Drug Discovery*, *3*(11), 935–949. doi:10.1038/nrd1549 PMID:15520816

Klawe, M., Whitney, T., & Simard, C. (2009, February). Women in computing-take 2. *Communications of the ACM*, *57*(2), 68–76. doi:10.1145/1461928.1461947

Klebe, G., & Mietzner, T. (1994). A fast and efficient method to generate biologically relevant conformations. *Journal of Computer-Aided Molecular Design*, *8*(5), 583–606. doi:10.1007/BF00123667 PMID:7876902

Kleinjung, J., Douglas, N., & Heringa, J. (2002). Parallelized multiple alignment. *Bioinformatics (Oxford, England)*, *18*(9), 1270–1271. doi:10.1093/bioinformatics/18.9.1270 PMID:12217922

Klepeis, J. L., & Floudas, C. A. (2003). ASTRO-FOLD: A combinatorial and global optimization framework for Ab initio prediction of three-dimensional structures of proteins from the amino acid sequence. *Biophysical Journal*, *85*(4), 2119–2146. doi:10.1016/S0006-3495(03)74640-2 PMID:14507680

Knott. (2007). *Verification, validation, and accreditation (VV&A), final report prepared for: Mr. Robert E. Miller, Jr. Contract Officer's Representative U.S. Army RDECOM, CERDEC and Dr. Alexander Kott Program Manager Defense Advanced Research Projects Agency, by: Evidence Based Research, Inc. 1595 Spring Hill Road, Suite 250 Vienna, Virginia 22182-2216, July 30, 2007, Contract: W15P7T-07-C-P209, [no author] pp. 123-125 EBASS description*. Retrieved 9 March 2014 from http://www.dtic.mil/cgi-bin/GetTRDoc?AD=ADA448132

Koch, C. (2013). The end of the beginning for the brain. *Science*, *339*(759), 759–760. doi:10.1126/science.1233813

Kofler, R., Pandey, R. V., & Schlotterer, C. (2011). PoPoolation2: Identifying differentiation between populations using sequencing of pooled DNA samples (Pool-Seq). *Bioinformatics (Oxford, England)*, *27*(24), 3435–3436. doi:10.1093/bioinformatics/btr589 PMID:22025480

Kogge, P. (2011). Next-generation supercomputers. *IEEE Spectrum*. Retrieved from http://spectrum.ieee.org/computing/hardware/nextgeneration-supercomputers/0

Kondo, J. (Ed.). (1991). *Supercomputing applications, algorithms, and architectures for the future of supercomputing*. Springer-Verlag Tokyo.

Koneck, C. M. (2006). *A study of women leadership styles and the glass ceiling*. (Unpublished doctoral dissertation). Capella University, Minneapolis, MN.

Koumoutsakos, P. (2013). *Scientists "burst" supercomputing record with bubble collapse simulation*. Retrieved 03/18, 2014, from http://phys.org/news/2013-11-scientists-supercomputing-collapse-simulation.html

Koyanagi, R., Takeuchi, T., Hisata, K., Gyoja, F., Shoguchi, E., Satoh, N., & Kawashima, T. (2013). MarinegenomicsDB: An integrated genome viewer for community-based annotation of genomes. *Zoological Science*, *30*(10), 797–800. doi:10.2108/zsj.30.797 PMID:24125644

Kramer, B., Beldica, C., Gropp, B., & Hwu, W. (2014). *Blue waters sustained petascale computing*. Retrieved May 21, 2014, Retrieved from https://bluewaters.ncsa.illinois.edu/team

Krieger, E., Koraimann, G., & Vriend, G. (2002). Increasing the precision of comparative models with YASARA NOVA--A self-parameterizing force field. *Proteins, 47*(3), 393–402. doi:10.1002/prot.10104 PMID:11948792

Krivobok, S., Kuony, S., Meyer, C., Louwagie, M., & Wilson, J. C. (2003). Identification of pyrene-induced proteins in *Mycobacterium* spp. strain 6PY1: Evidence for two ring-hydroxylating dioxygenas-es. *Journal of Bacteriology, 185*(13), 3828–3841. doi:10.1128/JB.185.13.3828-3841.2003 PMID:12813077

Krivov, G. G., Shapovalov, M. V., & Dunbrack, R. L. Jr. (2009). Improved prediction of protein side-chain conformations with SCWRL4. *Proteins, 77*(4), 778–795. doi:10.1002/prot.22488 PMID:19603484

Krogh, A. (1998). An introduction to hidden Markov models for biological sequences. In Computational methods in molecular biology (pp. 45-63). Amsterdam: Elsevier. doi:10.1016/S0167-7306(08)60461-5

Krogh, A. (1997). Two methods for improving performance of an HMM and their application for gene finding. *Proceedings of the International Conference on Intelligent Systems for Molecular Biology, 5*, 179–186. PMID:9322033

Krogh, A. (2000). Using database matches with for HMMGene for automated gene detection in Drosophila. *Genome Research, 10*(4), 523–528. doi:10.1101/gr.10.4.523 PMID:10779492

Kuhn, T. (1962). *The structure of scientific revolutions.* Chicago: University of Chicago Press.

Kundur, D., & Ahsan, K. (2003). *Practical internet steganography: Data hiding in IP.* Proc. Texas Wksp. Security of Information Systems.

Kuntz, I. D., Blaney, J. M., Oatley, S. J., Langridge, R., & Ferrin, T. E. (1982). A geometric approach to macromolecule–ligand interactions. *Journal of Molecular Biology, 161*(2), 269–1288. doi:10.1016/0022-2836(82)90153-X PMID:7154081

Kurzweil, R. (2013). *How to create a mind: The secret of human thought revealed.* Retrieved 9 March 2014 from http://en.wikipedia.org/wiki/How_to_Create_a_Mind

Kurzweil, R. (2013). *Ray Kurzweil: Future predictions.* Retrieved 9 March 2014 from http://en.wikipedia.org/wiki/Ray_Kurzweil#Future_predictions

Kuznetsova, A. S. (2005). *The concept of harmony in ancient philosophy.* (Thesis). Philosophy Department of Novosibirsk State University.

Labana, S., Pandey, G., Paul, D., Sharma, N. K., Basu, A., & Jain, R. K. (2005). Plot and field studies on bioremediation of *p*-nitrophenol contaminated soil using *Arthrobacter protophormiae* RKJ100. *Environmental Science & Technology, 39*(9), 3330–3337. doi:10.1021/es0489801 PMID:15926586

Labana, S., Singh, O. V., Basu, A., Pandey, G., & Jain, R. K. (2005). A microcosm study on bioremediation of p-nitrophenol-contaminated soil using *Arthrobacter protophormiae* RKJ100. *Applied Microbiology and Biotechnology, 68*(3), 417–424. doi:10.1007/s00253-005-1926-1 PMID:15806356

Lacy, R. C. (2012). Extending pedigree analysis for uncertain parentage and diverse breeding systems. *The Journal of Heredity, 103*(2), 197–205. doi:10.1093/jhered/esr135 PMID:22275398

Lamoureux, K., Campbell, M., & Smith, R. (2009, April). *High-impact succession management.* Bersin & Associates and Center for Creative Leadership Industry Study, V.1.0.

Langley, P., Simon, H. A., Bradshaw, G. L., & Zytkow, J. M. (1987). *Scientific discovery: Computational explorations of the creative processes.* Cambridge, MA: MIT Press.

Lapointe, F.-J., Legendre, P., & Casgrain, P. (2013). *Permute! Version 3.4 alpha 9: Multiple regression over distance, ultrametric and additive matrices with permutation test.* Academic Press.

Lapointe, F.-J., & Legendre, P. (1992). A statistical framework to test the consensus among additive trees (cladograms). *Systematic Biology, 41*(2), 158–171. doi:10.1093/sysbio/41.2.158

Larkin, M. A., Blackshields, G., Brown, N. P., Chenna, R., McGettigan, P. A., & McWilliam, H. et al. (2007). Clustal W and Clustal X version 2.0. *Bioinformatics (Oxford, England), 23*(21), 2947–2948. doi:10.1093/bioinformatics/btm404 PMID:17846036

Lasch, C. (1979). *The culture of narcissism: American life in an age of diminishing expectations*. New York: W. W. Norton.

Laskowski, R. A. (1995). SURFNET: A program for visualizing molecular surfaces, cavities, and intermolecular interactions. *Journal of Molecular Graphics, 13*(5), 323-330, 307-328.

Laskowski, R. A., Luscombe, N. M., Swindells, M. B., & Thornton, J. M. (1996). Protein clefts in molecular recognition and function. *Protein Science: A Publication of the Protein Society, 5*(12), 2438-2452. doi: 10.1002/pro.5560051206

Latour, R. A. (2008). Molecular simulation of protein-surface interactions: Benefits, problems, solutions, and future directions. *Biointerphases, 3*(3), FC2–FC12. doi:10.1116/1.2965132 PMID:19809597

Lau, D., Liu, J., Majumdar, S., Nandy, B., St-Hilaire, M., & Yang, C. S. (2013). A cloud-based approach for smart facilities management. In *Proceedings of 2013 IEEE Conference on Prognostics and Health Management (PHM)*. Gaithersburg, MD: IEEE. Doi:10.1109/ICPHM.2013.6621459

Laurie, A. T., & Jackson, R. M. (2005). Q-SiteFinder: An energy-based method for the prediction of protein-ligand binding sites. *Bioinformatics (Oxford, England), 21*(9), 1908–1916. doi:10.1093/bioinformatics/bti315 PMID:15701681

Lawrence Livermore Laboratory. (2013). *100 teraFLOPS Dedicated to capability computing*. Lawrence Livermore Laboratory: Advanced Simulation and Computing Purple. Retrieved 9 March 2014 from https://asc.llnl.gov/computing_resources/purple/

Lawson, D. J., Hellenthal, G., Myers, S., & Falush, D. (2012). Inference of population structure using dense haplotype data. *PLOS Genetics, 8*(1), e1002453. doi:10.1371/journal.pgen.1002453 PMID:22291602

Leibniz Supercomputing Centre. (2014). *Leibniz supercomputing centre of the Bavarian academy of sciences and humanities*. Retrieved from http://www.lrz.de/services/compute/supermuc/systemdescription/

Leibniz, G. (1703). *Explication de larithmetique binaire*. Retrieved 9 March 2014 from http://ads.ccsd.cnrs.fr/docs/00/10/47/81/PDF/p85_89_vol3483m.pdf

Lengauer, T., & Rarey, M. (1996). Computational methods for bimolecular docking. *Current Opinion in Structural Biology, 6*(3), 402–406. doi:10.1016/S0959-440X(96)80061-3 PMID:8804827

Leung, R. (2009, February 11). The echo boomers. *CBS News*. Retrieved May 28, 2013 from http://www.cbsnews.com/8301-18560_162-646890.html?pageNum=2

Levesque, J., & Wagenbreth, G. (2011). *High performance computing: Programming and applications*. Chapman & Hall/CRC.

Levitt, D. G., & Banaszak, L. J. (1992). POCKET: A computer graphics method for identifying and displaying protein cavities and their surrounding amino acids. *Journal of Molecular Graphics, 10*(4), 229–234. doi:10.1016/0263-7855(92)80074-N PMID:1476996

Levitt, M. (1992). Accurate modeling of protein conformation by automatic segment matching. *Journal of Molecular Biology, 226*(2), 507–533. doi:10.1016/0022-2836(92)90964-L PMID:1640463

Lewin, T. (2012, November 2). Digital Natives and their customs. *NY Times*. Retrieved May 28, 2013 from http://www.nytimes.com/2012/11/04/education/edlife/arthur-levine-discusses-the-new-generation-of-college-students.html?_r=0

Lewis-Rogers, N., Crandall, K. A., & Posada, D. (2004). Evolutionary analyses of genetic recombination. In V. Parisi, V. De Fonzo, & F. Aluffi-Pentini (Eds.), *Dynamical genetics* (p. 50). Kerala, India: Research Signpost.

Lewontin, R. C. (2000). What do population geneticists know and how do they know it? In Creath & Mainschein (Eds.), Biology and epistemology. Cambridge, UK: Cambirdge University Press.

Li, A., Yang, X., Kandula, S., & Zhang, M. (2010). CloudCmp: Comparing public cloud providers. In *Proceedings of 10th International ACM SIGCOMM Conference on Internet Measurements*, (pp. 1 – 14). ACM.

Li, Y.-S. (2010). The ancient Chinese super state of primary societies: Taoist philosophy for the 21st century. *Wikipedia: 300.* Retrieved March 10, 2014 from: http://en.wikipedia.org/wiki/Taoism

Librado, P., & Rozas, J. (2009). DnaSP v5: A software for comprehensive analysis of DNA polymorphism data. *Bioinformatics (Oxford, England), 25*(11), 1451–1452. doi:10.1093/bioinformatics/btp187 PMID:19346325

Lichtarge, O., Bourne, H. R., & Cohen, F. E. (1996). An evolutionary trace method defines binding surfaces common to protein families. *Journal of Molecular Biology, 257*(2), 342–358. doi:10.1006/jmbi.1996.0167 PMID:8609628

Li, J. Z., Absher, D. M., Tang, H., Southwick, A. M., Casto, A. M., & Ramachandran, S. et al. (2008). Worldwide human relationships inferred from genome-wide patterns of variation. *Science, 319*(5866), 1100–1104. doi:10.1126/science.1153717 PMID:18292342

Lin, H., Ma, X., Chandramohan, P., Geist, A., & Samatova, N. (2005). *Efficient data access for parallel BLAST.* Academic Press.

Linnola, R. J., Werner, L., Pandey, S. K., Escobar-Gomez, M., Znoiko, S. L., & Apple, D. J. (2000). Adhesion of fibronectin, vitronectin, laminin, and collagen type IV to intraocular lens materials in pseudophakic human autopsy eyes. Part 1: histological sections. *Journal of Cataract and Refractive Surgery, 26*(12), 1792-1806. doi: S0886335000007483

Lipman, D. J., & Pearson, W. R. (1985). Rapid and sensitive protein similarity searches. *Science, 227*(4693), 1435–1441. doi:10.1126/science.2983426 PMID:2983426

Lipson, M., Loh, P. R., Levin, A., Reich, D., Patterson, N., & Berger, B. (2013). Efficient moment-based inference of admixture parameters and sources of gene flow. *Molecular Biology and Evolution, 30*(8), 1788–1802. doi:10.1093/molbev/mst099 PMID:23709261

Lischer, H. E., & Excoffier, L. (2012). PGDSpider: An automated data conversion tool for connecting population genetics and genomics programs. *Bioinformatics (Oxford, England), 28*(2), 298–299. doi:10.1093/bioinformatics/btr642 PMID:22110245

List of Sequence Alignment Software. (2014). Retrieved June 17, 2014 from http://en.wikipedia.org/wiki/List_of_sequence_alignment_software

Li, T. T., & Chou, K. C. (1976). The quantitative relations between diffusion-controlled reaction rate and characteristic parameters in enzyme-substrate reaction systems. I. Neutral substrates. *Scientia Sinica, 19*(1), 117–136. PMID:1273571

Liu, J., Xiao, H., Huang, S., & Li, F. (2014). OMIGA: Optimized maker-based insect genome annotation. *Molecular Genetics and Genomics, 289*(4), 567–573. doi:10.1007/s00438-014-0831-7 PMID:24609470

Livingstone, D. J. (2000). The characterization of chemical structures using molecular properties. A survey. *Journal of Chemical Information and Computer Sciences, 40*(2), 195–209. doi:10.1021/ci990162i PMID:10761119

Liwo, A., Lee, J., Ripoll, D. R., Pillardy, J., & Scheraga, H. A. (1999). Protein structure prediction by global optimization of a potential energy function. *Proceedings of the National Academy of Sciences of the United States of America, 96*(10), 5482–5485. doi:10.1073/pnas.96.10.5482 PMID:10318909

LLNL. (2012). Nuclear weapons simulations push supercomputing limits. *InnovationNewsDaily Supercomputers Simulation.* Retrieved March 10, 2014 from: http://www.livescience.com/20810-nuclear-weapons-simulations-limits.html?utm_source=feedburner&utm_medium=feed&utm_campaign=Feed%3A+Livesciencecom+%28LiveScience.com+Science+Headline+Feed%29

Lloyd, S. (2010). *Parallel multiple sequence alignment: An overview.* Retrieved January 6, 2013, from http://dna.cs.byu.edu/msa/overview.pdf

Lobley, A., Sadowski, M. I., & Jones, D. T. (2009). pGenTHREADER and pDomTHREADER: New methods for improved protein fold recognition and superfamily discrimination. *Bioinformatics (Oxford, England), 25*(14), 1761–1767. doi:10.1093/bioinformatics/btp302 PMID:19429599

Loewe, L. (2008). Genetic mutation. *Nature Education, 1*(1).

Loh, P. R., Lipson, M., Patterson, N., Moorjani, P., Pickrell, J. K., Reich, D., & Berger, B. (2013). Inferring admixture histories of human populations using linkage disequilibrium. *Genetics*, *193*(4), 1233–1254. doi:10.1534/genetics.112.147330 PMID:23410830

Lohse, M., Nagel, A., Herter, T., May, P., Schroda, M., & Zrenner, R. et al. (2014). Mercator: A fast and simple web server for genome scale functional annotation of plant sequence data. *Plant, Cell & Environment*, *37*(5), 1250–1258. doi:10.1111/pce.12231 PMID:24237261

Lombardi, C. (2010). *Energy department awards supercomputing time*. Retrieved on July 6, 2014 from http://www.cnet.com/news/energy-department-awards-supercomputing-time/

Lou, J., Wang, M., Hu, J., & Shi, Z. (2007). Distributed data mining on agent grid: Issues, platform and development toolkit. *Future Generation Computer Systems*, *23*(1), 61–68. doi:10.1016/j.future.2006.04.015

Love, D. (2013). 9 facts about quantum computing that will melt your mind. *Business Insider*. Retrieved March 18, 2014, from http://www.businessinsider.com/what-is-quantum-computing-2013-7?op=1#ixzz2birUQ5xZ

Lovley, D. R. (2003). Cleaning up with genomic: Applying molecular biology to bioremediation. *Nature Reviews. Microbiology*, *1*(1), 35–44. doi:10.1038/nrmicro731 PMID:15040178

Loytynoja, A. (2014). Phylogeny-aware alignment with PRANK. *Methods in Molecular Biology (Clifton, N.J.)*, *1079*, 155–170. doi:10.1007/978-1-62703-646-7_10 PMID:24170401

Loytynoja, A., & Goldman, N. (2010). webPRANK: A phylogeny-aware multiple sequence aligner with interactive alignment browser. *BMC Bioinformatics*, *11*(1), 579. doi:10.1186/1471-2105-11-579 PMID:21110866

Lu, Y. (2014). *Overview of tianhe-2 (MilkyWay-2) supercomputer*. Retrieved from http://www.slideshare.net/ultrafilter/th2-isc13inspurlyt

Lu, Y., Gao, P., Lv, R., Su, Z., & Yu, W. (2007). Study of content-based image retrieval using parallel computing technique. In *Proceedings of the 2007 Asian Technology Information Program's (ATIP's) 3rd Workshop on High Performance Computing in China: Solution Approaches to Impediments for High Performance Computing*. New York: ACM. doi:10.1145/1375783.1375820

Lucifredi, F. (2013). *Supercomputing on the cheap with parallella*. Retrieved from http://programming.oreilly.com/2013/12/supercomputing-on-the-cheap-with-parallella.html

Lukashin, A. V., & Borodovsky, M. (1998). GeneMark. hmm: New solutions for gene finding. *Nucleic Acids Research*, *26*(4), 1107–1115. doi:10.1093/nar/26.4.1107 PMID:9461475

Lund, M., & Jonsson, B. (2005). On the charge regulation of proteins. *Biochemistry*, *44*(15), 5722–5727. doi:10.1021/bi047630o PMID:15823030

Maccoby, M. (2004, January). Narcissistic leaders: The incredible pros, the inevitable cons. *Harvard Business Review*, *82*(1), 92–101.

MacColl, H. (1906). *Symbolic logic and its applications*. New York: Longmans, Green, and Co.

MacKay, C., McKee, S., & Mulholland, A. J. (2006). Diffusion and convection of gaseous and fine particulate from a chimney. *IMA Journal of Applied Mathematics*, *71*(5), 670–691. doi:10.1093/imamat/hxl016

MacManes, M. D., & Lacey, E. A. (2012). Is promiscuity associated with enhanced selection on MHC-DQalpha in mice (genus Peromyscus)? *PLoS ONE*, *7*(5), e37562. doi:10.1371/journal.pone.0037562 PMID:22649541

Magalhaes, W. C., Rodrigues, M. R., Silva, D., Soares-Souza, G., Iannini, M. L., & Cerqueira, G. C. et al. (2012). DIVERGENOME: A bioinformatics platform to assist population genetics and genetic epidemiology studies. *Genetic Epidemiology*, *36*(4), 360–367. doi:10.1002/gepi.21629 PMID:22508222

Mahadevan, P., King, J. F., & Seto, D. (2009a). CGUG: In silico proteome and genome parsing tool for the determination of "core" and unique genes in the analysis of genomes up to ca. 1.9 Mb. *BMC Research Notes*, *2*(1), 168. doi:10.1186/1756-0500-2-168 PMID:19706165

Mahadevan, P., King, J. F., & Seto, D. (2009b). Data mining pathogen genomes using GeneOrder and Core-Genes and CGUG: Gene order, synteny and in silico proteomes. *International Journal of Computational Biology and Drug Design*, 2(1), 100–114. doi:10.1504/IJCBDD.2009.027586 PMID:20054988

Mahadevan, P., & Seto, D. (2010). Rapid pair-wise synteny analysis of large bacterial genomes using web-based GeneOrder4.0. *BMC Research Notes*, 3(1), 41. doi:10.1186/1756-0500-3-41 PMID:20178631

Mahony, P. (2013). *Raijin supercomputer cooks up a storm*. Retrieved 03/18, 2014, from http://www.ecosmagazine.com/print/EC13223.htm

Mainframes and Supercomputers. (2012). Retrieved 03/23, 2014, from http://maintec.com/blog/mainframes-andsupercomputers/.ecosmagazine.com/temp/EC13223_Fb.gif

Ma, J., Wang, S., Wang, Z., & Xu, J. (2014). MRFalign: Protein homology detection through alignment of markov random fields. *PLoS Computational Biology*, 10(3), e1003500. doi:10.1371/journal.pcbi.1003500 PMID:24675572

Manyika, J., Chui, M., Brown, B., Bughin, J., Dobbs, R., Roxburgh, C., & Byers, A. H. (2011). *Big data: The next frontier for innovation, competition, and productivity. Tech. rep.* McKinsey Global Institute.

Mariana, C., Paula, K., & Alta, M. (2012). Securing virtual and cloud environments. In *Cloud computing and services science: Research and innovations in the service economy*. Springer Science and Business Media, LLC. Retrieved on October 16, 2014 from http://books.google.com/books?id=ZCWIHhwxc_gC&pg=PA73&lpg=PA73&dq=Securing+virtual+and+cloud+environments.+In:+Cloud+computing+and+services+science:+Research+and+Innovations+in+the+Service+Economy&source=bl&ots=bj3-SI-21J&sig=30xeMoh9MXl1eiSFlm9MQWGRxzA&hl=en&sa=X&ei=dydCVPvxHO76iAKh3YCABQ&ved=0CDUQ6AEwAw#v=onepage&q=Securing%20virtual%20and%20cloud%20environments.%20In%3A%20Cloud%20computing%20and%20services%20science%3A%20Research%20and%20Innovations%20in%20the%20Service%20Economy&f=false

Markovits, M., & Donop, K. (2007, Winter). Collaborate for growth: Deepening involvement through hope. *Organization Development Journal*, 25(4), 13–18.

Marlow, S. (2013). *Parallel and concurrent programming in Haskell: Techniques for multicore and multithreaded programming*. Sebastopol, CA: O'Reilly.

Marmur, J., & Doty, P. (1961). Thermal renaturation of deoxyribonucleic acids. *Journal of Molecular Biology*, 3(5), 585–594. doi:10.1016/S0022-2836(61)80023-5 PMID:14470100

Marques, V. C. (2011). *Emerging leadership styles: Women's success strategy in engineering organizations and the new management paradigm*. (Unpublished doctoral dissertation). Capella University, Minneapolis, MN.

Massaro, K. (2013). *Re-creating earth's oceans inside a supercomputer*. Retrieved 03/18, 2014, from https://www.nas.nasa.gov/publications/articles/feature_ecco.html

Matlis, J. (2005). *A brief history of supercomputers*. Retrieved May 28, 2014 from http://www.computerworld.com.au/article/132504/brief_history_supercomputers/

Matsuzaki, Y., Uchikoga, N., Ohue, M., Shimoda, T., Sato, T., Ishida, T., & Akiyama, Y. (2013). MEGADOCK 3.0: A high-performance protein-protein interaction prediction software using hybrid parallel computing for petascale supercomputing environments. [MEGADOCK 3.0: a high-performance protein-protein interaction prediction software using hybrid parallel computing for petascale supercomputing environments.] *Pubmed*, 8(18). doi:10.1186/1751-0473-8-18

Mattos, C., & Ringe, D. (1996). Locating and characterizing binding sites on proteins. *Nature Biotechnology*, 14(5), 595–599. doi:10.1038/nbt0596-595 PMID:9630949

Maxam, A. M., & Gilbert, W. (1977). A new method for sequencing DNA. *Proceedings of the National Academy of Sciences of the United States of America*, 74(2), 560–564. doi:10.1073/pnas.74.2.560 PMID:265521

Mayer-Schonberger, V., & Cukier, K. (2012). *Big data: A revolution that will transform how we live, work, and think*. Boston: Hughton Mifflin Publishing Company.

Mazumder, R., Kolaskar, A., & Seto, D. (2001). Gene-Order: Comparing the order of genes in small genomes. *Bioinformatics (Oxford, England)*, *17*(2), 162–166. doi:10.1093/bioinformatics/17.2.162 PMID:11238072

McBride, B. T., Peterson, G. L., & Gustafson, S. C. (2005). A new blind method for detecting novel steganography. *Digital Investigation*, *2*(1), 50–70. doi:10.1016/j.diin.2005.01.003

McGann, M. R., Almond, H. R., Nicholls, A., Grant, J. A., & Brown, F. K. (2003). Gaussian docking functions. *Biopolymers*, *68*(1), 76–90. doi:10.1002/bip.10207 PMID:12579581

McKeown, N., Anderson, T., Balakrishnan, H., Parulkar, G., Peterson, L., Rexford, J., et al. (2008). OpenFlow: Enabling innovation in campus networks. ACM SIG-COMM Computer Communication Review Archive, 38(April 2008), 69-74.

McLeod, D., & Heimbigner, D. (1980). A federated architecture for database systems. In *Proceedings of the AFIPS National Computer Conference* (Vol. 39). AFIPS Press.

Measurement from a Practical Point of View. (n.d.). Retrieved 9 March 2014 from http://en.wikipedia.org/wiki/Measurement_in_quantum_mechanics#Measurement_from_a_practical_point_of_view

Medline, L. K., Lange, M., & Nothig, E.-M. (2000). Genetic diversity in the marine phytoplankton:a review and a consideration of Antarctic phytoplankton. *Antarctic Science*, *12*(3), 325–333.

Meglicki, Z. (2004). *The history of MPI*. Retrieved May 31, 2014 from http://beige.ucs.indiana.edu/I590/node54.html

Meier, A. (2006). Operating building during temporary electricity shortage. *Energy & Buildings*, *38*(11), 1296-1301. Retrieved on October 16, 2014 from http://www.sciencedirect.com/science/article/pii/S0378778806000922

Meirmans, P. (2013). *GenoDive (version 2.0b23, manual): Software for analysis of population genetic data*. Universiteit van Amsterdam.

Meirmans, P. G. (2012). AMOVA-based clustering of population genetic data. *The Journal of Heredity*, *103*(5), 744–750. doi:10.1093/jhered/ess047 PMID:22896561

Meirmans, P. G., & Tienderen, V. (2004). GENOTYPE and GENODIVE: Two programs for the analysis of genetic diversity of asexual organisms. *Molecular Ecology Notes*, *4*(4), 792–794. doi:10.1111/j.1471-8286.2004.00770.x

Mell, P., & Grance, T. (2011). *The NIST definition of cloud computing*. Retrieved May 21, 2013, from: http://csrc.nist.gov/publications/nistpubs/800-145/SP800-145.pdf

Mendelson, E. (1997). *Introduction to mathematical logic* (4th ed.). London: Chapman & Hall.

Mendoza-Barrera, C., Hernandez-Santoyo, A., Tenorio-Barajas, A. Y., & Altuzar, V. (2013). *Protein-protein and protein-ligand docking*. Retrieved June 17, 2014 from http://www.intechopen.com/books/protein-engineering-technology-and-application/protein-protein-and-protein-ligand-docking

Meng, E. C., Shoichet, B. K., & Kuntz, I. D. (2004). Automated docking with grid-based energy evaluation. *Journal of Computational Chemistry*, *13*(4), 505–524. doi:10.1002/jcc.540130412

Meng, T. C., Somani, S., & Dhar, P. (2004). Modeling and simulation of biological systems with stochasticity. *In Silico Biology*, *4*(3), 293–309. PMID:15724281

Milanesi, L. K. N. A., Rogozin, I. B., Ischenko, I. V., Kel, A. E., Orlov Yu, L., Ponomarenko, M. P., & Vezzoni, P. (1993). GenView: A computing tool for protein-coding regions prediction in nucleotide sequences. In *Proceedings of the Second International Conference on Bioinformatics, Supercomputing and Complex Genome Analysis*. Singapore: World Scientific Publishing. doi:10.1142/9789814503655_0048

Milojicic, D. (2012). *High performance computing (HPC) in the cloud*. Retrieved 03/18, 2014, from http://www.computer.org/portal/web/computingnow/archive/september2012

Minnesota Supercomputer Center. (1994). Retrieved May 31, 2014 from http://www.auditor.leg.state.mn.us/ped/1994/backgrd.htm

Minnesota Supercomputing Institute-Cascade. (2014). Retrieved May 28, 2014 from https://www.msi.umn.edu/hpc/cascade

Mintseris, J., Pierce, B., Wiehe, K., Anderson, R., Chen, R., & Weng, Z. (2007). Integrating statistical pair potentials into protein complex prediction. *Proteins*, *69*(3), 511–520. doi:10.1002/prot.21502 PMID:17623839

Miranker, G. S. (1992). *Titan III supercomputer architectural overview*. Retrieved from http://link.springer.com/article/10.1007%2FBF02241705

Mironov, A. A., Roytberg, M. A., Pevzner, P. A., & Gelfand, M. S. (1998). Performance-guarantee gene predictions via spliced alignment. *Genomics*, *51*(3), 332–339. doi:10.1006/geno.1998.5251 PMID:9721203

Misner, C. W., Thorne, K. S., & Wheeler, J. A. (1973). *Gravitation*. New York: W.H. Freeman and Company.

Miyazaki, H., Kusano, Y., Shinjou, N., Shoji, F., Yokokawa, M., & Watanabe, T. (2012). *Overview of the K computer system*. Retrieved from http://www.fujitsu.com/downloads/MAG/vol48-3/paper02.pdf

Modeling and Simulation Coordination Office. (2014). Retrieved 9 March 2014 from www.msco.mil

Moin, P., & Kim, J. (n.d.). *Tackling turbulence with supercomputers*. Retrieved 03/18, 2014, from http://www.stanford.edu/group/ctr/articles/tackle.html

Moitessier, N., Englebienne, P., Lee, D., Lawandi, J., & Corbeil, C. R. (2008). Towards the development of universal, fast and highly accurate docking/scoring methods: A long way to go. *British Journal of Pharmacology*, *153*(S1Suppl 1), S7–S26. doi:10.1038/sj.bjp.0707515 PMID:18037925

Molecular Electronics. (2013). Retrieved 9 March 2014 from http://en.wikipedia.org/wiki/Molecular_electronics

Mollin, R. A. (2003). *RSA and public-key cryptography*. Boca Raton, FL: Chapman & Hall/CRC.

Moltke, I., & Albrechtsen, A. (2013). RelateAdmix: A software tool for estimating relatedness between admixed individuals. *Bioinformatics (Oxford, England)*. doi:10.1093/bioinformatics/btt652 PMID:24215025

Montgomery, R. (2013). Consortium for advanced simulation of light water reactors. *ORNL-TechNotes Product Description -Rev.1*. Retrieved March 10, 2014 from: http://www.casl.gov/docs/CASL%20Product%20Applications%2003252013.pdf)

Morgenstern, B. (2014). Multiple sequence alignment with DIALIGN. *Methods in Molecular Biology (Clifton, N.J.)*, *1079*, 191–202. doi:10.1007/978-1-62703-646-7_12 PMID:24170403

Moritz, M. (2010). *Verteilte Dateisysteme in der cloud: Cloud Data Management*. Seminar presented at Leipzig University. Retrieved May 21, 2013, from: http://dbs.uni-leipzig.de/file/seminar_0910_maria_moritz_ausarbeitung.pdf

Morris, G. M., Goodsell, D. S., Halliday, R. S., Huey, R., Hart, W. E., Belew, R. K., & Olson, A. J. (1998). Automated docking using a Lamarckian genetic algorithm and an empirical binding free energy function. *Journal of Computational Chemistry*, *19*(14), 1639–1662. doi:10.1002/(SICI)1096-987X(19981115)19:14<1639::AID-JCC10>3.0.CO;2-B

Morris, J. A., & Barrett, J. C. (2012). Olorin: Combining gene flow with exome sequencing in large family studies of complex disease. *Bioinformatics (Oxford, England)*, *28*(24), 3320–3321. doi:10.1093/bioinformatics/bts609 PMID:23052039

Mortenson, D., & Cabrera-Cordon, L. (n.d.). *The past and present of supercomputing*. Retrieved May 28, 2014 from https://www.google.co.in/url?sa=t&rct=j&q=&esrc=s&source=web&cd=10&cad=rja&uact=8&ved=0CJcBEBYwCQ&url=http%3A%2F%2Fcourses.cs.washington.edu%2Fcourses%2Fcsep590%2F06au%2Fprojects%2Fsupercomputing.doc&ei=lmiFU-ymN4_78QXProKoBw&usg=AFQjCNGEijiGGowF-qq15ySWjoCcTkUf_Q&sig2=vK0Uyg2AptSQaHYJXR-2eA&bvm=bv.67720277,d.dGc

Moss, J. A., & Barbuto, J. E. Jr. (2010, January). Testing the relationship between interpersonal political skills, altruism, leadership success and effectiveness: A multilevel model. *Journal of Behavioral and Applied Management*, *11*(2), 155–174.

Moult, J. (2005). A decade of CASP: Progress, bottlenecks and prognosis in protein structure prediction. *Current Opinion in Structural Biology*, *15*(3), 285–289. doi:10.1016/j.sbi.2005.05.011 PMID:15939584

Mount, D. M. (2004). *Bioinformatics: sequence and genome analysis* (2nd ed.). Cold Springs Harbor, NY: Cold Springs Harbor Laboratory Press.

MSU Supercomputers: "Lomonosov ". (n.d.). Retrieved May 29, 2014 from http://hpc.msu.ru/?q=node/59

MSU's HPC History. (n.d.). Retrieved May 31, 2014 from http://hpc.msu.ru/?q=node/57

Mullender, S. J., Van Rossum, G., Tanenbaum, A. S., Van Renesse, R., & Van Staverene, H. (1990). Amoeba: A distributed operating system for the 1990s. *IEEE Computer, 23*(5), 44–53. doi:10.1109/2.53354

Muller, T., Rahmann, S., Dandekar, T., & Wolf, M. (2004). Accurate and robust phylogeny estimation based on profile distances: A study of the Chlorophyceae (Chlorophyta). *BMC Evolutionary Biology, 4*(1), 20. doi:10.1186/1471-2148-4-20 PMID:15222898

Mulzer, S. R., & Brash, J. L. (1989). Identification of plasma proteins adsorbed to hemodialyzers during clinical use. *Journal of Biomedical Materials Research, 23*(12), 1483–1504. doi:10.1002/jbm.820231210 PMID:2621220

Murray, M. (2012). Comparing ivy bridge vs. sandy bridge. *PC Magazine.* Retrieved March 18, 2014, from http://www.pcmag.com/article2/0,2817,2405317,00.asp(JUNE 7)

Murray, D., Hermida-Matsumoto, L., Buser, C. A., Tsang, J., Sigal, C. T., & Ben-Tal, N. et al. (1998). Electrostatics and the membrane association of Src: Theory and experiment. *Biochemistry, 37*(8), 2145–2159. doi:10.1021/bi972012b PMID:9485361

Myers, A. (2013). *Stanford researchers break million-core supercomputer barrier.* Retrieved 03/18, 2014, from http://engineering.stanford.edu/news/stanford-researchers-break-million-core-supercomputer-barrier

National Geographic. (2010). *Faster supercomputers aiding weather forecasts.* Retrieved on July 8, 2011 from http://news.nationalgeographic.com

National Institutes of Mental Health. (2013). *Research domain criteria.* Retrieved 9 March 2014 from http://www.nimh.nih.gov/about/strategic-planning-reports/index.shtml#strategic-objective1, http://www.nimh.nih.gov/research-funding/rdoc/nimh-research-domain-criteria-rdoc.shtml

National Renewable Energy Laboratory Supercomputer Tackles Power Grid Problems. (2014). Retrieved from http://windenergy.einnews.com/article__detail/211389116?lcode=Tn13hwnNZM_1i4zS4PmnUQ%3D%3D

National Science Board. (2012). Science and engineering indicators 2012. Arlington, VA: National Science Foundation (NSB 12-01).

National Science Foundation. (2012, August). *Age of recent graduates with bachelor's degrees in science, engineering, or health, by major field of degree: October 2008, table 13.* Characteristics of Recent Science and Engineering Graduates: 2008, (NSF 12-328). Retrieved June 7, 2013 from http://www.nsf.gov/statistics/nsf12328/pdf/nsf12328.pdf

National Science Foundation. (2013). *Computing and networking capacity increases at academic research institutions.* Retrieved 20 October 2014, from http://www.nsf.gov/statistics/infbrief/nsf13329/

National Science Foundation. (2013). Retrieved from http://www.nsf.org

Neisser, U. (Ed.). (1998). *The rising curve: Long-term gains in IQ and related measures.* Washington, DC: American Psychological Association; doi:10.1037/10270-000

Network Centric. (2013). Retrieved 9 March 2014 from http://en.wikipedia.org/wiki/Net-centric

Neuroquantology. (2013). Retrieved 9 March 2014 from http://www.neuroquantology.com/index.php/journal

New Supercomputing Method Helps Energy and Materials Research. (2014). Retrieved from http://tntoday.utk.edu/2014/01/15/capability-helps-overcome-limitations-study-energy-materials-applications/

Ng, E. S., & Sears, G. J. (2012). CEO leadership styles and the implementation of organizational diversity practices: Moderating effects of social values and age. *Journal of Business Ethics, 105*(1), 41–52. doi:10.1007/s10551-011-0933-7

Nietzsche, F. W. (1913). Beyond good and evil. (H. Zimerman, Trans.). In *The complete works of Friedrich Nietzsche.* Retrieved 9 March 2014 from http://www.gutenberg.org/files/4363/4363-h/4363-h.htm

Nietzsche, F. W. (1974). *The gay science (The joyful wisdom)* (W. Kaufmann, Ed.). New York: Vintage.

Nikravesh, M. (2010). *Yahoo! Expands Its M45 cloud computing initiative, adding top universities to supercomputing research cluster*. Retrieved March 9, 2013, from http://citris-uc.org/news/2010/11/29/yahoo_expands_its_m45_cloud_computing_initiative_adding_top_universities_supercomputing_research_cluster

Ning, Z., Cox, A. J., & Mullikin, J. C. (2001). SSAHA: A fast search method for large DNA databases. *Genome Research*, *11*(10), 1725–1729. doi:10.1101/gr.194201 PMID:11591649

NIST. (2011). *NIST definition of cloud computing*. National Institute of Standards and Technology. Retrieved on July 24, 2011 from http://www.nist.gov

Noe, L., & Kucherov, G. (2005). YASS: Enhancing the sensitivity of DNA similarity search. *Nucleic Acids Research, 33*(Web Server issue), W540-543. doi: 10.1093/nar/gki478

Nolan, S. A., Buckner, J. P., Marzabadi, C. H., & Kuck, V. J. (2008). Training and mentoring of chemists: A study of gender disparity. *Sex Roles*, *58*(3-4), 235–250. doi:10.1007/s11199-007-9310-5

Novakovic, N. (2011). Chinese high end CPUs are now in the game. *vr-zone*. Retrieved March 18, 2014, from http://vr-zone.com/articles/chinese-high-end-cpus-are-now-in-the-game-details-part-2-alpha/14347.html(December 26)

Nusca, A. (2010). Scientists use world's fastest supercomputer to model, simulate nuclear reactors. *Smart Planet Blog*. Retrieved March 10, 2014 from: http://www.smartplanet.com/blog/smart-takes/scientists-use-worlds-fastest-supercomputer-to-model-simulate-nuclear-reactors/

NVIDIA. (2011). *China's investment in GPU supercomputing begins to pay off big time*. Retrieved on July 8, 2011 from http://blogs.nvidia.com

Nvidia. (2014). TESLA GPU accelerators for workstations. *NVIDIA.com*. Retrieved March 18, 2014, from http://www.nvidia.com/object/tesla-workstations.html

Nyberg, P. (2008). *Cray supercomputers in climate, weather and ocean modeling*. Retrieved 03/18, 2014, from http://www.cray.com/Assets/PDF/products/xt/WP-XT02-1010.pdf

Oden, T., & Ghattas, O. (2012). *Computational science: The "third pillar" of science*. Retrieved May 30, 2014 from http://blog.tamest.org/tag/supercomputing/

Oestreich, K. (2010). Converged infrastructure. *CTO Forum*. Retrieved on December 2, 2011 from http://www.thectoforum.com

O'Fallon, B. (2010). TreesimJ: A flexible, forward time population genetic simulator. *Bioinformatics (Oxford, England)*, *26*(17), 2200–2201. doi:10.1093/bioinformatics/btq355 PMID:20671150

OLCF. (2013). Introducing titan: Advancing the era of supercomputing. *ORNL-TechNotes*. Retrieved March 18, 2014, from http://www.olcf.ornl.gov/titan/

One Year of Hermit. (2013). Retrieved May 29, 2014 from http://www.hlrs.de/news/press/for-journalists/1-year-of-hermit/

O'Neal, T. (2014). *Novel analyses improve identification of cancer-associated genes*. Retrieved June 16, 2014 from http://www.supercomputingonline.com/latest/topics/this-month/57971-novel-analyses-improve-identification-of-cancer-associated-genes

OpenFlow. (n.d.). Retrieved April 5, 2014 from Wikipedia: http://en.wikipedia.org/wiki/OpenFlow

Ophir, D. (1970). *Language for processes of numerical solutions to differential equations*. (Unpublished Doctoral Dissertation). Dept. of App. Math., The Weizmann Institute of Science, Rehovot, Israel.

Ophir, D. (2010). Walking language recognition. In *Proceedings of the Fourth Conference of the International Society for Gesture Studies* (pp.340-342). European University Viadrina.

Ophir, D. (2011). DDDL: A descriptive, didactic and dynamic programming language. In *Proceedings of Israeli-Polish Mathematical Meeting*. Łódź, Poland: Academic Press.

Ophir, D. (2013). An analysis of palindromes and n-nary tracts' frequencies applied in a genomic sequence. In *Proceedings of International Conference on Integrative Biology Summit*. Publishing OMICS Group, Inc.

Ophir, D., & Gera, A. E. (2008). Calculus: The dynamical and visual description. In *Proceedings of the 12th World Multi-Conference on Systemic, Cybernetics and Informatics* (Vol. 7, p. 141). Orlando, FL: Academic Press.

Ophir, D., Yahalom, A., Pinhasi, G. A., & Kopylenko, M. (2012). A combined variational and multi-grid approach for fluid dynamics simulation. In *Proceedings of the ICE - Engineering and Computational Mechanics* (pp.3–14). Academic Press. doi:10.2514/6.2006-695

Ophir, D. (2013). Computerized legilinguistics and psychology - Overriding the polygraph's drawbacks. In *Proceedings of Eighth Conference on Legal Translation, Court Interpreting and Comparative Legilinguistics.* Poznań, Poland: Academic Press.

Ophir, D., & Dekel, D. (2013). SNOBOL-Tone - The sound pattern-matching programming language. In *Proceedings of 2013 Speech Processing Conference at the Afeka Academic College of Engineering.* Academic Press.

Ophir, D., & Gera, A. E. (2005). Analysis of n-nary tract frequency in the genome. *Journal of Bioinformatics, 6*(2), 149–161.

Oracle. (2010). *Understanding basic multithreading concepts: Multithreaded programming guide.* Retrieved March 18, 2014, from http://docs.oracle.com/cd/E19455-01/806-5257/6je9h032e/index.html

ORNL. (2010). Nuclear energy - Supercomputer speeds path forward. *Science And Technology.* Retrieved March 10, 2014 from: http://www.casl.gov/highlights/supercomputer.shtml

ORNL. (2012). *Introducing Titan: Advancing the era of accelerated computing.* Retrieved March 1, 2014, from http://www.olcf.ornl.gov/titan/

ORNL_Info. (2013). Potent partnerships: CASL simulations add insight into operating nuclear reactor cores. *Ornl Review.* Retrieved March 10, 2014 from: http://web.ornl.gov/info/ornlreview/v46_2-3_13/article07.shtml#sthash.LqCPwgIb.dpuf

OSC. (2014). *The Ohio supercomputing center.* Retrieved February 28, 2014, from http://www.osc.edu/

Oshagbemi, T. (2003, June). Age influences on the leadership styles and behavior of managers. *Employee Relations, 26*(1), 14–29. doi:10.1108/01425450410506878

Otto, J. S., Stanojevic, R., & Laoutaris, N. (2012). Temporal rate limiting: Cloud elasticity at a flat fee. In *Proceedings of NetEcon Workshop (INFOCOM WKSHPS),* (pp. 151-156). Academic Press.

Ovcharenko, I., Loots, G. G., Hardison, R. C., Miller, W., & Stubbs, L. (2004). zPicture: Dynamic alignment and visualization tool for analyzing conservation profiles. *Genome Research, 14*(3), 472–477. doi:10.1101/gr.2129504 PMID:14993211

Overview of Sunway Bluelight Computer. (2012). Retrieved May 29, 2014 from http://hpc.inspur.com/images/News/2012/11/23/E34520689DA74A0F-A3360192582FDD7A.pdf

Overview of the ARCHER System. (2013). Retrieved May 29, 2014 from http://www.epsrc.ac.uk/SiteCollectionDocuments/Publications/tenders/PR120039Hardware-Overview.pdf

Oyonagi, Y. (2002). *Future of supercomputing.* Retrieved May 28, 2014 from http://www.sciencedirect.com/science/article/pii/S0377042702005265

Pacheco, P. S. (2011). *An introduction to parallel programming.* Boston: Morgan Kaufmann.

Pachter, L., Batzoglou, S., Spitkovsky, V. I., Banks, E., Lander, E. S., Kleitman, D. J., & Berger, B. (1999). A dictionary-based approach for gene annotation. *Journal of Computational Biology, 6*(3-4), 419–430. doi:10.1089/106652799318364 PMID:10582576

Palamara, P. F., Lencz, T., Darvasi, A., & Pe'er, I. (2012). Length distributions of identity by descent reveal finescale demographic history. *American Journal of Human Genetics, 91*(5), 809–822. doi:10.1016/j.ajhg.2012.08.030 PMID:23103233

Palmer J. (2012). Quantum computing: Is it possible, and should you care? *BBC News Science and Technology.*

Pandey, G., Paul, D., & Jain, K. (2003). Branching of *o*-nitrobenzoate degradation pathway in *Arthrobacter protophormiae* RKJ100: Identification of new intermediates. *FEMS Microbiology Letters, 229*(2), 231–236. doi:10.1016/S0378-1097(03)00844-9 PMID:14680704

Pandey, U. B., & Nichols, C. D. (2011). Human disease models in Drosophila melanogaster and the role of the fly in therapeutic drug discovery. *Pharmacological Reviews*, *63*(2), 2411–2436. doi:10.1124/pr.110.003293 PMID:21415126

Paquete, L., Matias, P., Abbasi, M., & Pinheiro, M. (2014). MOSAL: Software tools for multiobjective sequence alignment. *Source Code for Biology and Medicine*, *9*(1), 2. doi:10.1186/1751-0473-9-2 PMID:24401750

Paradis, E. (2010). pegas: An R package for population genetics with an integrated-modular approach. *Bioinformatics (Oxford, England)*, *26*(3), 419–420. doi:10.1093/bioinformatics/btp696 PMID:20080509

Param. (2014). Retrieved May 29, 2014 from http://en.wikipedia.org/wiki/PARAM

Parca, L., Gherardini, P. F., Helmer-Citterich, M., & Ausiello, G. (2011). Phosphate binding sites identification in protein structures. *Nucleic Acids Research*, *39*(4), 1231–1242. doi:10.1093/nar/gkq987 PMID:20974634

Parra, G., Blanco, E., & Guigo, R. (2000). GeneID in drosophila. *Genome Research*, *10*(4), 511–515. doi:10.1101/gr.10.4.511 PMID:10779490

Pasetto, D., Petrini, F., & Virat, A. (2010). Tools for very fast regular expression matching. *Computer*, *43*(3), 50–58. doi:10.1109/MC.2010.80

Pasquill, F. (1961). The estimation of the dispersion of windborne material. *The Meteorological Magazine*, *90*(1063), 33-49. Retrieved from http://www.researchgate.net/publication/231221906_The_Estimation_of_the_Dispersion_of_Windborne_Material

Pasquill, F. (1974). *Atmospheric diffusion* (2nd ed., p. 429). New York, NY: Halsted Press, John Wiley & Sons.

Patterson, N., Moorjani, P., Luo, Y., Mallick, S., Rohland, N., & Zhan, Y. et al. (2012). Ancient admixture in human history. *Genetics*, *192*(3), 1065–1093. doi:10.1534/genetics.112.145037 PMID:22960212

Patterson, N., Price, A. L., Reich, D., Plenge, R. M., Weinblatt, M. E., Shadick, N. A., & Reich, D. (2013). *EIGENSOFT version 5.01*. Harvard University.

Pavlopoulou, A., & Michalopoulos, I. (2011). State-of-the-art bioinformatics protein structure prediction tools. *International Journal of Molecular Medicine*, *28*(3), 295–310. doi:10.3892/ijmm.2011.705 PMID:21617841

Peacock, E., & Whiteley, P. (2005). Perlegen sciences, inc. *Pharmacogenomics*, *6*(4), 439–442. doi:10.1517/14622416.6.4.439 PMID:16004563

Peakall, R., & Smouse, P. E. (2012). GenAlEx 6.5: Genetic analysis in Excel. Population genetic software for teaching and research--An update. *Bioinformatics (Oxford, England)*, *28*(19), 2537–2539. doi:10.1093/bioinformatics/bts460 PMID:22820204

Peano, G. (1889). *Arithmetices principia novo methodo exposita*. Roma: Ediderunt Fratres Bocca.

Pearlman, D. A., & Connelly, P. R. (1995). Determination of the differential effects of hydrogen bonding and water release on the binding of FK506 to native and Tyr82-->Phe82 FKBP-12 proteins using free energy simulations. *Journal of Molecular Biology, 248*(3), 696-717. doi:10.1006/jmbi.1995.0252

Pearson, W. (1991). *LALIGN - Find mulitple matching subsegments in two sequences*. Retrieved December 29, 2012, from http://www.ch.embnet.org/software/LALIGN_form.html

Pearson, W. R. (2006a). *FASTA sequence comparison at the University of Virginia*. Retrieved December 30, 2012, from http://fasta.bioch.virginia.edu/fasta_www2/fasta_www.cgi?rm=lalign

Pearson, W. R. (2006b). *LALIGN/PLALIGN*. Retrieved December 30, 2012, from http://fasta.bioch.virginia.edu/fasta_www2/fasta_www.cgi?rm=lalign

Pearson, W. R., & Lipman, D. J. (1988). Improved tools for biological sequence comparison. *Proceedings of the National Academy of Sciences of the United States of America*, *85*(8), 2444–2448. doi:10.1073/pnas.85.8.2444 PMID:3162770

Pedersen, B. S., Yang, I. V., & De, S. (2013). CruzDB: Software for annotation of genomic intervals with UCSC genome-browser database. *Bioinformatics (Oxford, England)*, *29*(23), 3003–3006. doi:10.1093/bioinformatics/btt534 PMID:24037212

Pei, J., & Grishin, N. V. (2007). PROMALS: Towards accurate multiple sequence alignments of distantly related proteins. *Bioinformatics (Oxford, England)*, *23*(7), 802–808. doi:10.1093/bioinformatics/btm017 PMID:17267437

Pekerti, A. A., & Sendjaya, S. (2010, April). Exploring servant leadership across cultures: Comparative study in Australia and Indonesia. *International Journal of Human Resource Management*, *21*(5), 754–780. doi:10.1080/09585191003658920

Pembleton, L. W., Cogan, N. O., & Forster, J. W. (2013). StAMPP: An R package for calculation of genetic differentiation and structure of mixed-ploidy level populations. *Molecular Ecology Resources*, *13*(5), 946–952. doi:10.1111/1755-0998.12129 PMID:23738873

Penn, O., Privman, E., Ashkenazy, H., Landan, G., Graur, D., & Pupko, T. (2010). GUIDANCE: A web server for assessing alignment confidence scores. *Nucleic Acids Research, 38*(Web Server issue), W23-28. doi: 10.1093/nar/gkq443

Pennell, M. W., Stansbury, C. R., Waits, L. P., & Miller, C. R. (2013). Capwire: A R package for estimating population census size from non-invasive genetic sampling. *Molecular Ecology Resources*, *13*(1), 154–157. doi:10.1111/1755-0998.12019 PMID:22995036

Perez-Figueroa, A., Rodriguez-Ramilo, S. T., & Caballero, A. (2012). Analysis and management of gene and allelic diversity in subdivided populations using the software program METAPOP. *Methods in Molecular Biology (Clifton, N.J.)*, *888*, 261–275. doi:10.1007/978-1-61779-870-2_15 PMID:22665286

Peters, K. P., Fauck, J., & Frommel, C. (1996). The automatic search for ligand binding sites in proteins of known three-dimensional structure using only geometric criteria. *Journal of Molecular Biology*, *256*(1), 201–213. doi:10.1006/jmbi.1996.0077 PMID:8609611

Petitcolas, F. A. P., Anderson, R. J., & Kuhn, M. G. (1999). Information hiding: A survey. *Proceedings of the IEEE*, *87*(7), 1062–1078. doi:10.1109/5.771065

Pevsner, J. (2009). *Bioinformatics and functional genomics*. Hoboken, NJ: Wiley-Blackwell. doi:10.1002/9780470451496

Piaget, J. (1958). *Logic and psychology*. New York: Basic Books, Inc.

Pickrell, J. K., & Pritchard, J. K. (2012). Inference of population splits and mixtures from genome-wide allele frequency data. *PLOS Genetics*, *8*(11), e1002967. doi:10.1371/journal.pgen.1002967 PMID:23166502

Pietrokovski, S., Henikoff, J. G., & Henikoff, S. (1996). The Blocks database--A system for protein classification. *Nucleic Acids Research*, *24*(1), 197–200. doi:10.1093/nar/24.1.197 PMID:8594578

Plewniak, F., Bianchetti, L., Brelivet, Y., Carles, A., Chalmel, F., & Lecompte, O. et al. (2003). PipeAlign: A new toolkit for protein family analysis. *Nucleic Acids Research*, *31*(13), 3829–3832. doi:10.1093/nar/gkg518 PMID:12824430

Plimpton, S., Thompson, A., & Crozier, P. (2013). *LAMMPS*. Retrieved from http://lammps.sandia.gov/

Plutynski, A., & Evans, W. (2005). Population genetics. In S. Sarkar & J. Pheiffer (Eds.), *Routledge encyclopedia of science* (pp. 578–585). London: Routledge.

Podlaski, B. (2014). *The age of the supercomputer*. Retrieved May 30, 2014 from http://asutriplehelix.org/node/127

Ponder, B. A. (2001). Cancer genetics. *Nature*, *411*(6835), 336–341. doi:10.1038/35077207 PMID:11357140

Popa, B. M. (2013). Risks resulting from the discrepancy between organizational culture and leadership. *Journal of Defense Resources Management*, *4*(1), 179–182.

Popa-Simil, L. (2008a). Direct energy conversion nano-hetero fuel. *MRS Procedings NN(Spring)*, 6.

Popa-Simil, L. (2011a). *Micro-nano hetero structured fuel pellet's impact on nuclear reactor's performances*. Paper presented at the Water Reactor Fuel Performance Meeting, Chengdu, China.

Popa-Simil, L. (2011c). Advanced space nuclear reactors from fiction to reality. In *Proceedings of Space, Propulsion & Energy Sciences International Forum (Space, Propulsion & Energy Sciences International Forum)*. AIP. doi:10.1016/j.phpro.2011.08.025

Popa-Simil, L. (2012). The harmony between nuclear reactions and nuclear reactor structures and systems. In *Proceedings of ICAPP'12*. Retrieved March 18, 2014 from http://icapp.ans.org/icapp12/official%20program. pdf(12080)

Popa-Simil, L. (2008). Micro-structured nuclear fuel and novel nuclear reactor concepts for advanced power production. *Progress in Nuclear Energy, 50*(2–6), 539–548. doi:10.1016/j.pnucene.2007.11.041

Popa-Simil, L. (2010a). *Quasi-nano-clustered fuel for enhanced transmutation products separation.* OECD-NEA.

Popa-Simil, L. (2010b). The use of plutonium and micro-hetero structures. In *Novel nuclear reactors modifies the actual fuel cycle, plutonium futures.* ANS Tranzactions.

Popa-Simil, L. (2011b). *The drastic increase of safety and performances in nuclear power by implementing nano-engineered materials.* Washington, DC: Knowledge Foundation.

Popa-Simil, L. (2012). *Applied nano-technologies improves nuclear power safety and performances.* Los Alamos, CA: Amazon, Kindle.

Popek, G. J., & Walker, B. J. (1985). *The LOCUS distributed system architecture.* Cambridge, MA: MIT Press.

Porras-Hurtado, L., Ruiz, Y., Santos, C., Phillips, C., Carracedo, A., & Lareu, M. V. (2013). An overview of STRUCTURE: Applications, parameter settings, and supporting software. *Frontiers in Genetics, 4*, 98. doi:10.3389/fgene.2013.00098 PMID:23755071

Portal, E. B. R. (n.d.). *SIM - Alignment tool for protein sequences.* Retrieved December 30, 2012, from http://web.expasy.org/sim/

Powell, M. L., & Miller, B. P. (1983). Process migration in DEMOS/MP. In *Proceedings of the 9th ACM Symposium on Operating System Principles.* Association for Computing Machinery. doi:10.1145/800217.806619

Power, D. (2012). *The Boston viridis ARM server: Addressing the power challenges of exascale.* Retrieved 05/31, 2014, Retrieved from http://ukhpc.co.uk/files/2013/12/White-paper-The-Boston-Viridis-ARM%C2%AE-Server. pdf

Prescott, B. (2012). Gene helps predict time of death common gene variant influences when you will wake up each day—and the time of day you will die. *Harvard Medical School News.* Retrieved 9 March 2014 from http://hms.harvard.edu/news/gene-helps-predict-time-death-11-26-12

Price, A. L., Patterson, N. J., Plenge, R. M., Weinblatt, M. E., Shadick, N. A., & Reich, D. (2006). Principal components analysis corrects for stratification in genome-wide association studies. *Nature Genetics, 38*(8), 904–909. doi:10.1038/ng1847 PMID:16862161

Prodan, R. (2007). Grid computing: Experiment management, tool integration, and scientific workflows. Fahringer & Thomas.

Proffitt, B. (2012). Peta, Exa, Yotta and beyond: Big data reaches cosmic proportions. *readwrite enterprise.* Retrieved March 18, 2014, from http://readwrite.com/2012/11/23/peta-exa-yotta-and-beyond-big-data-reaches-cosmic-proportions-infographic#awesm=~oegH00ZWlbJMVt

Project on the Decade of the Brain. (n.d.). Retrieved 9 March 2014 from http://www.loc.gov/loc/brain/

Prottman, C. L. L. (2011). *Computational thinking and women in computer science.* (Unpublished Master's Thesis). University of Oregon, Eugene, OR.

Przestalski, S., Hladyszowski, J., Kuczera, J., Rozycka-Roszak, B., Trela, Z., Chojnacki, H., … Fisicaro, E. (1996). Interaction between model membranes and a new class of surfactants with antioxidant function. *Biophysical Journal, 70*(5), 2203-2211. doi: 10.1016/S0006-3495(96)79786-2

PTI. (2012, September 17). India plans 61 times faster supercomputer by 2017. *The Times of India.* Retrieved May 25, 2104 from http://articles.timesofindia.indiatimes.com/2012-09-17/hardware/33901529_1_first-supercomputers-petaflop-fastest-supercomputer

Puckelwartz, M. J., Pesce, L. L., Nelakuditi, V., Dellefave-Castillo, L., Golbus, J. R., & Day, S. M. et al. (2014). Supercomputing for the parallelization of whole genome analysis. *Bioinformatics (Oxford, England), 30*(11), 1508–1513. doi:10.1093/bioinformatics/btu071 PMID:24526712

Purcell, S., Neale, B., Todd-Brown, K., Thomas, L., Ferreira, M. A., & Bender, D. et al. (2007). PLINK: A tool set for whole-genome association and population-based linkage analyses. *American Journal of Human Genetics*, *81*(3), 559–575. doi:10.1086/519795 PMID:17701901

Qi, H., Ghodousi, M., Du, Y., Grun, C., Yin, P., & Khademhosseini, A. (2013). DNA-directed self-assembly of shape-controlled hydrogels. *Nature Communications*, *4*, 2275. doi:10.1038/ncomms3275

Qingzhong, L., Andrew, H. S., Bernardete, R., Mingzhen, W., Zhongxue, C., & Jianyun, X. (2008). Image complexity and feature mining for steganalysis of least significant bit matching steganography. *Information Sciences*, *178*(1), 21–36. doi:10.1016/j.ins.2007.08.007

Quantum Computer. (2013). Retrieved 9 March 2014 from http://en.wikipedia.org/wiki/Quantum_computer

Ramaswami, A. R., Dreher, G. F., Bretz, R., & Wiethoff, C. (2010). Gender, mentoring, and career success: The importance of organizational context. *Personnel Psychology*, *63*(2), 385–405. doi:10.1111/j.1744-6570.2010.01174.x

Rapoport, S. (2013). *Stephen Wolfram*. Retrieved 9 March 2014 from www.stephenwolfram.com/

Rapoport, D. L. (2009). Surmounting the Cartesian cut. *Foundations of Physics*, *41*(1), 33–76. doi:10.1007/s10701-009-9334-5

Rath, J. (2014). *NERSC flips the switch on new Edison supercomputer*. Retrieved April 17, 2014, from http://www.datacenterknowledge.com/archives/2014/01/31/nersc-flips-switch-new-edison-supercomputer/

Ratner, B. D. (1996). The engineering of biomaterials exhibiting recognition and specificity. *Journal of Molecular Recognition*, *9*(5-6), 617-625. doi: 10.1002/(SICI)1099-1352(199634/12)9:5/6<617::AID-JMR310>3.0.CO;2-D

Raut, V. P., Agashe, M. A., Stuart, S. J., & Latour, R. A. (2005). Molecular dynamics simulations of peptide-surface interactions. *Langmuir*, *21*(4), 1629–1639. doi:10.1021/la047807f PMID:15697318

Ravaoarimanana, I. B., & Montagnon, D. (2006). *Nucleotide sequences analyzer (NSA) version 3.3*. France: Institut d'Embryologie, Faculté de Médecine.

Raymond, M., & Rousset, F. (1995). GENEPOP (version 1.2) population genetic software for exact tests and ecumenicism. *The Journal of Heredity*, *86*, 248–249.

Read, J. (1957). *From alchemy to chemistry*. New York: Courier Dover Publications.

Rea, M. C. (2006). Polytheism and Christian belief. *Journal of Theological Studies*, *57*(Pt 1), 133–148. doi:10.1093/jts/flj007

Reed, L., Vidaver-Cohen, D., & Colwell, S. (2011, July). A new scale to measure executive servant leadership: Development, analysis, and implications for research. *Journal of Business Ethics*, *101*(3), 415–434. doi:10.1007/s10551-010-0729-1

Reese, M. G., Kulp, D., Tammana, H., & Haussler, D. (2000). Genie--gene finding in Drosophila melanogaster. *Genome Research*, *10*(4), 529–538. doi:10.1101/gr.10.4.529 PMID:10779493

Reimhult, E., Hook, F., & Kasemo, B. (2002). Temperature dependence of formation of a supported phospholipid bilayer from vesicles on SiO2. *Physical Review E: Statistical, Nonlinear, and Soft Matter Physics*, *66*(5 Pt 1), 051905. doi:10.1103/PhysRevE.66.051905 PMID:12513521

Reppell, M., Boehnke, M., & Zollner, S. (2012). FTEC: A coalescent simulator for modeling faster than exponential growth. *Bioinformatics (Oxford, England)*, *28*(9), 1282–1283. doi:10.1093/bioinformatics/bts135 PMID:22441586

Research Institutions Push the Boundaries of Supercomputing with Dell. (2013). Retrieved May 28, 2014 from http://pbdj.sys-con.com/node/2875456

Reumann, M., Holt, K. E., Inouye, M., Stinear, T., Goudey, B. W., Abraham, G., et al. (2011). *Precision medicine: Dawn of supercomputing in 'omics' research*. Paper presented at the 5th eResearch Australasia Conference, Melbourne, Australia.

Rice, P., Longden, I., & Bleasby, A. (2000). EMBOSS: The European molecular biology open software suite. *Trends in Genetics*, *16*(6), 276–277. doi:10.1016/S0168-9525(00)02024-2 PMID:10827456

Richmond, C. S., Glasner, J. D., Mau, R., Jin, H., & Blattner, F. R. (1999). Genome-wide expression profiling in *Escherichia coli* K-12. *Nucleic Acids Research, 27*(19), 3821–3835. doi:10.1093/nar/27.19.3821 PMID:10481021

Riedel, E., Gibson, G., & Faloutsos, C. (1998). Active storage for large-scale data mining and multimedia applications. In *Proceedings of VLDB '98 Proceedings of the 24rd International Conference on Very Large Data Bases* (pp. 62-73). Academic Press.

Rig Veda, Hymn CXXIX – Creation, Book the Tenth. (n.d.). Oxford Companion to Philosophy. Retrieved 9 March 2014 from http://www.answers.com/topic/ancient-philosophy#Indian_philosophy

Ripphausen, P., Nisius, B., Peltason, L., Bajorath, J., Quo, & Vadis. (2010). Virtual screening? A comprehensive survey of prospective applications. *Journal of Medicinal Chemistry, 53*, 8461-8467.

Rise, M. L., Jones, S. R., Brown, G. D., Von Schalburg, K. R., Davidson, W. S., & Koop, B. F. (2004). Microarray analyses identify molecular biomarkers of Atlantic salmon macrophage and hematopoietic kidney response to *Piscirickettsia salmonis* infection. *Physiological Genomics, 20*(1), 21–35. doi:10.1152/physiolgenomics.00036.2004 PMID:15454580

Rivoire, S. (2010). A breadth-first course in multicore and manycore programming. In *Proceedings of the 41st ACM Technical Symposium on Computer Science Education.* New York, NY: ACM. doi:10.1145/1734263.1734339

Robat, C. (2013). *Introduction to supercomputers.* Retrieved May 28, 2014 from http://www.thocp.net/hardware/supercomputers.htm

Roberts, R. J. (2004). Identifying protein function--A call for community action. *PLoS Biology, 2*(3), E42. doi:10.1371/journal.pbio.0020042 PMID:15024411

Robinson, K. (2011). *Out of our minds.* Westford, MA: Courier Westford, Inc.

Rodrigo, A., Drummond, A., & Goode, M. (2010). *Pebble, version 1.0, (phylogenetics, evolutionary biology, and bioinformatics in a modular environment).* Auckland, New Zealand: University of Auckland.

Rosencrance, L. (2014). Intel heralds new Xeon server chip, most powerful ever. *CIO Today.* Retrieved on October 16, 2014 from http://www.cio-today.com/article/index.php?story_id=12100006PL28

Rosser, J. B. (1953). *Logic for mathematicians.* New York: Chelsea Publishing Company.

Rost, B., & Sander, C. (1993). Prediction of protein secondary structure at better than 70% accuracy. *Journal of Molecular Biology, 232*(2), 584–599. doi:10.1006/jmbi.1993.1413 PMID:8345525

Rousset, F. (2008). genepop'007: A complete re-implementation of the genepop software for Windows and Linux. *Molecular Ecology Resources, 8*(1), 103–106. doi:10.1111/j.1471-8286.2007.01931.x PMID:21585727

Rowley, J. D. (1973). A new consistent chromosomal abnormality in chronic myelogenous leukemia identified by quina-crine fluorescence and Giemsa staining. *Nature, 243*(5405), 290–293. doi:10.1038/243290a0 PMID:4126434

Rozas, J., & Rozas, R. (1999). DnaSP version 3: An integrated program for molecular population genetics and molecular evolution analysis. *Bioinformatics (Oxford, England), 15*(2), 174–175. doi:10.1093/bioinformatics/15.2.174 PMID:10089204

Rubia, T. (2000). *Following materials over time and space.* Retrieved 03/18, 2014, from https://www.llnl.gov/str/Diaz.html

Ruch, P., Paredes, S., Meijer, I., & Bruno, M. (2013). Roadmap towards ultimately-efficient zeta-scale datacenters. In *Proceedings of Design, Automation & Test in Europe Conference & Exhibition (DATE)* (pp. 1339-1344). Academic Press.

Russell, R. (1977). *The cray-1 computer system.* Cray Research, Inc. Retrieved on May 25, 2011 from https://www.cs.auckland.ac.nz/courses/compsci703s1c/archive/2008/resources/Russell.pdf

Russell, B. (1919). *Introduction to mathematical philosophy.* London: George Allen & Unwin, Ltd.

Russell, D. J. (2014). GramAlign: Fast alignment driven by grammar-based phylogeny. *Methods in Molecular Biology (Clifton, N.J.), 1079*, 171–189. doi:10.1007/978-1-62703-646-7_11 PMID:24170402

Rutherford, K., Parkhill, J., Crook, J., Horsnell, T., Rice, P., Rajandream, M. A., & Barrell, B. (2000). Artemis: Sequence visualization and annotation. *Bioinformatics (Oxford, England), 16*(10), 944–945. doi:10.1093/bioinformatics/16.10.944 PMID:11120685

Sadana, A., & Sii, D. (1992). Binding kinetics of antigen by immobilized antibody: Influence of reaction order and external diffusional limitations. *Biosens Bioelectron, 7*(8), 559-568.

Sadana, A. (1992a). Inactivation of proteins and other biological macromolecules during chromatographic methods of bioseparation. *Bioseparation, 3*(2-3), 145–165. PMID:1369239

Sadana, A. (1992b). Interfacial protein adsorption and inactivation. *Bioseparation, 3*(5), 297–320. PMID:1369429

Sagan, C. (2010). *What is life?* Retrieved 9 March 2014 from http://www.aim.univ-paris7.fr/enseig/exobiologie_PDF/Biblio/Sagan%20Definitions%20of%20life.pdf

Sagoo, G. (2007). Glossary of terms. In D. J. Balding, M. Bishop, & C. Cannings (Eds.), *Handbook of statistical genetics* (3rd ed.; Vol. 1). West Sussex, UK: John Wiley & Sons.

Salamov, A. A., & Solovyev, V. V. (2000). Ab initio gene finding in Drosophila genomic DNA. *Genome Research, 10*(4), 516–522. doi:10.1101/gr.10.4.516 PMID:10779491

Salvatores, M. (2006). Advanced fuel cycles and R&D needs in the nuclear data field. In *Proceedings of Nuclear Physics and Related Computational Science R&D for Advanced Fuel Cycle Workshop*. Bethesda, MD: Academic Press.

San Diego Supercomputing Center. (2008, May 15). *Introduction to clusters and rocks overview: Rocks for noobs*. University of California, San Diego, CA. Retrieved May 28, 2013 from http://www.rocksclusters.org/presentations/tutorial/

San Lucas, F. A., Rosenberg, N. A., & Scheet, P. (2012). Haploscope: A tool for the graphical display of haplotype structure in populations. *Genetic Epidemiology, 36*(1), 17–21. doi:10.1002/gepi.20640 PMID:22147662

Sanders, J., & Kandrot, E. (2011). CUDA by example: An introduction to general-purpose GPU programming. Reading, MA: Addison- Wesley.

Sanderson, K. (2006). Sharpest cut from nanotube sword: Carbon nanotech may have given swords of Damascus their edge. *Nature News*. Retrieved March 10, 2014 from: http://www.nature.com/news/2006/061113/full/news061113-11.html

Sandhu, A. (2006). Who invented nano? *Nature Nanotechnology, 1*(87).

Sanger, F., Nicklen, S., & Coulson, A. R. (1977). DNA sequencing with chain-terminating inhibitors. *Proceedings of the National Academy of Sciences of the United States of America, 74*(12), 5463–5467. doi:10.1073/pnas.74.12.5463 PMID:271968

Sanghvi, A. P. (1991). Power shortages in developing countries: Impacts and policy implications. *Energy Policy, 19*(5), 425–440. doi:10.1016/0301-4215(91)90020-O

Santos, A. R., Barbosa, E., Fiaux, K., Zurita-Turk, M., Chaitankar, V., & Kamapantula, B. et al. (2013). PAN-NOTATOR: An automated tool for annotation of pan-genomes. *Genetics and Molecular Research, 12*(3), 2982–2989. doi:10.4238/2013.August.16.2 PMID:24065654

Satyanarayanan, M., Bahl, P., Caceres, R., & Davies, N. (2009). The case for VM-based cloudlets in mobile computing. *IEEE Pervasive Computing, 8*(4), 14–23. doi:10.1109/MPRV.2009.82

Scarpino, M. (2011). *OpenCL in action: How to accelerate graphics and computations*. Shelter Island, NY: Manning Publications Co.

Schadt, E. E., Linderman, M. D., Sorenson, J., Lee, L., & Nolan, G. P. (2010). Computational solutions to large-scale data management and analysis. *Nature Reviews. Genetics, 11*(9), 647–657. doi:10.1038/nrg2857 PMID:20717155

Schagrin, M. L., & Rapaport, W. J. (1985). *Logic: A computer approach*. New York: McGraw-Hill.

Schein, E. (2010). *Organizational culture and leadership* (4th ed.). San Francisco, CA: Jossey-Bass.

Schena, M., Shalon, D., Heller, R., Chai, A., Brown, P. O., & Davis, R. W. (1996). Parallel human genome analysis: Microarray-based expression of 1000 genes. *Proceedings of the National Academy of Sciences of the United States of America*, *93*(20), 10539–11286. doi:10.1073/pnas.93.20.10614 PMID:8855227

Schlegel H.B., (2003). Ab initio molecular dynamics with born-oppenheimer and extended lagrangian methods using atom centered basis functions. *Ab Initio Molecular Dynamics Bulletin, 24*(6).

Schmid, A. (2005). What is the truth of simulation? *Journal of Artificial Societies and Social Simulation, 8*(4).

Schmutz, J., Grimwood, J., & Myers, R. M. (2004). Sequence finishing. *Methods in Molecular Biology (Clifton, N.J.)*, *255*, 333–342. doi:10.1385/1-59259-752-1:333 PMID:15020836

Schnattinger, T., Schoning, U., Marchfelder, A., & Kestler, H. A. (2013). RNA-Pareto: Interactive analysis of Pareto-optimal RNA sequence-structure alignments. *Bioinformatics (Oxford, England)*, *29*(23), 3102–3104. doi:10.1093/bioinformatics/btt536 PMID:24045774

Schneidman-Duhovny, D., Inbar, Y., Nussinov, R., & Wolfson, H. J. (2005). PatchDock and SymmDock: Servers for rigid and symmetric docking. *Nucleic Acids Research, 33*, W363-367. doi: 10.1093/nar/gki481

Schrödinger, E. (1944). *What Is Life? The physical aspect of the living cell*. Retrieved 9 March 2014 from http://whatislife.stanford.edu/LoCo_files/What-is-Life.pdf

Schuler, G. D. (1997). Sequence mapping by electronic PCR. *Genome Research, 7*(5), 541–550. PMID:9149949

Schut, G. J., Zhou, J., & Adams, M. W. (2001). DNA microarray analysis of the hyperthermophilic archaeon *Pyrococcus furi-osus*: Evidence for a new type of sulfur-reducing enzyme complex. *Journal of Bacteriology, 183*(24), 7027–7036. doi:10.1128/JB.183.24.7027-7036.2001 PMID:11717259

Schwartz, E. (2013, October 28). Supercomputing inches toward mHealth. *Mhealthnews.*

Schwartz, S., Zhang, Z., Frazer, K. A., Smit, A., Riemer, C., & Bouck, J. et al. (2000). PipMaker--a web server for aligning two genomic DNA sequences. *Genome Research, 10*(4), 577–586. doi:10.1101/gr.10.4.577 PMID:10779500

Scott, S. (2007). *Future supercomputer architectures*. Paper presented at Frontiers of Extreme Computing 2007, Santa Cruz, CA.

Scrofano, R., Gokhale, M., Trouw, F., & Prasanna, V. K. (2006). A hardware/software approach to molecular dynamics on reconfigurable computers. In *Proceedings of FCCM '06 - Field-Programmable Custom Computing Machines 14th Annual IEEE Symposium on Date of Conference* (pp. 23-34). IEEE. doi:10.1109/FCCM.2006.46

SDSC. (2014). *San Diego supercompuer center*. Retrieved April 17, 2014, from http://www.sdsc.edu/supercomputing/gordon/

SDSC. (2014). *San Diego supercompuer center*. Retrieved February 28, 2014, from http://www.sdsc.edu

Second Life. (2013). Retrieved 9 March 2014 http://secondlife.com/

Seemann, T. (2014). Prokka: Rapid prokaryotic genome annotation. *Bioinformatics (Oxford, England)*, *30*(14), 2068–2069. doi:10.1093/bioinformatics/btu153 PMID:24642063

Segall, R. S. (2013a). Dimensionalities of computation: From global supercomputing to data, text and web mining. *Invited Plenary Address at International Institute of Informatics and Systemics (IIIS) Conference, 17th World Multi-conference on Systemics, Cybernetics and Informatics (WMSCI 2013)*. Retrieved from http://www.iiis.org/ViewVideo2013.asp?id=14

Segall, R. S., & Cook, J. (2014). Data visualization and information quality by supercomputing. In *Proceedings of the Forty-Fifth Meeting of Southwest Decision Sciences Institute (SWDSI)*. Dallas, TX: Academic Press.

Segall, R. S., & Zhang, Q. (2013). Information quality and supercomputing. In *Proceedings of the 18th International Conference on Information Quality (ICIQ 2013)* (pp. 400-446). Academic Press.

Segall, R. S., Zhang, Q., & Cook, J. S. (2013). Overview of current research in global supercomputing. In *Proceedings of Forty-Fourth Meeting of Southwest Decision Sciences Institute (SWDSI)*. Albuquerque, NM: Academic Press.

Segall, R. S., Zhang, Q., & Pierce, R. (2010a). Data mining supercomputing with SAS JMP® genomics. In *Proceedings of 14th World Multi-Conference on Systemics, Cybernetics and Informatics: WMSCI 2010*. Orlando, FL: Academic Press.

Segall, R. S., Zhang, Q., & Pierce, R. M. (2009). Visualization by supercomputing data mining. In *Proceedings of the 4th INFORMS Workshop on Data Mining and System Informatics*. San Diego, CA: Academic Press.

Segall, R. S., Zhang, Q., & Pierce, R. M. (2010b). Data mining supercomputing with SAS JMP® genomics: Research-in-Progress. In *Proceedings of 2010 Conference on Applied Research in Information Technology*. University of Central Arkansas.

Segall, R. S. (2013b). Computational dimensionalities of global supercomputing. *Journal of Systemics, Cybernetics, and Informatics*, *11*(9), 75–86.

Segall, R. S., Zhang, Q., & Pierce, R. (2011). Data mining supercomputing with SAS JMP® genomics. *Journal of Systemics, Cybernetics and Informatics*, *9*(1), 28–33.

Seinfeld, J. H. (1986). *Atmospheric chemistry and physics of air pollution*. John Wiley & Sons. Retrieved on October 16, 2014 from http://pubs.acs.org/doi/abs/10.1021/es00151a602

Seruwagi, L., Khanh, L. Z., & Nguyen, N. (2012). Resource location transparency in clouds. *Project Report presented at Worcester Polytechnic Institute*.

Seymour Cray Facts. (2014). Retrieved May 30, 2014 from http://www.yourdictionary.com/seymour-cray

Shadbolt, P. J., Verde, M. R., Peruzzo, A., Politi, A., Laing, A., & Lobino, M. et al. (2011). Generating, manipulating and measuring entanglement and mixture with a reconfigurable photonic circuit. *Nature Photonics*, *6*(1), 45–49. doi:10.1038/nphoton.2011.283

Shah, A. (2013). *Dell working on ARM supercomputer prototypes*. Retrieved May 28, 2014 from http://www.pcworld.com/article/2032568/dell-working-on-arm-supercomputer-prototypes.html

Shahid, S., & Axtell, M. J. (2013). Identification and annotation of small RNA genes using ShortStack. *Methods (San Diego, Calif.)*. doi:10.1016/j.ymeth.2013.10.004 PMID:24139974

Shalon, D., Smith, S. J., & Brown, P. O. (1996). A DNA microarray system for analyzing complex DNA samples using two-color fluorescent probe hybridization. *Genome Research*, *6*(7), 639–645. doi:10.1101/gr.6.7.639 PMID:8796352

Shannon, C. (1948). A mathematical theory of communication. *The Bell System Technical Journal*, *27*(3), 379–423. doi:10.1002/j.1538-7305.1948.tb01338.x

Sheffer, H. M. (1913). A set of five independent postulates for Boolean algebras, with application to logical constants. *Transactions of the American Mathematical Society*, 14.

Sheldrake, R. (2013). *Rupert Sheldrake: Biologist and author*. Retrieved 9 March 2014 from http://www.sheldrake.org/homepage.html

Sheng, C., Sarwal, S. N., Watts, K. C., & Marble, A. E. (1995). Computational simulation of blood flow in human systemic circulation incorporating an external force field. *Medical & Biological Engineering & Computing*, *33*(1), 8–17. doi:10.1007/BF02522938 PMID:7616787

Shepler, B. (2006). *Introduction to computational quantum chemistry*. Retrieved 03/19, 2014, from http://public.wsu.edu/~pchemlab/documents/Intro-QM-Chem.ppt

Sherlock, R., & Morrey, J. D. (2002). *Ethical issues in biotechnology*. Maryland: Rowman and Littlefield Publishers.

Shi, Z. (2013). *Multi-agent environment - MAGE*. Intelligent Science Research Group, at Key Lab of IIP, ICT CAS, China. Retrieved December 2013. http://www.intsci.ac.cn/en/research/mage.html

Shielding Analysis Modular System (SAMSY). (n.d.). *OECD nuclear energy agency*. Retrieved on May 25, 2011 from http://www.oecd-nea.org/tools/abstract/detail/iaea0837

Shirk, A. J., & Cushman, S. A. (2011). sGD: Software for estimating spatially explicit indices of genetic diversity. *Molecular Ecology Resources*, *11*(5), 922–934. doi:10.1111/j.1755-0998.2011.03035.x PMID:21679313

Shvachko, K., Kuang, H., Radia, S., & Chansler, R. (2010). The Hadoop distributed file system. In *Proceedings of 26ᵗʰ IEEE Symposium on Mass Storage Systems and Technologies (MSST)* (pp. 1-10). IEEE. doi:10.1109/MSST.2010.5496972

Siebens, J. & Ryan, C. L. (2012, February). *Field of bachelor's degree in the United States: 2009*. U.S. Census Bureau.

Sievers, F., Wilm, A., Dineen, D., Gibson, T. J., Karplus, K., & Li, W. et al. (2011). Fast, scalable generation of high-quality protein multiple sequence alignments using Clustal Omega. *Molecular Systems Biology*, *7*(1), 539. doi:10.1038/msb.2011.75 PMID:21988835

Sim, L. (2014). *Introduction to ARCHER and Cray MPI*. Retrieved May 29, 2014 from http://www.archer.ac.uk/training/courses/introandmpi.php

Simons, K. T., Kooperberg, C., Huang, E., & Baker, D. (1997). Assembly of protein tertiary structures from fragments with similar local sequences using simulated annealing and Bayesian scoring functions. *Journal of Molecular Biology*, *268*(1), 209–225. doi:10.1006/jmbi.1997.0959 PMID:9149153

Simossis, V. A., & Heringa, J. (2005). PRALINE: A multiple sequence alignment toolbox that integrates homology-extended and secondary structure information. *Nucleic Acids Research, 33*(Web Server issue), W289-294. doi: 10.1093/nar/gki390

Singh, A. et al. (2013). A review on DNA microarray technology. *International Journal of Current Research and Review*, *05*(22), 5.

Singh, N., & Krishnan, V. R. (2008). Self-sacrifice and transformational leadership: Mediating role of altruism. *Leadership and Organization Development Journal*, *29*(3), 261–274. doi:10.1108/01437730810861317

Singh, N., & Warshel, A. (2010). Absolute binding free energy calculations: On the accuracy of computational scoring of protein-ligand interactions. *Proteins*, *78*(7), 1705–1723. doi:10.1002/prot.22687 PMID:20186976

Sivasankar, S., Subramaniam, S., & Leckband, D. (1998). Direct molecular level measurements of the electrostatic properties of a protein surface. *Proceedings of the National Academy of Sciences of the United States of America*, *95*(22), 12961–12966. doi:10.1073/pnas.95.22.12961 PMID:9789023

Skotte, L., Korneliussen, T. S., & Albrechtsen, A. (2013). Estimating individual admixture proportions from next generation sequencing data. *Genetics*, *195*(3), 693–702. doi:10.1534/genetics.113.154138 PMID:24026093

Slade, D. H. (Ed.). (1986). *Meteorology and atomic energy*. U.S. Atomic Energy Commission, Air Resources Laboratories, Research Laboratories, Environmental Science Services Administration, U.S Department of Commerce. Retrieved on October 16, 2014 from http://www.orau.org/ptp/PTP%20Library/library/Subject/Meteorology/meteorology%20and%20atomic%20energy.pdf

Smith, C., Heyne, S., Richter, A. S., Will, S., & Backofen, R. (2010). Freiburg RNA Tools: A web server integrating INTARNA, EXPARNA and LOCARNA. *Nucleic Acids Research, 38*(Web Server issue), W373-377. doi: 10.1093/nar/gkq316

Smolin, L. (2001). *Three roads to quantum gravity*. New York: Basic Books.

Smotherman, M. (2013). *S1 supercomputer (1975-1988)*. Retrieved May 30, 2014 from http://people.cs.clemson.edu/~mark/s1.html

Snider, L. (2012). *NCAR's new supercomputer set to run models by summer's end*. Retrieved May 29, 2014 from http://www.dailycamera.com/ci_20817203/ncars-new-supercomputer-set-run-models-by-summers

Sodan, A. C., Machina, J., Deshmeh, A., Macnaughton, K., & Esbaugh, B. (2010). Parallelism via multithreaded and multicore CPUs. *Computer*, *43*(3), 24–32. doi:10.1109/MC.2010.75

Softberry, I. (2007). *SCAN2*. Mount Kisco, NY: Softberry, Inc. Retrieved April 17, 2014, from http://linux1.softberry.com/

Sokal, R. R. (1991). The continental population-structure of Europe. *Annual Review of Anthropology*, *20*(1), 119–140. doi:10.1146/annurev.an.20.100191.001003

Solovyev, V. V., Salamov, A. A., & Lawrence, C. B. (1994). Predicting internal exons by oligonucleotide composition and discriminant analysis of spliceable open reading frames. *Nucleic Acids Research, 22*(24), 5156–5163. doi:10.1093/nar/22.24.5156 PMID:7816600

Solovyev, V. V., Salamov, A. A., & Lawrence, C. B. (1995). Identification of human gene structure using linear discriminant functions and dynamic programming. *Proceedings of the International Conference on Intelligent Systems for Molecular Biology, 3*, 367–375. PMID:7584460

Spencer-Brown, G. (1972). *Laws of form.* New York: The Julian Press, Inc.

Staff, I. E. P. (2014). Deductive and inductive arguments. *Internet Encyclopedia of Philosophy.* Retrieved 9 March 2014 from http://www.iep.utm.edu/ded-ind/

Stanford Project. (n.d.). *Investigating the cosmos.* Retrieved from http://setistars.org/

Stein, J. (2013, May 20). Millennials: The me, me, me generation. *Time, 181*(19), 26–34.

Stein, L. (2001). Genome annotation: From sequence to biology. *Nature Reviews. Genetics, 2*(7), 493–503. doi:10.1038/35080529 PMID:11433356

Stern. (1988). *Matrix logic.* Amsterdam: North Holland.

Stone, J., Phillips, J., Hardy, D., Roberts, E., & Saam, J. (n.d.). *GPU acceleration of molecular modeling applications.* Retrieved 03/18, 2014, from http://www.ks.uiuc.edu/Research/gpu/

Straatsma, T. P. (2013). *A vision for eXtreme scale computing at Pacific northwest national laboratory.* Retrieved March 18, 2014, from http://xsci.pnnl.gov/

Stranger, B. E., Stahl, E. A., & Raj, T. (2011). Progress and promise of genome-wide association studies for human complex trait genetics. *Genetics, 187*(2), 367–383. doi:10.1534/genetics.110.120907 PMID:21115973

Stratton, J. A., Rodrigues, C., Sung, I., Chang, L., Anssari, N., & Liu, G. et al. (2012). Algorithm and data optimization techniques for scaling to massively threaded systems. *Computer, 45*(8), 26–32. doi:10.1109/MC.2012.194

Stroschein, J., Jennewein, D., & Reynoldson, J. (2005). Building a bioinformatics supercomputing cluster. *Linux Journal, (133).*

Structure Based drug Design and Molecular Modeling. (n.d.). Retrieved June 16, 2014 from http://www.imb-jena.de/~rake/Bioinformatics_WEB/dd_tools.html

STScI. (2012). *Space telescope science institute.* Retrieved 20 October 2014, from http://www.stsci.edu/portal/

Sturrock, S., & Collins, J. (1993). *MPsrch version 1.3.* Biocomputing Research Unit University of Edinburgh. Retrieved April 17, 2014, from http://www.ebi.ac.uk/Tools/MPsrch/

Subramanian, A. R., Kaufmann, M., & Morgenstern, B. (2008). DIALIGN-TX: Greedy and progressive approaches for segment-based multiple sequence alignment. *Algorithms for Molecular Biology; AMB, 3*(1), 6. doi:10.1186/1748-7188-3-6 PMID:18505568

Sullivan, T. (2014). *Can blackberry advance supercomputing in healthcare?* Retrieved May 30, 2014 from http://www.mhealthnews.com/news/can-blackberry-supercomputing-healthcare-nanthealth-mhealth-mobile-cloud

Sundberg, S. A., Chow, A., Nikiforov, T., & Wada, G. (2001). Microchip-based systems for biomedical and pharmaceutical analysis. *European Journal of Pharmaceutical Sciences, 14*(1), 1–12. doi:10.1016/S0928-0987(01)00153-1 PMID:11457644

Sunway BlueLight Supercomputer in Operation. (2012, January 19). *Chinadaily.*

Supercomputer Hermit. (2013). Retrieved May 29, 2014 from http://www.gauss-centre.eu/gauss-centre/EN/AboutGCS/Locations/HLRS/hermit.html?nn=1282612

Supercomputer. (2014). Retrieved May 30, 2014 from http://encyclopedia2.thefreedictionary.com/High+performance+computer

Supercomputer. (n.d.). Retrieved 9 March 2014 from http://en.wikipedia.org/wiki/Supercomputer

Supercomputing in China. (2014). Retrieved from http://en.wikipedia.org/wiki/Supercomputing_in_China

Supercomputing in Europe. (2014). Retrieved from http://en.wikipedia.org/wiki/Supercomputing_in_Europe

Supercomputing in India. (n.d.). In *Wikipedia*. Retrieved from http://en.wikipedia.org/wiki/Supercomputing_in_India

Supercomputing in Japan. (2014). Retrieved from http://en.wikipedia.org/wiki/Supercomputing_in_Japan

Supercomputing in Pakistan. (2014). Retrieved from http://en.wikipedia.org/wiki/Supercomputing_in_Pakistan

Superimpose. (2010). Retrieved June 16, 2014 from http://www.scfbio-iitd.res.in/software/utility/Superimpose.jsp

Su, X., Pan, W., Song, B., Xu, J., & Ning, K. (2014). Parallel-META 2.0: Enhanced metagenomic data analysis with functional annotation, high performance computing and advanced visualization. *PLoS ONE, 9*(3), e89323. doi:10.1371/journal.pone.0089323 PMID:24595159

Swarm Intelligence. (n.d.). Retrieved 9 March 2014 from http://en.wikipedia.org/wiki/Swarm_intelligence

Swiss National Supercomputing Centre. (2014). *Piz daint.* Retrieved from http://www.cscs.ch/computers/piz_daint/index.html

Szczepariski, A. F., Huang, J., Baer, T., Mack, Y. C., & Ahern, S. (2013). Data analysis and visualization in high-performance computing. *Computer, 46*(May), 84–92. doi:10.1109/MC.2012.192

Szczypiorski, K. (2003). *Steganography in TCP/IP networks: State of the art and a proposal of a new system - HICCUPS.* Paper presented at the Institute of Telecommunications Seminar. New York, NY.

Sze, S. H., & Pevzner, P. A. (1997). Las Vegas algorithms for gene recognition: Suboptimal and error-tolerant spliced alignment. *Journal of Computational Biology, 4*(3), 297–309. doi:10.1089/cmb.1997.4.297 PMID:9278061

Tae-il, K. et al. (2013). Injectable, cellular-scale optoelectronics with applications for wireless optogenetics. *Science, 211*(340). doi:10.1126/science.1232437

Takamatsu, Y., & Itai, A. (1998). A new method for predicting binding free energy between receptor and ligand. *Proteins, 33*(1), 62–73. doi:10.1002/(SICI)1097-0134(19981001)33:1<62::AID-PROT6>3.0.CO;2-N PMID:9741845

Takezaki, N., Nei, M., & Tamura, K. (2010). POPTREE2: Software for constructing population trees from allele frequency data and computing other population statistics with Windows interface. *Molecular Biology and Evolution, 27*(4), 747–752. doi:10.1093/molbev/msp312 PMID:20022889

Talia, D. (2006). Grid-based distributed data mining systems, algorithms and services. In *Proceedings of HPDM 2006: The 9th International Workshop on High Performance and Distributed Mining.* Bethesda, MD: Academic Press.

Tallent, N. R., & Mellor-Crummey, J. M. (2009). Identifying performance bottlenecks in work-stealing computations. *Computer, 42*(12), 44–50. doi:10.1109/MC.2009.396

Taniguchi, N. (1974). On the basic concept of nanotechnology. In *Proc. Intl. Conf. Prod. Eng. Tokyo:* Japan Society of Precision Engineering.

Tao, H., Bausch, C., Richmond, C., Blattner, F. R., & Conway, T. (1999). Functional genomics: Expression analysis of *Escherichia coli* growing on minimal and rich media. *Journal of Bacteriology, 181*, 6425–6440. PMID:10515934

Tapscott, D., & Williams, W. (2006). *Wikinomics.* New York: Penguin Group.

Taylor, B. W., & Dunbar, A. M. (1975). *Achievement in foundations courses related to cognitive level or major?.* ERIC Clearinghouse.

Taylor, E. (2010). *Using supercomputers to explore nuclear energy.* Retrieved March 10, 2014 from: http://www.anl.gov/articles/using-supercomputers-explore-nuclear-energy#sthash.ILDPRyIl.dpufanl.gov.

Taylor, K. (2014). Altera announces high-efficiency power conversion solution for high-performance FPGAs. *Market Watch.* Retrieved March 18, 2014, from http://www.marketwatch.com/story/altera-announces-high-efficiency-power-conversion-solution-for-high-performance-fpgas-2014-04-07?reflink=MW_news_stmp

Taylor, B. W., &Dunbar, A. M. (1983). An investigation of college students' academic achievement based on their Piagetian cognitive level and ACT scores. *Psychological Reports, 53*(3). doi:10.2466/pr0.1983.53.3.923

Taylor, P., Blackburn, E., Sheng, Y. G., Harding, S., Hsin, K. Y., & Kan, D. et al. (2008). Ligand discovery and virtual screening using the program LIDAEUS. *British Journal of Pharmacology*, *153*, 555–567. PMID:18037921

Taylor, R. D., Jewsbury, P. J., & Essex, J. W. (2003). FDS: Flexible ligand and receptor docking with a continuum solvent model and soft-core energy function. *Journal of Computational Chemistry*, *24*(13), 1637–1656. doi:10.1002/jcc.10295 PMID:12926007

Team, M. R. C. (2012). *Supercomputers on demand with Windows Azure*. Retrieved September 22, 2013, from http://blogs.msdn.com/b/msr_er/archive/2012/11/12/affordable-supercomputing-with-windows-azure.aspx

Technology Leadership and Strategy Initiative. (2012). Retrieved May 28, 2013 from http://www.compete.org/about-us/initiatives/tlsi

Templeton, A. R. (2006). *Population genetics and micro-evolutionary theory*. New Jersey: John Wiley and Sons. doi:10.1002/0470047356

Tennessen, J. A., Bigham, A. W., O'Connor, T. D., Fu, W., Kenny, E. E., & Gravel, S. et al. (2012). Evolution and functional impact of rare coding variation from deep sequencing of human exomes. *Science*, *337*(6090), 64–69. doi:10.1126/science.1219240 PMID:22604720

Tewari, S., & Spouge, J. L. (2012). Coalescent: An open-source and scalable framework for exact calculations in coalescent theory. *BMC Bioinformatics*, *13*(1), 257. doi:10.1186/1471-2105-13-257 PMID:23033878

Texas Multicore Technologies, Inc. (2012). *SequenceL*. Retrieved 20 October 2014, from http://www.texasmulticoretechnologies.com/

The International HapMap Consortium. (2005). A haplotype map of the human genome. *Nature*, *437*(7063), 1299–1320. doi:10.1038/nature04226 PMID:16255080

Theimer, M. M., Lantz, K. A., & Cheriton, D. R. (1985). Preemptable remote execution facilities for the V system. In *Proceedings of the 10th ACM Symposium on Operating System Principles*. Association for Computing Machinery. doi:10.1145/323647.323629

Thompson, J. D., Plewniak, F., Thierry, J., & Poch, O. (2000). DbClustal: Rapid and reliable global multiple alignments of protein sequences detected by database searches. *Nucleic Acids Research*, *28*(15), 2919–2926. doi:10.1093/nar/28.15.2919 PMID:10908355

Thornton, K. (2003). Libsequence: A C++ class library for evolutionary genetic analysis. *Bioinformatics (Oxford, England)*, *19*(17), 2325–2327. doi:10.1093/bioinformatics/btg316 PMID:14630667

Thornton, K. (2013). *Libsequence (version 1.7.9)*. University of Chicago.

Thorsen, O., Smith, B., Sosa, C. P., Jiang, K., Lin, H., Peters, A., & Feng, W. (2007). Parallel genomic sequence-search on a massively parallel system. New York, NY: Academic Press. doi:10.1145/1242531.1242542

Tian, Mulè, Paskevicius, & Dhal. (2008). Preparation, microstructure and hydrogen sorption properties of nanoporous carbon aerogels under ambient drying. *Nanotechnology IOP Science*, (19).

Tipler, F. (1994). *The physics of immortality: Modern cosmology and the resurrection of the dead*. New York: Doubleday.

Tittel, E. (2012). *Clusters for dummies*. New York: John Wiley.

Todd, T. (2013). *Harvard uses IBM supercomputer crowdsourcing to unearth new solar energy potential*. Retrieved on July 6, 2014 from http://turbotodd.com/blog/2013/06/24/harvard-uses-ibm-supercomputer-crowdsourcing-to-unearth-new-solar-energy-potential/

Tononi, G. (2008). Consciousness as integrated information: A provisional manifesto. *The Biological Bulletin*, *215*(3), 216–242. doi:10.2307/25470707 PMID:19098144

Top500. (2008). *Top500 June 2008: Roadrunner - BladeCenter QS22/LS21 cluster, PowerXCell 8i 3.2 Ghz/Opteron DC 1.8 GHz, Voltaire infiniband*. Retrieved April 17, 2014, from http://www.top500.org/system/176026

Top500. (2012, November). Retrieved from http://www.top500.org/lists/2012/11/

Top500. (2013). *Supercomputer sites*. Retrieved May 25, 2104 from http://www.top500.org/lists/2103/11

Top500. (2013). *Top500: Endeavor - Intel cluster*. Retrieved April 17, 2014, from http://www.top500.org/system/176908

Top500. (2013, November). Retrieved from http://www.top500.org/lists/2013/11/

Top500. (2013a). *Jade - SGI ICE 8200EX, Xeon E5450 4C 3.000GHz, Infiniband*. Retrieved February 28, 2014, from http://www.top500.org/system/176897

Top500. (2013b). *Titan - Cray XK7, Opteron 6274 16C 2.200GHz, Cray Gemini interconnect, NVIDIA K20x*. Retrieved March 1, 2014, from http://www.top500.org/system/177975

Top500. (2013c). *Top500 list supercomputer sites -June 2013*. Retrieved February 28, 2014, from http://www.top500.org/list/2013/06/?page=1

Top500. (2013d). *Top500 list supercomputer sites -November 2013*. Retrieved February 28, 2014, from http://www.top500.org/system/177455

Top500. (2013e). *Top 500 supercomputer site November 2013: CINECA*. Retrieved February 28, 2014, from http://www.top500.org/site/47495

Torrellas, J. (2009). Architectures for extreme-scale computing. *Computer*, 42(11), 28–35. doi:10.1109/MC.2009.341

Total, S. A. (2013). *Total inaugurates its new pangea supercomputer, ranking it among the global top ten in terms of computing power*. Retrieved May 22, 2014 from http://total.com/en/media/news/press-releases/20130321-Total-inaugurates-its-new-Pangea-supercomputer-ranking-it-among-the-global-top-ten-in-terms-of-computing-power

Totrov, M., & Abagyan, R. (2008). Flexible ligand docking to multiple receptor conformations: A practical alternative. *Current Opinion in Structural Biology*, 18(2), 178–184. doi:10.1016/j.sbi.2008.01.004 PMID:18302984

Trader, T. (2013). *Supercomputing raises materials science to new heights*. Paper presented at the International Supercomputing Conference, Leipzig, Germany.

Transhumanism. (n.d.). Retrieved 9 March 2014 from http://en.wikipedia.org/wiki/Transhumanism

Tretkoff, E. (2004). Dedicated supercomputers probe QCD theory. *APS Physics, 13*(3).

Troshin, P. V., Procter, J. B., & Barton, G. J. (2011). Java bioinformatics analysis web services for multiple sequence alignment--JABAWS:MSA. *Bioinformatics (Oxford, England)*, 27(14), 2001–2002. doi:10.1093/bioinformatics/btr304 PMID:21593132

Tuckerman, M. E., Berne, B. J., & Martyna, G. J. (1992). Reversible multiple time scale molecular dynamics. *The Journal of Chemical Physics*, 97(3), 1990–2001. doi:10.1063/1.463137

Tumeo, A., Simone, S., & Oreste, V. (2012). Designing next-generation massively multithreaded architectures for irregular applications. *Computer*, 45(8), 53–61. doi:10.1109/MC.2012.193

Turing, A. M. (1950). Computing machinery and intelligence. *Mind, 59*(236).

Turner, D. B. (1994). *Workbook of atmospheric dispersion estimates: An introduction to dispersion modeling* (2nd ed.). Lewis Publishers. Retrieved on October 16, 2014 from http://www.crcpress.com/product/isbn/9781566700238

Turner, D. B. (1979). Atmospheric dispersion modeling. *Journal of the Air Pollution Control Association*, 29(5), 502–519. doi:10.1080/00022470.1979.10470821

Turner, D. B., Bender, L. W., Pierce, T. E., & Petersen, W. B. (1989). Air quality simulation models from EPA. *Environmental Software*, 4(2), 52–61. doi:10.1016/0266-9838(89)90031-2

Tuulos, V. (2008). *The Hadoop distributed file system*. Retrieved February 13, 2013, from: http://commons.wikimedia.org/wiki/File:Mapreduce_(Ville_Tuulos).png

Tzeng, S., Brandon, L., & Owens, J. D. (2012). A GPU task-parallel model with dependency resolution. *Computer*, 45(8), 34–41. doi:10.1109/MC.2012.255

U.S. Census Bureau. (2011, September). *Doctorates awarded by field of study and year of study: 2000 to 2009, table 815*. Retrieved June 7, 2013, from www.census.gov/compendia/statab/2012/tables/12s0815.pdf

U.S. Census Bureau. (2011, September). *Doctorates conferred by recipients' characteristics: 2009, table 814*. Retrieved June 6, 2013, from www.census.gov/compendia/statab/2012/tables/12s0814.xls

U.S. Department of Education, National Center for Education Statistics. (2012, June) *Bachelor's degrees conferred by degree-granting institutions, by race/ethnicity and field of study: 2009-10 and 2010-11, Table 301*. Retrieved June 7, 2013 from nces.ed.gov/programs/digest/d12/tables/xls/tabn301.xls

U.S. Department of Education, National Center for Education Statistics. (2012, May). *Number of master's and doctor's degrees awarded by degree-granting institutions, percentage of total, number and percentage awarded to females, and percent change, by selected fields of study: Academic years 1999–2000 and 2009–10*. Condition of Education 2012 (NCES 2012-045), Indicator 39, Table A-39-1. Retrieved June 7, 2013 from http://nces.ed.gov/pubs2012/2012045_5.pdf

U.S. Department of Education. (2011). *Bachelor's degrees conferred by degree-granting institutions, by race/ethnicity and field of study: 2009-10 and 2010-11, table 301*. Digest of Education Statistics. Retrieved June 7, 2013 from http://nces.ed.gov/programs/digest/2011menu_tables.asp

Uberbacher, E. (n.d.). *Computing the genome*. Retrieved 03/19, 2014, from http://web.ornl.gov/info/ornlreview/v30n3-4/genome.htmhttp://web.ornl.gov/info/ornlreview/v30n3-4/digital/p63b.gif

Uberbacher, E. C., & Mural, R. J. (1991). Locating protein-coding regions in human DNA sequences by a multiple sensor-neural network approach. *Proceedings of the National Academy of Sciences of the United States of America*, 88(24), 11261–11265. doi:10.1073/pnas.88.24.11261 PMID:1763041

Uberbacher, E. C., Xu, Y., & Mural, R. J. (1996). Discovering and understanding genes in human DNA sequence using GRAIL. *Methods in Enzymology*, 266, 259–281. doi:10.1016/S0076-6879(96)66018-2 PMID:8743689

Union of Concerned Scientists. (n.d.). Retrieved 9 March 2014 from http://www.ucsusa.org/

United States Environment Protection Agency. (n.d.). Retrieved from http://www.epa.gov

United States Environmental Protection Agency. (1982). *Policy on excess emissions during startup, shutdown, maintenance, and malfunction*. Retrieved on October 16, 2014 from http://www2.epa.gov/sites/production/files/documents/excess-start-rpt.pdf

University of Texas at Austin Supercomputing Center to Receive $10 million in Private Funding. (2012, February 21). *Primeur Weekly Magazine*.

Valafar, F. (2002). Pattern recognition techniques in microarray data analysis: A survey. *Annals of the New York Academy of Sciences*, 980(1), 41–64. doi:10.1111/j.1749-6632.2002.tb04888.x PMID:12594081

van Aalten, D. M., Findlay, J. B., Amadei, A., & Berendsen, H. J. (1995). Essential dynamics of the cellular retinol-binding protein--evidence for ligand-induced conformational changes. *Protein Engineering*, 8(11), 1129–1135. doi:10.1093/protein/8.11.1129 PMID:8819978

van der Steen, A. J. (2005). *Overview of recent supercomputers*. Retrieved from http://citeseerx.ist.psu.edu/viewdoc/download?doi=10.1.1.63.3326&rep=rep1&type=pdf

Van Nooten, B. (2010). Binary numbers in Indian antiquity. *Journal of Indian Philosophy*, 21(1), 31–50. doi:10.1007/BF01092744

Varadarajan, S. (2004). *System X: Building the Virginia Tech supercomputer*. Paper presented at the 13th International Conference on Computer Communications and Networks. New York, NY. doi:10.1109/ICCCN.2004.1401571

Veda, R. (n.d.). Hymn CXXIX – Creation, Book the tenth. Rig Veda. *Oxford Companion to Philosophy*. Retrieved 9 March 2014 from http://www.answers.com/topic/ancient-philosophy#Indian_philosophy

Venter, J. C., Adams, M. D., Myers, E. W., Li, P. W., Mural, R. J., & Sutton, G. G. et al. (2001). The sequence of the human genome. *Science*, 291(5507), 1304–1351. doi:10.1126/science.1058040 PMID:11181995

Vermij, E. P. (2011). *Genetic sequence alignment on a supercomputing platform*. Netherlands: TU Delft.

Vetter, J. S. (2013). Contemporary high performance computing: From petascale toward exascale. Chapman & Hall/CRC Computational Science.

Viennas, E., Gkantouna, V., Ioannou, M., Georgitsi, M., Rigou, M., & Poulas, K. et al. (2012). Population-ethnic group specific genome variation allele frequency data: A querying and visualization journey. *Genomics*, *100*(2), 93–101. doi:10.1016/j.ygeno.2012.05.009 PMID:22659238

Vieru, T. (2010). New computer model shows nuclear fission. *Softpedia World Nuclear News*. Retrieved March 10, 2014 from: http://news.softpedia.com/news/New-Computer-Model-Shows-Nuclear-Fission-132990.shtml

Vilella, A. J., Severin, J., Ureta-Vidal, A., Heng, L., Durbin, R., & Birney, E. (2009). EnsemblCompara GeneTrees: Complete, duplication-aware phylogenetic trees in vertebrates. *Genome Research*, *19*(2), 327–335. doi:10.1101/gr.073585.107 PMID:19029536

Villegas, D., Rodero, I., Fong, L., Bobroff, N., Liu, Y., Parashar, M., & Sadjadi, M. (2010). The role of grid computing technologies in cloud computing. In *Handbook of cloud computing* (pp. 183–218). Springer; doi:10.1007/978-1-4419-6524-0_8

Vitalis, R. (2012). DETSEL: An R-package to detect marker loci responding to selection. *Methods in Molecular Biology (Clifton, N.J.)*, *888*, 277–293. doi:10.1007/978-1-61779-870-2_16 PMID:22665287

Vitkup, D., Melamud, E., Moult, J., & Sander, C. (2001). Completeness in structural genomics. *Nature Structural Biology*, *8*(6), 559–566. doi:10.1038/88640 PMID:11373627

Voelz, V. A., Bowman, G. R., Beauchamp, K., & Pande, V. S. (2010). Molecular simulation of ab initio protein folding for a millisecond folder NTL9(1–39). *Journal of the American Chemical Society*, *132*(5), 1526–1528. doi:10.1021/ja9090353 PMID:20070076

Voinova, M. V., Jonson, M., & Kasemo, B. (2002). Missing mass effect in biosensor's QCM applications. *Biosensors and Bioelectronics*, *17*(10), 835-841.

von Haeseler, A., Sajantila, A., & Paabo, S. (1996). The genetical archaeology of the human genome. *Nature Genetics*, *14*(2), 135–140. doi:10.1038/ng1096-135 PMID:8841181

Voorrips, R. E., & Maliepaard, C. A. (2012). The simulation of meiosis in diploid and tetraploid organisms using various genetic models. *BMC Bioinformatics*, *13*(1), 248. doi:10.1186/1471-2105-13-248 PMID:23013469

Wagstaff, K. (2012). What exactly is a supercomputer? *Time*, *19*(June). Retrieved from http://techland.time.com/2012/06/19/what-exactly-is-a-supercomputer/

Wakeley, J. (2004). Recent trends in population genetics: More data! More math! Simple models? *The Journal of Heredity*, *95*(5), 397–405. doi:10.1093/jhered/esh062 PMID:15388767

Wall, M., Rechtsteiner, A., & Rocha, L. (n.d.). *Singular value decomposition and principal component analysis*. Retrieved June 16, 2014 from http://public.lanl.gov/mewall/kluwer2002.html

Wang, Z., Liu, Z., & Liu, F. (2013). Engineers show feasibility of superfast materials: 'Organic topological insulators' for quantum computing. *Science News Web*. Retrieved March 18, 2014, from http://www.sciencedaily.com/releases/2013/02/130213132431.htm

Wang, Q., & Pang, Y. P. (2007). Preference of small molecules for local minimum conformations when binding to proteins. *PLoS ONE*, *2*(9), e820. doi:10.1371/journal.pone.0000820

Warren, A. S., Archuleta, J., Feng, W. C., & Setubal, J. C. (2010). Missing genes in the annotation of prokaryotic genomes. *BMC Bioinformatics*, *11*(1), 131. doi:10.1186/1471-2105-11-131 PMID:20230630

Warren, P., & Streeter, M. (2013). *Cyber crime & warfare: All that matters*. London: Hodder & Stoughton.

Washington Times. (2005, November 18). *Gen Y knocking on at the door of ownership*. Retrieved May 28, 2013 from http://www.washingtontimes.com/news/2005/nov/17/20051117-083543-6983r/?page=all

Wass, M. N., Kelley, L. A., & Sternberg, M. J. (2010). 3DLigandSite: Predicting ligand-binding sites using similar structures. *Nucleic Acids Research*, *38*, W469-473. doi: 10.1093/nar/gkq406

Watson, J. D. (2003). *DNA: The secret of life*. New York: Random House.

Webb, Z., & Childs, A. (2013). Researchers propose breakthrough architecture for quantum computers. *R&D Magazine*. Retrieved March 18, 2014, from http://www.rdmag.com/news/2013/02/researchers-propose-break-through-architecture-quantum-computers

Webb-Roberts, B.-J. (2004). *Protein & DNA sequence analysis*. Retrieved February 10, 2013, from http://www.sysbio.org/resources/tutorials/sequence_analysis_webb.pdf

Weber, M. (2003). *The protestant ethic and the spirit of capitalism*. New York: Charles Scribner and Sons.

Wei, B. Q., Weaver, L. H., Ferrari, A. M., Matthews, B. W., & Shoichet, B. K. (2004). Testing a flexible-receptor docking algorithm in a model binding site. *Journal of Molecular Biology*, *337*(5), 1161–1182. doi:10.1016/j.jmb.2004.02.015 PMID:15046985

Wei, H., Wang, C. H., Du, Q. S., Meng, J., & Chou, K.-C. (2009). Investigation into adamantane-based M2 inhibitors with FB-QSAR. *Journal of Medicinal Chemistry*, *5*(4), 305–317. doi:10.2174/157340609788681430 PMID:19689387

Weiner, N. (1948). *Cybernetics, or communication and control in the animal and the machine*. Cambridge, MA: MIT Press.

Weir, B. S. (1996). Intraspecific differentiation. In D. M. Hillis, C. Moritz, & B. K. Mable (Eds.), *Molecular systematics* (2nd ed.; pp. 385–406). Massachusetts: Sinauer Associates.

Weiser, E. L., Grueber, C. E., & Jamieson, I. G. (2012). AlleleRetain: A program to assess management options for conserving allelic diversity in small, isolated populations. *Molecular Ecology Resources*, *12*(6), 1161–1167. doi:10.1111/j.1755-0998.2012.03176.x PMID:22925629

Werner, T., Morris, M. B., Dastmalchi, S., & Church, W. B. (2012). Structural modelling and dynamics of proteins for insights into drug interactions. *Advanced Drug Delivery Reviews*, *64*(4), 323–343. doi:10.1016/j.addr.2011.11.011 PMID:22155026

What is a Beowulf?. (n.d.) Retrieved May 30, 2014 from http://yclept.ucdavis.edu/Beowulf/aboutbeowulf.html

What is Cloud Computing ?. (2014). Retrieved on July 6, 2014 from http://www.amazon.com/what-is-cloud-computing/

What's Next in Medical Imaging. (2007). *High-Def Ultra-sounds*. Pharma Investments, Ventures, and Law Weekly.

Wheeler, J. A. (1973). *Gravitation. San Fransisco*. W.H. Freeman and Company.

Wheeler, J. A. (1990). Information, physics, quantum: The search for links. In W. Zurek (Ed.), *Complexity, entropy, and the physics of information*. Redwood City, CA: Addison-Wesley.

Wheeler, J. A., & Ford, K. (1998). *Geons, black holes, and quantum foam: A life in physics*. New York: W. W. Norton & Co.

White, T. (2010). *Hadoop: The definitive guide*. Sebastopol, CA: O'Reilly Media, Inc.

Whittaker, Z. (2012). *U.S. IBM supercomputer is world's fastest: Does it matter?* Retrieved from http://www.zdnet.com/blog/btl/u-s-ibm-supercomputer-is-worlds-fastest-does-it-matter/80122

Whorf. (1959). *Language thought and reality*. MIT Press.

Wikipedia. (2012). *Control theory*. Retrieved March 10, 2014 from: http://en.wikipedia.org/wiki/Control_theory

Wikipedia. (2013). *Molecular dynamics*. Retrieved March 10, 2014 from: http://en.wikipedia.org/wiki/Molecular_dynamics

Wikipedia. (2013). *Orders of magnitude (computing)*. Retrieved March 18, 2014, from http://en.wikipedia.org/wiki/Orders_of_magnitude_%28computing%29

Wikipedia. (2013). *Quantum computer*. Retrieved March 18, 2014, from http://en.wikipedia.org/wiki/Quantum_computer

Wikipedia. (2014a). *Cray*. Retrieved May 25, 2014 from http://en.wikipedia.org/wiki/Cray

Wikipedia. (2014b). *Flynn's taxonomy*. Retrieved May 25, 2014 from http://en.wikipedia.org/wiki/Flynn%27s_taxonomy

Wikipedia. (2014c). *Human Brian project*. Retrieved May 25, 2014 from http//en.wikipedia.org/wiki/Human_Brian_Project

Wikipedia. (2014d). *Jungle computing*. Retrieved May 25, 2014 from http://en.wikipedia.org/wiki/Jungle_computing

Wikipedia. (2014e). *Multiprocessing*. Retrieved May 25, 2104 from http://en.wikipedia.org/wiki/Multiprocessing

Wikipedia. (2014f). *Supercompter*. Retrieved 5/25, 2014 from http://en.wikipedia.org/wiki/Supercomputer

Wikipedia. (2014g). *Tianhe-2, or Milky Way-2*. Retrieved May 25, 2014 from http://en.wikipedia.org/wiki/Tianhe-2

Wikipedia. (2014h). *Top500*. Retrieved 5/25, 2014 from http://en.wikipedia.org/wiki/Top500

Wikipedia. (2014i). *Vector processing*. Retrieved May 25, 2014 from http://en.wikipedia.org/wiki/Vector_processing

Wikipedia.org. (2013). *Folding@home*. Retrieved March 10, 2014 from: http://en.wikipedia.org/wiki/Folding@home

Wilde, M., Foster, I., Iskra, K., Beckman, P., Zhang, A., & Espinosa, A. et al. (2009). Parallel scripting for applications at the petascale and beyond. *Computer*, *42*(11), 50–60. doi:10.1109/MC.2009.365

Wilkins, J. F. (2006). Unraveling male and female histories from human genetic data. *Current Opinion in Genetics & Development*, *16*(6), 611–617. doi:10.1016/j.gde.2006.10.004 PMID:17067791

Willighagen, E. (2011). *An ontology for QSAR and cheminformatics*. Retrieved June 16, 2014 from http://chem-bla-ics.blogspot.in/2011/10/ontology-for-qsar-and-cheminformatics.html

Wilson, M. C. (2004). *Closing the leadership gap: Why women can and must help run the world*. New York: Viking.

Wilson, M., DeRisi, J., Kristensen, H. H., Imboden, P., Rane, S., Brown, P. O., & Schoolnik, G. K. (1999). Exploring drug-induced alterations in gene expression in *Mycobacterium tuberculosis* by microarray hybridization. *Proceedings of the National Academy of Sciences of the United States of America*, *96*(22), 12833–12838. doi:10.1073/pnas.96.22.12833 PMID:10536008

Wilt, N. (2013). *CUDA handbook: A comprehensive guide to GPU programming*. Upper Saddle River, NJ: Pearson Education, Inc.

WintelGuy.com. (2014). *Gigabyte (GB) to Gibibyte (GiB) and Megabyte (MB) to Mibibyte (MiB) converter*. Retrieved from http://wintelguy.com/gb2gib.html

Winter, D. J. (2012). MMOD: An R library for the calculation of population differentiation statistics. *Molecular Ecology Resources*, *12*(6), 1158–1160. doi:10.1111/j.1755-0998.2012.03174.x PMID:22883857

Winztum, D. (1980). *The additional dimension, about the two-dimensional writing of the Genesis*. Jerusalem: The Organization of Bible Research Press.

Wolf, K., & Schaefer, B. (2004). The mitochondrial genetics of the budding yeast. In K. Esser (Ed.), The mycota: A comprehensive treatise on fungi as experimental systems for basic and applied research (2nd ed.; Vol. 2, p. 82). Germany: Springer-Verlag.

Wolf, M., Ruderisch, B., Dandekar, T., Schultz, J., & Muller, T. (2010). *ProfDistS version 0.9.9: A tool for the construction of large phylogenetic trees based on profile distances*. Department of Bioinformatics, University Würzburg.

Wolf, M., Ruderisch, B., Dandekar, T., Schultz, J., & Muller, T. (2008). ProfDistS: (profile-) distance based phylogeny on sequence--structure alignments. *Bioinformatics (Oxford, England)*, *24*(20), 2401–2402. doi:10.1093/bioinformatics/btn453 PMID:18723521

Wolfram, S. (2013). *Stephen Wolfram*. Retrieved 9 March 2014 from www.stephenwolfram.com/

Wood, D. E., & Salzberg, S. L. (2014). Kraken: Ultrafast metagenomic sequence classification using exact alignments. *Genome Biology*, *15*(3), R46. doi:10.1186/gb-2014-15-3-r46 PMID:24580807

Wuensche, A. (1993). The ghost in the machine: Basins of attraction of random Boolean networks. *Cognitive Science Research Papers CSRP 281*. Brighton, UK: University of Sussex.

Wuensche, Discrete Dynamics Lab. (n.d.). Retrieved 9 March 2014 from http://www.ddlab.com/

Wu, S., Skolnick, J., & Zhang, Y. (2007). Ab initio modeling of small proteins by iterative TASSER simulations. *BMC Biology*, 5(1), 17. doi:10.1186/1741-7007-5-17 PMID:17488521

Xilnix. (2014). *Field programmable gate array (FPGA)*. Retrieved March 18, 2014, from http://www.xilinx.com/training/fpga/fpga-field-programmable-gate-array.htm

Xu, D., Xu, Y., & Uberbacher, E. C. (2000). Computational tools for protein modeling. *Current Protein & Peptide Science*, 1(1), 1–21. doi:10.2174/1389203003381469 PMID:12369918

Xu, J., Li, M., Kim, D., & Xu, Y. (2003). RAPTOR: Optimal protein threading by linear programming. *Journal of Bioinformatics and Computational Biology*, 1(1), 95–117. doi:10.1142/S0219720003000186 PMID:15290783

Xu, Y., Mural, R., Shah, M., & Uberbacher, E. (1994). Recognizing exons in genomic sequence using GRAIL II. *Genetic Engineering*, 16, 241–253. PMID:7765200

Yamada, M. (2014). *Supercomputing pioneer*. Retrieved May 30, 2014 from http://www.fujitsu.com/global/solutions/business-technology/tc/hpc/

Yang, Y. (2006). *Bioinformatics resources for microarray data analysis, protein function/structure prediction, and protein-protein interaction*. Retrieved June 16, 2014 from http://dragon.bio.purdue.edu/bioinfolinks/

Yang, Z. (2007). PAML 4: Phylogenetic analysis by maximum likelihood. *Molecular Biology and Evolution*, 24(8), 1586–1591. doi:10.1093/molbev/msm088 PMID:17483113

Ye, X., Chen, J., & Xing, G. (2013). Research helps make advance in "programmable matter" using nanocrystals. *Phys.org*. Retrieved March 10, 2014 from:http://phys.org/news/2013-07-advance-programmable-nanocrystals.html

Yeh, R. F., Lim, L. P., & Burge, C. B. (2001). Computational inference of homologous gene structures in the human genome. *Genome Research*, 11(5), 803–816. doi:10.1101/gr.175701 PMID:11337476

Yellowstone (Supercomputer). (2013). Retrieved May 29, 2014 from http://en.wikipedia.org/wiki/Yellowstone_(supercomputer)

Ye, R. W., Tao, W., Bedzyk, L., Young, T., Chen, M., & Li, L. (2000). Global gene expression profiles of *Bacillus subtilis* grown under anaerobic conditions. *Journal of Bacteriology*, 182(16), 4458–4465. doi:10.1128/JB.182.16.4458-4465.2000 PMID:10913079

Ye, Y., Wei, B., Wen, L., & Rayner, S. (2013). BlastGraph: A comparative genomics tool based on BLAST and graph algorithms. *Bioinformatics (Oxford, England)*, 29(24), 3222–3224. doi:10.1093/bioinformatics/btt553 PMID:24068035

Yilmaz, A., & Yang, K. (2013). *Supercomputer simulations reveal mysteries of specific microwave effect*. Retrieved 03/18, 2014, from https://www.ices.utexas.edu/about/news/251/

Yoshida, K., Kobayashi, K., Miwa, Y., Kang, C. M., Matsunaga, M., & Yamaguchi, H. et al. (2001). Combined transcriptome and proteome analysis as a powerful approach to study genes under glucose repression in *Bacillus subtilis*. *Nucleic Acids Research*, 29(3), 683–692. doi:10.1093/nar/29.3.683 PMID:11160890

Young, R. A. (2000). Biomedical discovery with DNA arrays. *Cell*, 102(1), 9–15. doi:10.1016/S0092-8674(00)00005-2 PMID:10929708

Yue, F. (2013). *Network functions virtualization—Everything old is new again* (White Paper). Academic Press.

Yu, H., & Miller, P. (2005). Leadership style: The X generation and baby boomers compared in different cultural contexts. *Leadership and Organization Development Journal*, 26(1), 35–50. doi:10.1108/01437730510575570

Yuichiro, A., Sumimoto, S., & Toshiyuki, S. (2009). Tofu: A 6D mesh/torus interconnect for exascale computers. *Computer*, 42(11), 36–40. doi:10.1109/MC.2009.370

Zafar, N., Mazumder, R., & Seto, D. (2001). Comparisons of gene colinearity in genomes using GeneOrder2.0. *Trends in Biochemical Sciences*, *26*(8), 514–516. doi:10.1016/S0968-0004(01)01881-3 PMID:11504629

Zafar, N., Mazumder, R., & Seto, D. (2002). CoreGenes: A computational tool for identifying and cataloging "core" genes in a set of small genomes. *BMC Bioinformatics*, *3*(1), 12. doi:10.1186/1471-2105-3-12 PMID:11972896

Zammataro, L., DeMolfetta, R., Bucci, G., Ceol, A., & Muller, H. (2014). AnnotateGenomicRegions: A web application. *BMC Bioinformatics*, *15*(Suppl 1), S8. doi:10.1186/1471-2105-15-S1-S8 PMID:24564446

Zanini, F., & Neher, R. A. (2012). FFPopSim: An efficient forward simulation package for the evolution of large populations. *Bioinformatics (Oxford, England)*, *28*(24), 3332–3333. doi:10.1093/bioinformatics/bts633 PMID:23097421

Zax, R., & Adelstein, F. (2009). FAUST: Forensic artefacts of uninstalled steganography tools. *Digital Investigation*, *6*(1-2), 25–28. doi:10.1016/j.diin.2009.02.002

Zemke, R., Raines, C., & Filipczak, R. (1999). *Generations at work: Managing the clash of veterans, boomers, Xers and nexters in your workplace*. New York: AMACOM.

Zhang, C. (2013). *Tianhe-2: More than super computing*. Retrieved March 18, 2014, from http://heim.ifi.uio.no/xingca/201309.html

Zhang, C., Li, P., Rajendran, A., Deng, Y., & Chen, D. (2006). *Parallelization of multicategory support vector machines (PMC-SVM) for classifying microarray data*. Retrieved June 16, 2014 from http://link.springer.com/article/10.1186%2F1471-2105-7-S4-S15

Zhang, M. Q. (1997). Identification of protein coding regions in the human genome by quadratic discriminant analysis. *Proceedings of the National Academy of Sciences of the United States of America*, *94*(2), 565–568. doi:10.1073/pnas.94.2.565 PMID:9012824

Zhang, X., & Wang, S. (2004). Vulnerability of pixel-value differencing steganography to histogram analysis and modification for enhanced security. *Pattern Recognition Letters*, *25*(3), 331–339. doi:10.1016/j.patrec.2003.10.014

Zhang, Y. (2008a). Progress and challenges in protein structure prediction. *Current Opinion in Structural Biology*, *18*(3), 342–348. doi:10.1016/j.sbi.2008.02.004 PMID:18436442

Zhang, Y. (2009). Protein structure prediction: When is it useful? *Current Opinion in Structural Biology*, *19*(2), 145–155. doi:10.1016/j.sbi.2009.02.005 PMID:19327982

Zhang, Y., & Skolnick, J. (2004). Automated structure prediction of weakly homologous proteins on a genomic scale. *Proceedings of the National Academy of Sciences of the United States of America*, *101*(20), 7594–7599. doi:10.1073/pnas.0305695101 PMID:15126668

Zhang, Y., & Waterman, M. S. (2003). DNA sequence assembly and multiple sequence alignment by an Eulerian path approach. *Cold Spring Harbor Symposia on Quantitative Biology*, *68*(0), 205–212. doi:10.1101/sqb.2003.68.205 PMID:15338619

Zhao, K., & Chu, X. (2014). G-BLASTN: Accelerating nucleotide alignment by graphics processors. *Bioinformatics (Oxford, England)*, *30*(10), 1384–1391. doi:10.1093/bioinformatics/btu047 PMID:24463183

Zhou, H., Pandit, S. B., & Skolnick, J. (2009). Performance of the Pro-sp3-TASSER server in CASP8. *Proteins*, *77*(S9), 123–127. doi:10.1002/prot.22501 PMID:19639638

Zhou, X.-Q., Kalasuwan, P., Ralph, T. C., & O'Brien, J. L. (2013). Calculating unknown eigenvalues with a quantum algorithm. *Nature Photonics*, *7*(3), 223–228. doi:10.1038/nphoton.2012.360

Zhuo, L., & Prasanna, V. K. (2006). Scalable hybrid designs for linear algebra on reconfigurable computing systems. In *Proceedings of the 12th International Conference on Parallel and Distributed Systems*. Academic Press. doi:10.1109/ICPADS.2006.95

Zizzi, P. (2000). *Emergent consciousness: From the early universe to our mind*. arXiv:gr-qc/0007006.

Zizzi, P. (2004). *Spacetime at the Planck scale*. arXiv:gr-qc/0304032v2.

Zola, J., Yang, X., Rospondek, A., & Aluru, S. (2007). Parallel T-coffee: A parallel multiple sequence aligner. In *Proceedings of the ISCA 20th International Conference on Parallel and Distributed Computing Systems*. Academic Press.

Zoran, D. (2004). *Information hiding: Steganography & steganalysis*. George Mason University, Department of Computer Science.

Zsoldos, R. Z., Simon, D., Sadjad, A. S. B., & Johnson, A. P. (2007). eHiTS: A new fast, exhaustive flexible ligand docking system. *Journal of Molecular Graphics & Modelling, 26*(1), 198–212.

Zuegge, J., Ebeling, M., & Schneider, G. (2001). H-BloX: Visualizing alignment block entropies. *Journal of Molecular Graphics & Modelling, 19*(3-4), 304–306, 379. doi:10.1016/S1093-3263(00)00074-7 PMID:11449568

Zumbush, G. (2003). *Parallel multilevel methods: Adaptive mesh refinement and load balancing*. Wiesbaden, Germany: B.G. Teubner Verlag/GWV fachverlage GmbH.

Zumer, B. (2013). *New APG supercomputers can do a quadrillion operations in a second*. Retrieved May 28, 2014 from http://www.baltimoresun.com/news/maryland/harford/aberdeen-havre-de-grace/ph-ag-apg-supercomputer-0612-20130611,0,5032500.story

Zverina, J. (2014). *SDSC assists in whole-genome sequencing analysis under collaboration with Janssen*. Retrieved April 17, 2014, from http://ucsdnews.ucsd.edu/pressrelease/sdsc_assists_in_whole_genome_sequencing_analysis_under_collaboration_with_j

Zweden, S. (2012). *Computing degree and enrollment trends from the 2011-2012 CRA Taulbee survey*. Computing Research Association. Retrieved April 13, 2013 from http://cra.org/uploads/documents/resources/taulbee/CRA_Taulbee_CS_Degrees_and_Enrollment_2011-12.pdf

About the Contributors

Richard S. Segall is a Professor of Computer and Information Technology at Arkansas State University in Jonesboro. He holds a Bachelor of Science and Master of Science in Mathematics as well as a Master of Science in Operations Research and Statistics from Rensselaer Polytechnic Institute in Troy, New York. He also holds a PhD in Operations Research from University of Massachusetts in Amherst. He has served as a faculty member with Texas Tech University, University of Louisville, University of New Hampshire, University of Massachusetts-Lowell, and West Virginia University. Segall's publications have appeared in numerous journals including *International Journal of Information Technology and Decision Making* (IJITDM), *International Journal of Information and Decision Sciences* (IJIDS), *Applied Mathematical Modelling, Kybernetes: International Journal of Cybernetics, Systems and Management Science, Journal of Systemics, Cybernetics and Informatics (JSCI)*, and *Journal of the Operational Research Society* (JORS). He has published book chapters in *Encyclopedia of Data Warehousing and Mining, Handbook of Computational Intelligence in Manufacturing and Production Management, Handbook of Research on Text and Web Mining Technologies, Encyclopedia of Business Analytics & Optimization*, and *Encyclopedia of Information Science & Technology*. Segall's research interests include data mining, text mining, web mining, database management, and mathematical modeling, and supercomputing applications. His research has been funded by the U.S. Air Force, U.S. National Aeronautics and Space Administration (NASA), Arkansas Biosciences Institute (ABI), and Arkansas Science & Technology Authority (ASTA). Segall is a member of the Editorial Board of the *International Journal of Data Mining, Modelling and Management* (IJDMMM*), International Journal of Data Science* (IJDS*), Journal of Systemics, Cybernetics and Informatics (JSCI), The Open Cybernetics and Systemics Journal*, and *The Open Bioinformatics Journal*. He is also a member of the Arkansas Center for Plant-Powered Production (P3), recipient of Session Best Paper awards at the 2008, 2009, 2010, 2011 and 2013 World Multi-Conference on Systemics, Cybernetics and Informatics (WMSCI) conferences. He has served as Local Arrangements Chair of the 2010 MidSouth Computational Biology & Bioinformatics Society (MCBIOS) Conference. He was the co-editor of a book titled *Visual Analytics of Interactive Technologies: Applications to Data, Text and Web Mining* published in 2011 by IGI Global.

Jeffrey S. Cook lives in Jonesboro, Arkansas, where he is an entrepreneur in computer technology. He contributed a chapter entitled "Supercomputers and Supercomputing" in *Visual Analytics and Interactive Technologies: Data, Text and Web Mining Applications* edited by Qingyu Zhang, Richard Segall, and Mei Cao that was published by IGI Global in 2011. He worked as a BetaTester for the Microsoft Corporation in the development of Windows 2000 and Windows XP. Cook spent 9 years in the United States Army where he specialized in nuclear, biological, and chemical warfare agents as well as computer systems and foreign languages. He currently holds a patent in Aerospace-design that was adopted by Boeing Aerospace Corporation along with several other patents pertaining to software development. He is also a research writer who has published several books through McGraw-Hill College Division and Vantage Press. He has served for 6 years on the Republican National Committee (RNC) of The United States House of Representatives. Jeffrey S. Cook is listed in Cambridge's book of Who's Who for influential people.

Qingyu Zhang is a Professor of Management Science and Director of the Research Institute of Business Analytics and Supply Chain Management at Shenzhen University, China. He earned his Ph.D. in Manufacturing Management and Engineering from the College of Business Administration at the University of Toledo, USA. He is an APICS Certified Fellow in Production and Inventory Management (CFPIM). He is also a Microsoft certified MCSD, MCSE, and MCDBA. His work was featured in the *Journal of Operations Management, European Journal of Operational Research, International Journal of Production Research, International Journal of Production Economics, International Journal of Operations and Production Management, International Journal of Logistics Management, Journal of Systems Science and Systems Engineering, Kybernetes: International Journal of Systems and Cybernetics, Industrial Management & Data Systems, International Journal of Information Technology and Decision Making, International Journal of Product Development, International Journal of Quality and Reliability Management, and European Journal of Innovation Management.* Dr. Zhang's research interests include supply chain management, value chain flexibility, product development, and data mining. He serves on the Editorial Boards of the *Transportation Research Part E Logistics and Transportation Review, International Journal of Integrated Supply Management, Information Resource Management Journal, International Journal of Data Analysis Techniques and Strategy, Iranian Journal of Management Studies*, and *International Journal of Information Technology Project Management.*

* * *

Tianxing Cai is a Researcher in the Dan. F. Smith Department of Chemical Engineering at Lamar University. Tianxing specializes in the research fields of modeling, simulation and optimization for the industrial operation, process safety, and environment protection. His research focuses on the development of optimization models to realize the synthesis of energy and water systems, manufacturing, planning, and scheduling, and plant-wide optimization. Additionally, Tianxing has assisted in the development of numerous software applications, including Aspen, HYSYS, ProII, MATLAB and gPROMS. He conducts simulations of these applications to optimize their designs, reduce their environmental impact, and assess their safety for users.

Gerard G. Dumancas is a Chemistry Lecturer and Laboratory Stockroom Manager at the Oklahoma Baptist University. He previously worked as Postdoctoral Fellow at Oklahoma Medical Research Foundation from 2012-2014. He holds a PhD in Chemistry at Oklahoma State University (OSU) and a BS in Chemistry (cum laude) from the University of the Philippines, where he is also a Presidential Leadership Scholar. He was awarded the 2005 International Eco-Minds Pathfinder Award in Asia-Pacific for his research plan involving the utilization of cottonseed oil wastes as diesel replacement fuel. In 2009, he won the American Oil Chemists' Society's (AOCS) Analytical Division Student Award for Excellence in Analytical Chemistry Research. In 2010, he was awarded the 2010 AOCS Honored Student Award, the 2010 AOCS Analytical Division Student Award for Excellence in Analytical Chemistry Research, and the 2010 AOCS Hans Kaunitz Award for outstanding research, academics, and leadership involvement. In 2011, he won the 2011 Tony B. Award as one of the upcoming 51 scientists and engineers in the world recognized by the Laboratory Automation Organization in California. Gerard has published eight papers to date in international scientific journals. He has also co-authored six book chapters and has presented in both national and international conferences. His research interests include statistical genetics and chemometrics.

Venkat N. Gudivada, Ph.D., is a Professor and Interim Chair of the Weisberg Division of Computer Science at Marshall University, Huntington, West Virginia. He received his Ph.D. in Computer Science from the University of Louisiana at Lafayette. His current research interests encompass Big Data Analytics, Verification and Validation of SQL Queries, HPC-driven applications, and Personalized eLearning. He has published over sixty peer-reviewed technical papers. His industry experience includes over six years of tenure as a Vice President for numerous Wall Street companies, including Merrill Lynch and Financial Technologies International. Previous academic appointments include work at the University of Michigan, University of Missouri, and Ohio University. He is also a member of the IEEE Computer Society.

Neha Gupta was born and raised in Hyderabad, India. She holds a Bachelors of Science in Microbiology, Chemistry, and Genetics from the Nizam College of Osmania University, India. She holds a Masters of Science in Genetics from Osmania University, India, and a Masters of Science in Bioinformatics from Northeastern University, USA. Gupta has four years of research experience in Bioinformatics. She has also organized and presented for numerous research conferences within her field. Post-graduation, she has gained Bioinformatics industry experience through companies such as Knome Inc. and the Boston Children's Hospital, aiding in human genome research and interpretations. Her research interests include Bioinformatics, Human Genome Analysis, Next Generation Sequencing Analysis, big data, programming, machine learning, medical informatics, and data mining.

Kim Grover-Haskin received her B.A. in Dance and Psychology from the State University of New York, Potsdam, NY, in 1982. In 1986, she completed her M.S. in Dance at the University of Oregon, Eugene, Oregon, and in 2001, earned her Ph.D. in Dance and Related Arts from Texas Woman's University, Denton, TX. Kim worked for Texas Woman's University (TWU) for 24 years. Kim's expertise in Technology and Information Services included directing the management of classroom instructional technology, video technology services, and end-user support services. Over the course of 15 years with Information Technology, Kim managed classroom, service desk, and video operations. Kim focused on Learning Space design as well as an interactive classroom implementing Clickers (Classroom Response Systems) and Lecture Capture. In addition to a dynamic learning environment, Kim wanted faculty to have the support they needed in the classroom, and she pursued the integration of a touch panel help button for classrooms. Faculty could request assistance directly to the Information Technology (IT) Help Desk through the touch panel. As a result, Kim's classroom support team put TWU among the top 10 contenders for AMX Innovation Award in 2011 for its use of AMX in the classrooms. She assessed new videoconferencing technologies, H.264, for more flexible learning environments with both Quality of Service and Non-Quality of Service technologies. In her investigation of mobile videoconferencing and grants, Kim developed *A Videoconference Roadmap: Moving to H.264*. Research and computing were united in Kim's last years at TWU when she was assigned High Performance Computing (HPC) for Bioinformatics. Unfamiliar with HPC, Kim studied Linux, supporting the open source Rocks platform on a small cluster. She attended the National Computational Science Institute Workshop: Introduction to Parallel Processing and Cluster Computing July/August 2012. Kim's experience with HPC was the inspiration for her interest in women and leadership development in technology. Kim currently teaches as an Adjunct Professor in the Department of Dance and Theatre at the University of North Texas, Denton, TX.

Jeremy Horne received his Ph.D. in Philosophy from Florida State University in 1988, concentrating in Political Philosophy, Logic, the History of Philosophy, and Philosophy of Education. He also holds a Masters in Political Science from Southern Connecticut State University and a Bachelors from Johns Hopkins University. Horne's current research interests include the cosmological and quantum semantics of binary logic, modeling and simulation, the relationship of first and second order logic to modeling theories, the effect of millimeter wave radiation on transitional states of consciousness, and consciousness studies, particularly the structure, role, and philosophy of bi-valued logic in consciousness. Horne is President Emeritus of the Southwest Area Meeting division of the American Association for the Advancement of Science (AAAS). His professional associations include the International Institute for Informatics and Systemics (IIIS), the International Institute of Electrical and Electronic Engineers (IEEE), and the Bioelectromagnetics Society. Currently, he is the CEO, consultant Science Advisor, and Curriculum Coordinator for the Inventors Assistance League.

Manzoor A. Khan received his Ph.D. in Computer Science from the Technical University of Berlin, Germany. He completed his Masters in Computer Science from Balochistan University of Information Technology and Management Sciences, Pakistan. He served in the Deployment and Optimization Departments of a major mobile operator in Pakistan. He is currently the Vice-Director of Competence Centre Network and Mobility at DAI-Labor. His main research interests include cloud federations, Software Defined Networking, learning within heterogeneous wireless networks, learning within agent-based autonomic networking, experimental research focusing on LTE, LTE protocols & operations, SAE, MPTCP/IP Protocols, IMS architecture, user-centric network selection, resource allocation, and Quality of Experience in future wireless networks. He is the author of several book chapters and numerous research papers.

Shen Lu is the founder of Soft Challenge LLC. She is also the company's Lead Software and Solution Developer. She received both her B.S and M.S in Computer Science at Tsinghua University, China. She also received a M.S in Computer Science at the University of Arkansas in Little Rock, USA. Shen has worked, researched, and published for many years within the fields of software and solution development. Her projects incorporate microarray gene expression data analysis, clinical data analysis, census data analysis, macro-economic data analysis, entity resolution, social network, text mining, distributed computing, and mobile computing. She has researched and developed the Apriori Association Rule model, Fellegi-Sunter model, expectation maximization, Latent Semantic Analysis (LSA), and several other statistical models. In 2005, Shen won first place in the Microsoft Innovation Cup Student Software Development Competition. She received the Best Paper Award at the World Multi-Conference on Systemics, Cybernetics and Informatics (WMSCI) in both 2011 and 2013. Her research interests include data mining and knowledge discovery through classification, associated rule learning, data clustering, and visualization as applied to text mining, entity resolution, microarray gene expression data analysis, distributed computing, and mobile computing.

Randall D Maples currently serves as the Chemistry Department Chair at Eastern Oklahoma State College in the Mathematics and Science Division. As a professor, he teaches the college's entire spectrum of general and organic chemistry, leading both lecture and laboratory courses. Dr. Maples graduated with a Chemistry B.S. from Southwestern Oklahoma State University in 2007, where he also earned his Chemistry PhD in May, 2012. Dr. Maples has worked in several areas of research including neurotoxicology, nanomaterials, forensic detection, and synthesis of medicinal tetraaza macrocycles. He has published articles in numerous journals, including the Journal of the American Chemical Society. He is also a member of the American Chemical Society (ACS) and the American Association for the Advancement of Science (AAAS).

Jagadeesh Nandigam, Ph.D., is a Professor of Computer Science in the School of Computing and Information Systems at Grand Valley State University (GVSU), Allendale, Michigan. He received his Ph.D. in Computer Science from the University of Louisiana, Lafayette in 1995. Since 1991, he has taught various undergraduate and graduate courses on the subjects of object-oriented programming, software engineering, and the principles of programming languages. Prior to joining GVSU, Nandigam worked for three years in the software industry, where he developed numerous web applications using Java, Microsoft.NET, and Web Services technologies. His current academic and research interests include software engineering, software engineering education, open source software tools, mock-object frameworks, and concurrent/parallel programming in functional languages. He is a member of the IEEE Computer Society.

Dan Ophir is currently a Senior Lecturer and Researcher at Ariel University. He earned his B.Sc. in Applied Mathmatics from the Technion Israel Institute of Technology, his M.Sc. in Computer Science from the Weizmann Institute of Science, and his Ph.D from the Afeka Academic College of Engineering. Dr. Ophir is an Advisor in leading institutions in Israel and abroad. He was a Guest Researcher for two years through the GMD Corporation for Mathematics and Data Processing Ltd. in Sankt Augustine, Germany. He is also a consultant and co-developer of software for the high-tech and defense industries. He has published scientific articles and participated in many international algorithmic-mathematical scientific conferences. Additionally, Dr. Ophir is a member of numerous professional societies, including the IIIS (International Institute of Informatics and Systemics) and KGCM (Knowledge, Generation, Communication, and Management). His research interests include applied algorithms in various fields such as bioinformatics, diffusion, fluids, games, robotics, and education.

Jordan Paris is an undergraduate Computer Science student at Marshall University. His research interests include verification and validation of SQL queries and high performance computing applications.

Sindhura Ramasahayam earned her Bachelors of Pharmacy from Osmania University, India and her PhD in Pharmacology and Toxicology from the University of Louisiana, Monroe. She completed post-doctoral training through the University of Pennsylvania, working in the Hematology and Genetics division of the Children's Hospital of Philadelphia. Her work focused on the effects of an investigational drug, Ataluren (or PTC 124), in facilitating the translational read-through of non-sense mutations in acquired genetic bone marrow failure disorder. She then completed her postdoctoral studies in Neurotoxicology at Oklahoma State University, focusing on mechanisms of cholinergic toxicity in organophosphate pesticides. Ramasahayam is a recipient of several graduate awards from the SOT, SCC-SOT, and ACT, all of which include her as a member. Her research focuses upon the hematotoxicity of munitions compounds, and intervention by myelostimulatory constituents of Echinacea in rodent and cell culture models.

Liviu Popa-Simil is the Executive director of the Los Alamos Academy of Science, and the President of LAVM LLC, a research company specializing in nuclear applications, THz imaging, security, and computers. He holds a PhD. in Nuclear, Atomic, and Molecular Physics from the Institute of Atomic Physics in Bucharest, Romania. There, he completed his dissertation on the subject of material characterization with nuclear methods. Popa-Simil has traveled throughout Europe, Asia, and the U.S. for his research. He served as a Senior Researcher and Project Manager at NIPNE-HH (Nuclear Institute for Physics and Nuclear Engineering – Horia Hulubei in Bucharest Romania), managing special applications of nuclear methods in both industrial and military domains. He also served as an Associate Professor of Physics with the Polytechnic Institute of Bucharest. He then moved on to the United States, where he worked as a Technical Director for a number of private companies active in Industrial Process Automation. Between 2002-2005 he worked with the Los Alamos National Laboratory in New Mexico (LANL) as a Technical Staff Member (TSM-PRA) moving between the company's Environment, Materials Science and Technology, and Decision Application Divisions. Between 2006 and 2007 he acted as a consultant for energy related applications with Los Alamos companies. Since 2007, he has served as the President of LAVM LLC. Popa-Simil is a Life Member of the ANS and a Senior Member IEEE and CAP. He has also served as a member of the PMI (PMP), ASNT, MRS, AIAA, NACE, APS, and numerous other scientific organizations. He has published over two-hundred peer reviewed articles and presented in over five-hundred international conferences, seminaries, and workshops. He has granted four patents and has ten patents of his own. He has also authored four books chapters and six books.

Anamika Singh is currently working as an Assistant Professor in Botany at the University of Delhi's Maitreyi College in India. She earned her Masters in Botany from the University of Allahabad and completed her Ph.D. in Bioinformatics through the Indian Institute of Information Technology, Allahabad (IIIT-A). Dr. Singh was awarded a Student National Fellowship in 2012. Since then, she has taught for three years within numerous institutions. Her research interests include Genetic Engineering, Molecular Biology, Bioinformatics, Biological Databases, Phylogeny, Molecular Modeling, Proteomics, Genomics, Drug Designing, Computer-based Drug Designing, Computational Biology, Sequence Analysis, and Evolutionary Computing. Dr. Singh is member of the Bioinformatics Society of India, International Society for Infectious Diseases (ISID), Asian Pacific Bioinformatics Network (APBioNet), European Federation of Biotechnology (EFB), and International Association of Engineers (IAENG). She also a research reviewer for several major journals. In her spare time, she enjoys writing and painting.

Rajeev Singh is presently working as a scientist and member of the Indian Council of Medical Research (ICMR) in New Delhi. He had obtained his post-graduation degree in Biotechnology with a specialization in Medical Genetics. In 2010, he completed his PhD in Zoology from the University of Delhi, where he specialized in Comparative Immuno-Endocrinology. Singh was awarded Senior Research Fellowships by the Council for Scientific and Industrial Research (CSIR), New Delhi, and the Indian Council for Medical Research (ICMR), New Delhi. He was also awarded a Gold Medal from the

Federation of European Microbiological Societies (FEMS) and a Young Scientist Meeting Grant. He has published several research papers in the reputed journals of *Developmental and Comparative Immunology, Peptides, General and Comparative Endocrinology,* and *Journal of Endocrinology.* He has also published several book chapters in the areas of biotechnology, bioinformatics, immunotechnology and nanotechnology.

Fikret Sivrikaya received his Ph.D. in Computer Science from Rensselaer Polytechnic Institute, NY, USA. Before joining TU Berlin, he worked as a Research Assistant with the Rensselaer Polytechnic Institute and an ICT company in Istanbul, Turkey. He is currently the Director of the Network and Mobility Group at DAI-Labor, where he is responsible for coordinating project and research activities in telecommunication technologies. Through DAI-Labor, Dr. Sivrikaya has presented and coordinated many national and international ICT projects. His research interests include wireless communication protocols, medium access control, routing issues in multi-hop ad-hoc networks, and distributed algorithms and optimisation.

Index

Q

R

S